Engineering Design with SolidWorks 2006

A Step-by-Step Project Based Approach Utilizing 3D Solid Modeling

David C. Planchard & Marie P. Planchard

ISBN: 1-58503-258-1

Schroff Development Corporation

www.schroff.com
www.schroff-europe.com

Trademarks and Disclaimer

SolidWorks and its family of products are registered trademarks of the Dassault Systemes. Microsoft Windows and its family of products are trademarks of the Microsoft Corporation. Other software applications and parts described in this book are trademarks or registered trademarks of their respective owners.

When parts from companies are used, dimensions may be modified for illustration purposes. Every effort has been made to provide an accurate text. The authors and the manufacturers shall not be held liable for any parts developed or designed with this book or any responsibility for inaccuracies that appear in the book.

Introduction

Engineering Design with SolidWorks 2006 is written to assist students, designers, engineers and professionals. The book provides a solid foundation in SolidWorks by utilizing projects with Step-by-Step instructions for the beginning to intermediate SolidWorks user. Explore the user interface, menus, toolbars and modeling techniques to create parts, assemblies and drawings in an engineering environment.

Follow the Step-by-Step instructions and develop multiple parts and assemblies that combine machined, plastic and sheet metal components. Formulate the skills to create, modify and edit sketches and solid features. Learn the techniques to reuse features, parts and assemblies through symmetry, patterns, copied components, Design tables, Bill of materials, properties and configurations.

FLASHLIGHT Assembly
Project 4 and Project 5

Desired outcomes and usage competencies are listed for each project. Know your objective up front. Follow the steps in Project 1 through Project 6 to achieve the design goals. Work between multiple documents, features, commands and custom properties that represent how engineers and designers utilize SolidWorks in industry.

Review individual features, commands and tools for each project with the Multimedia CD. The projects contain exercises. The exercises analyze and examine usage competencies. Collaborate with leading industry suppliers such as SMC Corporation of America, Boston Gear, DE-STA-CO, Emerson-EPT, Emhart, Enerpac, Reid Tool and Die and 80/20 Inc. Collaborative information translates into numerous formats such as paper drawings, electronic files, rendered images and animations. On-line intelligent catalogs guide designers to the product that meets both their geometric requirements and performance functionality.

AIR CYLINDER SUPPORT Assembly
Exercises Project 4

The authors developed the industry scenarios by combining their own industry experience with the knowledge of engineers, department managers, vendors and manufacturers. These professionals are directly involved with SolidWorks everyday. Their responsibilities go far beyond the creation of just a 3D model.

The book is designed to compliment the Online Tutorials and Online Help contained in SolidWorks 2006. Our goal is to illustrate how multiple design situations and systematic steps combine to produce successful projects.

About the Cover:

Displayed on the front cover is the GUIDE-CYLINDER assembly manufactured by SMC Corporation of America, Indianapolis, IN, USA. All parts are used with permission.

About the Authors:

Marie Planchard is an engineering professor at Mass Bay College in Wellesley Hills, MA. Before developing the CAD program, she spent 13 years in industry and held a variety of management and engineering positions including Beta Test Manager for CAD software at Computervision Corporation.

Marie is an active member of the SolidWorks Educational Advisory Board and the SolidWorks Drawing Advisory Board. As a Certified SolidWorks Professional (CSWP), she presented at SolidWorks World 2003 & 2004. Marie is the founder and coordinator of the New England SolidWorks Users Group.

David Planchard is the President of D & M Education, LLC. Before starting D & M Education LLC, he spent over 23 years in industry and academia holding various Engineering and Marketing positions. He has five U.S. patents and one International patent. He has published and authored numerous papers on equipment design. David is also a technical editor for Cisco Press. He is a member of the New England Pro/Users Group, New England SolidWorks Users Group and the Cisco Regional Academy Users Group.

David and Marie Planchard are Co-founders of D & M Education LLC and are active industry and education consultants. They are SolidWorks Research Partners, SolidWorks Solution Partners, and co-authors of the following SDC Publications books:

- **Assembly Modeling with SolidWorks 2001Plus, 2003 and 2004-2005.**
- **Engineering Design with SolidWorks 1999, 2000, 2001, 2001Plus, 2003, 2004, 2005, and 2006.**
- **Drawing and Detailing with SolidWorks 2001/2001Plus, 2003, 2004, and 2005.**
- **SolidWorks Tutorial 2001/2001Plus, 2003, 2004, and 2005.**
- **SolidWorks 2004, and 2005: The Basics.**
- **Applications in Sheet Metal Using Pro/SHEETMETAL & Pro/ENGINEER.**
- **An Introduction to Pro/SHEETMETAL.**

Acknowledgement

The authors would like to acknowledge the following professionals for their contribution to the enhancements made to this revision and the corresponding instructors guide. Their assistance has been invaluable.

- Mike Bastoni and Mark Newby, Gears Educational Design Systems, LLC.
- Dave Kempski, Steve Hoffer and the Etech Team, SMC Corp. of America.
- Rosanne Kramer and the SolidWorks Educational Team.
- The SolidWorks Solution Partners Team.
- Computer Aided Products Application Engineers: Jason Pancoast, Keith Pederson, Adam Snow, Joe St Cyr.
- Dave Pancoast and the SolidWorks Training Team.
- Mike J. Wilson, Devon Sowell, Scott Baugh, Paul Salvador and Matt Lombard, Gene Dimonte and Wayne Tiffany for their support of engineering education.
- SDC Publications: Stephen Schroff, Mary Schmidt and the SDC team.

For this 8th edition of Engineering Design with SolidWorks we realize that keeping software application books current is imperative to our customers.

We value the hundreds of professors, students, designers and engineers that have provided us input to enhance our books. We value your suggestions and comments.

Please contact us with any comments, questions or suggestions on this book or any of our other SolidWorks SDC Publications.

Marie P. Planchard
Mass Bay College
mplanchard@massbay.edu

David C. Planchard
D & M Education, LLC
dplanchard@msn.com

Note to Instructors

Please contact the publisher **www.schroff.com** for additional materials and the Instructor's Guide that support the usage of this text in the classroom.

Trademarks, Disclaimer and Copyrighted Material

Information in this text is provided from the ASME Engineering Drawing and Related Documentation Publications:

ASME Y14.1 1995
ASME Y14.2M-1992 (R1998)
ASME Y14.3M-1994 (R1999)
ASME Y14.41 2003
ASME Y14.5M-1994

References:

- SolidWorks Help Topics, SolidWorks Corporation, 2006.
- NBS Handbook 71, Specifications for Dry Cells and Batteries.
- Beers & Johnson, Vector Mechanics for Engineers, 6th ed. McGraw Hill, Boston, MA.
- Betoline, Wiebe, Miller, Fundamentals of Graphics Communication, Irwin, 1995.
- Earle, James, Engineering Design Graphics, Addison Wesley, 1999.
- Gradin, Hartley, Fundamentals of the Finite Element Method, Macmillan, NY 1986.
- Hibbler, R.C, Engineering Mechanics Statics and Dynamics, 8th ed, Prentice Hall.

References Continued:

- Hoelscher, Springer, Dobrovolny, Graphics for Engineers, John Wiley, 1968.
- Jensen & Helsel, Engineering Drawing and Design, Glencoe, 1990.
- Lockhart & Johnson, Engineering Design Communications, Addison Wesley, 1999.
- Olivo C., Payne, Olivo, T, Basic Blueprint Reading and Sketching, Delmar 1988.
- Walker, James, Machining Fundamentals, Goodheart Wilcox, 1999.
- 80/20 Product Manual, 80/20, Inc., Columbia City, IN, 2006.
- GE Plastics Product Data Sheets, GE Plastics, Pittsfield, MA. 2006.
- Reid Tool Supply Product Manual, Reid Tool Supply Co., Muskegon, MI, 2006.
- Simpson Strong Tie Product Manual, Simpson Strong Tie, CA, 2006.
- Ticona Designing with Plastics – The Fundamentals, Summit, NJ, 2006.
- SMC Corporation of America, Product Manuals, Indiana, USA, 2006.
- Gears Educational Design Systems, Product Manual, Hanover, MA, USA 2006.
- Emerson-EPT Bearing Product Manuals and Gear Product Manuals, Emerson Power Transmission Corporation, Ithaca, NY, 2006.
- Emhart – A Black and Decker Company, On-line catalog, Hartford, CT, 2006.
- DE-STA-CO Industries, On-line catalog, 2006.
- Boston Gear, On-line catalog, 2006.
- Enerpac a Division of Actuant, Inc., On-line catalog, 2006.

Table of Contents

Introduction **I-1**
About the Cover I-2
About the Authors I-2
Note to Instructors I-3
Acknowledgement, Trademarks and Disclaimer I-4
References I-4
Table of Contents I-6
Overview of Projects I-11
What is SolidWorks? I-14
Command Syntax I-16
Windows Terminology in SolidWorks I-16

Project 1 - Fundamentals of Part Modeling **1-1**
Project Objective 3
Project Situation 4
Project Overview 6
File Management 7
Start SolidWorks 9
User Interface and CommandManager 12
System Options 17
Part Document Template and Document Properties 19
PLATE Part Overview 23
Machined Part 26
Reference Planes and Orthographic Projection 27
PLATE Part-Extruded Base Feature 31
PLATE Part-Modify Dimensions and Rename 39
Display Modes, View Modes and Viewport 41
Fasteners 43
View Orientation 44
PLATE Part-Extruded Cut Feature 45
PLATE Part-Fillet Feature 52
PLATE Part-Hole Wizard 54
ROD Part Overview 57
ROD Part-Extruded Base Feature 59
Rod Part-Extruded Cut Feature 61
ROD Part-Chamfer Feature 62
ROD Part-Extruded Cut Feature & Convert Entities Sketch Tool 63
ROD Part-View Orientation, Named Views & Viewport Option 68
ROD Part-Copy/Paste Function 69
ROD Part-Design Changes with Rollback 72
ROD Part-Recover from Rebuild Errors 73
ROD Part-Edit Part Color 78
GUIDE Part Overview 81
GUIDE Part-Extruded Base Feature and Dynamic Mirror 83
GUIDE Part-Extruded Cut Slot Profile 86
GUIDE Part-Mirror Feature 90
GUIDE Part-Holes 91
GUIDE PART-Linear Pattern Feature 91

GUIDE Part-Materials Editor and Mass Properties 96
Manufacturing Considerations 98
Sketch Entities and Sketch Tools 101
Project Summary 102
Project Terminology 102
Questions / Exercises 105

Project 2 - Fundamentals of Assembly Modeling **2-1**
Project Objective 3
Project Situation 4
Project Overview 5
Assembly Modeling Approach 5
Linear Motion and Rotational Motion 6
GUIDE-ROD Assembly 7
GUIDE-ROD Assembly - Insert Components 11
FeatureManager Syntax 14
Mate Types 16
GUIDE-ROD Assembly-Mate the ROD Component 18
GUIDE-ROD Assembly-Mate the PLATE Component 22
GUIDE-ROD Assembly-Mate Errors 26
Collision Detection 30
Modify Component Dimension 31
Design Library 32
Inert Mates 35
Socket Head Cap Screw Part 39
SmartMates 44
Coincident/Concentric SmartMate 44
Tolerance and Fit 47
Exploded View 51
Section View 56
Analyze an Interference Problem 58
Save As Copy Option 59
GUIDE-ROD Assembly-Component Pattern 62
Redefining Mates and Linear Components Pattern 64
Folders and Suppressed Components 68
Make-Buy Decision: 3D ContentCentral 69
CUSTOMER Assembly 74
Copy the CUSTOMER Assembly 80
COSMOSXpress 84
Project Summary 95
Project Terminology 96
Questions / Exercises 99

Project 3 - Fundamentals of Drawing **3-1**
Project Objective 3
Project Situation 4
Project Overview 4
Drawing Template and Sheet Format 5
Sheet Format and Title Block 13
Company Logo 17

Save Sheet Format and Save As Drawing Template	20
GUIDE Part-Modify	23
GUIDE Part-Drawing	24
Move Views and Properties of the Sheet	27
Auxiliary View, Section View and Detail View	30
Display Modes and Performance	34
Detail Drawing	36
Move Dimensions in the Same View	39
Partial Auxiliary View-Crop View	41
Move Dimensions to a Different View	45
Dimension Holes and the Hole Callout	46
Center Marks and Centerlines	49
Modify the Dimension Scheme	51
GUIDE Part-Insert an Additional Feature	55
General Notes and Parametric Notes	57
Revision Table	60
Part Number and Document Properties	62
Exploded View	68
Balloons	70
Bill of Materials	72
Associative Part, Assembly and Drawing	77
Project Summary	78
Project Terminology	79
Questions / Exercises	81
Project 4 - Extrude and Revolve Features	**4-1**
Project Objective	3
Project Overview	4
Design Intent	6
Project Situation	9
Part Template	11
BATTERY Part	16
BATTERY Part-Extruded Base Feature	17
BATTERY Part-Fillet Feature Edge	22
BATTERY Part-Extruded Cut Feature	23
BATTERY Part-Fillet Feature Face	25
BATTERY Part-Extruded Boss Feature	26
Injection Molded Process	32
BATTERYPLATE Part	33
Save As, Delete, Modify and Edit Feature	34
BATTERYPLATE Part-Extruded Boss Feature	36
BATTERYPLATE Part-Fillet Features-Full Round, options	37
Multibody Parts and the Extruded Boss Features	40
LENS Part	42
LENS Part-Revolved Base Feature	43
LENS Part-Shell Feature	46
Extruded Boss Feature and Convert Entities Sketch Tool	47
LENS Part-Hole Wizard	48
LENS Part-Revolved Boss Thin Feature	51
LENS Part-Extruded Boss Feature and Offset Entities	53
LENS Part-Extruded Boss Feature and Transparent Property	55

BULB Part 57
BULB Part-Revolved Base Feature 58
BULB Part-Revolved Boss Feature and Spline Sketch Tool 60
BULB Part-Revolved Cut Thin Feature 62
BULB Part-Dome Feature 64
BULB Part-Circular Pattern Feature 65
Customizing Toolbars and Short Cut Keys 68
Design Checklist and Goals before Plastic Manufacturing 70
Mold Base 72
Applying SolidWorks Features for Mold Tooling Design 72
Manufacturing Design Issues 82
Mold Analysis Issues with MoldflowXpress 83
Project Summary 84
Project Terminology 85
Questions / Exercises 88

Project 5 – Sweep, Loft and Additional Features **5-1**
Project Objective 3
Project Overview 4
O-RING Part- Sweep Base Feature 7
O-RING Part-Design Table 9
SWITCH Part-Loft Base Feature 13
SWITCH Part-Shape Feature 18
Four Major Categories of Solid Features 20
LENSCAP Part 20
LENSCAP Part-Extruded Base, Extruded Cut and Shell Features 21
LENSCAP Part-Revolved Cut Thin Feature 24
LENSCAP Part-Thread, Sweep Feature and Helix/Spiral Curve 25
HOUSING Part 31
HOUSING Part-Loft Boss Feature 34
HOUSING Part-First Extruded Boss Feature 38
HOUSING Part-Shell Feature 39
HOUSING Part-Second Extruded Boss Feature 40
HOUSING Part-Draft Feature 41
HOUSING Part-Thread with Sweep Feature 42
HOUSING Part-Handle with Sweep Feature 46
HOUSING Part-Extruded Cut Feature with UpToSurface 51
HOUSING Part-First Rib and Linear Pattern Feature 52
HOUSING Part-Second Rib Feature 56
HOUSING Part-Mirror Feature 59
FLASHLIGHT Assembly 62
Assembly Template 63
LENSANDBULB Sub-assembly 63
BATTERYANDPLATE Sub-assembly 68
CAPANDLENS Sub-assembly 70
FLASHLIGHT Assembly 74
Addressing Interference Issues 81
Export Files and eDrawings 82
Project Summary 85
Project Terminology 86
Questions / Exercises 87

Project 6 - Top Down Assembly Modeling **6-1**
Project Objective 3
Project Situation 5
Top Down Design Approach 6
BOX Assembly Overview 8
InPlace Mates and In-Context features 10
Part Template and Assembly Template 12
Box Assembly and Layout Sketch 13
Link Values and Equations 17
MOTHERBOARD-Insert Component 20
POWERSUPPLY-Insert Component 26
Sheet Metal Overview 32
Bends 32
Relief 35
CABINET-Insert Component 35
CABINET-Rip Feature and Sheet Metal Bends 38
CABINET-Edge Flange 40
CABINET-Hole Wizard and Linear Pattern 43
CABINET-Sheetmetal Library Feature 47
CABINET-Louver Forming Tool 51
Manufacturing Considerations 52
Additional Pattern Options 58
CABINET-Formed and Flat States 60
CABINET-Sheet Metal Drawing with Configurations 62
PEM Fasteners and IGES Components 69
Derived Component Pattern 74
MOTHERBOARD-Assembly Hole Feature 76
Assembly FeatureManager and External References 77
Replace Components 79
Equations 82
Design Table 86
BRACKET Part-Sheet Metal Features 89
BRACKET Part-In-content Features 91
BRACKET Part-Edge, Tab, Break Corner and Miter Features 93
BRACKET Part-Mirror Component 98
MirrorBRACKET Part-Bends, Fold, Unfold and Jog Features 102
Project Summary 107
Project Terminology 108
Questions / Exercises 110

Appendix
ECO Form A1
Feature Toolbar and Insert menu A2
SolidWorks Shortcut Keys A3
Types of Decimal Dimensions A5
Helpful Online Information A6

Index

Overview of Projects

Project 1: Fundamentals of Part Modeling.

Project 1 introduces the basic concepts behind SolidWorks and the SolidWorks 2006 user interface.

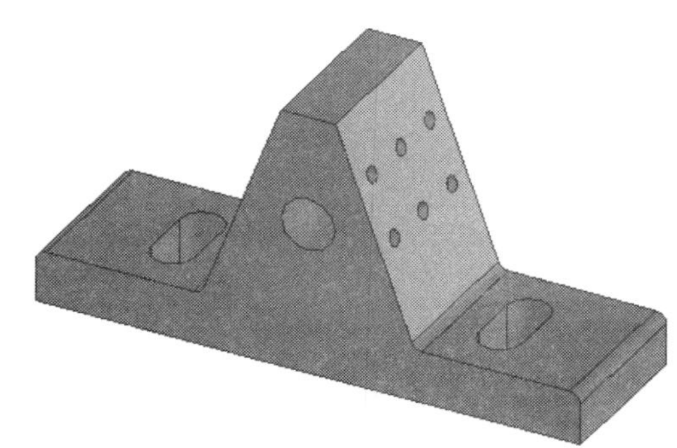

Create file folders and sub-folders to manage projects. Develop custom templates for part documents. Create three parts: PLATE, ROD and GUIDE.

Utilize the following features: Extruded-Base, Extruded-Boss, Extruded-Cut, Fillet, Chamfer, Hole Wizard and Linear Pattern.

Project 2: Fundamentals of Assembly Modeling.

Project 2 introduces the fundamentals of Assembly Modeling.

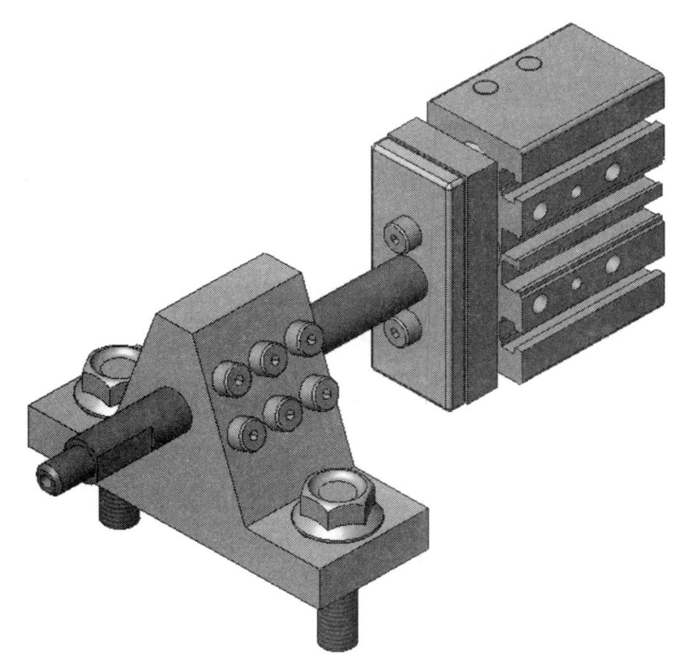

Create an Assembly template. Review the FeatureManager syntax. Create two assemblies. Edit component dimensions and address tolerance and fit.

Incorporate design changes into an assembly. Obtain additional SolidWorks parts from the World Wide Web and the Feature Palette.

Apply COSMOSXpress, a software application analysis tool to view VonMises stress plot and deflection animation.

Project 3: Fundamentals of Drawing.

Project 3 covers the development of a customized drawing template.

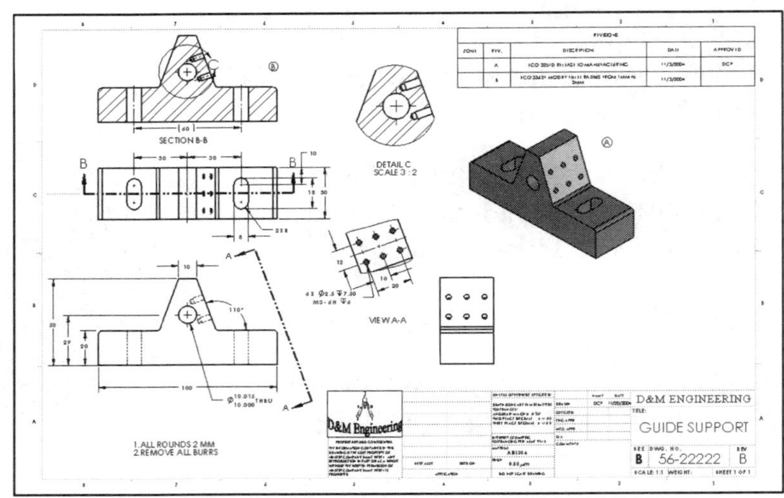

Review the differences between the sheet and the sheet format.

Develop a company logo from a bitmap or picture file.

Create a GUIDE drawing with seven views. Develop and incorporate a Bill of Materials into the drawing.

Project 4: Extrude and Revolve Features.

Project 4 focuses on the customer's design requirements. Create four key FLASHLIGHT components.

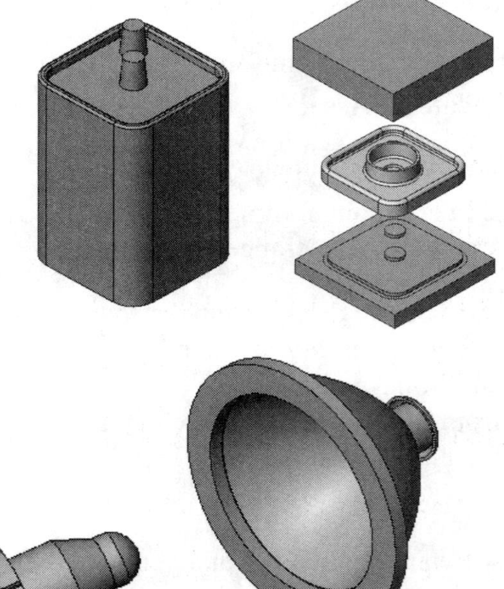

Develop an English part template.

Create the BATTERY and BATTERYPLATE parts with the Base-Extrude feature.

Create the LENS and BULB parts with the Base-Revolve feature.

Utilize the following features: Extruded Boss, Extruded Base, Extruded Cut, Revolved Base, Revolved Cut, Dome, Shell, Fillet and Circular Pattern.

Utilize the Mold tools to create the cavity plate for the BATTERYPLATE.

Project 5: Sweep, Loft and Additional Features.

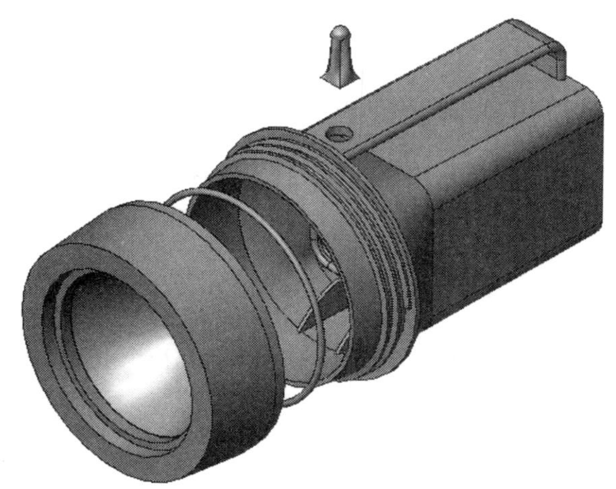

Project 5 develops four additional components to complete the FLASHLIGHT assembly.

Utilize the following features: Sweep, Loft, Rib, Linear Pattern, Circular Pattern, Draft and Dome.

Create an English assembly template.

Insert the parts and sub-assemblies to create the final FLASHLIGHT assembly.

Project 6: Top Down assembly and Sheet Metal parts.

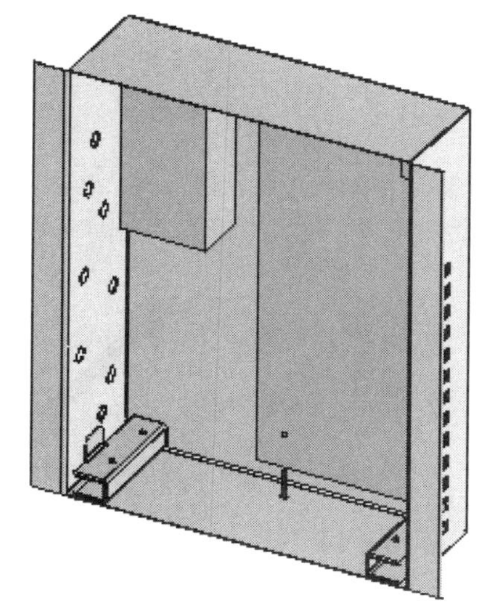

Project 6 focuses on a Top Down assembly modeling approach. Develop a Layout Sketch.

Create components and modify them In Context of the assembly.

Create Sheet metal features.

Utilize the following features: Rip, Insert Sheet metal Bends, Base Flange, Edge Flange, Miter Flange, Break Corners and Hem.

Utilize the Die Cut Feature and Louver Form Tool.

Add IGES format part files from World Wide Web.

Replace fasteners in the assembly and redefine Mates.

Utilize equations, link values and a Design Table to create multiple configuration of the BOX assembly.

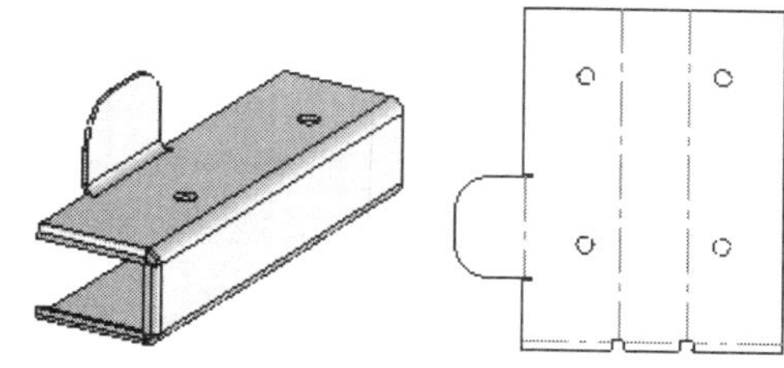

What is SolidWorks?

SolidWorks is a design automation software package used to produce parts, assemblies and drawings. SolidWorks is a Windows native 3D solid modeling CAD program. SolidWorks provides easy to use, highest quality design software for engineers and designers who create 3D models and 2D drawings ranging from individual parts to assemblies with thousands of parts.

The SolidWorks Corporation, headquartered in Concord, Massachusetts, USA develops and markets innovative design solutions for the Microsoft Windows platform. Additional information on SolidWorks and its family of products can be obtained at their URL, www.SolidWorks.com.

In SolidWorks, you create 3D parts, assemblies and 2D drawings. The part, assembly and drawing documents are related.

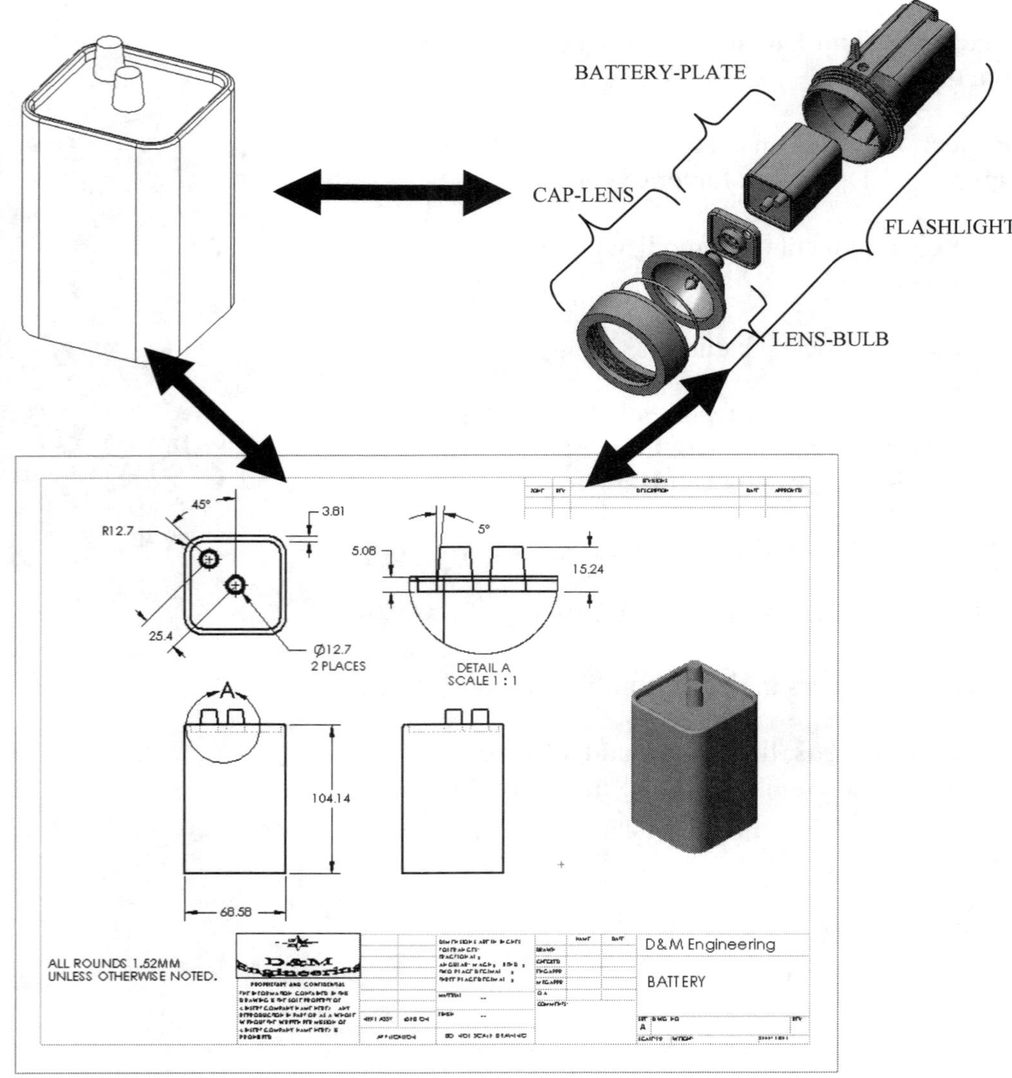

Features are the building blocks of parts. Use features to create parts, such as: Extruded-Boss and Extruded-Cut. Extruded features begin with a 2D sketch created on a sketch plane.

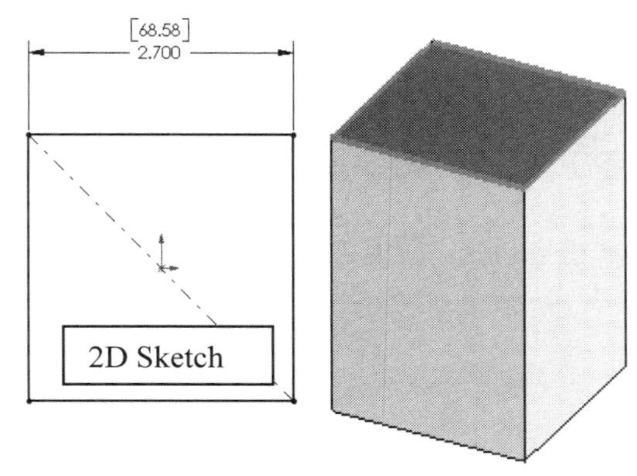

The 2D sketch is a profile or cross section. Sketch tools such as: lines, arcs, and circles are used to create the 2D sketch. Sketch the general shape of the profile. Add geometric relationships and dimensions to control the exact size of the geometry.

Create features by selecting edges or faces of existing features, such as a Fillet. The Fillet feature rounds sharp corners.

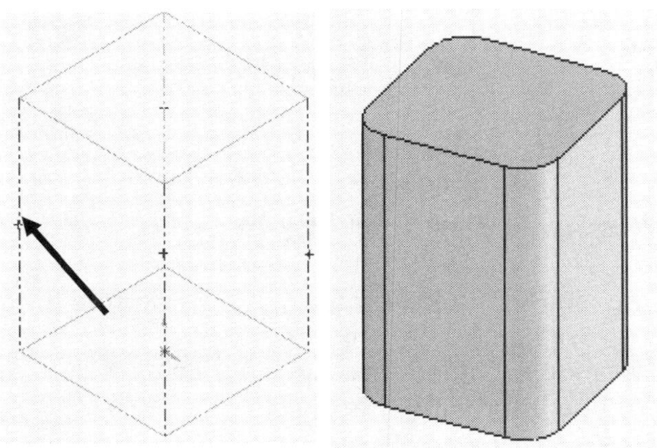

Dimensions drive features. Change a dimension, and you change the size of the part.

Use geometric relationships to maintain the design intent.

Create a hole that penetrates through a part. SolidWorks maintains relationships through the change.

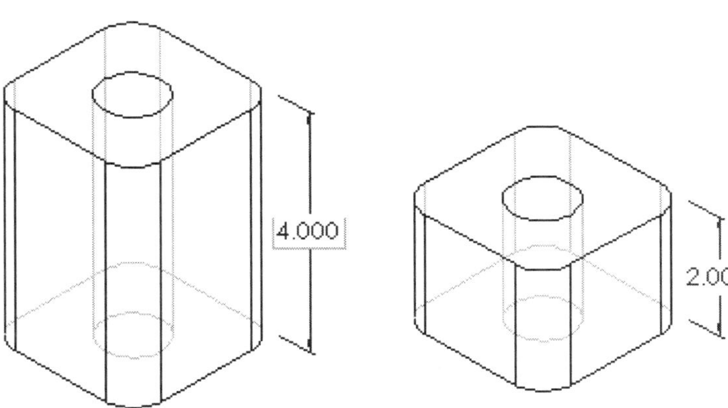

The step-by-step approach used in this text allows you to create parts, assemblies and drawings.

The text allows you to modify and change all components of the model. Change is an integral part of design.

Command Syntax

The following command syntax is used throughout the text. Commands that require you to perform an action are displayed in **Bold** text.

Format:	Convention:	Example:
Bold	• All commands actions. • Selected icon button. • Selected geometry: line, circle. • Value entries.	• Click **Tools**, **Options** from the Main menu. • Click **Rectangle** from the Sketch toolbar. • Select the **centerpoint**. • Enter **3.0** for Radius.
Capitalized	• Filenames. • First letter in a feature name.	• Save the FLASHLIGHT assembly. • Click the **Fillet** feature.

Windows Terminology in SolidWorks

The mouse buttons provide an integral role in executing SolidWorks commands.

The mouse buttons execute commands, select geometry, display Shortcut menus and provide information feedback.

A summary of mouse button terminology is displayed below:

Item:	Description:
Click	Press and release the left mouse button.
Double-click	Double press and release the left mouse button.
Click inside	Press the left mouse button. Wait a second, and then press the left mouse button inside the text box. Use this technique to modify Feature names in the FeatureManager design tree.
Drag	Point to an object, press and hold the left mouse button down. Move the mouse pointer to a new location. Release the left mouse button.
Right-click	Press and release the right mouse button. A Shortcut menu is displayed. Use the left mouse button to select a menu command.
ToolTip	Position the mouse pointer over an Icon (button). The tool name is displayed below the mouse pointer.
Large ToolTip	Position the mouse pointer over an Icon (button). The tool name and a description of its functionality are displayed below the mouse pointer.

Item:	Description:
Mouse pointer feedback	Position the mouse pointer over various areas of the sketch, part, assembly or drawing. The cursor provides feedback depending on the geometry.

A mouse with a center wheel provides additional functionality in SolidWorks.

Roll the center wheel downward to enlarge the model in the Graphics window.

Hold the center wheel down. Drag the mouse in the Graphics window to rotate the model.

Review various Windows terminology that describes: menus, toolbars and commands that constitute the graphical user interface in SolidWorks.

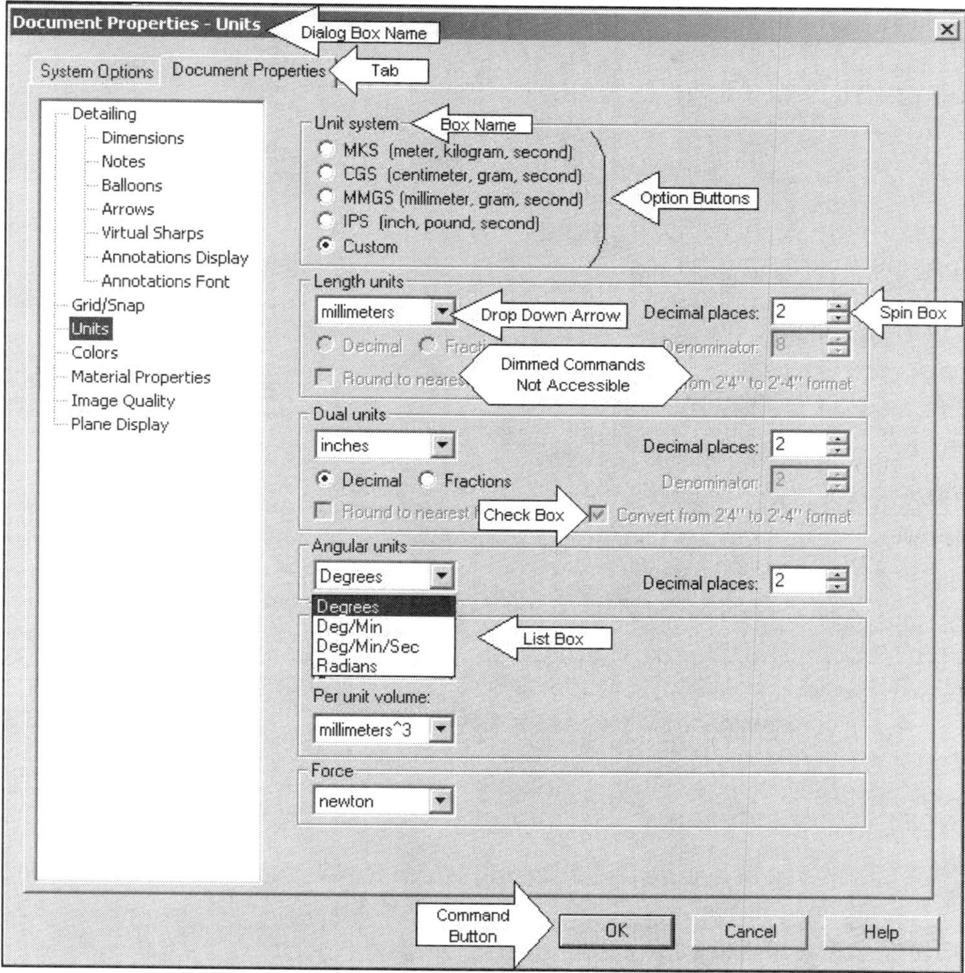

Item:	Description:
Property Manager/ Dialog box name	Name of a window in which to enter information.
Box name	Name of a sub-window area inside the dialog box.
Check box	A square box. Click to turn on/off an option.
Spin box	A box in which to type values or scroll by numerical increments.
Dimmed command	A menu command that is not currently available (light gray).
Tab	Dialog box sub-headings to simplify complex menus.
Option button	A small circle to activate/deactivate a single dialog box option.
Drop down arrow	Opens a cascading list containing additional options.
List box	A box containing a list of items. Click the list drop down arrow. Click the desired option.
Text box	A box to type text.
OK	Executes the command and closes the dialog box.
CANCEL	Closes the dialog box and leaves the original dialog box settings.
APPLY	Executes the command. The dialog box remains open.

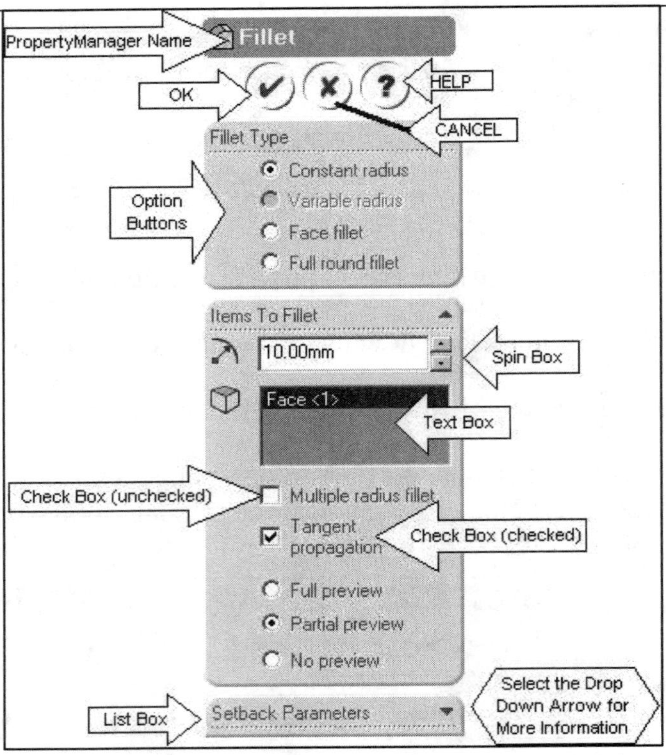

Project 1

Fundamentals of Part Modeling

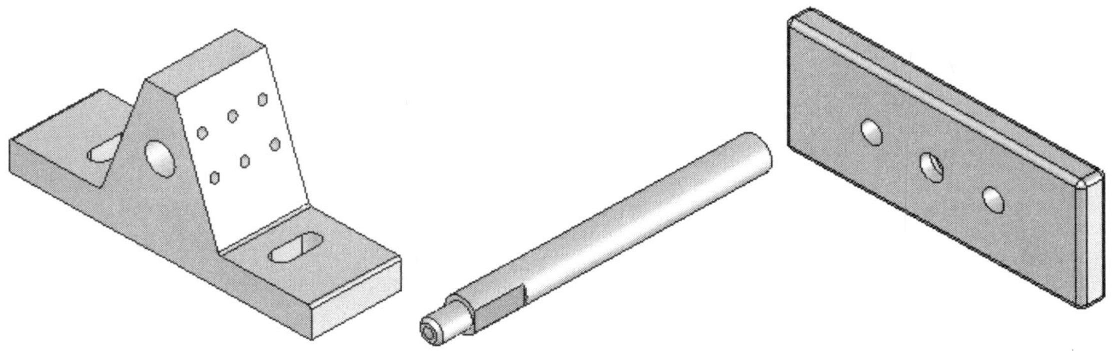

Below are the desired outcomes and usage competencies based on the completion of Project 1.

Project Desired Outcomes:	Usage Competencies:
• A comprehensive understanding of the SolidWorks user interface.	• Ability to establish and setup a SolidWorks session.
• Address File Management with folders.	• Aptitude to create folders for various projects and templates.
• Create the PART-ANSI-MM Part Template.	• Skill to apply Document Properties to create a Part Template.
• Create three new parts: ○ PLATE. ○ ROD. ○ GUIDE.	• Knowledge to create and modify SolidWorks features: Extruded Base, Extruded Cut, Extruded Boss, Fillet, Mirror, Chamfer, Hole Wizard and Linear Pattern.

Notes:

Project 1-Fundamentals of Part Modeling

Project Objective

Provide a comprehensive understanding of the SolidWorks user interface: Menus, Keyboard Shortcuts, Toolbars, System feedback, System Options, Document Properties, Part Templates and File Management.

Create three folders: PROJECTS, MY-TEMPLATES and VENDOR COMPONENTS.

Create the PART-MM-ANSI Template utilized for all parts in this project.

Create three parts:

- PLATE.
- ROD.
- GUIDE.

On the completion of this project, you will be able to:

- Create folders to manage projects.
- Set System Options and Document Properties.
- Create a part template.
- Create and modify parts.
- Open, Close and Save documents.
- Utilize Rectangle, Circle, Arc and Line Sketch tools.
- Utilize Trim Entities, Convert Entities and Mirror Entities Sketch tools.
- Add Dimensions.
- Add Relations.
- Create and modify the following SolidWorks features:
  - Extruded Base.
  - Extruded Cut.
  - Extruded Boss.
  - Fillet.
  - Mirror.
  - Hole Wizard.
  - Chamfer.
  - Linear Pattern.

Project Situation

You receive a fax from a customer. The customer is retooling an existing assembly line.

You are required to design and manufacture a ROD. The ROD part is 10mm in diameter x 100mm in length.

One end of the ROD connects to an existing customer GUIDE CYLINDER assembly.

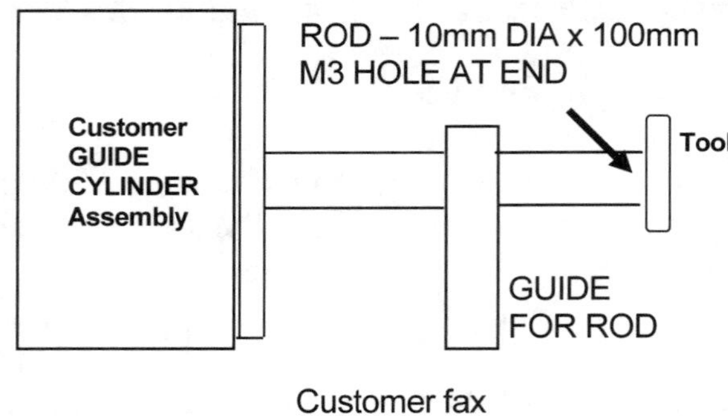

Customer fax

The other end of the ROD connects to the customer's tool. The ROD contains a 3mm hole and a key-way to attach the tool.

The ROD requires a support GUIDE. The ROD travels through the support GUIDE. The GUIDE-ROD assembly is the finished customer product.

The GUIDE-ROD assembly is a component used in a low volume manufacturing environment.

Investigate a few key design issues:

- How will the customer use the GUIDE-ROD assembly?
- How are the parts; PLATE, ROD and GUIDE used in the GUIDE-ROD assembly?
- Does the GUIDE-ROD assembly affect other components?
- Identify design requirements for load, structural integrity or other engineering properties.
- Identify cost effective materials.
- How will the parts be manufactured and what are their critical design features?
- How will each part behave when modified?

You may not have access to all of the required design information. Placed in a concurrent engineering situation, you are dependent on others and are ultimately responsible for the final design.

Dimensions for this project are in millimeters. Design information is provided from various sources. Ask questions. Part of the learning experience is to know which questions to ask and who to ask.

The ROD part requires support. During the manufacturing operations, the ROD exhibits unwanted deflection.

The engineering group calculates working loads on test samples. Material test samples include: 8086 Aluminum, 303 Stainless Steel and a machinable plastic acetal.

The engineering group recommends 303 Stainless Steel for the ROD and GUIDE parts.

In the real world, there are numerous time constraints. The customer requires a quote, design sketches and a delivery schedule, YESTERDAY! If you wait for all of the required design information, you will miss the project deadline.

You create a rough concept sketch with notes in a design review meeting.

Your colleagues review and comment on the concept sketch.

The ROD cannot mount directly to the customer's GUIDE CYLINDER assembly without a mounting PLATE part.

The PLATE part mounts to the customer's PISTON PLATE part in the GUIDE CYLINDER assembly.

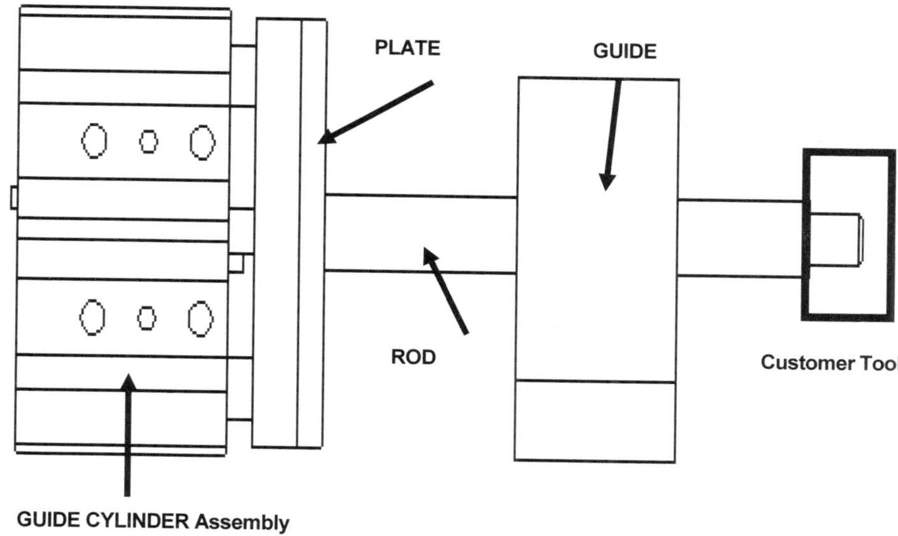

Concept Sketch

Project Overview

A key goal in this project is to create three individual parts, PLATE, ROD and GUIDE, for the requested GUIDE-ROD assembly.

Incorporate the three parts into the GUIDE-ROD assembly in Project 2.

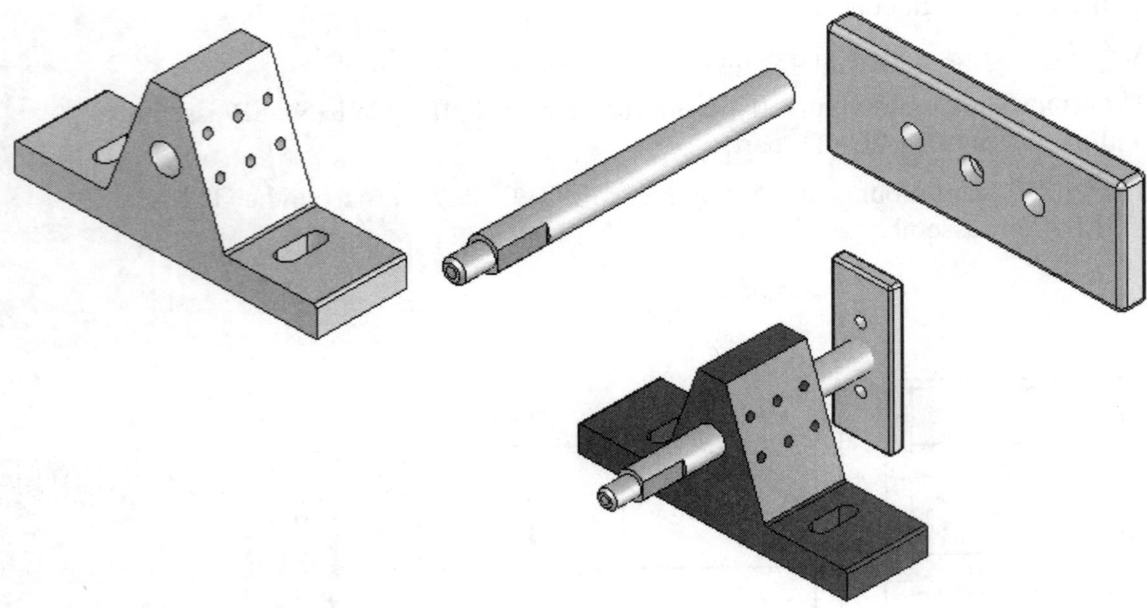

File Management organizes documents. The GUIDE-ROD assembly consists of numerous documents.

Create folders to organize parts, assemblies, drawings, templates and vendor components.

Drawing standards such as ANSI or ISO and units such as millimeters or inches are defined in the Document Properties and are stored in the Part Template.

Plan file organization and templates before you create parts.

Create the PART-MM-ANSI template for the metric parts required for the GUIDE-ROD assembly.

File Management

File management organizes parts, assemblies and drawings. Why do you need file management? A large assembly contains hundreds or even thousands of parts.

Parts and assemblies are distributed between team members to save time. Design changes occur frequently in the development process. How do you manage and control changes? Answer: Through file management. File management is a very important tool in the development process.

The GUIDE-ROD assembly consists of many files. Utilize folders to organize projects, vendor parts and assemblies, templates and libraries.

Folders exist on the local hard drive, example C:\. Folders also exist on a network drive, example Z:\. The letters C:\ and Z:\ are used as examples for a local drive and a network drive respectfully. The following example utilizes the folder, My Documents to contain the folders for your projects.

Activity: File Management

Create a new folder in Windows.

1) Click **Start** start from the Windows Taskbar.

2) Click **My Documents** My Documents in Windows.

3) Click **File**, **New**, **Folder** Folder from the Main menu.

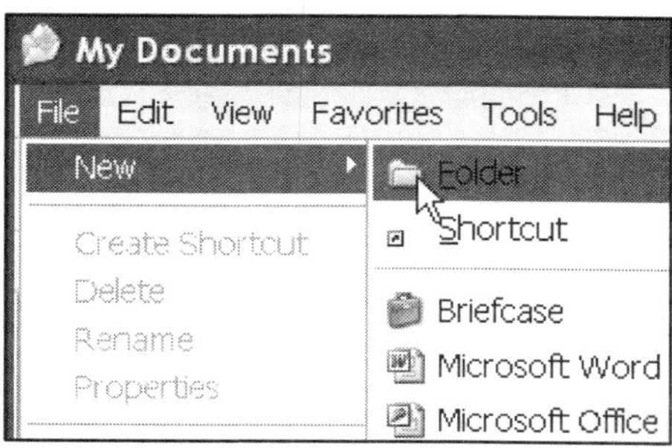

Enter the new folder name.

4) Enter **ENGDESIGN-W-SOLIDWORKS**.

Note: Select the Microsoft Windows commands from the Main menu, toolbar icons and with the right mouse button.

Create the first sub-folder.

5) Double-click on the **ENGDESIGN-W-SOLIDWORKS** file folder.

6) Right-click in the **ENGDESIGN-W-SOLIDWORKS** folder.

7) Click **New**, **Folder**. A New Folder icon is displayed.

8) Enter **MY-TEMPLATES** for the folder name.

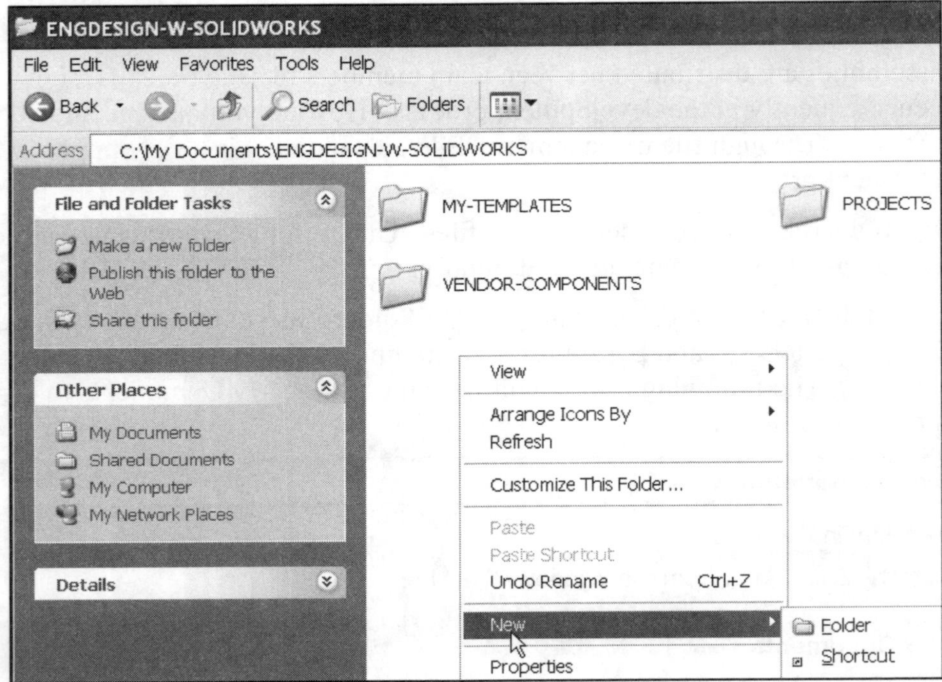

Create the second sub-folder.

9) Right-click in the **ENGDESIGN-W-SOLIDWORKS** Graphics window.

10) Click **New**, **Folder**.

11) Enter **PROJECTS** for the second sub-folder name.

Create the third sub-folder.

12) Right-click in the **ENGDESIGN-W-SOLIDWORKS** Graphics window.

13) Click **New**, **Folder**.

14) Enter **VENDOR-COMPONENTS** for the third sub-folder name.

Return to the EngDesign-W-SolidWorks folder.

15) Click the **Back** ⇦ Back icon.

Utilize the MY-TEMPLATES folder and the PROJECTS folder throughout the text. Store the Part Template, Assembly Template and Drawing Template in the MY-TEMPLATES folder. Store the parts, assemblies and drawings that you create in the PROJECTS folder.

Store the parts and assemblies that you download from the World Wide Web in the VENDOR-COMPONENTS folder. Note: The pathname to the MY-TEMPLATES folder utilized in the text is as follows: C:\My Documents\ENGDESIGN-W-SOLIDWORKS\MY-TEMPLATES.

Start SolidWorks

Start a SolidWorks session. The SolidWorks application is located in the Programs folder. SolidWorks displays the Tip of the Day box. Read the Tip of the Day every day to obtain additional information on SolidWorks.

Open a new part. Select File, New from the Main Pull Down menu. There are two options for new documents: Novice and Advanced. Select the Advanced option. Select the Part document.

Activity: Start SolidWorks

Start a SolidWorks 2006 session.

16) Click **Start** start on the Windows Taskbar.

17) Click **All Programs** All Programs .

18) Click the **SolidWorks 2006** SolidWorks 2006 folder.

19) Click **SolidWorks 2006** SolidWorks 2006 application. The SolidWorks program window opens. Note: Do not open a document.

Read the Tip of the Day dialog box.

20) Click the **Collapse arrow** in the Task Pane to close the Tip of the Day. Note: If you do not see this screen, click the SolidWorks **Resources** icon on the right side of the Graphics window.

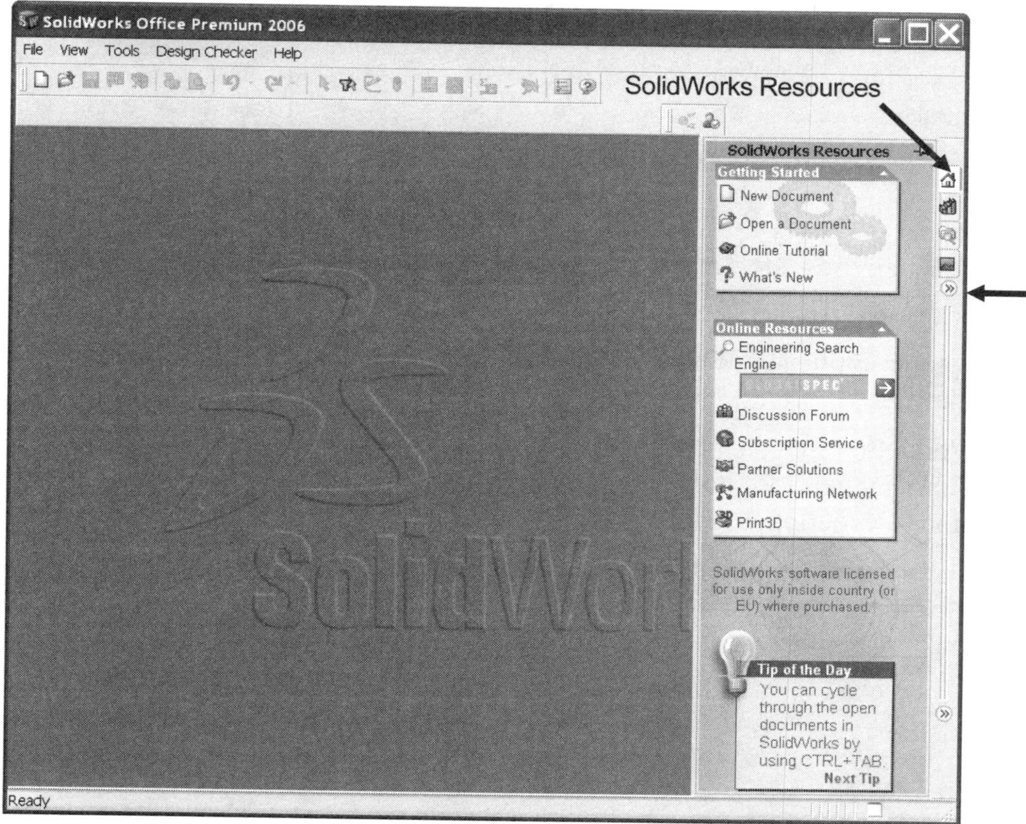

The SolidWorks 2006 Task Pane contains four options:

- SolidWorks Resources.
- Design Library.
- File Explorer.
- PhotoWorks Items.

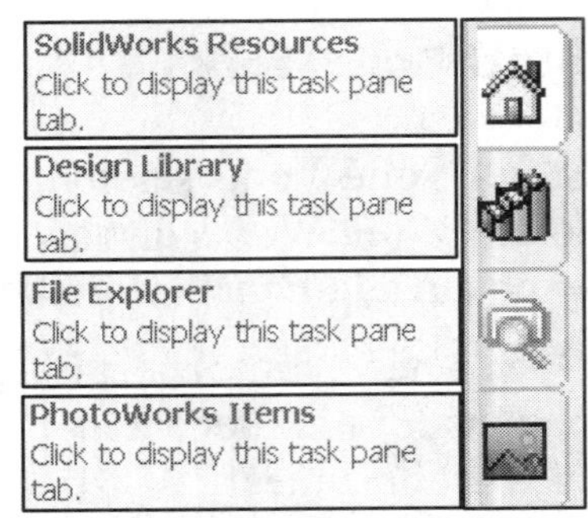

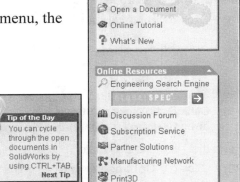

Utilize the left/right arrows to Expand or Collapse the Task Pane options.

SolidWorks Resources contains the Getting Started menu, the Online Resources menu and the Tip of the Day.

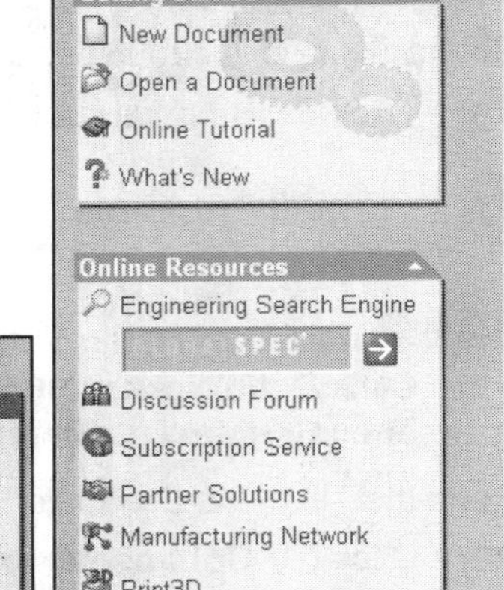

The Design Library includes entries for the design library, Toolbox and 3D ContentCentral. The Design Library contains the following folders: annotations, assemblies, features, forming tools parts routing and smart components.

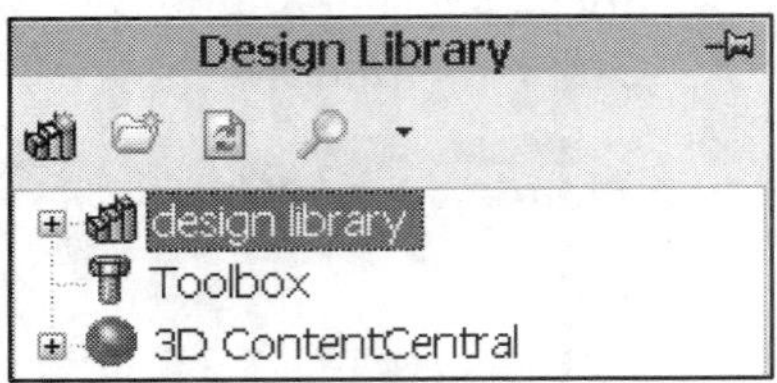

To access the Design Library folders, click Add File Location , enter: C\Programs Files\SolidWorks\data\design library. Click OK.

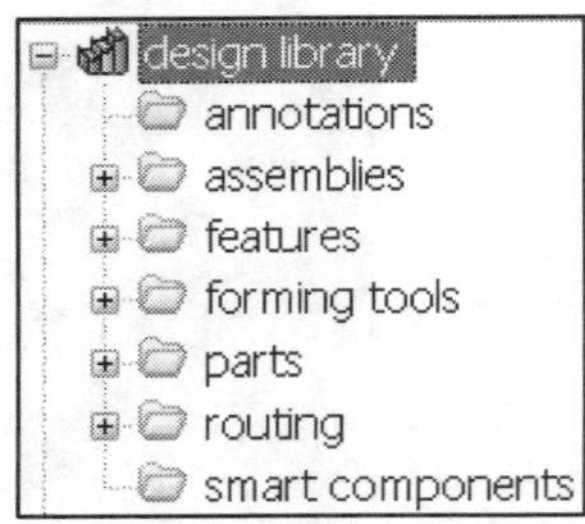

File Explorer duplicates Windows Explorer in functionality.

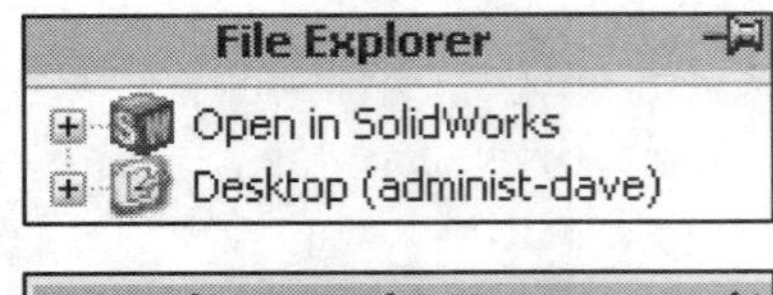

PhotoWorks Items create photo-realistic images of SolidWorks models. PhotoWorks provides many professional rendering effects.

You will explore the options in SolidWorks Resources, Design Library, File Explorer and PhotoWorks as you use this book.

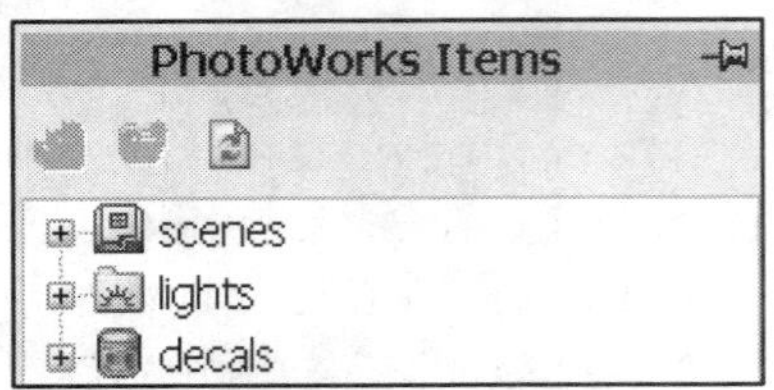

There are two modes in the New SolidWorks Document dialog box: Novice and Advanced. The Novice option is the default option with three templates. The Advanced option contains access to more templates.

Create a new part.

21) Click **File**, **New** from the Main menu.

Select Advanced Mode.

22) Click the **Advanced** button to display the New SolidWorks Document dialog box in Advanced mode.

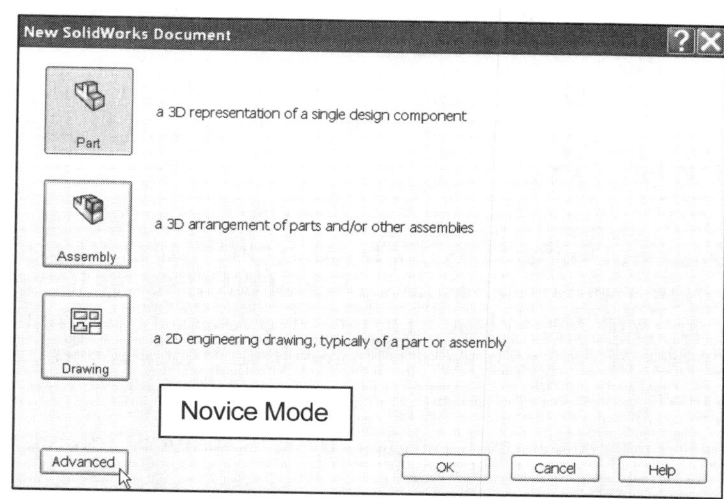

23) The Templates tab is the default tab. Part is the default template from the New SolidWorks Document dialog box. Click **OK**.

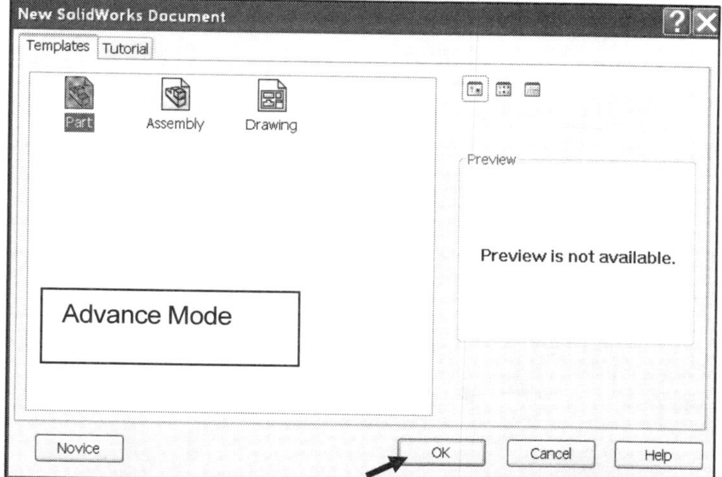

The Advanced mode remains selected for all new documents in the current SolidWorks session. When you exit SolidWorks, the Advanced mode setting is saved.

The default SolidWorks installation contains two tabs in the New SolidWorks Document dialog box, Templates and Tutorial. The Templates tab corresponds to the default SolidWorks templates. The Tutorial tab corresponds to the templates utilized in the Online Tutorials.

Note: The MY-TEMPLATES tab is not displayed in the New SolidWorks Document dialog box when the folder is empty. Save your templates to the MY-TEMPLATES folder. In some network installations, you are required to reference the MY-TEMPLATES folder at the beginning of each SolidWorks session. The System Option, File Locations, Document Templates option sets the pathname to additional template folders. File Locations is explored in this Project.

User Interface and CommandManager

The user interface combines the menus, toolbars and commands with graphic display and Microsoft Windows properties.

Part1 is displayed. Part1 is the new default part window name. The Main menu, Standard Toolbar, View Toolbar and CommandManager are displayed above the Graphics window.

The part Origin is displayed in blue in the center of the Graphics window. The Origin represents the intersection of the three default reference planes: Front Plane, Top Plane and Right Plane. The positive X-axis is horizontal and points to the right of the Origin in the Front view. The positive Y-axis is vertical and point upward in the Front view.

The FeatureManager contains a list of features, reference geometry, and settings utilized in the part.

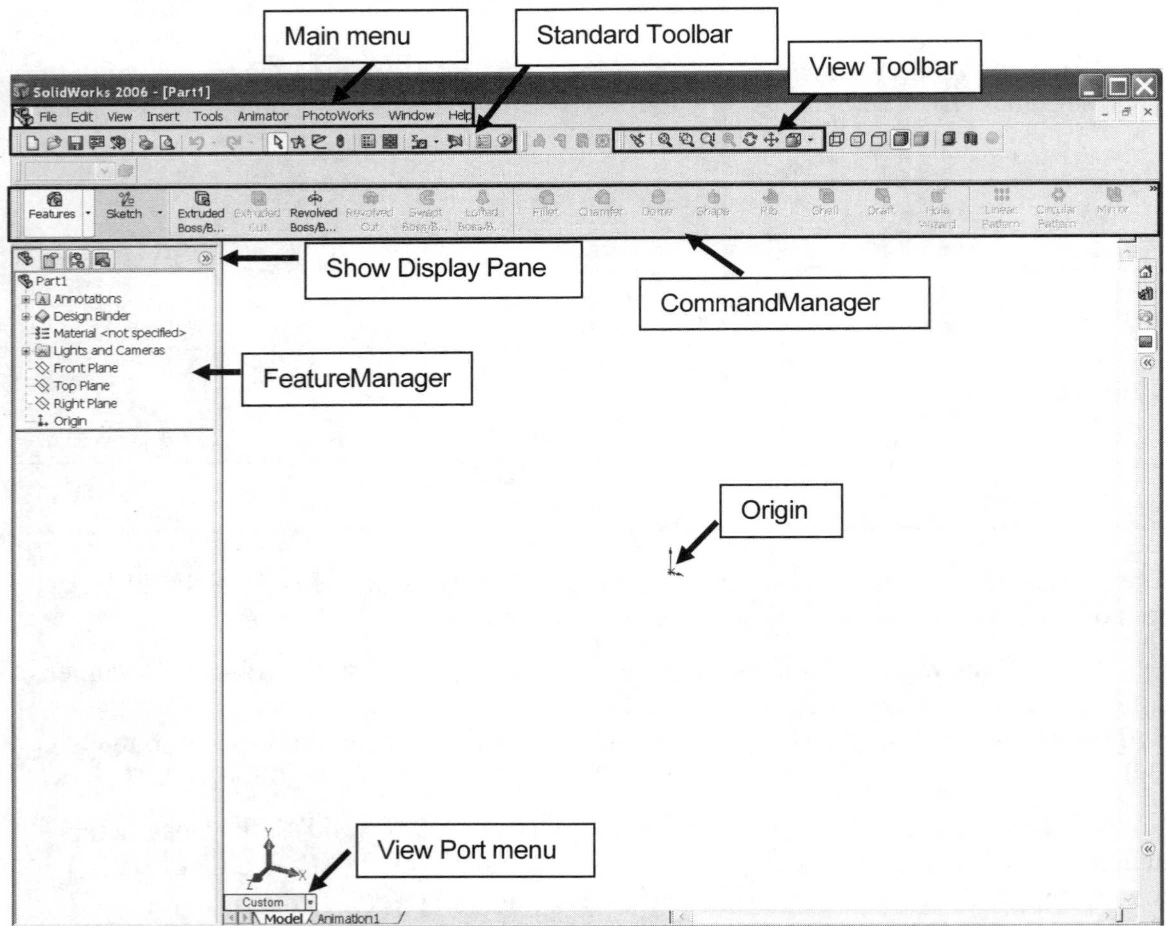

The CommandManager is divided into the Control Area and an expanded Toolbar. Select a Control Area icon to display the corresponding toolbar. The Features icon and Features Toolbar are selected by default in Part mode.

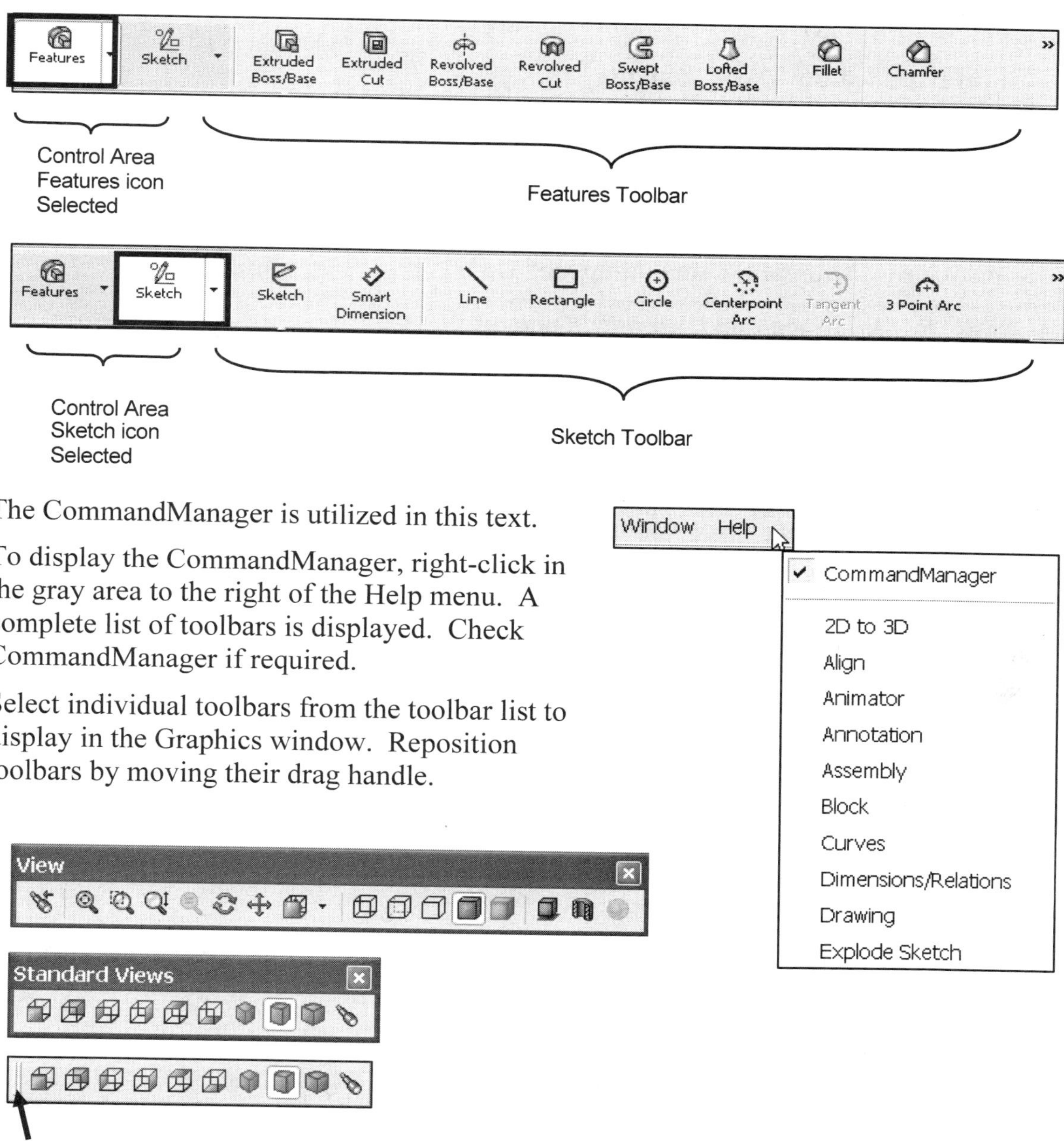

The CommandManager is utilized in this text.

To display the CommandManager, right-click in the gray area to the right of the Help menu. A complete list of toolbars is displayed. Check CommandManager if required.

Select individual toolbars from the toolbar list to display in the Graphics window. Reposition toolbars by moving their drag handle.

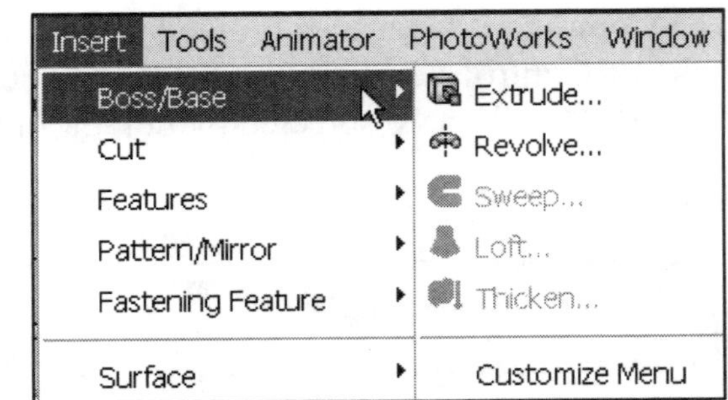

Enter commands from the CommandManager, individual toolbars and Main menus.

Example:

- Select Extruded Boss/Base in the CommandManager.
- Select Extruded Boss/Base from the Features toolbar.
- Select Insert, Boss/Base, Extrude from the Main menu.

Enter additional commands through Shortcut keys and the Right Mouse button Pop-up menus.

Activity: User Interface and CommandManager

Maximize the Graphics window.

24) Click the **Maximize** button in the top right corner of the SolidWorks window.

Display Tools and Toolbars.

25) Position the **mouse pointer** on the Standard Views icon. **Read** the Large ToolTip.

26) Click **Standard Views** from the View toolbar to list the default views. The small down arrow icon indicates additional information is available.

Display the Standard Views toolbar.

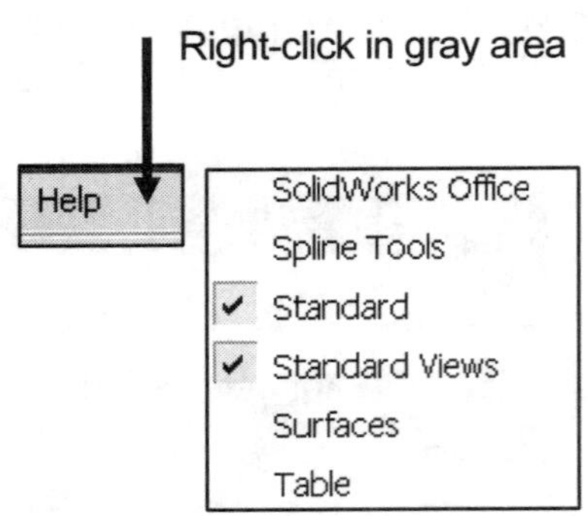

27) Right-click in the **gray area** of the Main menu, to the right of Help. Displayed toolbars are checked.

28) Check **Standard Views**. The Standard Views toolbar is displayed in the SolidWorks window.

29) Position the **mouse pointer** on the Front icon to display the Large Tool tip.

30) Click **Front view** from the Standard Views toolbar.

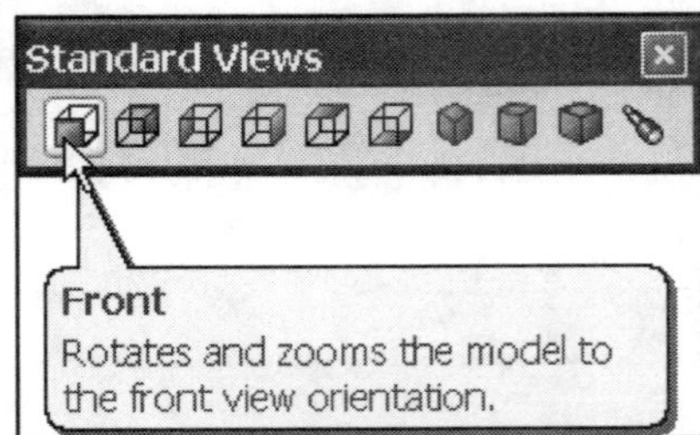

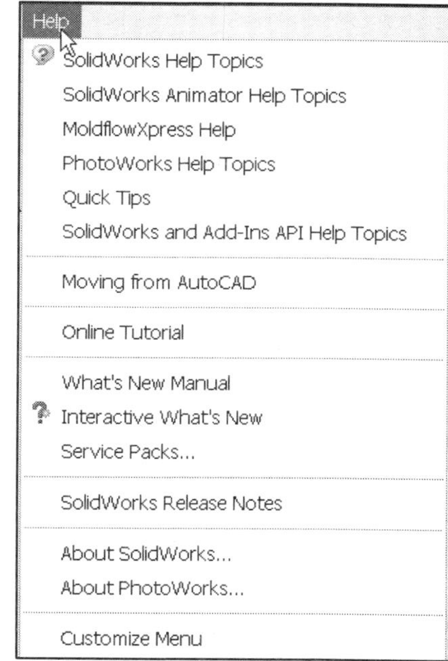

The SolidWorks Help Topics SolidWorks Help Topics contains step-by-step instructions for various commands. The Help icon appears in the dialog box or PropertyManager for each tool.

Display Help for a rectangle.

31) Click **Help** from the Main menu.

32) Select **SolidWorks Help Topics** SolidWorks Help Topics.

33) Click the **Index** tab.

34) Enter **rectangle**. The description appears in the right window.

35) Click **Close** to close the Help window.

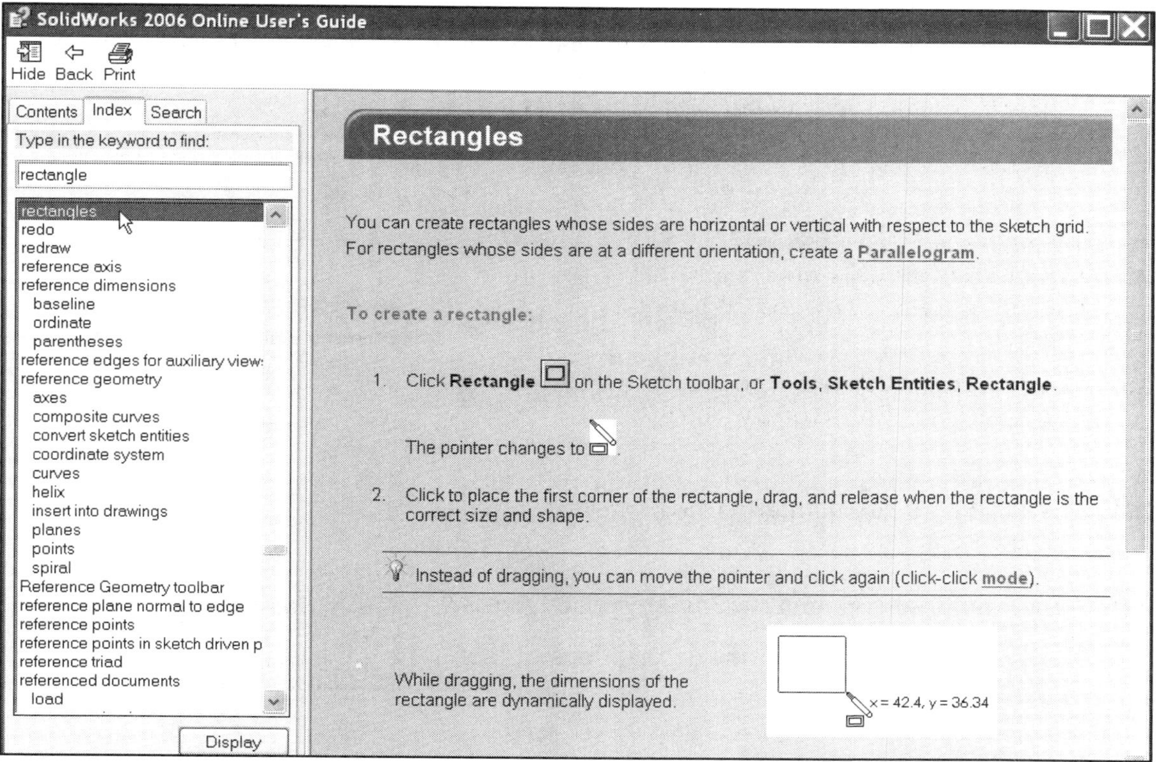

The Help menu contains the SolidWorks Online Tutorial, Introducing SolidWorks and Design Portfolio documents. These documents include additional information on using SolidWorks.

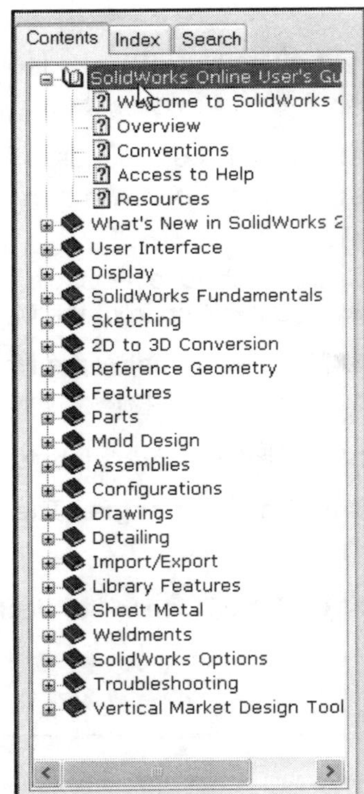

The Closer Look symbol indicates additional information about a tool or command is available from Help.

The Help option contains tools to assist the user.

The SolidWorks Help Topics contains:

- Contents tab containing the SolidWorks Online User's Guide documents.
- Index tab containing more information on key words.
- Search tab for finding information.

Quick Tips are a set of pop-up hints that appear as you create parts, assemblies and drawings. The messages are based on what tool or function is selected. The messages contain hyperlinks to associated areas in the Graphics window or additional files.

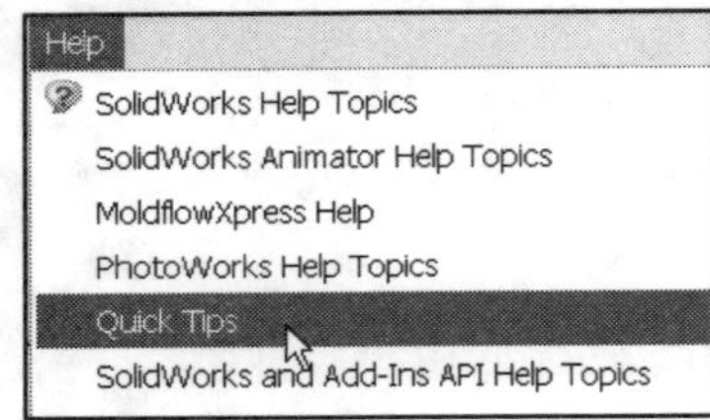

Activate Quick Tips by checking the Quick Tips entry in the Help Main menu.

The Pop-up Quick Tip windows contain a blue header with the question, "What would you like to do?" Read the options and select a statement for additional instructions.

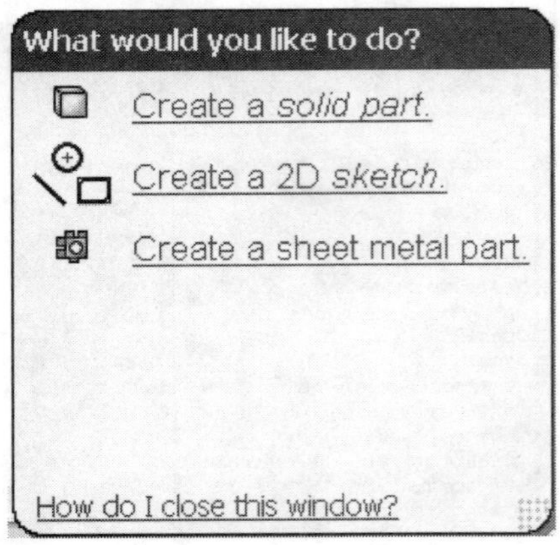

Introducing SolidWorks and the Design Portfolio are great electronic documents for the new SolidWorks user.

The Online Tutorial contains step-by-step examples.

The What's New Manual contains descriptions of the new functionality in SolidWorks since the last major revision.

System Options

System Options are stored in the registry of the computer. System Options are not part of the document. Changes to the System Options affect current and future documents.

Review and modify the System Options. If you work on a local drive C:\, the System Options are stored on the computer.

If you work on a network drive Z:\, set System Options for each SolidWorks session.

Set the System Options before you start a project. The File Locations Option contains a list of folders referenced during a SolidWorks session.

Add the ENGDESIGN-W-SOLIDWORKS\MY-TEMPLATES folder path name to the Document Templates File Locations list.

Activity: System Options

Set the System Options.

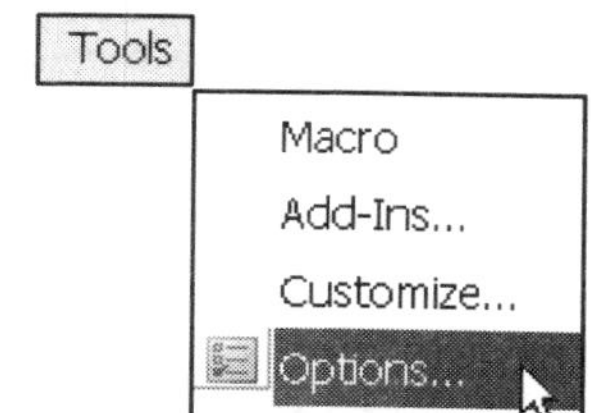

36) Click **Tools**, **Options** Options... from the Main menu. The System Options General dialog box is displayed.

37) Click **File Locations** to set the folder path for custom Document Templates. Click the **Add** button.

38) Select the **ENGDESIGN-W-SOLIDWORKS\MY-TEMPLATES** folder in the Browse For Folder dialog box.

39) Click **OK**.

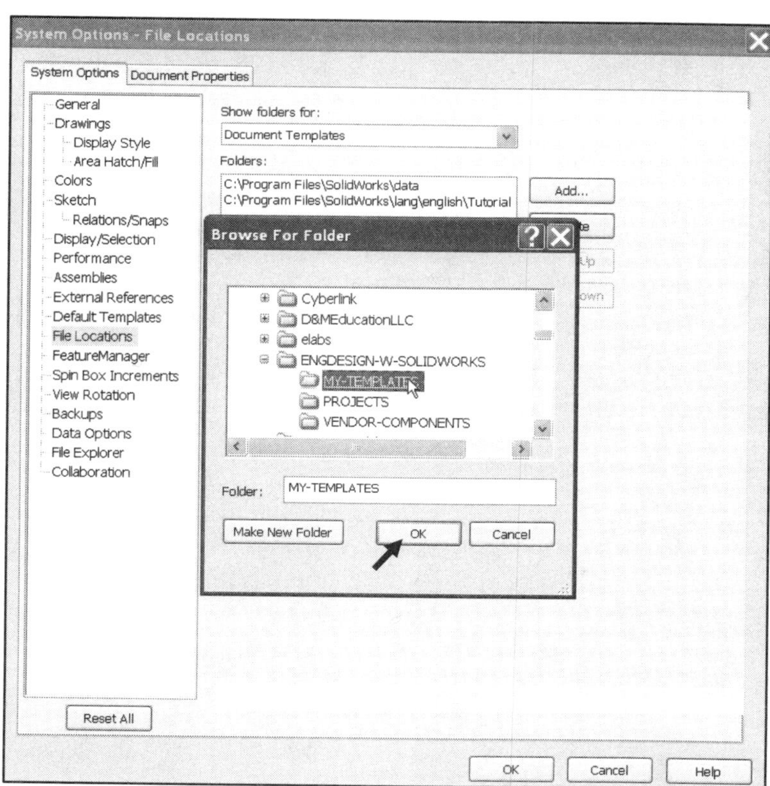

Each folder listed in the System Options, File Locations, Document Templates, Show Folders For option produces a corresponding Tab in the New SolidWorks Document dialog box.

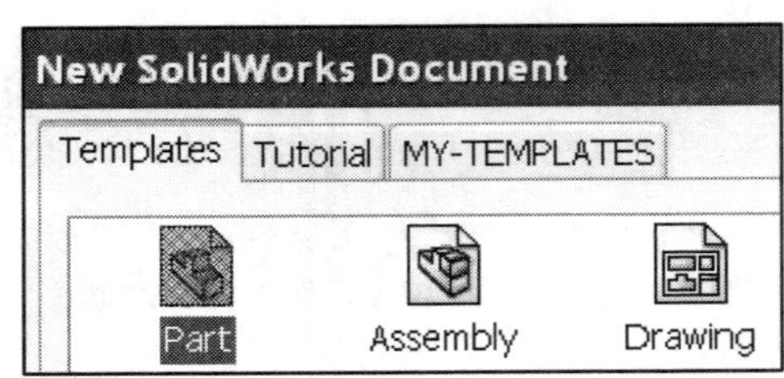

The default Templates folder is called: C:\Program Files\SolidWorks\data. The entry \SolidWorks\ is the SolidWorks load point. By default, the SolidWorks application is located in the Program Files folder.

Verify the General options.

40) Click the **General** option.

41) **Review** the default values. The Input dimension value option is checked.

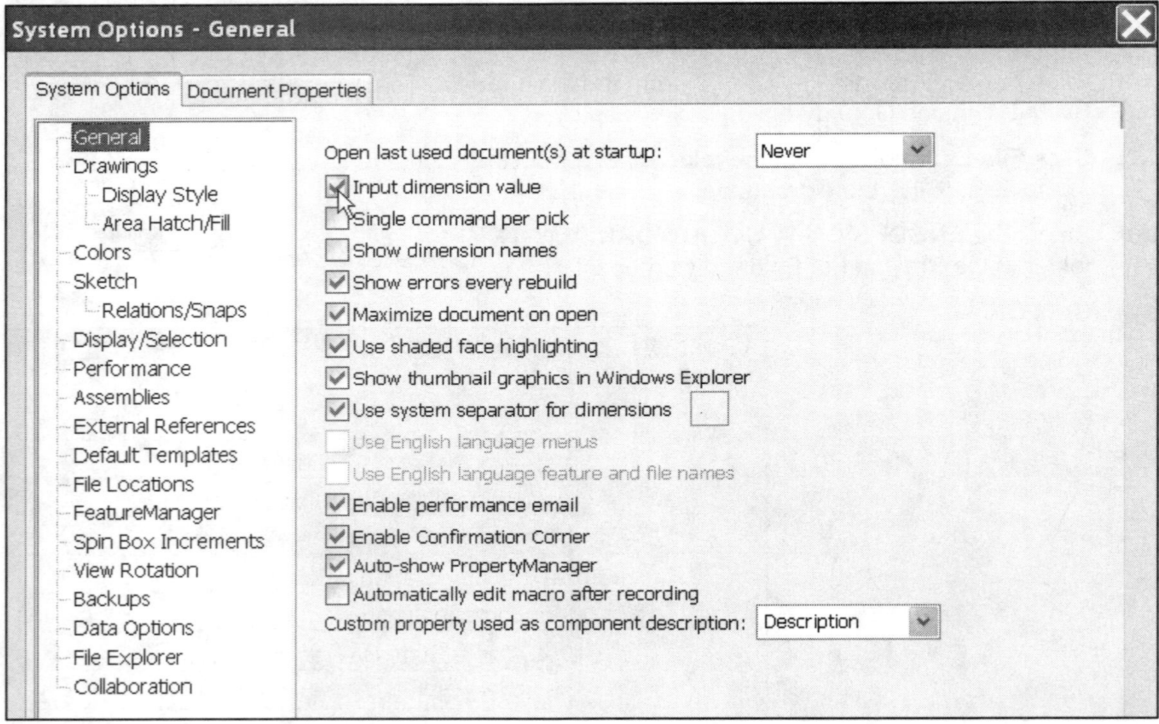

Part Document Template and Document Properties

The Part Template is the foundation for a SolidWorks part. Part1 displayed in the Graphics window utilizes the Part.prtdot Default Template located in the New dialog box.

Document Properties contain the default settings for the Part Template. The Document Properties include the dimensioning standard, units, dimension decimal display, grids, note font and line styles.

The Dimensioning Standard determines the display of dimension text, arrows, symbols and spacing. Units are the measurement of physical quantities. Millimeter dimensioning and decimal inch dimensioning are the two most common unit types specified for engineering parts and drawings.

Document Properties are stored with the document. Apply the Document Properties to the Part Template.

Create a Part Template named PART-MM-ANSI from the Default Part Template. Save the Custom Part Template in the ENGDESIGN-W-SOLIDWORKS\MY-TEMPLATES folder. Utilize the PART-MM-ANSI Part Template for all metric parts.

Conserve modeling time. Set the Document Properties and create the required templates before starting a project.

The Dimensioning standard options are: ANSI, ISO, DIN, JIS, BSI, GOST and GB.

Dimensioning standard options:	Abbreviation:	Description:
ANSI	ANSI	American National Standards Institute.
ISO	ISO	International Standards Organization
DIN	DIN	Deutsche Institute für Normumg (German)
JIS	JIS	Japanese Industry Standard
BSI	BSI	British Standards Institution
GOST	GOST	Gosndarstuennye State Standard (Russian)
GB	GB	Guo Biao (Chinese)

Display the parts, assemblies and drawings created in the GUIDE-ROD assembly in the ANSI standard.

The Units Document Property assists the designer by defining the Unit System, Length unit, Angular unit, Density unit and Force unit of measurement for the Part document.

The Decimal Place option displays the number of decimal places for the Length unit and Angular unit of measurement.

Activity: Part Document Template and Document Properties

Set the Document Properties.

42) Click the **Document Properties** tab.

43) Select **ANSI** from the Dimensioning standard drop down list. Various Detailing options are available depending on the selected standard.

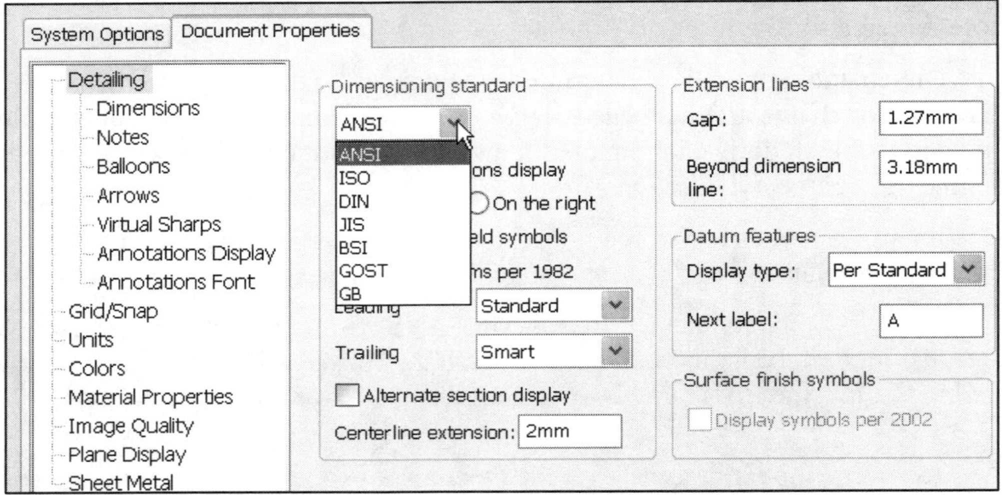

Set the document units.

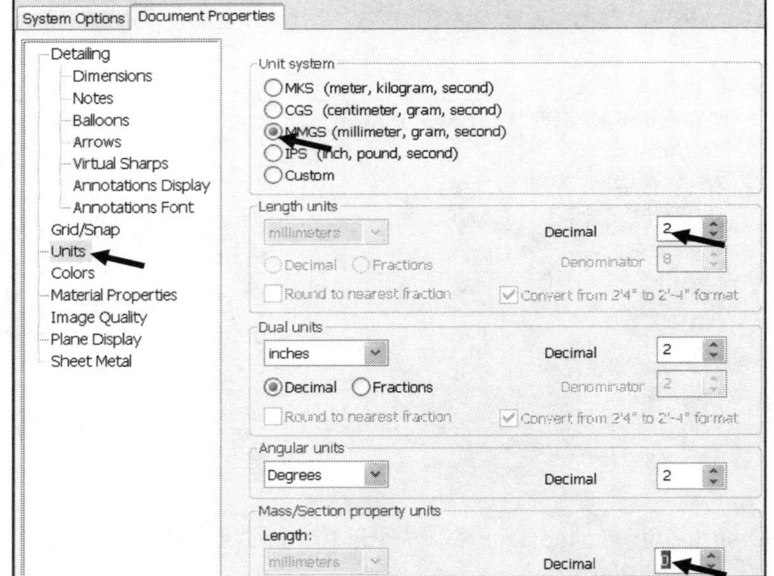

44) Click the **Units** option from the Document Properties tab.

45) Click **MMGS** for Unit system.

46) Select **2** in the Decimal places spin box.

47) Select **0** for Decimal places in the Angular units box.

48) Click **OK**.

Create the part document template.

49) Click **File**, **Save As** from the Main menu.

50) Select **Part Templates *.prtdot** from the Save as type list box. The default Templates folder is displayed.

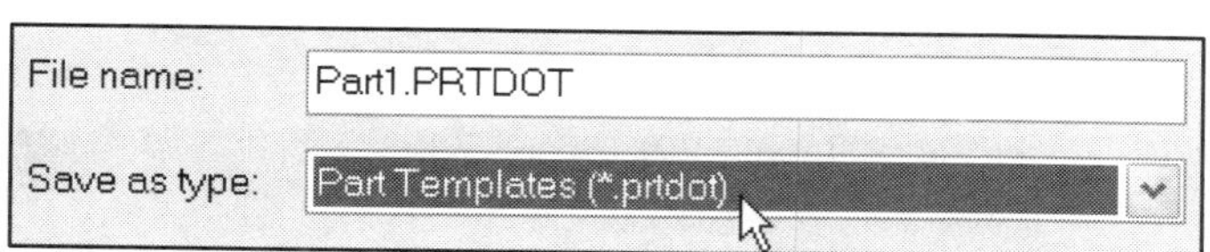

51) Click the **drop down arrow** in the Save in list box.

52) Select the **ENGDESIGN-W-SOLIDWORKS\MY-TEMPLATES** folder.

53) Enter **PART-MM-ANSI** in the File name text box.

54) Click **Save**. The PART-MM-ANSI.prtdot Part Template is displayed in the FeatureManager.

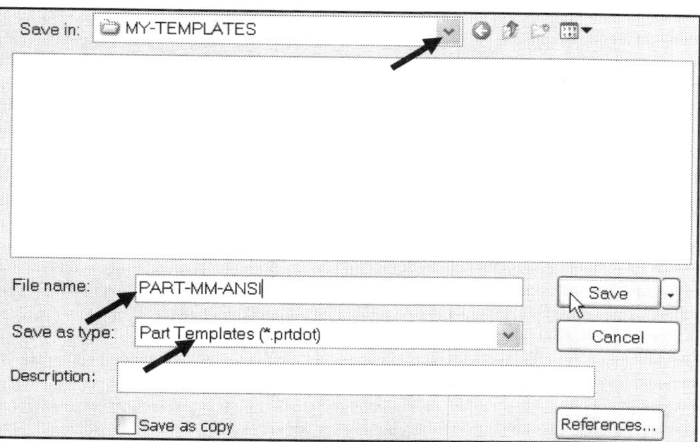

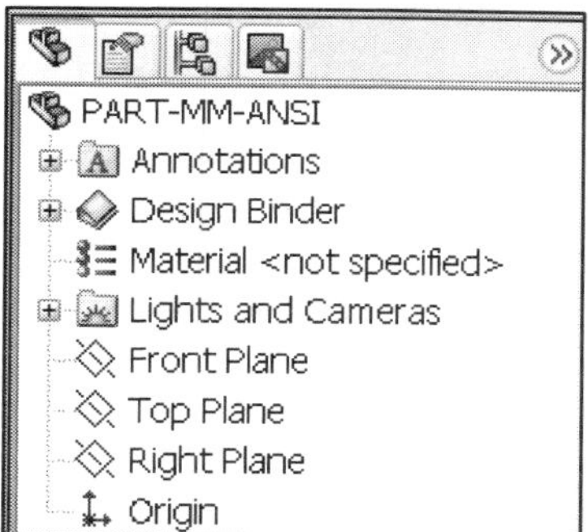

Close the PART-MM-ANSI Part Template.

55) Click **Window**, **Close All** from the Main menu. All SolidWorks documents are closed and the Graphics window and is displayed in gray.

Additional details on System Options and Document Properties are available using the Help option. Index keyword: System Options and Document Templates.

Review of the Part Templates.

You created the following folders: PROJECTS, MY-TEMPLATES and VENDOR-COMPONENTS to manage the documents for this project.

System Options, File Locations directed SolidWorks to open Document Templates from the MY-TEMPLATES folder. System Options are stored in the registry of the computer.

You created a custom part template, PART-MM-ANSI.prtdot from the default Part document. Document Properties control the Dimensioning Standard, Units, Tolerance and other properties. Document Properties are stored in the current document. The part template file extension is ".prtdot".

PLATE Part Overview

Determine the functional and geometric requirements of the PLATE.

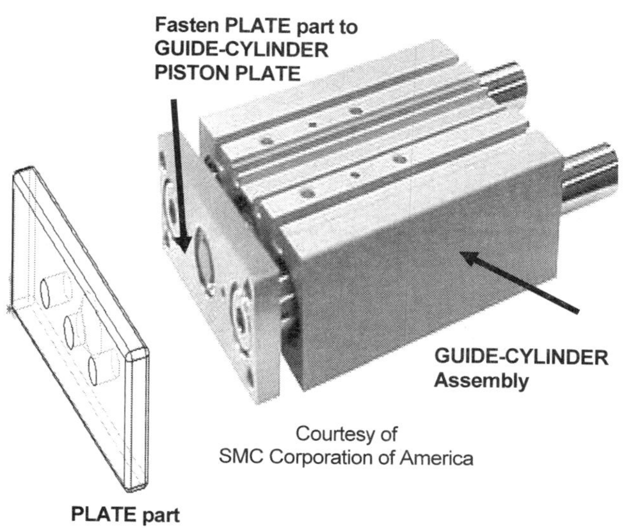

Functional:

The PLATE part fastens to the customer's PISTON PLATE part in the GUIDE-CYLINDER assembly.

Fasten the PLATE part to the ROD part with a countersunk screw.

Geometric:

The dimensions of the PISTON PLATE part are 56mm x 22mm.

The dimensions of the PLATE part are 56mm x 22mm.

Locate the 4mm mounting holes with respect to the PISTON PLATE mounting holes. The mounting holes are 23mm apart.

The PLATE part requires a Countersink Hole to fasten the ROD part to the PLATE part.

Review the mating part dimensions before creating the PLATE part.

The GUIDE-CYLINDER assembly dimensions referenced in this project are derived from the SMC Corporation of America (www.smcusa.com).

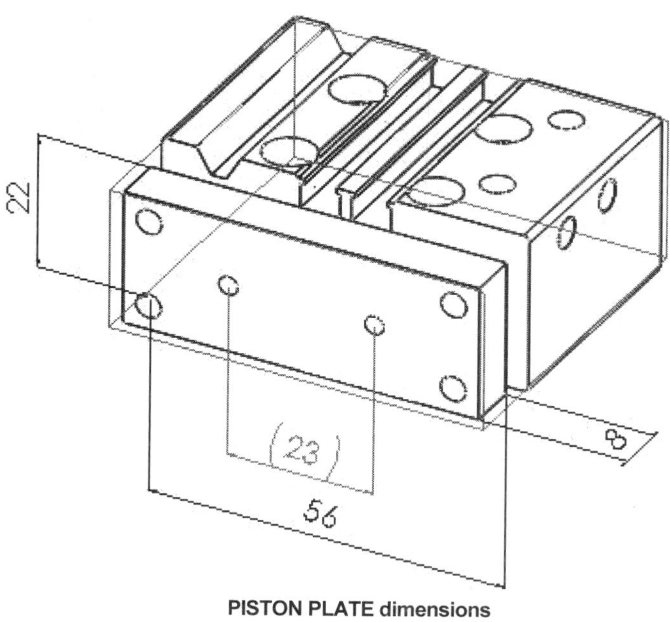

PISTON PLATE dimensions
GUIDE-CYLINDER
Assembly

Start the translation of the initial design functional and geometric requirements into SolidWorks features. What are features?

- Features are geometry building blocks.
- Features add or remove material.
- Features are created from sketched profiles or from edges and faces of existing geometry.

Utilize the following features to create the PLATE part:

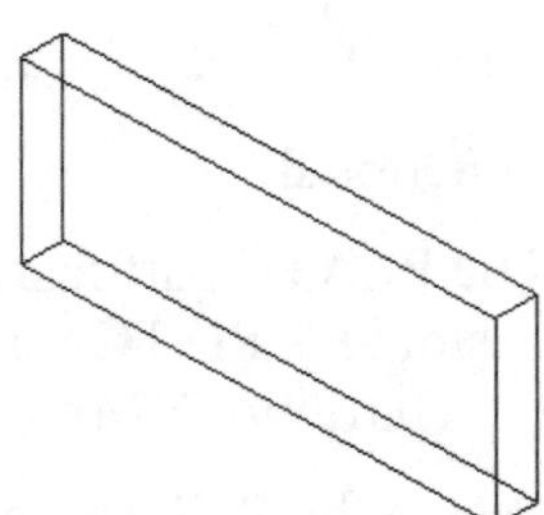

Extruded Boss/Base: The Extruded Boss/Base feature adds material to the part. The Extruded Base feature is the first feature of the PLATE. An extrusion extends a rectangular profile along a path normal to the profile plane for some distance. The movement along that path becomes the solid model. The 2D rectangle is sketched on the Front Plane.

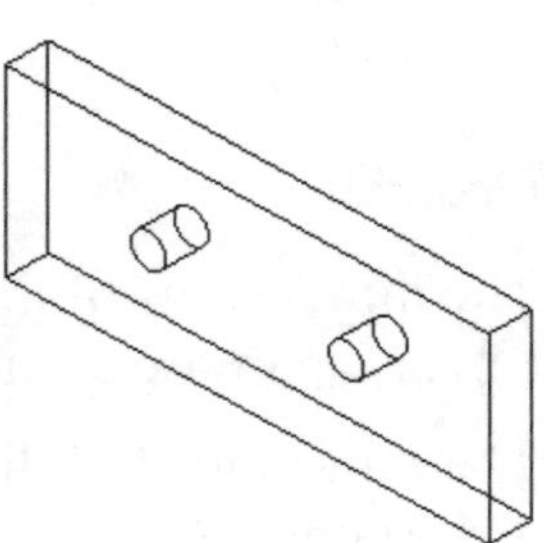

Extruded Cut: The Extruded Cut feature removes material. The Extruded Cut begins with a 2D circle sketched on the front face. Copy the sketch circle to create the second circle. The Extruded Cut utilizes the Through All option. The holes extend through the entire Extruded Base feature. Utilize the Extruded Cut feature to create the two holes for the PLATE.

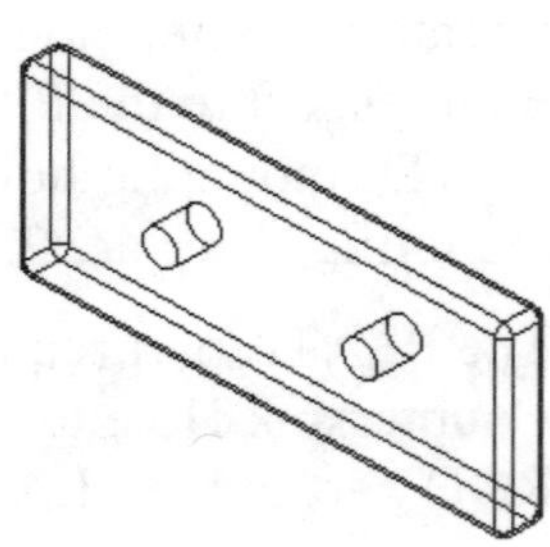

Fillet: The Fillet feature removes sharp edges of the PLATE. Fillets are generally added to the solids, not the sketch. Small corner edge Fillets are grouped together. Tangent edge Fillets are grouped together.

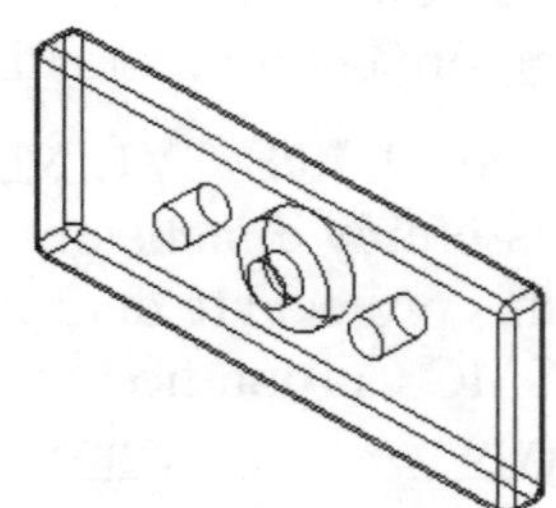

Hole Wizard: The Hole Wizard feature creates a countersink hole at the center of the PLATE. The Hole Wizard requires a sketch plane. The back face is the sketch plane.

Activity: PLATE Part-New SolidWorks Document

Create a new part.

56) Click **File**, **New** from the Main menu.

57) Click the **MY-TEMPLATES** tab. Double-click the **PART-MM-ANSI** PART-MM-A... icon. The FeatureManager is displayed.

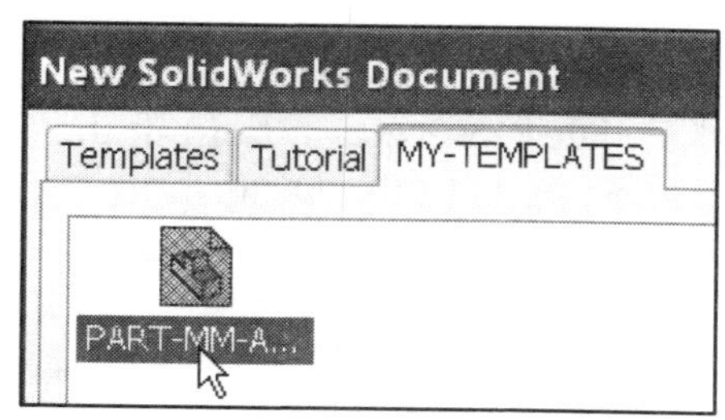

Note: In the New SolidWorks Document, Advanced option, Large icons are displayed by default. Utilize the List option or List Detail option in the New dialog box to view the complete template name.

In a SolidWorks session, the first system default part filename is named: Part1.sldprt. The system attaches the .sldprt suffix to the created parts. The second created part in the same session, increments to the filename: Part2.sldprt.

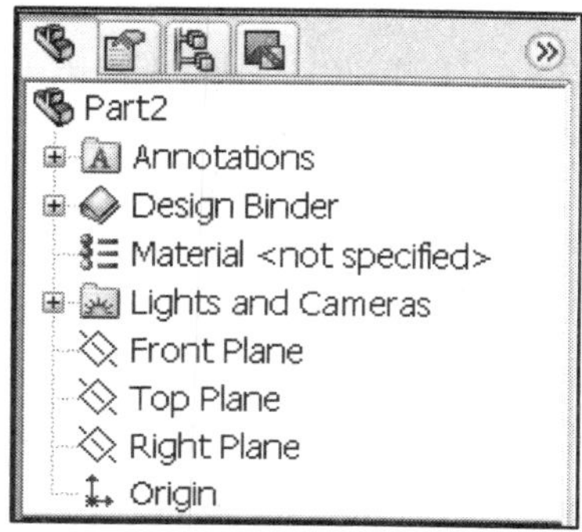

There are numerous ways to manage a part. Use Project Data Management (PDM) systems to control, manage and document file names and drawing revisions. Use appropriate filenames that describe the part.

Save the empty part.

58) Click **Save**.

59) Click the **Drop down arrow** in the Save in list box.

60) Select the **ENGDESIGN-W-SOLIDWORKS\PROJECTS** folder.

61) Enter **PLATE** for File name.

62) Enter **PLATE 56MM x 22MM** for Description.

63) Click **Save**.

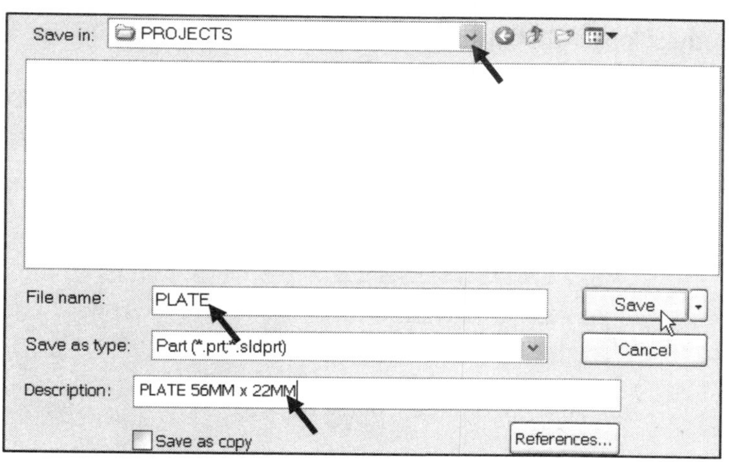

The part name PLATE is displayed in the SolidWorks FeatureManager. The part icon is displayed at the top of the FeatureManager.

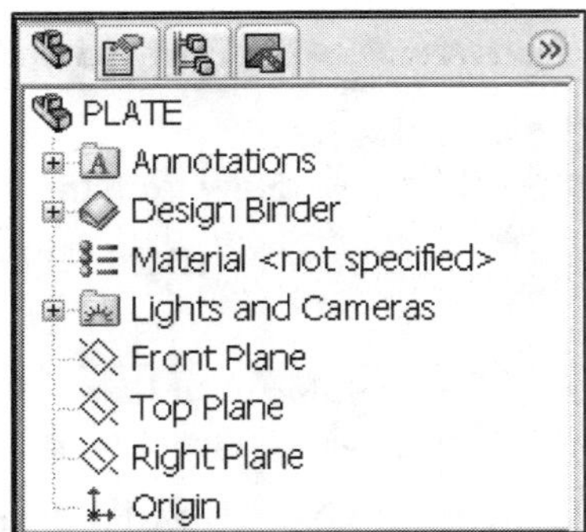

The Description field in the Save As dialog box corresponds to the Description field in the Bill of Materials. Utilize upper case.

Machined Part

As a designer, review your manufacturing options, before you design a part in SolidWorks. In earlier conversations with manufacturing, you decide to machine the parts.

Your material supplier stocks raw material in rod, sheet, plate, angle and block forms.

You select a standard plate form for the PLATE part, a standard rod form for the ROD part and a standard block form for the GUIDE part. A standard plate form will save time and money. To reduce cost, you utilize standard size holes and slot cuts. Square internal cuts are too costly to manufacture from machined stock.

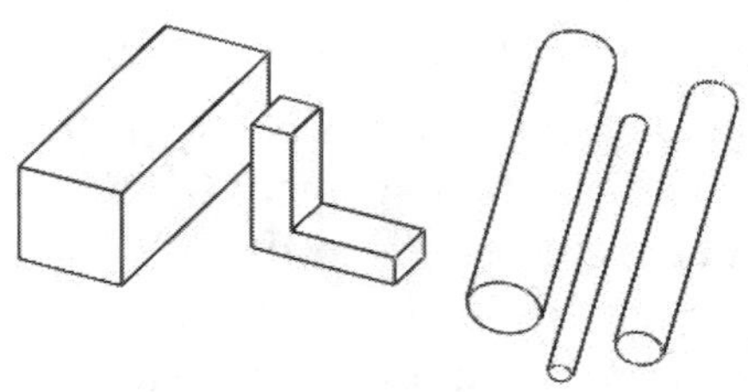

Block, Angle and Rod Stock

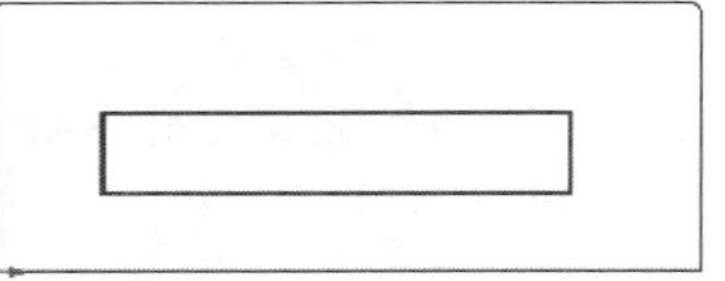

Internal Square Cut (expensive)

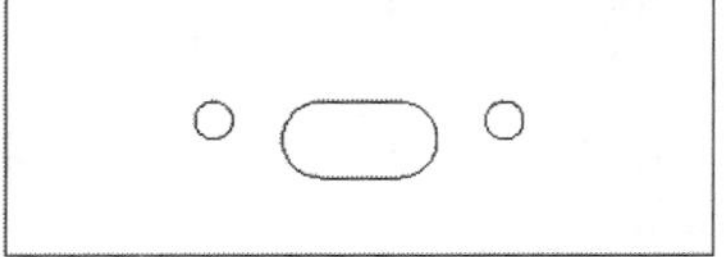

Holes and Slots (less expensive)

Machined parts require dimensions to determine the overall size and shape. Datum planes determine the location of referenced dimensions.

Understanding reference planes and views is important as you design machined parts. Before you create the PLATE, review the next topic on Reference Planes and Orthographic Projection.

Reference Planes and Orthographic Projection

The three default ⊥ reference planes represent infinite 2D planes in 3D space:

- Front.
- Top.
- Right.

Planes have no thickness or mass. Orthographic projection is the process of projecting views onto parallel planes with ⊥ projectors.

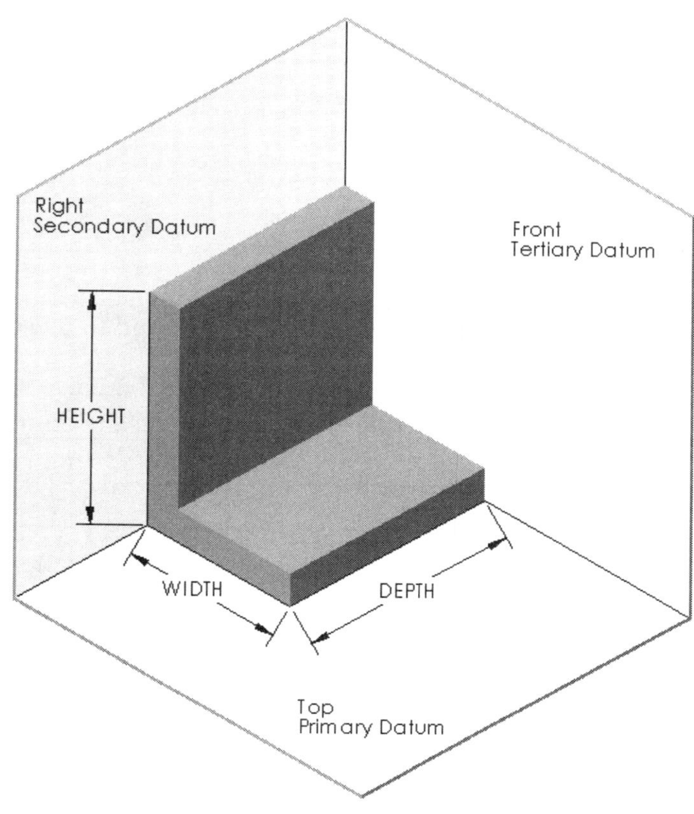

Default ⊥ datum Planes are:

- Primary.
- Secondary.
- Tertiary.

Use the following Planes in manufacturing:

- Primary datum Plane: Contacts the part at a minimum of three points.
- Secondary datum Plane: Contacts the part at a minimum of two points.
- Tertiary datum Plane: Contacts the part at a minimum of one point.

The part view orientation depends on the sketch plane. Compare the Front, Top and Right sketch planes for an L-shaped profile in the following figures:

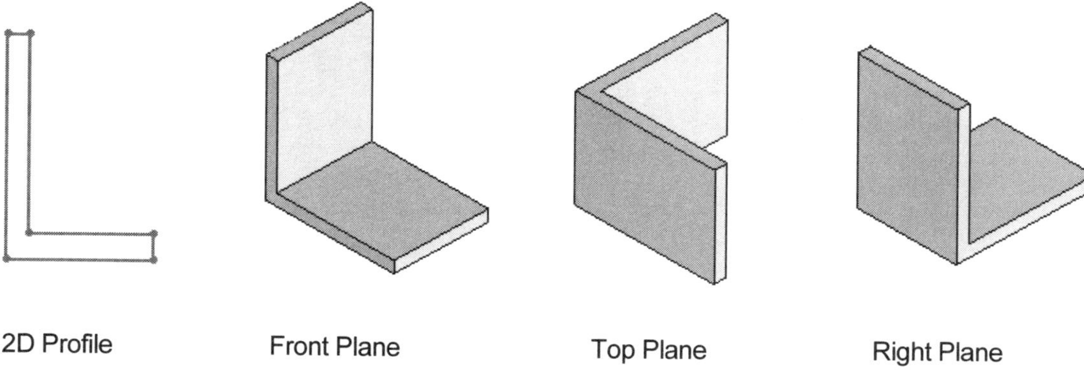

2D Profile | Front Plane | Top Plane | Right Plane

The six principle views of Orthographic projection listed in the ASME Y14.3M standard are:

- Top.
- Front.
- Right side.
- Bottom.
- Rear.
- Left side.

SolidWorks Standard view names correspond to these Orthographic projection view names.

ASME Y14.3M Principle View Name:	SolidWorks Standard View:
Front	Front
Top	Top
Right side	Right
Bottom	Bottom
Rear	Back
Left side	Left

The standard drawing views in third angle Orthographic projection are:

- Front.
- Top.
- Right.
- Isometric.

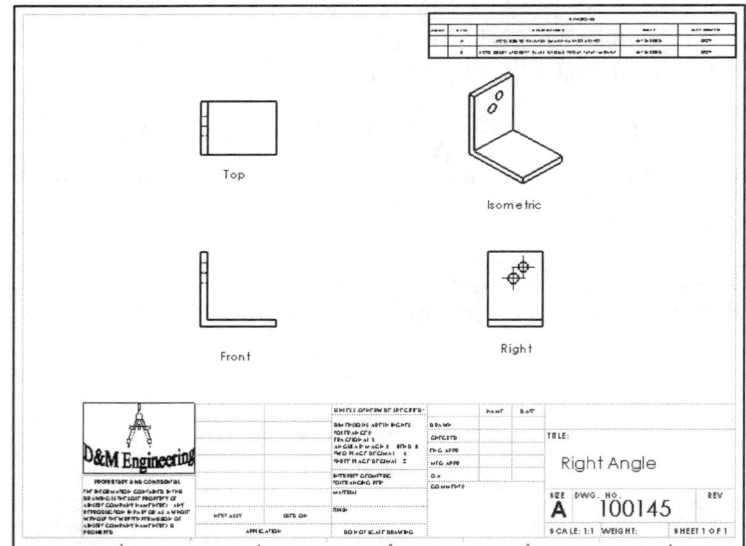

There are two Orthographic projection drawing systems. The first Orthographic projection system is called the third angle projection. The second Orthographic projection system is called the first angle projection. The systems are derived from positioning a 3D object in the third or first quadrant.

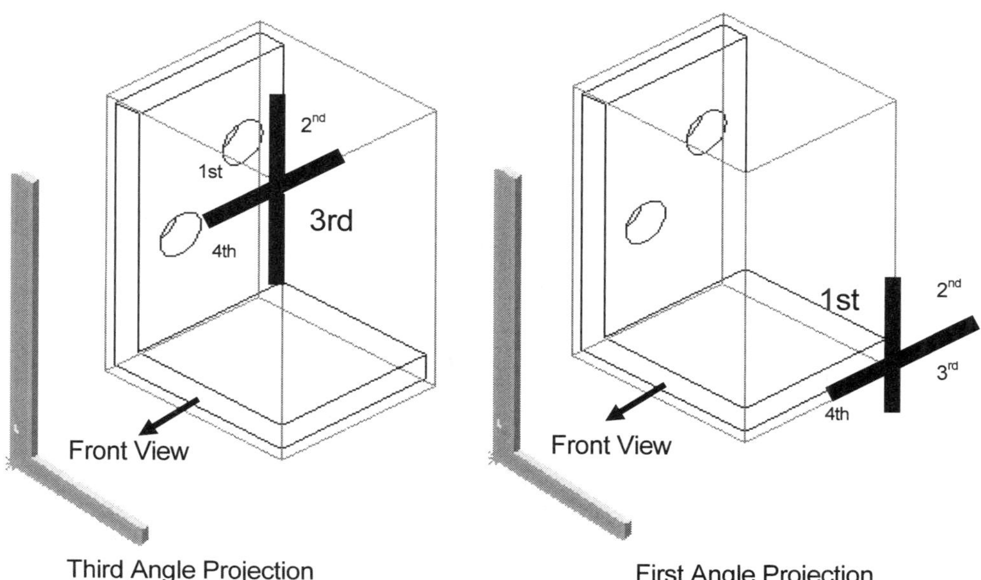

Third Angle Projection First Angle Projection

Third Angle Projection

The part is positioned in the third quadrant in third angle projection. The 2D projection planes are located between the viewer and the part. The projected views are placed on a drawing.

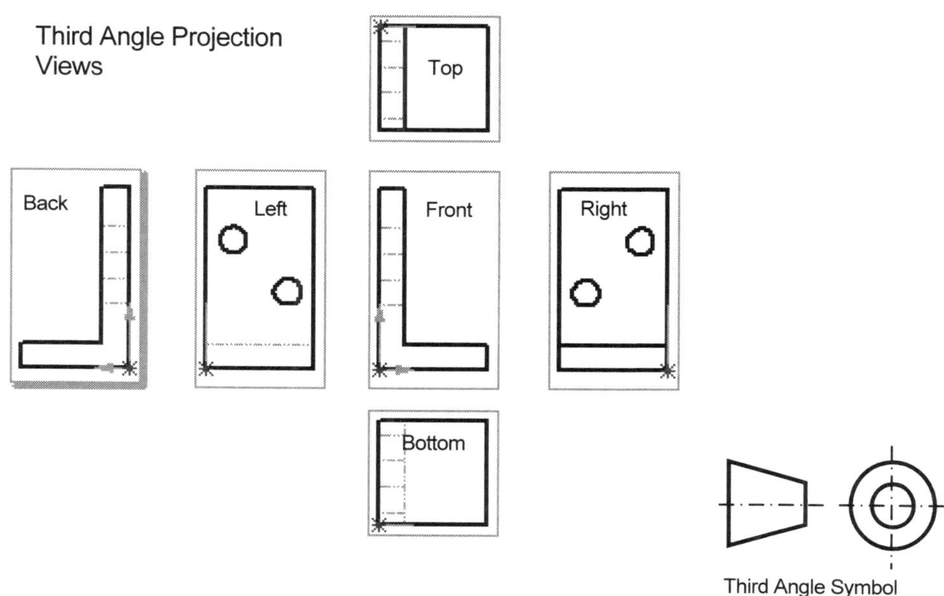

Third Angle Symbol

First Angle Projection

The part is positioned in the first quadrant in first angle projection. Views are projected onto the planes located behind the part. The projected views are placed on a drawing. First angle projection is primarily used in Europe and Asia.

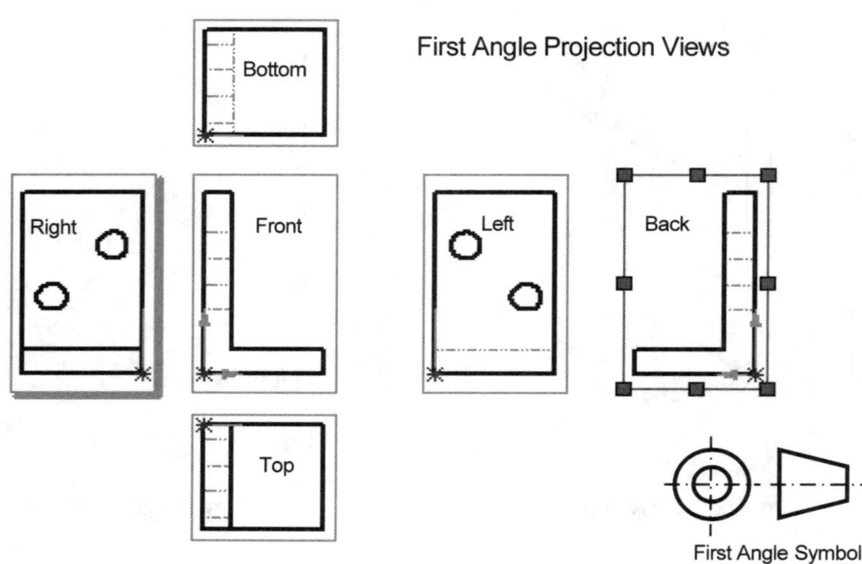

Third angle projection is primarily used in the U.S. & Canada and is based on the ASME Y14.3M Multi and Sectional View Drawings standard. Designers should have knowledge and understanding of both systems.

There are numerous multi-national companies. Example: A part is designed in the U.S., manufactured in Japan and destined for a European market.

Third angle projection is used in this text. A truncated cone symbol, appears on the drawing to indicate the projection system:

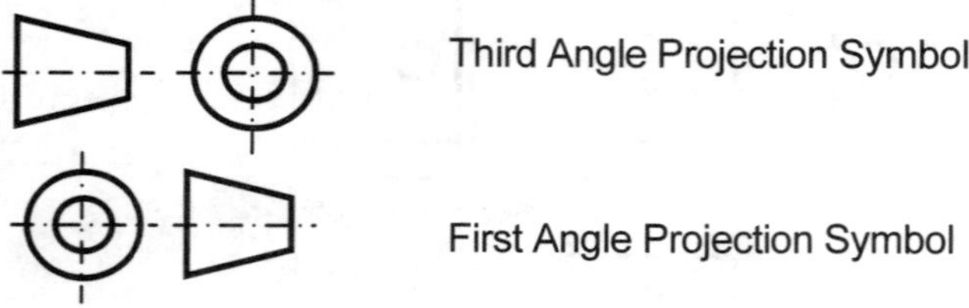

Utilize the Standard Views: Front, Back, Left, Right, Top, Bottom, Isometric, Trimetric, Dimetric, Normal To and View Orientation to orient the part.

Front
Back
Left
Right
Top
Bottom
Isometric
Trimetric
Dimetric
View Orientation

Before incorporating your design ideas into the Sketch plane, ask a question: How will the part be oriented in the assembly?

Answer: Orient or align the part to assist in the final assembly. Utilize the Front Plane to create the Extruded Base feature.

PLATE Part-Extruded Base Feature

An Extruded Base feature is a feature in SolidWorks that utilizes a sketched profile and extends the profile perpendicular (⊥) to the Sketch plane. The Base feature is the first feature that is created. Keep the Base feature simple!

How do you create a solid Extruded Base feature?

- Sketch a profile on a flat 2D plane.
- Extend the profile perpendicular (⊥) to the Sketch plane.
- The Extruded Base feature is the 3D block.

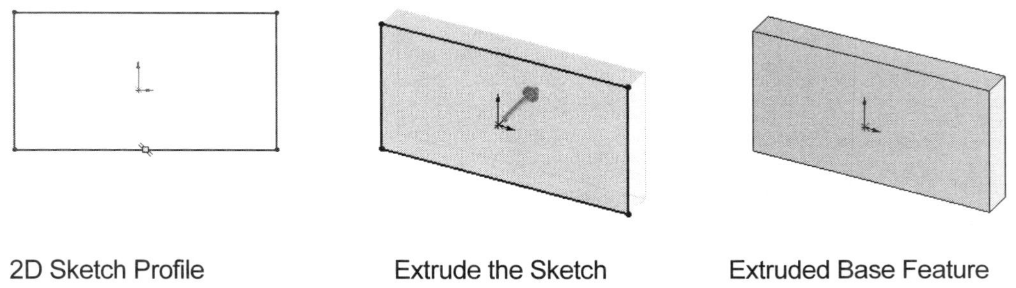

2D Sketch Profile — Extrude the Sketch — Extruded Base Feature

The Front Plane's imaginary boundary is represented on the screen with four visible edges. Planes are flat and infinite. Planes are used as the primary sketch surface for creating Base/Boss and Cut features. The Origin represents the intersection of the Front, Top and Right planes. The left corner point of the rectangle is coincident with the Origin.

In SolidWorks, the name used to describe a 2D profile is called a Sketch. A Sketch requires a Sketch plane and a 2D profile. The Sketch uses the Front Plane. The 2D profile is a rectangle. Geometric relationships and dimensions define the exact size of the rectangle. The rectangle is extruded perpendicular to the Sketch plane.

The Extruded Base feature utilizes the Depth option that corresponds to the thickness of the PLATE.

Activity: PLATE Part-Extruded Base Feature

Select the Sketch Plane.

64) Click the **Front Plane** from the FeatureManager.

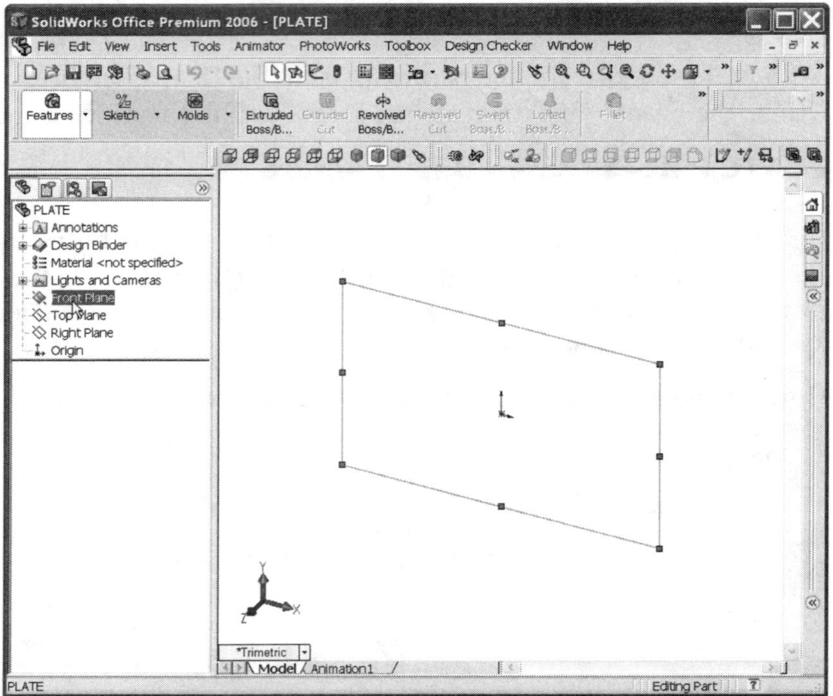

Insert a new Sketch.

65) Click **Sketch** Sketch from the Control Area. The Sketch toolbar is displayed in the CommandManager.

Sketch a Rectangle.

66) Click **Rectangle** Rectan... from the Sketch toolbar. The Sketch opens on the Front plane in the Front view. The mouse pointer displays the rectangle feedback symbol .

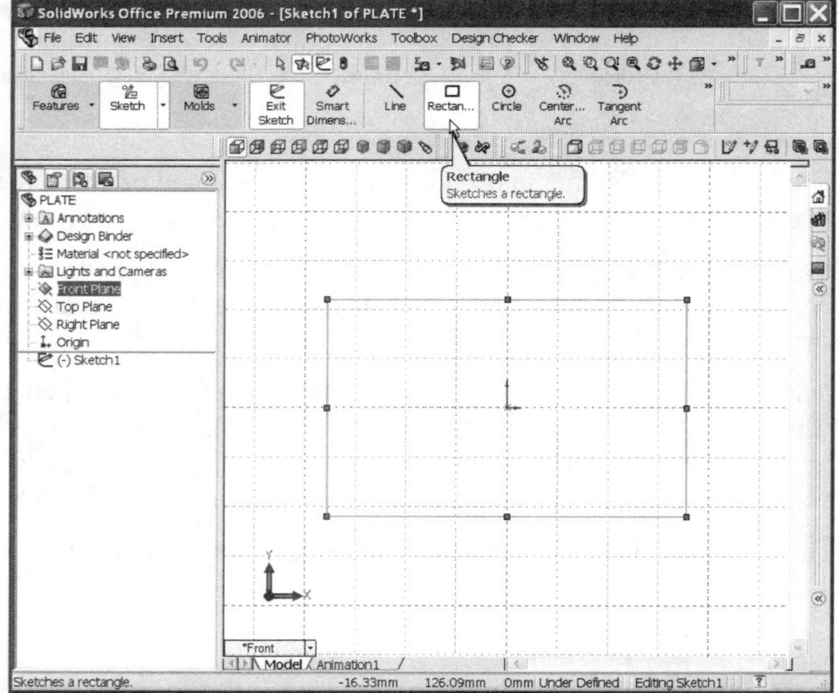

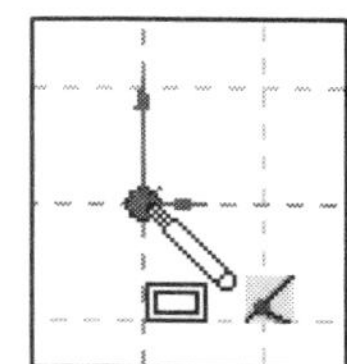

67) Click the **Origin**. This is the first point of the rectangle. The red dot feedback indicates the Origin point location. The mouse pointer displays the coincident to point feedback symbol.

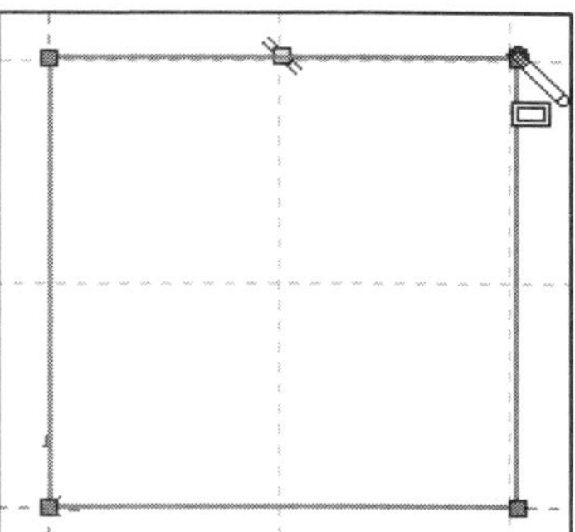

68) Drag the **mouse pointer** up and to the right.

69) Click a **position** to create the second point of the rectangle.

The rectangle sketch contains predefined geometric Sketch relations: two Horizontal relations and two Vertical relations. The first point of the rectangle contains a Coincident relation at the Origin. To control the Sketch relation display, click View, Sketch Relations from the Main menu.

If you make a mistake, select the UNDO

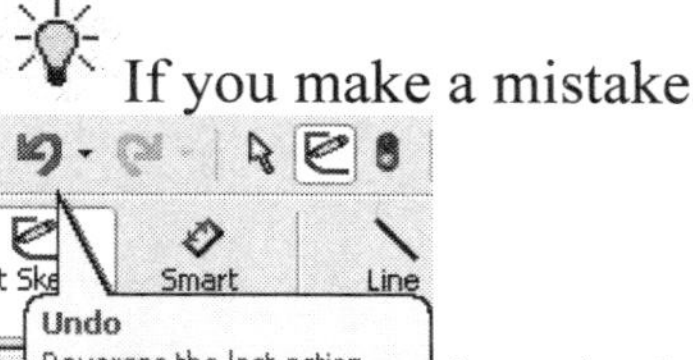

icon in the Standard toolbar.

The rectangle tool remains active until you select another tool or click the Select tool. The right mouse button contains additional tools.

Select sketch geometry.

70) Right-click a **position** in the Graphics window. The Shortcut menu is displayed.

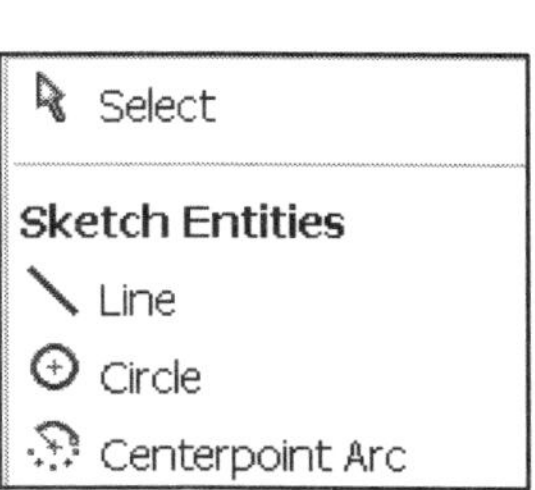

71) Click **Select** Select. The mouse pointer displays the Select icon and the Rectangle tool is deactivated.

Note: The phrase, "Right-click Select" Select from the Shortcut menu means right click the mouse in the Graphics window. Click Select.

Size the geometry of the rectangle.

72) Click and drag the **top horizontal line** of the rectangle upward. Release the **mouse button**.

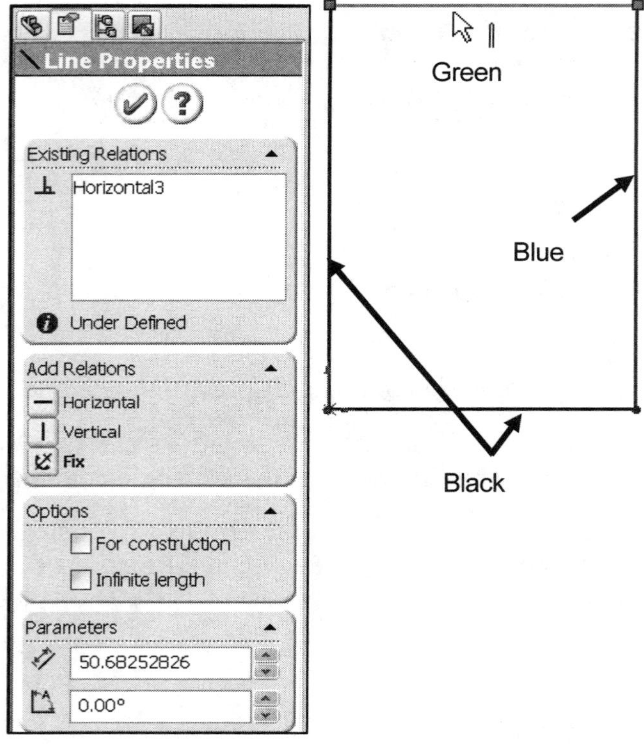

The Line Properties PropertyManager appears to the left of the Graphics window. The selected green line displays a Horizontal relation in the Existing Relations box.

SolidWorks colors aid in the sketching process. The rectangular sketch is displayed in three colors: green, blue and black. The geometry consists of four lines and four points.

The selected top horizontal line is displayed in green.

Selected geometry is displayed in green.

The right vertical line is displayed in blue.

The left vertical line and the bottom horizontal line are displayed in black.

Black sketches are fully defined with dimensions and geometric relationships. The black horizontal and vertical lines each contain a Coincident relation with the Origin.

Shortcut menus save time. Commands and tools vary depending on the mouse position in the SolidWorks window and the active Sketch tool.

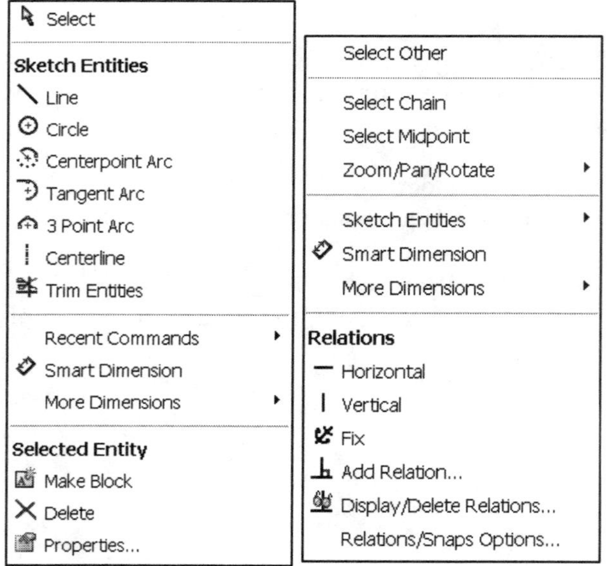

Add a dimension.

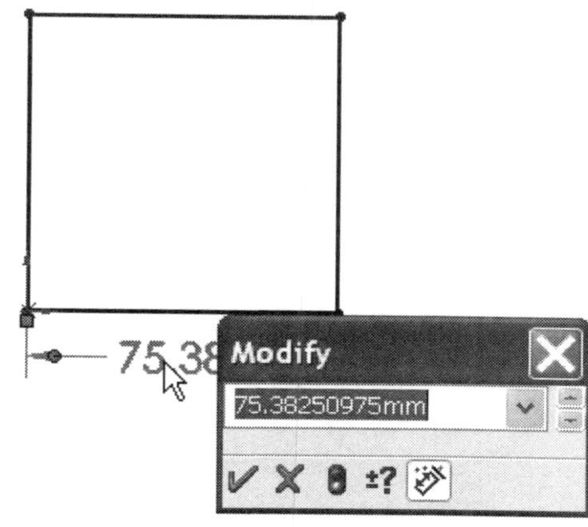

73) Click **Smart Dimension** Smart Dimens... from the Sketch toolbar. The pointer displays the dimension feedback symbol, .

Right-click Smart Dimension from the Pop up menu.

Dimension the bottom horizontal line.

74) Click the **bottom horizontal line** of the rectangle. A dimension value appears.

75) Click a **position** below the bottom horizontal line. The Modify dialog box appears.

76) Enter **56** in the Modify text box.

77) Click the **Green Check mark** in the Modify dialog box. Note: You can either press the enter key or click the Green Check mark to accept the dimension value.

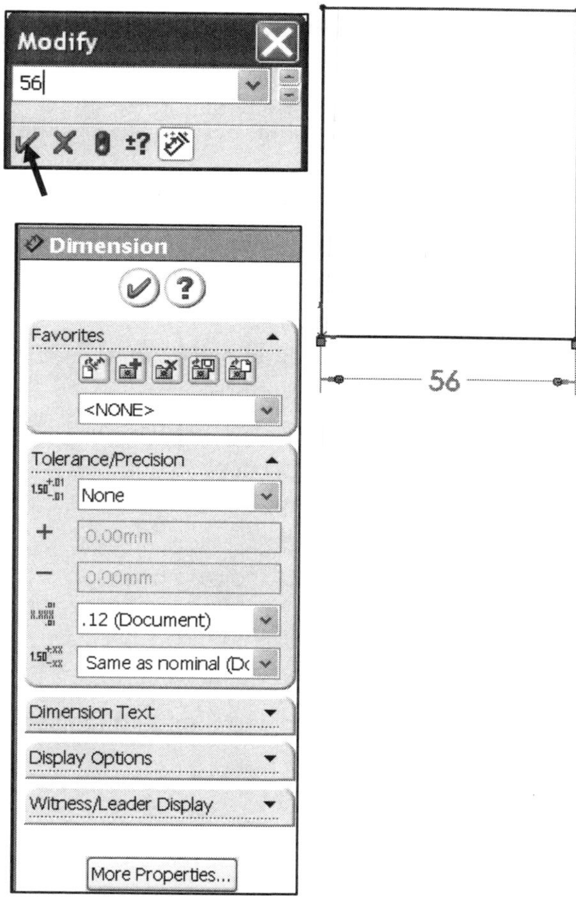

The Dimension PropertyManager is displayed when a dimension is selected. Change Dimension properties such as Tolerance/Precision, Font and Text in the Dimension PropertyManager.

Dimension the vertical line.

78) Click the **left most vertical line**.

79) Click a **position** to the left of the vertical line.

80) Enter **22**.

81) Click the **Green Check mark** ✔ in the Modify dialog box. The Sketch is fully defined. All lines and vertices are displayed in black.

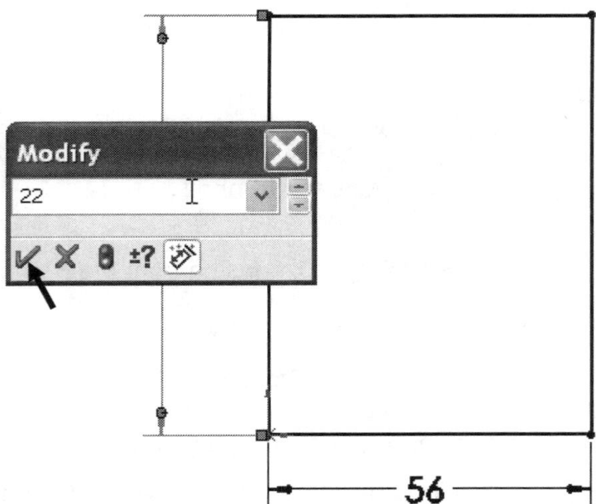

Select the dimension value.

82) Right-click **Select** Select from the Shortcut menu.

83) Position the **mouse pointer** over the dimension text. The pointer changes to a linear dimension symbol, with a displayed text box. D2 represents the second linear dimension created in Sketch1.

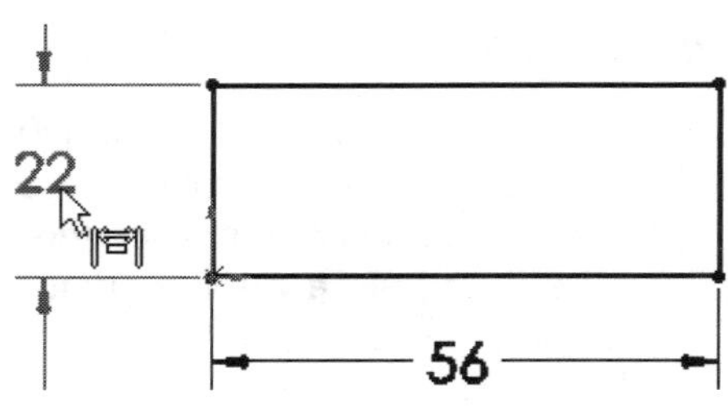

Modify the dimension text.

84) Double-click the **22** dimension text.

85) Click the **Spin Box Arrows** to increase or decrease dimensional values. Note: The default spin box increment is 2.5mm.

86) Enter **42** in the Modify dialog box.

87) Click the **Green Check mark** ✔

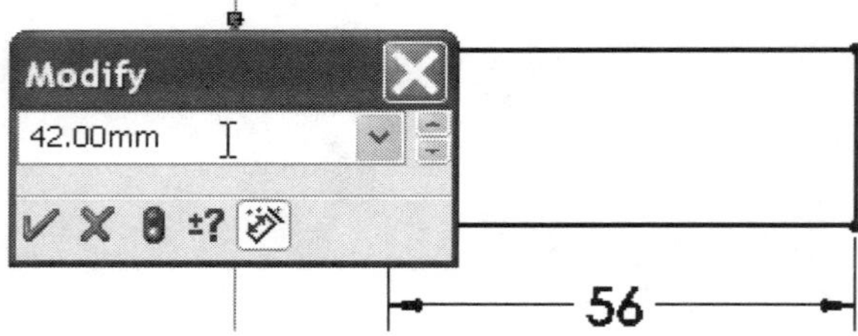

Return to the original vertical dimension.

88) Click **Undo** from the Standard toolbar.

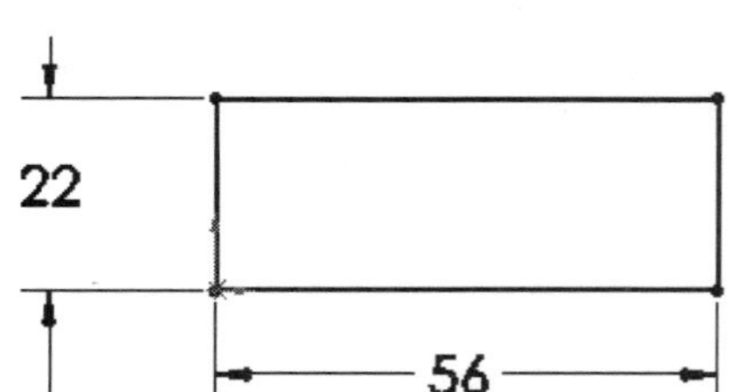

Options in the Modify dialog box:

- Green Check mark ✔, saves the current value and exits the Modify dialog box.
- Restore ✖, restores the original value and exits.
- Rebuild, rebuilds the model with the current value.
- Reset ±?, modifies the spin box increment.
- Mark for Drawing, set by default inserts part dimensions into the drawing.

Note: Undo from the Standard toolbar reverses changes to the sketch.

The System displays Fully Defined in the Status bar located in the lower right corner of the Graphics window. In a fully defined Sketch, entities are displayed in black. All entities are defined through position, dimensions or geometric relationships.

In an Under Defined Sketch, the entities that require position, dimensions or geometric relations are displayed in blue.

In an Over Defined Sketch, there is geometry conflict with the dimensions and or relationships. In an over defined Sketch, entities are displayed in red.

Although dimensions are not required to create features in SolidWorks, dimensions provide location and size information. Dimension the rectangle with horizontal and vertical dimensions.

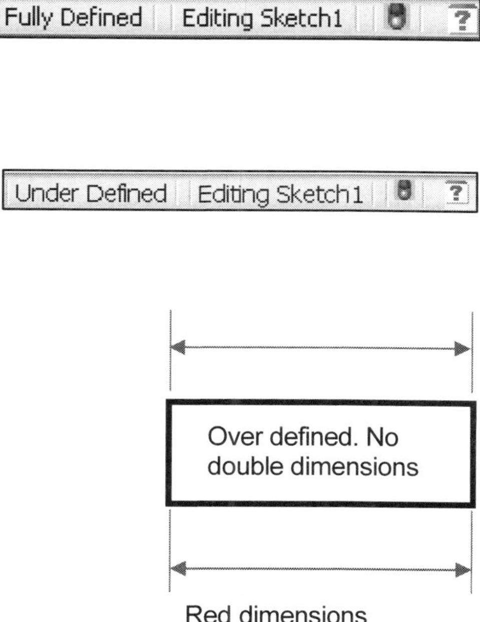

Insert an Extruded Base feature.

89) Click **Features** Features from the Control Area.

90) Click **Extruded Boss/Base** Extruded Boss/B... from the Features toolbar in the CommandManager. The Extrude PropertyManager is displayed on the left side of the Graphics window. The extruded Sketch is previewed in a Trimetric view. The preview displays the direction of the feature creation.

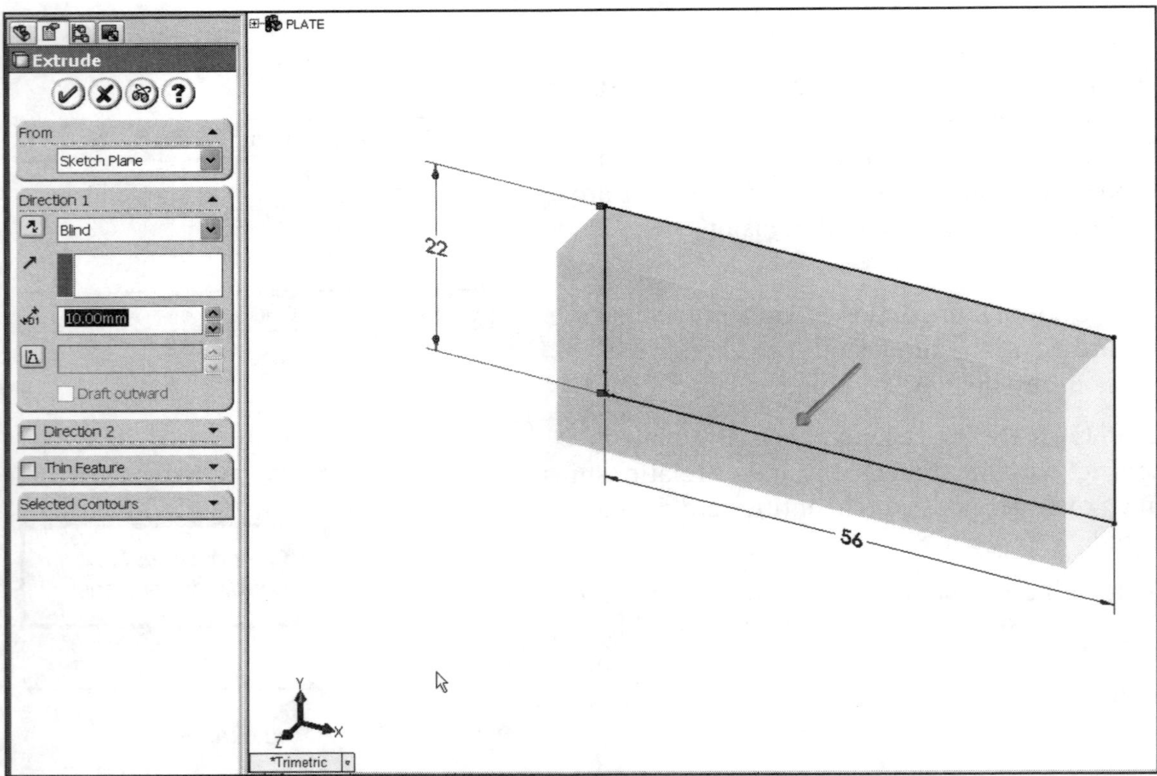

Reverse the direction of the extruded depth.

91) Click **Reverse Direction** . Blind is the default depth End Condition.

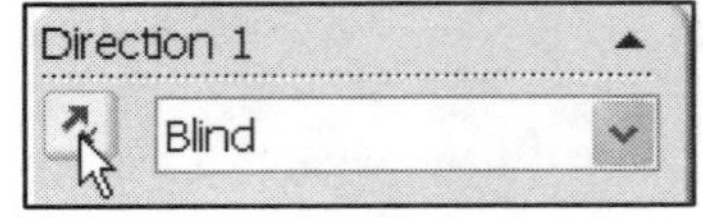

92) Click and drag the **Handle** in the extrusion direction and review the mouse pointer feedback for depth. The depth of the extrusion increases respectively with the depth spin box value. The feature expands towards the back. The Origin is displayed in the lower left corner.

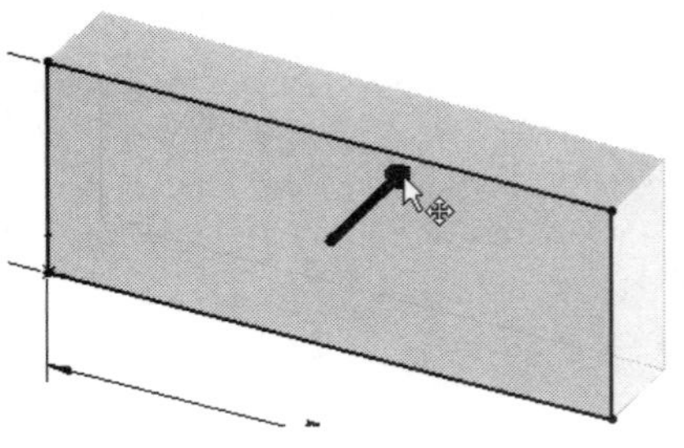

93) Enter **10** in the Depth spin box.

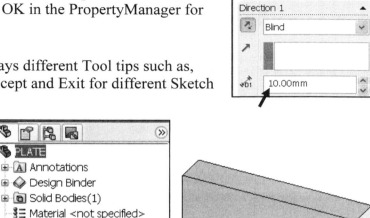

94) Click **OK** from the Extrude PropertyManager.

Note: The OK button accepts and completes the Feature process. The Tool tip displays OK in the PropertyManager for Feature tools.

The OK button also displays different Tool tips such as, Apply, Close Dialog, Close Accept and Exit for different Sketch tools.

The Extrude1 feature is displayed in the Graphics window. The name Extrude1 is listed in the PLATE FeatureManager.

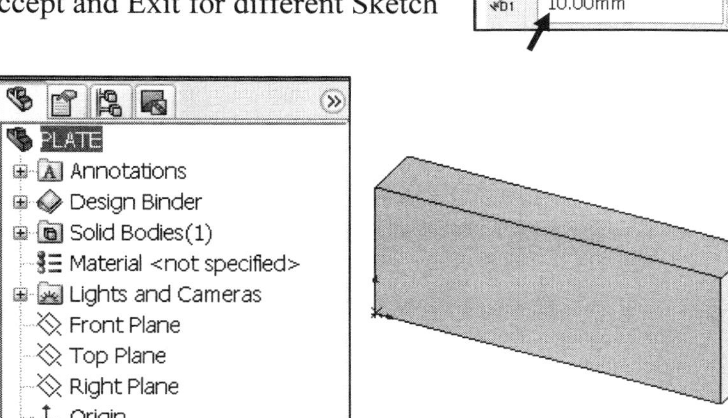

If you exit the Sketch before selecting Extruded Boss/Base from the Features toolbar, Sketch1 is displayed in the FeatureManager. To create the Extruded Base, click Sketch1 from the FeatureManager.

Click Extruded Boss/Base Extruded Boss/B... to create the feature.

PLATE Part-Modify Dimensions and Rename

Incorporate design changes into the PLATE. Modify dimension values in the Modify dialog box. Utilize Rebuild to update the Base Extrude feature.

The FeatureManager contains the entry, Extrude1. Expand Extrude1 to display the entry, Sketch1. The Plus Sign icon indicates that additional feature information is available. Rename entries by selecting on the text in the FeatureManager.

Activity: PLATE Part-Modify Dimensions and Rename

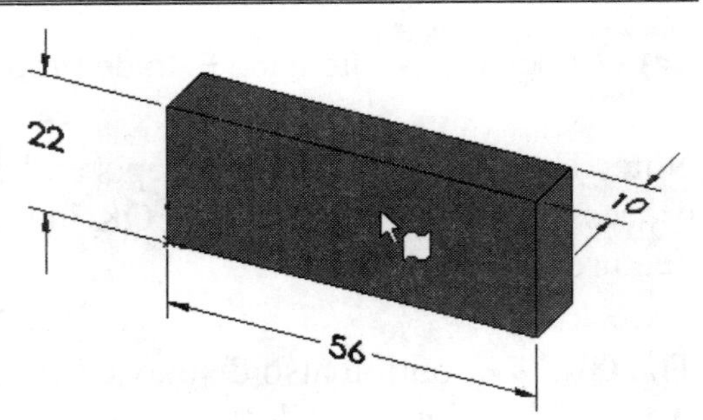

Modify the PLATE.

95) Double-click on the **Extrude1** front face in the Graphics window.

Fit the Model to the screen.

96) Press the **f** key.

Modify the width dimension.

97) Double-click **10**. The Dimension PropertyManager is displayed.

98) Enter **5** in the Modify dialog box.

99) Click **Rebuild** in the Modify dialog box.

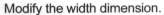

100) Click the **Green Check mark** ✔ in the Modify dialog box.

101) Click **OK** from the Dimension PropertyManager.

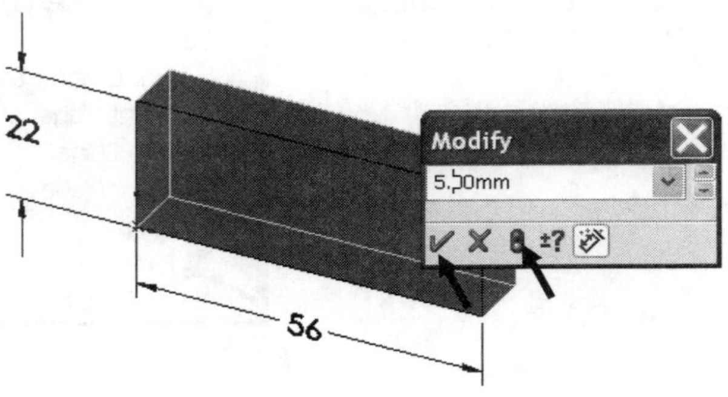

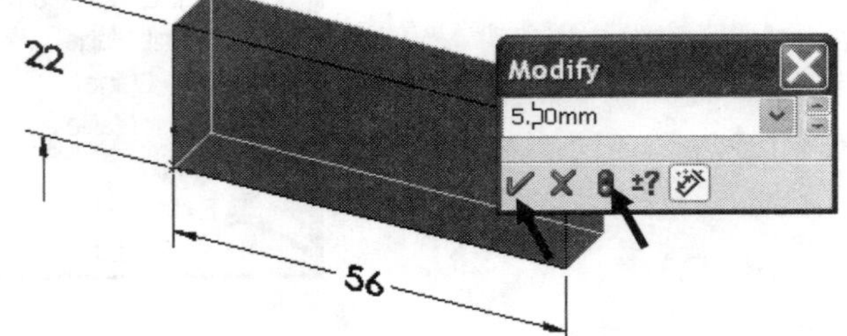

If you exit the Modify dialog box without selecting Rebuild, click Rebuild from the Standard toolbar to update the part.

Expand the Extrude1 entry.

102) Click **Plus Sign** of the Extrude1 entry in the FeatureManager.

Rename Sketch1.

103) Click **Sketch1** in the FeatureManager. Click a **position** inside the **Sketch1** text.

104) Enter **Sketch-Base** for the sketch name. The Minus Sign icon indicates that the feature information is expanded.

105) Click **Minus Sign** to collapse the Extrude1 feature.

Rename Extrude1.

106) Click **Extrude1** in the FeatureManager.

107) Enter **Base-Extrude** for the feature name.

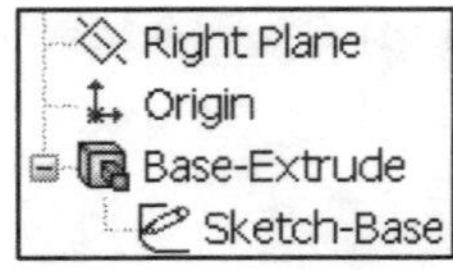

Save the PLATE.

108) Click **Save**.

Additional details on Rectangle, Dimension and Extrude feature are available in the SolidWorks Help Topics, SolidWorks Online Users Guide. Index keyword: Rectangle. Dimensions, Modify, Extrude (Boss/Base) and Sketch (Color).

Display Modes, View Modes and Viewport

The Display modes specify various model appearances in the Graphics window. The View modes manipulate the model in the Graphics window.

The Viewport provides an alterative to the Standard Views toolbar and provides a multi-view Graphics window option.

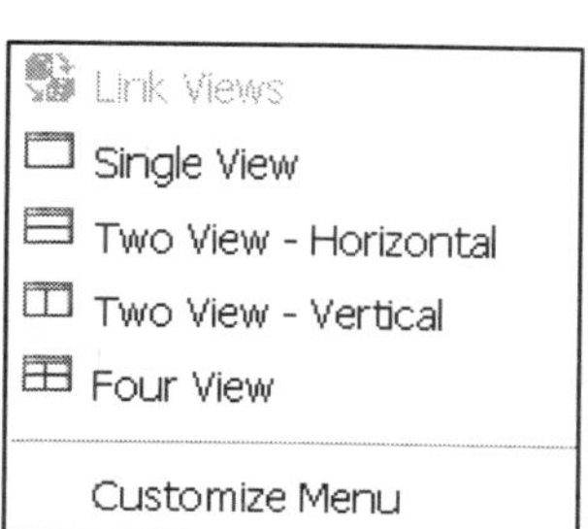

Activity: Display Modes, View Modes and Viewport

View the Display modes:

109) Click **Wireframe**.

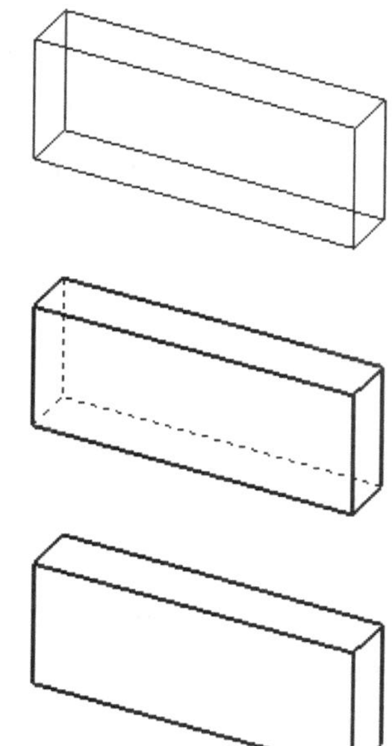

110) Click **Hidden Lines Visible**.

111) Click **Hidden Lines Removed**.

112) Click **Shaded with Edges**.

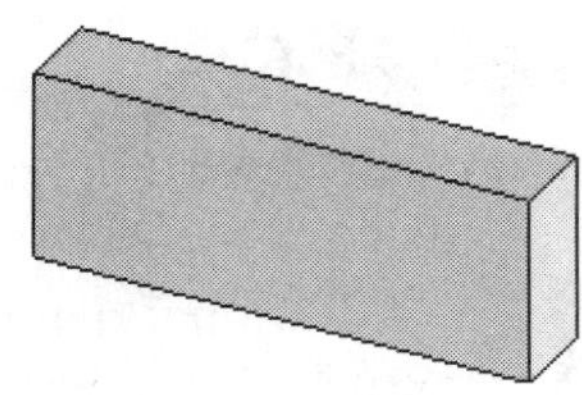

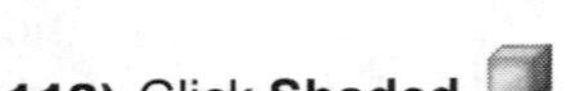

113) Click **Shaded**.

114) Click **Shadows in Shaded Mode**.

Display modes and View modes remain active until deactivated from the View toolbar or deactivated from the Shortcut menu.

Display the View modes.

115) Click **Previous View** to display the previous view of the part in the current window.

116) Click **Zoom to Fit** to display the full size of the part in the current window.

117) Click **Zoom to Area**.

118) Select two **opposite corners** of a rectangle to define the boundary of the view. The defined view fits to the current window.

119) Click **Zoom In/Out**.

120) Drag upward to **zoom in**.

121) Drag downward to **zoom out**.

122) Press the **z** key to zoom out.

123) Press the **Shift z** key to zoom in.

124) Right-click **Select** Select from the Shortcut menu.

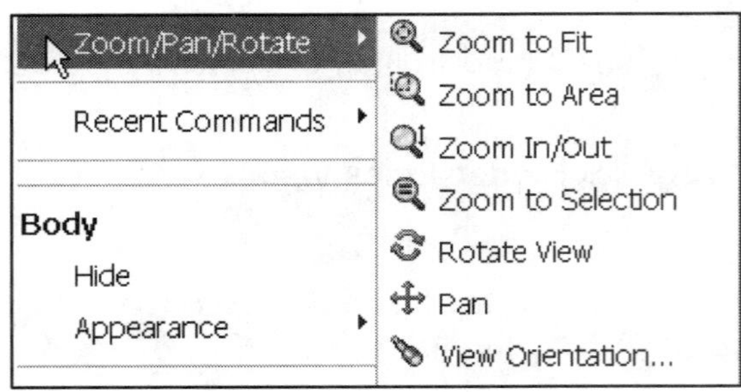

125) Click the **front edge** of Base-Extrude.

126) Click **Zoom to Selection**. The selected geometry fills the current window.

127) Click **Rotate**. Drag the **mouse pointer** to rotate about the screen center.

128) Use the computer keyboard **arrow keys** to rotate in 15-degree increments.

129) Click **Pan** ✥.

130) Drag the **mouse pointer** up, down, left, or right. The model scrolls in the direction of the mouse.

131) Right-click in the **Graphics window** area to display the zoom options.

132) Click **Zoom to Fit** .

Return to the standard Isometric view.

133) Click **Isometric view** from the Standard Views toolbar.

The "f" key is the Shortcut key for Zoom to Fit.

Display the Viewport options from the Graphics window.

134) Click the **View** *Front icon in the lower left corner of the Graphics window. The Viewport displays the current orientation.

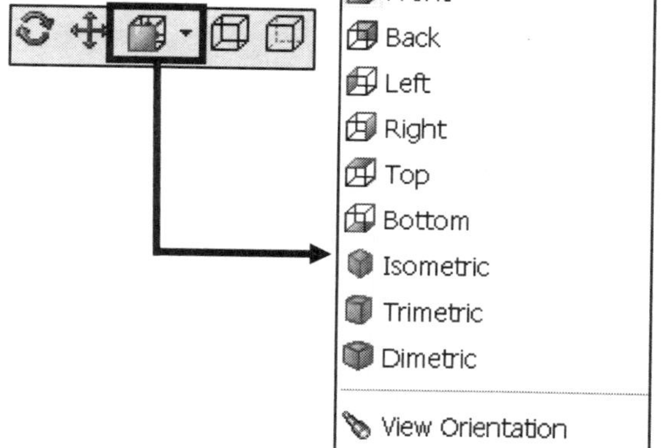

Fasteners

Screws, bolts and fasteners are used to join parts together. Use standard available fasteners whenever possible. Using standard available fasteners will decrease product cost and reduce component purchase lead times.

The American National Standard Institute (ANSI) and the International Standardization Organization (ISO) provide standards on various hardware components. The SolidWorks Library contains a variety of standard fasteners.

Below are a few general selection and design guidelines utilized in this text:

- Use standard industry fasteners where applicable.
- Reuse the same fastener types where applicable. Dissimilar screws and bolts require different tools for assembly, additional part numbers and increase inventory storage and cost.
- Decide on the fastener type before creating holes. Dissimilar fastener types require different geometry.
- Create notes on all fasteners. Notes will assist in the development of a Parts list and Bill of Materials.

- Use caution when positioning holes. Do not position holes too close to an edge. Stay one radius head width at a minimum from an edge or between holes. Review manufacturer's recommended specifications.
- Design for service support. Insure that the model can be serviced in the field and or on the production floor.

Use standard M4x8 Socket head cap screws in this exercise.

- M4 represents a metric screw.
- 4mm represents the major outside diameter.
- 8mm represents the overall length of the thread.

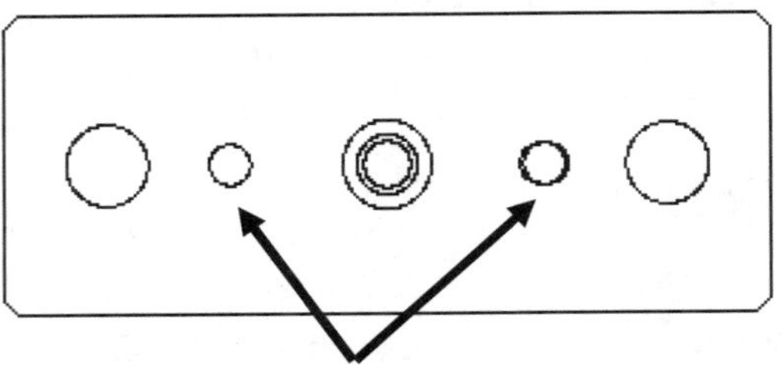

Determine the dimensions for the mounting holes from the drawing of the GUIDE CYLINDER assembly.

The customer attaches the PLATE to the GUIDE CYLINDER assembly with the two M4 Socket head cap screws.

View Orientation

The View Orientation tool defines the preset position of the model in the Graphics window.

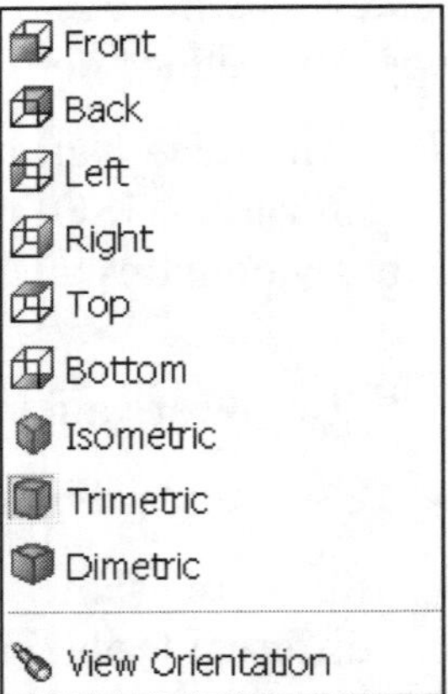

The Standard Views contain eleven view options: Front, Back, Left, Right, Top, Bottom, Isometric, Trimetric, Dimetric, Normal To and View Orientation.

The Isometric view displays the part in 3D with two equal projection angles.

The Normal To view displays the part perpendicular, $\perp$ to the selected plane.

The View Orientation tool also creates and displays custom named views.

To access View Orientation tools, utilize the View toolbar, Standard Views toolbar, lower left corner of the Graphics window or Space Bar key.

PLATE Part-Extruded Cut Feature

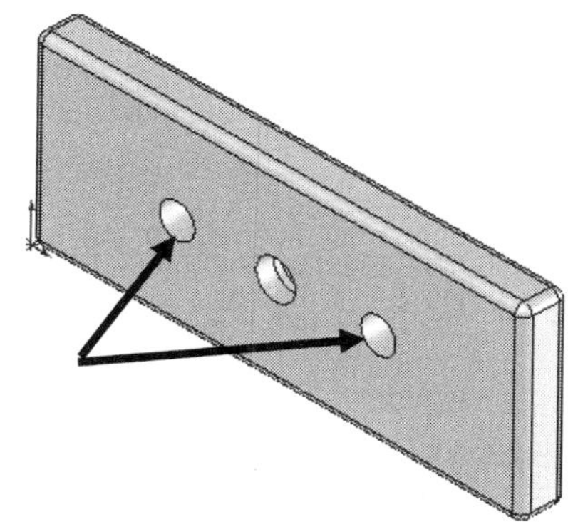

An Extruded Cut feature removes material, perpendicular, ⊥ to the Sketch for a specified depth. The Through All end condition option creates the holes through the entire PLATE depth.

Utilize the Circle Sketch tool to create the hole profile on the front face. The first circle is defined with a center point and a point on its circumference. The second circle utilizes the Ctrl-C (Copy) key to create a copy of the first circle.

Geometric relations are constraints between one or more entities. The holes may appear aligned and equal, but they are not! Add two relations: Insert an Equal relation between the two circumferences and a Horizontal relation between the two center points.

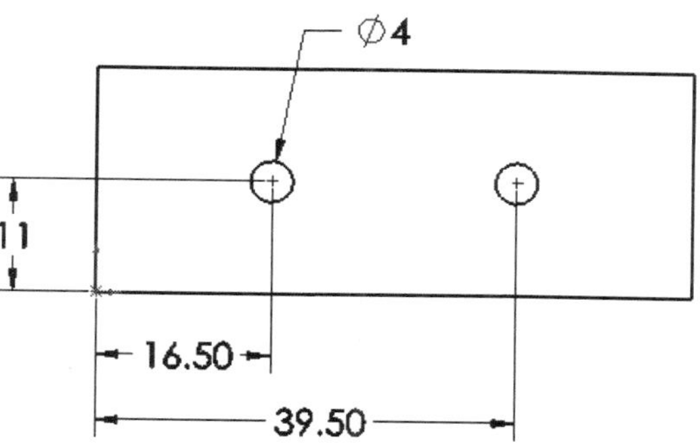

The machinist references all dimensions from the reference datum planes to produce the PLATE holes. Reference all three linear dimensions from the Right datum plane (left vertical edge) and the Top datum plane (bottom horizontal edge). Utilize a dimension to define the diameter of the circle.

The linear dimensions are positioned to the left and below the Base-Extrude feature. You will learn more about dimensioning to a drawing standard in Project 3.

Position the dimensions off the sketch profile. Place smaller dimensions to the inside. These dimensioning techniques in the part sketch will save time in dimensioning the drawing.

How a sketch or feature changes with modifications is called design intent. Dimension schemes vary depending on the design intent of the part. There are alternate dimensions schemes to define the position of the two circles.

The following two examples are left as a project exercise.

Example A: The center points of the holes reference a horizontal centerline created at the Midpoint of the two vertical lines. A dimension is inserted between the two center points.

Example B: The center points of the circles reference the horizontal line. Insert a vertical line at the Midpoint of the two horizontal lines. The center points of the circles utilize a Symmetric relation with the vertical centerline.

Dimension schemes defined in the part can also be redefined in the future drawing.

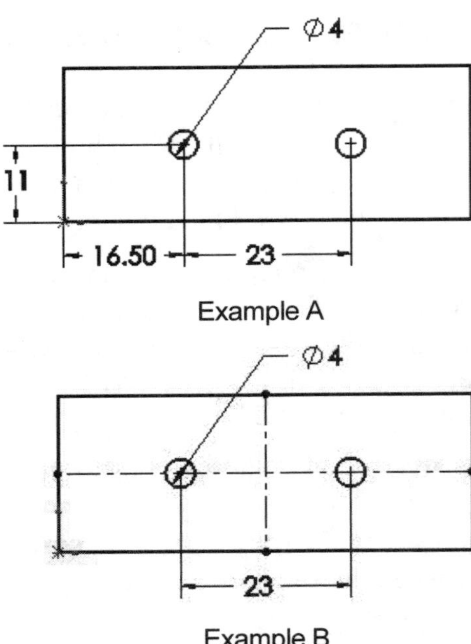

Example A

Example B

Activity: PLATE Part-Extruded Cut Feature

View the mouse pointer feedback.

135) Position the mouse pointer on the **front face**. View the Select Face icon. The mouse pointer provides various icons depending on the selected geometry.

136) Position the mouse pointer on the **right edge**. View the Select Line icon.

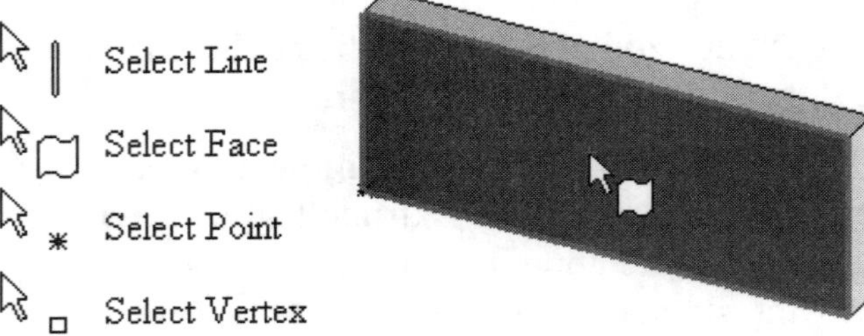

Select a Sketch plane for the holes.

137) Click the **front face** of the Base-Extrude feature for the Sketch plane. The face is displayed in green.

Insert a Sketch.

138) Click **Sketch** Sketch from the Sketch toolbar.

Display the Front view.

139) Click **Front view** from the Standard Views toolbar or Select Front view from the left corner of the Graphics window. The Origin is located in the lower left corner.

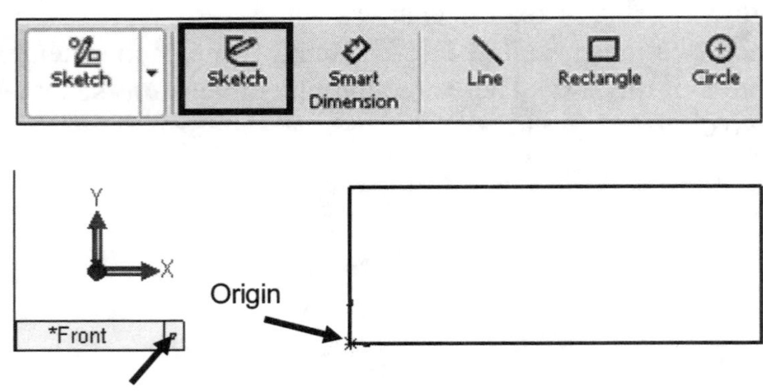

140) Click **Hidden Lines Visible**.

Sketch the first circle.

141) Click **Circle** from the Sketch toolbar. The cursor displays the Circle feedback symbol. The Circle PropertyManager is displayed.

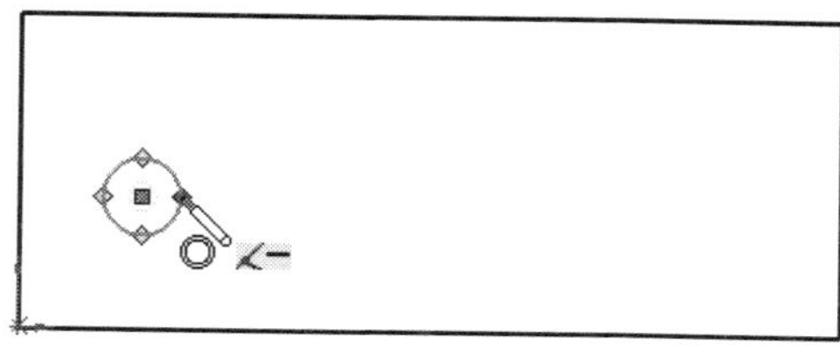

142) Click a **center point** on the front face diagonally to the right of the Origin.

143) Click a **position** to the right of the center point.

The circle is displayed in green. The circumference and the center point are currently selected.

Copy the first circle.

144) Right-click **Select**.

145) Hold the **Ctrl** key down.

146) Click and drag the **circumference** of the first circle to the right. The Circle icon is displayed on the mouse pointer.

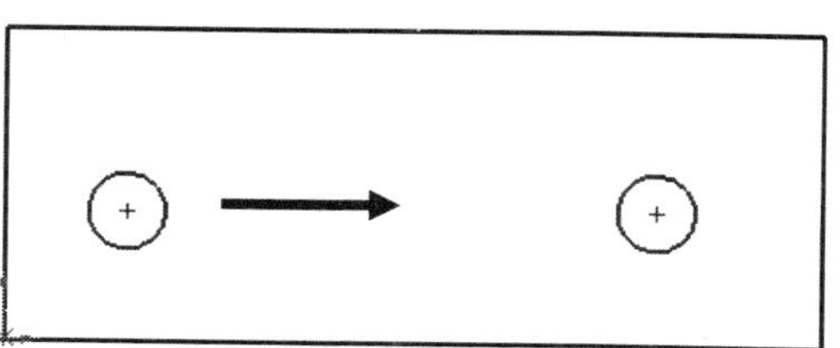

147) Release the **mouse button**.

148) Release the **Ctrl** key. The second circle is displayed in green.

149) Click a position in the **Graphics window**, off the sketch. The first and second circle is displayed in blue.

Add an Equal Relation.

150) Click the **first circle circumference**.

151) Hold the **Ctrl** key down.

152) Click the **second circle circumference**. Both selected circles are displayed in green.

153) Release the **Ctrl** key. Arc1 and Arc2 are displayed in the Selected Entities text box in the Properties PropertyManager.

154) Click **Equal** from the Add Relations box. The Equal radius/length is displayed in the Existing Relations text box.

155) Click **OK** from the Properties PropertyManager.

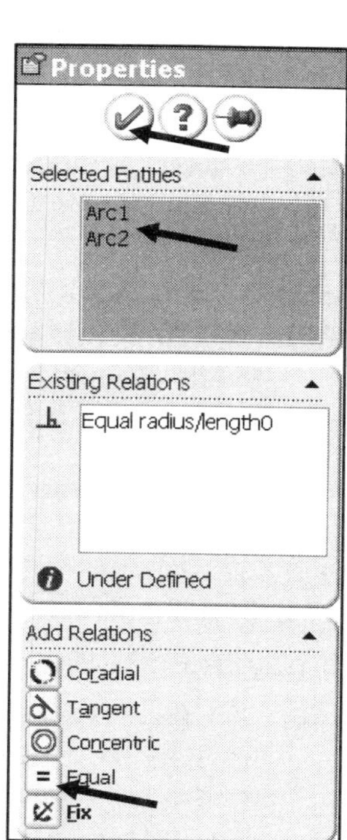

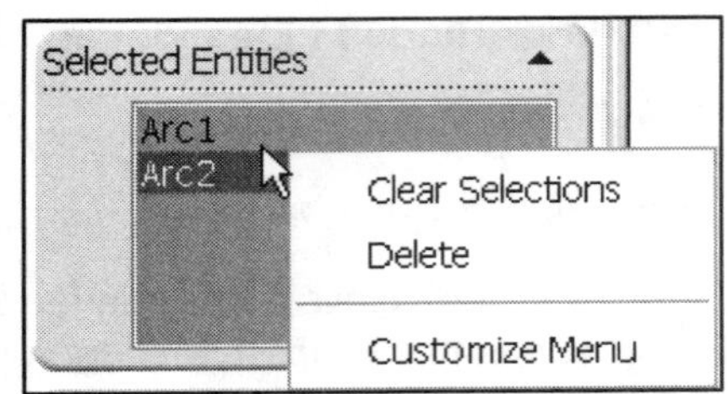

The SolidWorks default name for curve entities is Arc#. There is an Arc# for each circle. The default name for any point is Point#. The two center points are entities named Point2 and Point4.

To remove unwanted entities from the Selected Entities box, right-click in the Selected Entities window. Click Clear Selections.

The Selected Entities # differs if geometry was deleted and recreated. The Existing Relations box lists Equal radius/length0.

Add a Horizontal Relation.

156) Click the first circle **center point**.

157) Hold the **Ctrl** key down.

158) Click the second circle **center point**.

159) Release the **Ctrl** key.

160) Click **Horizontal** from the Add Relations box.

161) Click **OK**  from the Properties PropertyManager.

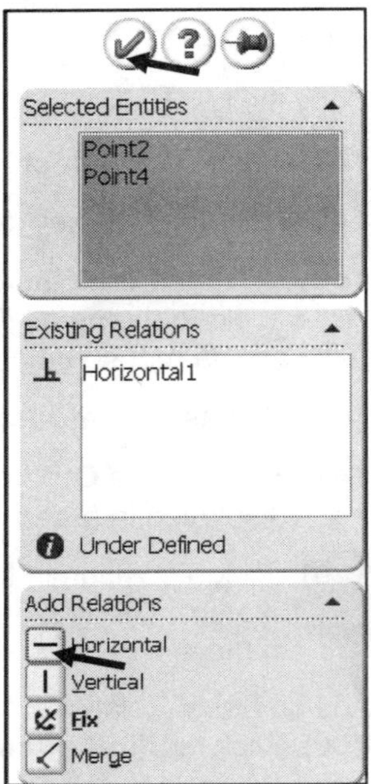

 Apply geometry relations quickly. Click inside the Graphics window to apply the geometric relation and to close the Properties PropertyManager. Clicking inside the Graphics window replaces the step, Click OK .

Add a dimension.

162) Click **Smart Dimension** Smart Dimens... from the Sketch toolbar.

163) Click the **circumference** of the first circle.

164) Click a **position** diagonally upward.

165) Enter **4**.

166) Click the **Green Check mark** ✔.

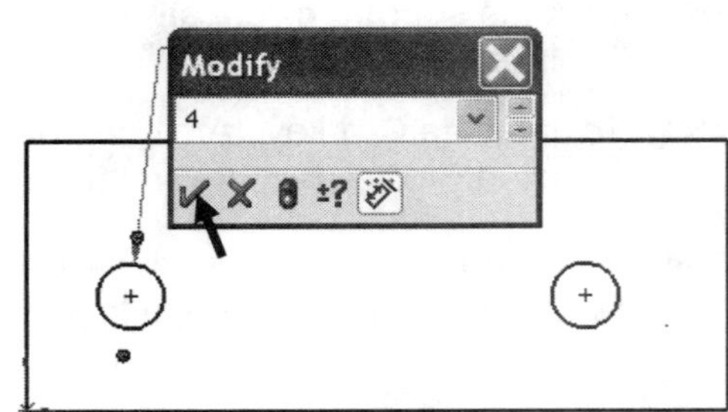

Add a vertical dimension.

167) Click the **bottom horizontal** line of the Base-Extrude feature.

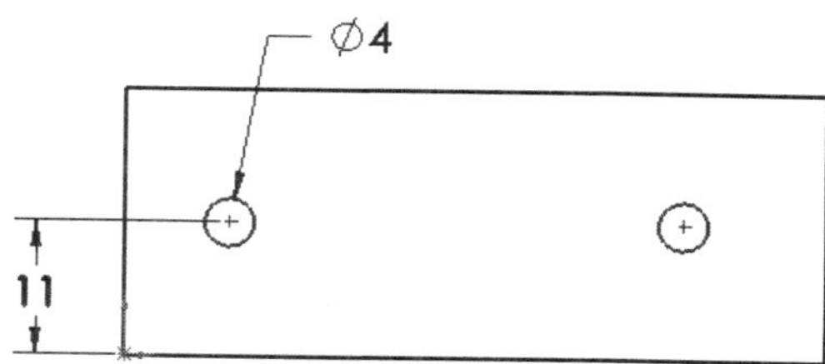

168) Click the **center point** of the first circle.

169) Click a **position** to the left of the profile.

170) Enter **11**.

171) Click the **Green Check mark** ✔.

Add a horizontal dimension.

172) Click the **left vertical** line of the Base-Extrude feature.

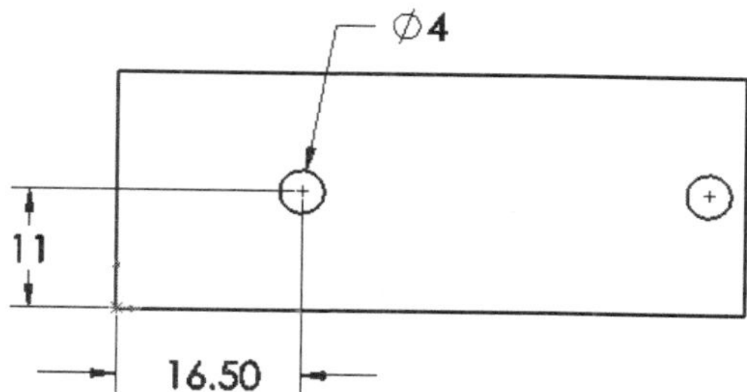

173) Click the **center point** of the first circle.

174) Click a **position** below the profile.

175) Enter **16.5**.

176) Click the **Green Check mark** ✔.

Add a second horizontal dimension.

177) Click the **left vertical** line of the Base-Extrude feature.

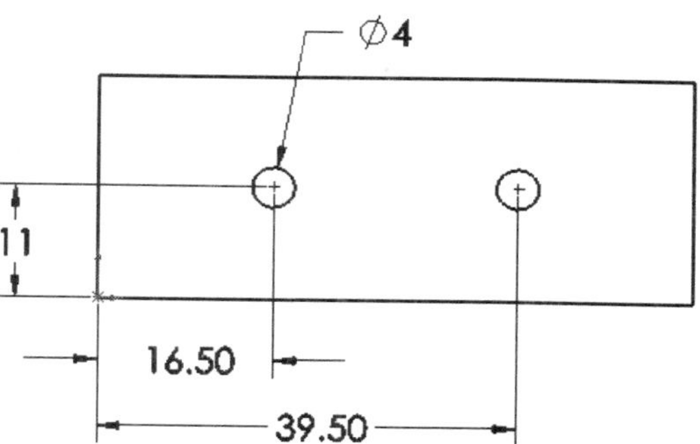

178) Click the **center point** of the second circle.

179) Click a **position** below 16.50.

180) Enter **39.5**.

181) Click the **Green Check mark** ✔.

Fit the Model to the Graphics window.

182) Press the **f** key.

The Dimensioning Standard preference is to place arrows to the inside of the extension lines. Select the arrowhead green dots to alternate the arrowhead position.

Flip the dimension arrows to the inside.

183) Click the **16.50** dimension text.

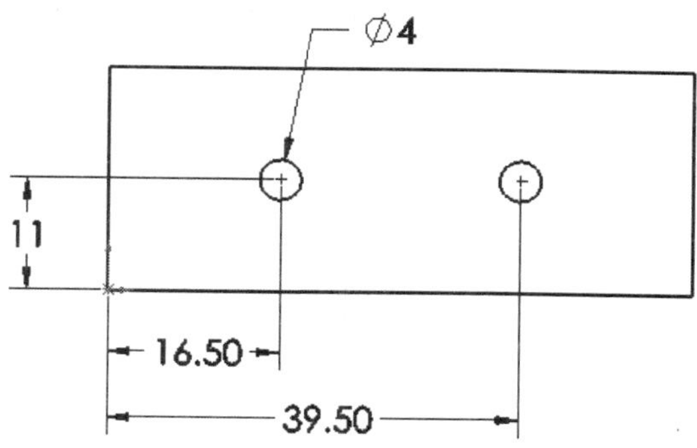

184) Click the **arrowhead green dot** to display the arrows inside the extension lines.

185) Repeat the flip dimension arrow procedure for the **39.50** dimension text.

Fit the PLATE to the Graphics window.

186) Press the **f** key.

187) Click **Isometric view**.

188) Click **Shaded With Edges**.

Display the Features toolbar.

189) Click **Features** from the Control Area.

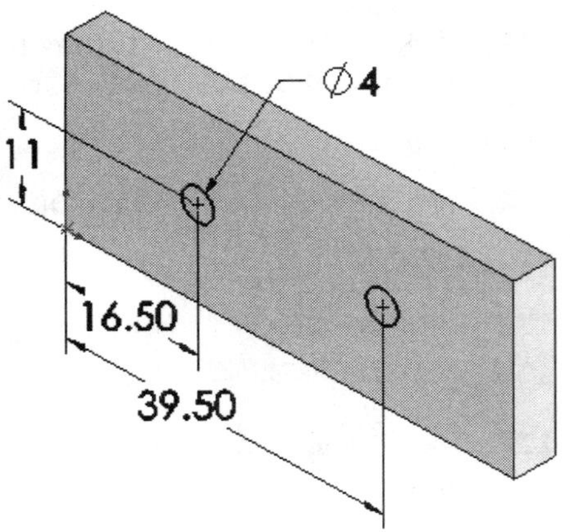

Create the Extruded Cut feature.

190) Click **Extruded Cut** from the Features toolbar. The Cut-Extrude PropertyManager is displayed. Note: The direction handle, "arrow" points into the Extruded Base feature.

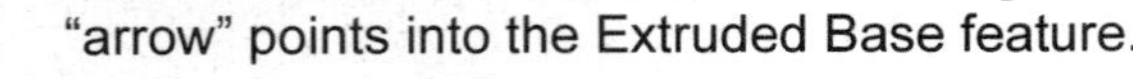

191) Click the **drop down arrow** from the End Condition list box.

192) Select the **Through All** option for Depth.

193) Click **OK** from the Cut-Extrude PropertyManager.

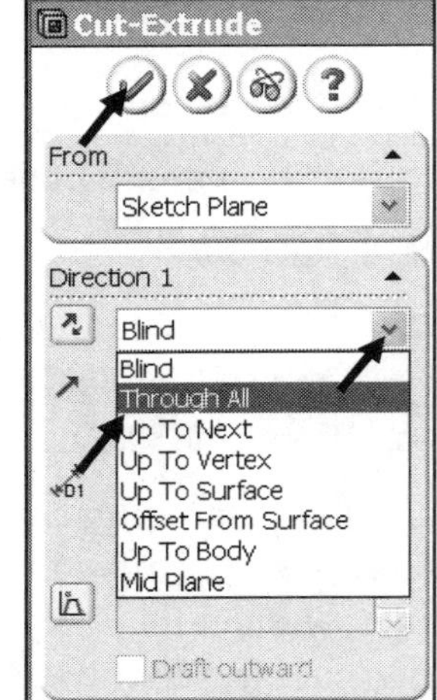

Fit the Plate to the Graphics window.

194) Press the **f** key.

Save the Plate.

195) Click **Save**.

Note: The Through All End Condition parameter creates the Mounting Holes feature through the Base Extrude feature. As you modify the depth dimension of the Base Extrude, the Mounting Holes update to reflect the change.

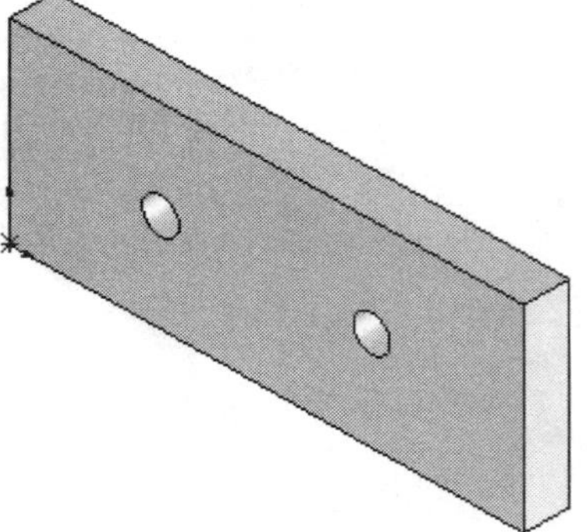

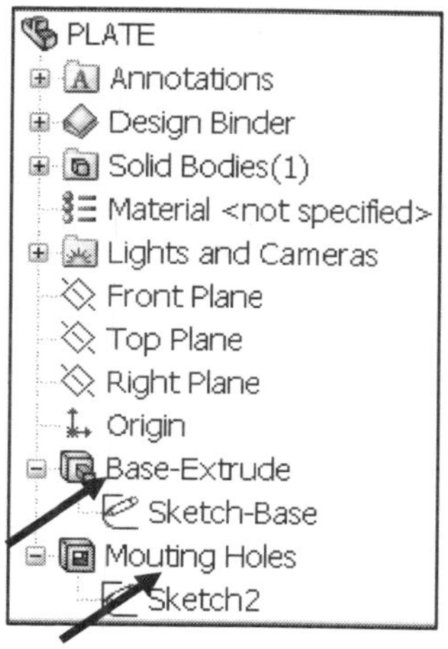

Rename the Cut-Extrude1 feature.

196) Click the **Cut-Extrude1** to **Mounting Holes** in the FeatureManager.

Modify the Base-Extrude depth.

197) Double-click **Base-Extrude** in the Graphics window.

Modify the depth dimension.

198) Click **Hidden Lines Visible**.

199) Double-click **5**.

200) Enter **30**.

201) Click **Rebuild** from the Modify dialog box.

202) Click the **Green Check mark**.

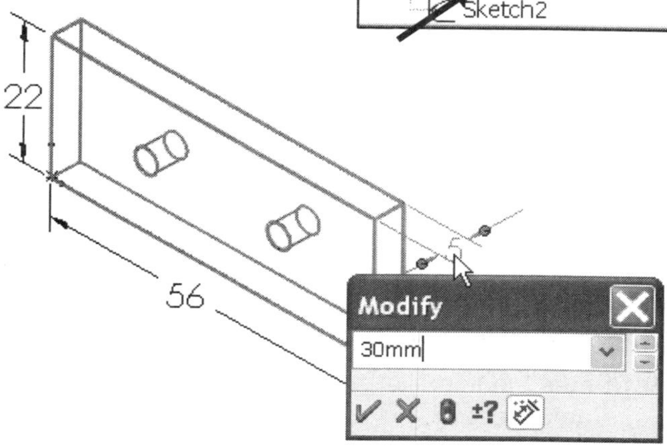

Return to the original dimension.

203) Click **Undo**.

Save the PLATE.

204) Click **Shaded With Edges**.

205) Click **Save**.

PLATE
Annotations
Design Binder
Solid Bodies(1)
Material <not specified>
Lights and Cameras
Front Plane
Top Plane
Right Plane
Origin
Base-Extrude
Sketch-Base
Mouting Holes
Sketch2

22
56
Modify
30mm

Additional details on Circles, Dimension, Geometric Relations and Extrude-Cut feature are available in SolidWorks Help Topics, SolidWorks Online Users Guide. Index keyword: Circles, Circle(Dimension), Add (Relations in Sketch) and Extrude Cut.

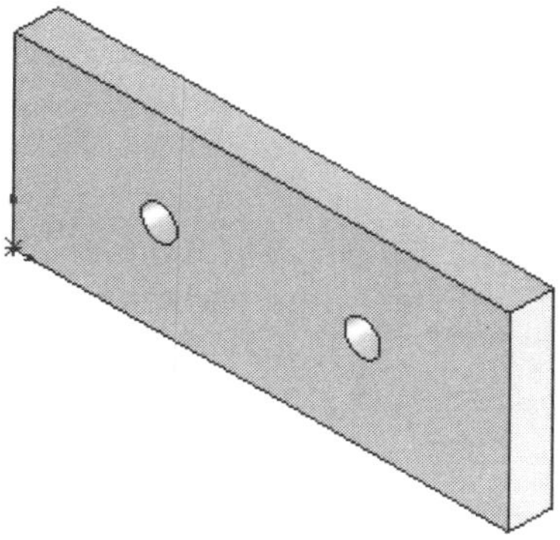

Review the Extruded Boss/Base and Extruded Cut Features.

An Extruded Boss/Base feature added material. An Extruded Cut feature removed material. Extrude features required the following:

- Sketch Plane.
- Sketch.
- Geometric Relations and Dimensions.
- Depth or End Condition.

PLATE Part-Fillet Feature

The Fillet feature removes sharp edges, strengthens corners and or cosmetically improves appearance. Fillets blend inside and outside surfaces. Fillet features are applied features. Applied features require edges or faces from existing features.

There are many fillet options. In the next activity, select single edges for the first Fillet. Select the Tangent propagation option for the second Fillet.

On castings, heat-treated machined parts and plastic molded parts, implement Fillets into the initial design. If you are uncertain of the exact radius value, input a small test radius of 1mm. It takes less time for the manufacturing supplier to modify an existing Fillet dimension than to create a new one.

Activity: PLATE Part-Fillet Feature

Insert an Edge Fillet.

206) Click **Hidden Lines Visible**.

207) Click **Fillet** from the Features toolbar.

208) Enter **1** in the Fillet Radius list box.

209) Click the **4 small corner edges**. Each edge is added to the Items to Fillet list.

210) Click **OK** from the Fillet PropertyManager.

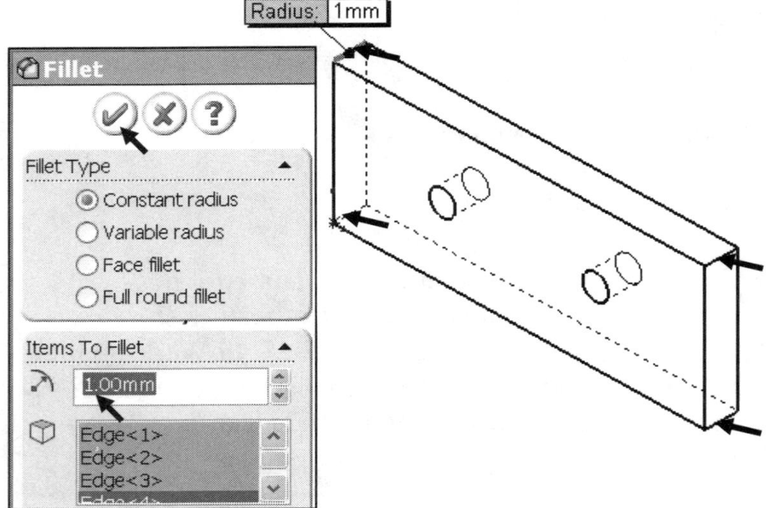

Rename Fillet1.

211) Rename **Fillet1** to **Small Edge Fillet**.

Save the PLATE.

212) Click **Save**.

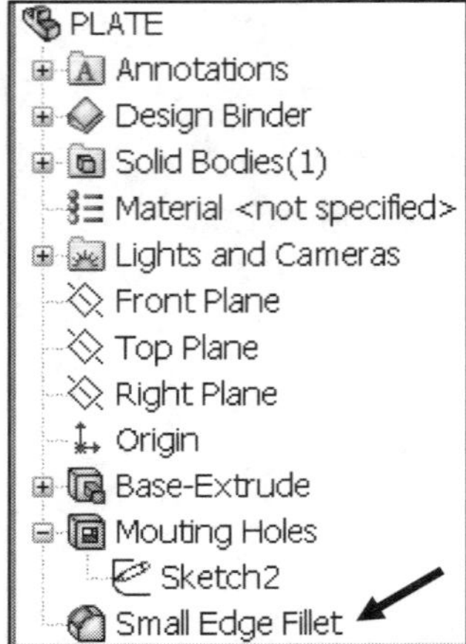

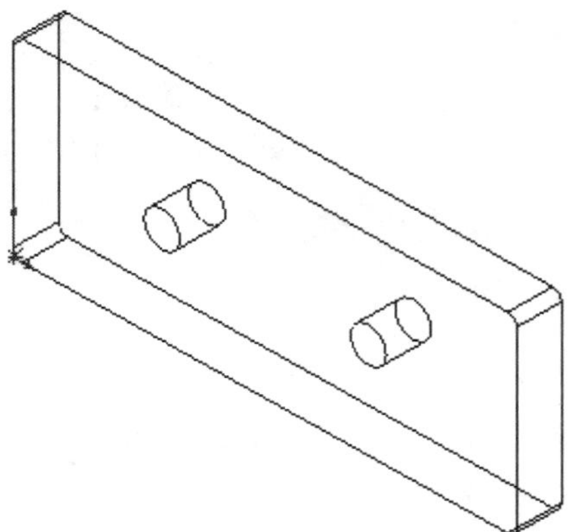

Insert a Tangent Edge Fillet.

213) Click the **front top horizontal edge**.

214) Click **Fillet** Fillet from the Features Toolbar. The Tangent propagation check box is checked.

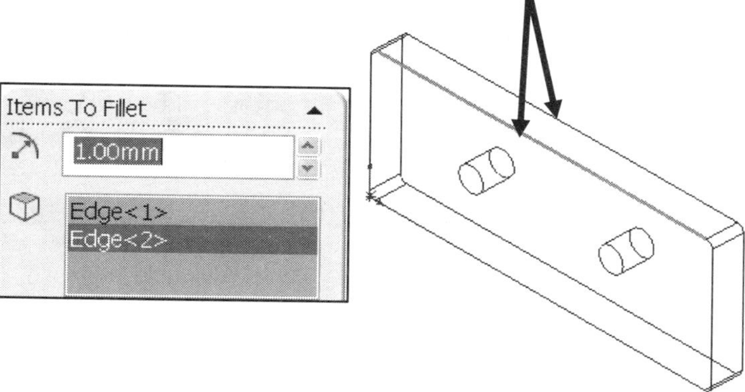

215) Click the **back top horizontal edge**. The default radius is 1 mm. All tangent edges are selected.

216) Click **OK** from the Fillet PropertyManager.

Rename Fillet2.

217) Rename **Fillet2** to **Front-Back Edge Fillet**.

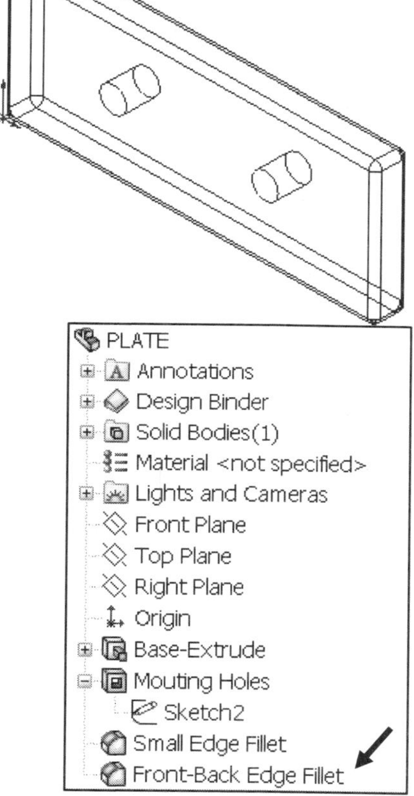

Save the PLATE.

218) Click **Save**.

Save selection time. Utilize Ctrl-Select and choose all edges to fillet. Select the Fillet feature. All Ctrl-Select edges are displayed in the Items to Fillet box.

Minimize the number of Fillet Radius sizes created in the FeatureManager. Combine Fillets and Rounds that have a common radius. Select all Fillet/Round edges. Add edges to the Items to Fillet list in the Fillet PropertyManager. Select the small edges, then fillet the larger edges.

Additional details on Fillet are available in SolidWorks Help Topics, SolidWorks Online Users Guide. Index keyword: Fillet. Review Fillet types.

PLATE Part-Hole Wizard

The PLATE part requires a Countersink Hole. Use the Hole Wizard. The Hole Wizard creates complex and simple Hole features by stepping through a series of options to define the hole type and hole placement. The Hole Wizard requires a face or plane to position the Hole feature. Select the back face; then click the Hole Wizard icon.

Activity: PLATE Part-Hole Wizard

Rotate the view.

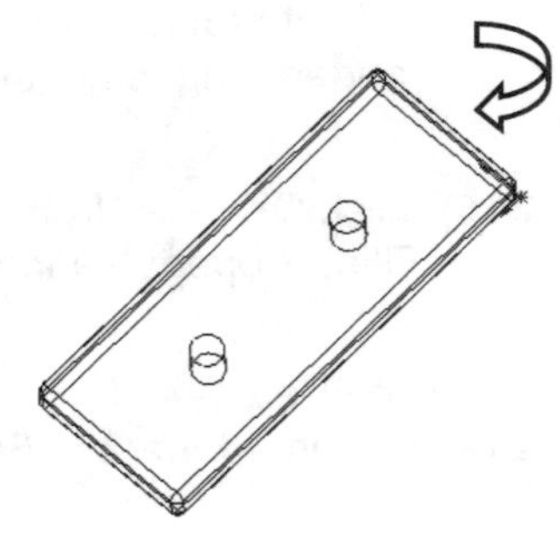

219) Click **Rotate view**. Click and drag the **mouse pointer** to the left to rotate the part.

220) Click **Rotate view** to deactivate.

Display the Back view.

221) Click **Back view**. The Origin is displayed at the lower right corner.

Select the Sketch plane for the Hole Wizard.

222) Click **Shaded With Edges** . Click the **middle Back face** of Base-Extrude.

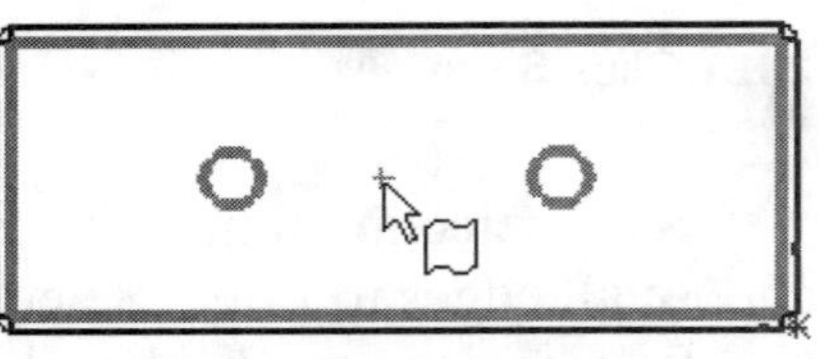

Insert the Countersink Hole.

223) Click **Hole Wizard** from the Feature Toolbar. The Hole Specification dialog box is displayed.

224) Click the **Type** tab.

225) Click the **Countersink** icon.

226) Select **ANSI Metric** for the Standard.

227) Select **Flat Head Screw – ANSI B18.6.7M** for Screw type.

228) Select **M4** for Size.

229) Select **Through All** from the drop down list for End Condition & Depth. Accept the other default values.

230) Click the **Positions** tab.

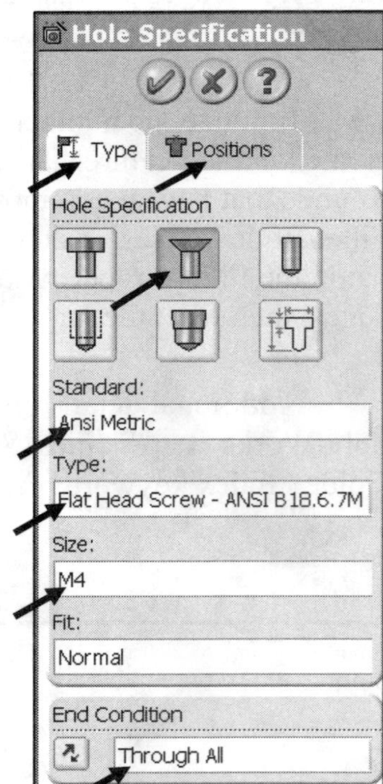

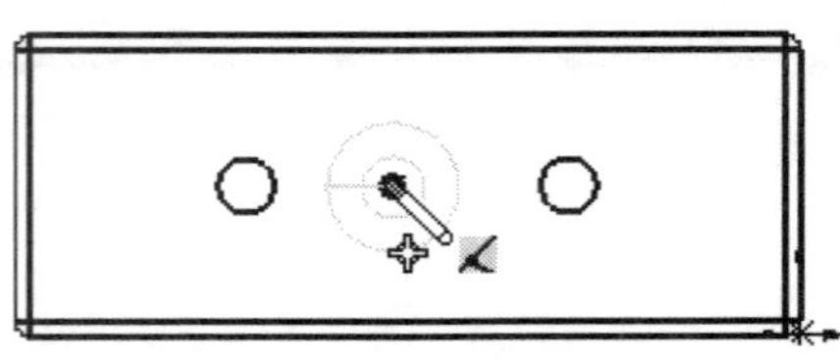

Add a horizontal dimension.

231) Click **Smart Dimension**  Smart Dimens... from the Sketch toolbar.

232) Click the **center point** of the countersink hole.

233) Click the far **right vertical line**.

234) Click a **position** below the bottom horizontal edge.

235) Enter **56/2**. The dimension value 28 is calculated.

236) Click the **Green Check mark** ✔.

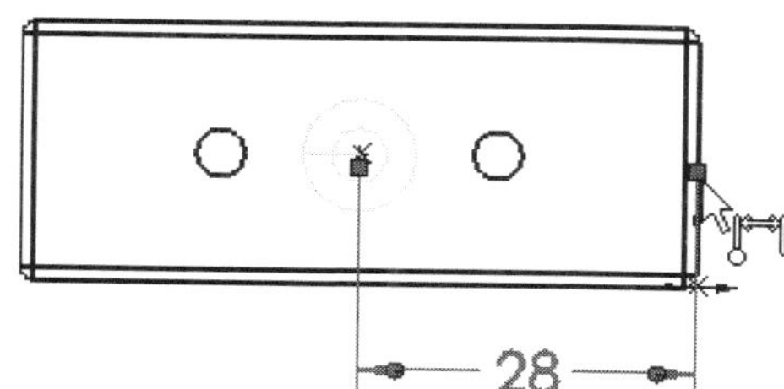

Add a vertical dimension.

237) Click the **center point** of the countersink hole.

238) Click the **bottom horizontal line**.

239) Click a **position** to the right of the profile.

240) Enter **11**.

241) Click the **Green Check mark** ✔.

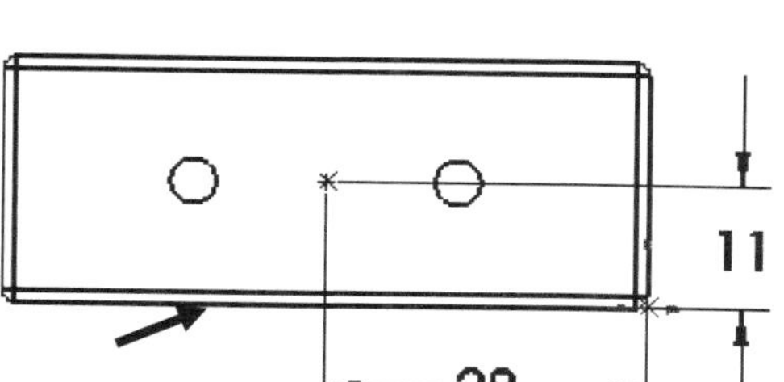

242) Click **OK** from the Dimension PropertyManager.

243) Click **OK** from the Hole Position PropertyManager.

Fit the Plate to the Graphics window.

244) Press the **f** key.

The Countersink Hole is named CSK for M4 Flat Head in the FeatureManager.

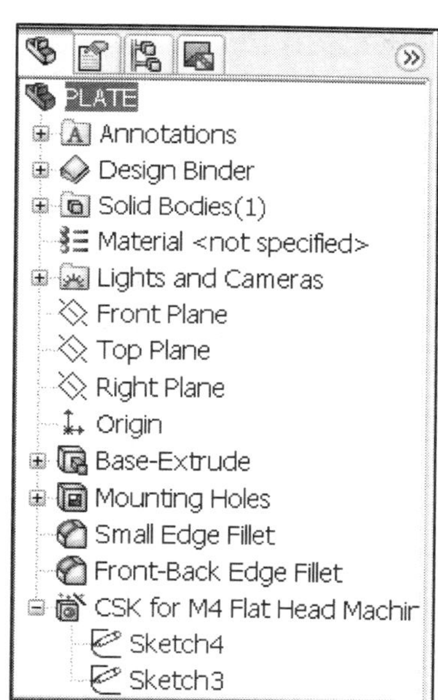

Enter dimensions as a formula in the Modify Dialog Box. Example 56/2 calculates 28.

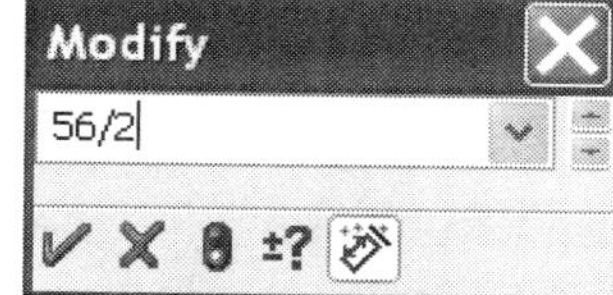

Enter dimensions for automatic unit conversion. Example 2.0in calculates 50.8mm when primary units are set to millimeters (1in = 25.4mm).

View the PLATE.

245) Click **Isometric view** from the Standard View toolbar.

246) Click **Shaded With Edges** .

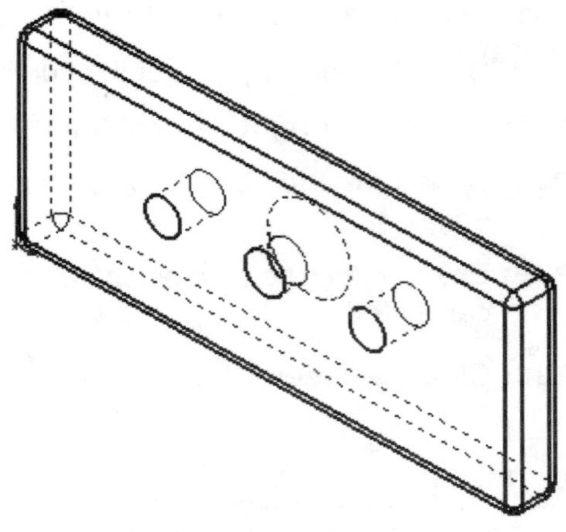

Save the PLATE.

247) Click **Save** .

Close the PLATE.

248) Click **File**, **Close** from the Main menu.

Display in the Shaded, Isometric view before you save and close the part. A bitmap image of the model is saved. To preview the image in the SolidWorks Open dialog box, select View menu, Thumbnails option.

Additional details on the Hole Wizard are available in SolidWorks Help Topics, SolidWorks Online Users Guide. Index keyword: Hole Wizard Overview. Review Hole Wizard types.

Review the PLATE Part.

The PLATE part utilized an Extruded Base feature. An Extruded Base feature consisted of a rectangular profile sketched on the Front Plane. You added linear dimensions to correspond to the overall size of the PLATE based on the GUIDE-CYLINDER assembly, Piston Plate.

The two holes utilized an Extruded Cut feature. You sketched two circles on the front face and added Equal and Horizontal relations. You utilized geometric relations in the sketch to reduce dimensions and to maintain the geometric requirements of the part. Linear dimension defined the diameter and position of the circles.

You created fully defined sketches in both the Extruded Base and Extrude Cut to prevent future rebuild problems and obtain faster rebuild times. The Fillet feature inserted the edge Fillets and tangent edge Fillets to round the corners of the Extruded Base feature.

The Hole Wizard Countersink Hole created the M4 Flat Head Countersink on the back face of the PLATE. You renamed all features in the PLATE FeatureManager.

Rename features in parts to locate quickly in the FeatureManager and in the assembly. Set up standard company feature names such as Mounting Holes when sharing models on a project.

ROD Part Overview

Recall the functional requirements of the customer:

- The ROD is part of a sub-assembly that positions materials onto a conveyor belt.
- The back end of the ROD fastens to the PLATE.
- The front end of the ROD mounts to the customer's components.
- The customer supplies the geometric requirements for the keyway cut and hole.

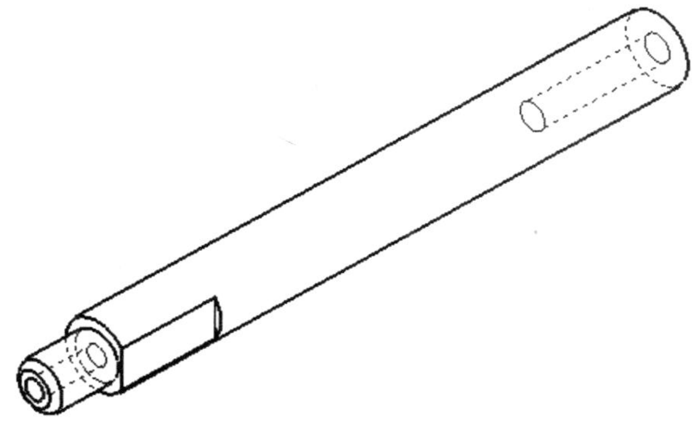

The ROD utilizes an Extruded Base feature with a circular profile sketched on the Front Plane. The ROD also utilizes the Extruded Cut feature with different options. Explore new features and techniques with the ROD.

Utilize the following features to create and modify the ROD part:

- Extruded Base: Create the Extruded Base feature on the Front Plane with a circular sketched profile.

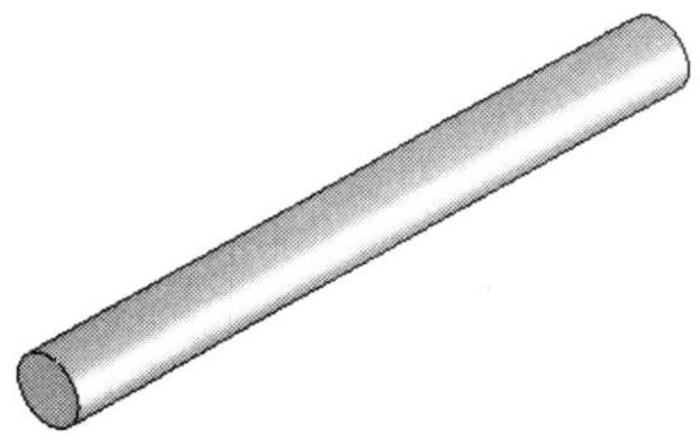

- Extruded Cut: Create the Extruded Cut feature by sketching a circle on the front face to form a hole.

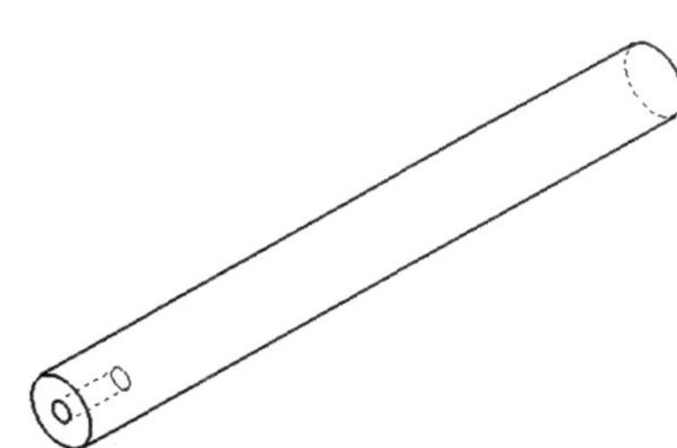

- Chamfer: Create the applied Chamfer feature from the circular edge of the front face.

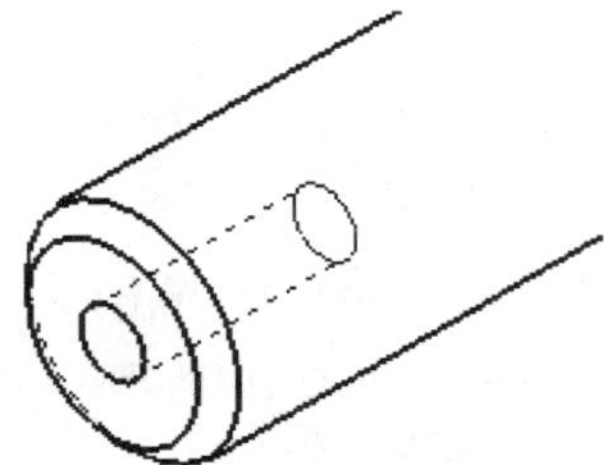

- Extruded Cut: Create the Extruded Cut feature from a sketched, converted edge of the Extruded Base feature to form a Keyway.

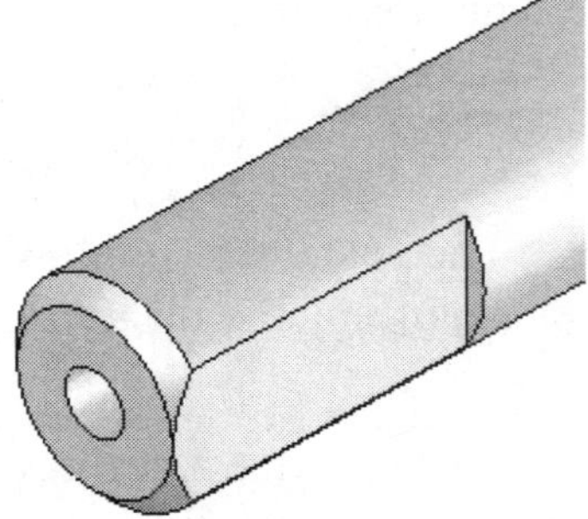

- Extruded Cut: Create the back hole with the Copy/Paste function. Copy the front hole to the back face. Modify the diameter to 4mm.

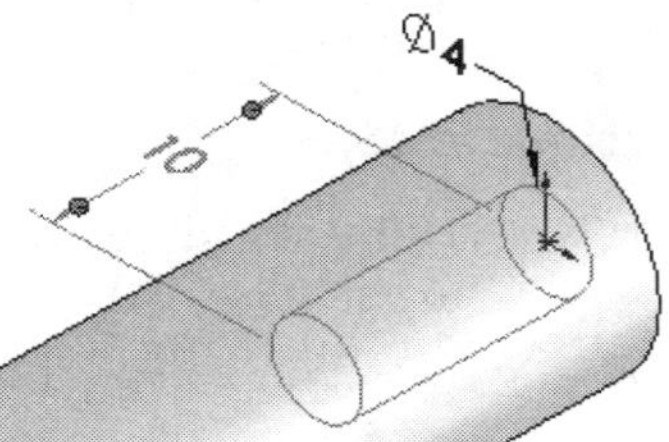

- Extruded Cut: Add a new Extruded Cut to the front face.

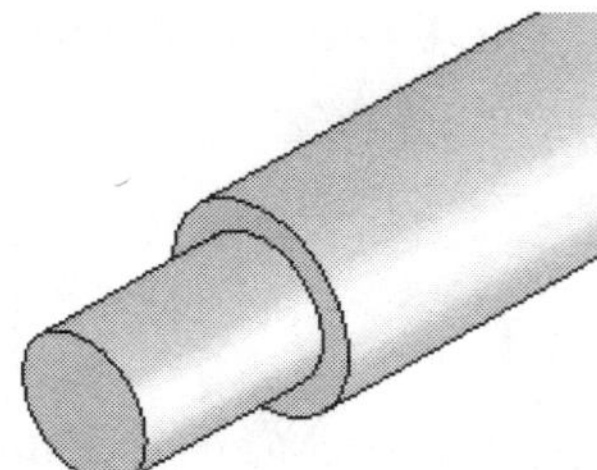

- Redefine the Chamfer and Keyway Cut.

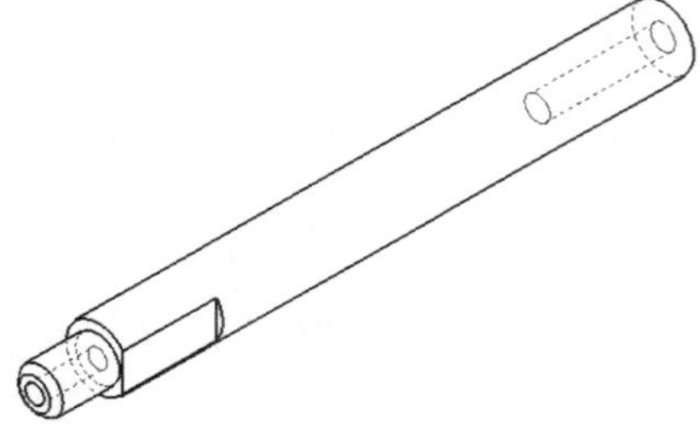

ROD Part-Extruded Base Feature

The geometry of the Base feature is a cylindrical extrusion. The Extruded Base feature is the foundation for the ROD.

What is the Sketch plane? Answer: The Front Plane is the Sketch plane.

What is the shape of the sketched 2D profile? Answer: A circle.

Activity: ROD Part-Extruded Base Feature

Create a new part.

249) Click **File**, **New** from the Main menu.

250) Click the **MY-TEMPLATES** tab. The New SolidWorks Document dialog displays the PART-MM-ANSI Part Template.

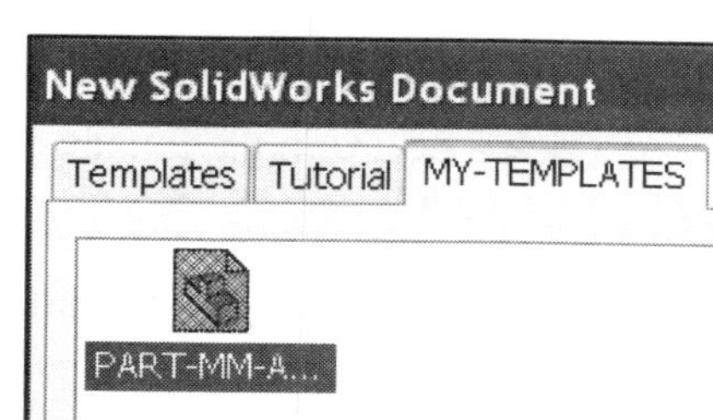

251) Double-click the **PART-MM-ANSI** template.

Note: If the MY-TEMPLATES tab is not displayed, select Tools, Options, System Options, File Locations. Add the full pathname to the MY-TEMPLATES folder to the Document Templates box.

Save the new part.

252) Click **Save**.

253) Click the **drop down arrow** in the Save in list box.

254) Select **ENGDESIGN-W-SOLIDWORKS\PROJECTS**.

255) Enter **ROD** for File name.

256) Enter **ROD 10MM DIA x 100MM** for Description.

257) Click **Save**.

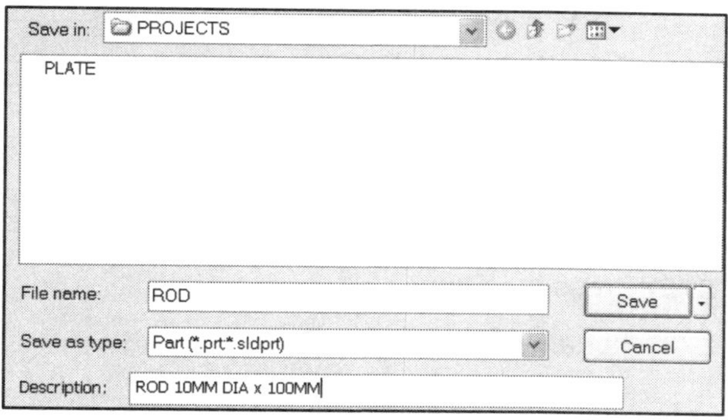

Select the Sketch plane.

258) Click the **Front Plane** from the FeatureManager.

259) Click **Sketch** from the Sketch toolbar.

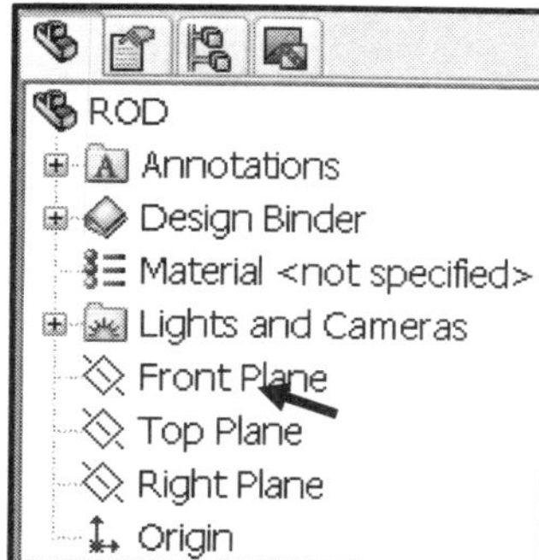

Create a circle.

260) Click **Circle** Circle from the Sketch toolbar.

261) Click the **Origin** .

262) Click a **position** to the right of the Origin.

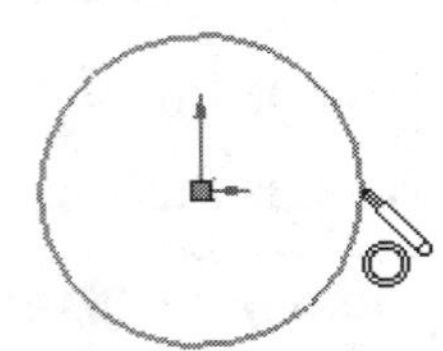

Add a dimension.

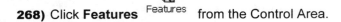

263) Click **Smart Dimension**  Smart Dimens... from the Sketch toolbar.

264) Click the **circumference** of the circle.

265) Click a **position** diagonally off the profile.

266) Enter **10**.

267) Click the **Green Check mark** ✔.

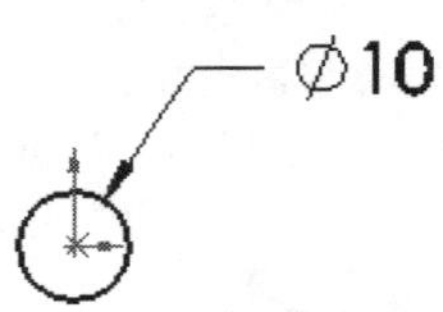

Insert an Extruded Boss feature.

268) Click **Features** Features from the Control Area.

269) Click **Extruded Boss/Base**  Extruded Boss/B... from the Features toolbar. Blind is the default End Condition.

270) Enter **100** in the Depth text box.

271) Click **OK** from the Extrude PropertyManager.

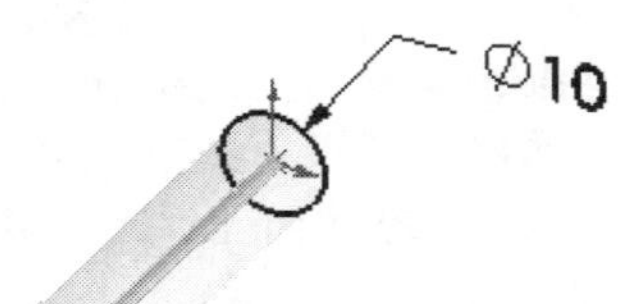

Fit the model to the Graphics window.

272) Press the **f** key.

273) Rename **Extrude1** to **Base Extrude**.

Save the ROD.

274) Click **Save** .

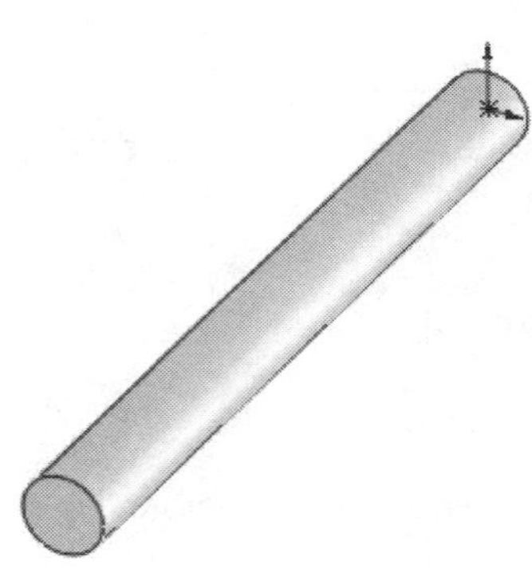

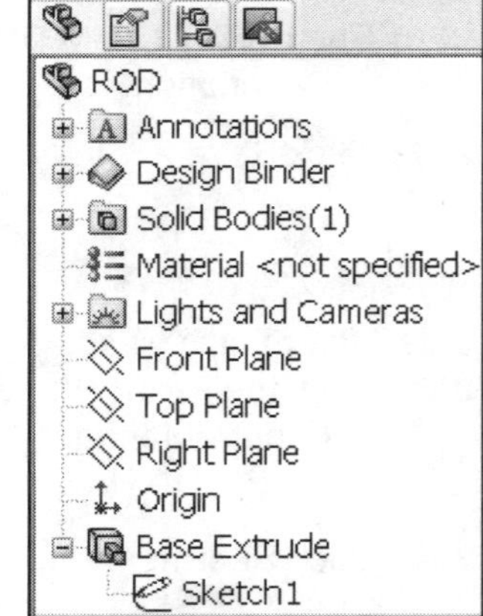

ROD Part-Extruded Cut Feature

The PLATE utilized an Extruded Cut to create two holes. Utilize an Extruded Cut to create the hole on the front face of the ROD.

What is the Sketch plane? Answer: The front face.

What is the shape of the sketched 2D profile? Answer: A circle.

Fully define the circular profile with a diameter dimension and a Coincident relation between the Origin and its center point.

Activity: ROD Part-Extruded Cut Feature

Select the Sketch plane.

275) Click the **front circular face** of the ROD. The front face turns green.

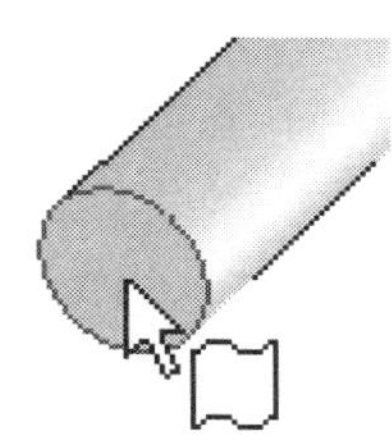

276) Click **Sketch** Sketch from the Sketch toolbar.

277) Click **Normal To view** Normal To from the Standard Views toolbar. The front face of the ROD is displayed.

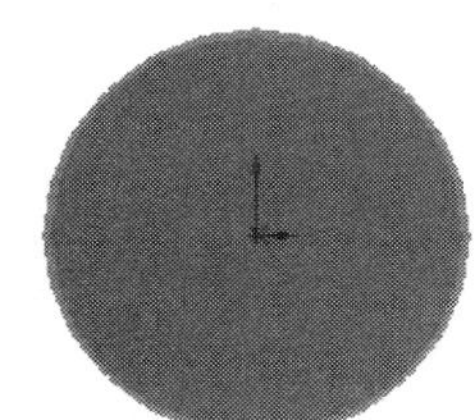

Create a circle.

278) Click **Circle** Circle from the Sketch toolbar.

279) Click the **Origin**.

280) Click a **position** to the right of the Origin.

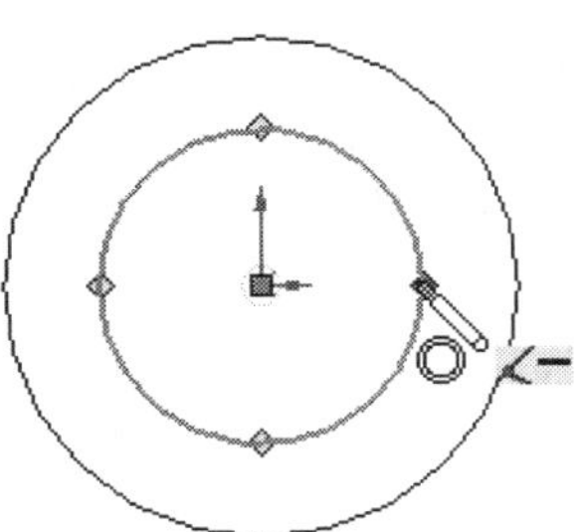

Add a dimension.

281) Click **Smart Dimension** .

282) Click the **circumference** of the circle.

283) Click a **position** off the profile, diagonally to the right of the Origin.

284) Enter **3**.

285) Click the **Green Check mark** ✔.

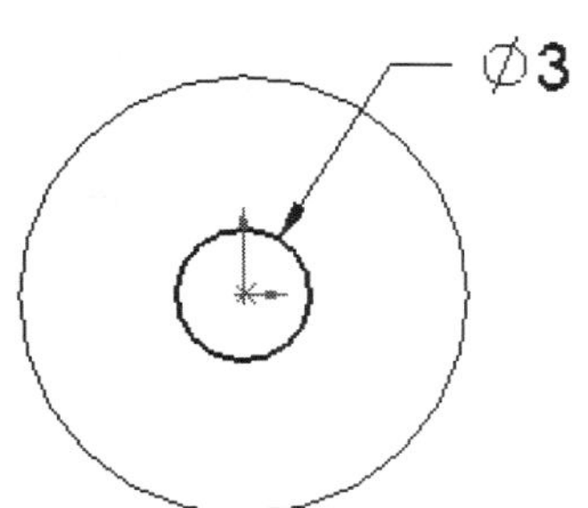

Insert an Extruded Cut feature.

286) Click **Features**  from the Control Area.

287) Click **Extruded Cut**  from the Features toolbar. Blind is the default End Condition. The Direction arrow points towards the back face of the ROD.

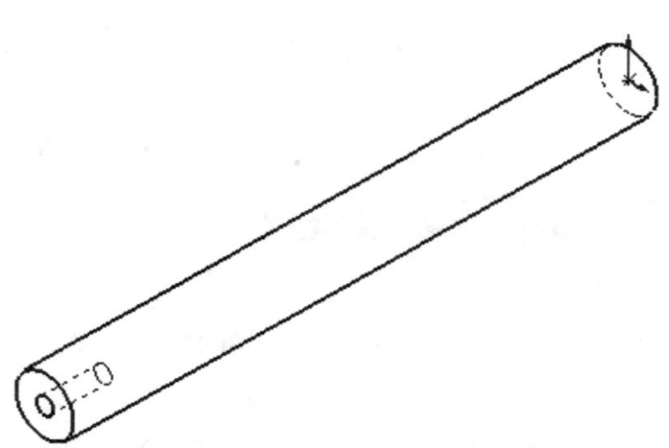

288) Enter **10** for Depth.

289) Click **OK** from the Cut-Extrude PropertyManager.

290) Click **Isometric view**.

291) Click **Hidden Lines Visible**.

Rename the feature.

292) Rename **Cut-Extrude1** to **Front Hole**.

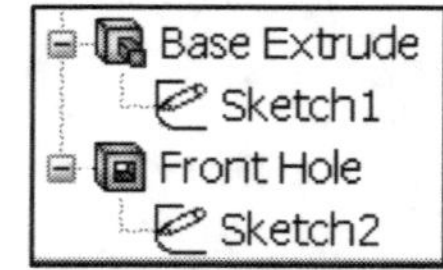

Save the ROD.

293) Click **Save**.

ROD Part-Chamfer Feature

The Chamfer feature removes material along an edge or face. The Chamfer feature is an applied feature. The Chamfer feature assists the ROD by creating beveled edges for ease of movement in the GUIDE-ROD assembly.

There are two options to specify for the Chamfer feature:

- Angle-Distance.
- Distance-Distance.

Chamfer the front circular edge and utilize the Angle-Distance option in the next activity.

Note: Selection order does not matter for the Chamfer and Fillet features.

Example 1: Select edges and faces. Select the feature tool.

Example 2: Select the feature tool. Select edges and faces.

Activity: ROD Part-Chamfer Feature

Insert a Chamfer feature.

294) Click the **front outer circular edge**. The edge turns green.

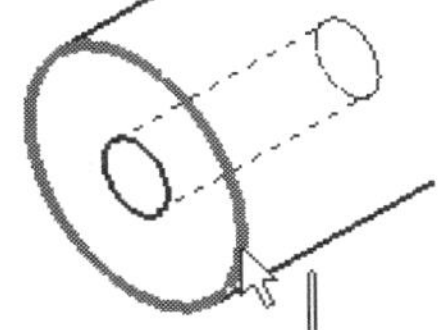

295) Click **Chamfer** from the Features toolbar. An arrow indicates the direction in which the distance of the chamfer is measured.

296) Enter **1** for Distance.

297) Accept the default **45** degree Angle.

298) Click **OK** from the Chamfer PropertyManager.

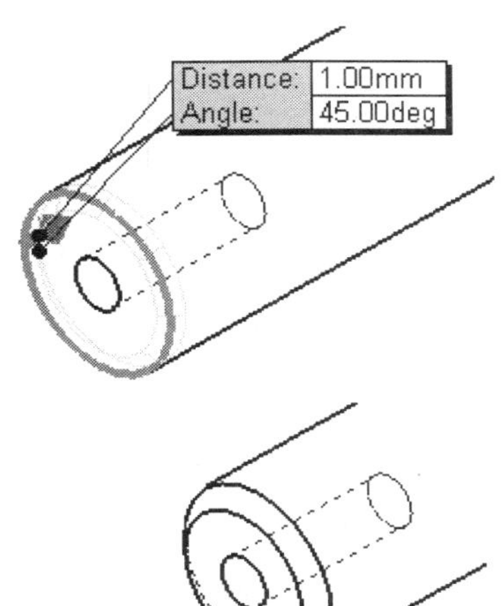

Save the ROD.

299) Click **Save**.

To deselect geometry inside the Chamfer Parameters box, right-click Clear Selections. Enter values for Distance-Angle in the Chamfer Property Manager or inside the Distance-Angle Pop-up box.

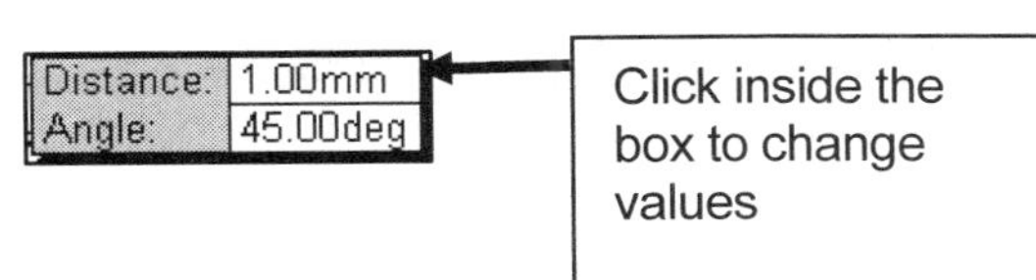

Additional details on Chamfer are available in Help, SolidWorks Help Topics. Index keyword: Chamfer.

ROD Part-Extruded Cut Feature & Convert Entities Sketch Tool

The Extruded Cut feature removes material from the front of the ROD to create a keyway. A keyway locates the orientation of the ROD into a mating part in the assembly.

Utilize the Convert Entities Sketch tool in the Sketch Tools toolbar to extract existing geometry to the selected Sketch plane. The Trim Entities Sketch tool deletes sketched geometry. Utilize the Power Trim option from the Trim Entities PropertyManager.

Convert Entities and Trim Entities require a selected Sketch icon from the Sketch toolbar or the Standard toolbar.

Activate the Sketch and then select the individual Sketch tool.

Activity: ROD Part-Extruded Cut Feature and Convert Entities Sketch Tool

Select the Sketch plane for the keyway.

300) Click **Shaded With Edges**.

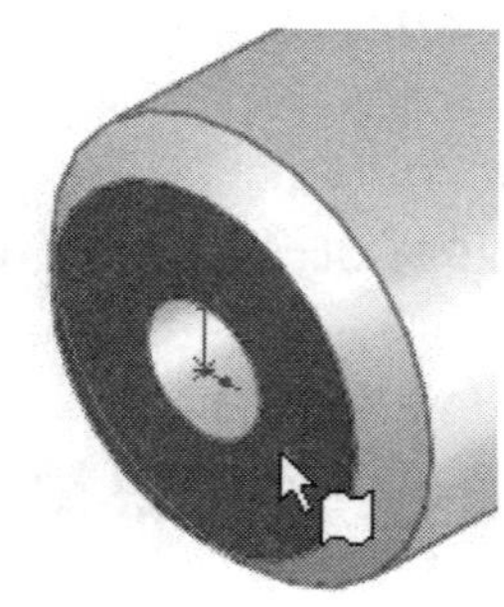

301) Click the **front circular face** of the ROD for the Sketch plane.

Create a Sketch.

302) Click **Sketch**.

Zoom in on the front face.

303) Click **Zoom to Area**.

304) **Zoom in** on the front face.

305) Click **Zoom to Area** to deactivate.

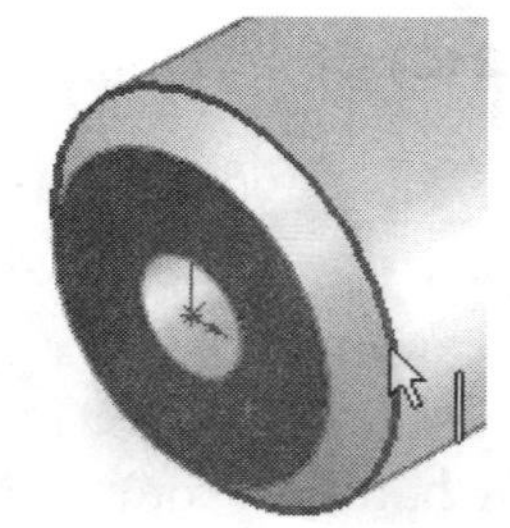

Convert the outside edge to the sketch plane.

306) Click the **outside front circular edge** of the Base Extrude.

307) Click **More Arrow** from the right side of the CommandManager. Additional Sketch Tools are displayed.

308) Click **Convert Entities** Convert Entities from the Sketch toolbar. The system extracts the outside edge and positions it on the Sketch plane.

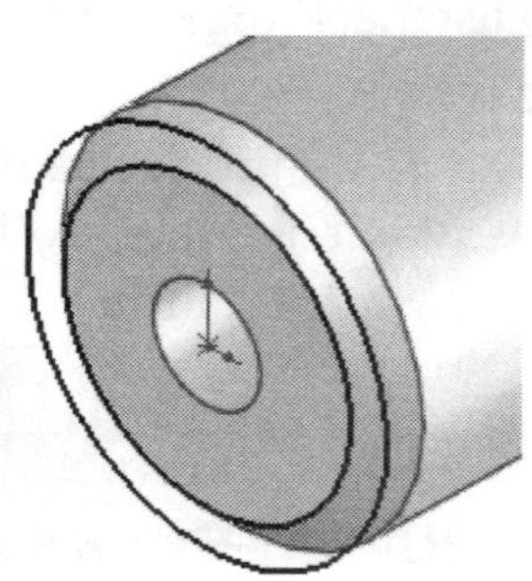

309) Click **Normal To** view from the Standard Views toolbar. The front face of the ROD is displayed.

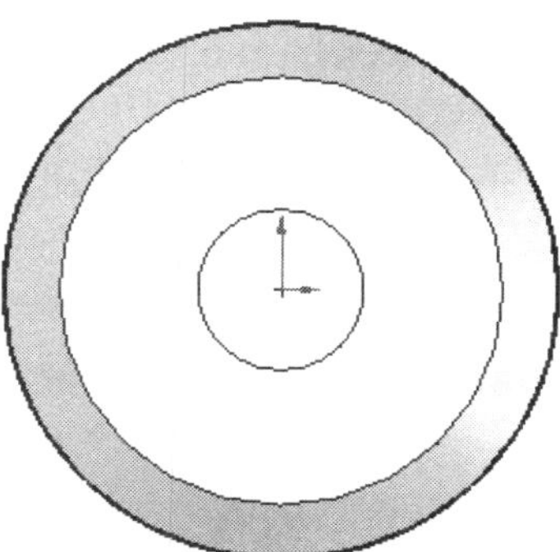

Sketch a vertical line.

310) Click **Line** from the Sketch toolbar.

311) Sketch a **vertical line**. The end points of the line extend above and below the diameter of the circle. Note: Click Vertical in the Add Relations box to add a vertical relation if required.

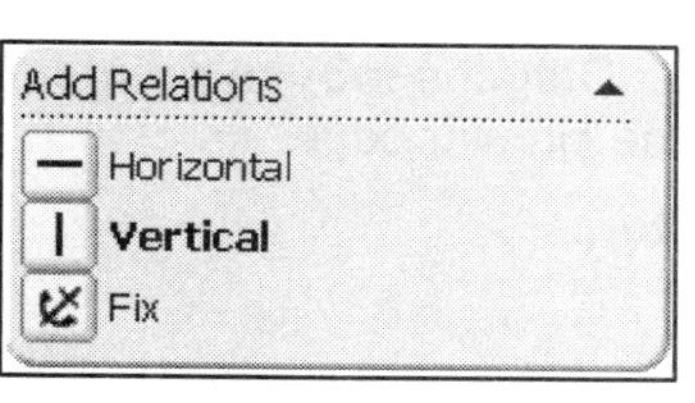

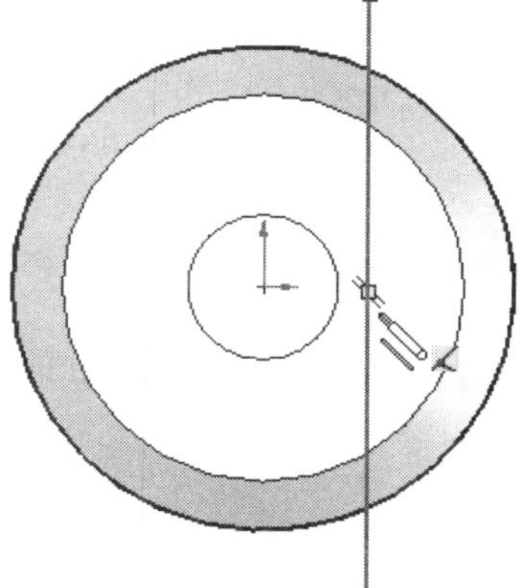

Trim the sketch.

312) Click **More Arrow** from the right side of the Sketch toolbar to view additional tools.

313) Click **Trim Entities** .

314) Click **Power trim** from the Trim PropertyManager Options box.

315) Click a **position** to the right of the vertical line, above the circular edge. Drag the **mouse pointer** to intersect the vertical line above the circular edge.

316) Release the **mouse button** when you intersect the vertical line. Note: SolidWorks displays a light gray line as you drag.

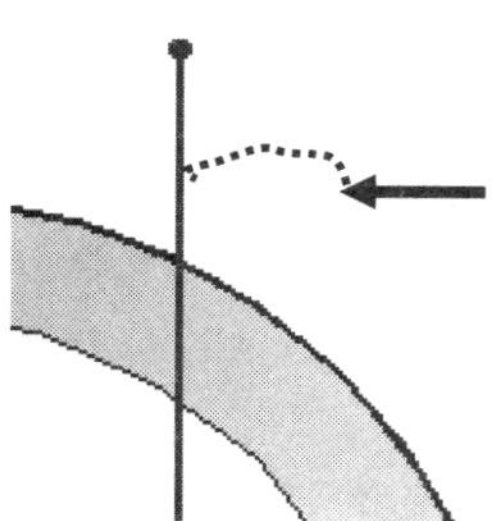

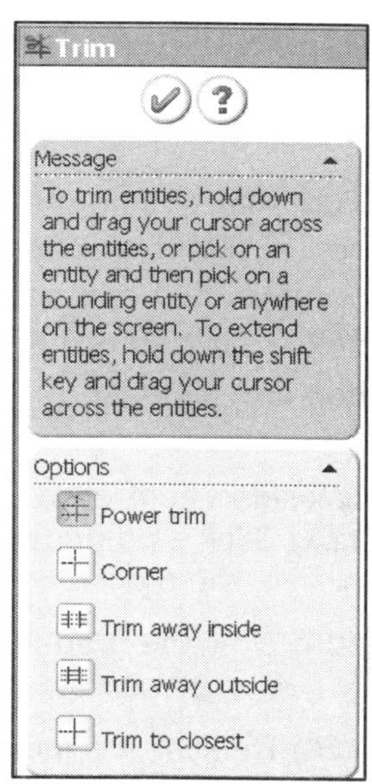

The Power trim option trims the vertical line to the converted circular edge and adds a Coincident relation between the endpoint of the vertical line and the circle.

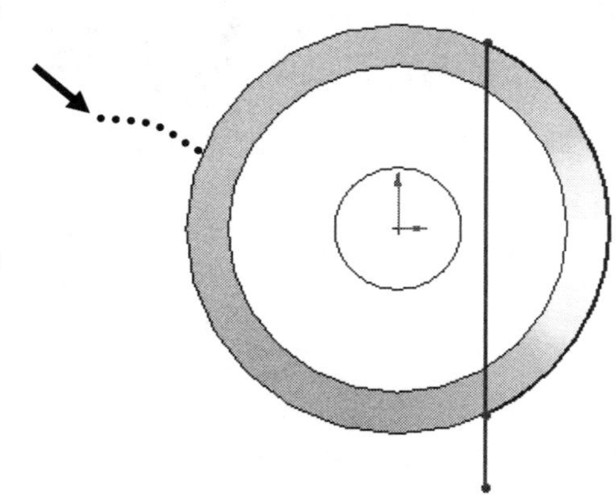

317) Click a **position** to the left of the circular edge.

318) Click and drag the **mouse pointer** to intersect the left circular edge.

319) Release the **mouse button**. The left circular edge displays the original profile.

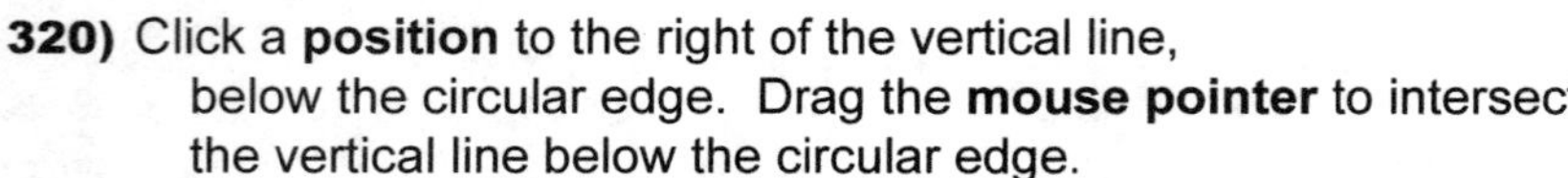

320) Click a **position** to the right of the vertical line, below the circular edge. Drag the **mouse pointer** to intersect the vertical line below the circular edge.

321) Release the **mouse pointer**.

322) Click **OK** from the Trim PropertyManager.

A selection box allows selection of multiple entities at one time.

To Box-select, click the upper left corner of the box in the Graphics window. Drag the mouse pointer to the lower right corner. A green box is displayed. Release the mouse pointer. If you create the box from left to right, the entities completely inside the box are selected.

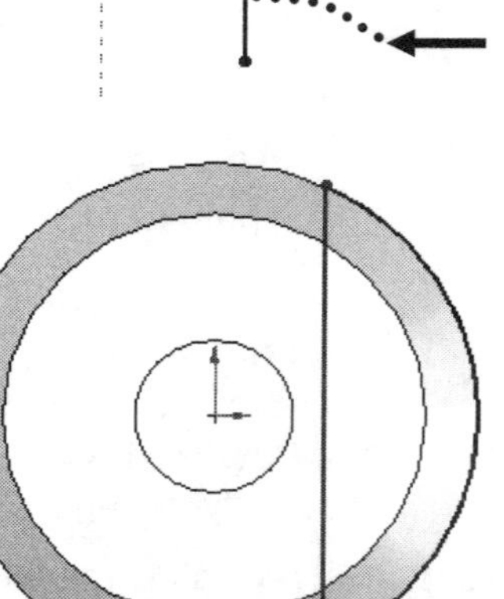

To Cross-select, click the lower right corner of the box in the Graphics window. Drag the mouse point to the upper right corner. If you create the box from right to left, the entities that cross the box are selected.

Box-select from left to right.

323) Click a **position** to the upper left hand corner of the profile.

324) Drag the **mouse pointer** diagonally to the lower right corner.

325) Release the **mouse pointer**. The Arc and Line sketched entities are displayed in the Selected Entities box.

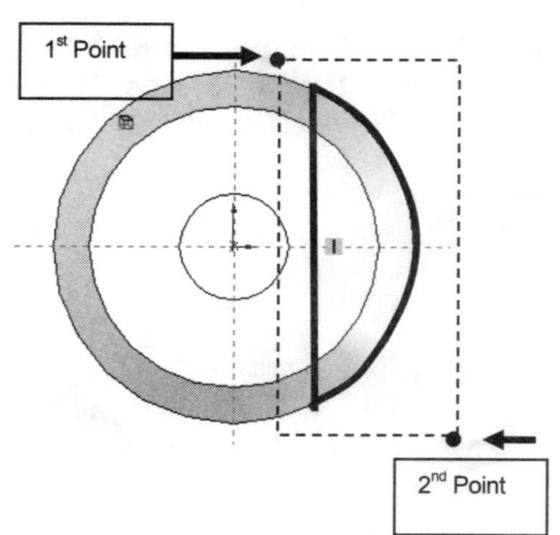

Cross-select from right to left.

326) Click a **position** in the Graphics window to de-select the sketch.

327) Click a **position** to the lower right of the profile.

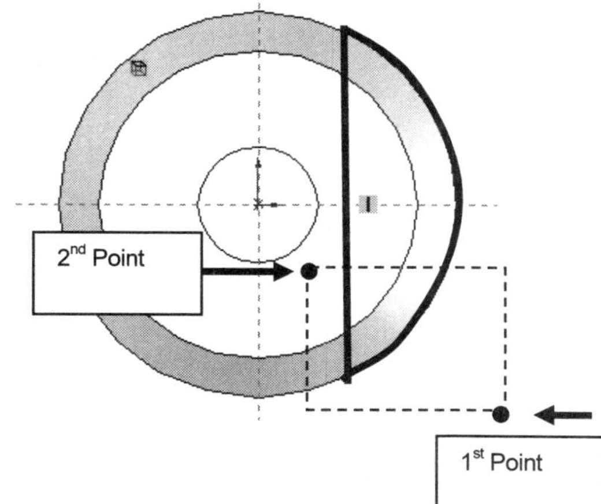

328) Drag the **mouse pointer** diagonally to the left below the Origin. Release the **mouse pointer**. The Arc and Line sketched entities are displayed in the Selected Entities box.

Add a dimension.

329) Click **Smart Dimension**  Smart Dimens... .

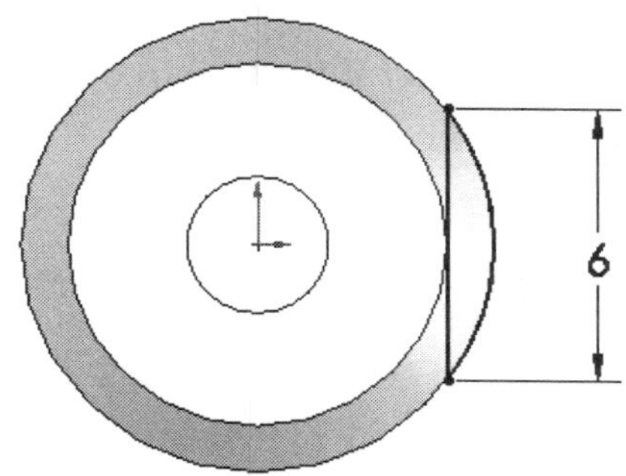

330) Click the vertical **line**. Click a **position** to the right of the profile. Enter **6.0**.

331) Click the **Green Check mark** ✔. The vertical line endpoints are coincident with the circle outside edge. The profile is a single closed loop.

Fit the Sketch to the Graphics window.

332) Press the **f** key.

Insert an Extruded Cut feature.

333) Click **Features**  Features from the Control Area.

334) Click **Extruded Cut**  Extruded Cut .

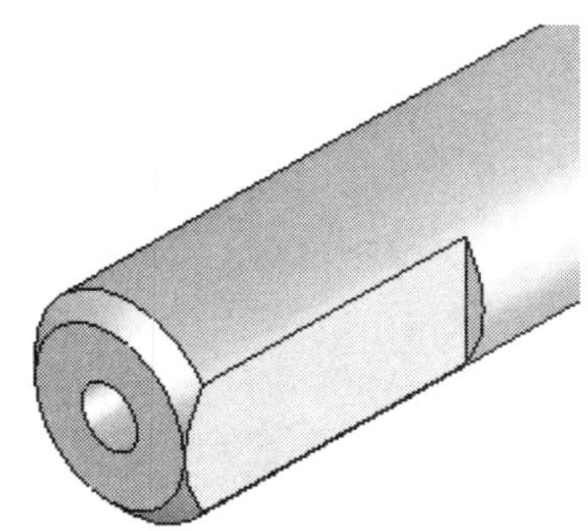

335) Enter 15 for the Depth.

336) Click **Isometric view** .

337) Click **OK** from the Cut-Extrude PropertyManager.

Rename the Extruded-Cut and Sketch.

338) Rename **Cut-Extrude2** to **Keyway Cut**. The selected Keyway Cut is green.

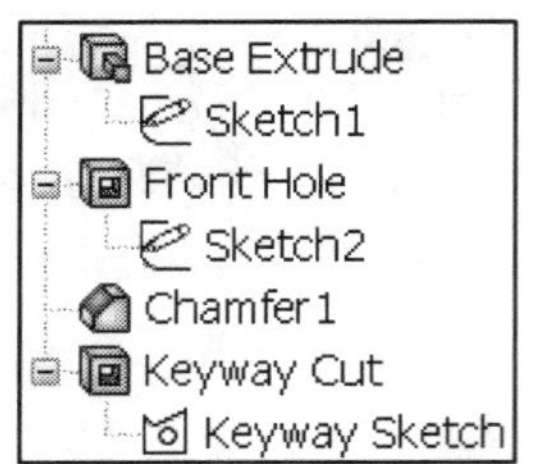

339) Expand **Keyway Cut**.

340) Rename **Sketch3** to **Keyway Sketch**.

Fit the Keyway Sketch to the Graphics window.
341) Press the **f** key.

Save the ROD.

342) Click **Save** .

Additional details on Trim Entity, Convert Entity, Extruded Cut, Relations are available in Help, SolidWorks Help Topics. Index keyword: Trim (Sketch), Cut (Extrude) and Coincident Relations.

The Extruded Cut feature created the Keyway Cut by converting existing geometry. The Extruded Cut feature also created the Front Hole on the front face.

The Convert Entities tool extracts feature geometry. Features are copied utilizing Copy/Paste Edit options.

ROD Part-View Orientation, Named Views & Viewport Option

The View Orientation defines the preset position of the ROD in the Graphics window. It is helpful to display various views when creating and editing features. The View Orientation options provide the ability to perform the following tasks:

- Create a named view.
- Select a standard view.
- Combine views by using the Viewport option.

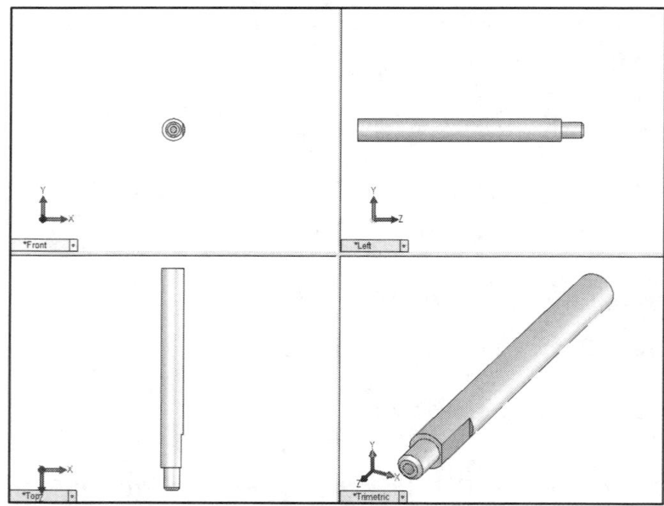

Shift key + Up arrow rotates the model in 90° increments. Start in an Isometric view. Hold the Shift key down and press the Up arrow key two times to create a Back Isometric view.

Activity: ROD Part-View Orientation and Named Views

Rotate the ROD.

343) Hold the **Shift** key down.

344) Press the **Up arrow** key.

345) Release the **Shift** key.

Insert a New View.

346) Click **View Orientation** from the Standard Views Toolbar.

347) Click **Push Pin** from the Orientation dialog box to maintain the displayed menu.

348) Click **New view** in the Orientation menu.

349) Enter **back iso** in the View name text box.

350) Click **OK**.

Close the Orientation menu.

351) Click **Close**.

Save the ROD.

352) Click **Save** .

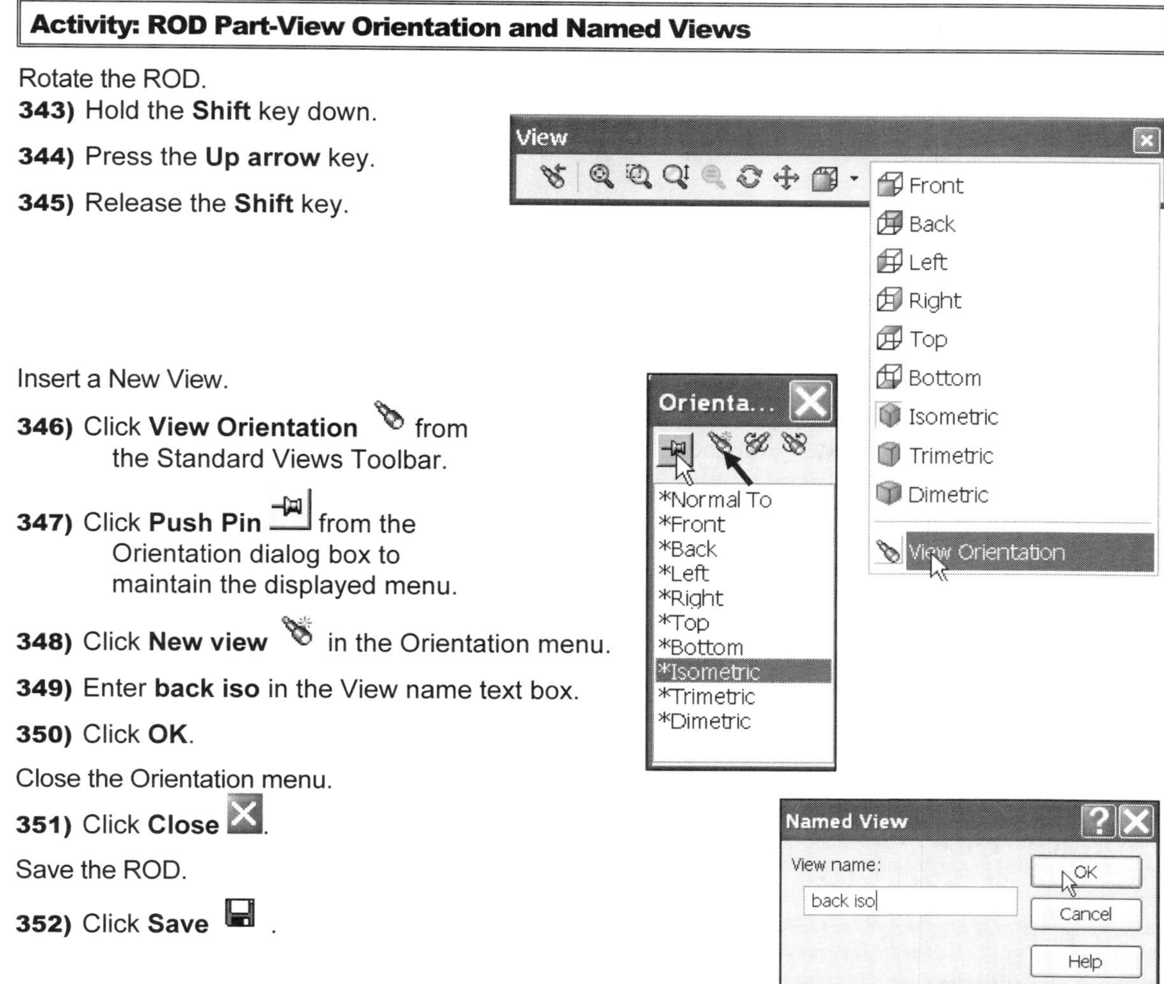

ROD Part-Copy/Paste Function

Copy and paste functionality allows you to copy selected sketches and features from one face to another face or from one model to different models.

The ROD requires an additional hole on the back face. Copy the Front Hole feature to the back face. Edit the sketch and modify the dimensions and geometric relations.

Activity: ROD Part-Copy/Paste Function

Copy the Front Hole to the Back Face.

Front Hole to Copy

Select back face to Paste

353) Click **Front Hole** Front Hole from the FeatureManager.

354) Click **Edit**, **Copy** from the Main menu.

355) Click the **back face** of the ROD. View the mouse pointer for face feedback.

356) Click **Edit**, **Paste** from the Main menu.

Note: The Copy Confirmation dialog box appears automatically. The box states that there are external constraints in the feature being copied. External constraints are the dimensions used to place the Front Hole.

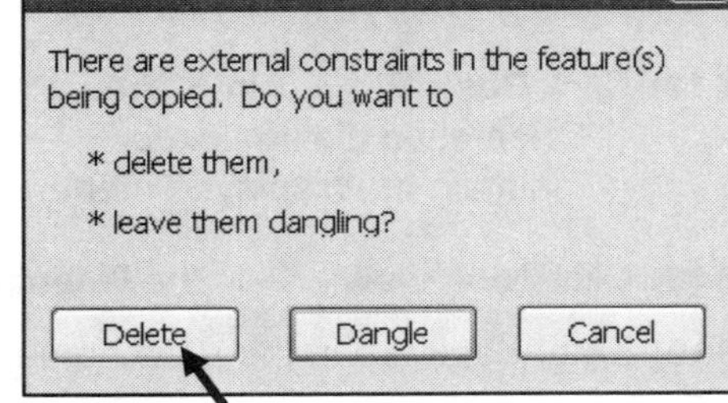

Delete the old dimensions.

357) Click **Delete** from the Copy Confirmation dialog box. The back face of the ROD contains a copy of the Front Hole feature.

358) Rename **Cut-Extrude3** to **Back Hole**.

Locate the Back Hole.

359) Right-click **Back Hole** from the FeatureManager.

360) Click **Edit Sketch**.

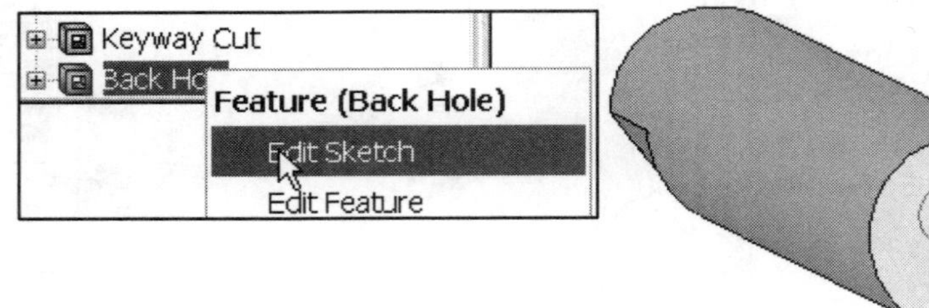

Display the Back view.

361) Click **Back view** . The Back Hole's center point is not coincident with the Origin.

Insert a Coincident Relation.

362) Click the **center point** of the 3mm circle.

363) Hold the **Ctrl** key down.

364) Click the **Origin** of the ROD.

365) Release the **Ctrl** key.

366) Click **Coincident** .

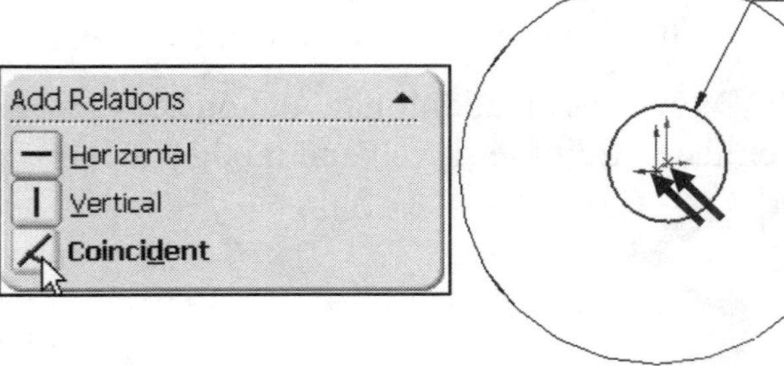

367) Click **OK** from the Properties PropertyManager.

Modify the diameter dimension.

368) Double-click the diameter dimension **3**.

369) Enter **4**.

370) Click **Rebuild** from the Modify dialog box.

371) Click the **Green Check mark**.

Exit the Sketch and return to the ROD Part.

372) Click **Exit Sketch**.

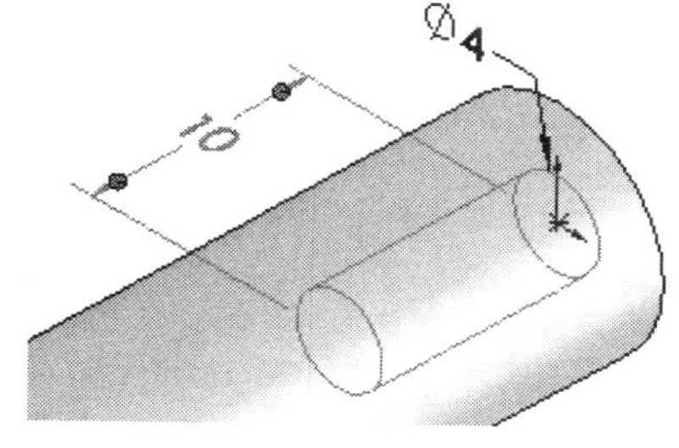

373) Click **Isometric view**.

374) Double-click **Back Hole** in the FeatureManager to display the dimensions.

375) Drag the **dimensions** off the profile.

376) Click **OK** from the Dimension PropertyManager.

Save the ROD.

377) Click **Save**.

The Confirmation corner in the Sketch Graphics window indicates that a sketch is active. The Save and Exit Sketch and Cancel Sketch short cut icons are located in the Confirmation corner.

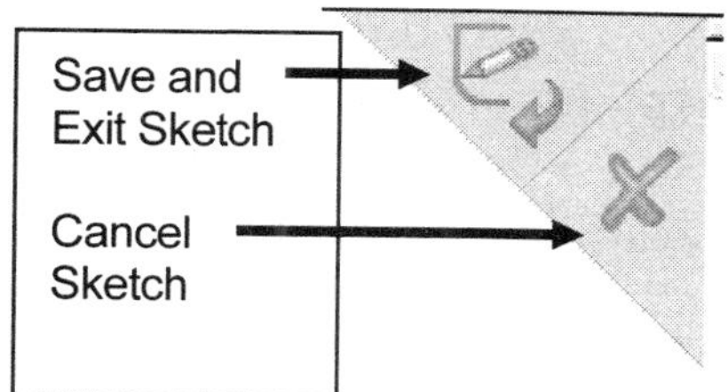

ROD Part-Design Changes with Rollback

You are finished for the day. The phone rings. The customer voices concern with the GUIDE-ROD assembly. The customer provided incorrect dimensions for the mating assembly to the ROD. The ROD must fit into a 7mm hole. The ROD fastens to the customer's assembly with a 4mm Socket head cap screw.

You agree to make the changes at no additional cost since the ROD has not been machined. You confirm the customer's change in writing.

The customer agrees but wants to view a copy of the GUIDE-ROD assembly design by tomorrow! You are required to implement the design change and to incorporate it into the existing part.

Use the Rollback and Edit Feature functions to implement the design change. The Rollback function allows a feature to be redefined in any state or order. Reposition the Rollback bar in the FeatureManager.

The Edit Feature function allows feature parameters to be redefined. Implement the design change.

- Add the new Extruded Cut feature to the front face of the ROD.
- Edit the Chamfer feature to include the new edge.
- Redefine a new Sketch Plane for the Keyway Cut feature.

In this procedure, you develop rebuild errors and correct rebuild errors.

Activity: ROD Part-Design Changes with Rollback

Position the Rollback bar.

378) Place the **mouse pointer** over the yellow Rollback bar at the bottom of the FeatureManager design tree. The mouse pointer displays a symbol of a hand.

379) Drag the **Rollback** bar upward to below the Base Extrude feature. The Base Extrude feature is displayed.

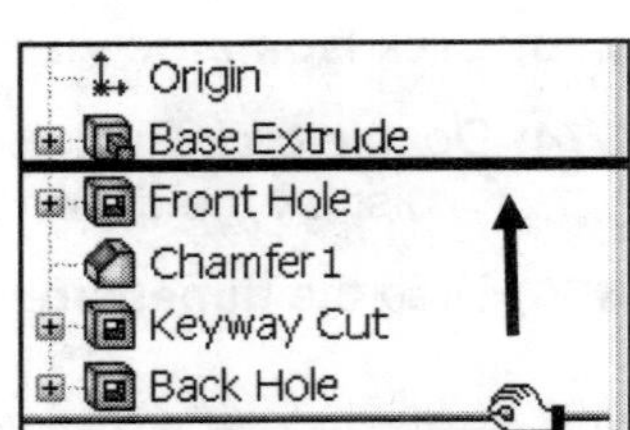

Select the Sketch Plane.

380) Click the **Front face** of the Base Extrude feature for the Sketch plane.

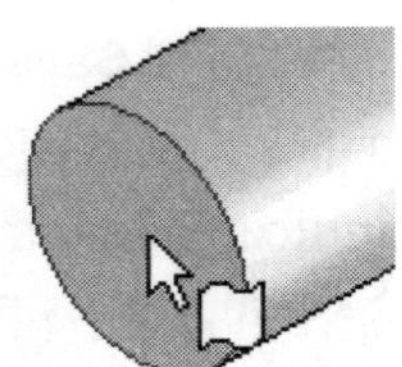

381) Click **Sketch** Sketch from the Sketch toolbar.

Sketch a circle.

382) Click **Circle** Circle from the Sketch toolbar.

383) Click the **Origin** of the Base Extrude.

384) Click a **position** to the right of the Origin.

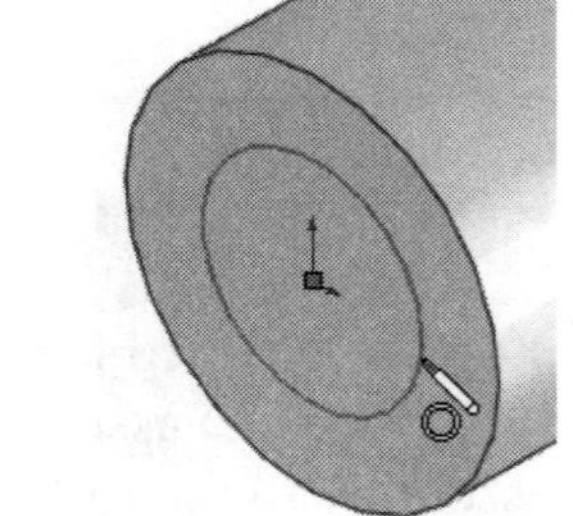

Add a dimension.

385) Click **Front view** .

386) Click **Smart Dimension**  Smart Dimens... .

387) Click the **circumference** of the circle.

388) Click a **position** diagonally off the profile.

389) Enter **7**.

390) Click the **Green Check mark** ✔.

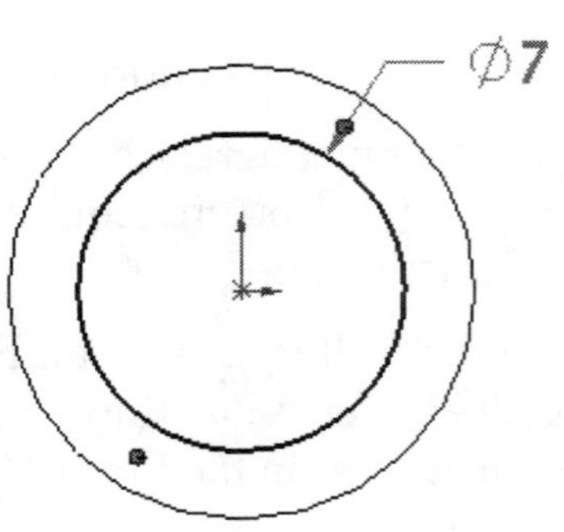

Fit the ROD to the Graphics window.

391) Press the **f** key.

Insert an Extruded Cut feature.

392) Click **Features** Features from the Control Area.

393) Click **Extruded Cut** Extruded Cut .

394) Click the **Flip side to cut** check box. The direction arrow points outward. Blind is the default End Condition.

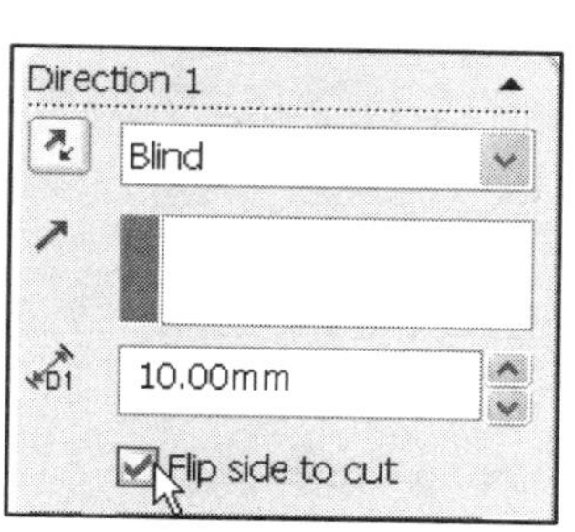

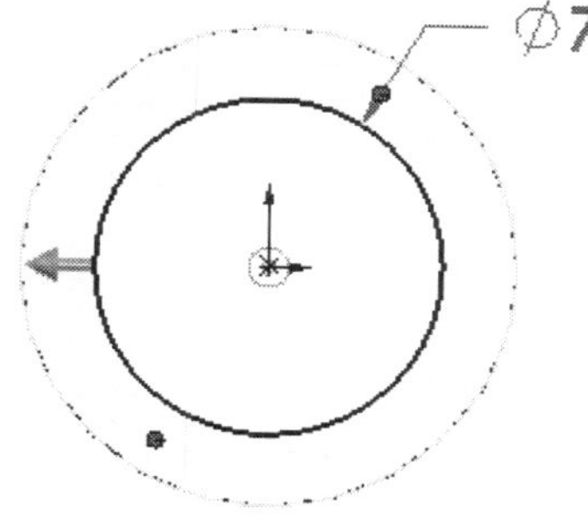

395) Enter **10** for Depth.

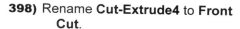

396) Click **OK**  from the Cut-Extrude PropertyManager.

397) Click **Isometric view** .

398) Rename **Cut-Extrude4** to **Front Cut**.

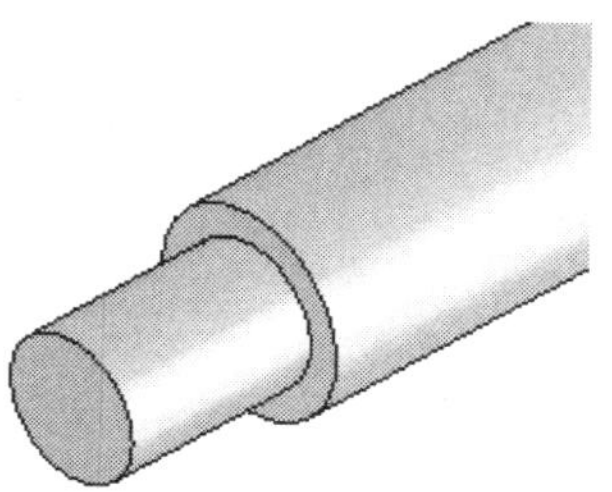

ROD Part-Recover from Rebuild Errors

Rebuild errors can occur when using the Rollback function. A common error occurs when an edge or face is missing. Redefine the edge for the Chamfer feature. When you delete sketch reference, Dangle dimensions, sketches and plane errors occur. Redefine the face for the Keyway Sketch plane and the Keyway Sketch.

Activity: ROD Part-Recover from Rebuild Errors

Redefine the Chamfer feature.

399) Drag the **Rollback** bar downward below the Chamfer1 feature. A red x Chamfer1 is displayed next to the name of the Chamfer1 feature. A red arrow is displayed Rod: next to the ROD part icon. Red indicates a model Rebuild error.

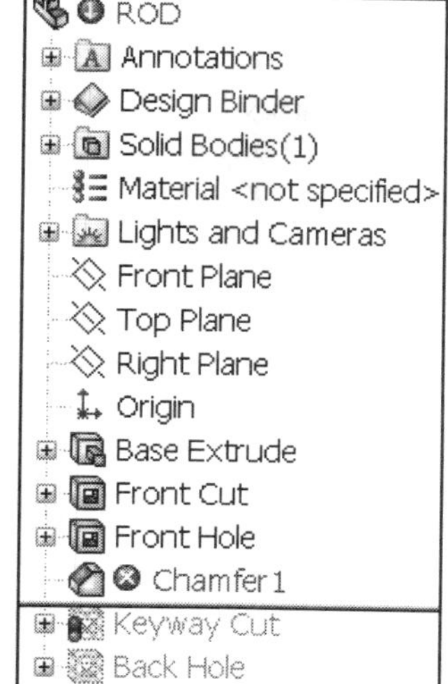

400) The ROD Rebuild Error dialog box is displayed. Click **Close**. When you created the Front Cut, you deleted the original edge from the Extruded-Base feature.

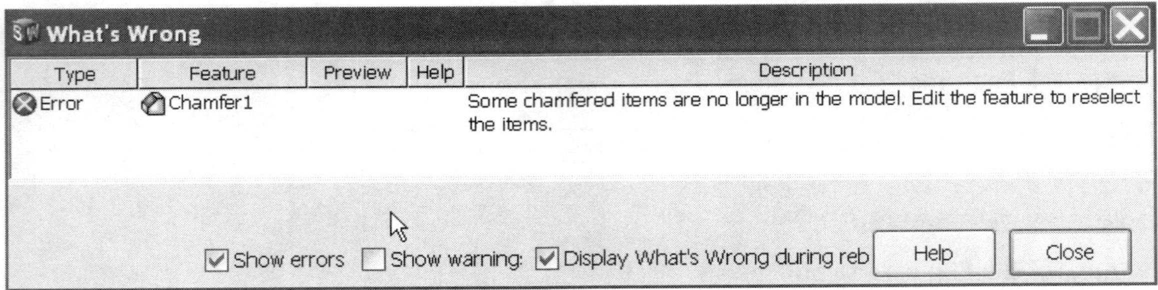

Insert the Chamfer feature on the Front Cut edge.

401) Right-click **Chamfer1** in the FeatureManager.

402) Click **Edit Feature** from the Shortcut menu. The Caution dialog box displays the message, "Chamfer1 is missing 1 edge".

403) Click **OK**. The Chamfer1 Feature PropertyManager appears.

404) Click the **front edge** of the Base Extrude feature. Edge<1> appears inside the Items to Chamfer list box.

405) Enter **1.0**mm for Distance.

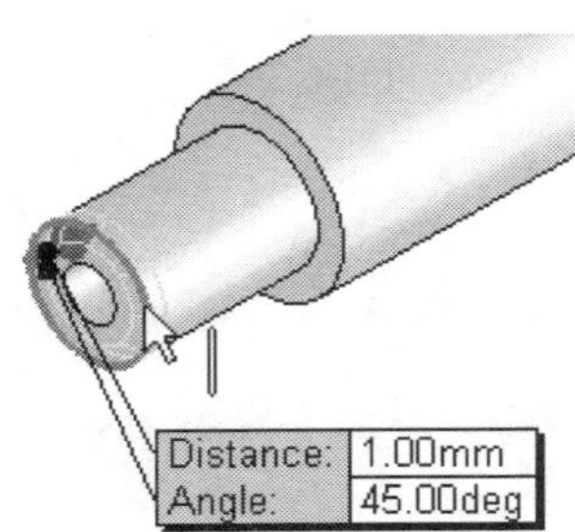

Update the Chamfer feature.

406) Click **OK** from the Chamfer1 PropertyManager.

Redefine the face for the Keyway Sketch Plane.

407) Drag the **Rollback** bar downward below the Keyway Sketch. The Rod Rebuild Error box is displayed. The Keyway Cut and the Keyway Sketch indicate a dangling sketch plane. The Front Cut deleted the original sketch plane.

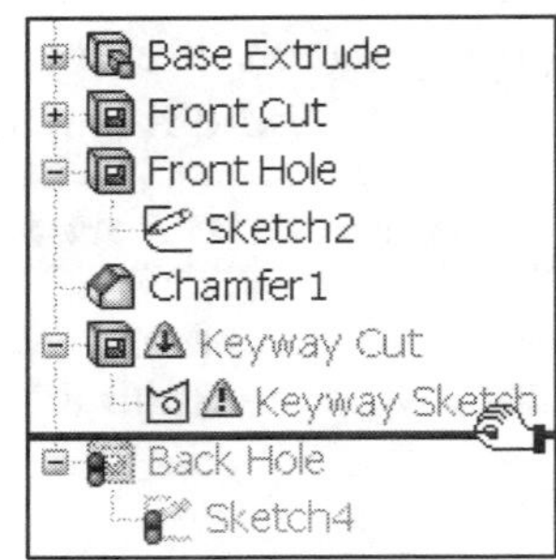

Redefine the sketch plane and sketch relations to correct the rebuild errors.

408) Right-click **Keyway Sketch** Keyway Sketch in the FeatureManager.

409) Click **Edit Sketch Plane**. The Sketch Plane dialog box appears.

410) Click the **large circular face** of the Front Cut.

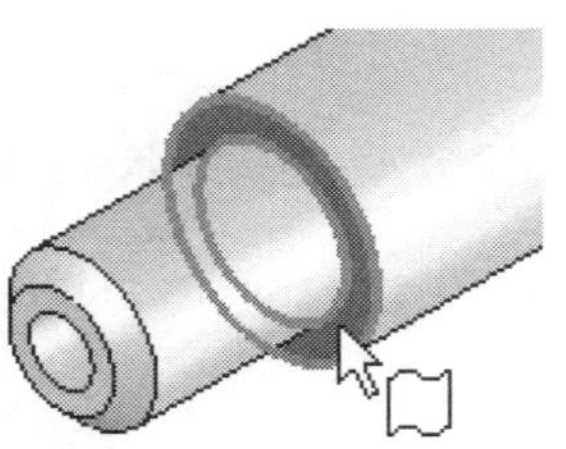

411) Click **OK** from the Sketch Plane PropertyManager. Note: The Keyway Sketch error is displayed until all entities are redefined.

The Keyway Sketch moves to the new Sketch plane. To access the Edit Sketch Plane option, right-click the Sketch entry in the FeatureManager.

Redefine the sketch relations and dimensions to correct the two build errors. Dangling sketch entities result from a dimension or relation that is unresolved. An entity becomes dangling when you delete previously defined geometry.

Brown indicates the sketch geometry is dangling. The Display/Delete Relations sketch tool lists dangling geometry.

Edit the Keyway Sketch.

412) Right-click **Keyway Cut** from the FeatureManager.

413) Click **Edit Sketch**. Display the Sketch relations.

414) Click the **Display/Delete Relations** 

icon from the Sketch toolbar.

415) Right-click the **On Edge 1** relation.

416) Click **Delete**. The Dangling status is replaced by Satisfied. The sketch is under defined and is displayed in blue.

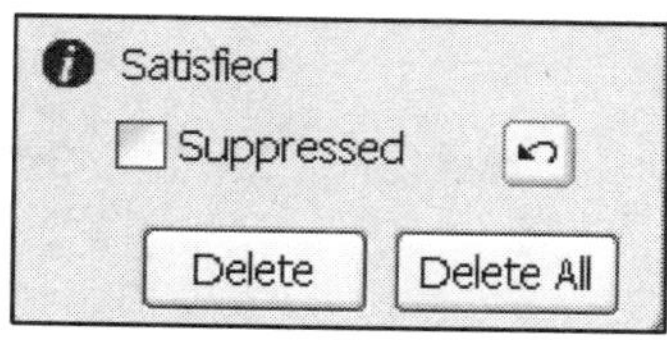

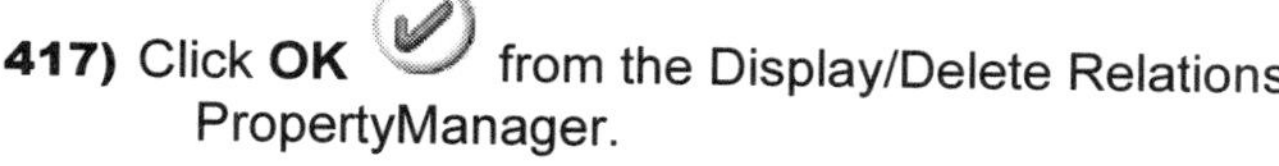

417) Click **OK** from the Display/Delete Relations PropertyManager.

Display the Front view.

418) Click **Front view** from the Standard View toolbar.

Add a Coradial Relation.

419) Click the **right blue arc**.

420) Hold the **Ctrl** key down.

421) Click the **outside circular edge**.

422) Release the **Ctrl** key.

423) Click **Coradial** from the Properties PropertyManager. The sketch is fully defined and is displayed in black.

424) Click **OK** from the Properties PropertyManager.

Exit the Sketch.

425) Click **Rebuild** from the Main menu.

426) Click **Isometric view**.

Save the ROD.

427) Click **Save**.

428) Click **Yes**.

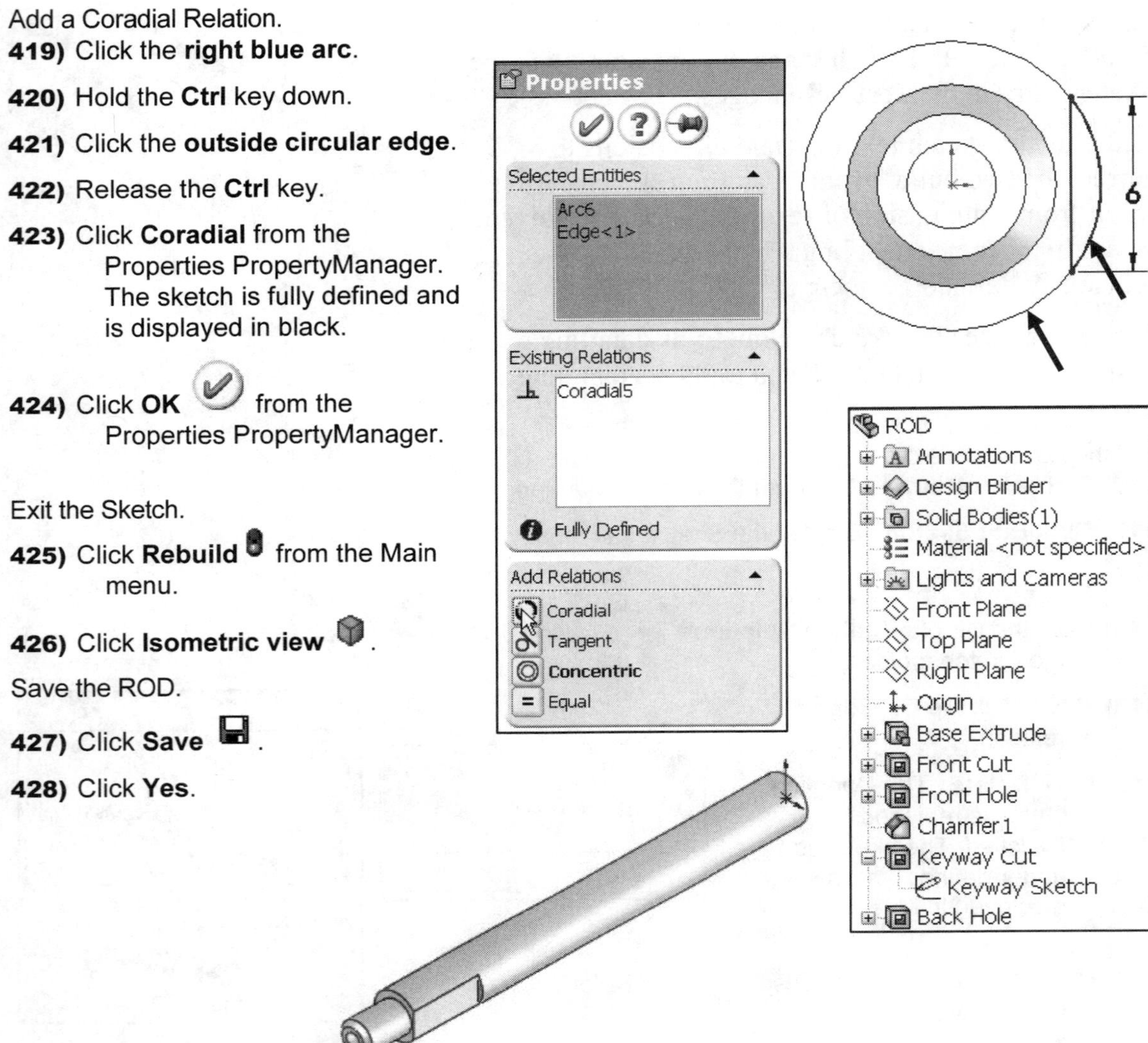

There are two ways to add geometric relations. Utilize the Add Relations Sketch Tool or the Properties PropertyManager.

Utilize the Properties PropertyManager when you select multiple sketch entities in the graphics area. Select the first entity. Hold the Ctrl key down and select the remaining geometry to create Sketch relations. The Properties technique requires fewer steps. View the mouse pointer feedback icon to confirm selection of points, edges and faces.

On a Rebuild, the Rollback bar is displayed at the bottom of the FeatureManager. The ROD FeatureManager displays no errors or warnings.

Modify the depth of the back hole.

429) Double-click **Back Hole** from the FeatureManager.

430) Double-click Depth, **10** in the Graphics window.

431) Enter **20** for Depth.

432) Click the **Green Check mark**.

433) Click in the **Graphics window**. A Rebuild icon is displayed before the Back Hole entry Back Hole.

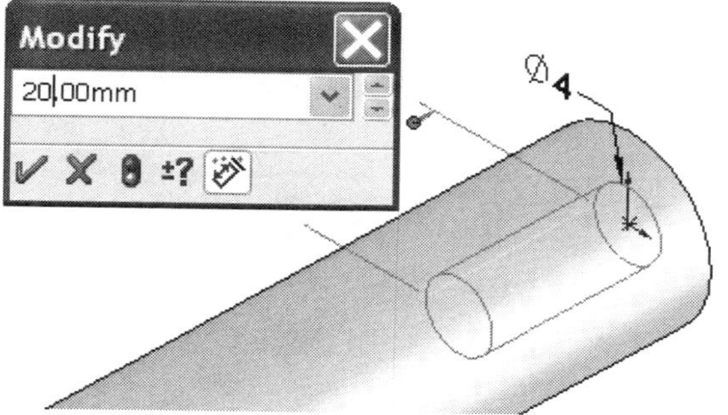

Rebuild all features.

434) Click **Rebuild** from the Main menu.

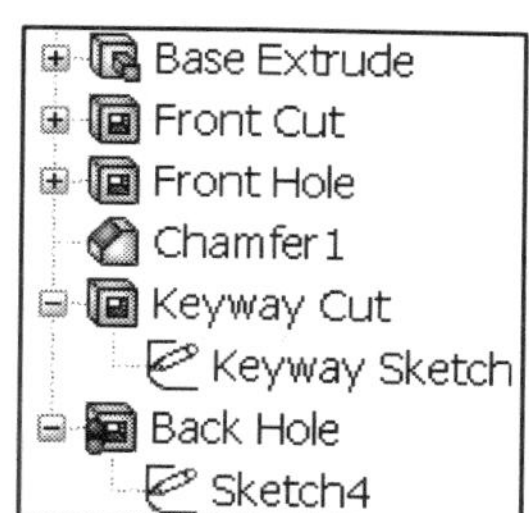

Save the ROD part.

435) Click **Save**.

Additional details on Rollback bar, Edit Feature, Display/Delete Relations and Add Relations in Sketch are available in Help, SolidWorks Help Topics.

A machinist rule of thumb states that the depth of a hole does not exceed 10 times the diameter of the hole.

A Countersunk screw fastens the PLATE to the ROD. The depth of the PLATE and the depth of the Back Hole determine the length of the Countersunk screw. Utilize standard length screws.

ROD Part-Edit Part Color

Parts are shaded gray by system default. The Edit Part Color option provides the ability to modify part, feature and face color. In the next activity, modify the part color and the machined faces.

Activity: ROD Part-Edit Part Color

Edit the part color.

436) Click **Shaded with Edges** from the View Manager.

437) Click the **ROD Part** ROD icon on the top of the FeatureManager design tree.

438) Click **Edit Color**. Basic colors are displayed in small squares, called swatches.

439) Click a **color swatch** from the Basic color palette. Example: Light blue.

440) Right-click **ROD** inside the Selection box.

441) Click **Clear Selections**.

Modify machined surfaces.

442) Click **Select Faces** in the Selection box.

443) Click the **flat Keyway Cut** face.

444) Click the **Front Hole** inside the cylindrical face.

445) Click **Back view**.

446) Click the **Back Hole** inside cylindrical face.

447) Click a **color swatch** for the faces. Example: Blue.

448) Click **OK** from the Color And Optics PropertyManager.

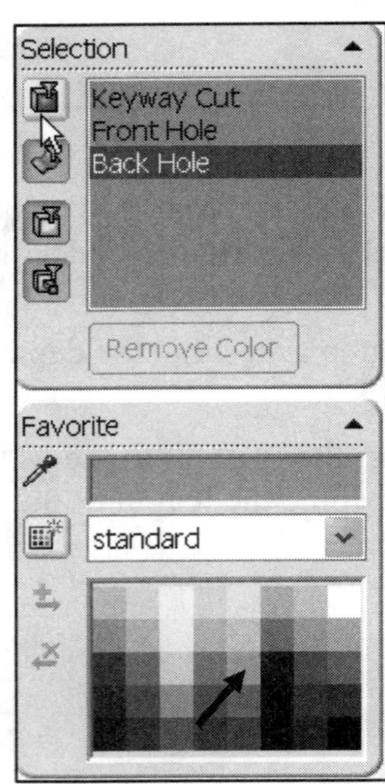

Expand the Show Display Plane.

449) Click the **Show Display Plane arrow**. **View** the results.

Collapse the Show Display Plane.

450) Click the **Hide Display Plane arrow** to collapse the FeatureManager.

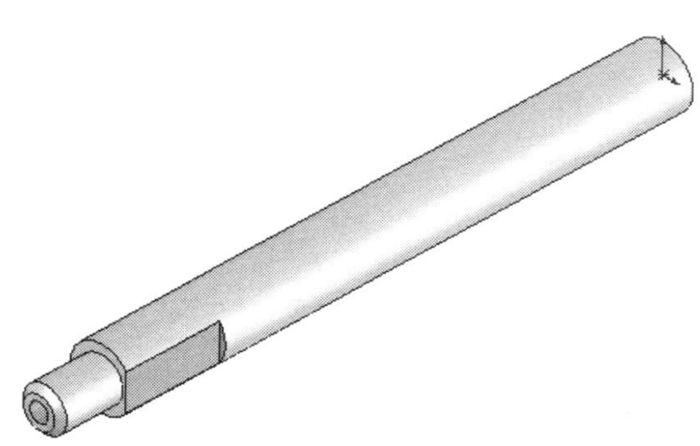

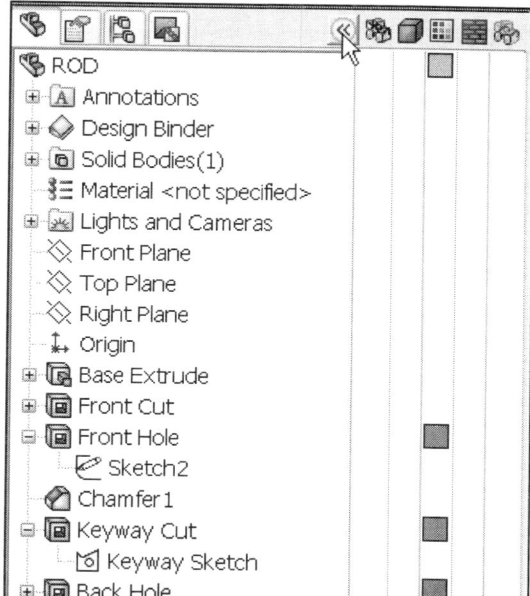

View model orientation from the Graphics window.

451) Click the **View** *Front icon in the lower left corner of the Graphics window. The model orientation options are displayed.

452) Click the **menu** to choose an orientation.

Display the Multi view modes.

453) Click **Two View – Horizontal** for a Top and Front horizontal view in the Graphics window.

454) Click **Two View – Vertical** for a Top and Front vertical view in the Graphics window.

455) Click **Four View** for a Front, Left, Top and Trimetric view in the Graphics window.

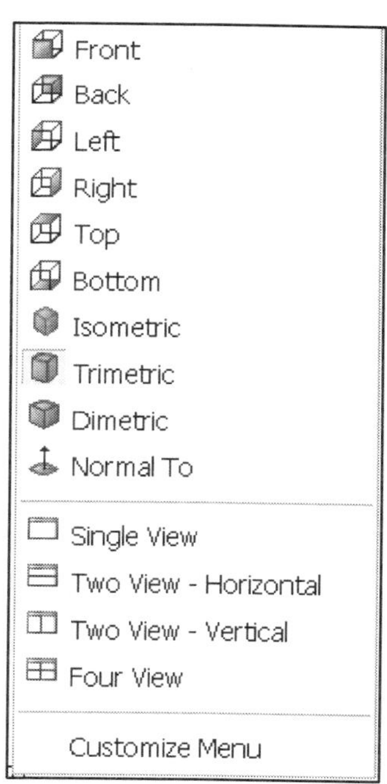

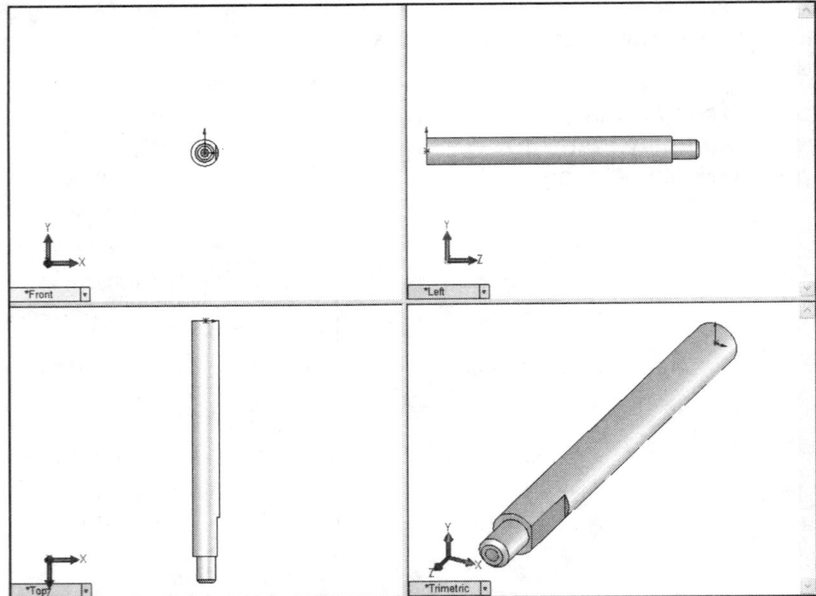

Display the Single view mode.

456) Click **Single View** to display a single view in the Graphics window.

457) Click **Isometric view** .

The ROD part is complete. Save the ROD.

458) Click **Save** .

Close the ROD.

459) Click **File**, **Close** from the Main menu.

Standardize the company part colors. Example: Color red indicates a cast surface. Color blue indicates a machined surface. Green is the selection color in SolidWorks. Minimize the use of the color green to avoid confusion.

Additional details on Colors are available in Help, SolidWorks Help Topics. Index keywords: Colors, Edit and Colors, Color and Optics PropertyManager.

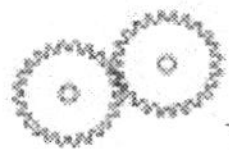 Review of the ROD Part.

The ROD part utilized an Extruded Base feature with a circular profile sketched on the Front Plane. Linear and diameter dimensions corresponded to the customer's requirements.

The Chamfer feature removed the front circular edge. The Chamfer required an edge, distance and angle parameters. The Extruded Cut utilized a converted edge of the Extruded Base to form a Keyway. Reuse geometry with the Convert Entity Sketch tool.

You utilized an Extruded Cut on the front face to create the Front Hole. Reuse geometry. The Front Hole was copied to the back face to create the Back Hole.

The Display\Delete Sketch Tool deleted dangling dimensions of the copied feature. You inserted an Extruded Cut by moving the Rollback Bar to a new position in the FeatureManager. You recovered from the errors that occur with Edit Feature, Edit Sketch and Edit Sketch Plane by redefining geometry.

GUIDE Part Overview

The GUIDE part supports the ROD. The ROD moves linearly through the GUIDE. Two slot cuts provide flexibility in locating the GUIDE in the final assembly.

The GUIDE supports a small sensor mounted on the angled right side. You do not have the information on the exact location of the sensor. During the field installation, you receive additional instructions.

Create a pattern of holes on the angled right side of the GUIDE to address the functional requirements.

Address the geometric requirements with the GUIDE features:

- Extruded Base: Create a symmetrical sketched profile with the Extruded Base feature.

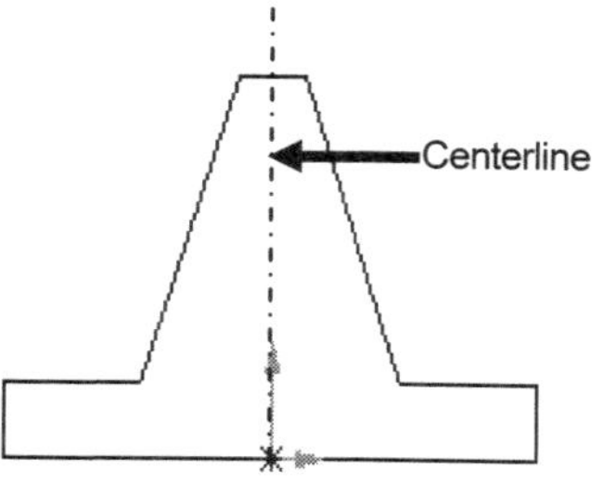

Extruded Base

Utilize a centerline and the Dynamic Mirror Sketch tool. The centerline acts as the mirror axis. The copied entity becomes a mirror image of the original across the centerline.

A centerline is a line with a property that makes it exempt from the normal rules that govern sketches. When the system validates a sketch, it does not include centerlines when determining if the profile is disjoint or self-intersecting.

- Extruded Cut: The Extruded Cut utilizes two lines and two arcs sketched on the top face to form the slot.

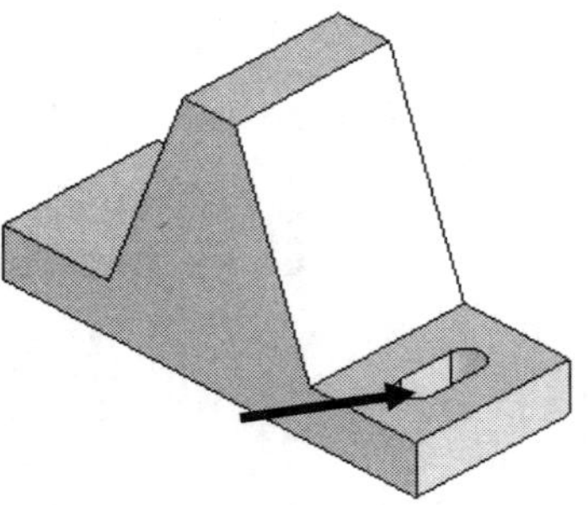

- Mirror: Use the Mirror feature to create a second slot about the Right plane. Reuse geometry with the Mirror feature.

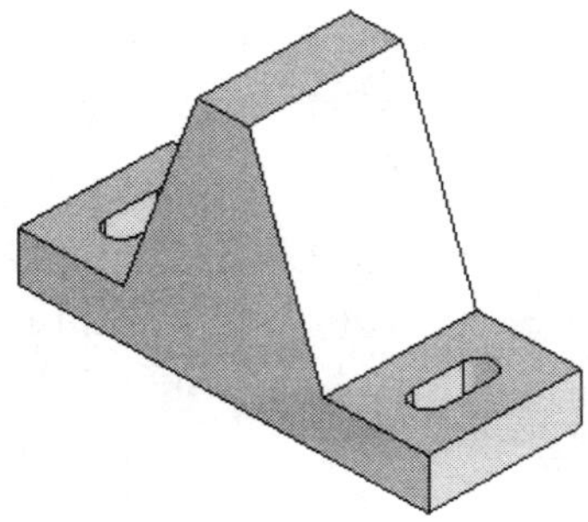

- Extruded Cut: Use the Extruded Cut feature to create the Guide Hole. The ROD glides through the Guide Hole.

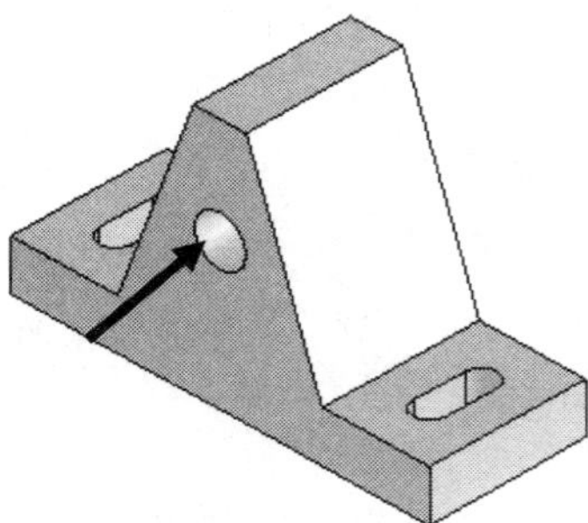

- Hole Wizard and Linear Pattern: Use the Hole Wizard to create a M3 tapped hole. Use the Linear Pattern to create multiple instances of the M3 tapped hole. Reuse geometry with the Linear Pattern feature.

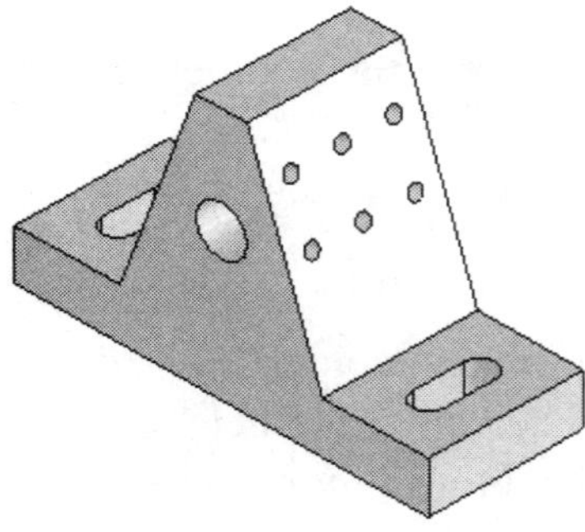

GUIDE Part-Extruded Base Features and Dynamic Mirror

The GUIDE utilized and Extruded Base feature. The geometry of the Extruded Base feature is a symmetric.

What is the Sketch plane? Answer: The Front Plane is the Sketch plane. The Mid Plane depth option extrudes the sketch symmetric about the Front Plane.

How do you sketch a symmetrical 2D profile? Answer: Use a sketched centerline and the Dynamic Mirror Sketch tool.

Sketching lines and centerlines produces different behavior depending on how you sketch. Review sketching line techniques before you begin the GUIDE part.

There are two methods to create a line:

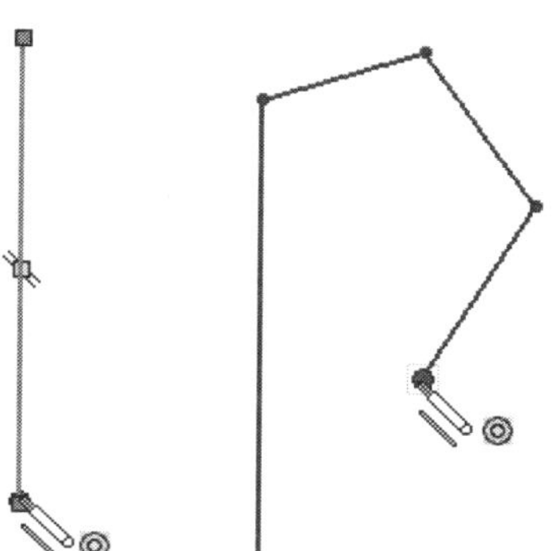

- Method 1: Click the first point of the line. Drag the mouse pointer to the end of the line and release. Utilize this technique to create an individual line segment.
- Method 2: Click the first point of the line. Release the left mouse button. Move to the end of the line and click again. The endpoint of the first line segment becomes the start point of the second line segment. Move to the end of the second line and click again.

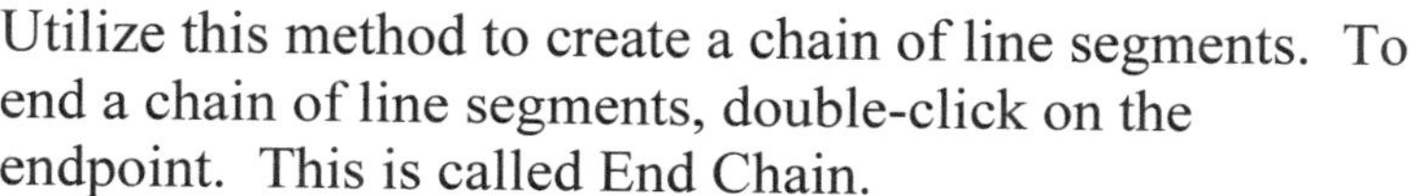

Utilize this method to create a chain of line segments. To end a chain of line segments, double-click on the endpoint. This is called End Chain.

Utilize Method 1 to create the individual centerline.

Utilize Method 2 to create the chained profile lines.

Activity: GUIDE Part-Extruded Base Feature and Dynamic Mirror

Create a new part.

460) Click **File**, **New** from the Main menu.

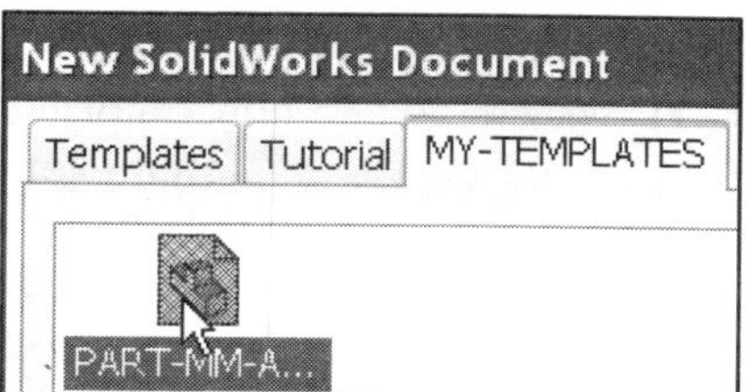

461) Click the **MY-TEMPLATES** tab.

462) Double-Click **PART-MM-ANSI** in the New SolidWorks Document Template dialog box.

Save the part.

463) Click **Save** .

464) Click the **drop down arrow** in the Save in list box.

465) Select **ENGDESIGN-W-SOLIDWORKS\PROJECTS**.

466) Enter **GUIDE** for the File name.

467) Enter **GUIDE SUPPORT** for the Description.

468) Click **Save**.

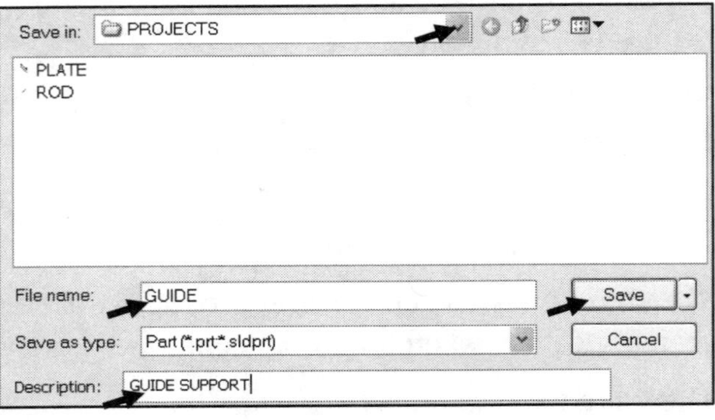

Create the Sketch.

469) Click the **Front Plane** from the FeatureManager.

470) Click **Sketch** Sketch from the Sketch toolbar.

Sketch a centerline.

471) Click **Centerline** Centerline from the Sketch toolbar. A Centerline is drawn with a series of long and short dashes.

472) Click the **Origin** .

473) Drag and click a **point** above the Origin.

Activate the Mirror Sketch Tool.

474) Click **Tools, Sketch Tools**, **Dynamic Mirror** Dynamic Mirror from the Main menu.

475) Click the **vertical centerline**.

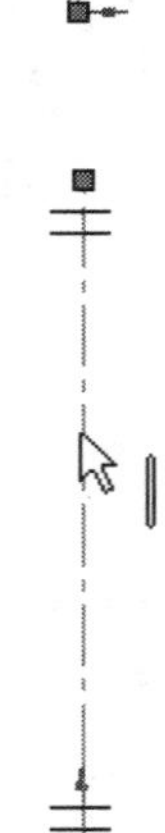

Sketch the profile.

476) Click **Line** Line from the Sketch toolbar.

477) Sketch the first horizontal line from the **Origin** to the right. The mirror of the Sketch appears on the left side of the centerline. Note: Click the endpoint of the line. Do not drag the mouse.

478) Sketch the **four additional line segments** to complete the sketch. The last point is coincident with the centerline. The profile is continuous; there are no gaps or overlaps.

479) Double-click the **end of the line** to end the Sketch.

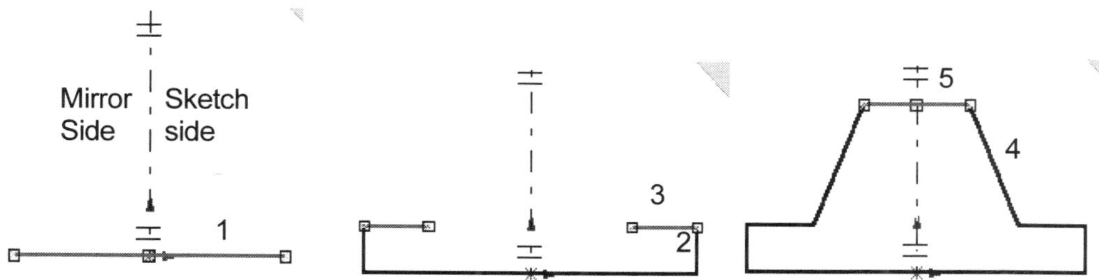

Add dimensions.

480) Click **Smart Dimension** Smart Dimens... .

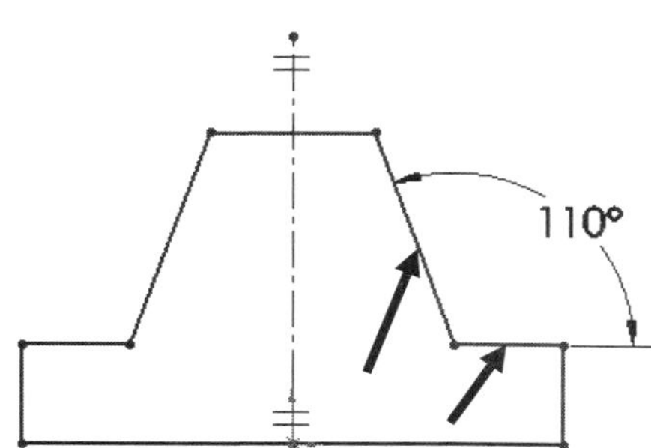

Create an angular dimension.

481) Click the **right horizontal line**.

482) Click the **right-angled line**.

483) Click a **position** between the two lines.

484) Enter **110**.

485) Click the **Green Check mark** ✔.

Create two vertical dimensions.

486) Click the **left small vertical line**.

487) Click a **position** to the left of the profile.

488) Enter **10**. Click the **Green Check mark** ✔.

489) Click the **bottom horizontal line**.

490) Click the **top horizontal line**.

491) Click a **position** to the left of the profile. Enter **50**. Click the **Green Check mark** ✔.

Create two linear horizontal dimensions.

492) Click the **top horizontal line**.

493) Click a **position** above the profile.

494) Enter **10**. Click the **Green Check mark** ✔.

495) Click the **bottom horizontal line**.

496) Click a **position** below the profile.

497) Enter **80**. Click the **Green Check mark** ✔.

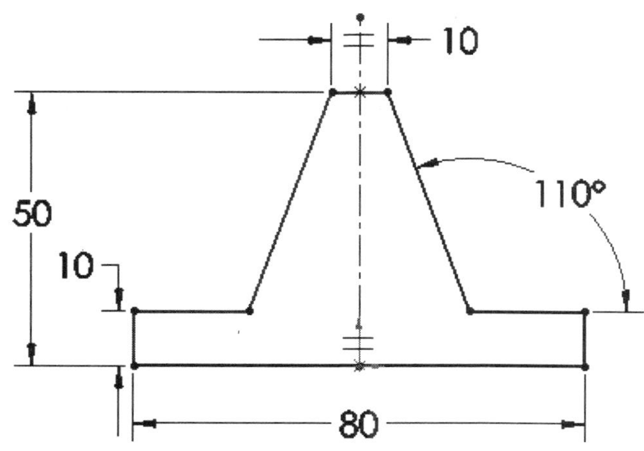

Select edges instead of points to create linear dimensions. Points are removed when Fillet and Chamfer features are added.

Dimension angles, smaller line segments, and then larger line segments to maintain the profile shape.

Insert an Extruded Base feature.

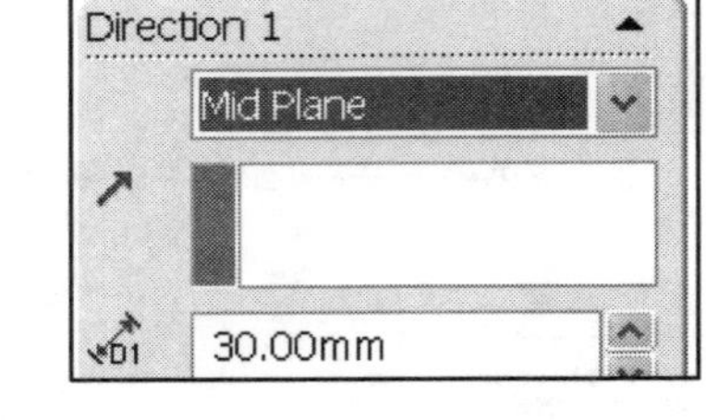

498) Click **Features** from the Control Area.

499) Click **Extruded Boss/Base**.

500) Enter **30** for Depth.

501) Select **Mid Plane** for End Condition.

502) Click **OK** from the Extrude PropertyManager.

503) Rename **Extrude1** to **Base Extrude**.

Save the GUIDE.

504) Click **Save**.

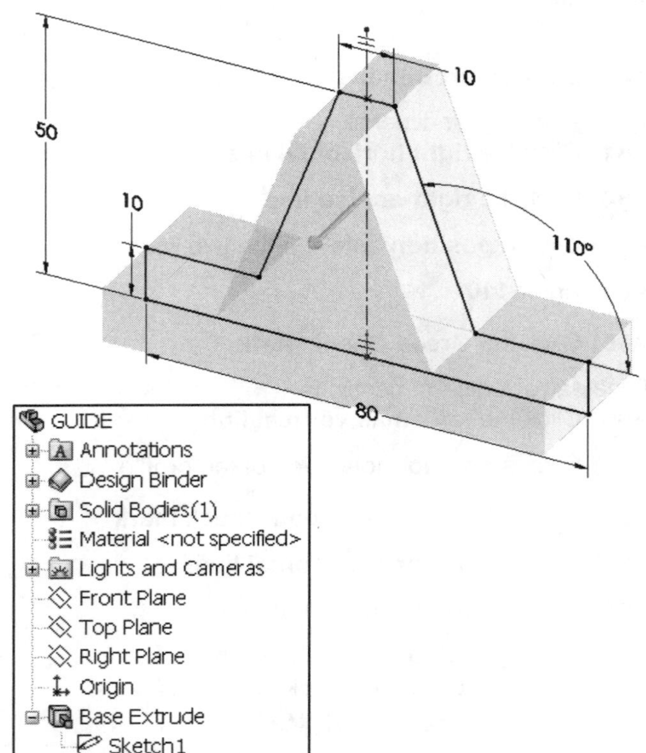

Note: There are two Mirror Sketch tools in SolidWorks: Dynamic Mirror and Mirror Entities.

Dynamic Mirror requires a centerline. As you sketch, entities are created about the centerline.

Mirror Entities requires a predefined profile and a centerline. Select Mirror Entities, then select the profile and the centerline.

GUIDE Part-Extruded Cut Slot Profile

Create an Extruded Cut feature. The 2D profile of the slot utilizes a sketch with two lines and two 180° Tangent Arcs.

Activity: GUIDE Part-Extruded Cut Slot Profile

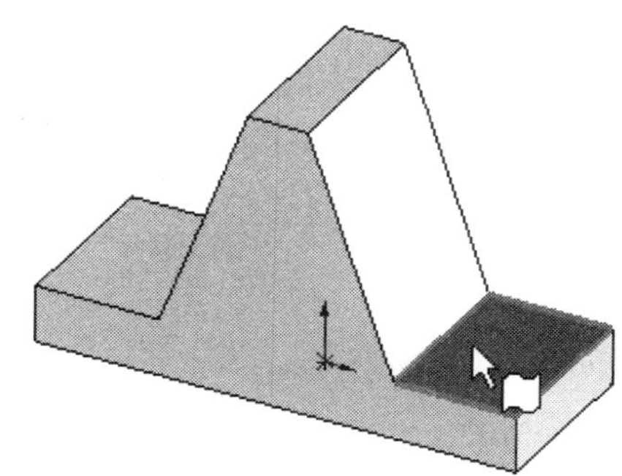

Create the Sketch.

505) Click the **top right face** of the GUIDE for Sketch plane.

506) Click **Sketch** Sketch .

507) Click **Top view** . The top right face of the GUIDE is displayed.

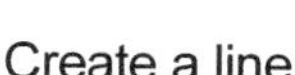

Create a line.

508) Click **Line** Line from the Sketch toolbar.

509) Sketch a short **vertical line** on the selected face. Note: The selected face is the top right face of the GUIDE.

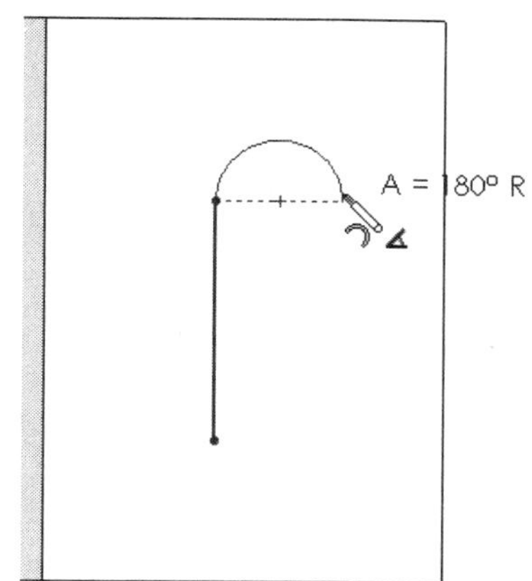

Create the first Arc.

510) Click **Tangent Arc** Tangent Arc from the Sketch toolbar.

511) Click the **endpoint** of the vertical line.

512) Drag the **arc** upward and to the right until the mouse pointer displays 180°.

513) **Click** to end the Arc. The three arc points are aligned horizontally.

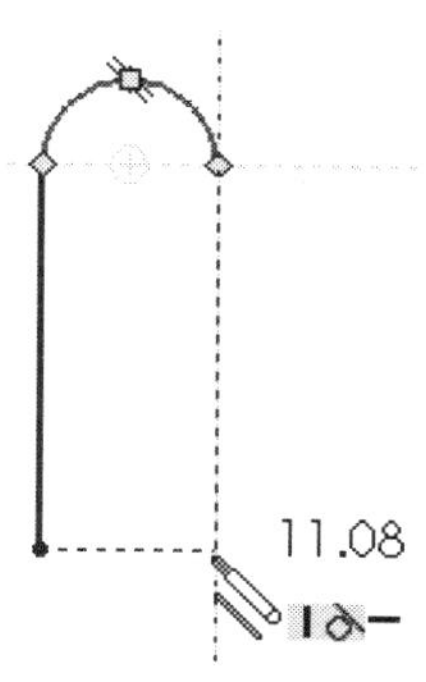

Create a second vertical line.

514) Click **Line** Line from the Sketch toolbar.

515) Sketch a **vertical line** parallel and equal in length to the first line. The sketch displays a dashed blue line when the endpoint of the second line is aligned to the endpoint of the first line.

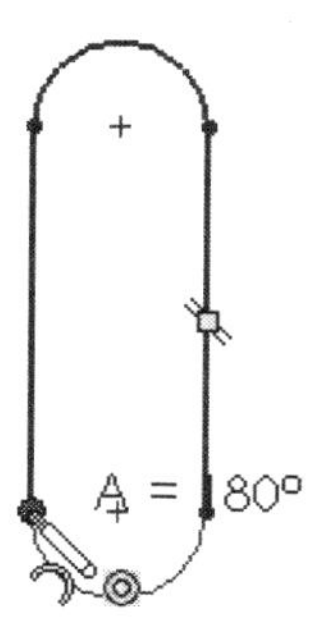

Create the second Arc.

516) Click **Tangent Arc** Tangent Arc from the Sketch toolbar.

517) Click the **endpoint** of the second vertical line.

518) Drag the **arc** downward and to the left.

519) Click the **first point** of the left vertical line.

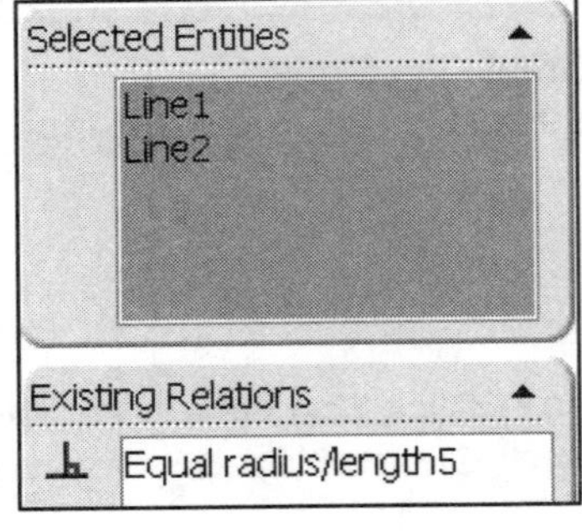

Add an Equal Relation.

520) Right-click **Select**.

521) Click the **first** vertical line. Hold the **Ctrl key** down.

522) Click the **second** vertical line. Release the **Ctrl** key.

523) Click **Equal** in the Add Relations box.

524) Click **OK**  from the Properties PropertyManager.

Add dimensions.

525) Click **Smart Dimension** Smart Dimens... .

526) Click the **Origin**. Click the **center point** of the first Arc. Note: When the mouse pointer is positioned over the center point, the center point is displayed in red.

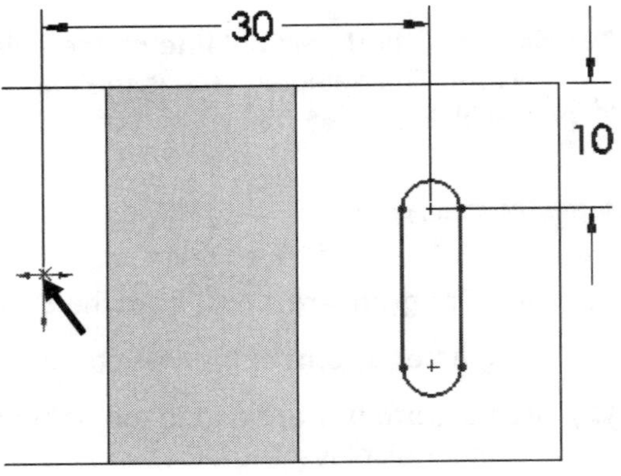

527) Click a **position** above the profile.

528) Enter **30**.

529) Click the **Green Check mark** ✔.

Create a vertical dimension.

530) Click the **top horizontal edge** of the GUIDE. Click the **center point** of the first arc. Click a **position** to the right of the profile.

531) Enter **10**.

532) Click the **Green Check mark** ✔.

Create a dimension between the two arc center points.

533) Click the first Arc **center point**. Click the second Arc **center point**.

534) Click a **position** to the right of the profile.

535) Enter **10**.

536) Click the **Green Check mark** ✔.

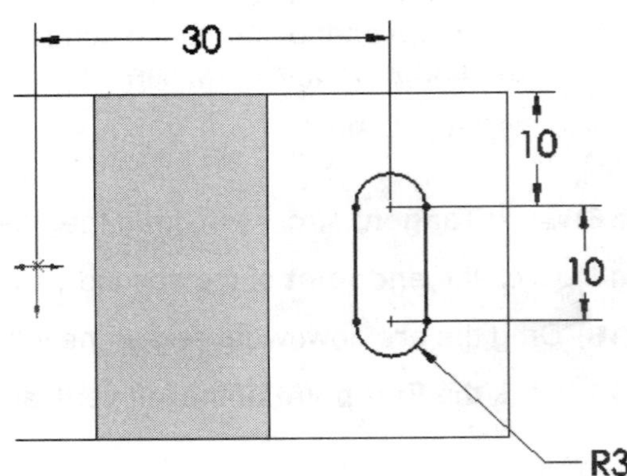

Create a radial dimension.

537) Click the **second Arc** radius.

538) Click a **position** diagonally below the profile.

539) Enter **3**.

540) Click the **Green Check mark** ✔. The is fully defined and is displayed in black.

Insert an Extruded Cut feature.

541) Click **Features** Features.

542) Click **Extruded Cut** Extruded Cut.

543) Enter **Through All** for the End Condition.

544) Click **OK** from the Cut-Extrude PropertyManager.

545) Click **Isometric view**.

546) Rename **Cut-Extrude1** to **Slot Cut**.

Save the GUIDE.

547) Click **Save**.

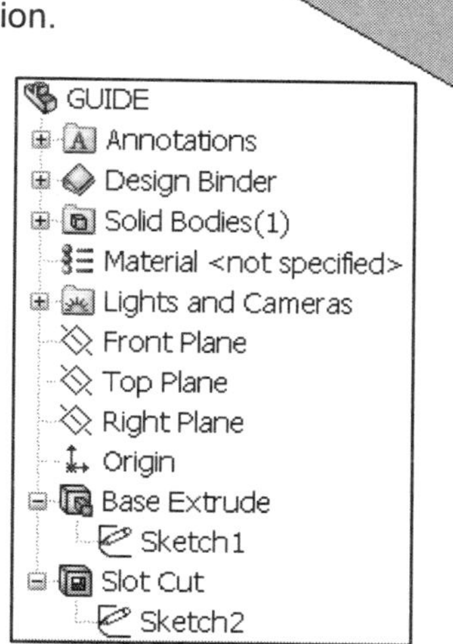

SolidWorks contains additional methods to create sketch slots. Here are three examples that you can explore as an exercise:

- Sketch a rectangle. Delete two opposite line segments. Insert two arcs. Extrude the profile.
- Sketch a single vertical centerline. Utilize Offset Entities, Bidirectional option and Cap Ends option. Extrude the profile.
- Utilize a Design Library Feature.

The machined, metric, straight slot feature provides both the Slot sketch and the Extruded-Cut feature. You define the references for dimensions, overall length and width of the Slot. Explore Design Library Features in Project 6.

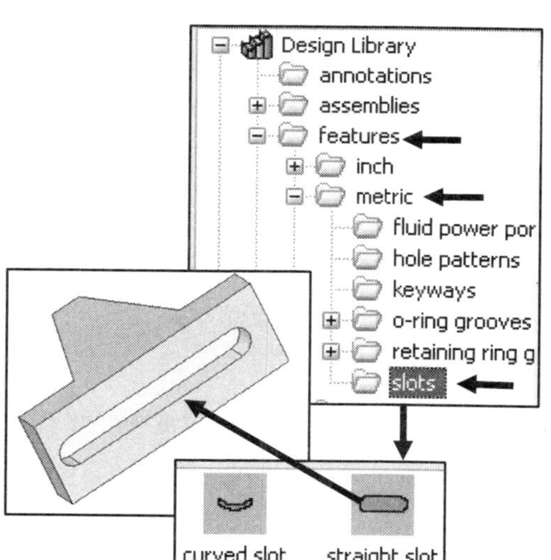

GUIDE Part-Mirror Feature

The Mirror feature mirrors a selected feature about a mirror plane. Utilize the Mirror feature to create the Slot Cut on the left side of the GUIDE. The mirror plane is the Right Plane.

Activity: GUIDE Part-Mirror Feature

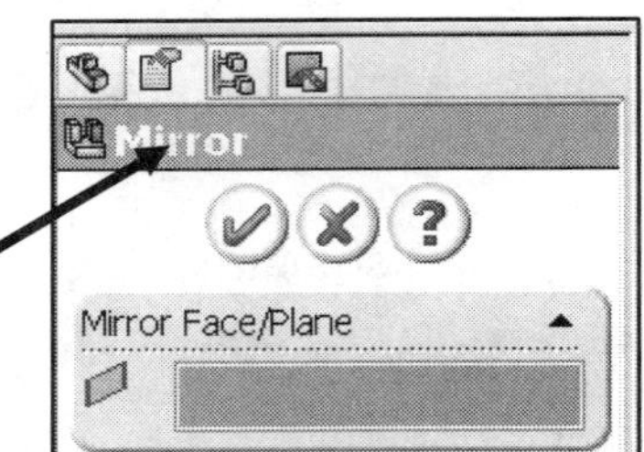

Insert a Mirror feature.

548) Click **Mirror**  from the Features toolbar.

549) Click the **Mirror Feature Property button** to expand the FeatureManager in the Graphics window.

550) Click the **Right Plane** from the FeatureManager for the Mirror plane. Click **Slot Cut** from the FeatureManager for the Features to Mirror.

551) Click the **Geometric Pattern** check box.

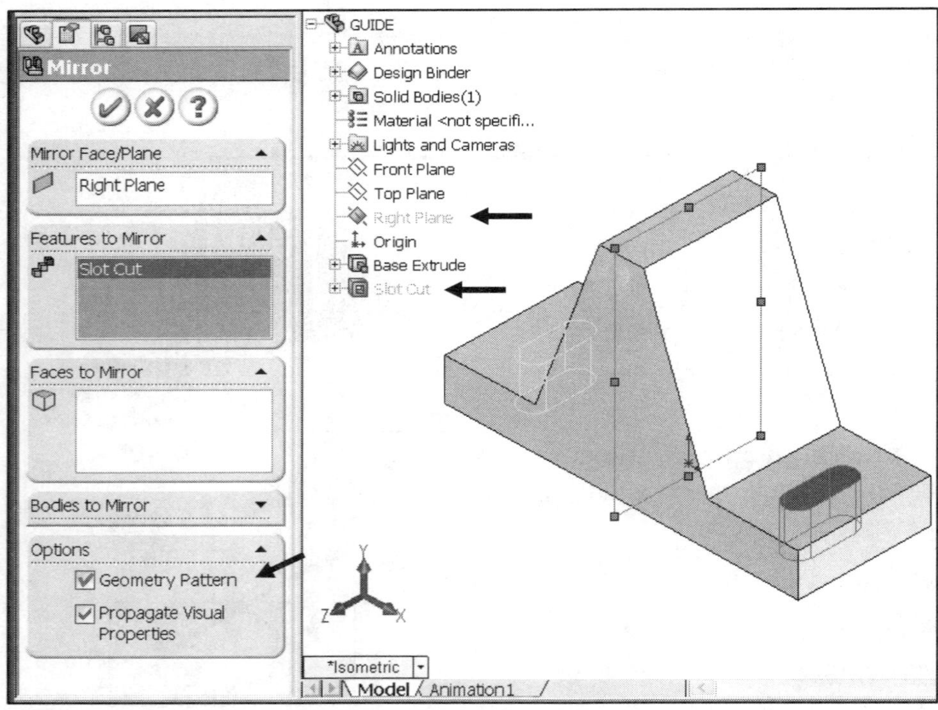

552) Click **OK** from the Mirror PropertyManager.

Save the GUIDE part.

553) Click **Save** .

Fit the GUIDE part to the Graphics window.

554) Press the **f** key.

To save Rebuild time, check the Geometry pattern option in the Mirror Feature PropertyManager. Each instance is an exact copy of the faces and edges of the original feature.

Additional details on Geometry Pattern, Mirror Feature and Sketch Mirror are available in Help, SolidWorks Help Topics. Index keywords: Geometry, Mirror Features and Mirror Entities.

GUIDE Part-Holes

The Extruded Cut feature removes material from the front face of the GUIDE to create a Guide Hole. The ROD moves through the Guide Hole.

Create the tapped holes with the Hole Wizard and a Linear Pattern. Dimension the tapped holes relative to the Guide Hole.

Activity: GUIDE Part-Holes

Create the Sketch.

555) Click the **front face** of the GUIDE for Sketch plane.

556) Click **Sketch** Sketch.

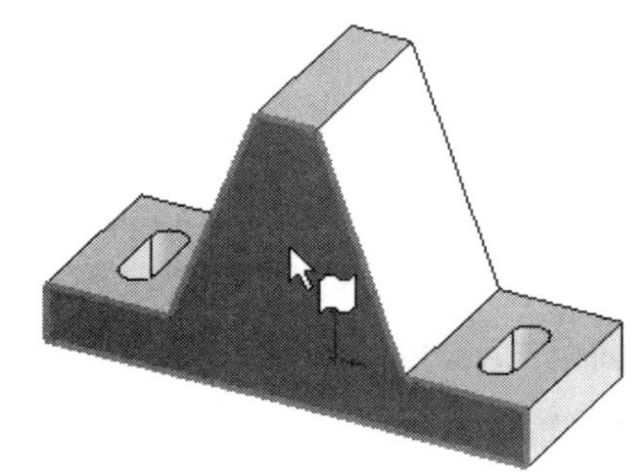

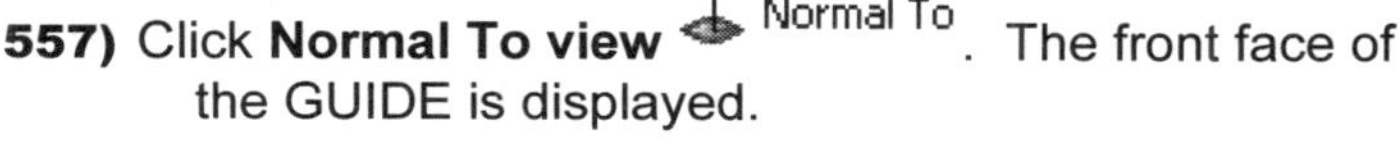

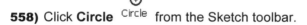

557) Click **Normal To view** Normal To. The front face of the GUIDE is displayed.

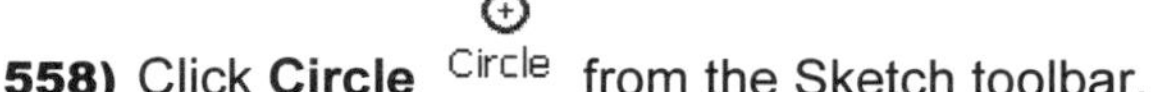

558) Click **Circle** Circle from the Sketch toolbar.

559) Sketch a **circle** in the middle of the GUIDE.

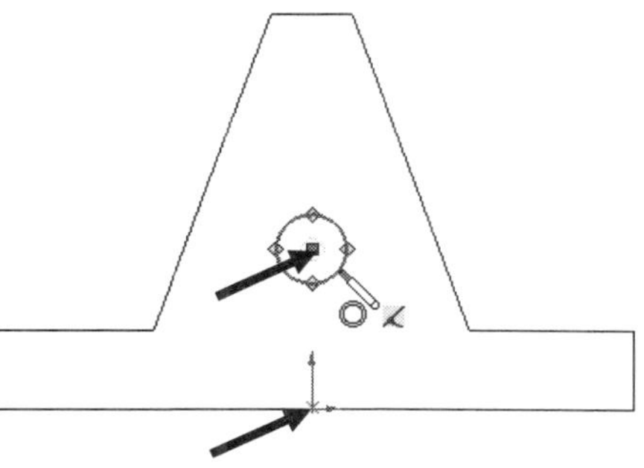

Add a Vertical Relation.

560) Right-click **Select**.

561) Click the **Origin**.

562) Hold the **Ctrl** key down.

563) Click the **center point** of the circle.

564) Release the **Ctrl** key. Click **Vertical** from the Add Relations box.

565) Click **OK** from the Properties PropertyManager.

Add a dimension.

566) Click **Smart Dimension** Smart Dimens... .

567) Click the circle **circumference**.

568) Click a **position** below the horizontal line.

569) Enter **10**.

570) Click the **Green Check mark** ✔.

571) Click the **center point** of the circle.

572) Click the **Origin**.

573) Click a **position** to the right of the profile.

574) Enter **29**.

575) Click the **Green Check mark** ✔.

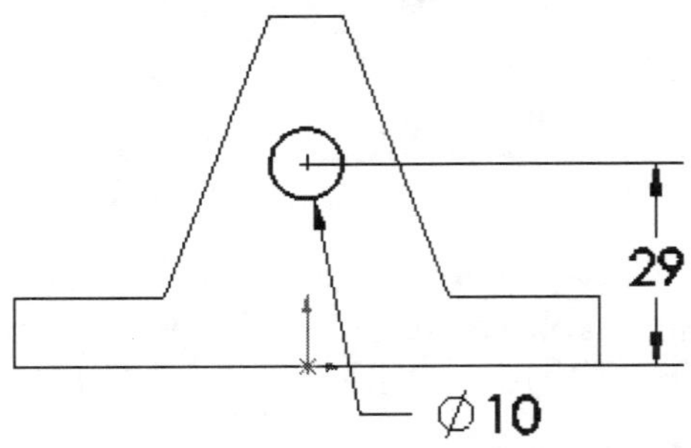

Create an Extruded Cut feature.

576) Click **Features** Features from the Control Area.

577) Click **Extruded Cut** Extruded Cut .

578) Enter **Through All** for End Condition.

579) Click **OK** from the Cut-Extrude PropertyManager.

580) Click **Isometric view** .

581) Rename **Cut-Extrude2** to **Guide Hole**.

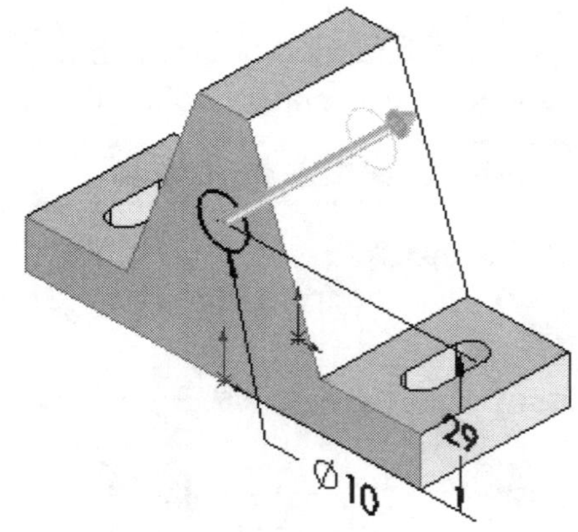

Display the Temporary Axes.

582) Click **View**, check **Temporary Axes** from the Main menu.

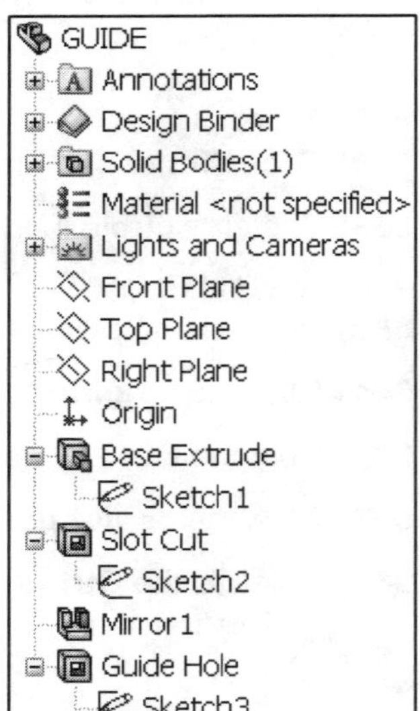

Create the Tapped Hole.

583) Click the **right angled face** below the Guide Hole Temporary Axis.

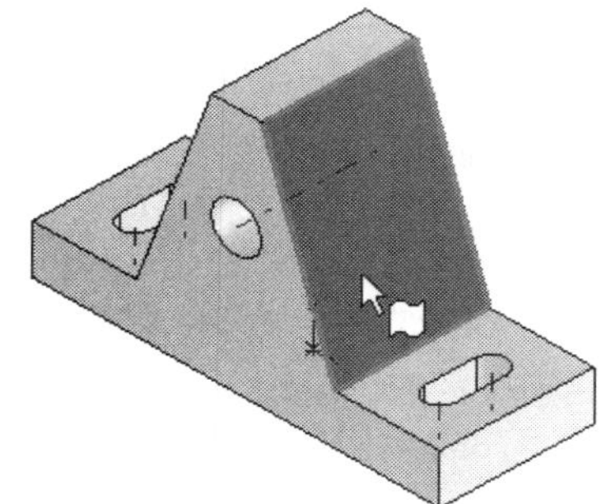

584) Click **Hole Wizard**  Hole Wizard. The Hole Definition dialog box is displayed.

585) Click the **Type** tab.

586) Click **Tap** Hole Specification.

587) Select **ANSI Metric** for Standard.

588) Select **Bottoming Tapped hole** for Screw type.

589) Select **M3x0.5** for Size.

590) Select **Blind** from the drop down list for Tap Drill Type/Depth. Accept the other default values in the table.

591) Click the **Positions** tab.

592) Click **Normal To view** Normal To to view the Sketch plane. Note: The Point icon is selected in the Sketch toolbar.

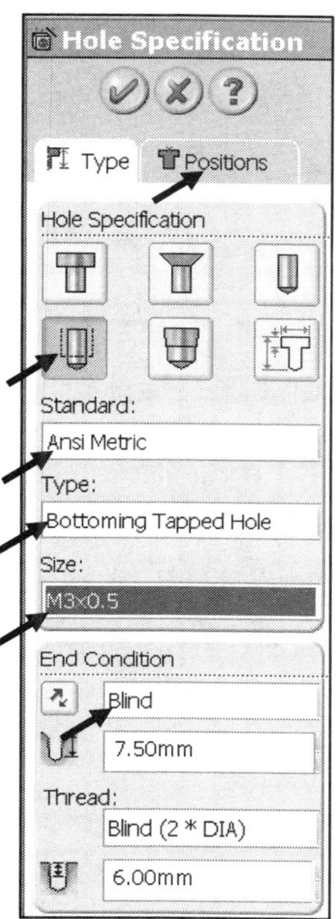

Dimension the tapped hole relative to the Guide Hole axis. Add the horizontal dimension.

593) Click **Smart Dimension**  Smart Dimens... .

594) Click the **center point** of the tapped hole.

595) Click the **right vertical edge**.

596) Click a **position** above the profile.

597) Enter **25**.

598) Click the **Green Check mark** ✔.

Add a vertical dimension.

599) Click the **center point** of the tapped hole.

600) Click the horizontal **Temporary Axis**.

601) Click a **position** to the right of the profile.

602) Enter **4**.

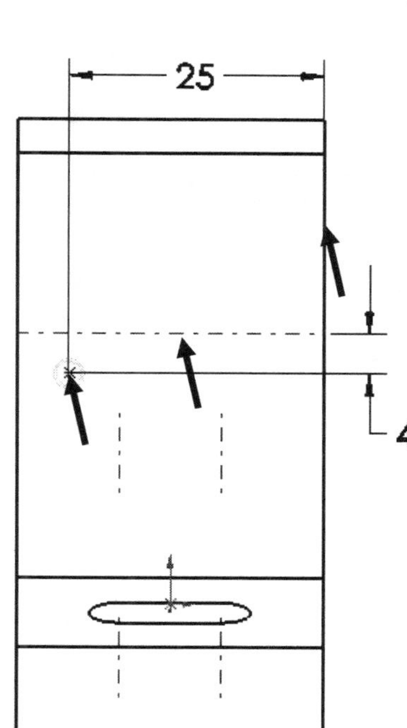

Display the tapped hole.

603) Click **OK** from the Dimension PropertyManager

604) Click **OK** from the Hole Position PropertyManager.

Hide the Temporary Axes.

605) Click **View**, uncheck **Temporary Axes** from the Main menu.

Fit GUIDE to the Graphics window.

606) Press the **f** key.

Save the GUIDE.

607) Click **Save** .

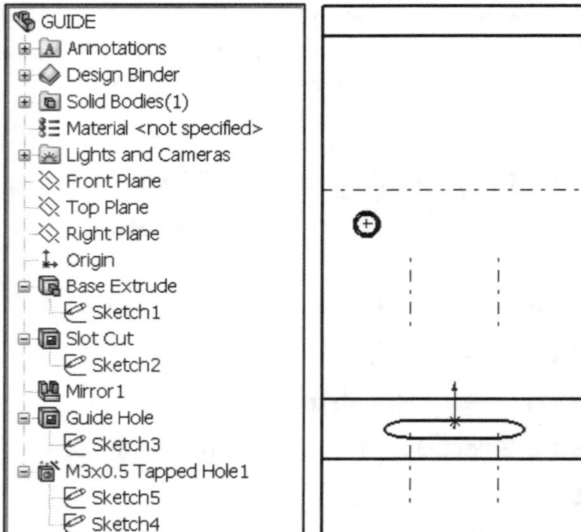

GUIDE Part-Linear Pattern Feature

A Linear Pattern creates multiple copies of a feature in an array. A copy of a feature is called an instance. A Linear Pattern requires:

- One or two directions.
- Distance between instances.
- Number of instances.

Insert a Linear Pattern of Tapped Holes on the right angled face of the GUIDE.

Activity: GUIDE Part-Linear Pattern Feature

Display the Right view.

608) Click **Right view** from the Standard Views toolbar.

Insert the Linear Pattern.

609) Click **Linear Pattern** Linear Pattern from the Features Toolbar.

610) Expand **GUIDE** in the Graphics window.

611) Click the **Features to Pattern** box. Click the **M3X0.5 Tapped Hole1** from the Graphics window for the Features to Pattern.

612) Click the **Pattern Direction** box for Direction1.

613) Click the top **horizontal edge** for Direction 1.

614) Enter **10** in the Direction1 Spacing box. The direction arrow points to the right.

615) Enter **3** in the Number of Instances box.

616) Click the **Pattern Direction** box for Direction 2.

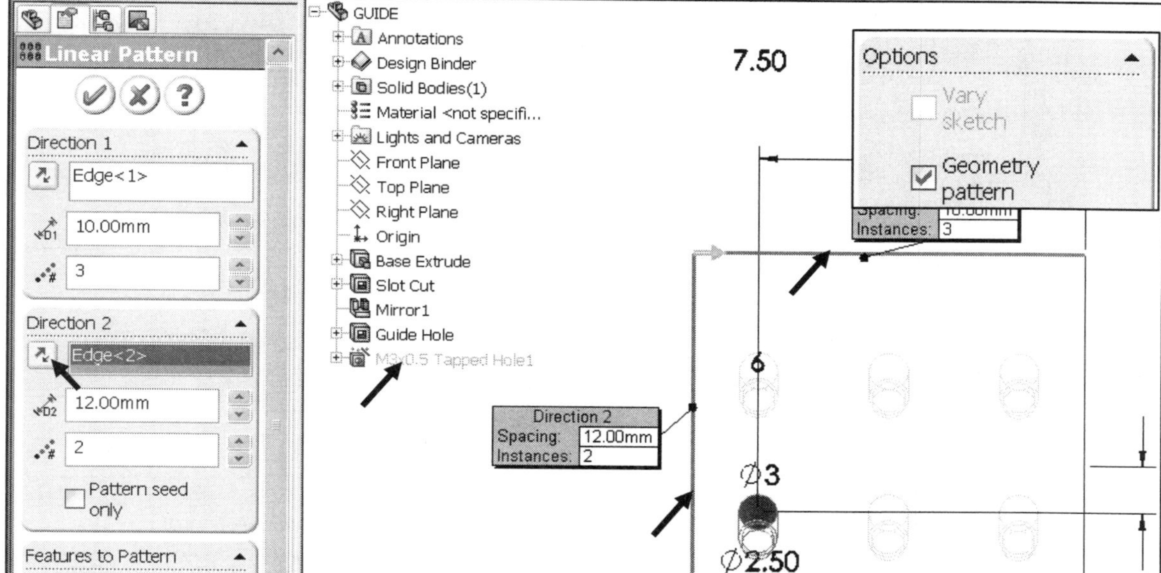

617) Click the **left vertical edge** for Direction 2. The direction arrow points upward.

618) Click the **Reverse Direction** button on the Direction2 text box if required.

619) Enter **12** for Distance in the Direction 2 Distance spin box.

620) Enter **2** in the Number of Instances spin box.

621) Check **Geometry Pattern** in the Options box at the bottom of the Linear Pattern PropertyManager.

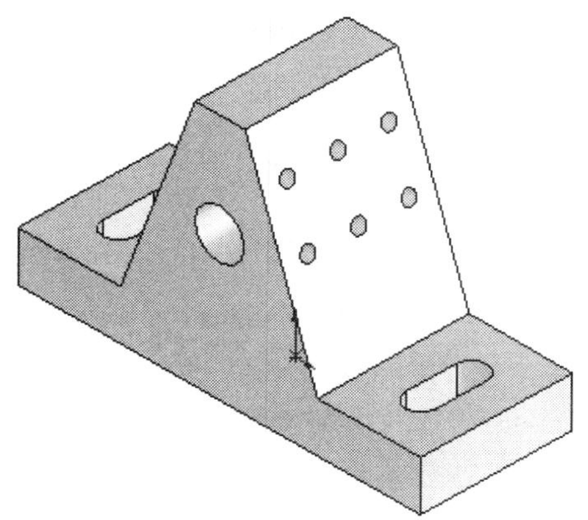

Display the Pattern.

622) Click **OK** from the Linear Pattern PropertyManager. Click **Isometric view**.

Save the GUIDE.

623) Click **Save**.

Reuse geometry. Linear Patterns with the Geometry Pattern option save rebuild time. Rename the seed feature in the part pattern. The seed feature is the first feature, Example: M3x0.5 Tapped Hole1. Assemble additional parts to the seed feature in the assembly.

Additional details on Linear Pattern are available in Help, SolidWorks Help Topics.

Save time when sketching by utilizing the Grid. Utilize Tools, Options, Document Properties, Grid/Snap to control display and spacing settings. The Display grid check box turns on/off the Grid in the Sketch.

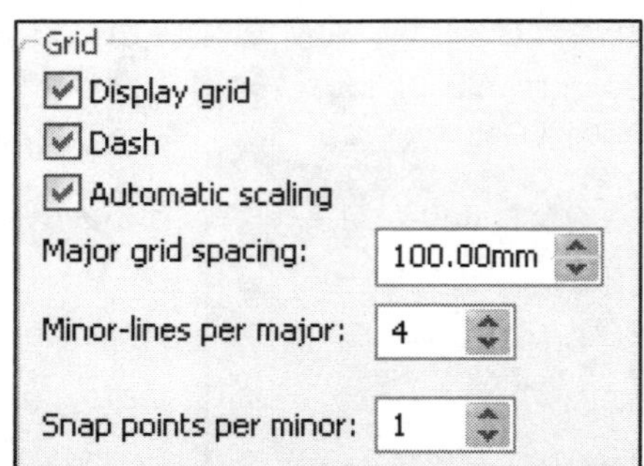

Hide geometric relations to clearly display profile lines in the Sketch. Check View, Sketch Relations to hide/display geometric relations in the sketch.

GUIDE Part-Materials Editor and Mass Properties

Apply Materials such as steel, aluminum and iron to a SolidWorks part through the Material entry in the FeatureManager. Visual Properties and Physical Properties are dispalyed in the Materials Editor. Visual Properties are displayed in the Graphics window and section views of the part. The Physical Property value for Density, 8000 kg/m^3 propogates to the Mass Properties Tool.

Activity: GUIDE Part-Materials Editor and Mass Properties

Apply AISI 304 Stainless Steel Material.

624) Right-click **Materials** in the FeatureManager.

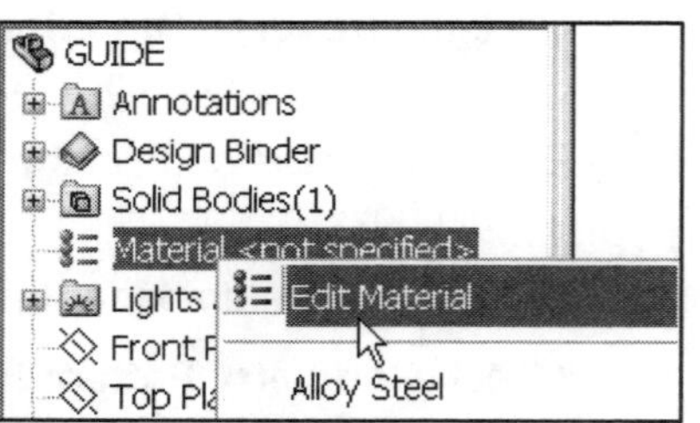

625) Click **Edit Material** Edit Material. The Materials Editor PropertyManager is displayed.

Expand Steel.

626) Click **Plus** ⊞.

627) Select **AISI 304**.

628) Click **OK** from the Materials Editor PropertyManager.

Calculate MassProperties.

629) Click **Tools, Mass Properties** Mass Properties... from the Main menu.

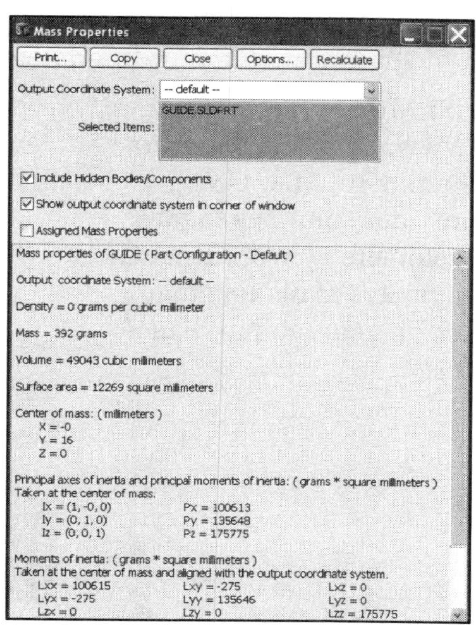

Set the units to display.

630) Click **Options**.

631) Click the **Use custom settings** Use custom settings button.

632) Enter **4** in the Decimal places spin box.

633) Click **OK**.

634) Drag the **right slide bar** downward to review the complete list of Mass Properties for the GUIDE.

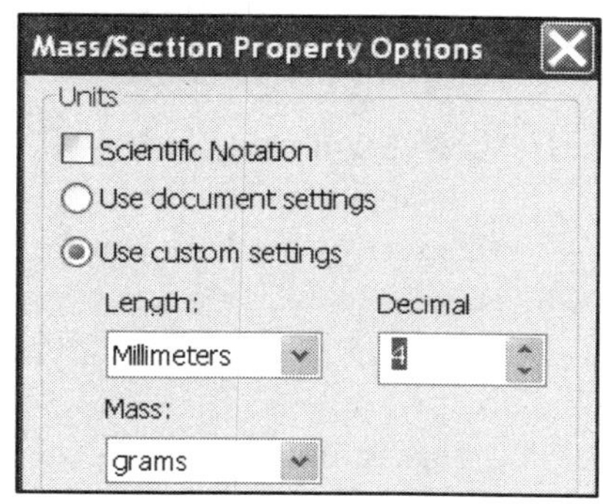

635) **Review** the Mass properties of the GUIDE.

636) Click **Close**.

Save the GUIDE.

637) Click **Save**.

Close the GUIDE.

638) Click **File**, **Close** from the Main menu.

Additional details on the Materials Editor and Mass Properties are available in Help, SolidWorks Help Topics.

The Materials Editor properties propagate to other SolidWorks applications: Mass Properties, COSMOSXpress, COSMOSWorks and PhotoWorks. Specify materials early in the design process. To define your own materials, utilize Create/Edit Material Create/Edit Material... to create a new Materials library.

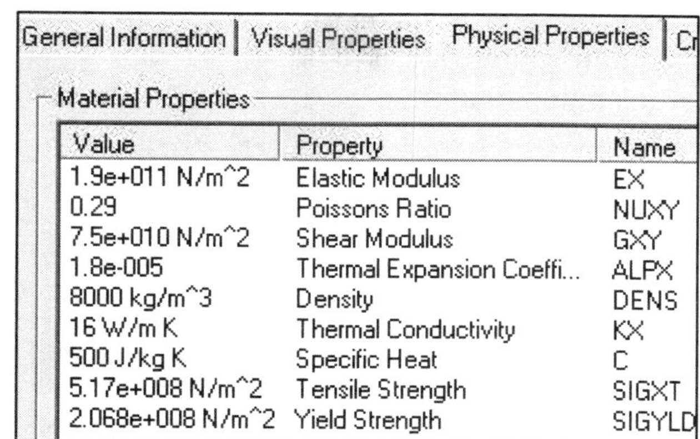

General Information | Visual Properties | Physical Properties | C

Material Properties

Value	Property	Name
1.9e+011 N/m^2	Elastic Modulus	EX
0.29	Poissons Ratio	NUXY
7.5e+010 N/m^2	Shear Modulus	GXY
1.8e-005	Thermal Expansion Coeffi...	ALPX
8000 kg/m^3	Density	DENS
16 W/m K	Thermal Conductivity	KX
500 J/kg K	Specific Heat	C
5.17e+008 N/m^2	Tensile Strength	SIGXT
2.068e+008 N/m^2	Yield Strength	SIGYLD

Manufacturing Considerations

CSI Mfg. (www.compsources.com) Southboro, MA, USA provides solutions to their customers by working with engineers to obtain their design goals and to reduce cost.

Customer Focus
Courtesy of CSI Mfg (www.compsources.com)
Southboro, MA

High precision turned parts utilize a variety of equipment such as single and multi-spindle lathes for maximum output.

MultiDECO 20/8b, 8 spindle, full CNC 23 axis automatic
Courtesy of Tornos USA (www.tornosusa.com)

Obtain knowledge about the manufacturing process from your colleagues before you design the part.

Ask questions on material selection, part tolerances, machinability and cost. A good engineer learns from past mistakes of others.

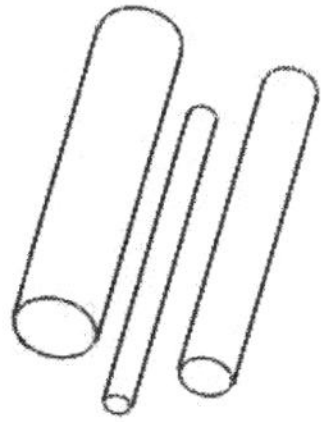

Examples of Cost Effective Materials

- AISI 303
- BRASS
- AL 2011

Review the following design guidelines for Turned Parts.

Guideline 1: Select the correct material.

Consider part functionality, operating environment, cost, "material and machine time", machinability and surface finish. Utilize standard stock sizes and material that is readily available. Materials are given a machinability rating. Brass (100), AISI303(65) and AISI304(30).

Example: Using AISI304 vs. AISI303. AISI303 is easier to machine due to its higher sulfur content.

Guideline 2: Minimize tool changes. Maximize feature manufacturability.

The Extrude Cut, Hole, Chamfer and Fillet features require different tooling operations. Will changes in form or design reduce the number of operations and the cost of machining?

Example:

- Avoid Fillets on inside holes to remove sharp edges. Utilize the Chamfer feature to remove sharp edges.

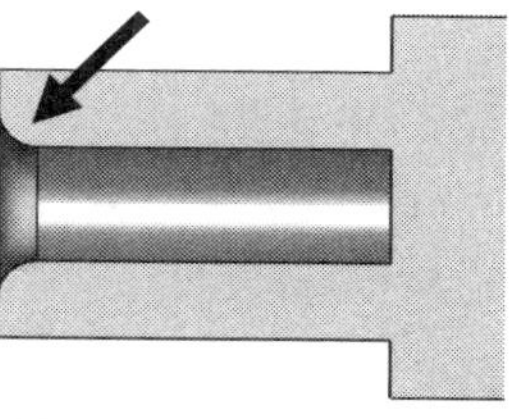

Fillet Edge Expensive

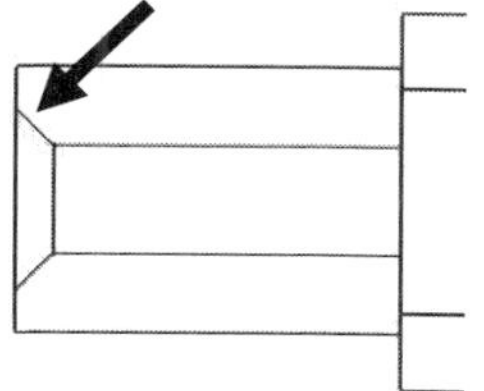

Chamfer Edge Preferred

- Utilize common size holes for fewer tool changes.
- Leave space between the end of an external thread and the shoulder of the rod. Rule of thumb: 1-2 pitch of thread, minimum.

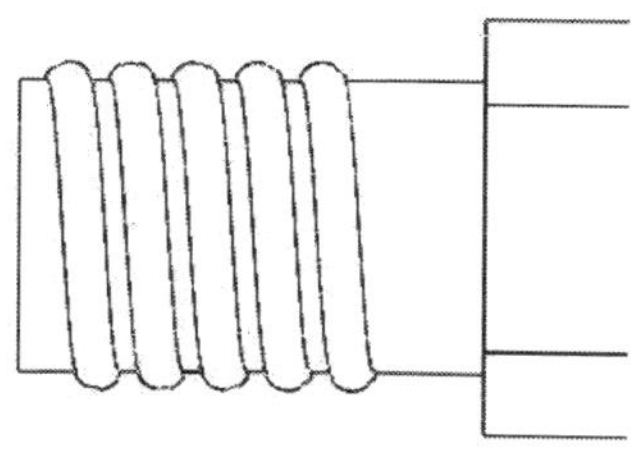

- Leave space at the end of an internal thread for the tool tip endpoint.

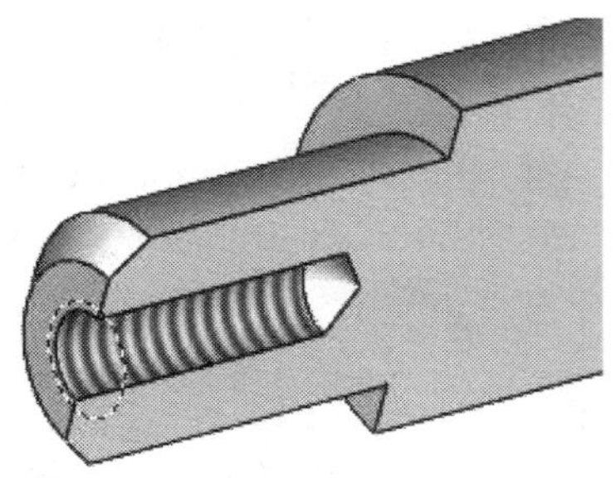

Guideline 3: Optimize the design for production. Provide dimension, tolerance and precision values that can be manufactured and inspected.

- Check precision on linear, diameter and angular dimensions. Additional non-needed decimal places increase cost to a part.

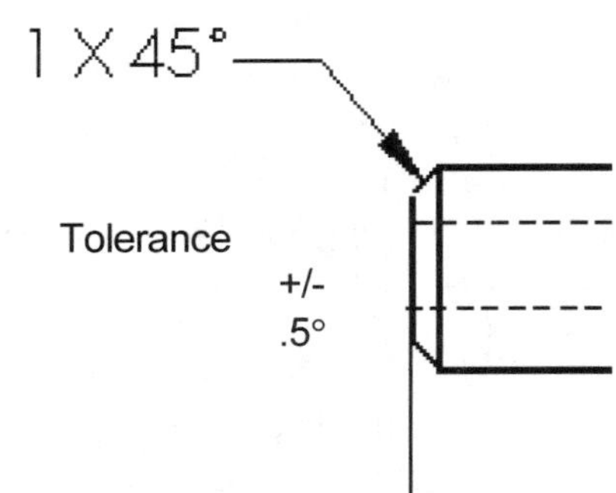

Example:

The dimension 45 at +/- .5° indicates the dimension is machined between 44.5° and 45.5.

The dimension 45.00 at +/- .05° indicates the dimension is machined between 44.95 and 45.05.

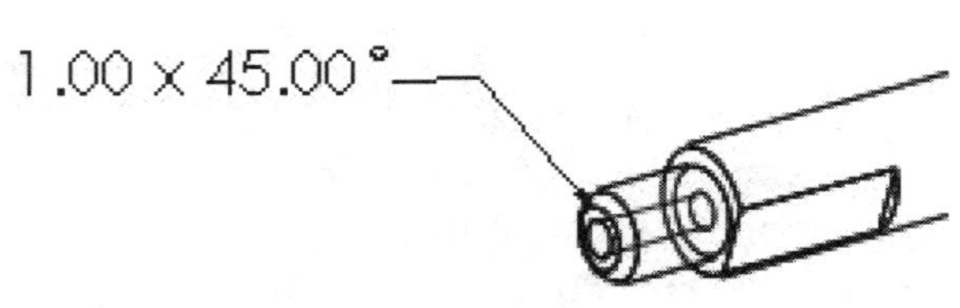

This range of values adds additional machining time and cost to the final product.

Modify the dimension decimal display in the Tolerance/Precision box in the part, assembly or drawing.

Set Document Properties, Dimensions, Tolerance and Precision for the Tolerance... Precision... entire document.

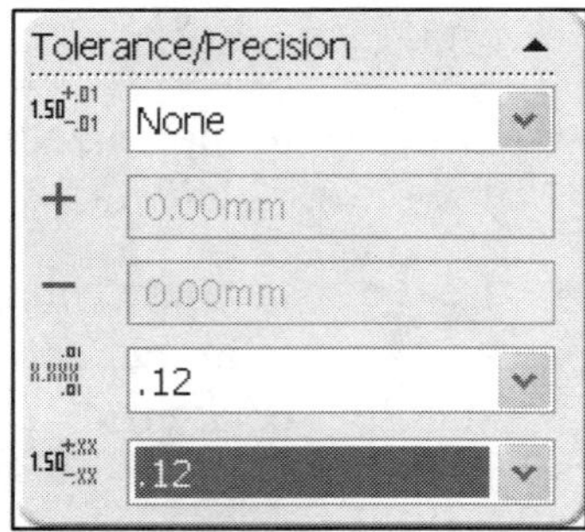

In Project 3, you will create drawings for the GUIDE part. Modify the dimension values and tolerance on the ROD and GUIDE to create a clearance fit.

Sketch Entities and Sketch Tools

The Sketch Entities and Sketch Tools entries in the Tools menu contain additional options not displayed in the default Sketch toolbar. Each option contains information in Help, SolidWorks Help Topics.

If a sketch produces errors during the feature creation process, utilize the Tools, Sketch Tools, Check Sketch for Feature option.

Example: Select Base Extrude for Feature usage. Click the Check button. The error message, “The sketch has more than one open contour” is displayed.

The most common errors are open contours (gaps) or overlapping contours. Edit the sketch and correct the error. Click the Check button. The message, “No problems found” is displayed for a valid sketch.

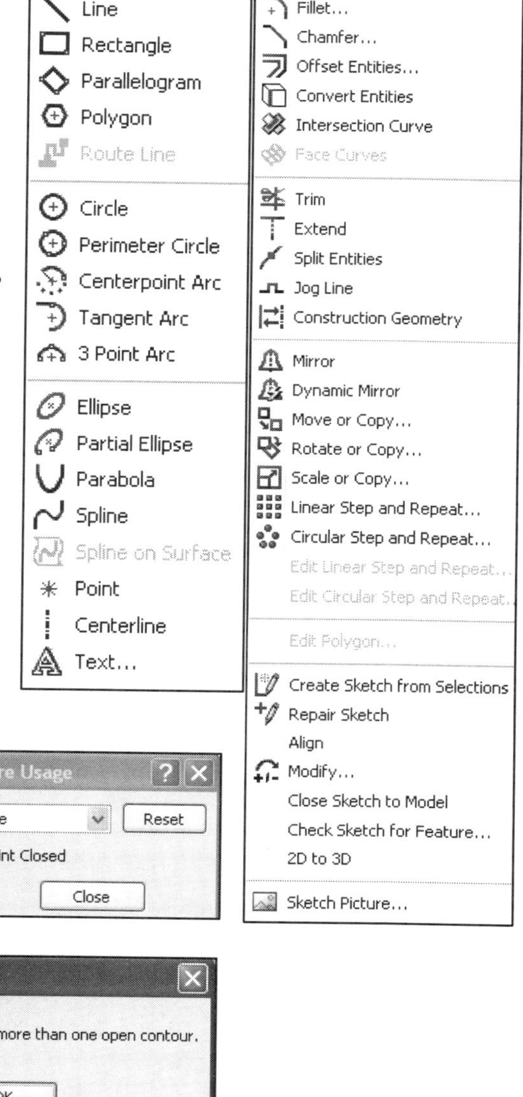

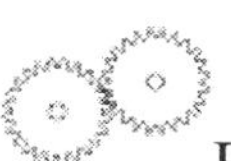

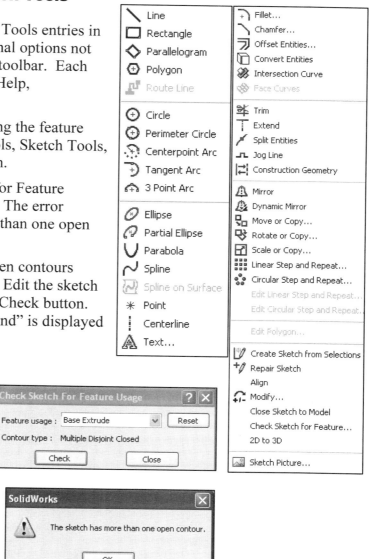

Review of the GUIDE Part.

The GUIDE part utilized an Extruded Base feature. The 2D sketched profile utilized the Dynamic Mirror Sketch tool to build symmetry into the part. The linear and diameter dimensions corresponded to the ROD and GUIDE-CYLINDER assembly.

The Extruded Cut feature created the Slot-Cut. The Mirror feature created a second Slot-Cut symmetric about the Right plane. The Guide Hole utilized the Extruded Cut feature with the Through All option.

The Hole Wizard created the M3 x0.5 tapped hole, the seed feature in the Linear Pattern. The Linear Pattern created multiple instances of the M3 x0.5 tapped hole.

You reused geometry to save design time and rebuild time. Mirror Feature, Linear Pattern, Geometry Pattern Option and Sketch Mirror are time saving tools. You defined materials in the part used by other software applications.

Refer to Help, Online Tutorial, Lesson1-Parts exercise for additional information.

Project Summary

You created three file folders to manage your project models, document templates and vendor components. The PART-ANSI-MM Part Template was developed and utilized for three parts: ROD, GUIDE and PLATE.

The PLATE part consisted of the Extruded Base, Extruded Cut, Fillet and HoleWizard features. The ROD consisted of the Extruded Base, Chamfer, and multiple Extrude Cut features. The ROD illustrated the process to manipulate design changes with the Rollback bar and Edit Sketch and Edit Feature commands. The GUIDE part utilized an Extrude Base feature sketch with the Dynamic Mirror Entities tool. The GUIDE also utilized the Extruded Cut, Mirror and Linear Pattern features.

All sketches for the Extruded Base and Extruded Cut features utilized geometric relationships. Incorporate geometric relations such as horizontal, vertical, symmetric, equal, collinear and coradial into your sketches.

In Project 2, you will incorporate the ROD, GUIDE and PLATE into an assembly. In Project 3, you will create an assembly drawing and a detailed drawing of the GUIDE.

Are you ready to start Project 2? Stop! Examine and create additional parts. Perform design changes. Take chances, make mistakes and have fun with the various features and commands in the project exercises.

Project Terminology

Add Relations: A Sketch tool that provides a way to connect related geometry. Some common relations in this book are concentric, tangent, coincident and collinear.

Applied Feature: A classification of a feature type that utilizes a model's existing edges or faces. Fillets and chamfers are examples of this type of feature.

Base Feature: The Base feature is the first feature that is created in a part. The Base feature is the foundation of the part. Keep the Base feature simple. The Base feature geometry for the PLATE is an extrusion. An Extruded-Base feature requires a sketch plane, sketch and extruded depth.

Centerline: A centerline is a construction line utilized for symmetry and revolved features.

Chamfer feature: An applied feature used to create a beveled edge. The front face of the ROD utilized the Chamfer.

Copy and Paste: Copy and paste simple sketched features and some applied features onto a planar face. Multi-sketch features such as sweeps and lofts cannot be copied. Utilize the Ctrl C / Ctrl V keys to Copy/Paste.

Dimensions: Dimensions measured geometry. A dimension consists of dimension text, arrows, dimensions lines, extension lines and or leader lines.

Extruded Boss/Base: Extends a profile along a path normal to the profile plane for some depth. The movement along that path becomes the solid model. An Extruded Boss/Base adds material. The Extruded Base feature is the first feature in a part. The PLATE utilized an Extruded Base feature. The profile was a rectangle sketched on the Front Plane.

Extruded Cut: Removes material from a solid. The Extruded Cut extends a profile along a path for some depth. The PLATE utilized an Extruded Cut to create two holes on the front face. The Through All end condition linked the depth of the Extruded Cut to the depth of the Extruded Base.

Features: Features are geometry building blocks. Features add or remove material. Create features from sketched profiles or from edges and faces of existing geometry. Features are classified as either sketched or applied.

Fillet: Removes sharp edges. Fillets are generally added to the solids, not to the sketch. By the nature of the faces adjacent to the selected edge, the system knows whether to create a round (removing materials) or a fillet (adding material). Some general filleting design rules:

- Leave cosmetic fillets until the end.
- Create multiple fillets that will have the same radius in the same command.
- Fillet order is important.
- Fillets create faces and edges that are used to generate more fillets.
- In the PLATE part you created the small edge fillets first.

Geometric Relations: A relation is a geometric constraint between sketch entities or between a sketch entity and a plane, axis, edge, or vertex. Relations force a behavior on a sketch element to capture the design intent.

Hole Wizard: The Hole Wizard feature is used to create specialized holes in a solid. Create simple, tapped, counterbore and countersink holes using a step by step procedure. Use the Hole Wizard to create a countersink hole at the center of the PLATE. Use the HoleWizard to create tapped holes in the GUIDE.

Linear Pattern: Repeats features or geometry in an array. Linear Pattern requires the number of instances and the spacing between instances.

Mass Properties: A tool used to reports the part density, mass, volume, moment of inertia and other physical properties.

Materials Editor: The Materials Editor provides visual properties and physical properties for a part. AISI 304 Stainless Steel was applied to the GUIDE. The cross hatching display propagate to the drawing. The physical properties propagate to COSMOSXpress and other applications.

Menus: Menus provide access to the SolidWorks commands.

Mirror Entities: Involves creating a centerline and using the Dynamic Mirror option. The centerline acts as the mirror axis. Sketch geometry on one side of the mirror axis. The copied entity becomes a mirror image of the original across the centerline. Mirror Entities requires a predefined centerline and a sketched profile.

Mirror Feature: Creates an instance (copy) of features about a plane. The GUIDE Slot Cut utilized the Mirror feature.

Mouse Buttons: The left and right mouse buttons have distinct meanings in SolidWorks. The left button is used to select geometry and commands. The right mouse button displays pop-up menus. The middle mouse button rotates the model in the Graphics window.

Plane: A plane is an infinite and flat surface. They display on the screen with visible edges. The PLATE, ROD, and GUIDE all utilize the Front Plane for the Extruded-Base feature.

Rebuild: Regenerates the model from the first feature to the last feature. After a change to the dimensions, rebuild the model to cause those changes to take affect.

Sketch: The name to describe a 2D profile is called a sketch. 2D Sketches are created on flat faces and planes within the model. Typical geometry types are lines, arcs, rectangles, circles and ellipses.

Sketched Features: The Sketched feature is based on a 2-D sketch. The sketch is transformed into a solid by extrusion, rotation, sweeping or lofting.

Status of a Sketch: Four states are utilized in this Project:

- Under Defined: There is inadequate definition of the sketch, (Blue).
- Fully Defined: Has complete information, (Black).
- Over Defined: Has duplicate dimensions, (Red).
- Dangling: Geometry or Sketch Plane has been deleted, (Mustard Yellow-Brown).

System Feedback: System feedback is provided by a symbol attached to the cursor arrow indicating your selection. As the cursor floats across the model, feedback is provided in the form of symbols, riding next to the cursor.

Toolbars: The toolbar menus provide shortcuts enabling you to quickly access the most frequently used commands.

Questions

1. Identify at least four key design areas that you should investigate before starting a project.
2. Why is file management important?
3. Describe the procedure to create a folder in Microsoft Windows.
4. Identify the steps in starting a SolidWorks session.
5. Describe the default reference planes.
6. What is the Base feature? Provide an example. Why should the Base feature be kept simple?
7. How do you recover from Rebuild errors?
8. When do you use the Hole Wizard feature?
9. Describe the difference between an Extruded Base feature and an Extruded Cut feature.
10. Describe a Fillet feature. Provide an example.
11. Name the command keys used to Copy sketched geometry.
12. Describe the difference between Edit Feature and Edit Sketch.
13. Describe a Chamfer feature. Provide an example.
14. Describe the Rollback function. Provide an example.
15. Identify the type of Geometric Relations added to a Sketch.
16. Describe the procedure in creating a part document template.
17. Identify the produce to modify the material assigned to a part.
18. List three guidelines for designing turned parts.
19. Identify the Menu name to locate additional Sketch Tools.
20. Where would you find out more information about the Sketch Entity named, Ellipse? Describe the procedure to sketch an elliptical profile.
21. Identify the following Shortcut Keys:

Shortcut Key	Command
f	
z	
Shift+z	
Ctrl+s	

22. Review the Features toolbar. Identify the name of each feature.

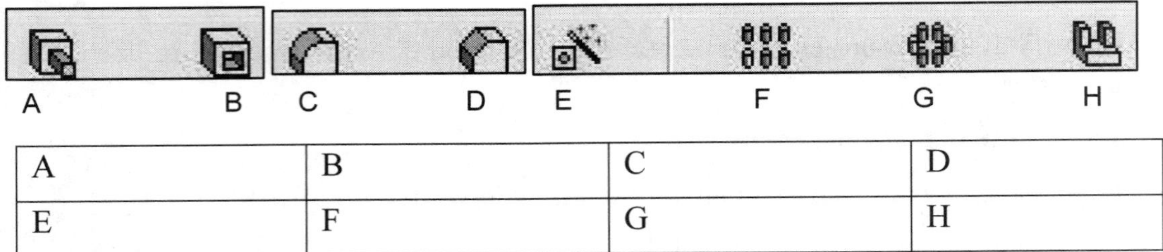

A	B	C	D
E	F	G	H

23. Identify the following icons in the Sketch Tools toolbar.

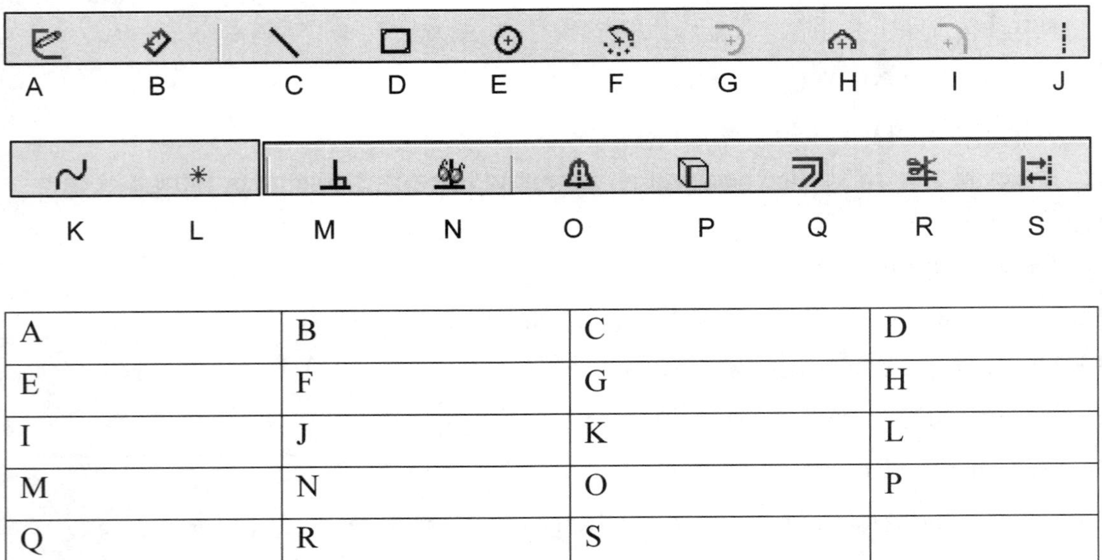

A	B	C	D
E	F	G	H
I	J	K	L
M	N	O	P
Q	R	S	

Exercises

Exercise 1.1 and Exercise 1.2

A fast and economical way to manufacture parts is to utilize Steel Stock, Aluminum Stock, Cast Sections, Plastic Rod and Bars, and other stock materials. Stock materials are available in different profiles and various dimensions from tool supply companies.

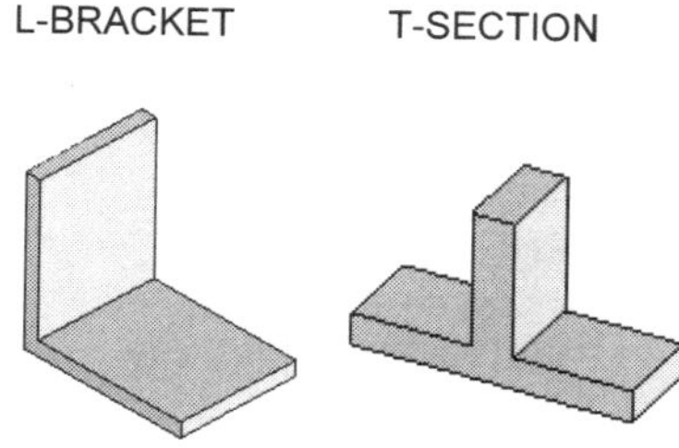

- Create a new part. Each part contains an Extrude feature. Select units.
- Utilize the Front Plane for the Sketch Plane.

Exercise 1.1: L-BRACKET

Ex.:	A:	B:	C:	LENGTH:	Units:
1.1a	3	3	5/8	10	IN
1.1b	4	4	3/4	10	
1.1c	6	4	1/2	25	
1.1d	8	6	3/4	25	
1.1e	12	12	3/2	25	
1.1f	7	4	3/4	30	
1.1g	75	75	10	250	MM
1.1h	75	100	10	250	
1.1i	200	100	25	500	

Exercise 1.2: T-SECTION

Ex.:	A:	B:	C:	LENGTH:	Units:
1.2a	3	3	5/8	30	IN
1.2b	4	4	3/4	30	
1.2c	6	6	1	30	
1.2d	75	75	10	250	MM
1.2e	75	100	10	250	
1.2f	200	100	25	500	

Parts manufactured from machine stock save design time and money. Machine stock is purchased from material supply companies. Machine stock sizes vary from supplier.

- Utilize the World Wide Web and determine common sizes for other machine stock. Example: 1/4in Aluminum Rod or 10mm Steel Plate.

Part information courtesy of the Reid Tool Supply Co. Muskegon, MI USA (www.reidtool.com).

Exercise 1.3: JOINING PLATE

Create the JOINING PLATE part.

- Use symmetry and geometric relations.
- Create a 6mm extruded plate.
- The 8.3mm thru holes are spaced 40mm apart.

The company, 80/20 Inc., manufactures modular aluminum structural extrusions to reduce fabrication time and cost. 80/20 manufacturers both Metric and English products.

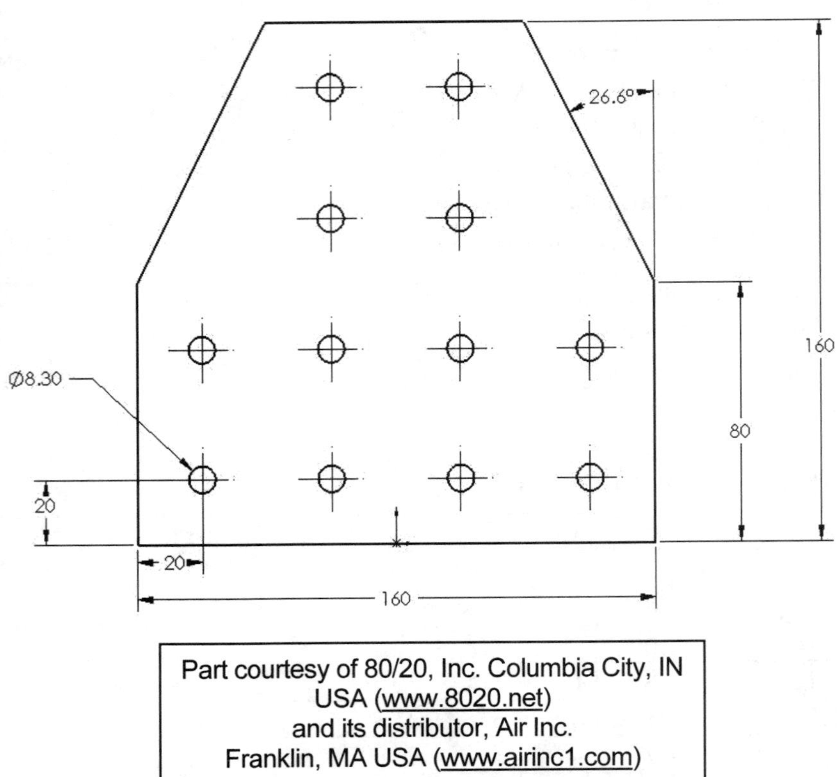

Exercise 1.4a: PART DOCUMENT TEMPLATES

Create a Metric part document template.

- Use an ISO dimension standard.
- Set the Drawing/Units to the appropriate values.
- Name the template, PART-MM-ISO.

Exercise 1.4b: PART DOCUMENT TEMPLATES

Create an English part document template.

- Use an ANSI dimension standard.
- Set Drawing/Units to the appropriate values.
- Name the template, PART-IN-ANSI.

Exercise 1.5: LINKAGE assembly

The LINKAGE assembly is a sub-assembly of the PNEUMATIC TEST MODULE assembly.

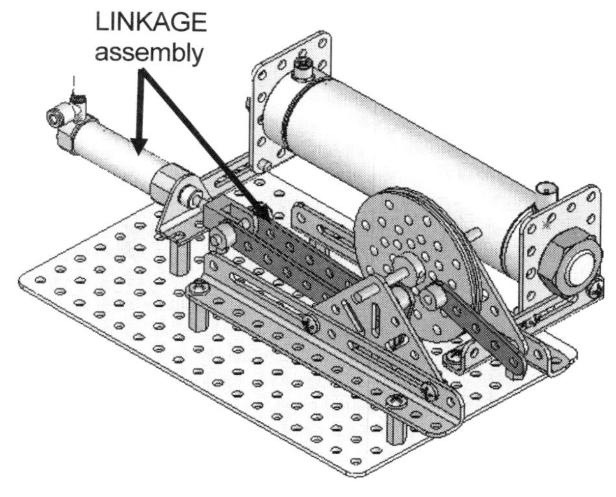

Develop the mechanical parts required for a LINKAGE assembly. The LINKAGE assembly contains four machined parts:

1. AXLE.
2. SHAFT COLLAR.
3. FLAT BAR - 3 HOLE.
4. FLAT BAR - 9 HOLE.

The pneumatic air cylinder is utilized to translate the LINKAGE assembly. The pneumatic air cylinder is a purchased part manufactured by SMC Corporation of America.

In Exercises 1.5a through 1.5d, create the four parts required for the LINKAGE assembly.

Provide the primary units in inches. Provide the secondary units in [millimeters].

The exercises in Projects 2 through 6 contain directions for the additional parts, assemblies and drawings for the PNEUMATIC TEST MODULE assembly.

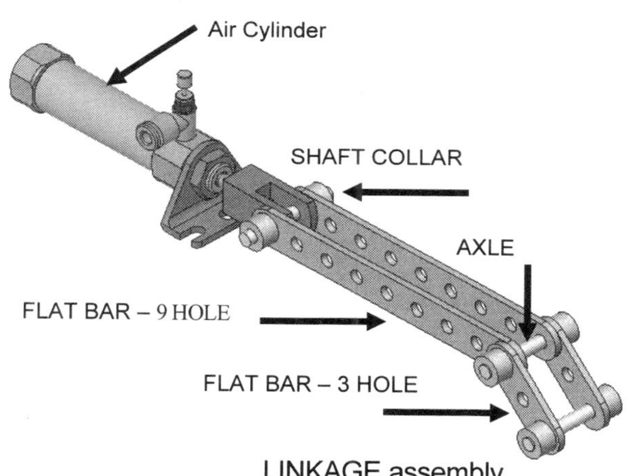

LINKAGE assembly
Complete in Project 2
Courtesy of
Gears Education Systems, LLC and
SMC Corporation of America.

Exercise 1.5a: AXLE

Create the AXLE part.

- Utilize the Front Plane for the Sketch plane.
- Utilize the MidPlane option. The AXLE is symmetric about the Front Plane.

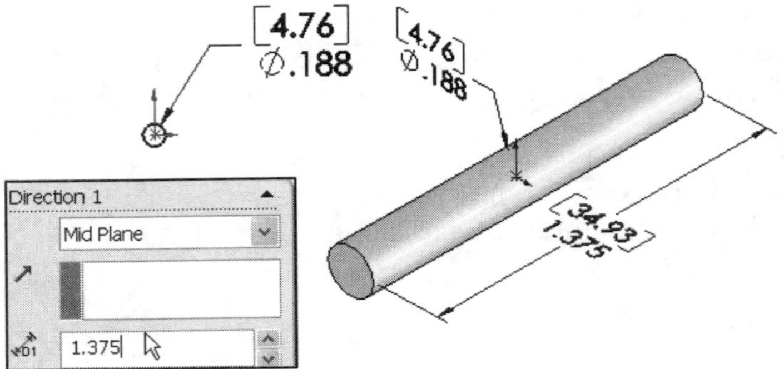

Exercise 1.5b: SHAFT COLLAR

Create the SHAFT COLLAR part.

- Utilize the Front Plane for the Sketch plane.

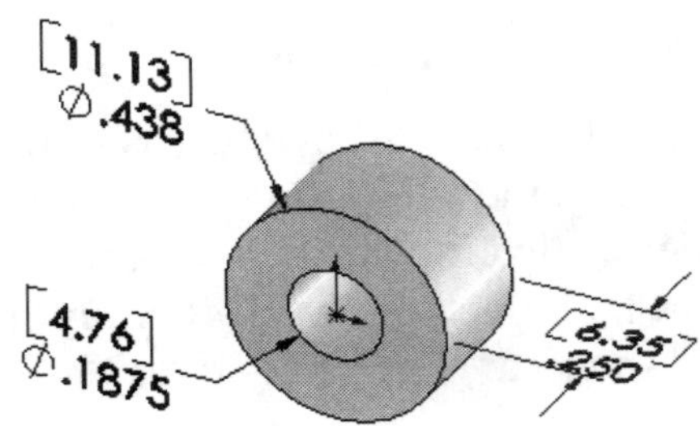

Exercise 1.5c: FLAT BAR - 3 HOLE

Create the FLAT BAR - 3 HOLE part.

- Utilize the Front Plane for the Sketch Plane.
- Utilize a Linear Pattern for the three holes. The FLAT BAR – 3 HOLE part is manufactured from 0.060in [1.5mm] Stainless Steel.

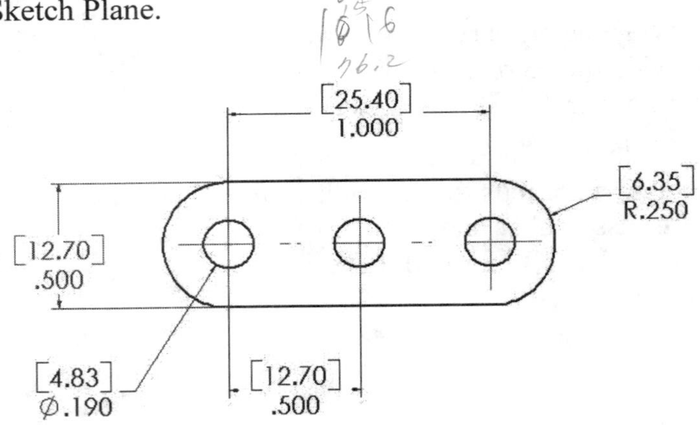

FLATBAR-3HOLE

Exercise 1.5d: FLAT BAR - 9 HOLE.

Design the FLAT BAR, 9 HOLE part.

- Manually sketch the 2D profile. The dimensions for hole spacing, height and end arcs are the same as the FLAT BAR, 3 HOLE part.
- Create the part.
- Utilize the Front Plane for the Sketch Plane.
- Utilize the Linear Pattern feature to create the hole pattern. The FLAT BAR – 9 HOLE part is manufactured from 0.060in [1.5mm] Stainless Steel.

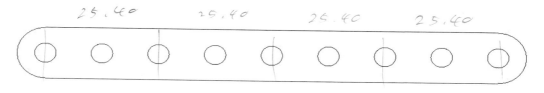

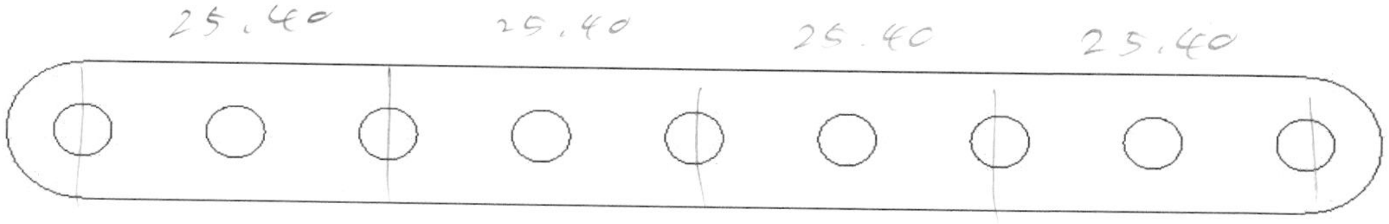

FLAT BAR, 9 HOLE

Exercise 1.6: Modify PLATE.

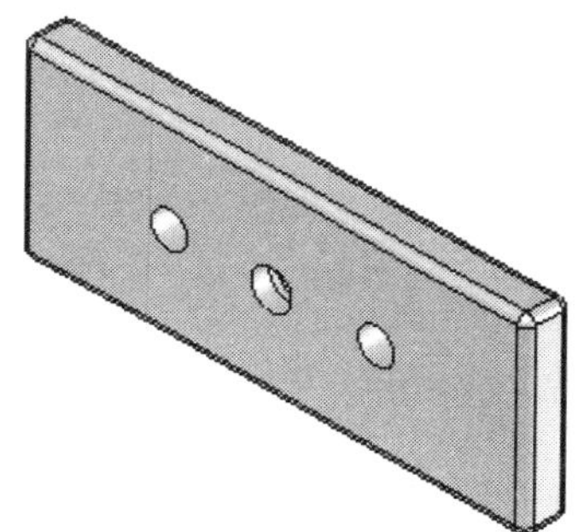

An Engineering Change Order (ECO) is issued for the PLATE. An Engineering Change Order or Engineering Change Notice (ECO/ECN) is required when a part is created or modified. A blank ECO form is contained in the Appendix. Review this form.

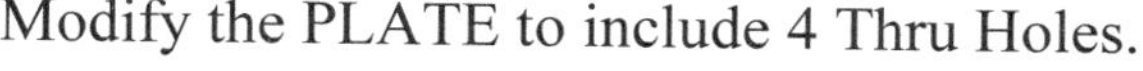

Modify the PLATE to include 4 Thru Holes.

- Use the Hole Wizard and a Linear Pattern. The 4 holes of the PLATE correspond to the 4 corner mounting holes on the Piston Plate.
- Review the dimensions from the Piston Plate drawing. Identify the required dimensions to create the SolidWorks features.
- A drawing number is required. Drawings are an integral part of the design process.
- Create the drawing at the end of Project 3.

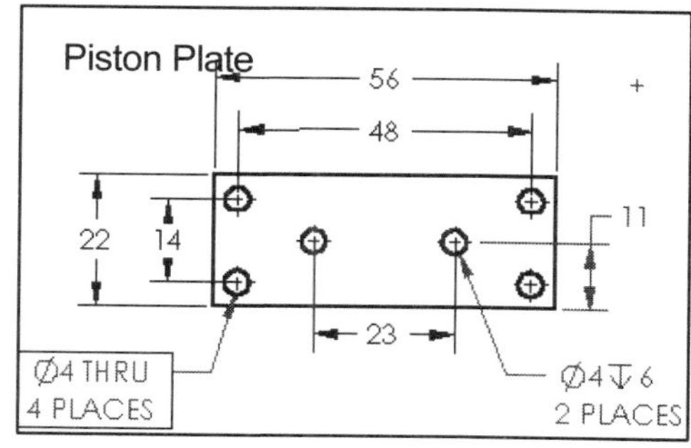

Exercise 1.7: PhotoWorks.

PhotoWorks Add-In is required to complete this exercise. Select Tools, Add-Ins. Select PhotoWorks. The PhotoWorks toolbar is added to the Main menu.

Create picture images of the GUIDE and PLATE parts. Incorporate the new images into a PowerPoint presentation.

PhotoWorks software application renders photo-realistic images of SolidWorks 2005 parts and assemblies. PhotoWorks generates an image directly from the view in the active SolidWorks Graphics window.

Rendering effects include materials, lighting, image background, image quality and image output format. A scene contains a combination of these rendering effects.

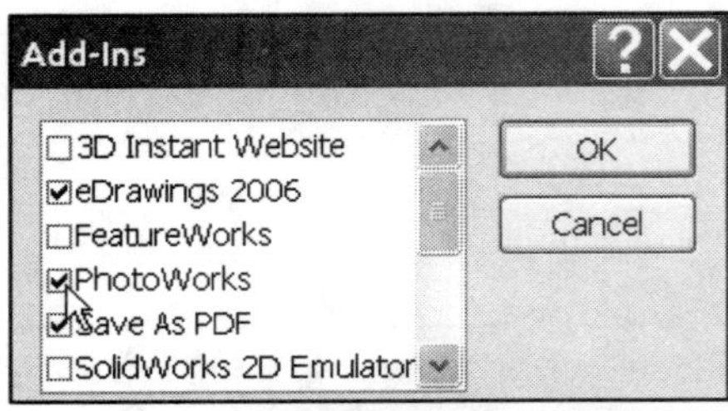

Add PhotoWorks.

- Open the GUIDE part.
- Click Tools, Add-Ins from the Main menu.
- Click PhotoWorks.
- Click OK.
- Click the PhotoWorks Items icon from the PhotoWorks toolbar.

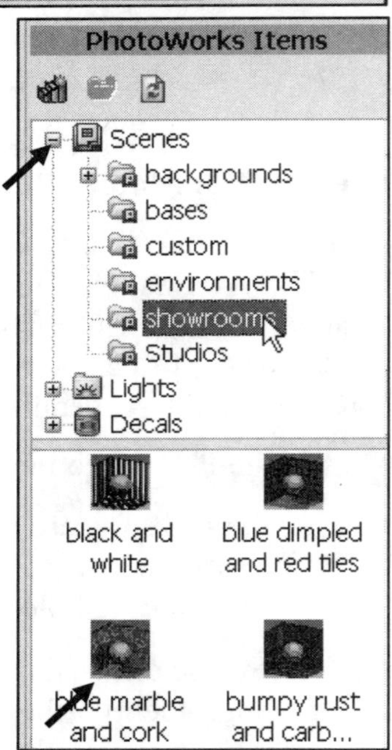

Create a Scene.

- Expand the Scene icon. Double-click showrooms.
- Double-click the blue marble and cork icon.
- Click Render from the PhotoWorks toolbar.

Note: The Preview screen displays a smaller view for faster rendering.

Modify the Material.

- Click Material from the PhotoWorks toolbar or click PhotoWorks, Material from the Main menu.
- Expand metals.
- Select aluminum. Click brushed aluminum.
- Click Render .
- Click Apply.
- Click Close.

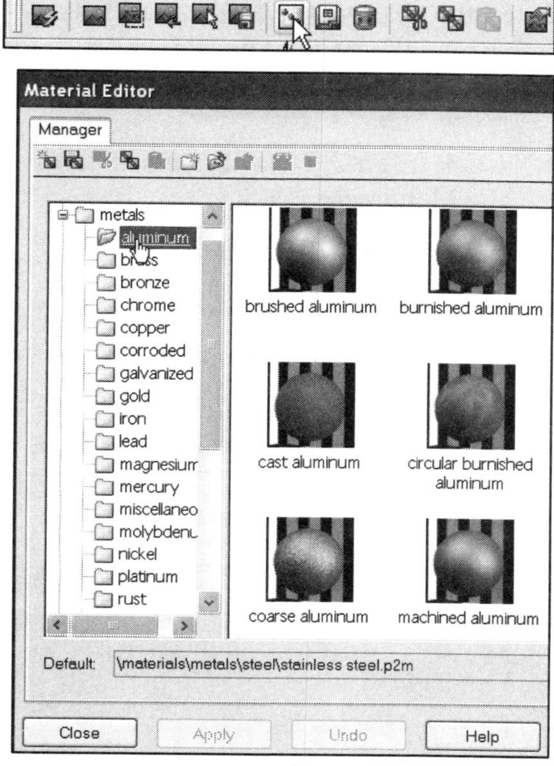

Save the image in JPEG format.

- Select Render to File .
- Select JPEG for Format. The default picture size is 320x240 pixels.
- Enter File name, GUIDE.
- Select file location, PROJECTS.
- Click Render.
- Click OK.

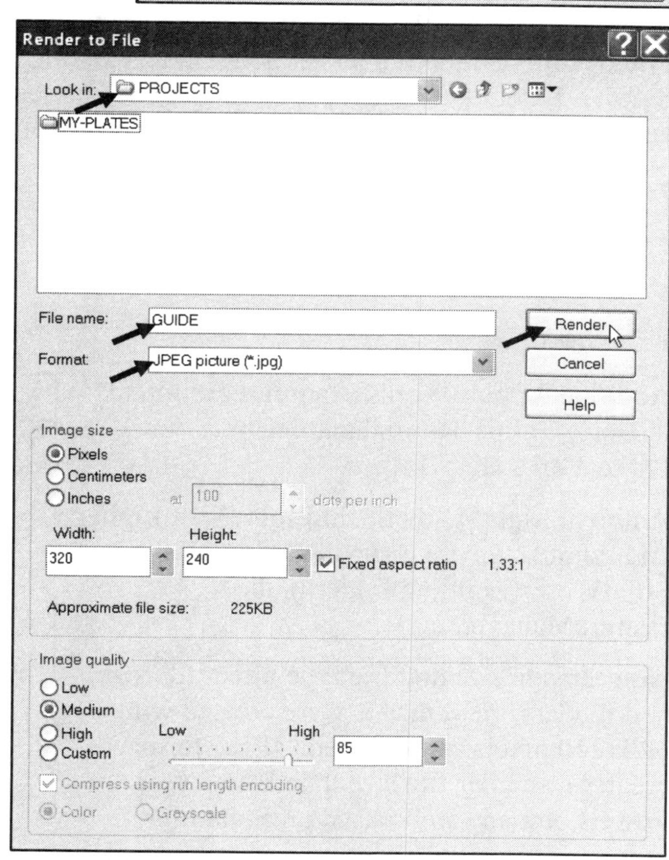

Insert the GUIDE.JPEG file as a Picture into a new PowerPoint document.

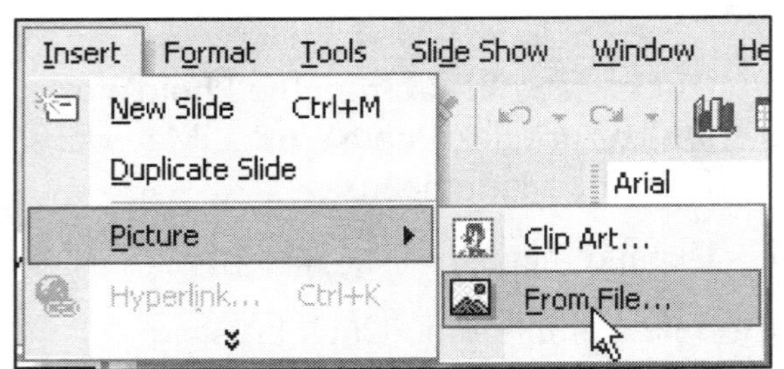

- Open Microsoft PowerPoint.
- Click Insert, Picture, From File from the Main menu.
- Select the PROJECTS folder.
- Double-click on the GUIDE.JPG file.
- Repeat the above procedure for the PLATE.
- Select a different material and scene.

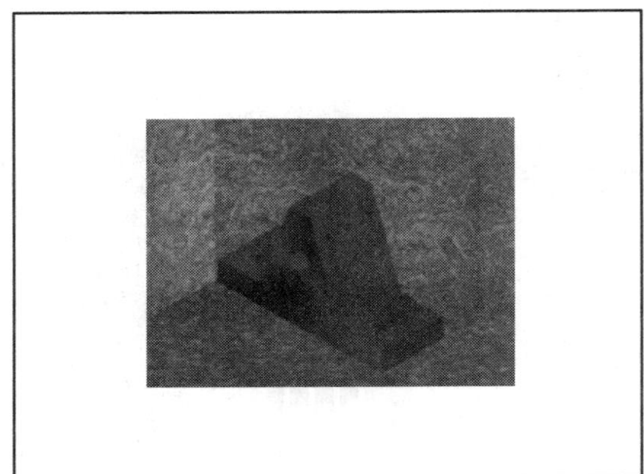

Return to SolidWorks. Address lighting for the GUIDE part. PhotoWorks Studio renders a model in an existing scene with lights. Select a Studio type, example Dark Room. The scene and lights are automatically added, scaled and sized to the model.

- Click PhotoWorks Studio.
- Select Dark Room.
- Click Render.
- Click OK.

Additional PhotoWorks examples are found in Help, Online Tutorial and Help PhotoWorks Help Topics.

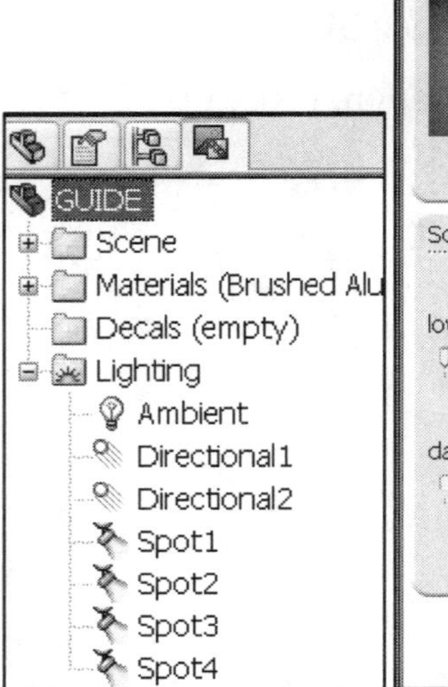

Ambient Light, Directional Light, Spot Light and Point Light are controlled through the SolidWorks Lighting folder in the FeatureManager.

Note: Image size and file type affect file size and render time. Images were created with 320x240 pixels and cropped. JPEG format creates a smaller file size than Bitmap for PowerPoint and web-based presentations.

Project 2

Fundamentals of Assembly Modeling

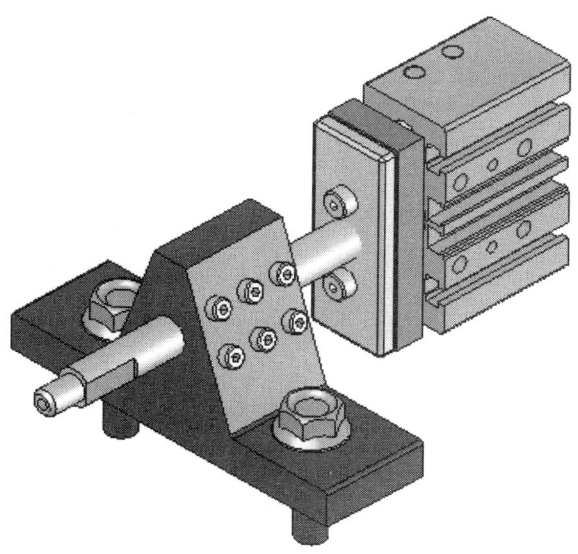

Below are the desired outcomes and usage competencies based on the completion of Project 2.

Project Desired Outcomes:	Usage Competencies:
• Create two assemblies: ○ GUIDE-ROD assembly. ○ CUSTOMER assembly.	• Ability to Insert, Mate and Modify components utilizing a Bottom-Up assembly design approach.
• Obtain an assembly from SMC USA. ○ GUIDE-CYLINDER.	• Aptitude to obtain and assemble components from the World Wide Web.
• Assemble the Flange Bolt part.	• Skill to assemble components from the Design Library.
• Create the 4MMCAPSCREW part. • Create the 3MMCAPSCREW part.	• Ability to apply the Revolve Base feature, the Save As Copy option and the Component Pattern.
• COSMOSXpress analysis for a MGPMROD part.	• Knowledge of simple applied FEA: Material, Restraints, Loads and Analysis.

Notes:

Project 2-Fundamentals of Assembly Modeling

Project Objective

Provide an understanding of the Bottom-Up assembly design approach. Insert existing parts into an assembly. Orient and position the components in the assembly using Mates.

Create the GUIDE-ROD assembly. Utilize the ROD, GUIDE and PLATE parts. The ROD, GUIDE and PLATE parts were created in Project 1.

Create the CUSTOMER assembly. The CUSTOMER assembly consists of two sub-assemblies: GUIDE-ROD and GUIDE-CYLINDER. Download the GUIDE-CYLINDER assembly from SMC USA.

Insert the FLANGE BOLT Design Library part into the GUIDE-ROD assembly.

Utilize a Revolve Base feature to create the 4MMCAPSCREW. Copy the 4MMCAPSCREW and modify dimensions to create the 3MMCAPSCREW.

On the completion of this project, you will be able to:

- Understand the FeatureManager Syntax in the assembly.
- Insert components into an assembly and apply and edit Mates.
- Rename parts and copy assemblies with references.
- Incorporate design changes into an assembly.
- Add a component from the Design Library.
- Utilize Component Pattern.
- Modify, Edit and Suppress features.
- Recover from Mate Errors.
- Suppress/Unsuppress features.
- Create an Exploded View.
- Create a Section View.
- Apply Materials.
- Apply COSMOSXpress.
- Use the following SolidWorks features:
  - Revolved Base.
  - Extruded Cut.
  - Chamfer.

Project Situation

The PLATE, ROD and GUIDE parts were created in Project 1. Perform the following steps:

Step 1: Assemble the ROD, GUIDE and PLATE into a GUIDE-ROD assembly.

Step 2: Obtain the customer's GUIDE-CYLINDER assembly from SMC USA. The assembly is obtained to insure proper fit between the GUIDE-ROD assembly and the customer's GUIDE-CYLINDER assembly.

Step 3: Create the CUSTOMER assembly. The CUSTOMER assembly combines the GUIDE-ROD assembly with the GUIDE-CYLINDER assembly.

Review the GUIDE-ROD assembly design constraints:

- The ROD requires the ability to travel through the GUIDE.
- The ROD keyway is parallel to the right surface of the GUIDE. The top surface of the GUIDE is parallel to the work area.
- The ROD mounts to the PLATE. The GUIDE mounts to a flat work surface.

The PISTON PLATE is the front plate of the GUIDE-CYLINDER assembly. The PLATE from the GUIDE-ROD assembly mounts to the PISTON PLATE. Create a rough sketch of the conceptual assembly.

Rough Sketch of Design Situation: CUSTOMER assembly

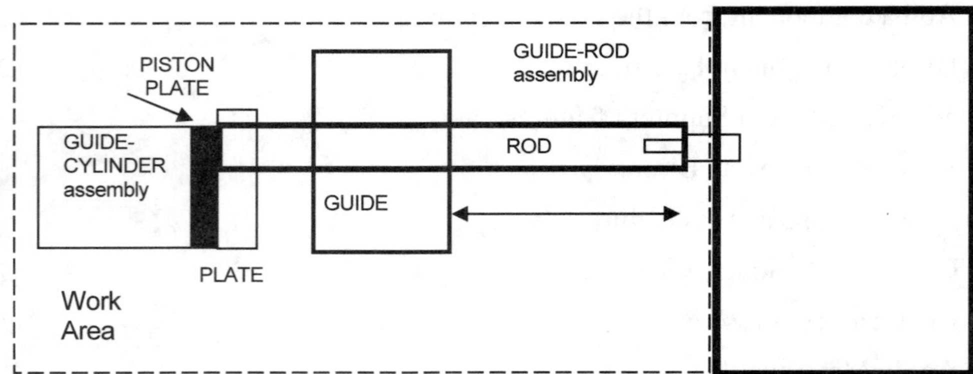

An assembly combines two or more parts. In an assembly, parts are referred to as components. Design constraints directly influence the assembly design process. Other considerations indirectly impact the assembly design, namely: cost, manufacturability and serviceability.

Project Overview

Translate the rough conceptual sketch into a SolidWorks assembly.

The GUIDE-ROD is the first assembly.

Determine the first component of the assembly.

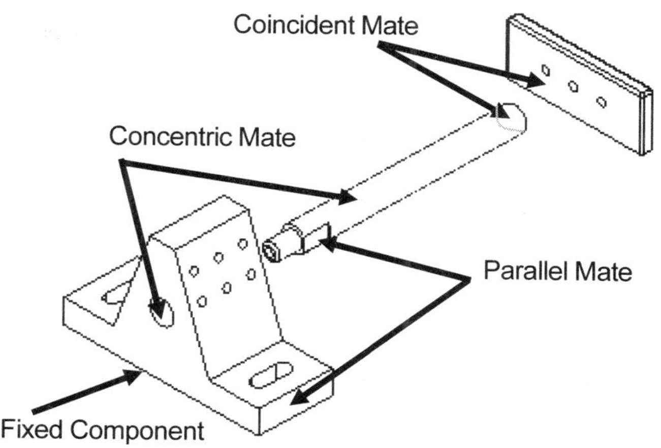

GUIDE-ROD assembly

The first component is the GUIDE. The GUIDE remains stationary. The GUIDE is a fixed component.

The action of assembling components in SolidWorks is defined as Mates.

Mates are relationships between components that simulate the construction of the assembly in a manufacturing environment.

The CUSTOMER assembly combines the GUIDE-CYLINDER assembly with the GUIDE-ROD assembly.

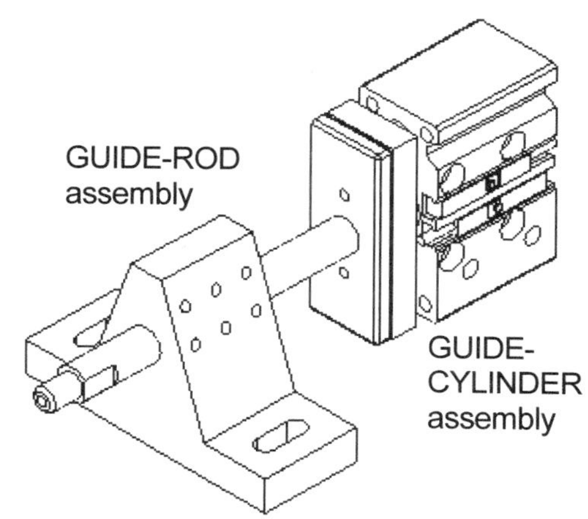

CUSTOMER assembly

Assembly Modeling Approach

In SolidWorks, components and their assemblies are directly related through a common file structure. Changes in the components directly affect the assembly and vise a versa. SolidWorks provides two assembly-modeling techniques:

- Top Down.
- Bottom Up.

In the Top Down approach, major design requirements are translated into assemblies, sub-assemblies and components.

Note: You do not need all of the required component design details. Individual relationships are required.

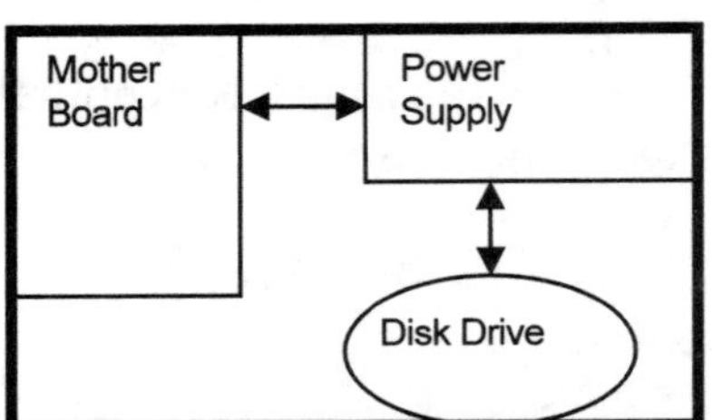

Example: A computer. The inside of a computer can be divided into individual key sub-assemblies such as a: motherboard, disk drive, power supply, etc.

Relationships between these sub-assemblies must be maintained for proper fit.

In the Bottom Up approach, components are assembled using part dependencies. In the Bottom Up approach, you possess all of the required design information for the individual components.

Use the Bottom Up design approach for the GUIDE-ROD assembly and the CUSTOMER assembly.

Linear Motion and Rotational Motion

In dynamics, motion of an object is described in linear and rotational terms. Components possess linear motion along the x, y and z-axes and rotational motion around the x, y and z-axes.

In an assembly, each component has 6 degrees of freedom: 3 translational (linear) and 3 rotational.

Mates remove degrees of freedom. All components are rigid bodies. The components do not flex or deform.

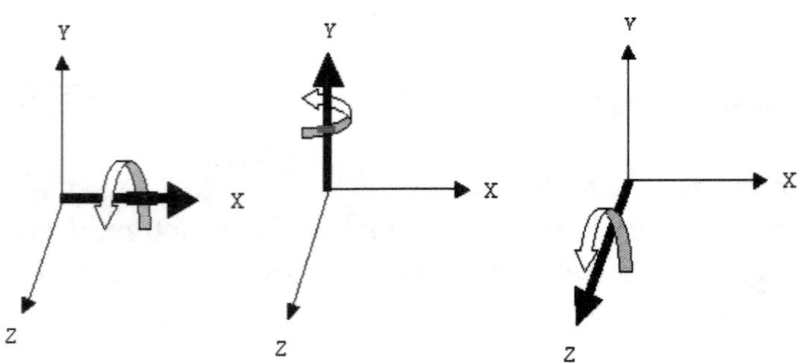

GUIDE-ROD assembly

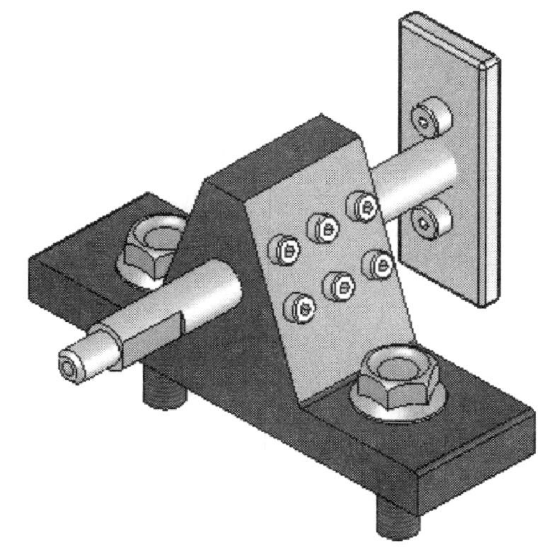

The GUIDE-ROD assembly consists of six components.

- GUIDE.
- ROD.
- PLATE.
- Flange Bolt.
- 4MMCAPSCREW.
- 3MMCAPSCREW.

The first component is the GUIDE. The GUIDE is the fixed component in the GUIDE-ROD assembly.

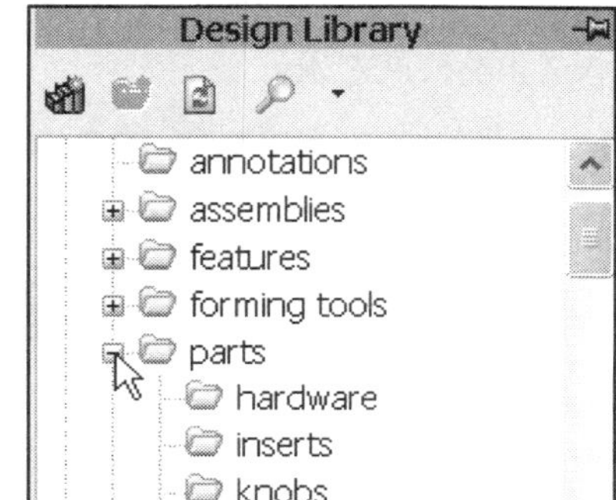

The second component is the ROD. The ROD translates linearly through the GUIDE.

The third component is the PLATE. The PLATE is assembled to the ROD and the GUIDE-CYLINDER assembly.

The forth component is the Flange Bolt. The Flange Bolts are obtained from the Design Library.

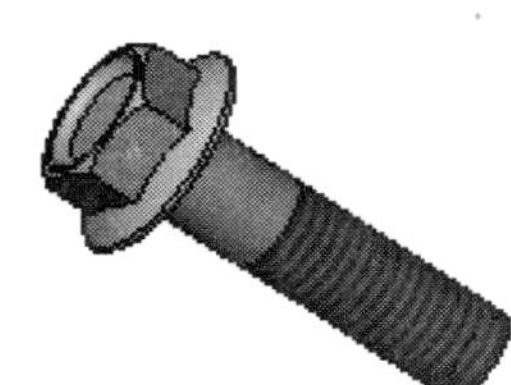

The fifth component is a 4MM CAPSCREW created with a Revolved-Base feature.

A Revolved-Base feature requires a centerline for an axis and a sketched profile. The profile is rotated about the axis to create the feature.

The sixth component is a 3MMCAPSCREW. Create the 3MMCAPSCREW from the 4MMCAPSCREW. Reuse geometry to save time.

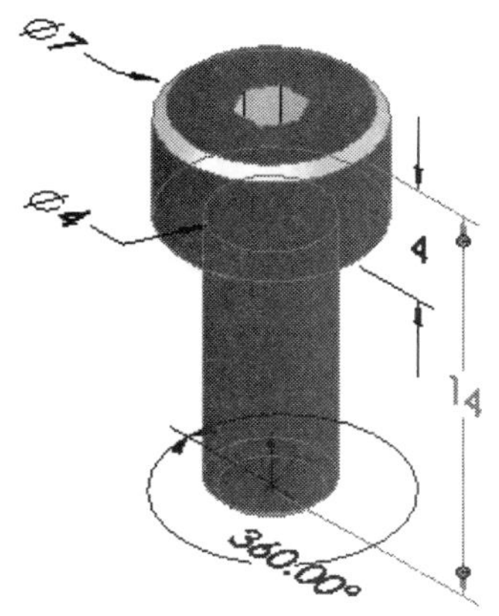

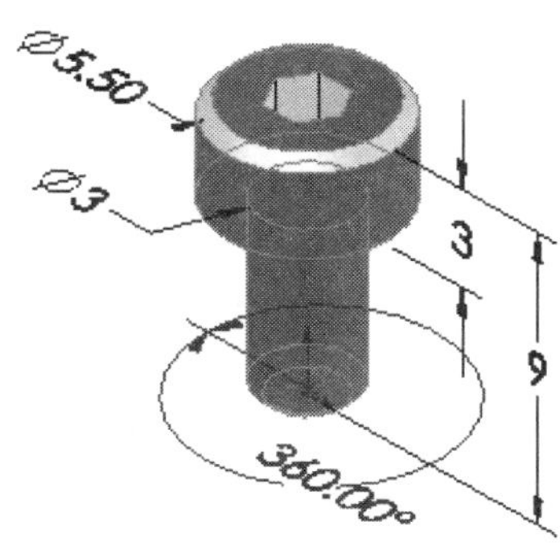

Insert a Component Pattern of 3MMCAPSCREWs. A Component Pattern is created in the assembly. Reference the GUIDE Linear Pattern of Tapped Holes to locate the 3MMCAPSCREWs.

Activity: GUIDE-ROD Assembly

Close all SolidWorks documents.

1) Click **Windows**, **Close All** from the Main menu before you begin this project.

Open the GUIDE part.

2) Click **File**, **Open** from the Main menu.

3) Select the **ENGDESIGN-W-SOLIDWORKS\PROJECTS** file folder.

4) Click **Part** for Files of Type.

5) Click **View Menu** .

6) Click **Thumbnails** to preview the bitmaps.

7) Double-click **GUIDE**.

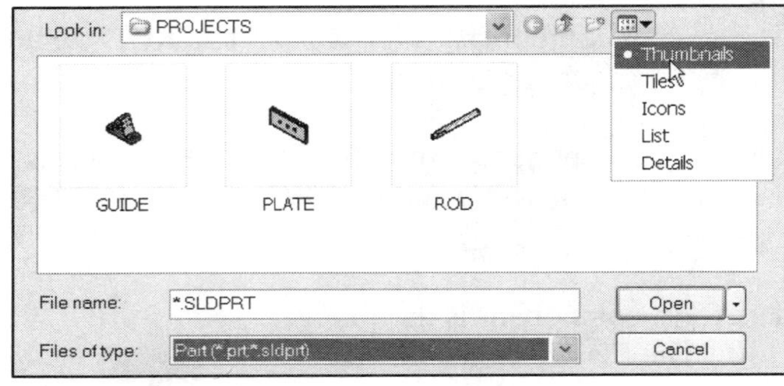

Create the GUIDE-ROD assembly.

8) Click **File**, **New** from the Main menu. The New SolidWorks Documents dialog box is displayed.

9) Double-click **Assembly** from the default Templates folder. The Insert Component PropertyManager is displayed.

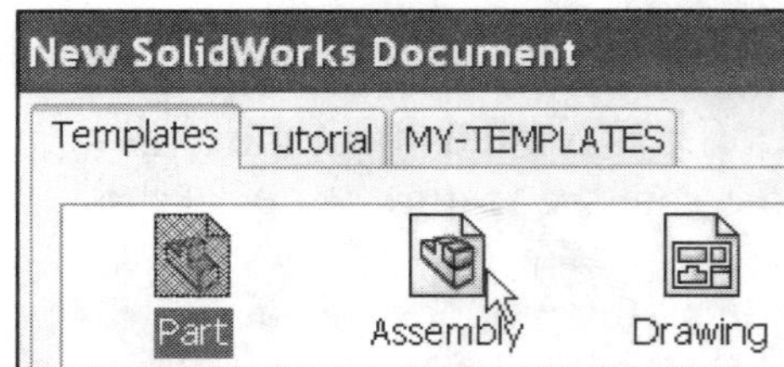

When a part is inserted into an assembly it is called a component. The Insert Component PropertyManager is displayed to the left of the Graphics window. GUIDE is listed in the Part/Assembly to Insert, Open documents box.

Insert the GUIDE and fix it to the assembly Origin.

10) Click **GUIDE** in the Open documents box.

11) Click **View**. Check **Origins** from the Main menu.

12) Click the assembly **Origin** in the Graphics window. The mouse pointer displays the Insert Component (Fixed at Origin) feedback symbol when the GUIDE Origin is coincident with the assembly Origin. The GUIDE part icon (f) GUIDE<1> is displayed in the assembly FeatureManager

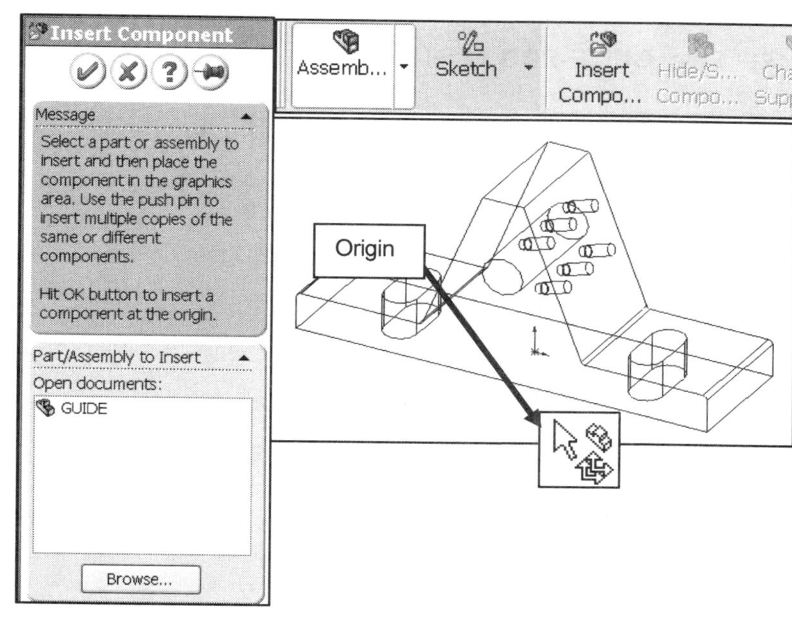

The GUIDE name is added to the assembly FeatureManager with the symbol (f).

The symbol (f) represents a fixed component.

A fixed component cannot move and is locked to the assembly Origin.

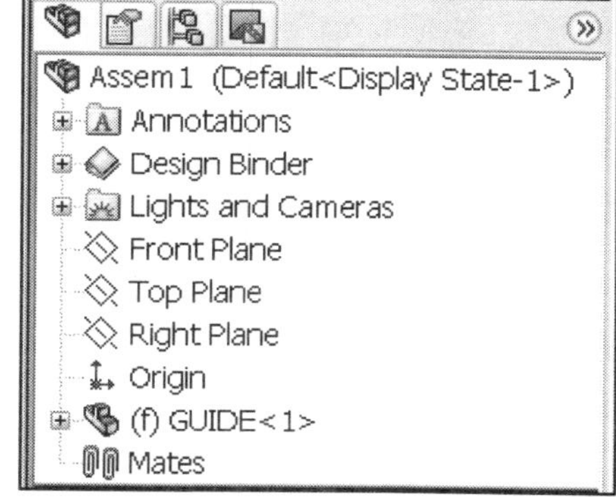

To remove the fixed state, Right-click a component name in the FeatureManager. Click Float. The component is free to move.

Save the assembly.

13) Click **File**, **Save As** from the Main menu.

14) Select **ENGDESIGN-W-SOLIDWORKS\PROJECTS** for Save in folder.

15) Enter **GUIDE-ROD** for File name.

16) Click **Save**.

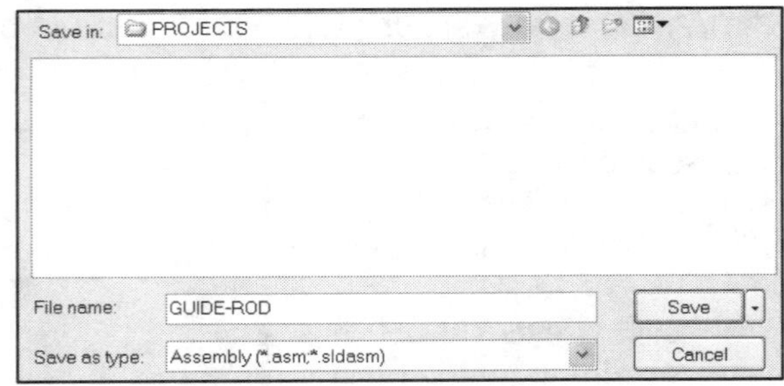

Close the GUIDE part.

17) Click **Window**, **GUIDE** from the Main tool bar.

18) Click **File**, **Close** from the Main menu. The GUIDE-ROD assembly is the open document.

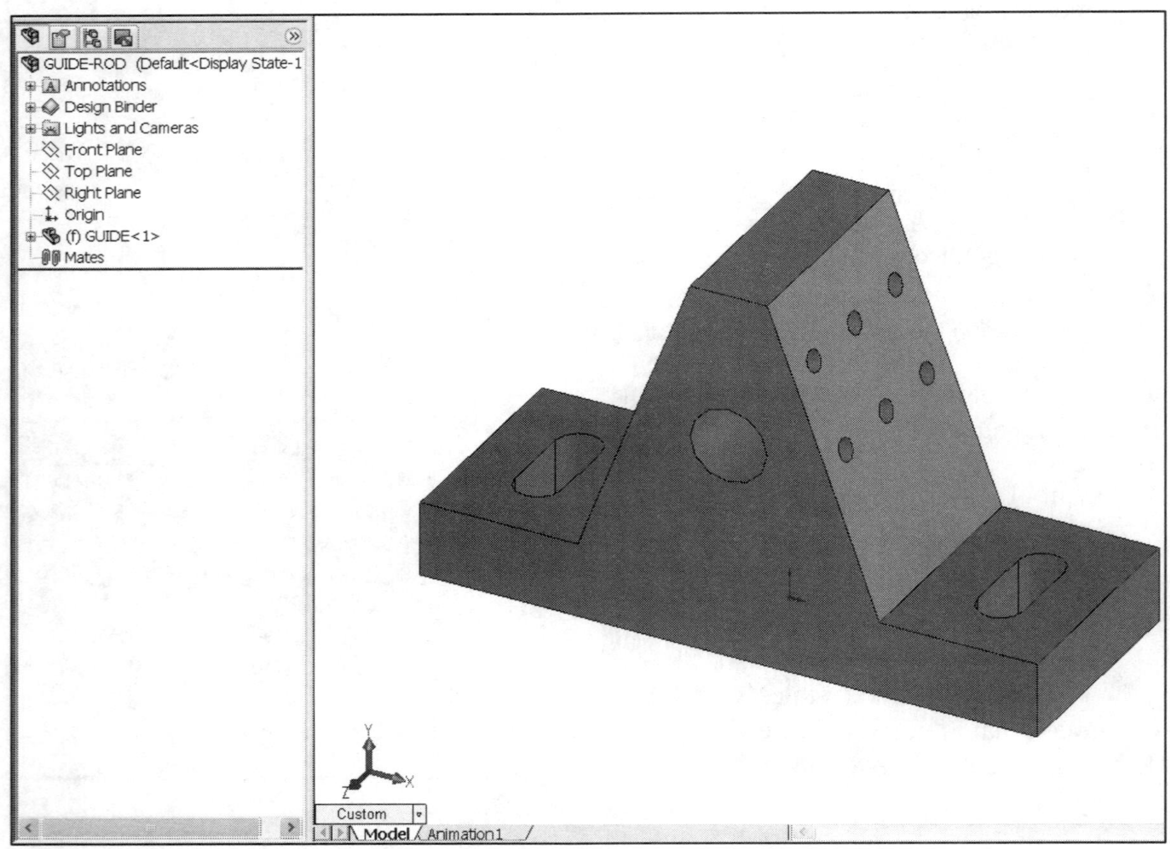

Select the Ctrl-Tab keys to quickly alternate between open SolidWorks documents. Select inside Close to close the current SolidWorks document. The outside Close exits SolidWorks.

Select the GUIDE-ROD assembly units.

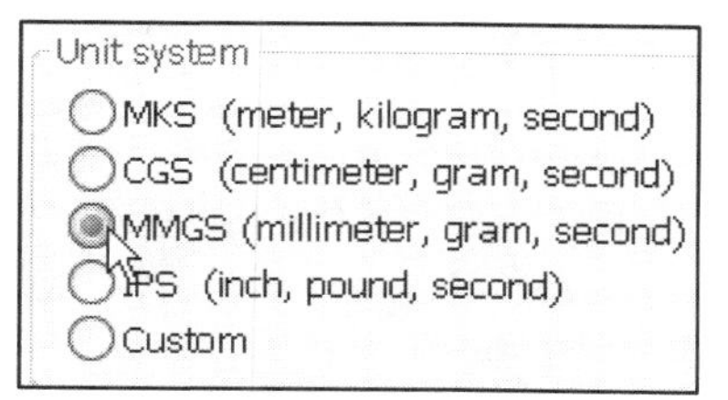

19) Click **Tools**, **Options** Options... from the Main menu.

20) Click the **Document Properties** tab.

21) Click **Units**.

22) Click **MMGS** for Unit system.

23) Click **OK**.

Save the GUIDE-ROD assembly.

24) Click **Save**.

The CommandManager displays the Assemblies icon and Sketch icon in the Control Area.

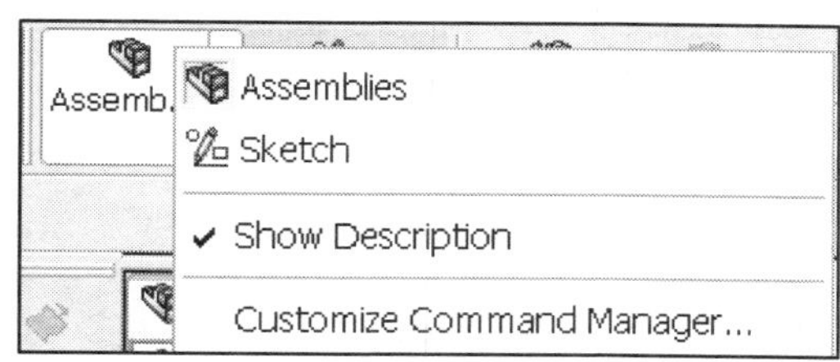

To customize the Control Area, right-click on the Assemblies icon. Click Customize Command Manager. Check the options to display in the Control Area. The options you select are based on the tool types you require for a design. Example: If notes are required in your assembly, check the Annotations option. Utilize the Sketch and Assemblies option for this project.

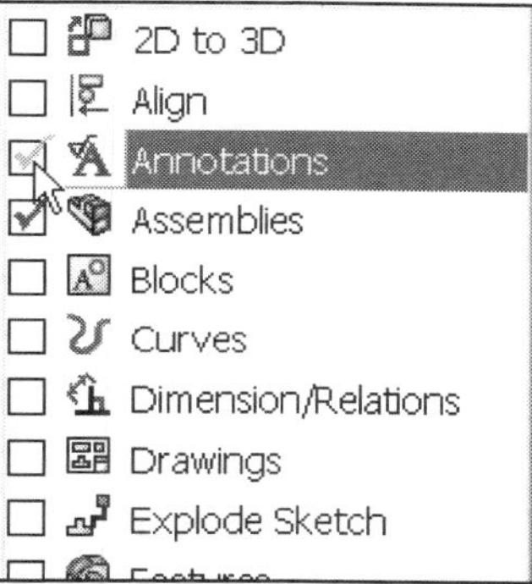

Assembly is the default toolbar in the CommandManager. The first icon is Insert Component.

Select this tool to insert a new component into the assembly that already exists in a project folder such as the PLATE or ROD.

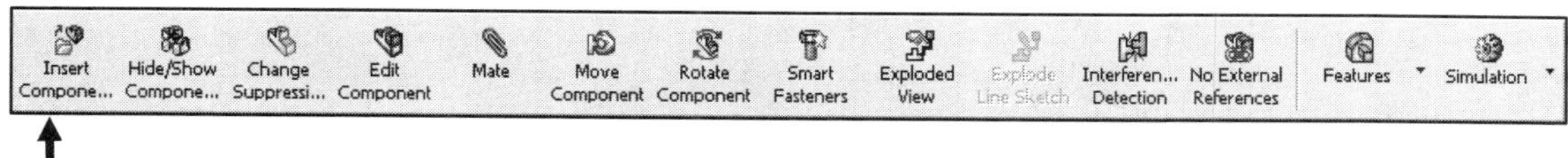

GUIDE-ROD Assembly-Insert Component

The first component is the foundation of the assembly. The GUIDE is the first component in the GUIDE-ROD assembly. The ROD is the second component in the GUIDE-ROD assembly. Add components to assemblies utilizing the following techniques:

- Utilize the Insert Component Property Manager.
- Utilize Insert, Component from the Main menu.
- Drag the components from the Windows Explorer.
- Drag the components from the Design Library.
- Drag the components from the Open part files.

Activity: GUIDE-ROD Assembly-Insert Component

Insert the ROD component.

25) Click **Inset Component**  from the Assemblies toolbar.

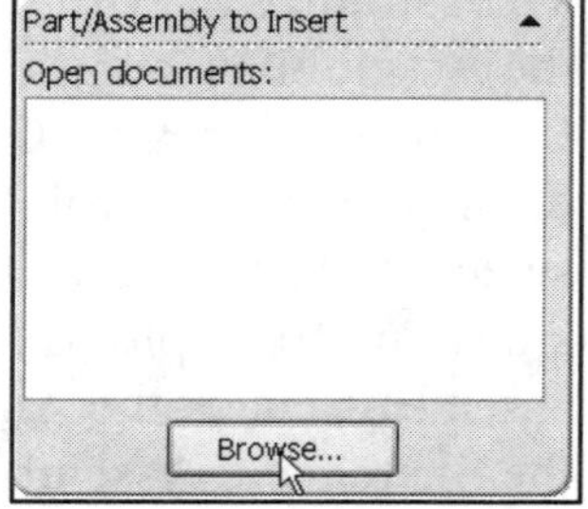

26) Click **BROWSE** from the Insert Component PropertyManager.

27) Click **Part** for Files of Type.

28) Click the **ROD** part in the Open dialog box.

29) Click **Open**.

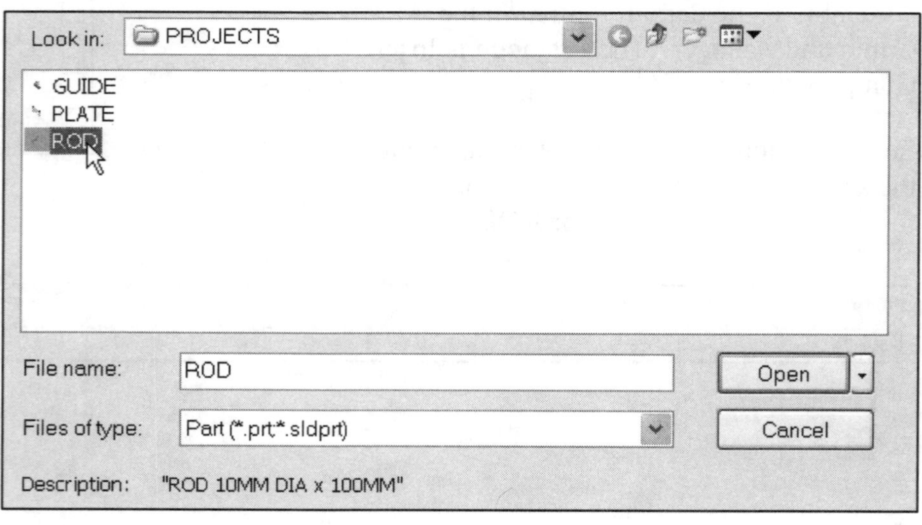

The ROD part icon is displayed in the Open documents text box. The mouse pointer displays the ROD component when positioned inside the GUIDE-ROD Graphics window.

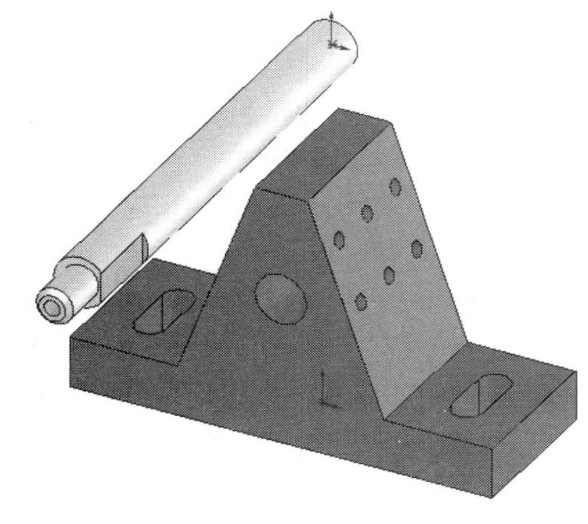

30) Click a **position** for the ROD to the left of the GUIDE.

Move the ROD component.

31) Click and drag the **shaft** of the ROD in the Graphic window.

32) Release the **mouse pointer** on the right side of the GUIDE.

Fit the model to the Graphics window.

33) Press the **f** key.

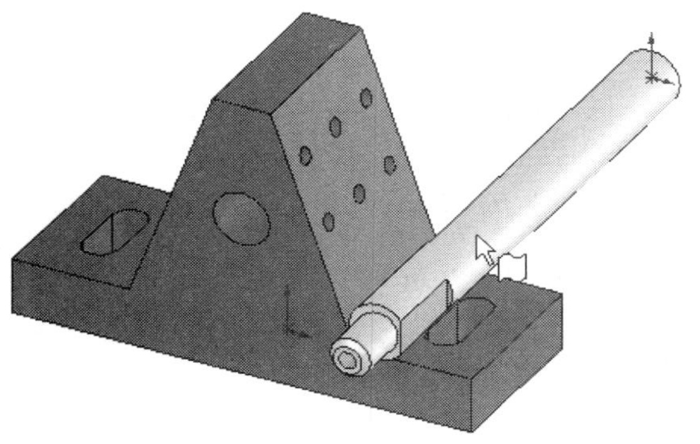

The component movement in the assembly is determined by its degrees of freedom.

Save the GUIDE-ROD assembly.

34) Click **Save** .

35) Click **Yes** to the question, “Save the document and the referenced models now?”

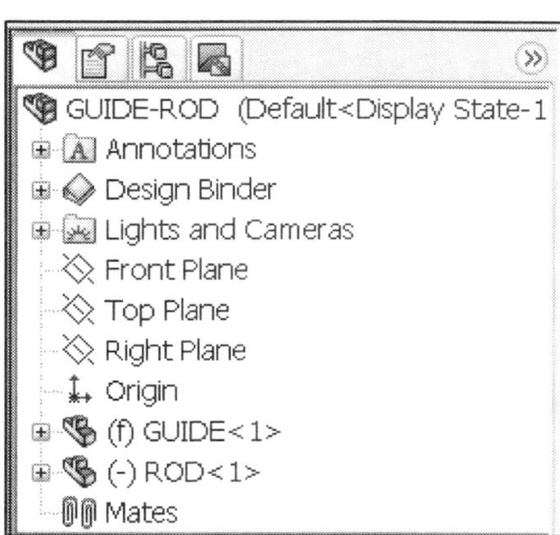

The “Save the document and the referenced models now?” question refers to the current assembly document and the GUIDE part and ROD part as the referenced models.

This message appears when the models referenced in the assembly have been modified.

Review the FeatureManager Syntax.

36) Click **Plus** (f) GUIDE<1> to the left of the GUIDE entry in the FeatureManager. The GUIDE component lists the features. Note: Base-Extrude, Slot-Cut, GuideHole and M3x0.5 Tapped Hole1 contain additional sketches. Recall features were renamed in Project 1. Example: Extrude1 was renamed to Base-Extrude.

37) Click **Plus** (-) ROD<1> to the left of the ROD entry in the FeatureManager.

38) Click **Minus** to the left of the GUIDE entry and ROD entry to collapse the list.

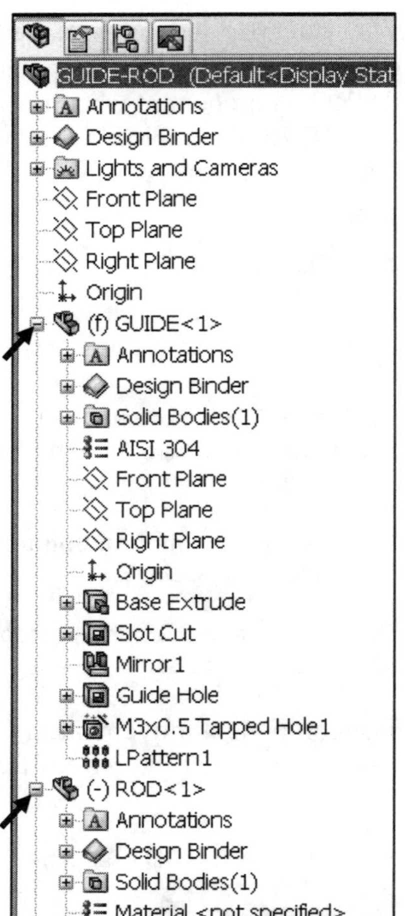

A Plus icon indicates that additional feature information is available. A Minus icon indicates that the feature list is fully expanded. Manipulating the FeatureManager is an integral part of the assembly. In the step-by-step instructions, Expand and Collapse are used as follows:

- Expand – Click Plus icon.
- Collapse – Click Minus icon.

FeatureManager Syntax

Entries in the FeatureManager design tree have specific definitions. Understanding syntax and states saves time when creating and modifying assemblies. Review the four columns of the ROD part syntax in the FeatureManager.

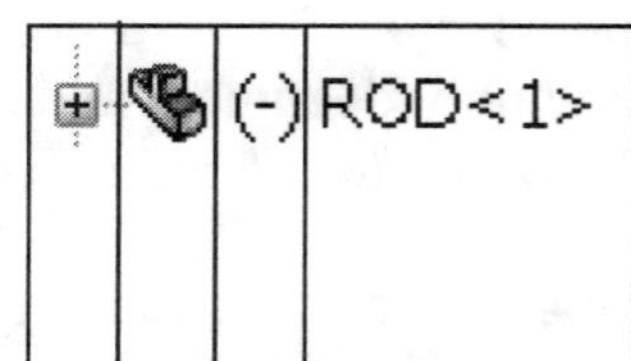

1. Column1: Identifies if the component is a part or assembly and determines the component's state. The ROD is a part in the Resolved state. Review the Component State options.

Component States:	
Symbol:	**State:**
	Resolved part. A yellow part icon indicates a resolved state. A blue part icon indicates a selected, resolved part.
	Lightweight part. A blue feather on the part icon indicates a lightweight state.
	Suppressed. A gray icon indicates the part is not resolved in the active configuration.
	Hidden. A clear icon indicates the part is resolved but invisible.
	Rebuild required.
	Resolved assembly. The part states also apply to an assembly.

2. Column 2: Identifies a component's (part or assembly) relationship with other components in the assembly. The ROD part is free to move and rotate (-). Review other relations between components in an assembly:

Component relationship with other components in the assembly:	
Symbol:	**Relationship:**
(-)	A minus sign (–) indicates that the part or assembly is under-defined and requires additional information.
(+)	A plus sign (+) indicates that the part or assembly is over-defined.
(f)	A fixed symbol (f) indicates that the part or assembly does not move.
(?)	A question mark (?) indicates that additional information is required on the part or assembly.

3. ROD - Name of the part.

4. The symbol <#> indicates the particular inserted instance of a component. The symbol <1> indicates the first inserted instance of a component, "ROD" in the assembly. If you delete a component and reinsert the same component again, the <#> symbol increments by one.

Mate Types

Mates reflect the physical behavior of a component in an assembly. The components in the GUIDE-ROD assembly utilize Standard Mate types. Review the Standard and Advanced Mates types.

Standard and Advanced Mates:

The Mate Property Manager displays Standard Mate Types and Advanced Mate Types. Components are assembled with various Mate Types. The Standard Mate Types are:

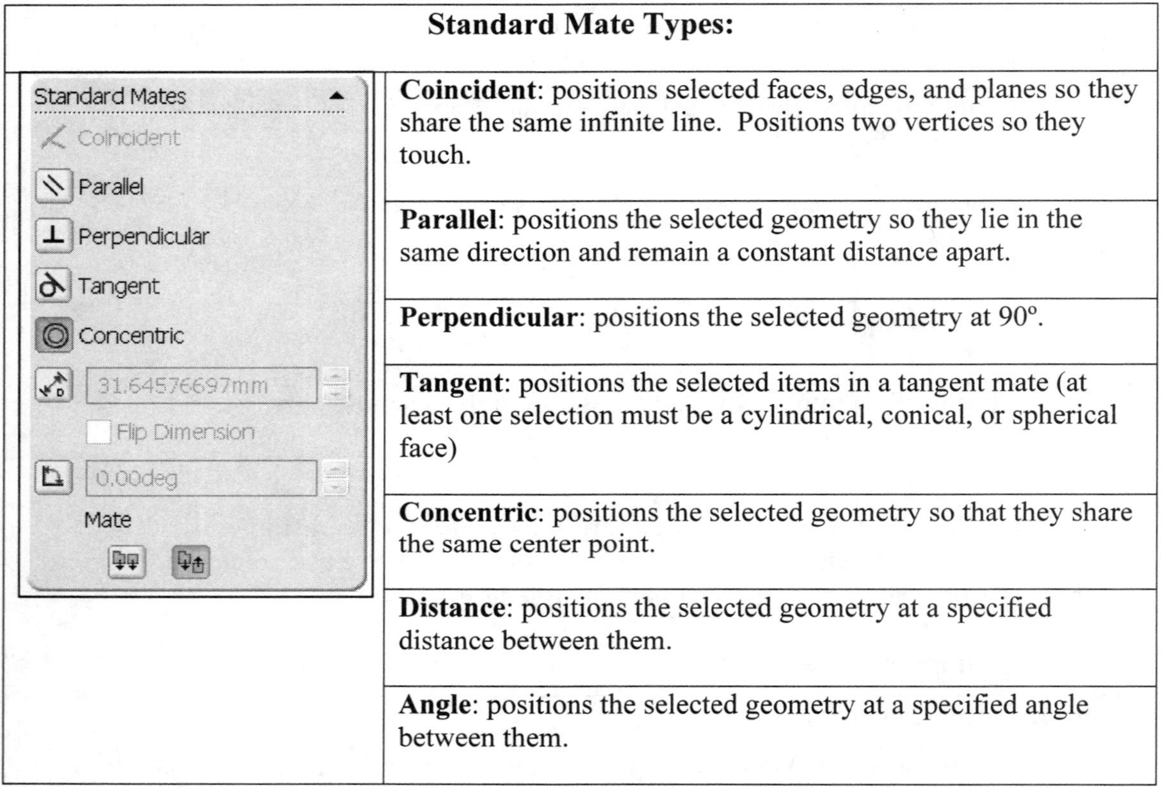

Standard Mate Types:
Coincident: positions selected faces, edges, and planes so they share the same infinite line. Positions two vertices so they touch.
Parallel: positions the selected geometry so they lie in the same direction and remain a constant distance apart.
Perpendicular: positions the selected geometry at 90°.
Tangent: positions the selected items in a tangent mate (at least one selection must be a cylindrical, conical, or spherical face)
Concentric: positions the selected geometry so that they share the same center point.
Distance: positions the selected geometry at a specified distance between them.
Angle: positions the selected geometry at a specified angle between them.

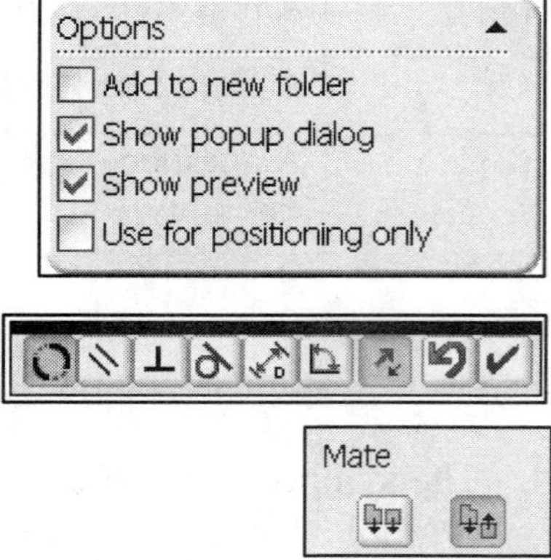

The Mate, Show popup dialog box, displays the Pop-up toolbar during the Mate options. The Standard Mate Types, Aligned/Anti-Aligned, Undo and OK are displayed in the Pop-up toolbar.

There are two Mate Alignment options. The Aligned option positions the components so that the normal vectors from the selected faces point in the same direction. The Anti-Aligned option positions the components so that the normal vectors from the selected faces point in opposite directions.

Advanced Mates:

The Advanced Mate Types are:

Advanced Mate Types:	
	**Symmetric**: Positions two selected entities to be symmetric about a plane or planar face. A Symmetric Mate does not create a Mirrored Component.
	Cam: A cam-follower mate is a type of tangent or coincident mate. It positions a cylinder, plane, or point to a series of tangent extruded Cam faces. The Cam profile is comprised of tangent lines, arcs, and/or splines in a closed loop.
	Width: Centers a tab within the width of a groove.
	Gear: Positions two components to rotate relative to one another about selected axes. The axis of rotation includes: cylindrical and conical faces, axes, and linear edges. Gear components are not required for a Gear Mate. Example, two rolling cylinders
	Limit: Defines a range of motion for a Distance Mate or Angle Mate. Specify a starting value, minimum value and maximum value.

SolidWorks Help Topics list the rules governing Mate Type valid geometry. The valid geometry selection between components in a Coincident Mate is displayed in the Coincident Mate Combinations Table.

SolidWorks Help Topics also display Standard Mates by Entity. Specific combinations of geometry create valid Mates.

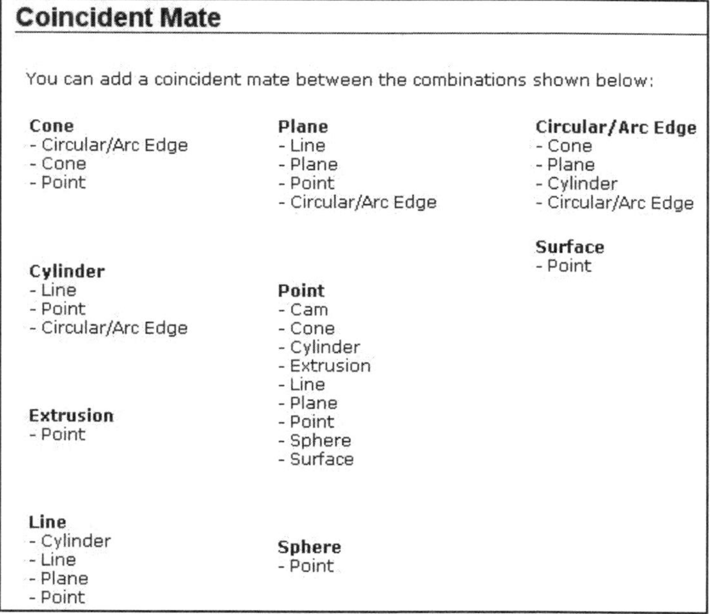

Coincident Mate

You can add a coincident mate between the combinations shown below:

Cone
- Circular/Arc Edge
- Cone
- Point

Cylinder
- Line
- Point
- Circular/Arc Edge

Extrusion
- Point

Line
- Cylinder
- Line
- Plane
- Point

Plane
- Line
- Plane
- Point
- Circular/Arc Edge

Point
- Cam
- Cone
- Cylinder
- Extrusion
- Line
- Plane
- Point
- Sphere
- Surface

Sphere
- Point

Circular/Arc Edge
- Cone
- Plane
- Cylinder
- Circular/Arc Edge

Surface
- Point

Mates reflect the physical behavior of a component in an assembly. In this project, the two most common Mate Types are Concentric and Coincident.

GUIDE-ROD Assembly-Mate the ROD Component

Recall the initial assembly design constraints:

- The ROD requires the ability to travel through the GUIDE.
- The Keyway Cut face of the ROD is parallel to the right face of the GUIDE.

Utilize Concentric and Parallel Mates between the ROD and GUIDE. The Concentric Mate utilizes the cylindrical face of the ROD's shaft with the cylindrical face of the GUIDE Hole. The Parallel Mate utilizes two planar faces from the ROD keyway cut and the right face of the GUIDE.

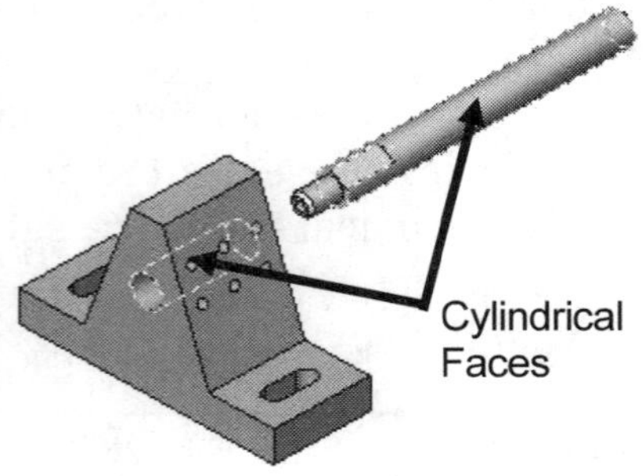

Concentric Mate – 2 Cylindrical faces

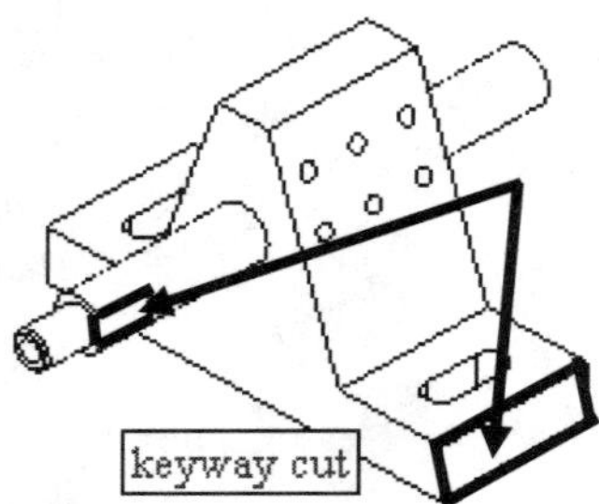

Parallel – 2 Planar faces

The Concentric Mate and the Parallel Mate allows the ROD to linearly translate through the GUIDE Hole. The ROD does not rotate.

Use the following steps to create a Mate:

1. Select Mate from the Assembly toolbar.
2. Select the geometry from the first component (usually the Part).
3. Select the geometry from the second component (usually the Assembly).
4. Select the Mate Type.
5. Select OK.

Activity: GUIDE-ROD Assembly-Mate the ROD Component

Insert a Concentric Mate.

39) Click **Mate** Mate from the Assembly toolbar. The Mate PropertyManager is displayed.

40) Click the **cylindrical face** of the ROD.

41) Click the **cylindrical face** of the Guide Hole. The faces are added to the Mate Selections list. Concentric is selected by default.

42) Click the **Green Check mark** ✔ in the Mates Pop-up toolbar to add a Concentric Mate. The Mate PropertyManager remains open on the left side of the Graphics window.

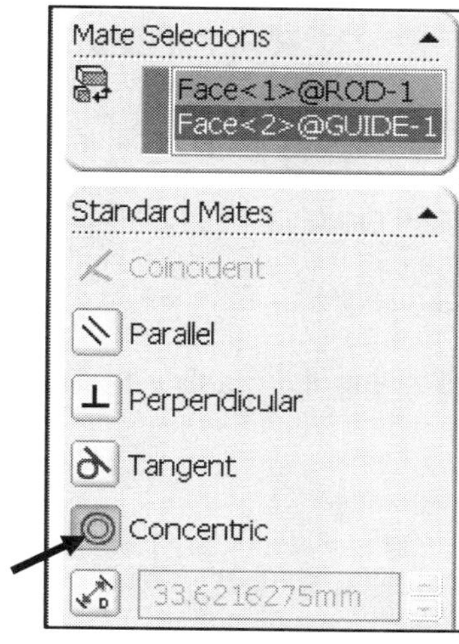

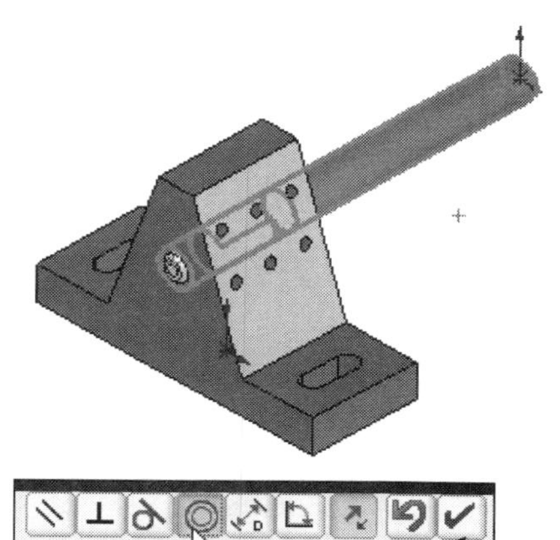

Review the Mate Selections, the cylindrical face of the Guide Hole and the cylindrical face of the ROD. If the Mate Selections are not correct, right-click a position inside the Mate Selections box and select Clear All.

The Mate Pop-up toolbar minimizes the time required to create a Standard Mate. Utilize the Mate Pop-up toolbar for this project.

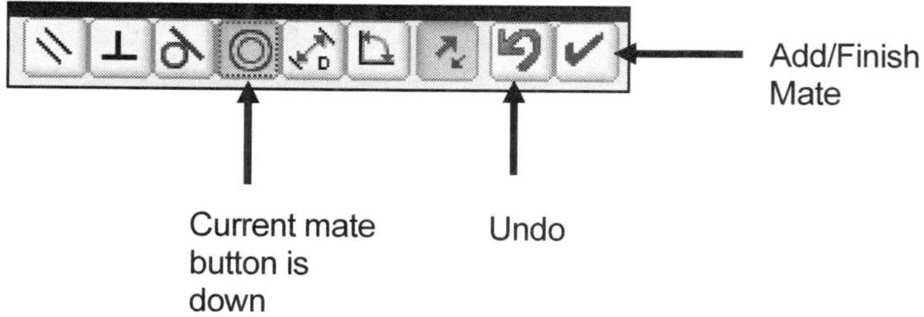

When selecting faces, position the mouse pointer in the middle of the face. Do not position the mouse pointer near the edge of the face. If the wrong face or edge is selected, perform one of the following actions:

- Click the face or edge again to remove it from the Mate Selections box.
- Right-click in the Mate Selections box. Click Clear Selections to remove all geometry from the Mate Selections box.
- Utilize the UNDO button to begin the Mate command again.

The ROD is concentric with the GUIDE. The ROD has the ability to move and rotate while remaining concentric to the GUIDE hole.

Move and rotate the ROD.

43) Click and drag the **ROD** in a horizontal direction. The ROD travels linearly in the GUIDE.

44) Click and drag the **ROD** in a vertical direction. The ROD rotates in the GUIDE.

45) Rotate the **Rod** until the keyway cut is approximately parallel to the Right face of the GUIDE.

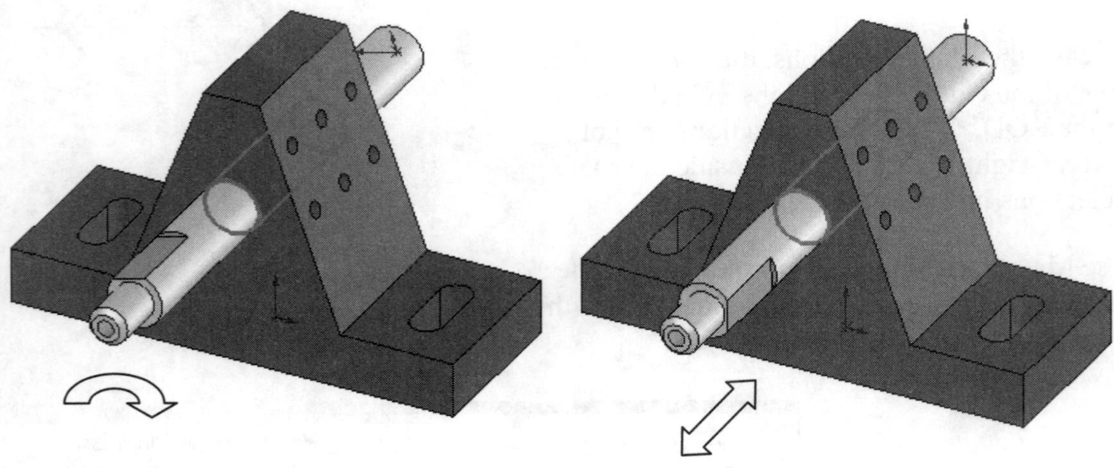

Recall the second assembly design constraint. The flat end of the ROD must remain parallel to the right surface of the GUIDE.

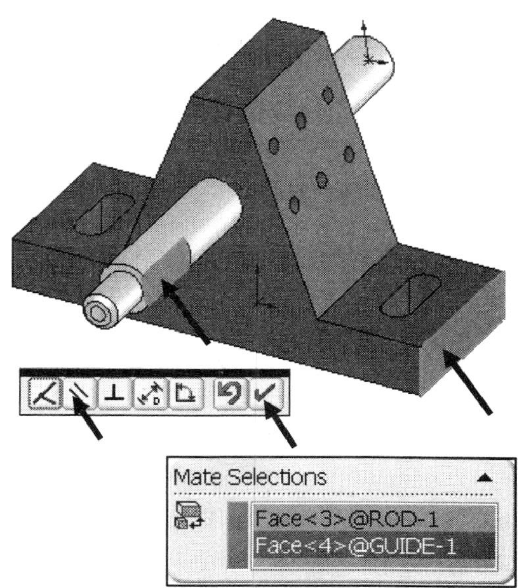

Insert a Parallel Mate.

46) Click the **Keyway face** of the ROD.

47) Click the **flat right face** of the GUIDE. Both faces are added to the Mate Selections list.

48) Click **Parallel** from the Mate Pop-up toolbar.

49) Click the **Green Check mark** to add a Parallel Mate.

50) Click **OK** from the Mate PropertyManager.

Move the ROD.

51) Click and drag the **ROD** in a horizontal direction and position it approximately in the center of the GUIDE.

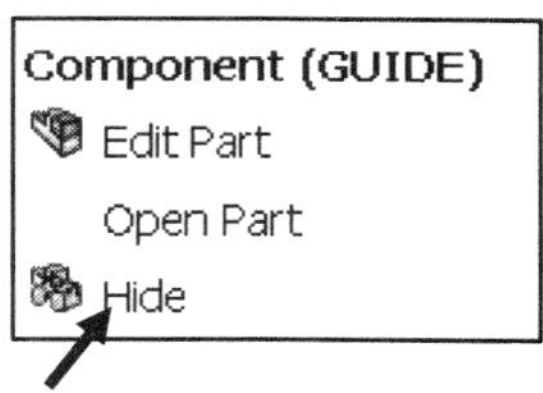

Hide the GUIDE component.

52) Right-click on the front face of the **GUIDE**.

53) Click **Hide** Hide .

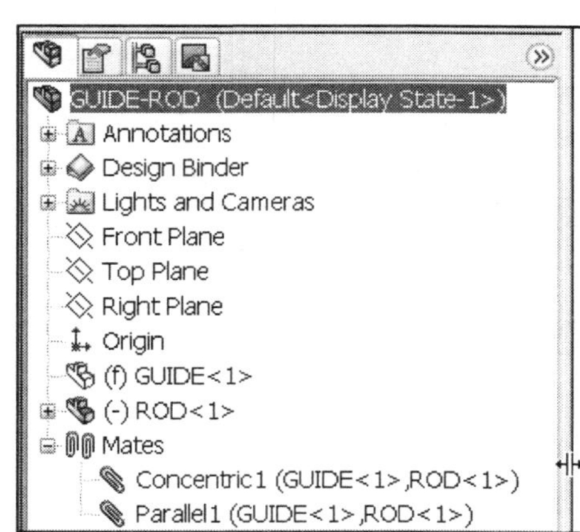

Display the Mate types.

54) Expand the **Mates** entry in the FeatureManager.

Display the full Mate names.

55) Drag the **vertical FeatureManager border** to the right.

Save the GUIDE-ROD assembly.

56) Click **Save** .

The ROD Mates reflect the physical constraints in the GUIDE-ROD assembly. The ROD is under defined, indicated by a minus sign (-).

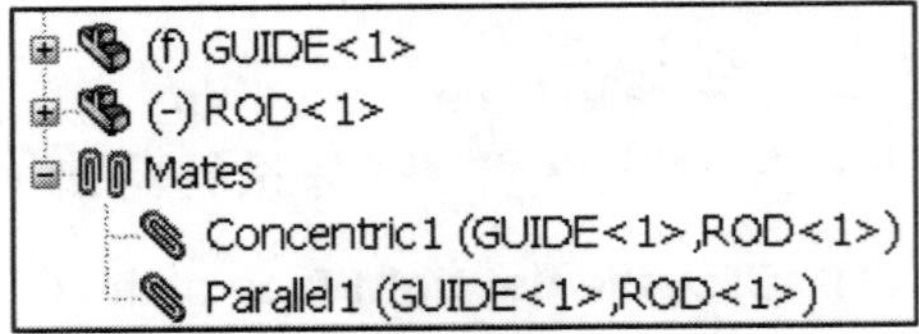

The Concentric Mate allows the ROD to translate freely in the Z direction through the Guide Hole. The Parallel Mate prevents the ROD from rotating in the Guide Hole.

The Guide part icon (f) GUIDE<1> is displayed with no color in the FeatureManager to reflect the Hide state.

GUIDE-ROD Assembly-Mate the PLATE Component

Recall the initial design constraints.

- The ROD is fastened to the PLATE.
- The PLATE part mounts to the GUIDE-CYLINDER PISTON PLATE part.

Use the Rotate Component command to position the PLATE before applying the Mates.

Activity: GUIDE-ROD Assembly-Mate the PLATE Component

Insert the PLATE component.

57) Click **Insert Component** from the Assemblies toolbar.

58) Click **BROWSE** from the Open documents box.

59) Double-click the **PLATE** part in the Open dialog box.

60) Click a **position** behind the ROD.

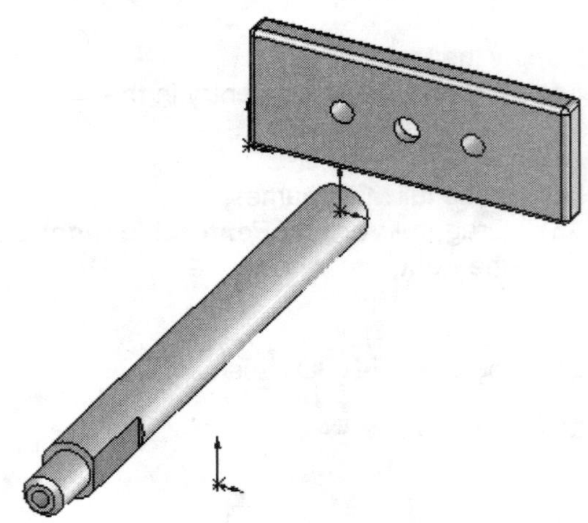

Fit the Model to the Graphics window.

61) Press the **f** key.

Rotate the PLATE.

62) Click **Rotate Component** Rotate Compo... from the Assemblies toolbar.

63) Click and drag the **front face** of the PLATE downward until the PLATE rotates approximately 90°.

64) Click **Rotate Component** Rotate Compo... to deactivate.

65) Click a **position** in the Graphics window, to the right of the PLATE, to deselect any faces or edges.

66) Click **View**, uncheck **Origins** from the Main menu.

Selection Filters are used to select difficult individual features such as: faces, edges and points. Utilize the Face Selection Filter to select the hidden ROD Back Hole face.

Activate the face Selection Filter.

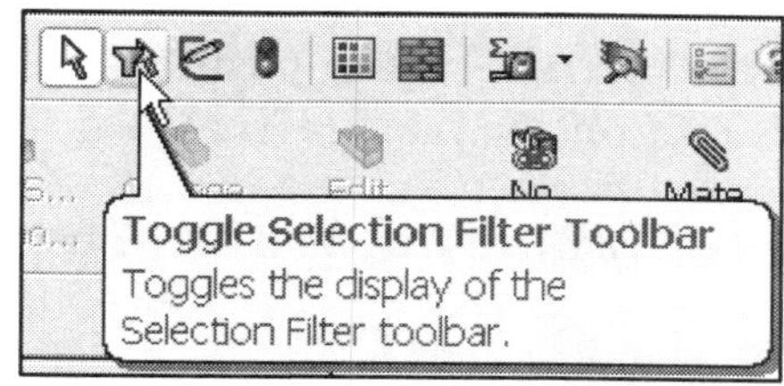
Toggle Selection Filter Toolbar
Toggles the display of the Selection Filter toolbar.

67) Click **Toggle Selection Filter Toolbar** from the Standard Toolbar.

68) Click **Filter Faces** from the Selection Filter toolbar.

Filter Faces
Allows selection of faces only.
Selection Filter

Insert a Concentric Mate.

69) Click **WireFrame**.

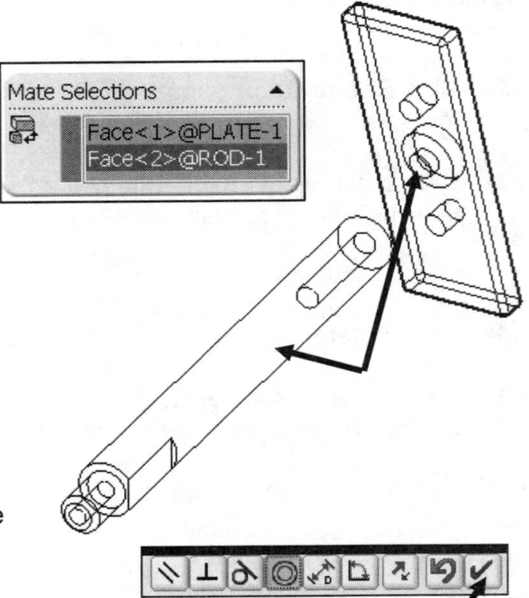

70) Click **Mate** from the Assemblies toolbar.

71) Click the **center cylindrical face** from the PLATE Countersink hole. The center-cylindrical face turns green.

72) Click the **cylindrical face** of the ROD. The ROD face and the Countersink hole of the PLATE face are added to the Mate Selections. Concentric is selected by default.

73) Click the **Green Check mark** ✔ from the Mate Pop-up toolbar.

Note: Review the Mate Selections, the cylindrical face of the PLATE and the cylindrical face of the ROD. If the Mate Selections are not correct, right-click a position inside the Mate Selections box and select Clear All.

74) Click and drag the **PLATE** behind the ROD.

Insert a Coincident Mate.

75) Press the **left arrow** key to rotate the view until the back face of the ROD is visible.

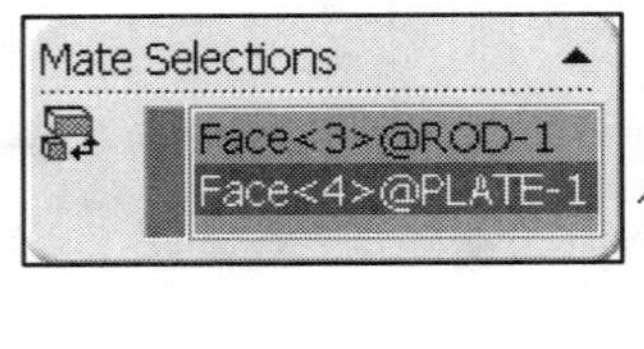

76) Click the **ROD back circular face**.

77) Press the **right arrow** key to rotate the view until the PLATE front face is visible.

78) Click the **front rectangular face** of the PLATE. Coincident is selected by default.

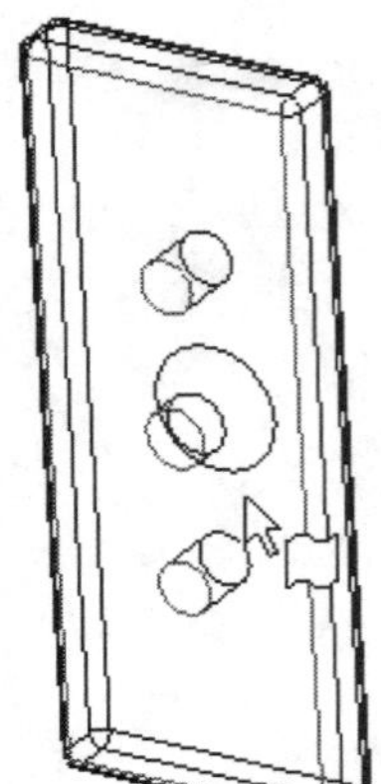

79) Click the **Green Check mark** ✔ from the Mate Pop-up toolbar.

80) Click **Shaded With Edges**.

81) Click **Isometric view**.

Insert a Parallel Mate.

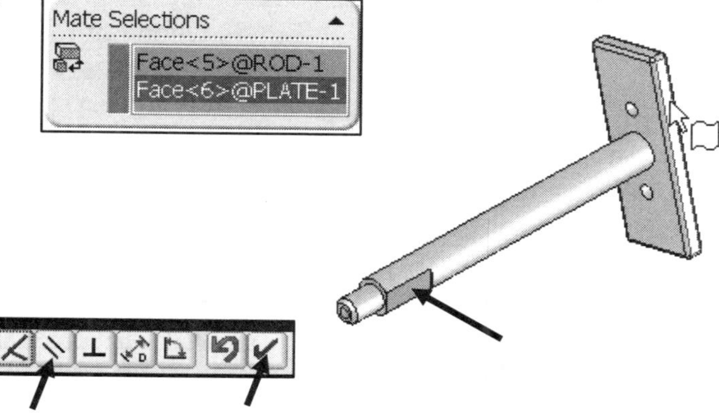

82) Press the **Shift + z** keys to Zoom in on the ROD.

83) Click the ROD **Keyway Cut flat face**.

84) Click the PLATE **right rectangular face**.

85) Click **Parallel** from the Mate Pop-up toolbar.

86) Click the **Green Check mark** ✔ from the Mate Pop-up toolbar.

87) Click **OK** from the Mate PropertyManager.

Reset the Filters.

88) Click the **Clear All Filters** icon from the Selection Filters toolbar.

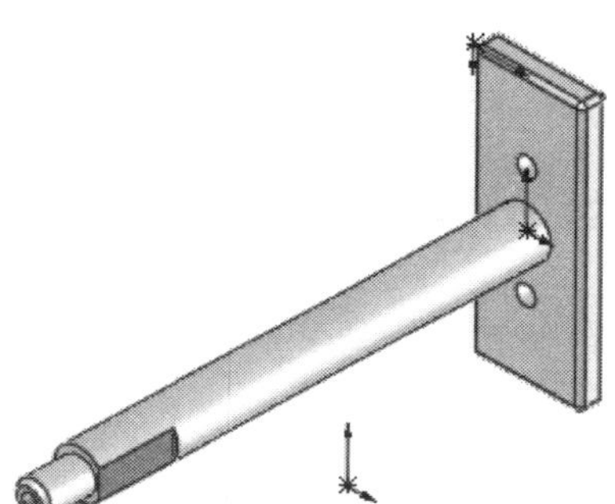

View the Origins.

89) Click **View**, check **Origins** from the Main menu.

Save the GUIDE-ROD assembly.

90) Click **Save**.

Note: View, Origins and Shaded, Hidden Lines Removed and Hidden Lines Visible are utilized in the remaining illustrations for clarity. Individual commands are not provided.

The Mates reflect the physical relations bewteen the PLATE and the ROD. The Concentric Mate aligns the PLATE Countersink Hole and the ROD cylindrical face. The Concentric Mate eliminates translation between the PLATE front face and the ROD back face. The Parallel Mate removes PLATE rotation about the ROD axis. Create the Parallel Mate.

A Distance Mate of 0 provides additional flexibility than a Coincident Mate. The Distance Mate value can be modified. Utilize a Coincident Mate when mating faces remain coplanar.

The mouse pointer displays the Filter On icon when the Selection Filters are activated. Deactivate Selection Filters when not required.

Activate/Deactive Filters using the following keys:

Filter for edges	Press e
Filter for faces	Press x
Filter for vertices	Press v
Hide/Show all Filters	F5
Off/On all Selected Filters	F6

Accidentally pressing the e, x or v keys activates a Filter. If the mouse pointer displays the Filter On icon, you cannot select geometry, dimensions or text. Press the F5 key to display the Selection Filter toolbar. Select Clear All Filters .

GUIDE-ROD Assembly-Mate Errors

Mate errors occur when component geometry is over defined.

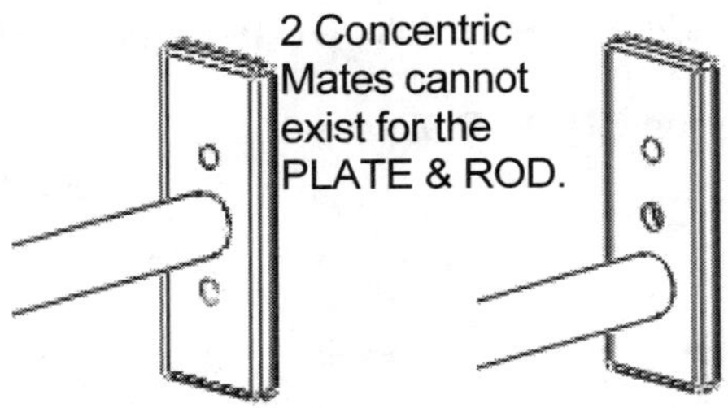
2 Concentric
Mates cannot
exist for the
PLATE & ROD.

Example: You added a new Concentric Mate between the PLATE bottom Mounting Hole and the ROD cylindrical face.

The ROD Back Hole cannot physically exist with a Concentric Mate to both the PLATE middle CSK Hole and bottom Mounting Hole.

- Review the design intent. Know the behavior of the components in the assembly.
- Review the messages in the dialog box and the symbols in the FeatureManager.
- Utilize Delete, Edit Feature and Undo commands to recover from Mate errors.

Insert a second Concentric Mate that creates a Mate error in the following steps. You will recover from the Mate error in the next activity.

Activity: GUIDE-ROD Assembly-Mate Errors

Insert a Concentric Mate.

91) Click **Mate** from the Assemblies toolbar.

92) Click the **ROD outside cylindrical face**.

93) Click the **PLATE bottom Mounting Hole cylindrical face**. Concentric is selected by default.

94) Click the **Green Check mark** ✔ from the Mate Pop-up toolbar to accept the Concentric Mate.

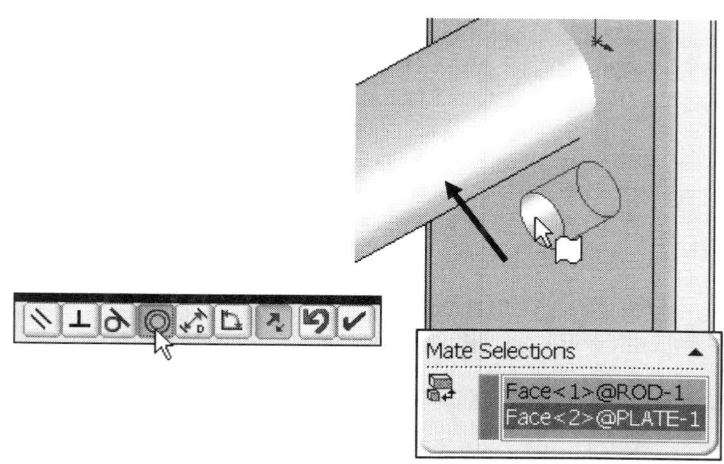

95) Click **OK** from the Mate PropertyManager.

Review the Mates.

96) **Expand** Mates in the FeatureManager.

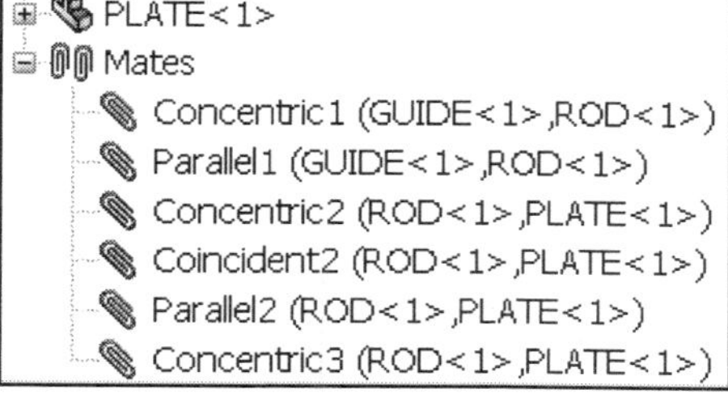

Recover from the Mate errors.

97) Right-click on **Concentric3**.

98) Click **Delete**.

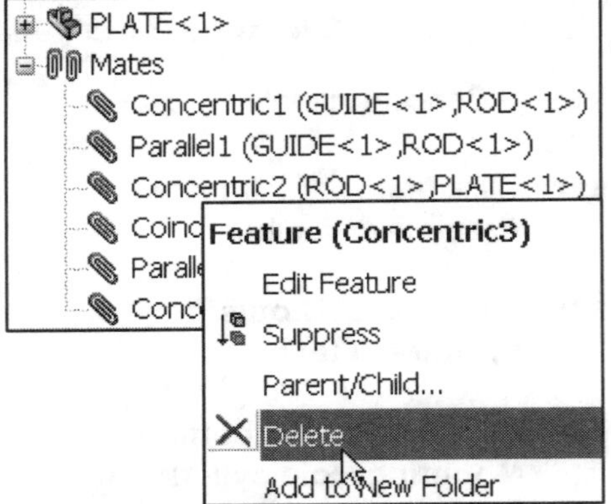

99) Click **Yes** to delete the Mate. The ROD is concentric with the bottom Mounting Hole.

Return to the Original Mates.

100) Click **Undo** from the Standard toolbar.

101) Click **Close** from the Rebuild Errors menu.

102) Click **Undo** from the Standard toolbar. The ROD is concentric with the PLATE Hole.

103) Click **Isometric view** .

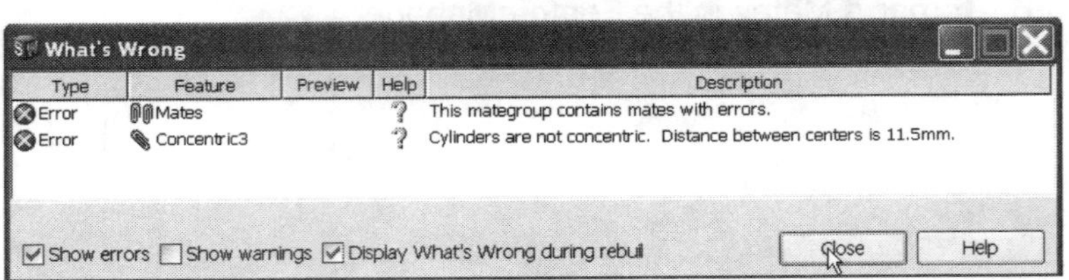

Save the GUIDE-ROD assembly.

104) Click **Save**.

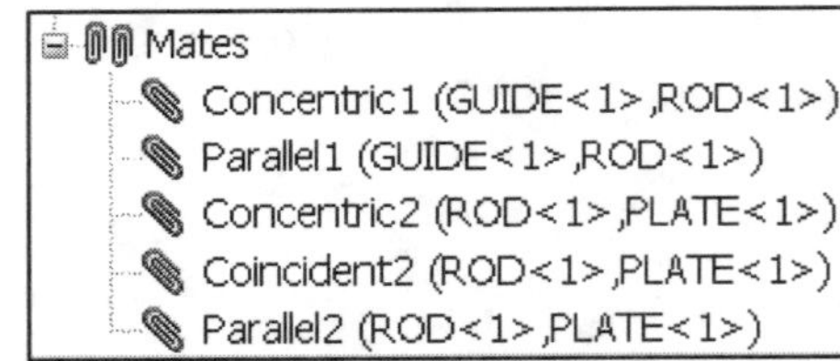

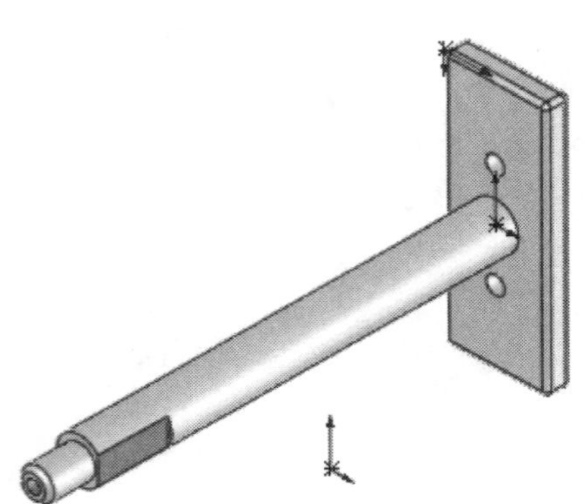

Mate flags

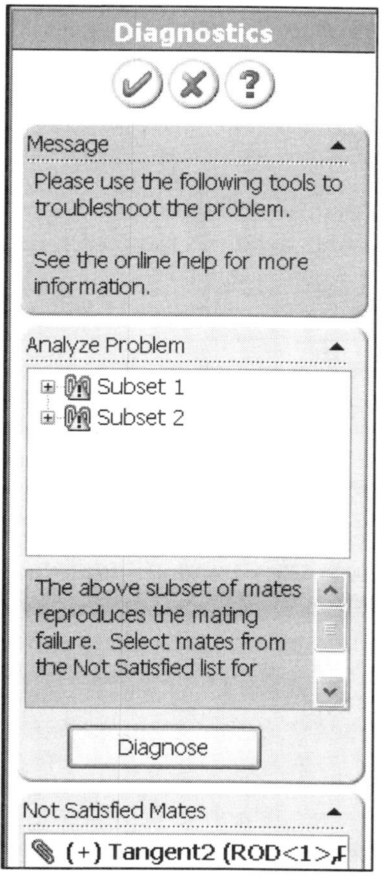

The red flags indicate Mate errors:

One or more Mates are not satisfied in a Mate Group.

Mate is satisfied but over defined.

Mate is not satisfied and over defined.

The Mate Diagnostics tool provides additional details about the Mate Errors.

Right-click on an over defined Mate in the FeatureManager. Run Mate Diagnostics .

The yellow box displays the names of the Mated entities and the problem, in the Diagnostics Property Manager.

If you delete a Mate, and recreate the same Mate Type, the Mate number increments.

Organize the Mates names. Rename Mate names with descriptive names for clarity.

Learn how to recover from a Mate error. Do not leave Mate errors in the sub-assembly. Mate errors propagate to the next assembly level and create additional design issues and longer Rebuild times.

The Undo Button in the Mate Property Manager removes the current over defined Mate.

Right-click Edit Feature in the FeatureManager to return to the Mate Property Manager to edit an individual Mate.

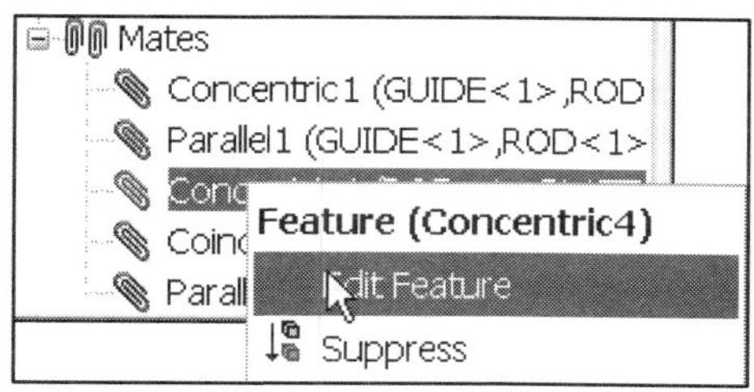

Collision Detection

The Collision Detection assembly function detects collisions between components as they move or rotate.

A collision occurs when geometry on one component coincides with geometry on another component. Place components in a non-colliding position; then test for collisions.

Activity: Collision Detection

Display the GUIDE.

105) Right-click **GUIDE** (f) GUIDE<1> from the FeatureManager.

Component (GUIDE)
Open Part
Show
Component Display

106) Click **Show** Show.

107) Click **Shaded with Edges**.

Move the PLATE behind the GUIDE.

108) Click **Move Component** Move Compo... from the Assemblies toolbar. The Move Component PropertyManager is displayed.

109) Drag the **PLATE** backward until the PLATE clears the GUIDE. The PLATE is free to translate along the Z-axis.

Display Collision Detection.

110) Click the **Collision Detection** checkbox. The Stop at collision check box is selected by default from the Move Component Options.

111) Drag the **PLATE** forward. The GUIDE back, top and angled right faces turns green when the PLATE front face collides with the back face of the GUIDE.

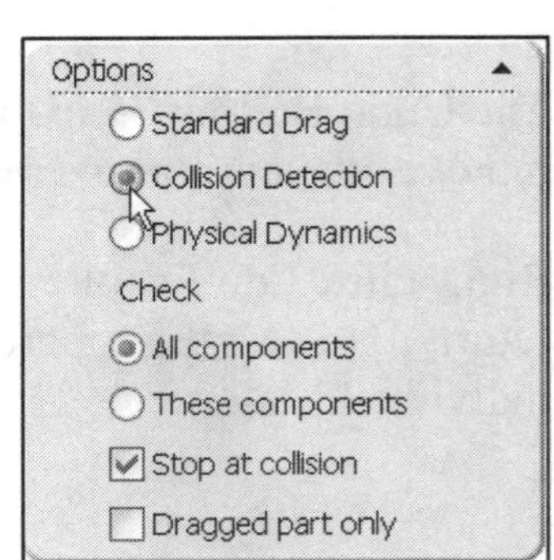

Return the PLATE to the original position.

112) Drag the **PLATE** backward until the ROD is approximately halfway through the GUIDE.

113) Click **OK** from the Move Component PropertyManager.

Save the GUIDE-ROD assembly.

114) Click **Save** .

115) Click **Yes** to Rebuild now.

Modify Component Dimension

Modify part dimensions in the assembly. Utilize Rebuild to update the part and the assembly. You realize from additional documentation that the Slot in the GUIDE is 4mm. Modify the right Slot Cut feature dimensions in the GUIDE-ROD assembly. Rebuild the assembly. The left Mirror Slot Cut and right Slot Cut update with the new value.

Activity: Modify Component Dimension

Modify the Slot of the Guide.

116) Double-click on the right **Slot Cut** of the GUIDE in the Graphics window.

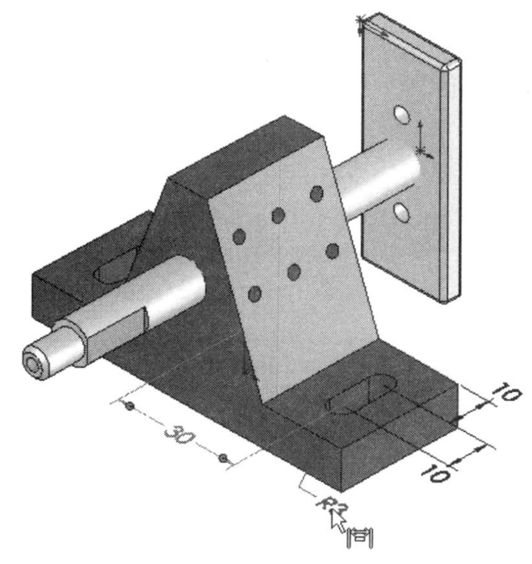

Modify the radial dimension.

117) Double-click **R3**.

118) Enter **4**.

119) Click **Rebuild** from the Modify dialog box.

120) Click the **Green Check mark** ✔ from the Modify dialog box. Note: R4 is displayed in Green.

121) Click **OK** from the Dimension PropertyManager.

Save the GUIDE-ROD assembly.

122) Click **Save** .

123) Click **Yes**.

Additional details on Assembly, Mates, Mate Errors, Collision Detection, Selection Filters are available in SolidWorks Help Topics.

Keywords: Standard Mates, Mate PropertyManager, Mates (Diagnostics), Collision Detection, Design Methods in Assembly and Selection Filters.

Additional information on Assemblies is available in Help, Introducing SolidWorks and Help, Online Tutorials. Additional information on Mate Diagnostics is found in Help, *What's New Manual.*

Design Library

A parts library contains components used in a design creation. The SolidWorks Design Library provides examples of common industry components for design creation.

The Design Library consists of annotations, assemblies, features, forming tools, parts, routing (add-in), Toolbox (add-in) and 3D ContentCentral (models from suppliers). SolidWorks add-ins are software applications.

Your company issued a design policy. The policy states that you are required to only use parts that are presently in the company's parts library. The policy is designed to lower inventory cost, purchasing cost and design time.

In this project, the Design Library parts simulate your company's part library. Utilize a hex flange bolt located in the Hardware folder. Specify a new folder location in the Design Library to quickly locate all the components utilized in this project.

The Design Library saves time locating and utilizing components in an assembly. Note: In some network installations, depending on your access rights, additions to the Design Library are only valid in new folders.

Activity: Design Library

Open the Design Library.

124) Click **Design Library**. The Design Library menu is displayed in the Graphics window.

Pin the Design Library to remain open.

125) Click **Pin**.

126) Expand design library.

Select the Flange Bolt from the parts folder.

127) Expand **parts**.

128) Double-click the **hardware** folder. The hardware components are displayed. The flange bolt icon represents a family of similar shaped components in various configurations.

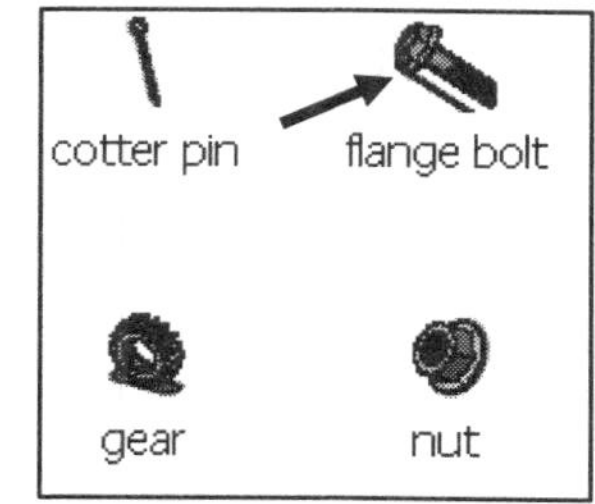

Add the first flange bolt to the assembly.

129) Click and drag the **flange bolt** icon to the right of the GUIDE-ROD assembly into the Graphics window.

130) Release the **mouse button**.

131) Select the 8mm flange bolt, **M8-1.25 x 30** from the configuration list.

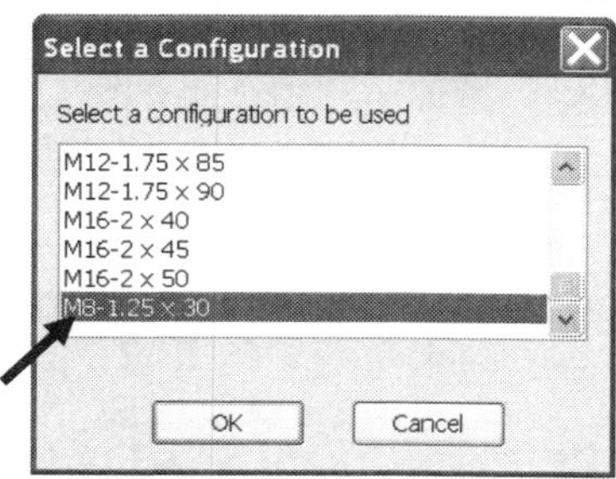

132) Click **OK**.

Add the second flange bolt to the assembly.

133) Click a **position** to the left of the GUIDE-ROD assembly.

134) Click Cancel from the Insert Component PropertyManager to exit the flange bolt placement and to close the PropertyManager.

Rotate the flange bolts.

135) Click **Rotate Component** Rotate Compo... .

136) Click and drag the **shaft** of the first flange bolt in a vertical direction. The flange bolt rotates.

137) Click and drag the **shaft** of the second flange bolt in a vertical direction.

138) Click **Rotate Component** Rotate Compo... to deactivate.

Add a new file location to the Design Library.

139) Click **Add File Location** from the Design Library.

140) Click the **drop down arrow** from the Look in box.

141) Select the **PROJECTS** folder in the Choose Folder dialog box.

142) Click **OK**. The PROJECTS folder is located in the Design Library.

143) Click the **PROJECTS** folder to display your parts and assemblies.

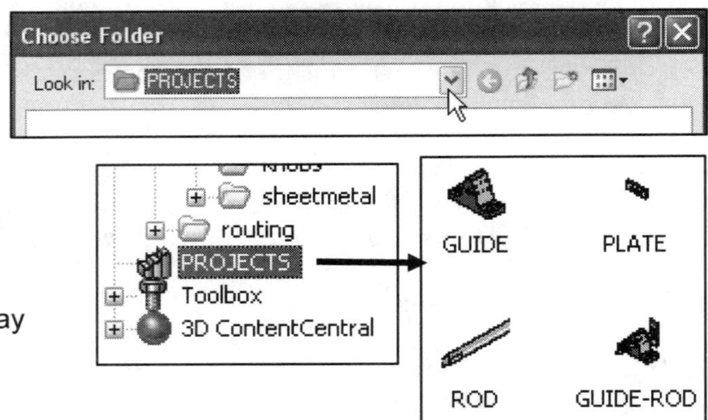

Add a new folder to the Design Library Parts.

144) Click the **PROJECTS** folder in the Design Library.

145) Click **Create New Folder**.

146) Enter **MY-PLATES** for folder name.

147) Click the **MY-PLATES** folder. The folder is empty.

Unpin the Design Library.

148) Click **Pin** .

Save the GUIDE-ROD assembly.

149) Click **Isometric view** .

150) Click **Save** .

Caution: Do not drag the PLATE part into the MY-PLATES folder at this time. The GUIDE-ROD assembly references the PLATE in the PROJECTS folder. Insert parts into the Design Library when the assembly is closed. This action is left as an exercise.

Features, Parts and Assemblies can be dragged from the Graphics window into a folder in the Design Library. Documents contain different file types in the Design Library.

There are files of type Part (*.sldprt) and Lib Feat Part (*.sldlfp) (Library Feature Part). The flange bolt is a Lib Feature Part. The PLATE is a Part.

The PLATE cannot be saved as a Lib Feat Part because it contains a Hole Wizard feature. Save the PLATE as a Part (*.sldprt) when the assembly is not opened.

Insert Mates

Insert a Concentric Mate for the first FLANGE BOLT.

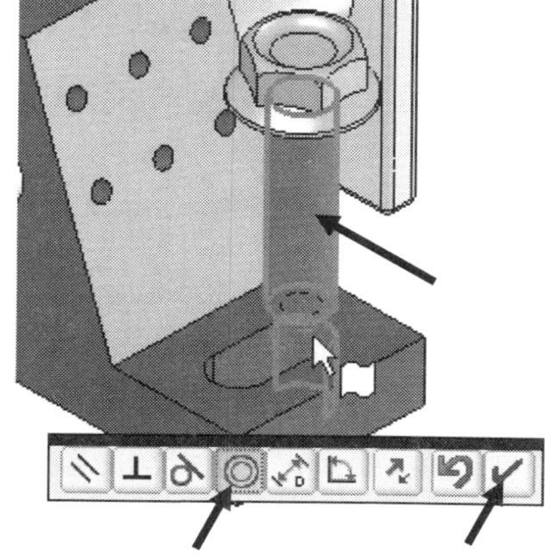

151) Click **Mate** Mate.

152) Click the FLANGE BOLT **cylindrical face**.

153) Click the **right Slot Cut back radial face**. Concentric is selected by default.

154) Click the **Green Check mark** ✔ from the Mate Pop-up toolbar.

Insert a Coincident Mate for the first FLANGE BOLT.

155) Rotate the view. Press the **up arrow key** until you display the flat bottom face of the bolt.

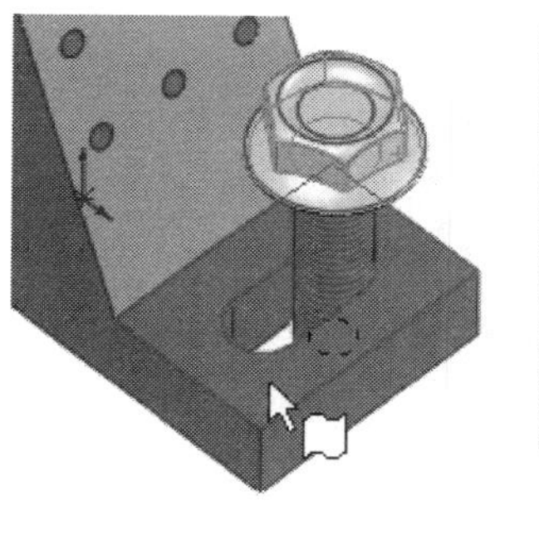

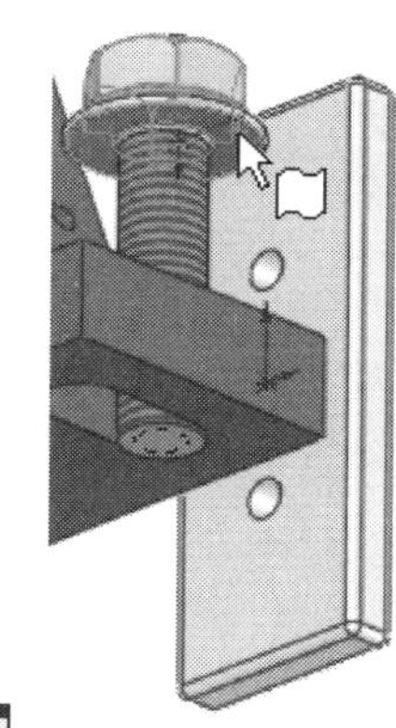

156) Click the FLANGE BOLT **flat bottom face.**

157) **Rotate** the view.

158) Click the **GUIDE top right face**. Coincident is selected by default in the Mate Pop-up toolbar.

159) Click the **Green Check mark** ✔.

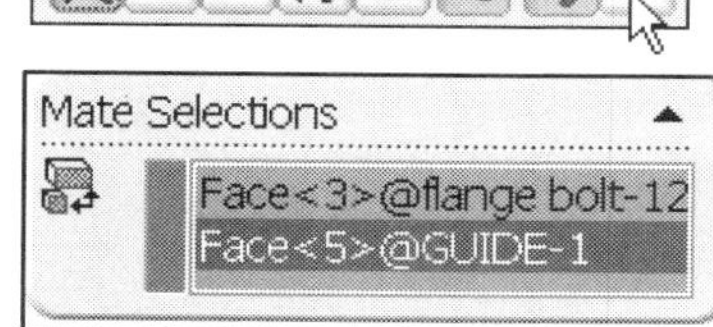

160) Click **Isometric view**. The first FLANGE BOLT is free to rotate about its centerline in the Slot Cut.

Insert a Parallel Mate.

161) Click the **front face** of the hex head.

162) Click the **front face** of the GUIDE.

163) Click **Parallel** ⫽.

164) Click the **Green Check mark** ✔ from the Pop-up toolbar. The FLANGE BOLT is fully defined.

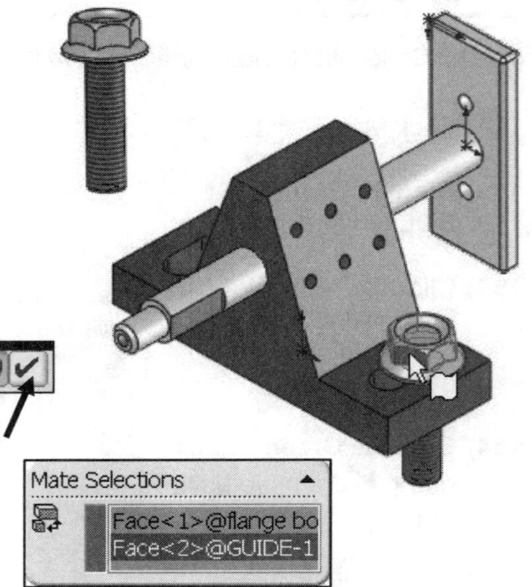

165) Click **OK** from the Mate PropertyManager.

Expand the Mates in the FeatureManager.

166) Click the **Plus sign** ⊞ in Mates.

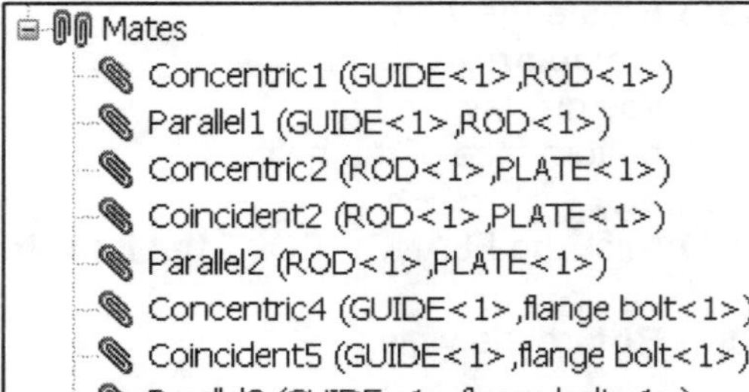

Display the Mates in the FeatureManager to check that the components and the Mate Types correspond to the design intent.

Note: If you delete a Mate and then recreate it, the Mate numbers will be different.

Insert a Concentric Mate for the second FLANGE BOLT.

167) Click **Mate** Mate .

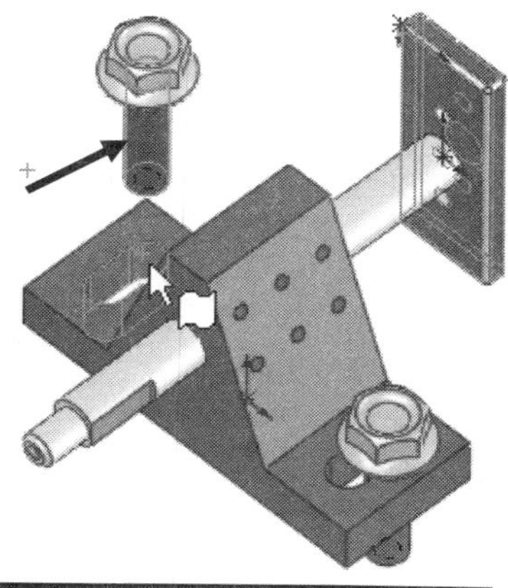

168) Rotate the view. Press the **arrow key** until you display the left Slot Cut back radial face.

169) Click the second FLANGE BOLT **cylindrical face**.

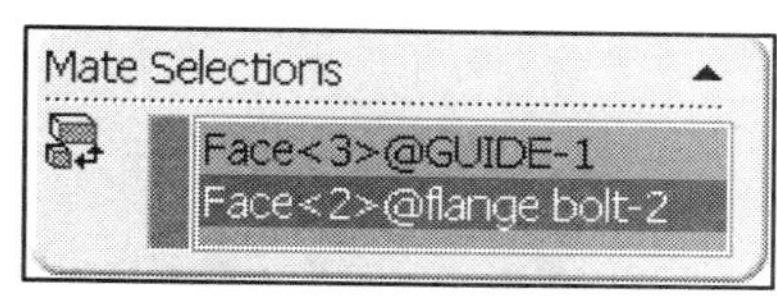

170) Click the **left Slot Cut back radial face**. Concentric is selected by default. Click the **Green Check mark** ✔ from the Mate Pop-up toolbar.

Insert a Coincident Mate.

171) Rotate the view. Press the **arrow key** until you display the flat bottom face of the bolt.

172) Click the FLANGE BOLT **flat bottom face. Rotate** the view.

173) Click the **GUIDE top left face**. Coincident is selected by default in the Mate Pop-up toolbar.

174) Click the **Green Check mark** ✔.

175) Click **Isometric view** .

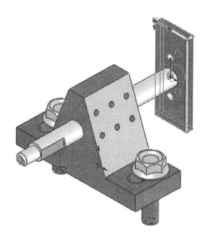

Insert a Parallel Mate.

176) Press the **direction arrows** to display the front face of the left Flange Bolt.

177) Click the **front face** of the left Flange Bolt hex head.

178) Click the **front face** of the GUIDE.

179) Click **Parallel** .

180) Click the **Green Check mark** . The second FLANGE BOLT is fully defined.

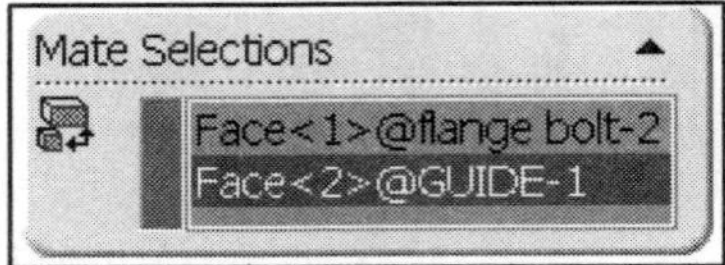

181) Click **OK** from the Mate PropertyManager.

182) Click **Isometric view** .

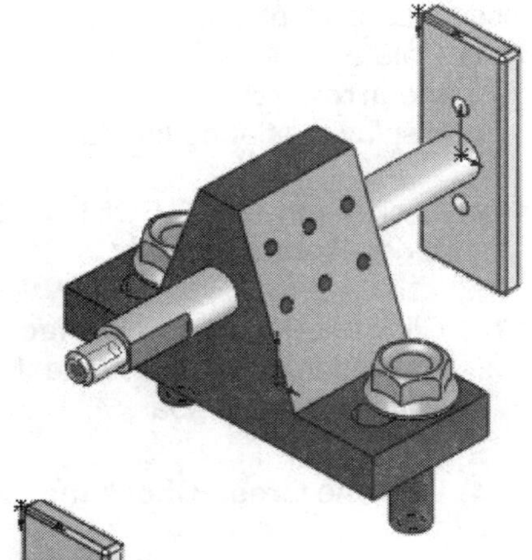

Save the GUIDE-ROD assembly.

183) Click **Save** .

Copy components directly in the Graphics window. Hold the Ctrl key down. Click and drag the component into the Graphic window to create a new instance (copy). Release the Ctrl key. Release the mouse button.

Socket Head Cap Screw Part

The PLATE mounts to the PISTON PLATE of the GUIDE CYLINDER assembly with two M4x0.7 Socket Head Cap Screws. Create a simplified version of the 4MMCAPSCREW based on the ANSI B 18.3.1M-1986 standard.

How do you determine the overall length of the 4MMCAPSCREW? Answer: The depth of the PLATE plus the required blind depth of the PISTON PLATE provided by the manufacturer.

When using fasteners to connect two plates, a design rule of thumb is to use a minimum of 75% to 85% of the second plate's blind depth. Select a common overall length available from your supplier.

The 4MMCAPSCREW is created from three features. The Base feature is a revolved feature. The Revolved Base feature creates the head and shaft of the 4MMCAPSCREW. The Chamfer feature inserts two end cuts. The Extrude-Cut feature utilizes a hex profile. Utilize the Polygon Sketch Tool to create the hexagon.

Activity: Socket Head Cap Screw Part

Create the 4MMCAPSCREW.

184) Click **File**, **New** from the Main menu.

185) Double-click **PART-MM-ANSI** for Template from the MY-TEMPLATES folder.

Save the part.

186) Click **Save** .

187) Select **ENGDESIGN-W-SOLIDWORKS\PROJECTS** for Save in file folder.

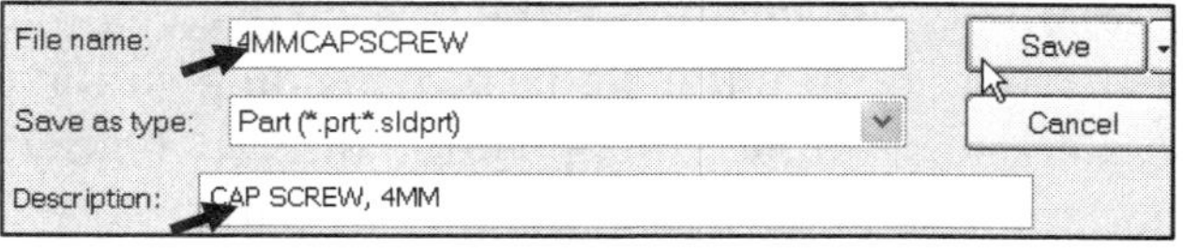

188) Enter **4MMCAPSCREW** for Filename.

189) Enter **CAP SCREW, 4MM** for Description.

190) Click **Save**.

Create the Sketch.

191) Click **Front Plane** from the FeatureManager.

192) Click **Sketch** Sketch .

193) Click **Centerline** Centerline from the Sketch toolbar.

194) Click **Front view** .

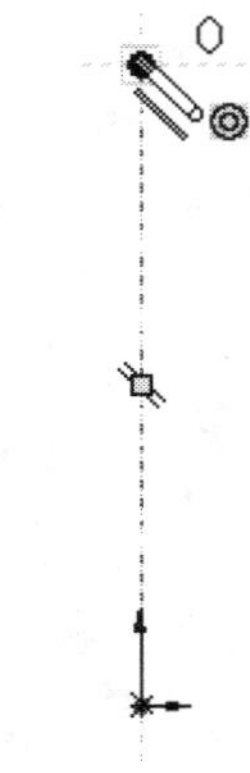

Sketch a vertical centerline.

195) Click the **Origin** .

196) Click a **position** directly above the Origin.

Sketch the profile.

197) Click **Line** Line from the Sketch toolbar.

198) Click **Origin** .

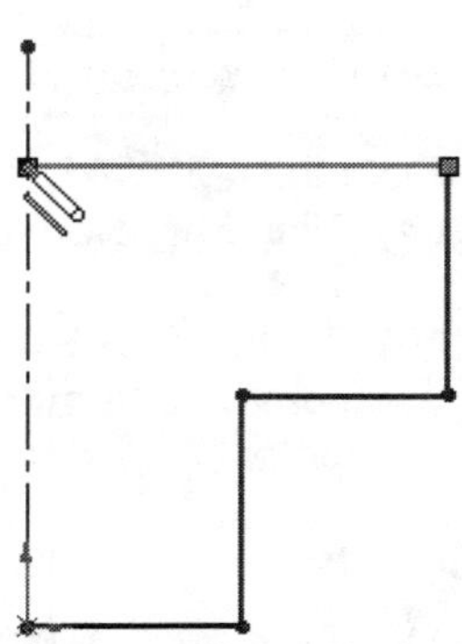

199) Click a **position** to the right of the Origin to create a horizontal line.

200) Sketch the first **vertical line** to the right of the centerline.

201) Sketch the second **horizontal line**. Sketch the second **vertical line**. Sketch the third **horizontal line**. The endpoint of the line is Coincident with the Centerline. The Centerline extends above the third horizontal line.

202) Double-click the last **endpoint** to end the Line tool.

A diameter dimension for the revolved sketch requires a centerline, profile line and a dimension position to the left of the centerline. A dimension position directly below the bottom horizontal line creates a radial dimension.

Insert smaller dimensions first, then larger dimensions to maintain the shape of the sketch profile.

Fit the sketch to the Graphics window.
203) Press the **f** key.

Add dimensions.

204) Click **Smart Dimension** Smart Dimens... .

Add a bottom diameter dimension.
205) Click the **centerline**.

206) Click the **first vertical line**.

207) Click a **position** below and to the left of the Origin to create a diameter dimension.

208) Enter **4**.

209) Click the **Green Check mark** ✔.

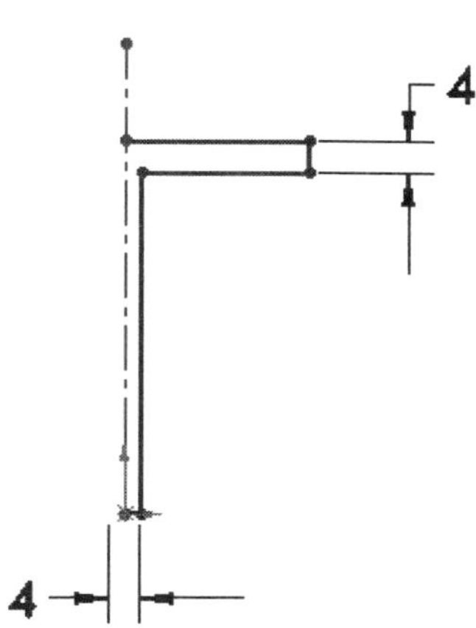

Add a vertical dimension.
210) Click the **second vertical line**.

211) Click a **position** to the right of the profile.

212) Enter **4**.

213) Click the **Green Check mark** ✔.

Add a top diameter dimension.
214) Click the **centerline**.

215) Click the **second vertical line**.

216) Click a **position** to the left of the Origin and above the second horizontal line to create a diameter dimension.

217) Enter **7**.

218) Click the **Green Check mark** ✔.

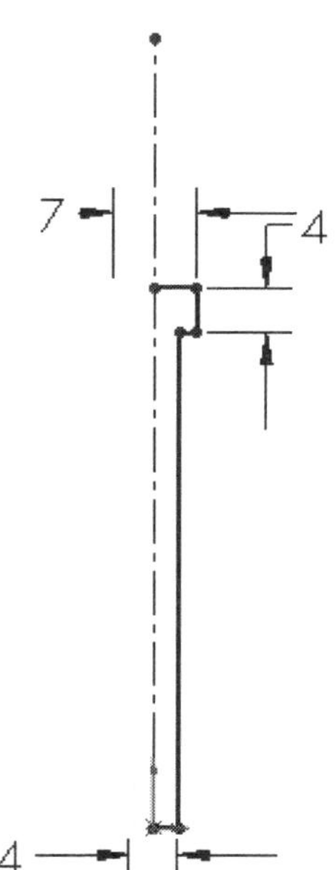

Create an overall vertical dimension.

219) Click the **top horizontal line**.

220) Click the **Origin**. Click a **position** to the right of the profile.

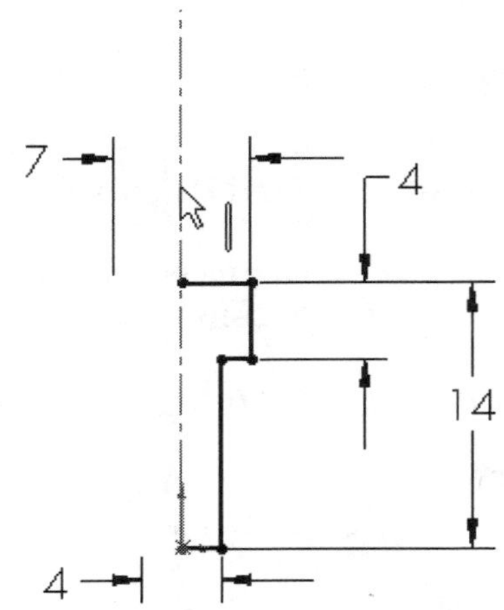

221) Enter **14**. Click the **Green Check mark** ✔.

Select the Centerline.

222) Right-click **Select** Select.

223) Click the **Centerline** for axis for revolution.

Insert the Revolved Base feature.

224) Click **Features** Features from the Control Area.

225) Click **Revolved Boss/Base** Revolved Boss/B... from the Features toolbar.

226) Click **Yes** to the question, "The sketch is currently open. A non-thin revolution feature requires a closed sketch. Would you like the sketch to be automatically closed?"

Note: The "Yes" button causes a vertical line to be automatically sketched from the top left point to the Origin. The Graphics window displays the Isometric view and a preview of the Revolved Base feature.

Revolve Parameters
Line1
One-Direction
360.00deg

227) Click **OK** from the Revolve PropertyManager.

Fit the Model to the Graphics window.

228) Press the **f** key.

Insert a Chamfer feature.

229) Click **Chamfer** Chamfer from the Features toolbar.

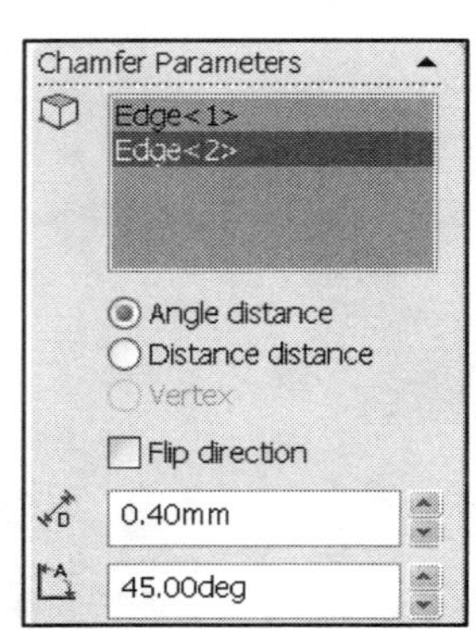

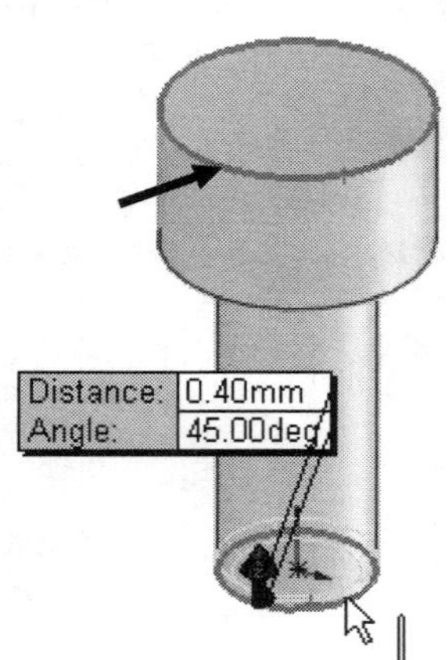

230) Click the **top circular edge** of the 4MMCAPSCREW head.

231) Select the **bottom circular edge** of the 4MMCAPSCREW shaft.

232) Enter **0.4** in the Distance box. Accept the default 45 degree Angle.

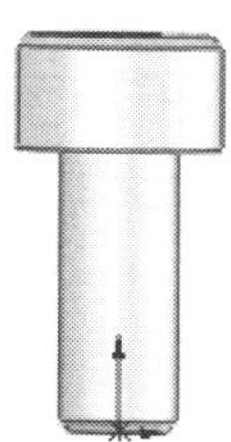

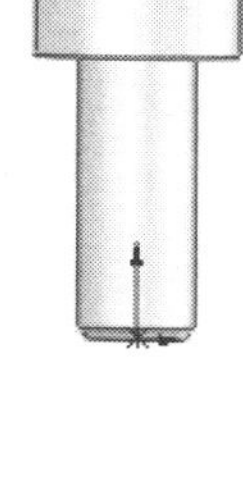

233) Click **OK** from the Chamfer PropertyManager.

Save the 4MMCAPSCREW part.

234) Click **Save**.

Distance and Angle values for the Chamfer feature can be entered in the Pop-up box Distance: 0.40mm Angle: 45deg.

Create the Hex Extruded Cut.

235) Rotate the view. Press the **direction arrows** to display the top circular face of the 4MMCAPASCREW.

Insert the Sketch.

236) Click the **top circular face** for sketch plane.

237) Click **Sketch** Sketch. Click **Top view**.

Sketch a hexagon.

Click **Tools**, **Sketch Entities**, **Polygon** Polygon from the Main menu.

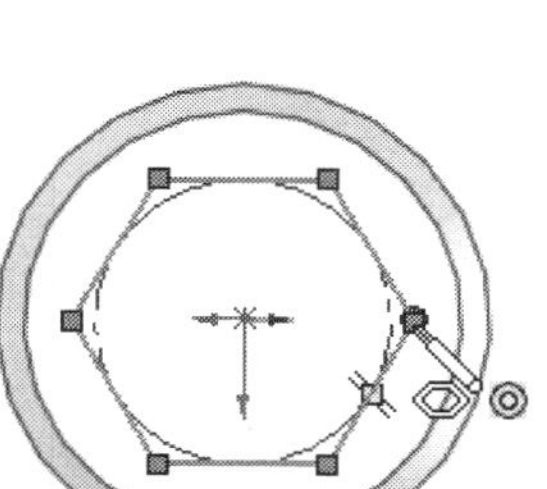

238) Click the **Origin**.

239) Click a **position** to the right.

Insert a Horizontal Relation.

240) Right-click **Select** Select.

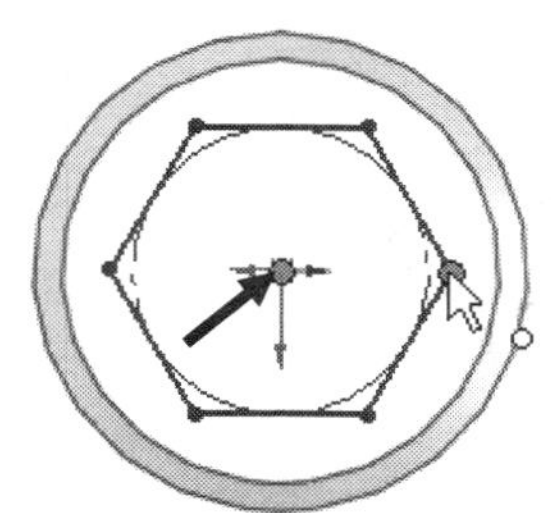

241) Click the **Origin**. Hold the **Ctrl** key down. Click the **right point** of the hexagon. Release the **Ctrl** key.

242) Click **Horizontal**.

Add a dimension.

243) Click **Smart Dimension** Smart Dimens... .

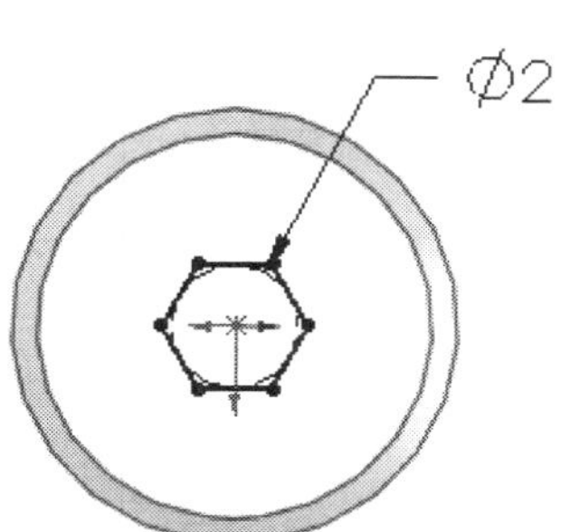

244) Click the **inscribed circle**.

245) Click a position **diagonally** to the right of the profile.

246) Enter **2.0**. Click the **Green Check mark**.

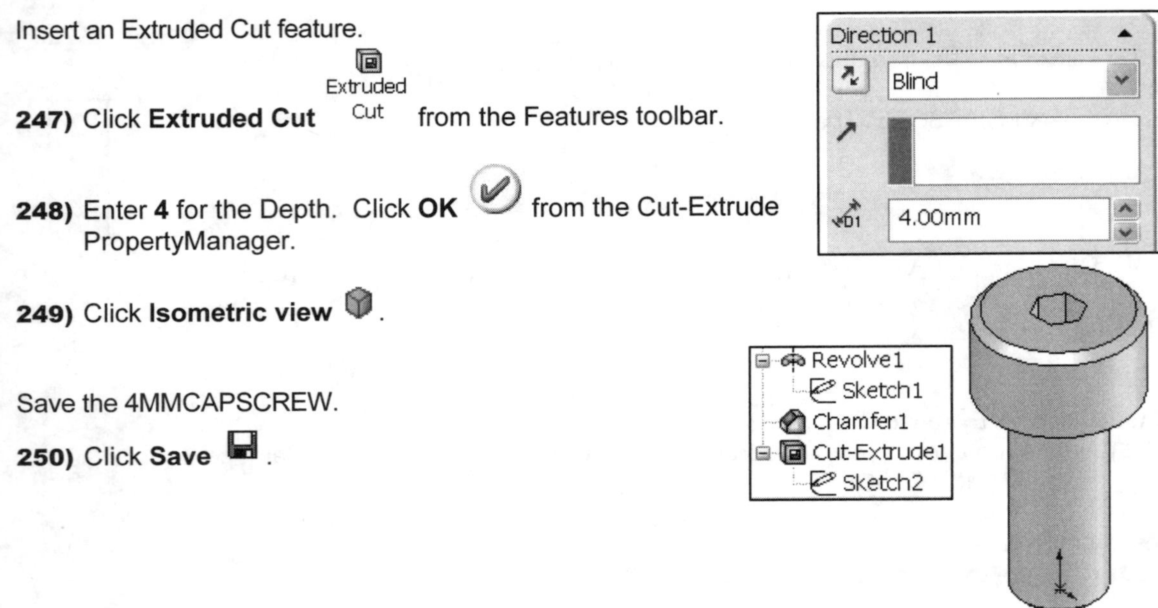

Insert an Extruded Cut feature.

247) Click **Extruded Cut** Extruded Cut from the Features toolbar.

248) Enter **4** for the Depth. Click **OK** from the Cut-Extrude PropertyManager.

249) Click **Isometric view**.

Save the 4MMCAPSCREW.

250) Click **Save**.

SmartMates

A SmartMate is a Mate that automatically occurs when a component is placed into an assembly. The mouse pointer displays a SmartMate feedback symbol when common geometry and relationships exist between the component and the assembly.

SmartMates are Concentric or Coincident. A Concentric SmartMate assumes that the geometry on the component has the same center as the geometry on an assembled reference. A Coincident Planes SmartMate assumes that a plane on the component lies along a plane on the assembly. As the component is dragged into place, the mouse pointer provides feedback such as:

- Concentric .
- Coincident .

Coincident/Concentric SmartMate

The most common SmartMate between a screw/bolt and a hole is the Coincident/Concentric SmartMate. The following technique utilizes two windows. The first window contains the 4MMCAPSCREW part and the second window contains the GUIDE-ROD assembly. Zoom in on both windows to view the Mate reference geometry. Drag the part by the shoulder edge into the assembly window.

View the mouse pointer for Coincident/Concentric feedback . Release the mouse pointer on the circular edge of the PLATE Mounting Hole.

Activity: Coincident/Concentric SmartMate

Display the 4MMCAPSCREW part and the GUIDE-ROD assembly.

251) Click **Window**, **Tile Horizontally** from the Main menu.

252) **Zoom in** on the PLATE to view the Mounting Holes.

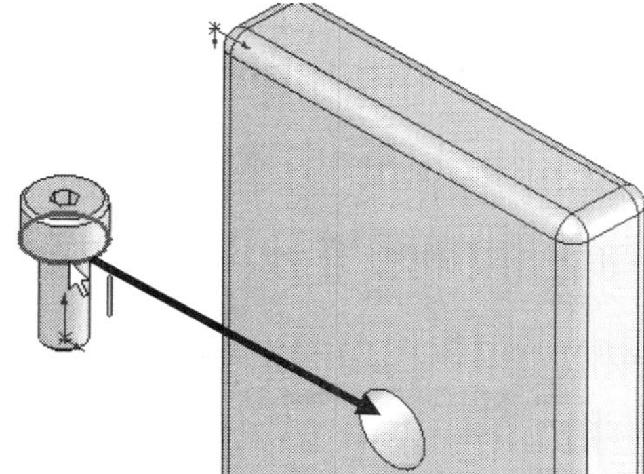

Insert the first 4MMCAPSCREW.

253) Click and drag the **circular edge** of the 4MMCAPSCREW part into the GUIDE-ROD assembly Graphic window.

254) Release the mouse pointer on the **top circular edge** of the PLATE. The mouse pointer displays the Coincident/Concentric Circular edges feedback symbol.

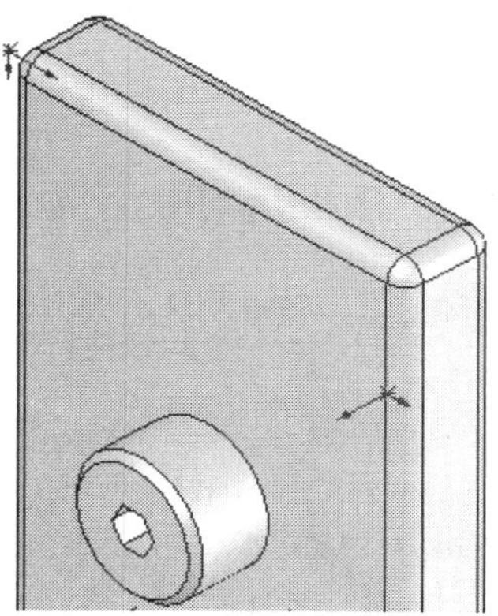

Insert the second 4MMCAPSCREW.

255) Click and drag the **circular edge** of the 4MMCAPSCREW part into the GUIDE-ROD assembly Graphic window.

256) Release the mouse pointer on the **bottom circular edge** of the PLATE. The mouse pointer displays the Coincident/Concentric Circular edges feedback symbol.

257) **Maximize** the GUIDE-ROD assembly.

Fit the GUIDE-ROD assembly to the Graphics window.

258) Press the **f** key.

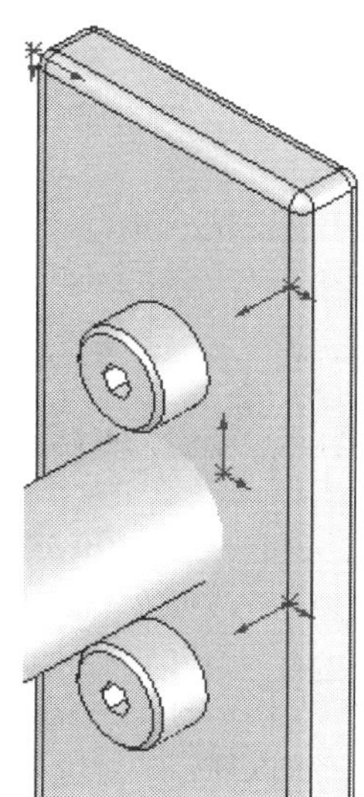

Zoom in before dragging a component into the assembly to select the correct circular edge for a Coincident/Concentric Mate.

The circular edge of the 4MMCAPSCREW produces both the Coincident/Concentric Mate. The cylindrical face of the 4MMCAPSCREW produces only a Concentric Mate. View the mouse pointer for the correct feedback.

Insert a Parallel Mate for the first 4MMCAPSCREW.

259) Click **Mate** Mate .

260) Expand the **GUIDE-ROD** GUIDE-ROD icon in the Graphics Window.

261) Click the **Right Plane** of the 4MMCAPSCREW<1> in the FeatureManager.

262) Click the **Right Plane** of 4MMCAPSCREW<2>.

263) Click **Parallel** .

264) Click the **Green Check mark** ✔. The two 4MMCAPSCREWS are free to rotate together.

265) Click **OK** from the Mate PropertyManager.

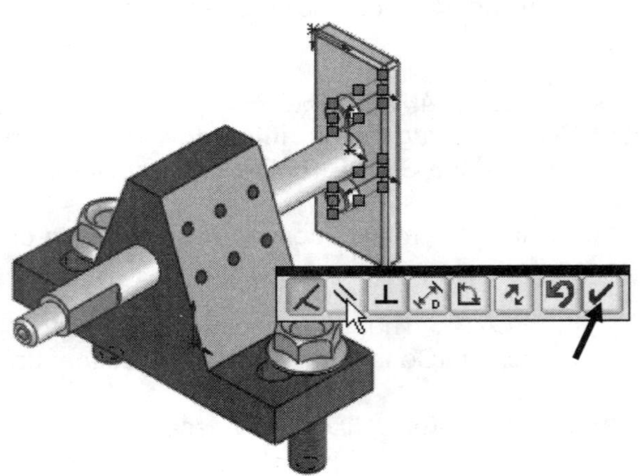

Fit the assembly to the Graphics window.
266) Press the **f** key.

267) Click **Isometric view** .

268) Click **View**, uncheck **Origins** from the Main menu.

Save GUIDE-ROD assembly.

269) Click **Save** .

270) Click **Yes** to the Rebuild question.

The PLATE, ROD and 4MMCAPSCREWS are free to translate along the z-axis. Their component status remains under defined in the GUIDE-ROD FeatureManager. The GUIDE is fixed to the assembly Origin. The FLANGE BOLTS are fully defined since they are mated only to the GUIDE.

Understand how Mates reflect the physical behavior in an assembly. Move and rotate components to test the mate behavior. The correct mate selection minimizes rebuild time and errors in the assembly.

Tolerance and Fit

The ROD travels through the GUIDE in the GUIDE-ROD assembly. The shaft diameter of the ROD is 10mm. The hole diameter in the GUIDE is 10mm. A 10mm ROD cannot be inserted into a 10mm GUIDE hole without great difficulty!

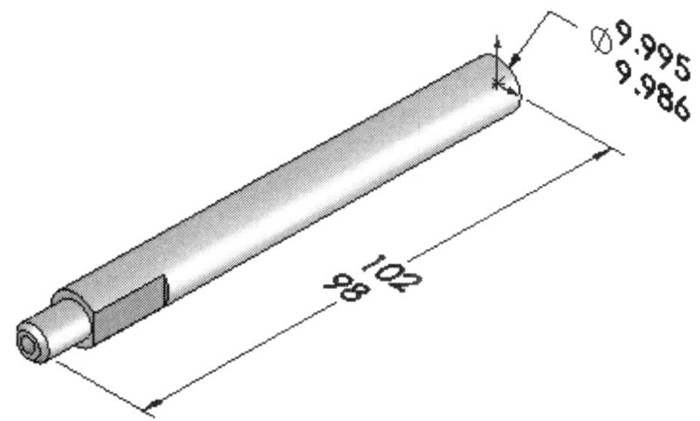

Note: The 10mm dimension is the nominal dimension. The nominal dimension is approximately the size of a feature that corresponds to a common fraction or whole number.

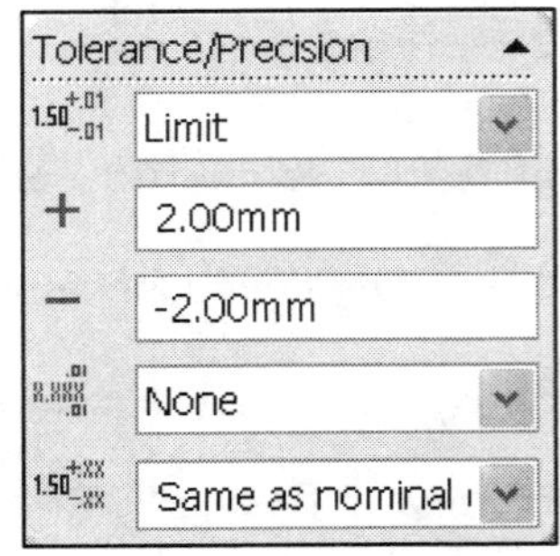

Tolerance is the difference between the maximum and minimum variation of a nominal dimension and the actual manufactured dimension.

Example: A ROD has a nominal dimension of 100mm with a tolerance of ± 2mm, (100mm ± 2mm). This translates to a part with a possible manufactured dimension range between 98mm to 102mm. The total ROD tolerance is 4mm. Note: Design rule of thumb: Design with the maximum permissible tolerance. Tolerance flexibility saves in manufacturing time and cost.

The assembled relationship between the ROD and the GUIDE is called the fit. The fit is defined as the tightness or looseness between two components. This project discusses three major types of fits:

- Clearance fit - The shaft diameter is less than the hole diameter.
- Interference fit – The shaft diameter is larger than the hole diameter. The difference between the shaft diameter and the hole diameter is called interference.
- Transition fit – Clearance or interference can exist between the shaft and the hole.

You require a Clearance fit between the shaft of the ROD and the Guide Hole of the GUIDE. There are multiple categories for Clearance fits.

Dimension the GUIDE hole and ROD shaft for a Sliding Clearance fit. All below dimensions are in millimeters.

Use the following values:

Hole	Maximum	10.015mm.	
	Minimum	10.000mm.	
Shaft	Maximum	9.995mm.	
	Minimum	9.986mm.	
Fit	Maximum	10.015 – 9.986 = .029	Max. Hole – Min. Shaft.
	Minimum	10.000 – 9.995 = .005	Min. Hole – Max. Shaft.

Calculate the maximum variation:

Hole Max: 10.015 – Hole Min: 10.000 = .015 Hole Max. Variation.

Select features from the FeatureManager and the Graphics window. In the next activity, locate feature dimensions with the FeatureManager for the GUIDE. Locate feature dimensions in the Graphics window for the ROD. Select the dimension text; then apply the Tolerance\Precision through options in the Dimension PropertyManager.

Activity: Tolerance and Fit

Locate the dimension in the FeatureManager.

271) Expand **GUIDE** in the GUIDE-ROD FeatureManager.

272) Double-click **Guide Hole** in the FeatureManager to display the dimensions.

Add the maximum and minimum Guide Hole dimensions.

273) Click the **∅10** dimension.

274) Select **Limit** from the Tolerance/Precision box in the Dimension PropertyManager.

275) Enter **0.015** in the plus box.

276) Enter **0.000** in the minus box.

277) Select **.123** for three place Precision.

278) Click **OK** from the Dimension PropertyManager.

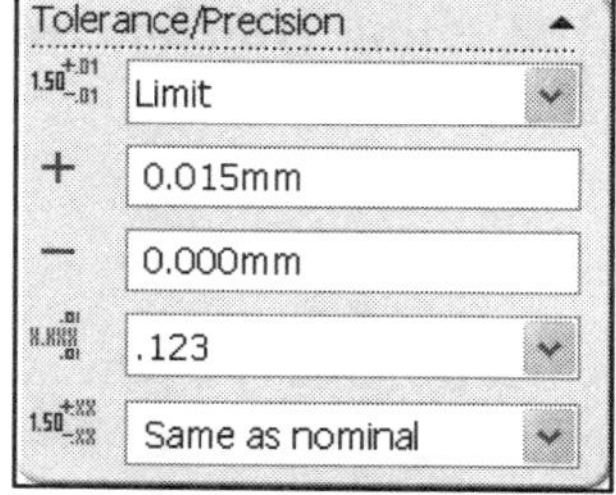

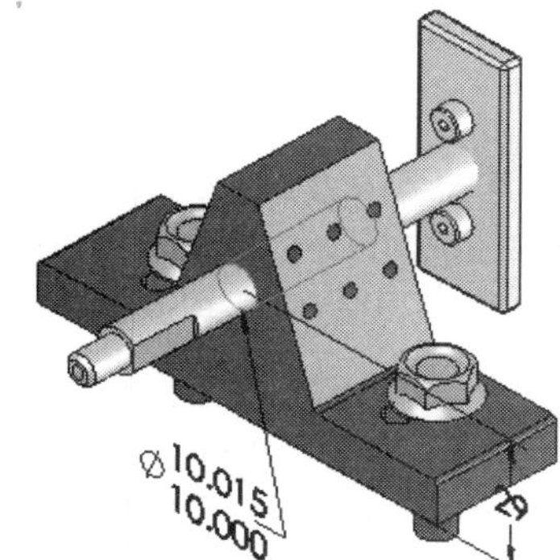

Add maximum and minimum Shaft dimensions.

279) Double-click on the **ROD** part in the Graphics window.

280) Click the **∅10** diameter dimension.

281) Select **Limit**.

282) Enter -**0.005** in the plus box.

283) Enter -**0.014** in the minus box.

284) Select **.123** for three place Precision.

285) Click **OK** from the Dimension PropertyManager.

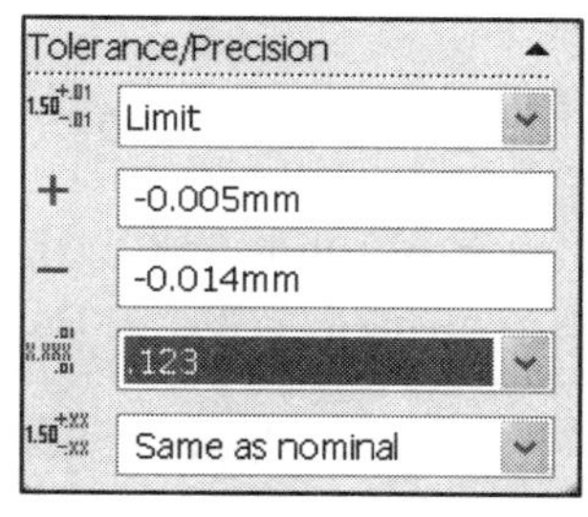

Save the GUIDE-ROD assembly.

286) Click **Save**. Click **Yes**.

Note: ISO symbol Hole/Shaft Classification is applied to an individual dimension for Fit, Fit with tolerance, or Fit (tolerance only) types.

Classification can be:

- User Defined.
- Clearance.
- Transitional.
- Press.

For a hole or shaft dimension, select a classification from the list. The Hole/Shaft designation for a Sliding Fit is H7/g6.

The values for Maximum and Minimum tolerances are calculated automatically based on the diameter of the Hole/Shaft and the Fit Classification. See the exercise at the end of this project.

Utilize Hole/Shaft Classification early in the design process. If the dimension changes, then the tolerance updates. The Hole/Shaft Classification propagates to the details in the drawing. You will create the drawing in Project 3.

Additional details on Tolerance, Precision, Smart Mates, Revolve Feature, and Design Library are available in Help, SolidWorks Help Topics. Keywords: Tolerances (Dimension), Fit Tolerance, Smart Mates, Feature Based Mates, Geometry Based Mates and Revolve Boss/Base.

Review of the GUIDE-ROD Assembly.

The GUIDE-ROD assembly combined the GUIDE, ROD and PLATE components. The GUIDE was the first component inserted into the GUIDE-ROD assembly.

Mates removed degrees of freedom. Concentric, Coincident and Parallel Mates were utilized to position the ROD and PLATE with respect to the GUIDE.

Flange Bolts were obtained from the Design Library. You utilize a Revolved feature to create the 4MMCAPSCREW. The Revolved feature contained an axis, sketched profile and an angle of revolution. The Polygon Sketch Tool was utilized to create the hexagon Extruded Cut. The 4MMCAPSCREW utilized the Concentric/Coincident SmartMate option.

Exploded View

The Exploded View illustrates how to assemble the components in an assembly. Create an Exploded View with four steps in the ROD-GUIDE assembly. Click and drag components in the Graphics window. The Manipulator icon indicates the direction to explode. Select an alternate component edge for the Explode direction. Drag the component in the Graphics window or enter an exact value in the Explode distance box. In this activity, manipulate the top-level components in the assembly.

In the project exercises, create exploded views for each sub-assembly and utilize the Re-use sub-assembly explode option in the top level assembly.

Access the Explode view option as follows:

- Right-click the configuration name in the ConfigurationManager.
- Select the Exploded View tool in the Assembly toolbar.
- Select Insert, Exploded View from the Main menu.

The Assembly Exploder utilizes a PropertyManager.

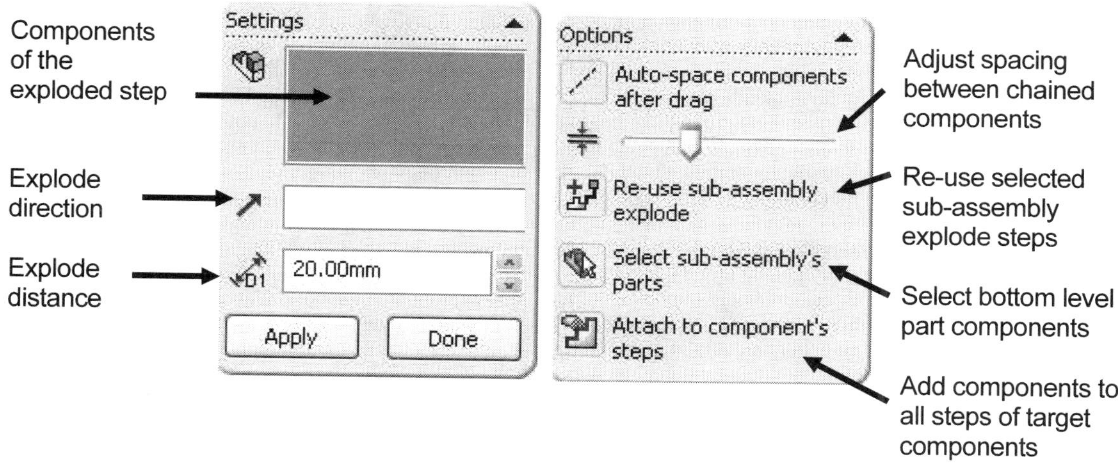

Activity: Exploded View

Insert an Exploded view.

287) Click **Assemblies**, Assemb... , **Exploded View** Exploded View .

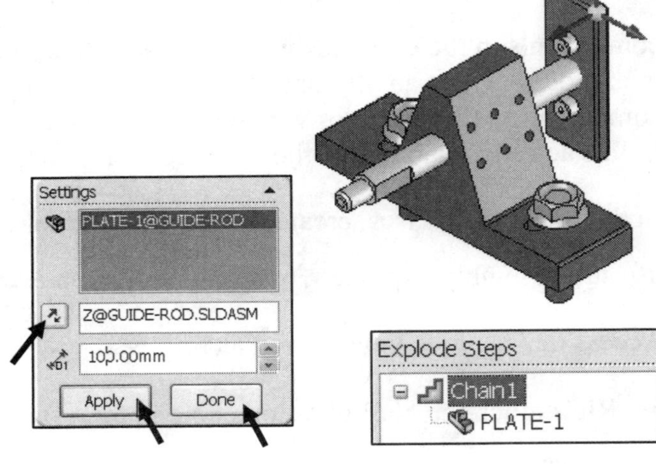

Fit the Model to the Graphics window.

288) Press the **f** key.

Create Explode Step 1.

289) Click the **PLATE**.

290) Enter **100mm** in the Explode distance box. If required, click **Reverse direction**.

291) Click **Apply**.

292) Click **Done**.

Note: The exact Explode distance value is not required. You can click and drag the Manipulator Handle. We will address this in the next step.

Create Explode Step2.

293) Click the **ROD**.

294) Press the **f** key.

295) Drag the **blue manipulator handle** backward to position between the PLATE and the GUIDE.

296) Click **Done**.

Create Explode Step3.

297) Click the **left flange bolt**.

298) Drag the **vertical green manipulator handle** upward above the GUIDE.

299) Click **Done**.

Create Explode Step4.

300) Click the **right flange bolt**.

301) Drag the **vertical green manipulator handle** upward above the GUIDE.

302) Click **Done**.

303) Click **OK** from the Explode PropertyManager.

304) Click **Isometric view**.

305) Click **Save**

.

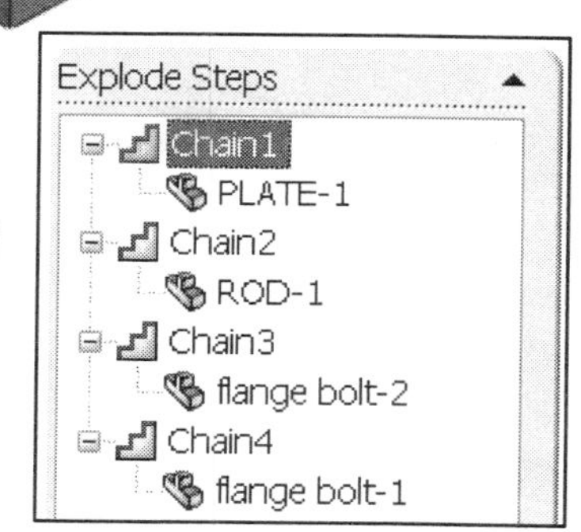

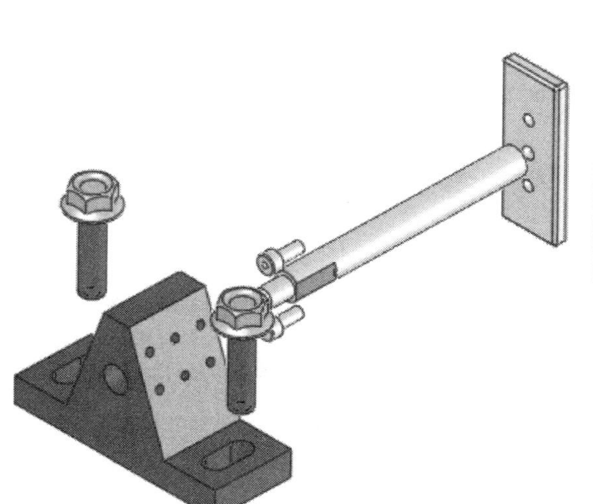

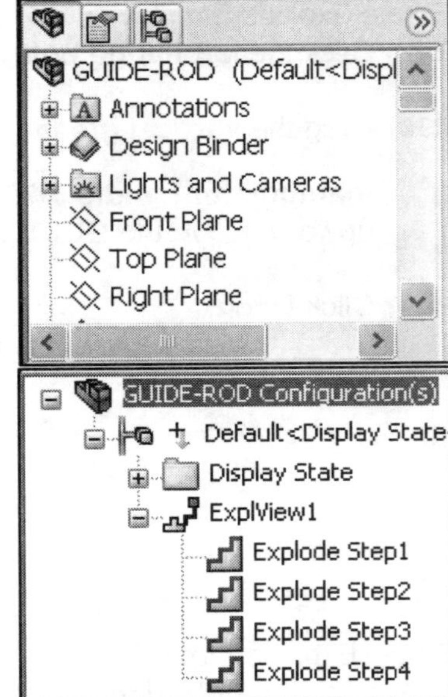

Split the FeatureManager to view the Exploded Steps.

306) Position the **mouse pointer** at the top of the FeatureManager. The mouse pointer displays the Split bar.

307) Drag the **Split bar** half way down to display two FeatureManager windows.

308) Click **ConfigurationManager** to display Default configuration in the lower window.

309) Expand **Default <Display State-1>**.

310) Expand **ExplView1** to display the 4 Exploded states.

Fit the Exploded view to the Graphics window.

311) Press the **f** key.

Remove the Exploded state.

312) Right-click in the **Graphic window**.

313) Click **Collapse** from the Pop-up menu.

314) Click **Isometric view** .

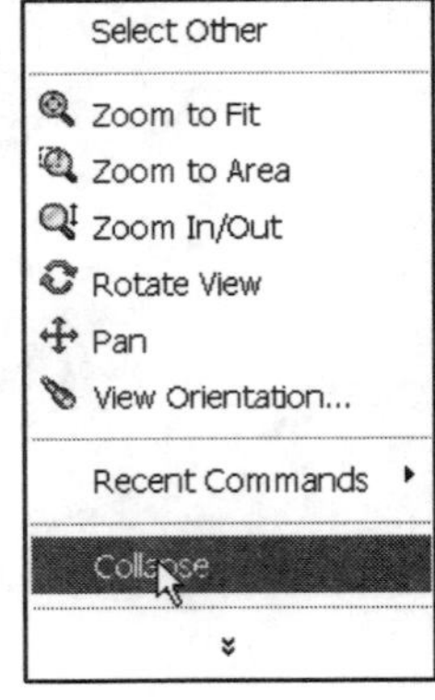

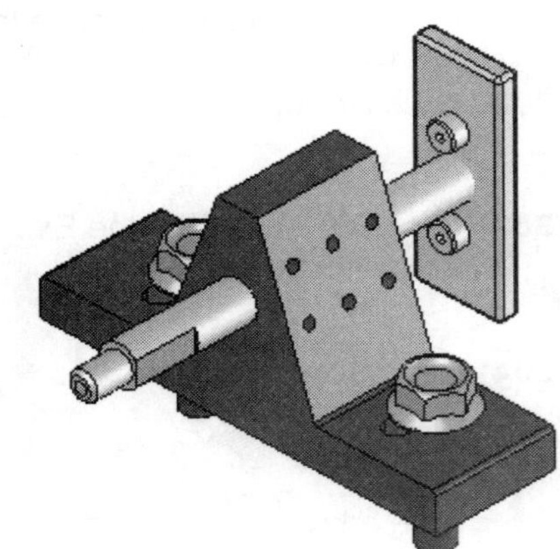

Animate the Exploded view.

315) Right-click **ExplView1**.

316) Click **Animate explode**. Play is selected by default. View the animation.

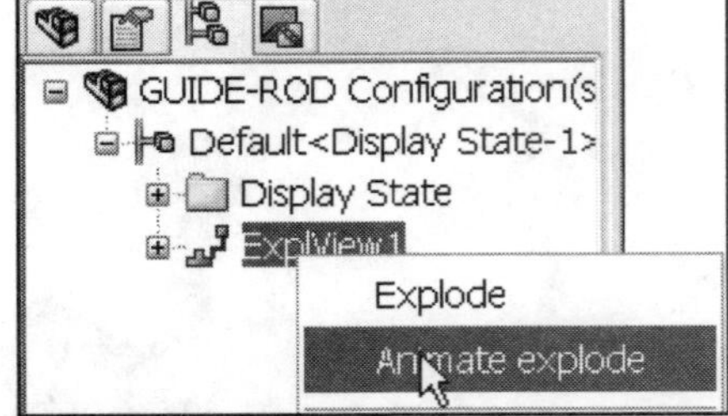

317) Click **Stop** to end the animation.

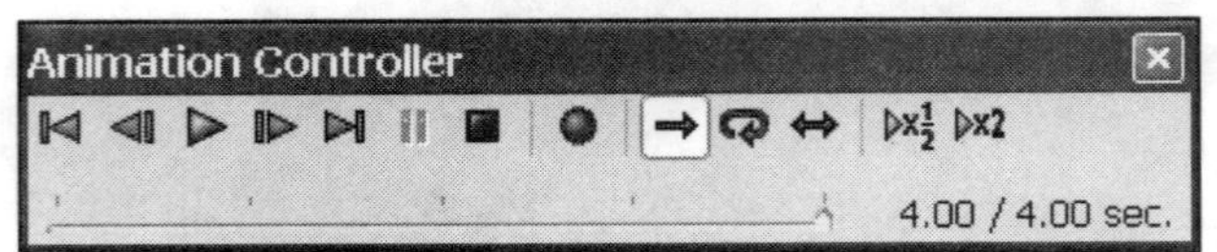

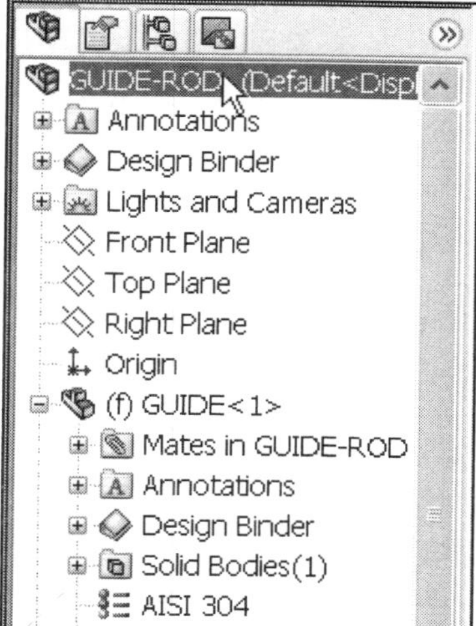

Close the Animation Controller.

318) Click **Close**. The GUIDE-ROD is in the Exploded state.

319) Right-click **Collapse** in the GUIDE-ROD Graphics window.

Display the FeatureManager.

320) Click the **FeatureManager** icon.

321) Drag the **Split bar** upward to display one FeatureManager window.

Save the GUIDE-ROD assembly.

322) Click **Save**.

Note: The SolidWorks Animator application is required to record an AVI file through the Animation Controller. Play the animation files through the Windows Media Player. The time required to create the animation file depends on the number of components in the assembly and the options selected.

Stop the animation before closing the Animation Controller toolbar to avoid issues. Utilize SolidWorks Animator for additional control over the Explode/Collapse motion in the assembly.

Create the Exploded steps in the order that you would disassemble the assembly. Collapse the assembly to return to the original assembled position. Your animations will appear more realistic based on the order of the Explode steps.

Review the exercises at the end of this project for additional examples on SolidWorks Animator.

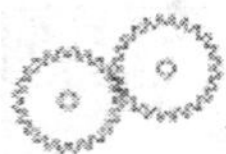
Review of the Exploded View.

You created an Exploded View in the GUIDE-ROD assembly. The Exploded View displayed the assembly with its components separated from one another.

The Exploded View animation illustrated how to assemble and disassemble the GUIDE-ROD assembly through the collapse and explode states.

Section View

Section Views display the internal cross section of a component or assembly. The Section View dissects a model like a knife slicing through a stick of butter. Section Views can be performed anywhere in a model. The location of the cut corresponds to the Section plane. A Section plane is a planar face or reference plane.

Use a Section View to determine the interference between the 10mm Guide Hole and the Linear Pattern of 3mm Holes in the GUIDE.

Activity: Section View

Open the GUIDE part.

323) Right-click **GUIDE** in the Graphics window.

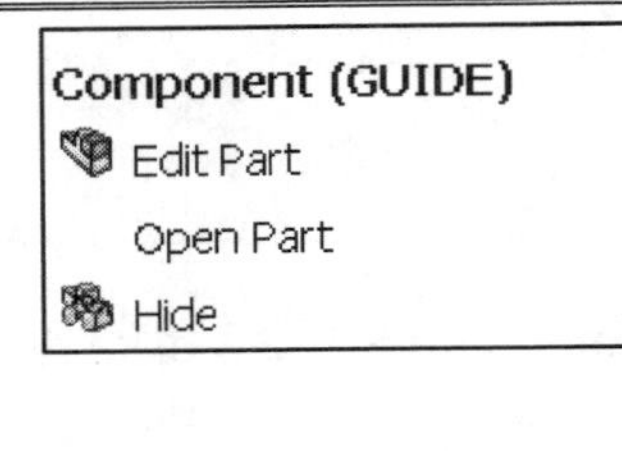

324) Click **Open Part**.

Insert the Section View on the Front Plane of the GUIDE.

325) Click **Front Plane** from the FeatureManager.

326) Click **Section View** from the View toolbar.

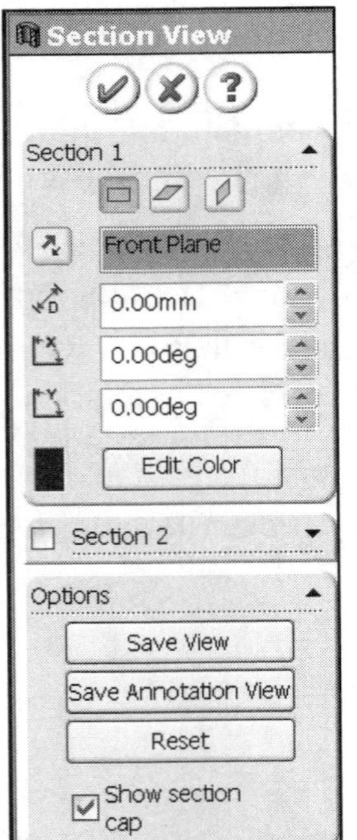

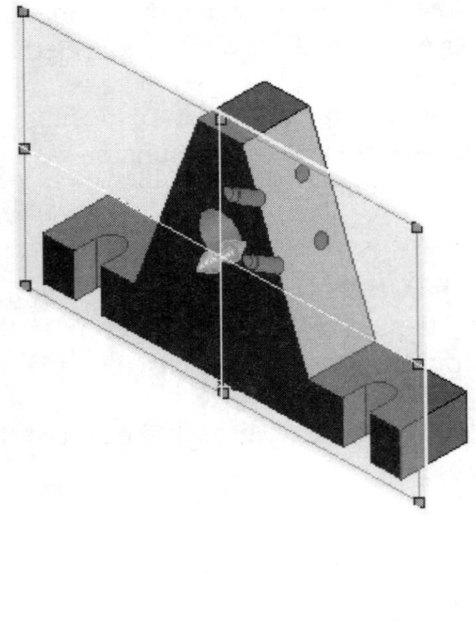

Save the Section View.

327) Click **Save View** [Save View]. SectionView1 is the default view name.

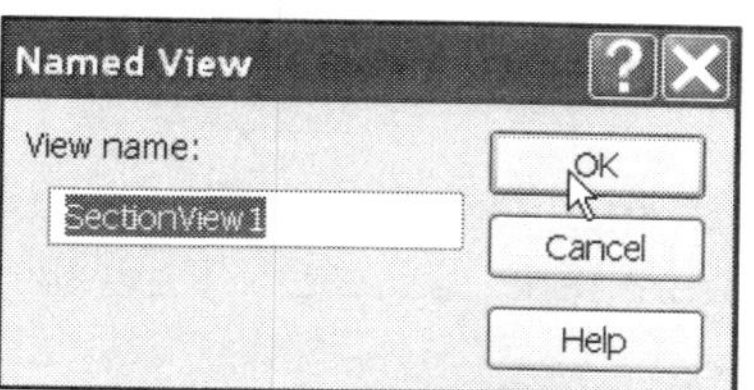

328) Click **OK**. SectionView1 is displayed in the View Orientation box.

Pin the View Orientation dialog box.

329) Click **Pin**.

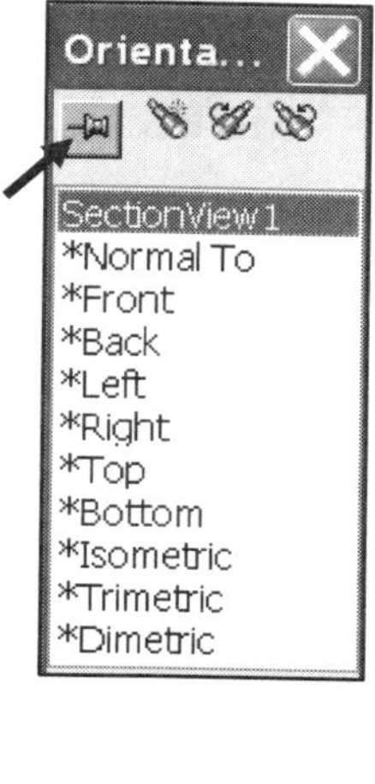

Close the Section View FeatureManager.

330) Click **OK** from the Section View FeatureManager.

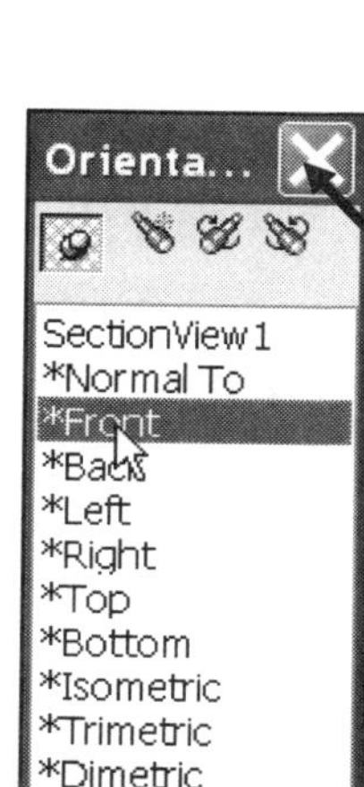

Display the Front view.

331) Click ***Front** from the Orientation box.

332) Click **Close** in the Orientation view box.

Display the Full view.

333) Click **Section view**.

334) Click **Front view**.

335) Click **Hidden Lines Visible**.

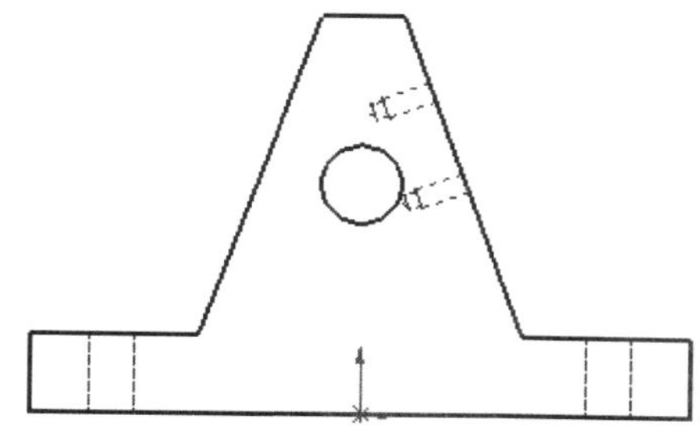

Save the GUIDE part.

336) Click **Save**.

The Section View detects potential problems before manufacturing. The Section View determines the interference between the 10mm Guide Hole and the Linear Pattern of 3mm Holes in the GUIDE.

The GUIDE, ROD and PLATE components all share a common file structure with the GUIDE-ROD assembly. What component do you modify? How will changes affect other components? Let's analyze the interference problem and determine a solution.

Analyze an Interference Problem

An interference problem exists between the 10mm Guide Hole and the 3mm tapped Holes. Review your design options:

- Reposition the Guide Hole.
- Modify the size of the Guide Hole.
- Adjust the length of the 3mm Holes.
- Reposition the Linear Pattern.

The first three options affect other components in the assembly. The GUIDE-CYLINDER assembly and PLATE determine the Guide Hole location.

The ROD diameter determines the size of the Guide Hole. The position sensor requires the current depth of the 3mm Holes. Reposition the Linear Pattern by modifying the first 3mm Thru Hole.

Activity: Analyze an Interference Problem

Modify the Thru Hole Dimensions.

337) Expand the **M3x0.5 Tapped Hole1** in the FeatureManager.

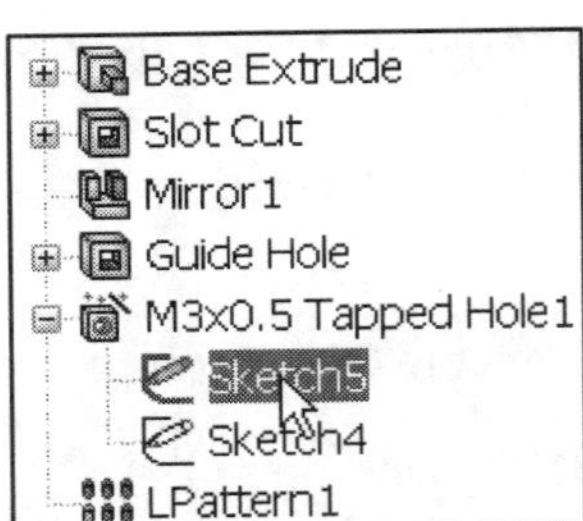

338) Click **Isometric view**.

339) Click **Shaded With Edges**.

340) Double-click **Sketch5** to display the position dimensions.

341) Double-click the **4** dimension created from the Temporary axis of the Guide Hole.

342) Enter **6**.

343) Click **Rebuild** from the Modify box.

344) Click the **Green Check mark**.

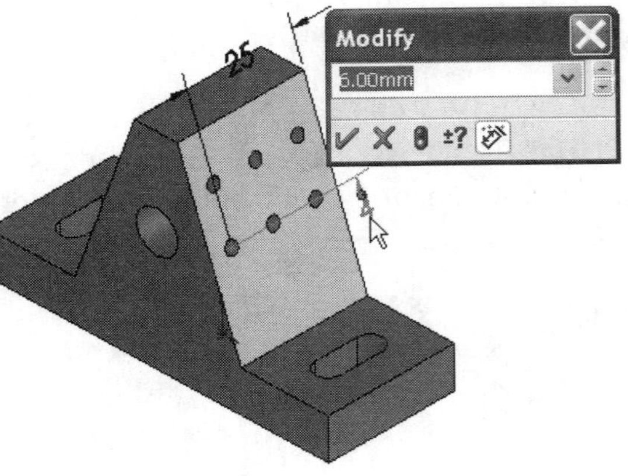

Close the GUIDE part.

345) Click **File**, **Close** from the Main menu.

346) Click **Yes** to Save changes to the GUIDE.

347) Click **Yes** to Rebuild.

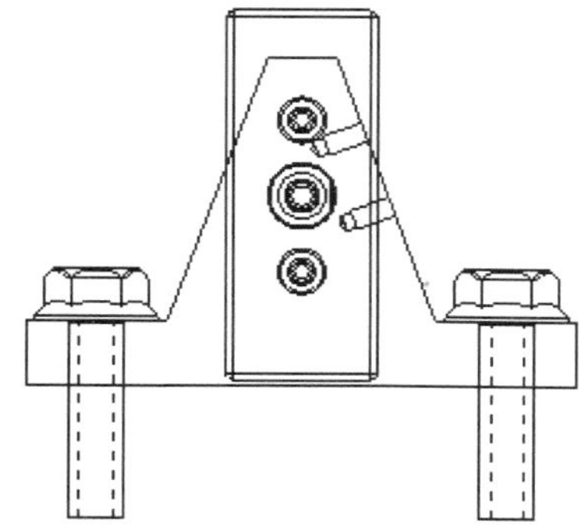

Display the Front view.

348) Click **Wireframe**.

349) Click **Front view**. The GUIDE-ROD assembly updates to display the changes to the GUIDE part.

Return to an Isometric view.

350) Click **Isometric view**.

351) Click **Shaded With Edges**.

Save the GUIDE-ROD assembly.

352) Click **Save**.

Analyze issues at the part level first. Working at the part level reduces rebuild time and complexity. Return to the assembly and review the modifications.

Additional details on Explode, Collapse and Section View are available in Help, SolidWorks Help Topics. Keywords: Exploded View (Collapse, Assemblies) and Section View.

The last component to insert to the GUIDE-CYLINDER is the 3MMCAPSCREW. Utilize the Save As Copy option to copy the 4MMCAPSCREW to the 3MMCAPSCREW.

Save As Copy Option

Conserve design time and cost. Modify existing parts and assemblies to create new parts and assemblies. Utilize the Save as copy option to avoid updating the existing assemblies with new file names.

The 4MMCAPSCREW was created earlier. The GUIDE requires 3MMCAPSCREWs to fasten the sensor to the 3MM Tapped Hole Linear Pattern.

Start with the 4MMCAPSCREW. Utilize the Save As Copy option. Enter the 3MMCAPSCREW for the new file name.

The Save As Copy option prevents the 3MMCAPSCREWS from replacing the 4MMCAPSCREWS in the GUIDE-CYLINDER assembly.

Important: Check the Save as copy check box. The Save as copy box check box creates a copy of the current part with no references to existing assemblies that utilize the part. The 3MMCAPSCREW is the new part name. Modify the dimensions of the Revolve Base feature to create the 3MMCAPSCREW.

Activity: Save as Copy Option

Open the 4MMCAPSCREW part.

353) Right-click the **4MMCAPSCREW front face** in the GUIDE-ROD assembly Graphics window.

354) Click **Open Part**.

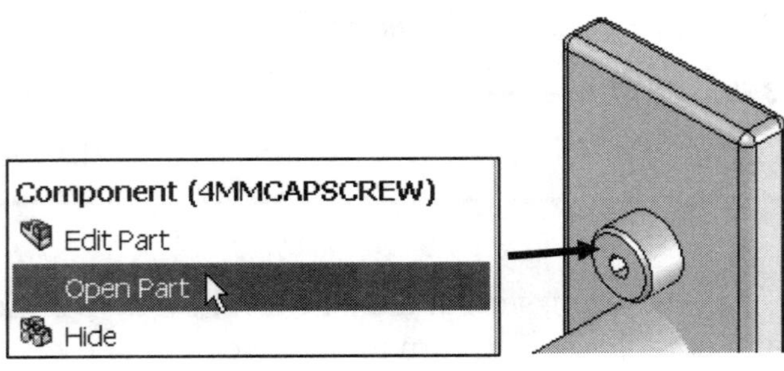

Use the Save As Copy option.

355) Select **File, Save As** from the Main menu.

356) Click **OK** to the warning message that the 4MMCAPSCREW is referenced by open documents.

357) Select **ENGDESIGN-W-SOLIDWORKS\ PROJECTS** for the Save in file folder.

358) Check **Save as copy**.

359) Enter **3MMCAPSCREW** for file name.

360) Enter **CAP SCREW**, **3MM** for Description.

361) Click **Save**. The 4MMCAPSCREW part remains open.

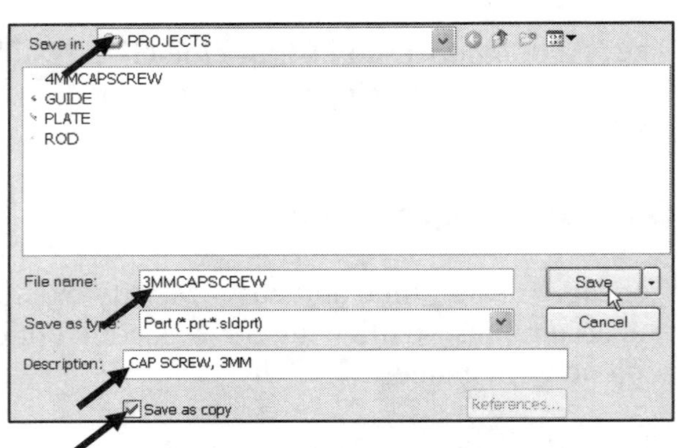

Close the 4MMCAPSCREW part.

362) Click **File**, **Close** from the Main menu.

Open the 3MMCAPSCREW part.

363) Click **File**, **Open** from the Main menu.

364) Click **Part** for Files of Type.

365) Double-click **3MMCAPSCREW** part.

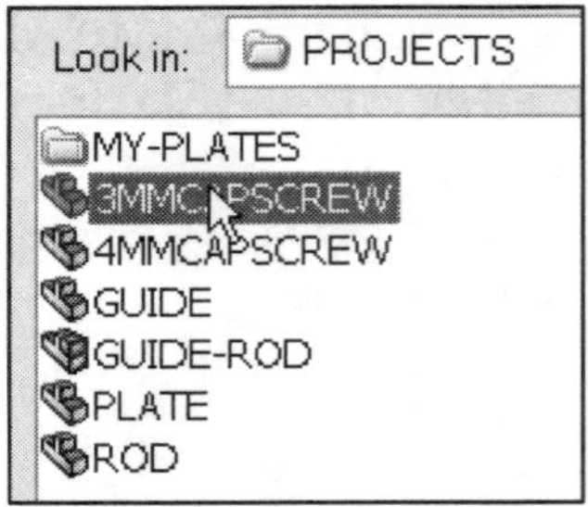

366) Double-click **Revolve1** in the FeatureManager.

Fit the Model to the Graphics window.

367) Press the **f** key.

Modify the Revolve dimensions.

368) Double click the vertical dimension **4**.

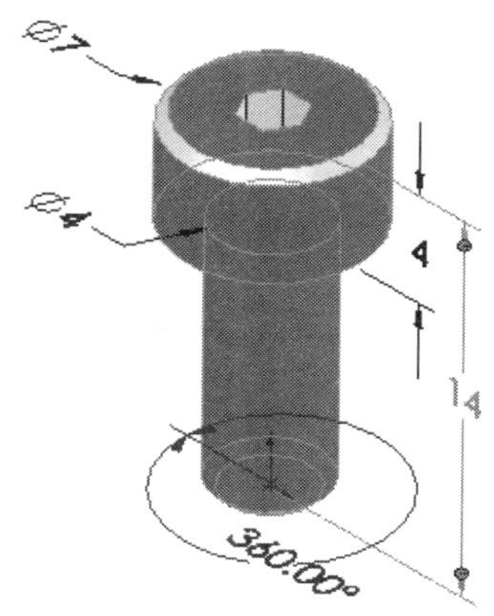

369) Enter **3**.

370) Double click the depth dimension **14**.

371) Enter **9**.

372) Double click the diameter dimension **4**.

373) Enter **3**.

374) Double click the diameter dimension **7**.

375) Enter **5.5**.

Update the feature dimensions.

376) Click **Rebuild** from the Main menu.

Save the 3MMCAPSCREW part.

377) Click **SAVE** .

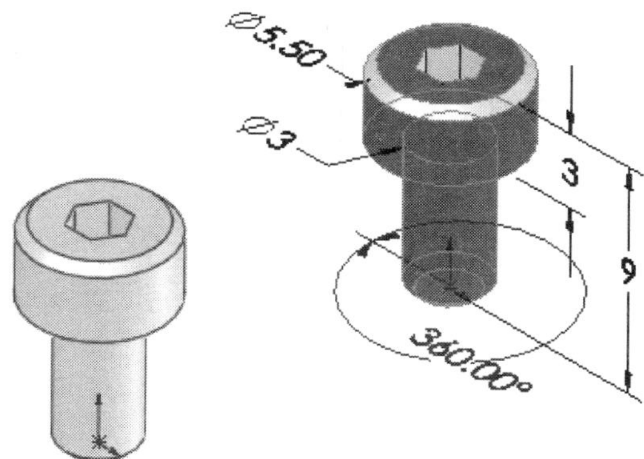

With the Save as Copy option the current document remains open. Close the open document. Select the copied document to open and modify.

The GUIDE Linear Pattern of 3MM Tapped Holes requires six 3MMCAPSCREWs. Do you remember the seed feature in the Linear Pattern?

The first 3MM Tapped Hole is the seed feature. The seed feature is required for a Component Pattern in the GUIDE-ROD assembly.

GUIDE-ROD Assembly-Component Pattern

There are three main methods to define a pattern in an assembly:

- Feature Pattern.
- Circular Pattern.
- Linear Pattern.

A derived Feature Pattern of components utilizes an existing pattern in the assembly.

A local Circular Pattern and Linear Pattern of components utilize geometry in the assembly. Utilized a Feature Pattern to create instances of the 3MMCAPSCREW. Insert the 3MMCAPSCREW part into the GUIDE-ROD assembly. Insert a Component Pattern of 3MMCAPSCREWS derived from the GUIDE Linear Pattern of Tapped Holes.

Activity: GUIDE-ROD Assembly-Component Pattern

Insert and Mate the 3MMCAPSCREW.

378) Click **Window**, **Tile Horizontally** from the Main menu.

Note: The 3MMCAPSCREW and the GUIDE-ROD assembly are the open documents. Close any other documents. Select the Close icon. Click Window, Tile Horizontally again to display the two open documents.

379) **Zoom in** on the bottom left circular edge of the GUIDE left Tapped Hole.

380) Click and drag the **bottom circular edge** of the 3MMCAPSCREW into the GUIDE-ROD assembly.

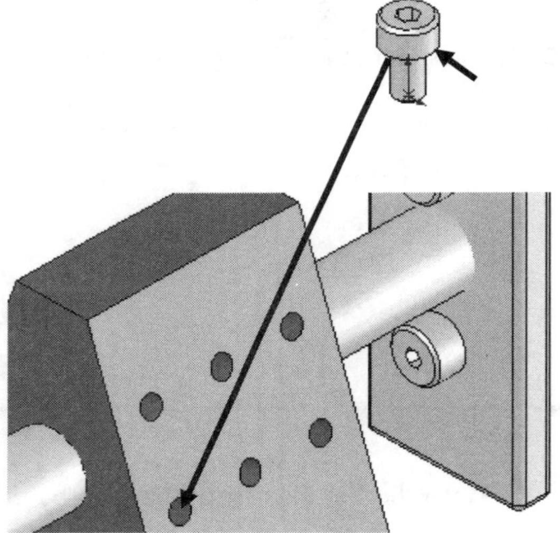

381) Release the mouse button on the **bottom left circular edge** of the GUIDE left Tapped Hole. The mouse pointer displays the Coincident/Concentric Circular edges feedback symbol. The 3MMCAPSCREW part is position in the bottom left Tapped Hole.

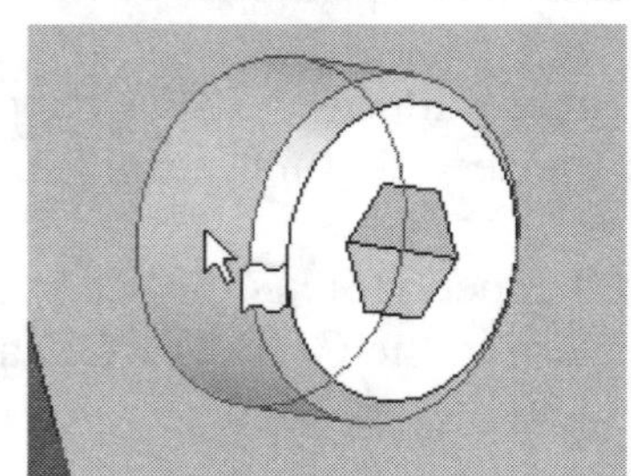

Insert a Feature Derived Component Pattern.

382) Maximize the GUIDE-ROD assembly.

Fit the GUIDE-ROD assembly to the Graphics window.

383) Press the **f** key.

384) Click **Insert**, **Component Pattern**, **Feature Driven** from the Main menu.

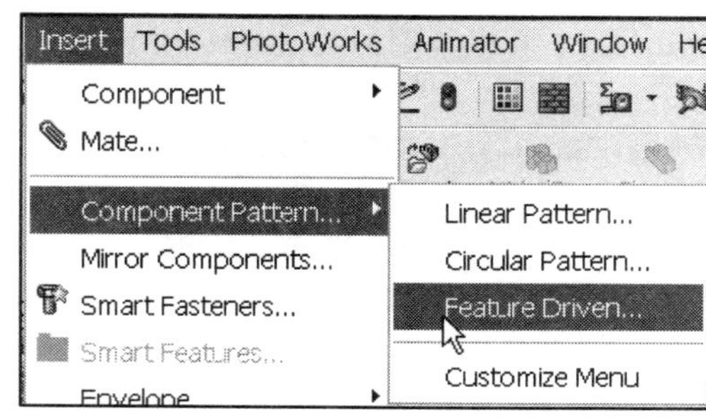

385) Click the **3MMCAPSCREW** that you inserted into the GUIDE from the Graphics window as the component to Pattern.

386) Click the **Driving Feature** text box.

387) Expand **GUIDE** in the GUIDE-ROD FeatureManager.

388) Click **LPattern1** under GUIDE<1> from the FeatureManager.

389) Click **OK** from the Feature Driven PropertyManager.

390) Click **Isometric view**.

Save the GUIDE-ROD assembly.

391) Click **Save**.

392) Click **Yes**.

Close all models.

393) Click **Window**, **Close All** from the Main menu.

Reuse geometry. Utilize patterns early in the design process. A Linear Pattern in the part is utilized as a Derived Feature Component Pattern in the assembly.

Review the Component Pattern for the 3MMCAPSCREWs.

You utilized the Save As Copy option to copy the 4MMCAPSCREW to the 3MMCAPSCREW. The 3MMCAPSCREW was mated to the GUIDE 3MM Tapped Hole. You utilized a Component Pattern to create an array of 3MMCAPSCREWs. The Component Pattern is derived from the GUIDE Linear Pattern of Tapped Holes.

Redefining Mates and Linear Component Pattern

In the modeling process, you modify and edit sketches and features. You are also required to redefine Mates. The two flange bolts are not centered with the GUIDE Slot Cut. Redefine the Mates to reposition the flange bolt at the center of the Slot Cut.

How do you redefine the existing Mates? Answer: First, review the Mates for an individual component with the View Mates option. Second, determine the Mates to redefine and the Mates to delete. Third, utilize Edit Feature to redefine a Mate.

No cylindrical face exists at the center of the Slot Cut. Delete the Concentric Mate and insert a new Coincident Mate between the Temporary Axis of the flange bolt and a sketched Point in the GUIDE Slot Cut.

The original Coincident Mate referenced an edge on the GUIDE. When you delete the Concentric Mate, this Coincident Mate acts like a hinge. Redefine the Coincident Mate between the bottom face of the flange bolt and the top face of the GUIDE.

Delete the second flange bolt. Utilize a Linear Component Pattern to create an instance of the flange bolt. A Linear Component Pattern developed in an assembly is called a Local Pattern. Note: If you delete a Mate and then recreate the Mate, your instance number will be different in the next activity. The View Mates option displays the Mate Type and instance number of the Mates utilized between the flange bolt and the GUIDE.

Activity: Redefining Mates and Linear Component Pattern

View the Mates.

394) **Open** the GUIDE-ROD assembly.

395) Expand **flange bolt<1>** in the GUIDE-ROD FeatureManager.

396) Expand **Mates in GUIDE-ROD**.

397) Click the **three Mates** to review their Mate references.

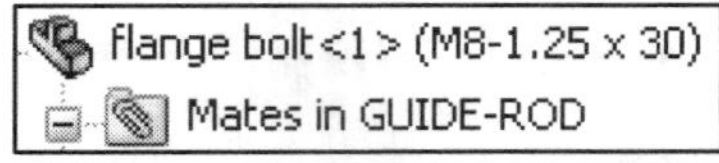

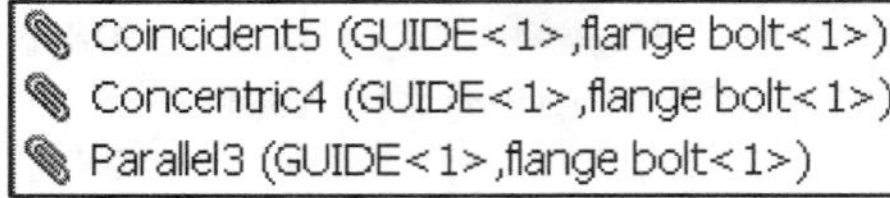

Delete the Concentric Mate.

398) Right-click the Concentric mate, **Concentric4** (GUIDE<1>, flange bolt<1>) in the FeatureManager.

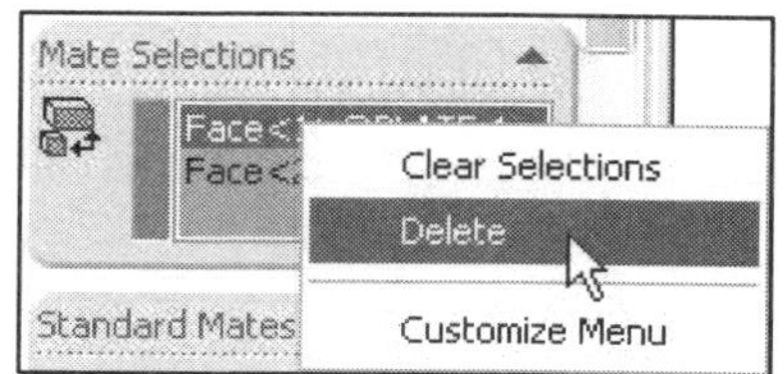

399) Click **Delete**. Click **Yes** to the question: Do you really want to delete this? The flange bolt is free to translate along the right top face of the GUIDE.

400) Click **OK** from the Mate PropertyManager.

Open the GUIDE part.

401) Right-click **GUIDE** in the FeatureManager.

402) Click **Open Part**.

Edit the Slot Cut. Insert a Sketch Point.

403) Right-click **Slot Cut** in the FeatureManager. Click **Edit Sketch**.

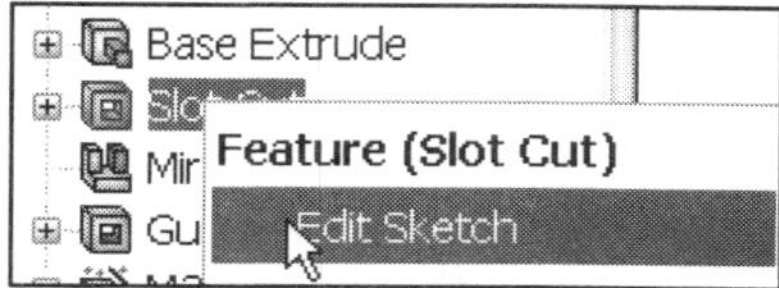

404) Click **Top view**. Click **Hidden Lines Visible**.

405) Click **Centerline** Centerl... from the Sketch tool bar. Sketch a **Centerline** between the two arc center points.

406) Click **Point** Point from the Sketch toolbar.

407) Click the **Midpoint** of the sketch centerline.

408) Click **OK** from the Point PropertyManager.

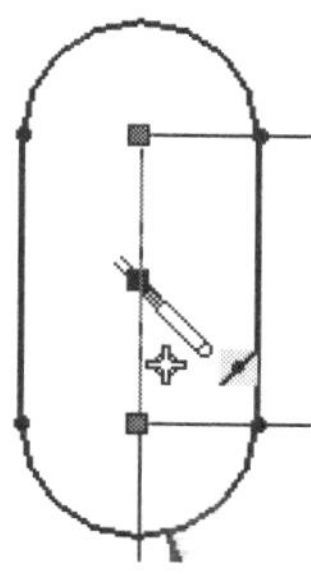

409) Click **Save**. Click **Yes** to rebuild.

Show the Sketch.

410) **Expand** Slot Cut in the FeatureManager. Right-click **Sketch2**. Click **Show**. Note: The Show command shows the Sketch in the GUIDE part, in order to select the Point in the GUIDE-ROD assembly.

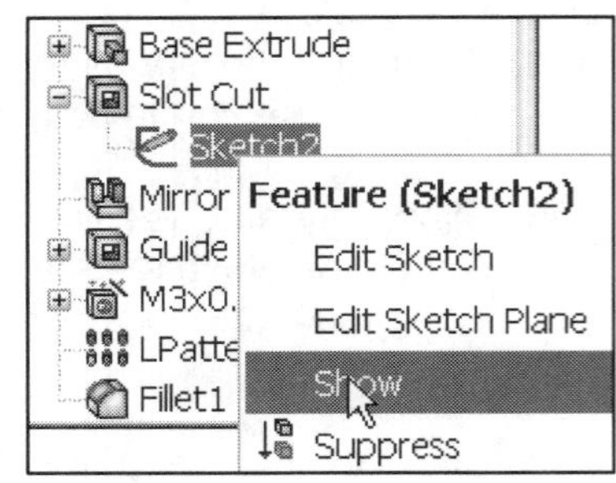

Save the GUIDE part.

411) Click **Isometric view** .

412) Click **Shaded with Edges** .

413) Click **Save** .

Open the GUIDE-ROD assembly.

414) Open the **GUIDE-ROD assembly**.

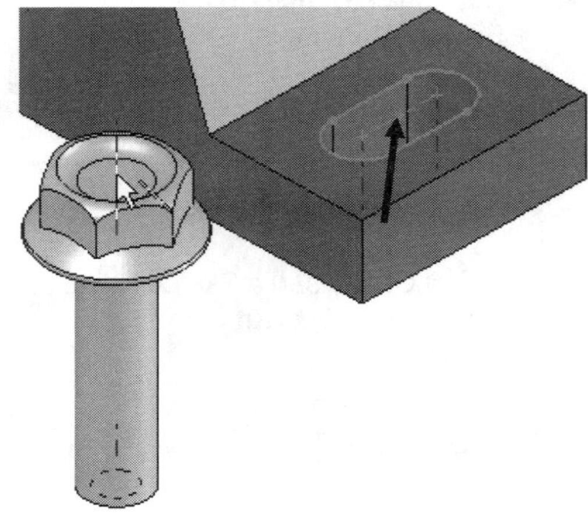

415) Click and drag the **first flange bolt** in front of the right Slot Cut.

Display the Temporary Axes and Sketches.

416) Click **View**, check **Temporary Axes** from the Main menu. Click **View**, check **Sketches** from the Main menu.

Insert a Coincident Mate.

417) Click **Mate** Mate . **Clear** all Mate Selections. Click the **flange bolt Axis**.

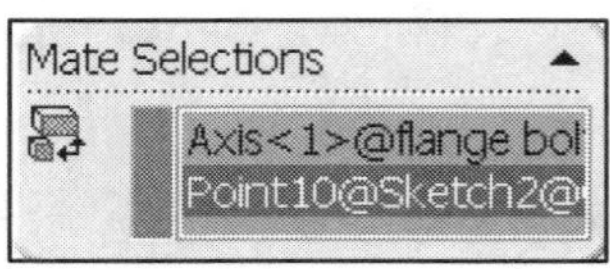

418) Click the **Point** in the Midpoint of the Slot Cut Sketch.

419) Click **Coincident**. Click the **Green Check mark** .

420) Click **OK** from the Mate PropertyManager.

Hide the reference geometry.

421) Click **View**, uncheck **Temporary Axes**. Click **View**, uncheck **Sketches** from the Main menu.

Hide the Slot Cut sketch.

422) Press **Ctrl Tab** to display the GUIDE. **Expand** Slot Cut.

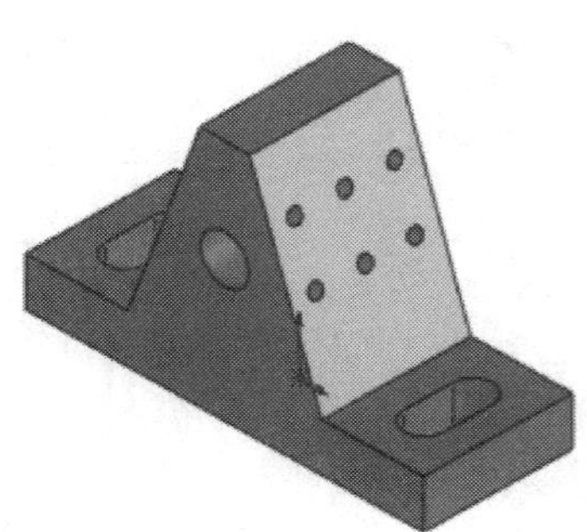

423) Right-click **Sketch2** in the FeatureManager.

424) Click **Hide**.

Close the GUIDE part.

425) Click **File**, **Close** from the Main menu. Click **Yes** to Save changes to GUIDE.

Delete the second flange bolt.

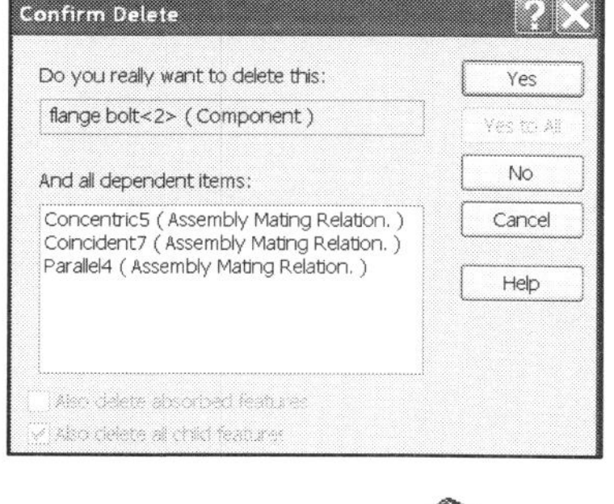

426) Right-click **flange bolt <2>** flange bolt<2> (M8-1.25 x 30) in the FeatureManager.

427) Click **Delete**. Click **Yes**.

Insert a Linear Component Local Pattern.

428) Click the **right flange bolt** in the GUIDE.

429) Click **Insert**, **Component Pattern**, **Linear Pattern** from the Main menu.

430) Click the **front horizontal edge** for Direction 1. The Direction arrow points to the left.

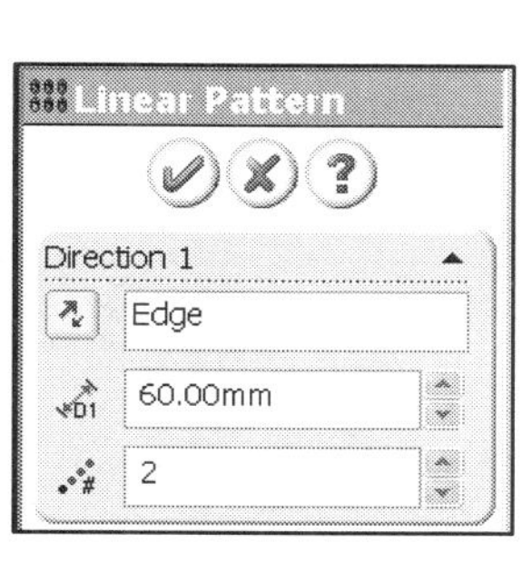

431) Enter **60** for Spacing. Enter **2** for Number of Instances

432) Click **OK** from the Linear Pattern PropertyManager.

The LocalPattern1 entry is displayed at the bottom of the GUIDE-ROD assembly FeatureManager.

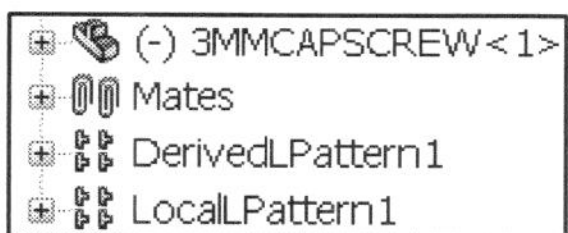

Save the GUIDE-ROD assembly.

433) Click **Isometric view** .

434) Click **Save** .

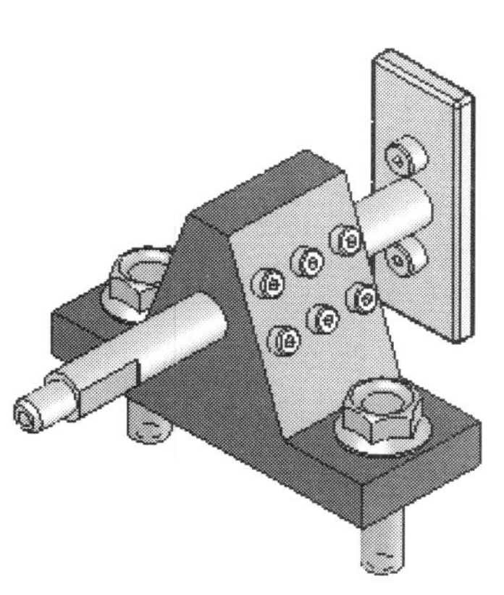

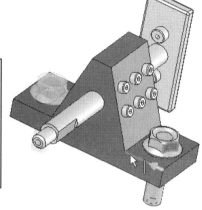

Before you redefine or edit a Mate, save the assembly. One Mate modification can lead to issues in multiple components that are directly related. Understand the Mate Selections syntax. The Mate PropertyManager lists the Mate Type, geometry selected and component reference (part/assembly and instance number).

The 3MM Tapped Holes utilizes a Derived Pattern. The flange bolts utilized a Local Pattern. Utilize Derived Pattern when a part contains a pattern to reference. Utilize Local Pattern when a part contains no pattern reference.

Folders and Suppressed Components

The FeatureManager entries increase as components are inserted into the Graphics window of an assembly. Folders reduce the length of the FeatureManager in the part and assembly. Folders also organize groups of similar components. Organize hardware in the assembly into Folders.

Suppress features, parts and assemblies that are not displayed. During model rebuilding, suppressed features and components are not calculated. This saves rebuilding time for complex models. The names of the suppressed features and components are displayed in light gray.

Create a Folder in the FeatureManager named Hardware. Drag all individual bolts and screws into the Hardware Folder. A Derived LPattern cannot be dragged into a Folder. Suppress the Hardware Folder. Suppress the Derived LPattern.

Activity: Folders and Suppressed Components

Create a Folder.

435) Right-click **flange bolt<1>** flange bolt<1> (M8-1.25 x 30) in the GUIDE-ROD FeatureManager.

436) Click **Create New Folder**. Folder1 appears in the FeatureManager

437) Enter **Hardware** for Folder Name.

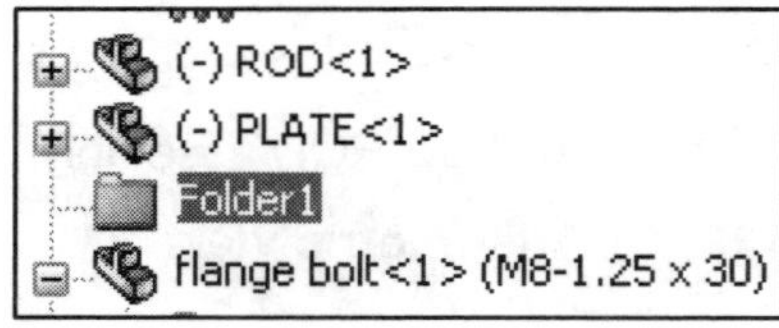

438) Click and drag **flange bolt<1>** in the FeatureManager into the Hardware Folder. The mouse pointer displays the Move Component in FeatureTree icon.

439) Repeat for the **4MMCAPSCREW<1>**, **4MMCAPSCREW<2>**, and **3MMCAPSCREW<1>**. All screws and bolts are located in the Hardware Folder.

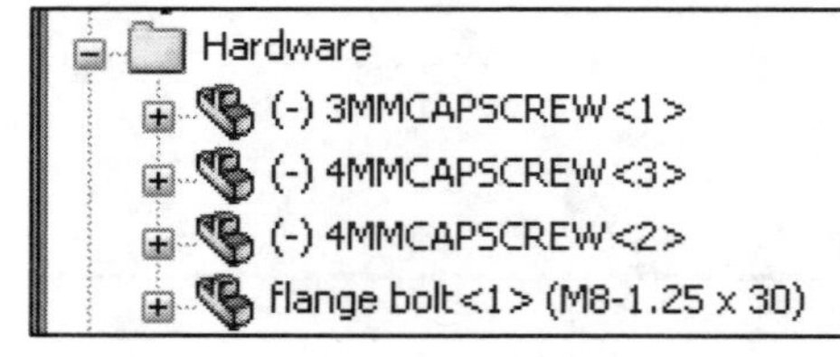

Suppress the Folder and Patterns.

440) Right-click on the **Hardware** Folder.

441) Click **Suppress.**

442) Right-click on **Derived LPattern1**.

443) Click **Suppress.**

444) Right-click on **LocalPattern1**.

445) Click **Suppress**.

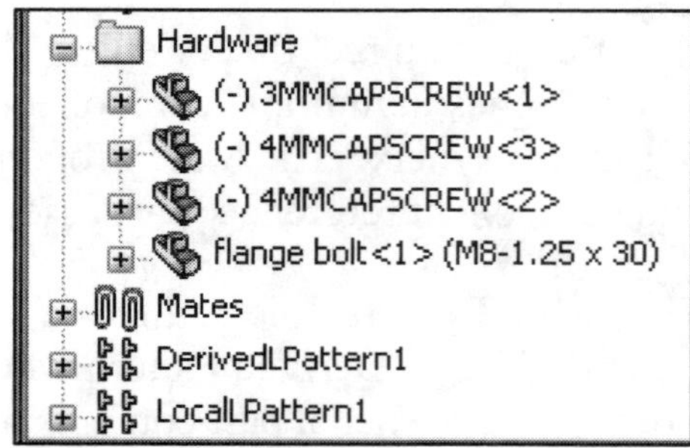

Display the GUIDE-ROD assembly.

446) Click **Isometric view** .

Save the GUIDE-ROD assembly.

447) Click **Save** .

Close all parts and assemblies.

448) Click **Window**, **Close All** from the Main menu.

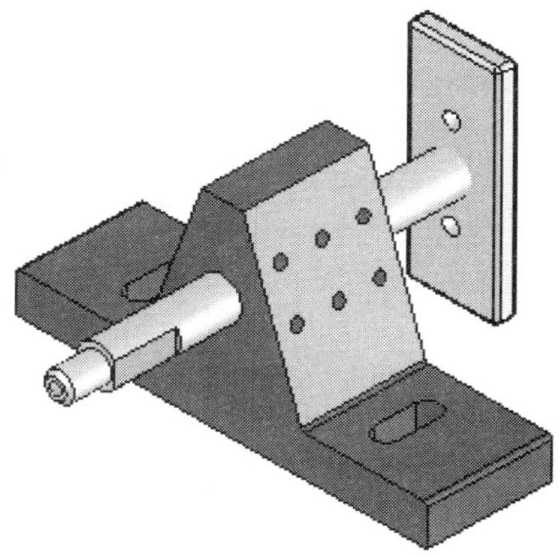

Standardize on Folder names such as Hardware or Fillets so colleagues recognize folder names. Place a set of continuous features or components into an individual folder.

Additional details on Save As, Component Pattern, View Mates and Folders are available in Help, SolidWorks Help Topics. Keywords: Save (Save as copy), Pattern (components in an assembly) and Folders.

Make-Buy Decision-3D ContentCentral

In a make-buy decision process, a decision is made on which parts to manufacture and which parts to purchase.

In assembly modeling, a decision is made on which parts to design and which parts to obtain from libraries and the World Wide Web. SolidWorks contains a variety of designed parts in the Design Library.

The SolidWorks Toolbox is a library of feature based design automation tools for SolidWorks. The Toolbox uses the window's drag and drop functionality with SmartMates. Fasteners are displayed with full thread detail.

The Toolbox library contains the following categories:

Toolbox Categories:				
Bearings. Bolts. Cams. Gears.	Jig Bushings Nuts. PEM® Inserts Pins.	Retaining rings. Screws. Sprockets. Structural shapes, including aluminum and steel.	Timing belt. Pulleys. Unistrut® Washers.	Beam Calculator for stress. Beam Calculator for bearing life. Structural steel cross sections. Groves to add standard groves to cylindrical parts.

SolidWorks SmartFastener uses the Hole Wizard to automatically SmartMate the corresponding Toolbox fasteners in an assembly. The fastener is sized and inserted into the assembly based on the Dimensioning Standard of the Hole.

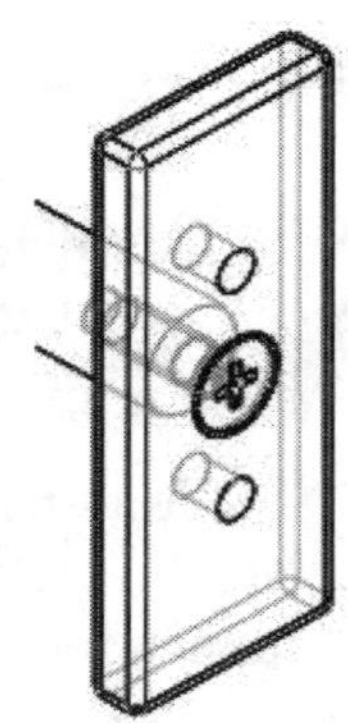

Additional details on Toolbox are available in Help, Toolbox.

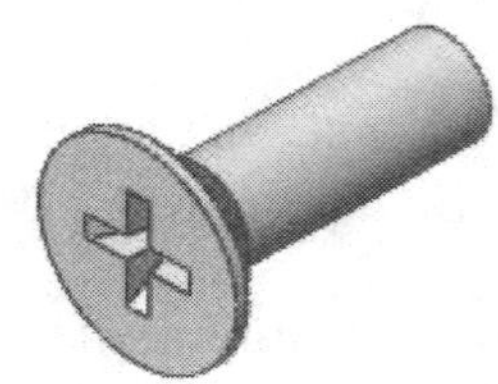

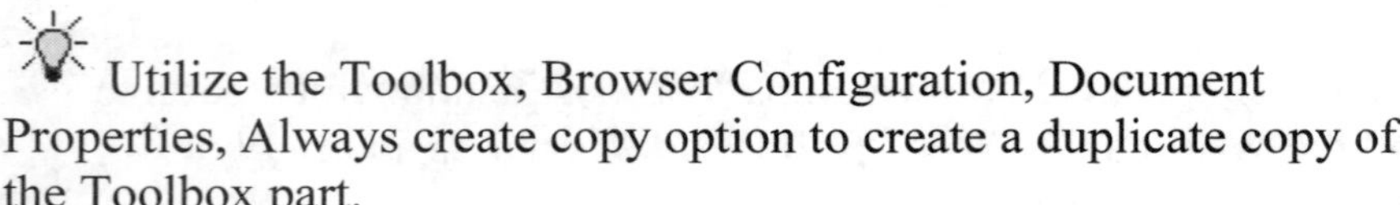

Utilize the Toolbox, Browser Configuration, Document Properties, Always create copy option to create a duplicate copy of the Toolbox part.

SolidWorks provides an Internet service, 3DContentCentral (www.3DContentCentral.com).

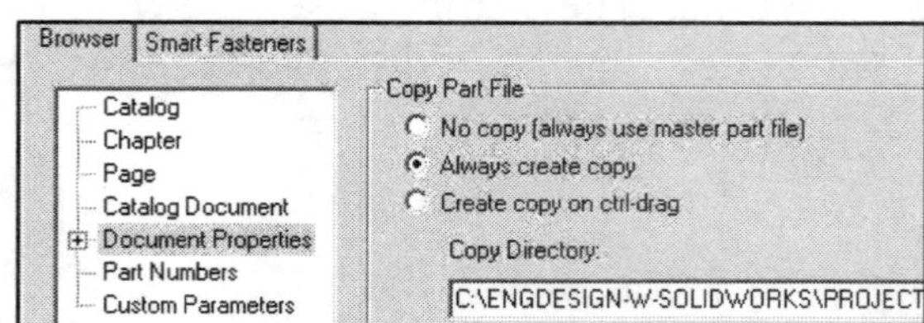

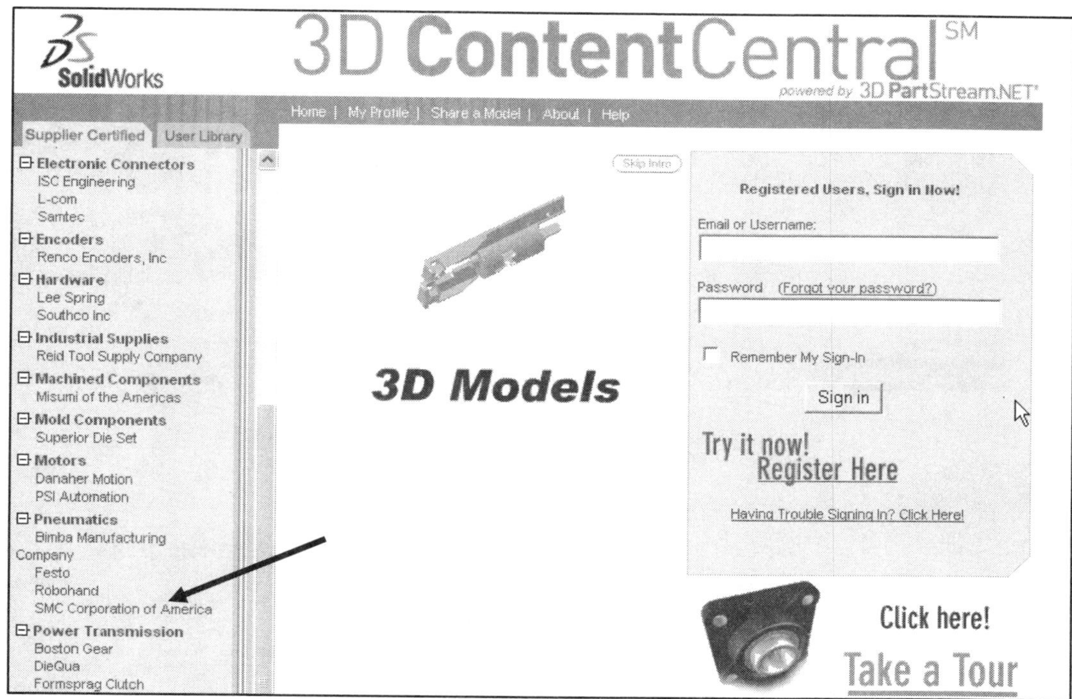

Vendors utilize this service to share model information with their customers. SolidWorks users share information through 3DContentCentral. Obtain models from SMC USA of America. Answer a series of questions on: working pressure, load conditions, travel, etc.

Note: If you do not have access to the Internet, the GUIDE-CYLINDER (MGPM12-10) assembly is available on the enclosed Multimedia CD.

An exercise on how to obtain an SMC component via 3DContentCentral is provided.

- Access to the World Wide Web is required for the following steps.
- Size and download a component for the CUSTOMER assembly.

Activity: Make or Buy Decision-3D ContentCentral

Obtain the GUIDE CYLINDER assembly from SMC USA.

449) **Invoke** a web browser.

450) Enter the following URL: **www.3DContentCentral.com**.

SMC Corporation of America and other suppliers are available via 3D Content Central. To access suppliers, the shared model user library, and share your own models, please register by clicking below. If you have already registered, please sign-in.

Try it now!
Register Here

451) Enter your **email address** and **password**. Note: If you are a new user, click the **Register button** and enter the **requested** information.

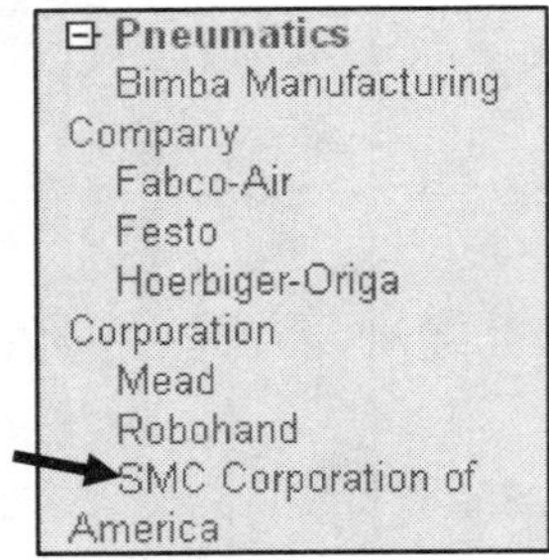

452) Click **SMC Corporation of America** under the Pneumatics category.

453) Select the **Product Selector** product selector button.

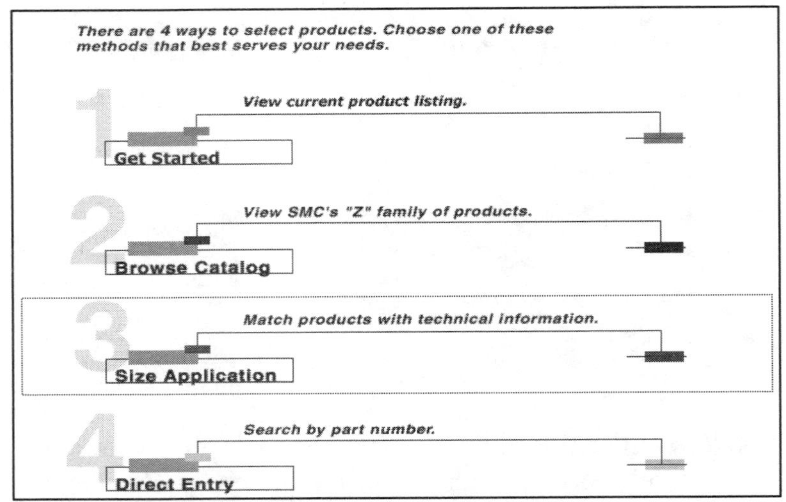

454) Click the **Size Application** button.

455) Click **Guided Actuators**.

456) **Read** the Sizing Disclaimer. **Accept** the Sizing Disclaimer.

Enter the design parameters.
457) Enter **10**mm for Stoke.

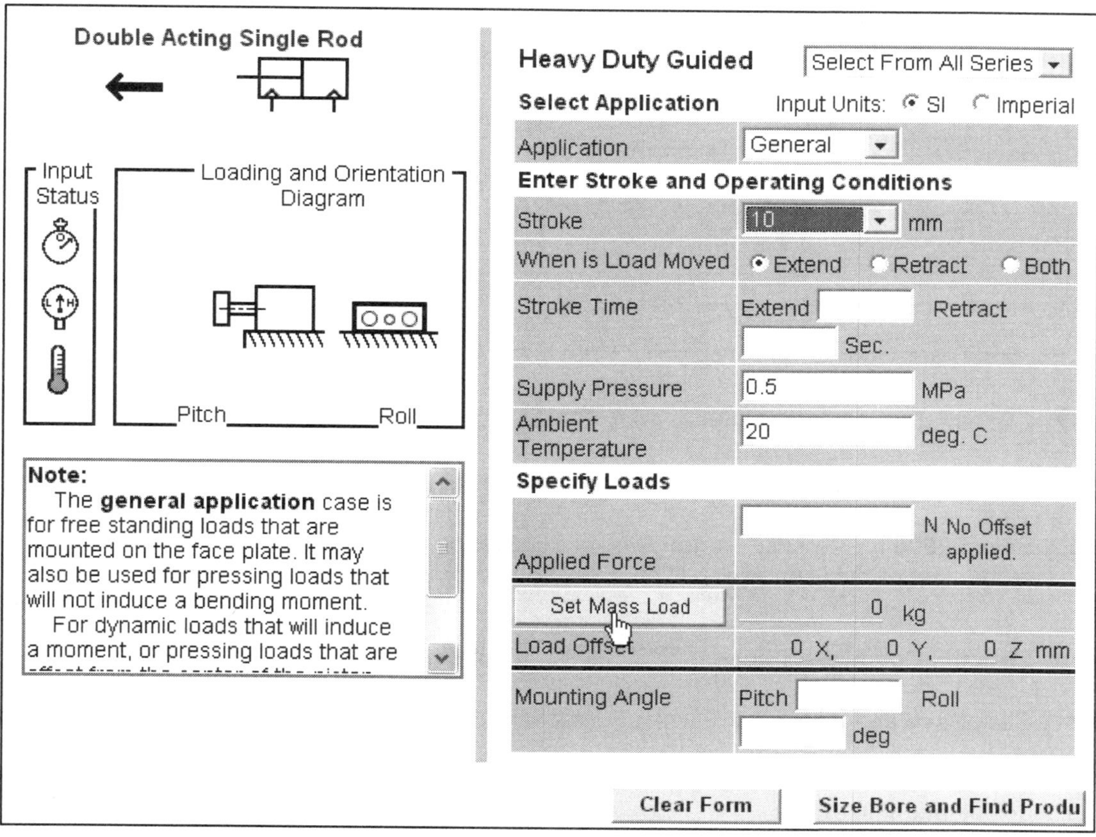

458) Enter **0.5** MPa for Supply Pressure.

459) Click the **Set Mass Load** Set Mass Load button.

460) Enter **0.3** for Weight (kg).

461) Enter **0** for X (mm).

462) Enter **0** for Y (mm).

463) Enter **0** for Z (mm).

464) Click **OK**.

465) Click the **Size Bore and Find Product** button.

466) Click the **MGPM, Compact Guide button**.

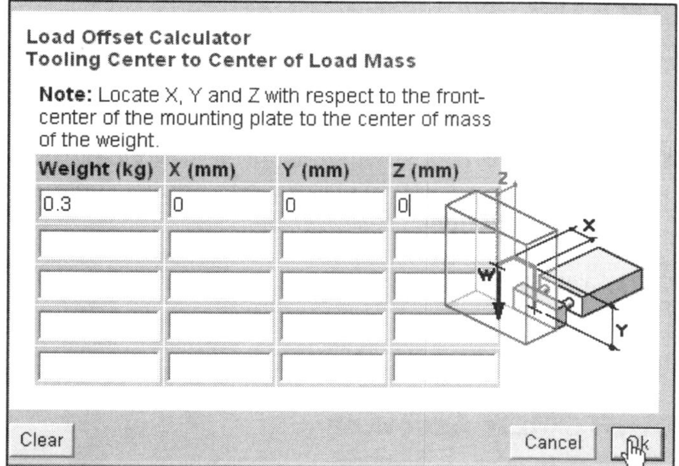

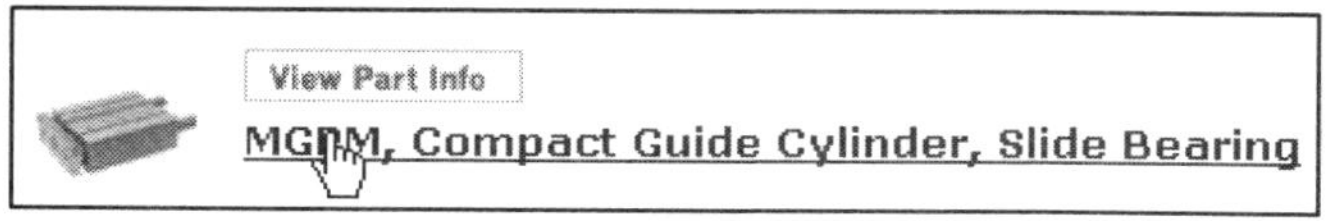

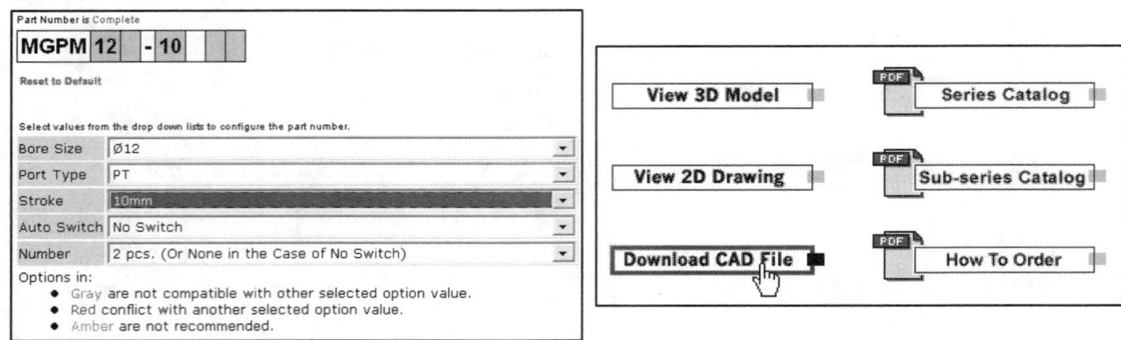

467) Click the **Download CAD File** [Download CAD File] button.

468) Select the 3D **SolidWorks Part/Assembly (.sldasm)**.

469) Select **2006** for Version. Note: Version 2003 is the default and at the time of publication and 2005 was the latest version.

470) Click the **Download Files** [Download Files] button.

471) Click **Save** and follow the download directions.

472) The zipped SolidWorks file is downloaded to your computer. Store the downloaded files.

473) Double-click the **MGPM12_10** [MGPM12-10] icon.

474) Click **Unzip.**

475) Select **ENGDESIGN-W-SOLIDWORKS\VENDOR COMPONENTS** file folder.

476) Click the **Unzip Now** button. Note: If your Zip/Unzip utility requires you to utilize the Extract option, select **Extract all files**.

477) Click **Close**.

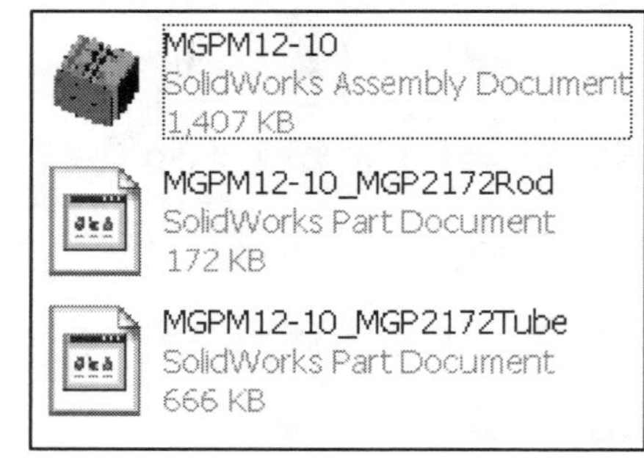

CUSTOMER Assembly

Three documents are contained in the unzipped folder:

- MGPM12-10.
- MGPM12-10_MGP2172Tube.
- MGPM12-10_MGP2172Rod.

The MGPM12-10_MGP2172Tube part and the MGPM12-10_MGP2172Rod part contain references to the MGPM12-10 assembly.

When parts reference an assembly, open the assembly first. Then open the individual parts from within the Assembly FeatureManager.

The CUSTOMER assembly combines the GUIDE-ROD assembly and the GUIDE-CYLINDER (MGPM12-10) assembly. The GUIDE-ROD assembly is fixed to the CUSTOMER assembly Origin.

Activity: CUSTOMER Assembly

Open the MGPM12-10 assembly.

478) Double-click the **MGPM12-10** assembly from the ENGDESIGN-W-SOLIDWORKS\VENDOR-COMPONENTS folder.

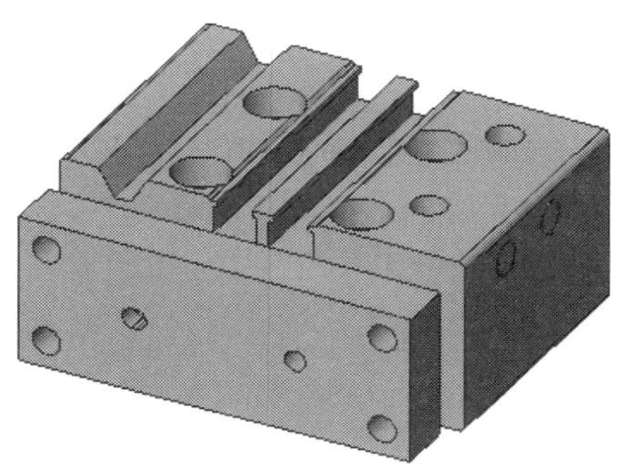

Fit the Model to the Graphics window.

479) Press the **f** key.

Open the GUIDE-ROD assembly.

480) Double-click the **GUIDE-ROD** assembly from the PROJECTS folder.

Create the CUSTOMER assembly.

481) Click **File**, **New** from the Main menu.

482) Double-click **Assembly** from the Templates tab.

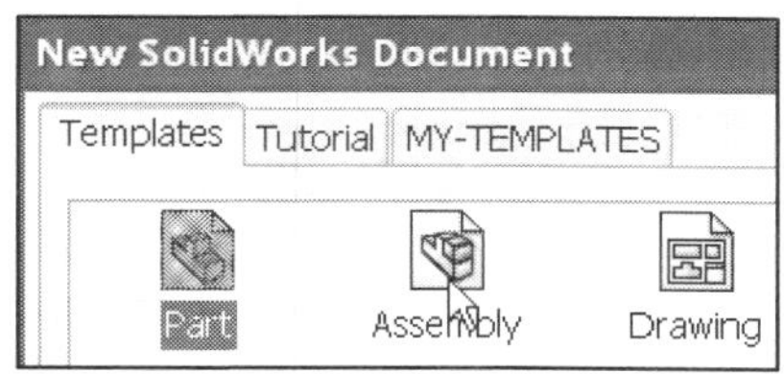

Display the Origin.

483) Click **View**, check **Origins** from the Main menu. The MGPM12-10 assembly and the GUIDE-ROD assembly are displayed in the Part/Assembly to Input box.

484) Click **GUIDE-ROD** from the Open documents list.

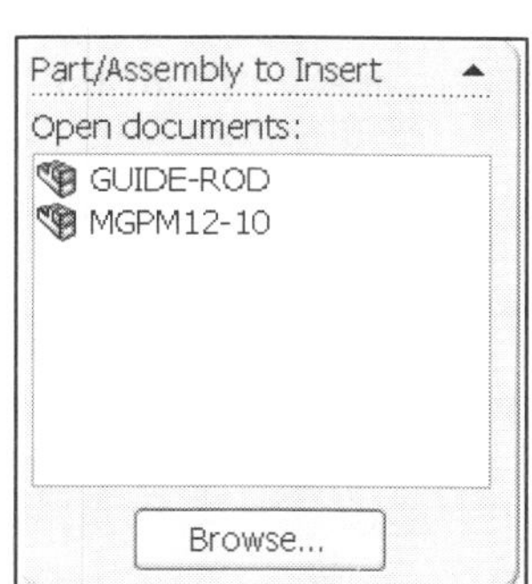

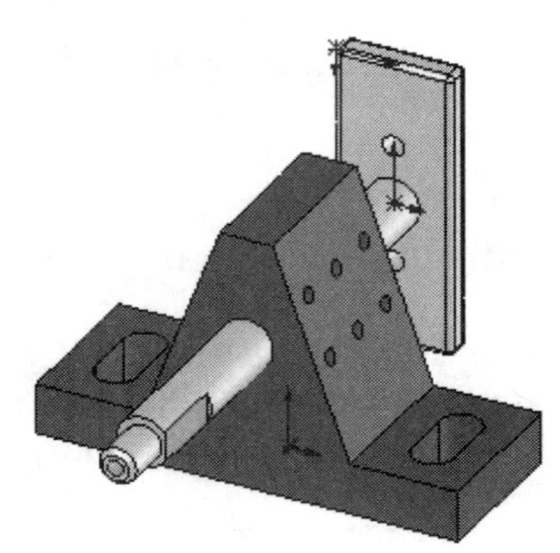

485) Click the Assem1 **Origin** .

Save the assembly.

486) Click **Save** .

487) Select **ENGDESIGN-W-SOLIDWORKS/PROJECTS** for Save in file folder.

488) Enter **CUSTOMER** for File name.

489) Enter **GUIDE-ROD AND GUIDE-CYLINDER ASSEMBLY** for Description.

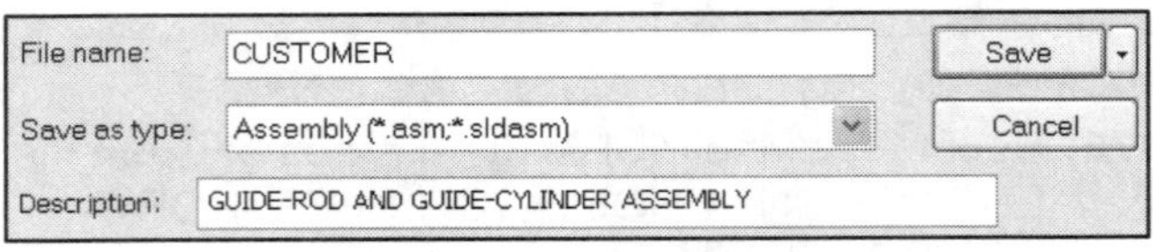

490) Click **Save**.

GUIDE-ROD is the first component in the CUSTOMER assembly. Inset the second component.

Insert the MGPM12-10 assembly.

491) Click **Assemblies** Assemb... from the Control Area.

492) Click **Insert Component** Insert Compo... from the Assembly toolbar.

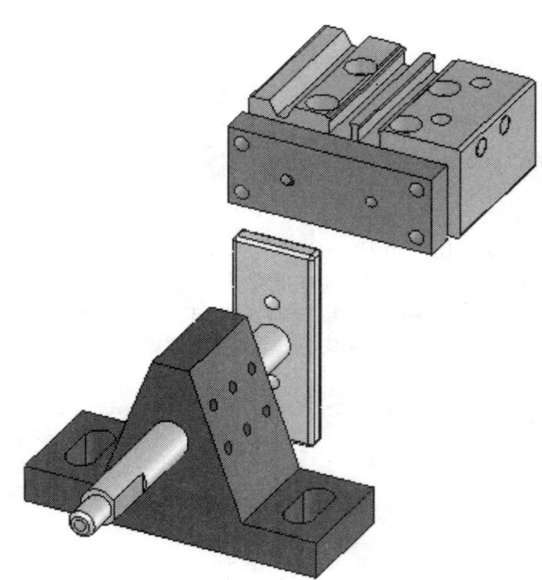

493) Click **MGPM12-10** from the Part/Assembly to Input box.

494) Click a **position** in the Graphics window behind the GUIDE-ROD assembly.

Fit the model to the Graphics window.

495) Press the **f** key.

Deactivate the Origins for clarity.

496) Click **View**, uncheck **Origins** from the Main menu.

Deactivate the Planes for clarity.

497) Click **View**, uncheck **Planes** from the Main menu.

Position the component.

498) Click the **MGPM12-10<1>** component in the FeatureManager.

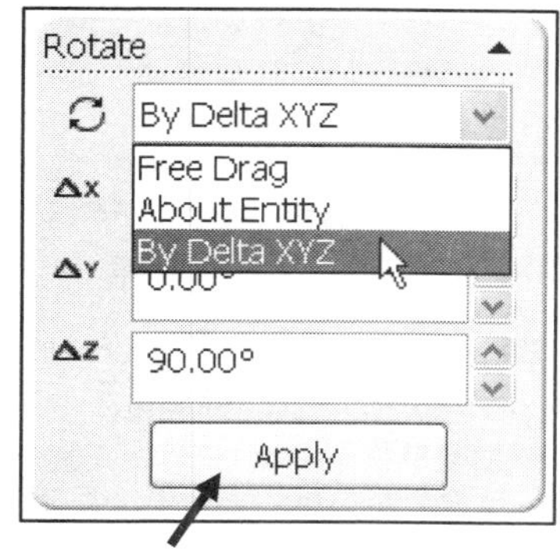

499) Click **Rotate Component** from the Assemblies toolbar.

500) Select **By Delta XYZ** from the Rotate box.

501) Enter **90** in the delta Z text box.

502) Click **Apply**.

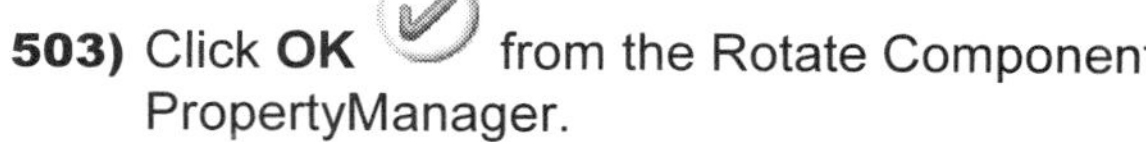

503) Click **OK** from the Rotate Component PropertyManager.

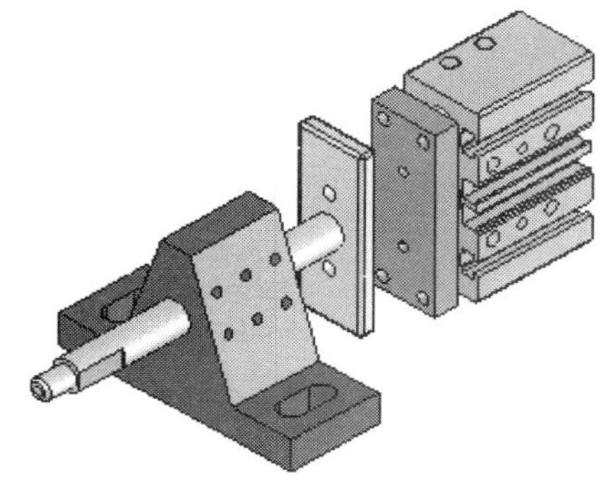

Fit the model to the Graphics window.

504) Press the **f** key.

505) Click and drag the **MGPM12-10 assembly** behind the GUIDE-ROD assembly. Note: The PISTON PLATE is behind the GUIDE-ROD assembly.

Zoom in on the component.

506) Click **Zoom to Area**. **Zoom in** on the PISTON PLATE and the top M4 hole face of the PLATE.

507) Click **Zoom to Area** to deactivate.

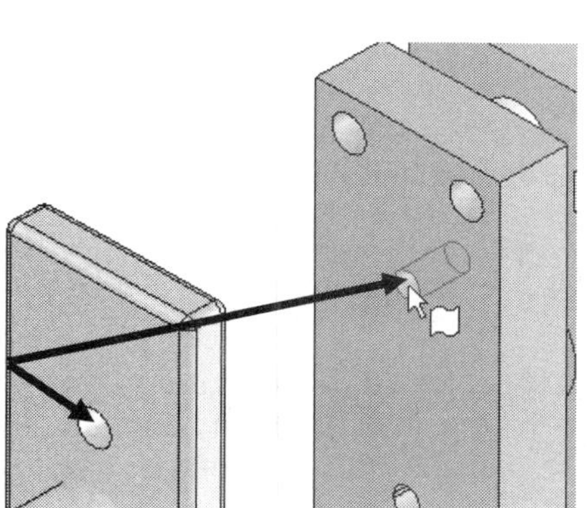

Insert a Concentric Mate.

508) Click **Mate**.

509) Click the **inside M4 hole face** of the PLATE.

510) Click the **inside M4 hole face** of the PISTON PLATE. Both faces are selected.

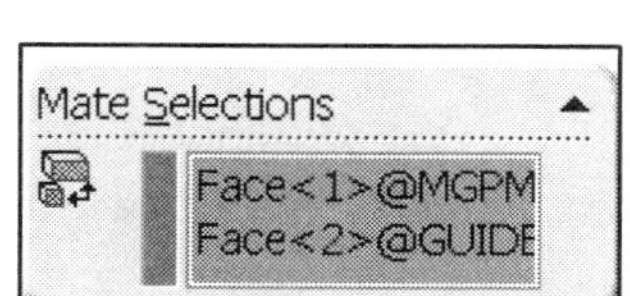

511) Click the **Green Check mark** ✔

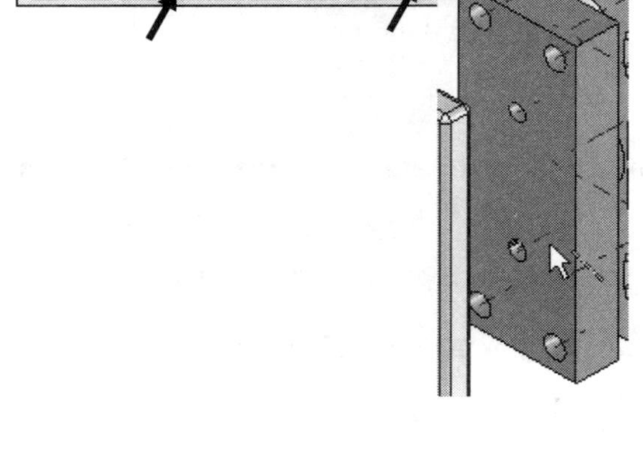

Note: The bottom hole feature contains a Slot Cut and an M4 Hole. The M4 Hole is hidden. Utilize the Select Other option to select the hidden M4 Hole.

Insert a Concentric Mate.

512) Click **View**, check **Temporary** axes from the Main menu.

513) Select the hidden M4 hole. Click **Zoom to Area** .

514) **Zoom in** on the bottom Slot and the M4 Hole. Do not select the Slot.

515) Click **Zoom to Area** to deactivate.

516) Right-click a **position** behind the Slot Cut on the Piston Plate.

517) Click **Select Other**. The Select Other dialog box is displayed. The Select Other box lists geometry in the selected region of the Graphics window. There are edges, faces and axes. The list order and geometry entries depend on the selection location of the mouse pointer.

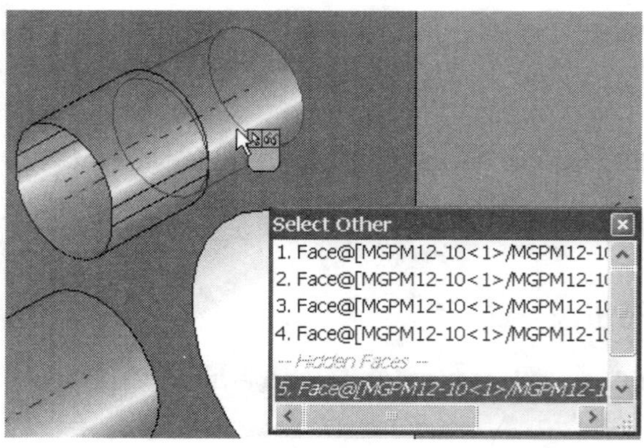

518) Position the **mouse pointer** over the M4 Hole.

519) Click the **M4 Hole**.

520) Click the **bottom inside M4 hole face** of the PLATE. Both faces are displayed in the Mate Selections box. Concentric is selected by default.

521) Click the **Green Check mark** ✔.

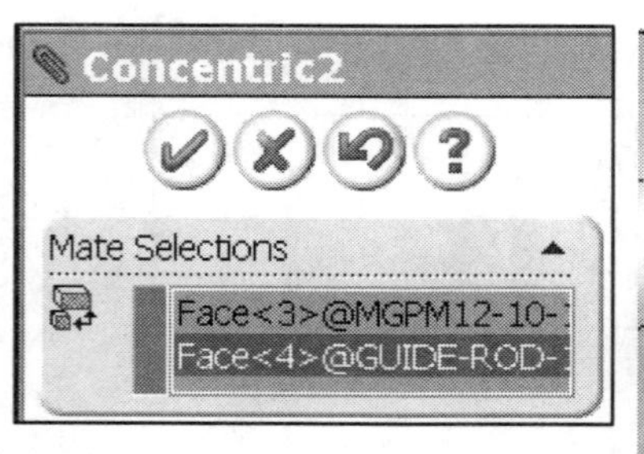

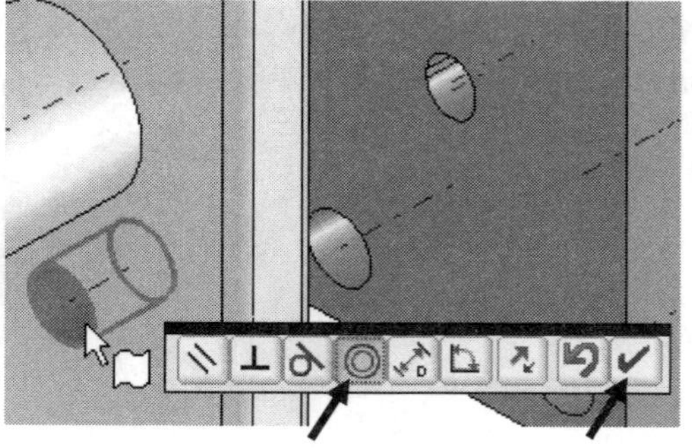

Fit the model to the Graphics window.

522) Press the **f** key.

Insert a Coincident Mate.

523) Click and drag the **PISTON PLATE** backward to create a gap.

524) Click the **front face** of the PISTON PLATE.

525) Press the **left arrow key** to rotate the view until you can see the back face of the PLATE.

526) Click the **back face** of the PLATE. Coincident is selected by default.

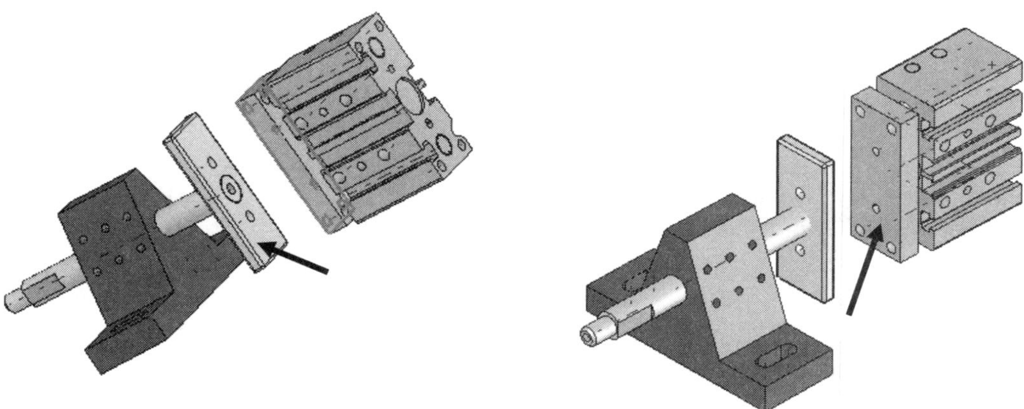

527) Click the **Green Check mark** ✔.

528) Click **OK** from the Mate PropertyManager.

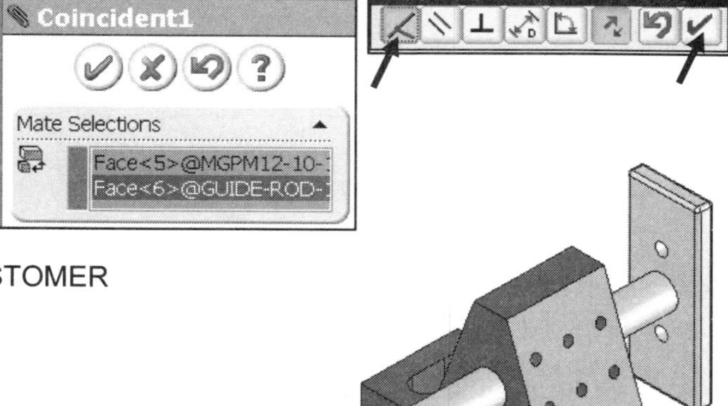

Unsuppress all components.

529) Right-click **GUIDE-ROD** in the CUSTOMER FeatureManager.

530) Click **Open Assembly**.

531) Right-click the **Hardware** folder in the FeatureManager.

532) Click **UnSuppress** Unsuppress.

533) Hold the **Ctrl** key down.

534) Click **Derived LPattern1** in the FeatureManager.

535) Click **LocalLPattern1**.

536) Release the **Ctrl** key.

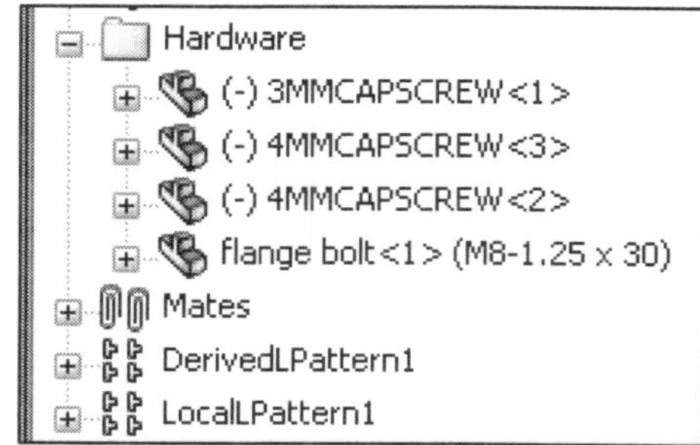

537) Right-click **UnSuppress** Unsuppress.

Return to the CUSTOMER assembly.
538) Press **Ctrl Tab**.

539) Click **Isometric view** . Click **View**, un-check **Temporary Axes** from the Main menu.

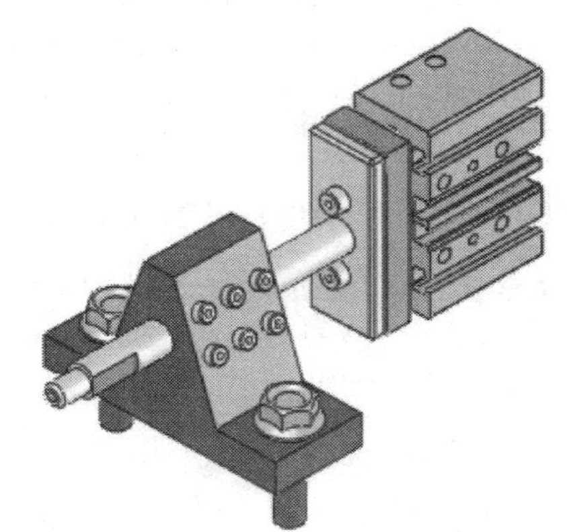

Save the CUSTOMER assembly in the ENGDESIGN-W-SOLIDWORKS/PROJECTS file folder.

540) Click **Save** .

541) Click **Yes** to update the assembly.

Copy the CUSTOMER Assembly

Copying and assembly in SolidWorks is not the same as copying a document in Microsoft Word. The customer assembly contains references to its parts and other sub-assemblies. You task is to provide a copy of the CUSTOMER assembly to a colleague for review. Copy the CUSTOMER assembly and all of the components into a different file folder named CopiedModels. Reference all component file locations to the new file folder.

Activity: Copy the CUSTOMER Assembly

Save the CUSTOMER assembly to a new file folder.
542) Select **File**, **SaveAs** from the Main menu.

543) Select **My Documents** for the Save in File Folder.

544) Click **References...** from the Save dialog box.

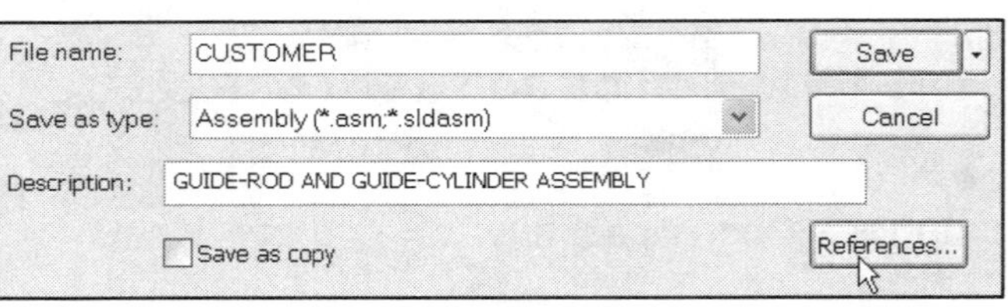

545) Click **Select All**.

546) Click **Browse**. Select **My Documents**.

547) Click the **Make New Folder** button.

548) Enter **CopiedModels** for Folder Name.

549) Click **inside** the Folder: box to display the CopiedModels folder name.

550) Click **OK** from Browse For Folder.

551) Click **OK** from the Edit Referenced File Locations to return to the Save As dialog box.

552) Double-click **CopiedModels** for the Save in folder.

553) Enter **CUSTOMER COPIED** for File name.

554) Check **Save As Copy**.

555) Click **Save**.

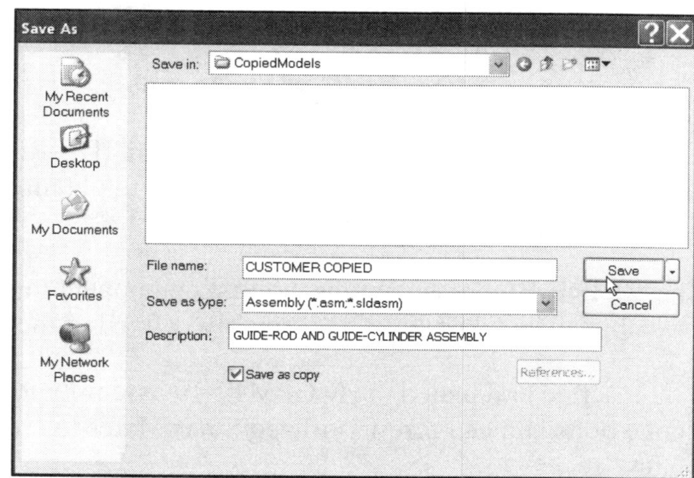

Close all files.

556) Click **Windows**, **Close All** from the Main menu.

557) Click **Yes**.

The CUSTOMER assembly is copied to CUSTOMER COPIED. All Reference documents are copied to the MY DOCUMENTS\CopiedModels folder.

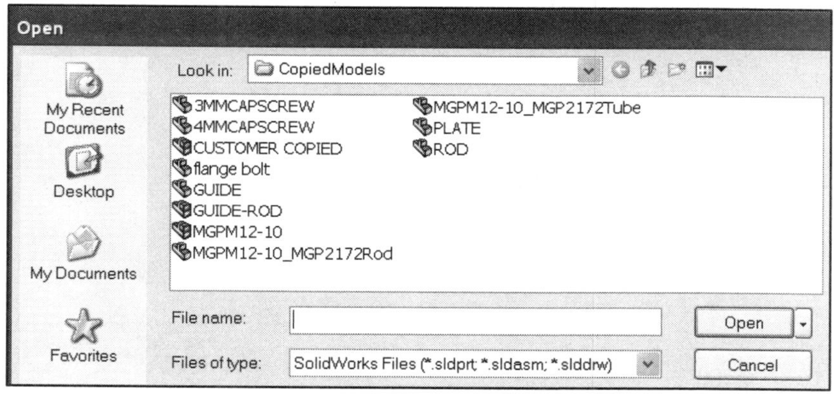

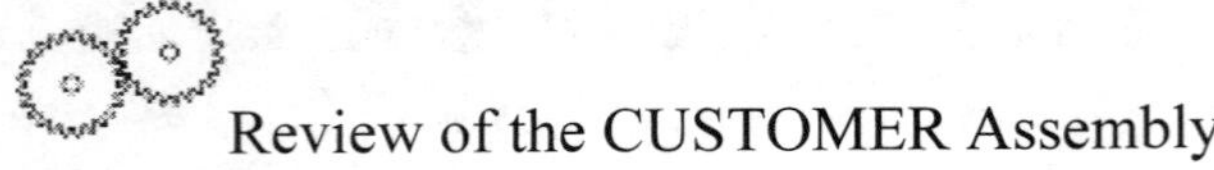

Review of the CUSTOMER Assembly.

The CUSTOMER assembly combined the GUIDE-ROD assembly and the MGPM12-10 assembly. In the design process you decide to obtain the MGPM12-10 assembly in SolidWorks format from the 3D ContentCentral.

The GUIDE-ROD assembly is the first component inserted into the CUSTOMER assembly. The GUIDE-ROD assembly is fixed to the CUSTOMER Origin.

You inserted and mated the MGPM12-10 assembly to the GUIDE-ROD assembly. The flange bolts and cap screws utilized SmartMates to create Concentric and Coincident Mates.

In the GUIDE-ROD assembly, you utilized a Local Pattern for the flange bolt and a Derived Pattern for the 3MMCAPSCREW. The flange bolt Mates were modified and redefined.

The Save As option with the Reference option copied the CUSTOMER assembly and all references to a new folder location.

Will the ROD experience unwanted deflection or stress? Insure a valid GUIDE-ROD assembly by using the COSMOSXpress tool.

In Project 1 you assigned Material AISI304 Stainless Steel to the GUIDE, ROD and PLATE. You also calculated the mass in grams of each part with the Mass Properties tool.

A newton is defined as the force acting on a mass of one kilogram at a location where the acceleration due to gravity is 1m/s^2. Weight equals mass * gravity. Weight is a Force.

$$1\ newton = \frac{1\,kg - m}{s^2}$$

How do you determine if the MGPM12-10 assembly supports the Weight under static load conditions? Answer: Utilize COSMOSXpress. Determine the engineering data required for the simplified static analysis.

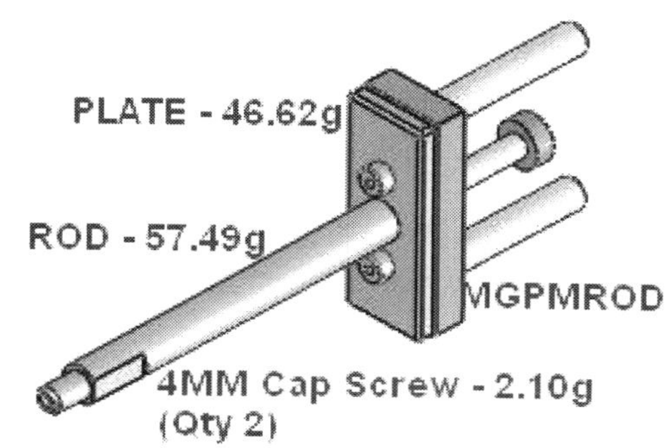

Analyze the MGPM12-10_MGP2172Rod<1> part.

Component:	MATERIAL:	Mass:
PLATE	AISI304	46.62g
ROD	AISI304	57.49g
2 – 4MMCAPSCREWS	AISI304	4.20g
Customer Component Fasten to Rod	Unknown	1500.00g
Total	**Total**	1608.31g ~1.61kg

Assume $g_c = 9.81\ \text{m/s}^2$.

$$Weight = mg = 1.61\ kg\ x\ 9.81\frac{m}{s^2}$$

$$Weight = 16.1\frac{kg - m}{s^2}$$

$$Weight = 16N$$

Reuse Material Properties. Assign a Material Property to the part through the FeatureManager. The same Material Property is automatically assigned in COSMOSXpress.

COSMOSXpress

COSMOSXpress is a Finite Element Analysis (FEA) tool.

COSMOSXpress calculates the displacement and stress in a part based on material, restraints and static loads.

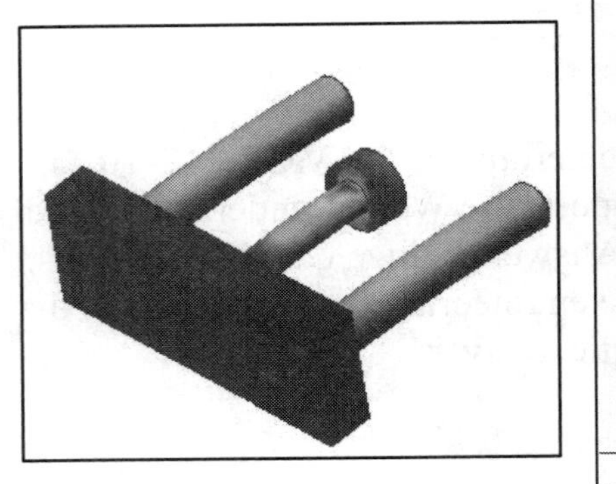

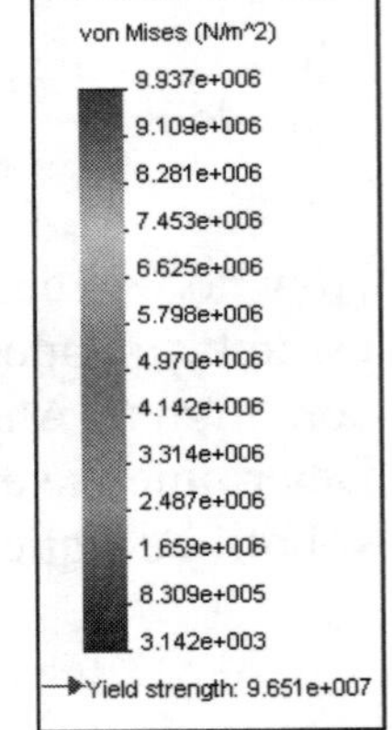

When loads are applied to a part, the part tries to absorb its effects by developing internal forces.

Stress is the intensity of these internal forces. Stress is defined in terms of Force per unit Area: $Stress = \frac{f}{A}$.

Different materials have different stress property levels. Mathematical equations derived from Elasticity theory and Strength of Materials are utilized to solve for displacement and stress. These analytical equations solve for displacement and stress for simple cross sections.

Example: Bar or Beam. In complicated parts, a computer based numerical method such as Finite Element Analysis is used.

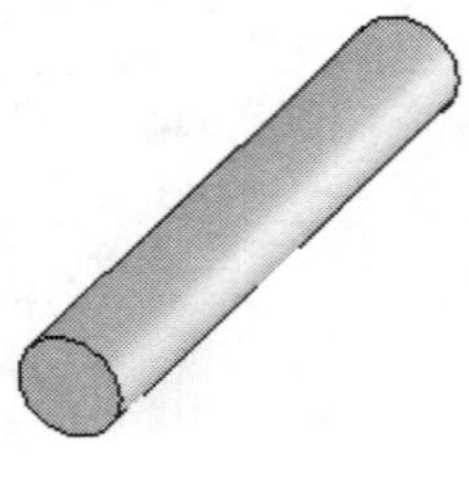

Bar

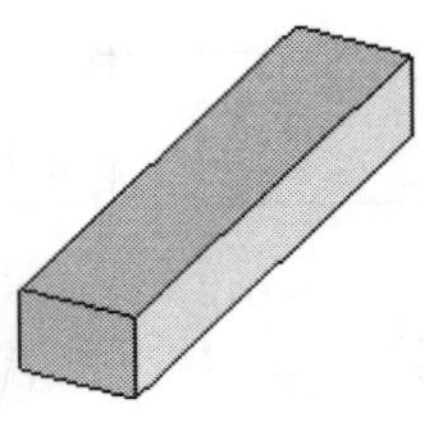

Beam

COSMOSXpress utilizes linear static analysis based on the Finite Element Method. The Finite Element Method is a numerical technique used to analyze engineering designs. FEM divides a large complex model into numerous smaller models. A model is divided into numerous smaller segments called elements.

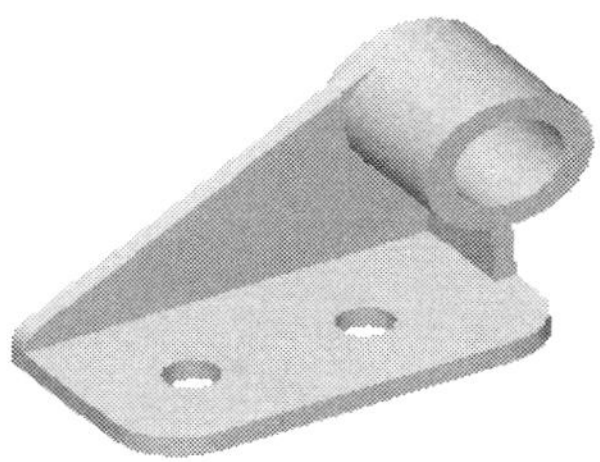

CAD model of a bracket

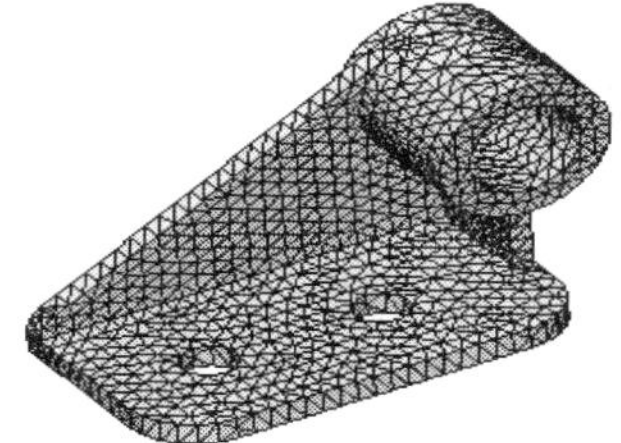

Model subdivided into small pieces (elements)

COSMOSXpress utilizes a tetrahedral element containing 10 nodes.

Each node contains a series of equations. COSMOSXpress develops the equations governing the behavior of each element.

The equations relate displacement to material properties, restraints, "boundary conditions" and applied loads.

The COSMOSXpress Solver organizes a large set of simultaneous algebraic equations.

The Finite Element Analysis (FEA) equation is:

[K]{U} = {F} where:

1. [K] is the structural stiffness matrix.
2. {U} is the vector of unknown nodal displacements.
3. {F} is the vector of nodal loads.

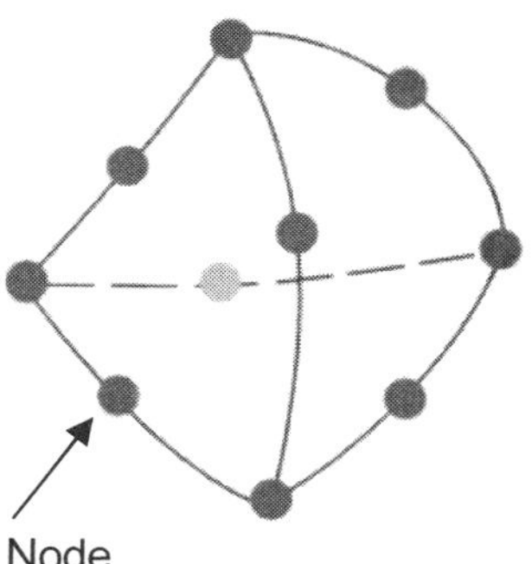

Tetrahedral Element

The COSMOSXpress Solver determines the X, Y and Z displacement at each node. This displacement is utilized to calculate strain.

Strain is defined as the ratio of the change in length, δL to the original length, L.

Stress is proportional to strain in a Linear Elastic Material.

The Elastic Modulus (Young's Modulus) is defined as stress divided by strain.

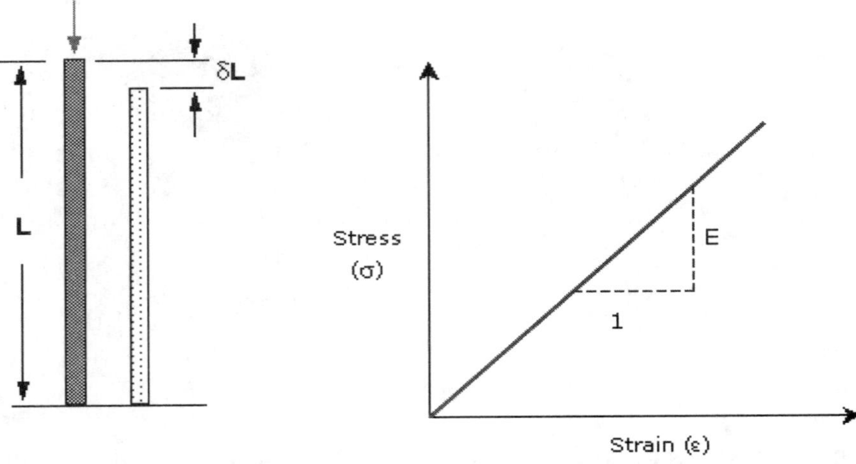

Strain = $\delta L / L$

Compression Force Applied
Original Length L
Change in Length δL

Elastic Modulus is the ratio of Stress to Strain for Linear Elastic Materials.

The COSMOSXpress Solver determines the stress for each element based on the Elastic Modulus of the material and the calculated strain.

The Stress versus Strain Plot for a Linearly Elastic Material provides information about a material.

The Elastic Modulus, E is the stress required to cause one unit of strain. The material behaves linearly in the Elastic Range.

The material remains in the Elastic Range until it reaches the elastic limit.

The point EL is the elastic limit. The material begins Plastic deformation.

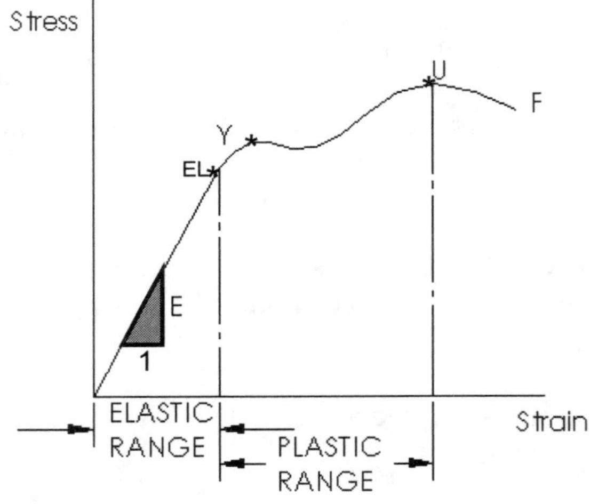

Stresss versus Strain Plot
Linearly Elastic Material

The point Y is called the Yield Point. The material begins to deform at a faster rate. The material behaves non-linearly in the Plastic Range. The point U is called the ultimate tensile strength. Point U is the maximum value of the non-linear curve. Point U represents the maximum tensile stress a material can handle before a facture or failure. Point F represents where the material will fracture.

Designers utilize maximum and minimum stress calculations to determine if a part is safe. COSMOSXpress reports a recommended Factor of Safety during the analysis.

The COSMOSXpress Factor of Safety is a ratio between the material strength and the calculated stress.

The von Mises stress is a measure of the stress intensity required for a material to yield. The COSMOSXpress Results plot displays von Mises stress.

The COSMOSXpress design analysis wizard steps through six task tabs. The tabs are defined as follows:

- Select the Welcome tab to set units and to store the results in a file folder.
- Select the Material tab to assign or input Material Properties to a part.
- Select the Restraint tab to apply boundary conditions to a face of a part.
- Select the Load tab to apply force or pressure to a face of a part.
- Select the Analyze tab to modify the default settings, run the analysis, automatically apply a mesh and solve a series of simultaneous equations to obtain displacement and stress results.
- Select the Results tab to view the analysis.

The Results are viewed as follows:

1. Show critical areas where the factor of safety is less than a specified value.
2. Show the stress distribution of a part.
3. Show the deformed shape of the part.
4. Generate an HTML report.
5. Generate eDrawing files for analysis.

Run the COSMOSXpress wizard: Analysis of the MGPM12-10_MGP2172Rod<1> -> part. The part is a reference part in the MGPM12-10 assembly. Add three Restraints to the back circular faces of the part. The three faces are fixed.

Apply a 100N Force on the front face of the part. The Force is perpendicular to the Top Plane.

Activity: Analyze the MGPMRod Part-COSMOSXpress

Close all documents.

558) Click **Window**, **Close All** from the Main menu.

Open the MGPM12-10 assembly.

559) Click **File**, **Open** from the Main menu.

560) Select **ENGDESIGN-W-SOLIDWORKS\VENDOR COMPONENTS** for Look In Folder.

561) Double-click the **MGPM12-10** assembly.

Open the part.

562) Right-click MGPM12-10_MGP2172Rod<1> -> from the FeatureManager.

563) Click **Open Part**.

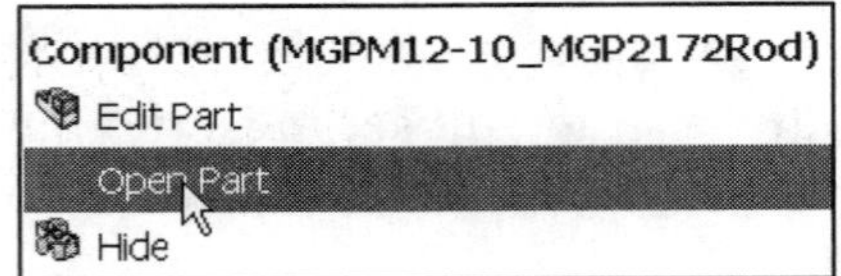

564) Click **Isometric view**.

565) Click **Tools, COSMOSXpress** COSMOSXpress... from the Main menu.

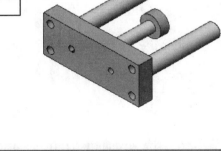

Define the Options.

566) Click **Options** Options... from the Welcome tab.

567) Select **SI** for Units.

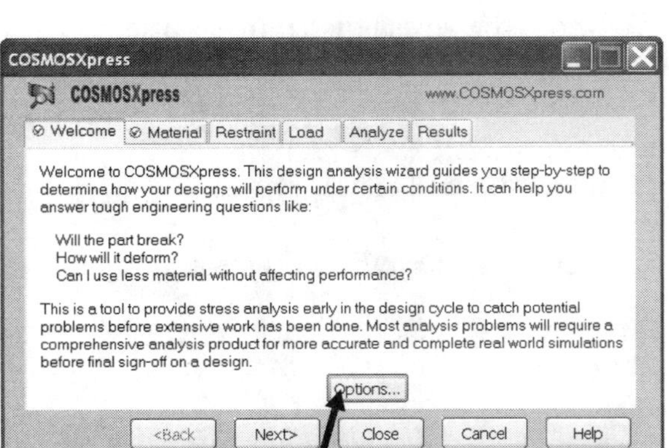
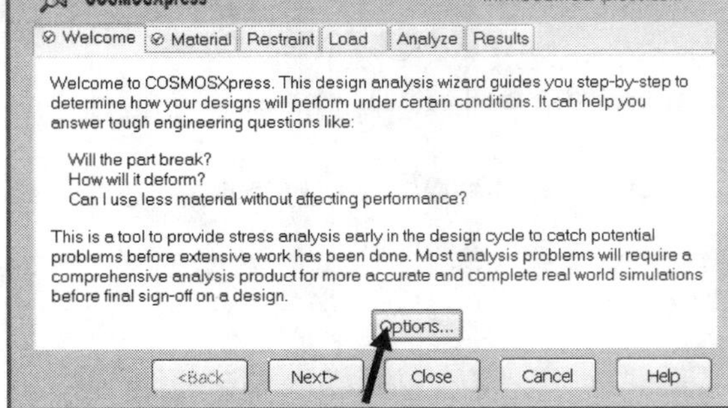

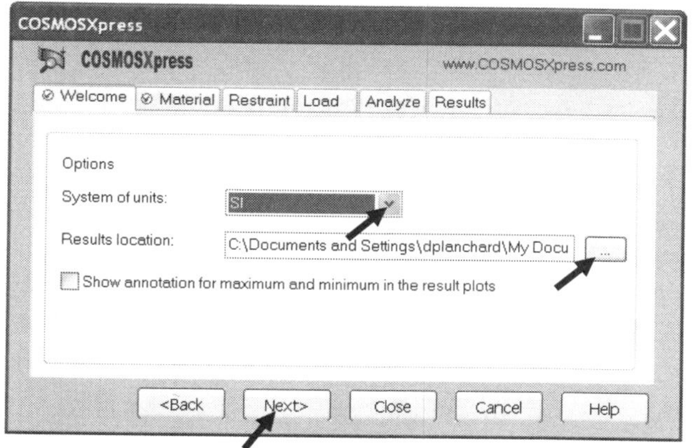

568) Click **Browse** .

569) Select the **ENGDESIGN-W-SOLIDWORKS\PROJECTS** file folder to store the results.

570) Click **OK**.

571) Click **Next>**. The Material tab is selected.

Select a Material.

572) Expand the **Aluminum Alloys** category.

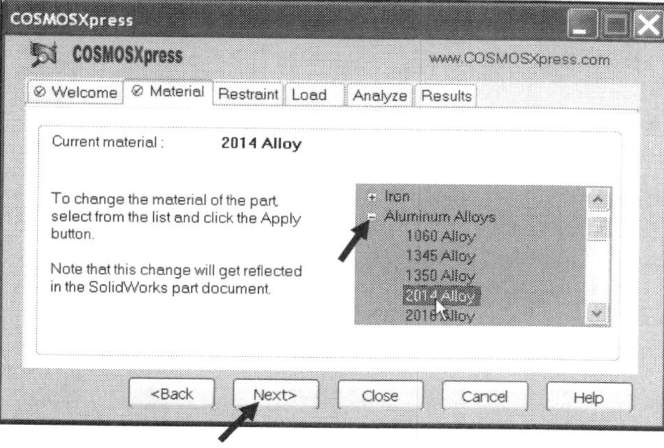

573) Select **Aluminum Alloy (2014 alloy)**.

574) Click **Apply**. The Current Material is Aluminum Alloy (2014 alloy). A green checkmark is displayed on the Materials tab.

575) Click **Next>**.

Four Material Properties for 2014 Aluminum are defined in the SolidWorks Materials Editor:

- Elastic Modulus.
- Poisson's ratio.
- Yield Strength.
- Mass Density.

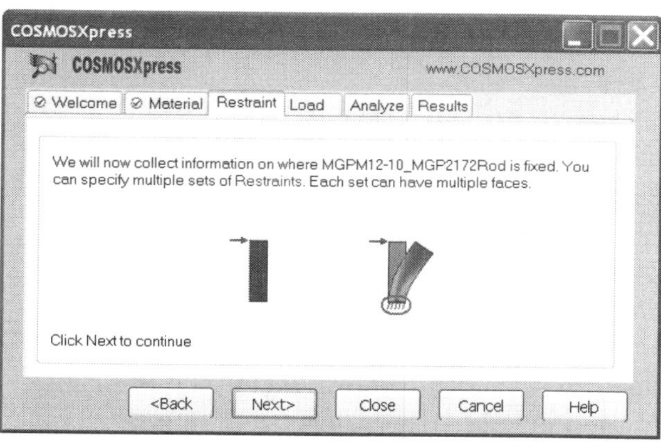

Note: Create Material properties in SolidWorks. Example: AISI304 Stainless Steel. The Material Properties transfer to COSMOSXpress.

COSMOSXpress utilizes Linear Elastic Isotropic materials. Add the Restraints to the three circular back part faces. The Restraints create fixed boundary conditions.

Define the Restraint.

576) The Restraint tab is selected. Click **Next>**.

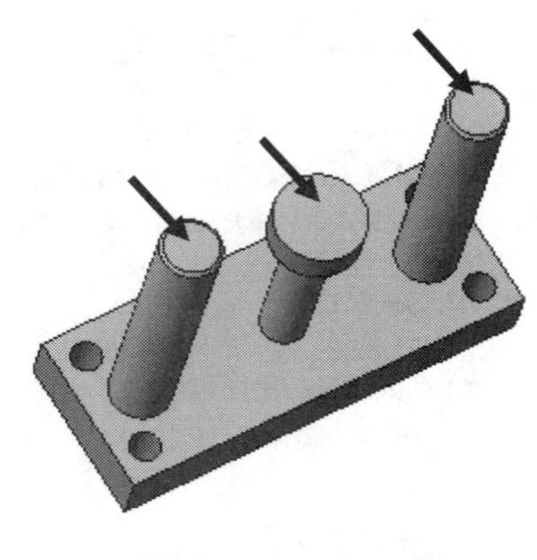

577) Drag the **COSMOSXpress** dialog box to the lower right corner of the Graphics window. Do not close the dialog box.

Add Restraints.

578) Click a **position** inside the Graphics window.

579) Press the **arrow keys** until the three circular back faces are displayed. The current restraint set is named Restraint1.

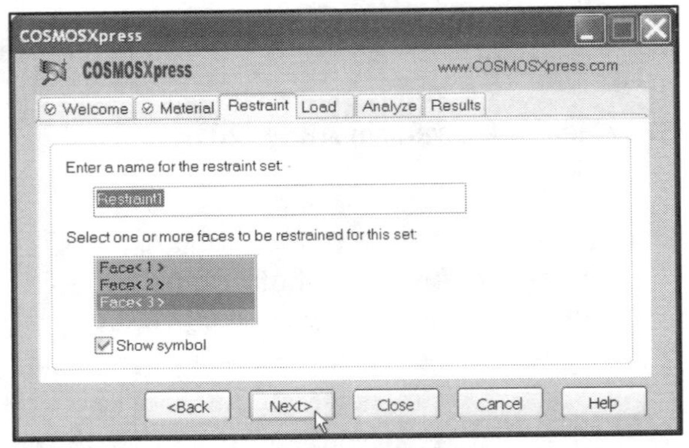

580) Click the **back middle circular face**. Small hatch symbols are displayed on the circular face.

581) Select the **back left circular face**.

582) Select the **back right circular face**.

583) Click **Next>** from the COSMOSXpress dialog box. Face <1>, Face<2> and Face<3> are added to the restraint set.

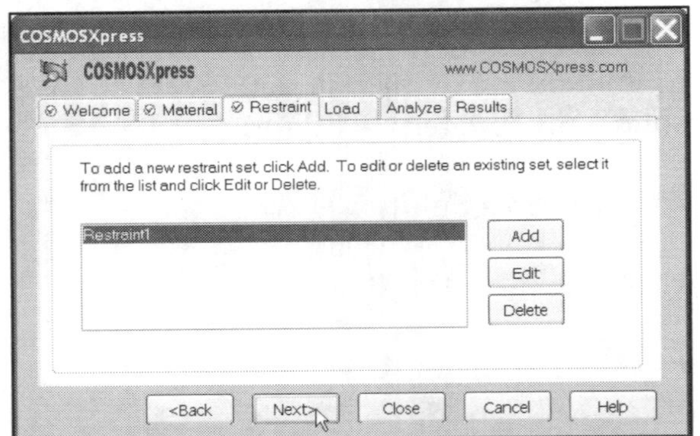

584) A checkmark is displayed on the Restraint tab. Restraint1 is listed in the Existing Restraint Set list box. Click **Next>**. The Load tab is selected.

The Add, Edit and Delete buttons are utilized to add a new restraint set, edit an existing restraint set or delete an existing restraint set, respectfully.

Apply a distributed load set to the part front face. The applied Force is 16N. The downward Force is Normal (Perpendicular) to the Plane2 (Top) Reference Plane.

Add Loads.

585) Add the Load set. Click **Next>**.

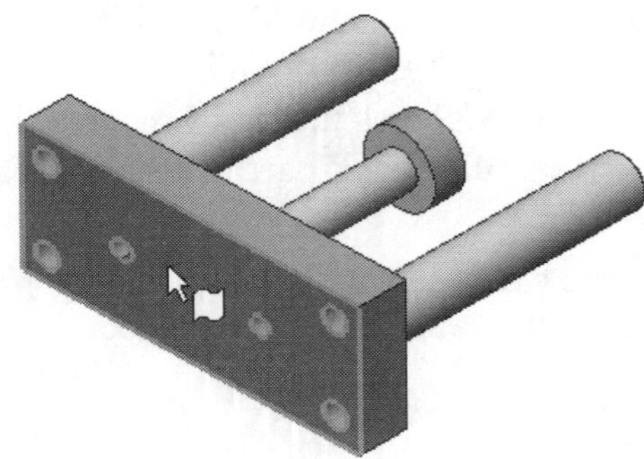

586) Click **Force**. Click **Next>**. Load1 is the default name for the first load set.

587) Click **Isometric view** .

588) Click the **front face**.

589) Click **Next>**.

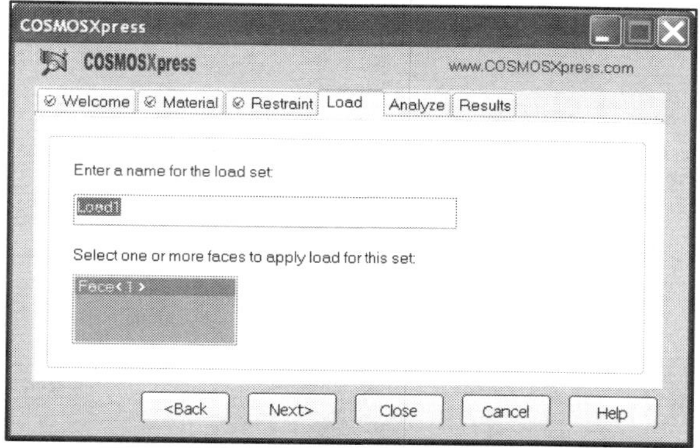

Select the direction for Load1.

590) Click **Normal to a reference plane**.

591) Click **Plane2** from the FeatureManager.

592) Enter **16**N for the Force value.

593) Click the **Flip direction** check box. The force symbols point downward.

594) Click **Next>**. Load1 is listed in the Load text box.

595) Click **Next>**. A checkmark is displayed on the Load tab.

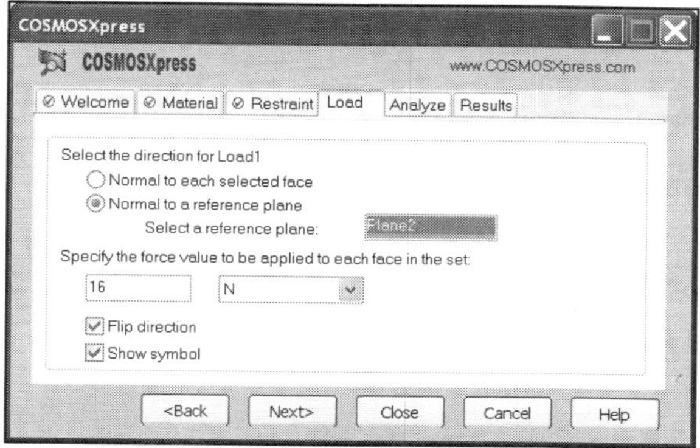

Run the Analysis.

596) The Yes button is selected to run the analysis with the default settings. Click **Next>** to utilize the default settings.

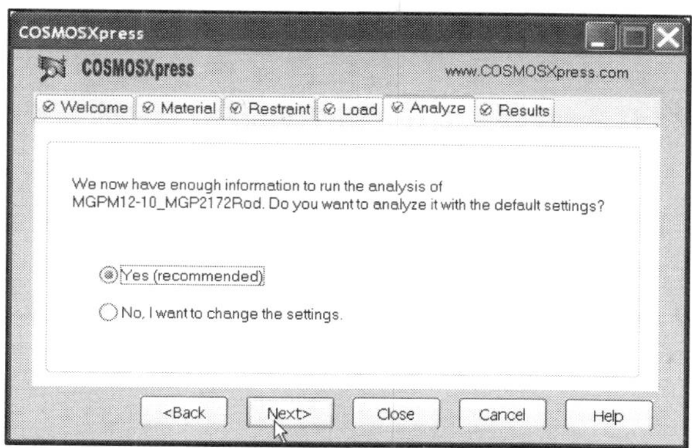

597) Click **Run** to apply the mesh and to calculate the results. A series of simultaneous equations is solved.

A checkmark is displayed on the Analysis tab. The Lowest Factor of Safety (FOS) for the part is 9.77947. Display the Results.

598) Click **Show me**. The model is displayed in blue. The model meets your lowest factor of safety.

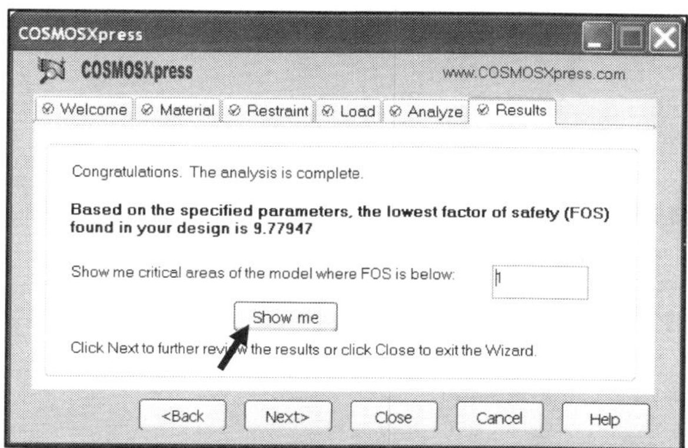

599) Click **Next>**.

600) Select the result type. Click the **Show me the stress distribution in the model** to displace the Stress plot in the Graphics window.

601) Click **Next>**.

Play the Deformation animation.

602) Click **Play** .

Stop the Deformation animation.

603) Click **Stop** .

Save the Animation.

604) Click **Save** .

605) Accept the default filename,. MGPM12-10_MGP2172Rod-COSMOSXpressStudy_stress_1. Click **Save**. Note: Do not click close.

The MGPM12-10_MGP2172Rod -> part is within the Factor of Safety default design criteria based on the 16N Force. The customer requires a second design application that utilizes a 100N Load. Return to the Load tab. Modify the Force to 100N. Run the analysis and review the results.

Modify the force.

606) Click the **Load** tab.

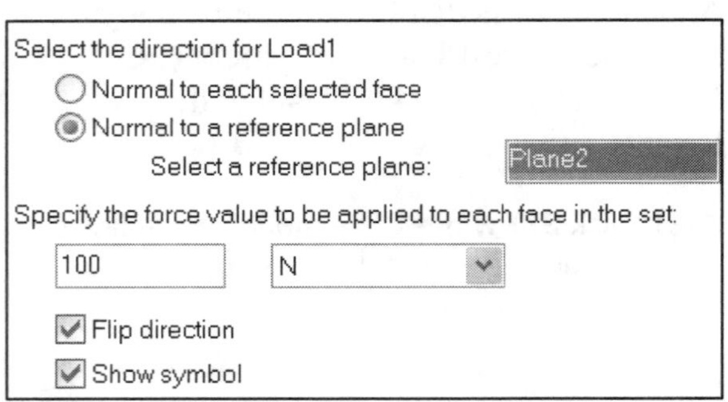

607) Click **Edit**.

608) Click **Next>**.

609) Select **Plane2** from the FeatureManager.

610) Enter **100N** for Force.

611) Click **Next>**.

Calculate the Analyze and Results for the new Force.

612) Click the **Analyze** tab.

613) Click **Next>**.

614) Click **Run**. Review the Results. The lowest Factor of Safety is 1.56471. Display the critical areas of the model.

615) Click **Show me**.

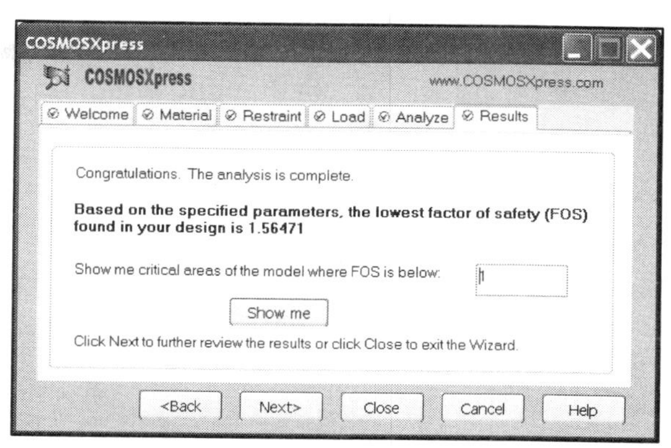

Close COSMOSXpress.

616) Click **Close**.

617) Click **Yes** to Save the COSMOSXpress data.

Close all parts and assemblies.

618) Click **Window**, **Close All** from the Main menu.

619) Click **Yes** to Save changes.

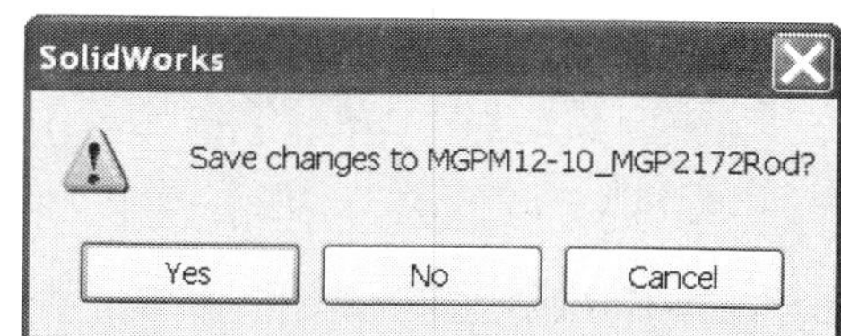

There is an area of concern near the back face of the Piston.

How do you increase the Factor of Safety? There are two suggestions:

- Modify the Material from Aluminum to Steel.
- Increase the piston diameter from 6mm to 10mm.

The MGPM12-10_MGP2172Rod -> part is a purchased part.

Property	Description	Value	Units
EX	Elastic modulus	2.1e+011	N/m^2
NUXY	Poisson's ratio	0.28	NA
SIGYLD	Yield strength	6.20422e+008	N/m^2
DENS	Mass density	7700	kg/m^3

Material Properties for Steel

Property	Description	Value	Units
EX	Elastic modulus	6.9e+010	N/m^2
NUXY	Poisson's ratio	0.33	NA
SIGYLD	Yield strength	27574200	N/m^2
DENS	Mass density	2700	kg/m^3

Material Properties for Aluminum

You return to SMCUSA.com to locate the GUIDE-CYLINDER with a larger bore size for your customer's second application.

Here are a few tips in performing the analysis. Remember you are dealing with thousands or millions of equations. These tips are a starting point. Every analysis situation is unique.

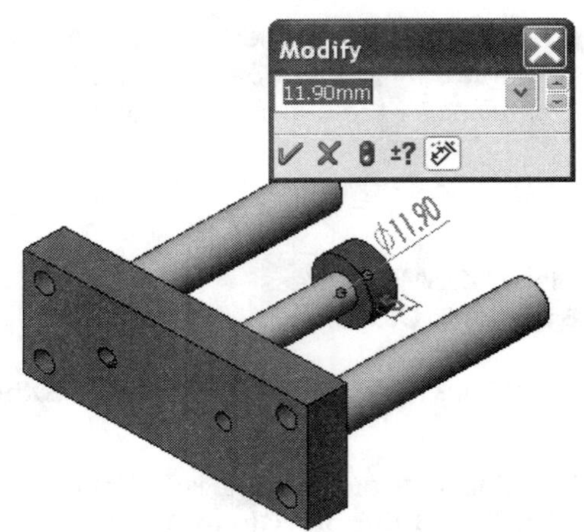

- Utilize symmetry. If a part is symmetric about a plane, utilize one half of the model for analysis. If a part is symmetric about two planes, utilize one fourth of the model for analysis.
- Suppress small fillets and detailed features in the part.
- Avoid parts that have aspect ratios over 100.
- Utilize consistent units.
- Estimate an intuitive solution based on the fundamentals of stress analysis techniques.
- Factor of Safety is a guideline for the designer. The designer is responsible for the safety of the part.

Additional details on COSMOSXpress are found through the Help button on the COSMOSXpress dialog box. Additional COSMOSXpress Tutorials are available in Help, Online Tutorials.

Additional analysis tools for static, dynamic, thermal and fluid analysis are available with the COSMOS software applications.

Review of COSMOSXpress.

COSMOSXpress is a Finite Element Tool that calculated the displacement and stress based on material, restraints and static loads.

You utilized COSMOSXpress to analysis the displacement and stress on the MGPM12-10_MGP2172Rod<1> part early in the design process.

You assigned the Material to be Aluminum, added restraints to three faces and applied a force of 16 N. Based on the inputs, the results provided visual representation of displacement and von Mises stress.

The applied force was modified to 100N. The material was modified from Aluminum to Steel.

Refer to Help, Online Tutorial, Lesson2-Assemblies exercise for additional information.

Project Summary

You created the GUIDE-ROD assembly from the following parts: GUIDE, ROD, PLATE, FLANGE BOLT, 3MMCAPSCREW and 4MMCAPSCREW. The components were oriented and positioned in the assembly using Mates.

Mates were redefined in the GUIDE-ROD assembly to center the FLANGE BOLT in the GUIDE Slot Cut. You created a Local Linear Pattern for the FLANGE BOLT and a Derived Component Pattern for the 3MMCAPSCREW.

The CUSTOMER assembly contained the MGPM12-10 assembly and the GUIDE-ROD assembly. The assemblies utilized a Bottom-Up design approach. In a Bottom-Up design approach you possess all the required design information for the individual components.

COSMOSXpress provided an analysis of a part during the development process. Specific Material, Restraints and Loads produced deflection and stress analysis plots.

Project 2 is completed. In Project 3, you will create an assembly drawing and a detailed drawing of the GUIDE.

Project Terminology

Add Relations: Constraints utilized to connect related geometry. Some common relations are horizontal, concentric, equal, coincident and collinear. The Add Relations tool is invoked through the Sketch Toolbar. Relations are also added by selecting the Ctrl key, geometric entities and then the relation through the Properties PropertyManager.

Assembly: An assembly combines two or more parts. In an assembly, parts are referred to as components. The file extension for an assembly is *.sldasm.

Bottom-Up assembly design approach: Components are assembled using part dependencies and parent-child relationships. In this approach, you possess all of the required design information for the individual components.

Chamfer: Removes material with a beveled cut from an edge or face. The Chamfer requires a distance and an angle or two distances.

Component Pattern, Derived: A pattern of components in an assembly based on a feature pattern of an existing component. The 3MMCAPSCREW pattern in the assembly was derived from the GUIDE Linear Pattern of 3MM Tapped Holes.

Component Pattern, Linear: A pattern of components in an assembly based on reference geometry in the assembly. A Linear Component Pattern is called a local pattern. The two flange bolts were redefined with a Linear Component Pattern.

Component: A part or sub-assembly inserted into an assembly. Changes in the components directly affect the assembly and vise a versa.

COSMOSXpress: A Finite Element Analysis (FEA) tool. COSMOSXpress calculates the displacement and stress in a part based on material, restraints and static loads. Results are displayed for von Mises stress and deflection.

Dimensions: Values that define the overall size and shape of a feature or the relationship between components.

Editing Component: Individual parts and sub-assemblies are edited in-context of the top-level assembly. Changes can be made to a part's dimensions while active in the assembly.

Elastic Modulus, E: The stress required to cause one unit of strain. Utilized in Material Properties.

Exploded view: Displays an assembly with its components separated from one another. An Exploded view is used to show how to assemble or disassemble the components. With SolidWorks Animator, exploded view collapse and explode animations are recorded to an avi file.

Extruded Cut: Cut features are used to remove material from a solid. This is the opposite of the Extruded Boss.

Fits: There are three major types of fits addressed in this Project:

- Clearance fit - The shaft diameter is less than the hole diameter.
- Interference fit – The shaft diameter is larger than the hole diameter. The difference between the shaft diameter and the hole diameter is called interference.
- Transition fit – Clearance or interference can exist between the shaft and the hole.

Geometric Relations: A relation is a geometric constraint between sketch entities or between a sketch entity and a plane, axis, edge, or vertex. Relations force a behavior on a sketch element to capture the design intent.

Hidden Geometry: Geometry that is not displayed. Utilize Hide/Show to control display of components in an assembly.

Mates: The action of assembling components in SolidWorks is defined as Mates. Mates are geometric relationships that align and fit components in an assembly. Mates remove degrees of freedom from a component. Mates require geometry from two different components. Selected geometry includes Planar Faces, Cylindrical faces, Linear edges, Circular/Arc edges, Vertices, Axes, Temporary axes, Planes, Points and Origins.

Modify Dimension: The act of changing a dimension. Double-click on a dimension. Enter the new value in the Modify dialog box. Click Rebuild.

Move Component/Rotate Component: Components in an assembly are translated by selecting the middle mouse button. To rotate a component in an assembly, utilize Rotate Component from the Assembly toolbar. Additional options for Collision Detection are available from the Move Component option on the Assembly toolbar.

Rebuild: After changes are made to the dimensions, rebuild the model to cause those changes to take affect.

Revolved Boss/Base: Creates a feature from an axis, a profile sketch and an angle of revolution. The Revolve Boss/Base feature adds material to the part. The 4MMCAPSCREW utilized a Revolve Base feature.

Save As: Utilize the References button to save all parts and subassemblies in a new assembly to a different file folder. Utilize the Save as copy option to create a copy of an existing part.

Section View: Displays the internal cross section of a component or assembly. Section views can be performed anywhere in a model. The location of the cut corresponds to the Section plane. A Section plane is a planar face or reference plane.

Sketch: The name to describe a 2D profile is called a sketch. 2D Sketches are created on flat faces and planes within the model. Typical geometry types are lines, arcs, circles, rectangles and ellipses.

SmartMates: A SmartMate is a Mate that automatically occurs when a component is placed into an assembly. The mouse pointer displays a SmartMate feedback symbol when common geometry and relationships exist between the component and the assembly. SmartMates are Concentric or Coincident.

- Coincident Planes SmartMate assumes that a plane on the component lies along a plane on the assembly.

- Concentric SmartMate assumes that the geometry on the component has the same center as the geometry on an assembled reference.

Sub-assemblies: Sub-assemblies are components inserted into an assembly. They behave as a single piece of geometry. When an assembly file is added to an existing assembly, it is referred to as a sub-assembly, (*.sldasm) or component.

Suppressed features and components: Suppressed features, parts and assemblies are not displayed. During model rebuilding, suppressed features and components are not calculated. Features and components are suppressed at the component or assembly level in the FeatureManager. The names of the suppressed features and components are displayed in light gray.

Tolerance: The difference between the maximum and minimum variation of a nominal dimension and the actual manufactured dimension.

Top-Down assembly design approach: Major design requirements are translated into assemblies, sub-assemblies and components. You do not need all of the required component design details. Individual relationships are required. See Project 6.

Questions

1. Describe an assembly or Sub-assembly.
2. What are Mates and why are they important in assembling components?
3. Name and describe the three major types of Fits.
4. Name and describe the two assembly modeling techniques in SolidWorks.
5. Describe Dynamic motion.
6. In an assembly, each component has_______# degrees of freedom? Name them.
7. True or False. A fixed component cannot move.
8. Identify the procedure to create a Revolved Base feature.
9. Describe the different types of SmartMates. Utilize on line help to view the animations for different Smart Mates.
10. How are SmartMates used?
11. Identify the process to insert a component from the Design Library.
12. Describe a Section view.
13. What are Suppressed features and components? Provided an example.
14. True or False. If you receive a Mate Error you should always delete the component from the assembly.
15. True or False. COSMOSXpress calculates the displacement and stress in a part based on material, restraints and static loads.
16. List the names of the following icons in the Assembly toolbar.

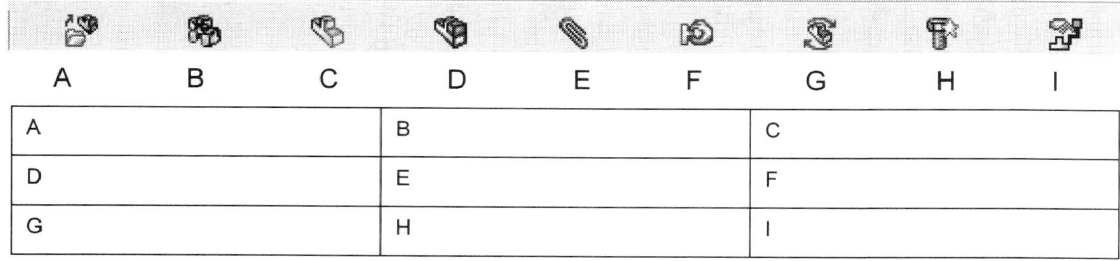

A	B	C
D	E	F
G	H	I

Exercises

Exercise 2.1: BASE-CUSTOMER Assembly.

- Design a BASE PLATE part to fasten three CUSTOMER assemblies. The BASE PLATE is the first component in the BASE-CUSTOMER assembly:

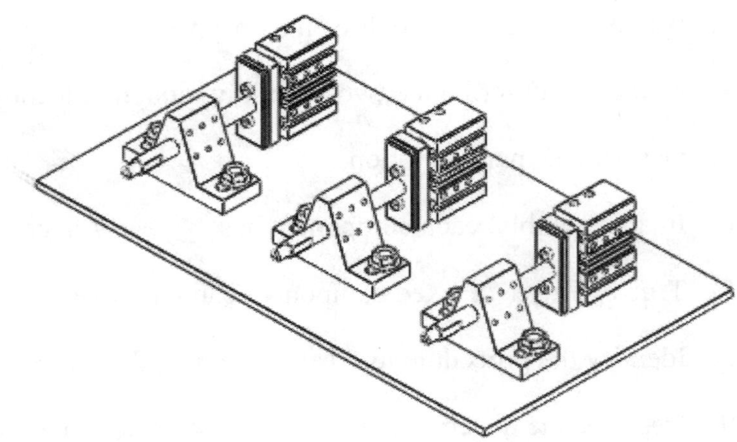

- Create six holes. Determine the hole location based on the CUSTOMER assembly.
- The BASE PLATE thickness is 10mm. The material is Aluminum.

Exercise 2.2: PLATE4H-Part & Assembly.

Create a PLATE4H part. Utilizes four front outside holes of the MGPM12-10 assembly.

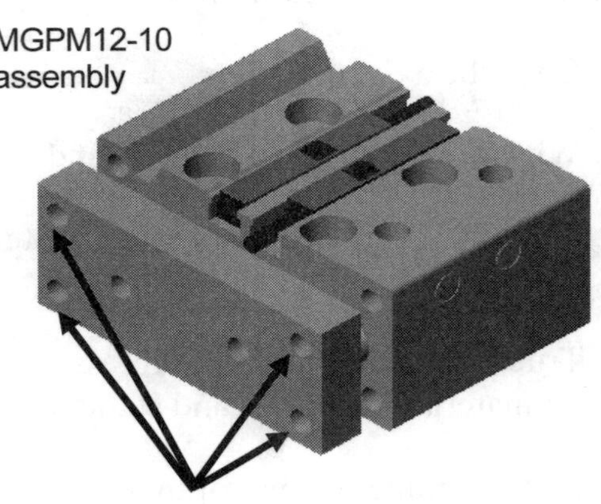

- Manually sketch the dimensions of the PLATE4H part.
- Dimension the 4 outside holes.
- The Material thickness is 10mm.
- Create the new assembly, PLATE4H-GUIDECYLINDER.
- Mate the PLATE4H part to the MGPM12-10 assembly.

Exercise 2.3a: LINKAGE Assembly.

CJ 2KL16-45S
Y-J016B

In Exercise 1.5, you created four machined parts for the LINKAGE assembly.

- AXLE.
- SHAFT COLLAR.
- FLAT BAR - 3 HOLE.
- FLAT BAR - 9 HOLE.

- The LINKAGE assembly incorporates an SMC Air Cylinder.

AIRCYLINDER
SHAFT COLLAR
ROD CLEVIS
AXLE
FLAT BAR – 9 HOLE
FLAT BAR – 3 HOLE

LINKAGE assembly

The AIRCYLINDER is the first component in the LINKAGE assembly. When compressed air goes in to the air in let, the Piston Rod is pushed out. Without compressed air, the Piston Rod is returned by the force of the spring.

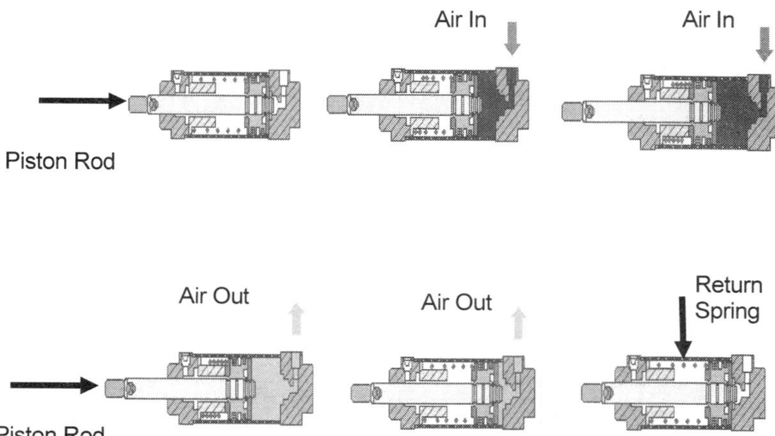

The Piston Rod linearly translates the ROD CLEVIS in the LINKAGE assembly.

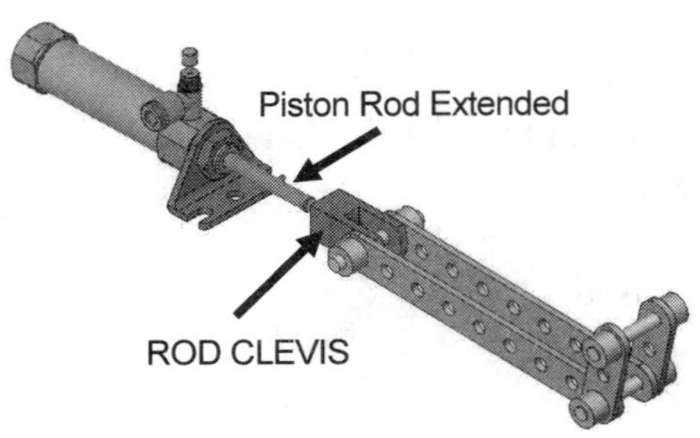

- Insert the AIRCYLINDER. The AIRCYLINDER is fixed to the LINKAGE assembly Origin.

The AIRCYLINDER information is available on the Multimedia CD.

- Insert the AXLE through the holes on the ROD CLEVIS.
- Utilize a Concentric Mate to align the AXLE in the ROD CLEVIS holes. The AXLE is symmetric about its Front Plane.

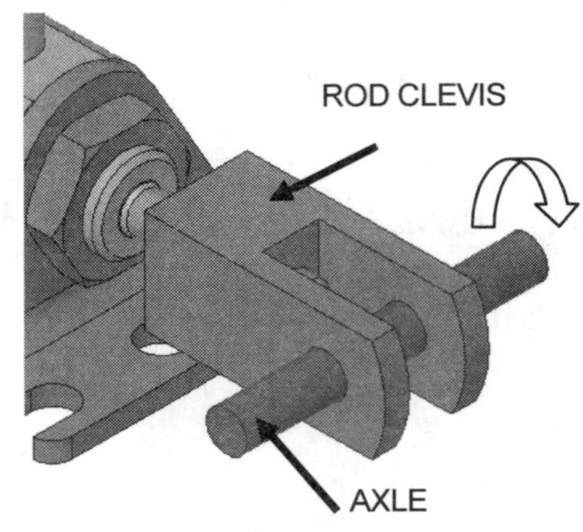

- Utilize a Coincident Mate between the Front Plane of the AXLE and the LINKAGE assembly.
- Position the FLAT BAR – 9 HOLE on the left side of the AXLE.
- Utilize a Concentric Mate and Coincident Mate. The FLAT BAR – 9 HOLE rotates about the AXLE.

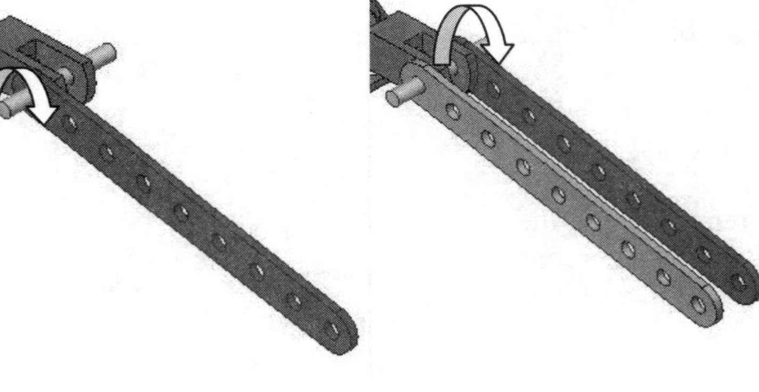

- Repeat the Concentric Mate and Coincident Mate for the second FLAT BAR – 9 HOLE. The second FLAT BAR – 9 HOLE is free to rotate about the AXLE, independent from the first FLAT BAR.
- Add a Parallel Mate between the two top narrow faces of the FLAT BAR – 9 HOLE. The two FLAT BAR – 9 HOLEs rotate together.
- Insert the second instance of the AXLE. Mate the AXLE to the right hole of the FLAT BAR – 9 HOLE.

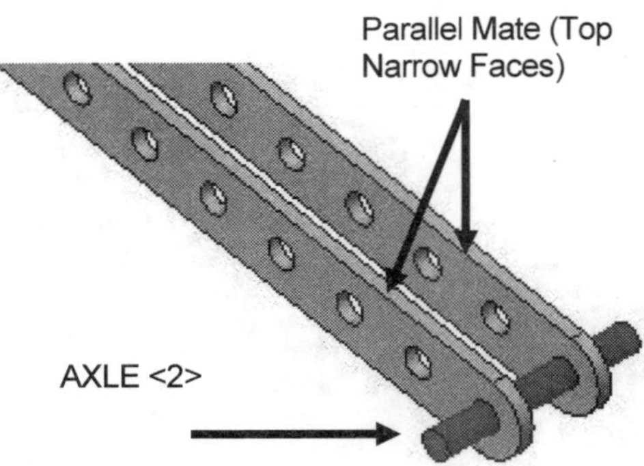

- Insert the first FLAT BAR – 3 HOLE.

- Add Mates. The back face of the FLAT BAR – 3 HOLE is coincident front face of the FLAT BAR – 9 HOLE.

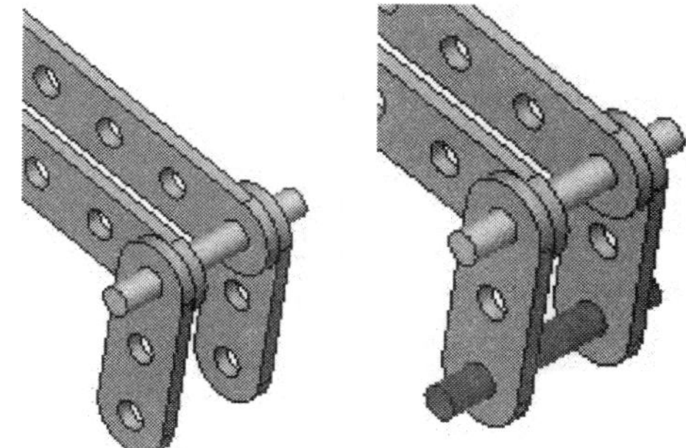

- Repeat for the second FLAT BAR – 3 HOLE. The two FLAT BAR – 3 HOLEs are free to rotate about AXLE <2>.

- Insert the third AXLE to complete the LINKAGE assembly.

Note: There is more than one mating technique to create the LINKAGE assembly. Utilize Mates that reflect the physical behavior of the assembly.

Exercise 2.3b: Physical Simulation.

The Physical Simulation tools represent the effects of motors, springs and gravity on an assembly. The Physical Simulation tools are combined with Mates and Physical Dynamics to translate and rotate components in an assembly. The Simulation toolbar contains four simulation tools: Linear Motor, Rotary Motor, Spring and Gravity.

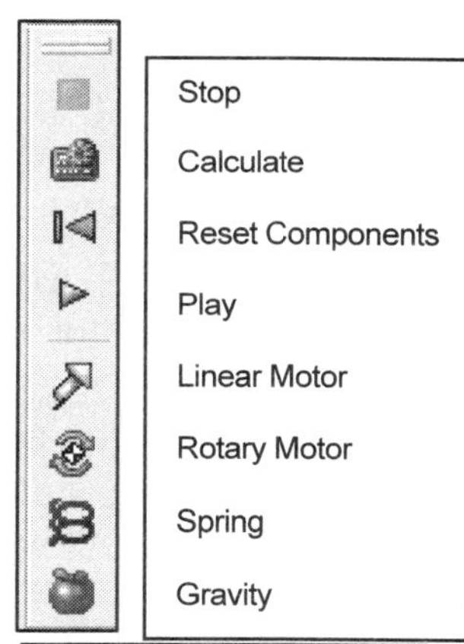

Physical Simulation Toolbar

The procedure to create a Rotary Motor Physical Simulation is as follows:

- Open an assembly.

- Review the Mates of the components that are free to translate and rotate.

- Apply a Physical Simulation tool, Rotary Motor to a face of a part in the assembly.

- Set the Velocity bar and Rotation direction.

- Press the Calculate button to determine the path of the Physical Simulation.

- Click the Play button and view the motion of the part with respect to other components in the assembly.

- Select the Stop Record button to complete the Physical Simulation.
- Select the Reset Components button to return to the original position.

Create a Physical Simulation for the LINKAGE assembly in Exercise 2.3a. The two FLATBAR – 3HOLEs are free to rotate about AXLE<2>. The FLATBAR – 9 HOLE is free to rotate about AXLE<1>.

AXLE<1>

AXLE<2>

AXLE<3>

Linkage assembly
Courtesy of
Gears Education Systems and
SMC Corporation of America.

- Position the FLATBAR-3HOLE to avoid interference.
- Utilize Rotate Component to position the AXLE<3> below AXLE <2>
- Apply a Rotary Motor Physical Simulation tool.
- Click Rotary Motor from the Simulation toolbar.

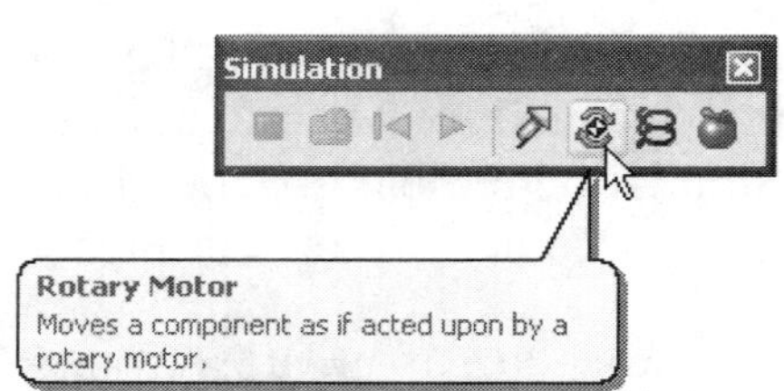

- Click the FLAT BAR – 3HOLE<1> front face. A red Rotary Motor icon is displayed.
- Click the Direction arrow button from the Rotary Motor Property Manager. The Direction arrow points counterclockwise.

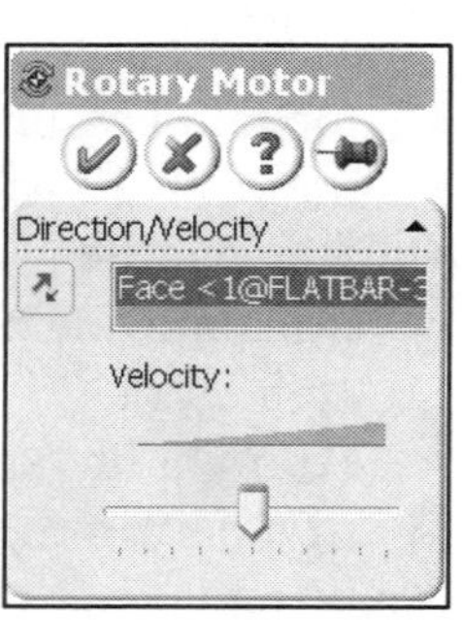

- Position the Velocity Slide bar in the middle of the PropertyManager.

- Click OK. The FLAT BAR – 3HOLE<1> rotates in a counterclockwise direction until collision with the FLAT BAR – 9 HOLE<1> component. The FLAT BAR – 9HOLE component begins to rotate in a counterclockwise direction.

- SolidWorks Animator is a separate software application required to record the animation. Load SolidWorks Animator (SolidWorks Animator is required to record the animation).

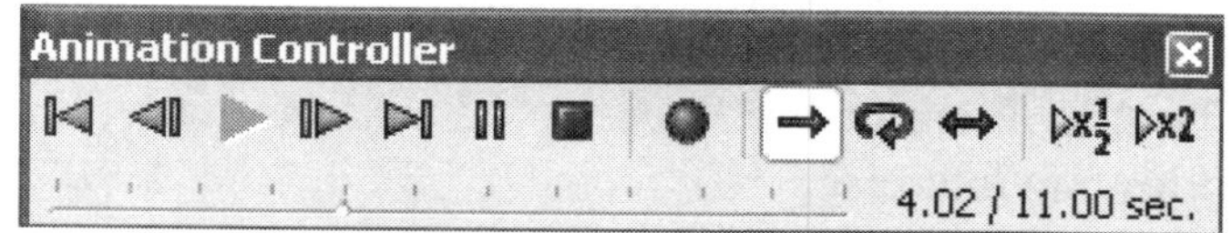

- Click Tools, Add Ins.
- Check the SolidWorks Animator check box.

Record and Save the Simulation

- Click Save. Select a File name for the .AVI file. The recording process takes a few seconds.
- Click OK to the default Microsoft Video Compression.
- Stop the Simulation. Click Stop.
- Return to SolidWorks. Click Close from the Animation Controller.

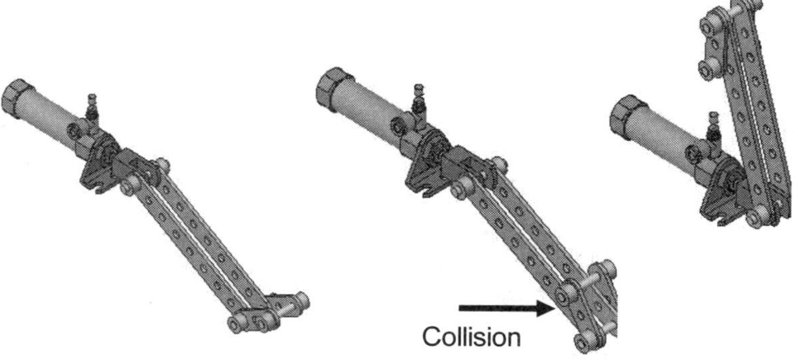

LINKAGE Assembly Simulations with SolidWorks Animator

Important: The toolbars and commands remain inactive until you close the Animation Controller.

Exercise 2.3c: Engineering Analysis.

The AXLE created in Exercise 1.5 and assembled in Exercise 2.3a is utilized in the following exercise.

- Determine the Factor of Safety, the von Mises Stress Plot and Deflection Plot utilizing COSMOSXpress.

The AXLE is fixed at both ends. A 100N load is applied along the entire cylindrical face perpendicular to the Top plane.

1. Utilize Aluminum.
2. Utilize Stainless Steel.

- Determine the modifications to the material, geometry, restraints and loading conditions that will increase the Factor of Safety in your design.

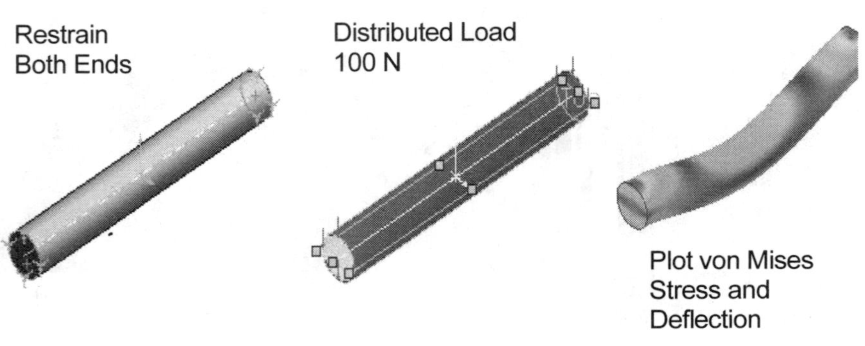

Exercise 2.3d: Exploded View and Animation.

Insert a new Exploded view for the LINKAGE assembly. The Exploded view represents how the components will be assembled.

- Create an animation of the LINKAGE assembly. Utilize the Animate collapse option.

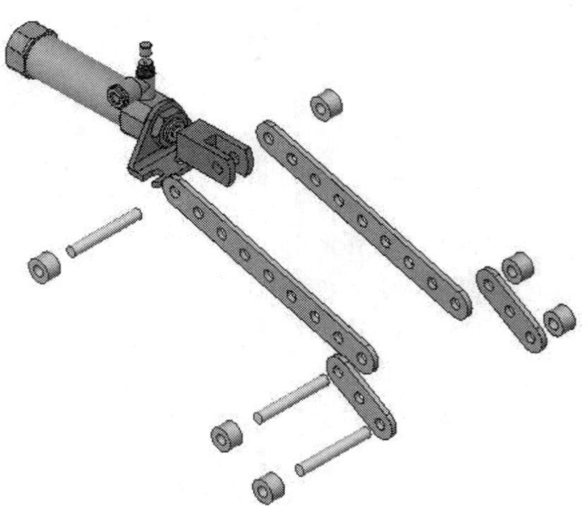

To record the animation, SolidWorks Animator is required.

- Load SolidWorks Animator
- Click Tools, Add Ins.
- Check the SolidWorks Animator check box.
- Create a collapse animation of the GUIDE-ROD assembly. Click the Animation1 tab.
- Click the Animator Wizard.
- Click Collapse.
- Click Next. Enter 20 seconds for Duration.
- Enter 0 for Start Time.
- Click Finish to view the collapse.
- Record the animation and create the .AVI file. Click Save. The Renderer is the SolidWorks screen.

Microsoft Video 1 is the Video Compression. Play the .AVI file with the Windows Media Player.

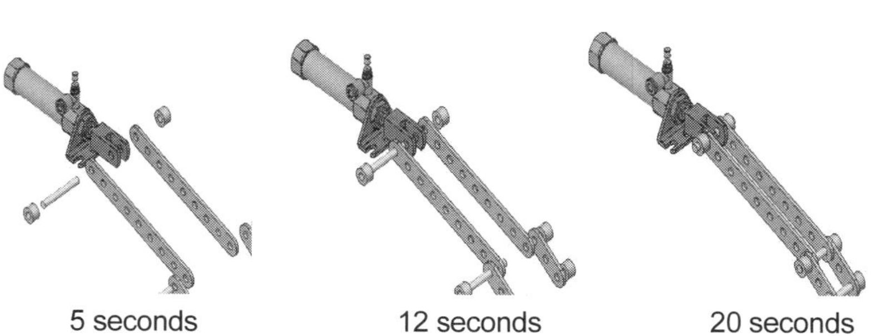

5 seconds 12 seconds 20 seconds

A manufacturing procedure can be created by combining parts and assemblies from SolidWorks and Animator in PowerPoint or HTML applications.

Immersive Design (www.immersivedesign.com) manufactures software applications to document manufacturing procedures in an automated process.

Refer to Help, Online Tutorial, SolidWorks Animator exercise for additional information.

Exercise 2.4: PNEUMATIC ON-OFF-PURGE VALVE Assembly.

Create the PNEUMATIC ON-OFF-PURGE VALVE assembly.

- The new assembly is comprised of the SERVO BRACKET and the SMC Purge Valve assembly. The SMC Purge Valve is contained on the Multimedia CD.

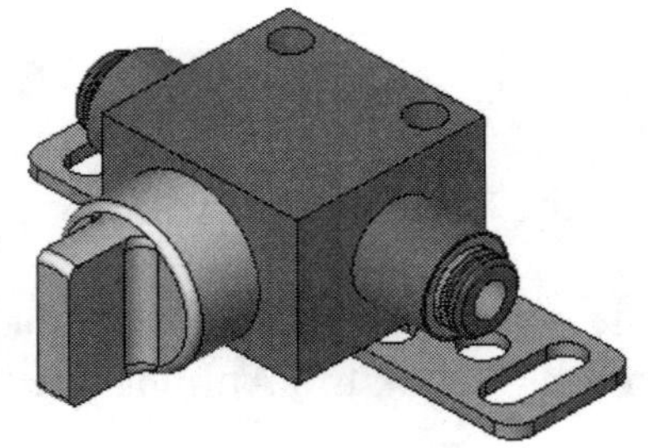

Pneumatic On-Off-Purge-Valve assembly
Component of the Pneumatic Test Module assembly

- The SERVO BRACKET part is machined from 0.06in [1.5mm] Stainless Steel flat stock. The default units are inches.

- The ∅4.2mm [.165in] Mounting Holes fasten to the back Slot Cuts of the SERVO BRACKET. The default units are millimeters.

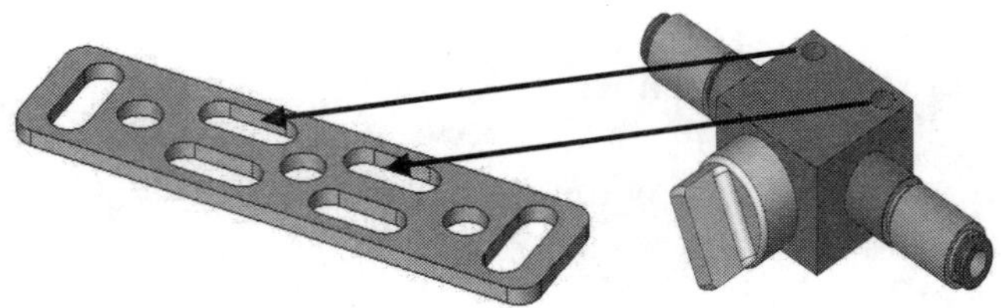

Servo Bracket Purge-Valve assembly
Courtesy of SMC Corporation of America and Gears Educational Systems

Engineers and designers work with components in multiple units such as inches and millimeters.

- Utilize Tools, Options, Document Properties, Units to check default units and precision.

The SERVO BRACKET illustration represents part dimensions, only.

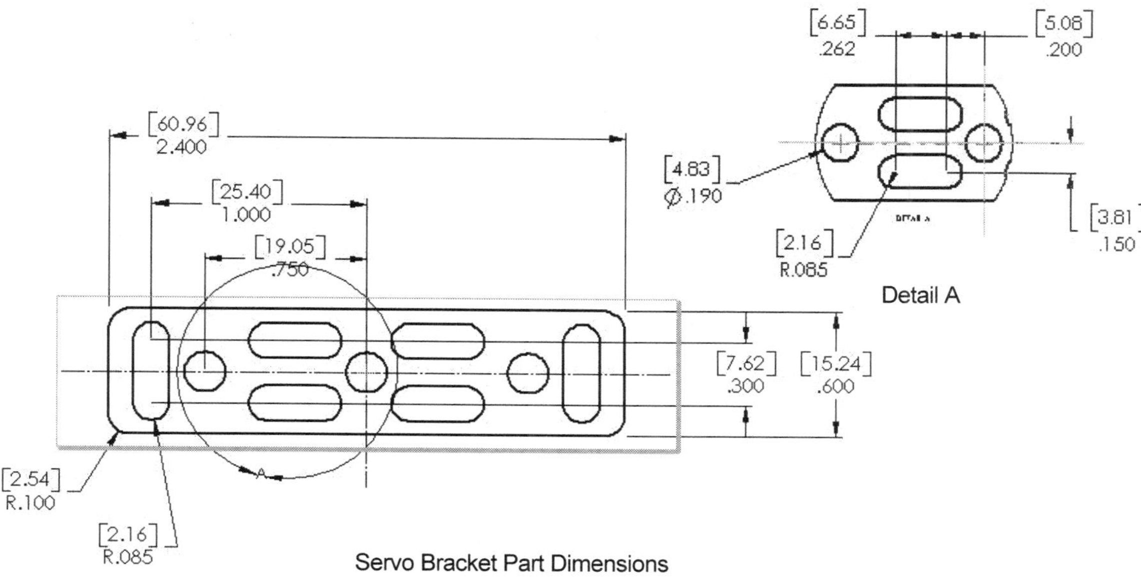

Servo Bracket Part Dimensions

- Locate the center circle at the part Origin.
- Utilize Mirror and Linear Pattern to create the features.
- Mate the Right planes to center the two components.
- Utilize a Distance Mate to align the Mounting Holes of the Purge Valve to the Slot Cuts of the SERVO BRACKET. The Shut Off Valve knob indiates the direction of flow.

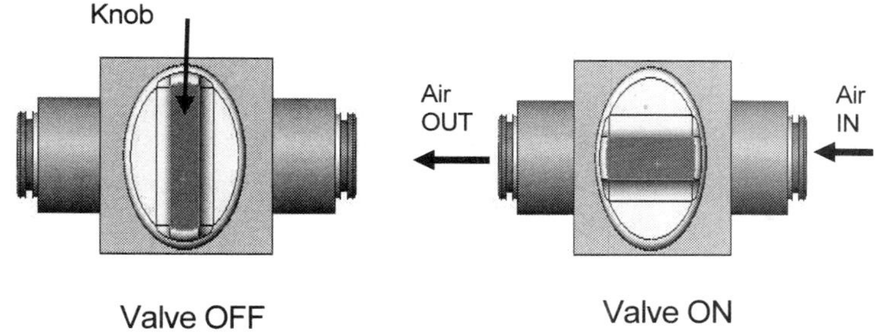

Exercise 2.5: Computer Aided Manufacturing.

How do you insure that the parts machined are the same as the parts modeled? CAMWorks, manufactured by TekSoft, Scottsdale, AZ USA (www.teksoft.com) is a fully integrated CAM (Computer Aided Manufacturing) application.

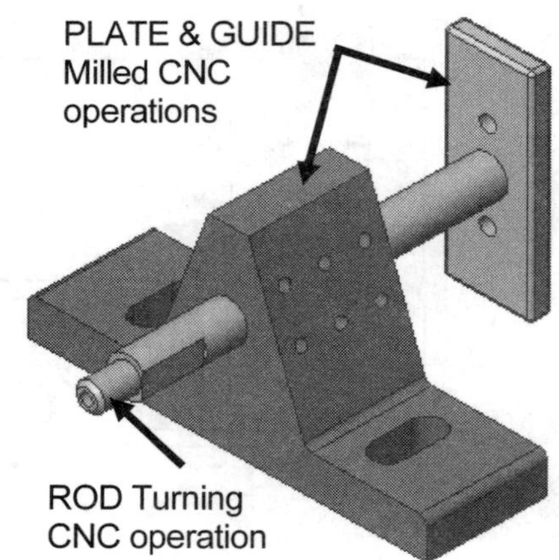

The GUIDE-ROD assembly requires Milling and Turning CNC (Computer Numerical Control) operations. CAMWorks offers knowledge-based, feature recognition and associate machining capabilities within SolidWorks.

- Research other Mill and Turning CNC Operations using the World Wide Web.

Exercise 2.6: 3-BEARING Assembly, L-SHAPE SUPPORT PLATE Part and COSMOSXpress.

In a make-buy decision process, you decide on which parts to manufacture and which parts to purchase. In assembly modeling, you decide on which parts to design and which parts to obtain from other sources.

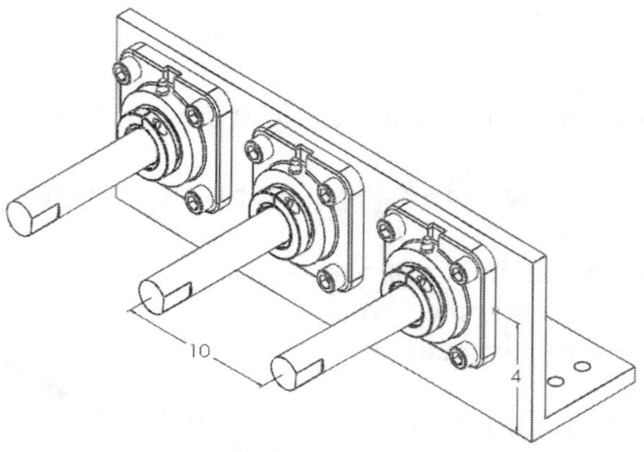

3-BEARING assembly
Model and Images
Courtesy of Emerson Power Transmission Corporation, Ithaca, NY a subsidiary of Emerson.

You now work with a team of engineers on a new project. The senior engineer has specified a steel shaft size of 1 in diameter, [25.4mm] by 12in length, [305mm] to be used in conjunction with a mounted ball bearing.

Three bearings are mounted to a support plate. Each shaft is separated by a minimum of 10 inches, [254mm]. The center of each shaft is located 4 inches, [100mm] about the bottom face of the support plate.

The senior engineer provides two key bearing requirements.

- The bearing contains a concentric collar.
- The bearing must be located in a 4-bolt flange block.

Time is critical. Obtain purchased components directly from the manufacturer, Emerson-EPT, website: http://www.emerson-ept.com.

Design the L-SHAPE SUPPORT PLATE to hold three bearings. Assemble the shaft to the bearing. Utilize SolidWorks Toolbox or create the fasteners for this project.

Note: Access is required to the World Wide Web with a valid email address to perform this exercise according to the instructions. The two components, VF4B-216 and VF4B-224 are available on the CD contained with the book.

- Size and download two components for the 3-BEARING assembly.
- Obtain the BEARING from EMERSON-EPT.
- Invoke a web browser.
- Enter the URL: www.emerson-ept.com.
- Enter your email address and password. If you are a new user to the web site, click the Register button and enter the requested information. You will be emailed with the required information.
- Select the Search area. Enter VF4B-216.
- Click VF4B-216 to display the part details. The Part Number and Description are displayed.
- View the 3D Image and display the file formats to download.
- Click the CAD button.
- Select SolidWorks Part/Assembly-2006
- Click the Download button.

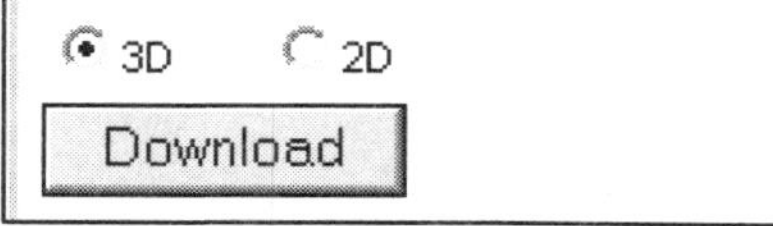

- Save the zipped file EPTCAD-VF4B-216.SLDPRT to the ENGDESIGN-W-SOLIDWORKS\VENDOR-COMPONENTS file folder. The zipped SolidWorks file is downloaded to your computer.

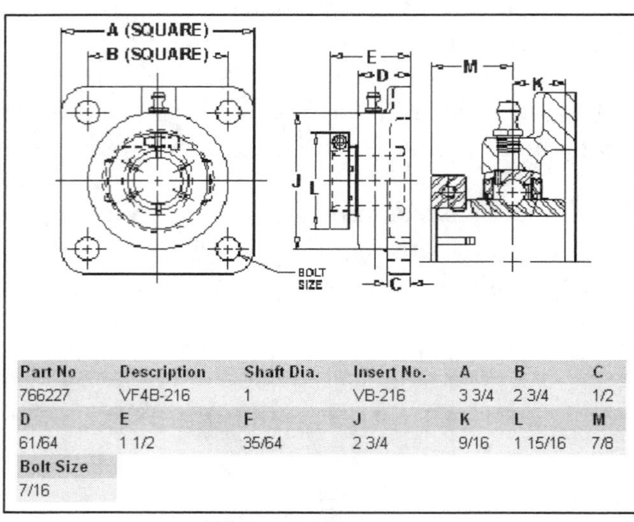

Part No	Description	Shaft Dia.	Insert No.	A	B	C
766227	VF4B-216	1	VB-216	3 3/4	2 3/4	1/2
D	**E**	**F**	**J**	**K**	**L**	**M**
61/64	1 1/2	35/64	2 3/4	9/16	1 15/16	7/8
Bolt Size						
7/16						

- Search and download the VF4B-224 part. Save the zipped file EPTCAD-VF4B-224 in the VENDOR-COMPONENT folder.
- Close the 3D View window.
- Utilize the bolt size required in the design.
- Unzip the files.
- Create the 3-BEARING assembly. The Shaft diameter requires a Close Running Fit H8/f7. Click Fit from the Tolerance/Precision box.
- Perform a static COSMOSXpress analysis.
- A 500lb (2224N) load is applied to the end of the 12in shaft fixed at the bearing. The engineer requires a factor of safety greater than 2.

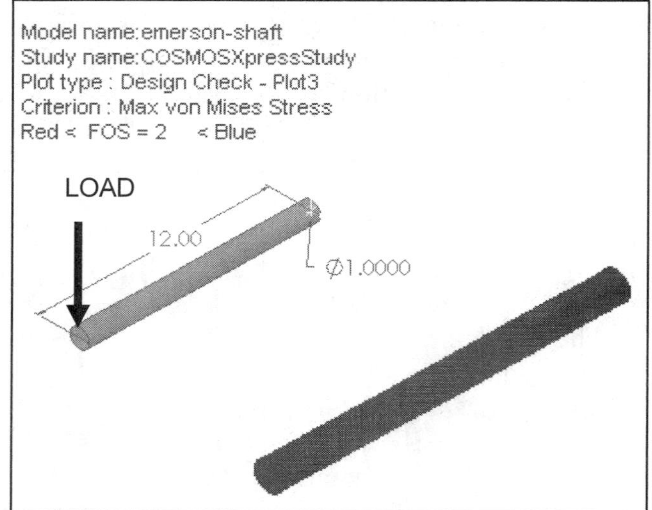

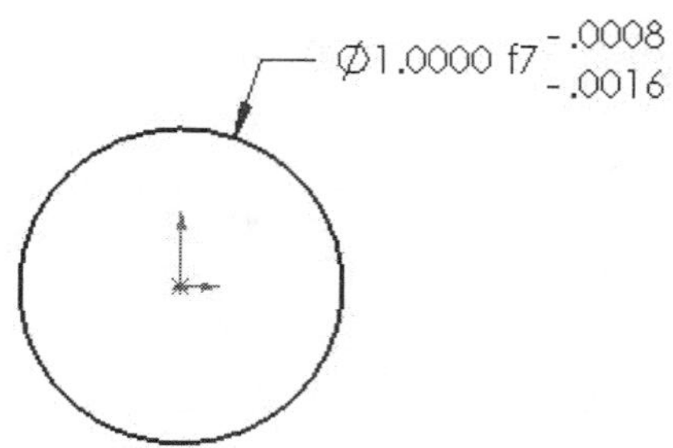

- Increase the shaft diameter from 1in (25.4mm) to 1.5in.

- Locate a 4Bolt Flange Ball Bearing for a 1.5in shaft.

- Identify the key dimensions in the new 4Bolt Flange Ball Bearing affect the overall assembly. Dimensions are provided in the table below.

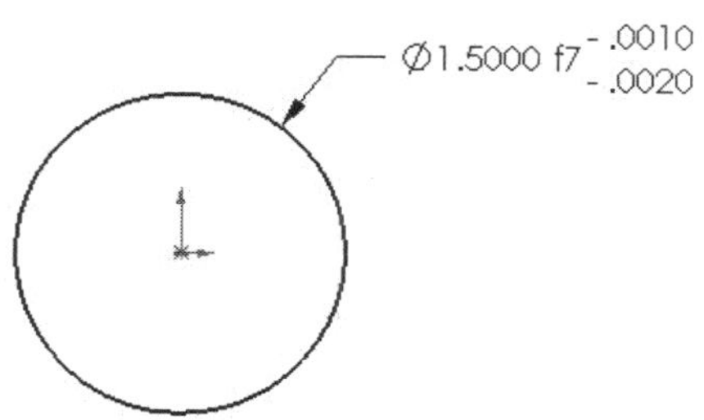

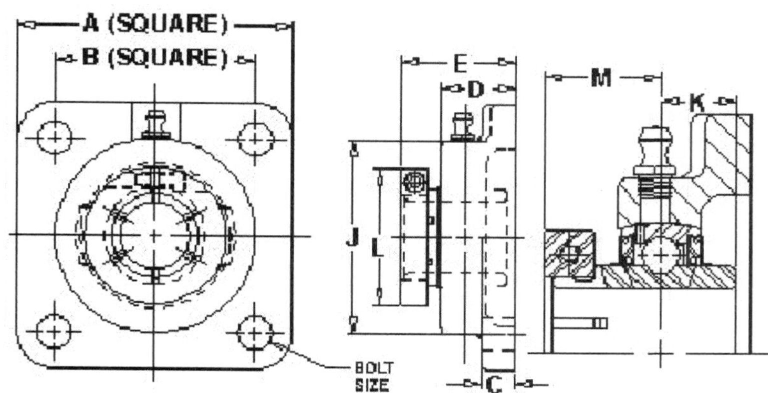

Part No	Description	Shaft Dia.	Insert No.	A	B	C
766234	VF4B-224	1.5000	VB-224	5 1/8	4	5/8
D	**E**	**F**	**J**	**K**	**L**	**M**
1 19/64	2 5/64	25/32	4 1/8	3/4	2 11/16	1 1/4
Bolt Size						
1/2						

Notes:

Project 3

Fundamentals of Drawing

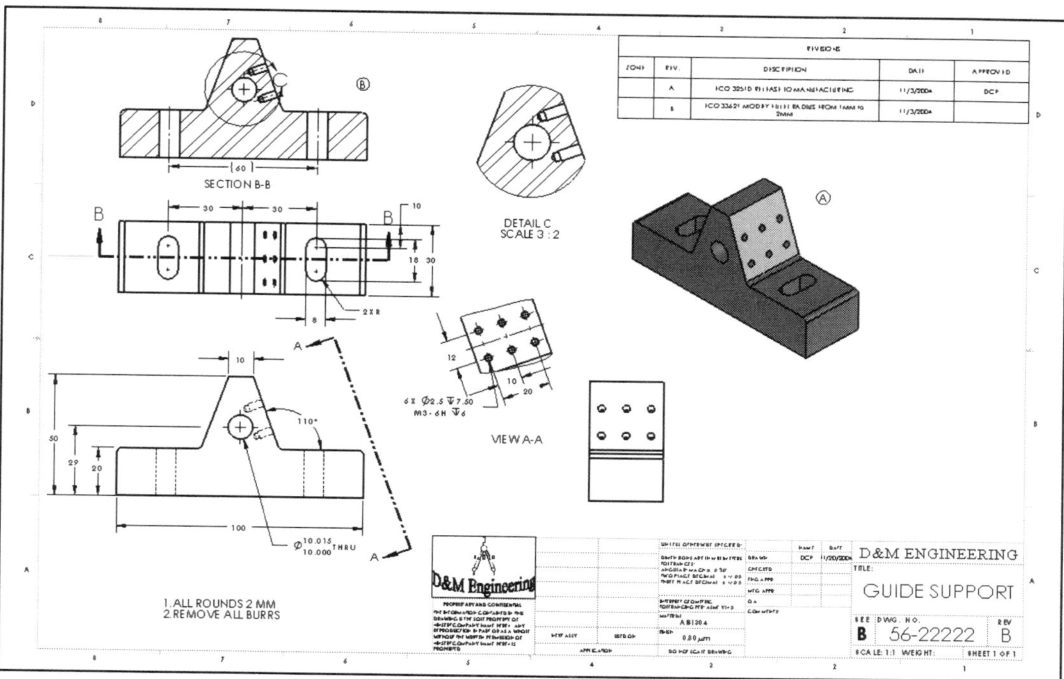

Below are the desired outcomes and usage competencies based on the completion of Project 3.

Project Desired Outcomes:	Usage Competencies:
• B-ANSI-MM Drawing Template.	• Ability to create a Drawing Template with Document Properties and Sheet Properties.
• CUSTOM-B Sheet Format.	• Aptitude to create a Sheet Format with Title block and company logo.
• GUIDE Drawing.	• An understanding of displaying Standard, Auxiliary, Detail and Section Views and the skill to insert, create and modify dimensions and annotations.
• A GUIDE-ROD assembly drawing with a Bill of Materials.	• Knowledge to develop and incorporate a Bill of Materials with Custom Properties.

Notes:

Project 3-Fundamentals of Drawing

Project Objective

Provide an understanding of Drawing Templates, part drawings, assembly drawings, details and annotations.

Create a B-ANSI-MM Drawing Template. Create the CUSTOM-B Sheet Format. The Drawing Template contains Document Property settings. The Sheet Format contains a company logo, Title block, Revision table and sheet information.

Create the GUIDE drawing. Display Standard, Section, Auxiliary and Detail drawing views. Insert, create and modify dimensions.

Create a GUIDE-ROD assembly drawing with a Bill of Materials.

Obtain knowledge to develop and incorporate a Bill of Materials with Custom Properties.

On the completion of this project, you will be able to:

- Create a new Drawing Template.
- Generate a customized Sheet Format with Custom Properties.
- Open, Close and Save Drawings.
- Produce a Bill of Materials with Custom Properties.
- Insert and position views on a drawing.
- Set the Dimension Layer.
- Insert, move and modify dimensions from the part.
- Insert Annotations: Center Mark, Centerline, Notes, Hole Callouts and Balloons.
- Use Edit Sheet Format and Edit Sheet.
- Insert a Revision table.
- Modify the dimension scheme.
- Create a parametric drawing note.
- Link notes in the Title block to SolidWorks properties.
- Rename parts and drawings.

Project Situation

The individual parts and assembly are completed. What is the next step? You are required to create drawings for various internal departments, namely: production, purchasing, engineering, inspection and manufacturing.

Each drawing contains unique information and specific footnotes. Example: A manufacturing drawing would require information on assembly, Bill of Materials, fabrication techniques and references to other relative documents.

Project Overview

Generate two drawings in this project:

- A GUIDE drawing with a customized Sheet Format.
- A GUIDE-ROD assembly drawing.

The GUIDE drawing contains three Standard Views, (Principle Views) and an Isometric View.

Do you remember what the three Principle Standard Views are? They are: Top, Front and Right side.

Three new views are introduced in this project: Detailed View, Section View and Auxiliary View. Orient the views to fit the drawing sheet. Incorporate the GUIDE dimensions into the drawing.

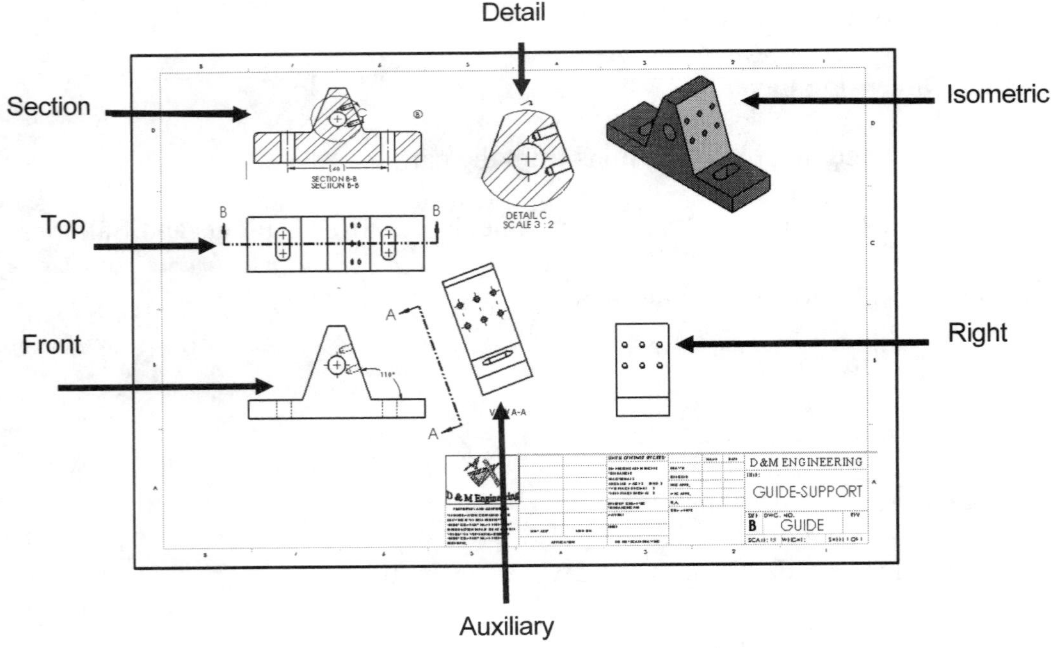

The GUIDE-ROD assembly drawing contains an Exploded View.

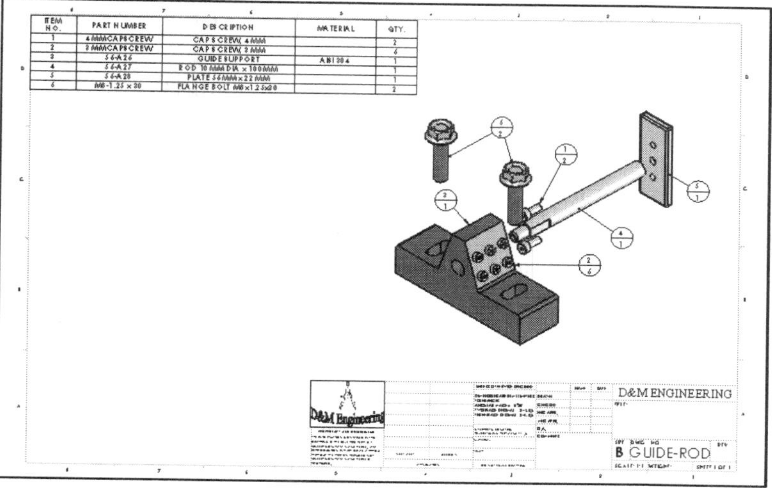

The drawing contains a Bill of Materials and balloon text.

Both drawings utilize a custom Sheet Format containing a company logo, Title block and sheet information.

There are two major design modes used to develop a drawing:

- Edit Sheet Format.
- Edit Sheet.

The Edit Sheet Format mode provides the ability to:

- Change the Title block size and text headings.
- Incorporate a company logo.
- Add a drawing, design or company text.

The Edit Sheet mode provides the ability to:

- Add or modify views.
- Add or modify dimensions.
- Add or modify text.

Drawing Template and Sheet Format

The foundation of a SolidWorks drawing is the Drawing Template. Drawing size, drawing standards, company information, manufacturing and or assembly requirements, units and other properties are defined in the Drawing Template.

The Sheet Format is incorporated into the Drawing Template. The Sheet Format contains the border, Title block information, revision block information, company name and or logo information, Custom Properties and SolidWorks Properties. Custom Properties and SolidWorks Properties are shared values between documents.

Utilize the standard B-size Drawing Template with no Sheet Format. Set the Units, Font and Layers. Modify a B-size Sheet Format to create a Custom Sheet Format and Custom Drawing Template.

1. Set Sheet Properties and Document Properties for the Drawing Template.
2. Add Custom Properties: Company Name, Tolerance Values and Company Logo to the Sheet Format.
3. Save the Custom Drawing Template and Custom Sheet Format in the MY-TEMPLATE file folder.

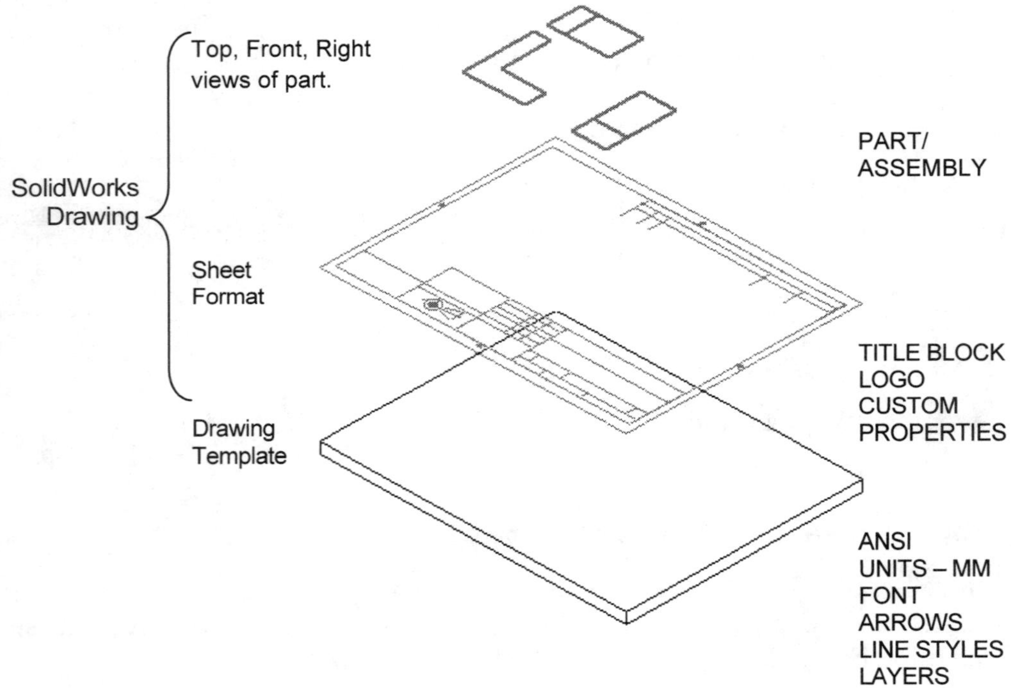

Views from the part or assembly are inserted into the SolidWorks Drawing.

A Third Angle Projection scheme is illustrated in this project.

For non-ANSI dimension standards, the dimensioning techniques are the same, even if the displayed arrows and text size are different.

For printers supporting millimeter paper sizes, select A3-Landscape (420mm x 297mm).

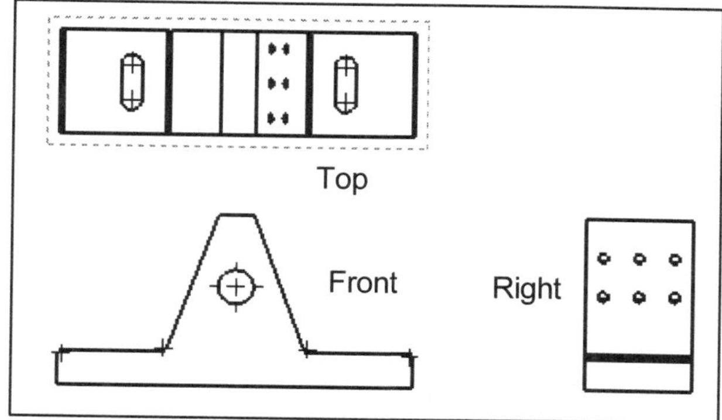

Third Angle Projection Scheme

The default Drawing Templates with Sheet Format displayed contain predefined Title block Notes linked to Custom Properties and SolidWorks Properties.

Activity: Drawing Template

Close all documents.

1) Click **Window**, **Close All** from the Main menu.

Open a B-size drawing.

2) Click **File**, **New** from the Main menu.

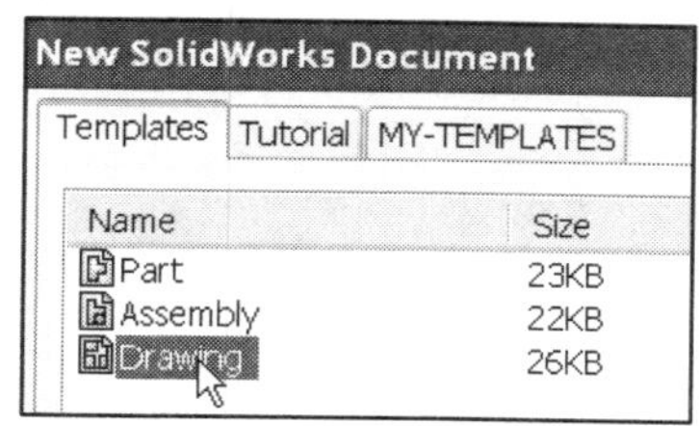

3) Double-click **Drawing** from the Templates tab.

4) Select **B-Landscape** from the Standard Sheet Size drop down list.

5) Uncheck **Display sheet format**.

6) Click **OK**.

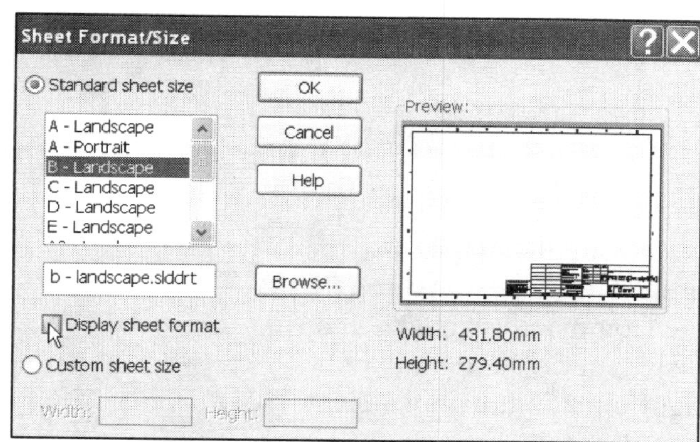

7) Click **Cancel** from the Model View PropertyManager.

Note: If the Start command when creating new drawing option is checked, the Model View PropertyManager is selected by default.

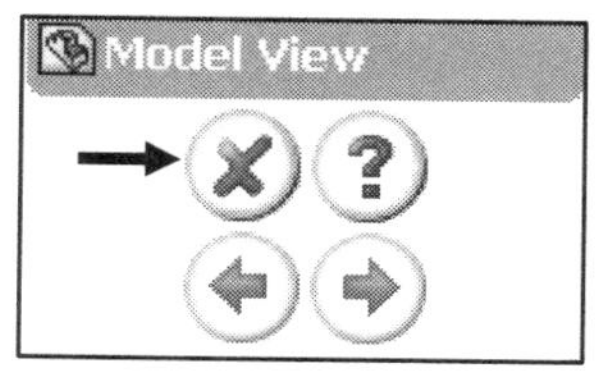

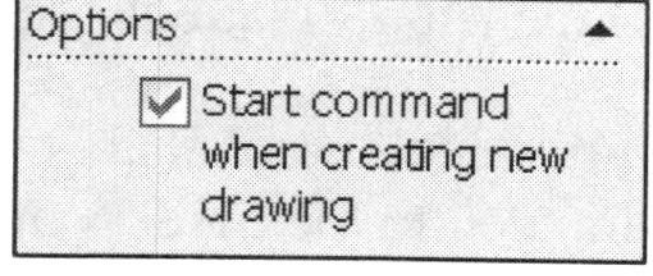

The B-Landscape Standard Sheet Size is displayed in the Graphics window. The sheet border defines the drawing size, 17" x 11", (431.8mm x 279.4mm). Draw1 is the default drawing name. Sheet1 is the default first sheet name. The Control Area alternates between Drawings, Sketch and Annotations toolbars. The Model View PropertyManager is selected by default.

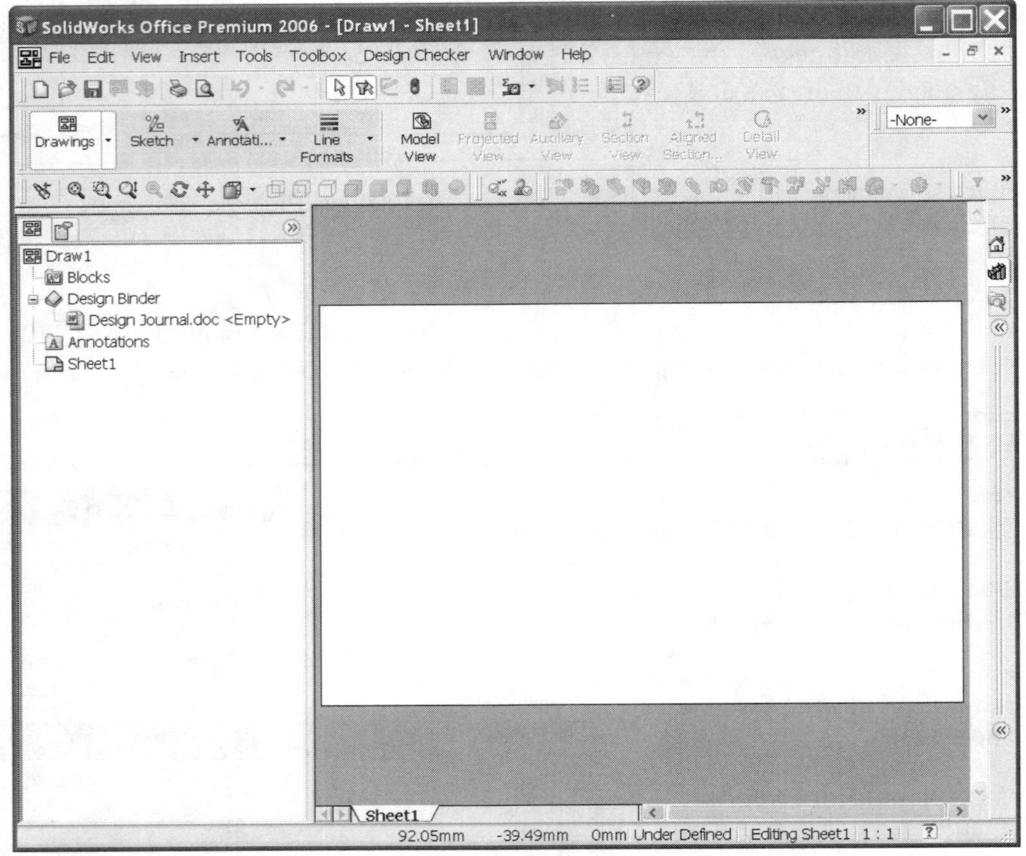

Note: Commands in this project are accessed through the Command Manager. To display individual toolbars, right-click in the gray area and check the Drawing, Annotation, Sketch, or Dimension/Relations toolbar.

Individual toolbars are dragged to the borders of the Graphics window. Utilize the CommandManager or individual toolbars.

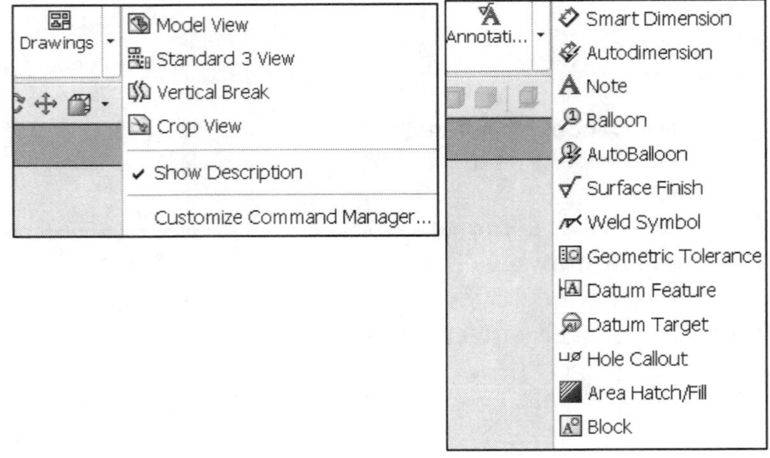

Set the Sheet Properties and Document Properties for the Drawing Template. Sheet Properties control Sheet Size, Sheet Scale and Type of Projection. Document Properties control the display of dimensions, annotations and symbols in the drawing.

Sheet (Sheet1)
Edit Sheet Format
Add Sheet...
Delete
Properties...

Set Sheet Properties.

8) Right-click in the **Graphics window**.

9) Click **Properties** Properties... . The Sheet Properties are displayed.

10) Select Sheet Scale **1:1**.

11) Select the **Third Angle** for Type of Projection.

12) Click **OK**.

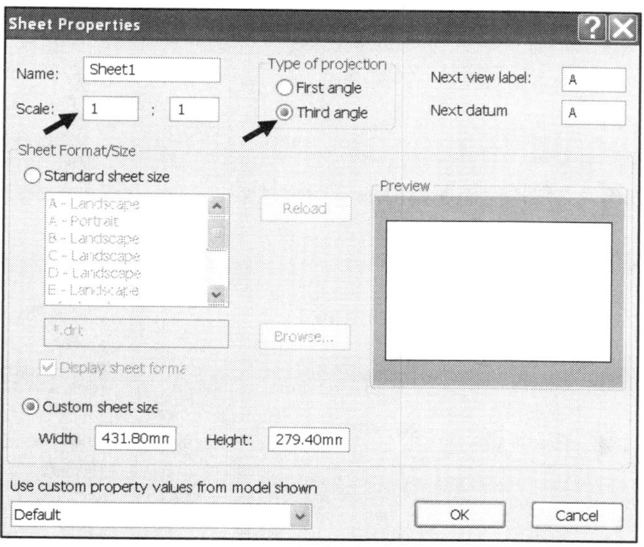

Set Document Properties.

13) Click **Tools**, **Options**, **Document Properties** tab from the Main menu.

14) Click **ANSI** for Dimensioning Standard.

15) Click **Units**.

16) Select **MMGS** for Unit system.

17) Enter **2** for Decimal places.

18) Enter **0** for Angular units Decimal places.

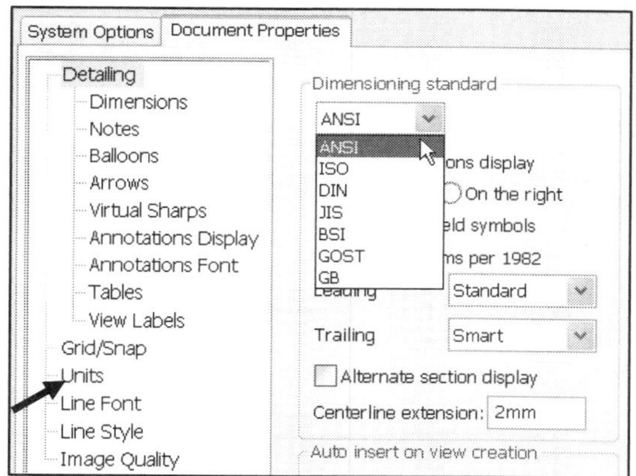

Detailing options provide the ability to address: dimensioning standards, text style, center marks, extension lines, arrow styles, tolerance and precision.

There are numerous text styles and sizes available in SolidWorks. Companies develop drawing format standards and use specific text height for Metric and English drawings.

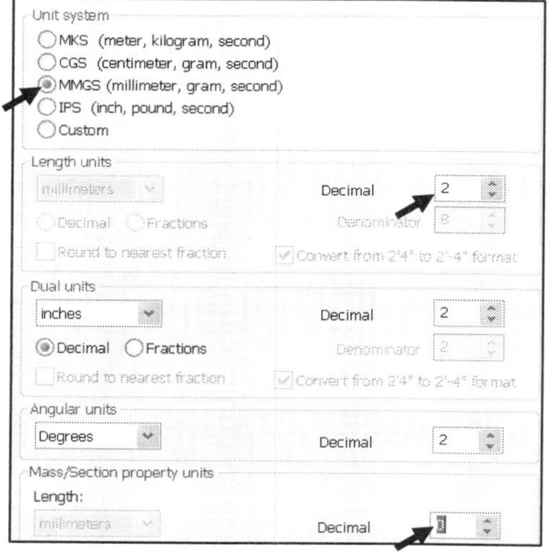

Utilize the Option icon from the Standard toolbar to quickly access Tools, Options.

Numerous engineering drawings use the following format:

- Font: Century Gothic – All capital letters.
- Text height: .125in. or 3mm for drawings up to B Size, 17in. x 22in.
- Text height: .156in. or 5mm for drawings larger than B Size, 17in x 22in.
- Arrow heads: Solid filled with a 1:3 ratio of arrow width to arrow height.

Set the dimension font height.

19) Click **Annotations Font**.

20) Click **Dimension**.

21) Click the **Units** button.

22) Enter **3.0** for Height.

23) Click **OK**.

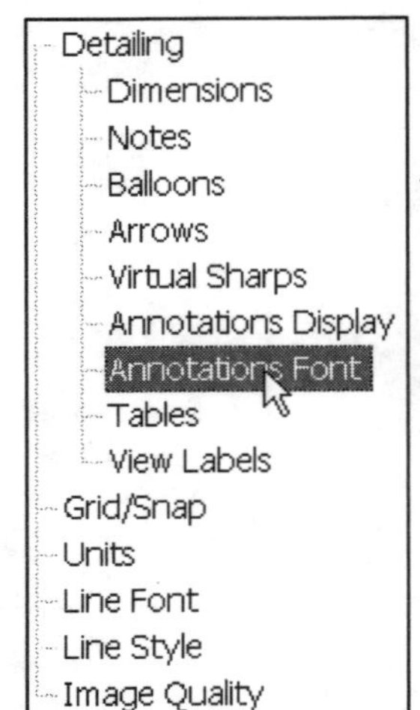

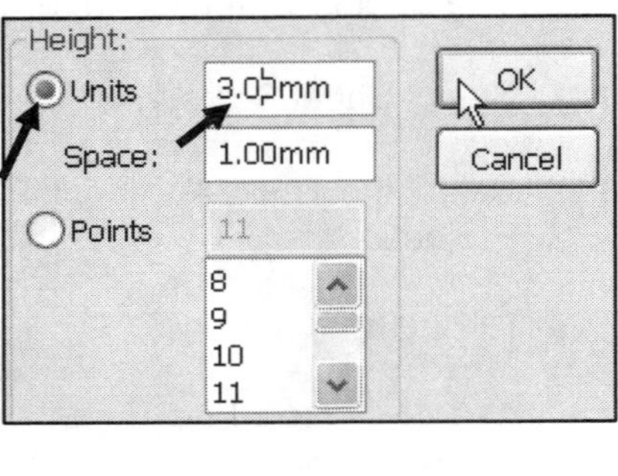

Change the Arrow Height.

24) Click the **Arrows** entry in the Documents Property.

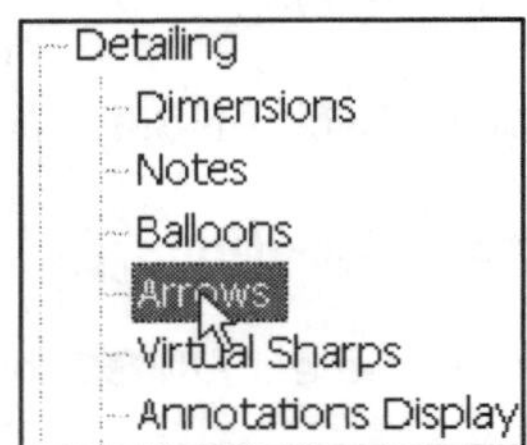

25) Enter **1** for arrow Height.

26) Enter **3** for arrow Width.

27) Enter **6** for arrow Length.

Set Section/View size.

28) Enter **2** for arrow Height.

29) Enter **6** for arrow Width.

30) Enter **12** for arrow Length.

31) Click **OK**.

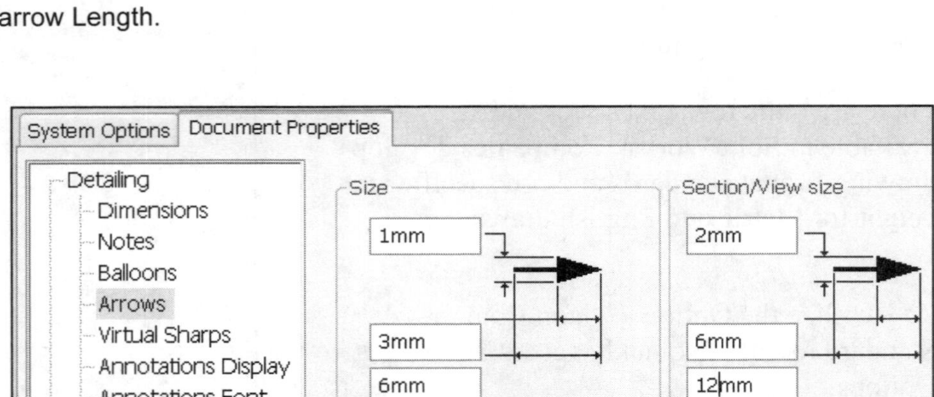

Drawing Layers organize dimensions, annotations and geometry. Create a new drawing layer to contain dimensions and notes. Create a second drawing layer to contain hidden feature dimensions.

Select the Light Bulb to turn On/Off Layers. Dimensions placed on the hidden are turned on and off for clarity and can be recalled for parametric annotations.

Display the Layer toolbar.

32) **Right-click** in the gray area to the right of the word Help in Main menu. Check **Layer** if Layer toolbar is not active.

33) Click the **Layer Properties** file folder from the Layer toolbar. The Layers dialog box is displayed.

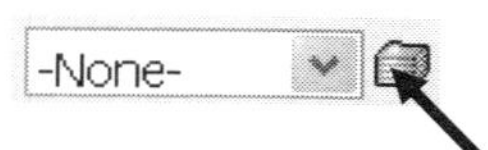

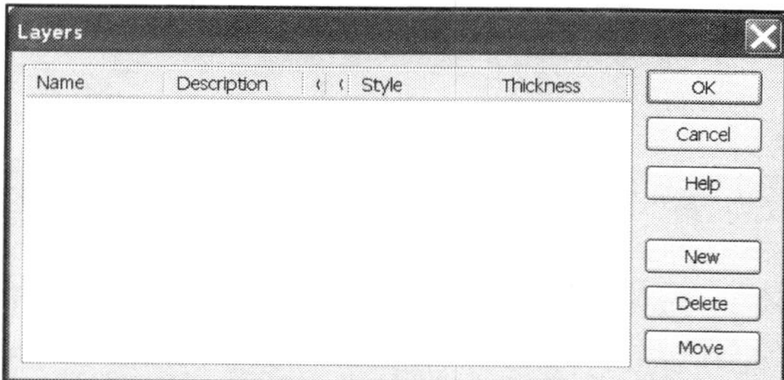

Create the Dimension Layer.

34) Click the **New** button. Enter **Dims** in the Name column.

35) **Double-click** under the Description column. Enter **Dimensions** in the Description column.

Create the Notes Layer.

36) Click the **New** button. Enter **Notes** for Name. **Double-click** under the Description column. Enter **General Notes** for Description.

Create the Hidden Dims Layer.

37) Click the **New** button. Enter **Hidden Dims** for Name. **Double-click** under the Description column. Enter **Hidden Insert Dimensions** for Description.

Dimensions placed on the Hidden Dims Layer are not displayed on the drawing until the Hidden Dims Layer status is On. Set the Layer Color to locate dimensions on this layer easily.

Turn the Hidden Insert Dimension Layer Off.

38) Click **On/Off**. The light bulb is displayed in light gray.

Set the Layer Color.

39) Click the **small black square** in the Hidden Dims row.

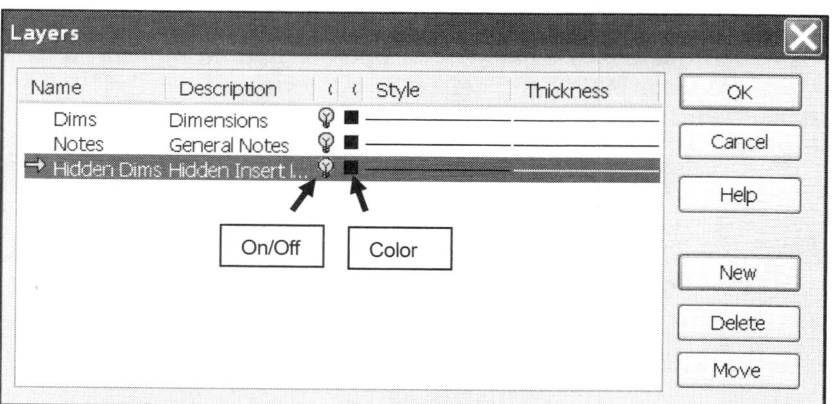

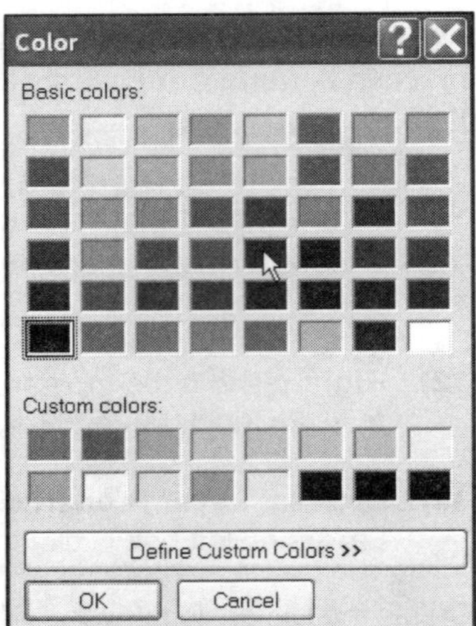

Select a Color Swatch.

40) Select **Dark Blue**.

41) Click **OK**.

42) Click **OK** from the Layers dialog box.

The current Layer is Hidden Dims. Set the current Layer to None before saving the Drawing Template.

Set None for Layer.

43) Click the **Layer drop down arrow**.

44) Click **None**. None is displayed in the Layer toolbar.

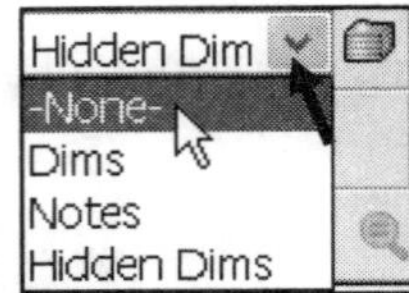

The Drawing Template contains the drawing Size, Document Properties and Layers. The Dimensioning standard is ANSI and the Units are in millimeters. The current Layer is set to None. The Drawing Template requires a Sheet Format. The Sheet Format contains Title block information. The Title block contains vital part or assembly information. Each company may have a unique version of a Title block.

Sheet Format and Title block

The Sheet Format contains the Title block, Revision block, Company logo and Custom Properties. The Title block contains text fields linked to System Properties and Custom Properties.

System Properties are determined from the SolidWorks documents. Custom Property values are assigned to named variables. Save time. Utilize System Properties and define Custom Properties in your Sheet Formats.

System Properties Linked to fields in default Sheet Formats:	**Custom Properties of drawings linked to fields in default Sheet Formats:**		**Custom Properties of parts and assemblies linked to fields in default Sheet Formats:**
SW-File Name (in DWG. NO. field):	CompanyName:	EngineeringApproval:	Description (in TITLE field):
SW-Sheet Scale:	CheckedBy:	EngAppDate:	Weight:
SW-Current Sheet:	CheckedDate:	ManufacturingApproval:	Material:
SW-Total Sheets:	DrawnBy:	MfgAppDate:	Finish:
	DrawnDate:	QAApproval:	Revision:
	EngineeringApproval:	QAAppDate:	

Utilize the standard landscape B Sheet Format (17in. x 11in.) or the standard-A3 Sheet Format (420mm x 297mm) to create a Custom Sheet Format.

Activity: Sheet Format and Title block

Display the standard B landscape Sheet Format.

45) Right-click in the **Graphics window**.

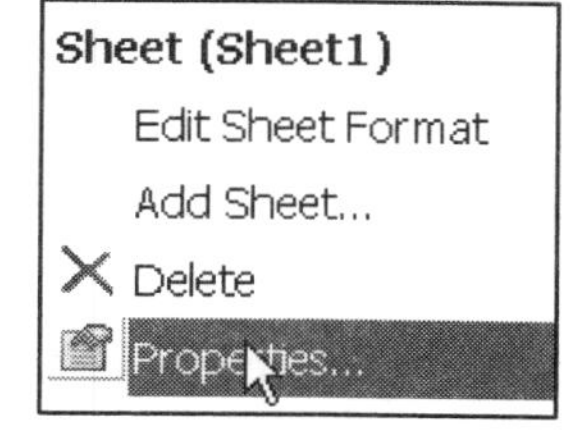

46) Click **Properties**. The Sheet Properties dialog box is displayed.

47) Click **Standard sheet size**.

48) Select **B-landscape**.

49) Check **Display sheet format**. The default Sheet Format, B-landscape.slddrt is displayed.

50) Click **OK**.

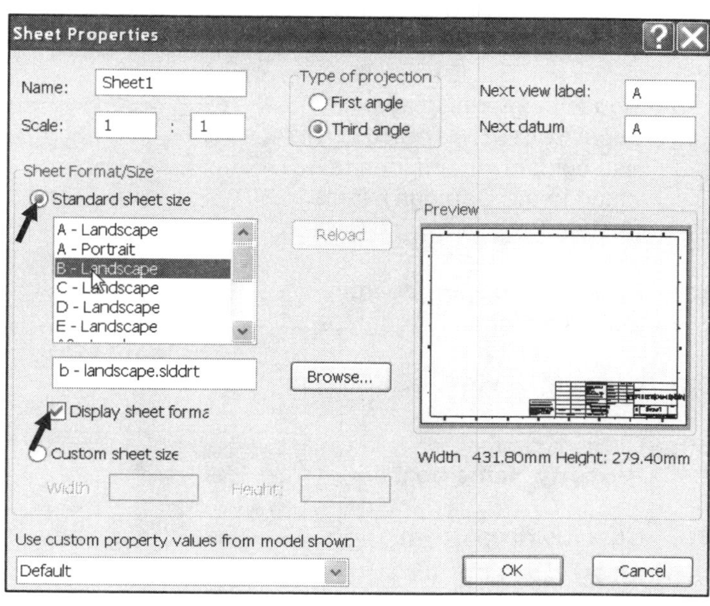

The default Sheet Format is displayed in the Graphics window. The FeatureManager displays Draw1, Sheet 1.

A Drawing contains two modes:

1. Edit Sheet.

2. Edit Sheet Format.

Insert views and dimensions in the Edit Sheet mode.

Modify the Sheet Format text, lines or Title block information in the Edit Sheet Format mode.

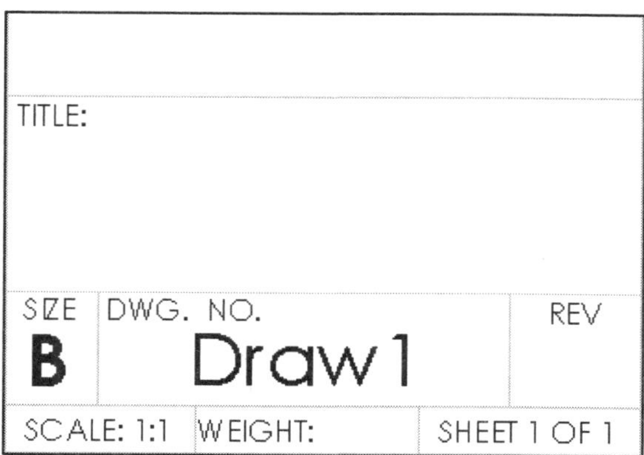

The CompanyName Custom Property is located in the Title block above the TITLE box. There is no value defined for CompanyName. A small text box indicates an empty field. Define a value for the Custom Property CompanyName. Example: D&M ENGINEERING.

Sheet (Sheet1)
Edit Sheet Format
Add Sheet...
Delete
Properties...

Activate the Edit Sheet Format Mode.

51) Right-click in the **Graphics window**.

52) Click **Edit Sheet Format**. The Title block lines turn blue.

View the right side of the Title block.

53) Click **Zoom to Area** .

54) **Zoom in** on the Sheet Format Title block.

55) Click **Zoom to Area** to deactivate.

Define CompanyName Custom Property.

56) Position the **mouse pointer** in the middle of the box above the TITLE box. The mouse pointer displays Sheet Format1. The box also contains the hidden text, linked to the CompanyName Custom Property.

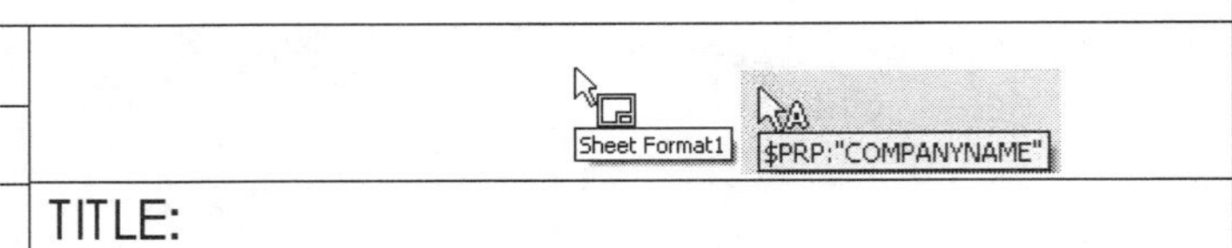

57) Click **File**, **Properties** from the Main menu.

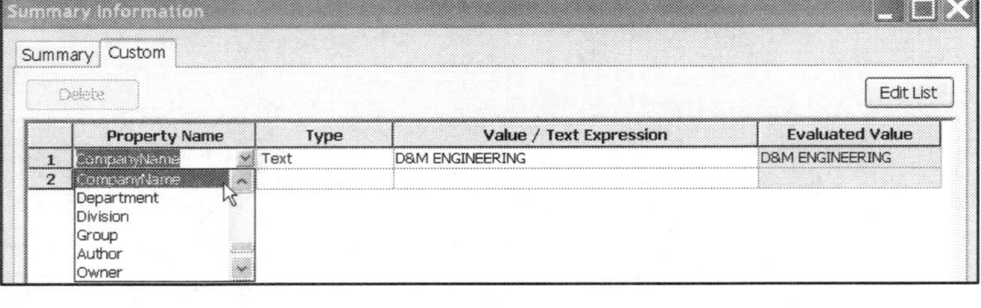

58) Click the **Custom** tab.

59) Click inside the **Property Name box**.

60) Click the **drop down arrow** in the PropertyName box.

61) Select **CompanyName** from the Property List.

62) Enter **D&M ENGINEERING** (or your company name) in the Value/Text Expression box. The CompanyName is displayed in the Evaluated Value box. Click **OK**. The Custom Property, "$PRP:COMPANYNAME", Value "D&M ENGINEERING" is displayed in the Title block.

Change the font size.

63) Double-click **D&M ENGINEERING**.

64) Click the **drop down arrows** to set the Text Font and Height from the Formatting toolbar. Click the **Style buttons** and **Justification buttons** to modify the selected text.

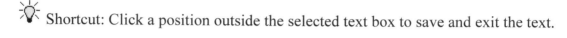

65) Click **OK** from the Note PropertyManager.

Shortcut: Click a position outside the selected text box to save and exit the text.

The Tolerance block is located in the Title block. The Tolerance block provides information to the manufacturer on the minimum and maximum variation for each dimension on the drawing. If a specific tolerance or note is provided on the drawing, the specific tolerance or note will override the information in the Tolerance block.

General tolerance values are based on the design requirements and the manufacturing process.

Create Sheet Formats for different parts types. Example: sheet metal parts, plastic parts and high precision machined parts. Create Sheet Formats for each category of parts that are manufactured with unique sets of Title block notes.

Modify the Tolerance block in the Sheet Format for ASME Y14.5 machined, millimeter parts. Delete unnecessary text. The FRACTIONAL text refers to inches. The BEND text refers to sheet metal parts. The Three Decimal Place text is not required for this millimeter part.

Modify the Tolerance Note.

66) Click and drag the **horizontal slider bar** to the left until the Tolerance block is displayed.

67) Double-click the text **INTERPRET GEOMETRIC TOLERANCING PER:**

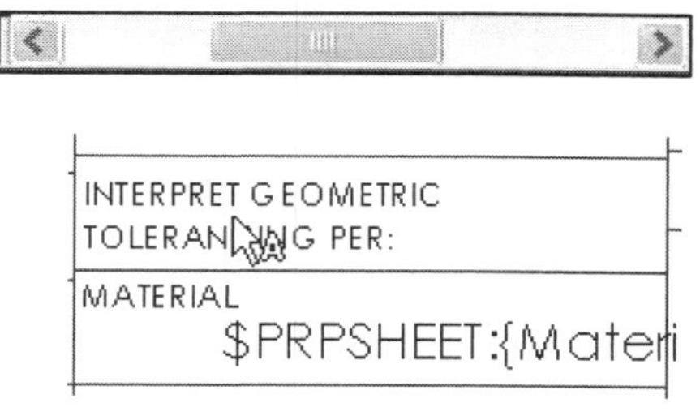

68) Enter **ASME Y14.5**. Click **OK** from the Note PropertyManager.

69) Right-click the **Tolerance block** text.

70) Click **Properties**.

71) Delete the text **INCHES**.

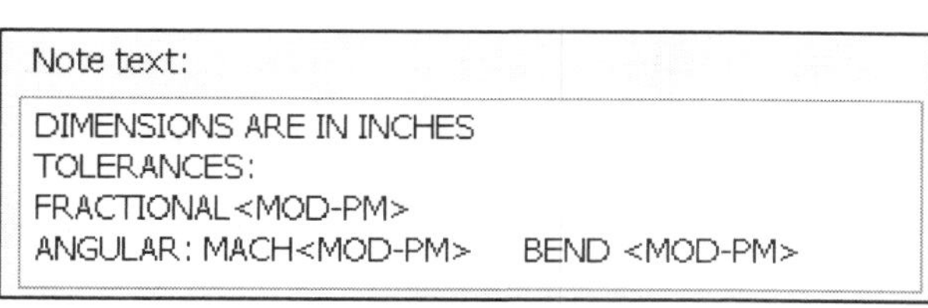

72) Enter **MILLIMETERS**.

73) Delete the lines **FRACTIONAL <MOD-PM>**.

74) Delete the text **BEND <MOD-PM>**.

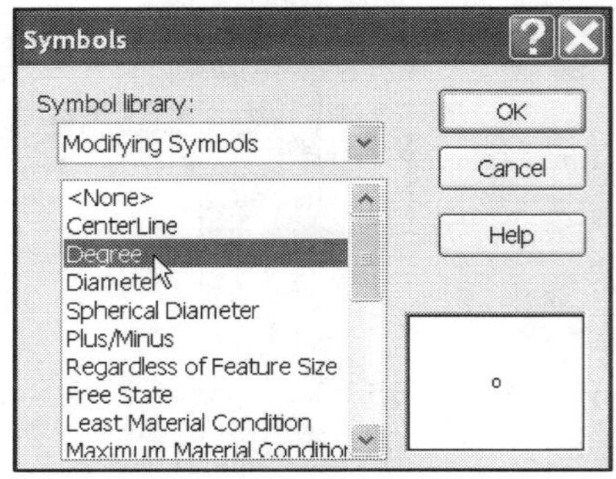

Enter ANGULAR tolerance.

75) Click a **position** at the end of the ANGULAR: MACH<MOD-PM> line.

76) Enter **0**. Click **Add Symbol** Add Symbol... . Select **Degree** from the Modifying Symbols library.

77) Click **OK**. Enter **30'** for minutes of a degree.

Modify the TWO and THREE PLACE DECIMAL LINES.

78) Delete the **TWO** and **THREE PLACE DECIMAL lines.**

79) Enter **ONE PLACE DECIMAL <MOD-PM> 0.5**.

80) Enter **TWO PLACE DECIMAL <MOD-PM> 0.15**.

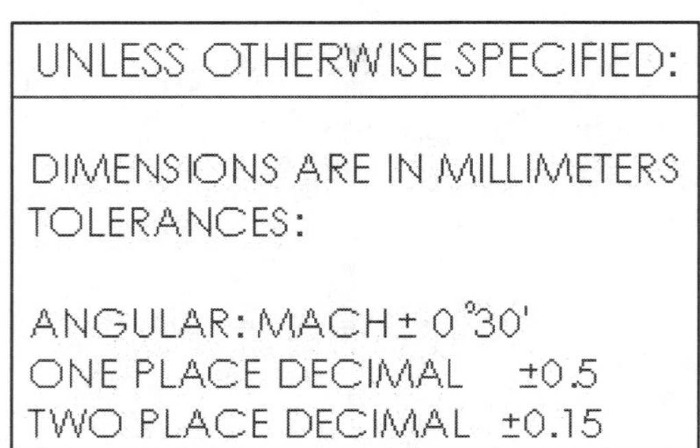

81) Click **OK** from the Note PropertyManager.

Save Draw1.

82) Press the **f** key.

83) Click **Save** .

Note: Draw1 is the default drawing file name. This name is temporary. In the next activity, invoke Microsoft Word. Always save before selecting another software application.

Various symbols are available through the Symbol button in the Text dialog box. The ± symbol is located in the Modify Symbols list. The ± symbol is displayed as <MOD-PM>. The degree symbol ° is displayed as <MOD-DEG>.

Interpretation of tolerances is as follows:

- The angular dimension 110 is machined between 109.5 and 110.5.
- The dimension 2.5 is machined between 2.0 and 3.0.
- The Guide Hole dimension 10.000/10.015 is machined according to the specific tolerance on the drawing.

Company Logo

A company logo is normally located in the Title block. Create a company logo. Copy a picture file from Microsoft ClipArt using Microsoft Word. Paste the logo into the SolidWorks drawing. Note: The following logo example was created in Microsoft Word XP using the COMPASS.wmf. You can utilize any ClipArt picture, scanned image or bitmap for a logo in this activity.

Activity: Company Logo

Create a New Microsoft Word Document.

84) Click **Start**.

85) Click Microsoft Word .

86) Click **File**, **New** from the Standard toolbar in MS Word.

87) Click **Insert**, **Picture**, **ClipArt** from the Draw toolbar. The Insert Clip Art menu appears.

88) In the Search text enter **compass**. Note: Enter any name for Clip Art to Search For. If you do not have the Clip Art loaded on your system, click **Clips Online** to obtain additional Clip Art. Follow the provided directions to select and download.

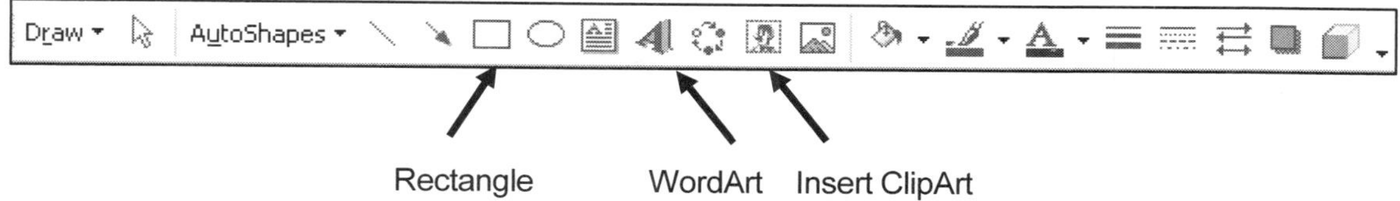

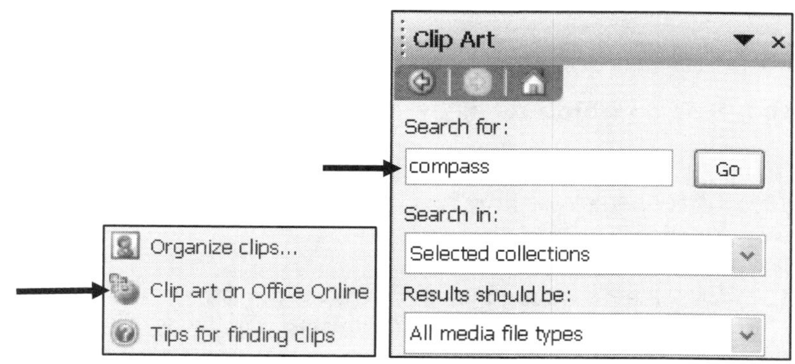

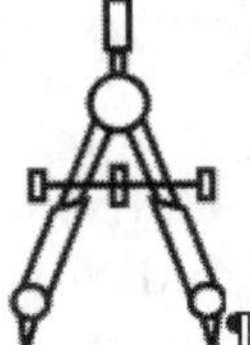

Locate the picture file.

89) Click **Go**. Locate the **Compass.wmf** file. **Double-click** the file. The picture appears in the Word document.

Redefine the picture layout.

90) Click the **picture**.

91) Right-click **Format Picture** Format Picture... .

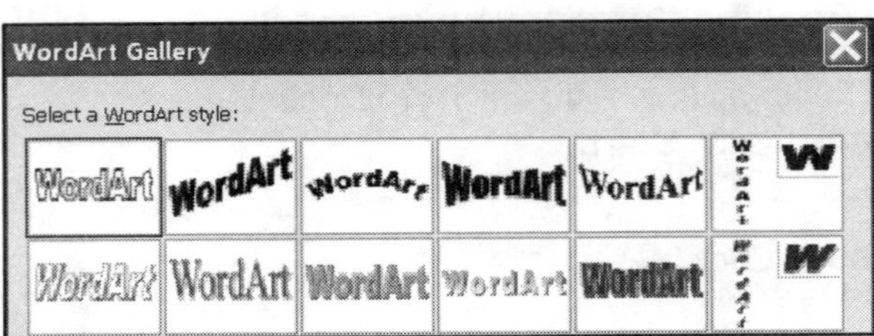

Display the drag handles.

92) Click **Layout**. Click **Square**.

93) Click **OK**.

Add text to the logo picture.

94) Click **Insert WordArt** from the Draw toolbar.

95) Click a **WordArt** style.

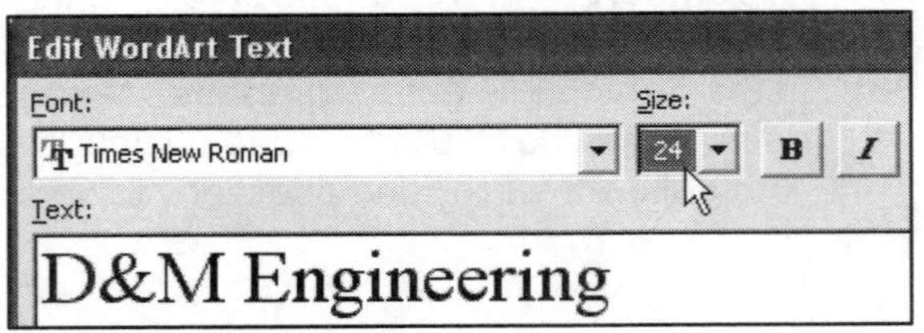

96) Click **OK**.

97) Enter **D&M Engineering** in the text box.

98) Click **24** from the Size drop down list.

99) Click **OK**.

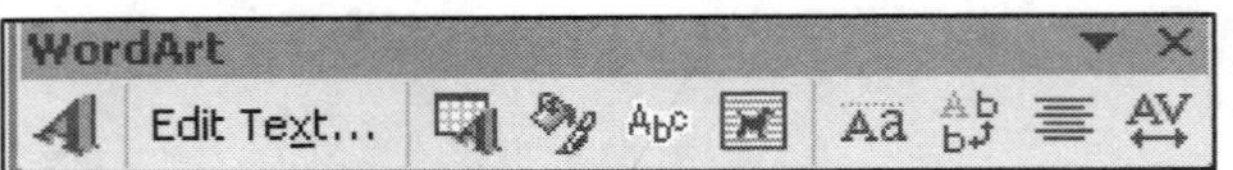

100) Click the **Word Art text**. A Word Art toolbar appears.

101) Click **Text Wrapping** .

102) Click **Square**.

103) Click and drag the **Word Art text** under the Compass picture.

104) Size the **Word Art text** by dragging the picture handles.

Group the Word Art text and the picture to create the logo.

105) Click on the **Word Art text**. Hold the **Ctrl** key down.

106) Click the **compass** picture. Release the **Ctrl** key. Right-click and select **Grouping**.

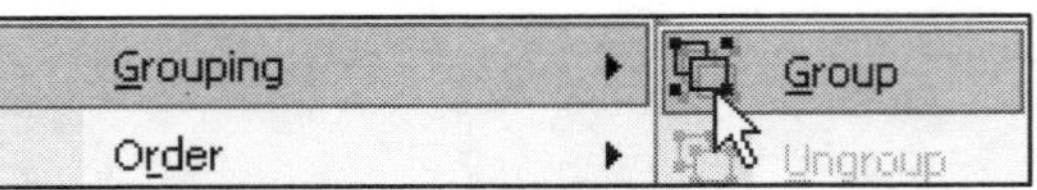

107) Click **Group**. The Word Art text and the picture is now grouped. The logo is created.

Copy the new logo.

108) Click **Copy** from the standards toolbar.

109) The logo is placed into the Clipboard. **Minimize** the Microsoft Word Graphics window.

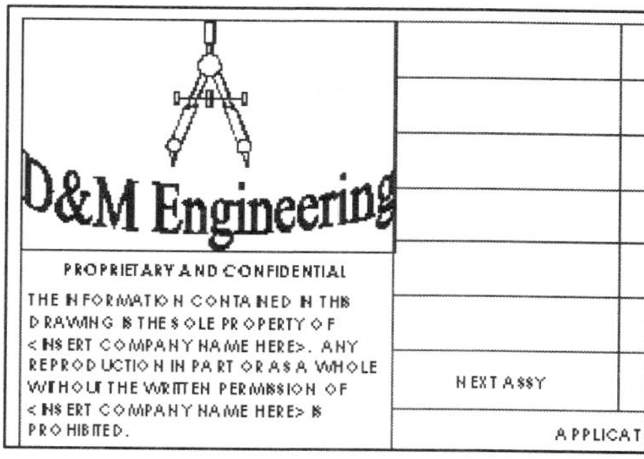

Return to the SolidWorks Title block.

110) Click a **position** on the left side of the Title block in the SolidWorks Graphics window.

111) **Zoom out** if required.

Paste the logo.

112) Click **Edit**, **Paste** from the Main menu.

113) **Move** and **Size** the logo to the SolidWorks Title block by dragging the picture handles.

Return to Edit Sheet mode.

114) Right-click in the **Graphics window**.

115) Click **Edit Sheet**. The Title block is displayed in black/gray.

Sheet (Sheet Format1)
Edit Sheet

Fit the Sheet Format to the Graphics window.

116) Press the **f** key.

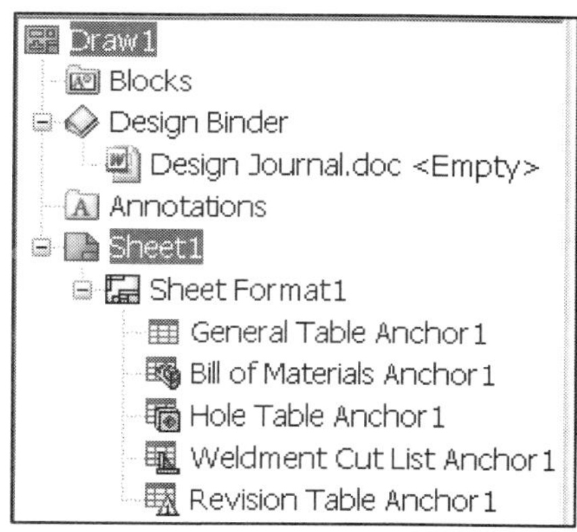

Draw1 displays Editing Sheet1 in the Status bar. The Title block is displayed in black when in Edit Sheet mode.

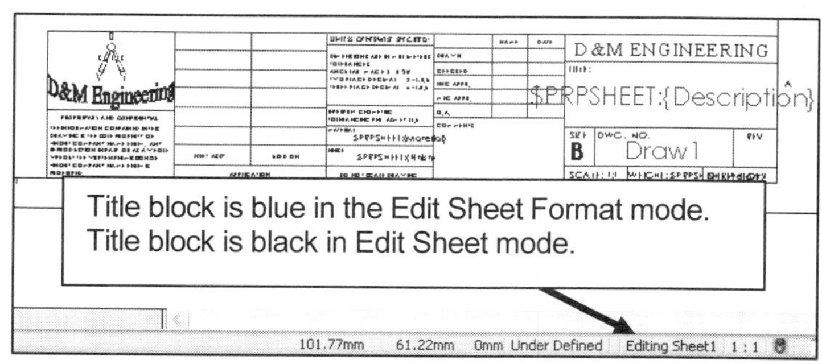

Save Sheet Format and Save As Drawing Template

Save the drawing document in the Graphics window in two forms: Sheet Format and Drawing Template. Save the Sheet Format as a custom Sheet Format named CUSTOM-B. Use the CUSTOM-B Sheet Format for the drawings in this project. The Sheet format file extension is .slddrt.

The Drawing Template can be displayed with or without the Sheet Format. Combine the Sheet Format with the Drawing Template to create a custom Drawing Template named B-ANSI-MM. Utilize the File, Save As option to save a Drawing Template. The Drawing Template file extension is .drwdot.

Always select the Save as type option first, then select the Save in folder to avoid saving in default SolidWorks installation directories.

The System Options, File Locations, Document Templates option is only valid for the current session of SolidWorks in some network locations. Set the File Locations option in order to view the MY-TEMPLATES tab in the New Document dialog box.

Activity: Save Sheet Format and Save As Drawing Template

Save the Sheet Format.

117) Click **File**, **Save Sheet Format** from the Main menu. The Save Sheet Format dialog box appears.

118) Click **Browse** from the Save Sheet Format dialog box.

The default Sheet Format file folder is called data. The file extension for Sheet Format is .slddrt.

119) Select **ENGDESIGN-W-SOLIDWORKS\ MY-TEMPLATES** for Save In File Folder.

120) Enter **CUSTOM-B** for File name.

121) Click **Save** from the Save Sheet Format dialog box.

Save the Drawing Template.

122) Click **File**, **Save As** from the Main menu.

123) Click **Drawing Templates[*.drwdot]** from the Save as type list.

124) Select **ENGDESIGN-W-SOLIDWORKS\MY-TEMPLATES** for Save In File Folder.

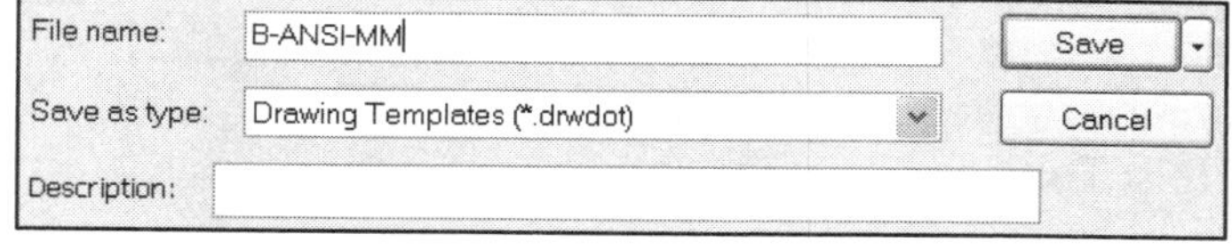

125) Enter **B-ANSI-MM** for File name.

126) Click **Save**.

Set System Options - File Locations.

127) Click **Tools**, **Options**, **File Locations** from the Main menu.

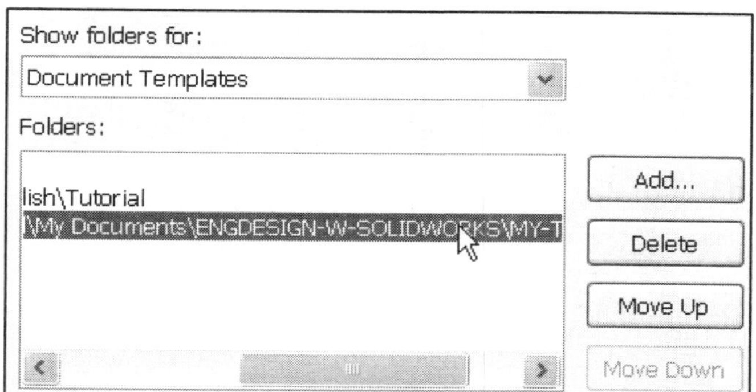

128) Click **Add**. Click **Browse**.

129) Select **ENGDESIGN-W-SOLIDWORKS\MY-TEMPLATES** for Folder. Click **OK** from the Browse For Folder menu.

130) Click **OK** to exit System Options.

Close all files.

131) Click **Window**, **Close All** from the Main menu. SolidWorks remains open, no documents are displayed.

Utilize Drawing Template descriptive filenames that contain the size, dimension standard and units.

Combine customize Drawing Templates and Sheet Formats to match your company's drawing standards. Save the empty Drawing Template and Sheet Format separately to reuse information.

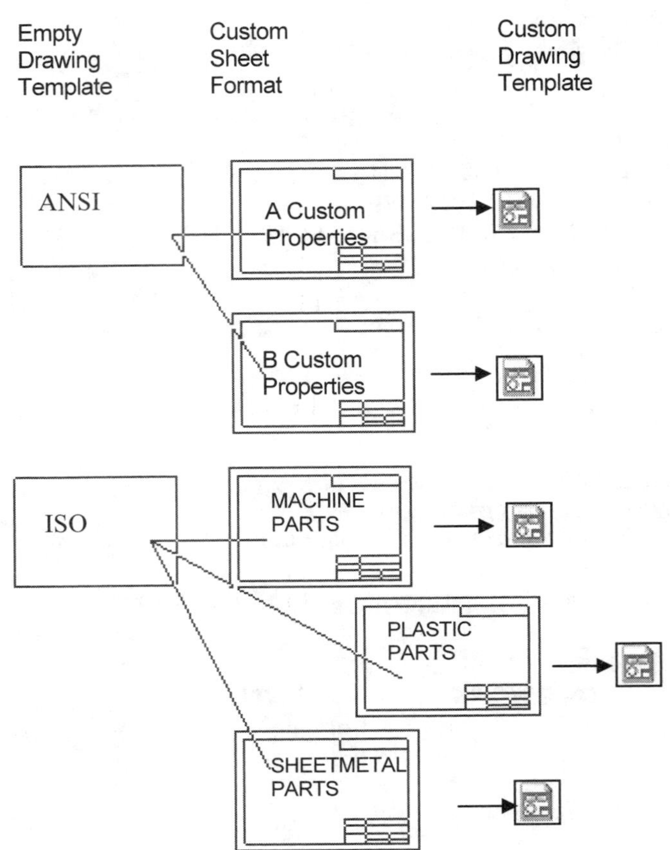

Additional details on Drawing Templates, Sheet Format and Custom Properties are available in SolidWorks Help Topics.

Keywords: Documents (templates, properties) Sheet Formats (new, new drawings, note text), Properties (drawing sheets), Customize Drawing Sheet Formats.

Review Drawing Templates.

A custom Drawing Template was created from the default Drawing Template. You modified Sheet Properties and Document Properties to control the sheet size, scale, annotations, dimensions and layers.

The Sheet Format contained Title block and Custom Property information. You inserted a Company Logo and modified the Title block.

The Save Sheet Format option was utilized to save the CUSTOM-B.slddrt Sheet Format. The File, Save As option was utilized to save the B-ANSI-MM.drwdot Template. The Sheet Format and Drawing Template were saved in the MY-TEMPLATES folder.

GUIDE Part-Modify

A drawing contains part views, geometric dimensioning and tolerances, notes and other related design information. Perform the following tasks before starting the GUIDE drawing:

- Verify the part. The drawing requires the associated part.
- View dimensions in each part. Step through each feature of the part and review all dimensions.
- Review the dimension scheme to determine the required dimensions and notes to manufacture the part.

Activity: GUIDE Part-Modify

Open the GUIDE part.

132) Click **File**, **Open** from the Main menu.

133) Select **ENGDESIGN-W-SOLIDWORKS\PROJECTS** for the Look in folder.

Modify the dimensions.

134) Select **Part** for Files of Type.

135) Double-click **GUIDE**. Click **Shaded With Edges** .

136) Double-click **Base Extrude** in the GUIDE FeatureManager.

137) Double-click **80**. Enter **100**.

138) Click **Rebuild** from the Modify toolbar. Click the **Green Check mark** .

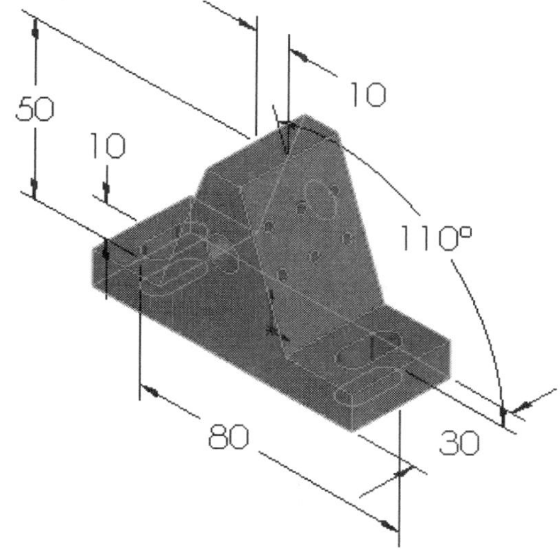

139) Click **OK** from the Dimension PropertyManager.

Save the GUIDE part.

140) Click **Save** .

Review part history with the Rollback bar to understand how the part was created. Position the Rollback bar at the top of the FeatureManager.

Drag the Rollback bar below each feature. When working between features, right-click in the FeatureManager. Select Roll to Previous\Roll to End.

GUIDE Part Drawing

The GUIDE drawing consists of multiple views, dimensions and annotations. The GUIDE part was designed for symmetry. Add or redefine dimensions in the drawing to adhere to a Drawing Standard. Add dimensions and notes to the drawing in order to correctly manufacture the part.

Address the dimensions for three features:

- The right Slot Cut is not dimensions to an ASME Y14 standard.
- No dimensions exist for the left Mirror Slot Cut.
- The Guide Hole and Linear Pattern of Tapped Holes require notes.

The GUIDE part remains open. Create a new GUIDE drawing. Utilize the B-ANSI-MM Drawing Template. Utilize the Model View (Model View) option in the Drawing toolbar to insert the Front view into Sheet1. Utilize the Auto-start Projected View option to project the Top, Right and Isometric views from the Front view.

Activity: GUIDE Part Drawing

Create the GUIDE Drawing.

141) Click **File**, **New** from the Main menu.

142) Double-click **B-ANSI-MM** from the MY-TEMPLATES tab.

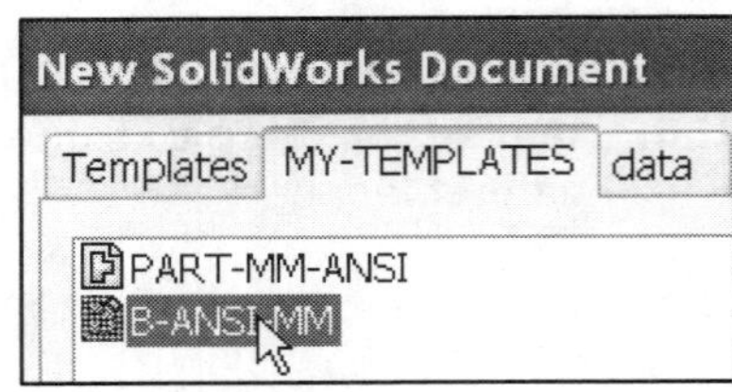

143) Click **Cancel** from the Model View PropertyManager.

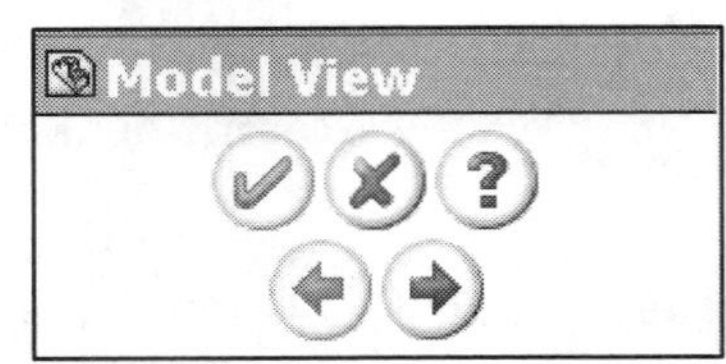

Review the Draw2 FeatureManager.

144) Click **Sheet1** from the FeatureManager.

Note: The current drawing name is Draw2 if the second new drawing is created in the same session of SolidWorks. The current sheet name is Sheet1. Sheet1 is the current Sheet.

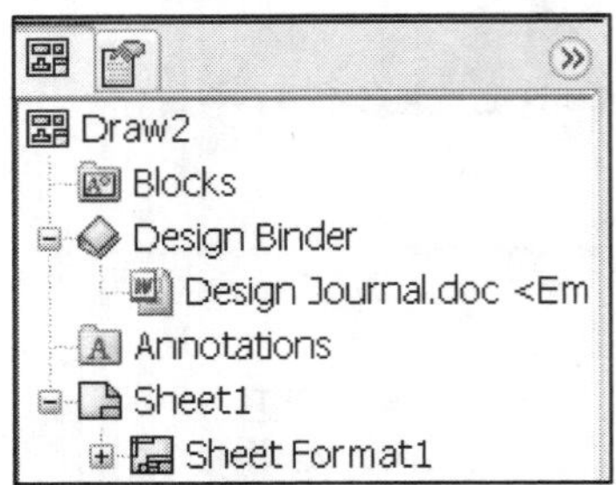

Insert four Drawing Views.

145) Click **Drawings** Drawings, **Model View** Model View from the FeatureManager.

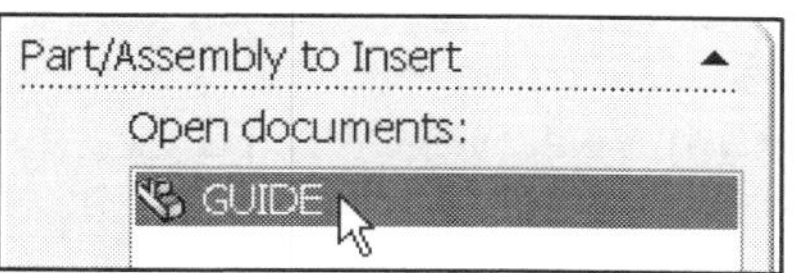

146) Double-click **GUIDE** from the Part/Assembly to Insert box.

Insert four views.

147) Click **Multiple views**.

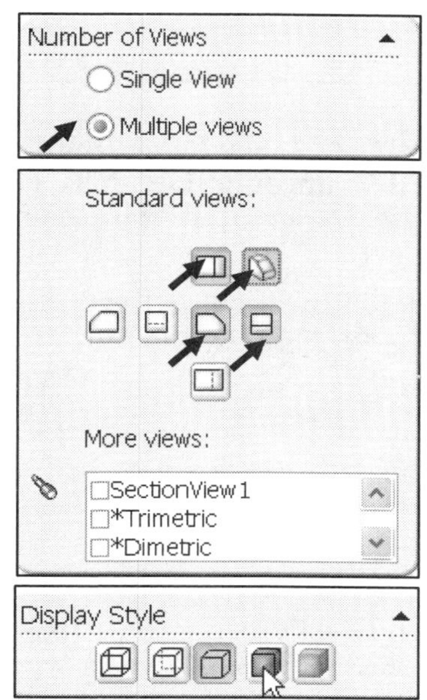

148) Click ***Front, *Top** and ***Right** from the Orientation list. Note: All four views are selected. *Isometric is selected by default.

149) Click **OK** from the Model View PropertyManager.

150) Click inside the **Isometric view boundary**.

151) Click **Shaded With Edges** in the Display Style box.

152) Click **OK** from the Drawing View4 PropertyManager.

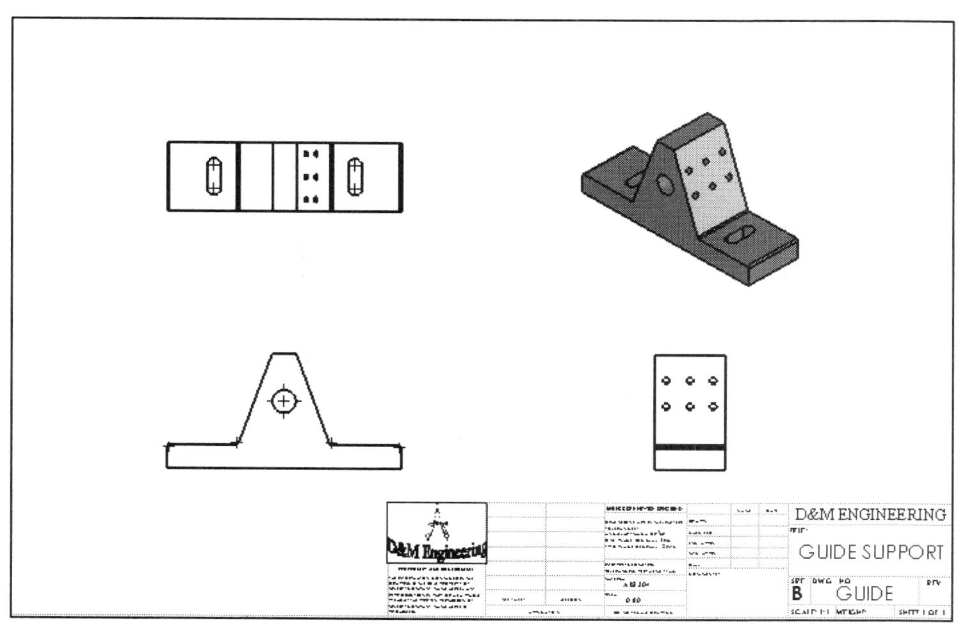

Hide the Origins.

153) Click **View**, uncheck **Origins** from the Main menu.

Save the GUIDE drawing.

154) Click **File**, **Save As** from the Main menu.

155) Select **PROJECTS** for Save in folder. GUIDE is the default filename. Drawing is the default Save as type.

156) Click **Save**.

The DWG. NO. box in the Title block displays the part File name, GUIDE. The TITLE: box in the Title block displays GUIDE SUPPORT.

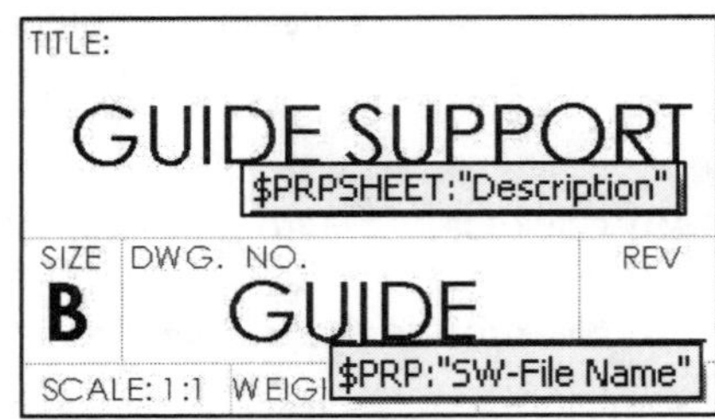

Predefined text in the CUSTOM-B Sheet Format links the Properties: $PRPSHEET:"Description" and $PRP:"SW-FileName". The Properties were defined in the GUIDE part utilizing File, Save As. Properties in the Title block are passed from the part to the drawing.

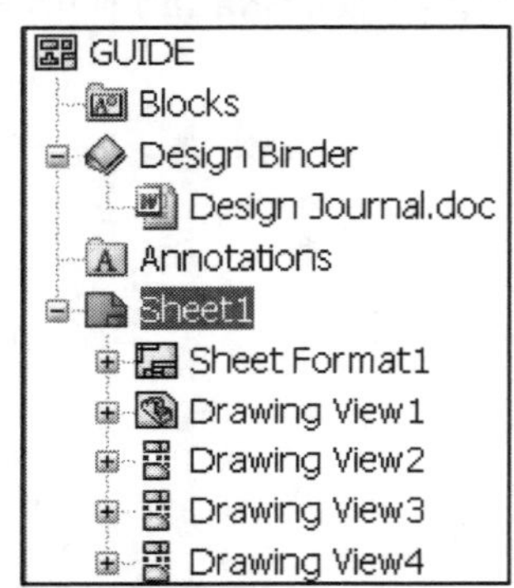

Always confirm your File name and Save in folder. Projects deal with multiple File names and folders. Select Save as type from the drop down list. Do not enter the extension. The file extension is entered automatically.

Each drawing has a unique file name. Drawing file names end with a .slddrw suffix. Part file names end with a .sldprt suffix. A drawing or part file can have the same prefix. A drawing or part file cannot have the same suffix.

Example: Drawing file name: GUIDE.slddrw. Part file name: GUIDE.sldprt. The current file name is GUIDE.slddrw.

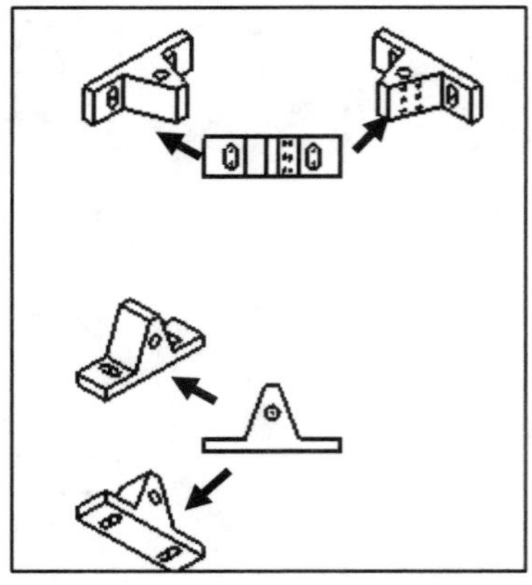

The GUIDE drawing contains three Principle Views (Standard Views): Front, Top and Right and an Isometric View. You created the views with the Model View option.

Drawing views are inserted as follows:

- Utilize the Model View option.
- Drag a part into the drawing to create three Standard Views.
- Predefine views in a custom Drawing Template.
- Drag a hyperlink through Internet Explorer.

Utilize the Projected View (Projected View) to insert additional Isometric views projected from the corner of a 2D View.

Move Views and Properties of the Sheet

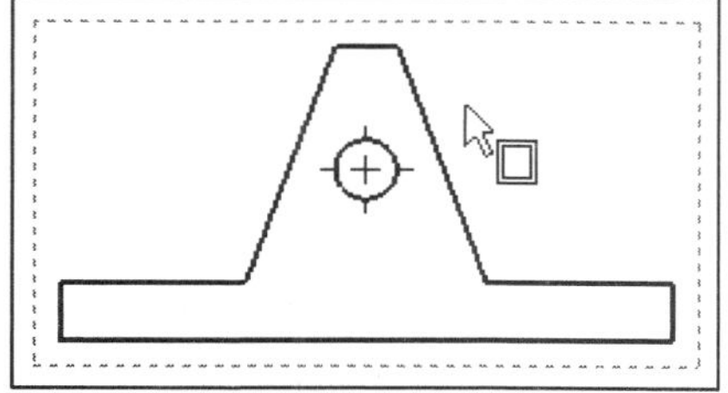

The GUIDE drawing contains four views. Reposition the view on a drawing. Provide approximately 1in. - 2in., (25mm – 50mm) between each view for dimension placement.

Move Views on Sheet1 to create space for additional Drawing View placement.

The mouse pointer provides feedback in both the Drawing Sheet and Drawing View modes.

The mouse pointer displays the Drawing Sheet icon when the Sheet properties and commands are executed. The mouse pointer displays the Drawing View icon when the View properties and commands are executed.

View the mouse pointer for feedback to select Sheet, View, Component and Edge properties in the Drawing.

Sheet Properties

- Sheet Properties display properties of the selected sheet.

  Right-click in the sheet boundary 

.

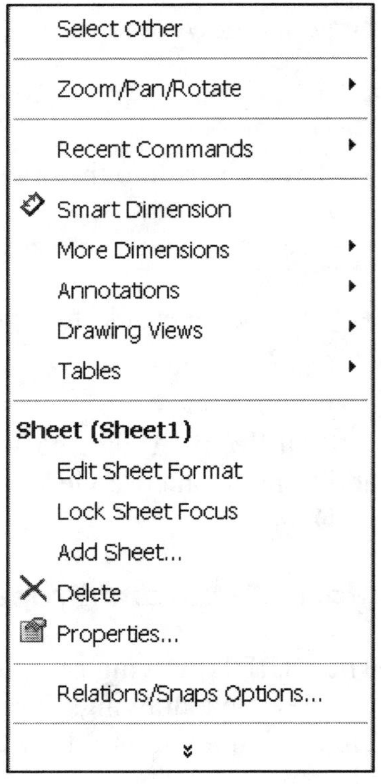

View Properties

- View Properties display properties of the selected view.

  Right-click on the view boundary Drawing View1. Modify the View Properties in the Display Style box or the View Toolbar.

View (Drawing View1)
Lock View Position
Lock View Focus
Alignment
Tangent Edge
Open guide.sldprt
Delete

Component Properties

- Component Properties display properties of the selected component. Right-click to on the face of the component.

Component (GUIDE)
Open Part
Show/Hide
Component Line Font...

Edge Properties

- Edge Properties display properties of the geometry.

  Right-click on an edge .

Edge
Hide Edge
Show Edge

Activity: Move Views and Properties of the Sheet

Move the View.

157) Click inside the **Drawing View1** (Front) view boundary. The mouse pointer displays the Drawing View Drawing View1 icon. The view boundary is displayed in green.

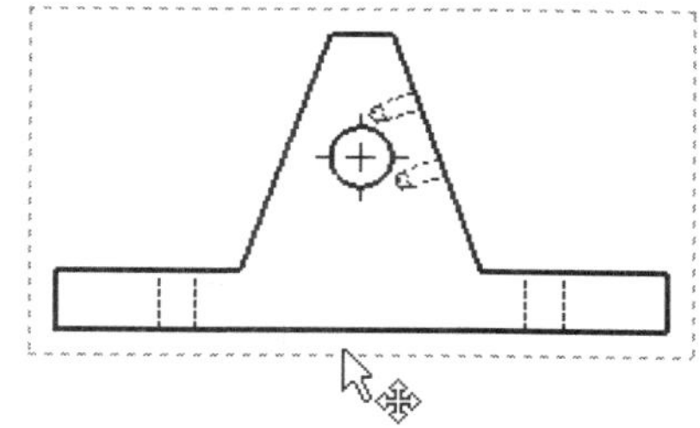

158) Click **Hidden Lines Visible**.

159) Position the **mouse pointer** on the edge of the view until the Drawing Move View icon is displayed.

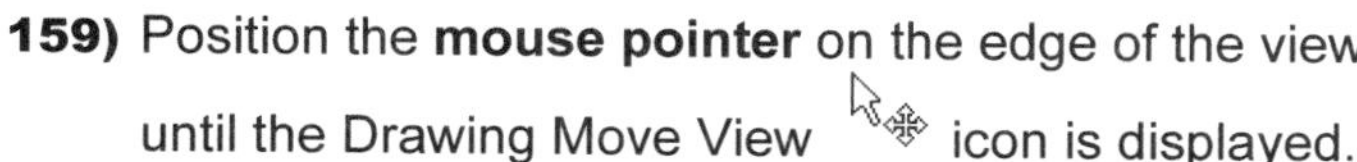

160) Click and drag **Drawing View1** in an upward vertical direction. The Top and Right view move aligned to Drawing View1 (Front).

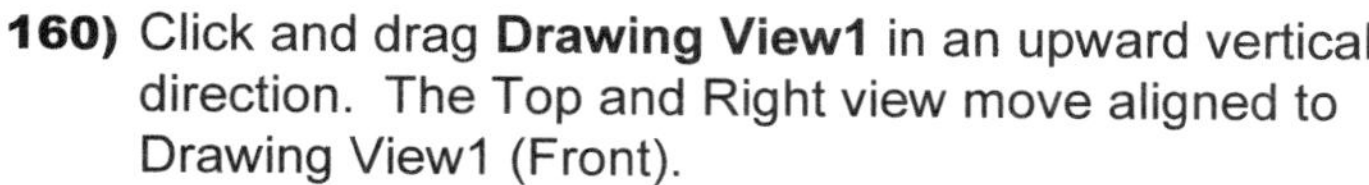

Modify the View Display.

161) Click inside the **Top view boundary**, (Drawing View3).

162) Click **Hidden Lines Removed**.

163) Click the **Right view boundary,** (Drawing View2).

164) Click **Hidden Lines Removed**.

165) Click **OK** from the Drawing View2 PropertyManager.

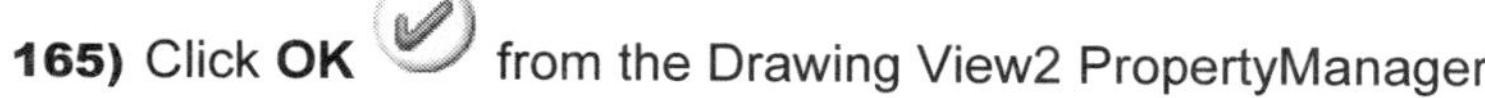

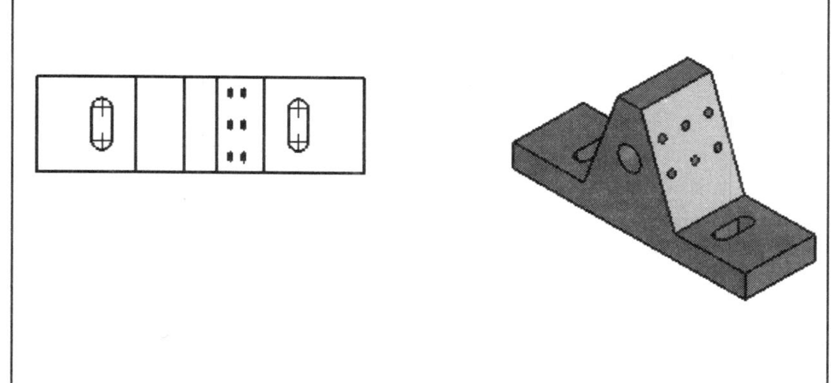

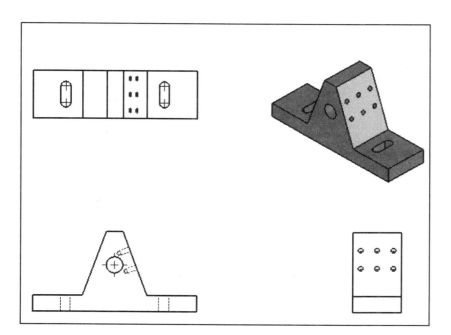

 Select the middle of the dashed green view boundary to move the view.

Auxiliary View, Section View and Detail View

The GUIDE drawing requires additional views to document the part. Insert an Auxiliary View, Section View and Detail View from the Drawing toolbar. Review the following view terminology before you begin the next activity.

Auxiliary View

An Auxiliary View displays a plane parallel to an angled plane with true dimensions.

A primary Auxiliary View is hinged to one of the six Principle Views. Create a Primary Auxiliary View that references the angled edge in the Front view.

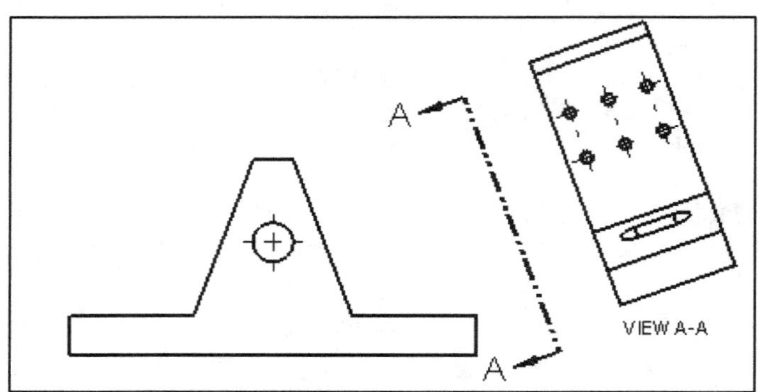

Section View

Section Views display the interior features of a part. Define a cutting plane with a sketched line in a view perpendicular to the Section View.

Create a full Section View by sketching a section line in the Top view.

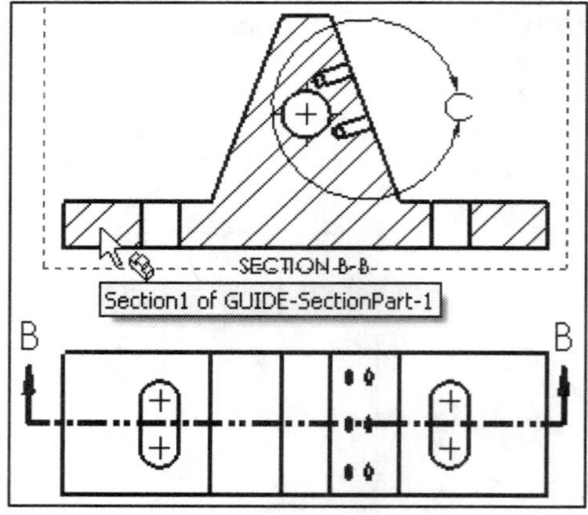

Detail View

Detailed Views enlarge an area of an existing view. Specify location, shape and scale.

Create a Detail View from a Section View with a 3:2 scale.

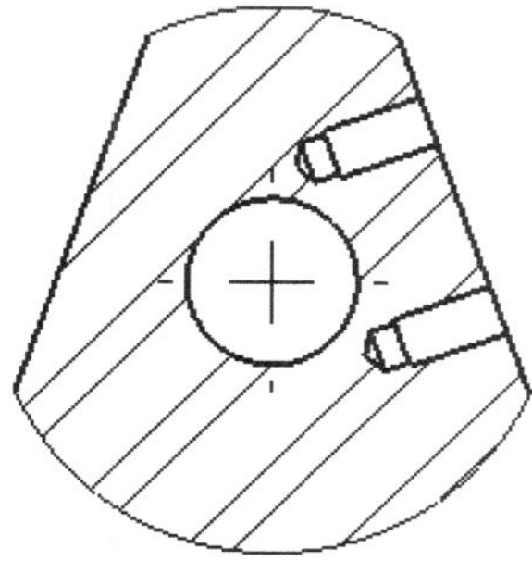

DETAIL C
SCALE 3 : 2

Activity: Auxiliary View

Insert an Auxiliary View.

166) Click **Drawings** Drawings.

167) Click **Auxiliary View** 

from the Drawing toolbar.

168) Click the **right angled edge** of the GUIDE in the Front view.

169) Click a **position** to the right of the Front view.

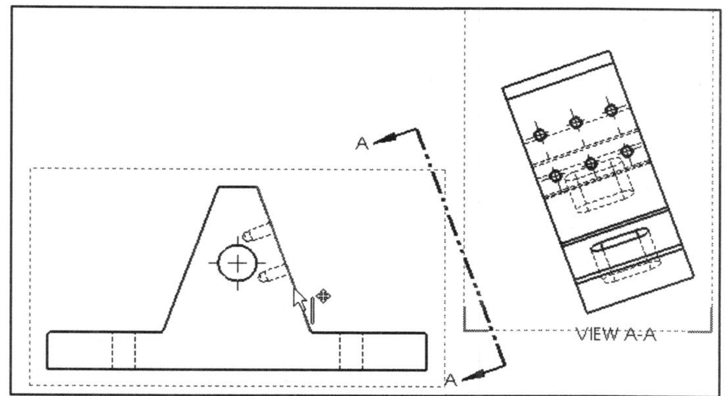

Position the Auxiliary View.

170) Click and drag the **section line A-A midpoint** toward Drawing View1. The default Label, A is displayed in the Arrow box.

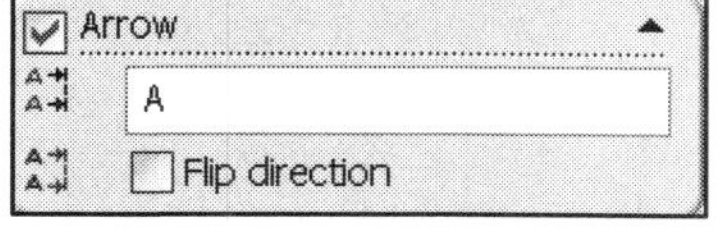

171) Click the **OK** from the Drawing View5 PropertyManager.

172) Rename the **Drawing View5** to **Auxiliary**.

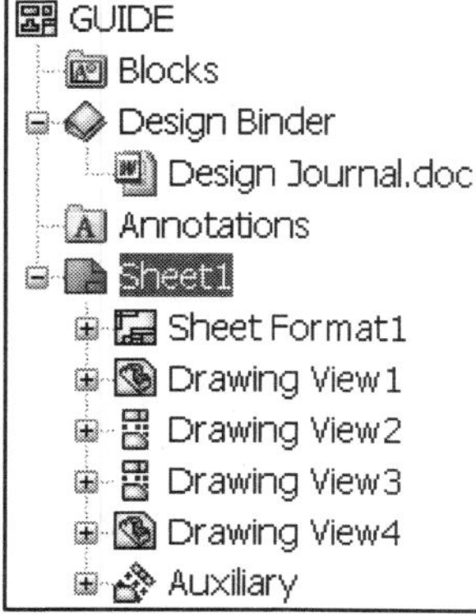

Activity: Section View

Insert a Section View.

173) Click **Section View** Section View from the Drawing toolbar. The Section View FeatureManager is displayed. Locate the midpoint of the left vertical line for a reference.

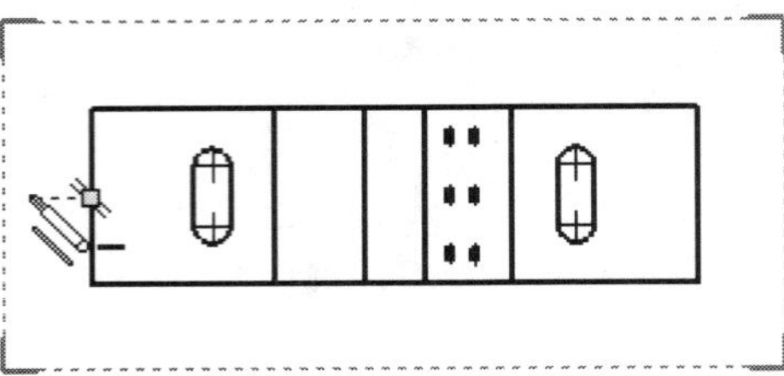

174) Position the **mouse pointer** over the center of the left vertical line. Do not click the midpoint.

175) Drag the **mouse pointer** to the left.

176) Click a **position** to the left of the profile.

177) Click a **position** horizontally to the right of the profile. The Section line extends beyond the left and right profile lines.

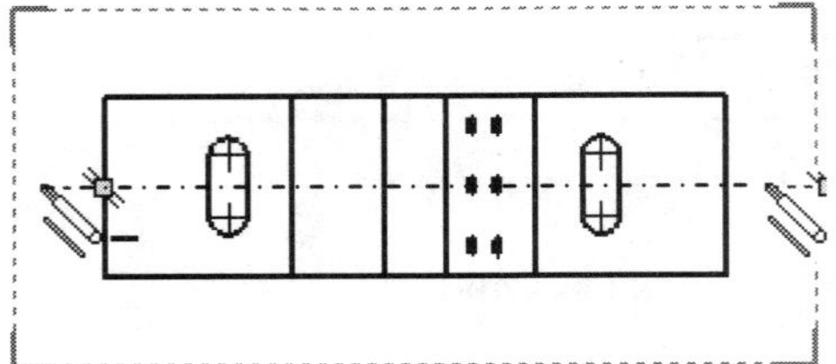

Position the Section View.

178) Click a **position** above the Top view. The section arrows point up.

179) Check **Flip direction** from the Section Line box. The arrows point upward.

180) If required, enter **B** for Section View Name in the Label text box.

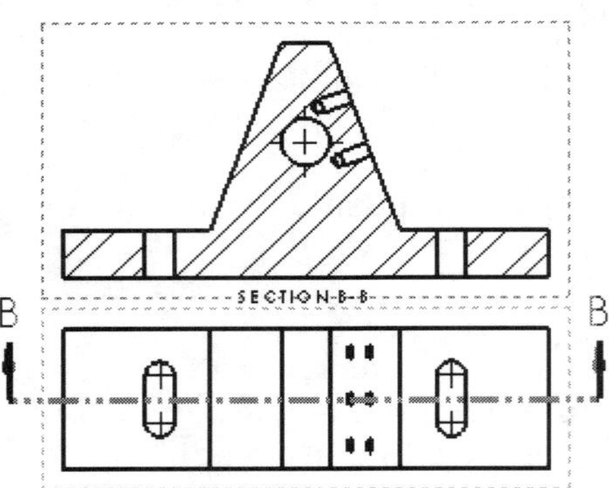

181) Click **OK** from the Section View B-B PropertyManager.

Save the drawing.

182) Click **Save** .

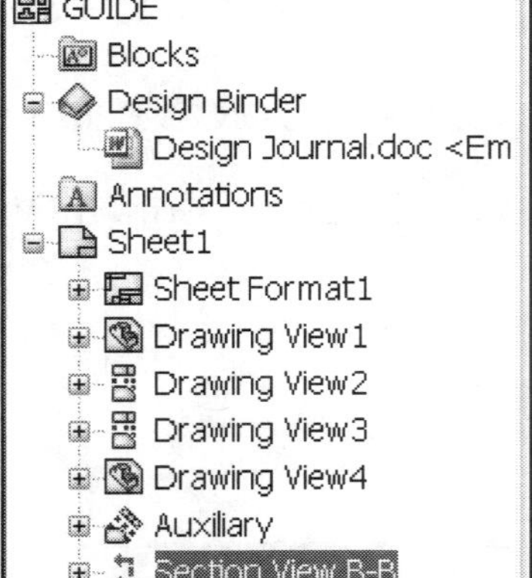

Note: The AISI 304 Material in the GUIDE part determines the hatch pattern in the GUIDE drawing.

Activity: Detail View

Insert a Detail View.

183) Click **Detail View** (Detail View) from the Drawing toolbar.

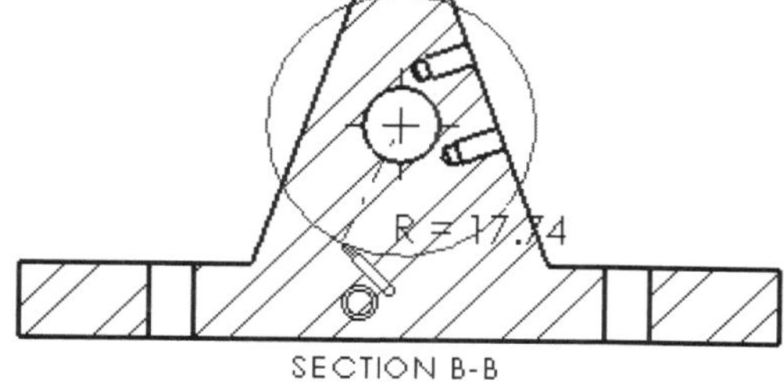

Sketch the Detail Circle.

184) Click the **centerpoint** of the Guide Hole in the Section view.

185) Click a **position** to the lower left of the Guide Hole to complete the circle.

Position the Detail View.

186) Click a **position** to the right of the Section View.

187) If required, enter **C** for Detail View Name in the Label text box.

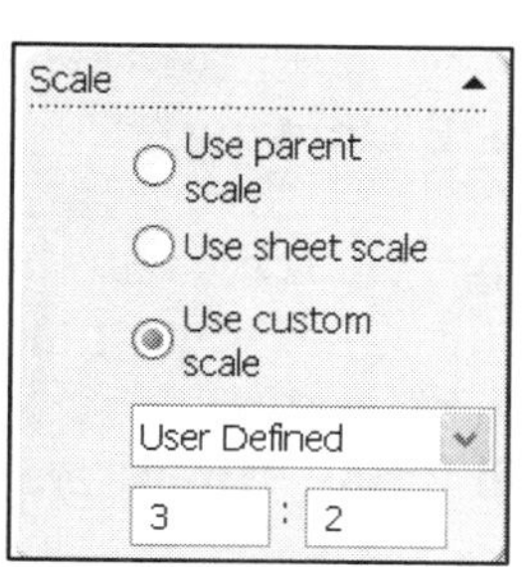

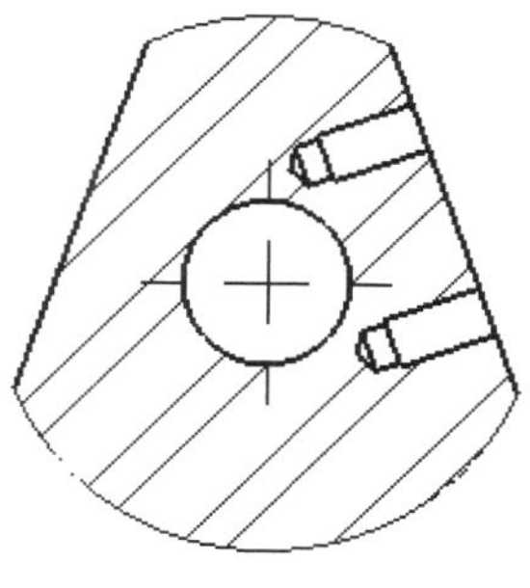

DETAIL C
SCALE 3 : 2

Change the View scale

188) Check **Use custom scale** option. Select **User Defined**. Enter **3:2** in the Use custom scale text box.

189) Click **OK** from the Detail View C PropertyManager.

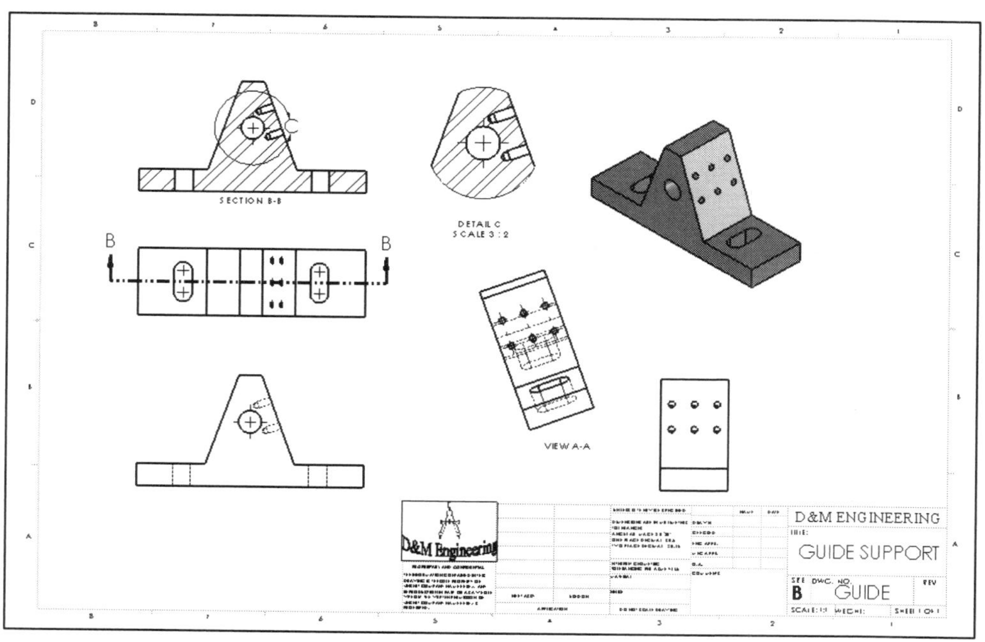

Save the GUIDE drawing.

190) Click **Save** .

The Drawing Views are complete. Move the views to allow for ample spacing for dimensions and notes.

Additional information on creating a New Drawing, Model View, Move View, Auxiliary View, Section View and Detail View are found in SolidWorks Help Topics. Keywords: New (drawing document), Drawing Views (overview), Drawing Views (model), Move (drawing views), Auxiliary Views, Detail Views and Section Views.

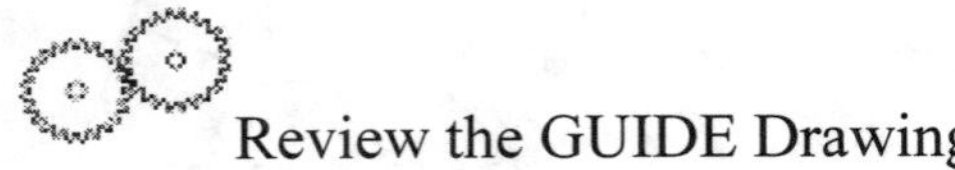

Review the GUIDE Drawing.

You created a new drawing, GUIDE with the B-ANSI-MM Drawing Template. The GUIDE drawing utilized the GUIDE part in the Model View PropertyManager. The Model View Property Manager allowed new views to be inserted with a View Orientation. You selected Front, Top, Right and Isometric to position the GUIDE views.

Additional views were required to fully detail the GUIDE. You inserted the Auxiliary, Section and Detail Views. You moved the views by dragging the green view boundary. The next step is to insert the dimensions and annotations to detail the GUIDE drawing.

Display Modes and Performance

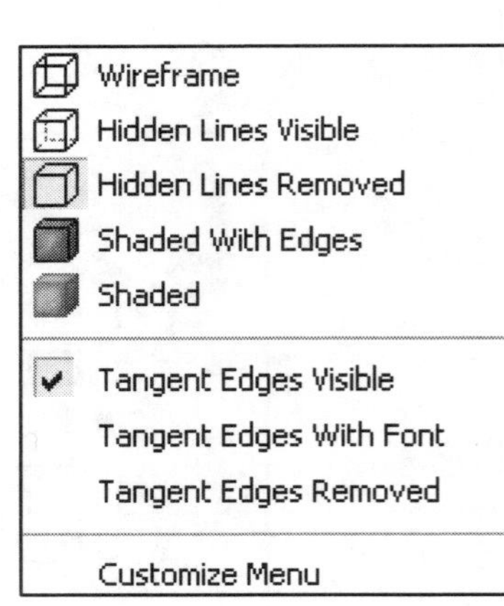

Display Modes for a Drawing View are similar to a part. Wireframe and Shaded Display Modes provide the best graphic performance.

Mechanical details require Hidden Lines Visible display and Hidden Lines Removed display. Select Shaded/Hidden Lines Removed to display Auxiliary Views to avoid confusion.

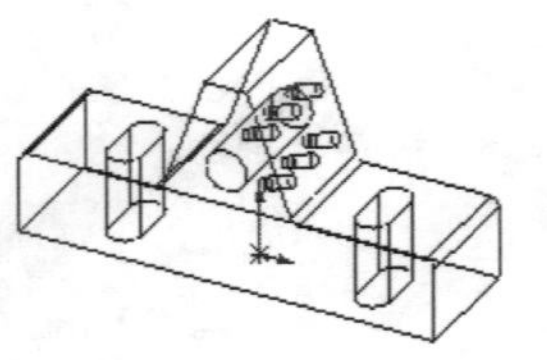

Wireframe

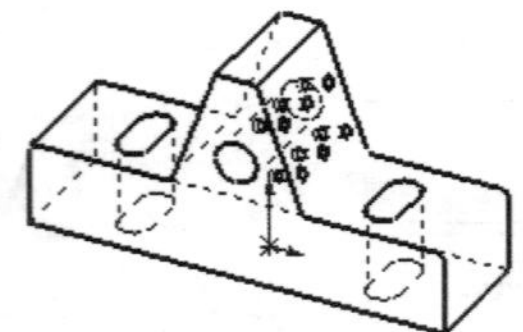

Hidden Line Visible

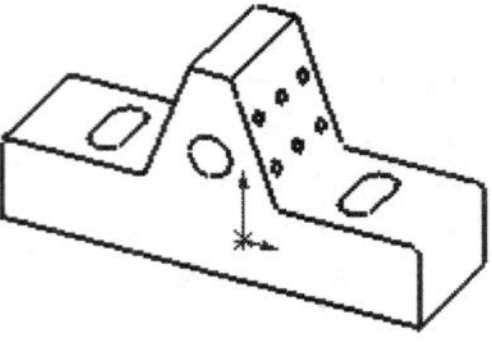

Hidden Line Remove

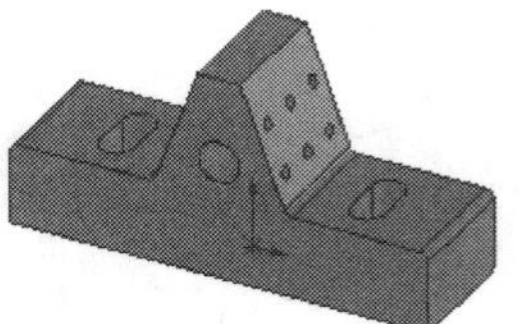

Shaded with Edges

Tangent Edges Visible provides clarity for the start of a Fillet edge. Tangent Edges Removed provides the best graphic performance.

Right-click in the view boundary to access the Tangent Edge options.

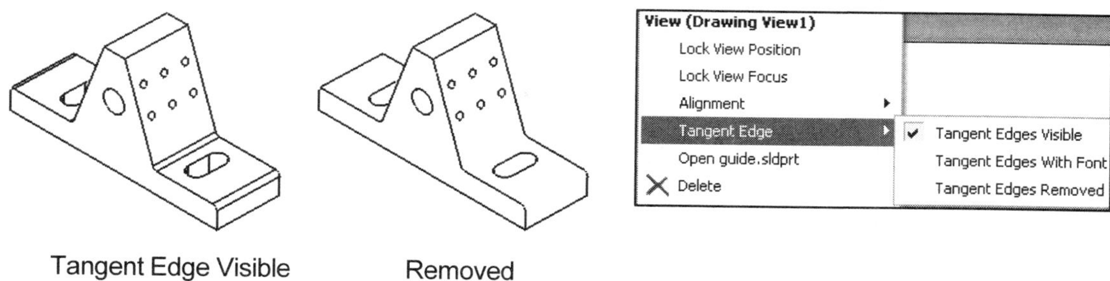

Tangent Edge Visible Removed

Drawing views can be displayed in High quality and Draft quality. In High quality, all model information is loaded into memory. By default, drawing views are displayed in High quality.

In Draft quality, only minimum model information is loaded into memory. Utilize Draft quality for large assemblies to increase performance.

Utilize Tools, Options, System Options, Display Style to control the quality of a view.

Detail Drawing

The design intent of this project is to work with dimensions inserted from parts and to incorporate them into the drawings. Explore methods to move, hide and recreate dimensions to adhere to a drawing standard.

There are other solutions to the dimensioning schemes illustrated in this project. Detail drawings require dimensions, annotations, tolerance, materials, Engineering Change Orders, authorization, etc. to release the part to manufacturing and other notes prior to production.

Review a hypothetical "worse case" drawing situation. You just inserted dimensions from a part into a drawing. The dimensions, extensions lines and arrows are not in the correct locations. How can you address the position of these details? Answer: Dimension to an ASME Y14.5M standard.

No.	Situation:
1	Extension line crosses dimension line. Dimensions not evenly spaced.
2	Largest dimension placed closest to profile.
3	Leader lines overlapping.
4	Extension line crossing arrowhead.
5	Arrow gap too large.
6	Dimension pointing to feature in another view. Missing dimension – inserted into Detail view (not shown).
7	Dimension text over centerline, too close to profile.
8	Dimension from other view – leader line too long.
9	Dimension inside section lines.
10	No visible gap.
11	Arrows overlapping text.
12	Incorrect decimal display with whole number (millimeter), no specified tolerance.

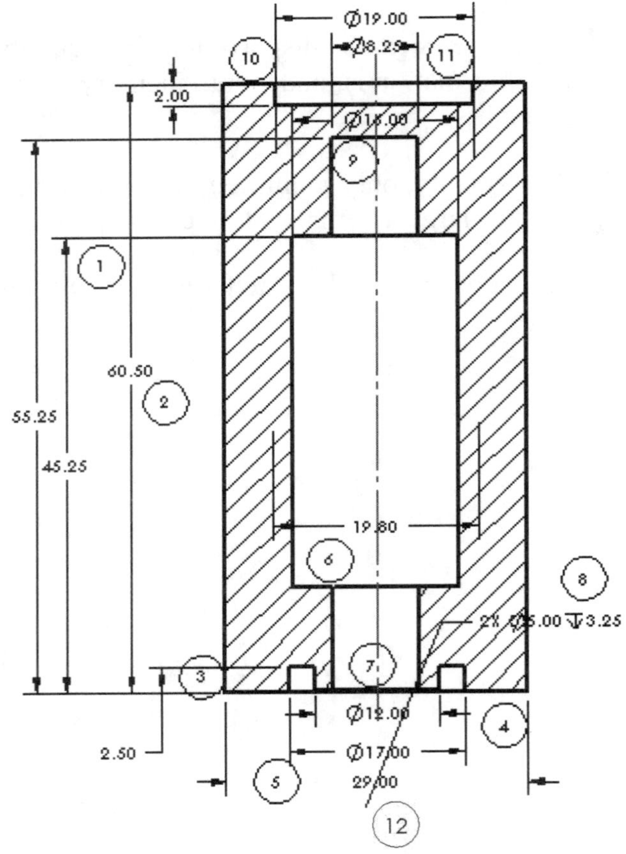

Worse Case Drawing Situation

The ASME Y14.5M standard defines an engineering drawing standard. Review the twelve changes made to the drawing to meet the standard.

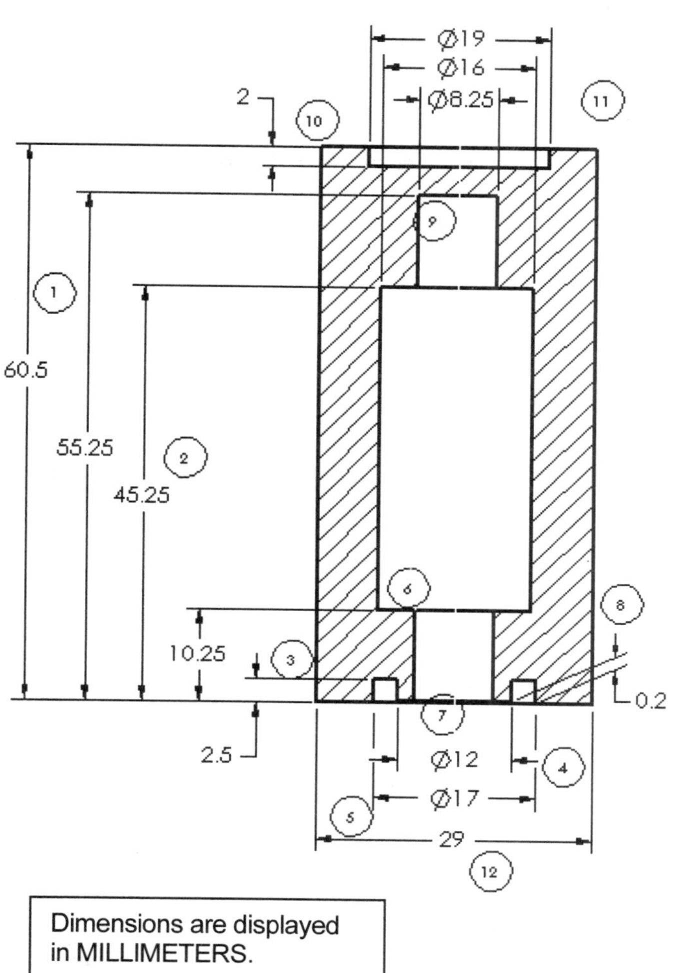

Dimensions are displayed in MILLIMETERS.

No.	Preferred Application of the Dimensions:
1	Extension lines do not cross unless situation is unavoidable. Stagger dimension text.
2	Largest dimension placed farthest from profile. Dimensions are evenly spaced and grouped.
3	Arrow heads do not overlap.
4	Break extension lines that cross close to arrowhead.
5	Flip arrows to the inside.
6	Move dimensions to the view that displays the outline of the feature. Insure that all dimensions are accounted for.
7	Move text off of reference geometry (centerline).
8	Drag dimensions into their correct view boundary. Create reference dimensions if required. Slant extension lines to clearly illustrate feature.
9	Locate dimensions outside off section lines.
10	Create a visible gap between extension lines and profile lines.
11	Arrows do not overlap the text.
12	Whole numbers displayed with no zero and no decimal point (millimeter).

Apply these dimension practices to the GUIDE drawing. Manufacturing utilizes detailed drawings. A mistake on a drawing can cost your company substantial loss in revenue.

The mistake could result in a customer liability lawsuit.

As the designer, dimension and annotate your parts clearly to avoid common problems and mistakes.

Insert Dimensions from the part. Dimensions you created for each part feature are inserted into the drawing.

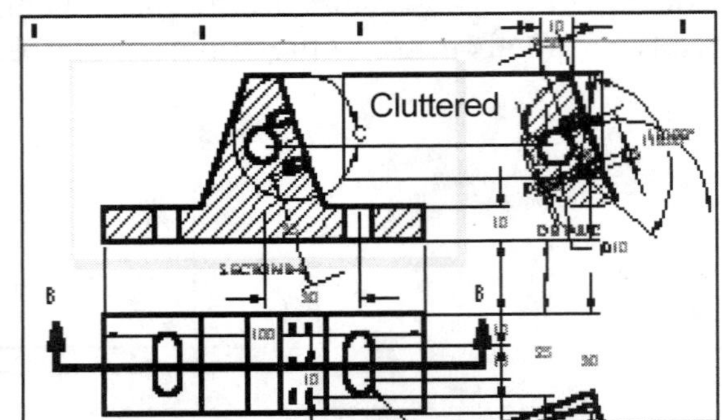

Select the first dimensions to display for the Front view. Do not select the Import Items into all Views option for complex drawings. Dimension text is cluttered and difficult to locate.

Follow a systematic, "one view at a time" approach for complex drawings. Insert part feature dimensions onto the Dims Layer for this project.

Activity: Detail Drawing-Insert Model Items

Set the Dimension Layer.

191) Click the **drop down arrow** from the Dims Layer list.

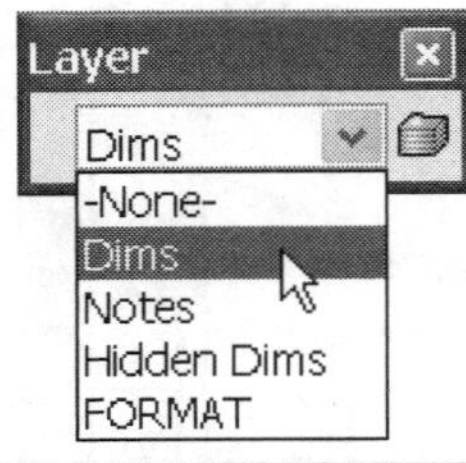

192) Click **DIMS**.

Insert dimensions into Drawing View1 (Front) view.

193) Click inside the **Drawing View1** boundary.

194) Click **Model Items** from the Annotations toolbar.

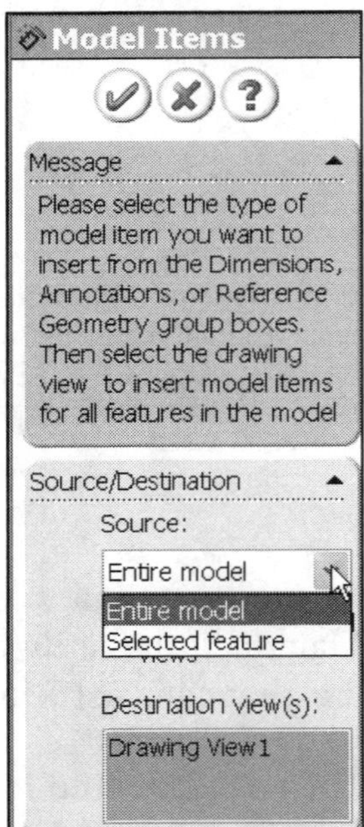

195) Select **Entire model** for the Import from box. The Model Items FeatureManager is displayed. Drawing View1 is displayed in the Import into drawing views. Accept the default settings.

196) Click **OK** from the Model Items PropertyManager.

The dimensions are located too far from the profile lines. Drawing dimension location is dependent on:

- Feature dimension creation.
- Selected drawing views.

Note: The Import items into all views option, first inserts dimensions into Section Views and Detail Views. The remaining dimensions are distributed among the visible views on the drawing.

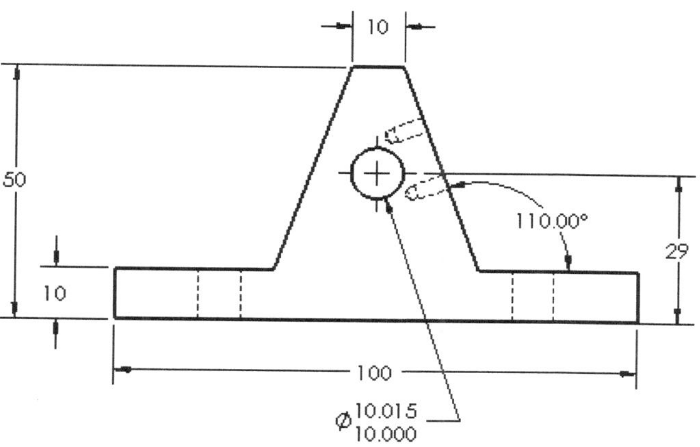

Move Dimensions in the Same View

Move dimensions within the same view. Use the mouse pointer to drag dimensions and leader lines to a new location.

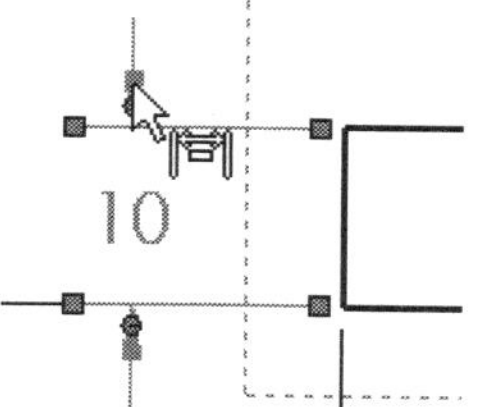

Leader lines reference the size of the profile. A gap must exist between the profile lines and the leader lines. Shorten the leader lines to maintain a drawing standard. Use the green Arrow buttons to flip the dimension arrows.

Insert part dimensions into the Top view. The Top view displays crowded dimensions. Move the overall dimensions. Move the Slot Cut dimensions.

Place dimensions in the view where they display the most detail. Move dimensions to the Auxiliary View. Hide the diameter dimensions and add Hole Callouts. Display the view with Hidden Lines Removed.

Activity: Detail Drawing-Move Dimensions

Move the linear dimensions in Drawing View1, (Front).

197) Zoom to area on Drawing View1.

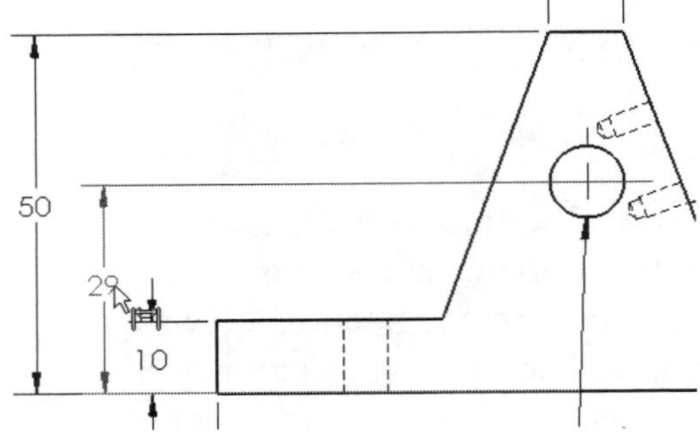

198) Click the vertical dimension text **29**.

199) Drag the **dimension text** to the left.

200) Click a **position** between the two arrowheads.

Create a gap between the extension lines and the profile lines.

201) Drag the lower **square green endpoint** to the vertex of the left corner. The vertex displays a red dot. A gap is created between the extension line and the profile.

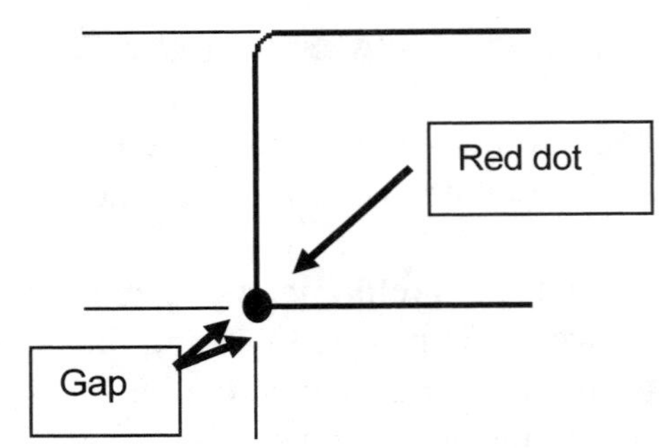

202) Click the vertical dimension **10**.

203) Drag the **text** approximately 10mm's from the profile. The smallest linear dimensions are closest to the profile.

A gap exists between the profile line and the leader lines. Drag the green endpoints to a vertex, to create a gap. Note: The 10.015/10.000 Limit tolerance propagates from the part to the drawing.

Display Hidden Lines in Drawing View1.

204) Position the **horizontal** and **angular** dimensions.

205) Flip the arrows if required.

Fit the drawing to the Graphics window.

206) Press the **f** key.

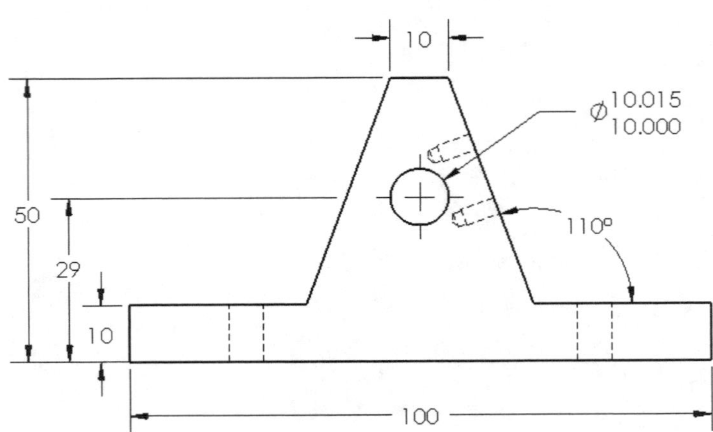

Insert dimensions into Drawing View3.

207) Click inside the **Top view** boundary.

208) **Zoom to Area** on Drawing View3.

209) Click **Model Items** from the Annotations toolbar.

210) Select **Entire model** for the Import from box. The Model Items FeatureManager is displayed. Drawing View3 is selected.

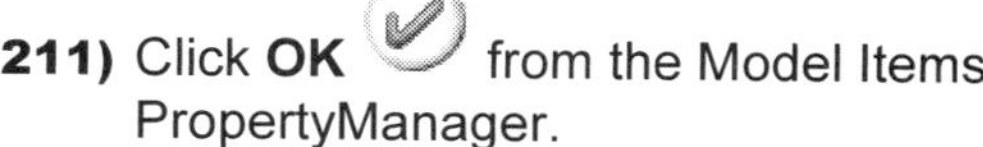

211) Click **OK** from the Model Items PropertyManager.

Move the vertical dimensions.

212) Click and drag the two vertical Slot Cut dimensions, **10** to the right of the Section arrow.

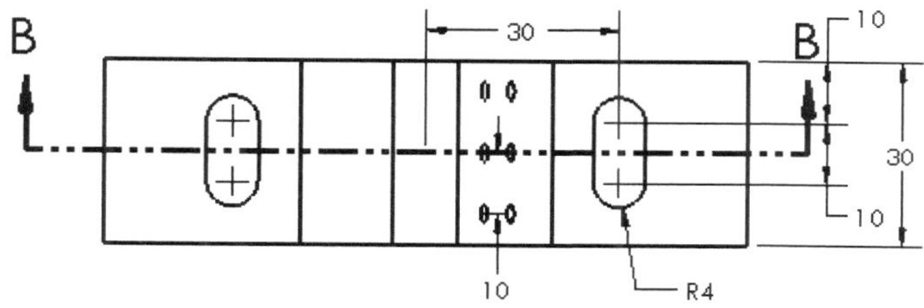

213) Flip the **arrows** to the inside. Click the **dimension text** and drag the text outside the leader lines.

Fit the drawing to the Graphics window.

214) Press the **f** key.

Save the GUIDE drawing.

215) Click **Save** .

Partial Auxiliary View–Crop View

Create a Partial Auxiliary View from the Full Auxiliary View. Sketch a closed profile in an active Auxiliary View. Create the Profile with a closed Spline. Create a Partial Auxiliary View. Crop the view. The 6mm dimension references the centerline from the Guide Hole.

For Quality Assurance and Inspection of the GUIDE part, add a dimension that references the Temporary Axis of the Guide Hole. Sketch a centerline collinear with the Temporary Axis.

Activity: Partial Auxiliary View-Crop View

Select the view.

216) Click **Zoom to Area** .

217) **Zoom in** on the Auxiliary view.

218) Click **Zoom to Area** to deactivate.

219) Click the **Auxiliary view boundary**.

220) Click **Hidden Lines Removed** .

Sketch a closed Spline.

221) Click **Sketch** Sketch .

222) Click **Spline** Spline from the Sketch tools toolbar.

223) Click seven **positions** clockwise to create the closed Spline. The first point is coincident with the last point.

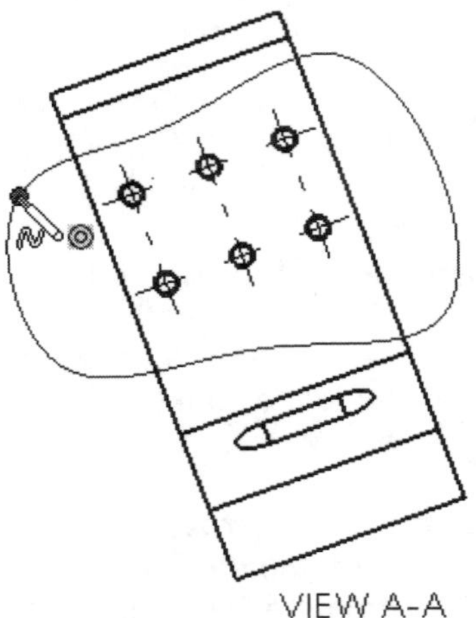

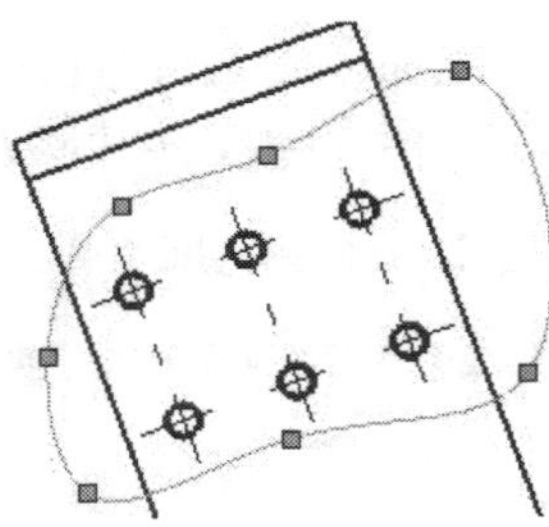

Insert a Partial Auxiliary View.

224) Click **Drawings** Drawings from the Control Area.

225) Click **Crop View** Crop View from the Drawings toolbar.

226) Click **OK** from the Spline PropertyManager.

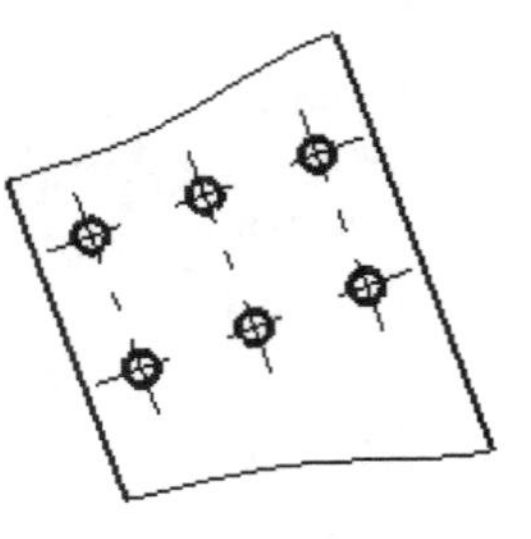

Insert a sketched Centerline.

227) Click inside the **Auxiliary View** boundary.

228) Check **View**, **Temporary Axis** from the Main menu. The Temporary Axis for the Guide Hole is displayed.

229) Click **Sketch** Sketch.

230) Click **Centerline** Centerl... from the Sketch toolbar. The Insert Line PropertyManager is displayed.

231) Sketch a **centerline** parallel, above the Temporary axis. The centerline extends approximately 5mm to the left and right of the profile lines.

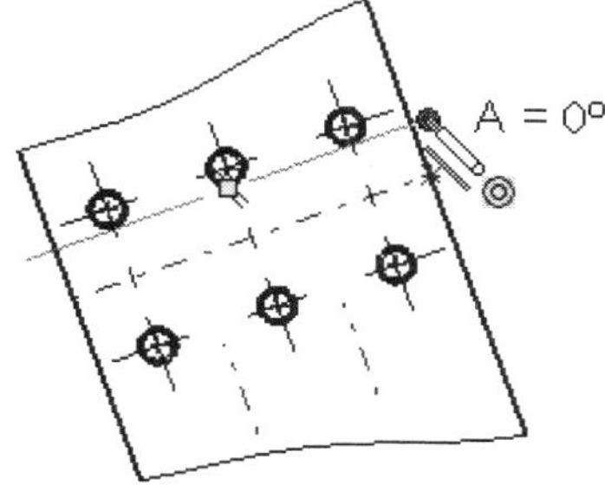

232) Click **OK** from the Insert Line PropertyManager.

Add a Collinear Relation.

233) Click the **centerline**. The centerline turns green.

234) Hold the **Ctrl** key down.

235) Click the **Temporary Axis**. The mouse pointer displays the Axis feedback icon. Axis<1> is added to the Add Relations Selected Entities box.

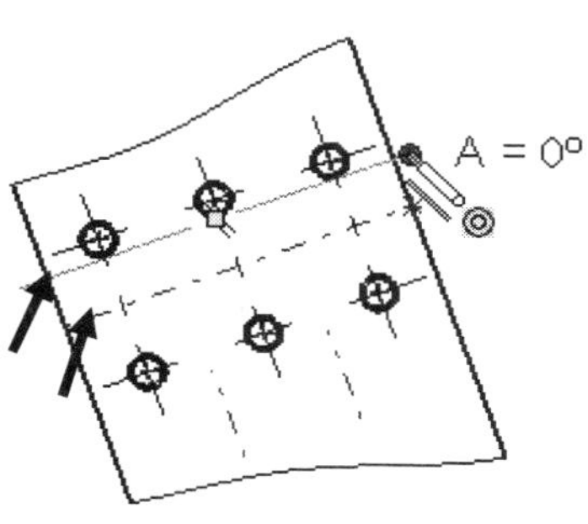

236) Release the **Ctrl** key.

237) Click **Collinear** in the Add Relations dialog box.

238) Click **OK** from the Properties PropertyManager.

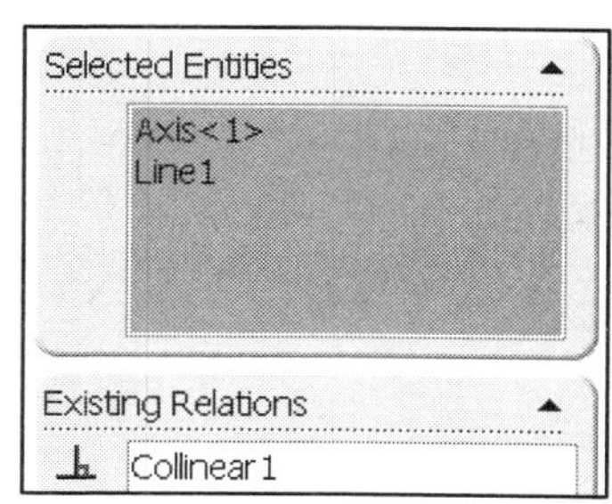

Hide the Temporary Axis.

239) Click **View**, uncheck **Temporary Axis** from the Main menu.

Insert dimensions into the Auxiliary View.

240) Click the **Auxiliary View** boundary.

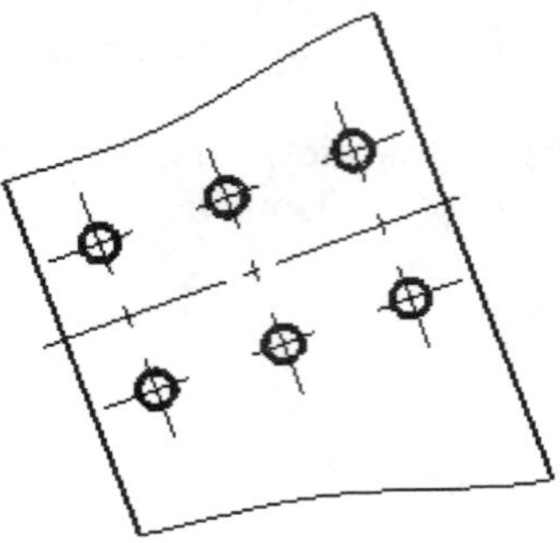

VIEW A-A

241) Click **Model Items** Model from the Annotations toolbar.

242) Select **Entire Model** in the Import from list box.

243) Click **Hole Wizard Locations** from the Dimensions box.

244) Check **OK** from the Model Items PropertyManager.

Note: The dimensions for the Linear Pattern of Holes are determined from the initial Hole Wizard position dimensions and the Linear Pattern dimensions. Your dimensioning standard requires the distance between the holes in a pattern.

Do not over dimension. In the next steps, you will hide the existing dimensions and add a new dimension.

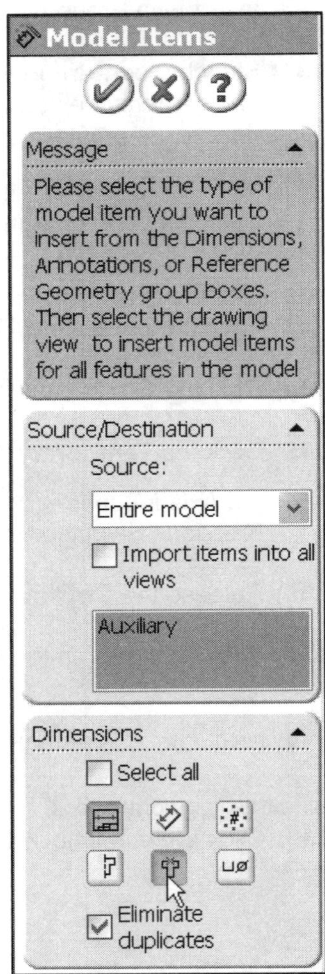

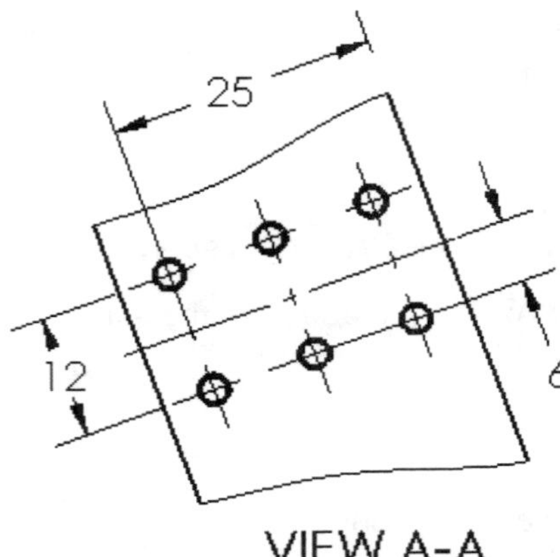

VIEW A-A

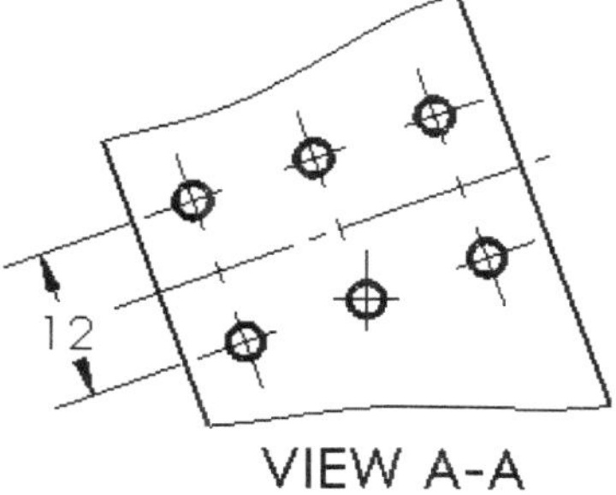

Hide the dimensions.

245) Right-click **25**.

246) Click **Hide**.

247) Right-click **6**.

248) Click **Hide**.

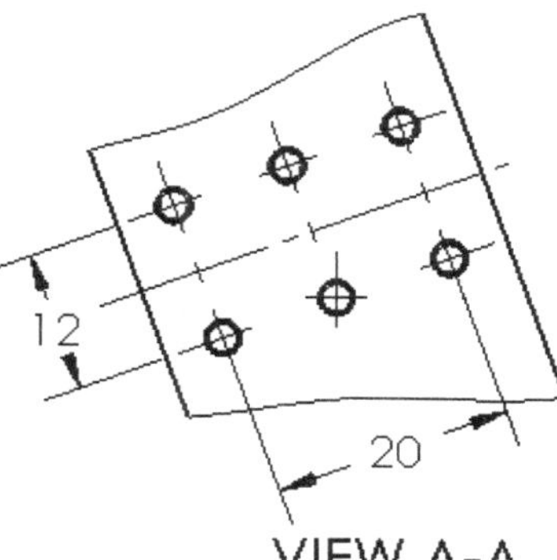

Add a dimension.

249) Click **Smart Dimension** 

250) Click the **center point** of the bottom left hole. Click a **center point** of the bottom right hole.

251) Click a **position** below the profile. Check **OK** from the Dimension PropertyManager.

252) Uncheck the **Parentheses** box.

Save the drawing.

253) Click **Save**.

Move Dimensions to a Different View

Move the linear dimension 10 that defines the Linear Hole Pattern from Drawing View3 (Top) to the Auxiliary View. When moving dimensions from one view to another, utilize the Shift key and only drag the dimension text.

Release the dimension text inside the view boundary. The text will not switch views if positioned outside the view boundary.

Activity: Move Dimensions to a Different View

Move dimensions from the Top view to the Auxiliary View.

254) Press the **z key** approximately 4 times to view the dimensions in the Top view.

255) Hold the **Shift** key down. Click and drag the vertical dimension **10**, between the 2 holes from the Top view to the Auxiliary View.

256) Release the **mouse button** and the **Shift** key when the mouse pointer is inside the Auxiliary view boundary.

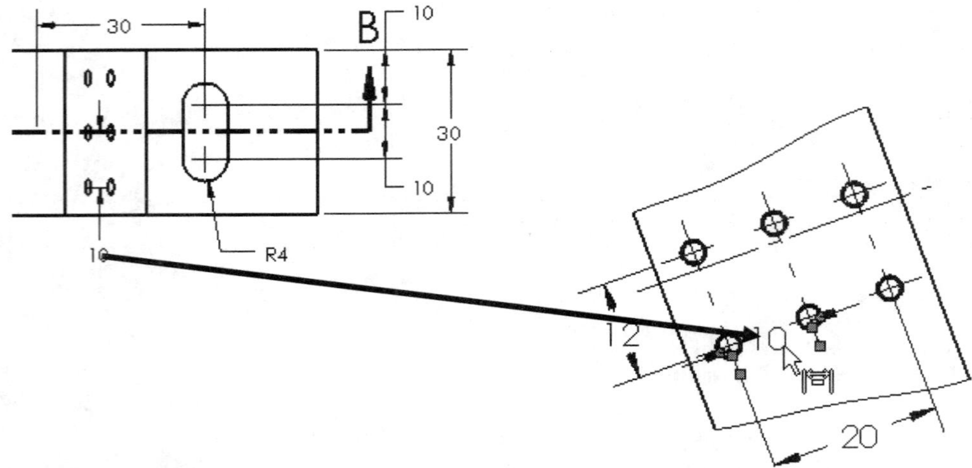

257) Click and drag the **dimensions** off the Auxiliary View.

258) Click and drag the **VIEW A-A** text off the view boundary.

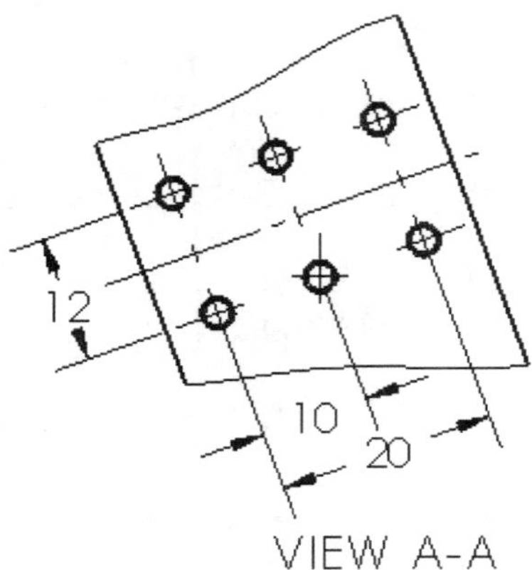

Save the drawing.

259) Click **Save** .

Dimension Holes and the Hole Callout

Simple Holes and other circular geometry are dimensioned in three ways: Diameter, Radius and Linear (between two straight lines).

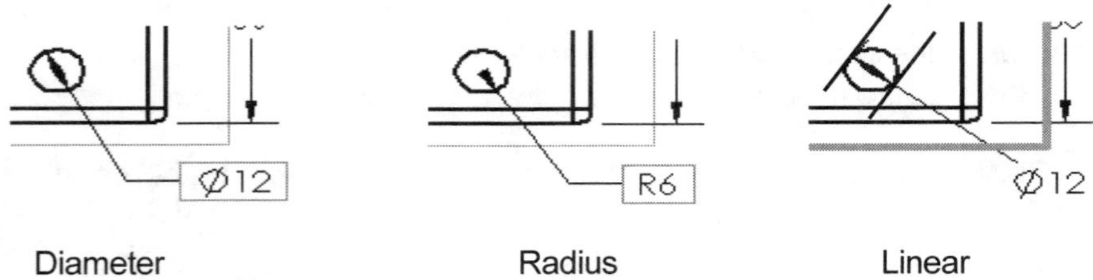

Diameter Radius Linear

The holes in the Auxiliary view require a diameter dimension and a note to represent the six holes. Use the Hole Callout to dimension the holes. The Hole Callout function creates additional notes required to dimension the holes.

The dimension standard symbols are displayed automatically when you use the Hole Wizard.

Activity: Dimension Holes and the Hole Callout

Dimension the Linear Pattern of Holes.

260) Click **Annotations** Annotati... from the Control Area.

261) Click **Hole Callout** Hole Callout in the Annotation Toolbar.

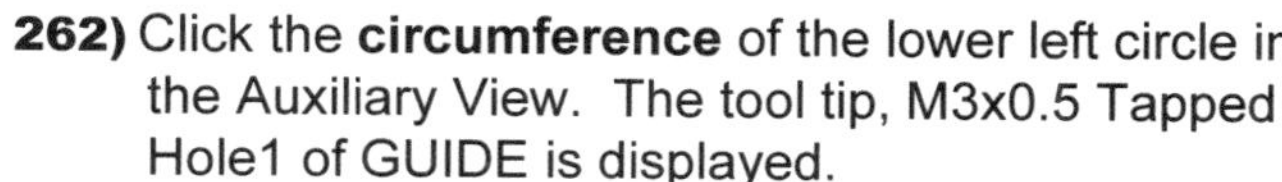

262) Click the **circumference** of the lower left circle in the Auxiliary View. The tool tip, M3x0.5 Tapped Hole1 of GUIDE is displayed.

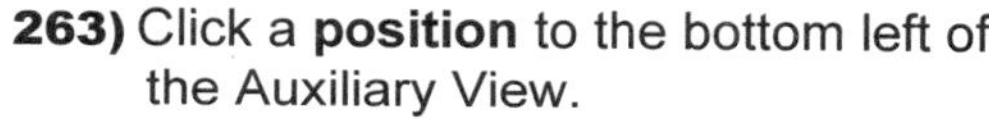

263) Click a **position** to the bottom left of the Auxiliary View.

Note: The Hole Callout text displayed in the Dimension Text box depends on the options utilized in the Hole Wizard and Linear Pattern.

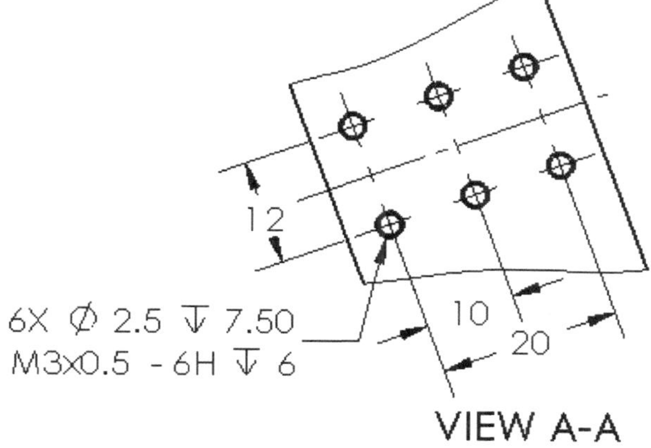

Remove the trailing zeros for ASME Y14 millimeter display.

264) Click **.1** from the Primary Unit Tolerance/Precision box.

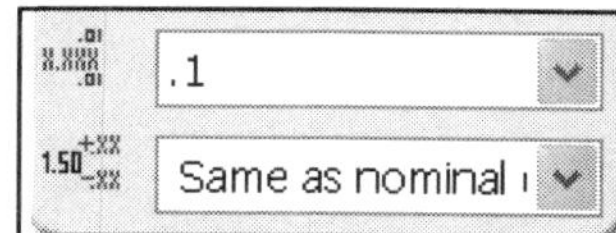

265) Click **OK** from the Dimension PropertyManager. The Hole Callout is deactivated.

 Know inch/mm decimal display. The ASME Y14.5 standard states:

- For millimeter dimensions <1, display the leading zero. Remove trailing zeros.
- For inch dimensions <1, delete the leading zero. The dimension is displayed with the same number of decimal places as its tolerance.

Symbols are located on the bottom of the Dimension Text dialog box.

The current text is displayed in the text box. Example:

- <NUM_INST>: Number of Instances in a Pattern.
- <MOD-DIAM>: Diameter symbol ∅.
- <HOLE-DEPTH>: Deep symbol ↧.
- <HOLE-SPOT>: Counterbore symbol ⌴.
- <DIM>: Dimension value 3.

Fit the Drawing to the Graphics window.

266) Press the **f** key.

Insert dimension text.

267) Click inside the **Drawing View1 boundary**.

268) Click **Zoom to select**. Click the Guide Hole dimension **∅10.015/10.000** in Drawing View1.

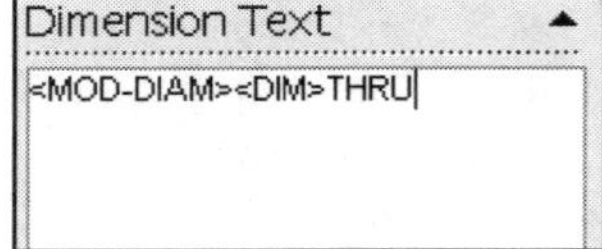

269) Enter text **THRU** in the Dimension Text box. THRU is displayed on the drawing in green.

270) Click **OK** from the Dimension PropertyManager.

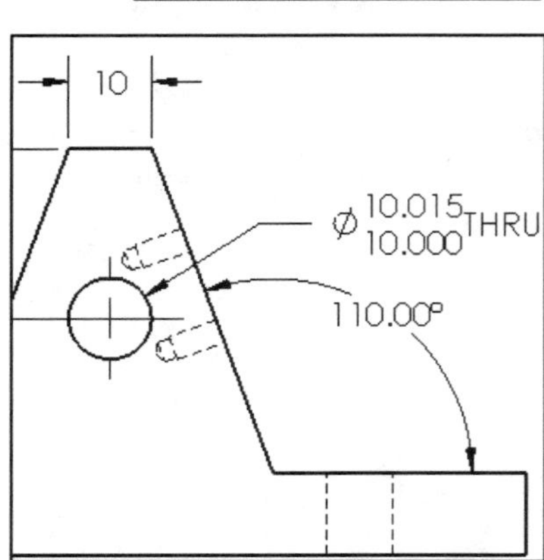

Save the drawing.

271) Click **Save**.

Access Notes, Hole Callouts and other Dimension Annotations through the Annotations toolbar menu. Access Annotations with the Right Mouse button, Annotations.

Center Marks and Centerlines

Hole centerlines are composed of alternating long and short dash lines. Centerlines indicate symmetry. Centerlines also identify the center of a circle, axes or cylindrical geometry.

Auto insert on view creation
Center marks
Centerlines
Balloons
Dimensions marked for drawing
Center marks
Size: 2.54mm
Extended lines
Centerline font

Center Marks represents two perpendicular intersecting centerlines. The default Size and display of the Center Mark is set in Tools, Options, Document Properties, Center marks check box. The option Auto insert on view creation controls the display of Center Marks within a new view. Center Marks are inserted on view creation by default. Modify the position and size of the Center Marks. The following three steps illustrate how to create a new Center Mark.

Note: If the Center Mark exists, skip the next four steps.

Activity: Center Marks and Centerlines

Insert a Center Mark.

272) Click **Annotations** Annotati... .

273) Click **Center Mark** Center from the Annotations toolbar. The Center Mark PropertyManager is displayed.

274) Click the **Guide Hole circumference**. The Center mark is inserted.

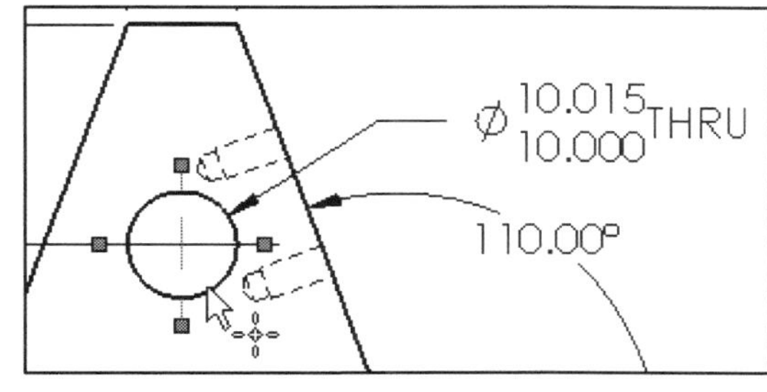

275) Click **OK** from the Center Mark PropertyManager.

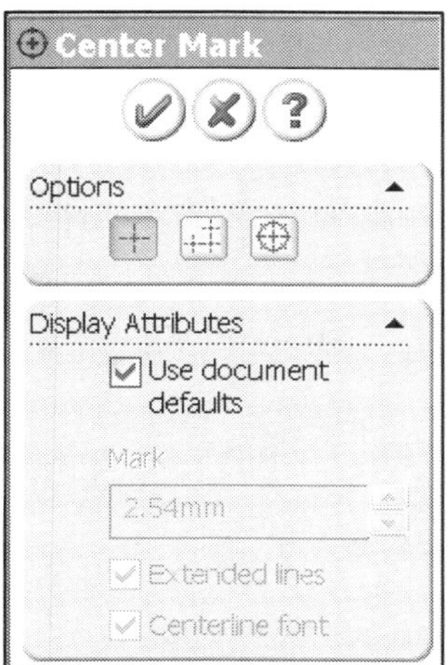

Dimension standards require a gap between the Center Mark and the end points of the leader line. Currently, the leader line overlaps the Center Mark.

Create a gap.

276) Click the vertical dimension **29** of the GUIDE.

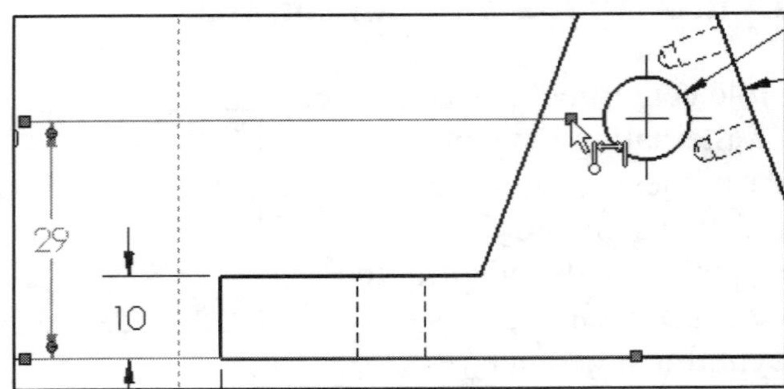

277) Click and drag the **green endpoint** to the left of the Center Mark.

278) Click **OK** from the Dimension PropertyManager.

Selection filters all you to select small Center Marks quickly. Activate the Selection Filter toolbar and resize the Center Marks in the Top view.

Activate the Selection Filter Center Marks.

279) Click **Filter Center Marks** from the Selection Filter toolbar.

Activate the Top view.

280) Click the **Top view boundary**.

281) Click **Zoom to Selection** .

Reduce the size of the Center Mark.

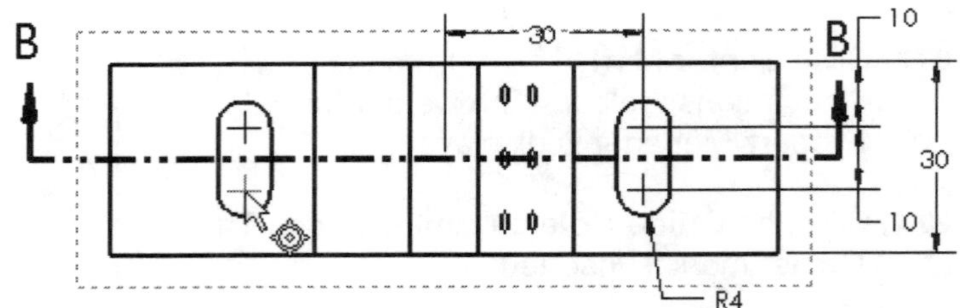

282) Click the bottom left **Center Mark**. The Filter Center Marks mouse feedback is displayed.

283) Hold the **Ctrl** key down. Click the other **three Center Marks**.

284) Release the **Ctrl** key. Enter **1** for Mark size. Click **OK** from the Center Mark PropertyManager.

285) Update the Center Mark size. Click **Rebuild** from the Main menu.

Save the drawing.

286) Click **Save** .

Deactivate the Selection Filter.

287) Click **Clear All Filters** from the Selection Filter toolbar.

Ctrl-Select Center Marks, dimensions, and annotations to modify the same property of the group.

Insert an Annotation Centerline.

288) Click **Annotations** Annotati... . Click **Centerline** Centerline from the Annotations toolbar.

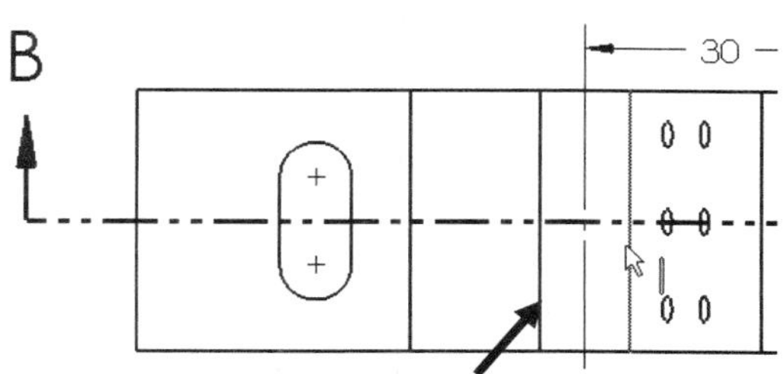

289) Click the **left edge** of the GUIDE hole.

290) Click the **right edge** of the GUIDE hole. The centerline is displayed in the Top view.

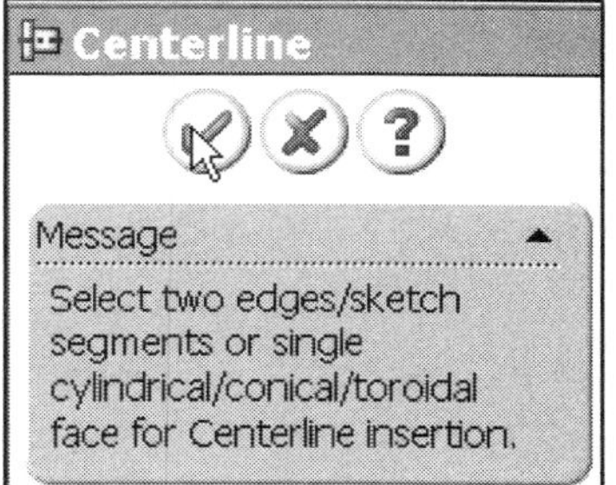

291) Click **OK** from the Centerline PropertyManager.

Save the drawing.

292) Click **Save** .

Modify the Dimension Scheme

The current feature dimension scheme represents the design intent of the GUIDE part. The Mirror Entities Sketch tool built symmetry into the Extruded Base sketch. The Mirror feature built symmetry into the Slot Cuts.

The current dimension scheme for the Slot Cut differs from the ASME 14.5M Dimension Standard for a slot. Redefine the dimensions for the Slot Cut according to the ASME 14.5M Standard.

The ASME 14.5M Standard requires an outside dimension of a slot. The Radius value is not dimensioned. The left Slot Cut was created with the Mirror feature.

Create a centerline and dimension to complete the detailing of the Slot Cut. Sketch the vertical dimension, 10. The default arc conditions are measured from arc center point to arc center point. The dimension extension lines are tangent to the top arc and bottom arc.

Activity: Modify the Dimension Scheme

Modify the Slot Cut Dimension scheme.

293) Click **Layer Properties** from the Layer Toolbar. The Layer Status is displayed.

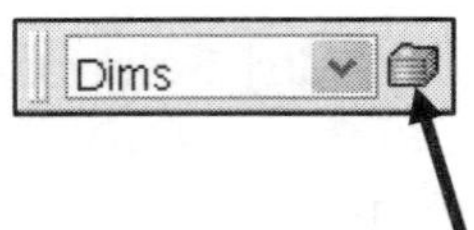

Set the On/Off icon to modify the status of the Layers.

294) Click **Dims Layer** On. Dims is the current layer.

295) Click the **Notes Layer** On. Click the **Hidden Dims Layer** Off.

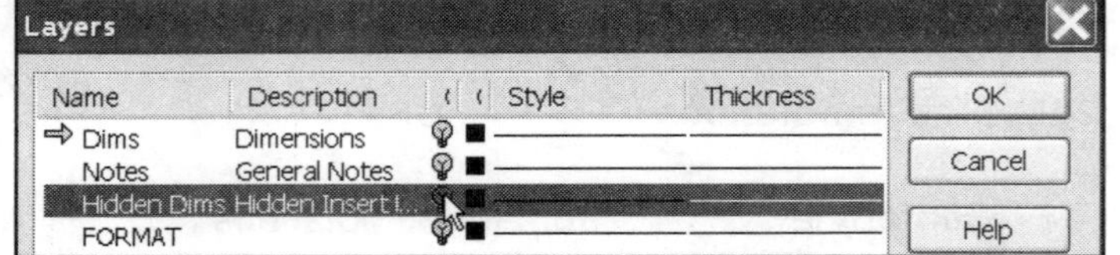

296) Click the **Format Layer** On.

297) Click **OK**.

298) Click **Zoom to Area** .

299) **Zoom in** on the right slot of the Top view.

300) Click **Zoom to Area** to deactivate.

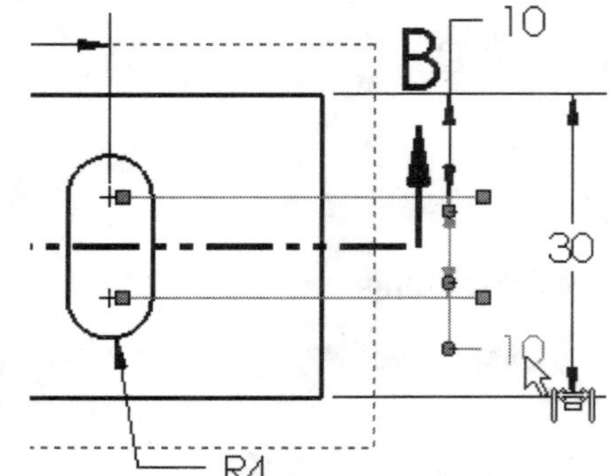

Hide the dimension between the two arc center points.

301) Click the **10** dimension on the right side of the Top view.

302) Select the **Hidden Dims** from the Layer box in the Dimension PropertyManager.

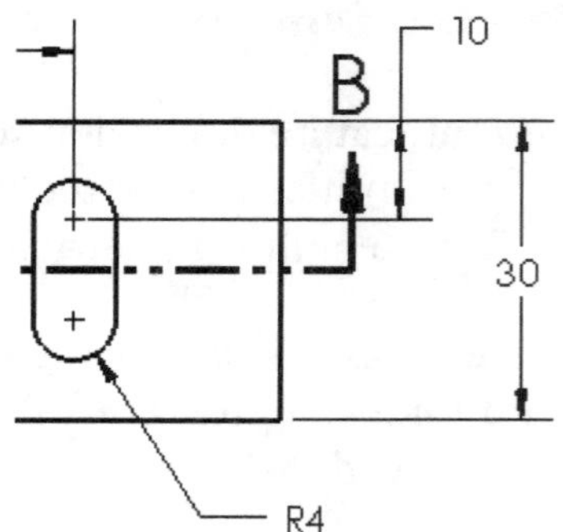

303) Click **OK** from the Dimension PropertyManager.

Create the vertical dimension.

304) Click **Smart Dimension**  .

305) Click the top of the **top left arc**. Click the bottom of the **bottom left arc**. Click a **position** to the right of the Top view. Right-click **Properties** on the 10 dimension. Click **Max** for First arc condition.

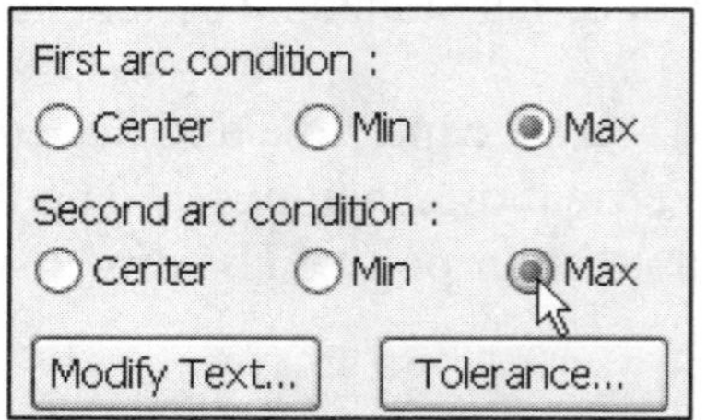

306) Click **Max** for Second arc condition.

307) Click **OK**.

Modify the Radius text.

308) Click **R4**.

309) Delete **R<DIM>** in the Dimension text box.

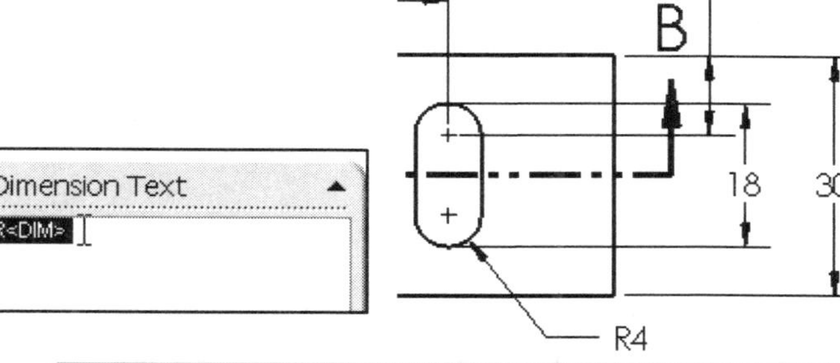

310) Click **Yes** to the Confirm dimension value text override message.

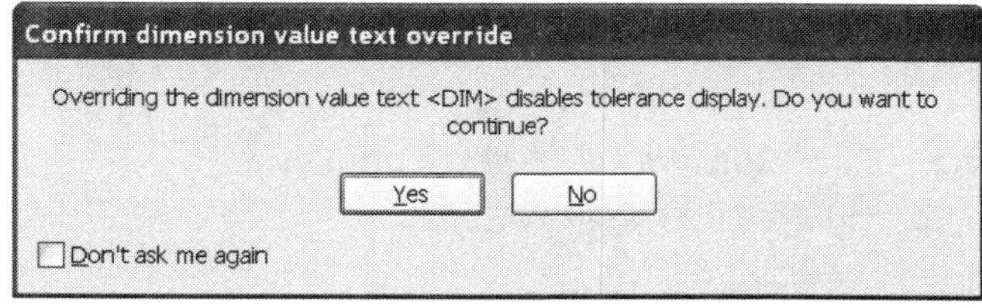

311) Enter **2X R** for Dimension text.

312) Click **OK**  from the Dimension PropertyManager.

Add a dimension.

313) Click **Smart Dimension** Smart Dimens....

314) Click the **left vertical line** of the Slot Cut.

315) Click the **right vertical line** of the Slot Cut.

316) Click a **position** below the horizontal profile line.

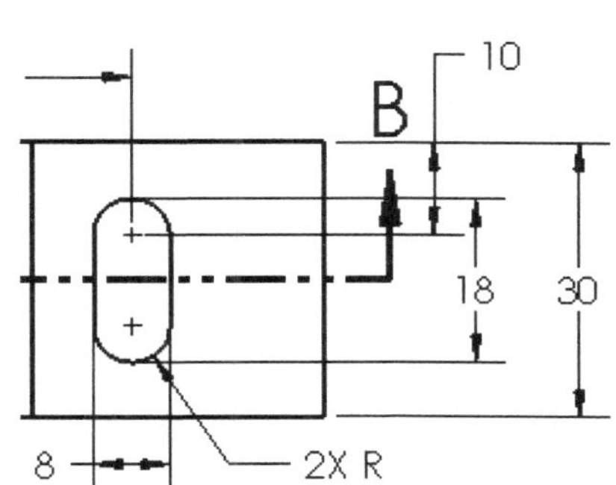

Drawing dimensions are added in the drawing document. Model dimensions are inserted from the part. Utilize Smart Dimension in the GUIDE drawing to create drawing dimensions.

317) Click the **centerline**. Click the left **Slot Cut arc center point**.

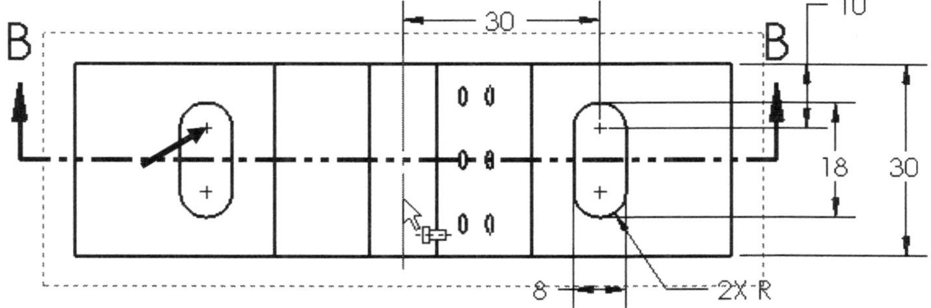

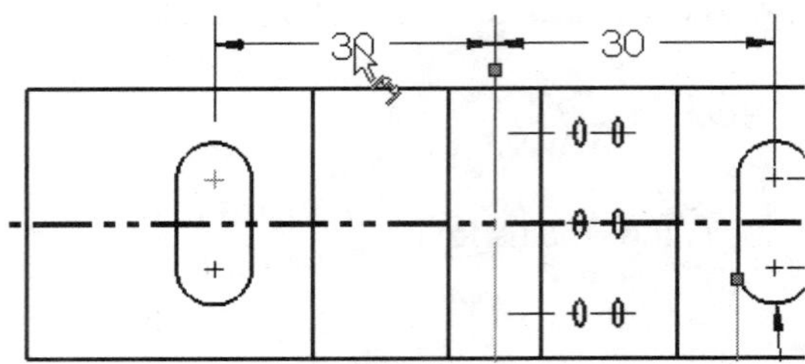

318) Click a **position** above the top horizontal line.

319) Enter **30**. Dimensions in this view contain no parentheses. Uncheck the Parentheses box if required.

Insert Centerlines.

320) Click **Annotations** Annotati... .

321) Click **Centerline** Centerline from the Annotations toolbar.

Activate the Section View.

322) Click inside the **Section View** boundary. Centerlines are inserted into the Section view.

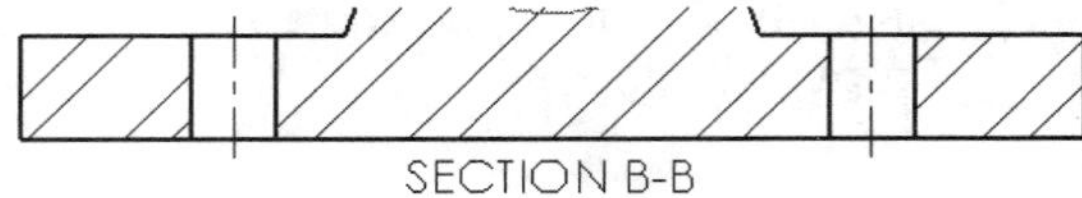

Add a reference dimension.

323) Click **Smart Dimension** Dimens... .

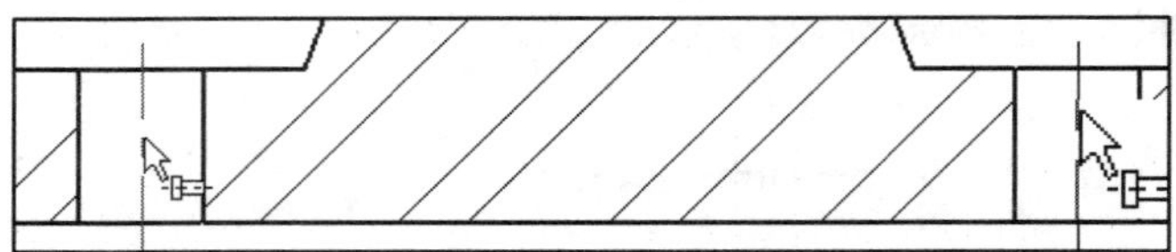

324) Click the **left centerline**.

325) Click the **right centerline**.

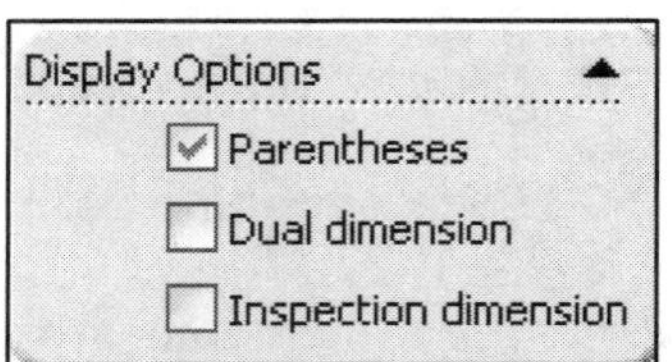

326) Click a **position** below the bottom horizontal line.

327) Check **Parentheses** in the Display Options box. The (60) reference dimension is displayed with parenthesis.

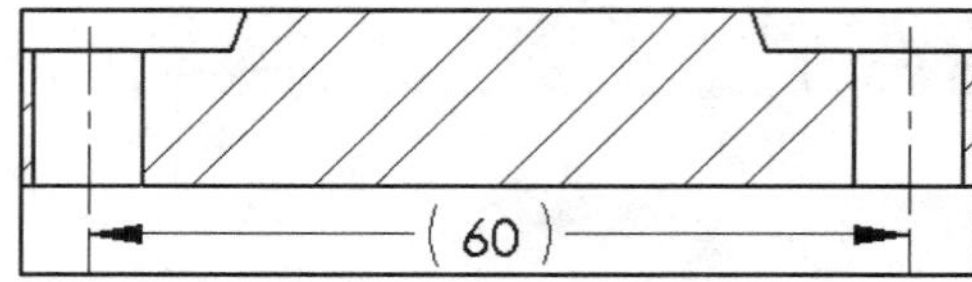

328) Click **OK** from the Dimension PropertyManager.

Save the drawing.

329) Click **Save** .

Design parts to maximize symmetry and geometric relations to fully define sketches. Minimize dimensions in the part. Insert dimensions in the drawing to adhere to machining requires and Dimension Standards.

Examples: Insert reference dimensions by adding par theses and redefine a slot dimension scheme according to the ASME Y14.5 standard.

Additional Information Dimensions and Annotations are found in SolidWorks Help Topics. Keywords: Dimensions (circles, extension lines, inserting into drawings, move, parenthesis), Crop view, Annotations (Hole Callout, Centerline, Centermark).

Review the Dimensions and Annotations.

You inserted part dimensions and annotations into the drawing. Dimensions were moved to new positions. Leader lines and dimension text were repositioned. Annotations were edited to reflect the drawing standard.

Centerlines and Center Marks were inserted into each view and were modified in the PropertyManager. You modified Hole Callouts, dimensions, annotations and referenced dimensions to conform to the drawing standard.

GUIDE Part-Insert an Additional Feature

The design process is dynamic. We do not live in a static world. Create and add an edge Fillet feature to the GUIDE part. Insert dimensions into the Drawing View1 (Front).

Activity: GUIDE Part-Insert an Additional Feature

Open the Guide part.

330) Right-click inside the **Drawing View1** boundary.

331) Click **Open guide.sldprt**.

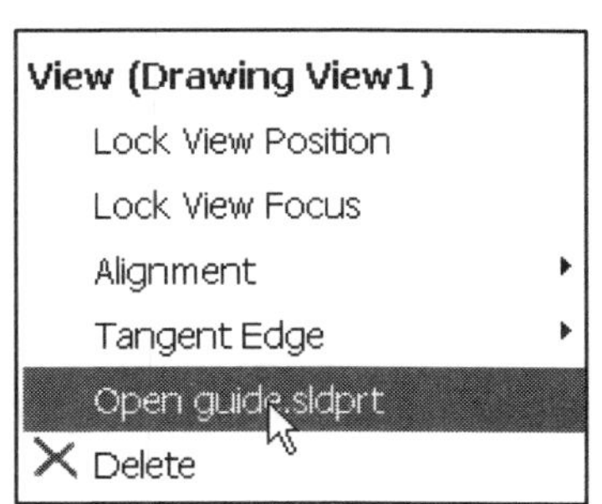

If the View menu is not displayed, right-click Select. Tools in the Annotations toolbar remain active until they are deactivated or an OK, Select or other command is issued.

Display Hidden Lines to select edges to fillet.

332) Click **Hidden Lines Visible**.

Display the Isometric view.

333) Click **Isometric view** .

Create a Fillet feature.

334) Click the hidden **edge**.

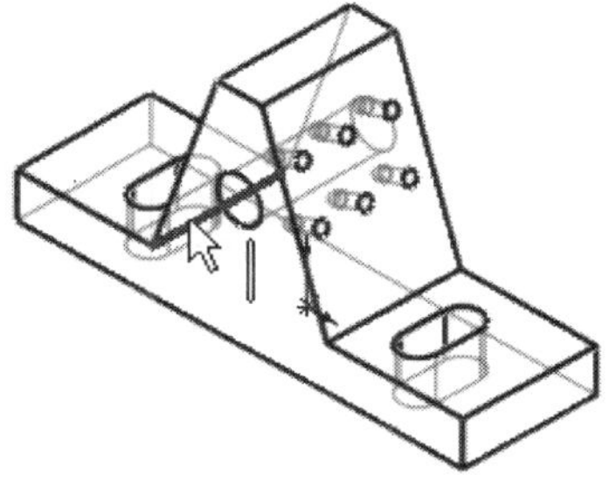

335) Click **Fillet** Fillet. The Fillet feature PropertyManager is displayed.

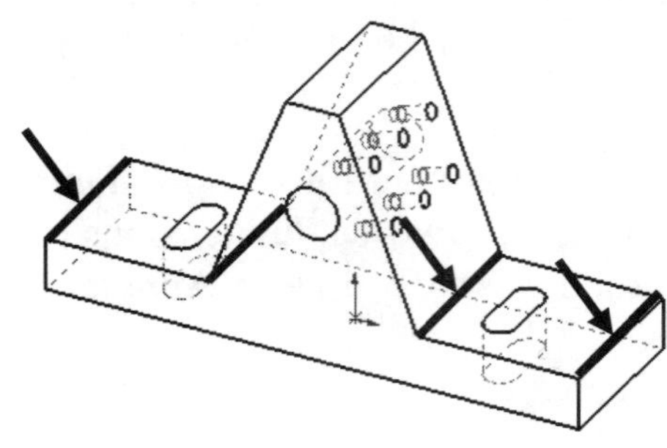

336) Enter **1** in the Fillet Radius list box.

337) Click the other **3 edges**. Each edge is added to the Items to Fillet list.

338) Click **OK** from the Fillet PropertyManager.

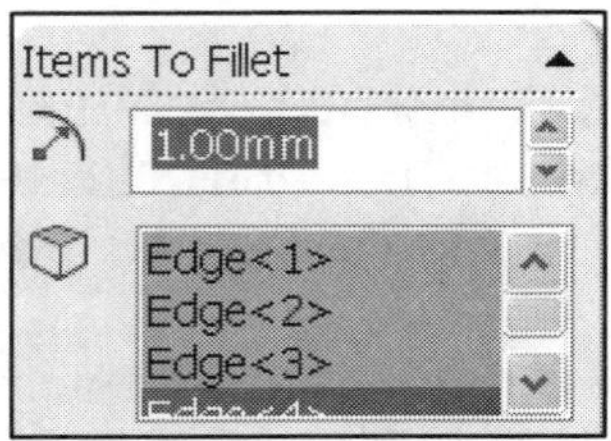

Save the GUIDE part.

339) Click **Save** .

Open the Drawing.

340) Right-click on the **GUIDE Part** GUIDE icon in the FeatureManager.

341) Click **Open Drawing**.

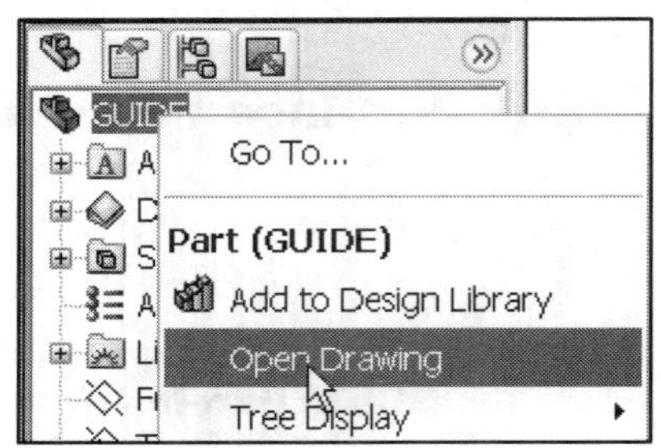

Fit the drawing to the Graphics window.

342) Press the **f** key.

Display the GUIDE features.

343) Click the **Drawing FeatureManager icon** .

344) Click **Plus** to expand Drawing View1.

345) Click **Plus** to expand the GUIDE part.

346) Click **Fillet1**.

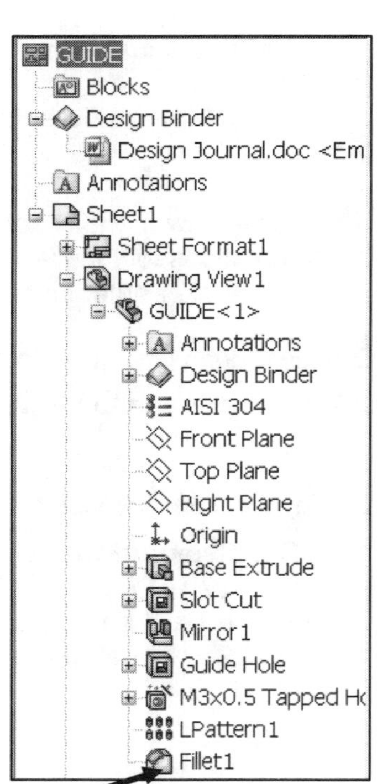

Insert the dimensions for the Fillet1 feature on the Dims Layer. The current layer should be Dims. Dims .

The Model Items, Import into drawing view, Import items into all views option insert dimensions into Section Views and Detail View before other types of views on the drawing. The Fillet feature dimension appears in the Section View.

Insert dimensions by Selected feature into Drawing View1 (Front).

347) Click **Model Items** from the Annotations toolbar. The Selected feature option and Import items into all views option are selected by default.

348) Click **OK** from the Model Items PropertyManager.

Position the Fillet text.

349) Click and Drag the **R1** text off the profile in the Section View. The R1 text is displayed on the left side or right side of the Section View.

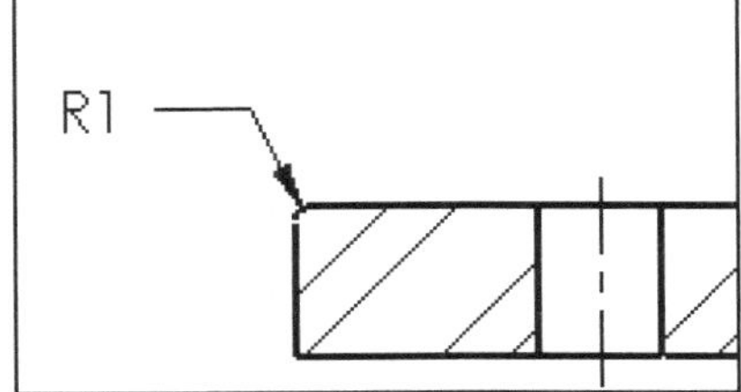

Save the GUIDE drawing.

350) Click **Save** .

General Notes and Parametric Notes

Plan ahead for general drawing notes. Notes provide relative part or assembly information. Example: Material type, material finish, special manufacturing procedure or considerations, preferred supplier, etc.

Below are a few helpful guidelines to create general drawing notes:

- Use capital letters.
- Use left text justification.
- Font size should be the same size as the dimension text.

Create parametric notes by selecting dimensions in the drawing. Example: Specify the Fillet Radius of the GUIDE as a note in the drawing. If the Radius is modified, the corresponding note is also modified.

Hide superfluous feature dimensions. Do not delete feature dimensions. Recall hidden dimension with the View, Show Hidden command. Utilize a Layer to Hide/Show superfluous feature dimensions with the Layer On/Off icon.

Locate the R1 text used to create the edge Fillet. The text is found in Drawing View1 (Front).

Activity: General Notes and Parametric Notes

Locate the R1 text.

351) Position the **mouse pointer** over the R1 text in the Section View. The text displays the dimension name.

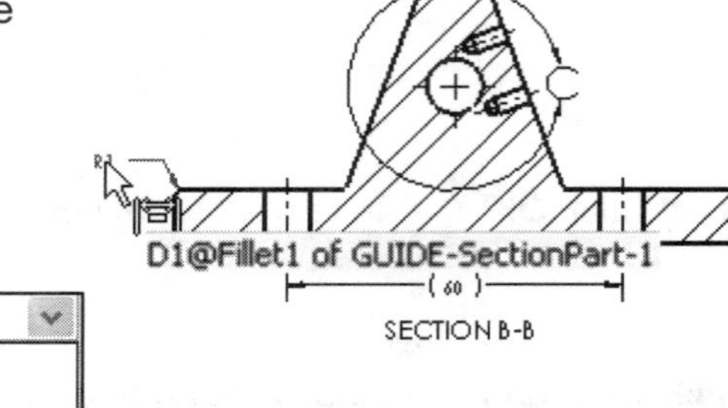

Insert a parametric drawing note.

352) Click the **Notes** Layer from the Layer drop down list.

Notes
-None-
Dims
Notes
Hidden Dims
FORMAT

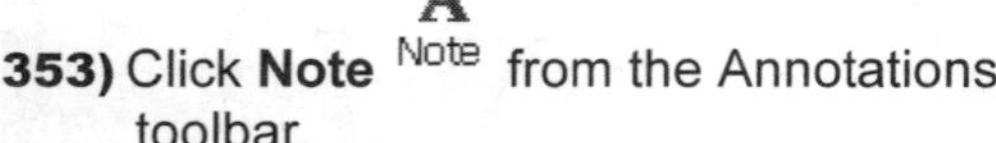

353) Click **Note** from the Annotations toolbar.

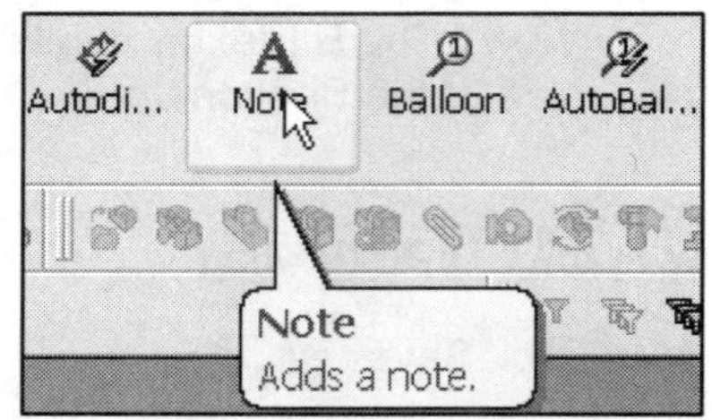

354) Click a **start point** in the lower left corner of the Graphics window, to the left of the Title block, below Drawing View1.

355) Type two lines of notes in the Note text box. Line 1: Enter **1. ALL ROUNDS**.

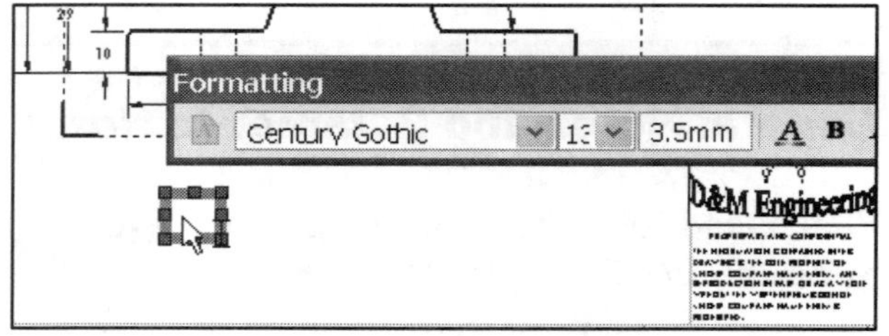

356) Press the **Space** key.

357) Click **R1**. The radius value 1 is added to the text box.

358) Press the **Space** key.

359) Enter **MM**.

360) Press **Enter**.

1. ALL ROUNDS 1 MM.
2. REMOVE ALL BURRS.

361) Line 2: Enter **2. REMOVE ALL BURRS**.

362) Click **OK** from the Note PropertyManager.

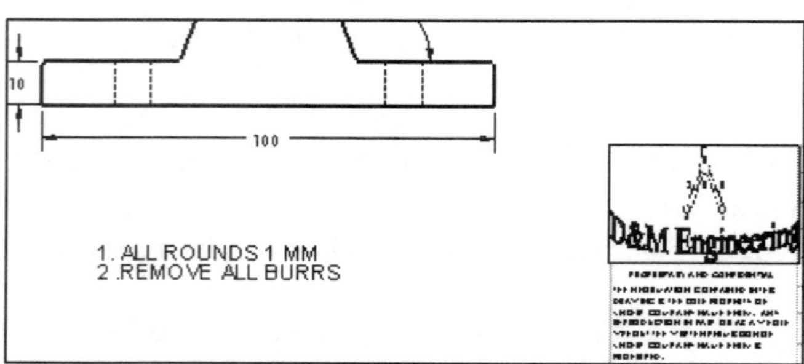

The parametric note specifies that the radius of all Rounds is 1MM. Modify the Fillet radius from 1MM to 2MM.

Do not double dimension a drawing with a note and the corresponding dimension. Hide the radial dimension.

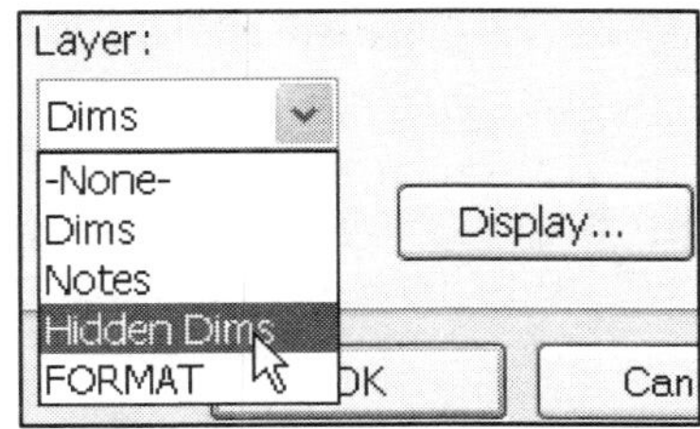

Hide the R1 dimension in the drawing.

363) Click the **R1** text in the Section View.

364) Right-click **Properties**.

365) Click **Hide Dims** from the Layer drop down list.

366) Click **OK**.

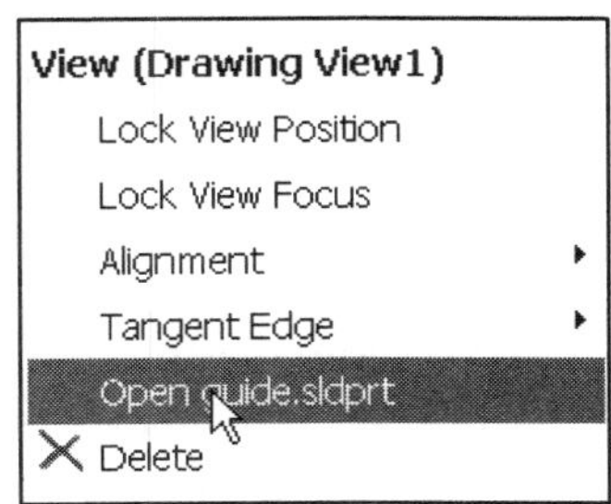

Open the GUIDE part.

367) Right-click **Open guide.sldprt** in the Front view of the GUIDE.

Modify the Fillet Radius.

368) Double-click **Fillet1** from the FeatureManager.

369) Double-click **R1** text.

370) Enter **2** in the Modify dialog box.

371) Click **Rebuild** .

372) Click the **Green Check mark** .

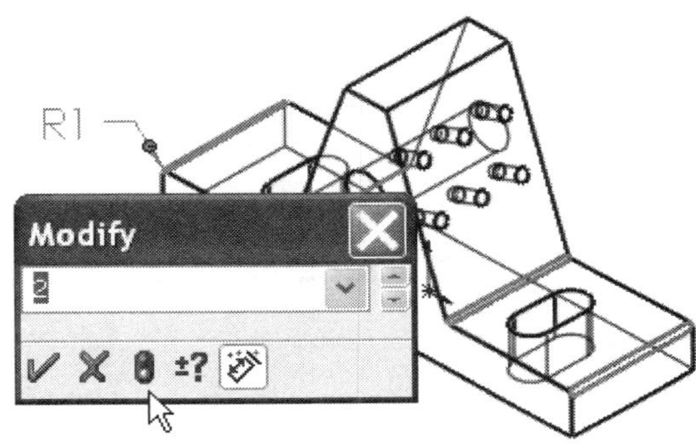

373) Click **OK** from the Dimension PropertyManager.

374) Click **Window**, **GUIDE –Sheet1** from the Main menu. The parametric note displays ALL ROUNDS 2 MM. The updated views reflect the new Fillet radius.

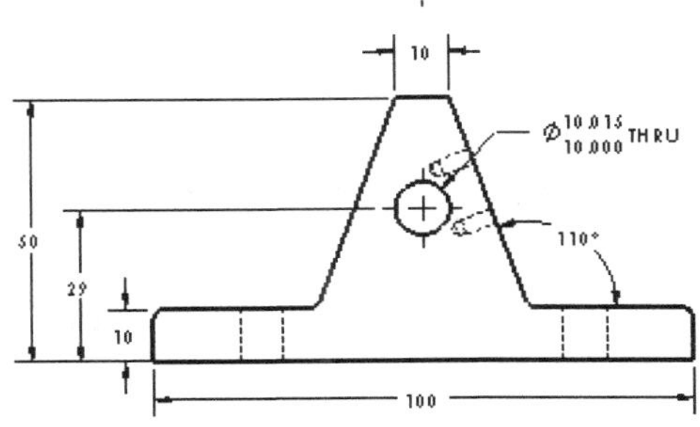

Fit the drawing to the Graphics window.

375) Press the **f** key.

Save the GUIDE drawing.

376) Click **Save** .

377) Click **Yes** to Save the Referenced model.

By modifying the Fillet radius from 1MM to 2MM, a change was made to the drawing. Changes made to the drawing require written documentation.

An Engineering Change Order (ECO) or Engineering Change Notice (ECN) is written for each modification in the drawing. Modifications to the drawing are listed in the Revision Table.

 Obtain the ECO number before you institute the change to manufacturing.

Revision Table

The Revision Table provides a drawing history. Changes to the document are recorded systematically in the Revision Table. Insert a Revision Table into the GUIDE drawing. The default columns are as follows: Zone, Rev, Description, Date and Approved.

Zone utilizes the row letter and column number contained in the drawing boarder. Position the Rev letter in the Zone area. Enter the Zone letter/number.

Enter a Description that corresponds to the ECO number. Modify the date if required. Enter the initials/name of the engineering manager who approved the revision.

Activity: Revision Table

Insert Revision Table.

378) Click **Insert**, **Tables**, **Revision Table** Revision Table from the Main menu. The Revision Table PropertyManager is displayed. Accept the default Table Template.

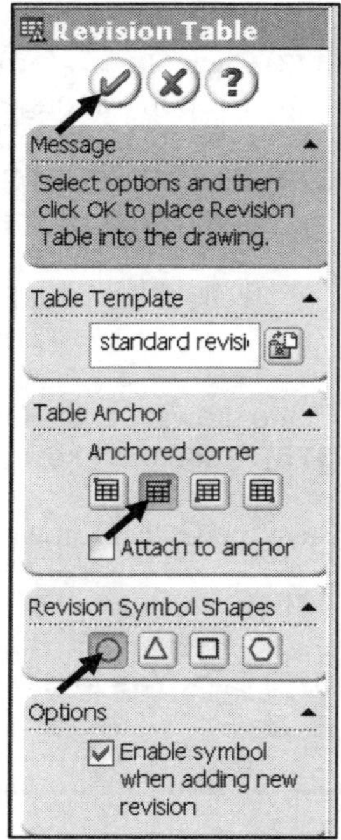

379) Click **Top Right** in the Table Anchor box.

380) Click **Circle** in the Revision Symbol Shapes menu.

381) Check **Enable symbol when adding new revision**.

382) Click **OK** from the Revision Table PropertyManager.

383) Click **Zoom to Area**. **Zoom in** on the first row in the drawing. Click **Zoom to Area** to deactivate.

Insert the first row. Create the first revision.

384) Right-click the **Revision Table**.

REVISIONS				
ZONE	REV.	DESCRIPTION	DATE	APPROVED

385) Click **Revisions**, **Add Revision**. The Revision letter, A and the current date are displayed. The Revision Symbol is displayed on the mouse pointer.

REVISIONS				
ZONE	REV.	DESCRIPTION	DATE	APPROVED
	A		7/1/2005	

386) Click a **position** in the Isometric view.

387) Click **OK** from the Revision Table PropertyManager.

388) Double-click the **text box** under the Description column.

389) Enter **ECO 32510 RELEASE TO MANUFACTURING** for DESCRIPTION.

390) Click **OK** from the Note PropertyManager.

391) Double-click the **text box** under the APPROVED.

392) Enter Documentation Control Manager's Initials, **DCP**.

REVISIONS				
ZONE	REV.	DESCRIPTION	DATE	APPROVED
	A	ECO 32510 RELEASE TO MANUFACTURING	7/1/2005	DCP

393) Click **OK** from the Note PropertyManager.

Insert the second row. Create the second revision.

394) Right-click the **Revision Table**. Click **Revisions**, **Add Revision**. The Revision letter B and the current date are displayed. Click a **position** at the corner of the Section View.

395) Click **OK** from the Revision Symbol PropertyManager.

396) Double-click the **text box** under the Description column.

397) Enter **ECO 33621 MODIFY FILLET RADIUS FROM 1MM to 2MM** for DESCRIPTION.

398) Click **OK** from the Note PropertyManager.

399) Double-click the **text box** under the APPROVED.

400) Enter Documentation Control Manager's Initials, **DCP**.

REVISIONS				
ZONE	REV.	DESCRIPTION	DATE	APPROVED
	A	ECO 32510 RELEASE TO MANUFACTURING	7/1/2005	DCP
	B	ECO 33621 MODIFY FILLET RADIUS FROM 1MM to 2MM	7/1/2005	DCP

401) Click **OK**  from the Note PropertyManager.

The Revision Property, $PRP:"Revision", in the Title block is linked to the REV. Property in the REVISIONS table. The latest REV. letter is displayed in the Title block.

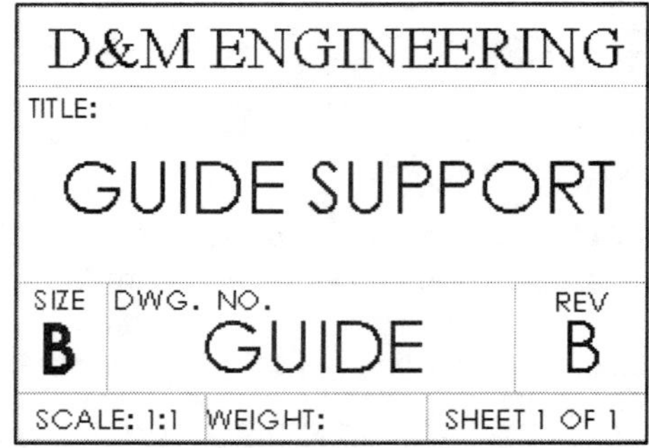

Revision Table Zone Numbers, Dates and Approved names are inserted as an exercise. The Revision Table and Engineering Change Order documentation are integrated in the drawing and the design process.

To save time, incorporate the Revision Table into your custom Sheet Formats.

Part Number and Document Properties

Engineers manage the parts they create and modify. Each part requires a Part Number and Part Name. A part number is a numeric representation of the part. Each part has a unique number. Each drawing has a unique number. Drawings incorporate numerous part numbers or assembly numbers.

There are software applications that incorporate unique part numbers to create and perform:

- Bill of Materials.
- Manufacturing procedures.
- Cost analysis.
- Inventory control / Just in Time, JIT.

You are required to procure the part and drawing numbers from the documentation control manager.

Utilize the following prefix codes to categories created parts and drawings. The part name, part number and drawing numbers are as follows:

Category:	Prefix:	Part Name:	Part Number:	Drawing Number:
Machined Parts	56-	GUIDE	56-A26	56-22222
		ROD	56-A27	56-22223
		PLATE	56-A28	56-22224
Purchased Parts	99-	FLANGE BOLT	99-FBM8x1.25	999-551-8
Assemblies	10-	GUIDE-ROD	10-A123	10-50123

Link notes in the Title block to SolidWorks Properties. The title of the drawing is linked to the GUIDE Part Description, GUIDE-SUPPORT. Create additional notes in the Title block that complete the drawing.

Additional notes are required in the Title block. The text box headings: SIZE B, DWG. NO., REV., SCALE, WEIGHT and SHEET OF are entered in the SolidWorks default Sheet Format.

Properties are variables shared between documents and applications. Define the Document Properties in the GUIDE drawing. Link the Document Properties to the notes in the Title block.

Activity: Part Number and Document Properties

Enter Summary information for the GUIDE drawing.

402) Click **File**, **Properties** from the Main menu. The Summary Information dialog box is displayed.

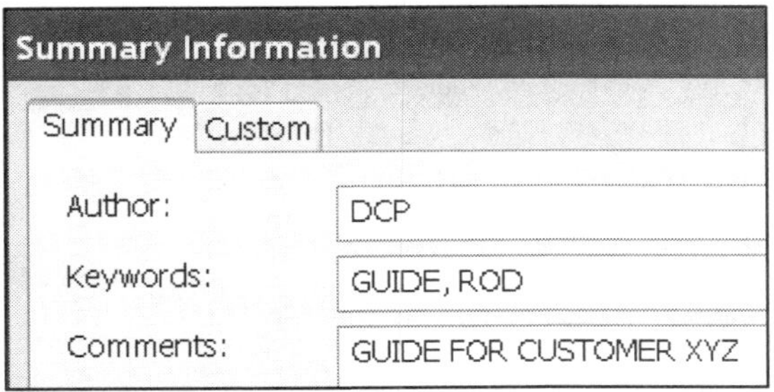

403) Click the **Summary Tab**.

404) Enter your **initials** for Author. Example: DCP.

405) Enter **GUIDE, ROD** for Keywords.

406) Enter **GUIDE FOR CUSTOMER XYZ** for Comments.

Select the Custom Tab.

407) Click the **Custom** tab. Row 1 contains the Company Name. Row 2 contains the latest Rev. Letter displayed in the Revisions Table.

408) Click the **third row** under the Property Name.

409) Select **Number** from the Name drop down list.

410) Click in the **Value/Text Expression box**.

411) Enter **56-22222** for Value. Click the **Evaluated Value** box.

Add DrawnBy and DrawnDate in Custom Properties.
412) Click the **forth row** under the Property Name.

413) Select **DrawnBy** from the Name drop down list.

414) Click in the **Value/Text Expression box**.

415) Enter **your initials** for Value.

416) Click in the **Evaluated Value** box.

417) Click the **fifth row** under the Property Name.

418) Select **DrawnDate** from the Name drop down list.

419) Enter **today's date** for Value. Click in the **Value/Text Expression box**.

420) Click **OK** from the Summary Information dialog box.

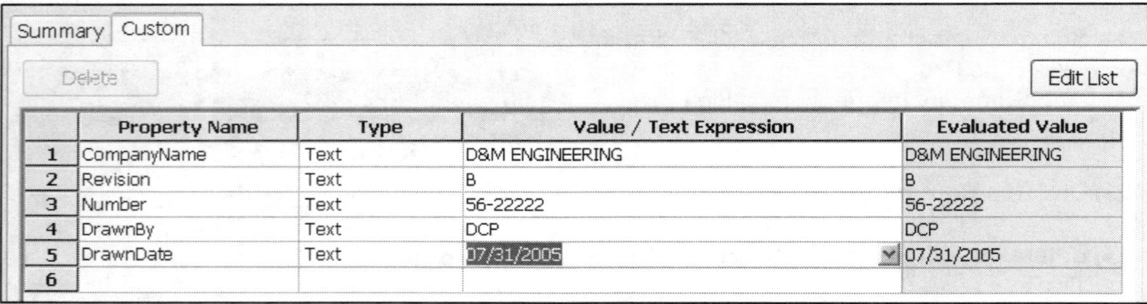

	Property Name	Type	Value / Text Expression	Evaluated Value
1	CompanyName	Text	D&M ENGINEERING	D&M ENGINEERING
2	Revision	Text	B	B
3	Number	Text	56-22222	56-22222
4	DrawnBy	Text	DCP	DCP
5	DrawnDate	Text	07/31/2005	07/31/2005
6				

The DrawnBy Property and DrawnDate Property are updated in the Title block. The current DWG NO. is the SolidWorks File Name. Assign the Number Property to the DWG NO. in the Title block.

	NAME	DATE
DRAWN	DCP	07/31/2005
CHECKED		
ENG APPR.		
MFG APPR.		
Q.A.		

Link the Properties to the Drawing Notes.
421) Click in the **Graphics window**.

422) Right-click **Edit Sheet Format**.

Edit the DWG NO.

423) Right-click the **GUIDE** text in the DWG NO. box. Click **Properties**.

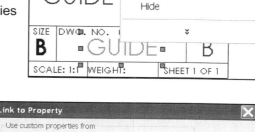

424) **Delete** the text $PRP:"SW-File Name" in the Properties Note text box.

425) Click **PropertyLink** .

426) Select **Number** from the Link to Property drop down list.

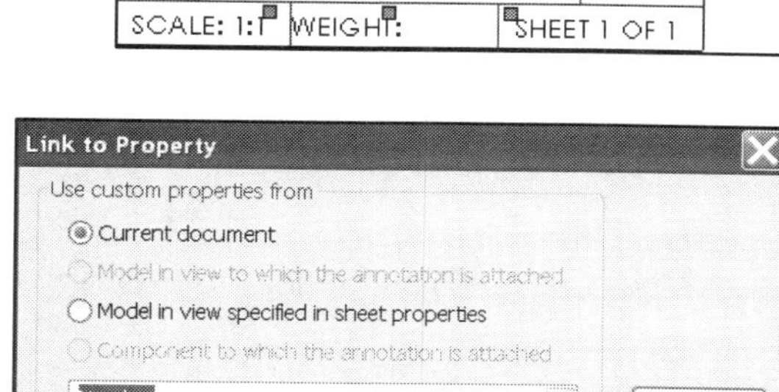

427) Click **OK** from the Link to Property box.

428) Click **OK** from the Properties box.

429) Click **OK** from the Note PropertyManager.

Fit the drawing to the Graphics window.

430) Press the **f** key. The drawing remains in Edit Sheet Format mode.

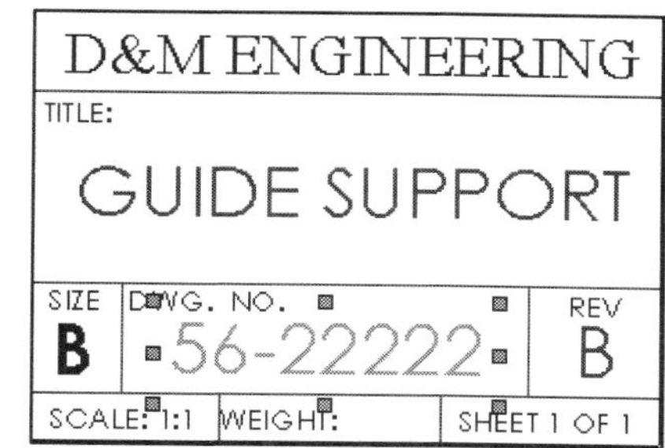

Save the Drawing.

431) Click **Save** .

Note: Remain in the Edit Sheet Format mode through the next few steps. Title block information is displayed in blue.

Define Custom Properties for Material and Surface Finish in the GUIDE part. Return to the GUIDE drawing to complete the Title block. The design team decided that the GUIDE part would be fabricated from 304 Stainless Steel. There are numerous types of Stainless steels for various applications. Select the correct material for the application. This is critical!

AISI 304 was set in the Materials Editor in the part. Open the GUIDE part and create the Material Custom Property. The AISI 304 value propagates to the drawing. Surface Finish is another important property in machining. The GUIDE utilizes an all around 0.80 μm high grade machined finish. The numerical value refers to the roughness height of the machined material. Surface finish adds cost and time to the part. Work with the manufacturer to specify the correct part finish for your application.

Create the Material Custom Property.

432) **Open** the GUIDE part.

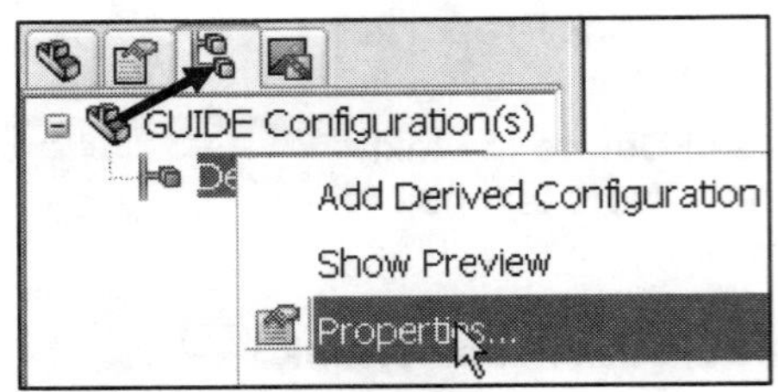

433) Click the **Configuration PropertyManager icon**.

434) Click **Default[GUIDE]**. Right-click **Properties**.

435) Click **Custom Properties** Custom Properties... .

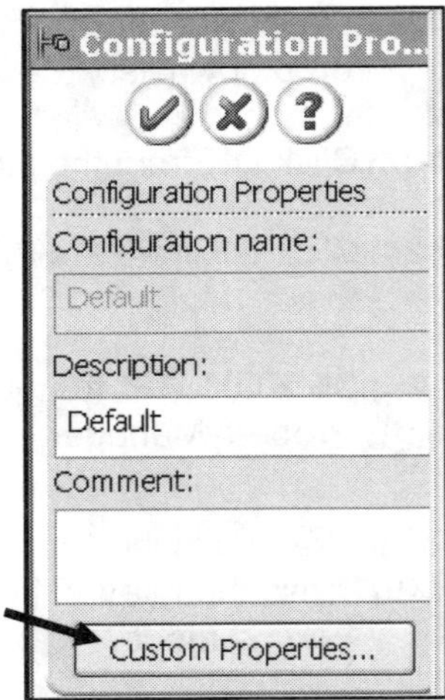

436) Click the **Configuration Specific** tab.

Specify the Material.

437) Click the **first row** under the Property Name.

438) Select **Material** from the Name list.

439) Click the **first row** under the Value/Text Expression. Select **Material**.

Determine the correct units before you create Custom Properties linked to Mass, Density, Volume, Center of Mass, Moment of Inertia etc. Recall Weight = Mass *Gravity. Modify the Title block text to include "g" for gravity, SI units in the Weight box.

Specify the Finish.

440) Click the **second row** under the Property Name.

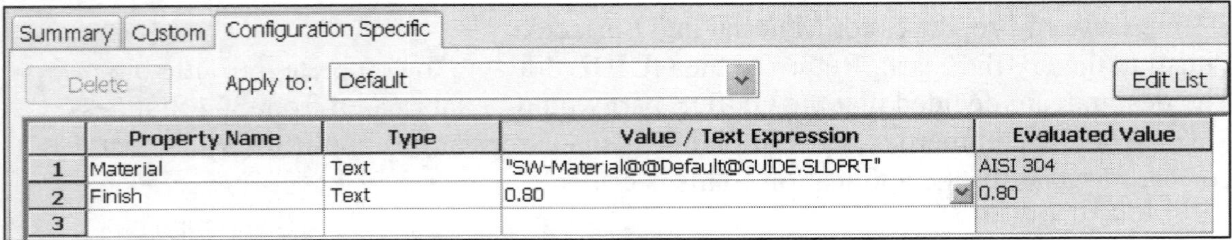

441) Select **Finish** from the Name list.

442) Enter **0.80** for Value/Text Expression.

443) Click **OK** from the Summary Information box.

444) Click **OK** from the Configuration Properties PropertyManager.

Return to the GUIDE drawing.

445) Press **Ctrl Tab**. The Material Custom Property displays AISI304 in the MATERIAL block and 0.80 in the FINISH block.

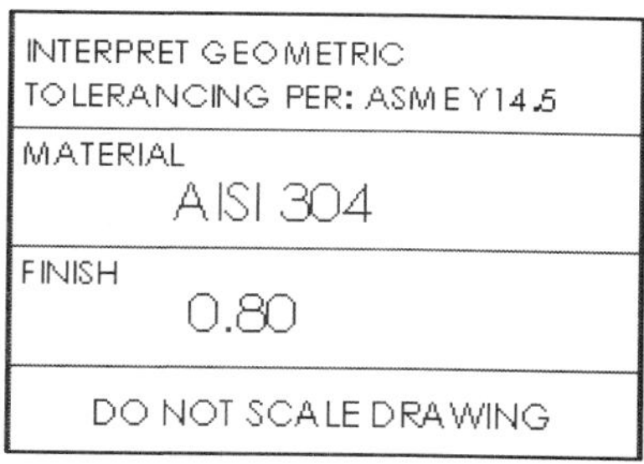

Insert a micrometer symbol.

446) Double-click **0.80**. Click **SWGrekC** from the Formatting toolbar for Font.

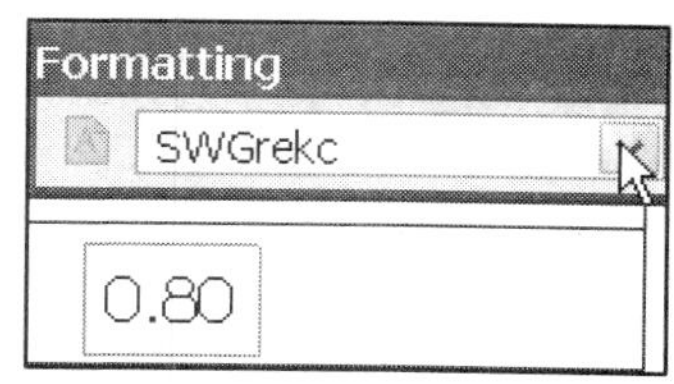

447) Press the **m** key to display the Greek letter μ. μ is the Greek letter for micro.

448) Click **Century Gothic** for Font. Enter **m** for meter. The text reads μm for micrometer. Click a **position** outside the text box.

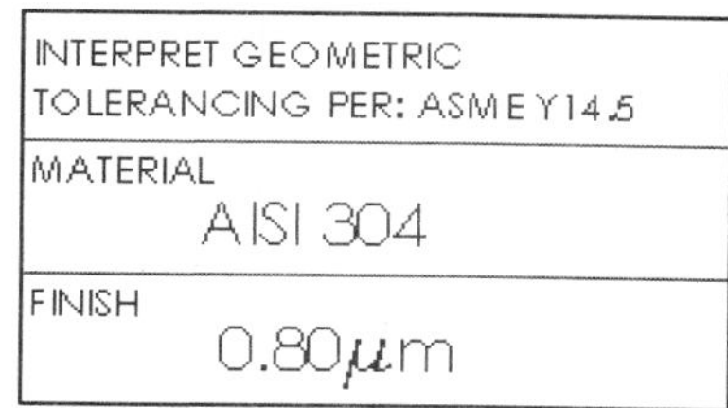

Invoke the Edit Sheet Mode.

449) Right-click in the **Graphics window**.

450) Click **Edit Sheet**. The Title block is displayed in black.

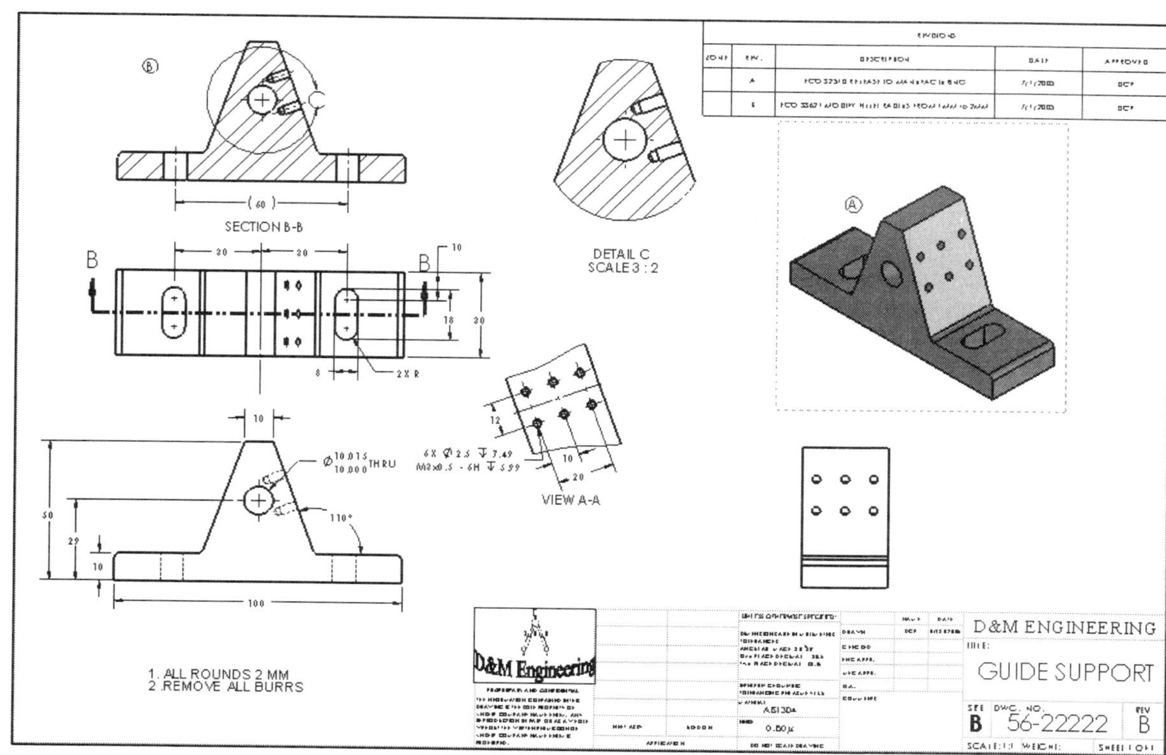

Fit the drawing to the Graphics window.
451) Press the **f** key.

452) Drag the **views** and **annotations** if required for spacing.

Save the GUIDE drawing.

453) Click **Save** .

Establish Custom Properties early in the design process. The MATERIAL and FINISH Custom Properties are established in the part and propagate to the Title block in the drawing. MATERIAL Custom Property is also listed in the default Bill of Material template and CosmosXpress Finite Element Analysis Tool.

Create engineering procedures to define the location and values of Custom Properties. The REVISION Custom Property was created in the drawing in the REVISION Table. The REVISION Custom Property can also be established in the part and propagate to the drawing. Does the part or the drawing control the revision? Your company's engineering procedures determine the answer.

Additional annotations are required for drawings. Utilize Annotations, Surface Finish Surface Finish to apply symbols to individual faces/edges in the part or in the drawing. When an assembly contains mating parts, document their relationship. Add part numbers in the Used On section. Additional annotations are left as an exercise.

Exploded View

Add an Exploded view and Bill of Materials to the drawing. Add the GUIDE-ROD assembly Exploded view. The Bill of Materials reflects the components of the GUIDE-ROD assembly. Create a drawing with a Bill of Materials.

Perform the following steps:

- Create a new drawing from the B-ANSI-MM Drawing Template.
- Display the Exploded view of the assembly.
- Insert the Exploded view of the assembly into the drawing.
- Label each component with Balloon text.
- Create a Bill of Materials.

Activity: Exploded View

Close all parts and drawings.
454) Click **Windows**, **Close All** from the Main menu.

Create a new drawing.
455) Click **File**, **New** from the Main menu.

456) Double-click **B-ANSI-MM** from the MY-TEMPLATES tab.

457) Click **Cancel** from the Model View PropertyManager.

Insert the GUIDE-ROD assembly.

458) Click **Drawings** Drawings .

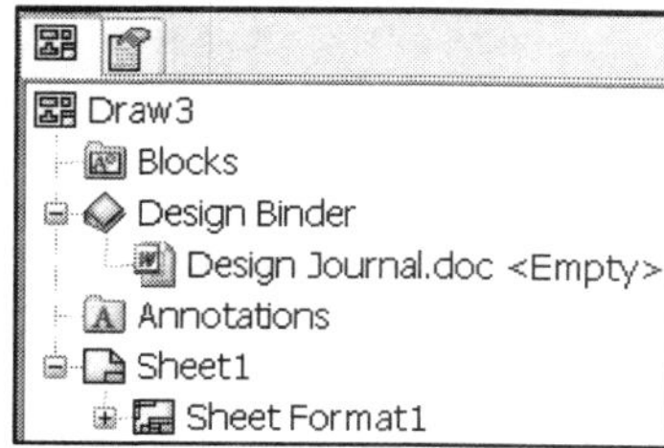

459) Double-click **Sheet1** in the FeatureManager

460) Click **Model View** Model View from the Drawings toolbar.

461) Click **Browse** from the Part/Assembly to Insert box.

462) Click **Assembly** for Files of type.

463) Double-click the **GUIDE-ROD** from the Open dialog box.

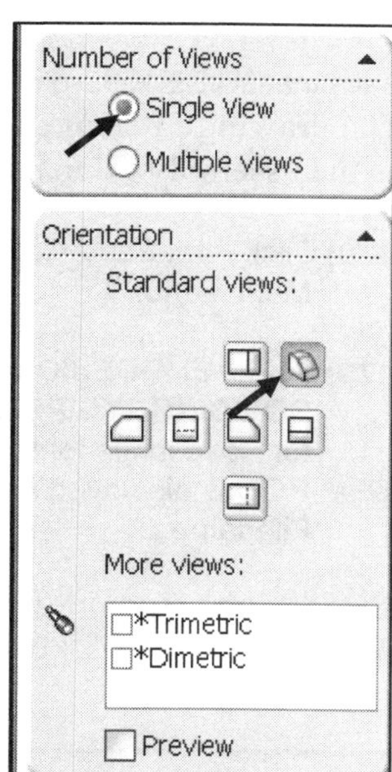

Select the View Orientation.
464) Click **Single View**.

465) Click ***Isometric**.

466) Click a position on the **right side of the drawing**.

467) Click **OK** from the Drawing View1 PropertyManager.

Display view shaded.
468) Click inside the **Isometric view** boundary.

469) Click **Shaded with Edges** in the Display Style box.

Hide the Origins.
470) Click **View**, uncheck **Origin** from the Main menu.

Display the Exploded view.

471) Click **inside** the Isometric view boundary. Right-click **Properties**.

Configuration information
Use model's "in-use" or last saved configuration
Use named configuration:
Default
Show in exploded state
Display State
Display State-1

472) Check **Show in exploded state**.

473) Click **OK** from the Drawing View Properties box.

474) Click **OK** from the Drawing View1 PropertyManager.

Note: The Explode view was created in Project 2. The Show in exploded state option is visible if an Exploded view exists in the assembly.

Fit the Drawing to the Graphics window.

475) Press the **f** key.

476) Move the **Isometric view** boundary into the drawing.

477) Click **OK** from the Drawing View1 PropertyManager.

Save the GUIDE-ROD drawing.

The drawing Filename is the same as the assembly Filename.

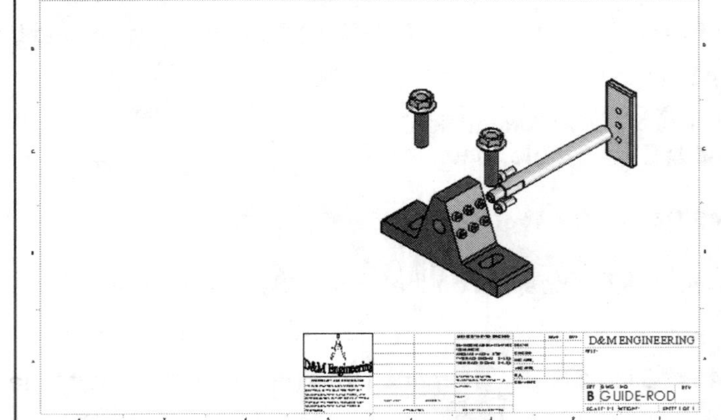

478) Click **File**, **Save As** from the Main menu.

479) Select **ENGDESIGN-W-SOLIDWORKS\PROJECTS** for Save in file folder. GUIDE-ROD is displayed for Filename.

Save the drawing.

480) Click **Save**. Click **Yes**.

Balloons

Label each component with a unique item number. The item number is placed inside a circle. The circle is called Balloon text. List each item in a Bill of Materials table.

Utilize Auto Balloon to apply Balloon text to all components. Utilize Insert, Table, Bill of Materials to apply a BOM to the drawing.

The Circle Split Line option contains the Item Number and Quantity. Item number is determined by the order listed in the assembly FeatureManager. Quantity lists the number of instances in the assembly.

Activity: Balloons

Insert the Automatic Balloons.

481) Click **Annotations** Annotati... from the Control Area. Click **Auto Balloon** AutoBal... from the Annotations toolbar. The Auto Balloon PropertyManager is displayed. Accept the Square default. Click **OK** from the Auto Balloon PropertyManager.

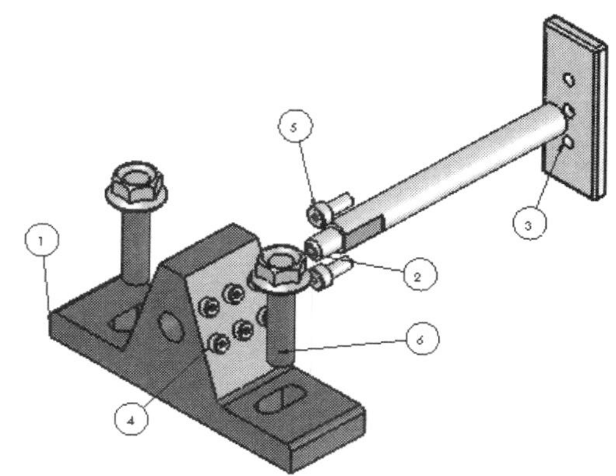

Reposition the Balloon text.

482) Click and drag each **Balloon** to the desired position.

483) Click the **Balloon arrowhead attachment** to reposition the arrow on a component edge.

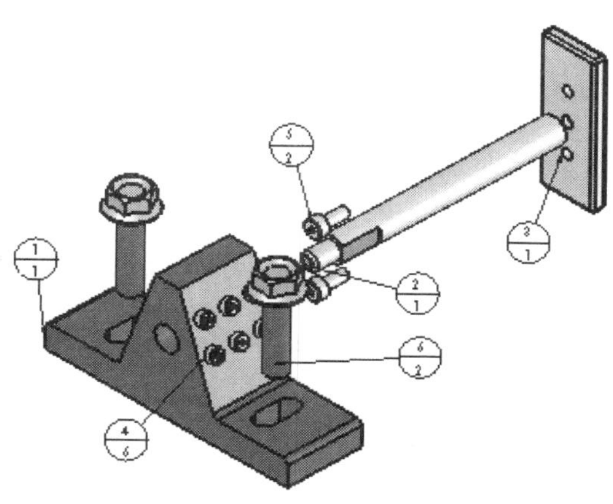

Display Item Number and Quantity.

484) Ctrl-Select all six **Balloon text**.

485) Select **Circle Split Line** for Style in the Balloon PropertyManager.

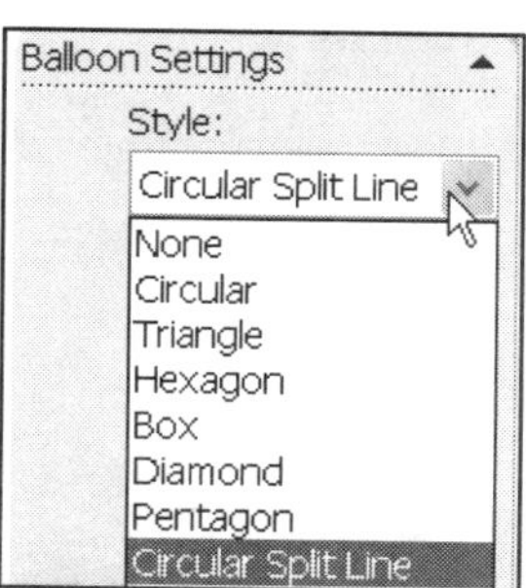

486) Click **OK** from the Balloon PropertyManager.

487) Click **Save**

The symbol "?" is displayed when the Balloon attachment is not coincident with an edge or face.

ASME Y14.2 defines the attachment display as an arrowhead for Edge and a dot for Face.

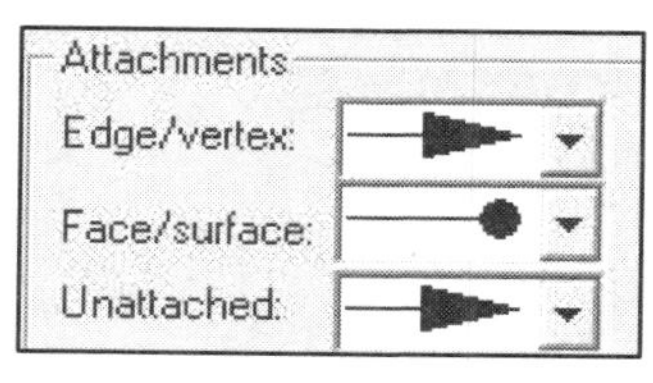

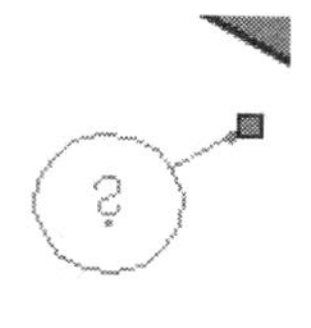

Arrowhead display is found in Tools, Options Document Properties, Arrows. Edge/vertex attachment is selected by default.

Each Balloon references a component with a SolidWorks File Name. The SolidWorks File Name is linked to the Part Name in the Bill of Materials by default. Customize both the Balloon text and the Bill of Materials according to your company's requirements.

Bill of Materials

The Bill of Materials reflects the components of the GUIDE-ROD assembly. The Bill of Materials is a table in the assembly drawing that contains Item Number, Quantity, Part Number and Description by default. Insert additional columns to customize the Bill of Materials.

Part Number and Description are Custom Properties entered in the individual part documents. Insert additional Custom Properties to complete the Bill of Materials.

Activity: Bill of Materials

Create a Bill of Materials.

488) Click inside the **Isometric view** in the GUIDE-ROD drawing.

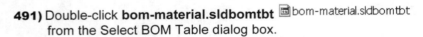

489) Click **Insert**, **Tables**, **Bill of Materials** Bill of Materials... from the Main menu. The Bill of Materials PropertyManager is displayed.

490) Click **Open Table Template for Bill of Materials**.

491) Double-click **bom-material.sldbomtbt** bom-material.sldbomtbt from the Select BOM Table dialog box.

492) Click **OK** from the Bill Of Materials PropertyManager

493) Click a **position** in the upper left corner of Sheet1.

The Bill of Materials requires some editing. The current part file name determines the PART NUMBER values. Material for the GUIDE was defined in the Material Editor and the Material Custom Property.

The current part description determines the DESCRIPTION values. Redefine the PART NUMBER for the Bill of Materials.

ITEM NO.	PART NUMBER	DESCRIPTION	MATERIAL	QTY.
1	GUIDE	GUIDE SUPPORT	AISI 304	1
2	ROD	ROD 10MM DIA x 100MM		1
3	PLATE	PLATE 56MM x 22MM		1
4	3MMCAPSCREW	CAP SCREW, 3MM		6
5	4MMCAPSCREW	CAP SCREW, 4MM		2
6	M8-1.25 x 30			2

Modify the GUIDE part number.

494) Click on the **GUIDE** in the Isometric view.

495) Right-click **Open Part**.

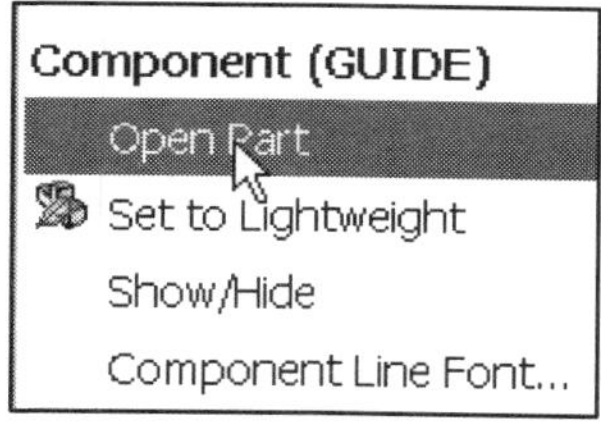

496) Click the GUIDE **ConfigurationManager**.

497) Right-click **Default** [**GUIDE**] in the ConfigurationManager.

498) Click **Properties**.

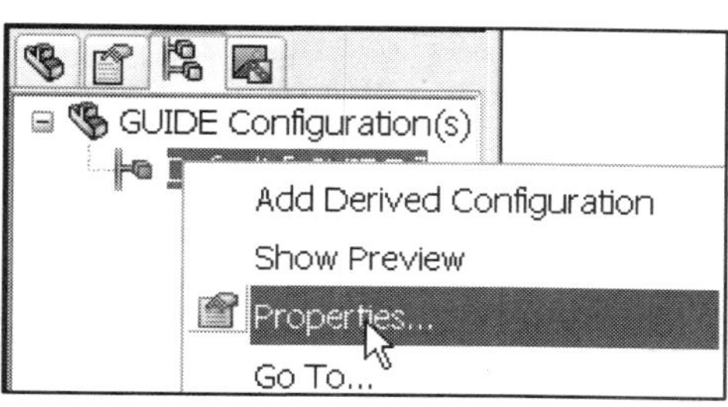

499) Select **User Specified Name** in the spin box from the Bill of Materials Options.

500) Enter **56-A26** for the Part Number in the Bill of Materials Options.

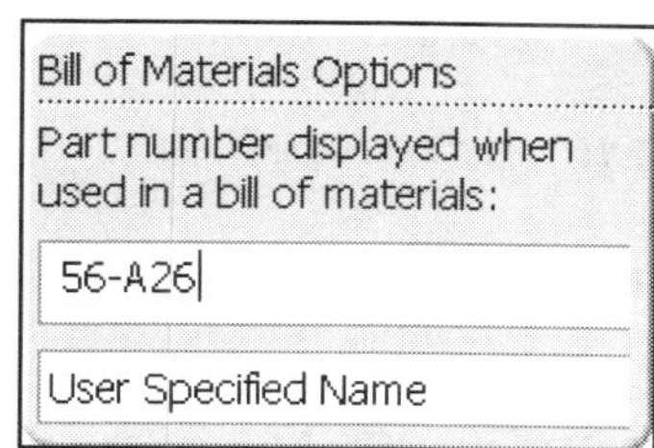

501) Click **OK** from the Configuration Properties PropertyManager. Default [56-A26] is displayed in the Configuration Manager.

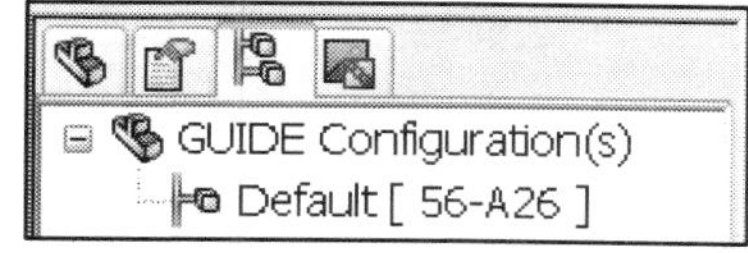

Return to the GUIDE-ROD drawing.

502) Click **Window**, **GUIDE-ROD – Sheet1** from the Main menu.

Modify the ROD part number.

503) Click on the **ROD** in the Isometric view.

504) Right-click **Open Part**.

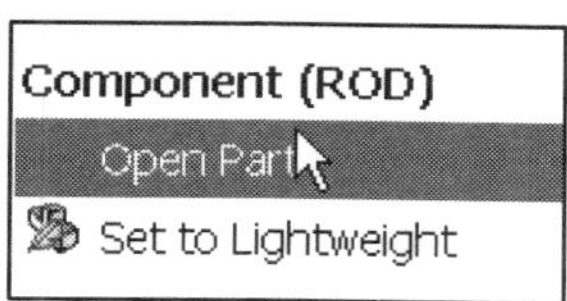

505) Click the ROD **ConfigurationManager** .

506) Right-click **Default[ROD]** from the Configuration Manager.

507) Click **Properties**.

508) Select **User Specified Name** in the spin box from the Bill of Materials Options. Enter **56-A27** for the Part Number in the Bill of Materials Options.

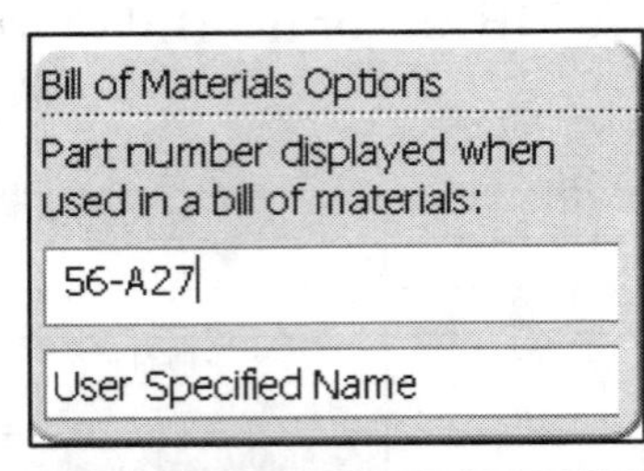

509) Click **OK** from the Configuration Properties PropertyManager.

Return to the GUIDE-ROD drawing.

510) Click **Window**, **GUIDE-ROD – Sheet1** from the Main menu.

Modify the PLATE part number.

511) Click on the **PLATE** in the Isometric view.

512) Right-click **Open Part**.

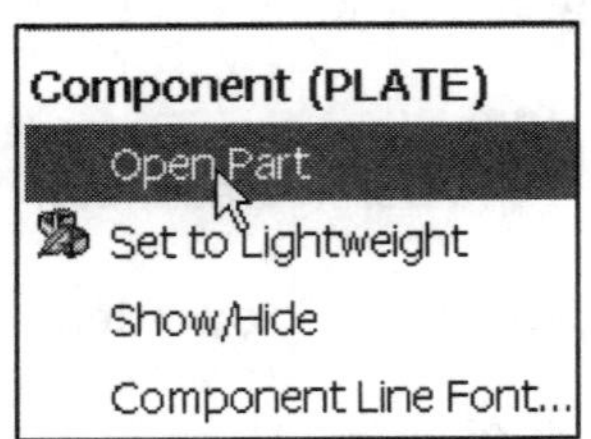

513) Click the PLATE **ConfigurationManager** .

514) Right-click **Default [PLATE]** from the ConfigurationManager.

515) Click **Properties**.

516) Select **User Specified Name** in the spin box from the Bill of Materials Options.

517) Enter **56-A28** for the Part Number in the Bill of Materials Options.

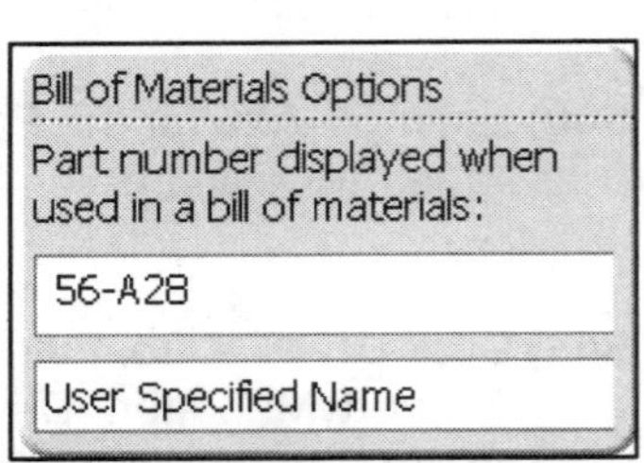

518) Click **OK** from the Configuration Properties PropertyManager.

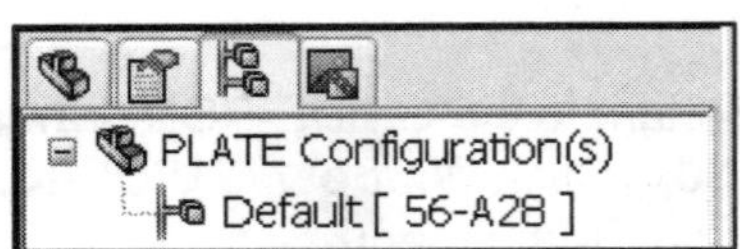

Return to the GUIDE-ROD drawing.

519) Click **Window**, **GUIDE-ROD – Sheet1** from the Main menu.

The FLANGE BOLT is a SolidWorks library part. Copy the part with a new name to the ENGDESIGN-W-SOLIDWORKS\PROJECTS file folder with the Save As command.

Utilize the FLANGE BOLT's Part Number for File name.

Modify the FLANGE BOLT.

520) Click on the **FLANGE BOLT** in the Isometric view.

521) Right-click **Open Part**.

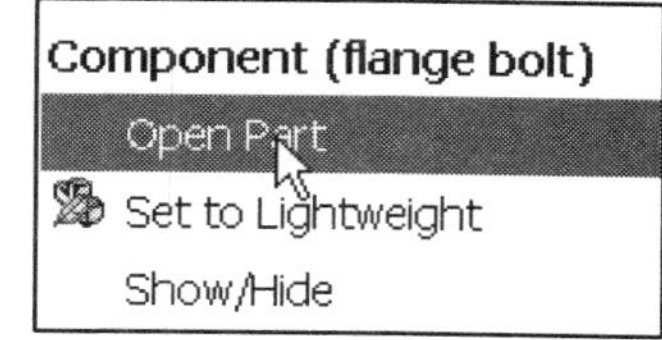

Save the FLANGE BOLT.

522) Click **File**, **Save As** from the Main menu.

523) Click **OK** to replace the FLANGE BOLT references in the GUIDE-ROD assembly with the new file name.

SolidWorks 2006

C:\Program Files\SolidWorks\data\design library\parts\hardware\flange bolt.sldprt is being referenced by other open documents. "Save As" will replace these references with the new name. Check "Save As Copy" in the "Save As" dialog if you wish to maintain existing references.

OK Cancel

Don't ask me again

524) Select the **ENGDESIGN-W-SOLIDWORKS\PROJECTS** file folder.

525) Enter **99-FBM8-1-25** for the File name.

526) Enter **FLANGE BOLT M8x1.25x30** for Description.

527) Click **Save**.

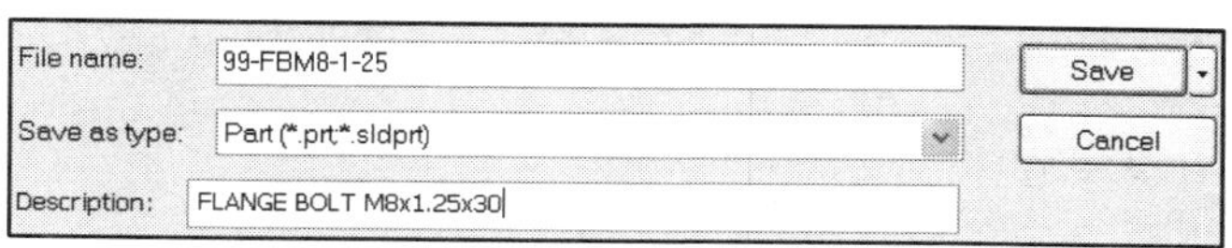

Return to the GUIDE-ROD drawing.

528) Press **Ctrl Tab**.

Open the GUIDE-ROD assembly.

529) Right-click in the **Isometric view**.

530) Click **Open guide-rod.sldasm**

Open guide-rod.sldasm

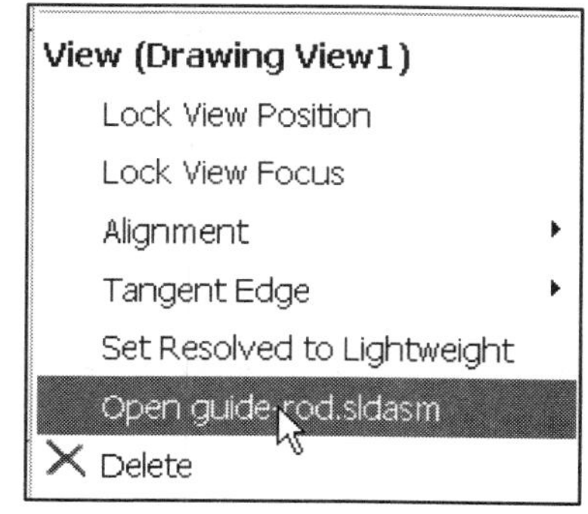

531) **Expand** the Hardware folder. The FLANGE BOLT displays the new name.

Return to the GUIDE-ROD drawing.

532) Press **Ctrl Tab**.

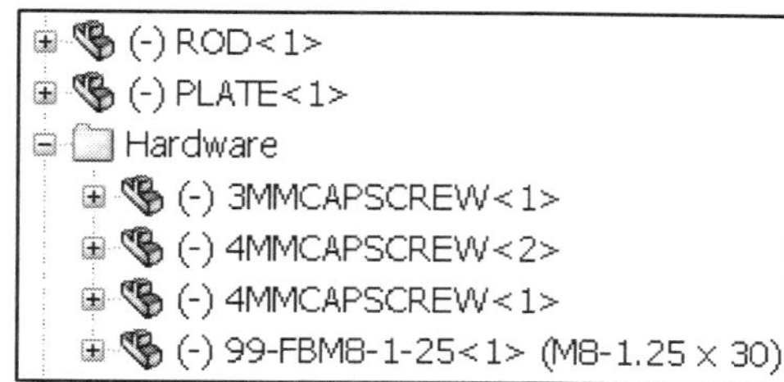

Update the Bill of Materials.

533) Click **Rebuild** from the Main menu.

Fit the drawing to the Graphics window.

534) Press the **f** key.

If the Bill of Materials does not update when changes to a part have been made, then open the assembly. Return to the drawing. Issue a Rebuild.

The FLANGE BOLT PART NUMBER, CAP SCREW PART NUMBER and MATERIAL Property for all items utilized in the Bill of Materials are explored in the project exercises.

ITEM NO.	PART NUMBER	DESCRIPTION	MATERIAL	QTY.
1	4MMCAPSCREW	CAP SCREW, 4MM		2
2	3MMCAPSCREW	CAP SCREW, 3MM		6
3	56-A26	GUIDE SUPPORT	AISI 304	1
4	56-A27	ROD 10MM DIA x 100MM		1
5	56-A28	PLATE 56MM x 22MM		1
6	M8-1.25 x 30	FLANGE BOLT M8x1.25x30		2

Save the GUIDE-ROD drawing.

535) Click **Save** .

536) Click **Yes** to update.

List assembly items such as: adhesives, oil and labels in the Bill of Materials. Select Insert, Row. Enter the information in each cell.

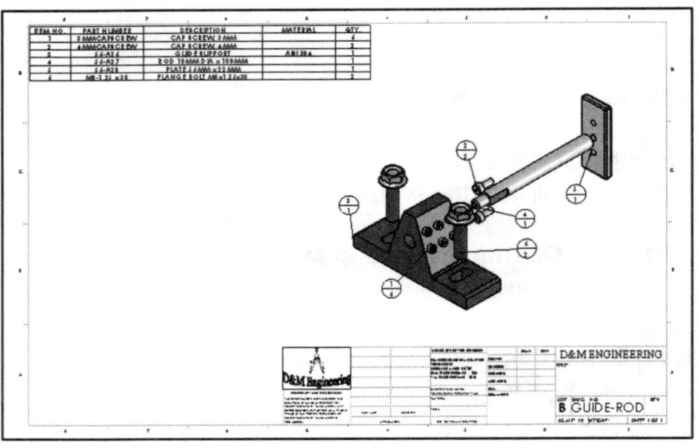

Additional details on Notes, Revision Tables, Properties, Bill of Materials are available in SolidWorks Help Topics. Keywords: Notes (linked to properties, in sheet formats, parametric), Revision Tables, Properties (configurations), Bill of Materials.

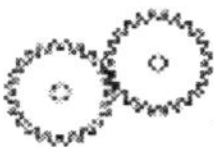

Review of the Parametric Notes, Revision Table and Bill of Materials.

You created a parametric Note in the drawing by inserting a part dimension into the Note text box. The Revision Table was inserted into the drawing to maintain drawing history.

The Bill of Materials listed the Item Number, Part Number, Description, Material and Quantity of components in the assembly.

You developed Custom Properties in the part and utilized the Properties in the drawing and Bill of Materials.

Associative Part, Assembly and Drawing

The associative part, assembly and drawing share a common database. Verify the association between the part, assembly and drawing.

Open the GUIDE part.

537) Open the GUIDE part.

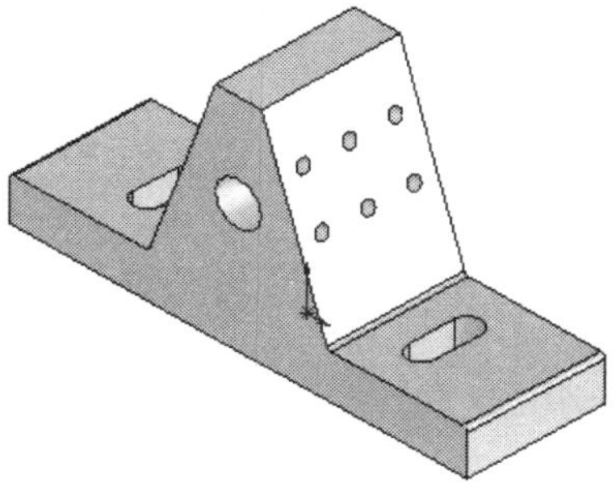

538) Click **Shaded with Edges**.

539) Double-click the **Base Extrude** from the FeatureManager.

540) Double click the vertical linear dimension **10**.

541) Enter **20** in the Modify box.

542) Click **Rebuild** from the Modify box.

543) Click the **Green Check mark**.

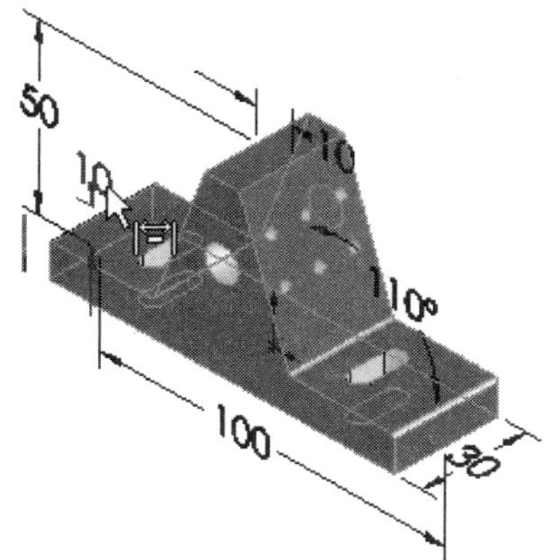

Open the GUIDE drawing.

544) Open the GUIDE drawing. **View** the update.

Open the GUIDE-ROD assembly.

545) Open the GUIDE-ROD assembly.

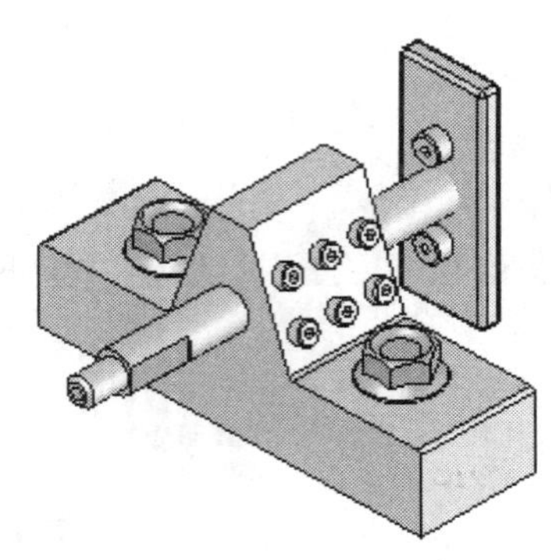

546) Click **Yes** to update the assembly.

Open the GUIDE-ROD drawing.

547) Open the GUIDE-ROD drawing. **View** the update.

Close all parts and assemblies.

548) Click **Window**, **Close All** from the Main menu.

549) Click **Yes to All**. The project is complete.

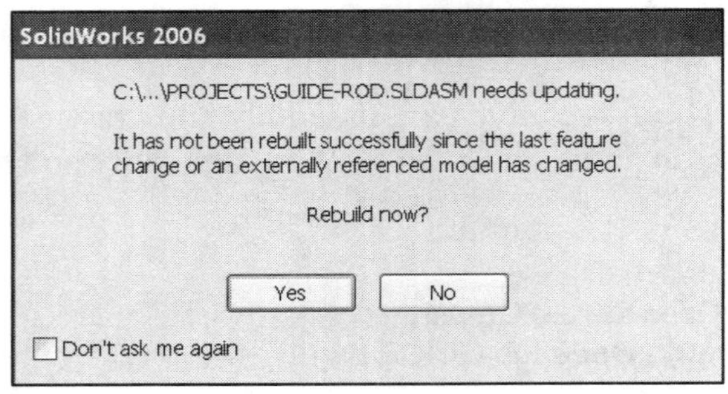

Drawings and Custom Properties are an integral part of the design process. Part, assemblies and drawings all work together.

From your initial design concepts, you created parts and drawings that fulfill the design requirements of your customer.

Refer to Help, Online Tutorial, Lesson3-Drawings exercise and Advanced Drawings exercise for additional information.

Project Summary

In this project you developed two drawings: GUIDE drawing and the GUIDE-ROD assembly drawing. The drawings contained three standard views, (principle views) and an Isometric view. The drawings utilized a custom Sheet Format containing a company logo, Title block and Custom Properties. You incorporated the GUIDE part dimensions into the drawing.

The Drawing toolbar contained Model View and Projected View to develop standard views. Additional views were required and utilized the Auxiliary, Detail and Section View tools. Dimension were inserted from the part and added in the drawing.

You used two major design modes in the drawings: Edit Sheet Format and Edit Sheet.

The detailed GUIDE drawing included annotations and Custom Properties. The GUIDE-ROD assembly drawing incorporated a Bill of Materials and additional Custom Properties.

Project Terminology

Annotations: Text note or a symbol that adds specific design intent to a part, assembly, or drawing. Annotations in the drawing include note, hole callout, surface finish symbol, datum feature symbol, datum target, geometric tolerance symbol, weld symbol, balloon, stacked balloon, center mark, area hatch, and block.

Associatively: The relationship between parts, assemblies, drawings and other SolidWorks documents that share a common file structure.

Auxiliary View: Displays a plane parallel to an angled plane with true dimensions. A primary Auxiliary View is hinged to one of the six principle views.

Balloon: Annotations on a drawing used to identify items in a Bill of Materials.

Bill of Materials: A table in an assembly drawing that contains the properties: Item Number, Part Number, Description and Quantity. Additional properties are added to a Bill of Materials.

Centerlines: Are composed of alternating long and short dash lines. The lines identify the center of a circle, axes or cylindrical geometry.

Center Marks: Represents two perpendicular intersecting centerlines.

Crop View: Displays only a bounded area from a view. Sketch a Spline for the boundary.

Custom Properties: Variables shared between documents. Custom Properties are defined in the part and utilized in the drawing through Linked Notes. Configuration Specific Properties are defined in a part or assembly.

Detailed View: Detailed Views enlarge an area of an existing view. Specify location, shape and scale.

Drawing file name: Drawing file names end with a .slddrw suffix.

Drawing Template: The foundation of a SolidWorks drawing. Defines sheet size, drawing standards, company information, manufacturing and or assembly requirements, units, layers and other properties

Edit Sheet Format Mode: Provides the ability to change the Title block, incorporate a company logo, and insert Custom Properties. Remember: A part cannot be insert into a drawing when the Edit Sheet Format mode is selected. Edit Sheet Format displays all lines in blue.

Edit Sheet Mode: Provides the ability to insert and modify views and dimensions.

General Notes: Text utilized on a drawing. In engineering drawings notes are usually all upper case letters, left justification and the same size as dimension text.

Hole Callout: The Hole Callout function creates additional notes required to dimension the holes.

Layers: Contain dimensions, annotations and geometry. Layers are assigned display properties and styles.

Leader lines: Reference the size of the profile. A gap must exist between the profile lines and the leader lines.

Notes: Text annotations inserted into a document. Notes are displayed with leaders or as a stand-alone text string. If an edge, face or vertex is selected prior to adding the note, a leader is created to that location. Link Notes to Custom Properties.

Revision Table: A table the documents the history of changes to a drawing. The Revision letter in the Table is linked to the Rev letter in the Title block.

Section View: Section Views display the interior features. Define a cutting plane with a sketched line in a view perpendicular to the Section View.

Sheet Format: The Sheet Format is incorporated into the Drawing Template. The Sheet Format contains the border, Title block information, revision block information, company name and or logo information, Custom Properties and SolidWorks Properties. In this project the Sheet Format contained the Title block information.

Title block: Contains vital part or assembly information. Each company can have a unique version of a Title block.

Questions

1. Describe a Bill of Materials and its contents.
2. Name the two major design modes used to develop a drawing in SolidWorks.
3. Identify seven components that are commonly found in a Title block.
4. How do you insert an Isometric view to the drawing?
5. In SolidWorks, drawing file names end with a ______ suffix.
6. In SolidWorks, part file names end with a ______ suffix.
7. Can a part and drawing have the same name?
8. True or False. In SolidWorks, if a part is modified, the drawing is automatically updated.
9. True or False. In SolidWorks, when a dimension in the drawing is modified, the part is automatically updated.
10. Name three guidelines to create General Notes.
11. True or False. Most engineering drawings use the following font: Time New Roman – All small letters.
12. What are Leader lines? Provide an example.
13. Name the three ways that Holes and other circular geometry can be dimensioned.
14. Describe Center Marks. Provide an example.
15. How do you calculate the maximum and minimum variation?
16. Describe the differences between a Drawing Template and a Sheet Format.
17. Describe the key differences between a Detail View and a Section View.
18. Describe a Revision table and its contents.
19. Identify the Drawing tools.

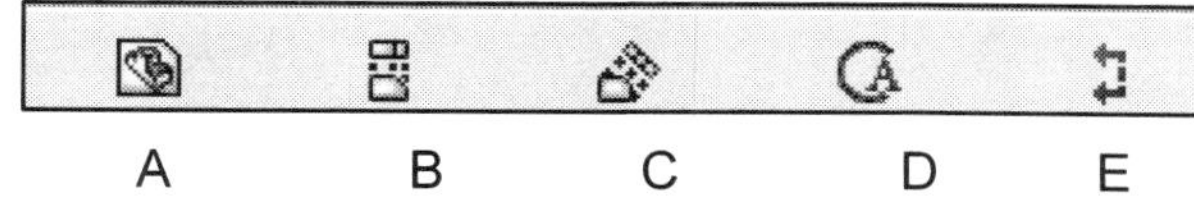

Exercises

Exercise 3.1: L-BRACKET Drawing.

Create the L-BRACKET drawing. The L-BRACKET part was created in Project 1, Exercise 1.1a – Exercise 1.1i.

- Open the L-BRACKET part.
- Utilize Tools, Options, Document Properties to set Units and Font size. Note: Dimensions are enlarged for clarity.
- Insert a Front, Top and Right view.
- Insert an Isometric view.
- Insert Dimensions from the part.
- Insert a Linked Note in the Title block.

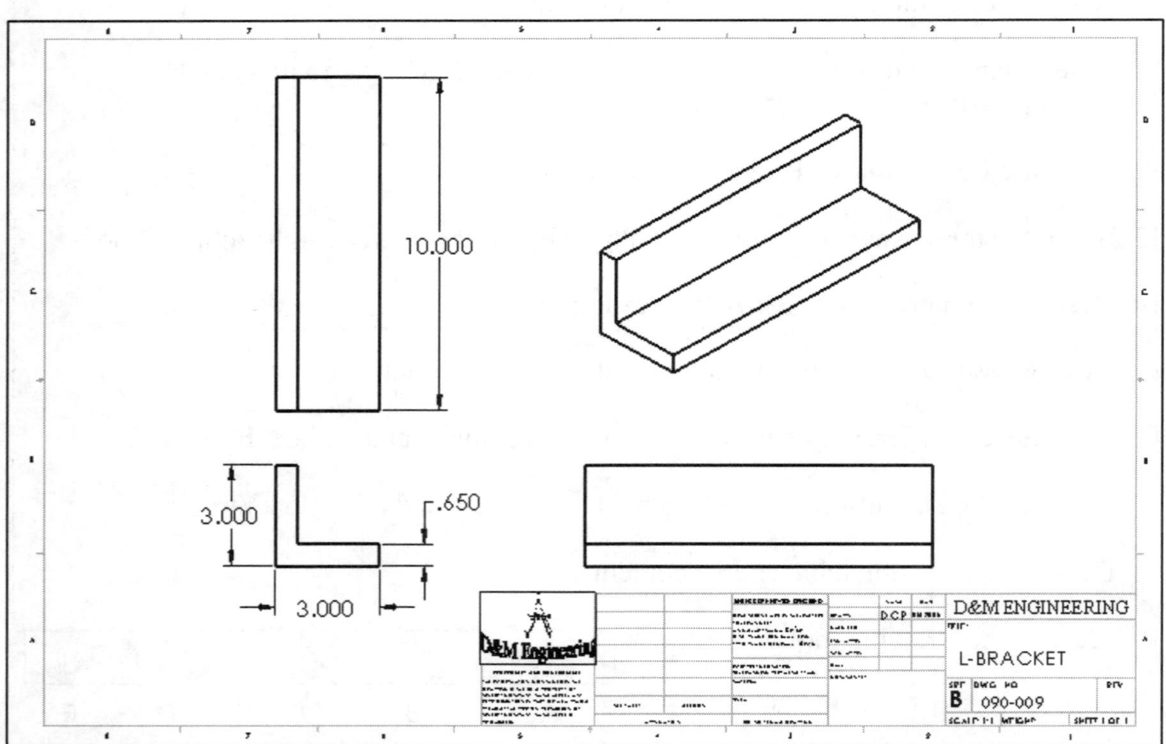

Exercise 3.2: T-SECTION Drawing.

Create the T-SECTION drawing. The T-SECTION part was created in Project 1, Exercise 1.2a – Exercise 1.2f.

- Open the T-SECTION part.
- Insert a Front, Top and Right view.
- Insert an Isometric view.
- Insert Dimensions from the part.
- Utilize Sketch Tools to add a centerline.
- Insert a Linked Note in the Title block.

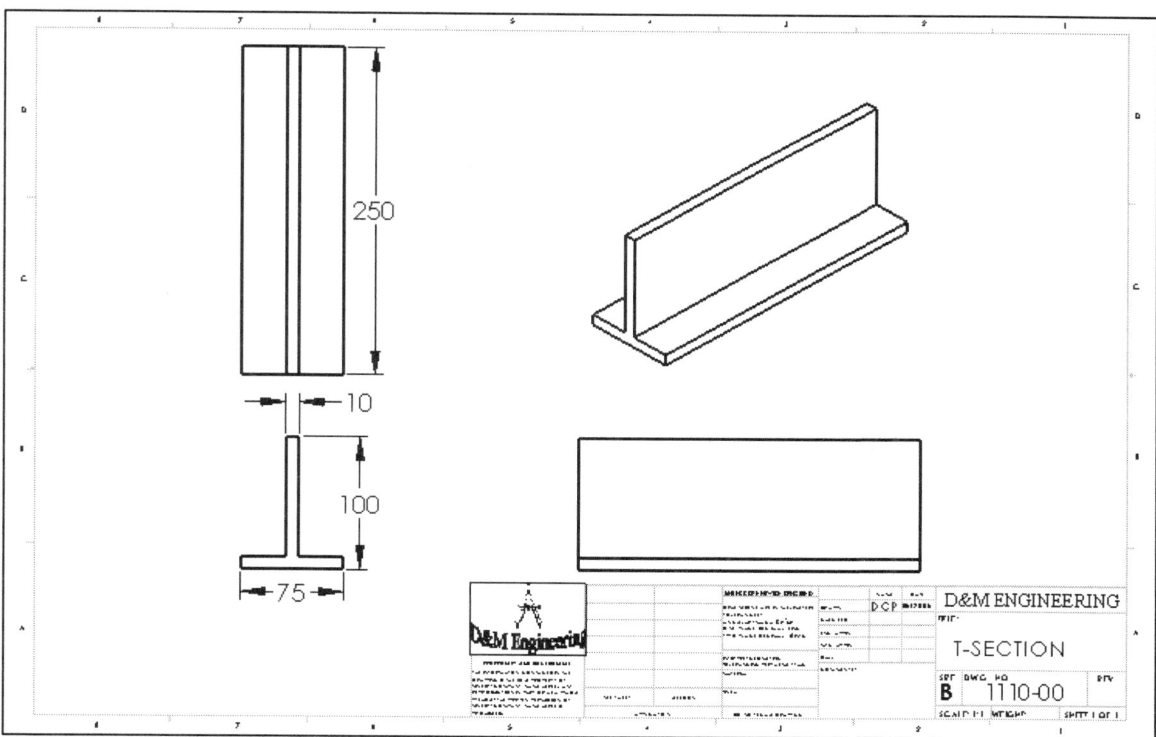

Exercise 3.3: LINKAGE Component Drawings.

Create four drawings of the mechanical components required for the LINKAGE assembly; AXLE, SHAFT COLLAR, FLAT BAR – 3 HOLE and FLAT BAR – 9 HOLE from Project 1, Exercise 1.5a – Exercise 1.5d. Note: Dimensions are enlarged for clarity.

- Utilize inch, millimeter or dual dimensioning.
- Insert a Shaded Isometric view in the lower right corner of each drawing.

Exercise 3.3a: FLAT BAR – 3HOLE Drawing.

Create the FLAT BAR – 3HOLE drawing.

- Open the FLAT BAR – 3HOLE part. Insert a Front view and a Shaded Isometric view.
- Insert dimensions from the part. Dual dimension the Drawing.
- Add a parametric note for MATERIAL THICKNESS. Modify the Hole dimension to include 3X.
- Insert a Linked Note in the Title block.

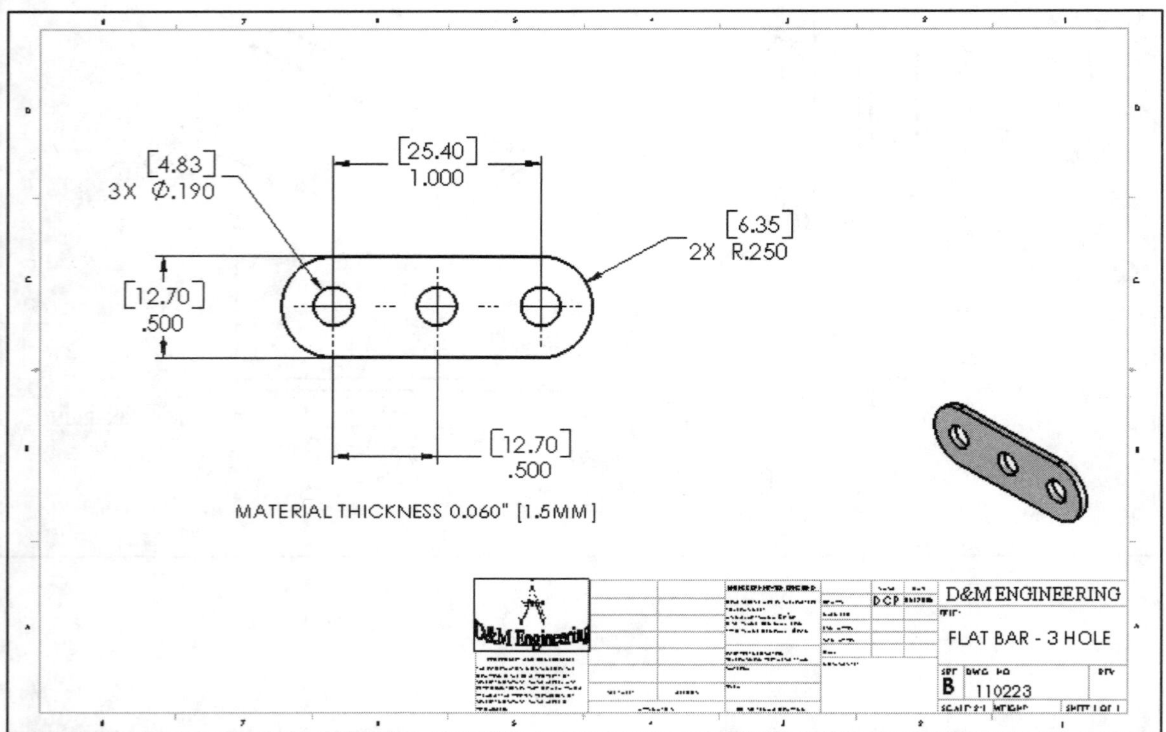

Exercise 3.3b: FLAT BAR – 9 HOLE Drawing.

Create the FLAT BAR – 9HOLE drawing.

- Open the FLAT BAR – 9HOLE drawing.
- Insert a Front and Shaded Isometric view.
- Insert dimensions from the part.
- Dual dimension the Drawing.
- Add a parametric note for MATERIAL THICKNESS.

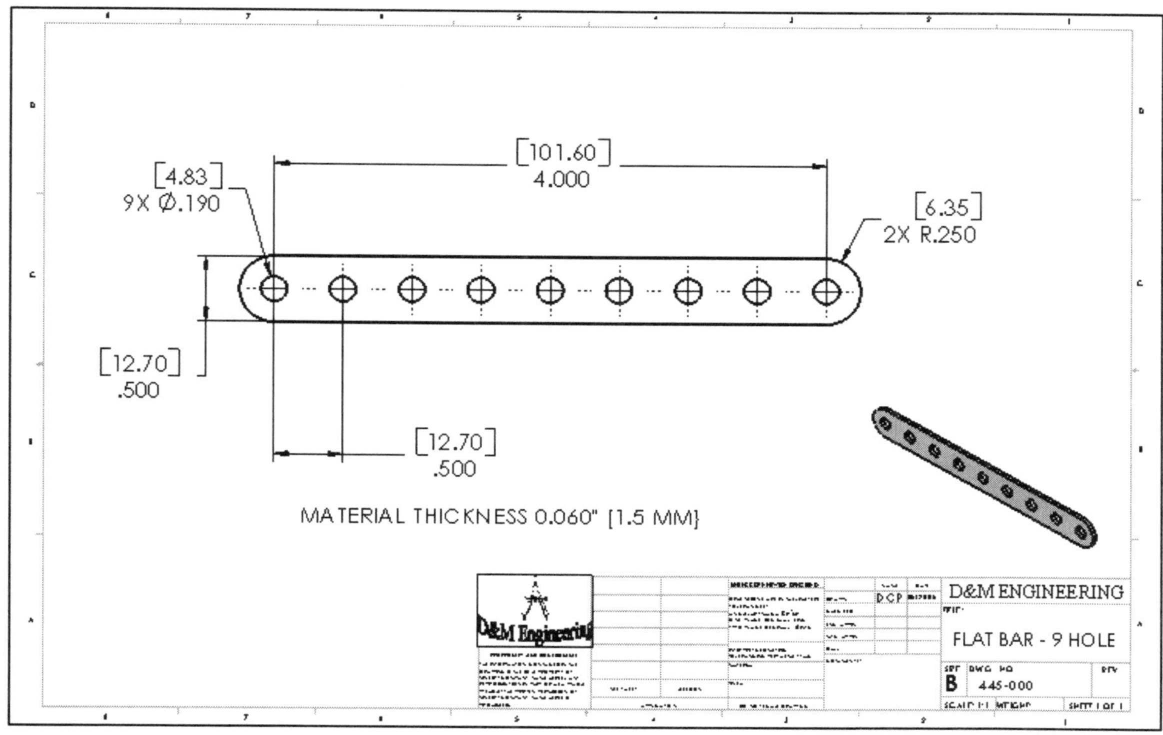

Exercise 3.3c: AXLE Drawing.

Create the AXLE drawing.

- Open the AXLE part.
- Insert a Front view, Right view and a Shaded Isometric view.
- Insert dimensions from the part. Dual dimension the Drawing.
- Insert a Linked Note in the Title block.
- Add a centerline in the Right view.

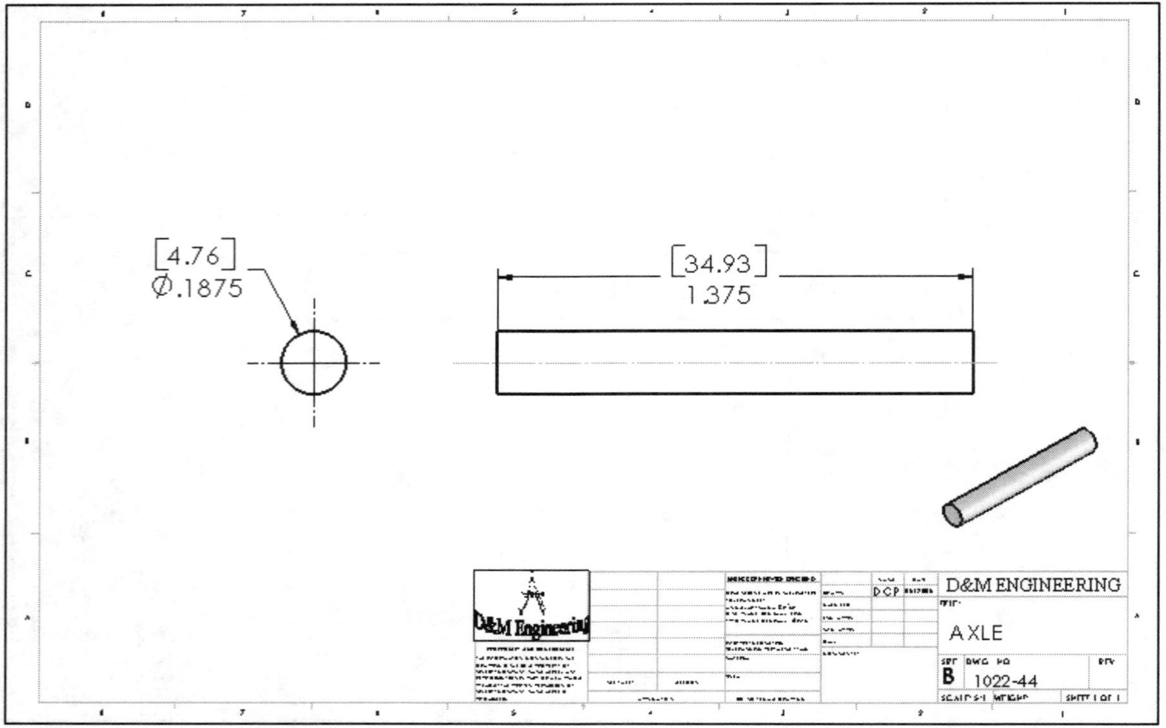

Exercise 3.3d: SHAFT COLLAR Drawing.

Create the SHAFT COLLAR drawing.

- Open the SHAFT COLLAR part.
- Insert a Front, Top and a Shaded Isometric view.
- Insert dimensions from the part.
- Dual dimension the Drawing.
- Add a 4:1 scale to the Isometric view.
- Add a centerline in the Isometric view.
- Insert a Linked Note in the Title block.

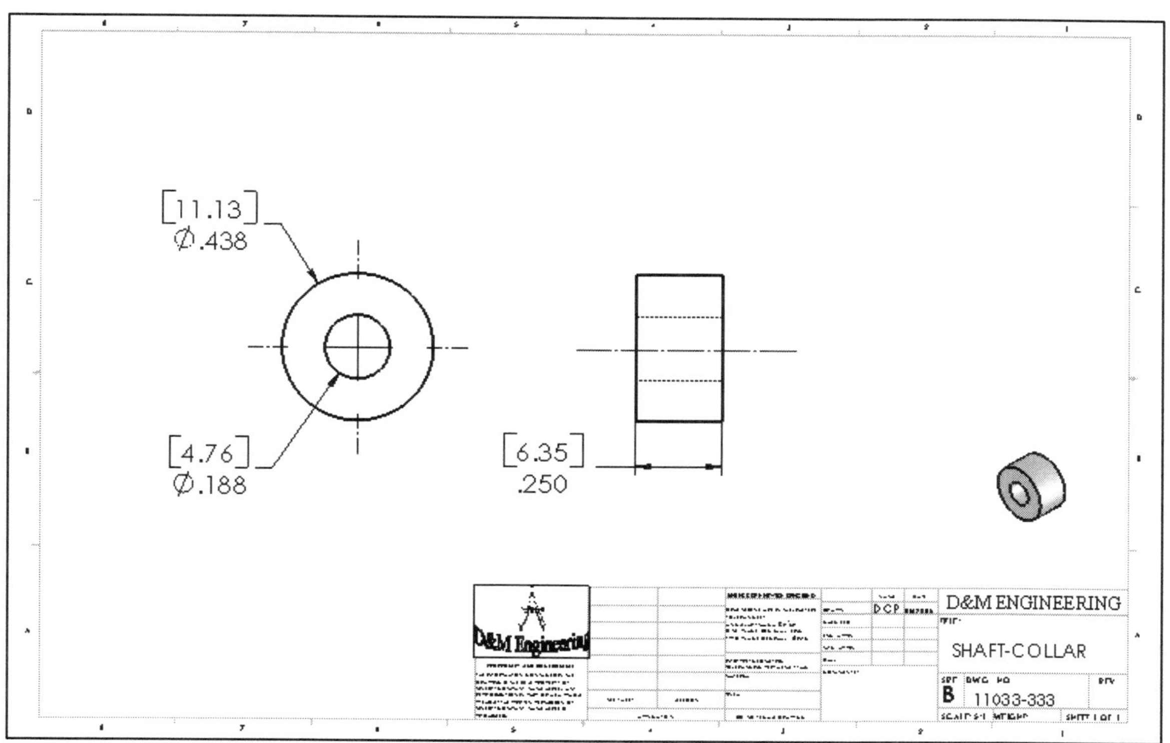

Exercise 3.4: LINKAGE Assembly Drawing.

Create the LINKAGE assembly drawing with a Bill of Materials. The LINKAGE assembly drawing utilizes the LINKAGE assembly created in Exercise 2.3a. The Bill of Materials requires the PART NO. Property and the DESCRIPTION Property. Define Properties in each part.

- Open each mechanical part in the LINKAGE assembly.
- Define the PART NO. Property and the DESCRIPTION Property for the AXLE, FLAT BAR- 9HOLE, FLAT BAR – 3HOLE and SHAFT COLLAR.

PART NO. Property:	DESCRIPTION Property:
GIDS-SC-10017	AXLE
GIDS-SC-10001-9	FLAT BAR – 9 HOLE
GIDS-SC-10001-3	FLAT BAR – 3 HOLE
GIDS-SC-10012-3-16	SHAFT COLLAR

- Open the LINKAGE assembly, created in Exercise 2.3a.
- Insert an Isometric view.
- Insert a Bill of Materials. Show the top level subassemblies and parts only in the Bill of Materials.

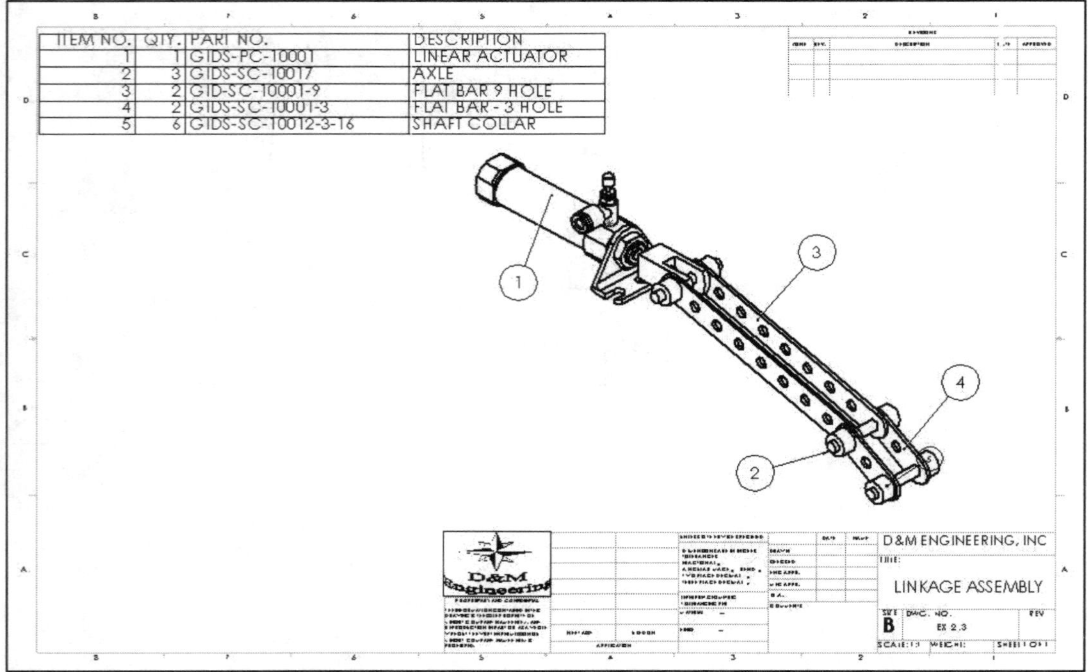

Exercise 3.5: Bill of Materials.

Modify the PART NUMBER for the FLANGE BOLT and 3MM CAP SCREW and 4MM CAP SCREW in the GUIDE-ROD Assembly Bill of Materials.

ITEM NO.	PART NUMBER	DESCRIPTION	MATERIAL	QTY.
1	56-A27	ROD 10MM DIA X 100MM	AISI 304	1
2	56-A28	PLATE 56MM X 22MM	AISI 304	1
3	56-A26	GUIDE-SUPPORT	AISI 304	1
4	99-SHCS-23	3MM CAP SCREW	AISI 304	6
5	99-SHCS-25	4MM CAP SCREW	AISI 304	2
6	99-FBM8-1-25	FLANGE BOLT	AISI 304	2

- Utilize the MATERIAL EDITOR to assign AISI 304.
- Add the Custom Property MATERIAL to the ROD and PLATE.
- Utilize User Defined for Part Number when used in Bill of Materials for the Flange Bolt.

Exercise 3.6: Sketching on Planes.

- Label the Front, Top and Right Planes.
- Sketch an L-shaped profile on the Front Plane.
- Sketch an L-shaped profile on the Top Plane.

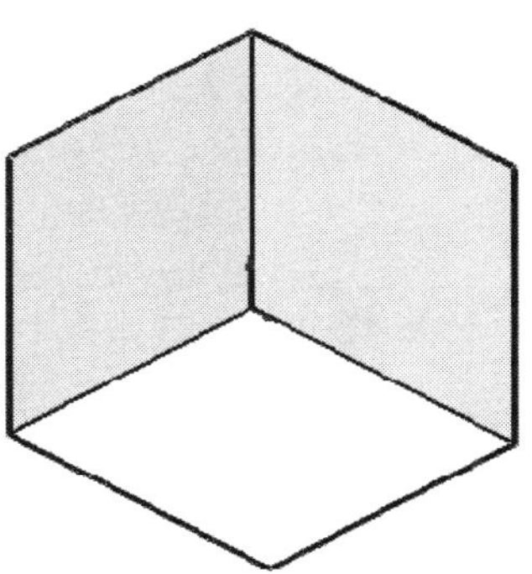

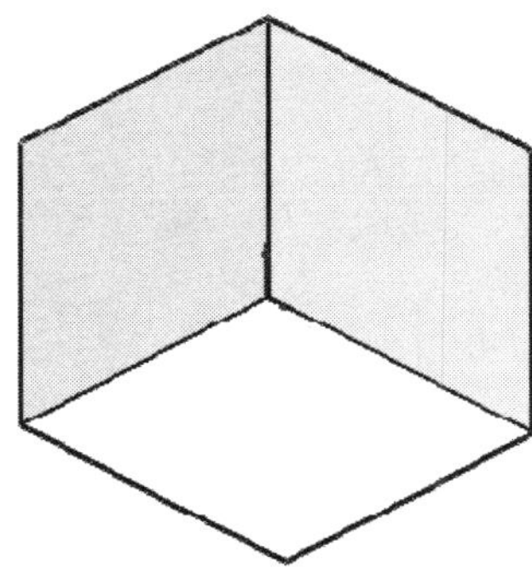

Exercise 3.7: VALVE PLATE Part and Drawing.

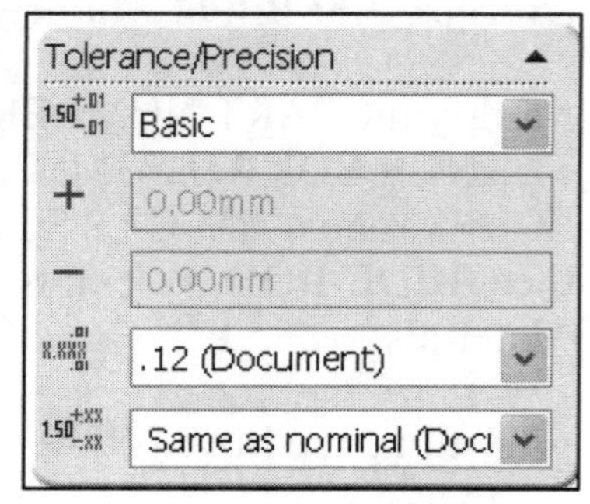

Create the VALVE PLATE part as illustrated in the ASME 14.5M Geometric Dimensioning and Tolerancing Standard.

Create the VALVE PLATE drawing according to the ASME 14.5M standard.

- Utilize the Tolerance/Precision option to modify the decimal place value.
- Utilize Surface Finish, Geometric Tolerance and Datum Feature tools in the Annotations menu.

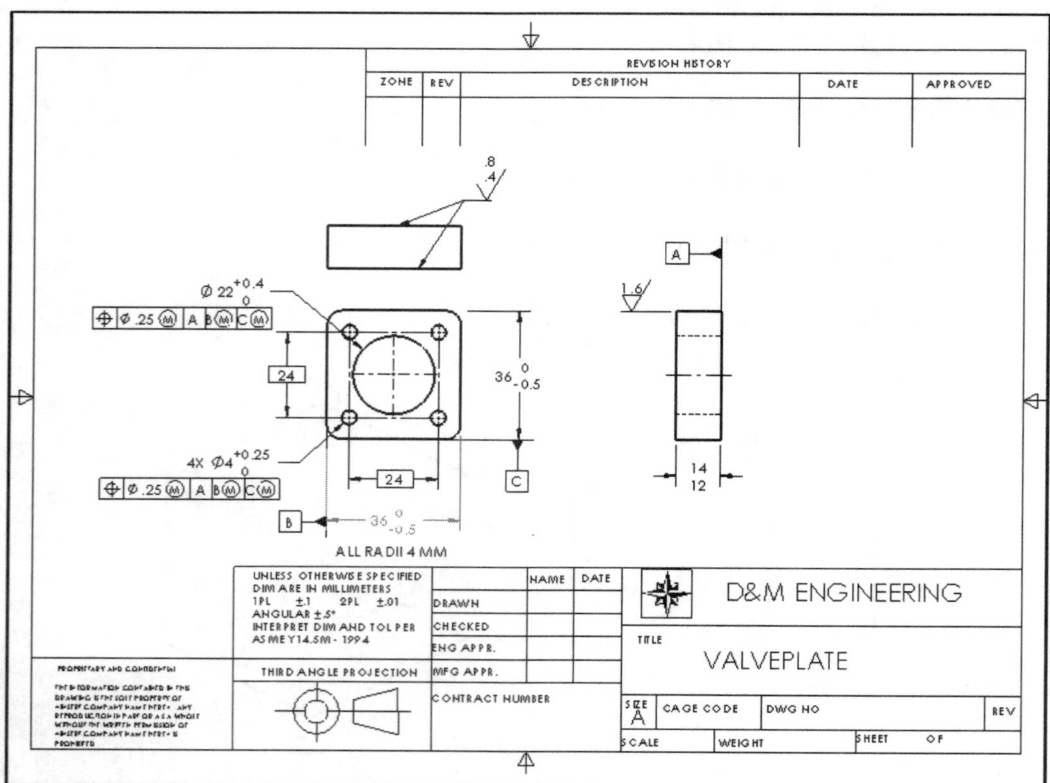

Drawing Exercise 3-7 and the Project 3 Slot Cut dimensioning scheme are reprinted from ASME Y14.5M- 1994 by permission of the American Society of Mechanical Engineers, New York, NY.

Exercise 3.8: SQUARE-PLATE Part and Drawing

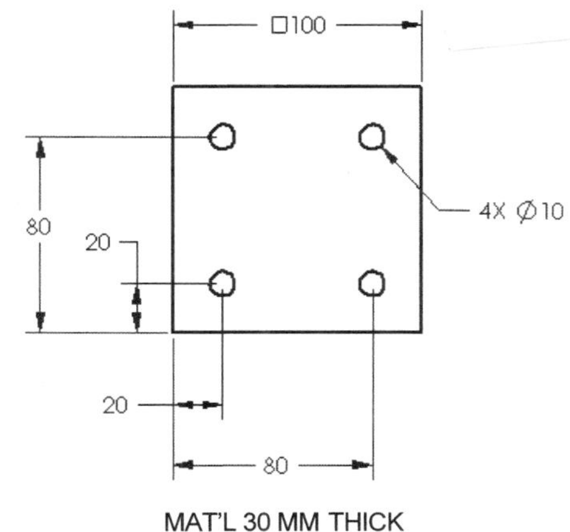

- Create the SQUARE-PLATE part. The SQUARE-PLATE is 100mm x 100mm x 30mm.
- Utilize the Hole Wizard to create the first M10 x 1.5 Thru hole.
- Utilize a Linear Pattern to create the other three holes.

Review the design with your teammates. An engineer on your team expresses concerns about the standard M10x1.5 screw fastener.

The engineer specifies a threaded insert to prevent the screws from loosening under vibration. The threaded insert must adhere to the following design considerations:

- M10 x 1.5 Thread Size (Nominal Diameter = 10 mm, Thread Pitch = 1.5).
- Free Running.
- Tapped depth less than 30mm.

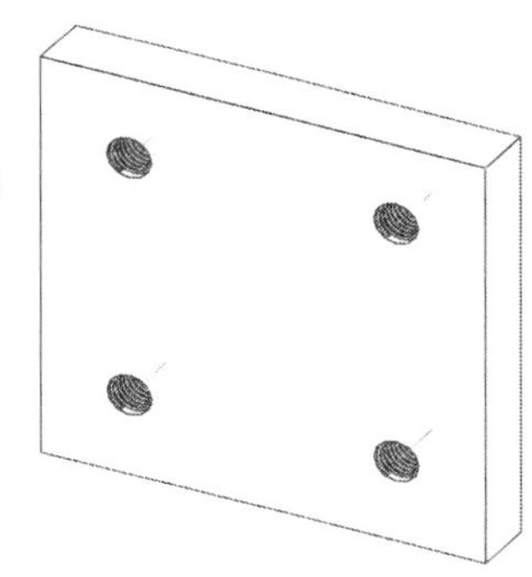

Tasks on this project are as follows:

- Locate a threaded insert and record the part number. Invoke a web browser. Enter the URL: http://:www.emhart.com. Note: Emhart Fastening Teknologies, A Black & Decker Company, manufactures Heli-Coil® Screw Thread Inserts.
- Select the Heli-Coil® Selector button. Select the Innovations button. Click Continue.
- Enter your email address and password. If you are a new user to the web site, click the Register button and enter the requested information. You will be emailed with the required information.

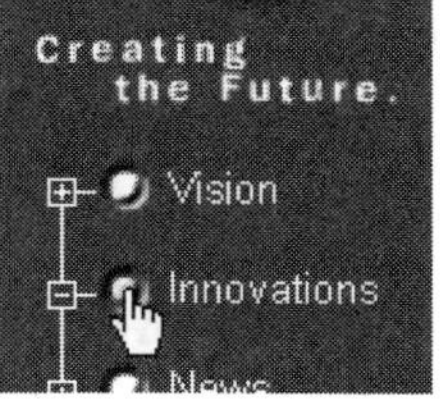

Components Courtesy of Emhart Teknologies New Haven, CT USA

Emhart® and Heli-Coil® are registered trademarks of the Black & Decker Company

- Click Heli-Coil®. Click the Search Selector.

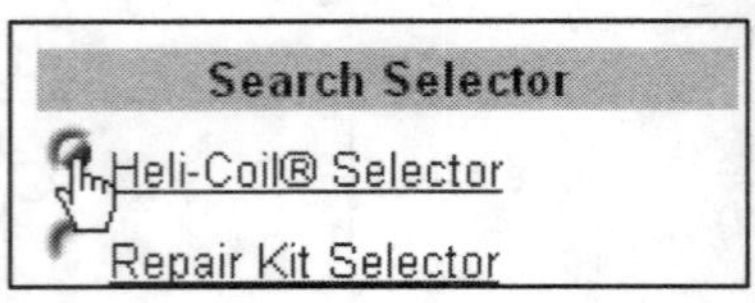

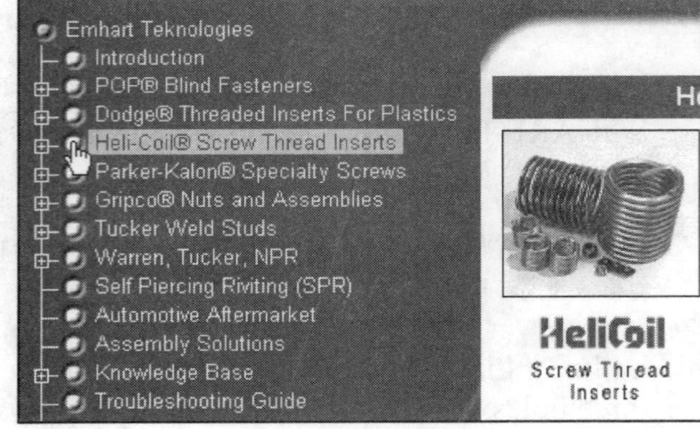

- Enter the following product requirements:
  - Thread size: M10x1.5
  - Type: FR
  - Length: 15
  - Packaging: B

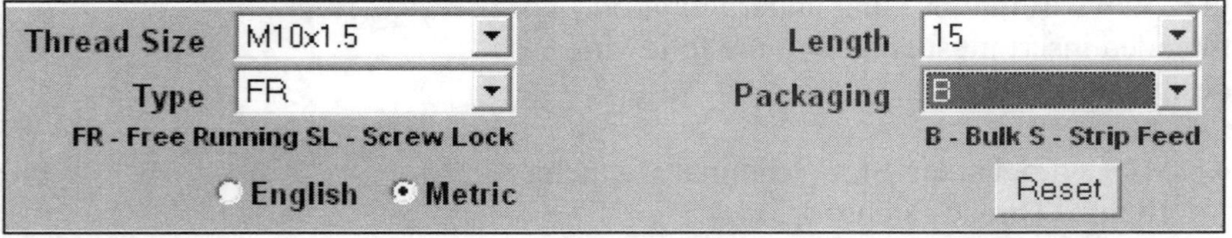

- Click Spec. Obtain the part number, min/max outside diameter.

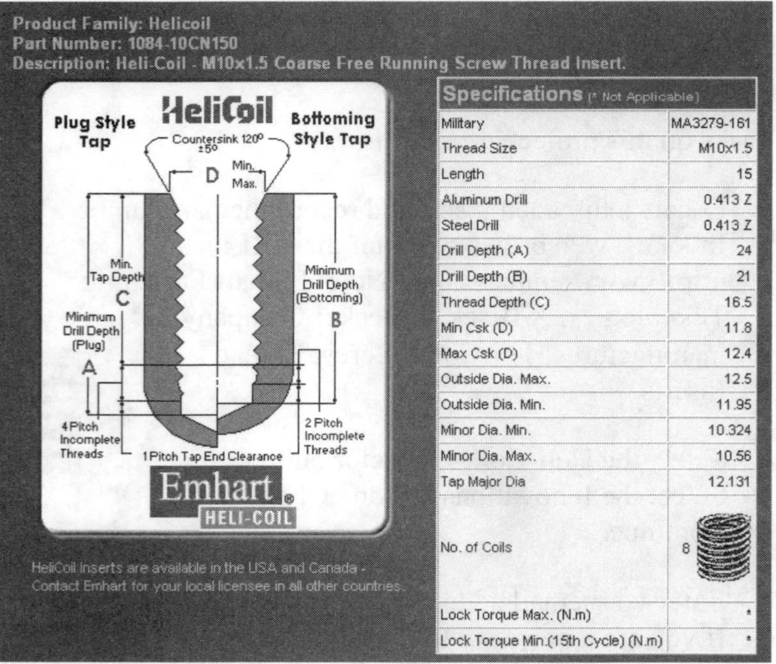

Specifications (* Not Applicable)

Military	MA3279-161
Thread Size	M10x1.5
Length	15
Aluminum Drill	0.413 Z
Steel Drill	0.413 Z
Drill Depth (A)	24
Drill Depth (B)	21
Thread Depth (C)	16.5
Min Csk (D)	11.8
Max Csk (D)	12.4
Outside Dia. Max.	12.5
Outside Dia. Min.	11.95
Minor Dia. Min.	10.324
Minor Dia. Max.	10.56
Tap Major Dia	12.131
No. of Coils	8
Lock Torque Max. (N.m)	*
Lock Torque Min.(15th Cycle) (N.m)	*

- Click the Product Tools button to obtain the drawing notes required for manufacturing.
- Click the CAD Drawings button to view and download the component. Down load SW3dPS-1084-10CN150.SLDPRT.
- Modify the SQUARE-PLATE. Edit the Thru Hole.

- Change the Standard to HeliCoil® Metric Tapped Hole.
- Enter 21 for Tap Drill Type & Hole Depth.
- Create a new assembly with the Heli-Coil® threaded insert and the SQUARE-PLATE. P is the Pitch of the thread. P = 1.5.
- Create a Distance Mate between the two components.
- Position the Heli-Coil® threaded insert between 0.75P to 1.5 P from the top face of the SQUARE-PLATE.
- Create a Coincident Mate between the Origin of the Heli-Coil® and Temporary Axis of the Tapped Hole.

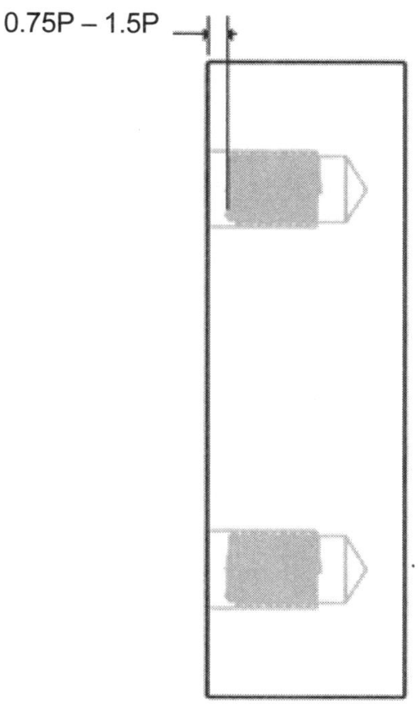

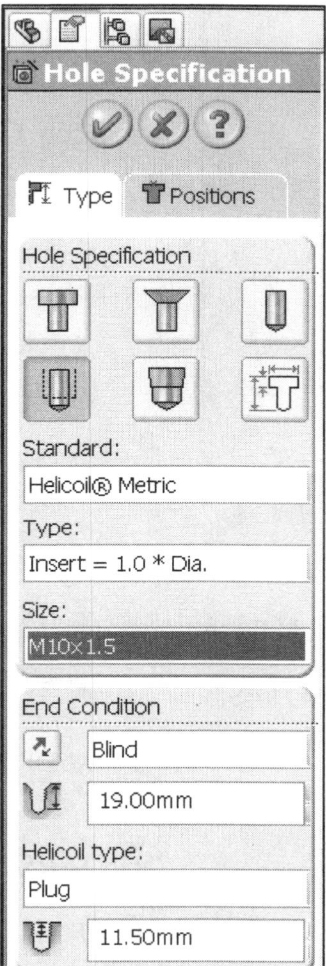

- Create the SQUARE-PLATE drawing.

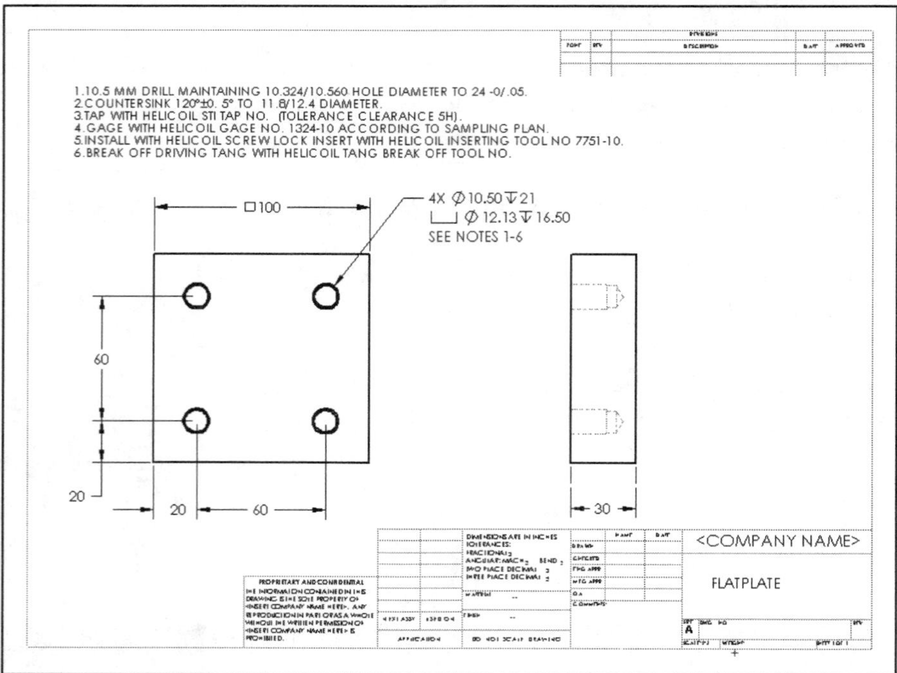

Add the following Notes to complete the drawing:

NOTES:

1. 10.5 MM DRILL MAINTAINING 10.324/10.560 HOLE DIAMETER TO 24 -0/.05.
2. COUNTERSINK 120°±0. 5° TO 11.8/12.4 DIAMETER.
3. TAP WITH HELICOIL STI TAP NO. 2087-10 (TOLERANCE CLEARANCE 5H).
4. GAGE WITH HELICOIL GAGE NO. 1324-10 ACCORDING TO SAMPLING PLAN.
5. INSTALL WITH HELICOIL SCREW LOCK INSERT 4184-10CN WITH HELICOIL INSERTING TOOL NO 7751-10.
6. BREAK OFF DRIVING TANG WITH HELICOIL TANG BREAK OFF TOOL NO. 4238-10.

Store Drawing notes for threaded inserts in a Notepad.txt document to conserve time.

Exercise 3.10: GUIDE eDrawing.

Create the GUIDE eDrawing. A SolidWorks eDrawing is a compressed document that does not require the corresponding part or assembly. SolidWorks eDrawing is animated to display multiple views and dimensions. Review the eDrawing SolidWorks Help Topics for additional functionality. The eDrawings Professional version contains additional options to mark up a drawing.

- Select the UI Mode button to toggle between Simple and Complete UI mode interface.
- Select Tools, Add-Ins, eDrawings.
- Click Publish eDrawing from the eDrawing toolbar.
- Click the Play button to animate the drawing views.
- Save the GUIDE eDrawing.

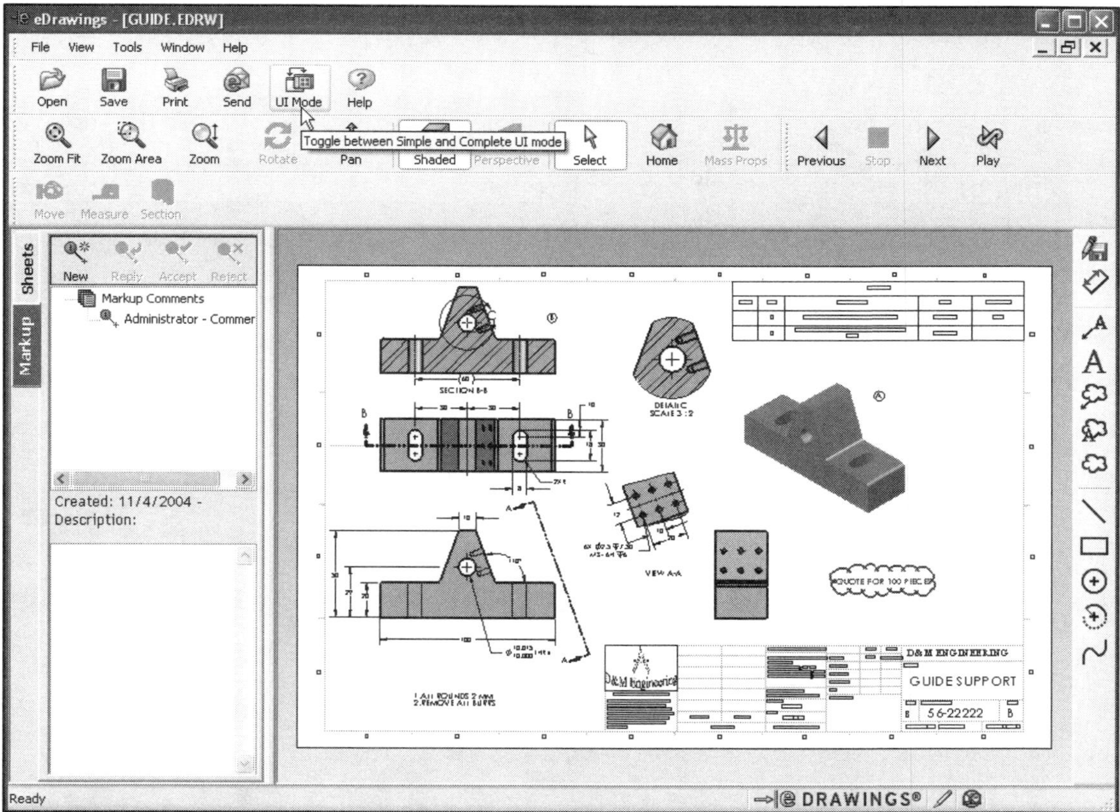

Refer to Help, Online Tutorial, eDrawings exercise for additional information.

Notes:

Project 4

Extrude and Revolve Features

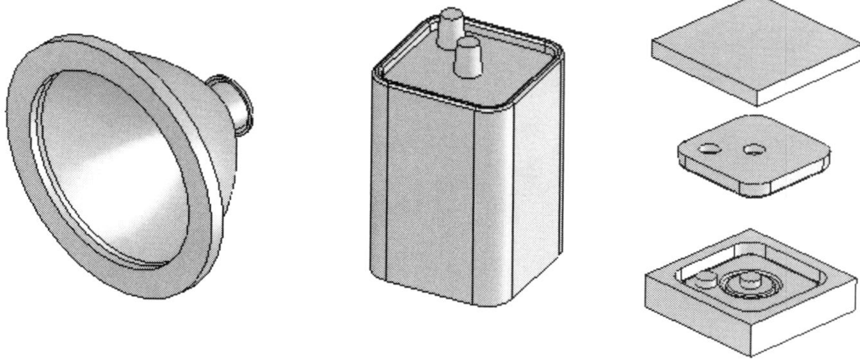

Below are the desired outcomes and usage competencies based on the completion of Project 4.

Project Desired Outcomes:	Usage Competencies:
• An understanding of the customer's requirements for the FLASHLIGHT assembly.	• Ability to apply design intent to sketches, features, parts and assemblies.
• Two Part Templates: o PART-IN-ANSI. o PART-MM-ISO.	• Ability to apply Document Properties and create custom Part Templates.
• Four key parts: o BATTERY. o BATTERYPLATE. o LENS. o BULB.	• Specific knowledge and understanding of the following Features: Extruded-Boss, Extruded Base, Extruded-Cut, Revolve Boss/Bass, Revolved Cut, Dome, Shell, Circular Pattern and Fillet.
• Core and Cavity Tooling for the BATTERYPLATE.	• Understanding of the Mold Tools: Scale, Parting Lines, Parting Surfaces, Shut-off Surfaces, Tooling Split and Draft Analysis to create a simple core and cavity.

Notes:

Project 4-Extrude and Revolve Features

Project Objective

Design a FLASHLIGHT assembly according to the customer's requirements. The FLASHLIGHT assembly will be cost effective, serviceable and flexible for future manufacturing revisions.

Design intent is the process in which the model is developed to accept future changes. Build design intent into the FLASHLIGHT sketches, features, parts and assemblies.

Create a custom Part Template. The Part Template is the foundation for the FLASHLIGHT parts.

Create the following parts:

- BATTERY.
- BATTERYPLATE.
- LENS.
- BULB.

The other parts for the FLASHLIGHT assembly are addressed in Project 5.

Create the Core and Cavity mold tooling required for the BATTERYPLATE.

On the completion of this project, you will be able to:

- Apply design intent to sketches, features and parts.
- Choose the best profile for sketching.
- Choose the proper sketch plane.
- Create a Template: English and Metric units.
- Set Document Properties.
- Customize Toolbars.
- Insert/Edit Dimensions.
- Insert/Edit Relations.
- Use the following SolidWorks features:
    - Extruded Boss/Base.
    - Extruded Cut.
    - Edge and Face Fillets.

- Revolved Boss/Base.
- Revolved Boss Thin.
- Revolved Cut Thin.
- Dome.
- Shell.
- Circular Pattern.

- Use the following Mold Tools:
  - Draft Analysis.
  - Scale.
  - Parting Lines.
  - Shut-off Surfaces.
  - Parting Surfaces.
  - Tooling Split.

Project Overview

In Project 4, you begin the design of a FLASHLIGHT assembly according to the customer's requirements. The FLASHLIGHT assembly will be cost effective, serviceable and flexible for future manufacturing revisions.

A template is the foundation for a SolidWorks document. A template contains settings for units, dimensioning standards and other properties. Create two part templates for the FLASHLIGHT Project:

- PART-IN-ANSI.
- PART-MM-ISO.

Create two parts for the FLASHLIGHT assembly in this Project:

- BATTERY.
- BATTERYPLATE.

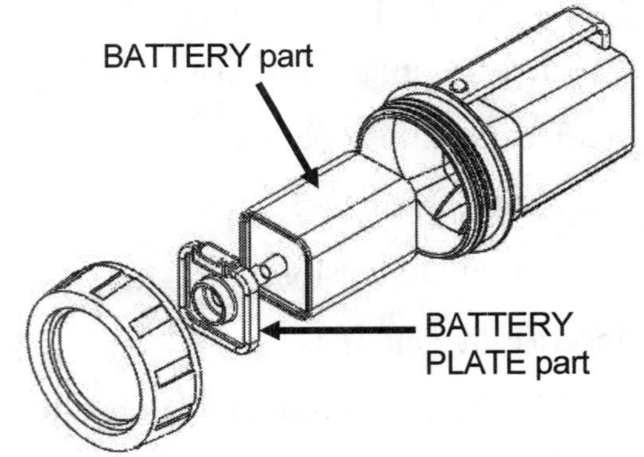

FLASHLIGHT Assembly

Parts models consist of 3D features. Features are the building blocks of a part.

A 2D sketch is required to create an Extruded feature. Utilize the sketch geometry and sketch tools to create the following features:

- Extruded Base.
- Extruded Boss.
- Extruded Cut.

Utilize existing faces and edges to create the following features:

- Fillet.
- Chamfer.

This project introduces you to the Revolved feature.

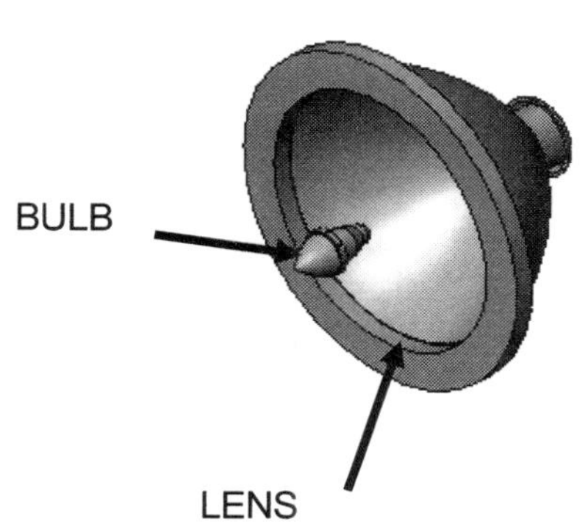

Create two parts for the FLASHLIGHT assembly in this section:

- LENS.
- BULB.

A Revolved feature requires a 2D sketch profile and a centerline. Utilize sketch geometry and sketch tools to create the following features:

- Revolved Base.
- Revolved Boss.
- Revolved Boss-Thin.
- Revolved Cut.

Utilize existing faces to create the following features:

- Shell.
- Dome.
- Hole Wizard.

Utilize the Extruded Cut feature to create a Circular Pattern.

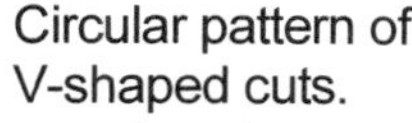

Utilize the Mold Tools to create the cavity tooling plates for the BATTERYPLATE part.

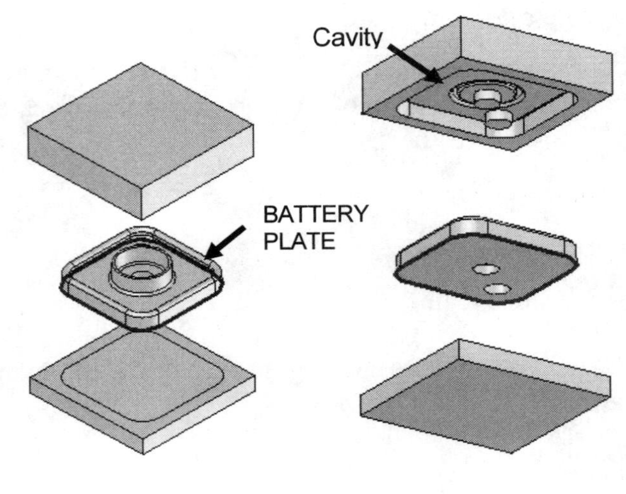

Mold Tools

Design Intent

The SolidWorks definition of design intent is the process in which the model is developed to accept future changes.

Models behave differently when design changes occur. Design for change. Utilize geometry for symmetry, reuse common features and reuse common parts.

Build change into the following areas:

1. Sketch.
2. Feature.
3. Part.
4. Assembly.
5. Drawing.

1. Design Intent in the Sketch.

Build the design intent in the sketch as the profile is created.

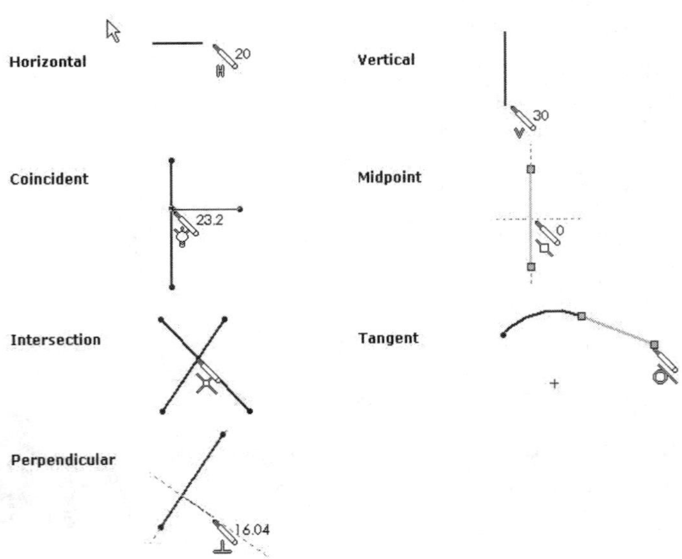

A profile is determined from the sketch tools, Example: rectangle, circle and arc.

Build symmetry into the profile through a sketch centerline, mirror entity and position about the reference planes and Origin.

Build design intent as you sketch with automatic relationships.

A rectangle contains horizontal, vertical and perpendicular automatic relations.

Build design intent using added geometric relations. Example: horizontal, vertical, coincident, midpoint, intersection, tangent and perpendicular.

Example A: Develop a square profile.

Build the design intent to create a square profile.

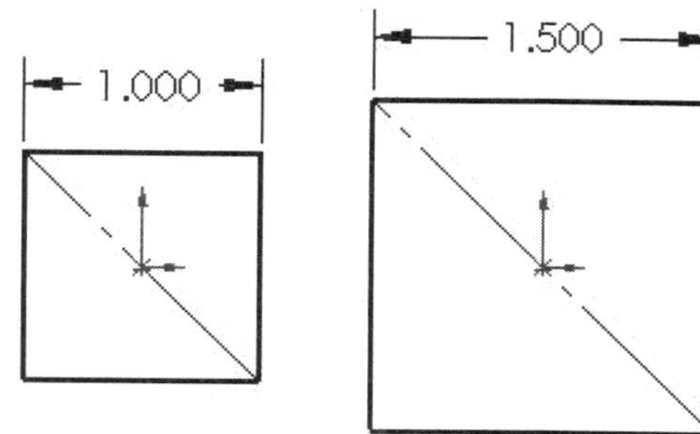

Sketch a rectangle with the Origin approximately in the center. Insert a centerline. Add a midpoint relation. Add an equal relation between the two perpendicular lines. Insert a dimension to define the exact width of the square.

Example B: Develop a rectangular profile.

The bottom horizontal midpoint of the rectangular profile is located at the Origin.

Sketch a rectangle. Add a midpoint relation between the horizontal edge of the rectangle and the Origin. Insert two dimensions to define the width and height of the rectangle.

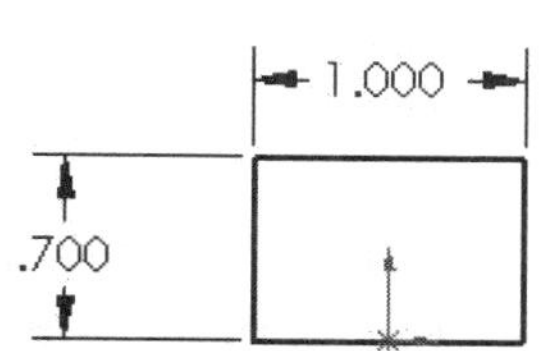

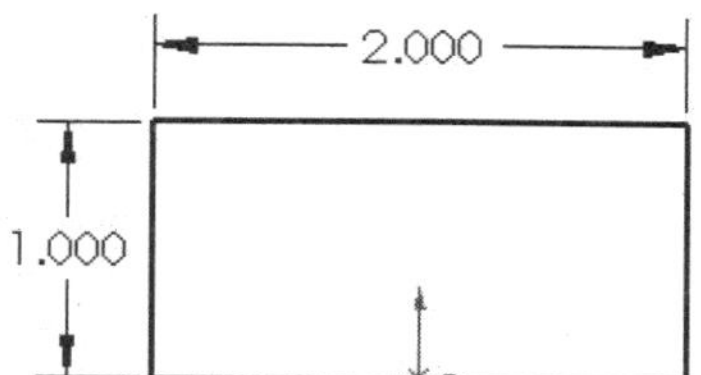

2. Design Intent in the Feature.

Build design intent into a feature by addressing symmetry, feature selection and the order of feature creations.

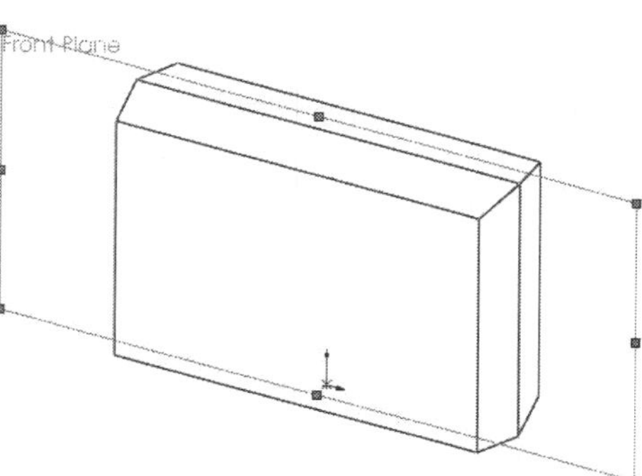

Example A: Extruded feature remains symmetric about a plane.

Utilize the Mid Plane Depth option.

Change the depth and the feature remains symmetric about the Front Plane. Example B: Part manufactured utilizing an injection-molded process.

Plastic parts require draft to remove the part from the mold. Utilize the Draft feature. Change the draft angle as determined by the manufacturer.

Example C: Six holes for a bolt circle.

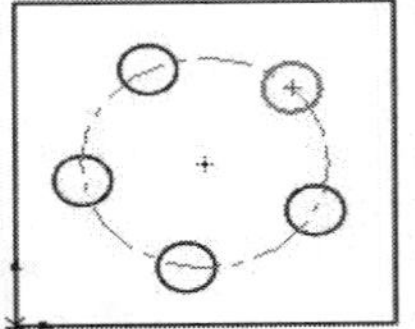
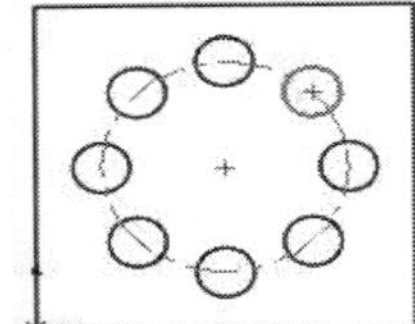

Do you create six separate Extruded Cuts? No. Create one hole with the Hole Wizard. Insert a Circular Pattern. Change the number of holes from five to eight. The holes remain centered on the bolt circle.

3. Design Intent in the Part.

Utilize symmetry, feature order and reusing common features to build design intent into the part.

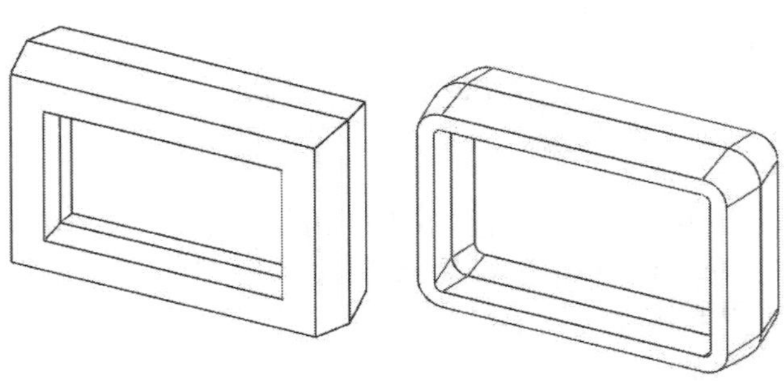

Example A: Feature Order.

Is the entire part symmetric?

Feature order affects the part.

Apply the Shell feature before the Fillet feature and the inside corners remain perpendicular.

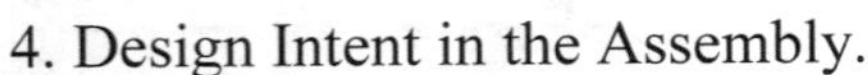

4. Design Intent in the Assembly.

Utilize symmetry, reuse common parts and use the Mate relationship between parts to build the design intent into an assembly.

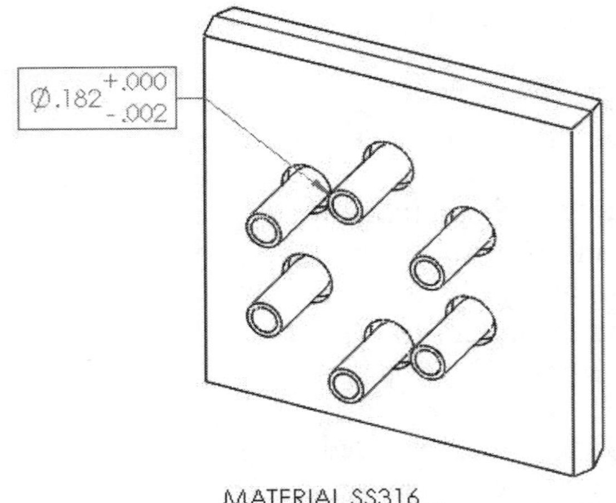

Example A: Reuse Geometry in the PLATE-TUBE assembly.

The PLATE part contains a Circular Pattern of six Holes. Insert one TUBE into the first Hole. Utilize Component Pattern to copy the TUBE to the other five holes.

5. Design Intent in the Drawing.

Utilize dimensions, tolerances and notes in parts and assemblies to build the design intent into the Drawing.

Example A: Tolerance and material in the drawing.

Insert an outside diameter tolerance +.000/-.002 into the TUBE part. The tolerance propagates to the drawing.

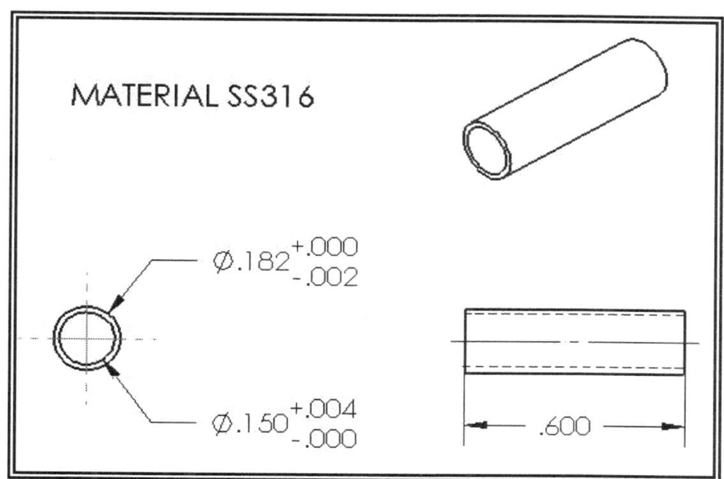

Additional information on the design process and design intent is available in SolidWorks Help Topics, *Introducing SolidWorks*.

Project Situation

You work for a company that specializes in providing promotional tradeshow products. The company is expecting a sales order for 100,000 flashlights with a potential for 500,000 units next year. Prototype drawings of the flashlight are required in three weeks.

You are the design engineer responsible for the project. You contact the customer to discuss design options and product specifications. The customer informs you that the flashlights will be used in an international marketing promotional campaign. Key customer requirements:

- Inexpensive reliable flashlight.
- Available advertising space of 10 square inches, 64.5 square centimeters.
- Lightweight semi indestructible body.
- Self standing with a handle.

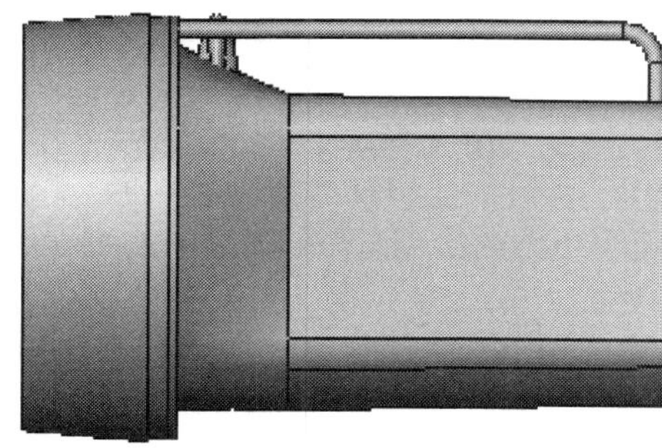

Your company's standard product line does not address the above key customer requirements. The customer made it clear that there is no room for negotiation on the key product requirements.

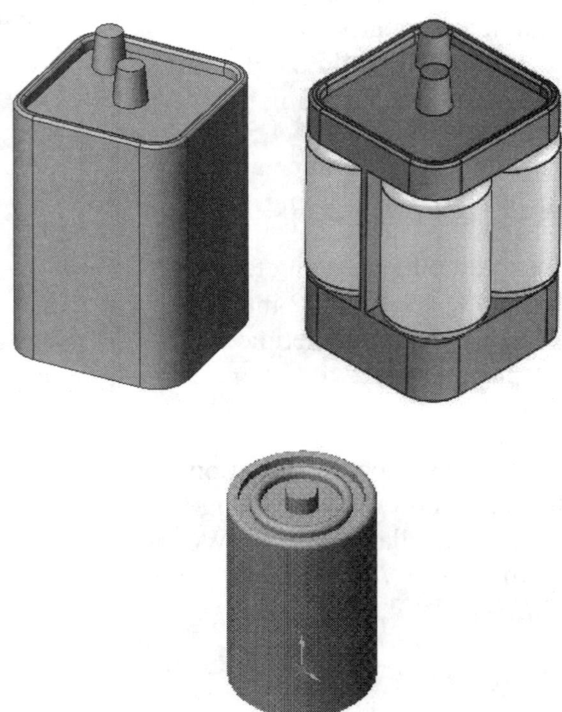

You contact the salesperson and obtain additional information on the customer and product. This is a very valuable customer with a long history of last minute product changes. The job has high visibility with great future potential.

In a design review meeting, you present a conceptual sketch. Your colleagues review the sketch. The team's consensus is to proceed with the conceptual design.

The first key design decision is the battery. The battery type directly affects the flashlight body size, bulb intensity, case structure integrity, weight, manufacturing complexity and cost.

Review two potential battery options:

- A single 6-volt lantern battery.
- Four 1.5-volt D cell batteries.

The two options affect the product design and specification. Think about it.

A single 6-volt lantern battery is approximately 25% higher in cost and 35% more in weight. The 6-volt lantern battery does provide higher current capabilities and longer battery life.

A special battery holder is required to incorporate the four 1.5 volt D cell configuration. This would directly add to the cost and design time of the FLASHLIGHT assembly.

Time is critical. For the prototype, you decide to use a standard 6-volt lantern battery. This eliminates the requirement to design and procure a special battery holder. However, you envision the four D cell battery model for the next product revision.

Design the FLASHLIGHT assembly to accommodate both battery design options. Battery dimensional information is required for the design. Where do you go? Potential sources: product catalogs, company web sites, professional standards organizations, design handbooks and colleagues.

The team decides to purchase the following parts: 6-volt BATTERY, LENS ASSEMBLY, SWITCH and an O-RING. Model the following purchased parts: BATTERY, LENS assembly, SWITCH and the O-RING. The LENS assembly consists of the LENS and the BULB.

Your company will design, model and manufacture the following parts: BATTERYPLATE, LENSCAP and HOUSING.

Purchased Parts:	Designed Parts:
BATTERY	BATTERYPLATE
LENS assembly	MOLD TOOLING
*SWITCH	*LENSCAP
*O-RING	*HOUSING

*Parts addressed in Project 5.

The BATTERYPLATE, LENSCAP and HOUSING are plastic parts. Review the injection molded manufacturing process and the SolidWorks Mold tools. Modify the part features to eject the part from the mold. Create the MOLD TOOLING for the BATTERYPLATE.

Part Template

Units are the measurement of physical quantities. Millimeter dimensioning and decimal inch dimensioning are the two most common unit types specified for engineering parts and drawings. The FLASHLIGHT project is designed in inch units and manufactured in millimeter units. Inch units are the primary unit and Millimeter units are the secondary unit.

Create two Part Templates:

- PART-IN-ANSI.
- PART-MM-ISO.

Save the Part Templates in the MY-TEMPLATES folder. System Options, File Locations option controls the file folder location of SolidWorks documents. Utilize the File Locations option to reference your Part Templates in the MY-TEMPLATES folder. Add the MY-TEMPLATES folder path name to the Document Templates File Locations list.

Activity: Part Template

Create the PART-IN-ANSI Template.

1) Click **File**, **New** from the Main menu.

2) Double-click **Part** from the default Templates tab.

Set the Dimensioning Standard to ANSI.

3) Click **Tools**, **Options** from the Main menu.

4) Click the **Document Properties** tab.

5) Select **ANSI** from the Dimensioning Standard list box.

6) Click the **System Options** tab.

7) Click **Spin Box Increments**.

8) Click the English units **text box**.

9) Enter **.100**.

10) Click the Metric units **text box**.

11) Enter **2.5**.

12) Click the **Document Properties** tab.

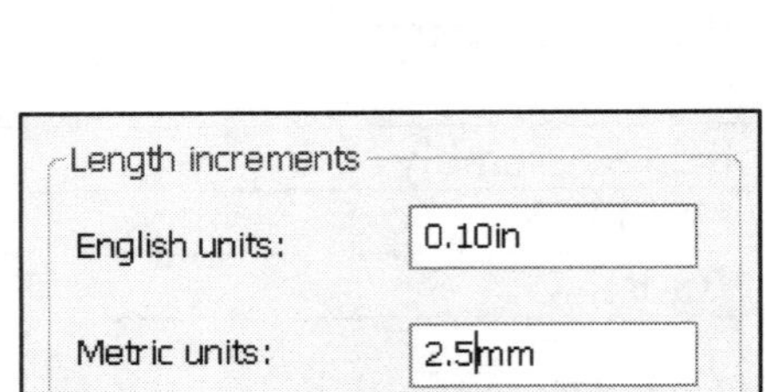

Set the part units for inch.

13) Click **Units**.

14) Select **IPS** for Unit system.

15) Select **3** for Length units Decimal places.

16) Select **millimeters** for Dual units.

17) Select **2** for Decimal places.

18) Select **0** for Angular units Decimal places.

19) Click **OK**.

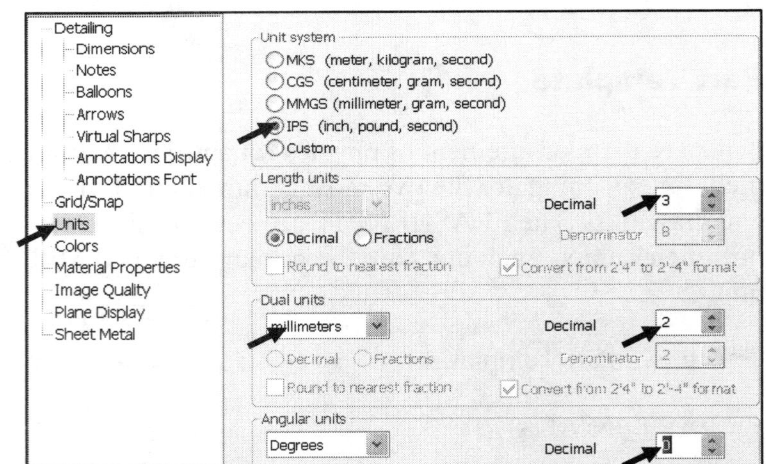

Save the part template.

20) Click **File**, **Save As** from the Main menu.

21) Click **Part Templates (*.prtdot)** from the Save As type list box.

22) Select **ENGDESIGN-W-SOLIDWORKS\MY-TEMPLATES** from the Save in list.

23) Enter **PART-IN-ANSI** in the File name text box.

24) Click **Save**.

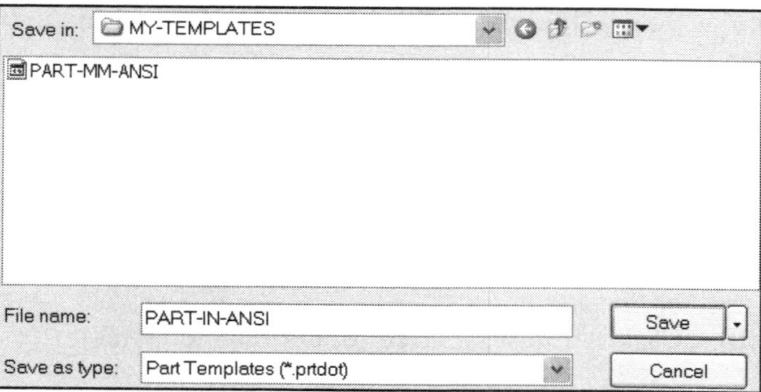

Utilize the PART-IN-ANSI template to create the PART-MM-ISO template.

25) Click **Tools**, **Options** from the Main menu.

26) Click the **Document Properties** Tab.

27) Select **ISO** from the Dimensioning standard list box.

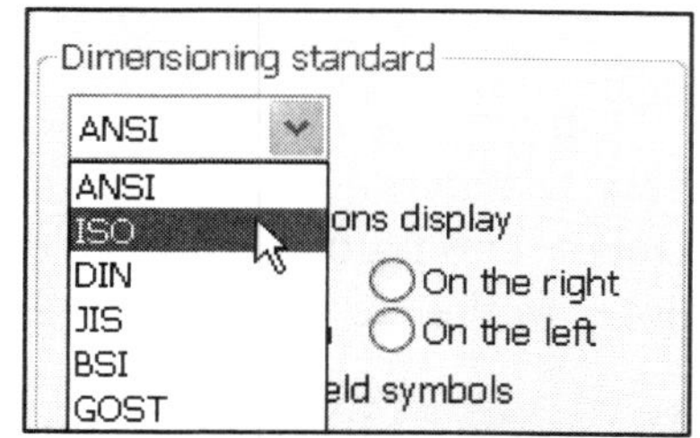

Set the part units for millimeter.

28) Click **Units**.

29) Select **MMGS** for Unit system.

30) Select **2** for Length units Decimal places.

31) Select **0** for Angular units Decimal places.

32) Click **OK**.

Save the part template.

33) Click **File**, **Save As** from the Main menu.

34) Click **Part Templates (*.prtdot)** from the Save As type list box.

35) Select **My Documents\ENGDESIGN-W-SOLIDWORKS\MY-TEMPLATES** from the Save in list.

36) Enter **PART-MM-ISO** in the File name text box.

37) Click **Save**.

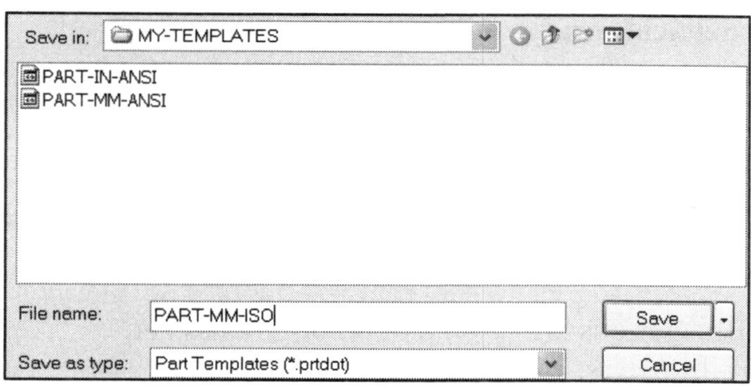

Set the System Options for File Locations to display in the New dialog box.

38) Click **Tools**, **Options** from the Main menu.

39) Click **File Locations** from the System Options tab.

External References
Default Templates
File Locations
FeatureManager

40) Select **Document Templates** from Show folders for.

41) Click the **Add** button.

42) Select the **MY-TEMPLATES** folder.

43) Click **OK** from Browse for Folder.

44) Click **OK** from System Options.

Close all documents.

45) Click **Windows**, **Close All** from the Main menu.

Each folder listed in the System Options, File Locations, Document Templates, Show Folders For option produces a corresponding Tab in the New SolidWorks Document dialog box. The order in the Document Templates box corresponds to the Tab order in the New dialog box.

The MY-TEMPLATES Tab is visible when the folder contains SolidWorks Template documents. Create the PART-MM-ANSI template as an exercise.

The PART-IN-ANSI Template contains Document Properties settings for the parts contained in the FLASHLIGHT assembly. Substitute the PART-MM-ISO or PART-MM-ANSI Template to create the identical parts in millimeters.

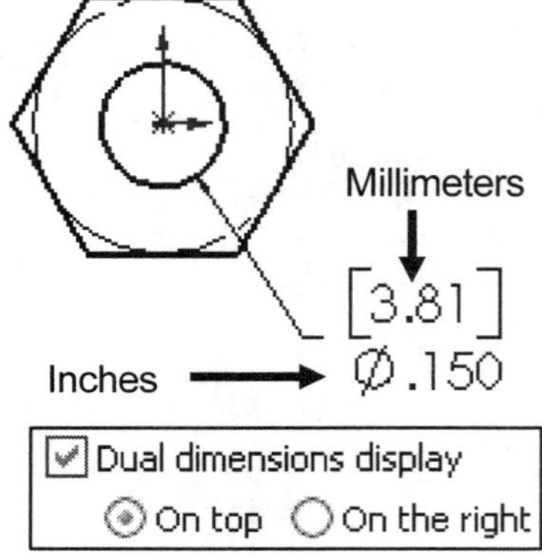

The primary units in this Project are IPS (inch, pound, seconds).

The optional secondary units are MMGS (millimeters, grams, second) and are indicated in brackets [ ].

Illustrations are provided in both inches and millimeters.

Utilize inches, millimeters or both.

To set dual dimensions, select Tools, Options, Document Properties.

Check the Dual dimension display box.

Select Toolbars, Features in SolidWorks Help Topic to review the function of each tool in the Features toolbar.

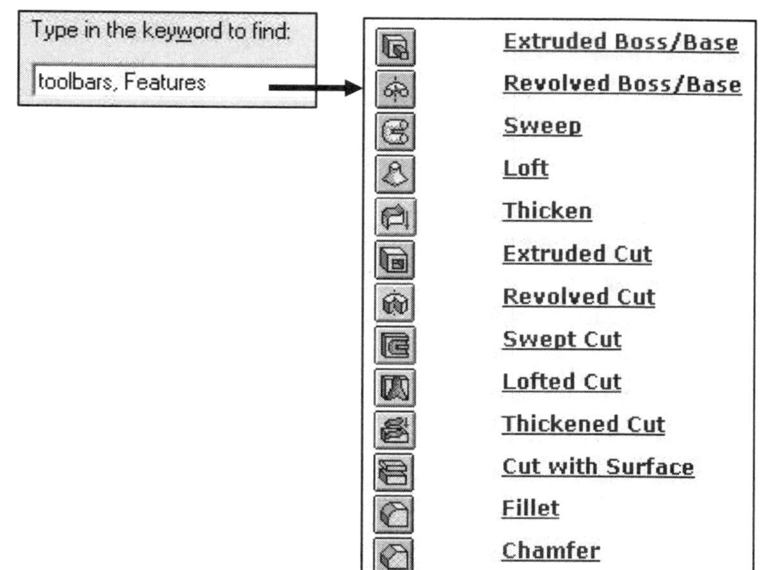

Additional information on System Options, Document Properties, File Locations and Templates is found in SolidWorks Help Topics. Keywords: Options (detailing, units), templates, Files (locations), menus and toolbars (features, sketch).

Review of the Part Templates.

You created two Part Templates: PART-MM-ISO and PART-IN-ANSI. The Document Properties Dimensioning Standard, Units and Decimal Places were stored in the Part Templates.

The File Locations System Option, Document Templates option controls the reference to the MY-TEMPLATES folder.

Note: In some network locations and school environments, the File Locations option must be set to MY-TEMPLATES for each session of SolidWorks.

You can exit SolidWorks at any time during this project. Save your document. Select File, Exit from the Main menu.

BATTERY Part

The BATTERY is a simplified representation of a purchased OEM part. Represent the battery terminals as cylindrical extrusions. The battery dimensions are obtained from the ANSI standard 908D.

A 6-Volt lantern battery weighs approximately 1.38 pounds, (0.62kg). Locate the center of gravity closest to the center of the battery.

Create the BATTERY part.

Use features to create parts. Features are building blocks that add or remove material.

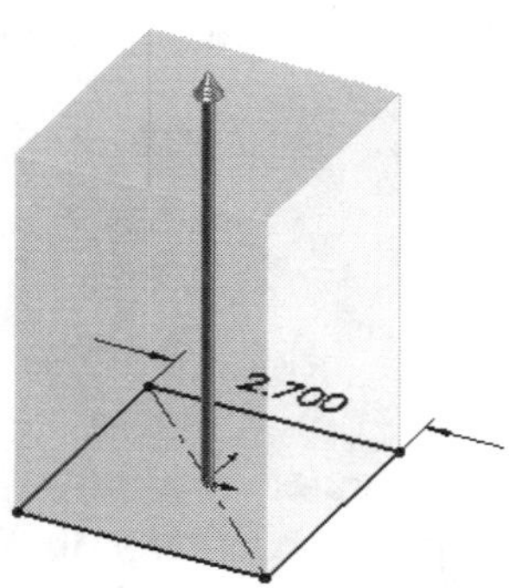

Utilize the Extruded Base feature. The Extrude Base features add material. The Base feature is the first feature of the part.

Utilize symmetry. Sketch a rectangle profile on the Top plane, centered at the Origin.

Extend the profile perpendicular (⊥) to the Top plane.

Utilize the Fillet feature to round four vertical edges.

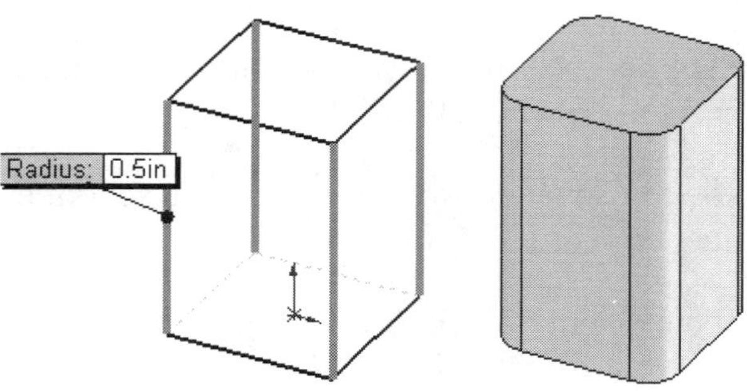

The Extruded Cut feature removes material from the top face. Utilize the top face for the Sketch plane. Utilize the Offset Entity Sketch tool to create the profile.

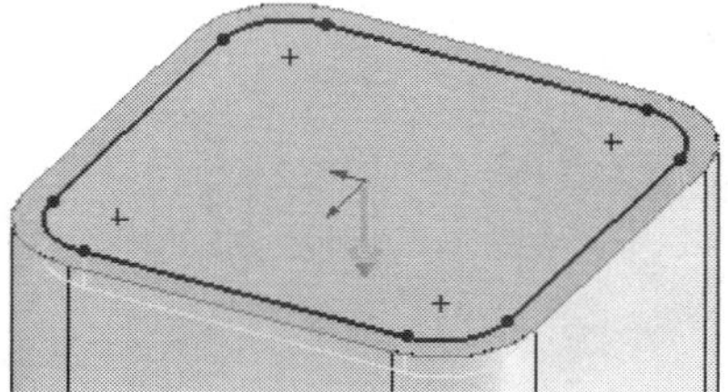

Utilize the Fillet feature to round the top narrow face.

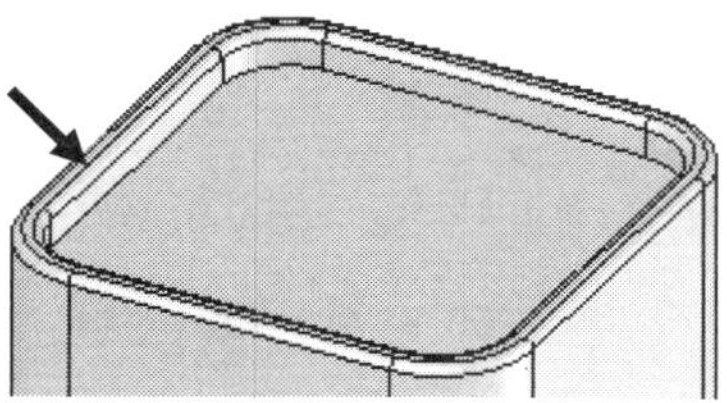

The Extruded Boss feature adds material. Conserve design time. Represent each of the terminals as a cylindrical Extruded Boss feature.

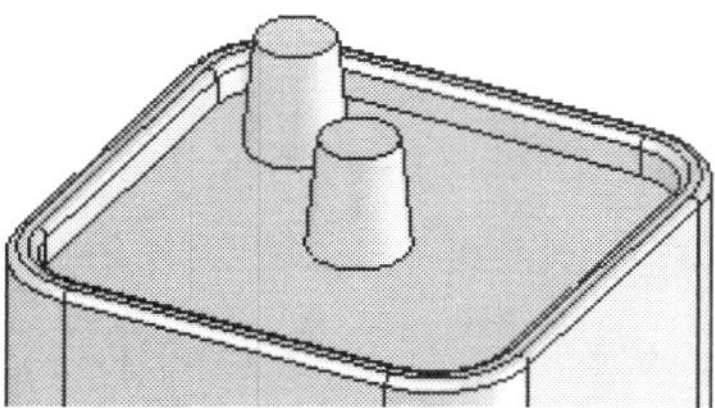

BATTERY Part-Extruded Base Feature

The Extruded Base feature requires:

- Sketch Plane (Top).
- Sketch Profile (Rectangle).
  - Geometric Relations and Dimensions.
- End Condition (Blind Depth).

Create a new part named, BATTERY. Insert an Extruded Base feature. Extruded features require a Sketch Plane. The Sketch Plane determines the orientation of the Extruded Base feature. The Sketch Plane locates the Sketch Profile on any plane or face.

The Top Plane is the Sketch Plane. The Sketch Profile is a Rectangle. The Rectangle consists of 2 horizontal lines and 2 vertical lines.

Geometric Relations and Dimensions constrain the sketch in 3D space. The Blind End Condition requires a Depth value to extrude the 2D Sketch Profile and complete the 3D feature.

Note: Alternate between Feature and Sketch in the Control Area to display the Features toolbar and Sketch toolbar or display the individual toolbars outside the Graphics window.

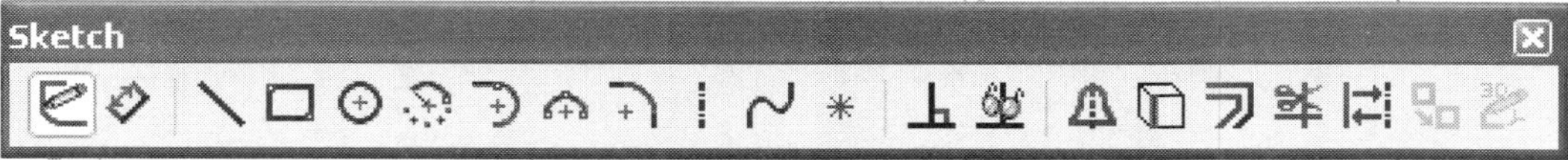

Activity: BATTERY Part-Extruded Base Feature

Create a new part.

46) Click **File**, **New** from the Main menu.

47) Click the **MY-TEMPLATES** tab.

48) Double-click **PART-IN-ANSI**, [**PART-MM-ISO**].

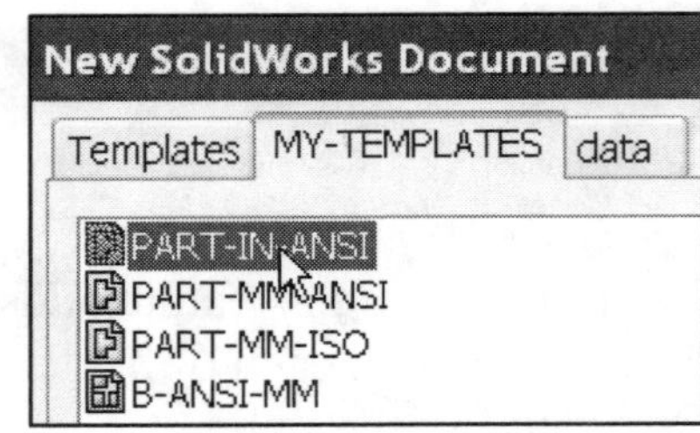

Save the empty part.

49) Click **Save**.

50) Select **PROJECTS** for Save in folder.

51) Enter **BATTERY** for file name.

52) Enter **BATTERY**, **6-VOLT** for Description.

53) Click **Save**.

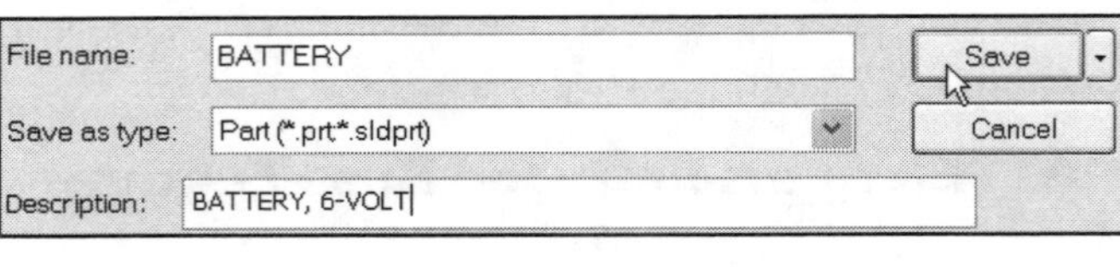

Select the Sketch plane.

54) Click the **Top Plane** from the FeatureManager.

Sketch the profile.

55) Click **Sketch** Sketch from the Sketch toolbar.

56) Click **Top view**.

57) Click **Rectangle** Rectan... from the Sketch toolbar.

58) Click the **first point** in the lower left quadrant.

59) Drag and click the **second point** in the upper right quadrant. The Origin is approximately in the middle of the Rectangle.

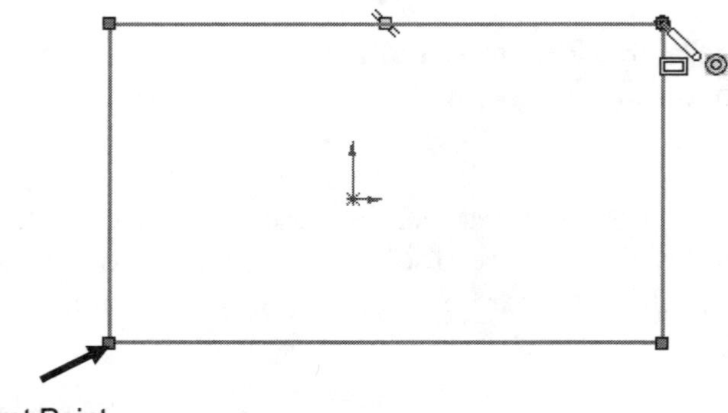

Sketch the Centerline.

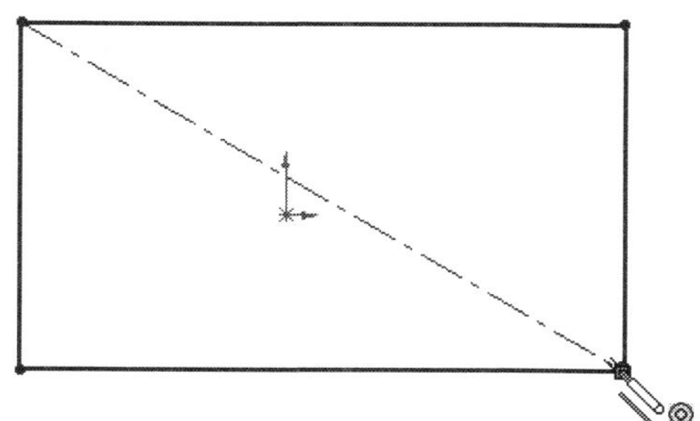

60) Click **Centerline** from the Sketch Tools toolbar.

61) Sketch a diagonal centerline from the **upper left corner** to the **lower right corner**. The endpoints of the centerline are coincident with the corner points of the Rectangle.

Add a Midpoint Relation.

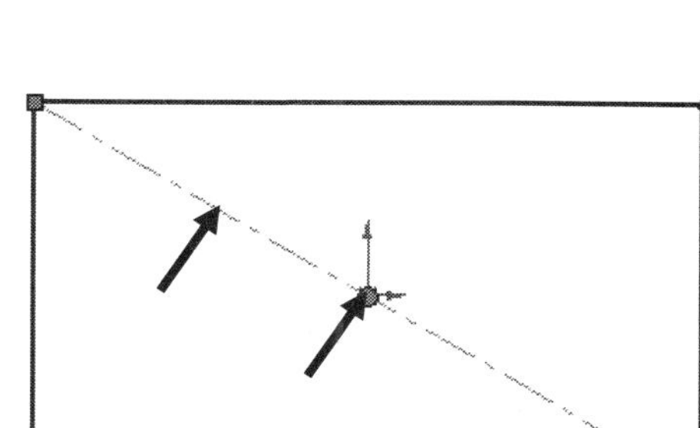

62) Right-click **Select** in the Graphics window.

63) Click the **centerline**.

64) Hold the **Ctrl** key down.

65) Click the **Origin**.

66) Release the **Ctrl** key.

67) Click **Midpoint** from the Add Relations box.

68) Click **OK** from the Properties PropertyManager. Note: The Line# may be different than the line numbers above. The Line# is dependent on the line number order creation.

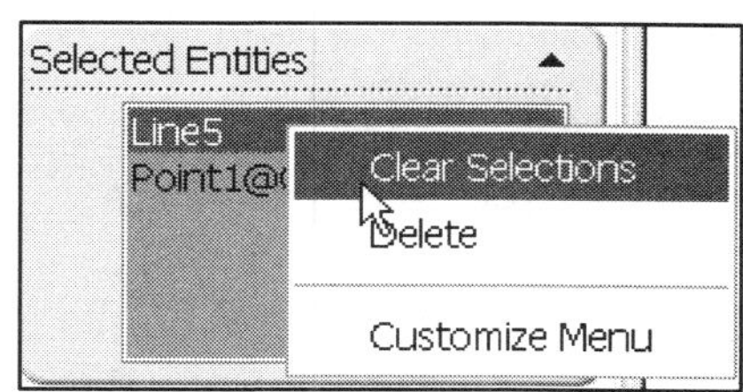

To clear entities from the Selected Entities box, right-click Clear Selections.

Create a square. Add an Equal Relation.

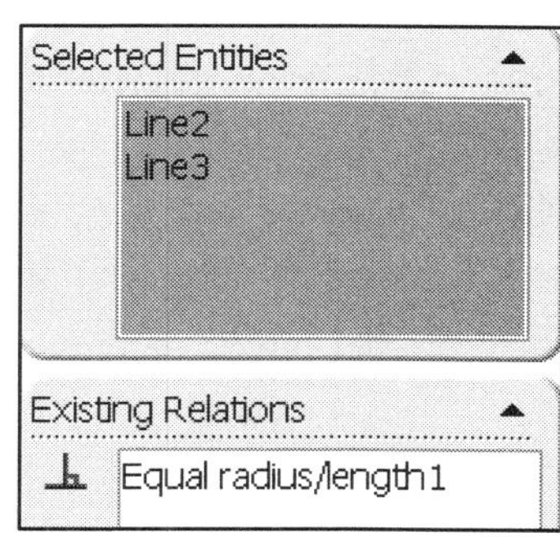

69) Click the **top horizontal line**.

70) Hold the **Ctrl** key down.

71) Click the **left vertical line**.

72) Release the **Ctrl** key.

73) Click **Equal** from the Add Relations box.

74) Click **OK** from the Properties PropertyManager.

Add a dimension.

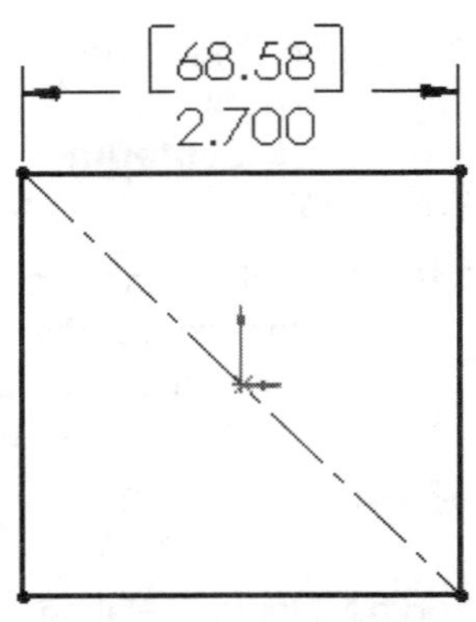

75) Click **Smart Dimension** Smart Dimens... from the Sketch toolbar.

76) Click the **top horizontal line**.

77) Click a **position** above the horizontal line.

78) Enter **2.700**, **[68.58]** for width.

79) Click the **Green Check mark** ✔. The black Sketch status is fully defined.

80) Click **OK** from the Dimension PropertyManager.

Display the Sketch Relations.

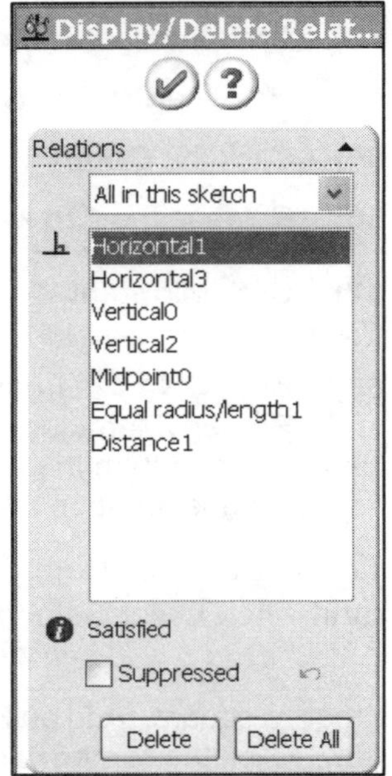

81) Click **Display/Delete Relations** Display... Relations from the Sketch toolbar. The Distance relation was created from the dimension. The Display/Delete Relations PropertyManager is displayed.

82) Click **OK** from the Display/Delete Relations PropertyManager.

Insert an Extruded Base feature.

83) Click **Features**  Features.

84) Click **Extruded Boss/Base** Extruded Boss/B... . The Extrude PropertyManager is displayed. Blind is the default option.

85) Enter **4.100**, **[104.14]** for Depth.

86) Click **OK** from the Extrude PropertyManager.

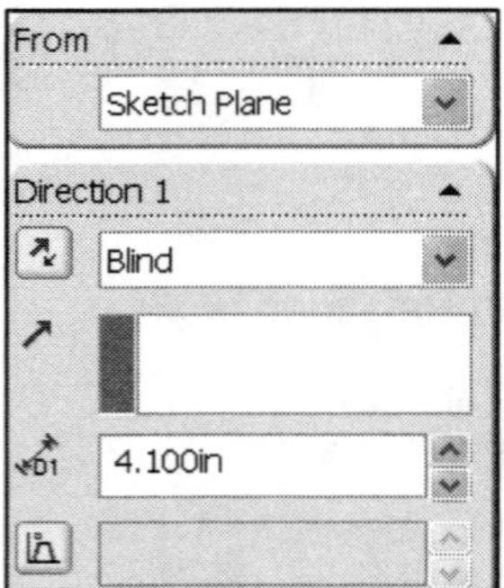

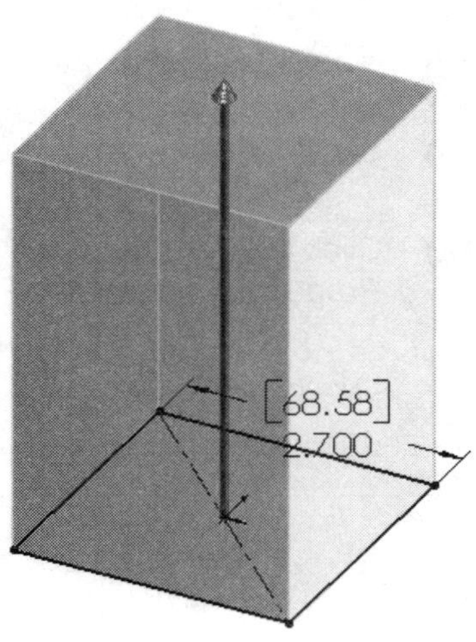

Fit the part to the Graphics window.

87) Press the **f** key.

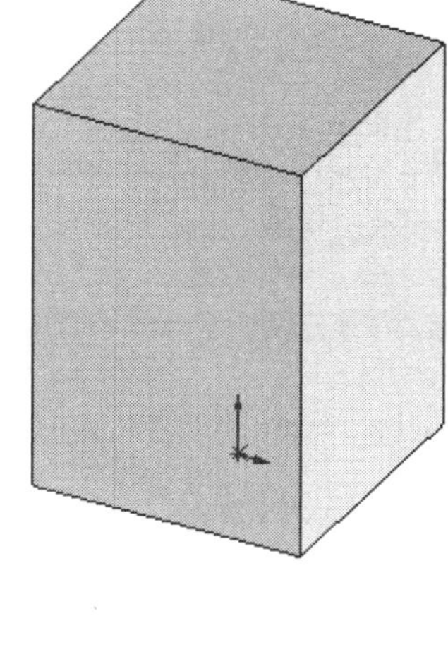

Rename the Extruded Base feature.

88) Rename **Extrude1** to **Base Extrude**.

Save the BATTERY.

89) Click **Save**.

Utilize an Equal relation versus two linear dimensions when a rectangular profile is square.

One dimension controls the size. The 6-Volt manufacturing standard determines the square profile.

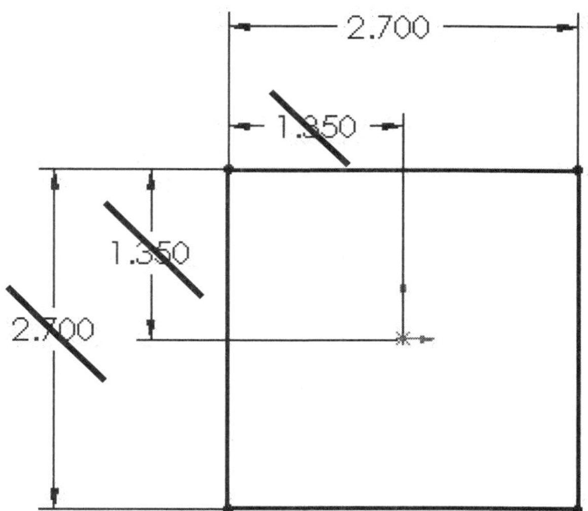

The Midpoint relation centers the square profile about the Origin.

One relation eliminates two dimensions to locate the profile with respect to the Origin.

The color of the sketch indicates the sketch status.

- Green: – Currently selected.
- Blue: – Under defined, requires additional Geometric Relations and dimensions.
- Black: – Fully defined.
- Red: – Over defined, requires Geometric Relations or dimensions to be deleted or redefined to solve the sketch.

 Short Cuts save time. Right-click Select Select to choose geometry.

Click inside the Graphics window to close the Properties PropertyManager or Dimension PropertyManager. Tools are located on the right mouse button and the toolbars. The Select icon is also located in the Standard toolbar.

BATTERY Part-Fillet Feature Edge

Fillets remove sharp edges. Utilize Hidden Lines Visible to display hidden edges.

An edge Fillet requires:

- Edge.
- Fillet Radius.

Select a vertical edge. Select the Fillet feature from the Features toolbar. Enter the Fillet radius. Add the other vertical edges to the Items to Fillet option.

The order of selection for the Fillet feature is not predetermined. Select edges to produce the correct result.

Activity: BATTERY Part-Fillet Feature Edge

Display the hidden edges.

90) Click **Hidden Lines Visible** from the View toolbar.

Insert the Fillet feature.

91) Click the **left vertical edge**.

92) Click **Fillet** Fillet from the Features toolbar. Edge<1> is displayed in the Items To Fillet box.

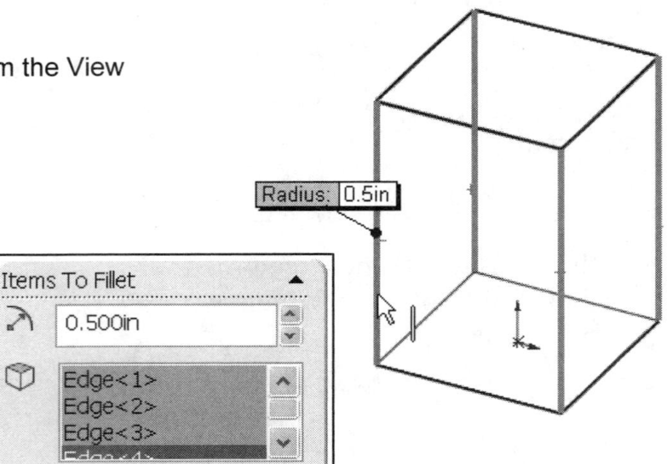

93) Click the remaining **3 vertical edges**.

94) Enter **.500**, [**12.7**] for Radius.

95) Click **OK** from the Fillet PropertyManager

96) Click **Isometric view**.

97) Click **Shaded With Edges**.

98) Rename **Fillet1** to **Side Fillets**.

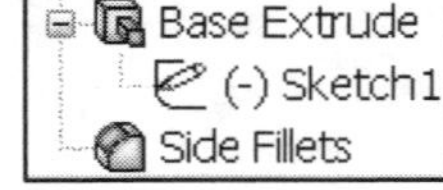

Save the BATTERY.

99) Click **Save**.

BATTERY Part-Extruded Cut Feature

An Extruded Cut feature removes material. An Extruded Cut requires:

- Sketch Plane (Top face).
- Sketch Profile (Offset Entities).
- End Condition (Blind Depth).

The Offset Entity Sketch tool uses existing geometry, extracts an edge or face and locates the geometry on the current sketch plane.

Offset the existing Top face for the 2D sketch. Utilize the Blind Depth for End Condition.

Activity: BATTERY Part-Extruded Cut Feature

Select the Sketch plane.

100) Click the **Top face** of the BATTERY.

Create a Sketch.

101) Click **Sketch** from the Sketch toolbar.

Display the face.

102) Click **Top view** from the Standards View toolbar.

Offset the existing geometry from the boundary of the Sketch plane.

103) Click **Offset Entities** from the Sketch Tools toolbar.

104) Enter **.150**, [**3.81**] for the Offset Distance.

105) Click the **Reverse** check box. The new Offset orange profile displays inside the original profile.

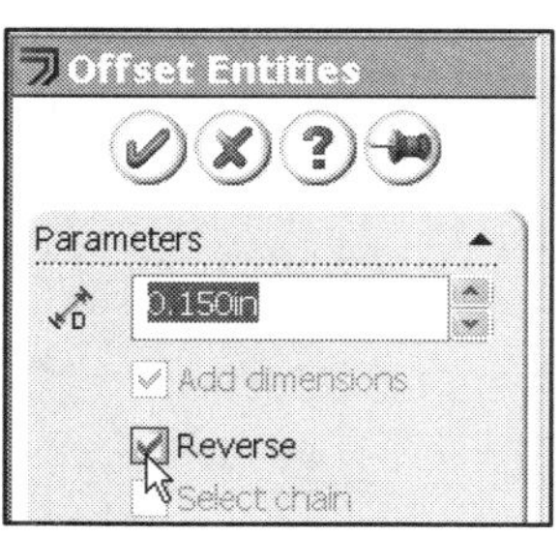

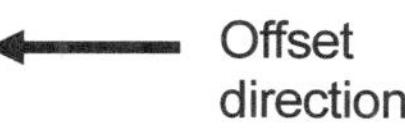

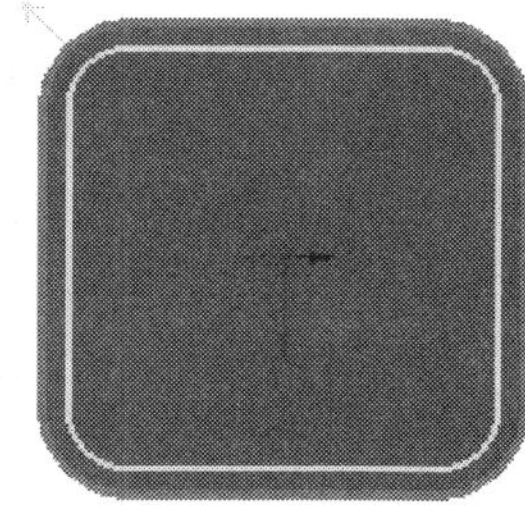

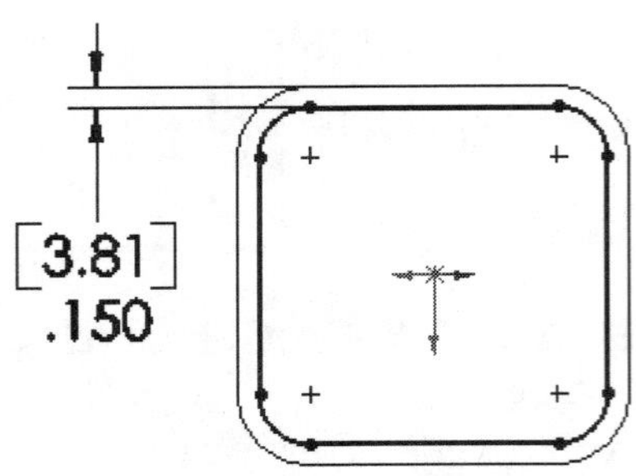

106) Click **OK** from the Offset Entities PropertyManager.

A leading zero is displayed in the spin box. For inch dimensions less than 1, the leading zero is not displayed in the part dimension in the ANSI standard.

Display the profile.

107) Click **Isometric view** .

Insert an Extruded Cut feature.

108) Click **Features** Features , **Extruded Cut** Extruded Cut from the Features toolbar.

109) Enter **.200**, [**5.08**] for Depth.

110) Click **OK** from the Cut-Extrude PropertyManager.

111) Rename **Cut-Extrude1** to **Top Cut**.

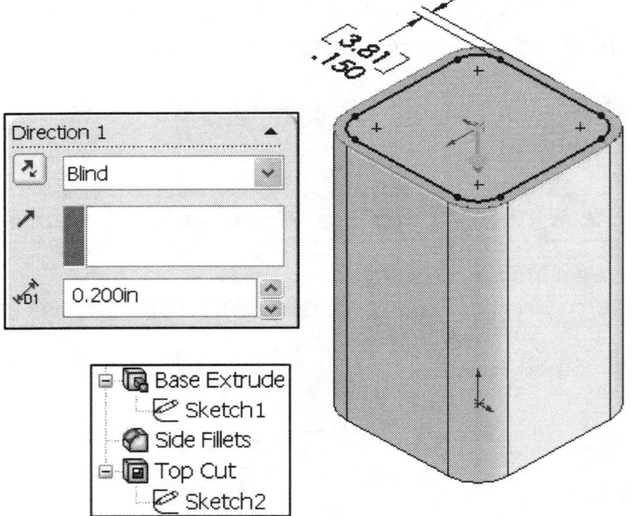

Save the BATTERY

112) Click **Save** .

The Cut-Extrude PropertyManager contains numerous options. The Reverse Direction option determines the direction of the Extruded Cut. The Extruded Cut is valid when the Direction arrow points into material to be removed.

Cut direction not valid, no material to remove

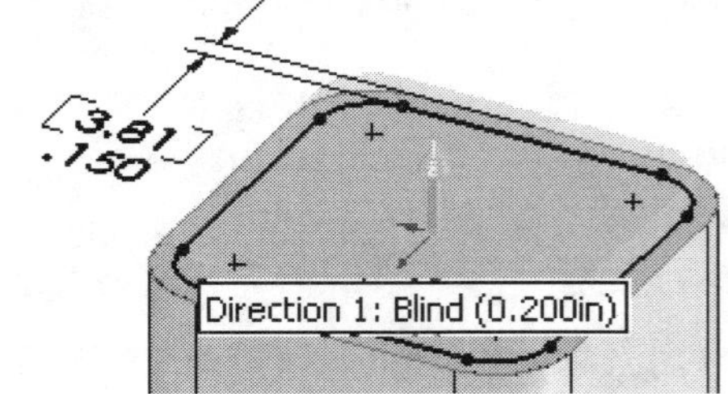

The Flip side to cut option determines if the cut is to the inside or outside of the Sketch Profile. The Flip side to cut arrow points outward. The Extruded Cut occurs on the outside.

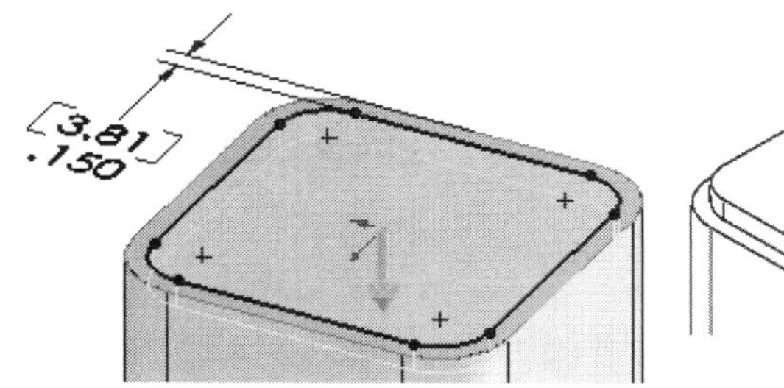

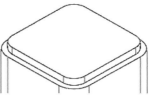

Extruded Cut with Flip side to cut option checked

BATTERY Part-Fillet Feature

The Fillet feature rounds sharp edges with a constant radius by selecting a face. A Fillet requires a:

- Face.
- Fillet Radius.

Activity: BATTERY Part-Fillet Feature Face

Insert the Fillet feature on the top face.

113) **Zoom to Area** on the Top face.

114) Click the **top thin face**.

115) Select **Fillet** Fillet from the Features toolbar. Face<1> is displayed in the Edge fillet items box.

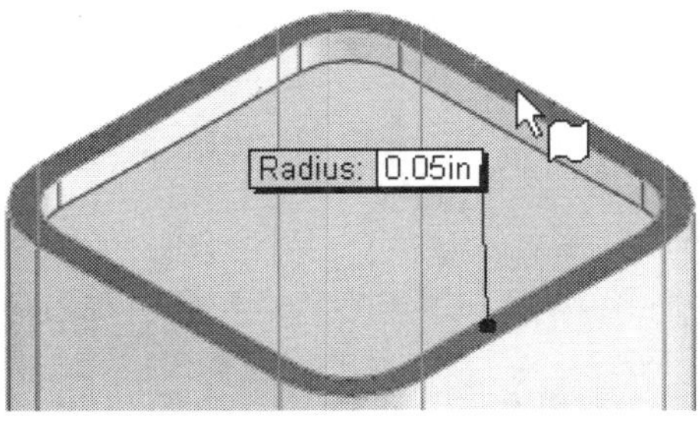

116) Click **Constant Radius** for Fillet Type.

117) Enter **.050**, [**1.27**] for Fillet Radius.

118) Click **OK** from the Fillet PropertyManager.

119) Rename **Fillet2** to **Top Face Fillet**.

120) Press the **f** key.

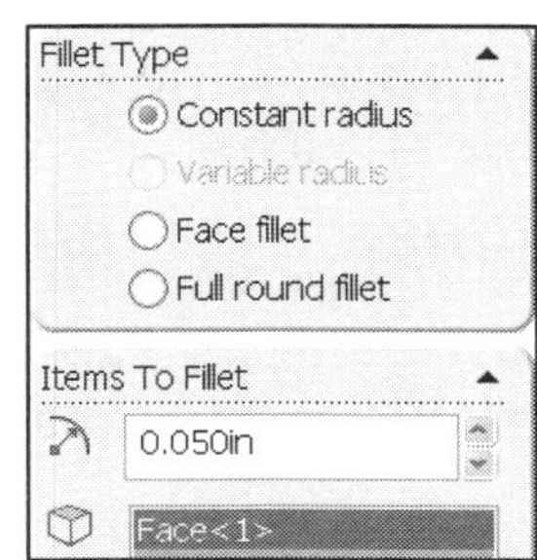

Save the BATTERY.

121) Click **Save** .

View the mouse pointer for feedback to select Edges or Faces for the Fillet.

 Do not select a Fillet radius which is larger then the surrounding geometry.

Example: The top edge face width is .150, [3.81]. The Fillet is created on both sides of the face. A common error is to enter a Fillet too large for the existing geometry. A minimum face width of .200, [5.08] is required for a Fillet radius of .100, [2.54].

The following error occurs when the Fillet radius is too large for the existing geometry:

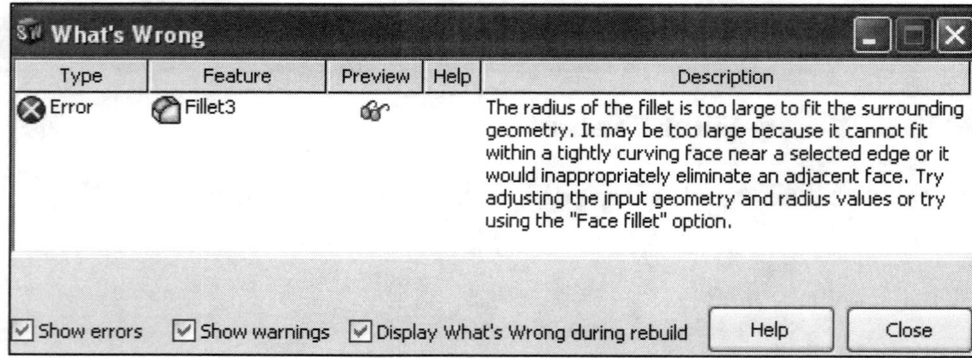

Avoid the Fillet Rebuild error. Reduce the Fillet size or increase the face width.

BATTERY Part-Extruded Boss Feature

The Extruded Boss requires a truncated cone shape to represent the geometry of the battery terminals. The Draft Angle option creates the tapered shape.

Sketch the first circle on the top face. Utilize the Ctrl key to copy the first circle.

The dimension between the center points is critical. Dimension the distance between the two center points with an aligned dimension. The dimension text toggles between linear and aligned. An aligned dimension is created when the dimension is positioned between the two circles.

An angular dimension is required between the Right plane and the centerline. Acute angles are less than 90°. Acute angles are the preferred dimension standard. The overall battery height is a critical dimension. The battery height is 4.500in, [114.30mm].

Calculate the depth of the extrusion: For inches: 4.500in – (4.100in Base-Extrude height – .200in Offset cut depth) = .600in The depth of the extrusion is .600in.

For millimeters: 114.3mm – (104.14mm Base-Extrude height – 5.08mm Offset cut depth) = 15.24mm. The depth of the extrusion is 15.24mm.

Activity: BATTERY Part-Extruded Boss Feature

Select the Sketch plane.

122) Click the **Top face** of the Top Cut feature.

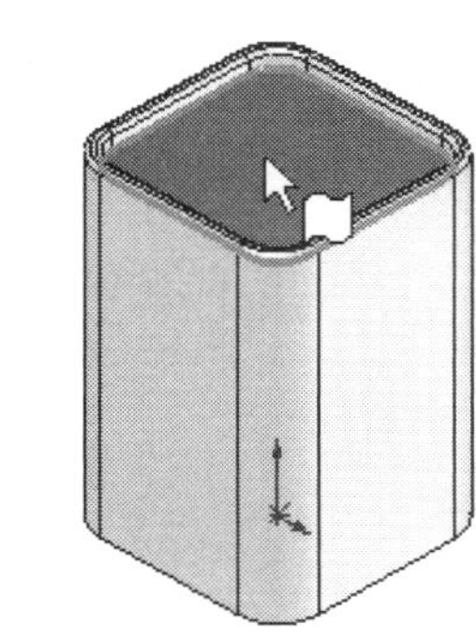

Create the Sketch.

123) Click **Sketch** Sketch from the Sketch toolbar.

124) Click **Top view** .

Sketch the profile.

125) Click **Circle** Circle from the Sketch Tools toolbar.

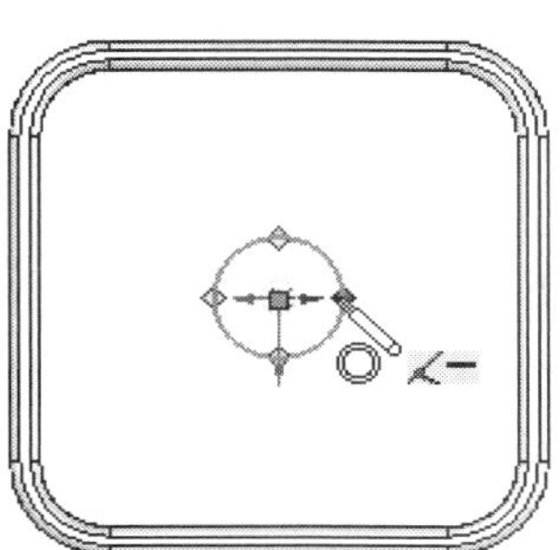

126) Click the **center point** of the circle coincident to the Origin .

127) Drag and click the **mouse pointer** to the right of the Origin.

Add a dimension.

128) Click **Smart Dimension** Smart Dimens....

129) Select the **circumference** of the circle.

130) Click a **position** diagonally to the right.

131) Enter **.500**, [**12.7**].

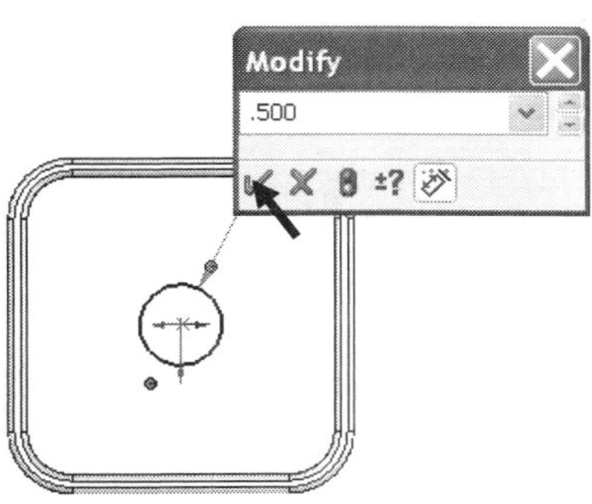

132) Click the **Green Check mark** . The black Sketch is fully defined.

Copy the sketched circle.

133) Right-click **Select** Select .

134) Hold the **Ctrl** key down.

135) Click and drag the **circumference** of the circle to the upper left quadrant.

136) Release the **mouse button**.

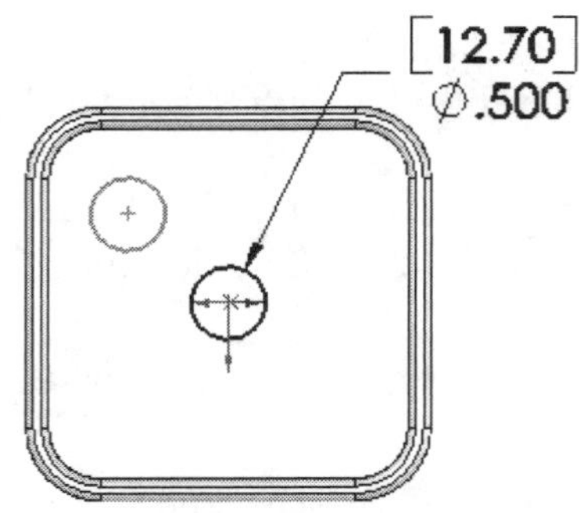

137) Release the **Ctrl** key. The second circle is selected and is displayed in green.

Add an Equal Relation.

138) Hold the **Ctrl** key down.

139) Click the **circumference of the first circle**. Note: Both circles are selected and are displayed in green.

140) Release the **Ctrl** key.

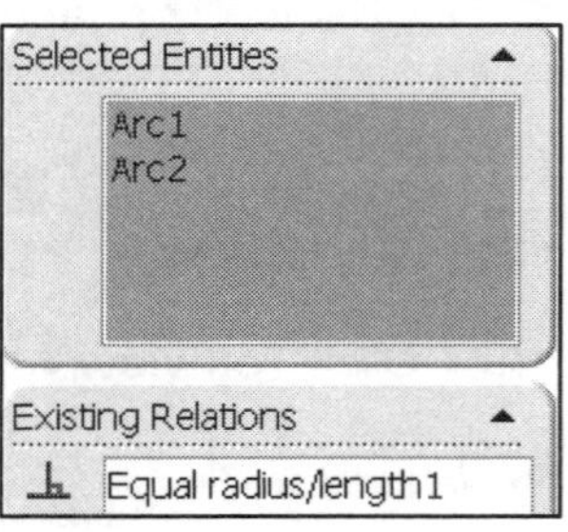

141) Click **Equal** = from the Add Relations box.

142) Click **OK** from the Properties PropertyManager.

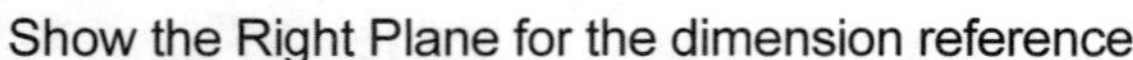

Show the Right Plane for the dimension reference.

143) Right-click the **Right Plane** from the FeatureManager.

144) Click **Show**.

Add an aligned dimension.

145) Click **Smart Dimension**  Smart Dimens....

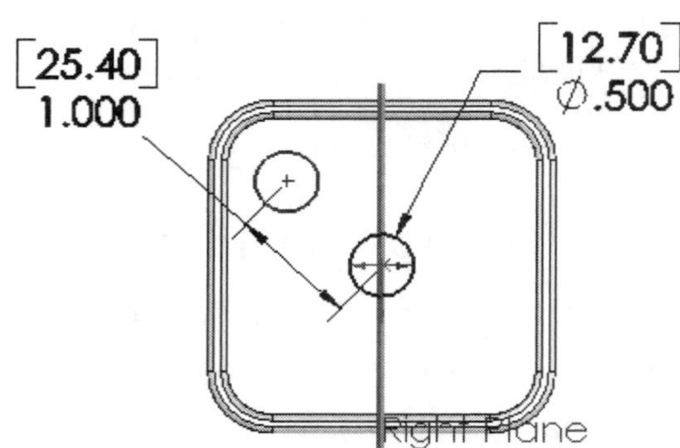

146) Click the **two center points** of the two circles.

147) Click a **position** off the profile in the upper left corner.

148) Enter **1.000**, [**25.4**] for the aligned dimension.

149) Click the **Green Check mark**.

Insert a centerline.

150) Click **Centerline** Centerl... from the Sketch toolbar.

151) Sketch a centerline between the **two circle center points**.

152) Right-click **End Chain** to end the line.

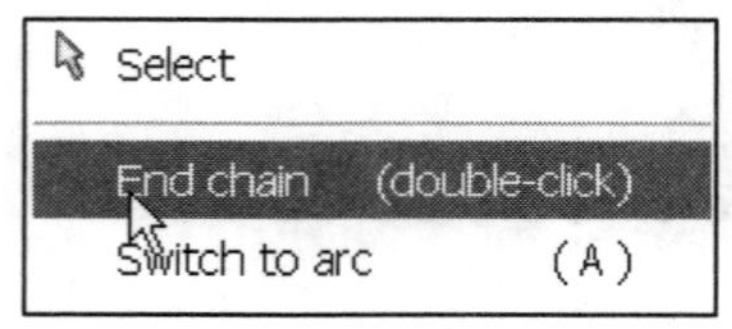

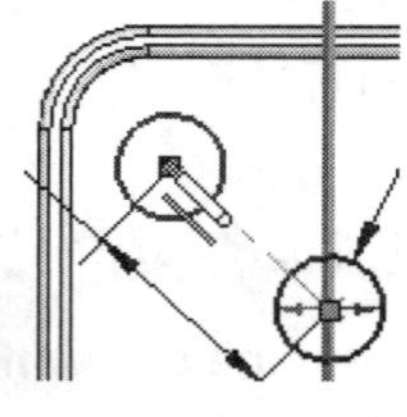

 Shortcut: Double-click to end the centerline.

Shortcut: Press the Enter key to accept the value in the Modify dialog box. The Enter key replaces the Green Check mark.

Add an angular dimension.

153) Click **Smart Dimension**  Smart Dimens....

154) Click the **centerline** between the two circles.

155) Click the **Right Plane** (vertical line). Click a **position** between the centerline and the Right plane, off the profile.

156) Enter **45**.

157) Click **OK** from the Dimension PropertyManager.

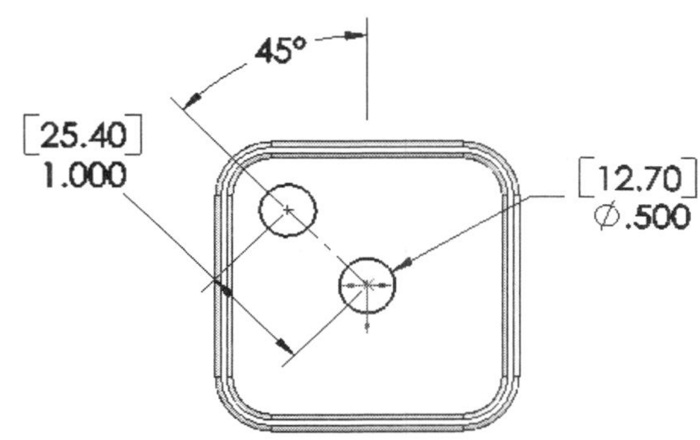

Fit the Model to the Graphics window.

158) Press the **f** key.

Hide the Right Plane.

159) Right-click **Right Plane** in the FeatureManager.

160) Click **Hide**. Click **Save** .

Create an angular dimension between three points or two lines. Sketch a centerline/construction line when an additional point or line is required.

Insert an Extruded Boss feature.

161) Click **Isometric view** .

162) Click **Extruded Boss/Base**  Extruded Boss/B... from the Features toolbar. Blind is the default Type option.

163) Enter **.600**, [**15.24**] for Depth.

164) Click the **Draft ON/OFF** button. Enter **5** in the Draft Angle box. Click **OK** from the Extrude PropertyManager.

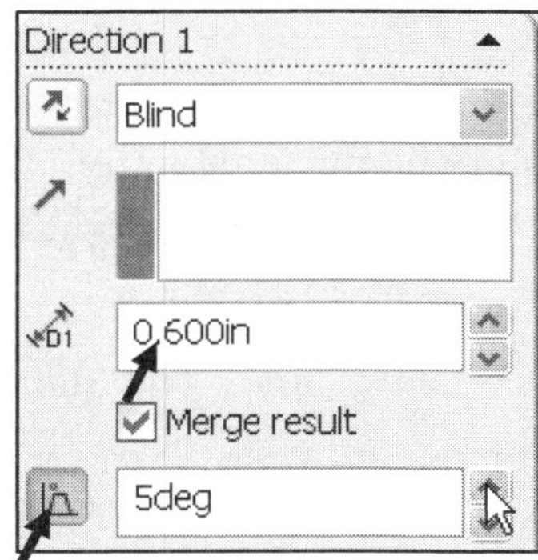

Rename the Feature and Sketch.

165) Rename **Extrude2** to **Terminals**.

166) Expand **Terminals**.

167) Rename **Sketch3** to **Sketch-TERMINALS**.

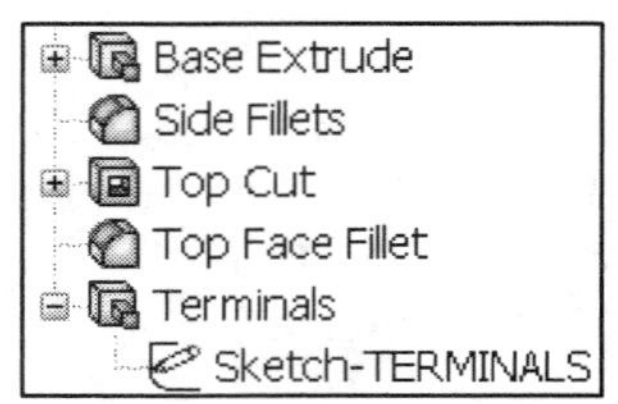

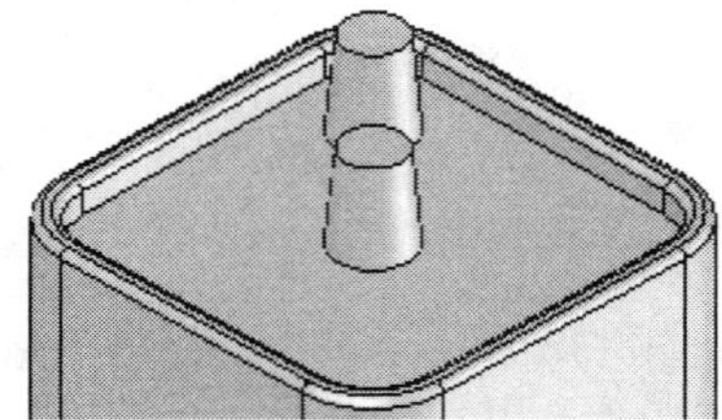

168) Click **Save**.

Each time you create a feature of the same feature type, the feature name is incremented by one. Example: Extrude1 is the first Extrude feature. Extrude2 is the second Extrude feature. If you delete a feature, rename a feature or exit a SolidWorks session, the feature numbers will vary from those illustrated in the text.

Rename your features with descriptive names. Standardize on feature names that are utilized in mating parts. Example: Mounting Holes.

Measure the overall BATTERY height.

169) Click **Right view** from the Standard Views toolbar.

170) Click **Tools**, **Measure** Measure... from Main menu.

171) Click the **top edge** of the battery terminal.

172) Click the **bottom edge** of the battery. The overall height, Delta Y is 4.500, [114.3].

173) Click **Close** from the Measure box.

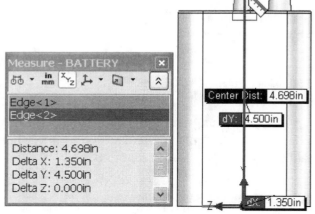

To measure a line or diameter quickly, click an entity. Read the measured value in the Status bar Length: 4.050in Editing Part in the right corner of the Graphics window.

Save time. The Standard toolbar contains quick access to the icons: Tools, Selection Filters and Help. The Tools icon displays the Measure, Equations, Analysis and other commands.

The Selection Filter option toggles the Selection Filter toolbar. When Selection Filters are activated, the mouse pointer displays the Filter icon . The Clear All Filters tool removes the current Selection Filters. The Help icon displays the SolidWorks Online Users Guide.

Display the Trimetric view.

174) Click **Trimetric view** from the view toolbar.

Save the BATTERY.

175) Click **Save** .

Additional information on Extrude Boss/Base Extrude Cut and Fillets is located in SolidWorks Help Topics. Keywords: Extrude (Boss/Base, Cut), Fillet (constant radius fillet), Geometric Relations (sketch, equal, midpoint), Sketch (rectangle, circle), Offset Entities and Dimensions (angular).

Refer to Help, Online Tutorial Fillets exercise for additional information.

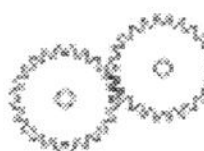

Review of the BATTERY Part.

The BATTERY utilized an Extruded Base feature sketched on the Top Plane. The rectangle was sketched with a diagonal centerline to build symmetry into the part. A Midpoint geometric relation centered the sketch on the Origin. The Equal relation created a square sketch.

The Fillet feature rounded sharp edges. All four edges were selected to combine common geometry into the same Fillet feature. The Fillet feature also rounded the top face. The Sketch Offset Entity created the profile for the Extruded Cut feature.

The Terminals were created with an Extruded Boss feature. You sketched a circular profile and utilized the Ctrl key to copy the sketched geometry.

A centerline was required to locate the two holes with an angular dimension. The Draft Angle option tapered the Extruded Boss feature. All feature names were renamed.

Injection Molded Process

Lee Plastics of Sterling, MA is a precision injection molding company. Through the World Wide Web (www.leeplastics.com), review the injection molded manufacturing process.

The injection molding process is as follows:

An operator pours the plastic resin in the form of small dry pellets, into a hopper. The hopper feeds a large augur screw. The screw pushes the pellets forward into a heated chamber. The resin melts and accumulates into the front of the screw.

At high pressure, the screw pushes the molten plastic through a nozzle, to the gate and into a closed mold, (Plates A & B). Plates A and B are the machined plates that you will design in this project.

The plastic fills the part cavities through a narrow channel called a gate.

The plastic cools and forms a solid in the mold cavity. The mold opens, (along the parting line) and an ejection pin pushes the plastic part out of the mold into a slide.

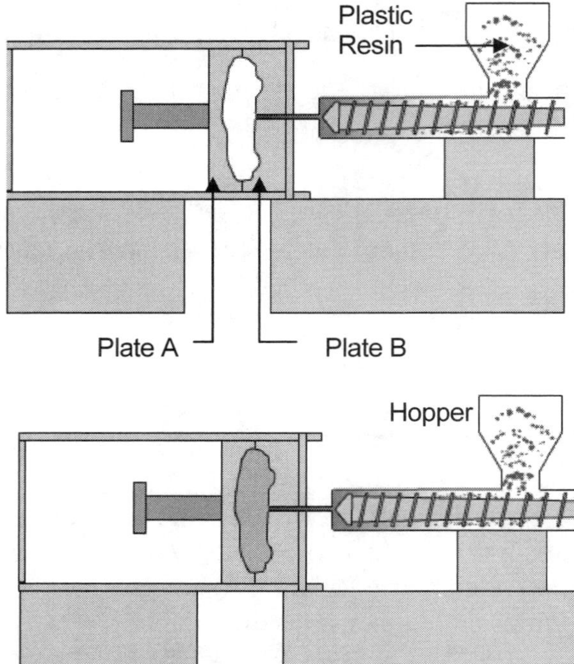

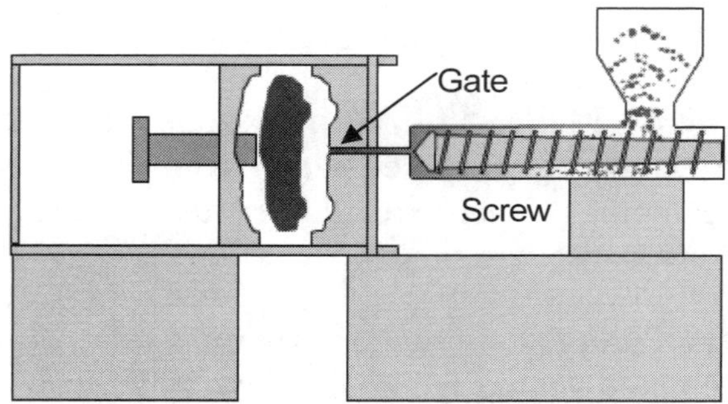

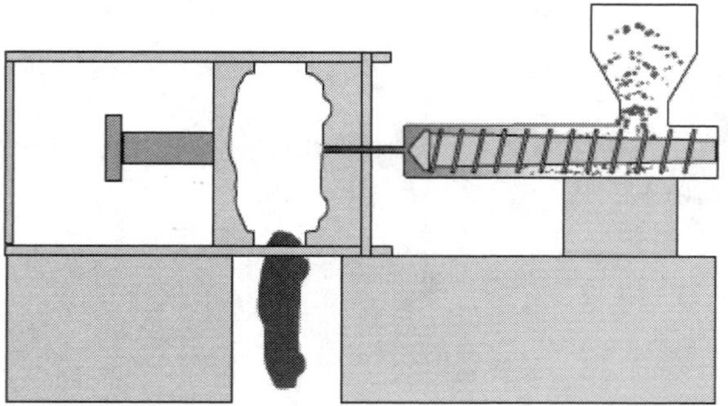

Injection Molded Process
(Courtesy of Lee Plastics, Inc.)

BATTERYPLATE Part

The BATTERYPLATE is a critical plastic part. The BATTERYPLATE:

- Aligns the LENS assembly.
- Creates an electrical connection between the BATTERY and LENS.

Design the BATTERYPLATE. Utilize features from the BATTERY to develop the BATTERYPLATE. The BATTERYPLATE is manufactured as an injection molded plastic part. Build Draft into the Extruded Base\Boss features.

Edit the BATTERY features. Create two holes from the original sketched circles. Use the Extruded Cut feature.

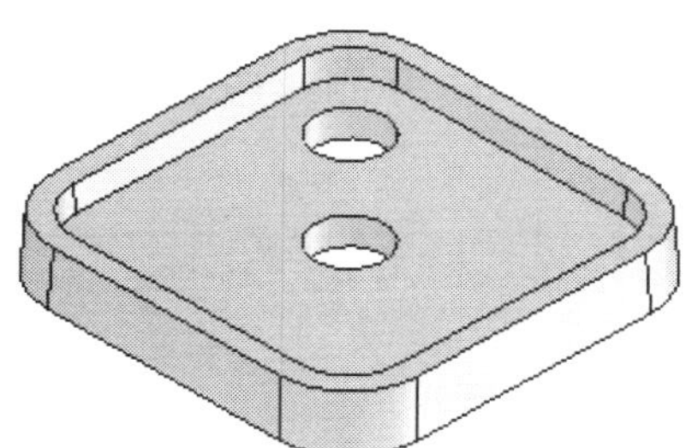

Modify the dimensions of the Base feature. Add a 3-degree draft angle.

Note: A sand pail contains a draft angle. The draft angle assists the sand to leave the pail when the pail is flipped upside down.

Insert an Extruded Boss feature. Offset the center circular sketch.

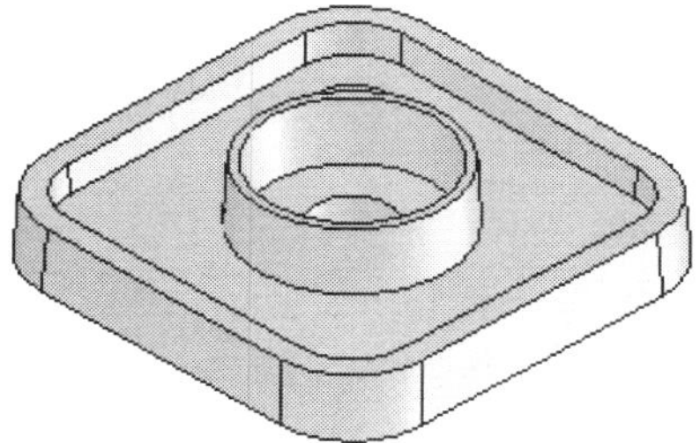

The Extruded Boss feature contains the LENS. Create an inside draft angle. The draft angle assists the LENS into the Holder.

Insert Face Fillet and a multi-radius Edge Fillet to remove sharp edges. Plastic parts require smooth edges. Group Fillet feature together into a Folder.

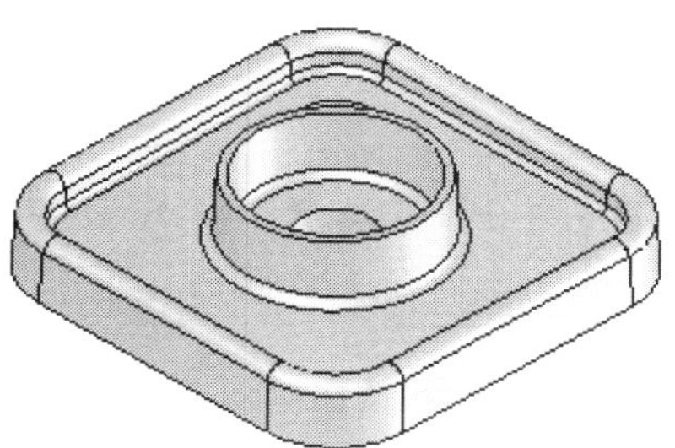

In this project you will perform a Draft Analysis on this part and create the Core and Cavity mold tooling.

Group fillets together into a folder to locate quickly. Features listed in the FeatureManager must be continuous in order to be placed as a group into a Folder.

Save As, Delete, Modify and Edit Feature

Create the BATTERYPLATE from the BATTERY. Utilize the File, Save As option to copy the BATTERY to the BATTERYPLATE.

Reuse existing geometry. Create two holes. Delete the Terminals feature and reuse the circle sketch. Select the sketch in the FeatureManager. Insert an Extruded Cut. The Through All Depth option creates two holes that cut through the entire Extruded Base.

Right-click the Extruded Cut in the FeatureManager. Select the Edit Feature option. The Edit Feature option returns to the Extruded Cut PropertyManager. Modify the End Condition from Blind to Through All.

Modify the depth dimension or the Extruded Base feature. Sketch dimensions are displayed in black. Feature dimensions are displayed in blue. Select Rebuild to update the part.

Activity: Save As, Delete, Modify and Edit Feature

Create a new part.

176) Click **File**, **Save As** from the Main menu.

177) Enter **PROJECTS** for Save In Folder.

178) Enter **BATTERYPLATE** for File name.

179) Enter **BATTERY PLATE, FOR 6-VOLT** for Description.

180) Click **Save**.

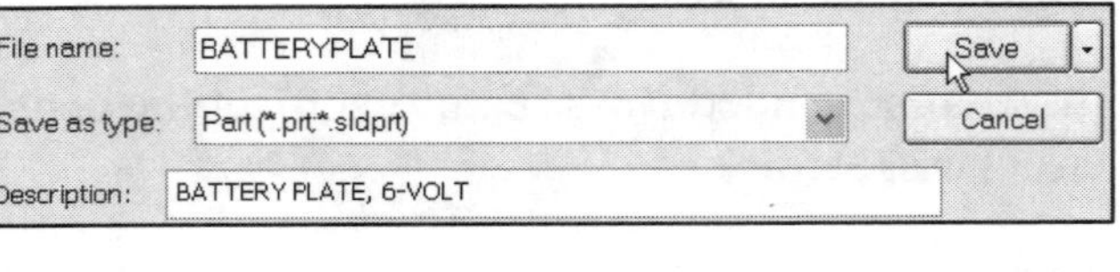

The BATTERYPLATE part icon is displayed at the top of the FeatureManager. The BATTERY part is closed.

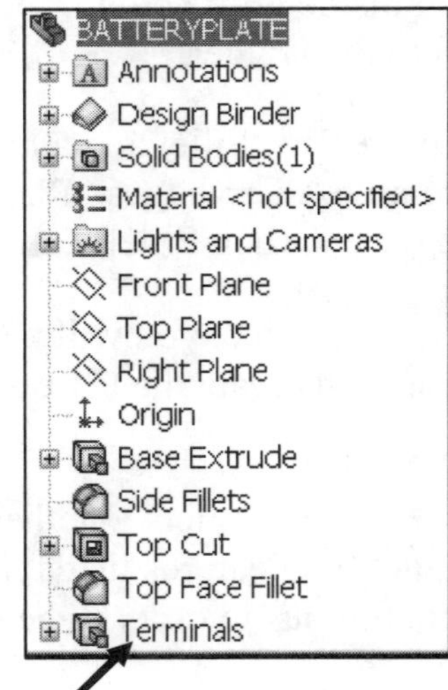

Delete the Terminals feature.

181) Right-click **Terminals** from the FeatureManager.

182) Click **Delete** ✕ Delete... .

183) Click **Yes** from the Confirm Delete dialog box. Do not delete the two-circle sketch, Sketch-TERMINALS.

Create an Extruded Cut feature from the Sketch–TERMINALS.

184) Click **Sketch-TERMINALS** from the FeatureManager.

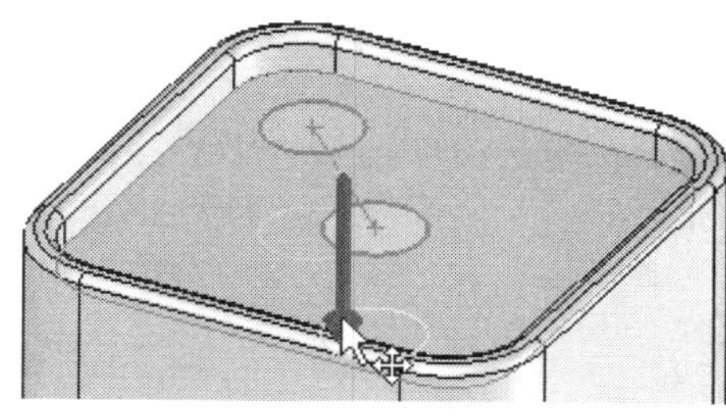

185) Click **Extruded Cut**  Extruded Cut from the Features toolbar.

186) Select **Through All** for End Condition.

187) Click **OK** from the Cut-Extrude PropertyManager.

188) Rename **Cut-Extrude2** to **Holes**.

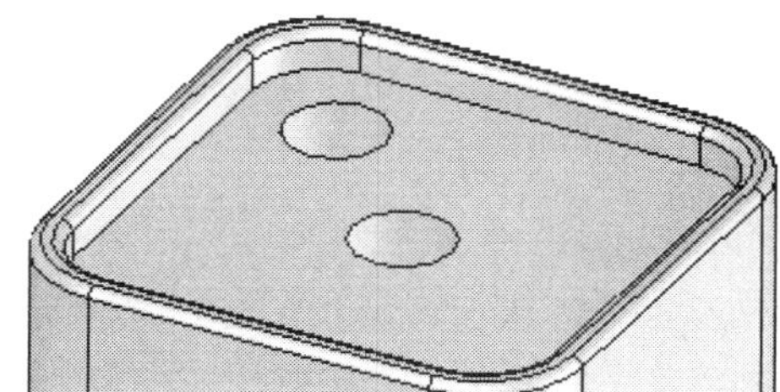

Edit the Base Extrude feature.

189) Right-click **Base Extrude** in the FeatureManager.

190) Click **Edit Feature** from the Pop-up menu.

Change the overall Depth.

191) Enter **.400**, [**10.16**] in Depth box.

192) Click the **Draft ON/OFF** button.

193) Enter **3.00** in the Angle text box.

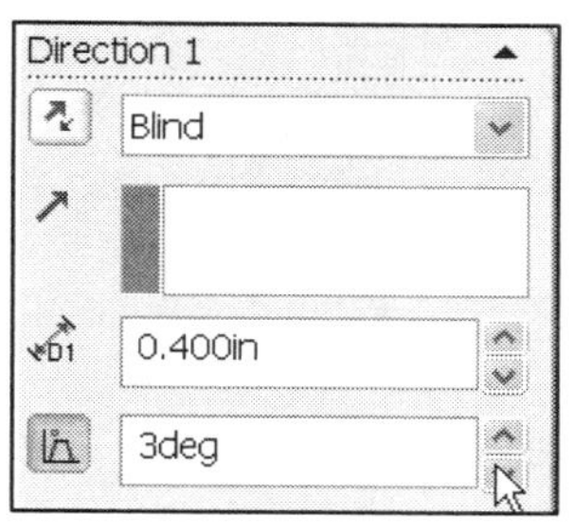

194) Click **OK** from the Base Extrude PropertyManager.

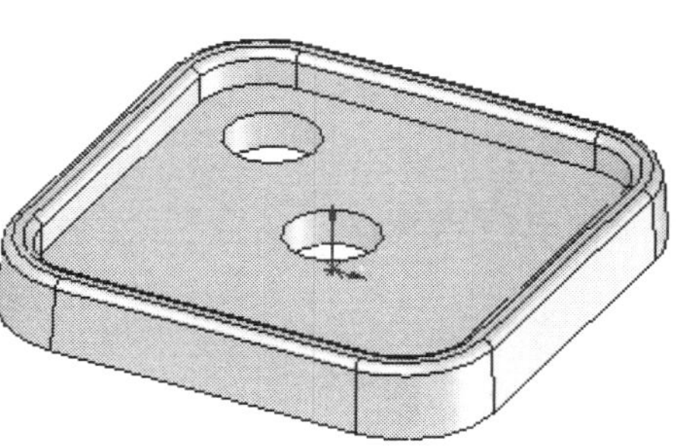

Fit the model to the Graphics window.

195) Press the **f** key.

Save the BATTERYPLATE.

196) Click **Save** .

To delete both the feature and the sketch at the same time, select the Also Delete Absorbed Feature check box from the Confirm Delete dialog box.

BATTERYPLATE Part-Extruded Boss Feature

The Holder is created with a circular Extruded Boss feature. Utilize Offset Sketch Entity to create the second circle. Utilize a Draft Angle of 3° in the Extrude Boss options.

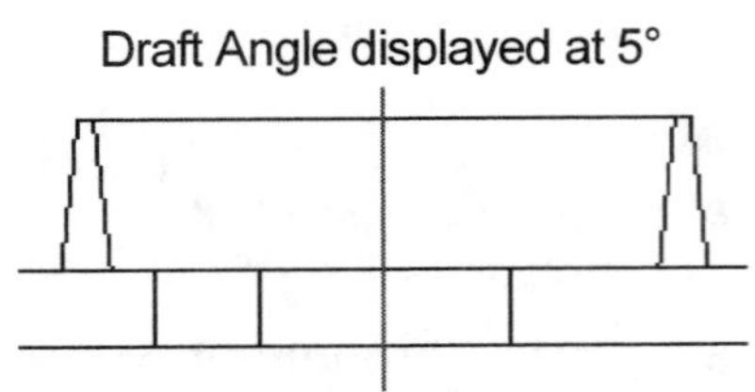

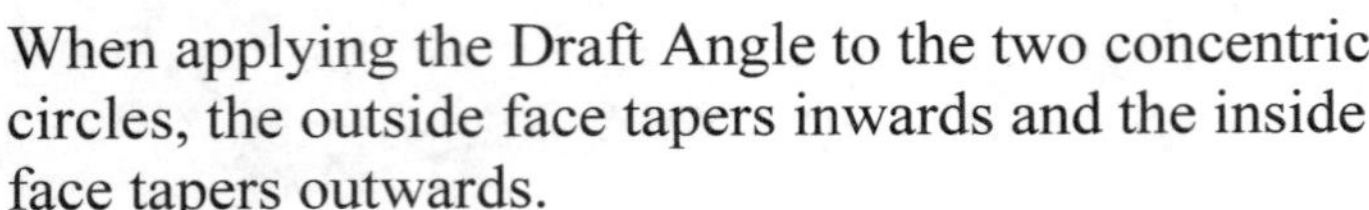

When applying the Draft Angle to the two concentric circles, the outside face tapers inwards and the inside face tapers outwards.

Plastic parts require a draft angle. A rule of thumb; 1° to 5° is the draft angle. The draft angle is created in the direction of pull from the mold. This is defined by geometry, material selection, mold production and cosmetics. Always verify the draft with the mold designer and manufacturer.

Activity BATTERYPLATE Part-Extruded Boss Feature

Select the Sketch plane.

197) Click the **top face** of Top Cut.

Top circular edge

Top face

Create the Sketch.

198) Click **Sketch** Sketch from the Sketch toolbar.

199) Click the **top circular edge** of the center Hole. Note: Use the keyboard arrow keys to rotate the sketch.

200) Click **Offset Entities** Offset from the Sketch toolbar.

201) Enter **.300**, **[7.62]** for Offset Distance.

202) Click **OK** from the Offset Entities PropertyManager.

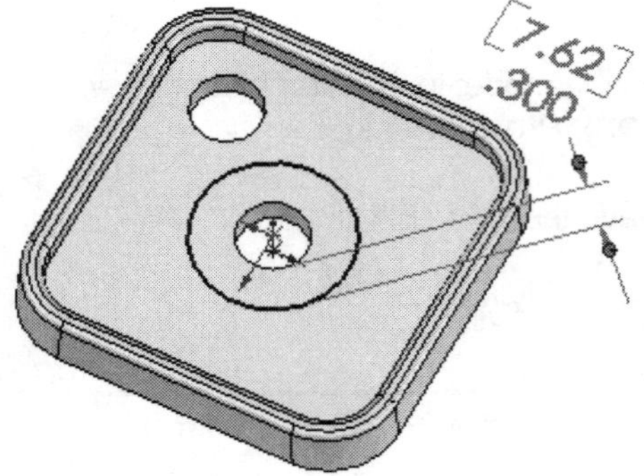

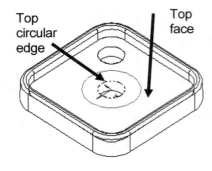

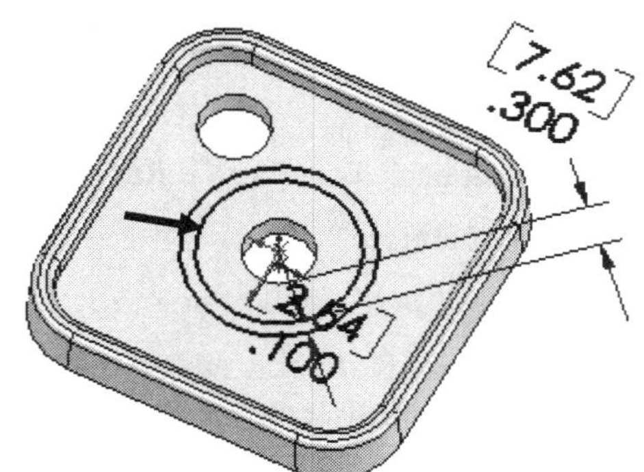

Create the second offset circle.

203) Select the **offset circle**.

204) Click **Offset Entities** Offset.

205) Enter **.100**, [**2.54**] for Distance.

206) Click **OK** from the Offset Entities PropertyManager.

Two offset concentric circles define the sketch.

Insert the Extruded Boss feature.

207) Click **Extruded Boss/Base** 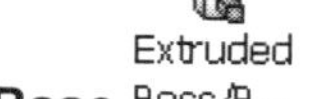.

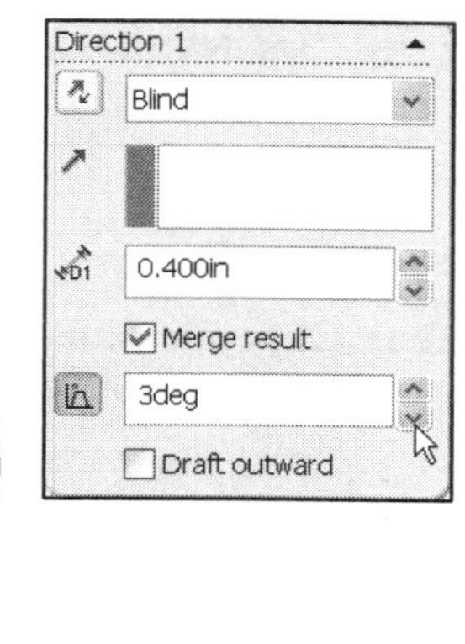

208) Enter **.400**, [**10.16**] for Depth.

209) Click the **Draft ON/OFF** button.

210) Enter **3** in the Angle text box.

211) Click **OK** from the Extrude PropertyManager.

212) Rename **Extrude3** to **Holder**.

213) Click **Save**.

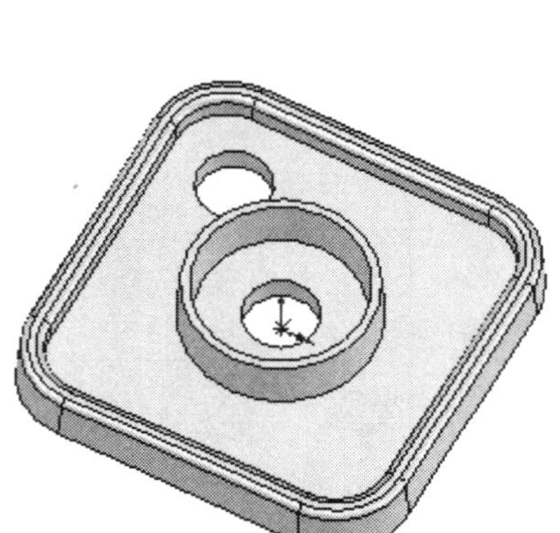

BATTERYPLATE Part-Fillet Features: Full Round, Multiple Radius Options

Fillet features are used to smooth rough edges. Plastic parts require fillets on sharp edges. Create two Fillets. Utilize different techniques. The current Top Face Fillet produced a flat face. Delete the Top Face Fillet. The first Fillet is a Full Round Fillet. Insert a Full Round Fillet on the top face for a smooth rounded transition.

The second Fillet is a Multiple Radius Fillet. Select a different radius value for each edge in the set. Select the inside and outside edge of the Holder. Select all inside tangent edges of the Top Cut. A Multiple Radius Fillet is utilized next as an exercise. There are machining instances were radius must be reduced or enlarged to accommodate tooling. Note: There are other ways to create Fillets.

Group Fillets into a Fillet folder. Placing Fillets into a folder reduces the time spent for your mold designer or toolmaker to look for each Fillet in the FeatureManager.

Activity: BATTERYPLATE Part-Fillet Features: Full Round, Multiple Radius Options

Delete the Top Edge Fillet.

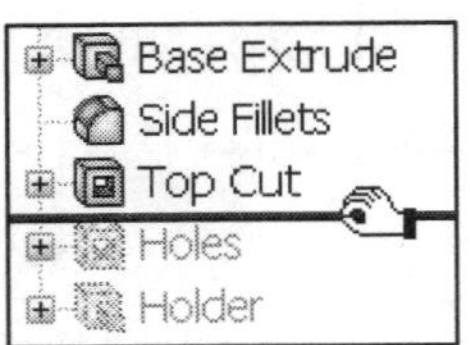

214) Right-click **Top Face Fillet** from the FeatureManager.

215) Click **Delete**.

216) Click **Yes** to confirm delete.

217) Drag the **Rollback** bar below Top Cut in the FeatureManager.

Insert the Full Round Fillet feature.

218) Click **Hidden Lines Visible**.

219) Click **Fillet** Fillet .

220) Click **Full round fillet**.

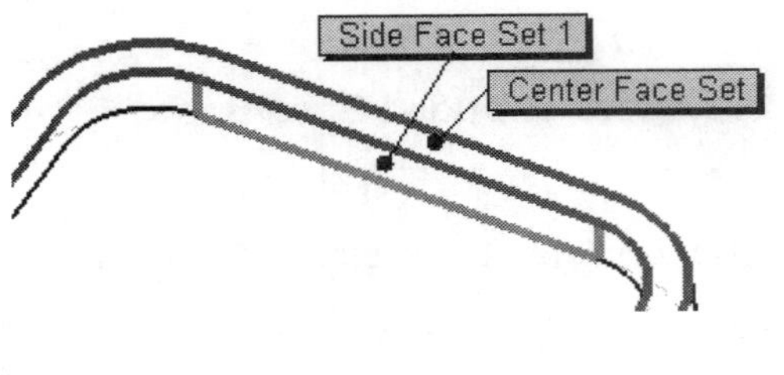

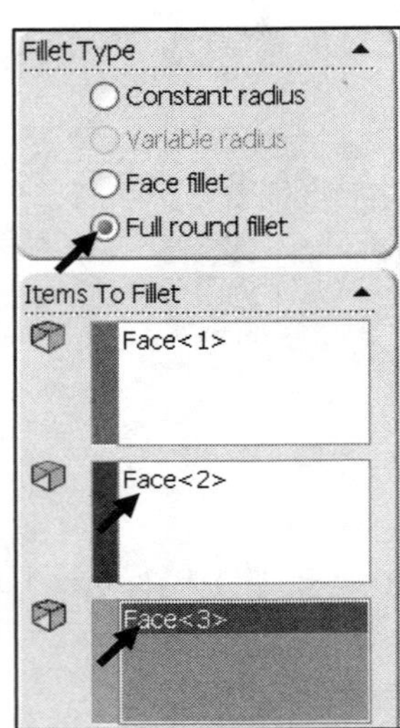

221) Click the **inside Top Cut face** for Side Face Set 1.

222) Click **inside** the Center Face Set box.

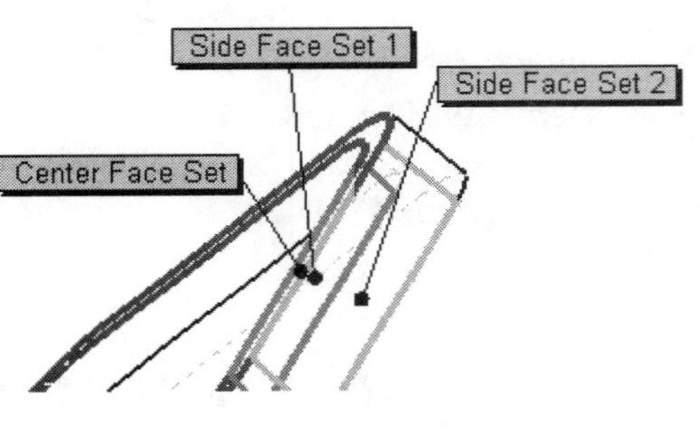

223) Click the **top face** for Center Face Set.

Rotate the part.

224) Press the **Left Arrow** key until you can select the outside Base Extrude face.

225) Click **inside** the Side Face Set 2 box.

226) Click the **outside Base Extrude face** for Side Face Set 2.

227) Click **OK** from the Fillet PropertyManager.

228) Rename **Fillet3** to **TopFillet**.

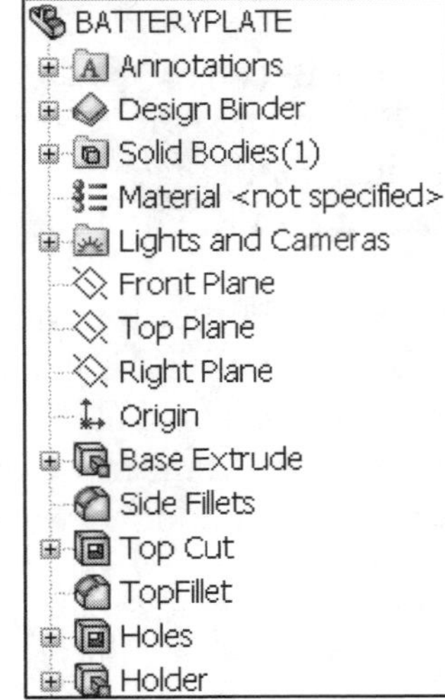

Save the BATTERYPLATE.

229) Click **Isometric view** .

230) Click **Hidden Lines Removed** .

231) Click **Save** .

232) Click **Yes** to rebuild the part.

Note: The Rollback bar is placed at the bottom of the FeatureManager during a Rebuild.

Insert a Multiple Radius Fillet feature.

233) Click the **bottom outside circular edge** of the Holder.

234) Click **Fillet** Fillet.

235) Enter **.050**, [**1.27**] for Radius.

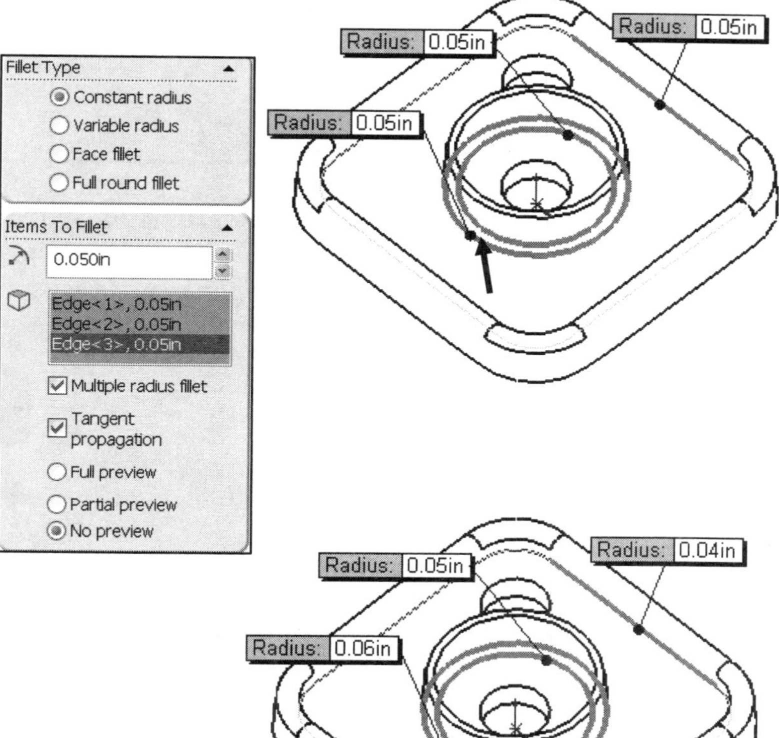

236) Click the **bottom inside circular edge** of the Holder.

237) Click the **inside edge** of the Top Cut.

238) Check **Tangent Propagation**.

239) Check **Multiple radius fillet**.

Modify the Fillet values.

240) Click the **Radius** box Radius: 0.05in for the Holder outside edge.

241) Enter **0.060**, [**1.52**].

242) Click the **Radius** box for the Top Cut inside edge.

243) Enter **0.040**, [**1.02**].

244) Click **OK** from the Fillet PropertyManager.

245) Rename **Fillet4** to **HolderFillet**.

246) Click **Shaded With Edges** .

Group the Fillets into a Folder.

247) Click **TopFillet** from the FeatureManager.

248) Drag the **TopFillet** feature directly above the HolderFillet in the FeatureManager.

249) Click the **HolderFillet** in the FeatureManager.

250) Hold the **Ctrl** key down.

251) Click the **TopFillet**.

252) Right-click **Add to New Folder**.

253) Release the **Ctrl** key.

254) Rename **Folder1** to **FilletFolder**.

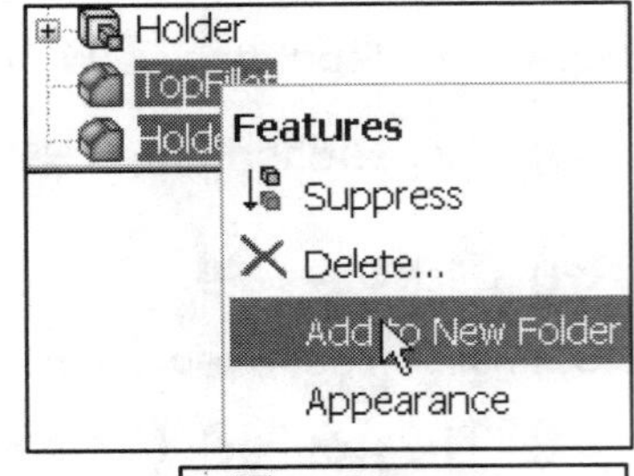

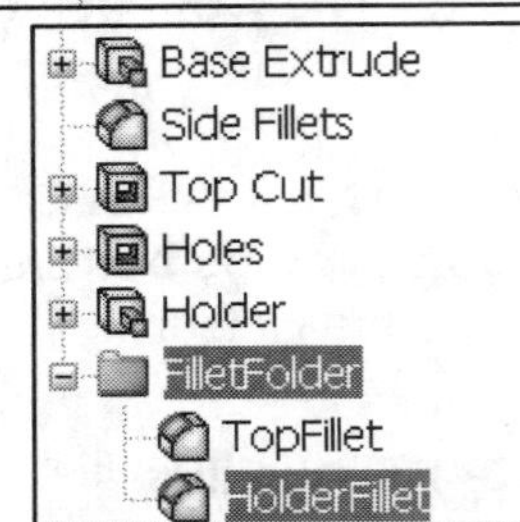

Save the BATTERYPLATE.

255) Click **Save**.

Multibody Parts and the Extruded Boss Feature

A Multibody part has separate solid bodies within the same part document.

A WRENCH consists of two cylindrical bodies. Each extrusion is a separate body. The oval profile is sketched on the right plane and extruded with the Up to Body End Condition option.

The BATTERY and BATTERYPLATE parts consisted of a solid body with one sketched profile. Each part is a single body part.

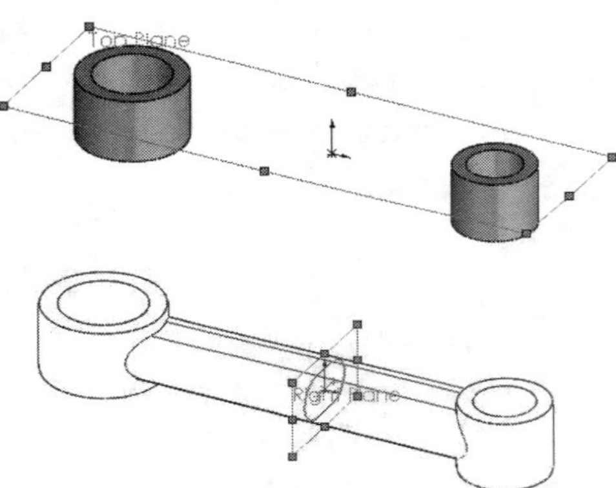

Multi-body part Wrench

Additional information on Save, Extrude Boss/Base, Extruded Cut, Fillets, Copy Sketched Geometry and Multi-body are located in SolidWorks Help Topics. Keywords: Save (save as copy), Extruded (Boss/Base, Cut), Fillet (face blends, variable radius), Chamfer, Geometric Relations (sketch), Copy (sketch entities), Multibody (extrude, modeling techniques).

Refer to Help, Online Tutorial Multibody Parts exercise for additional information.

Review of the BATTERYPLATE Part.

The File, Save As option was utilized to copy the BATTERY part to the BATTERYPLATE part. You modified and deleted features in the BATTERYPLATE.

The BATTERYPLATE is a plastic part. The Draft Angle option was added in the Extruded Base feature.

The Holder Extruded Boss utilized a circular sketch and the Draft Angle option. The Sketch Offset tool created the circular ring profile. Multi radius Edge Fillets and Face Fillets removed sharp edges. Similar Fillets were grouped together into a Folder. All features were renamed in the FeatureManager. The BATTERY and BATTERYPLATE utilized an Extruded Base feature.

LENS Part

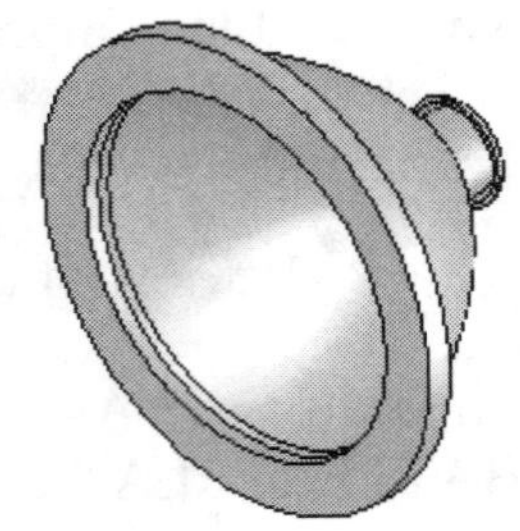

Create the LENS. The LENS is a purchased part.

The LENS utilizes a Revolved Base feature.

Sketch a centerline and a closed profile on the Right Plane. Insert a Revolved Base feature. The Revolved Base feature requires an axis of revolution and an angle of revolution.

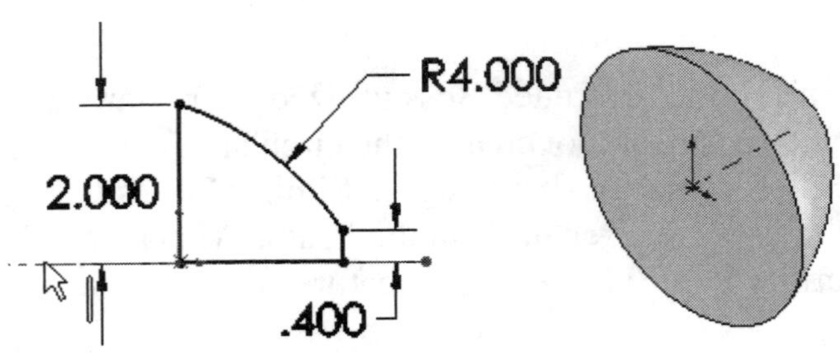

Insert the Shell feature. The Shell feature provides uniform wall thickness. Select the front face as the face to be removed.

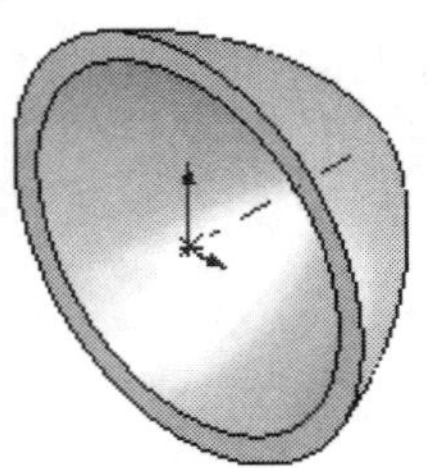

Utilize the Convert Entities sketch tool to extract the back circular edge for the sketched profile. Insert an Extruded Boss feature from the back of the LENS.

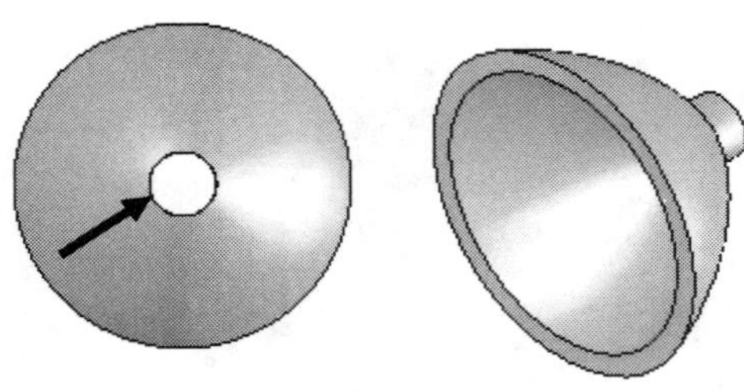

Sketch a single profile. Insert a Thin Revolved feature to connect the LENS to the BATTERYPLATE. The Thin Revolved feature requires a thickness.

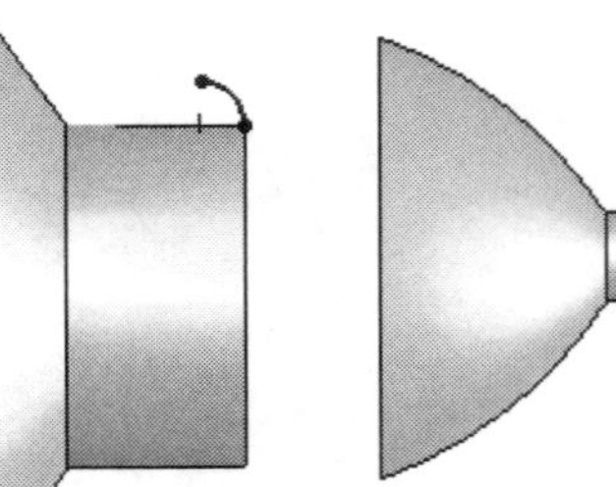

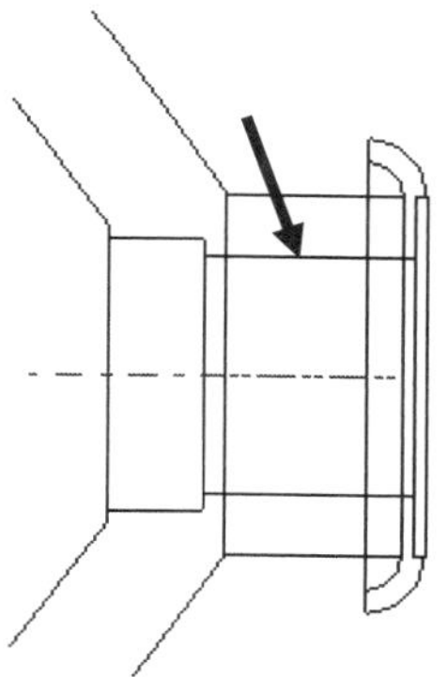

Insert a Counterbore Hole feature with the Hole Wizard.

The BULB is located inside the Counterbore Hole.

Insert the front Lens Cover with an Extruded Boss feature. The Extruded Boss is sketched on the Front Plane. Add a transparent Lens Shield with the Extruded Boss feature.

LENS Part-Revolved Base Feature

Create the LENS with a Revolved Base feature. The solid Revolved Base feature requires:

- Sketch Plane (Right).
- Sketch profile.
- Centerline.
- Angle of Revolution (360°).

The profile lines reference the Top and Front planes. Create the curve of the LENS with a 3-point arc.

Activity: LENS Part-Revolved Base Feature

Create the new part.

256) Click **File**, **New** from the Main menu.

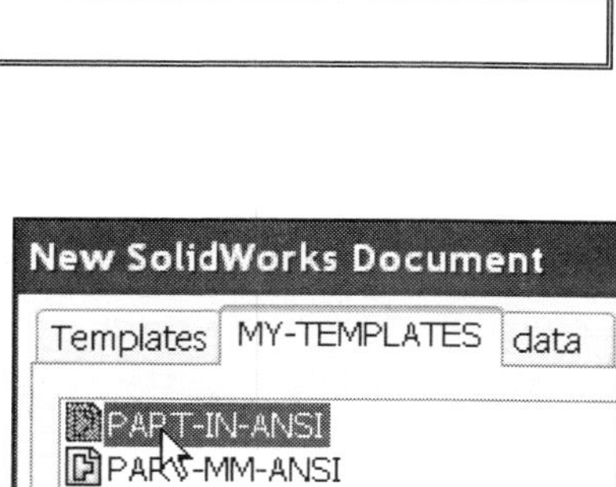

257) Click the **MY-TEMPLATES** tab.

258) Double-click **PART-IN-ANSI**, [**PART-MM-ISO**] from the Template dialog box.

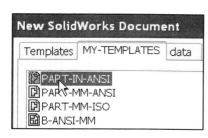

Save the part.

259) Click **Save**.

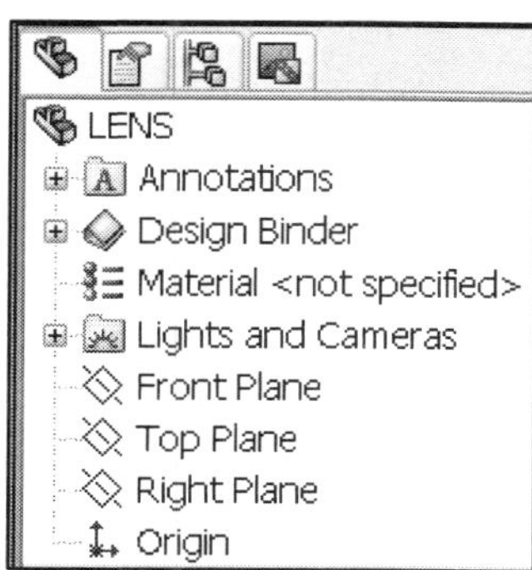

260) Select **PROJECTS** for Save in folder.

261) Enter **LENS** for the file name.

262) Enter **LENS WITH SHIELD** for Description.

263) Click **Save**.

View the planes.

264) Right click **Front Plane** in the FeatureManager.

265) Click **Show**.

Create the Sketch.

266) Click **Right Plane** from the FeatureManager.

267) Click **Sketch** Sketch from the Sketch toolbar.

268) Click **Centerline** Centerl... from the Sketch toolbar.

269) Sketch a horizontal **centerline** collinear to the Top Plane, through the Origin.

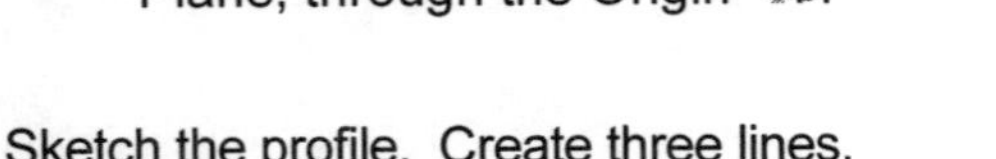

Sketch the profile. Create three lines.

270) Click **Line** Line from the Sketch toolbar.

271) Sketch a **vertical line** collinear to the Front plane coincident with the Origin.

272) Sketch a **horizontal line** coincident with the Top plane.

273) Sketch a **vertical line** approximately 1/3 the length of the first line.

274) Right-click **End Chain**.

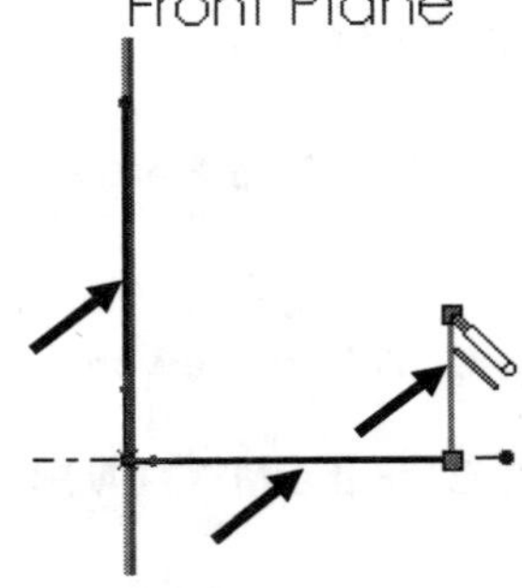

Create a 3 Point Arc.

275) Click **3Pt Arc** 3 Point Arc from the Sketch toolbar.

276) Click the **top point** on the left vertical line.

277) Drag the **mouse pointer** to the right.

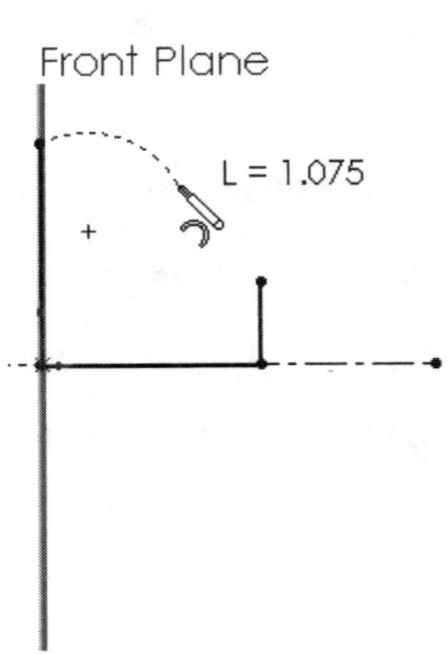

278) Click the **top point** on the right vertical line.

279) Drag the **mouse pointer** upward.

280) Click a **position** on the arc.

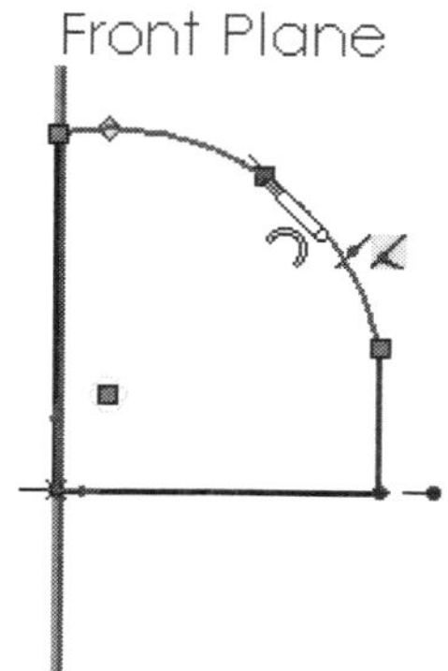

Add an Equal Relation.

281) Right-click **Select**.

282) Click the **left vertical** line.

283) Hold the **Ctrl** key down.

284) Click the **horizontal** line.

285) Release the **Ctrl** key.

286) Click **Equal** from the Add Relations box.

287) Click **OK**  from the Properties PropertyManager.

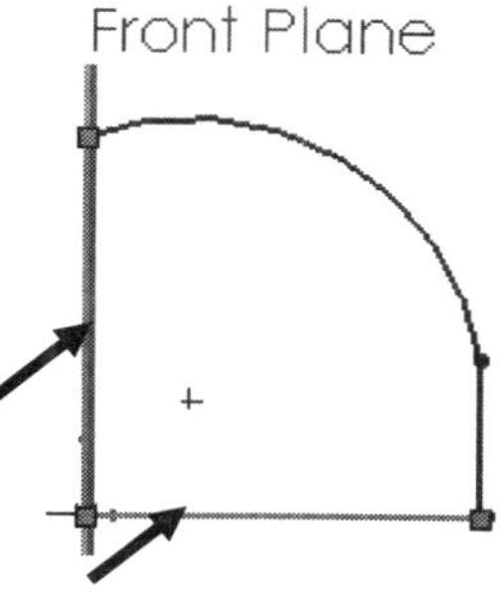

Add dimensions.

288) Click **Smart Dimension** Smart Dimens....

289) Click the **left vertical** line.

290) Click a **position** to the left of the profile.

291) Enter **2.000**, [**50.8**].

292) Click the **right vertical** line.

293) Click a **position** to the right of the profile.

294) Enter **.400**, [**10.16**].

295) Click the **arc**.

296) Click a **position** to the right of the profile.

297) Enter **4.000**, [**101.6**]. The black sketch is fully defined.

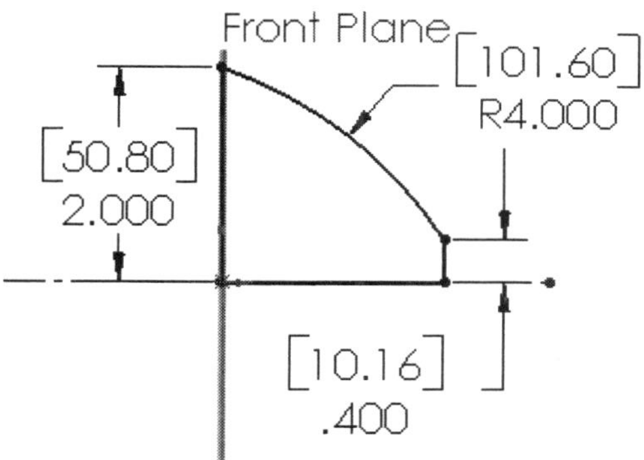

Utilize Tools, Sketch Tools, Check Sketch for Feature Usage option to determine if a sketch is valid for a specific feature and to understand what is wrong with a sketch.

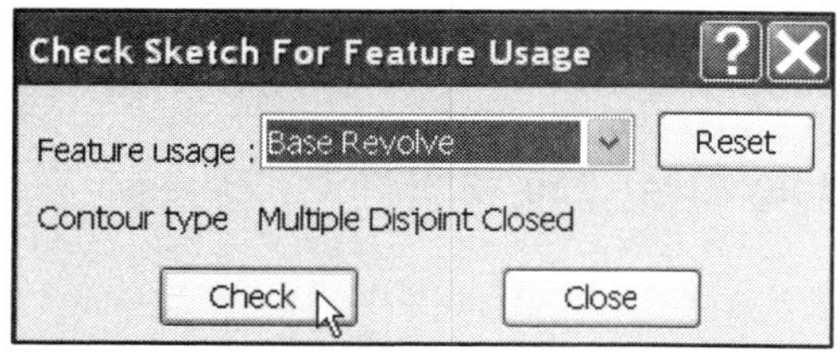

Insert the Revolved Base feature.

298) Click **Revolved Boss/Base** Revolved Boss/B... from the Feature toolbar.

299) Click the **horizontal centerline** for the axis of revolution. Note: The Direction arrow points clockwise.

300) Click **OK** from the Revolve PropertyManager.

301) Rename **Revolve1** to **BaseRevolve**.

302) Click **Save**.

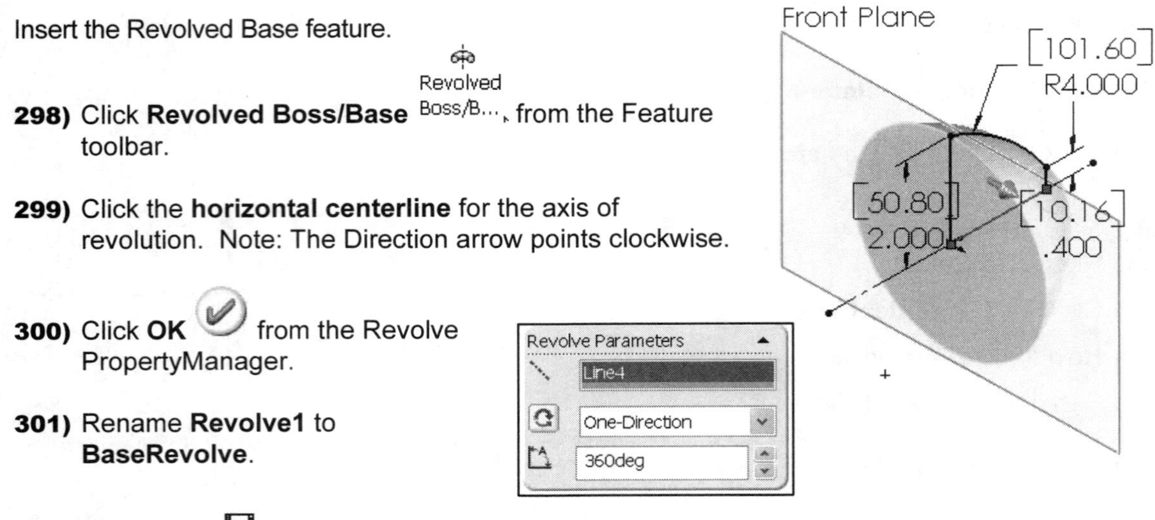

Display the axis of revolution.

303) Click **View**, check **Temporary Axis** from the Main menu.

Revolve features contain an axis of revolution. The axis of revolution utilizes a sketched centerline, edge or an existing feature/sketch or a Temporary Axis. The solid Revolved feature contains a closed profile. The Revolved thin feature contains an open or closed profile.

LENS Part-Shell Feature

The Revolved Base feature is a solid. Utilize the Shell feature to create a constant wall thickness around the front face. The Shell feature removes face material from a solid. The Shell feature requires a face and thickness. Use the Shell feature to create thin-walled parts.

Activity: LENS Part-Shell Feature

Insert the Shell feature.

304) Click the **front face** of the Revolved Base feature.

305) Click **Shell** Shell from the Feature toolbar.

306) Enter **.250**, [**6.35**] forThickness.

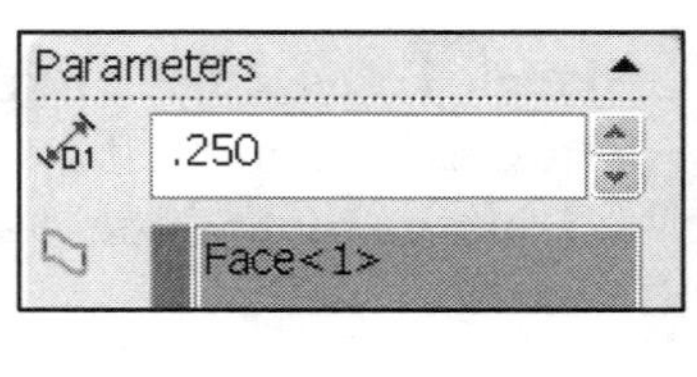

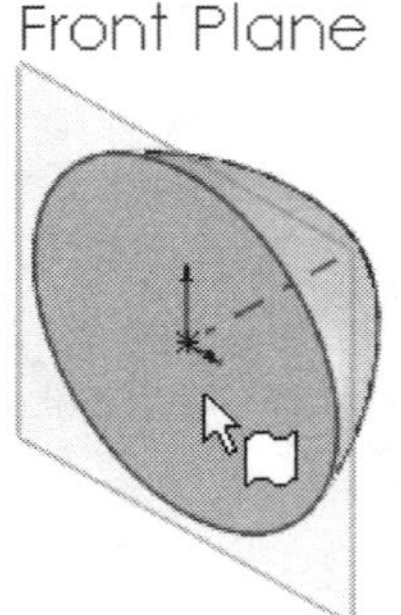

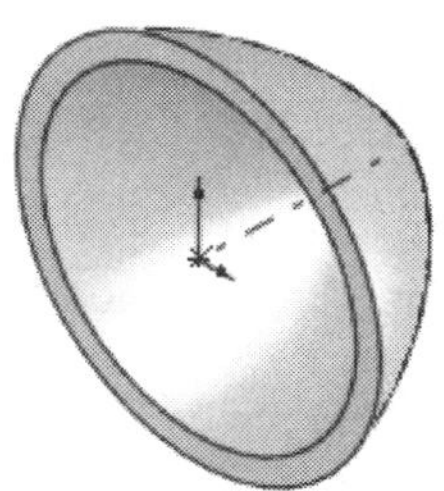

Display the Shell feature.

307) Click **OK** from the Shell1 PropertyManager.

308) Right-click **Front Plane** from the FeatureManager.

309) Click **Hide**.

310) Rename **Shell1** to **LensShell**.

311) Click **Save**.

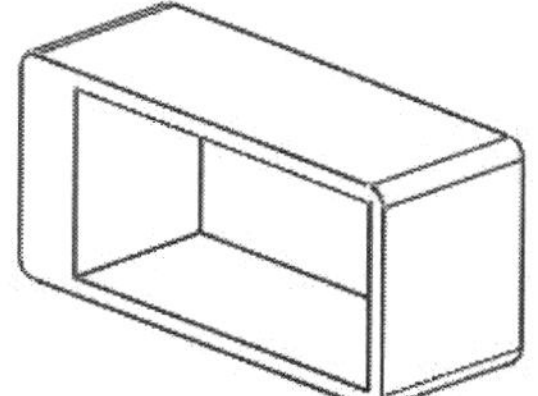

To insert rounded corners inside a shelled part, apply the Fillet feature before the Shell feature. Select the Multi-thickness option to apply different thicknesses.

Extruded Boss Feature and Convert Entities Sketch tool

Create the LensNeck. The LensNeck houses the BULB base and is connected to the BATTERYPLATE. Use the Extruded Boss feature. The back face of the Revolved Base feature is the Sketch plane.

Utilize the Convert Entities Sketch tool to extract the back circular face to the Sketch plane. The new curve develops an On Edge relation. Modify the back face, and the extracted curve updates to reflect the change. No sketch dimensions are required.

Activity: Extruded Boss Feature and Convert Entities Sketch tool

Rotate the Lens.

312) Press the **left arrow** key approximately 8 times to display the back face.

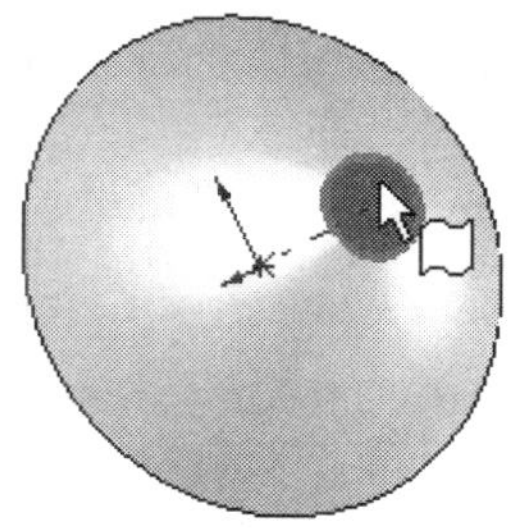

Sketch the profile.

313) Click the **back face** for the Sketch plane.

314) Click **Sketch**.

315) Click **Convert Entities** Convert from the Sketch Tools toolbar.

Insert an Extruded Boss feature.

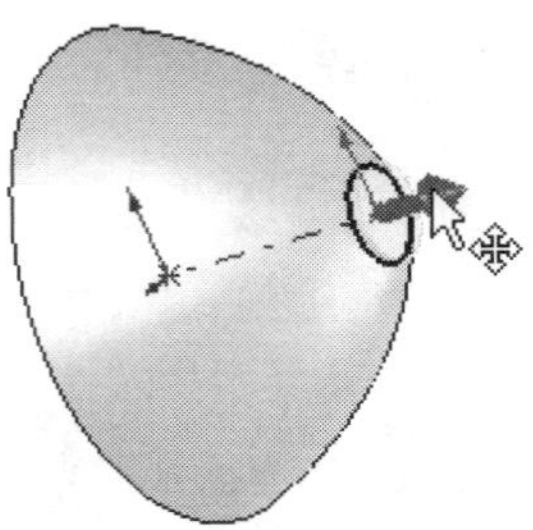

316) Click **Extruded Boss/Base** Extruded Boss/B... from the Features toolbar.

317) Enter **.400**, [**10.16**] for Depth.

318) Click **OK** from the Extrude PropertyManager.

319) Press the **right arrow** key to display the view.

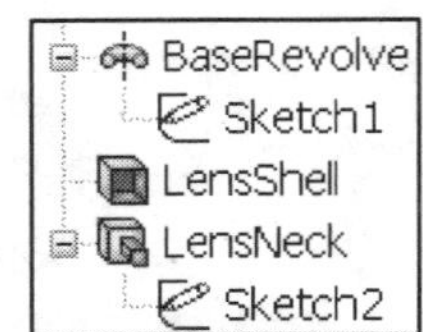

320) Rename **Extrude1** to **LensNeck**.

321) Click **Save** .

LENS Part-Hole Wizard

The LENS requires a Counterbore Hole feature. Use the Hole Wizard. The Hole Wizard assists in creating complex and simple Hole features. The Hole Wizard categories are: Counterbore, Countersink, Hole, Tapped, PipeTap and Legacy (Holes created before SolidWorks 2000).

Select the face or plane to locate the hole profile. Specify the user parameters for the custom Counterbore Hole. The parameters are: Description, Standard, Screw Type, End Condition, C'Bore diameter and depth.

Insert a Coincident Relation to position the hole center point. Dimensions for the Counterbore Hole are provided in both inches and millimeters.

Activity: LENS Part-Hole Wizard Counterbore Hole Feature

Create the Counterbore Hole.

322) Click **Front view** .

323) Click the small **inside back face** of the LensShell feature. Do not select the Origin.

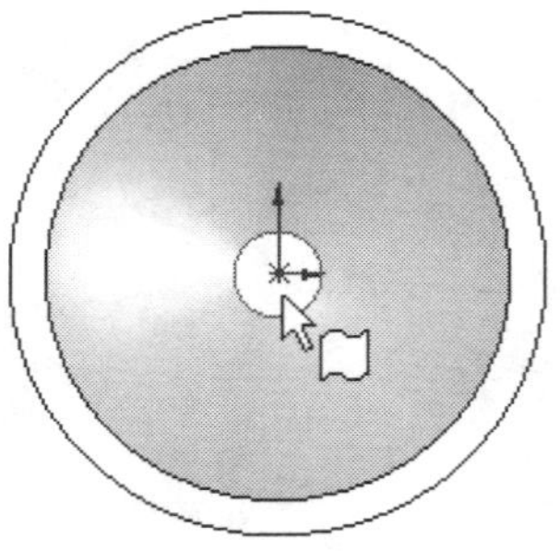

324) Click **Hole Wizard**  from the Features toolbar.

325) Click the **Counterbore** Icon.

Note: For a metric hole, skip the next few steps.

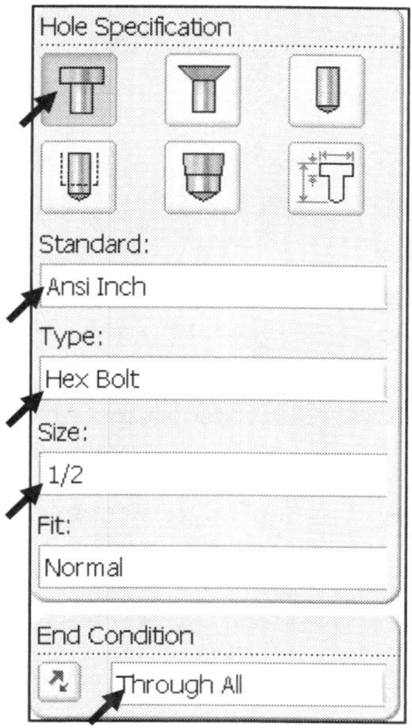

For inch Cbore Hole:

326) Select **Ansi Inch** for Standard.

327) Select **Hex Bolt** from the drop down list for Screw type.

328) Select ½ from the drop down list for Size.

329) Click **Through All** from the drop down list for End Condition & Depth.

330) Expand **Custom Sizing**.

331) Click the **Counterbore Diameter** value.

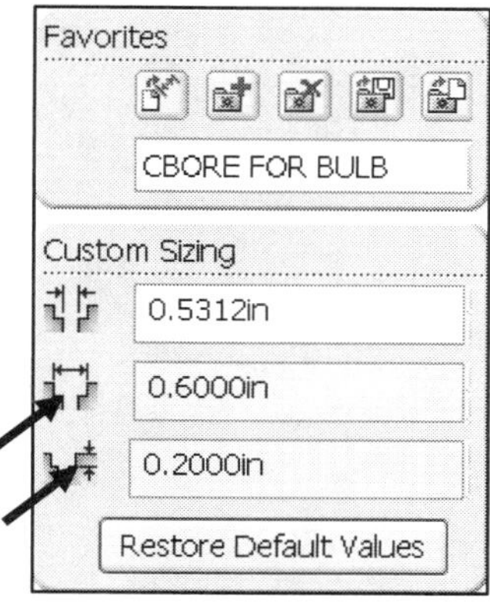

332) Enter **.600**.

333) Click the **Counterbore Depth** value.

334) Enter **.200**.

335) Click the **Position Tab**.

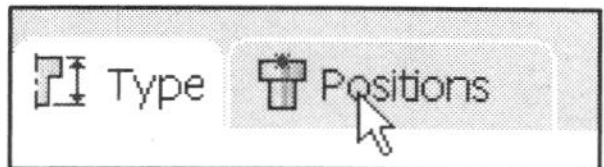

336) Right-click **Select**.

Note: For an inch hole, skip the next few steps.

For millimeter Cbore Hole:

337) Select **Ansi Metric** for Standard.

338) Enter **Hex Bolt** from the drop down list for Screw type.

339) Select **M5** from the drop down list for Size.

340) Click **Through All** from the drop down list for End Condition & Depth.

341) Click the **Hole Diameter** value.

342) Enter **13.5**.

343) Expand **Custom Sizing**.

344) Click the **Counterbore Diameter** value.

345) Enter **15.24**. Click the **Counterborebore Depth** value.

346) Enter **5**. Click the **Position Tab**.

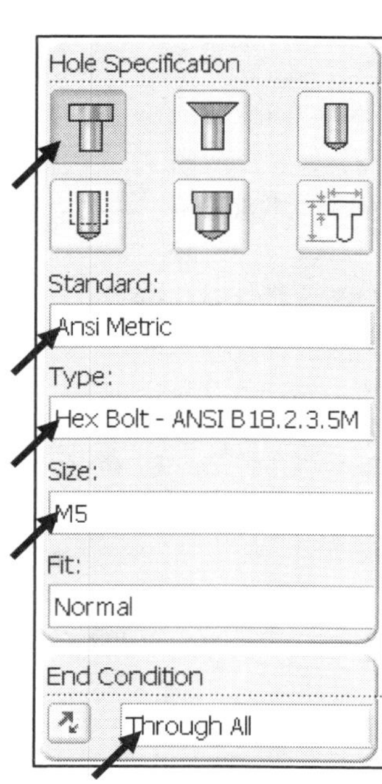

Add a Coincident Relation.

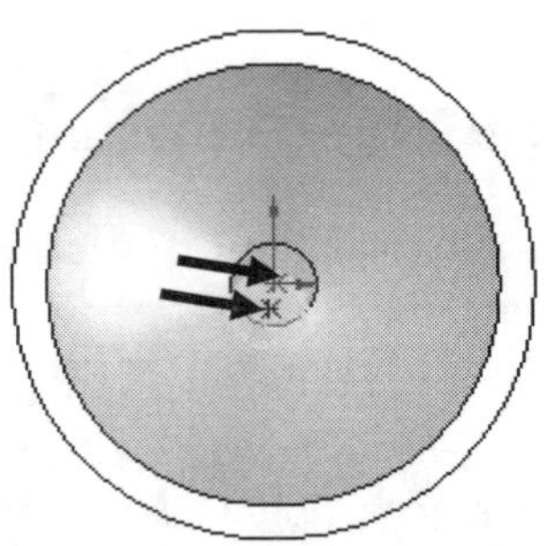

347) Click the **center point** of the Counterbore hole.

348) Hold the **Ctrl** key down.

349) Click the **Origin**.

350) Release the **Ctrl** key.

351) Click **Coincident** from the Add Relations box.

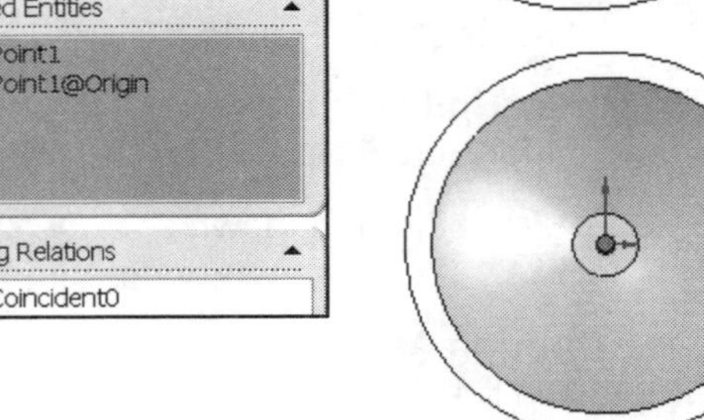

352) Click **OK** from the Properties PropertyManager.

353) Click the **Type** Tab.

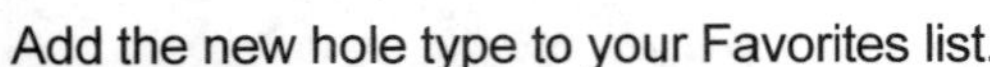

Add the new hole type to your Favorites list.

354) Click the **Add or Update Favorite** button.

355) Enter **CBORE FOR BULB**.

356) Click **OK**. Click **Yes** to update.

357) Click **OK** from the Hole Specification PropertyManager.

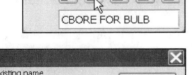

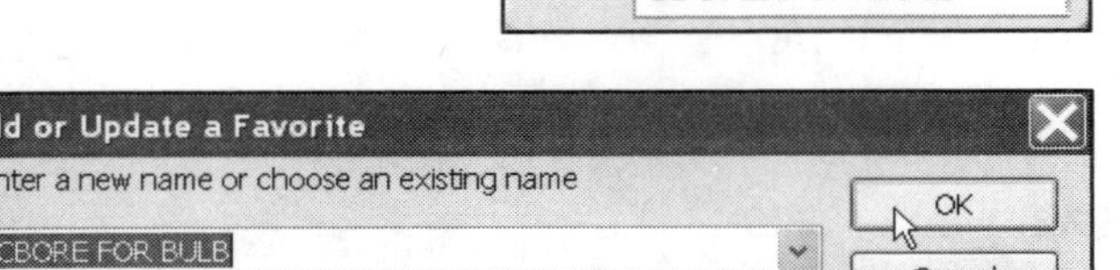

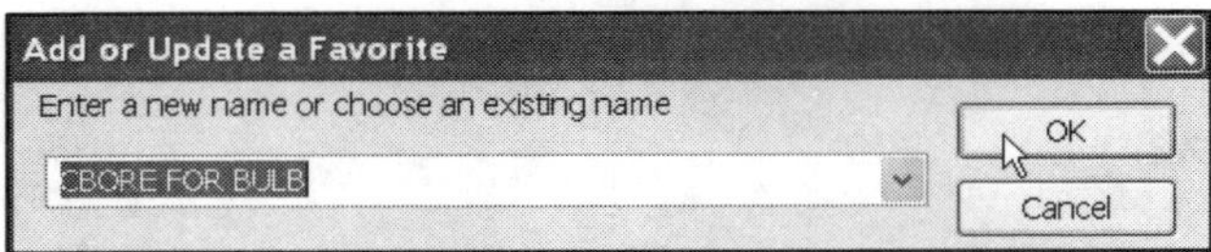

Expand the Hole feature.

358) Click the **Plus Sign** to the left of the CBORE feature. Note: Sketch3 and Sketch4 created the CBORE feature.

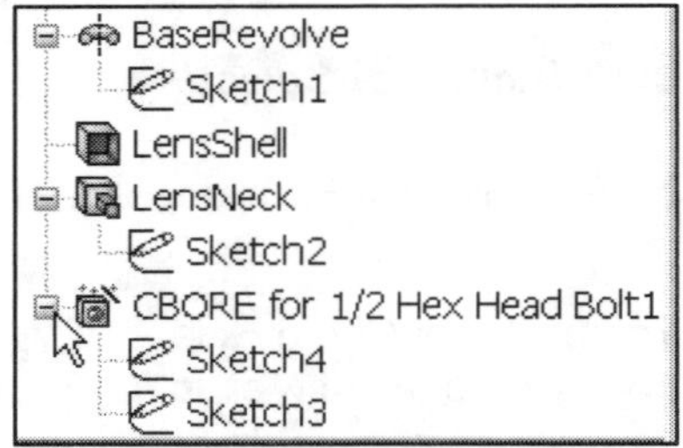

Display the Section view.

359) Click the **Right Plane** from the FeatureManager.

360) Click **Section view** from the View toolbar.

361) Click **OK** from the Section View PropertyManager.

362) Click **Isometric view**.

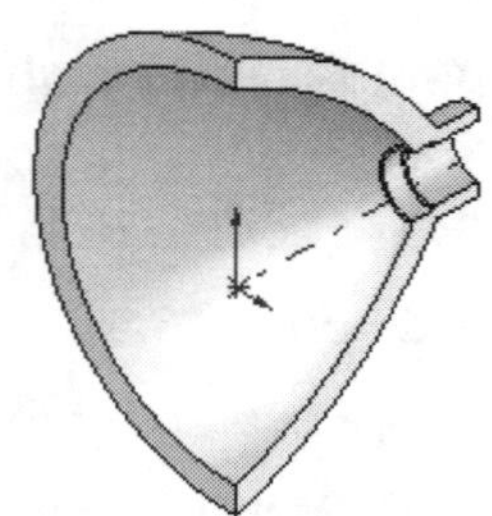

Display the Full view.

363) Click **Section view**.

364) Rename **CBORE for ½ Hex Head Bolt1** to **BulbHole**.

365) Click **Save**.

LENS Part-Revolved Boss Thin Feature

Create a Revolved Boss Thin feature. Rotate an open sketched profile around an axis. The sketch profile must be open and cannot cross the axis. A Revolved Boss Thin feature requires:

- Sketch Plane (Right Plane)
- Sketch Profile (Center point arc)
- Axis of Revolution (Temporary axis)
- Angle of Rotation (360)
- Thickness (.100in, 2.54mm)

Select the Right Plane for the Sketch Plane. Sketch a center point arc. The sketched center point arc requires three Geometric Relations: coincident, intersection and vertical.

The three Geometric Relations insure that the 90° center point of the arc is coincident with the horizontal silhouette edges of the Revolved feature. A Revolved feature produces silhouette edges in 2D views. A silhouette edge represents the extent of a cylindrical or curved face. Utilize silhouette edges for Geometric Relations.

Select the Temporary Axis for Axis of Revolution. Select the Revolved Boss feature. Enter .100in [2.54] for Thickness in the Revolve Boss PropertyManager. Enter 360° for Angle of Revolution. Note: If you cannot select a silhouette edge in Shaded mode, switch to Wireframe mode.

Activity: LENS Part-Revolved Boss Thin Feature

Create the Sketch.

366) Click the **Right Plane** from the FeatureManager.

367) Click **Sketch** Sketch. Click **Right view**.

368) Zoom in on the LensNeck.

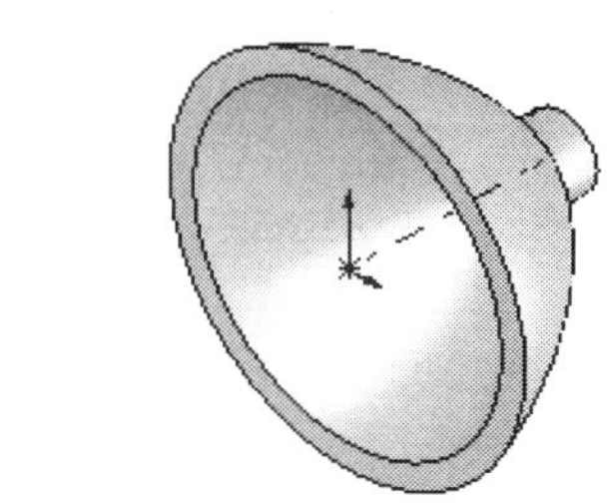

369) Click **Centerpoint Arc**  from the Sketch toolbar.

370) Click the **top horizontal silhouette edge** of the LensNeck. Do not select the midpoint of the silhouette edge.

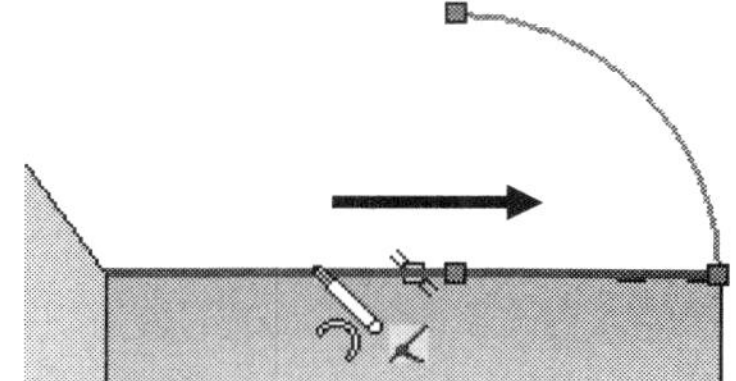

371) Click the **top right corner** of the LensNeck. Drag the **mouse pointer** counterclockwise to the left.

372) Click a **position** above the center point.

Add a dimension.

373) Click **Smart Dimension** Smart Dimens....

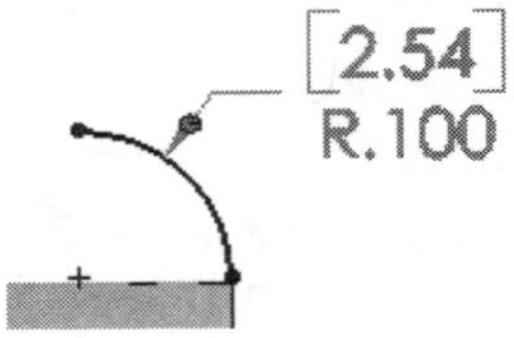

374) Click the **arc**.

375) Click a **position** to the right of the profile.

376) Enter **.100**, [**2.54**].

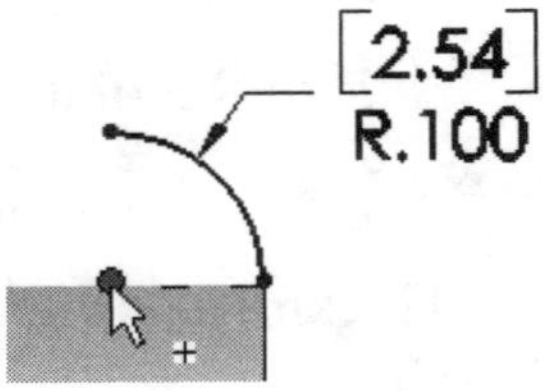

Add a Coincident Relation.

377) Right-click **Select**.

378) Click the **arc center point**.

379) Hold the **Ctrl** key down.

380) Click the **top horizontal** line (silhouette edge) of the LensNeck feature. Release the **Ctrl** key.

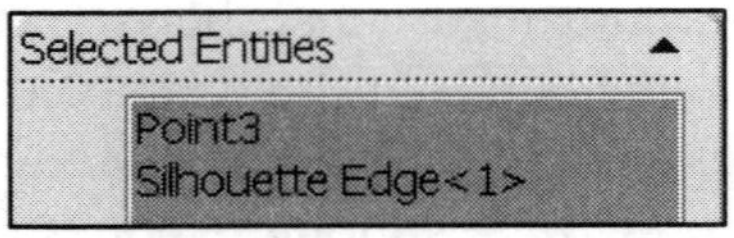

Selected Entities
Point3
Silhouette Edge<1>

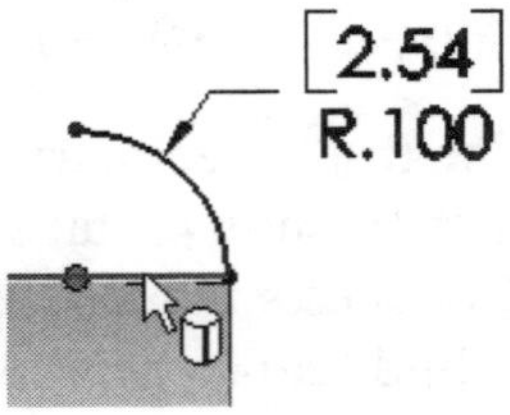

381) Click **Coincident** from the Add Relations box.

382) Click **OK** from the Properties PropertyManager.

Add an Intersection Relation.

383) Click the **arc start point**.

384) Hold the **Ctrl** key down.

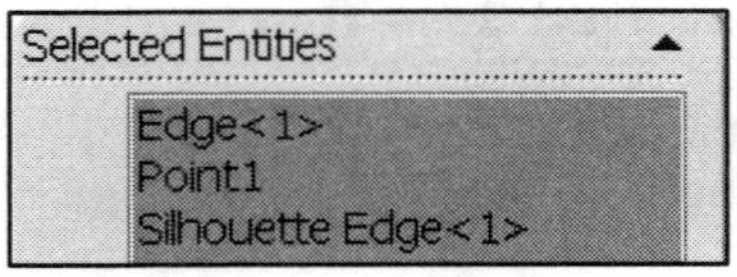

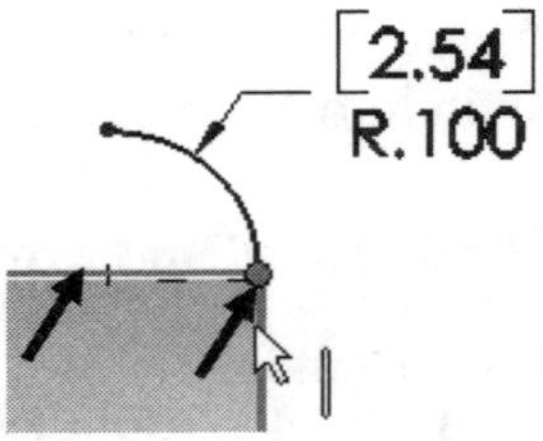

385) Click the **rightmost vertical line** of the LensNeck feature.

386) Click the **top horizontal line** (silhouette edge) of the LensNeck feature. Release the **Ctrl** key.

Selected Entities
Edge<1>
Point1
Silhouette Edge<1>

387) Click **Intersection** from the Add Relations box.

388) Click **OK** from the Properties PropertyManager.

Add a Vertical Relation.

389) Click the **arc center point**. Hold the **Ctrl** key down. Click the **arc end point**. Release the **Ctrl** key.

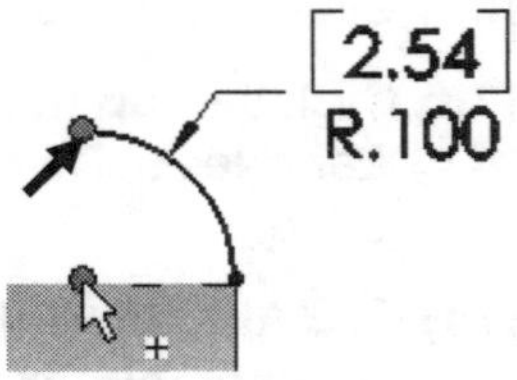

390) Click **Vertical** from the Add Relations box.

[2.54]
R.100

391) Click **OK** from the Properties PropertyManager.

Insert a Revolved Thin feature.

392) Click **Revolved Boss/Base** Revolved Boss/B... .

393) Select **Mid-Plane** from the Thin Feature Type box.

394) Enter **.050**, [**1.27**] for Direction1 Thickness.

395) Click the **Temporary Axis** for Axis of Revolution.

396) Click **OK** from the Revolve PropertyManager.

397) Rename **Revolve-Thin1** to **LensConnector**.

Fit the model to the Graphics window.

398) Press the **f** key.

399) Click **Save** .

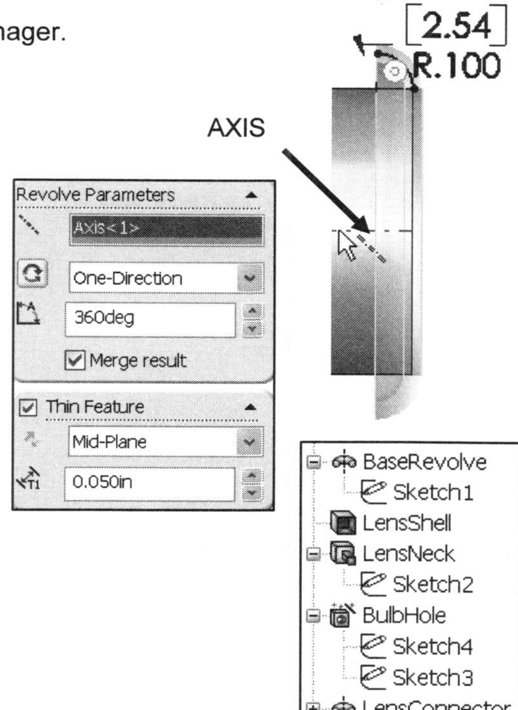

A Revolved sketch that remains open results in a Thin-Revolve feature . A Revolved sketch that is automatically closed, results in a line drawn from the start point to the end point of the sketch. The sketch is closed and results in a non-thin Revolve feature.

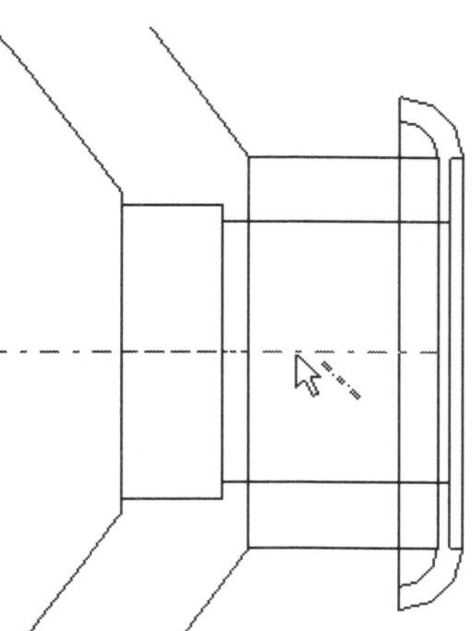

LENS Part-Extruded Boss Feature and Offset Entities

Use the Extruded Boss feature to create the front LensCover. Utilize the Offset Entities Sketch tool to offset the outside circular edge of the Revolved feature. The Sketch Plane for the Extruded Boss is the front circular face. The Offset Entities Sketch tool requires an Offset Distance and direction. Utilize the Bi-direction option to create a circular sketch in both directions. The Extrude Direction is away from the Front Plane.

Activity: LENS Part-Extruded Boss Feature and Offset Entities

Create the Sketch.

400) Click **Isometric view**.

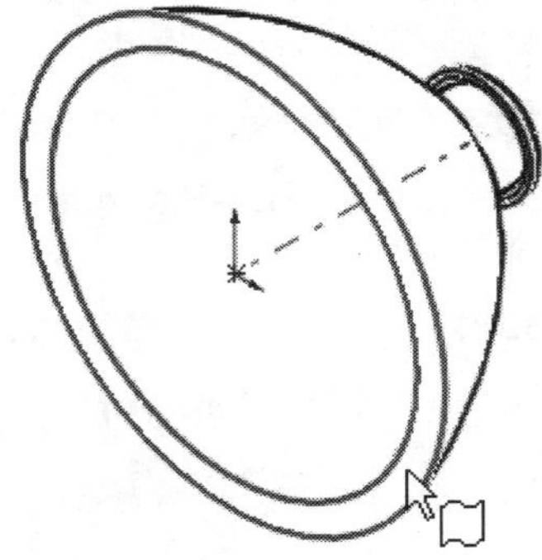

401) Click **Hidden Lines Removed**.

402) Click the **front circular face** for the Sketch plane.

403) Click **Sketch** Sketch.

404) Click **Front view**.

Offset the selected edge.

405) Click the **outside circular edge**.

406) Click **Offset Entities** Offset from the Sketch toolbar.

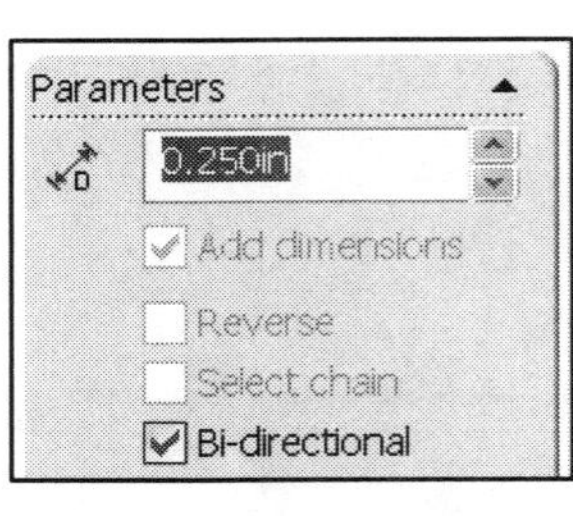

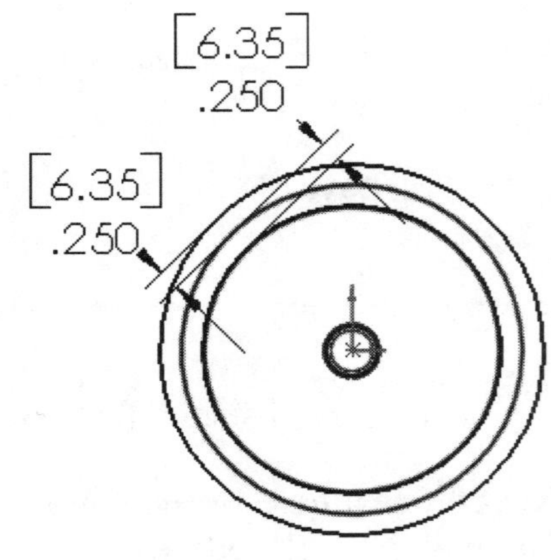

407) Click the **Bi-directional** check box.

408) Enter **.250**, [**6.35**] for Offset Distance.

409) Click **OK** from the Offset Entities PropertyManager.

410) Click **Isometric view**.

Insert an Extruded Boss feature.

411) Click **Extruded Boss/Base** Extruded Boss/B... .

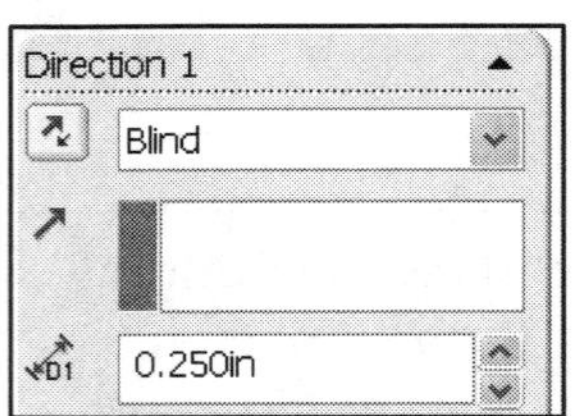

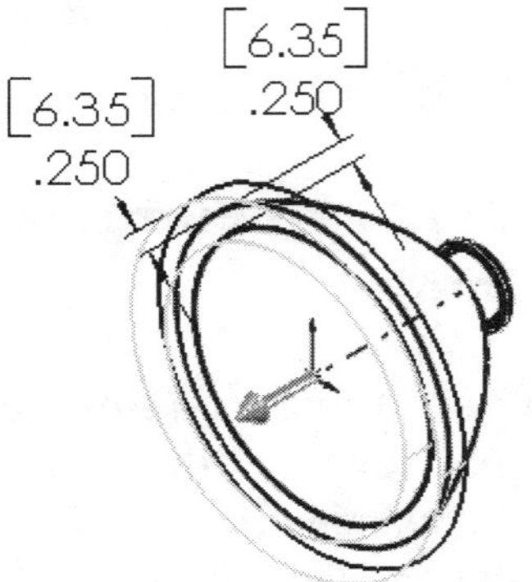

412) Enter **.250**, [**6.35**] for Depth.

413) Click **OK** from the Extrude PropertyManager.

Verify the position of the Extruded Boss.

414) Click the **Top view**.

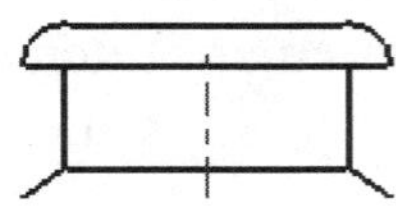

415) Rename **Extrude2** to **LensCover**.

416) Click **Isometric view** .

417) Click **Save** .

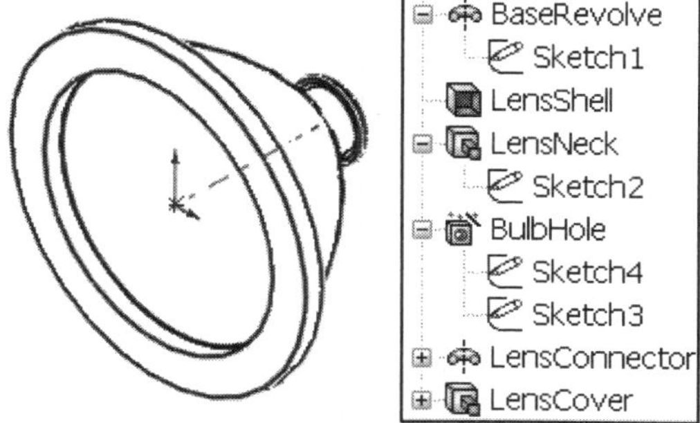

LENS Part-Extruded Boss Feature and Transparent Optical Property

Use an Extruded Boss feature to create the LensShield. Utilize the Convert Entities Sketch tool to extract the inside circular edge of the LensCover and place it on the Front Plane.

Apply the Transparent Optical property to the LensShield to control the ability for light to pass through the surface. Transparent is an Optical Property found in the Color PropertyManager. Control the following properties:

- **Transparency** - ability to pass light through the surface.
- **Ambience** - light reflected and scattered by other objects.
- **Diffusion** - light scattered equally in all directions on the surface.
- **Specularity** - ability to reflect light from a surface.
- **Shininess** - a glossy, highly reflective surface.
- **Emissivity** - ability to project light from the surface.

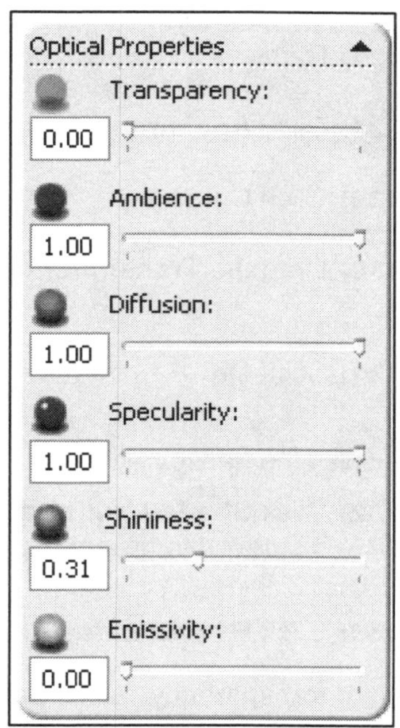

Activity: LENS Part-Extruded Boss Feature and Transparent Optical Property

Create the Sketch.

418) Click **Front Plane** Front Plane from the FeatureManager.

419) Click **Sketch** Sketch.

420) Click the **front inner circular edge** of the LensCover (Extrude2).

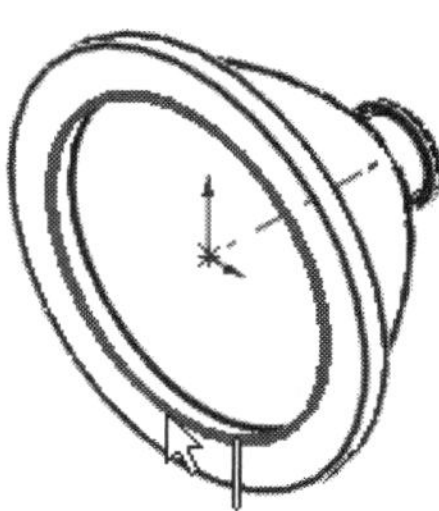

421) Click **Convert Entities** Convert from the Sketch Tool toolbar. The circle is projected onto the Front Plane.

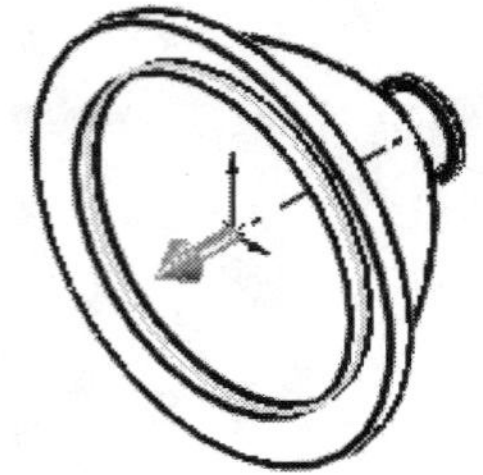

Insert an Extruded Boss feature.

422) Click **Extruded Boss/Base** Extruded Boss/B... .

423) Enter **.100**, **[2.54]** for Depth.

424) Click **OK** from the Extrude PropertyManager.

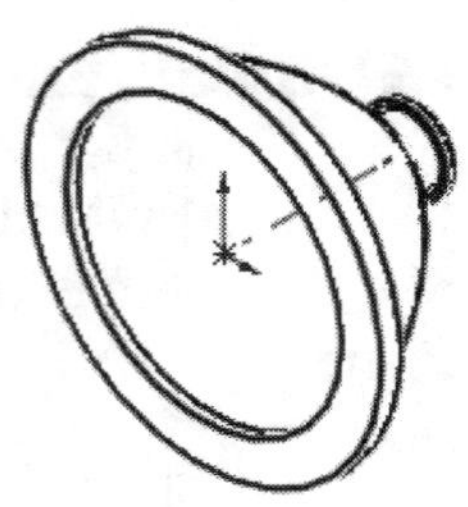

425) Rename **Extrude3** to **LensShield**.

426) Click **Save** .

Add transparency.

427) Right-click **LensShield** in the FeatureManager.

428) Click **Appearance** under the Feature (LensShield).

429) Click **Color**.

430) Drag the **Transparency slider** to the far right side.

431) Click **OK** from the PropertyManager.

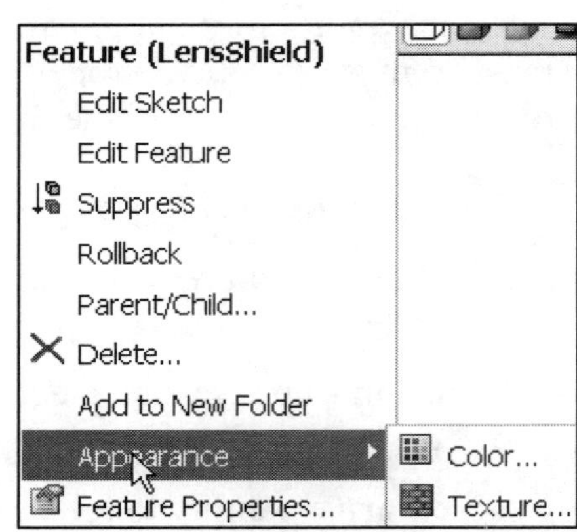

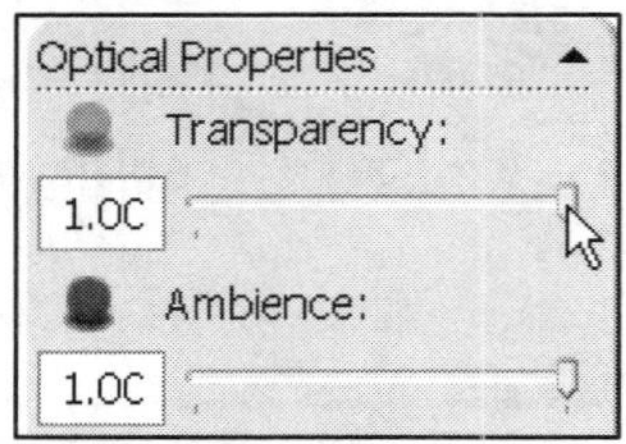

Display the transparent faces.

432) Click **Shaded With Edges** . Selected faces are displayed in green; they are not transparent.

433) Click **Hidden Lines Removed** to display the face transparency. Click **Save** .

Additional information on Revolved Boss/Base, Shell, Hole Wizard and Appearance is located in SolidWorks Help Topics. Keywords: Revolved (features), Shells, Hole Wizard (Counterbore), Color and Optics.

Refer to Help, Online Tutorial, Revolves exercise for additional information.

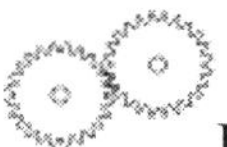 Review of the LENS Part.

The LENS feature utilized an Revolved Base feature. A Revolved feature required an axis, profile and an angle of revolution. The Shell feature created a uniform wall thickness.

You utilized the Convert Entities Sketch tool to create the Extruded Boss for the LensNeck. The Counterbore Hole feature was created with the HoleWizard.

The Revolved thin feature utilized a single 3 Point Arc. Geometric Relations were added to the Silhouette edge to define the arc. The LensCover and LensShield utilized existing geometry to Offset and Convert the geometry to the sketch. The Color and Optics PropertyManager determined the LensShield transparency.

BULB Part

The BULB fits inside the LENS. Use the Revolved feature as the Base feature for the BULB.

Insert the Revolved Base feature from a sketched profile on the Right Plane.

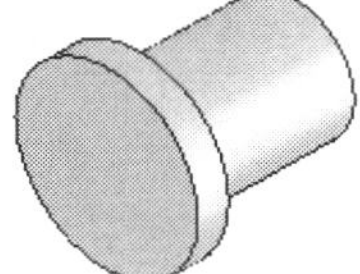

Insert a Revolved Boss feature using a Spline sketched profile. A Spline sketched profile is a complex curve.

Insert a Revolved Cut Thin feature at the base of the BULB.

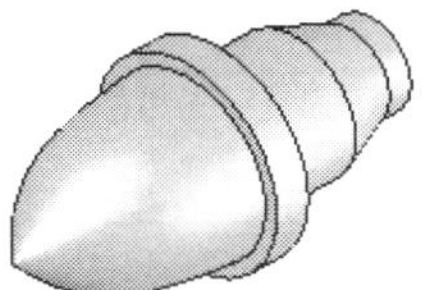

Insert a Dome feature at the base of the BULB.

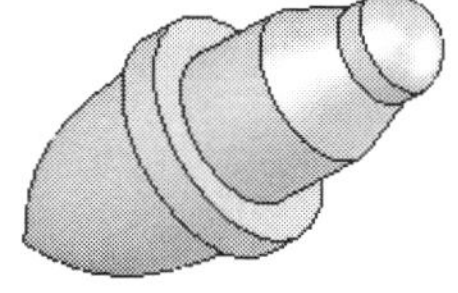

Insert a Circular Pattern feature from an Extruded Cut.

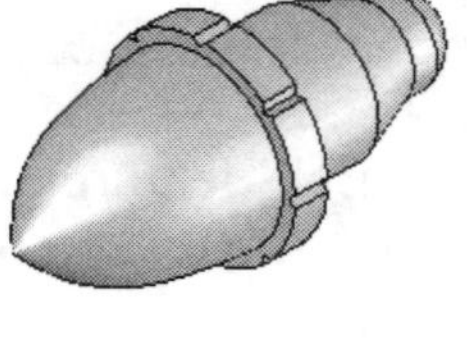

BULB Part-Revolved Base Feature

Create the new part, BULB. The BULB utilizes a solid Revolved Base feature.

The solid Revolved Base feature requires a:

- Sketch Plane (Right Plane).
- Sketch Profile (Lines).
- Axis of Revolution (Centerline).
- Angle of Rotation (360°).

Utilize the Centerline to create a diameter dimension for the profile. The flange of the BULB is located inside the Counterbore Hole of the LENS. Align the bottom of the flange with the Front Plane. The Front Plane mates against the Counterbore face.

Activity: BULB Part-Revolved Base Feature

Create the new part.

434) Click **File**, **New** from the Main menu.

435) Click the **MY-TEMPLATES** tab.

436) Double-click **PART-IN-ANSI**, [**PART-MM-ISO**].

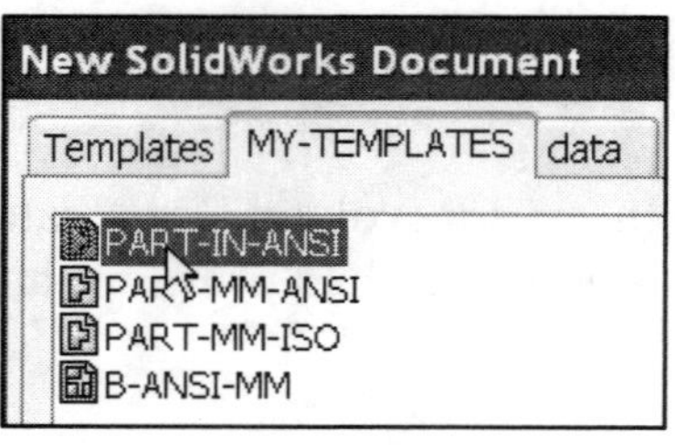

Save the part.

437) Click **Save**.

438) Select **PROJECTS** for Save in folder.

439) Enter **BULB** for Filename.

440) Enter **BULB FOR LENS** for Description.

441) Click **Save**.

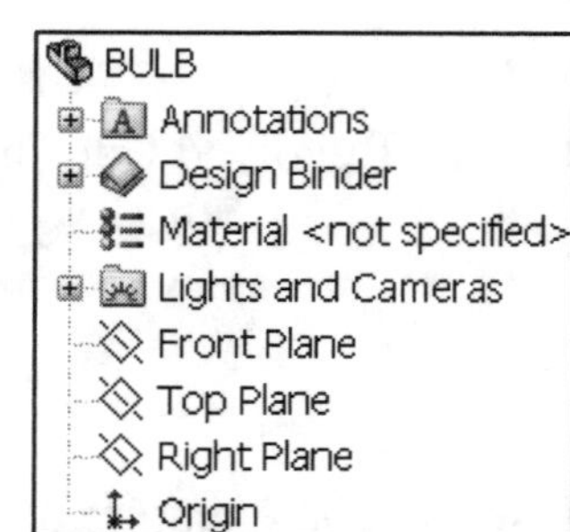

Select the Sketch plane.

442) Click the **Right Plane** from the FeatureManager.

Create the Sketch.

443) Click **Sketch** .

Sketch the Centerline.

444) Click **Centerline** Centerl... from the Sketch toolbar.

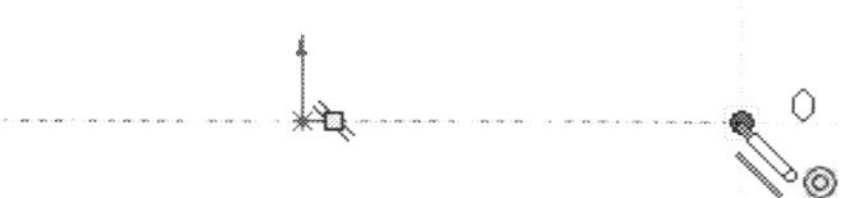

445) Sketch a horizontal **centerline** through the Origin.

Create six profile lines.

446) Click **Line** Line. Sketch a **vertical line** to the left of the Front Plane.

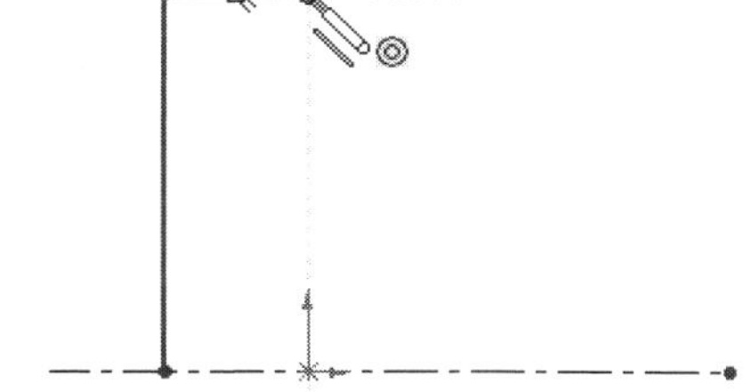

447) Sketch a **horizontal line** with the endpoint coincident to the Front Plane.

448) Sketch a short **vertical line** towards the centerline, collinear with the Front Plane.

449) Sketch a **horizontal line** to the right.

450) Sketch a **vertical line** with the endpoint collinear with the centerline.

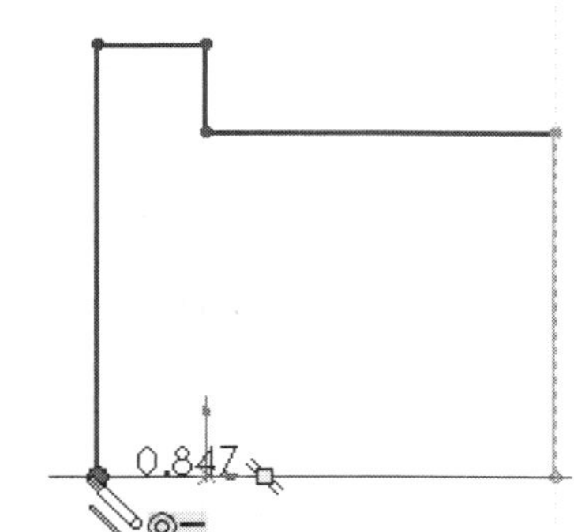

451) Sketch a **horizontal line** to the first point to close the profile.

Add dimensions.

452) Click **Smart Dimension** .

453) Click the **centerline**.

454) Click the **top right horizontal line**.

455) Click a **position** below the centerline and to the right.

456) Enter **.400** [**10.016**].

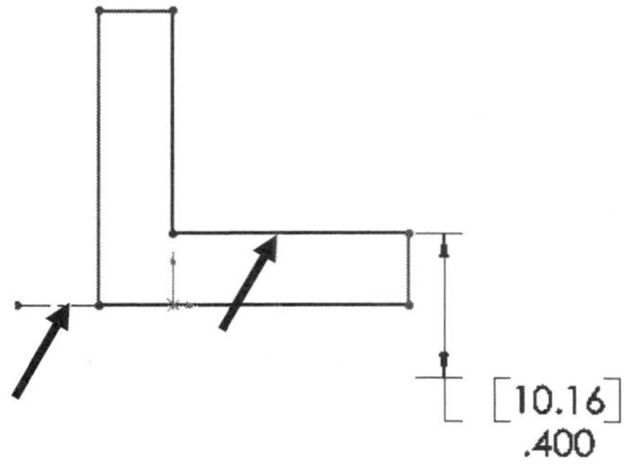

457) Click the **centerline**.

458) Click the **top left horizontal line**.

459) Click a **position** below the centerline and to the left.

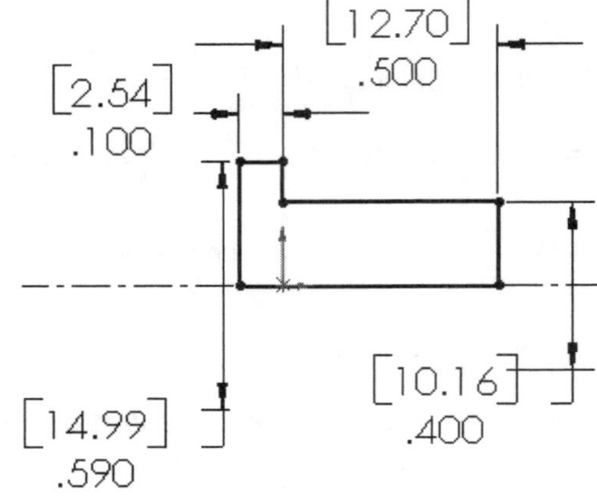

460) Enter **.590** [**14.99**].

461) Click the **top left horizontal line**.

462) Click a **position** above the profile.

463) Enter **.100** [**2.54**].

464) Click the **top right horizontal line**.

465) Click a **position** above the profile.

466) Enter **.500** [**12.7**].

Fit the Model to the Graphics window.

467) Press the **f** key.

Insert a Revolved Base feature.

468) Click **Revolved Boss/Base**  from the Feature toolbar. The Revolve Feature dialog box is displayed.

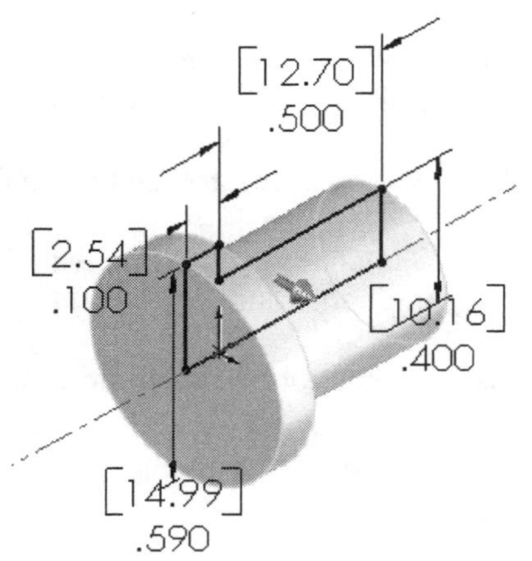

Accept the default option values.

469) Click **OK** from the Revolve PropertyManager.

470) Click **Isometric view**.

471) Click **Save**.

BULB Part-Revolved Boss Feature and Spline Sketch Tool

The BULB requires a second solid Revolved feature. The profile utilizes a complex curve called a Spline (Non-Uniform Rational B-Spline or NURB). Draw Splines with control points. Adjust the shape of the curve by dragging the control points.

Activity: BULB Part-Revolved Boss Feature and Spline Sketch Tool

Create the Sketch.

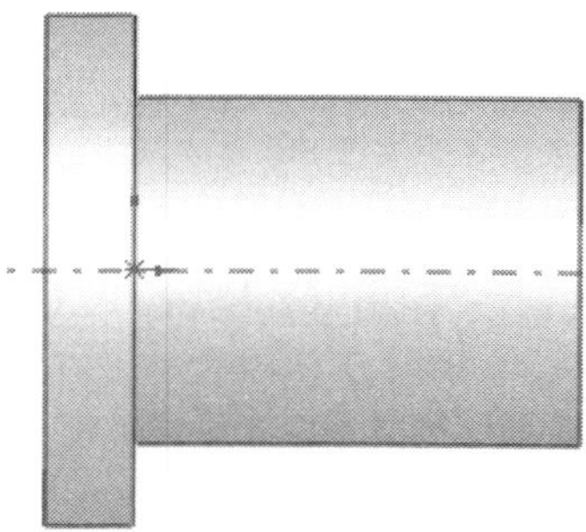

472) Click the **Right Plane** from the FeatureManager for the Sketch plane. Click **View**, check **Temporary Axes** from the Main menu.

473) Click **Sketch** Sketch. Click **Right view**. The Temporary Axis is displayed as a horizontal line.

474) Press the **z** key approximately five times to view the left vertical edge.

Sketch the profile.

475) Click **Spline** Spline.

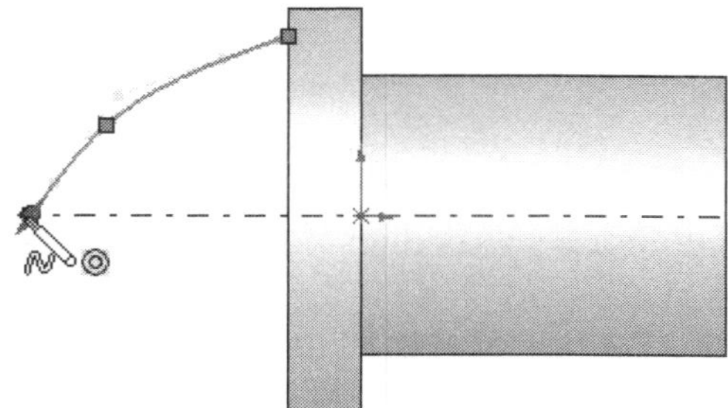

476) Click the **left vertical edge** of the Base feature for the Start point.

477) Drag the **mouse pointer** to the left.

478) Click a **position** above the Temporary Axis for the Control point. Double-click the **Temporary Axis** to create the End point and to end the Spline.

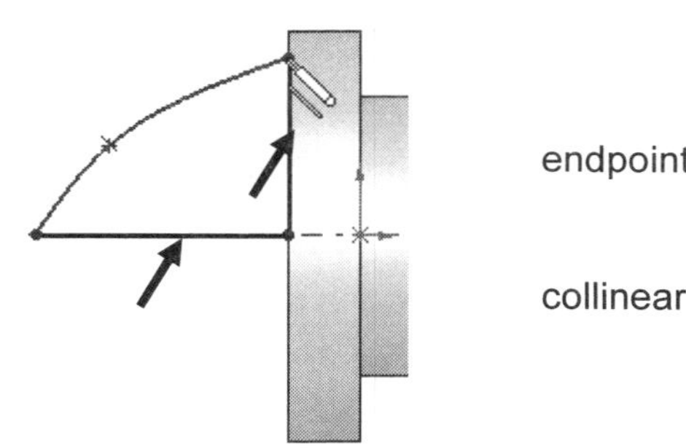

479) Click **Line** Line from the Sketch toolbar.

480) Sketch a **horizontal line** from the Spline to the left edge of the Revolved feature.

481) Sketch a **vertical line** to the Spline start point, with the left edge of the Revolved feature. Note: Dimensions are not required to create a feature.

Insert a Revolved Boss feature.

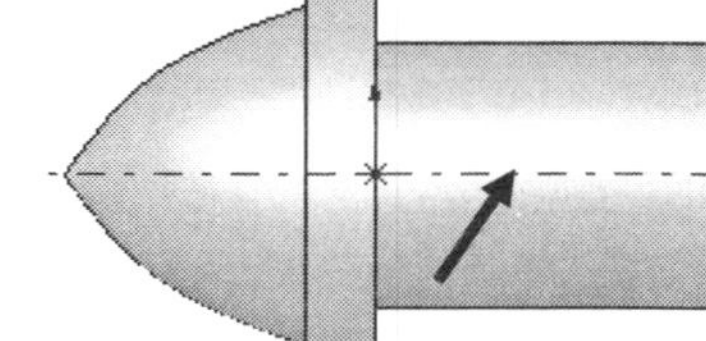

482) Right-click **Select**. Click the **Temporary Axis**.

483) Click **Revolved Boss/Base** Revolved Boss/B... from the Feature toolbar. Accept the default options.

484) Click **OK** from the Revolve PropertyManager.

485) Click **Isometric view** .

486) Click **Save** .

The points of the Spline dictate the shape of the Spline. Edit control points in the sketch to produce different results for the Revolved Boss feature.

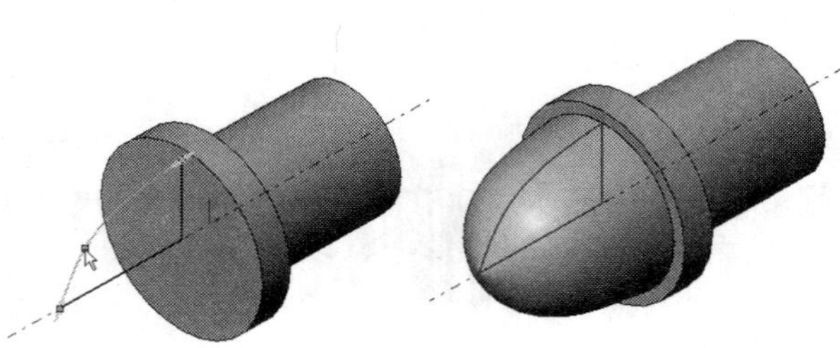

BULB Part-Revolved Cut Thin Feature

A Revolved Cut Thin feature removes material by rotating an open sketch profile around an axis. Sketch an open profile on the Right Plane. Add a Coincident relation to the silhouette and vertical edge. Insert dimensions.

Sketch a Centerline to create a diameter dimension for a revolved profile. The Temporary axis does not produce a diameter dimension.

Note: If lines snap to grid intersections, uncheck Tools, Sketch Settings, Enable Snapping for the next activity.

Activity: BULB Part-Revolved Cut Thin Feature

Create the Sketch.

487) Click the **Right Plane** from the FeatureManager.

488) Click **Sketch** Sketch. Click **Right view** .

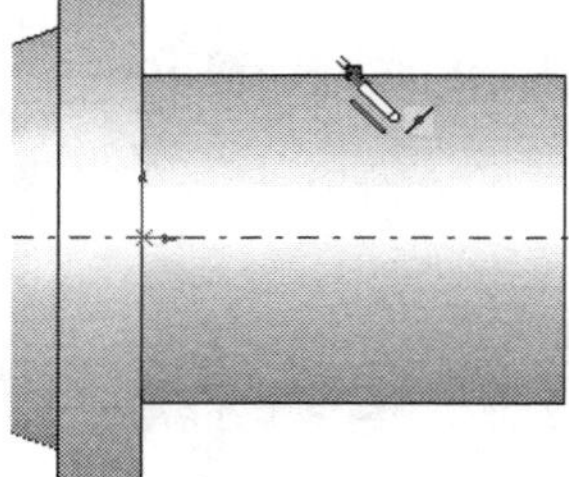

489) Click **Line** Line.

490) Click the **mid point** of the top silhouette edge. Sketch a **line** downward and to the right.

491) Sketch a horizontal **line** to the right vertical edge.

492) Right-click **Select**.

Add a Coincident Relation.

493) Click the **end point** of the line.

494) Hold the **Ctrl** key down.

495) Click the right **vertical edge**.

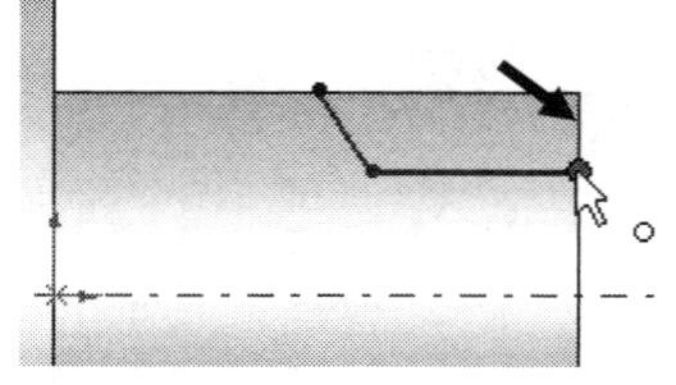

496) Release the **Ctrl** key.

497) Click **Coincident** from the Add Relations box.

498) Click **OK** from the Properties PropertyManager.

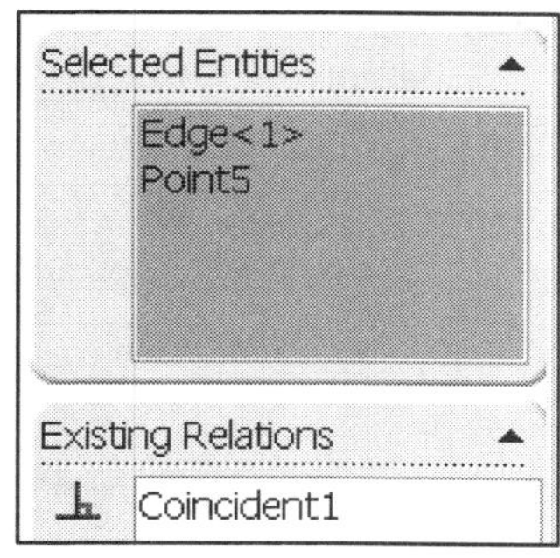

Sketch a Centerline.

499) Click **View**, uncheck **Temporary Axes** from the Main menu.

500) Click **Centerline** Centerl... from the Sketch toolbar.

501) Sketch a **horizontal Centerline** through the Origin.

Add dimensions.

502) Click **Smart Dimension** 

503) Click the **horizontal Centerline**. Click the **short horizontal line**. Click a **position** below the profile to create a diameter dimension.

504) Enter **.260**, [**6.6**].

505) Click the **short horizontal line**.

506) Click a **position** above the profile to create a horizontal dimension.

507) Enter **.070**, [**1.78**]. The Sketch is fully defined and is displayed in black.

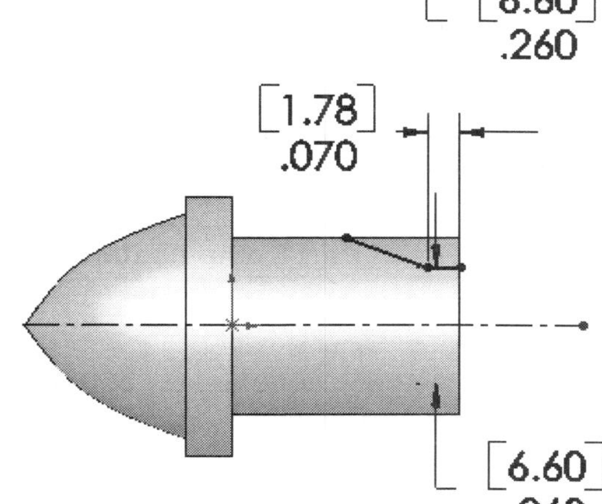

For Revolved features, the ∅ symbol is not displayed in the part. The ∅ symbol is displayed when inserted into the drawing.

Insert the Revolved Cut Thin feature.

508) Right-click **Select**. Click the **Centerline**.

509) Click **Revolved Cut** 

from the Feature toolbar.

510) Click **No** to the Warning Message, "Would you like the sketch to be automatically closed?"

511) Check the **Thin Feature** check box. Enter **.150**, [**3.81**] for Thickness. Click the **Reverse Direction arrow**.

512) Click **OK** from the Cut-Revolve PropertyManager.

513) Click **Save**.

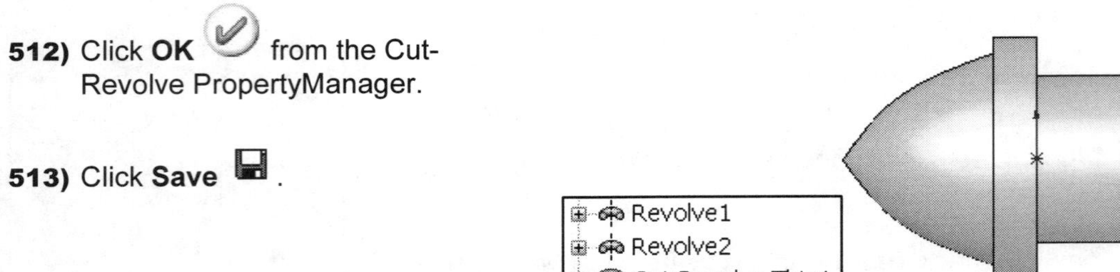

Toggle between the Line tool and the Arc tool with the A key. Press the A key to invoke the Arc tool while the Line tool is active.

Toggle between the Line tool and Tangent arc with the mouse to increase your sketching speed. Do not select the Line Tool or Tangent Arc tool. To toggle, select the endpoint of the line, then move the pointer away. The preview displays a new line. Move the pointer back to the endpoint, then away again. The preview displays a Tangent arc. Note: Practice sketch techniques in a new part. Create a new sketch. Toggle between the Line tool, Arc tool and Tangent arc tool.

BULB Part-Dome Feature

A Dome feature creates spherical or elliptical shaped geometry. Use the Dome feature to create the Connector feature of the BULB. The Dome feature requires a face and a Height value.

Activity: BULB Part-Dome Feature

Insert the Dome feature.

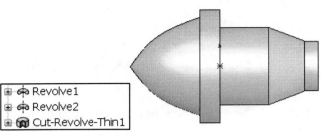

514) Click the **back circular face** of Revolve1. Revolve1 is highlighted in the FeatureManager.

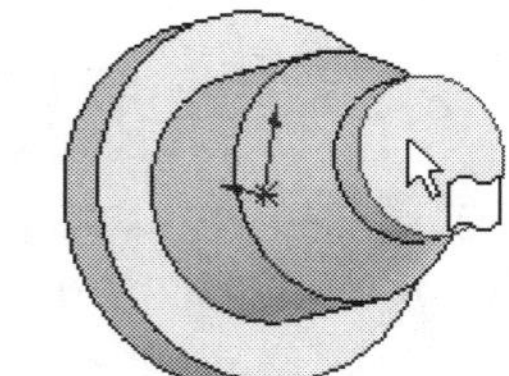

515) Click **Insert**, **Features, Dome** Dome... from the Main menu.

516) Enter **.100**, [**2.54**] for Distance.

517) Click **OK** from the Dome PropertyManager.

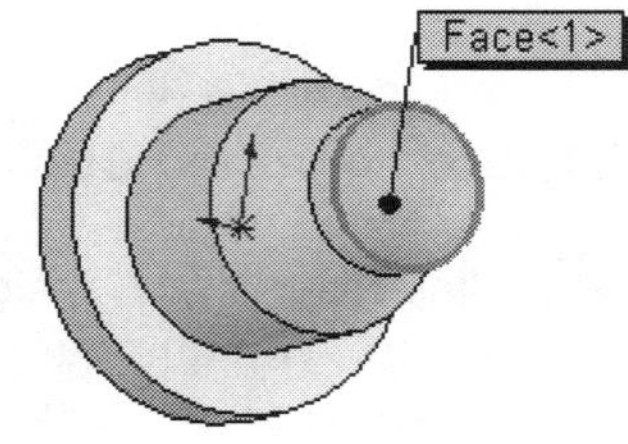

518) Click **Isometric view**.

519) Click **Save**.

BULB Part-Circular Pattern Feature

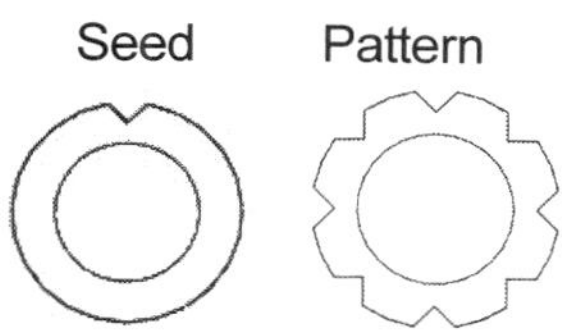

The Pattern feature creates one or more instances of a feature or a group of features. The Circular Pattern feature places the instances around an axis of revolution.

The Circular Pattern feature requires a seed feature. The seed feature is the first feature in the Pattern. The seed feature in this section is a V-shaped Extruded Cut feature.

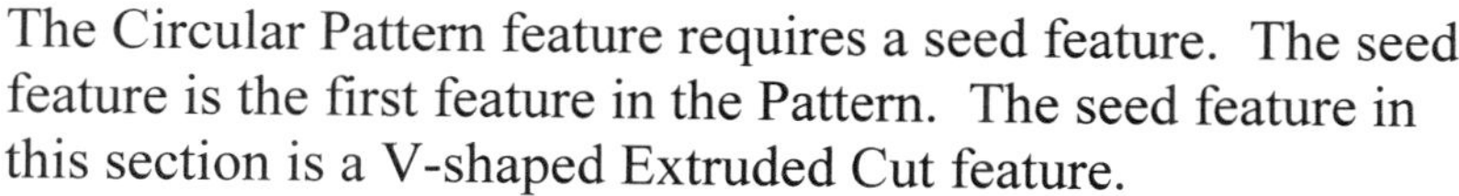

Activity: BULB Part-Circular Pattern Feature

Create the Seed Cut.

520) Click the **front face** of the Base feature for Sketch Plane. Revolve1 is highlighted in the FeatureManager.

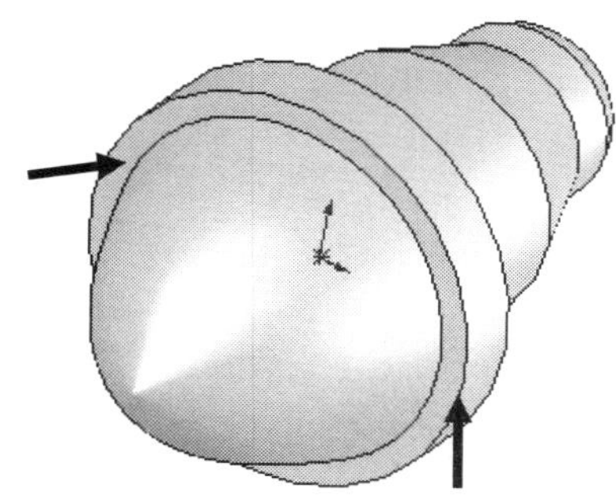

521) Click **Sketch** Sketch.

522) Click the **outside circular edge**.

523) Click **Convert Entities** Convert from the Sketch Tools toolbar.

524) Click **Front view**.

525) **Zoom in** on the top half of the BULB.

Sketch the Centerline.

526) Click **Centerline** Centerl... from the Sketch toolbar.

527) Sketch a **vertical centerline** coincident with the top and bottom circular circles and coincident with the Right Plane.

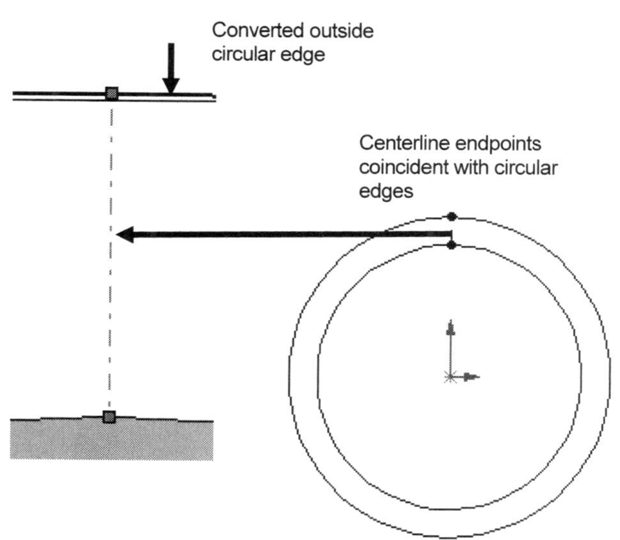

Sketch a V-shaped line.

528) Click **Tools, Sketch Tools, Dynamic Mirror** Dynamic Mirror from the Main menu.

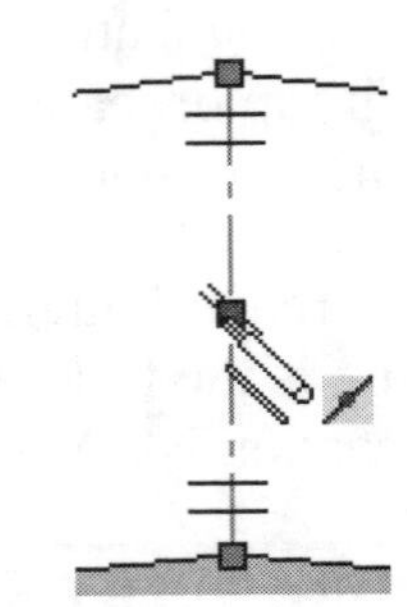

529) Click the **Centerline**.

530) Click **Line** Line from the Sketch toolbar.

531) Click the **midpoint** of the Centerline.

532) Click the coincident **outside circle edge to the left** of the centerline.

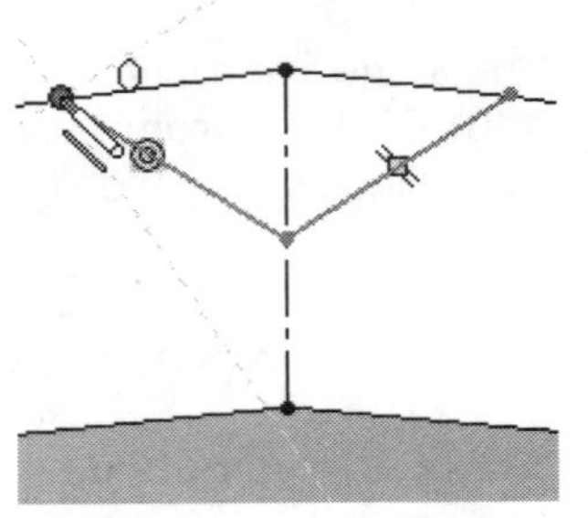

533) Click **Tools**, **Sketch Tools**, **Dynamic Mirror** Dynamic Mirror from the Main menu.

Trim unwanted geometry.

534) Click **Trim Entities** Trim from the Sketch toolbar.

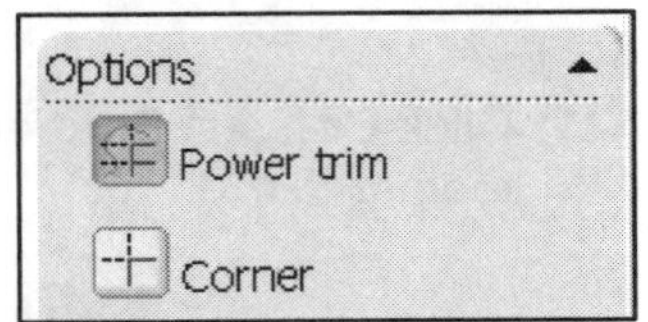

535) Click **Power trim** from the Options box.

536) Click a **position** in the Graphics window and drag the mouse pointer until it intersects the circle circumference.

537) Click **OK** from the Trim PropertyManager.

Add a Perpendicular Relation.

538) Click the **left** V shape line.

539) Hold the **Ctrl** key down.

540) Click the **right** V shape line.

541) Release the **Ctrl** key.

542) Click **Perpendicular** ⊥ from the Add Relations box.

543) Click **OK** from the Properties PropertyManager. The Sketch is fully defined.

Create an Extruded Cut feature.

544) Click **Extruded Cut** Extruded Cut . Click **Through All** from the End Condition list box.

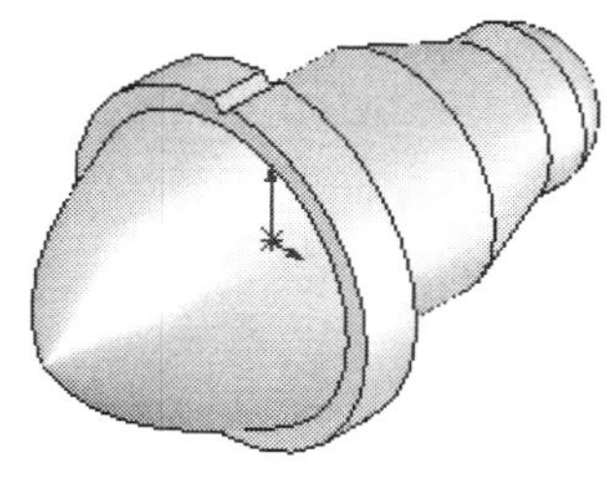

545) Click **OK** from the Cut-Extrude PropertyManager.

546) Click **Isometric view** .

Fit the drawing to the Graphics window.

547) Press the **f** key. Click **Save** .

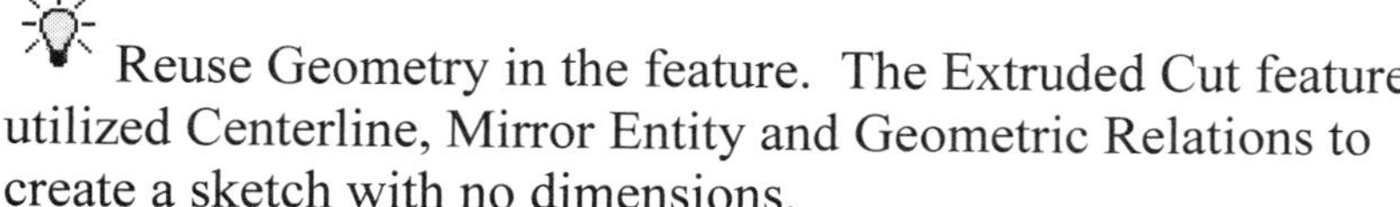

Reuse Geometry in the feature. The Extruded Cut feature utilized Centerline, Mirror Entity and Geometric Relations to create a sketch with no dimensions.

The Cut-Extrude is the seed feature for the Pattern. Create 4 copies of the seed feature. A copy of a feature is called an instance. Modify 4 instances to 8.

Insert the Circular Pattern feature.

548) Click **Cut-Extrude1** from the FeatureManager.

549) Click **Circular Pattern** Circular Pattern from the Features toolbar.

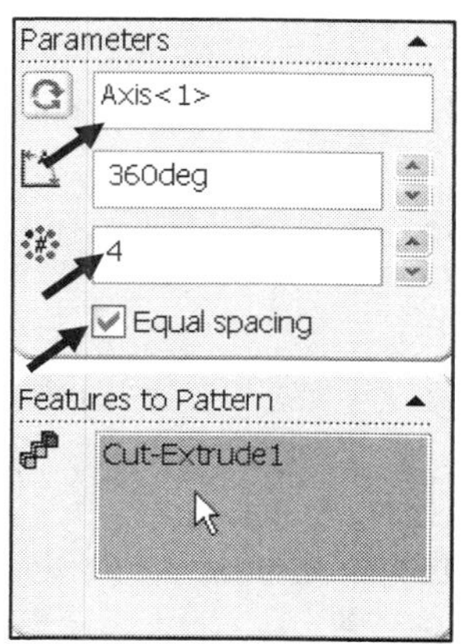

550) Click the **Pattern Axis** text box.

551) Click **View**, check **Temporary Axes** from the main menu.

552) Click the **Temporary Axis**.

553) Enter **4** in the Number of Instances spin box.

554) Check **Equal spacing** box.

555) Check the **Geometry pattern** box.

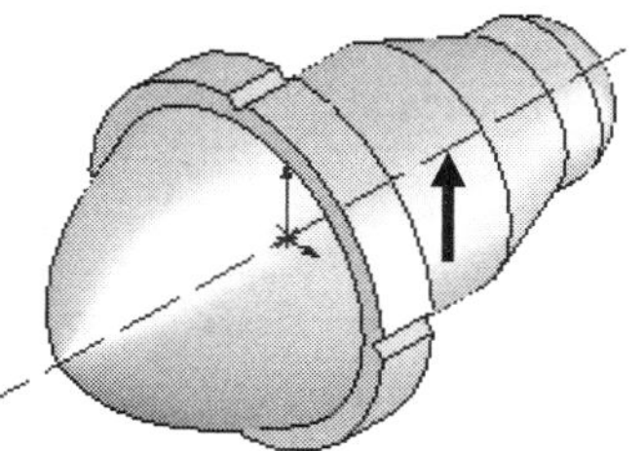

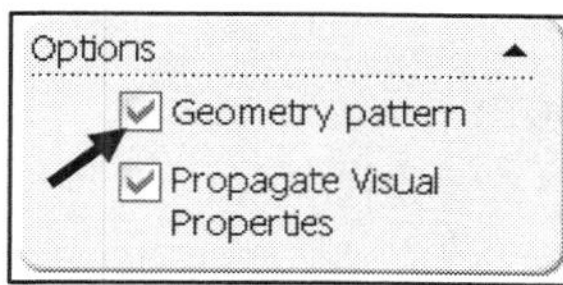

556) Click **OK** from the Circular Pattern PropertyManager.

Edit the Circular Pattern feature.

557) Right-click on the **CirPattern1** from the FeatureManager.

558) Click **Edit Feature**. Enter **8** in the Number of Instances box.

559) Click **OK** from the CirPattern1 PropertyManager.

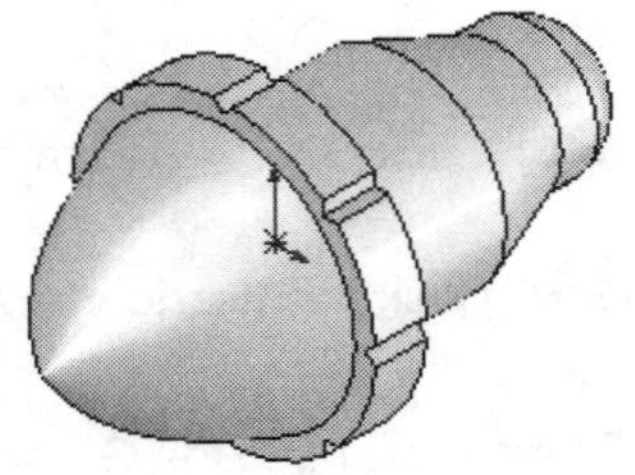

560) Rename **Cut Extrude1** to **Seed Cut**.

Hide the reference geometry.

561) Click **View**, uncheck **Temporary Axes** from the Main menu.

562) Click **Save**.

Locate the seed feature in Feature Pattern. Rename the seed feature of a Pattern to locate quickly for future assembly.

Customizing Toolbars and Short Cut Keys

The default Toolbars contains numerous icons that represent basic functions. Additional features and functions are available that are not displayed on the default Toolbars.

You have utilized the z key for Zoom In/Out, the f key for Zoom to Fit and Ctrl-C/Ctrl-V to Copy/Paste. Short Cut keys save time. Assign a key to execute a SolidWorks function. Create a Short Cut key for the Temporary Axis.

Activity: Customizing Toolbars and Short Cut Keys

Customize the Toolbar.

563) Click **Tools**, **Customize** from the Main menu.

Place the Shape icon on the Features Toolbar.

564) Click the **Commands** tab.

565) Click **Features** from the category text box.

566) Drag the **Shape** icon into the Features Toolbar.

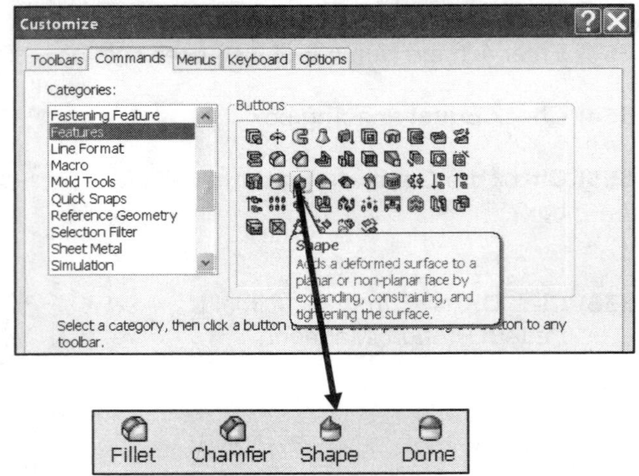

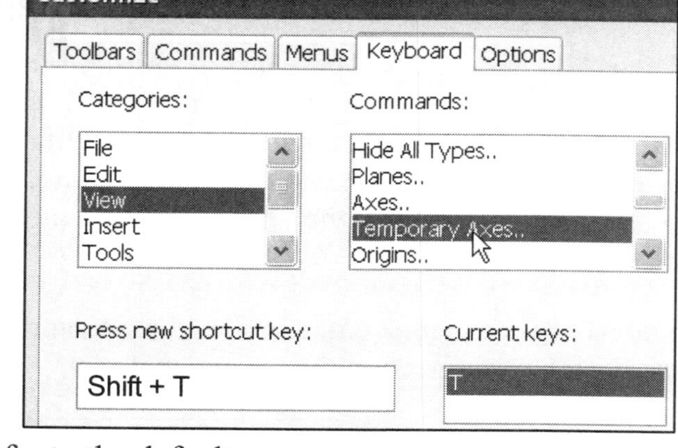

Customize the Keyboard for a Section View.

567) Click the **Keyboard** tab from the Customize dialog box.

568) Select **View** for Categories. Select **Temporary Axes** for Commands.

569) Enter **T** for Press new shortcut key. Click **Assign**. Click **OK**. Press the **T** key to toggle the display of the Temporary Axes.

Test the proposed Short Cut key, before you customize your keyboard. Refer to the default Keyboard Short Cut table in the Appendix.

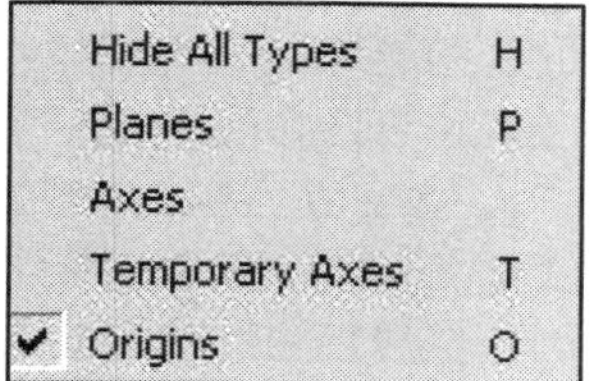

Set up View Short Cut keys for Planes (P), Origins (O), Temporary Axis (T) and Hide All Types (H). You utilize these view commands often. Short Cut keys are displayed to the right of the command.

Additional information on Revolved Boss/Base, Spline, Circular Pattern, Dome, Line/Arc Sketching is located in SolidWorks Help Topics. Keywords: Revolved (features), Spline, Pattern (Circular) and Dome.

Refer to Help, Online Tutorial, Pattern Features exercise for additional information.

Review of the BULB Part.

The Revolved Base feature utilized a sketched profile on the Right Plane and a centerline. The Revolved Boss feature utilized a Spline sketched profile. A Spline is a complex curve.

You created the Revolved Cut Thin feature at the base of the BULB to remove material. A centerline was inserted to add a diameter dimension. The Dome feature was inserted on the back face of the BULB. The Circular Pattern feature was created from an Extruded Cut. The Extruded Cut feature utilized existing geometry and required no dimensions.

Toolbars and keyboards were customized to save time. Always verify that a Short Cut key is not predefined in SolidWorks.

Design Checklist and Goals before Plastic Manufacturing

The BATTERYPLATE part is manufactured from a plastic resin. A plastic part requires mold base plates, named Plate A and Plate B, to create the mold. A plastic part also requires knowledge of the material and manufacturing process. Critical decisions need to be made. What type of plastic resin do you use? The answer is derived from the development team: designer, resin supplier, mold maker and mold base, (Plate A & Plate B) supplier.

Ticona (www.ticona.com) supplies their customers with a designer's checklist to assist the designer in selecting the correct material.

TICONA-Celanese Typical Design Checklist
1. What is the function of the part?
2. What is the expected lifetime of the part?
3. What agency approvals are required? (UL, FDA, USDA, NSF, USP, SAE, MIL spec)
4. What electrical characteristics are required and at what temperatures?
5. What temperature will the part see and for how long?
6. What chemicals will the part be exposed to?
7. Is moisture resistance necessary?
8. How will the part be assembled? Can parts be combined into one plastic part?
9. Is the assembly going to be permanent or one time only?
10. Will adhesives be used? Some resins require special adhesives.
11. Will fasteners be used? Will threads be molded in?
12. Does the part have a snap fit? Glass filled materials will require more force to close the snap fit, but will deflect less.
13. Will the part be subjected to impact? If so, radius the corners.
14. Is surface appearance important? If so, beware of weld lines, parting lines, ejector location and gate location.
15. What color is required for the part? Is a specific match required or will the part be color-coded? Some glass or mineral filled materials do not color as well as unfilled materials.
16. Will the part be painted? Is primer required? Will the part go through a high temperature paint oven?
17. Is weathering or UV exposure a factor?
18. What are the required tolerances? Can they be relaxed to make molding more economical?
19. What is the expected weight of the part? Will it be too light (or too heavy)?
20. Is wear resistance required?
21. Does the part need to be sterilized? With what methods (chemical, steam, radiation)?
22. Will the part be insert molded or have a metal piece press fit in the plastic part? Both methods result in continuous stress in the part.
23. Is there a living hinge designed in the part? Be careful with living hinges designed for crystalline materials such as acetal.
24. What loading and resulting stress will the part see? And, at what temperature and environment.
25. Will the part be loaded continuously or intermittently? Will permanent deformation or creep be an issue?
26. What deflections are acceptable?
27. Is the part moldable? Are there undercuts? Are there sections that are too thick or thin?
28. Will the part be machined?
29. What is the worst possible situation the part will be in? Worst-case environment.

In "Designing With Plastic – The Fundamentals", Ticona lists three design goals for creating injection molded parts:

Goal 1: Maximize Functionality

Mold bases are costly. Design functionality into the part. A single plastic chassis replaces several sheet metal components.

Reduce assembly time and part weight whenever it is appropriate.

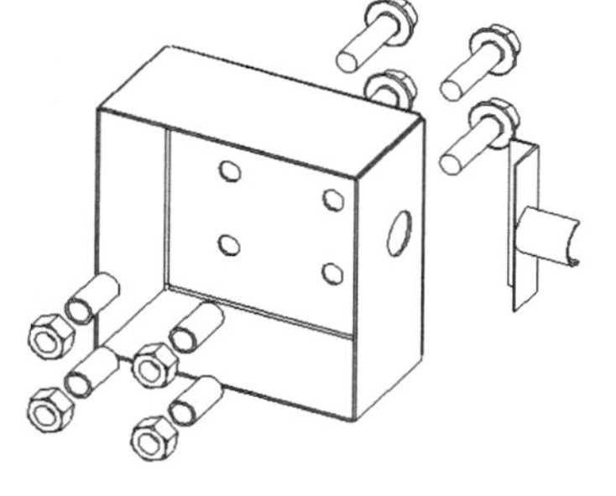
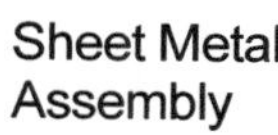

Sheet Metal Assembly

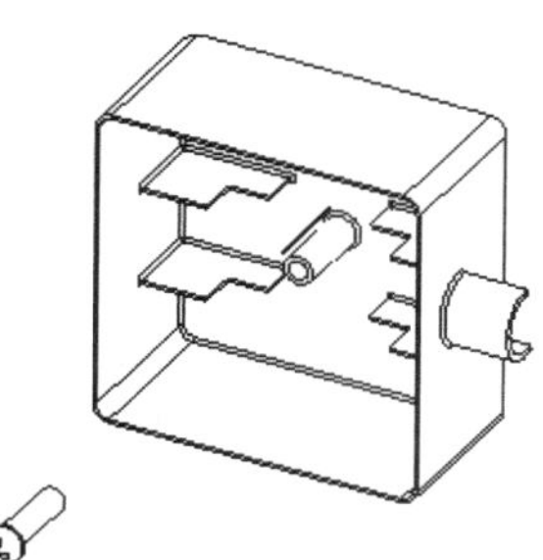

Injection Molded Thermoplastic

Goal 2: Optimize Material Selection

For material selection, consider the following elements: part functionality, operating environment, cost/price constraint and any special cosmetic requirements.

Several materials should be selected with a developed list of advantages and disadvantages for review.

For maximum product performance at a competitive cost in this project, use Celanese® (Nylon 6/6) (P/A 6/6), where:

- Celanese® is the registered trademark name.
- Nylon 6/6 is the common plastic name.
- P/A 6/6 (Polyhexamethyleneadipamide) is the chemical name.

Goal 3: Minimize Material Use

Optimize part wall thickness for cost and performance.

The minimum volume of plastic that satisfies the structural, functional, appearance and molding requirements of the application is usually the best choice.

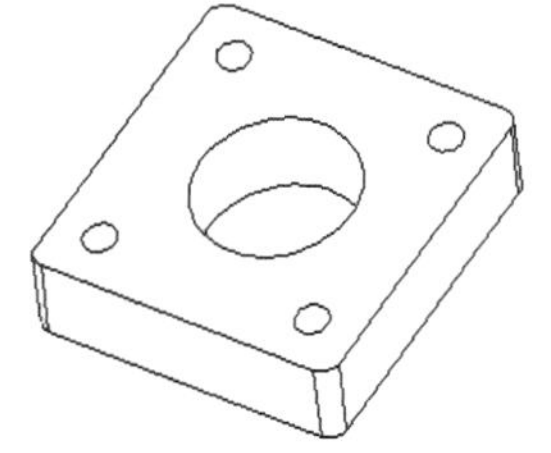
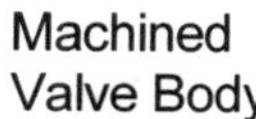

Machined Valve Body

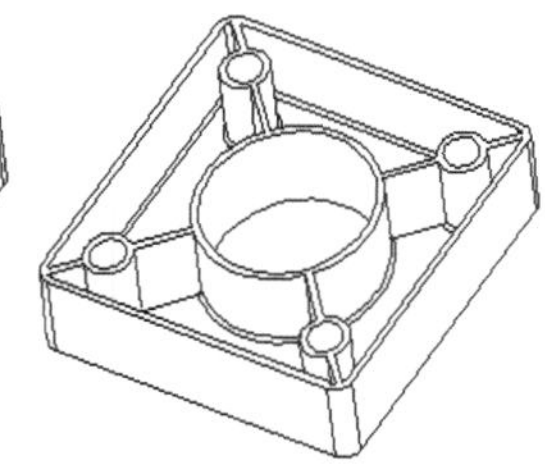

Injected Molded Valve Body

Mold Base

Designing a custom mold base is expensive and time consuming. An example of a mold base supplier is Progressive Components (www.procomps.com).

The mold base positions the mold cavities. The mold base plates are machined to create the mold cavities. The mold base is designed to withstand high pressure, heating and cooling sequences during the fabrication process.

The mold base assembly is composed of the following:

- PLATE A.
- PLATE B.

And a variety of support plates, ejector plates, pins and bushings.

Courtesy of Progressive Components
Wauconda, IL USA

Applying SolidWorks Features for Mold Tooling Design

SolidWorks features such as Draft, Fillet and Shell assist in the design of plastic parts. Utilize the Draft Analysis Tool in the part before creating the Mold Tooling, PLATE A and PLATE B.

Most molded parts require Draft. Plastic molded injection parts require a draft angle to eject the part from the mold. To properly eject the part, design parts with a draft angle in the direction of the mold movement. A draft angle of 1° – 3° is the design rule for most injection molded parts. There are exceptions based upon material type and draw depth. For illustration purposes, a draft angle of 1° is used in the BATTERYPLATE.

The draft angle is an option in both the Extruded Boss/Base and Extruded Cut features. The Draft feature adds a specified Draft Angle to faces of an existing feature.

Use the Fillet feature to remove sharp edges from plastic parts. For thin walled parts, insure that the inside sharp edges are removed. Sketch Arcs and 2D Fillets in the 2D profile to remove sharp edges. The Shell feature, Cut feature or Extruded Thin feature all provide Wall Thickness. Select the correct Wall Thickness for a successful part.

If the Wall Thickness is too thin, the part will structurally fail. If the Wall Thickness is too thick, the part will be overweight. This will increase cycle time and decrease profits.

There are numerous types of plastic molds. SolidWorks contains a variety of Mold Tools to assist the designer, mold maker and mold manufacturer. For a simple Cavity Mold follow the following steps:

- Perform a Draft Analysis on the part. A Draft Analysis determines the faces that require draft
- Follow the Mold Tool steps in sequence:
  - Scale.
  - Parting Lines.
  - Shut-off Surfaces.
  - Parting Surfaces. (The Parting Surfaces icon displays after defining the Shut-off Surfaces)
  - Tooling Split.
  - Hide the Surface Bodies used by the Mold tools.
  - Utilize Move\Copy to display the Tooling (PLATE A and PLATE B).

Activity: SolidWorks Features for Mold Tooling Design

Create the new part.

570) Click **File**, **New** from the Main menu.

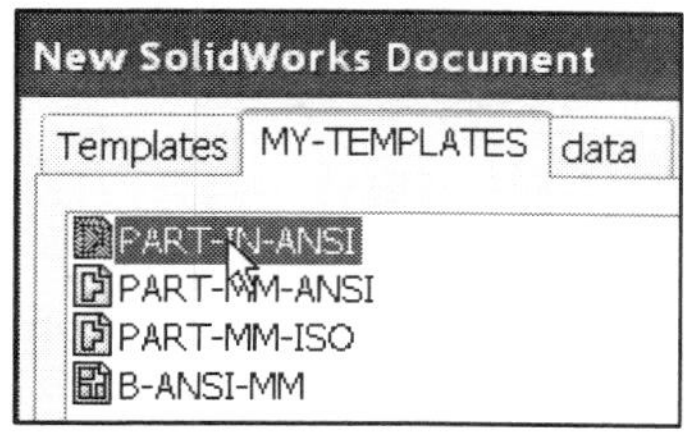

571) Click the **MY-TEMPLATES** tab.

572) Double-click **PART-IN-ANSI**, [**PART-MM-ISO**].

Save the part.

573) Click **Save**.

574) Select **PROJECTS** for Save in folder.

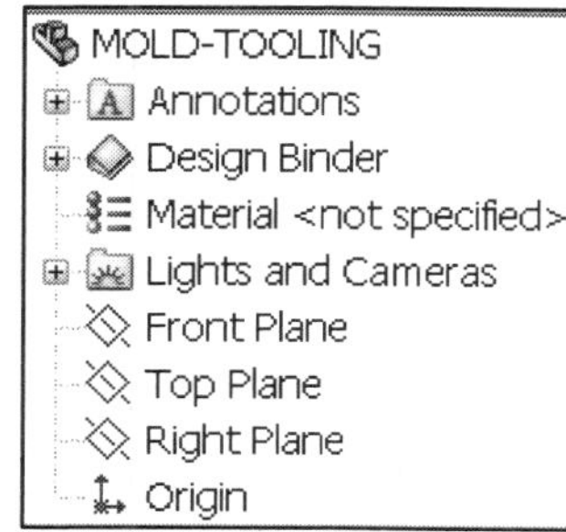

575) Enter **MOLD-TOOLING** for Filename.

576) Enter **MOLD FEATURES FOR TOOLING** for Description.

577) Click **Save**.

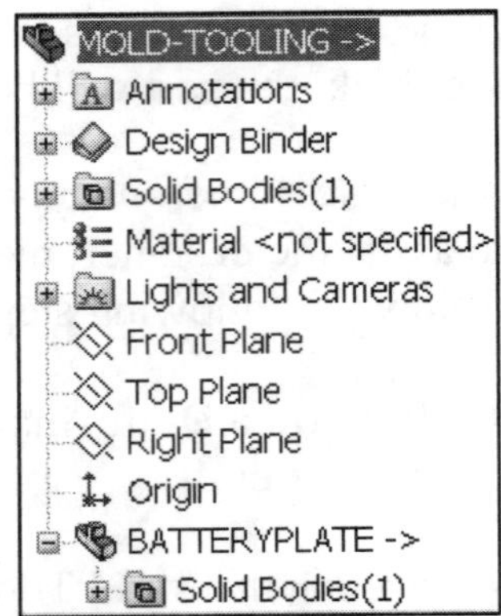

Insert a part.

578) Click **Insert**, **Part** Part... from the Main menu.

579) Double-click **BATTERYPLATE** for part.

580) Click the **Origin**. The BATTERYPLATE part is the first feature in the MOLD-TOOLING part.

Utilize the Insert Part option to maintain the original part and a simplified FeatureManager. The Insert Part maintains an external reference to the original part. Modify the original part and the Insert Part updates on a Rebuild. Apply the Insert Part option to SolidWorks parts and imported parts.

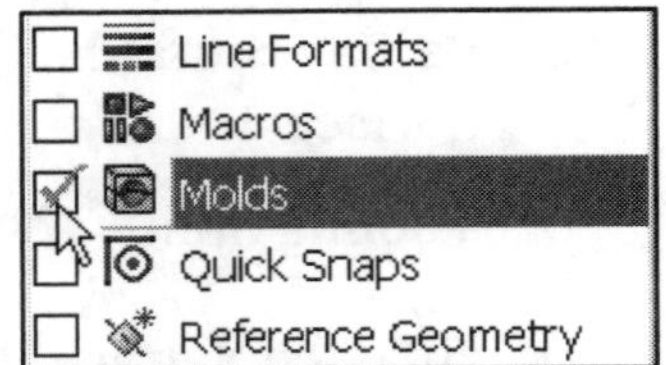

Display the Mold Toolbar.

581) Click the **drop down arrow** from the Features icon in the Control Area. Click **Customize CommandManager**. Check **Molds** Molds. Click in the **Graphics window**.

582) Click **Molds** Molds in the Control Area to display the Mold Tools toolbar in the CommandManager.

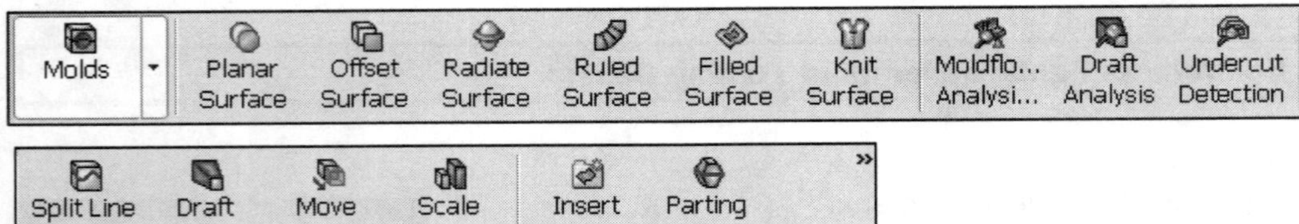

Display the Temporary Axes.

583) Click **View**, check **Temporary Axes** from the Main menu.

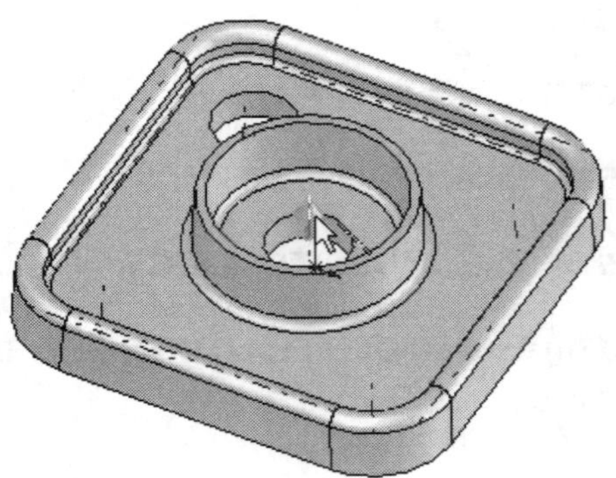

Perform a Draft Analysis

584) Click **Draft Analysis** Draft Analysis from the Mold toolbar.

585) Click the **Temporary Axis** at the center hole for the Direction of Pull. The Direction arrow points upward.

586) Enter **1** for Draft angle.

587) Click **Calculate**.

588) Rotate the **part** to display the faces that require draft.

589) Click **OK** from the Draft Analysis PropertyManager.

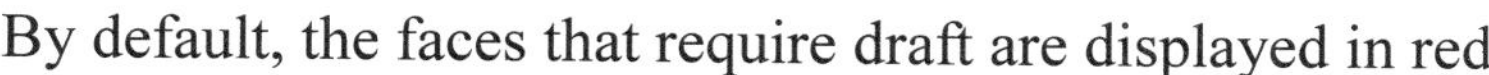

By default, the faces that require draft are displayed in red. The Top Cut Extruded Cut and the Holes Extruded Cut requires a draft. The bottom flat surface will become the parting surface.

Modify the BATTERYPLATE part In Context of the MOLD-TOOLING part. Both parts are open during the modification.

Modify the BATTERYPLATE In Context.
590) Right-click **BATTERYPLATE** in the FeatureManager.

591) Click **Edit In Context**.

Insert Draft into the Top Cut.
592) Right-click **Top Cut** in the BATTERYPLATE FeatureManager.

593) Click **Edit Feature**.

594) Click **Draft on/off**.

595) Enter **1** for Draft Angle.

596) Click **OK** from the Top Cut PropertyManager.

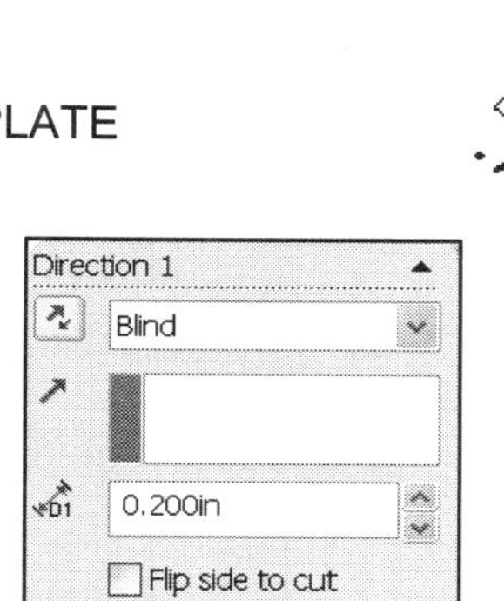

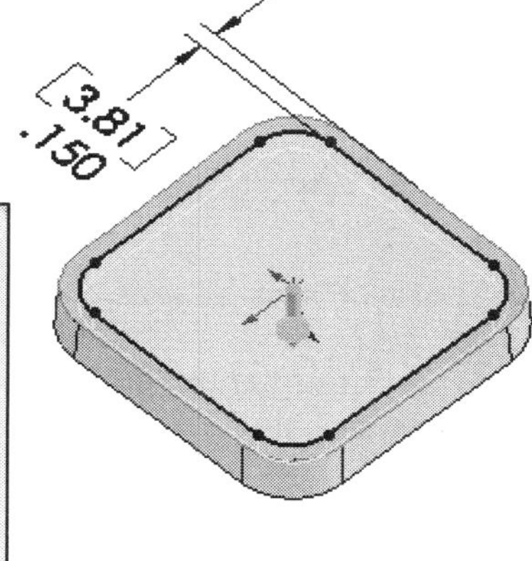

Insert Draft into the Holes.
597) Right-click **Holes** in the BATTERYPLATE FeatureManager.

598) Click **Edit Feature**. Click the **Draft on/off** button. Enter **1** for Draft Angle.

599) Click **OK** from the Holes PropertyManager.

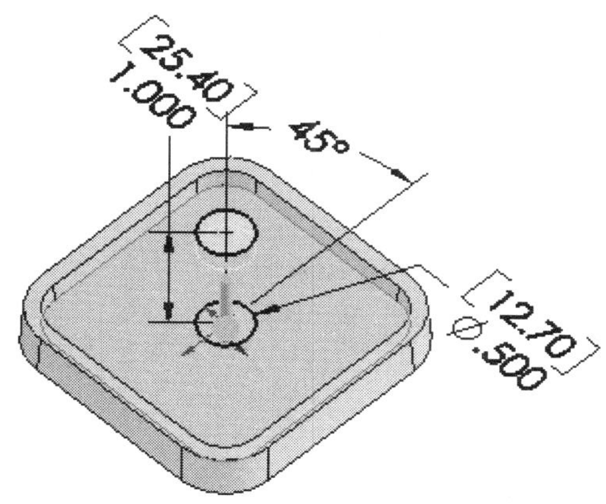

Return to the MOLD-TOOLING part.
600) Press **Ctrl-Tab**.

Scale:

The Scale feature increases or decreases the part's volume by a specified factor. The hot thermoplastic utilized in this part, cools during the molding process, hardens and shrinks. Increase the part with the Scale feature to compensate for shrinkage.

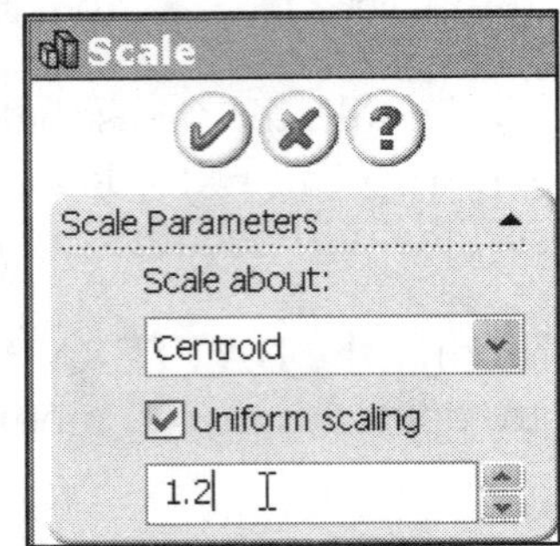

Insert the Scale.

601) Click **Scale** Scale from the Mold toolbar. Enter **1.2** for Scale Factor.

602) Click **OK** from the Scale PropertyManager.

Parting Lines:

The Parting Lines are the boundary between the core and cavity surfaces. The Parting Lines create the edges of the molded part. The Parting Lines consist of the bottom eight edges.

Insert the Parting Lines.

603) Click **Parting Lines** Parting Lines from the Mold toolbar.

604) Click the **Temporary Axis** displayed through the center hole for the Direction of Pull.

605) Click **Reverse Direction** if required. The direction arrow points upward.

606) Enter **1** for Draft Angle.

607) Click **Draft Analysis**. The Parting Lines box contains the eight bottom edges of the BATTERYPLATE.

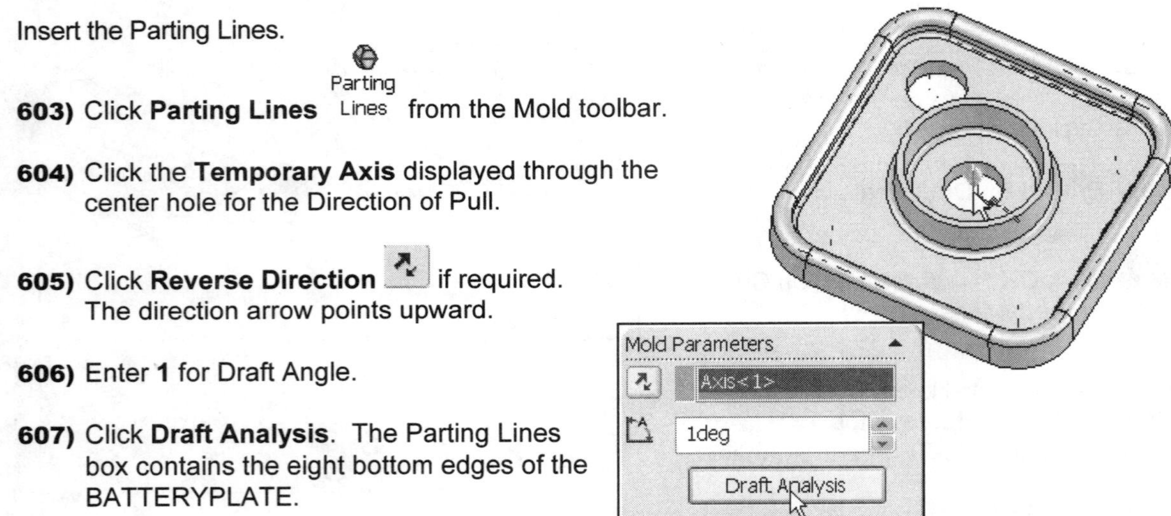

608) Click **OK** from the Parting Line PropertyManager.

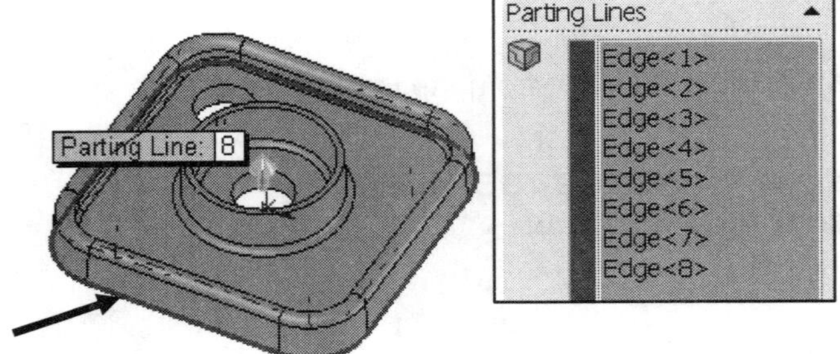

Parting Lines

Hide the Temporary Axes.
609) Click **View**, uncheck **Temporary Axes** from the Main menu.

Shut-off Surfaces:

Holes and windows that penetrate through an entire part require separate mold tooling. A shut-off area in a mold is where two pieces of the mold tooling contact each other. These areas require a Shut-off Surface. There are two Thru Holes in the BATTERYPLATE.

Insert the Shut-off Surfaces.

610) Click **Shut-off Surfaces** Shut-off from the Mold toolbar.

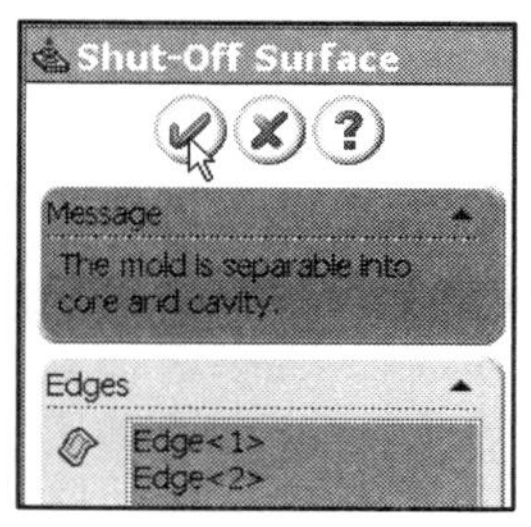

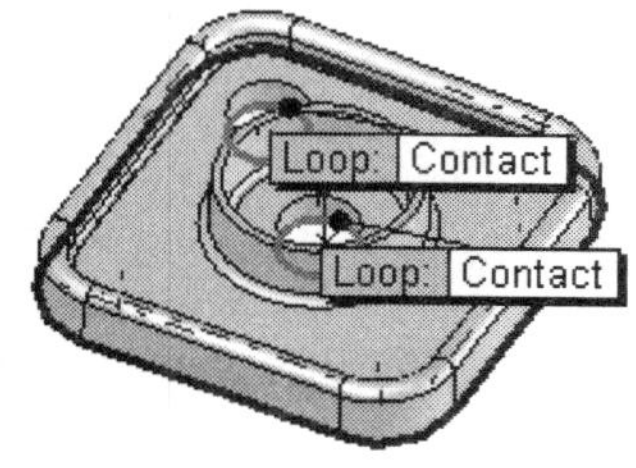

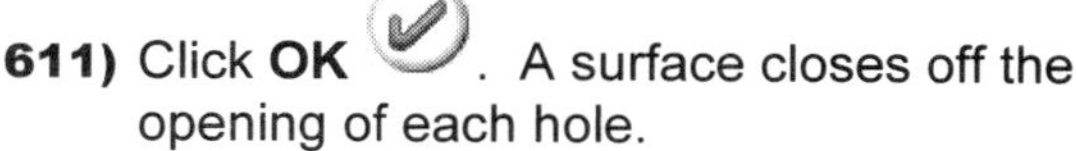

611) Click **OK**. A surface closes off the opening of each hole.

Parting Surface:

A Parting Surface is utilized to separate the mold tooling components. A Parting Surface extends radial, a specified distance from the Parting Lines. Usually, the surface is normal to the direction of pull for simple molds. The boundary of the Parting Surface must be larger than the profile for the Tooling Split.

Insert the Parting Suface.

612) Click **Parting Surfaces** Parting from the Mold toolbar.

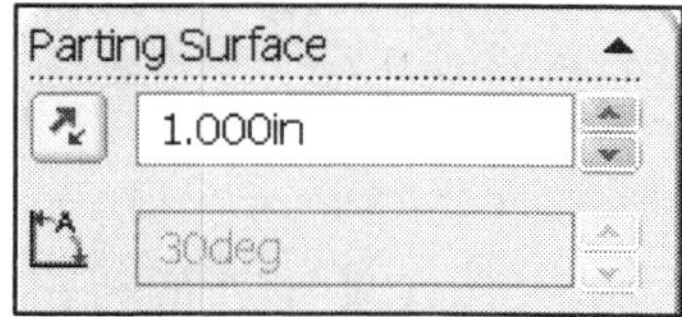

613) Click **Top view**.

614) Enter **1.000 [2.54]** for Distance.

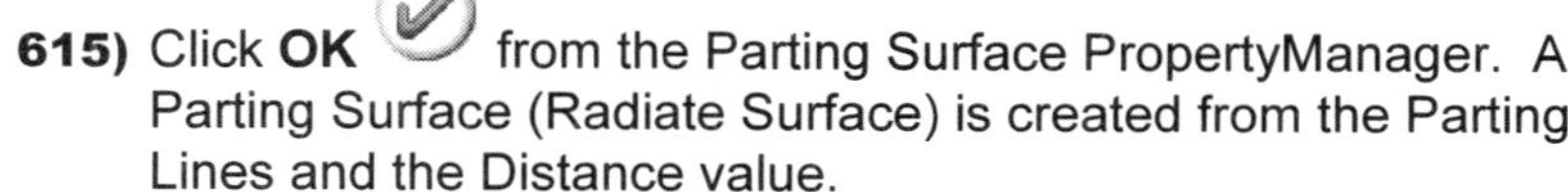

615) Click **OK** from the Parting Surface PropertyManager. A Parting Surface (Radiate Surface) is created from the Parting Lines and the Distance value.

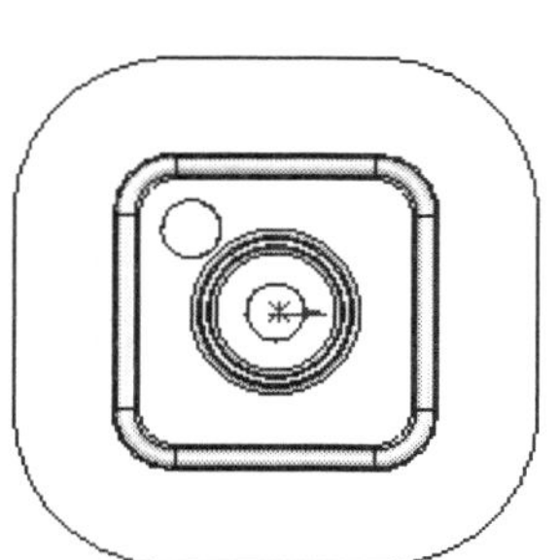

Fit the Model to the Graphics window.
616) Press the **f** key.

617) Click **Save**.

Tooling Split:

The Tooling Split separates the solid bodies from the parting surfaces. The solid bodies become the mold tooling and the molded part. The Tooling Split for the BATTERYPLATE creates two mold base plates named, Tooling Split1 and Tooling Split2.

Insert the Tooling Split.

618) Click **Parting Surface1** in the FeatureManager.

619) Click **Tooling Split** Tooling. Click the **front face** of Parting Surface1.

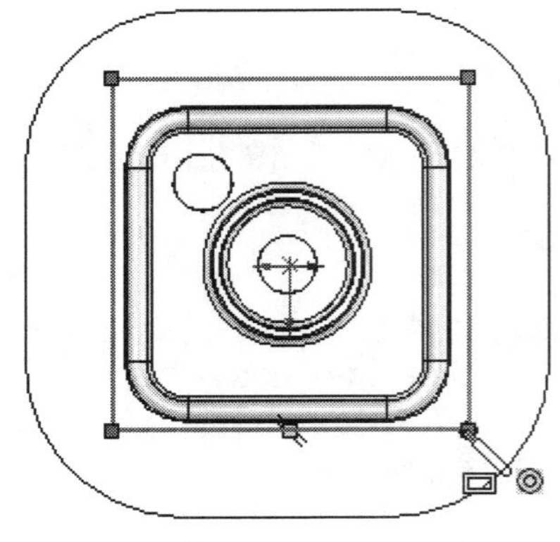

620) Click **Rectangle** Rectan... from the Sketch toolbar.

621) Sketch a **rectangle** between the Parting Surface outside profile and the BATTERYPLATE profile.

622) Click **Centerline** Centerl....

623) Sketch a **diagonal centerline** between the two corner points of the rectangle.

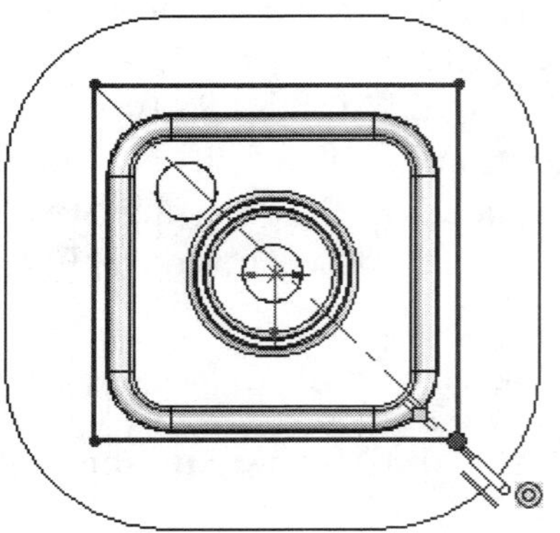

Add a MidPoint Relation.

624) Right-click **Select**. Click the **Origin**.

625) Hold the **Ctrl key down**.

626) Click the **Centerline**. Release the **Ctrl key**.

627) Click **MidPoint** from the Add Relations box.

628) Click **OK** from the Properties PropertyManager.

Add an Equal Relation.

629) Click the **top horizontal line** of the rectangle.

630) Hold the **Ctrl key** down.

631) Click the **vertical line** of the rectangle.

632) Release the **Ctrl key**.

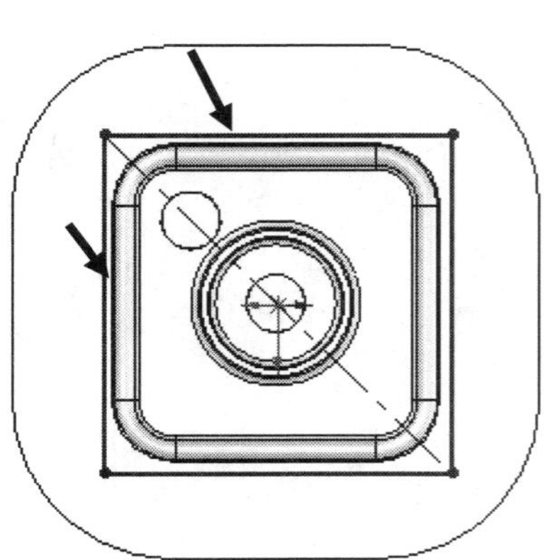

633) Click **Equal** = from the Add Relations box.

634) Click **OK** from the Properties PropertyManager.

Add a dimension.

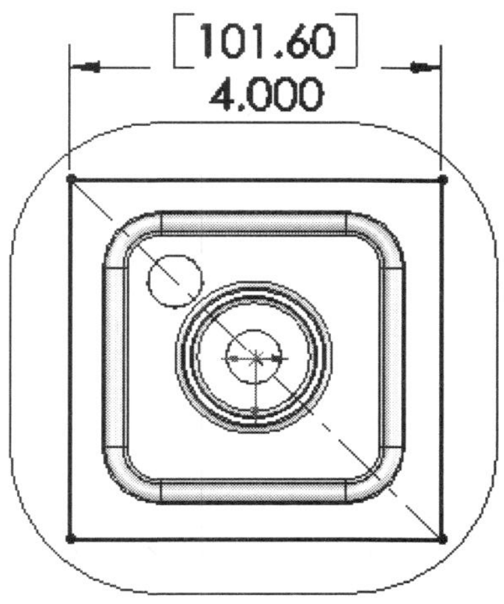

635) Click **Smart Dimension** 

636) Click the **top horizontal line**.

637) Enter **4.000 [101.60]**.

638) Click **Exit Sketch** Exit Sketch.

Enter values for the Block Size.

639) Click **Front view**.

640) Enter **1.000 [25.4]** for Depth in Direction 1.

641) Enter **.500 [12.7]** for Depth in Direction 2.

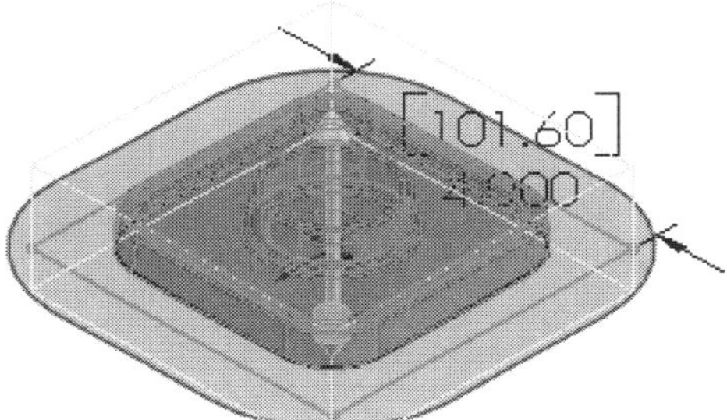

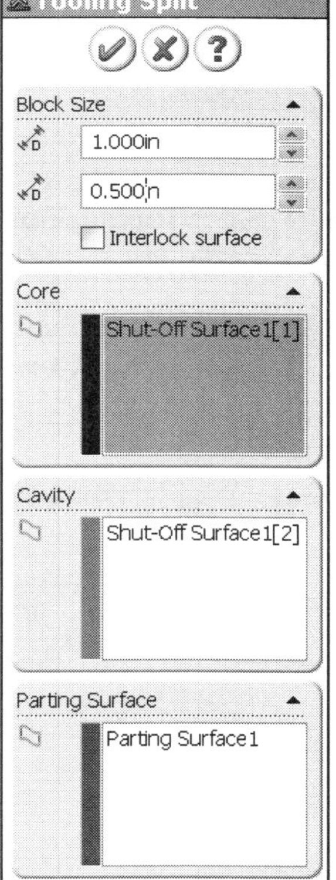

642) Click **Isometric view**.

643) Click **OK** from the Tooling Split PropertyManager.

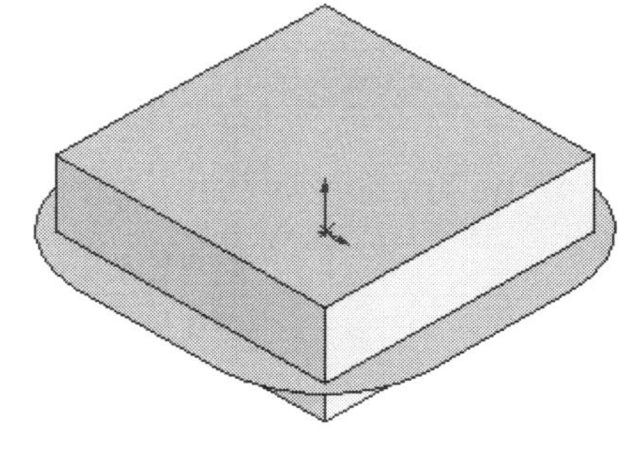

The Mold Tools produce Surface Bodies and Solid Bodies. The Solid Bodies are utilized in an assembly for the actual mold base. The Surface Bodies were utilized as interim features to create the mold tooling parts. Hide the Surface Bodies to display the solid mold tooling parts.

Hide the Surface Bodies.

644) **Expand** Surface Bodies folder in the FeatureManager.

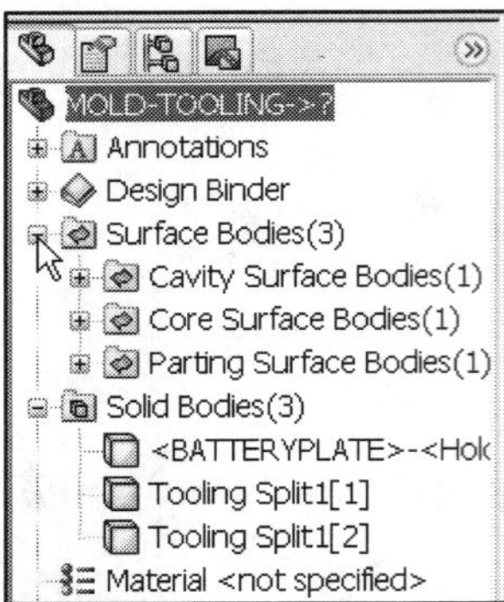

645) Right-click the **Surface Bodies** folder.

646) Click **Hide Bodies**.

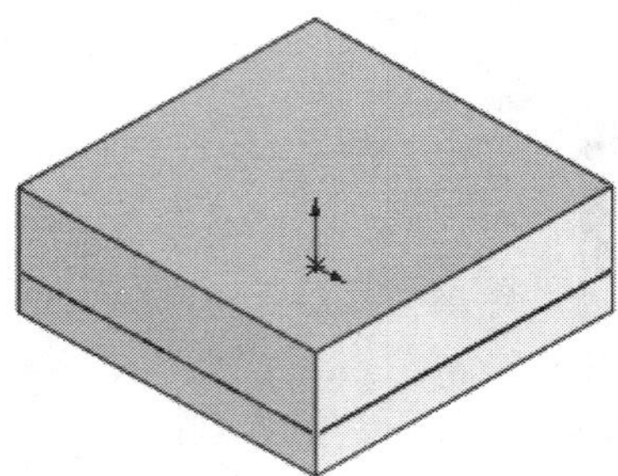

Display the Solid Bodies.

647) **Expand** the Solid Bodies folder in the FeatureManager.

View each entry.

648) Click each **entry** in the Solid Bodies folder.

Separate Tooling Split1.

649) Click **Tooling Split1** from the FeatureManager.

650) Click **Insert**, **Features**, **Move/Copy** Move/Copy... from the Main menu.

651) Click the **Translate/Rotate** Translate/Rotate button.

652) Drag the **vertical axis of the Triad** downward approximately 3inches (75mm) to display the BATTERYPLATE part.

653) Click **OK** .

Separate Tooling Split2.

654) Click **Tooling Split2** in the Graphics window.

655) Click **Insert**, **Features, Move/Copy** from the Main menu.

656) Drag the **vertical axis** of the Triad upward approximately 4inches (100mm) to display the BATTERYPLATE part.

657) Click **OK**.

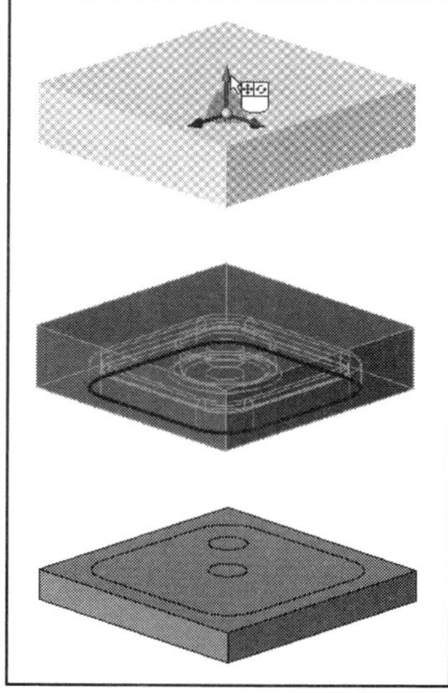

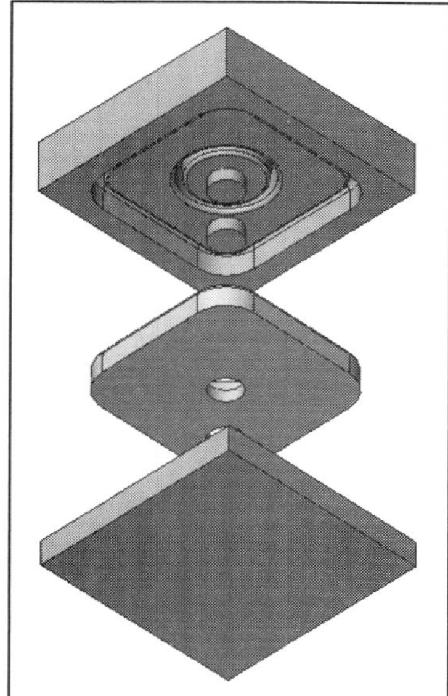

Rotate the view.

658) Click the **Up Arrow key** to display the in inside Tooling Split2 in the Graphics window.

Save the MOLD-TOOLING part.

659) Click **Save**.

660) Click **Yes** to save the referenced part (BATTERYPLATE).

Rename Tooling Split1 and Tooling Split2 to PLATE-A and PLATE-B in your mold base assembly.

Manufacturing Design Issues

For the experienced mold designer, the complete mold base requires additional mold tooling, lines and fittings. Utilize the Solid Bodies, Insert into New Part option to create the MOLD-TOOLING-CAVITY part from Body2 in the Solid Bodies folder.

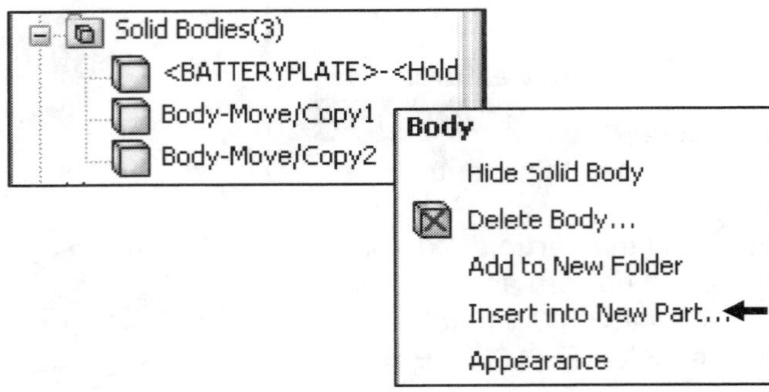

The mold designer works with a material supplier and mold manufacturer. For example, Bohler-Uddeholm provides mold steels in rod, bar and block form. Cutting operations include Milling, Drilling, Sawing, Turning and Grinding. A wrong material selection is a costly mistake.

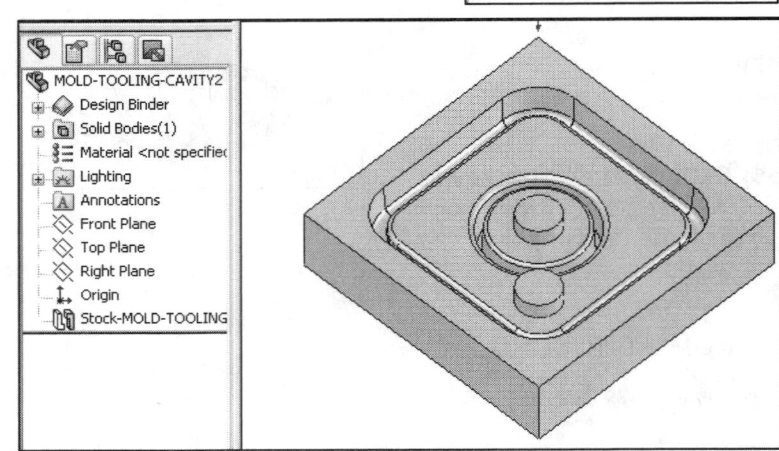

As a designer, you work with the material supplier to determine the best material for the project. For example, a material supplier application engineer asks the following questions:

- What is the plastic material utilized in this application?
- Will the material be corrosive or abrasive?
- Will the mold be textured?
- How important is the surface finish?
- What are the quantities of the part to be produced?
- Are part tolerances held within close limits?
- Have you inserted fillets on all sharp corners?
- Did you utilize adequate wall thickness and overall dimensions?

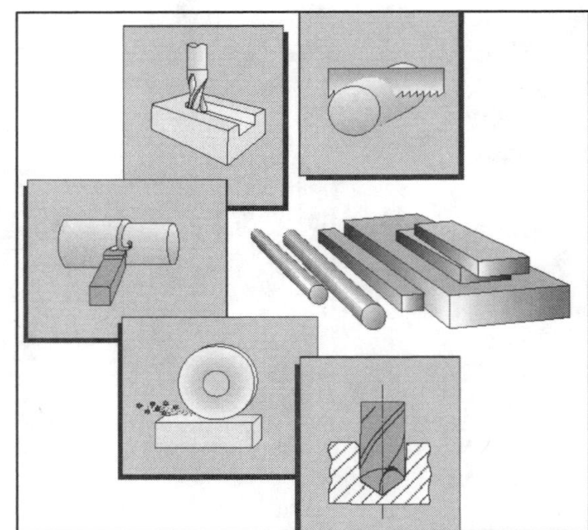

Cutting Operations for Tool Steels
Courtesy of Bohler-Uddeholm
www.bucorp.com

You send an eDrawing of your MOLD-TOOLING part for advice to the application engineer. Take the time early in the design process to determine the tooling material.

Mold Analysis Issues with MoldflowXpress

The mold designer utilizes a variety of analysis tools. SolidWorks Mold Tools contains the MoldflowXpress Analysis Wizard Moldflow... Analysis ... . MoldflowXpress is an entry-level plastics simulation filling tool that predicts if an injection molded part will fill with molten plastic. The designer enters criteria based on the part geometry, plastic injection location, type of plastic, melt temperature, mold temperature and injection time.

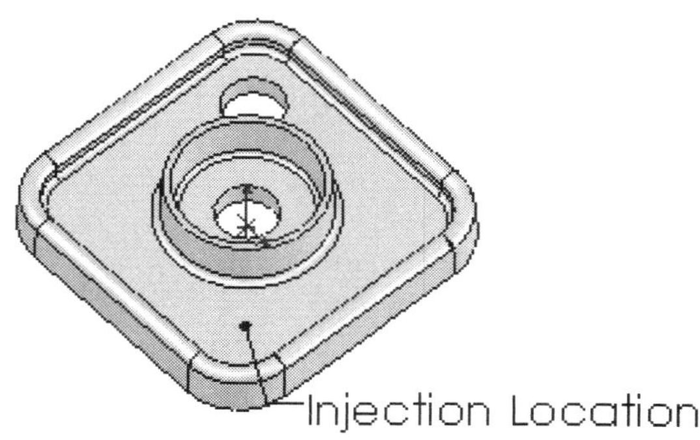

The analysis provides the designer feedback to minimize part wall thickness, reduce product development cycle time and optimize plastic part designer for manufacturing. MoldflowXpress also allows the designer to vary the Injection Location.

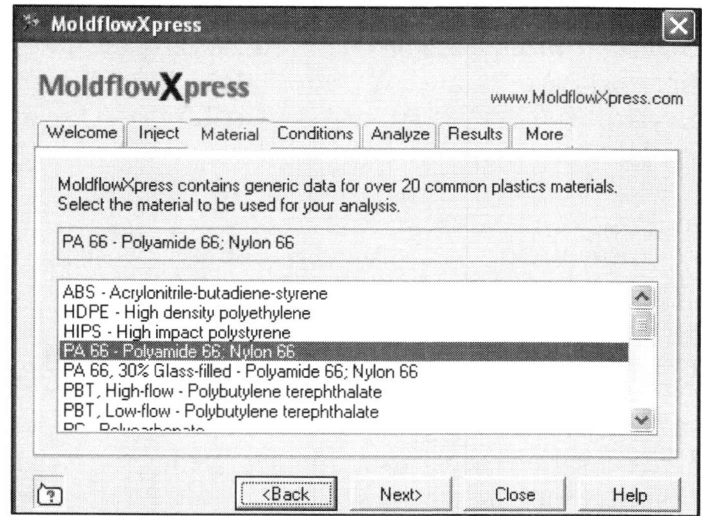

MoldflowXpress calculates a Fill time of 1.71 seconds for the BATTERYPLATE utilizing PA66 and default processing temperature conditions. The design engineer inserted a Shell feature on the bottom face to remove material. The resulting Fill time was .81 seconds. The part volume decreased from 1.73 cu in to 1.16 cu in.

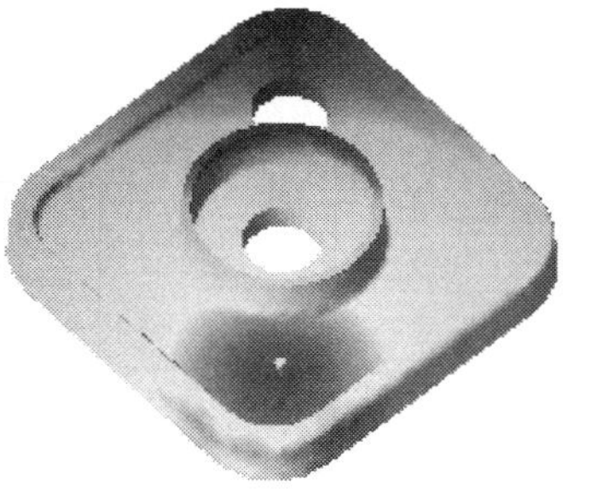

Original design
Fill time 1.71 seconds

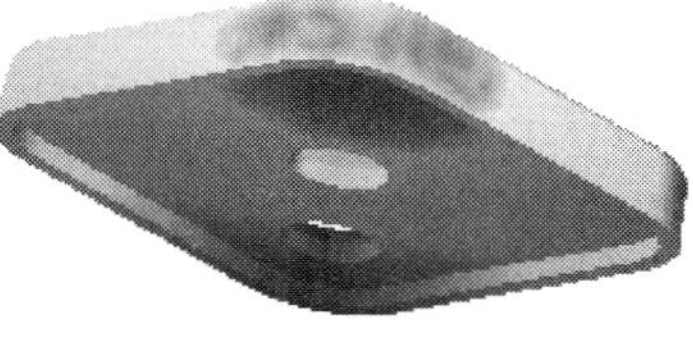

Shell feature
Fill time .81 seconds

Utilize MoldflowXpress early in the design process to reduce time and material cost.

Additional information on the Mold Tools is available in SolidWorks Help Topics. Keywords: Mold Tools, Draft, Draft Analysis.

MoldFlowXpress Help button is available in the Wizard dialog box.

Review the multimedia CD, Project 4, for additional information on MoldFlowXpress.

Refer to Help, Online Tutorial, Mold Design exercise and MoldflowXpress exercise for additional information.

Project Summary

You are designing a FLASHLIGHT assembly that is cost effective, serviceable and flexible for future design revisions. The FLASHLIGHT assembly consists of various parts. The BATTERY, BATTERYPLATE, LENS and BULB parts were modeled in this project.

Project 4 concentrated on the Extruded Base feature and the Revolved Base feature. The Extruded Base feature required a Sketch Plane, Sketch Profile and End Condition (Depth). The BATTERY and BATTERYPLATE parts incorporated an Extruded Base feature: A Revolved feature requires a sketch plane, sketch profile, axis of revolution and an angle of rotation.

You also utilized the Extruded Boss/Base, Extruded Cut, Fillet, Chamfer, Revolved Cut, Revolved Cut-Thin, Shell, Hole Wizard, Dome and Circular Pattern features.

You addressed the following Sketch tools in this project: Sketch, Smart Dimension, Line, Rectangle, Circle, Tangent Arc and Centerline. You addressed additional Sketch tools that utilized existing geometry: Add Relations, Display/Delete Relations, Mirror Entities, Convert Entities and Offset Entities. Geometric Relations were utilized to build symmetry into the sketches.

The BATTERYPLATE utilized Mold Tools to develop the core and cavity tooling plates required in the manufacturing process. Plastic parts require Draft. The Draft Analysis tool determines areas of positive and negative draft. Features were modified to accommodate the manufacturing process.

Practice these concepts with the project exercises. The other parts for the FLASHLIGHT assembly are addressed in Project 5.

Project Terminology

Assembly: An assembly is a document in which parts, features and other assemblies (sub-assemblies) are put together. The filename extension for a SolidWorks assembly file name is .SLDASM. The FLASHLIGHT is an assembly. The BATTERY is a part in the FLASHLIGHT assembly.

Centerpoint Arc: An arc Sketch tool that requires a centerpoint, start point and end point.

Chamfer: A feature that bevels sharp edges or faces by a specified distance and angle or by two specified distances.

Circular Pattern: A feature that creates a pattern of features or faces in a circular array about an axis.

Convert Entities: A sketch tool that projects one or more curves onto the current sketch plane. Select an edge, loop, face, curve, or external sketch contour, set of edges, or set of sketch curves.

Cursor Feedback: Feedback is provided by a symbol attached to the cursor arrow indicating your selection.

Dimension: A value indicating the size of feature geometry.

Dimensioning Standard: A set of drawing and detailing options developed by national and international organizations. A few key dimensioning standard options are: ANSI, ISO, DIN, JIS, BSI, GOST and GB.

Dome: A feature used to add a spherical or elliptical dome to a selected face.

Draft angle: A draft angle is the degree of taper applied to a face. Draft angles are usually applied to molds or castings.

Edit Feature: A tool utilized to modify existing feature parameters. Right-click the feature in the FeatureManager. Click Edit Feature.

Edit Sketch: A tool utilized to modify existing sketch geometry. Right-click the feature in the FeatureManager. Click Edit Sketch.

Extruded Boss/Base: A feature that adds material utilizing a 2D sketch profile and a depth perpendicular to the sketch plane. The Base feature is the first feature in the part.

Extruded Cut: A feature that removes material utilizing a 2D sketch profile and a depth perpendicular to the sketch plane.

Features: Features are geometry building blocks. Features add or remove material. Features are created from sketched profiles or from edges and faces of existing geometry.

Fillet: A feature that rounds sharp edges or faces by a specified radius.

Geometric relationships: Relations between geometry that are captured as you sketch.

Hole Wizard: The Hole Wizard feature is used to create specialized holes in a solid. The HoleWizard creates simple, tapped, counterbore and countersunk holes using a step-by-step procedure.

Mold Tools: The options available to develop the Parting Lines, Parting Surfaces and Shut-off Surfaces to create the core and cavity plates and additional mold tooling.

Menus: Menus provide access to the commands that the SolidWorks software offers.

Mirror Entities: A sketch tool that mirrors sketch geometry to the opposite side of a sketched centerline.

Mouse Buttons: The left and right mouse buttons have distinct meanings in SolidWorks. The left mouse button is utilized to select geometry. The right-mouse button is utilized to invoke commands.

Offset Entities: A sketch tool utilized to create sketch curves offset by a specified distance. Select sketch entities, edges, loops, faces, curves, set of edges or a set of curves.

Part: A part is a single 3D object that consists of various features. The filename extension for a SolidWorks part is .SLDPRT.

Plane: Planes are flat and infinite. Planes are represented on the screen with visible edges.

Relation: A relation is a geometric constraint between sketch entities or between a sketch entity and a plane, axis, edge or vertex. Utilize Add Relations to manually connect related geometry.

Revolved Base/Boss: A feature used to add material by revolutions. A Revolved feature requires a centerline, a sketch on a sketch plane and an angle of revolution. The sketch is revolved around the centerline.

Revolved Cut: A feature used to remove material by revolutions. A Revolved Cut requires a centerline, a sketch on a sketch plane and angle of revolution. The sketch is revolved around the centerline.

Shell: A feature used to remove faces of a part by a specified wall thickness.

Silhouette Edge: The imaginary edge of a cylinder or cylindrical face.

Sketch: The name to describe a 2D profile is called a sketch. 2D sketches are created on flat faces and planes within the model. Typical geometry types are lines, arcs, rectangles, circles, polygons and ellipses.

Spline: A complex sketch curve.

States of a Sketch: There are four key states that are utilized in this Project:

- Fully Defined: Has complete information, (Black).
- Over Defined: Has duplicate dimensions, (Red).
- Under Defined: There is inadequate definition of the sketch, (Blue).
- Selected: The current selected entity, (Green).

Template: A template is the foundation of a SolidWorks document. A Part Template contains the Document Properties such as: Dimensioning Standard, Units, Grid/Snap, Precision, Line Style and Note Font.

Thin option: The Thin option for the Revolved Boss and Revolved Cut utilizes an open sketch to add or remove material, respectively.

Toolbars: The toolbars provide shortcuts enabling you to access the most frequently used commands.

Trim Entities: A sketch tool used to delete selected sketched geometry.

Units: Used in the measurement of physical quantities. Decimal inch dimensioning and Millimeter dimensioning are the two types of common units specified for engineering parts and drawings.

Questions

1. Identify and describe the function of the following features:

Fillet	Extruded Cut	Draft	Scale
Extruded Boss	Revolved Base	Shell	Move/Copy
Revolved Cut Thin	Circular Pattern	Hole Wizard	Parting Surface

2. True of False. Design intent exists only in the sketch.
3. Describe a symmetric relation.
4. Describe an angular dimension.
5. What is a draft angle? When is a draft angle used? Provide an example.
6. When do you use the Mirror command? Utilize the SolidWorks Online Users Guide to determine the difference between the Sketch Mirror and the Dynamic Mirror Sketch tool.
7. What is a Spline?
8. How do you add the Shape feature icon to the Feature Toolbar?
9. How do you create a Short Cut key to Show/Hide Planes.
10. For a simple mold, describe the procedure to create the core and cavity mold tooling.
11. Identify the following Features.

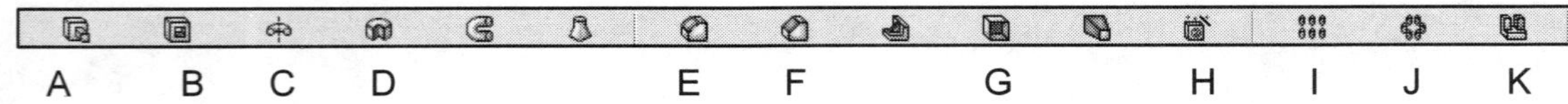

12. Identify the following Sketch Tools.

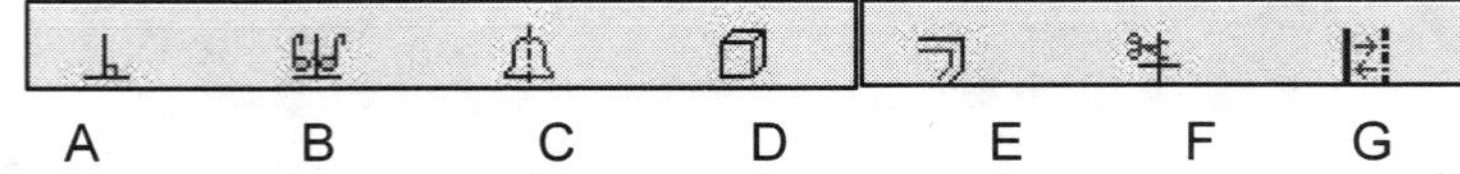

13. Identify the following Mold Tools.

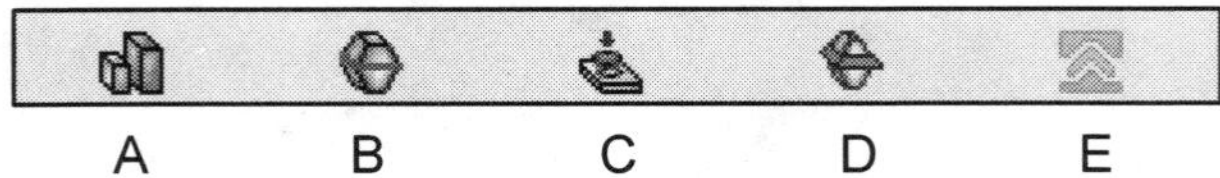

Exercises

Exercise 4.1: AIR RESERVOIR SUPPORT Assembly.

Create the AIR RESERVOIR SUPPORT assembly and components.

Create three new parts:

- FLAT PLATE.
- IM15-MOUNT.
- ANGLE BRACKET.

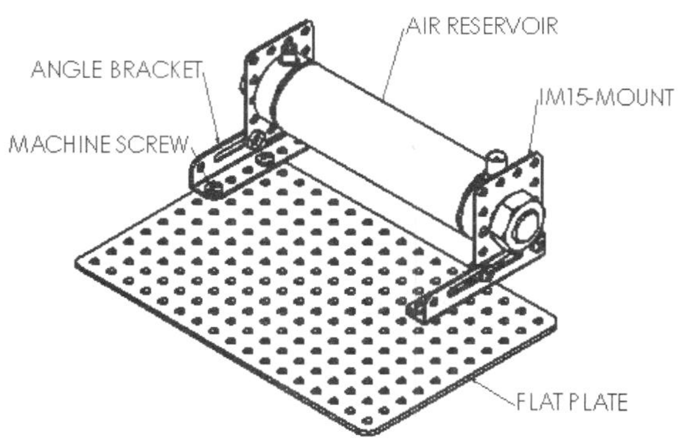

AIR RESERVOIR SUPPORT ASSEMBLY
Courtesy of Gears Educational Systems & SMC Corporation of America

The AIR RESERVOIR assembly is a purchased part. The assembly file is located in the CD-ENGDESIGN-W-SW2006 folder, or can be downloaded from Gears Educational Systems (www.gearseds.com).

- Two M15-MOUNT parts and two ANGLE-BRACKET parts hold the AIR RESERVOIR.
- The ANGLE-BRACKET parts are fastened to the FLAT-PLATE.

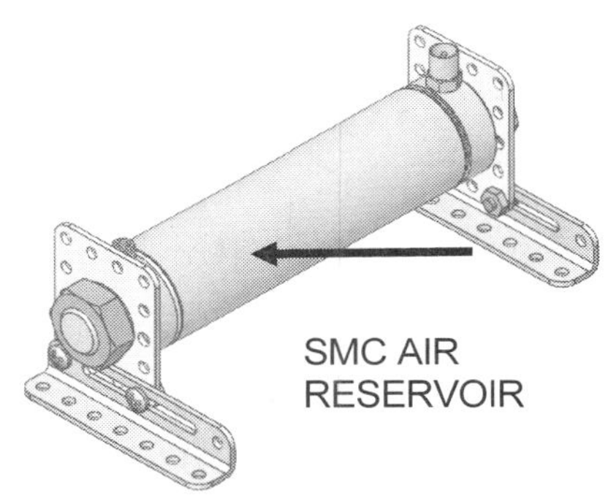

AIR RESERVOIR SUPPORT Assembly
Courtesy of Gears Educational Systems & SMC Corporation of America

Exercise 4.1a: FLAT PLATE Part and Drawing.

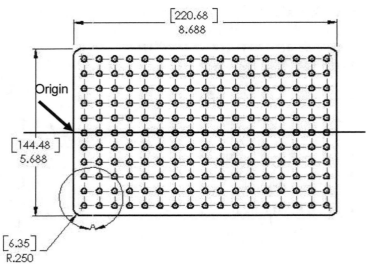

[220.68]
8.688
Origin
[144.48]
5.688
[6.35]
R.250

- Create the FLAT PLATE Part on the Top Plane. The FLAT PLATE is machined from 0.090 [2.3mm] Aluminum plate stock. The default units are inches. The default units are inches.
- The 8.688[220.68mm] x 5.688[144.48mm] FLAT PLATE contains a Linear Pattern of ∅.190[4.83mm] Thru Holes.
- The Holes are equally spaced, .500[12.70mm] apart. Utilize Geometric Pattern for the Linear Pattern Option.

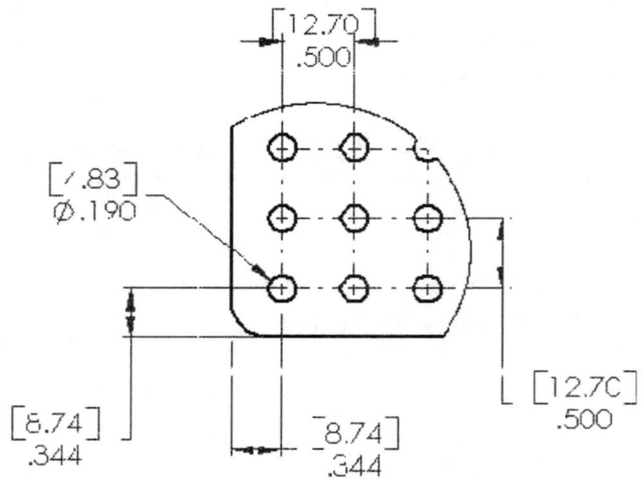

- Enter the FLAT PLATE Part Number in the Configuration Manager.
- Right-click Default. Click Properties.
- Enter GIDS-SC-10002 for Part number displayed when used in bill of materials.
- Select the User Specified Name from the list box.
- Click the Custom button from the Configuration Properties dialog box.

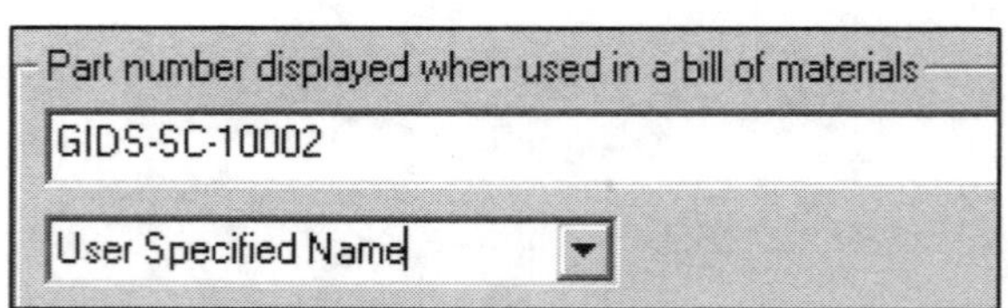

- Enter FLAT PLATE for Description.
- Create a FLAT PLATE drawing.

Exercise 4.1b: IM15-MOUNT Part and Drawing.

Create the IM15-MOUNT Part on the Right Plane. The IM15-MOUNT Part is machined from 0.060 [1.5mm] Stainless Steel flat stock. The default units are inches.

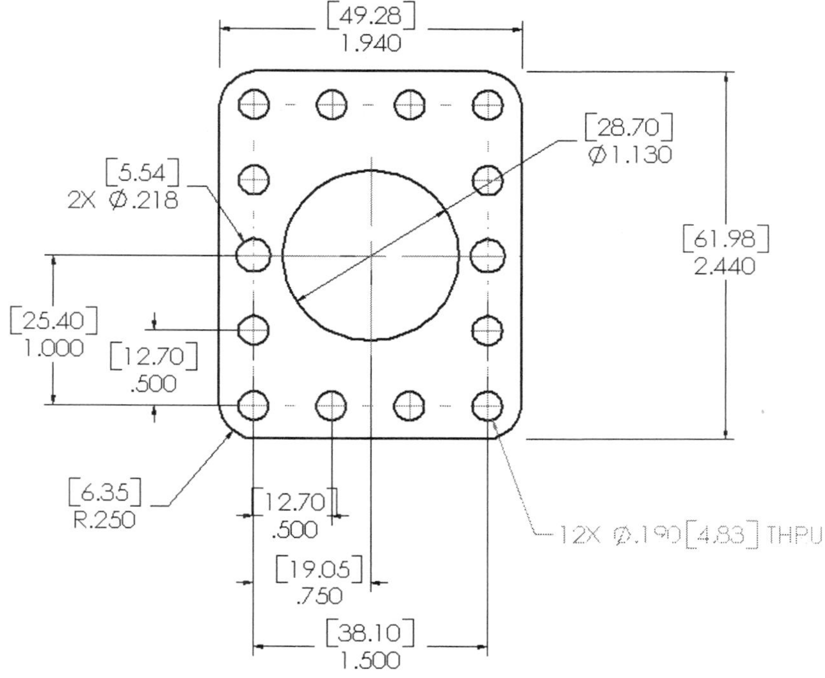

- Enter the IM15-MOUNT part number in the Configuration Manager.
- Right-click Default.
- Click Properties.
- Enter GIDS-SC-10009 for Part number displayed when used in bill of materials.

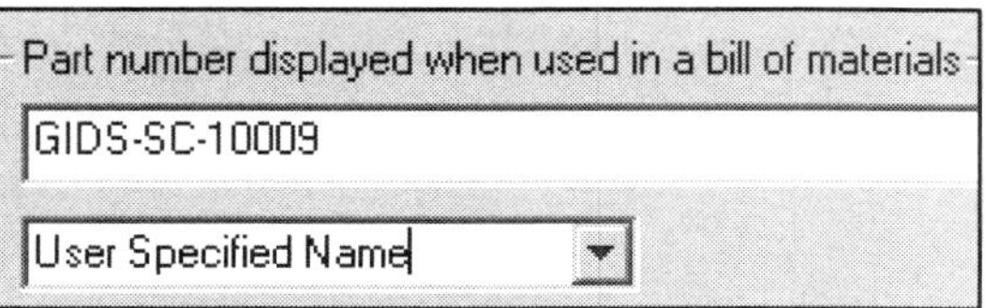

- Select User Specified Name from the list box.
- Click the Custom button from the Configuration Properties dialog box. Enter IM15 MOUNT for Description.
- Create IM15 MOUNT drawing.

Exercise 4.1c: ANGLE BRACKET 7-HOLE Part.

Create the ANGLE BRACKET Part. The Base Extrude feature is sketched with an L-Shaped profile on the Right Plane.

The ANGLE BRACKET Part is machined from 0.060 [1.5mm] Stainless Steel flat stock. The default units are inches.

- Create the Base Feature.
- Use the Mid Plane for Direction1 End Condition.

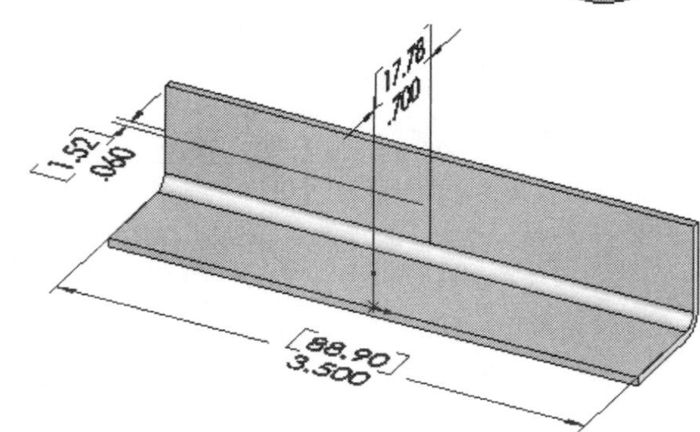

- Create the first Extruded Cut on the Top view for the hole.

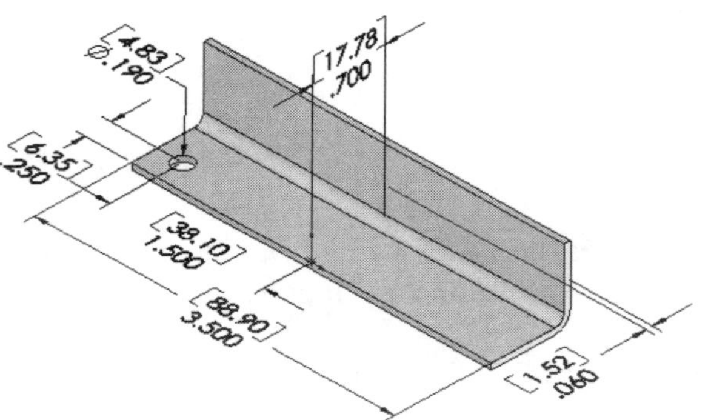

- Use the Linear Pattern Feature to create six additional holes.

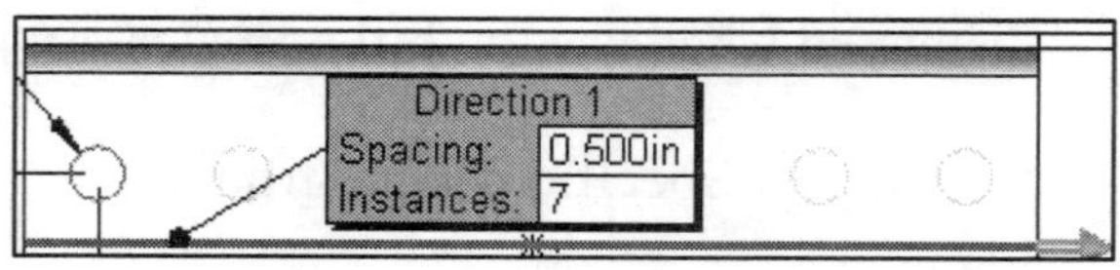

- Add Fillets to the four edges.

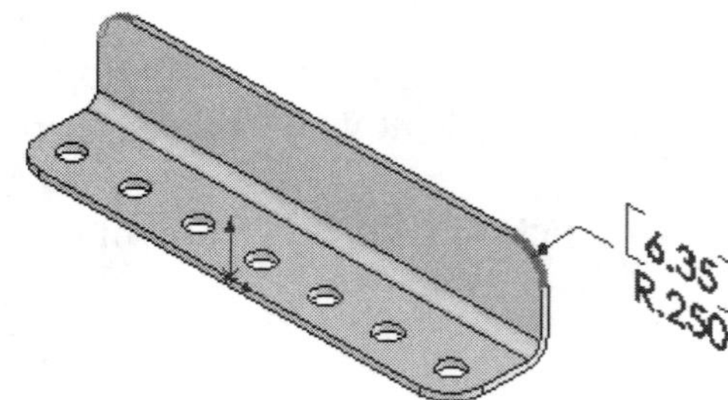

- Create the second Extruded Cut.

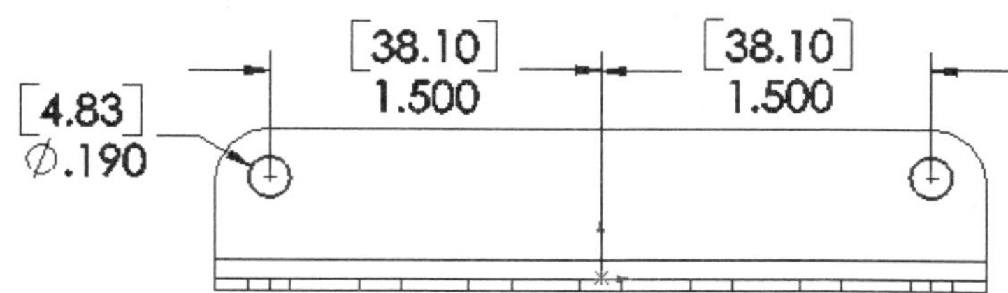

- Create the Center slot.

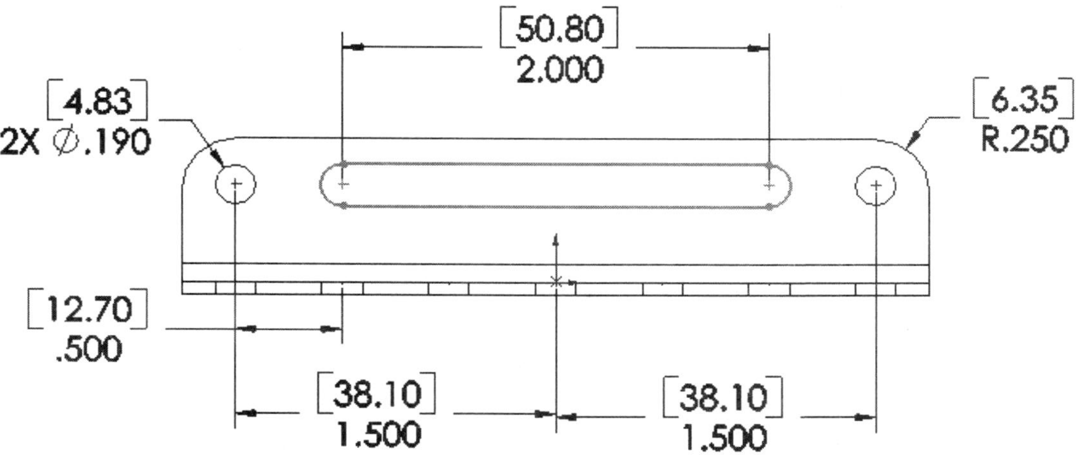

- Enter the ANGLE BRACKET part number in the Configuration Manager.
- Right-click Default. Click Properties.
- Enter GIDS-SC-10007 for Part number.
- Select User Specified Name from the list box.
- Click the Custom button from the Configuration Properties dialog box.
- Enter ANGLE BRACKET 7 HOLE for Description.

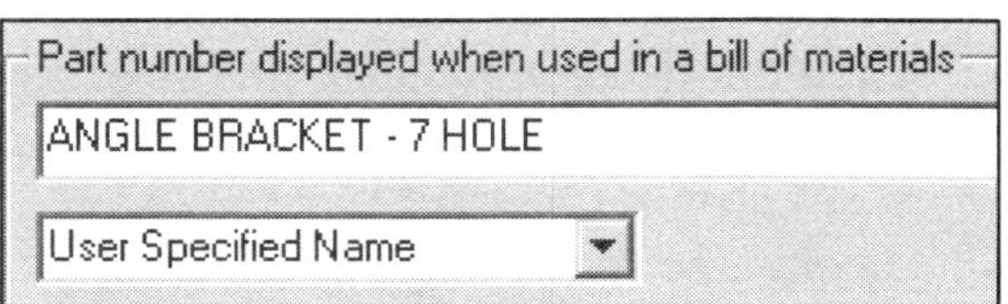

Exercise 4.1d: ANGLE BRACKET 7 HOLE Drawing and eDrawing.

Part 1: Create a new drawing named ANGLE BRACKET 7 - HOLE.

- Utilize the ANGLE BRACKET part created in Exercise 4.1c.
- Create a Front, Top, Righ and Isometric view.
- Add part dimensios.
- Modify the Hole text to contain the total number of holes.

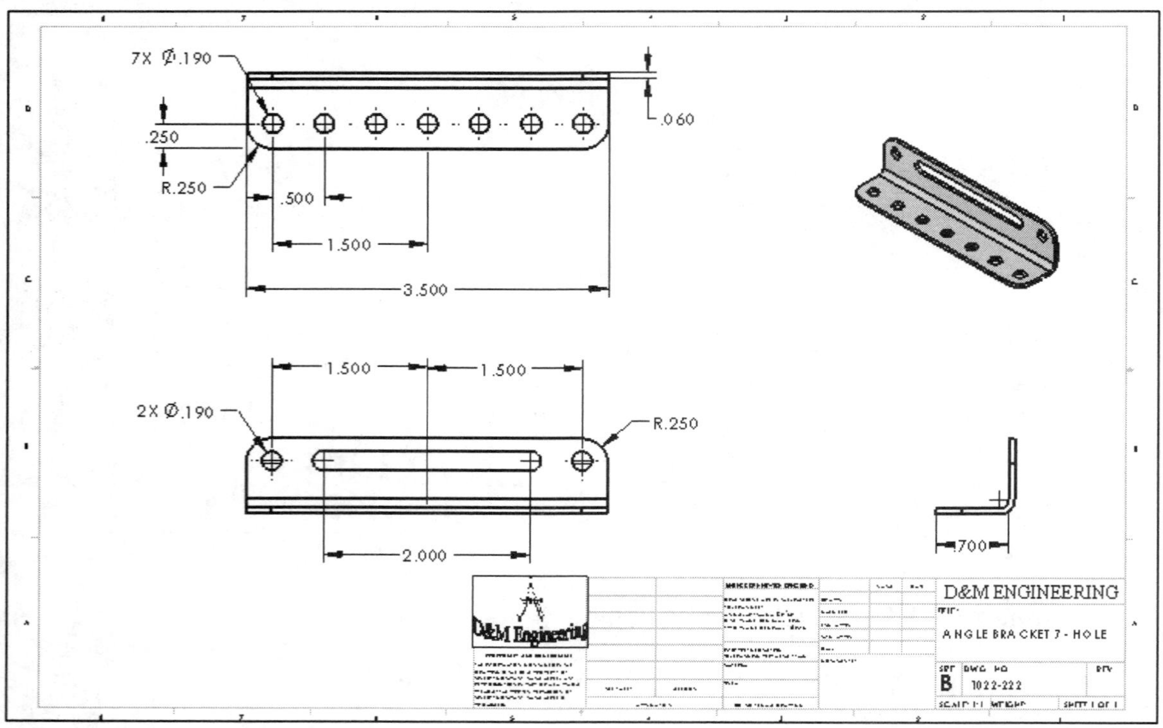

Create an eDrawings file. A SolidWorks eDrawings file is a compressed document that does not require the corresponding part or assembly. SolidWorks eDrawings file is animated to display multiple views and dimensions. Review the eDrawing on-line Help for additional functionality.

- Select Tools, Add-Ins, eDrawings. Click the Animate from the eDrawing toolbar.
- Click Publish eDrawing from the eDrawing toolbar. The Front view of the ANGLE BRACKET drawing is displayed. Click Next.
- Display the remaining views. Click Play.
- Save the ANGLE BRACKET eDrawing.

Exercise 4.1e: MACHINE SCREW Part.

SolidWorks Toolbox is utilized in this project for nuts and washers. Create the 10-24 x 3/8 MACHINE SCREW part. Note: A Simplified version.

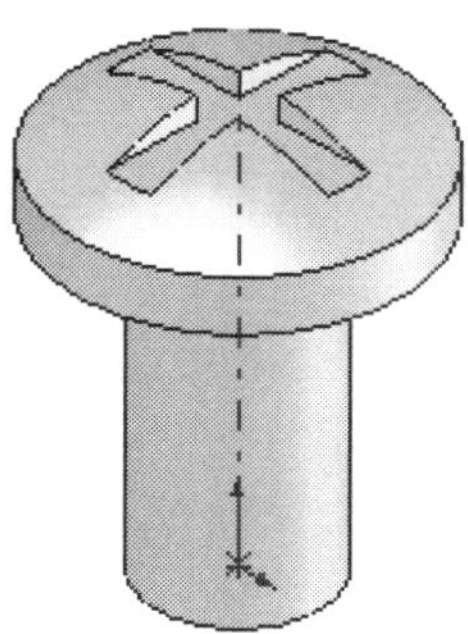

Simplified version

- Sketch a centerline on the Front sketch plane.
- Sketch a closed profile.
- Utilize a Revolved Feature. For metric size, utilize an M4x10 machine screw.

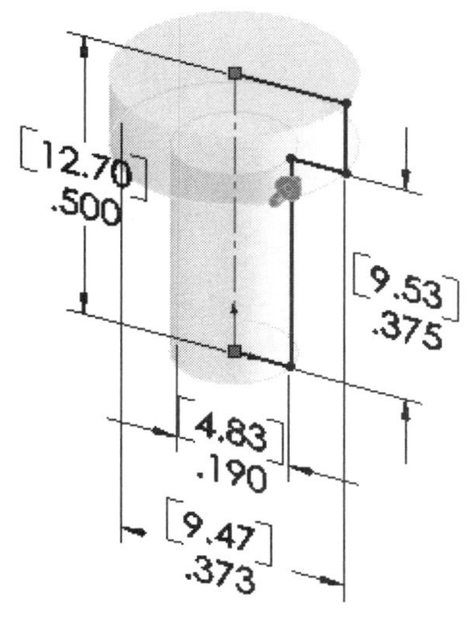

- Edit the Revolved Base Sketch. Use the Tangent Arc tool with Trim Entities. Enter an Arc dimension of .304 [7.72].

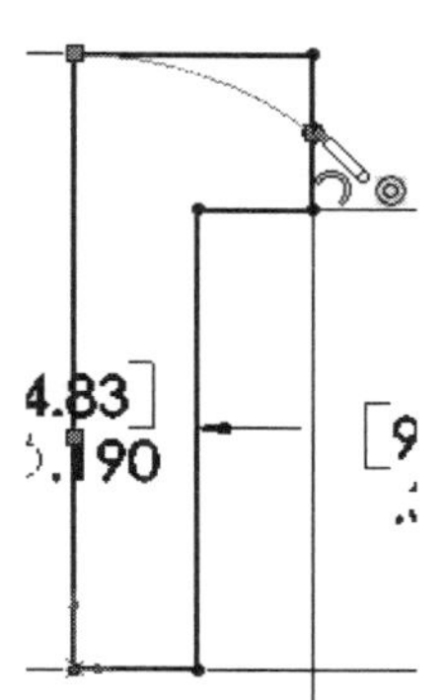

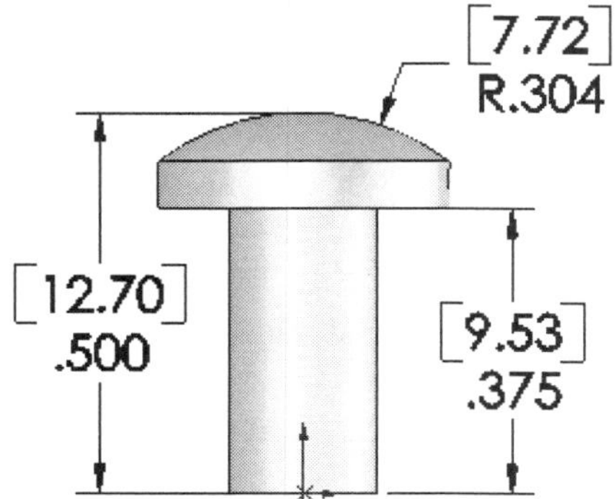

- Utilize an Extruded Cut feature with the Mid Plane option to create the Top Cut.
- The Top Cut is sketched on the Front Plane.

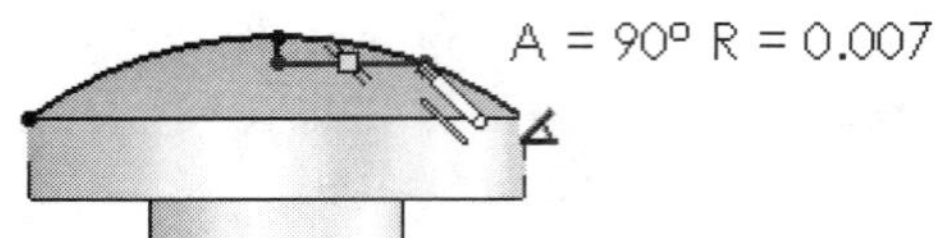

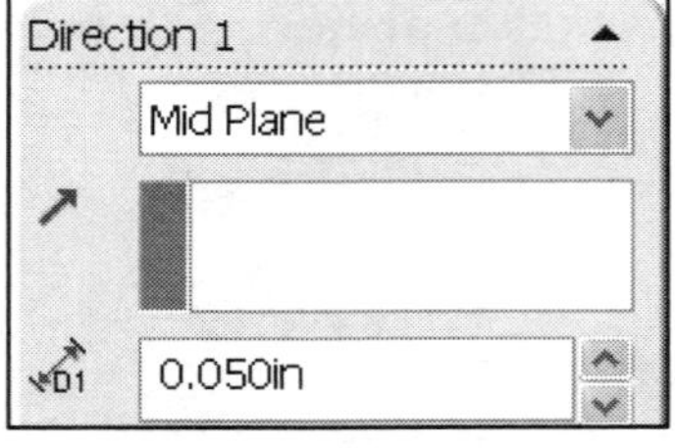

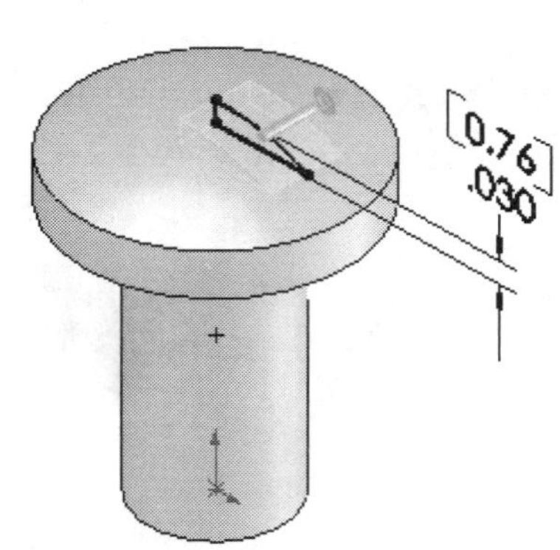

- Utilize the Convert Entities Sketch Tool to extract the left edge of the profile.
- Utilize Circular Pattern and the Temporary Axis to create 4 Top Cuts.

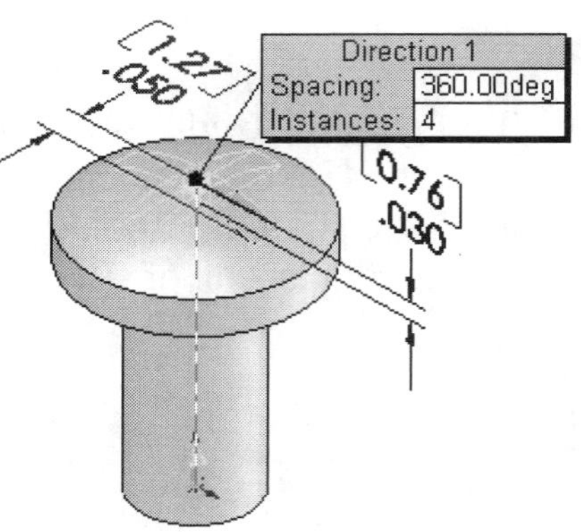

- Use the Fillet Feature on the top circular edge to finish the simplified version of the SCREW part.

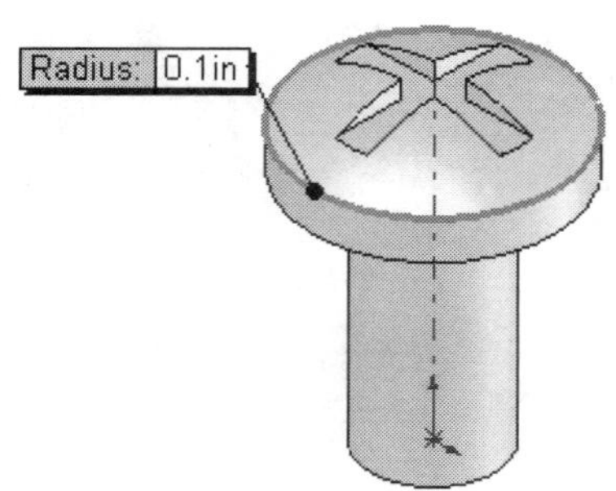

Exercise 4.1g: AIR RESERVOIR SUPPORT Assembly.

Create the AIR RESERVOIR SUPPORT Assembly. Note: There is more than one solution for the Mate types illustrated below.

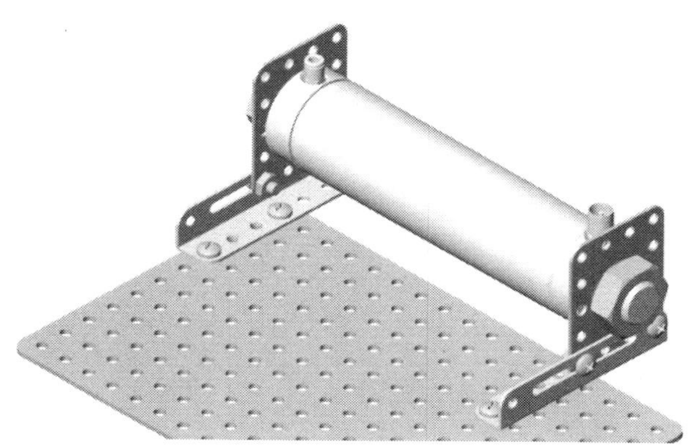

AIR RESERVOIR SUPPORT Assembly
Courtesy of Gears Educational Systems & SMC Corporation of America

The FLAT PLATE is the first component in the AIR RESERVOIR SUPPORT Assembly. Insert the FLAT PLATE. The FLAT PLATE is fixed to the Origin.

- Insert the ANGLE BRACKET.
- Mate the ANGLE BRACKET to the FLAT PLATE. The bottom flat face of the ANGLE BRACKET is coincident to the top face of the FLAT PLATE.

The center hole of the ANGLE BRACKET is concentric to the upper left hole of the FLAT PLATE.

- The first hole of the ANGLE bracket is concentric with the hole in the 8th row, 1st column of the FLAT PLATE.
- Insert the IM15-MOUNT.
- Mate the IM15-MOUNT. The IM15-MOUNT flat back face is coincident to the flat inside front face of the ANGLE BRACKET.
- The bottom right hole of the IM15-MOUNT is concentric with the right hole of the ANGLE BRACKET.

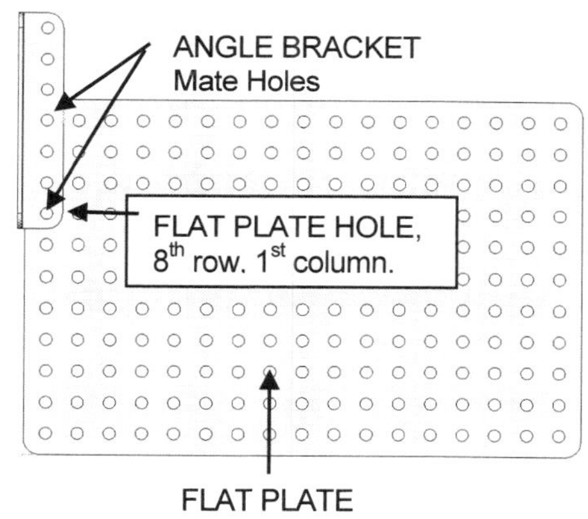

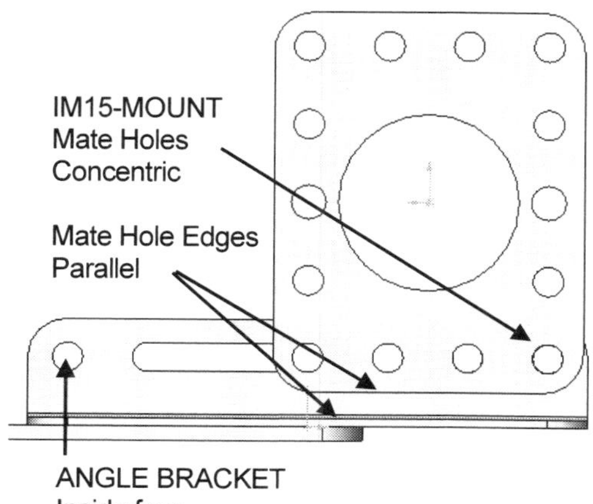

- The bottom edge of the IM15-MOUNT is parallel to bottom edge of the ANGLE BRACKET. Insert the Reservoir Assembly.
- Mate the Reservoir Assembly. The conical face of the Reservoir is concentric to the IM15-MOUNT center hole.

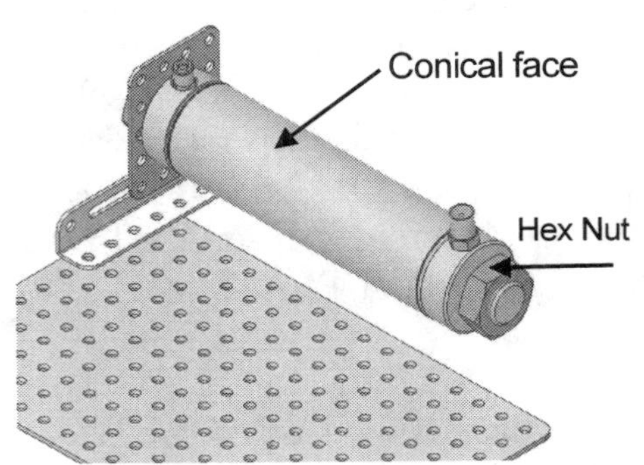

- The left end cap of the Reservoir Assembly is coincident to the front face of the IM15-MOUNT.
- The Hex Nut flat face is parallel to the top face of the FLAT PLATE.
- Insert the second ANGLE BRACKET.
- Mate the ANGLE BRACKET to the FLAT PLATE. The bottom flat face of the ANGLE BRACKET is coincident to the top face of the FLAT PLATE.

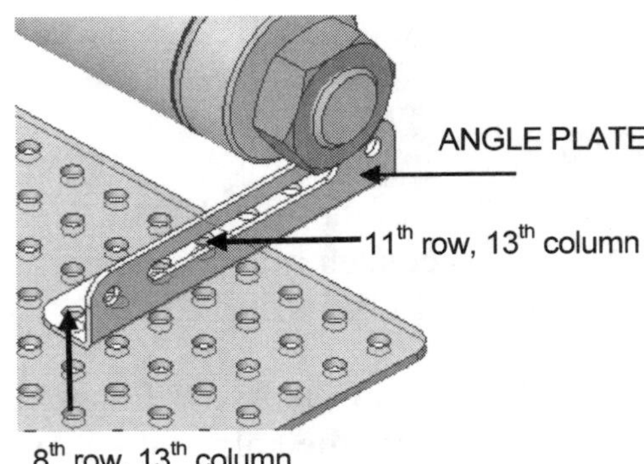

- The center hole of the ANGLE BRACKET is concentric with the hole in the 11th row, 13th column of the FLAT PLATE.
- The first hole of the ANGLE bracket is concentric with the hole in the 8th row, 13th column of the FLAT PLATE.
- Insert the second IM15-MOUNT.
- Mate the IM15-MOUNT to the outside face of the ANGLE BRACKET. The bottom right hole of the IM15-MOUNT is concentric with the right hole of the ANGLE BRACKET.

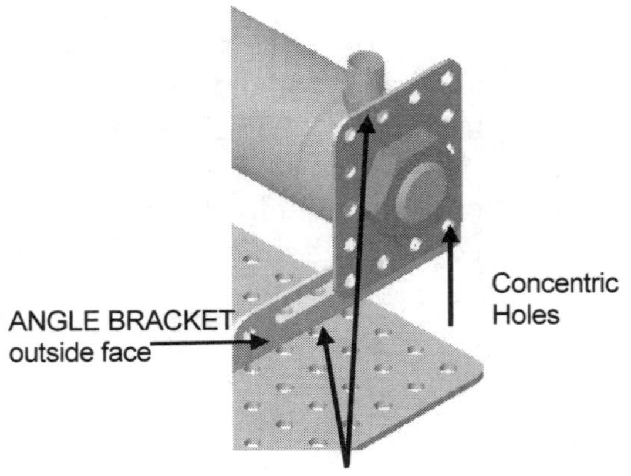

- The top edge of the IM15-MOUNT is parallel to the top edge of the ANGLE BRACKET.
- Save the assembly. The AIR RESERVOIR SUPPORT Assembly is complete.

Exercise 4.1f: RESERVOIR Assembly COSMOSXpress.

The RESERVOIR stores compressed air. Air is filled through a Schrader Valve. A Quick Connect Straight Fitting is utilized to supply air to the Pneumatic Test Module assembly. Quick Connect Fittings allow air tubing to be assembled and disassembled with out removing the fitting.

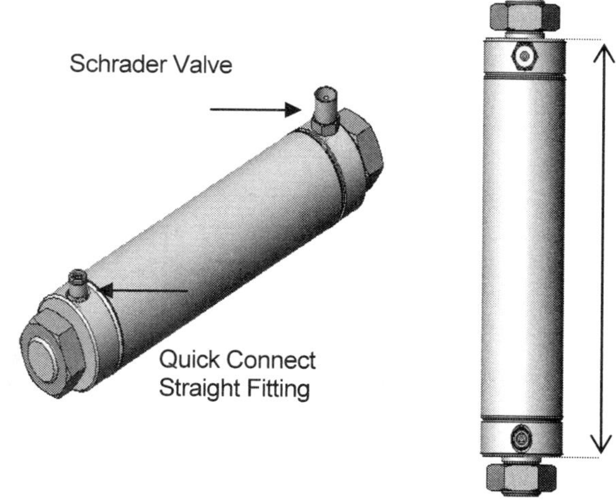

Reservoir and Fittings
Courtesy of SMC Corporation of America and Gears Educational Systems

- Open the part, RESERVOIR from the book's CD.
- Utilize Tools, Measure in the Top view to determine the distance between the two end caps. The distance determines the location of the ANGLE BRACKETS in the AIR RESERVOIR SUPPORT Assembly. The RESERVOIR default units are millimeters.

Engineers and Designers work in metric units and english units. Always verify your units for parts and other engineering data. In pneumatic systems, common units for volume , pressure and temperature are defined in the following table.

Magnitude	Metric Unit (m)	English (e)
Mass	kg g	pound ounce
Length	m m mm	foot yard inch
Temperature	°C	°F
Area, Section	m^2 cm^2	sq.ft sq.inch
Volume	m^3 cm^3 dm^3	cu.yard cu.inch cu.ft.
Volume Flow	m^3n / min dm^3n /min (ℓ/min)	scfm scfm
Force	N	pound force (ℓbf.)
Pressure	bar	ℓbf./sq.inch (psi)

Common Metric and English Units

The ISO unit of pressure is the Pa (Pascal). 1Pa = 1N/m.

Air is a gas. Boyle's Law states that with constant temperature, the pressure of a given mass of a gas is inversely proportional to its volume.

$P_1 / P_2 = V_2 / V_1$

$P_1 \times V_1 = P_2 \times V_2$

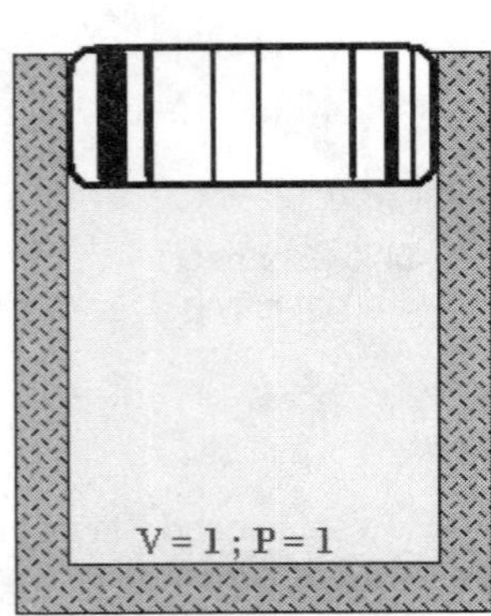

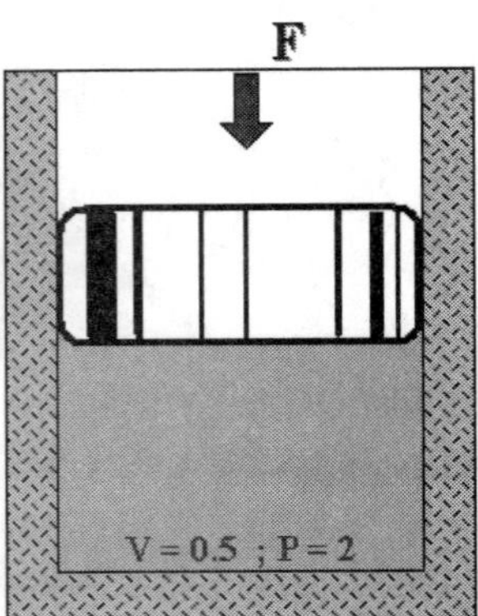

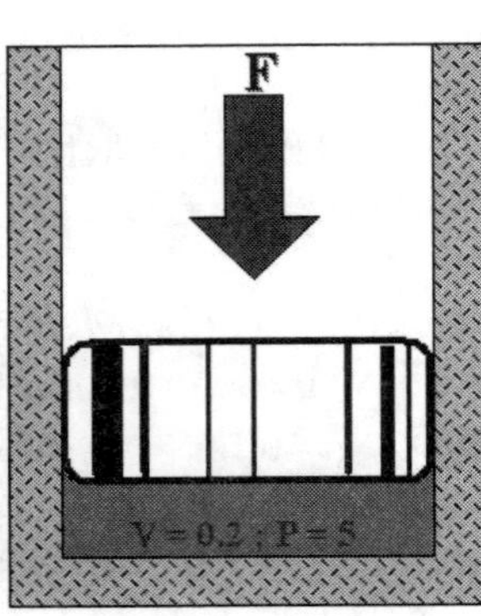

Illustration of Boyle's Law

Utilize COSMOSXpress to perform a simplified static analysis on the Reservoir.

- Open the part, NCMTube. This is the first component in the Reservoir assembly.
- Utilize Save As to copy NCMTube to NCMTube-Analysis. Suppress the Cut-Extrude1 and RodBore features.

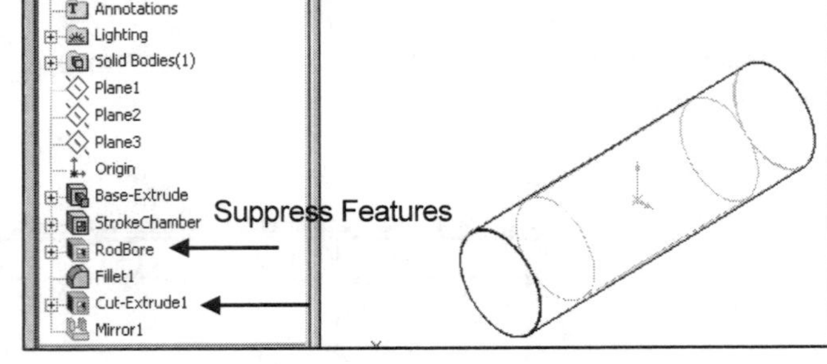

- Run COSMOSXpress.
- Select Aluminum Alloy 2014 for material. Restrain both end circular faces.
- Select Pressure for Type of Load. Select the outside cylindrical face. Enter 100 psi for Pressure Load. The direction arrow points outward.

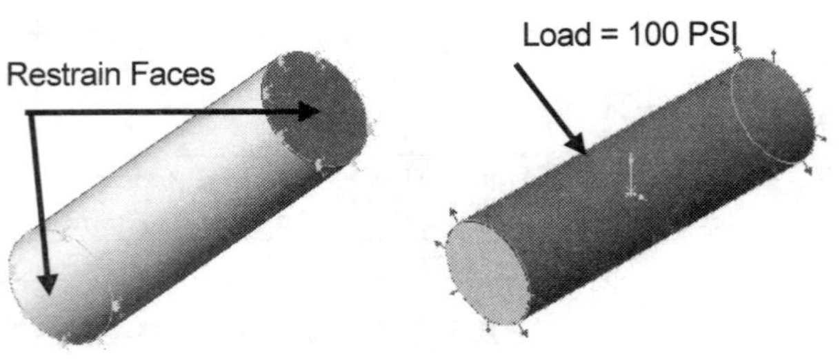

- Run an analysis. The NCMTube is within the Factor of Safety.
- Display the animation of the Deformation Plot and vonMises Stress Plot.

Animation of NCMTube part, magnified 2400 times

The maximum pressure rating on the SMC Air Reservoir is 250psi (1.70Mpa). Explain why the actual values vary from the NCMTube-Analysis part utilized with COSMOSXpress.

Exercise 4.2: EMBOSSED STAMP Part.

Create an EMBOSSED-STAMP with your initials.

- Click the Sketch plane.
- Sketch a Centerline.
- Click Tools, Sketch Entities, Text.
- Enter text.
- Click Help from the Sketch Text PropertyManager to explore additional options.

Exercise 4.3: FLYWHEEL Assembly.

Create a FLYWHEEL assembly. A SHAFT supports the WHEEL. The SHAFT connects two L-BRACKETS.

The L-BRACKETS are mounted to a SLOTPLATE. Use purchased parts to save time and cost. The only dimension provided is the WHEEL diameter.

FLYWHEEL Assembly

Select one WHEEL diameter:

1. 3in.
2. 4in.
3. 100mm

Identify the FLYWHEEL assembly parts.

Create FLYWHEEL Assembly Parts:

- SLOTPLATE.
- BUSHINGS.
- L-BRACKET.
- BOLTS.
- SHAFT.
- Create manual sketches of the SLOTPLATE and L-BRACKET.
- Create the FLYWHEEL Assembly.
- Create the FLYWHEEL Drawing with Bill of Materials.

Exercise 4.4: TRAY and GLASS Parts.

Create the TRAY and GLASS parts.

- Use real objects to determine the overall size and shape of the Base feature.
- Apply Materials.
- Optional: Utilize PhotoWorks Materials.

Exercise 4.6: PUMP Assembly and MOUNTINGPLATE Part.

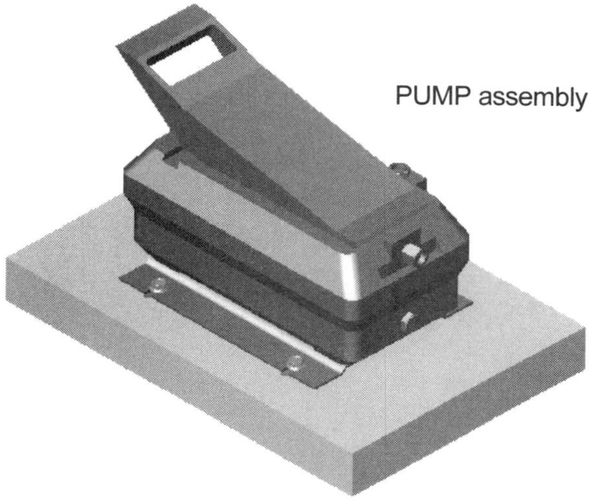

PUMP assembly

Enerpac (A Division of Actuant, Inc.) specializes in the manufacturing and distribution of high-pressure hydraulic tools and cylinders. Enerpac provides solutions for heavy lifting, pressing, pulling, and clamping for the construction, industrial maintenance and manufacturing industries.

Create the PUMP assembly. Locate the Turbo II® air hydraulic pump. Part number: PATG-3102-NB.

- Obtain pump information. Invoke a web browser.
- Enter the URL: http://www.enerpac.com. Select the part number to download the SolidWorks 2006 part file. Note: If you do not have access to the world wide web locate the pump in the Exercise folder on the CD.
- Create a new assembly that contains the MOUNTING PLATE, PUMP and flange bolts. What is the air pressure range required to operate this Turbo II® air-hydraulic pump?

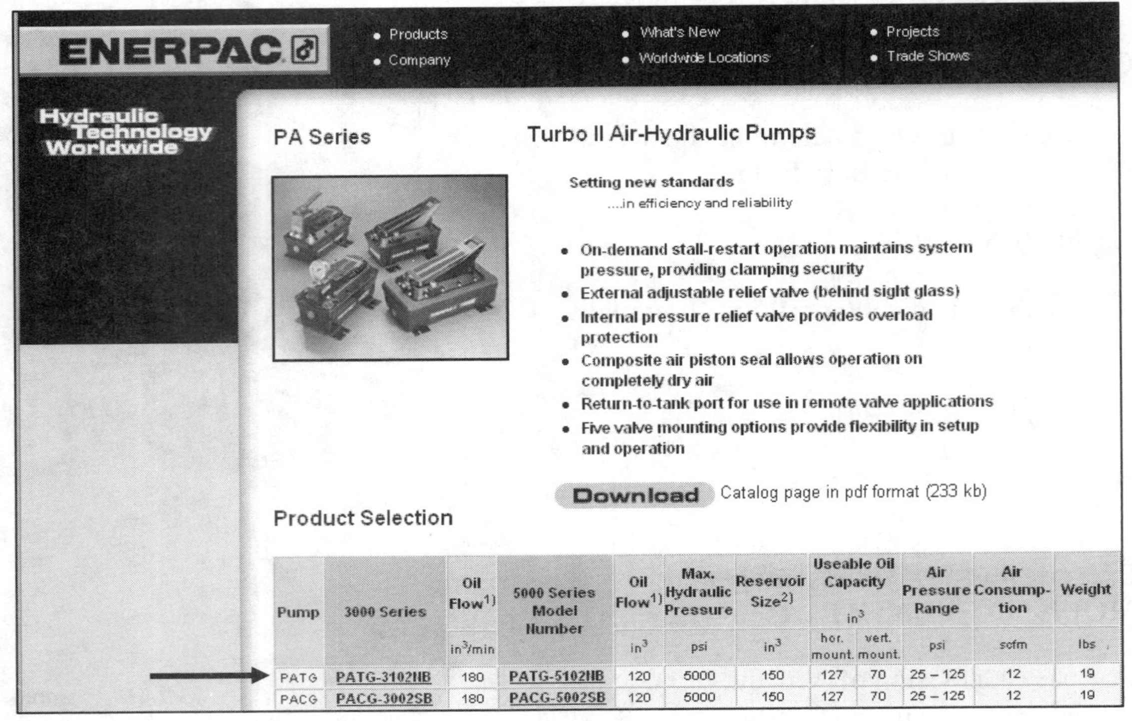
ENERPAC
Products
Company
What's New
Worldwide Locations
Projects
Trade Shows
Hydraulic Technology Worldwide
PA Series
Turbo II Air-Hydraulic Pumps
Setting new standards
....in efficiency and reliability
On-demand stall-restart operation maintains system pressure, providing clamping security
External adjustable relief valve (behind sight glass)
Internal pressure relief valve provides overload protection
Composite air piston seal allows operation on completely dry air
Return-to-tank port for use in remote valve applications
Five valve mounting options provide flexibility in setup and operation
Download
Catalog page in pdf format (233 kb)
Product Selection

Pump	3000 Series	Oil Flow[1]	5000 Series Model Number	Oil Flow[1]	Max. Hydraulic Pressure	Reservoir Size[2]	Useable Oil Capacity in^3		Air Pressure Range	Air Consump-tion	Weight
		in^3/min		in^3	psi	in^3	hor. mount.	vert. mount.	psi	scfm	lbs
PATG	PATG-3102NB	180	PATG-5102NB	120	5000	150	127	70	25 – 125	12	19
PACG	PACG-3002SB	180	PACG-5002SB	120	5000	150	127	70	25 – 125	12	19

Project 5

Sweep, Loft and Additional Features

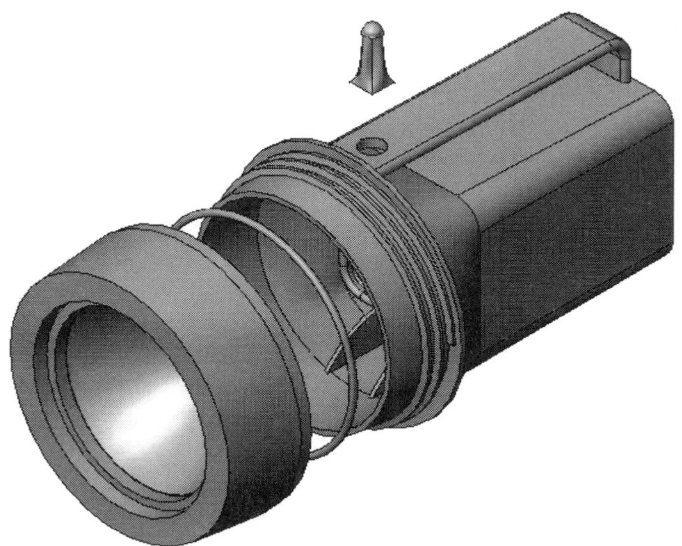

Below are the desired outcomes and usage competencies based on the completion of Project 5.

Project Desired Outcomes:	Usage Competencies:
• Model four FLASHLIGHT parts: ○ O-RING. ○ SWITCH. ○ LENSCAP. ○ HOUSING.	• Comprehension of the fundamental definitions and process of Feature-Based 3D Solid Modeling using Sweeps and Lofts.
• Develop three O-RING Configurations.	• Ability to create a Design Table.
• Create four assemblies: ○ LENSANDBULB assembly. ○ CAPANDLENS assembly. ○ BATTERYANDPLATE assembly. ○ FLASHLIGHT assembly.	• Ability to combine multiple features to create components. • Knowledge of additional assembly techniques.

Notes:

Project 5-Sweep, Loft and Additional Features

Project Objective

Create four parts: O-RING, SWITCH, LENSCAP and HOUSING of the FLASHLIGHT assembly.

Create four assemblies: LENSANDBULB, CAPANDLENS, BATTERYANDPLATE and the final FLASHLIGHT assembly.

On the completion of this project, you will be able to:

- Choose the best profile for sketching.
- Choose the proper sketch Plane.
- Develop O-RING configurations with a Design Table.
- Create an Assembly Template with Document Properties.
- Develop bottom up assembly modeling techniques.
- Calculate Interference.
- Export Files.
- Utilize the following SolidWorks features:
    - Sweep.
    - Loft.
    - Extruded and Revolved Boss/Base
    - Extruded and Revolved Cut.
    - Draft.
    - Shape.
    - Rib.
    - Circular Pattern and Linear Pattern.
    - Mirror.

Project Overview

Project 5 introduces the Sweep and Loft features. The O-RING utilizes a Sweep Base feature. The SWITCH utilizes the Loft feature. The LENSCAP and HOUSING utilize the Sweep Boss and Loft Boss features.

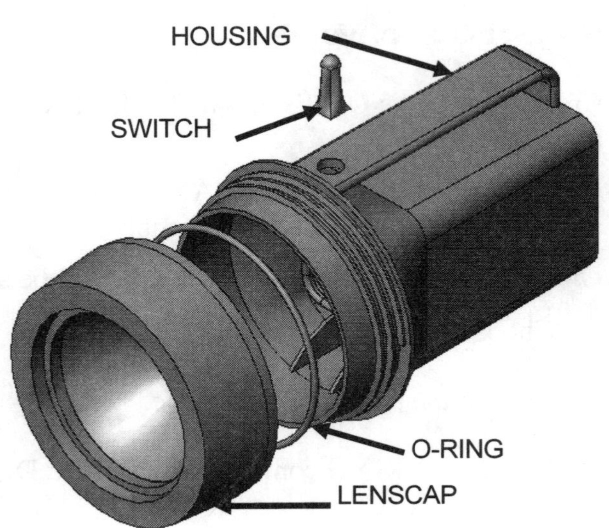

FLASHLIGHT assembly

A Sweep feature requires a minimum of two sketches: path and profile. Sketch the path and profile on different planes. The profile follows the path to create the following Sweep features:

- Sweep Base.
- Sweep Boss.

The Loft feature requires a minimum of two profiles sketched on different planes. The profiles are blended together to create the following Loft features:

- Loft Base.
- Loft Boss.

Utilize existing features to create the Rib, Linear Pattern and Mirror features.

Utilize existing faces to create the Draft and Shape features.

The LENSCAP and HOUSING combines the Extruded Boss/Base, Extruded Cut, Revolved Cut Thin, Shell and Circular Pattern with the Sweep and Loft.

Note: Features in the SWITCH, LENSCAP and HOUSING have been simplified for educational purposes.

Create four assemblies in this project:

1. LENSANDBULB assembly.
2. CAPANDLENS assembly.
3. BATTERYANDPLATE assembly.
4. FLASHLIGHT assembly.

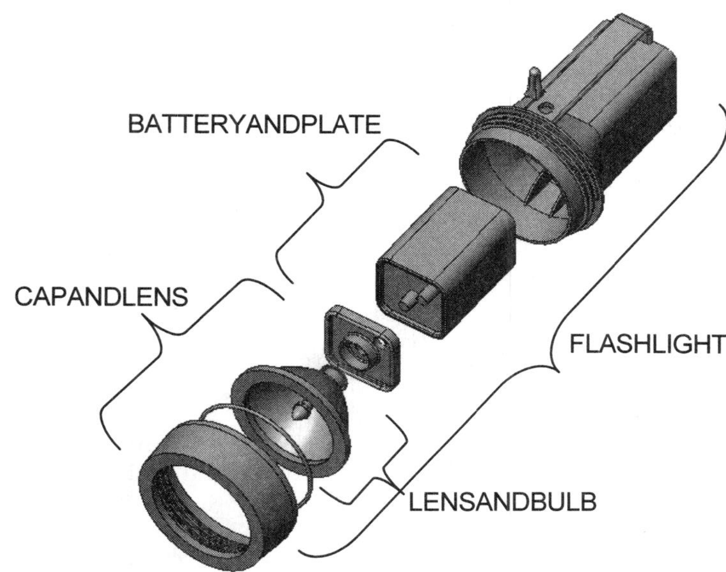

Create an inch and metric Assembly Template.

- ASM-IN-ANSI.
- ASM-MM-ISO.

Develop an understanding of assembly modeling techniques.

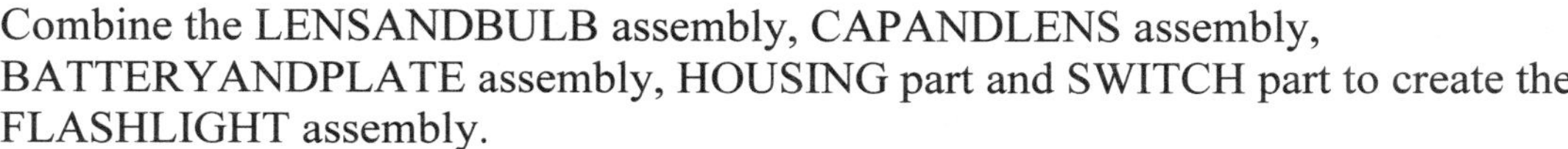

Combine the LENSANDBULB assembly, CAPANDLENS assembly, BATTERYANDPLATE assembly, HOUSING part and SWITCH part to create the FLASHLIGHT assembly.

Review Mate types. Create the following Mate relationships:

- Coincident.
- Concentric.
- Distance.

Utilize the Assembly tools: Insert Component, Hide/Show, Change Suppression, Mate, Move Component, Rotate Component, Exploded View and Interference Detection.

Project Situation

Communications is a major component to a successful development program. Provide frequent status reports to the customer and to your team members.

Communicate with suppliers. Ask questions. Check on details. What is the delivery time for the BATTERY, LENS and SWITCH parts? Talk to colleagues to obtain useful manufacturing suggestions and ideas. Your team decided that plastic injection molding is the most cost effective method to produce large quantities of the desired part.

Investigate surface finishes that support the customers advertising requirement. You have two fundamental choices:

- Adhesive label.
- Silk-screen.

There are time, quantity and cost design constraints. For the prototype, use an adhesive label. In the final product, create a silk screen.

Investigate the options on O-Ring material. Common O-Ring materials for this application are Buna-N (Nitrile®) and Viton®. Be cognizant of compatibility issues between O-RING materials and lubricants.

The LENSCAP encloses the LENS. The HOUSING protects the BATTERY. How do you design the LENSCAP and HOUSING to ease the transition from development to manufacturing? Answer: Review the fundamental design rules behind the plastic injection manufacturing process:

- Maintain a constant wall thickness. Inconsistent wall thickness creates stress.
- Create a radius on all corners. No sharp edges. Sharp edges create vacuum issues when removing the mold. Filleting inside corners on plastic parts will strength the part and improve plastic flow characteristics around corners in the mold.
- Understand the Draft feature. The Draft feature is commonly referred to as: plus draft or minus draft. Plus draft adds material. Minus draft removes material.
- Allow a minimum draft angle of 1 degree. Draft sides and internal ribs. Draft angles assist in removing the part from the mold.
- Ribs are often added to improve strength. Ribs must also be added to improve plastic flow to entirely fill the cavity and to avoid a short shot; not enough material to fill the mold.
- Generally use a 2:3 ratio for rib thickness compared to overall part thickness.
- Shrinkage of the cooling plastic requires that the cavity is larger than the finished part. Shrinkage around the core will cause the part to bind onto the core. The Draft feature helps eject the part from the mold. Shrinkage on the cavity side will cause the part to pull from the mold. Less draft is needed on the cavity faces than on the core faces.
- Sink marks occur where there is an area with thicker material than the rest of the part wall thickness. A problem may occur where a tall rib with draft meets a face of the part.
- Mold cavities should be vented to allow trapped gases to escape through the channels.

Obtain additional information on material and manufacturing from material suppliers or mold manufacturers. Example: GE Plastics of Pittsfield, MA (www.geplastics.com & www.gepolymerland.com) provides design guidelines for selecting raw materials and creating plastic parts and components.

O-RING Part-Sweep Base Feature

The O-RING part is positioned between the LENSCAP and the LENS.

Create the O-RING with a Sweep Base feature.

The Sweep-Base feature uses:

- A circular path sketched on the Front Plane.
- A small cross section profile sketched on the Right Plane.

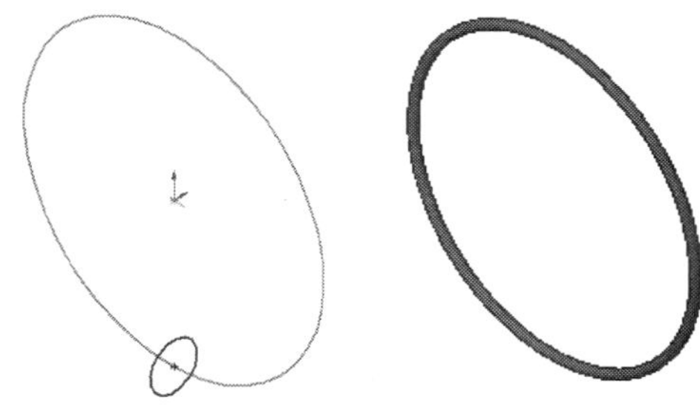

Path & Profile Sweep feature

The Pierce geometric relation positions the center of the cross section profile on the sketched path.

Utilize the PART-IN-ANSI Template created in Project 1 for inch units. Utilize the PART-MM-ISO Template for millimeter units. Millimeter dimensions are provided in brackets [x].

Activity: O-RING Part-Sweep Base Feature

Create the new part.

1) Click **File**, **New** from the Main menu.

2) Click the **MY-TEMPLATES** tab.

3) Double-click **PART-IN-ANSI**, **[PART-MM-ISO]**.

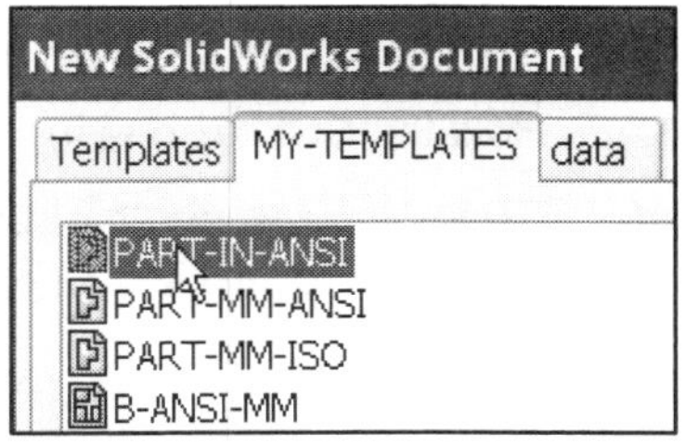

4) Click **Save**.

5) Select **PROJECTS** for the Save in folder.

6) Enter **O-RING** for file name.

7) Enter **O-RING FOR LENS** for Description.

8) Click **Save**.

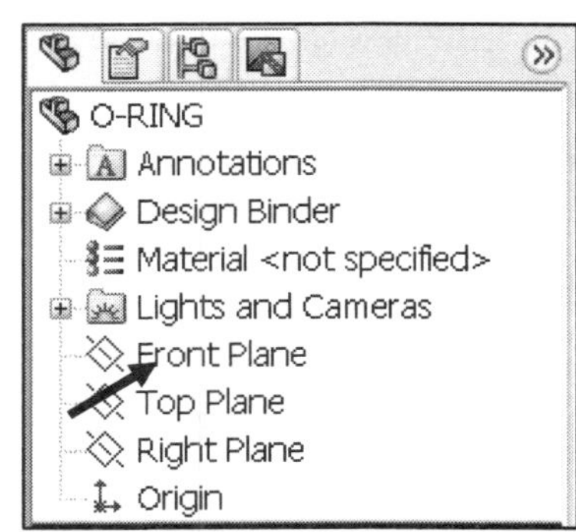

Create the Sweep path.

9) Click **Front Plane** from the FeatureManager for the Sketch plane.

10) Click **Sketch** Sketch.

11) Click **Circle** Circle from the Sketch toolbar.

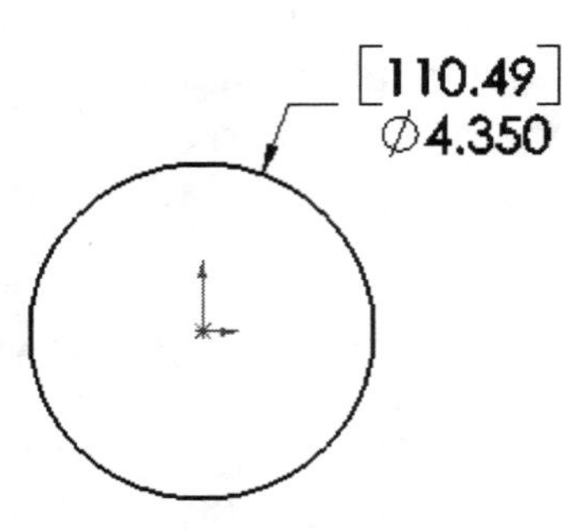

12) Sketch a circle centered at the **Origin**.

Add a dimension.

13) Click **Smart Dimension** Smart Dimens... . Click the **circumference** of the circle. Click a **position** off the profile.

14) Enter **4.350**, [**110.49**].

Close the Sketch.

15) Click **Exit Sketch** Exit Sketch . Sketch1 is displayed in the FeatureManager.

16) Rename **Sketch1** to **Sketch-path**.

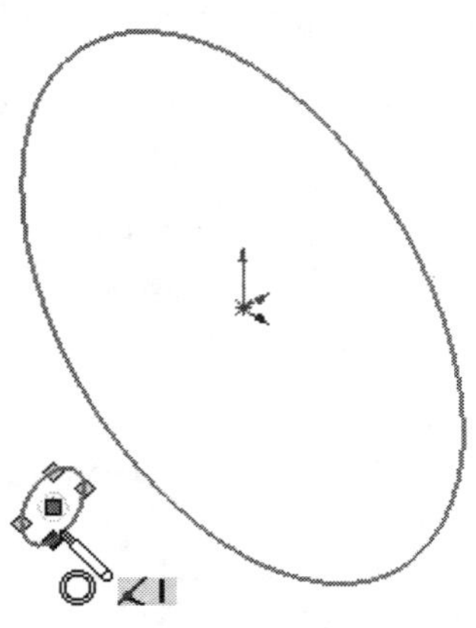

Create the Sweep profile.

17) Click **Isometric view** .

18) Click the **Right Plane** from the FeatureManager.

19) Click **Sketch** Sketch . Click **Circle** Circle from the Sketch toolbar.

20) Create a **small circle** left of the Sketch-path on the Right plane.

Add a Pierce Relation.

21) Right-click **Select** in the Graphics window.

22) Click the **small circle center point**.

23) Hold the **Ctrl** key down.

24) Click the **large circle circumference**. Release the **Ctrl** key.

25) Click **Pierce** from the Add Relations box. The center point of the small circle pierces the sketch-path (large circle).

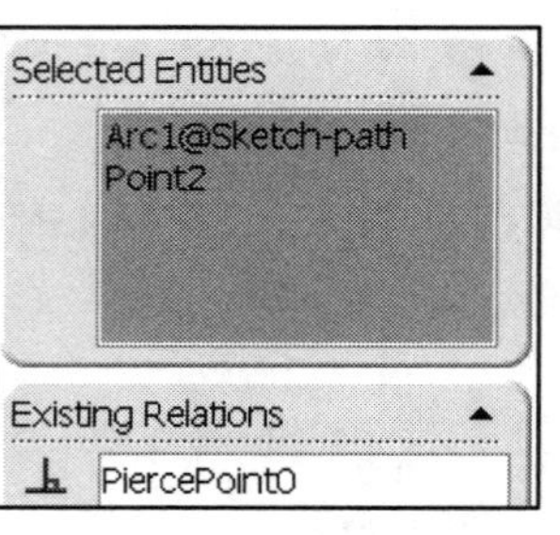

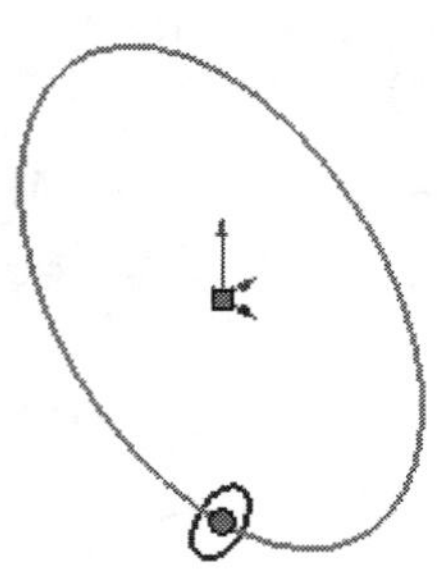

26) Click **OK** from the Properties PropertyManager.

Add a dimension.

27) Click **Smart Dimension** Smart Dimens... . Click the **circumference** of the small circle.

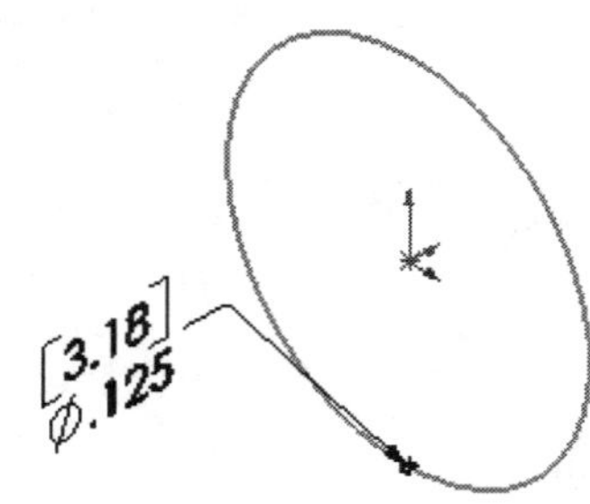

28) Click a **position** to the left of the profile.

29) Enter **.125**, [**3.18**].

Close the Sketch.

30) Click **Exit Sketch** Exit Sketch. Sketch2 is displayed in the FeatureManager.

31) Rename **Sketch2** to **Sketch-profile**.

The FeatureManager displays two sketches: Sketch-path and Sketch-profile. Create the path before the profile. The profile requires a Pierce relation to the path.

Improve visibility. Small profiles are difficult to dimension on large paths. Perform the following steps to create a detailed small profile:

- Create a large cross section profile that contains the required dimensions and relationships. The black profile is fully defined.
- Pierce the profile to the path. Add dimensions to reflect the true size.
- Rename the profile and path to quickly located sketches in the FeatureManager.

Insert the Sweep feature.

32) Click **Swept Boss/Base** Swept Boss/B... from the Features toolbar.

33) Expand the **O-RING icon** O-RING.

34) Click **Sketch-profile** from the FeatureManager.

35) Click inside the **Path** text box. Click **Sketch-path** from the FeatureManager.

36) Click **OK** from the Sweep PropertyManager.

37) Rename **Sweep1** to **Base-Sweep**.

38) Click **Isometric view**.

39) Click **Save**.

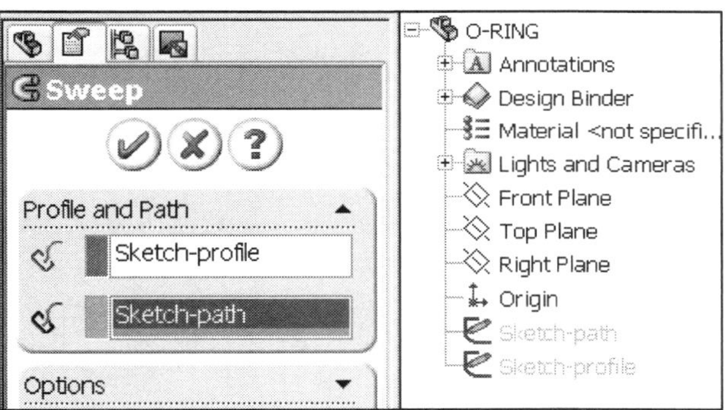

O-RING Part-Design Table

A Design Table is a spreadsheet used to create multiple configurations in a part or assembly. The Design Table controls the dimensions and parameters in the part. Utilize the Design Table to modify the overall path diameter and profile diameter of the O-RING.

Create three configurations of the O-RING:

- Small.
- Medium.
- Large.

Note: The O-RING contains two dimension names in the Design Tables. Parts contain hundreds of dimensions and values. Rename dimension names for clarity.

The part was initially designed in inches. You are required to manufacture the configurations in millimeters. Modify the part units to millimeters.

Activity: O-RING Part-Design Table

Modify the Primary Units.

40) Click **Tool**, **Options**, **Documents Properties** tab, **Units** from the Main menu.

41) Select **MMGS**. Enter **2** for Length units Decimal Places.

42) Click **OK**.

Insert a Design Table.

43) Click **Insert**, **Design Table** Design Table from the Main menu. The Auto-create option is selected.

44) Click **OK** from the Design Table PropertyManager.

45) Click **D1@Sketch-path**. Hold the **Ctrl** key down. Click **D1@Sketch-profile**. Release the **Ctrl** key. Click **OK**.

Note: The dimension variable name will be different if sketches or features were deleted.

The input dimension names and default values are automatically entered into the Design Table. The value Default is entered in Cell A3.

The values for the O-RING are entered in Cells B3 through C6. The sketch-path diameter is controlled in Column B. The sketch-profile diameter is controlled in Column C.

Enter the three configuration names.

46) Click **Cell A4**. Enter **Small**.

47) Click **Cell A5**. Enter **Medium**.

48) Click **Cell A6**. Enter **Large**.

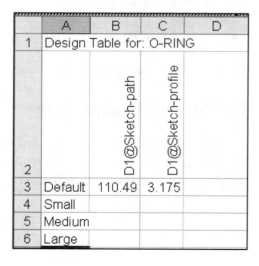

	A	B	C	D
1	Design Table for: O-RING			
2		D1@Sketch-path	D1@Sketch-profile	
3	Default	110.49	3.175	
4	Small			
5	Medium			
6	Large			

	A	B	C
1	Design Table for: O-RING		
2		D1@Sketch-path	D1@Sketch-profile
3	Default	110.49	3.175
4	Small	100	3
5	Medium	150	4
6	Large	200	10

Enter the dimension values for the Small configuration.

49) Click **Cell B4**. Enter **100**. Click **Cell C4**. Enter **3**.

Enter the dimension values for the Medium configuration.

50) Click **Cell B5**. Enter **150**. Click **Cell C5**. Enter **4**.

Enter the dimension values for the Large configuration.

51) Click **Cell B6**. Enter **200**. Click **Cell C6**. Enter **10**.

Build the three configurations.

52) Click a **position** inside the Graphics window.

53) Click **OK** to generate the three configurations. The Design Table icon is displayed in the FeatureManager.

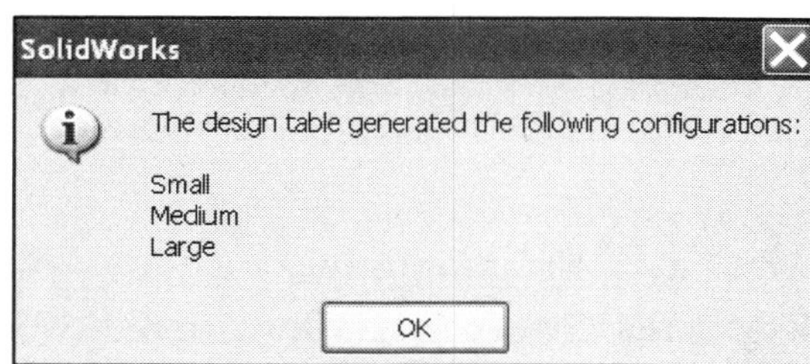

Display the configurations.

54) Click the **ConfigurationManager** icon.

View the three configurations.

55) Double-click **Small**.

56) Double-click **Medium**.

57) Double-click **Large**.

58) Double-click **Default**.

59) Click **Save** .

The O-RING is classified as a simple Sweep. Complex Sweeps utilize 3D curves and Guide Curves. Investigate additional Sweep features later in the project.

An example of a complex Sweep is a Thread. A Thread requires a Helical/Spiral curve for the path and a circular profile.

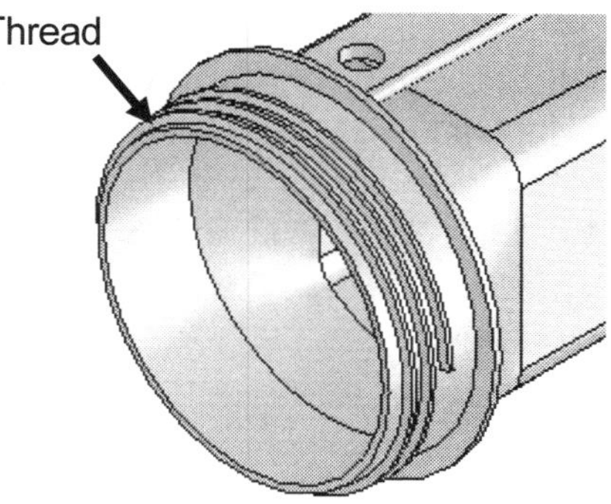

Another example of a complex Sweep is the violin body. The violin body requires Guide Curves control Sweep geometry. Without Guide Curves the profile follows the straight path to produce a rectangular shape.

With Guide Curves, the profile follows the path and the Guide Curve geometry to produce the violin body.

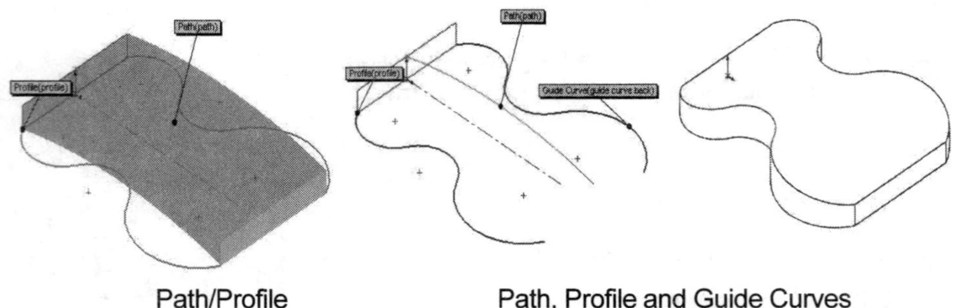

Path/Profile Path, Profile and Guide Curves

Additional information on Sweep and Pierce are found in SolidWorks Help Topics. Keywords: Sweep (overview, simple sweeps) and Pierce (relations).

Refer to Help, Online Tutorial Revolves and Sweeps exercise and Design Tables exercise for additional information.

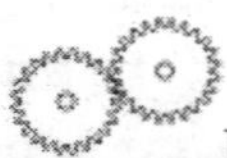

Review of the O-RING Part.

The O-RING utilized the Sweep feature. The Sweep feature required a sketched path and a sketched profile. The path was a large circle sketched on the Front Plane. The profile was a small circle sketched on the Right Plane. The Pierce Relation was utilized to attach the profile to the path.

The Sweep feature required a minimum of two sketches. You created a simple Sweep feature. Sweep features can be simple or complex. Small, Medium and Large configurations of the O-RING were developed with a Design Table. The Design Table is an EXCEL based spread sheet utilized to create variations of dimensions and features.

Recognize the properties and understand the order of the sketches to create successful simple Sweep features. The following are the steps to create successful Sweeps:

- Create the path as a separate sketch. The path is open or closed. The path is a set curves contained in one sketch. The path can also be one curve or a set of model edges.
- Create each profile as a separate sketch. The profile is closed for a Base/Boss Sweep.
- Fully define each sketch. The sketch is displayed in black.
- Sketch the profile last before inserting the Sweep feature.

- Position the start point of the path on the plane of the profile.
- Path, profile and solid geometry cannot intersect themselves.

The Sketch toolbar contains two areas, Sketch Entities and Sketch Tools. There are three ways to access these areas: Select the Sketch Sketch icon in the Standard toolbar to access both Sketch Entities and Sketch Tools. Select Sketch Sketch in the Control Area to access Sketch Entities. Select the Sketch Sketch icon from the Sketch toolbar to access the Sketch Entities and the Sketch Tools. Select Tools, Sketch Entities and Tools, Sketch Tools from the Main menu.

SWITCH Part-Loft Base Feature

The SWITCH is a purchased part. The SWITCH is a complex assembly. Create the outside casing of the SWITCH as a simplified part. Create the SWITCH with the Loft Base feature.

The orientation of the SWITCH is based on the position in the assembly. The SWITCH is comprised of three cross section profiles. Sketch each profile on a different plane.

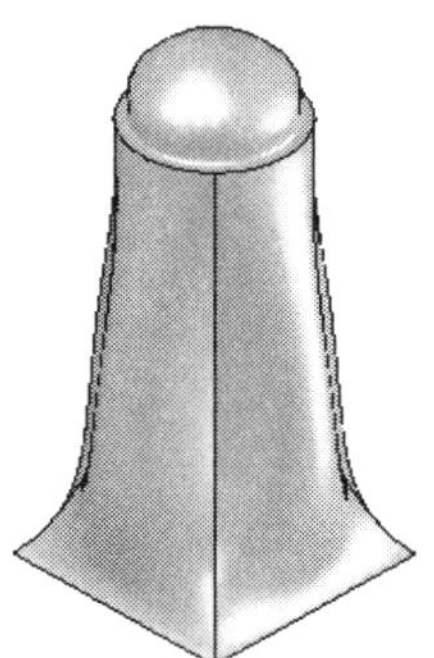

The first plane is the Top Plane. Create two reference planes parallel to the Top Plane.

Sketch one profile on each plane. The design intent of the sketch is to reduce the number of dimensions.

Utilize symmetry, construction geometry and Geometric Relations to control three sketches with one dimension.

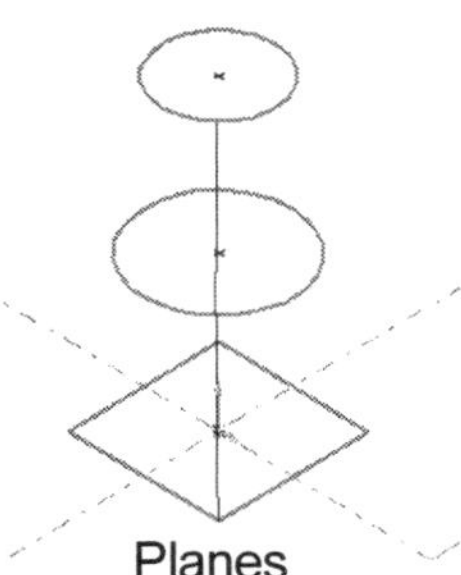

Insert the Loft feature. Select the profiles to create the Loft feature.

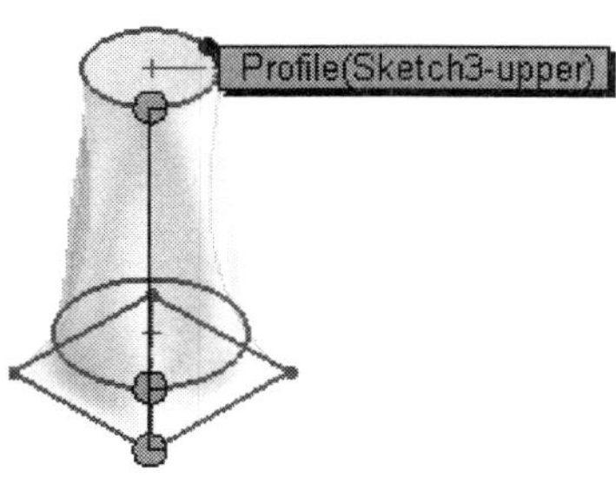

Insert the Shape feature to the top face of the Loft. Modify the dimensions to complete the SWITCH. The Shape feature is located in the Insert Pull down menu.

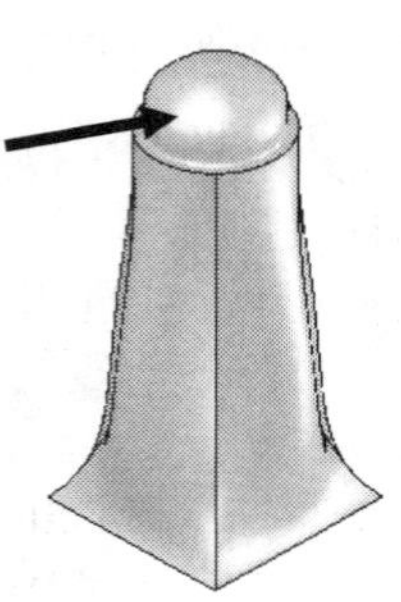

Activity: Switch Part-Loft Base Feature

Create a new part.

60) Click **File**, **New** from the Main menu. Click the **MY-TEMPLATES** tab.

61) Double-click **PART-IN-ANSI**, [**PART-MM-ISO**].

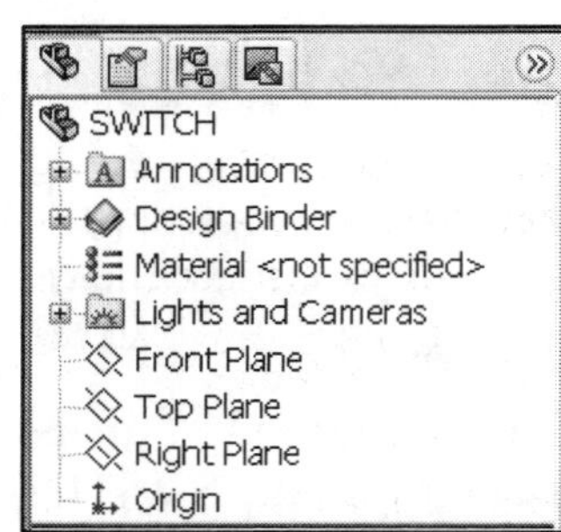

62) Click **Save** .

63) Select **PROJECTS** for the Save in folder.

64) Enter **SWITCH** for file name. Enter **BUTTON STYLE** for Description.

65) Click **Save**.

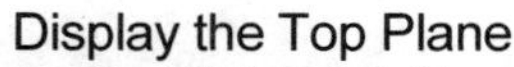

Display the Top Plane.

66) Right-click **Top Plane** from the FeatureManager.

67) Click **Show**.

68) Click **Isometric view** .

Hold the Ctrl key down and drag the Top Plane upward.
Pick an edge, not the handles.

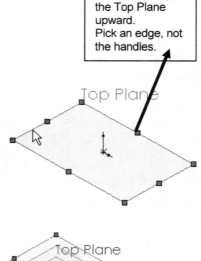

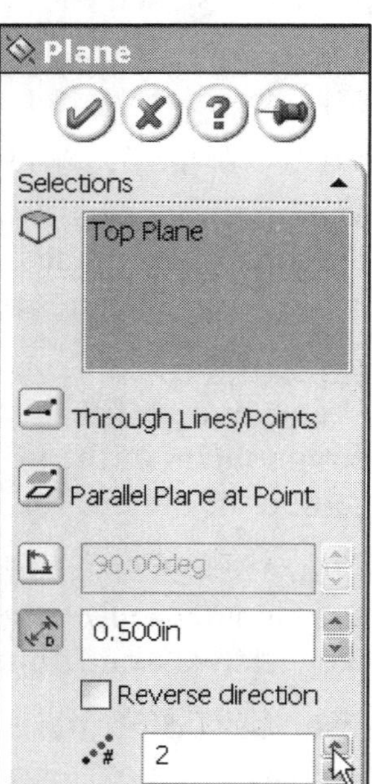

Insert two reference planes.

69) Hold the **Ctrl** key down. Click and drag the **Top Plane** upward. Release the **mouse button**. Release the **Ctrl** key.

70) Enter **.5**, [**12.7**] for Offset Distance. Enter **2** for # of Planes to Create.

71) Click **OK** from the Plane PropertyManager.

72) Click **Front view** to display the Plane1 and Plane2 offset from the Top plane.

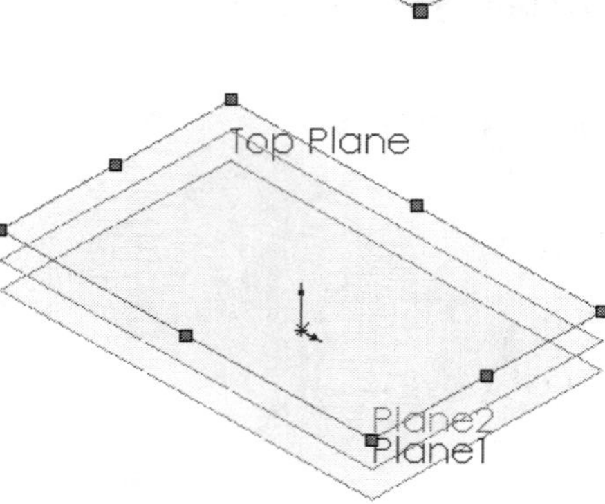

73) Click **Isometric view**.

Insert Sketch1. Sketch1 is a square on the Top Plane.

74) Click the **Top Plane** from the FeatureManager. Click **Sketch** Sketch.

75) Click **Rectangle** Rectan... from the Sketch toolbar. Sketch a **Rectangle** centered about the Origin.

Create a diagonal Centerline.

76) Click **Centerline** Centerl... .

77) Click the two **corner points** of the rectangle.

Add a Midpoint Relation.

78) Right-click **Select**. Click the **Origin**. Hold the **Ctrl** key down. Click the diagonal **centerline**. Release the **Ctrl** key.

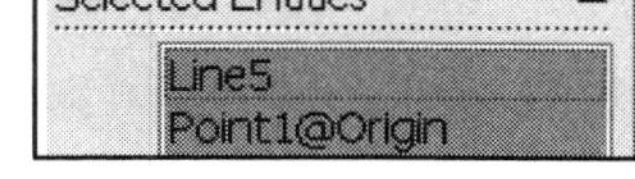

79) Click **Midpoint** from the Add Relations box.

80) Click **OK** from the PropertyManager.

Add an Equal Relation.

81) Click the **left vertical line**.

82) Hold the **Ctrl** key down.

83) Click the **top horizontal line**. Release the **Ctrl** key.

84) Click **Equal** = .

85) Click **OK** from the PropertyManager.

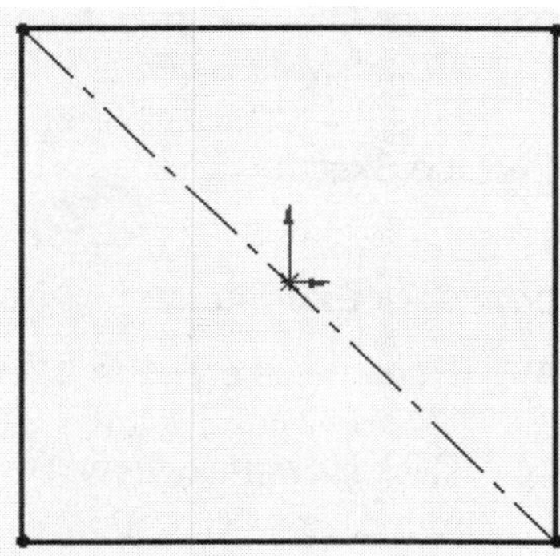

Add a dimension.

86) Click **Smart Dimension** Smart Dimens....

87) Click the **top horizontal line**. Click a **position** above the Profile.

88) Enter **.500**, [**12.7**].

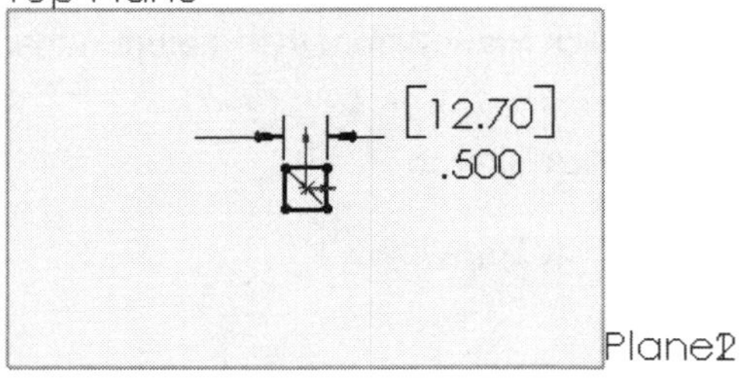

Close the Sketch.

89) Click **Exit Sketch** Exit Sketch .

90) Rename **Sketch1** to **Sketch1-lower**.

91) Click **Save** .

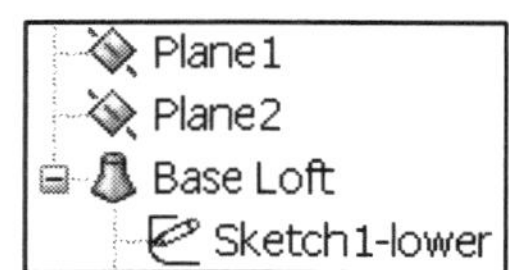

Insert Sketch2 on Plane1.

92) Click **Plane1** from the FeatureManager.

93) Click **Top view** .

94) Click **Sketch** Sketch .

95) Click **Circle** Circle from the Sketch toolbar.

96) Create a **Circle** centered at the Origin.

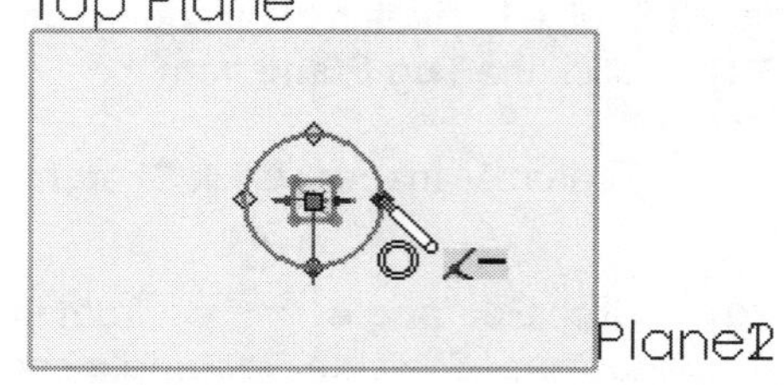

Add a Tangent Relation.

97) Right-click **Select**.

98) Click the **circumference** of the circle.

99) Hold the **Ctrl** key down.

100) Click the **top horizontal Sketch1-lower line**.

101) Release the **Ctrl** key.

102) Click **Tangent** from the Add Relations box.

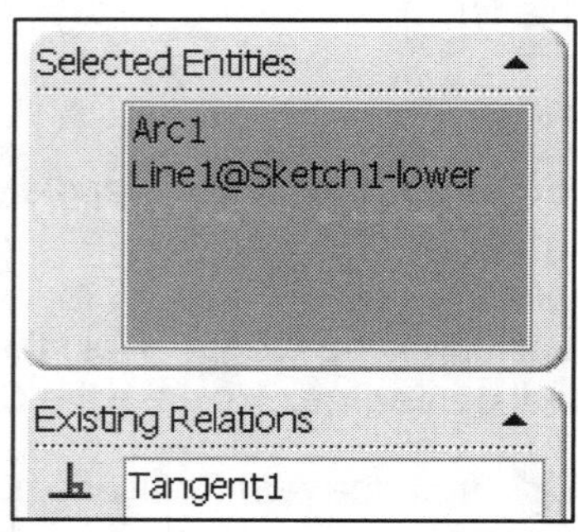

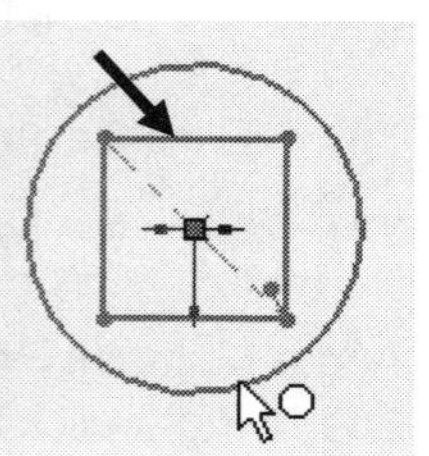

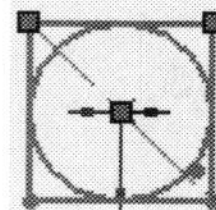

103) Click **OK**  from the Properties PropertyManager.

Close the Sketch.

104) Click **Exit Sketch** Exit Sketch .

105) Rename **Sketch2** to **Sketch2-middle**.

106) Click **Isometric view** .

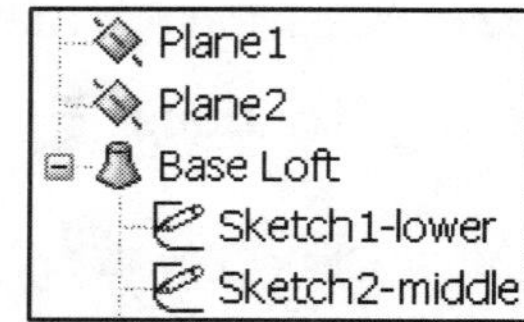

Insert Sketch3 on Plane2.

107) Click **Plane2** from the FeatureManager.

108) Click **Sketch** Sketch .

109) Click **Top view** .

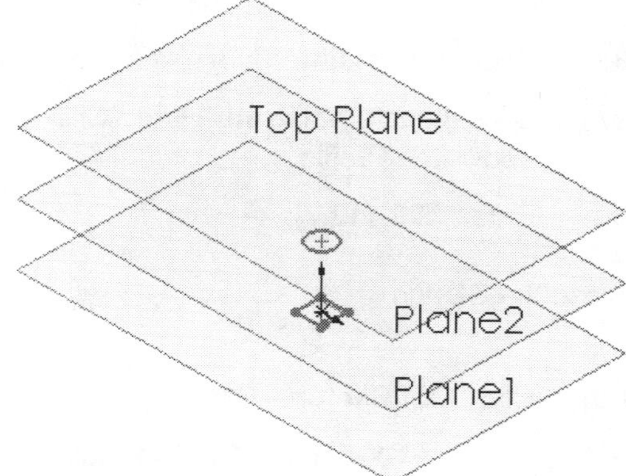

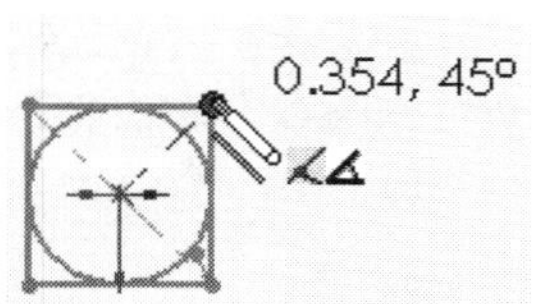

110) Click **Centerline** Centerline from the Sketch toolbar.

111) Sketch a **centerline** coincident with the Origin and the upper right corner point.

112) Click **Point** Point from the Sketch toolbar.

113) Click the **midpoint** of the right diagonal centerline.

114) Click **Circle** Circle from the Sketch toolbar.

115) Create a **Circle** centered at the Origin to the midpoint of the diagonal centerline.

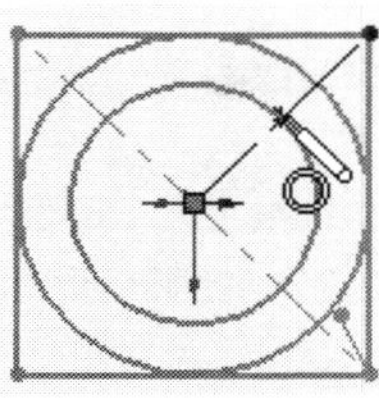

Close the Sketch.

116) Click **Exit Sketch**  Exit Sketch.

117) Rename **Sketch3** to **Sketch3-upper**.

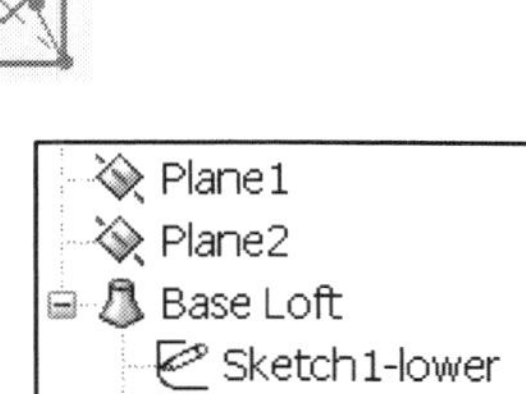

Insert the Loft feature.

118) Click **Lofted Boss/Base** Lofted Boss/B... from the Features toolbar.

119) Click **Isometric view**.

120) Right-click in the **Profiles box**. Click **Clear Selections**. Click the **front corner** of Sketch1-lower.

121) Click **Sketch2-middle**. Click **Sketch3-upper**.

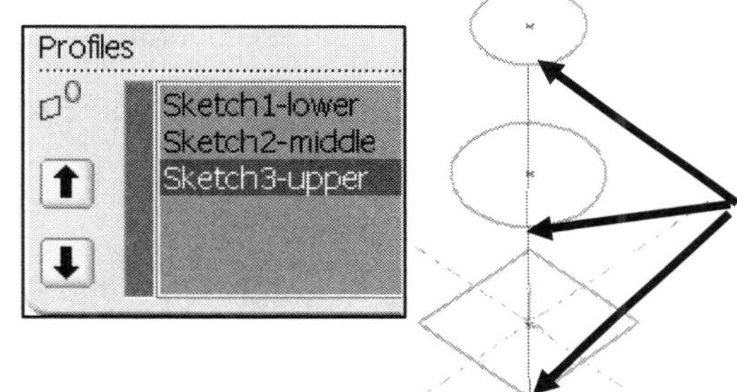

Click the front of Sketch1-lower, Sketch2-middle and Sketch3-upper.

122) Click **OK** from the Loft PropertyManager.

123) Rename **Loft1** to **Base Loft**.

Hide the planes.

124) Click **View**, uncheck **Planes** from the Main menu.

125) Click **Isometric view**.

Save the part.

126) Click **Save**.

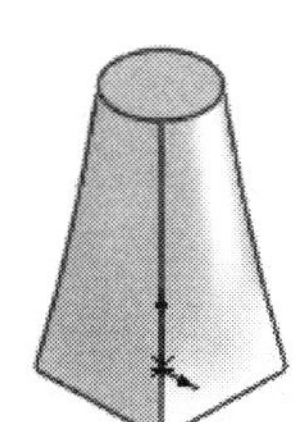

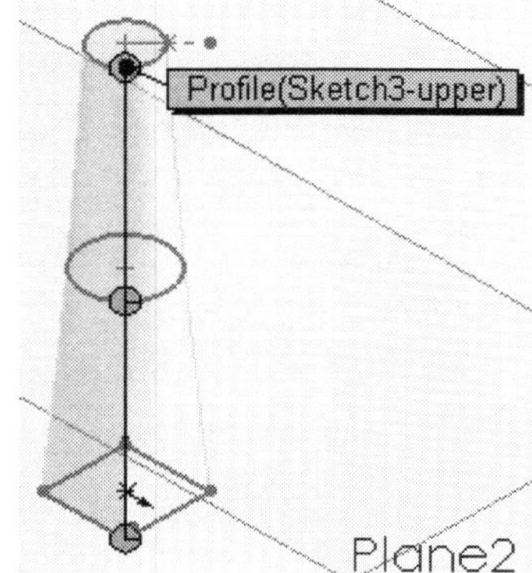

The system displays a preview curve and preview loft as you select the profiles. Use the Up button and Down button in the Loft PropertyManager to rearrange the order of the profiles.

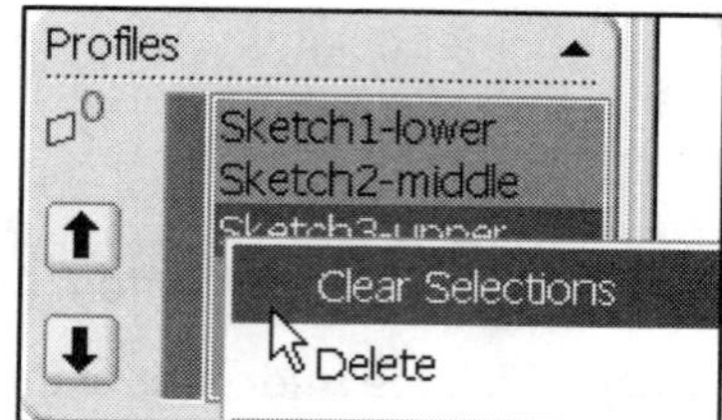

Redefine incorrect selections efficiently. Right-click in the Graphics window, click Clear Selections to remove selected profiles. Select the correct profiles.

SWITCH Part-Shape Feature

Insert the Shape feature on the top face of the Loft Base feature. The Shape feature deforms a surface. Control the surface deformation through the Pressure and Curve Influence sliders. Preview the results. Adjust the sliders to obtain a similar shape display in the illustrations.

Activity: SWITCH Part-Shape Feature

Insert the Shape feature.

127) Click the **top face** of the Base Loft feature.

128) Click **Insert**, **Features, Shape** Shape... from the Main menu.

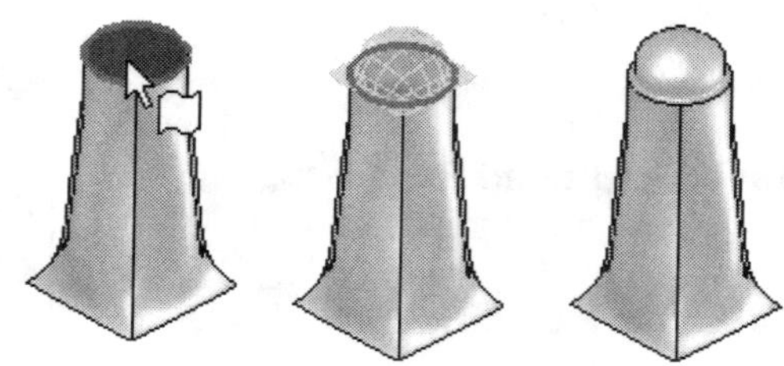

129) Click the **Controls** tab from the Shape Feature dialog box.

130) Drag the **Gains Pressure slider** to approximately 12. The Pressure slider deflates/inflates the shape of the surface.

131) Drag the **Advanced controls Resolution slider** to 8. The Resolution slider changes the number of points of the deformed face.

132) Click **OK** to display the Shape Feature.

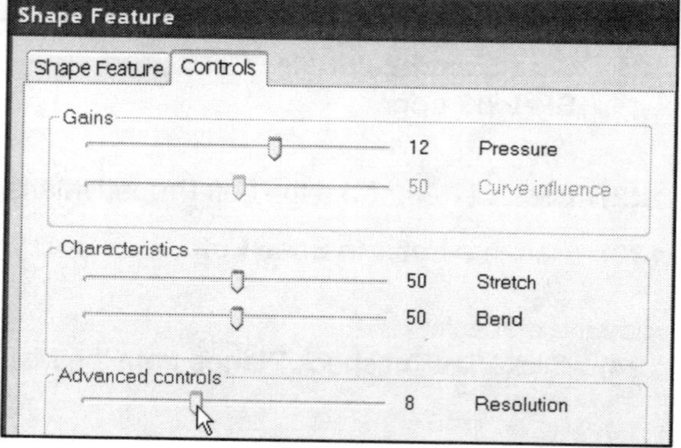

Experiment with the Shape feature to display different results. The Characteristics sliders adjust the degree of bend and stretch in the surface.

The top face of your Switch will vary depending on the Shape parameters.

The distance between the Loft planes contribute to the shape of the Loft feature. Modify the offset distance between the Top plane and Plane1.

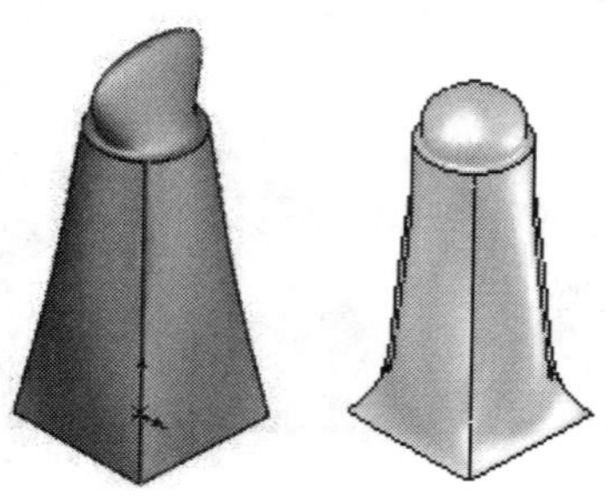

Modify the Loft Base feature.

133) **Expand** the Base Loft feature. Right-click on **Annotations** in the FeatureManager. Click **Show Feature Dimensions**.

134) Double-click on the Plane1 offset dimension, **.500**, [**12.700**].

135) Enter **.125**, [**3.180**]. Click **Rebuild**.

136) Click the **Green Check mark**.

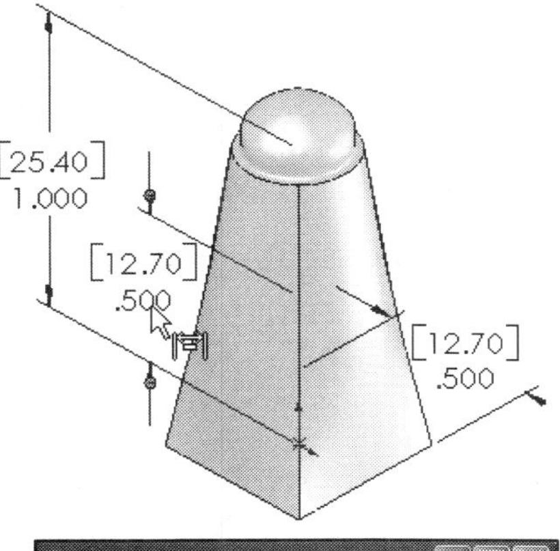

Hide Feature dimension.

137) Right-click on **Annotations** in the FeatureManager. Un-check **Show Feature Dimensions**.

Display Feature Statistics.

138) Click **Tools, Feature Statistics** Feature Statistics... from the Main menu.

View the SWITCH feature statistics.

139) Click **Close**.

140) Click **Save**.

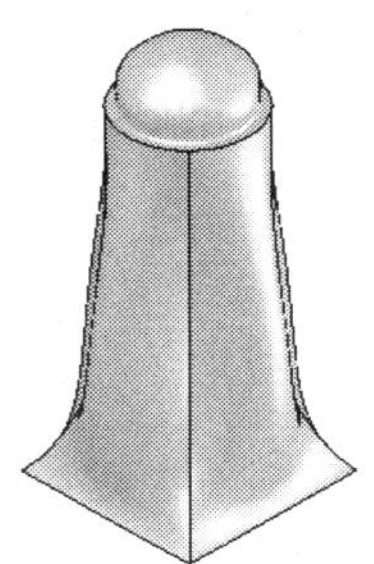

Feature Statistics

Print... Copy Refresh Close

SWITCH
Features 7, Solids 1, Surfaces 0

Feature Order	Time %	Time(s)
Shape Fea...	95.69	1.38
Base Loft	4.31	0.06
Plane1	0.00	0.00
Plane2	0.00	0.00
Sketch1-l...	0.00	0.00
Sketch2-...	0.00	0.00
Sketch3-u...	0.00	0.00

The Shape feature Control parameters produce various results. The Feature Statistics report displays the Rebuild time for the Shape feature and the other SWITCH features. As feature geometry becomes more complex, the rebuild time increases.

Additional information on Loft, Shape feature and Reference Planes are found in SolidWorks Help Topics. Keywords: Loft (simple), Shape (features) and Reference Geometry (Planes). Refer to Help, Online Tutorial, Lofts exercise for additional information.

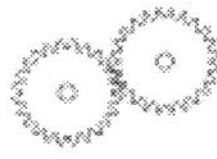

Review of the SWITCH Part.

The SWITCH utilized the Loft feature. The Loft feature required three planes. One profile was sketched on each plane. The three profiles were combined to create the Loft feature.

The Shape feature deformed geometry on the top face of the Loft. Through a series of sliding control parameters, the top faced deformed.

The SWITCH utilized a simple Loft. Lofts become more complex with additional Guide Curves. Complex Lofts contain hundreds of profiles.

Four Major Categories of Solid Features

The LENSCAP and HOUSING combine the four major categories of solid features:

- Extrude: Requires one profile.
- Revolve: Requires one profile and axis of revolution.
- Sweep: Requires one profile and one path sketched on different planes.
- Loft: Requires two or more profiles sketched on different planes.

Identify the simple features of the LENSCAP and HOUSING. Extrude and Revolve are simple features. Only a single sketch profile is required. Sweep and Loft are more complex features. Two or more sketches are required.

Example: The O-RING was created as a Sweep.

Could the O-RING utilize an Extruded feature?

Answer: No. Extruding a circular profile produces a cylinder.

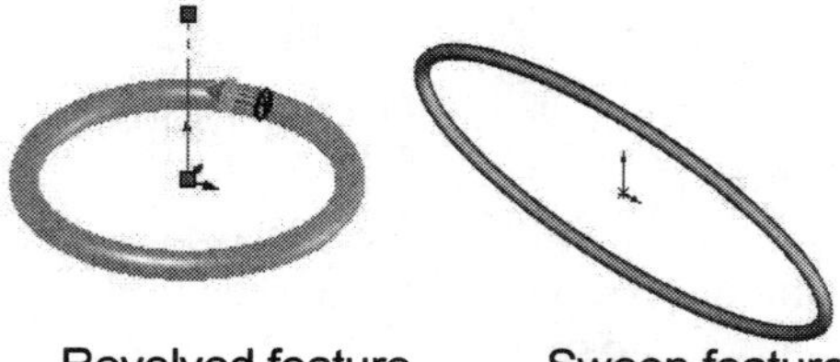

Revolved feature   Sweep feature

Can the O-RING utilize a Revolved feature? Answer: Yes. Revolving a circular profile about a centerline creates the O-RING.

A Sweep feature is required if the O-RING contained a non-circular path. Example: A Revolved feature does not work with an elliptical path or a more complex curve as in a paper clip. Combine the four major features and additional features to create the LENSCAP and HOUSING.

LENSCAP Part

The LENSCAP is a plastic part used to position the LENS to the HOUSING. The LENSCAP utilizes an Extruded Base, Extruded Cut, Extruded Thin Cut, Shell, Revolved Cut and Sweep features.

The design intent for the LENSCAP requires that the Draft Angle be incorporated into the Extruded Base and Revolved Cut feature. Create the Revolved Cut feature by referencing the Extrude Base feature geometry. If the Draft Angle changes, the Revolved Cut also changes.

Insert an Extruded Base feature with a circular profile on the Front Plane. Use a Draft option in the Extrude PropertyManager. Enter 5° for the Draft Angle.

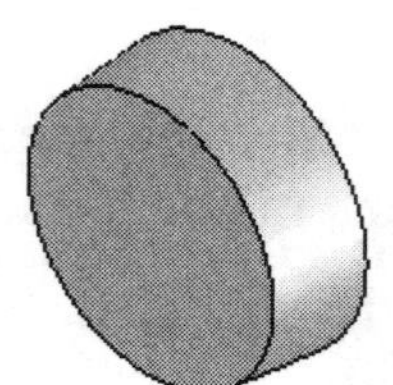

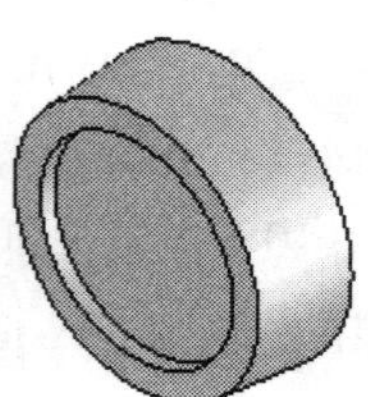

Insert an Extruded Cut feature. The Extruded Cut feature should be equal to the diameter of the LENS Revolved Base feature.

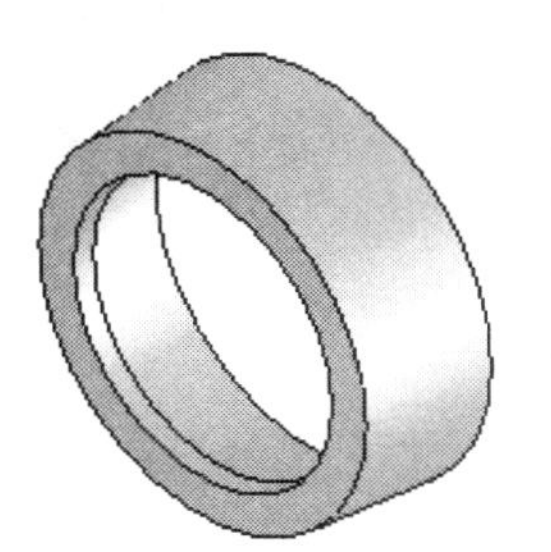

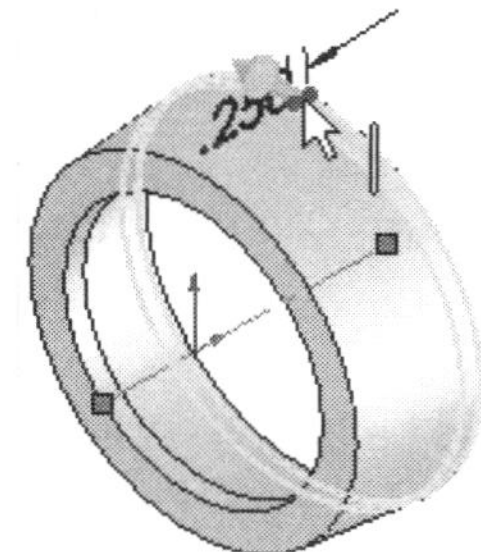

Insert a Shell feature. Use the Shell feature for a constant wall thickness.

Insert a Revolved Cut feature on the back face. Sketch a single line on the Silhouette edge of the Extruded Base. Utilize the Thin Feature option in the Revolved Cut PropertyManager.

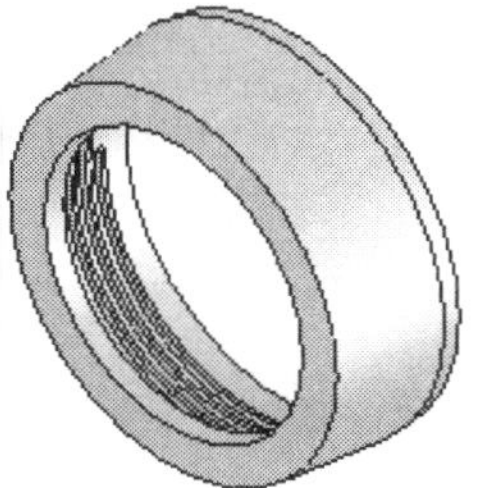

Utilize a Sweep feature for the thread.

Insert a new reference plane for the start of the thread. Insert a Helical Curve for the path. Sketch a trapezoid for the profile.

LENSCAP Part-Extruded Base, Extruded Cut and Shell Features

Create the LENSCAP. Review the Extruded Base, Extruded Cut and Shell features introduced in Project 4. The first feature is an Extruded Base feature. Select the Front Plane for the Sketch plane. Sketch a circle centered at the Origin for the profile. Utilize a Draft Angle of 5°.

Create an Extruded Cut feature on the front face of the Base feature. The diameter of the Extruded Cut equals the diameter of the Revolved Base feature of the LENS. The Shell feature removes the front and back face from the solid LENSCAP.

Activity: LENSCAP Part-LENSCAP, Extruded Base, Extruded Cut and Shell Features

Create a new part.

141) Click **File**, **New** from the Main menu. Click the **MY-TEMPLATES** tab.

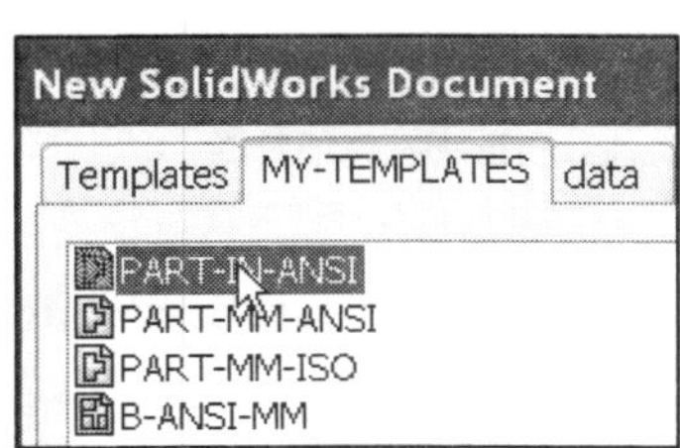

142) Double-click **PART-IN-ANSI**, [**PART-MM-ISO**].

143) Click **Save** .

144) Select **PROJECTS** for the Save in folder.

145) Enter **LENSCAP** for file name.

146) Enter **LENSCAP for 6V FLASHLIGHT** for Description.

147) Click **Save**.

Create the Sketch for the Extruded Base.

148) Click **Front Plane** from the FeatureManager.

149) Click **Sketch** Sketch. Click **Circle** Circle from the Sketch toolbar. Create a circle centered at the **Origin**.

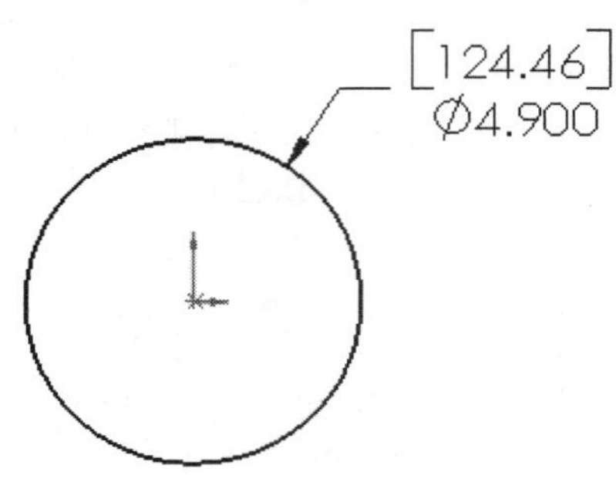

Add a dimension.

150) Click **Smart Dimension** Smart Dimens....

151) Click the **circumference** of the circle.

152) Click a **position** of the profile. Enter **4.900**, [**124.46**].

Insert an Extruded Base feature.

153) Click **Extruded Boss/Base** Extruded Boss/B... .

154) Click **Reverse Direction**.

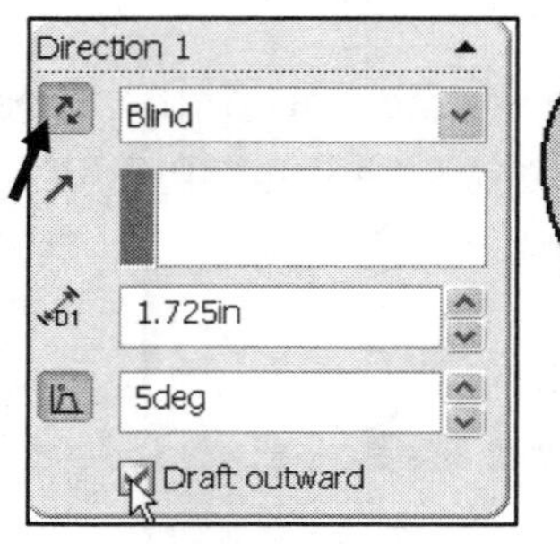

155) Enter **1.725**, [**43.82**] for Depth.

156) Click the **Draft On/Off** button.

157) Enter **5** deg for Angle.

158) Click the **Draft outward** check box. Click **OK** from the Extrude PropertyManager. Rename **Extrude1** to **Base Extrude**.

159) Click **Save**.

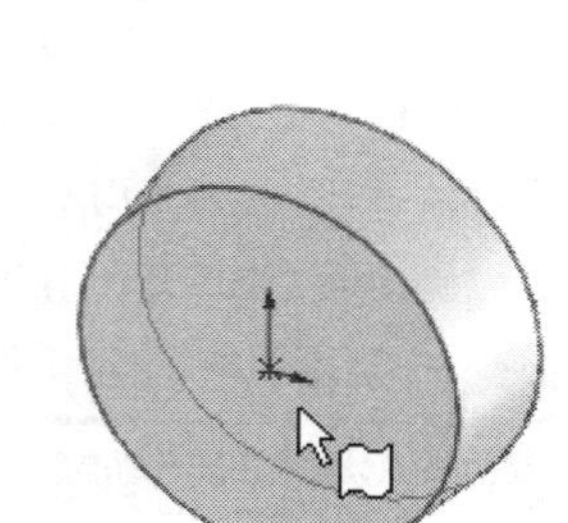

Create the Sketch for the Extruded Cut.

160) Click the **front face** for the Sketch plane.

161) Click **Sketch** Sketch. Click **Circle** Circle. Create a **circle** centered at the Origin.

Add a dimension.

162) Click **Smart Dimension** Smart Dimens....

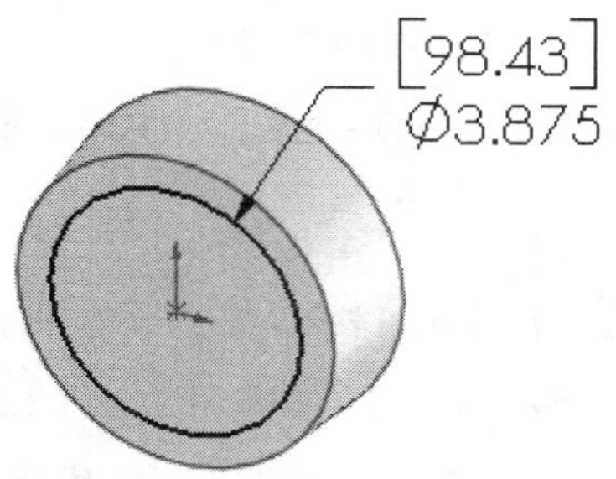

163) Click the **circumference** of the circle.

164) Click a **position** of the profile.

165) Enter **3.875**, [**98.43**].

Insert an Extruded Cut feature.

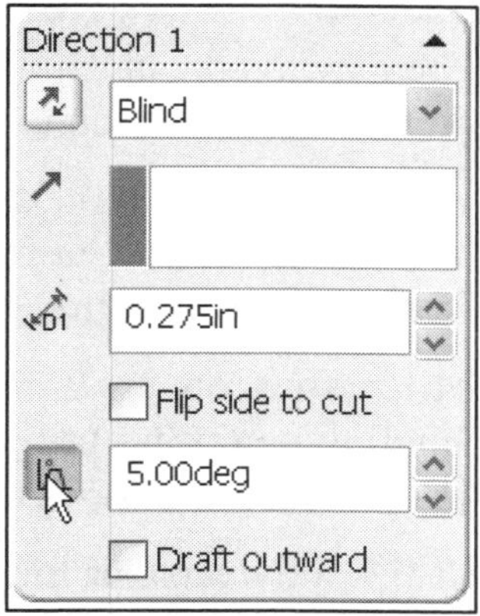

166) Click **Extruded Cut** Extruded Cut. Blind is the default Type option.

167) Enter **.275**, [**6.99**] for Depth.

168) Click the **Draft On/Off** button.

169) Enter **5** for Angle.

170) Click **OK** from the Cut-Extrude PropertyManager.

171) Rename **Cut-Extrude1** to **Front-Cut**.

172) Click **Save** .

Insert the Shell feature.

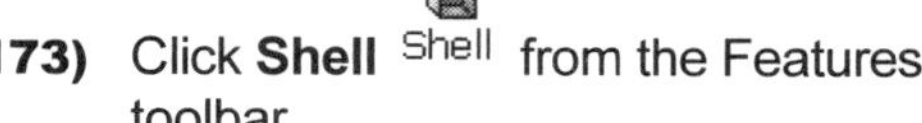

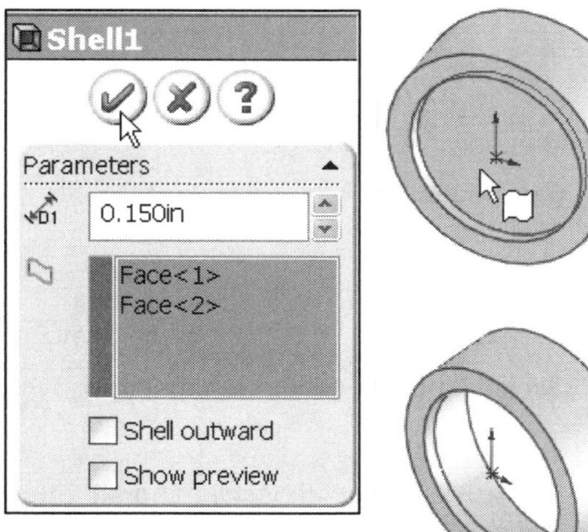

173) Click **Shell** Shell from the Features toolbar.

174) Click the **front face** of the Front-Cut.

175) Press the **left arrow** approximately 8 times to view the back face.

176) Click the **back face** of the Base Extrude.

177) Enter **.150**, [**3.81**] for Thickness.

178) Click **OK** from the Shell1 PropertyManager.

179) Click **Isometric view** .

Display the inside of the Shell.

180) Click **Right view** .

181) Click **Hidden Lines Visible** .

182) Click **Save** .

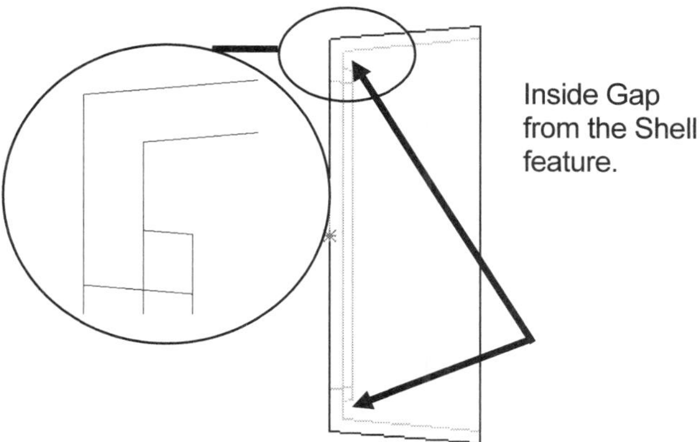

Inside Gap from the Shell feature.

Note: Use the inside gap created by the Shell feature to seat the O-RING in the assembly.

LENSCAP Part-Revolved Cut Thin Feature

The Revolved Cut Thin feature removes material by rotating a sketched profile around a centerline.

The Right Plane is the sketch plane. The design intent requires that the Revolved Cut maintains the same Draft Angle as the Extruded Base feature.

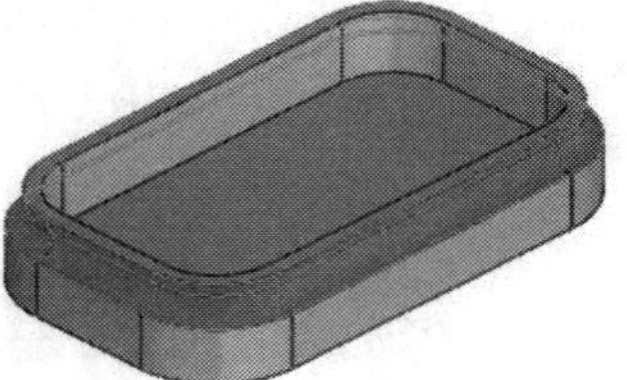

Sweep Cut Example

Utilize the Convert Entities Sketch tool to create the profile. Small thin cuts are utilized in plastic parts. Utilize the Revolved Thin Cut feature for cylindrical geometry in the next activity.

Utilize a Sweep Cut for non-cylindrical geometry. The semi-circular Sweep Cut profile is explored in the project exercises.

Activity: LENSCAP Part-Revolved Cut Thin Feature

Create the Sketch.

183) Click **Right Plane** from the FeatureManager.

184) Click **Sketch** Sketch.

Sketch the Centerline.

185) Click **Centerline** Centerl... from the Sketch toolbar.

186) Sketch a **horizontal centerline** through the Origin.

Create the profile.

187) Right-click **Select**. Select the **top silhouette outside edge**.

188) Click **Convert Entities** Convert from the Sketch toolbar.

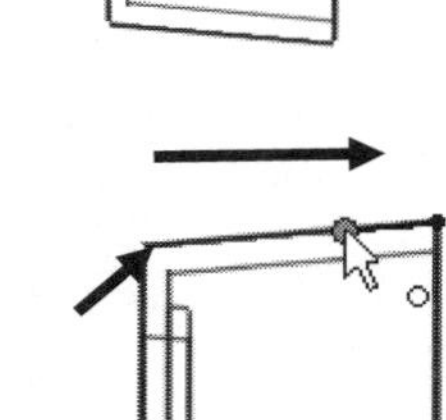

189) Click and drag the **left endpoint 2/3** towards the right endpoint. Release the **mouse button**.

Add a dimension.

190) Click **Smart Dimension** Smart Dimens....

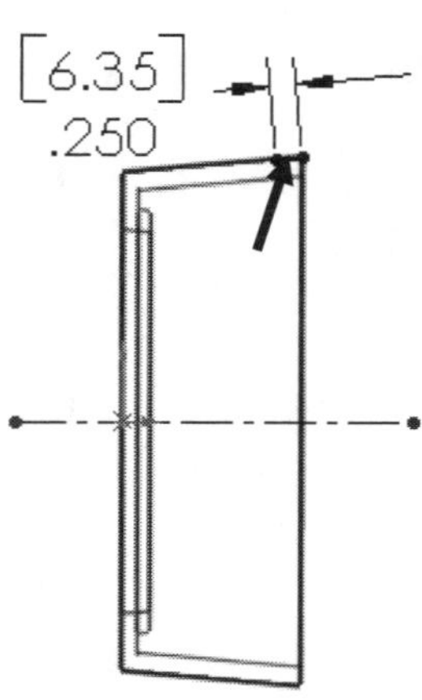

191) Click the **line**. The aligned dimension arrows are parallel to the profile line.

192) Drag the **text upward** and to the left.

193) Enter **.250**, **[6.35]**.

Insert a Revolved Cut feature.

194) Click **Revolved Cut** Revolved Cut from the Features toolbar. Do not close the Sketch. The warning message states; "The sketch is currently open."

195) Click **No**.

196) Click **Reverse Direction** in the Thin Feature box.

197) Enter **.050**, [**1.27**] for Direction 1 Thickness.

198) Click **OK** from the Cut-Revolve PropertyManager.

Display the Revolve-Thin Cut.

199) **Rotate** the part to view the back face.

200) Click **Isometric view**.

201) Click **Shaded With Edges**.

202) Rename **Cut-Revolve-Thin1** to **BackCut**.

203) Click **Save**.

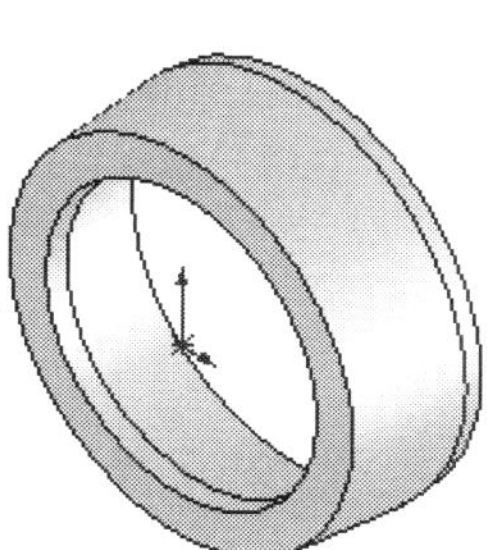

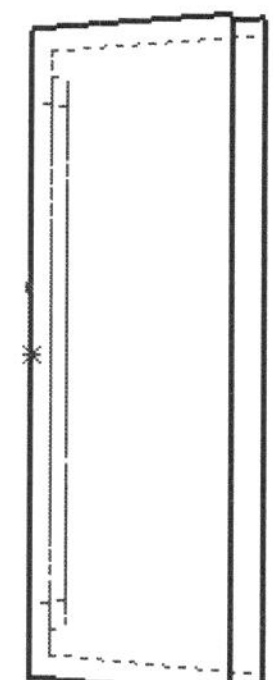

LENSCAP Part-Thread, Sweep Feature and Helix/Spiral Curve

Utilize the Sweep feature to create the required threads. The thread requires a spiral path. This path is called the ThreadPath. The thread requires a sketched profile. This cross section profile is called the ThreadSection.

The plastic thread on the LENSCAP requires a smooth lead in. The thread is not flush with the back face. Use an offset Plane to start the thread. There are numerous steps required to create a thread:

- Create a new Plane for the start of the thread.
- Create the thread path. Utilize Convert Entities and Insert, Curve Helix/Spiral.
- Create a large thread cross section profile for improve visibility.
- Insert the Sweep feature.
- Reduce the size of the thread cross section.

…vity: LENSCAP Part-Thread, Sweep Feature and Helix/Spiral Curve

…ate the offset plane.

204) Click **Rotate** and **Zoom to Area** on the back face of the LENSCAP.

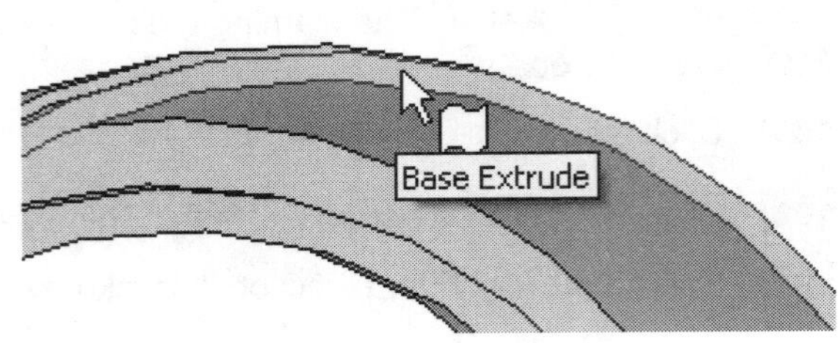

205) Click the **narrow back face** of the Base Extrude feature.

206) Click **Insert**, **Reference Geometry, Plane** Plane... from the Main menu.

207) Enter **.450**, **[11.43]** for Distance.

208) Click the **Reverse direction** checkbox.

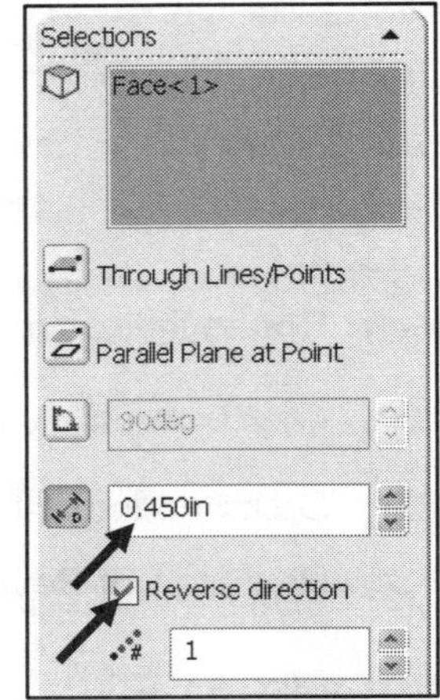

209) Click **OK** from the Plane PropertyManager.

210) Rename **Plane1** to **ThreadPlane**.

Display the Isometric view with Hidden Lines Removed.

211) Click **Isometric view**.

212) Click **Hidden Lines Removed**.

213) Click **Save**.

Utilize Convent Entities Sketch tool to extract the back circular edge of the LENSCAP to the ThreadPlane.

Create the Thread path.

214) Click **ThreadPlane** from the FeatureManager.

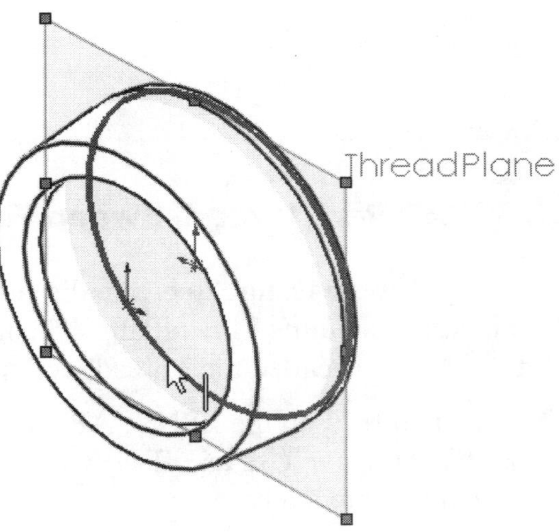

215) Click **Sketch** Sketch.

216) Click the **back inside circular edge** of the Shell.

217) Click **Convert Entities** Convert from the Sketch toolbar.

218) Click **Top view**. The circular edge is displayed on the ThreadPlane.

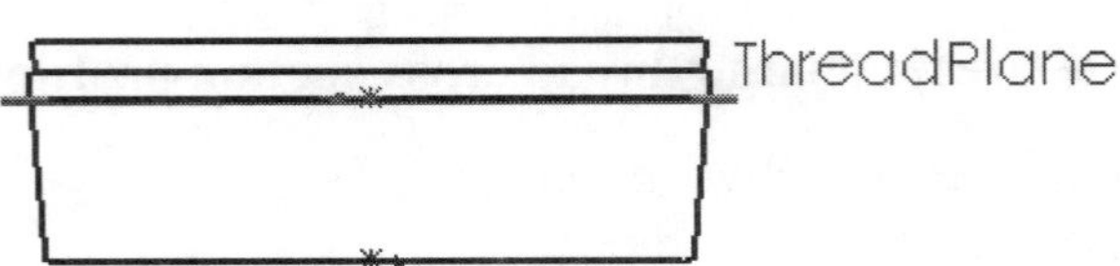

Insert the Helix/Spiral curve path.

219) Click **Insert, Curve, Helix/Spiral** Helix/Spiral... from the Main menu.

220) Enter **.250**, [**6.35**] for Pitch.

221) Check **Reverse direction**.

222) Enter **2.5** for Revolutions.

223) Enter **0** for Starting angle. The Helix start point and end point are Coincident with the Top Plane.

224) Check **Clockwise**.

225) Click the **Taper Helix** check box.

226) Enter **5** for Angle.

227) Uncheck the **Taper outward** check box.

ThreadPath
Defined By:
Pitch and Revolution
Parameters
Constant Pitch
Variable Pitch
Pitch:
0.250in
Reverse direction
Revolutions:
2.5
Start angle:
0deg
Clockwise
Counterclockwise
Taper Helix
5deg
Taper outward

228) Click **OK** from the Helix/Spiral PropertyManager.

229) Rename **Helix/Spiral1** to **ThreadPath**.

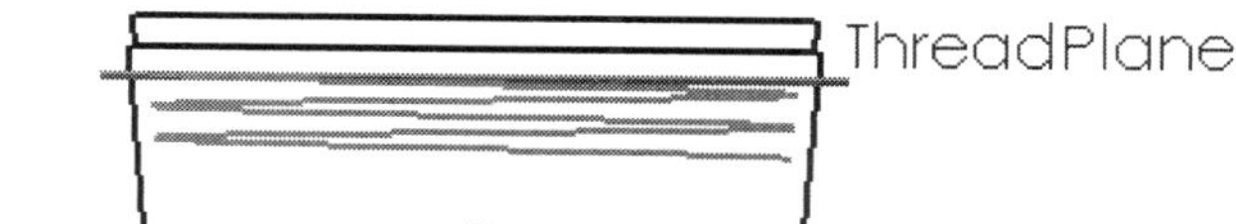
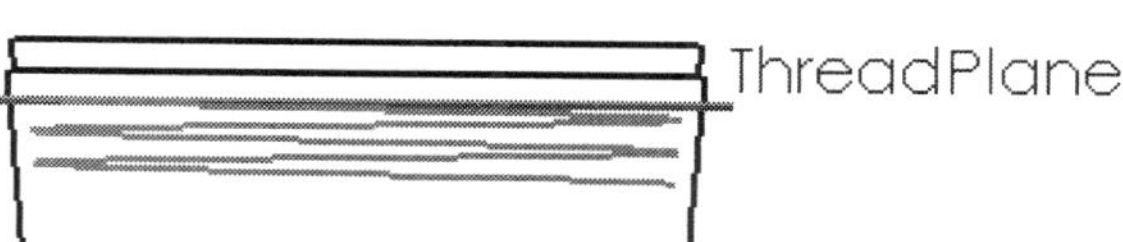

230) Click **Save**.

The Helix tapers with the inside wall of the LENSCAP. Position the Helix within the wall thickness to prevent errors in the Sweep.

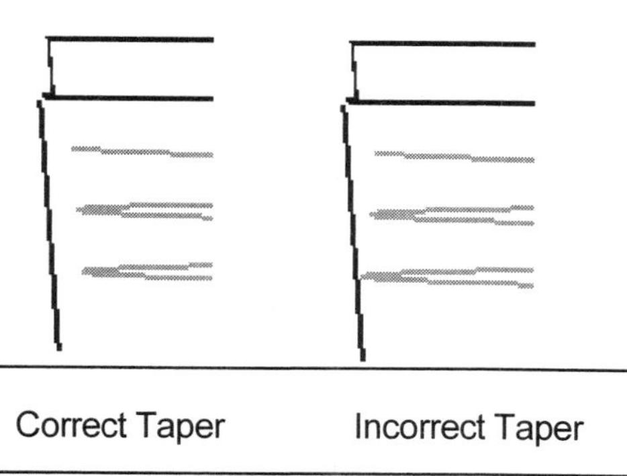

Correct Taper Incorrect Taper

Sketch the profile on the Top Plane. Position the profile to the Top right of the LENSCAP in order to pierce to the ThreadPath in the correct location.

Hide the ThreadPlane.

231) Right-click **ThreadPlane** from the FeatureManager.

232) Click **Hide**.

Sketch to the Top right

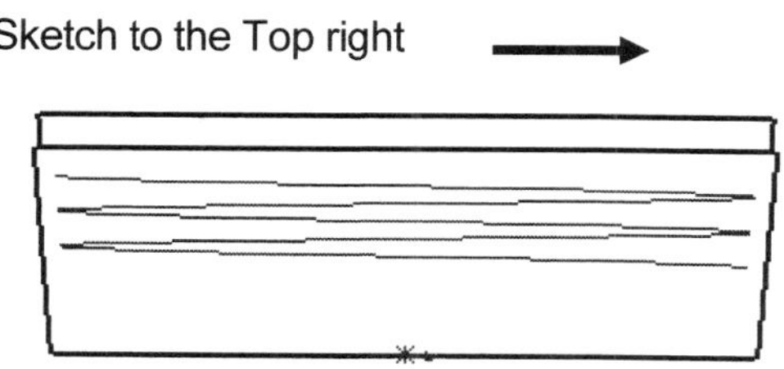

Select the Plane for the Thread.

233) Click the **Top Plane**.

Sketch the profile.

234) Click **Sketch** Sketch.

235) Click **Top view**.

236) Click **Centerline** Centerl... from the Sketch toolbar.

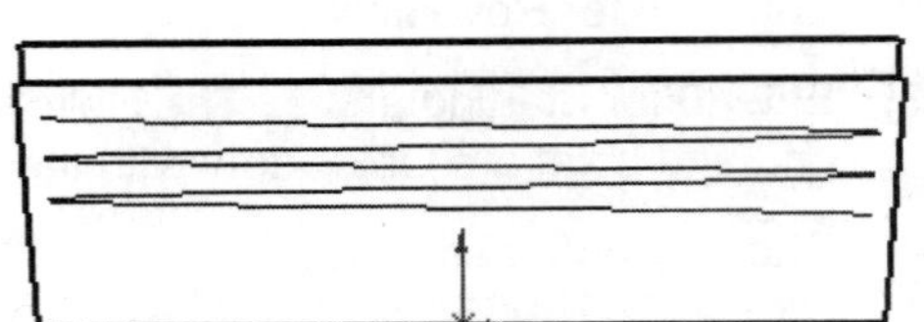

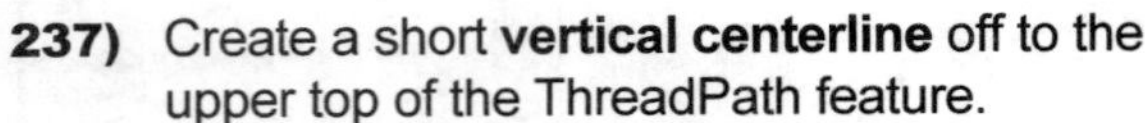

237) Create a short **vertical centerline** off to the upper top of the ThreadPath feature.

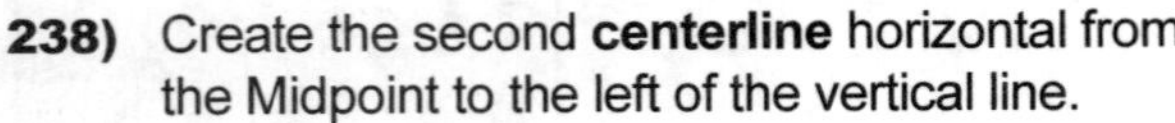

238) Create the second **centerline** horizontal from the Midpoint to the left of the vertical line.

239) Create the third centerline coincident with the left horizontal endpoint. Drag the **centerline upward** until it is approximately the same size as the right vertical line.

240) Create the fourth **centerline** coincident with the left horizontal endpoint. Drag the **centerline** downward until it is approximately the same size as the left vertical line.

Add an Equal Relation.

241) Right-click **Select**.

242) Click the **right vertical line**.

243) Hold the **Ctrl** key down.

244) Click the **two left vertical lines**.

245) Release the **Ctrl** key.

246) Click **Equal** = from the Add Relations box.

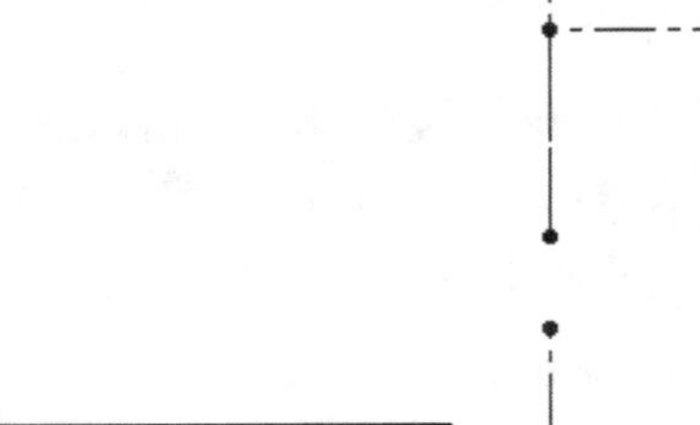

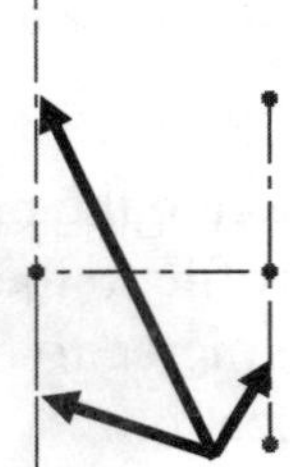

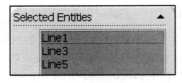

247) Click **OK** from the Properties PropertyManager.

Utilize centerlines and construction geometry with Geometric Relations to maintain relationships with minimal dimensions.

Check View, Sketch Relations from the Main toolbar to show/hide sketch relation symbols.

Add a dimension.

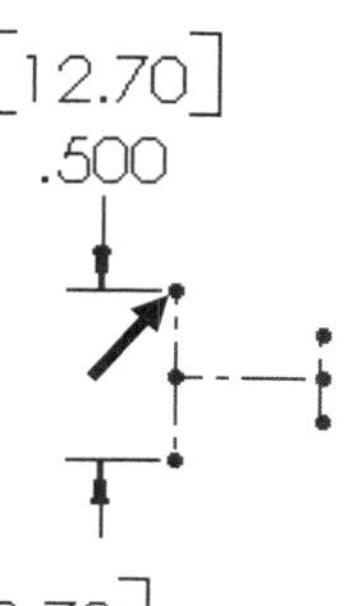

248) Click **Smart Dimension** .

249) Click the two **left vertical endpoints**. Click a **position** to the left.

250) Enter **.500**, [**12.7**].

Sketch the profile. The profile is a trapezoid.

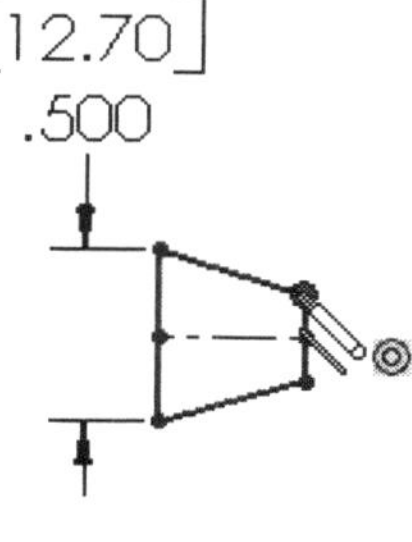

251) Click **Line** from the Sketch toolbar.

252) Click the **endpoints** of the vertical centerlines to create the trapezoid.

253) Double-click the **first point** to close and end the line.

Add an Equal Relation.

254) Right-click **Select**. Click the **left vertical line**. Hold the **Ctrl** key down.

255) Click the **top** and **bottom lines** of the trapezoid.

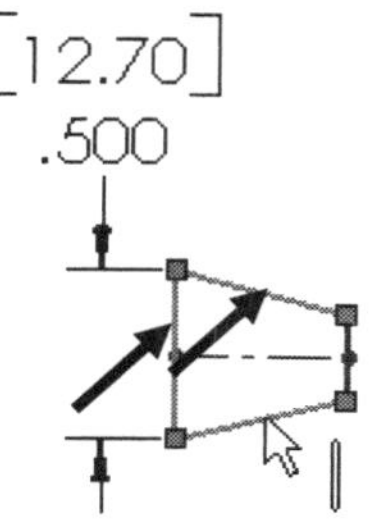

256) Release the **Ctrl** key. Click **Equal** = from the Add Relations box.

257) Click **OK** from the Properties PropertyManager.

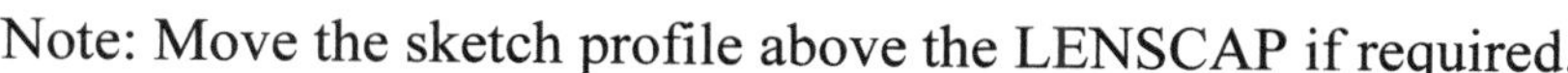

Note: Move the sketch profile above the LENSCAP if required.

Window-select the profile and dimension. Utilize Move/Copy from the Sketch toolbar. Click and drag the sketch to a position above the top right corner of the LENSCAP.

Add a Pierce Relation.

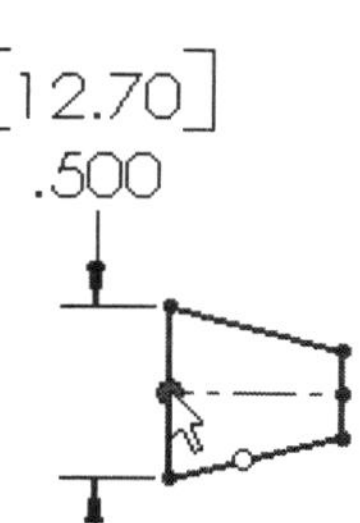

258) Click the **left midpoint** of the trapezoid. Hold the **Ctrl** key down.

259) Click the **starting left back edge** of the ThreadPath.

260) Release the **Ctrl** key.

261) Click **Pierce** from the Add Relations box.

262) Click **OK** from the Properties PropertyManager.

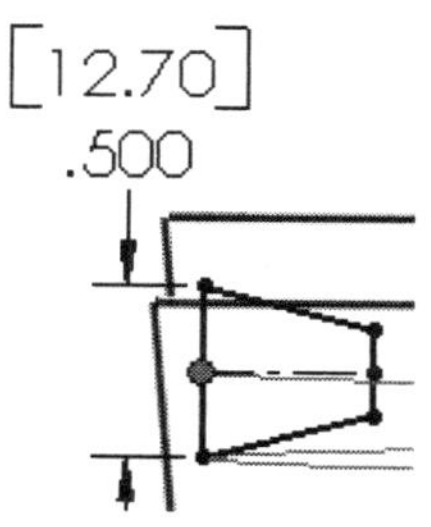

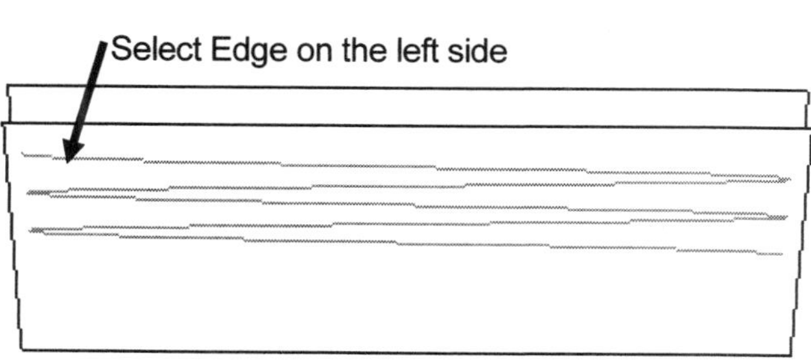

Display the sketch in an Isometric view.

263) Click **Isometric view** .

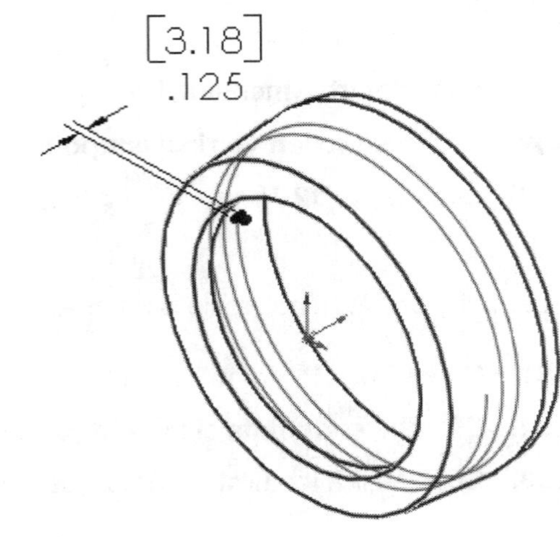

Modify the dimension.

264) Double click the **.500 dimension text**.

265) Enter **.125**, [**3.18**].

Close the Sketch.

266) Click **Exit Sketch**  Exit Sketch.

267) Rename **Sketch5** to **ThreadSection**.

268) Click **Save** .

Insert the Sweep feature.

269) Click **Swept Boss/Base** Swept Boss/B... from the Features toolbar.

270) If required, click **ThreadSection** for the Profile.

271) Click the **Path** box.

272) Click **ThreadPath** from the FeatureManager.

273) Click **OK** from the Sweep PropertyManager.

274) Rename **Sweep1** to **Thread**.

275) Click **Save** .

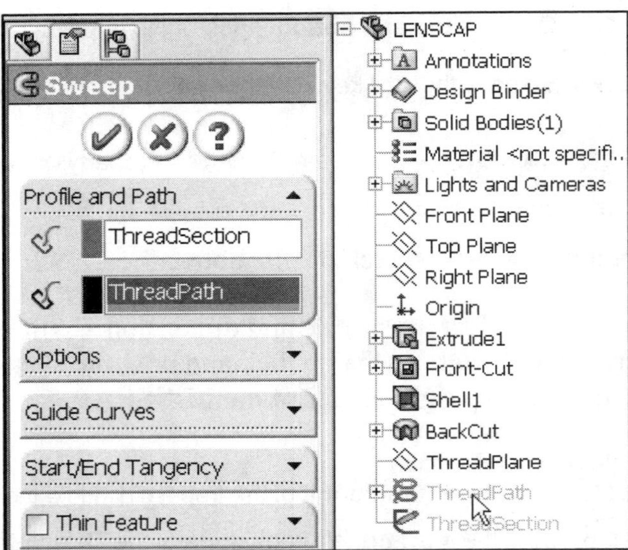

Sweep geometry cannot intersect itself. If the ThreadSection geometry intersects itself, the cross section is too large. Reduce the cross section size and recreate the Sweep feature.

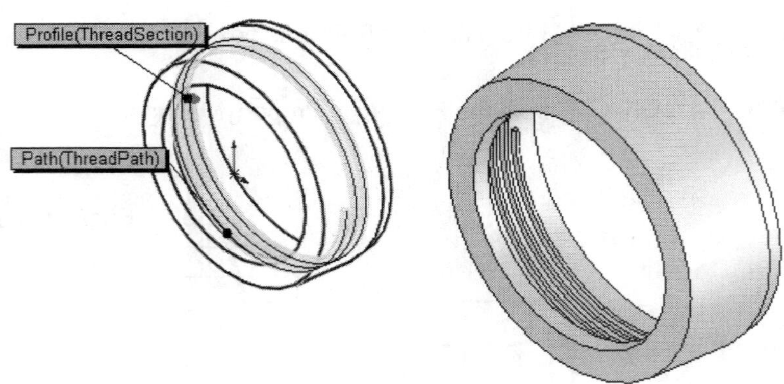

The Thread feature is composed of the following: ThreadSection and ThreadPath.

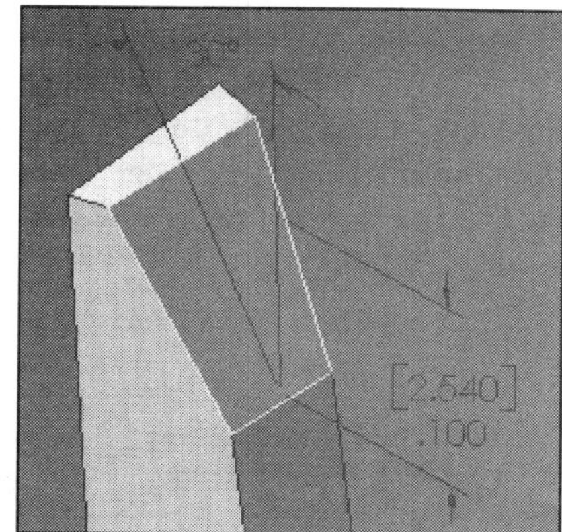

The ThreadPath contains the circular Sketch and the Helical curve.

Most threads require a beveled edge or smooth edge for the thread part start point. A 30° Chamfer feature can be utilized on the starting edge of the trapezoid face. This action is left as an exercise.

Create continuous Sweep features in a single step. Pierce the cross section profile at the start of the sweep path for a continuous Sweep feature.

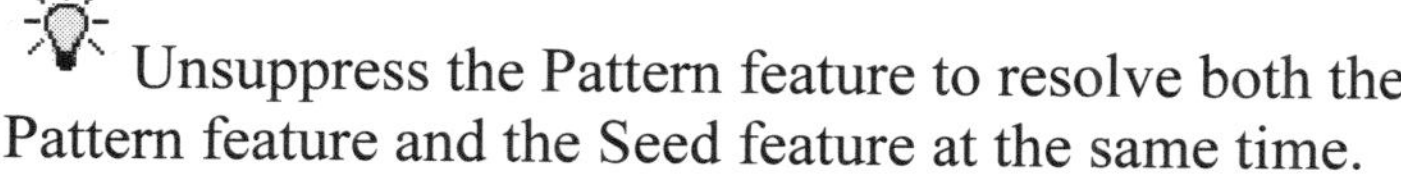

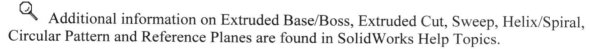

Unsuppress the Pattern feature to resolve both the Pattern feature and the Seed feature at the same time.

The LENSCAP is complete. Review the LENSCAP before moving onto the last part of the FLASHLIGHT.

Additional information on Extruded Base/Boss, Extruded Cut, Sweep, Helix/Spiral, Circular Pattern and Reference Planes are found in SolidWorks Help Topics.

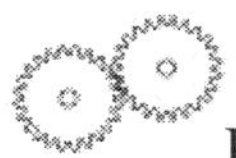

Review of the LENSCAP Part.

The LENSCAP utilized the Extruded Base feature with the Draft Angle option. The Extruded Cut feature created an opening for the LENS. You utilized the Shell feature with constant wall thickness to remove the front and back faces.

The Revolved Cut Thin feature created the back cut with a single line. The line utilized Convert Entities to maintain the same Draft Angle as the Extruded Base feature.

You utilized a Sweep with a Helical Curve and Thread profile to create the Thread.

HOUSING Part

The HOUSING is a plastic part utilized to contain the BATTERY and to support the LENS. The HOUSING utilizes an Extruded Base, Loft, Extruded Boss, Extruded Cut, Draft, Sweep, Rib, Mirror and Linear Pattern features.

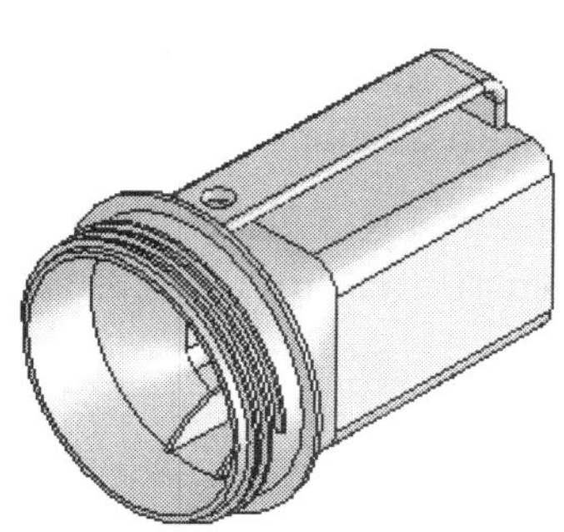

Insert an Extruded Base feature centered at the Origin.

Insert a Loft Boss feature. The first profile is the converted circular edge of the Extruded Base. The second profile is a sketched on the BatteryLoftPlane.

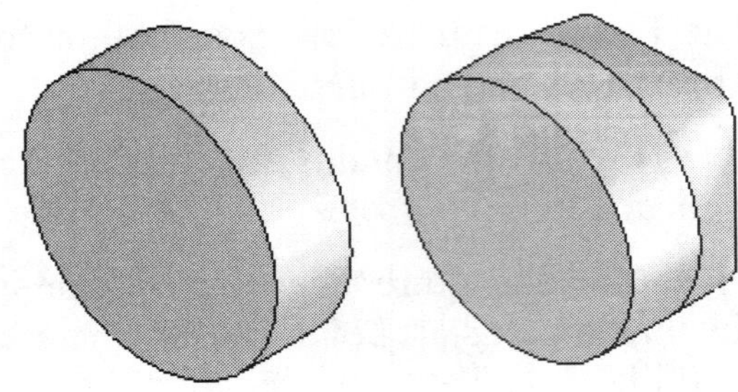

Insert an Extruded Boss. The sketch is a converted edge from the Loft Boss. The depth is determined from the height of the BATTERY.

Insert a Shell feature to create a thin walled part.

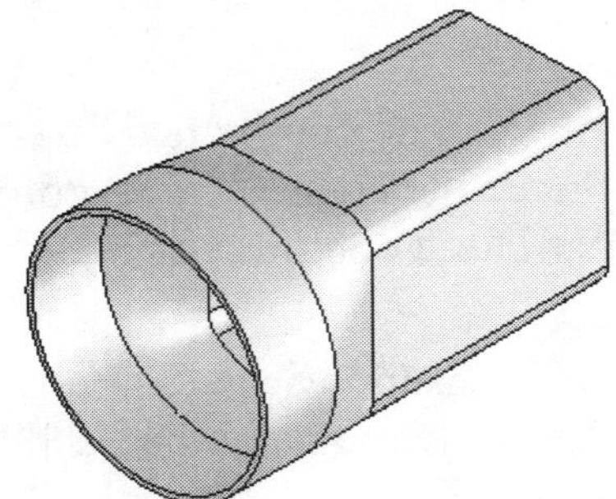

Insert the second Extruded Boss feature. Create a solid circular ring on the back circular face of the Extruded Base feature. Insert the Draft feature to add a Draft Angle to the circular face of the HOUSING. The design intent for the Extruded Base feature requires you to maintain the same LENSCAP Draft Angle.

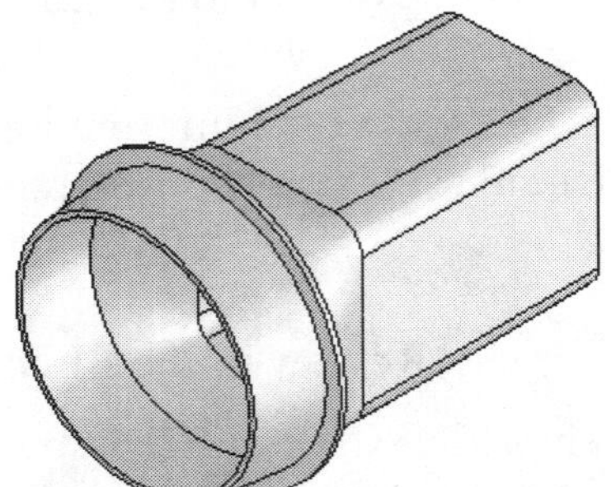

Insert a Sweep feature for the Thread. Insert a Sweep feature for the Handle. Reuse the Thread profile from the LENSCAP part. Insert an Extruded Cut to create the hole for the SWITCH.

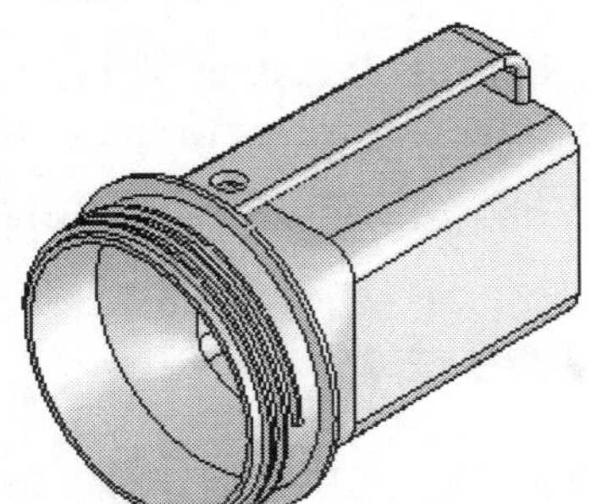

Insert the Rib feature on the back face of the HOUSING. Insert a Linear Pattern to create a row of Ribs.

Insert a Rib along the bottom of the HOUSING. Utilize the Mirror feature to create a second Rib.

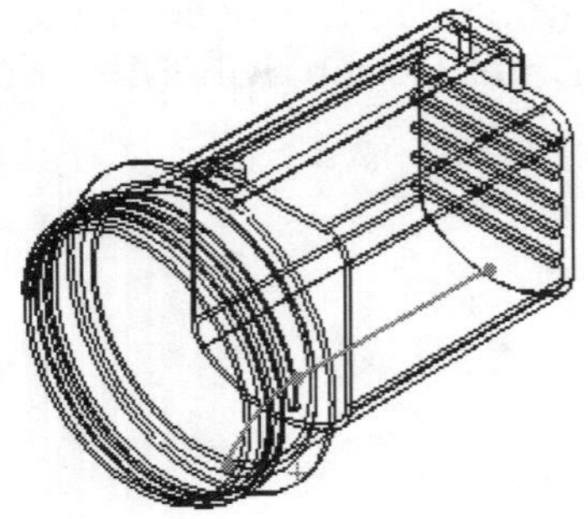

Reuse geometry between parts. The LENSCAP thread is the same as the HOUSING thread. Copy the ThreadSection from the LENSCAP to the HOUSING.

Reuse geometry between features. The Linear Pattern and Mirror Pattern utilized existing features.

Reuse geometry between sketches. The Convert Entities Sketch tool, symmetry and Geometric Relations are utilized in the HOUSING features.

Activity: HOUSING Part-Extruded Base Feature

Create the new part.

276) Click **File**, **New** from the Main menu. Click the **MY-TEMPLATES** tab.

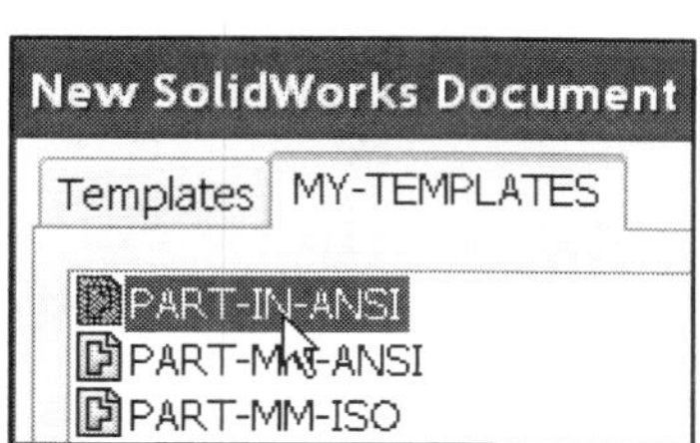

277) Double-click **PART-IN-ANSI**, [**PART-MM-ISO**].

278) Click **Save**. Select **PROJECTS** for the Save in folder.

279) Enter **HOUSING** for file name. Enter **HOUSING FOR 6VOLT FLASHLIGHT** for Description. Click **Save**.

Create the Sketch.

280) Click **Front Plane** from the FeatureManager.

281) Click **Sketch** Sketch. Click **Circle** Circle from the Sketch toolbar.

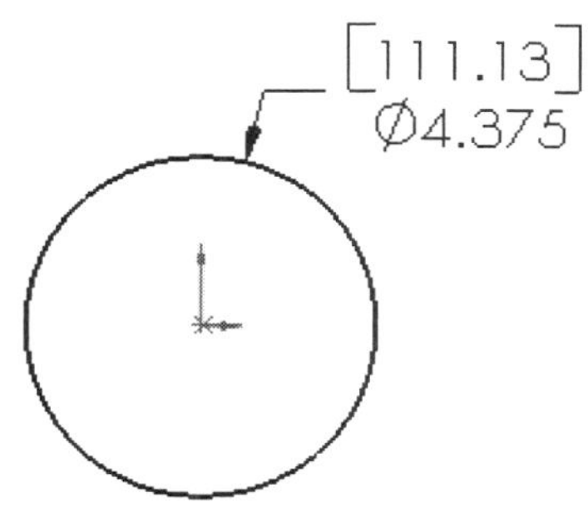

282) Create a circle centered at the **Origin**.

Add a dimension.

283) Click **Smart Dimension** .

284) Click the **circumference**.

285) Enter **4.375**, [**111.13**].

Insert an Extruded Base feature.

286) Click **Extruded Boss/Base** .

287) Enter **1.300**, [**33.02**] for Depth.

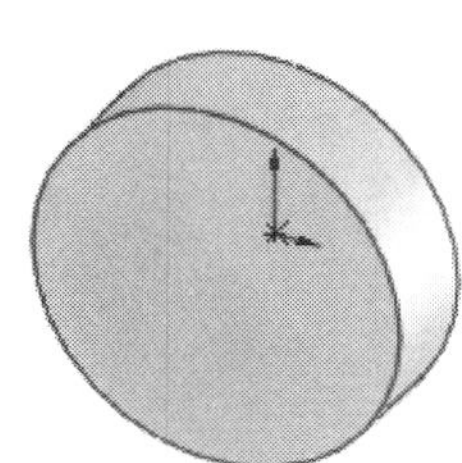

288) Click **OK** from the Extrude PropertyManager.

289) Rename **Extrude1** to **Base Extrude**.

290) Click **Save**.

HOUSING Part-Loft Boss Feature

The Loft Boss feature is composed of two profiles. The first sketch is named Sketch-Circle. The second sketch is named Sketch-Square.

Create the first profile from the back face of the Extruded feature.

Utilize the Convert Entities sketch tool to extract the circular geometry to the back face.

Create the second profile on an Offset Plane. The FLASHLIGHT components must remain aligned to a common centerline. Insert dimensions that reference the Origin and build symmetry into the sketch. Utilize the Mirror Entities Sketch tool.

Activity: HOUSING Part-Loft Boss Feature

Create the first profile.

291) Click the **back face** of the Base Extrude feature.

292) Click **Sketch** Sketch.

293) Click **Convert Entities** Convert from the Sketch toolbar to extract the face to the sketch plane.

Close the Sketch.

294) Click **Exit Sketch** Exit Sketch.

295) Rename **Sketch2** to **SketchCircle**.

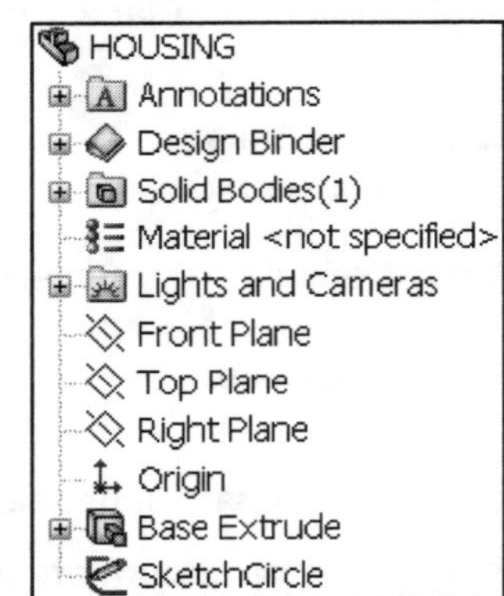

Create an offset plane.

296) Click the **back face** of the Base Extrude feature.

297) Click **Insert**, **Reference Geometry**, **Plane** from the Main menu.

298) Enter **1.300**, [**33.02**] for Distance.

299) Click **Top view** to verify the Plane position.

300) Click **OK** from the Plane PropertyManager.

301) Rename **Plane1** to **BatteryLoftPlane**.

302) Click **Rebuild** from the Main menu.

303) Click **Save**.

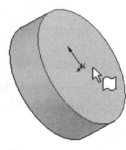

BatteryLoftPlane

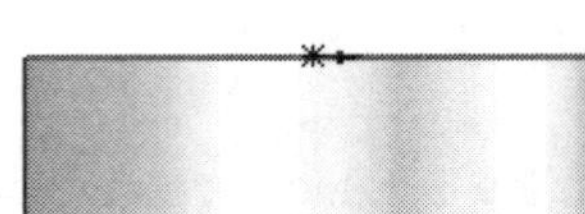

Create the second profile.

304) Click **BatteryLoftPlane** in the FeatureManager.

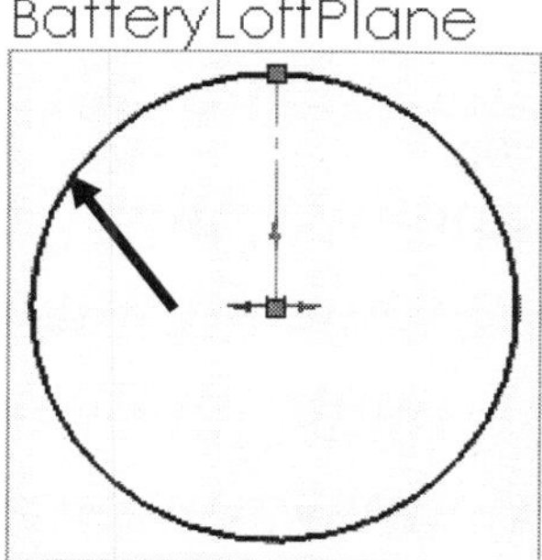

305) Click **Sketch** .

306) Click **Back view**.

307) Click the **circumference** of the circle.

308) Click **Convert Entities** Convert from the Sketch toolbar.

309) Click **Centerline** Centerl... from the Sketch toolbar.

310) Sketch a **vertical centerline** coincident to the Origin to the top edge of the circle.

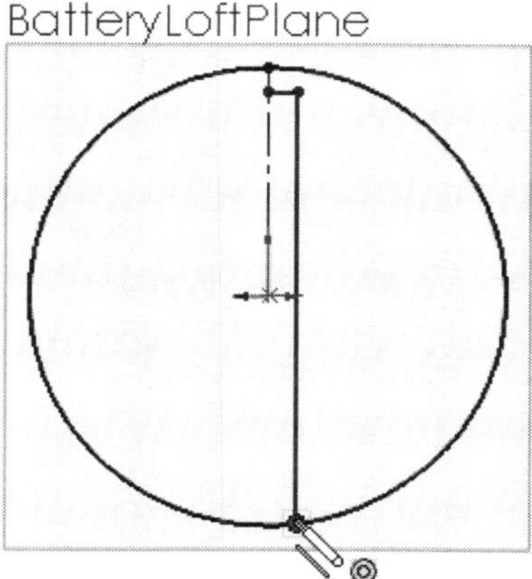

311) Click **Line** Line from the Sketch toolbar.

312) Sketch a **horizontal line** to the right side of the centerline.

313) Sketch a **vertical line** down to the circumference.

314) Click **Sketch Fillet** Sketch Fillet from the Sketch toolbar.

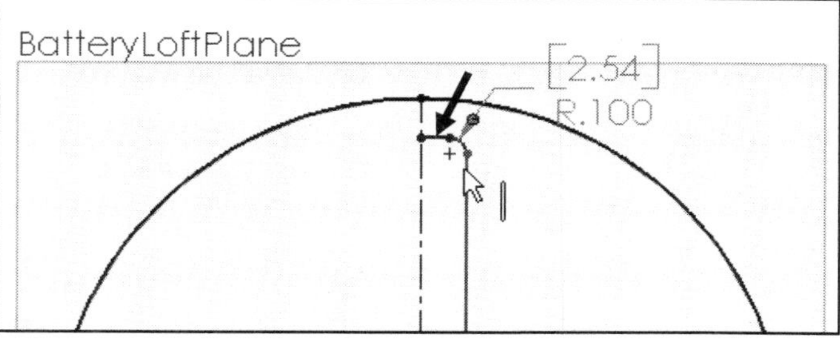

315) Click the **horizontal line**.

316) Click the **vertical line**.

317) Enter **.1** [**2.54**] for Radius.

318) Click **OK** from the Sketch Fillet PropertyManager.

Mirror the profile.

319) Click **Mirror Entities** Mirror from the Sketch toolbar.

320) Click the **horizontal line**, **fillet** and **vertical line**.

321) Click the **Mirror about** text box.

322) Click the **Centerline**.

323) Click **OK** from the Mirror Entities PropertyManager.

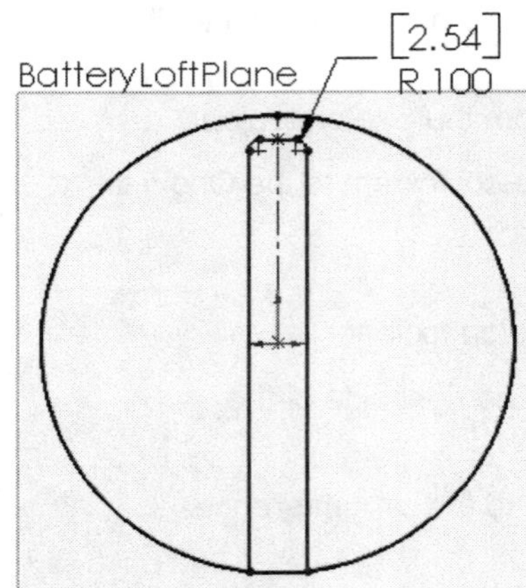

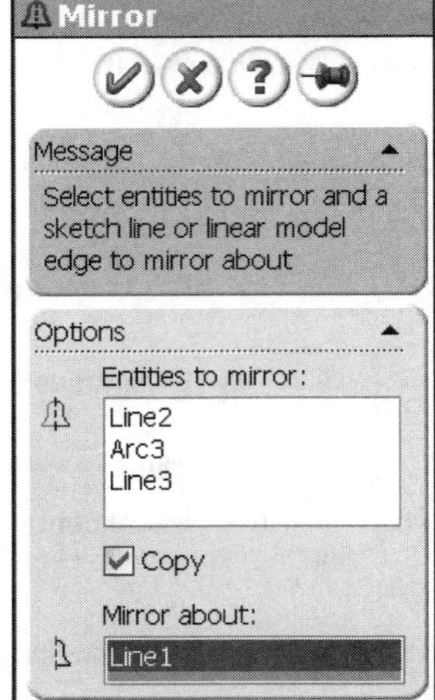

Trim unwanted geometry.

324) Click **Trim Entities** Trim from the Sketch toolbar.

325) Click **PowerTrim** from the Option box.

326) Click a **position** to the far right of the circle.

327) Drag the **mouse pointer** to intersect the circle.

328) Perform the same **actions** on the left side of the circle.

329) Click **OK** from the Trim PropertyManager.

Add dimensions.

330) Click **Smart Dimension** Smart Dimens... .

Create the horizontal dimension.

331) Click the **left vertical** line.

332) Click the **right vertical line**.

333) Click a **position** above the profile.

334) Enter **3.100**, [**78.74**].

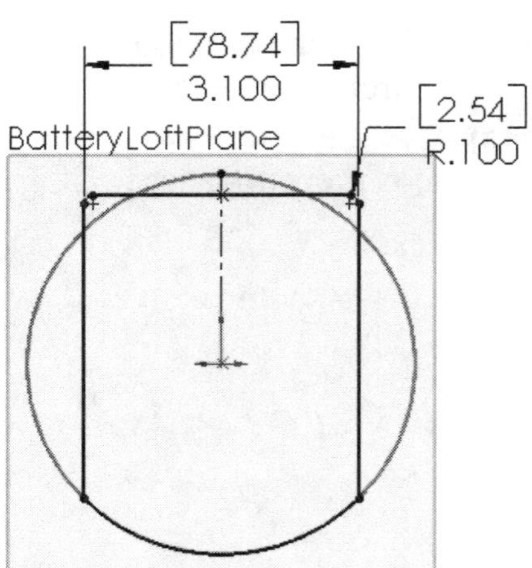

Create the vertical dimension.

335) Click the **Origin**.

336) Click the **top horizontal** line.

337) Click a **position** to the right of the profile.

338) Enter **1.600**, **[40.64]**.

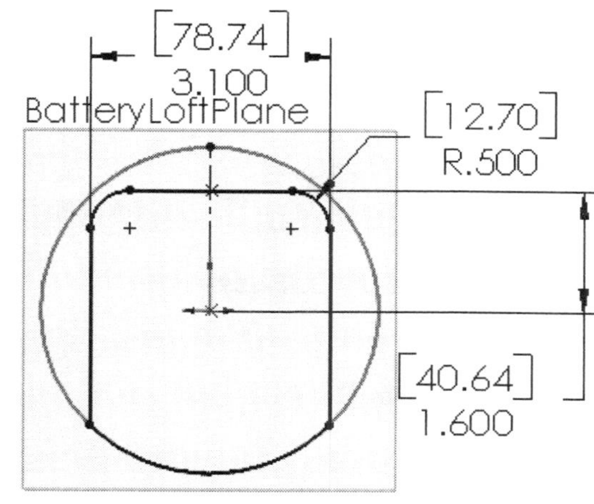

Modify the fillet dimension.

339) Double-click the **.100** fillet dimension.

340) Enter **.500**, **[12.7]**.

Remove all sharp edges.

341) Click **Sketch Fillet** Sketch Fillet from the Sketch toolbar.

342) Enter **.500**, **[12.7]** for Radius.

343) Click the **lower left corner point**.

344) Click the **lower right corner point**.

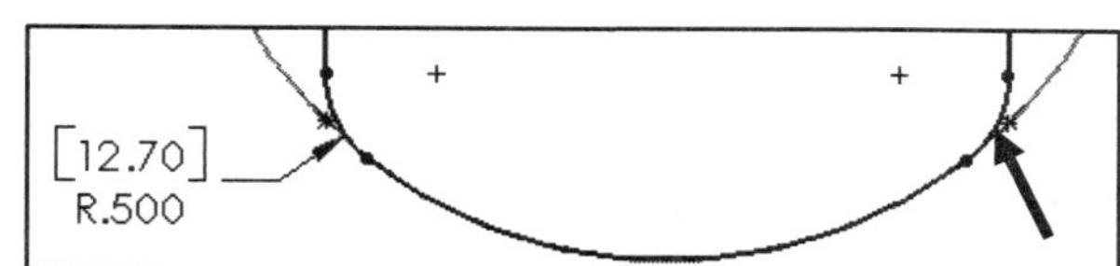

345) Click **OK** from the Sketch Fillet PropertyManager.

Close the Sketch.

346) Click **Exit Sketch** Exit Sketch.

347) Rename **Sketch3** to **SketchSquare**.

Base Extrude
SketchCircle
BatteryLoftPlane
SketchSquare

348) Click **Save** .

The Loft feature is composed of the SketchSquare and the SketchCircle. Select two individual profiles to create the Loft. The Isometric view provides clarity when selecting Loft profiles.

Display the Isometric view.

349) Click **Isometric view** .

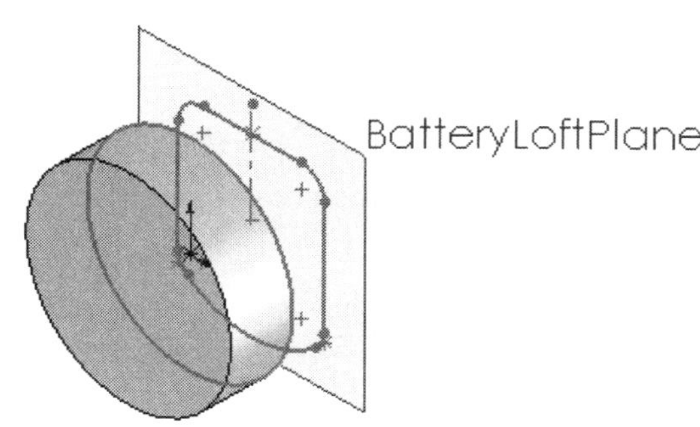

Insert a Loft feature.

350) Click **Lofted Boss/Base** Lofted Boss/B... from the Features toolbar.

351) Click the **top right corner** of the Sketch Square.

352) Click the **upper right side** of the Sketch Circle.

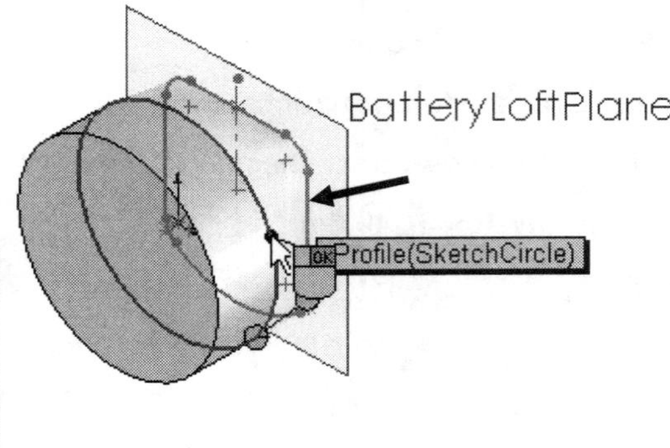

353) Click **OK** from the Loft PropertyManager.

354) Rename **Loft1** to **Boss-Loft1**.

355) Click **Save**.

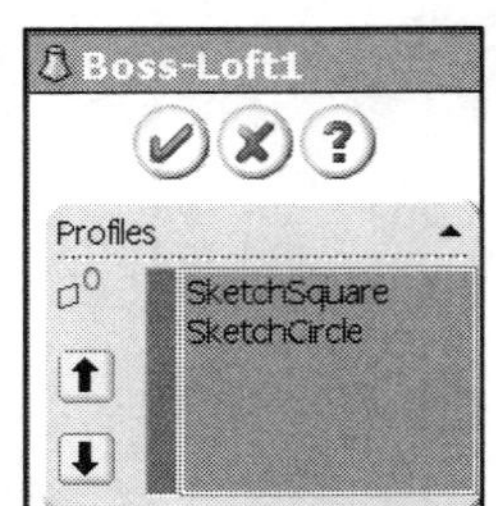

Organize the FeatureManager to locate Loft profiles and planes. Insert the Loft reference planes directly before the Loft feature. Rename the planes, profiles and guide curves with clear descriptive names.

HOUSING Part-First Extruded Boss Feature

Create the first Extruded Boss feature from the square face of the Loft. How do you estimate the depth of the Extruded Boss feature? Answer: The Extruded Base feature of the BATTERY is 4.1in, [104.14mm].

Ribs are required to support the BATTERY. Design for Rib construction. Ribs add strength to the HOUSING and support the BATTERY. Use a 4.4in, [111.76mm] depth as the first estimate. Adjust the estimated depth dimension later if required in the FLASHLIGHT assembly.

The Extruded Boss feature is symmetric about the Right Plane. Utilize Convert Entities to extract the back face of the Boss-Loft. No sketch dimensions are required.

Activity: HOUSING Part-First Extruded Boss Feature

Select the Sketch Plane.

356) Click **Back view**.

357) Click the **back face** of Boss-Loft1.

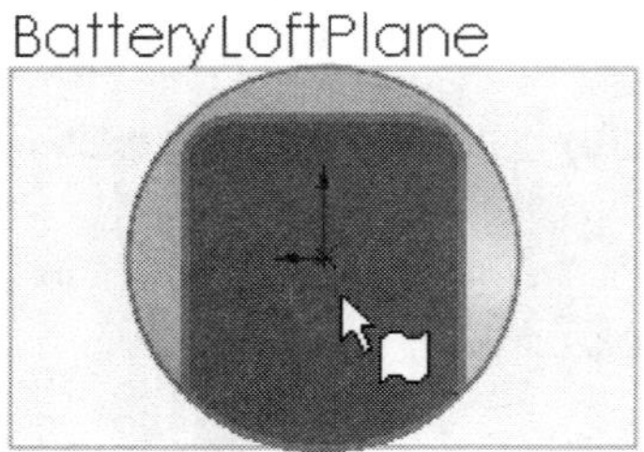

Insert the Sketch.

358) Click **Sketch** Sketch.

359) Click **Convert Entities** Convert from the Sketch toolbar.

Insert an Extruded Boss feature.

360) Click **Extruded Boss/Base** .

361) Enter **4.400**, [**111.76**] for Depth.

362) Check the **Draft On/Off** button.

363) Enter **1** for Draft Angle.

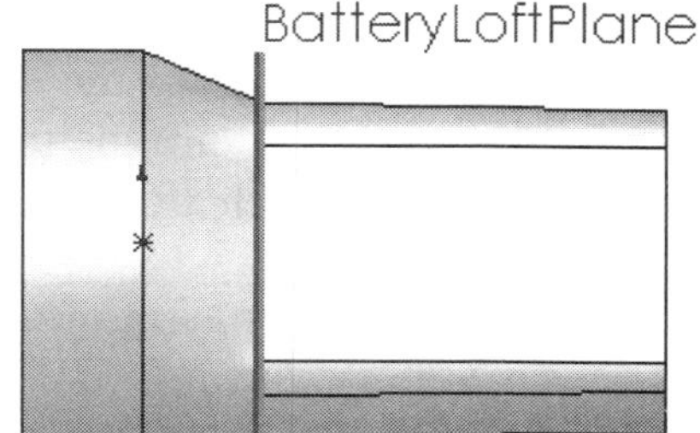

364) Click **OK** from the Extrude PropertyManager.

365) Click **Right view**.

366) Rename **Extrude2** to **Boss-Battery**.

367) Click **Save**.

HOUSING Part-Shell Feature

The Shell feature removes material. Use the Shell feature to remove the front face of the HOUSING. In the injection-molded process, the body wall thickness remains constant.

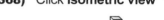

Activity: HOUSING Part-Shell Feature

Insert the Shell feature.

368) Click **Isometric view**.

369) Click **Shell** from the Features toolbar.

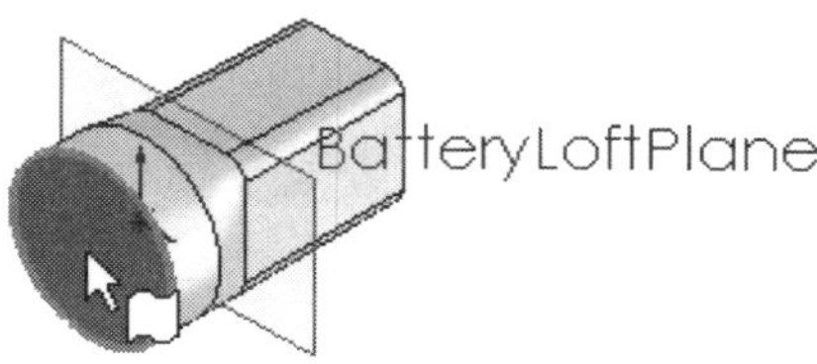

370) Click the **front face** of the Extruded feature.

371) Enter **.100**, [**2.54**] for Thickness.

372) Click **OK** from the Shell1 PropertyManager.

373) Click **Save**.

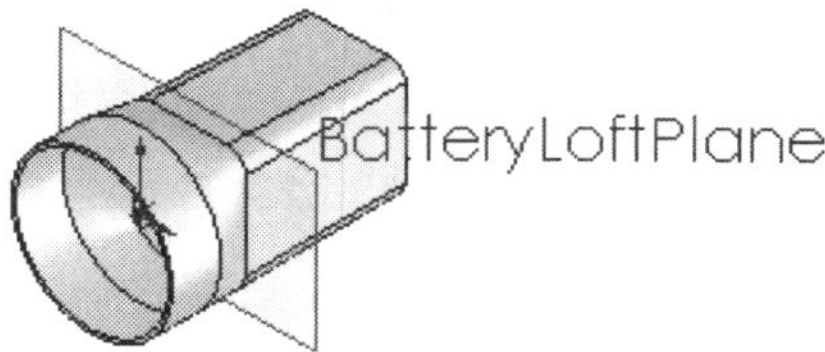

The Shell feature position in the FeatureManager determines the geometry of additional features. Features created before the Shell contained the wall thickness specified in the Thickness option. Position features of different thickness such as the Rib feature and Thread Sweep feature after the Shell. Features inserted after the Shell remain solid.

HOUSING Part-Second Extruded Boss Feature

The second Extruded Boss feature creates a solid circular ring on the back circular face of the Extruded Base feature. The solid ring is a cosmetic stop for the LENSCAP and provides rigidity at the transition of the HOUSING. Design for change. The Extruded Boss feature updates if the Shell thickness changes.

Utilize the Front Plane for the sketch. Select the inside circular edge of the Shell. Utilize Convert Entities to obtain the inside circle. Utilize the Circle Sketch tool to create the outside circle. Extrude the feature towards the front face.

Activity: HOUSING Part-Second Extruded Boss Feature

Select the Sketch Plane.

374) Click the **Front Plane** from the FeatureManager.

Create the Sketch.

375) Click **Sketch** Sketch.

376) Click the **front inside circular edge** of Shell1.

377) Click **Convert Entities** Convert from the Sketch toolbar.

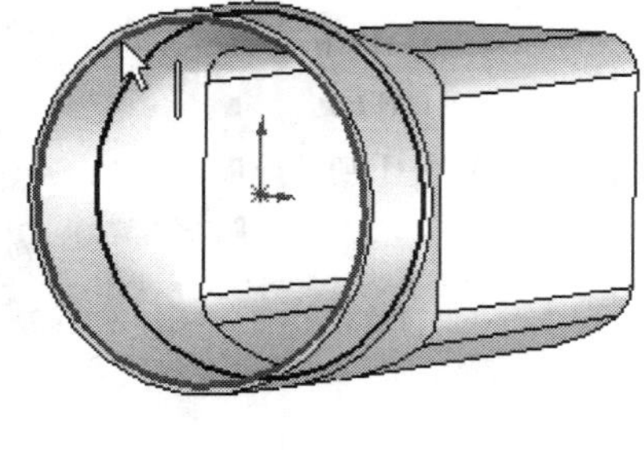

Create the outside circle.

378) Click **Front view**.

379) Click **Circle** Circle from the Sketch toolbar.

380) Create a **circle** centered at the Origin.

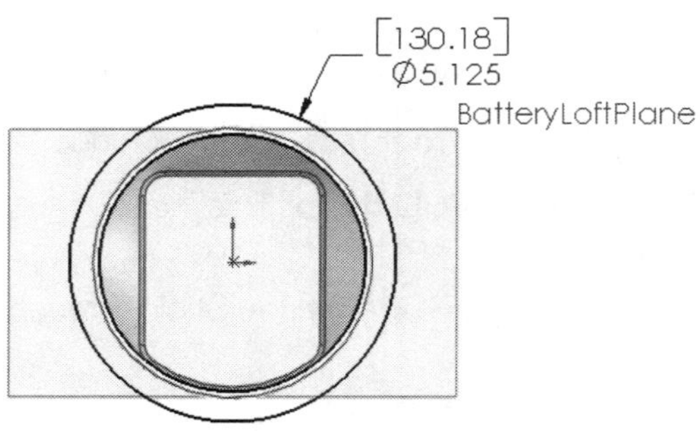

Add a dimension.

381) Click **Smart Dimension** Smart Dimens....

382) Click the **circumference** of the circle.

383) Enter **5.125**, **[130.18]**.

Insert an Extruded Boss feature.

384) Click **Extruded Boss/Base** Extruded Boss/B....

385) Enter **.100**, **[2.54]** for Depth.

386) Click **OK** from the Extrude PropertyManager.

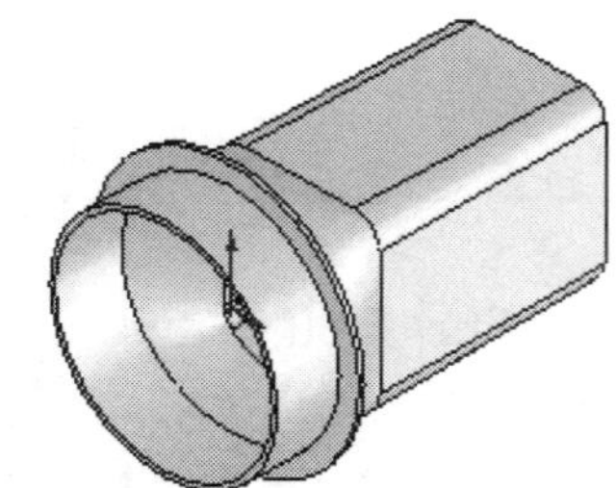

387) Click **Isometric view** .

388) Rename **Extrude3** to **Boss-Stop**.

389) Click **Save** .

HOUSING Part-Draft Feature

The Draft feature tapers selected model faces by a specified angle by utilizing a Neutral Plane or Parting Line. The Neutral Plane option utilizes a plane or face to determine the pull direction when creating a mold.

The Parting Line option drafts surfaces around a parting line of a mold. Utilize the Parting Line option for non-planar surfaces. Apply the Draft feature to solid and surface models.

A 5° draft is required to insure proper thread mating between the LENSCAP and the HOUSING. The LENSCAP Extruded Base feature has a 5° draft angle.

The outside face of the Extruded Base feature HOUSING requires a 5° draft angle. The inside HOUSING wall does not require a draft angle. The Extruded Base feature has a 5° draft angle. Use the Draft feature to create a draft angle. The front circular face is the Neutral Plane. The outside cylindrical surface is the face to draft.

You created the Extruded Boss/Base and Extrude Cut features with the Draft Angle option. The Draft feature differs from the Extruded feature, Draft Angle option. The Draft feature allows you to select multiple faces to taper.

Activity: HOUSING Part-Draft Feature

Insert the Draft feature.

390) Click the thin **front circular face** of the Base-Extrude.

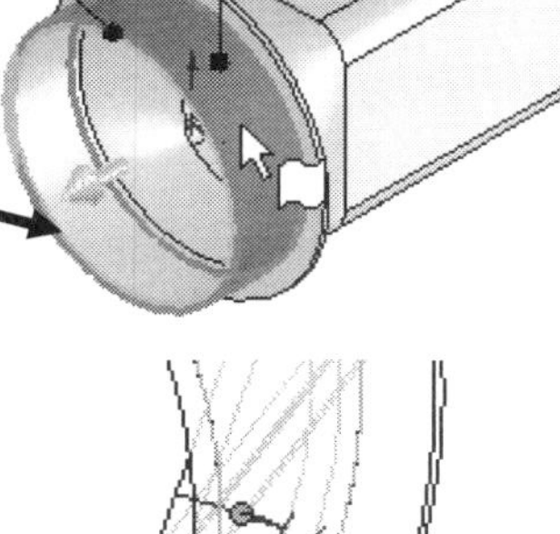

391) Click **Draft**  from the Feature toolbar.

392) The front circular face is displayed in the Neutral Plane text box. Click the **Faces to draft** box.

393) Click the **outside circular face**.

394) Enter **5** for Draft Angle.

395) Click **OK** from the Draft PropertyManager.

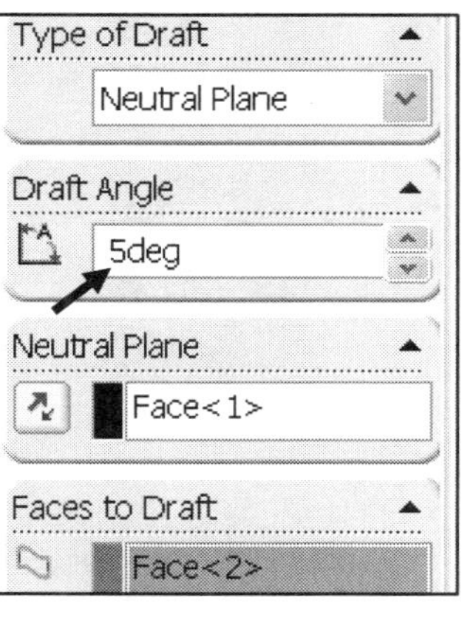

5°

Display the Draft Angle and the straight interior.

396) Click **Right view**.

397) Click **Hidden Lines Visible**.

398) Click **Save**.

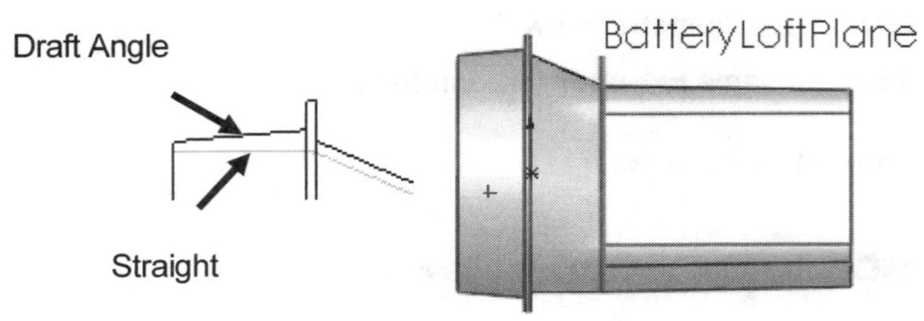

Order of feature creation is important. Apply threads after the Draft feature for plastic parts to maintain a constant thread thickness.

HOUSING Part-Thread with Sweep Feature

The HOUSING requires a thread. Create the threads for the HOUSING on the outside of the Draft feature. Create the thread with the Sweep feature. The thread requires two sketches: ThreadPath and ThreadSection. The LENSCAP and HOUSING Thread utilize the same technique. Create a ThreadPlane. Utilize Convert Entities to create a circular sketch referencing the HOUSING Base Extrude feature. Insert a Helix/Spiral curve to create the path.

Reuse geometry between parts. The ThreadSection is copied from the LENSCAP and is inserted into the HOUSING Top Plane.

Activity: HOUSING Part-Thread with Sweep Feature

Insert the ThreadPlane.

399) Click **Isometric view**.

400) Click the **thin front circular face,** Base Extrude.

401) Click **Insert**, **Reference Geometry, Plane** Plane... from the Main menu.

402) Click the **Reverse direction** check box. Enter **.125**, **[3.18]** for Distance.

403) Click **OK** from the Plane PropertyManager.

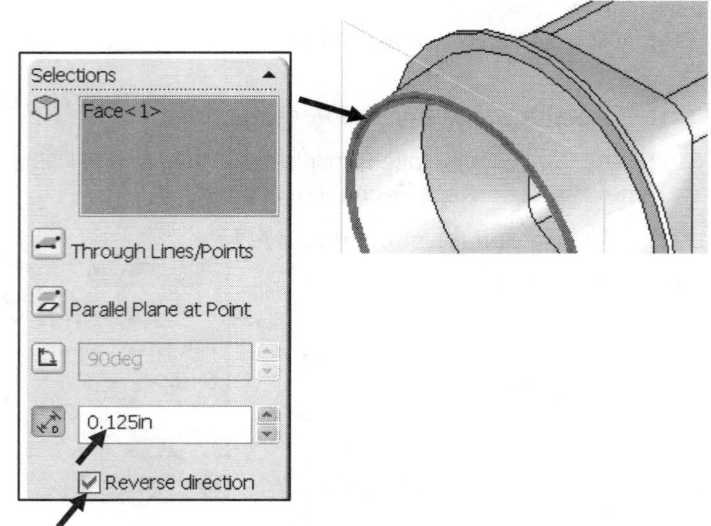

404) Click **Save** .

405) Rename **Plane2** to **ThreadPlane**.

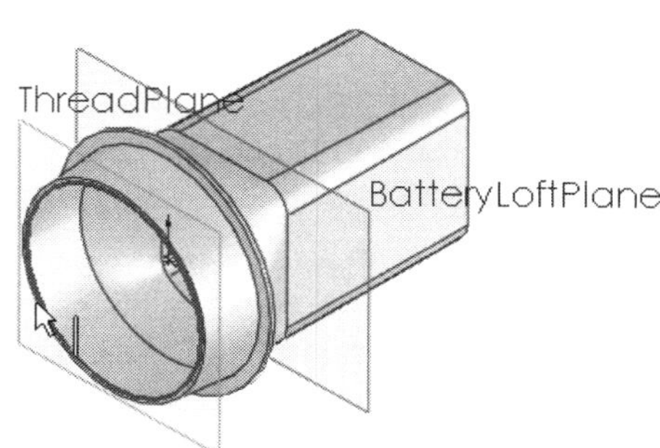

Insert the ThreadPath.

406) Click **Sketch** Sketch .

407) Select the **front outside circular edge** of the Base Extrude.

408) Click **Convert Entities** Convert . The circular edge is displayed on the ThreadPlane.

Insert the Helix/Spiral curve.

409) Click **Insert**, **Curve**, **Helix/Spiral** Helix/Spiral... from the Main menu.

410) Enter **.250**, [**6.35**] for Pitch.

411) Click the **Reverse direction** checkbox.

412) Enter **2.5** for Revolution.

413) Enter **180** in the Start angle spin box. The Helix start point and end point are Coincident with the Top Plane.

414) Click the **Taper Helix** check box.

415) Enter **5** for Angle.

416) Click the **Taper outward** check box.

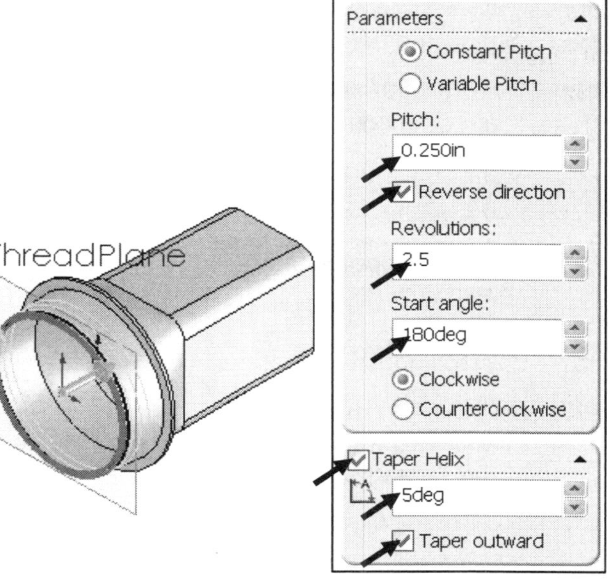

417) Click **OK** from the PropertyManager.

418) Click **Exit Sketch** Exit Sketch.

419) Rename **Helix/Spiral1** to **ThreadPath**.

420) Click **Isometric view** .

421) Click **Save** .

Copy the LENSCAP ThreadSection.

422) **Open** the LENSCAP. **Expand** the Thread feature from the FeatureManager. Click the **ThreadSection** sketch. Click **Edit**, **Copy** from the Main menu.

423) **Close** the LENSCAP.

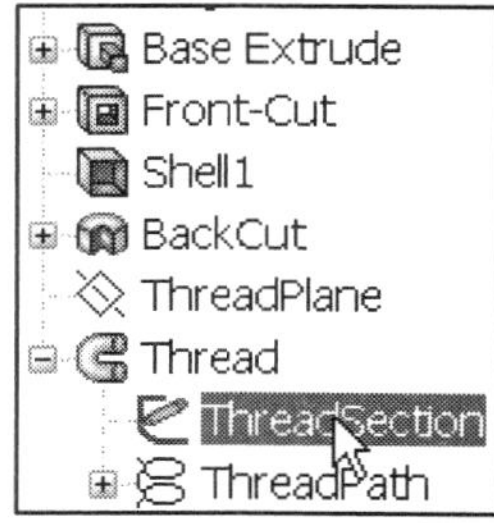

Open the HOUSING.

424) **Return** to the Housing.

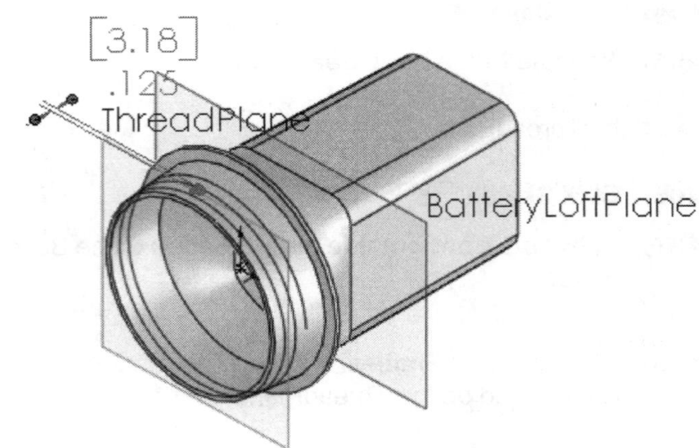

Paste the LENSCAP ThreadSection.

425) Click the **Top Plane** from the HOUSING FeatureManager.

426) Click **Edit**, **Paste** from the Main menu. The ThreadSection is displayed on the Top Plane. The new Sketch7 name is added to the bottom of the FeatureManager.

427) Rename **Sketch7** to **ThreadSection**.

428) Click **Save** .

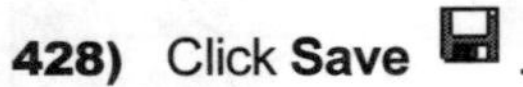

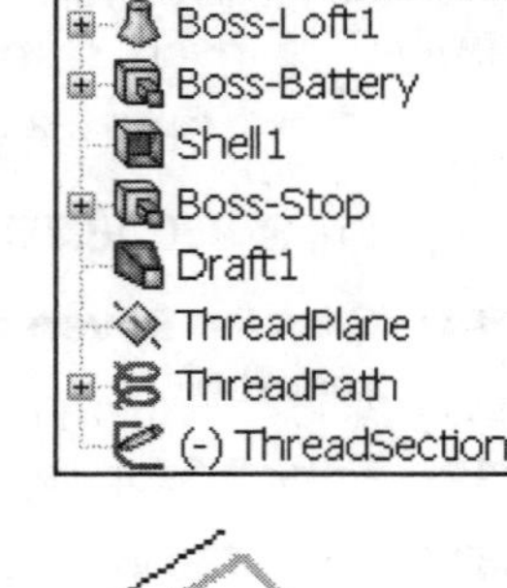

Add a Pierce Relation.

429) Right-click on **ThreadSection** from the FeatureManager.

430) Click **Edit Sketch**.

431) Click **ThreadSection** from the HOUSING FeatureManager.

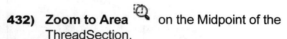

432) **Zoom to Area** on the Midpoint of the ThreadSection.

433) Click the **Midpoint** of the ThreadSection.

434) Click **Isometric view** .

435) Hold the **Ctrl** key down.

436) Click the **right back edge of the ThreadPath**.

437) Release the **Ctrl** key.

438) Click **Pierce** from the Add Relations box.

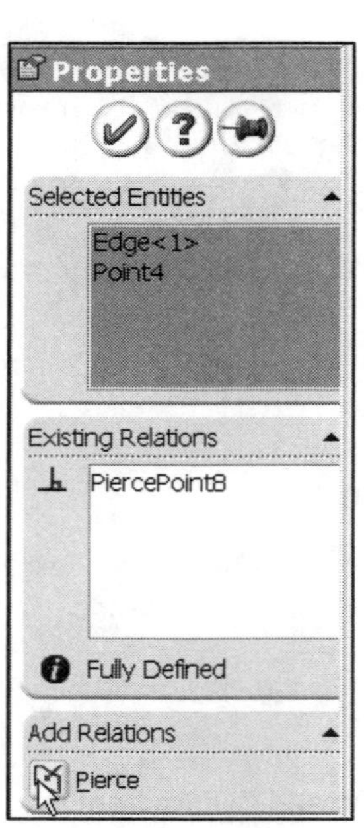

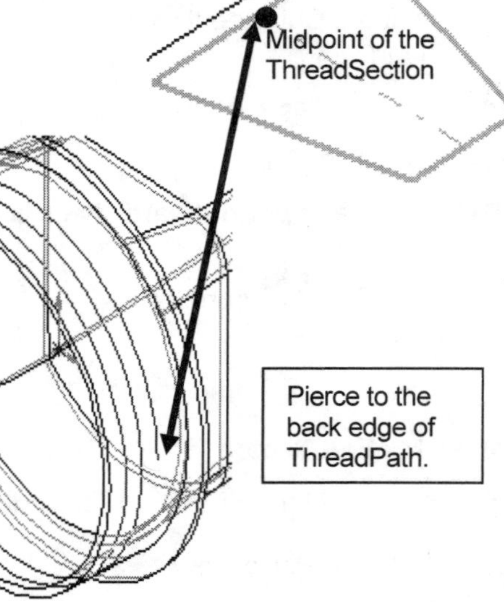

439) Click **OK** from the Properties PropertyManager.

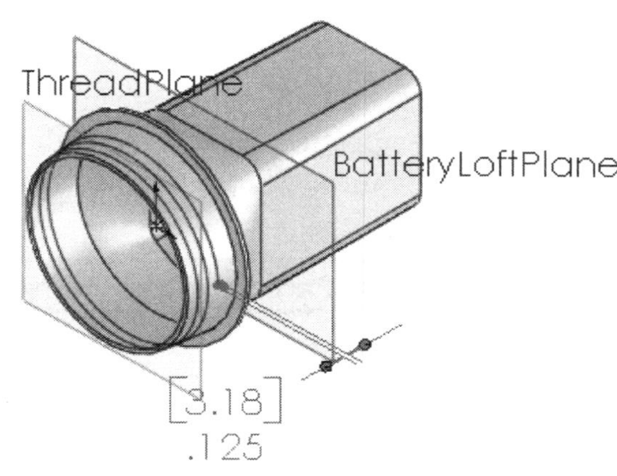

Caution: Do not click the front edge of the Thread path. The Thread is then created out of the HOUSING.

Close the Sketch.

440) Click **Exit Sketch** Exit Sketch.

Insert the Sweep feature.

441) Click **Swept** Boss/B... from the Feature toolbar.

442) **Expand** HOUSING in the Graphics window.

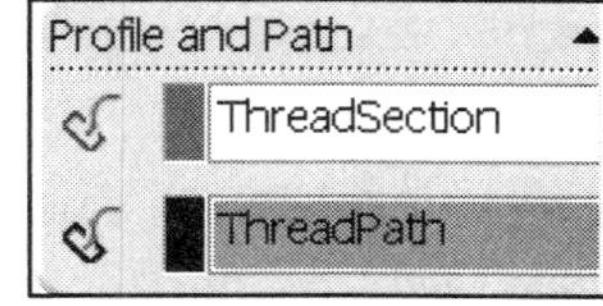

443) Click the **Profile** box.

444) Click **ThreadSection** from the FeatureManager.

445) Click the **Path** box.

446) Click **ThreadPath** from the FeatureManager.

447) Click **OK** from the Sweep PropertyManager.

448) Rename **Sweep1** to **Thread**.

449) Click **Save**.

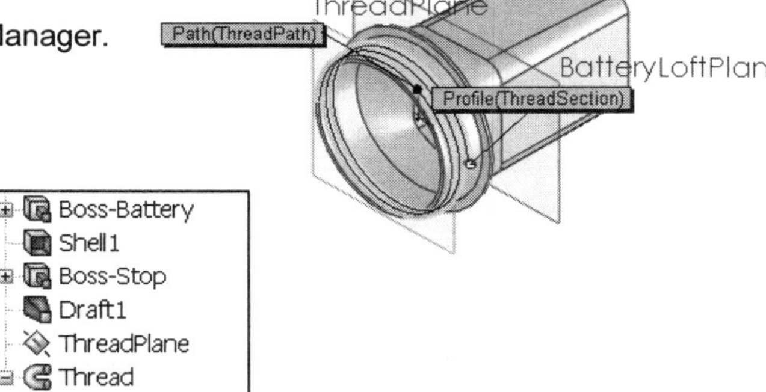

Creating a ThreadPlane provides flexibility to the design. The ThreadPlane allows for a smoother lead. Utilize the ThreadPlane offset dimension to adjust the start of the thread.

HOUSING Part-Handle with Sweep Feature

Create the handle with the Sweep feature. The Sweep feature consists of a sketched path and cross section profile. Sketch the path on the Right Plane. The sketch uses edges from existing features. Sketch the profile on the back circular face of the Boss-Stop feature.

Activity: HOUSING Part-Handle with Sweep Feature

Create the Sweep path sketch.

450) Click **Right Plane** from the FeatureManager.

451) Click **Sketch** Sketch.

452) Click **Right view**.

453) Click **Hidden Lines Removed**.

454) Click **Line** Line.

455) Sketch a **horizontal line** below the top of the Boss Stop.

456) Sketch a **vertical line** to the right top corner of the Housing.

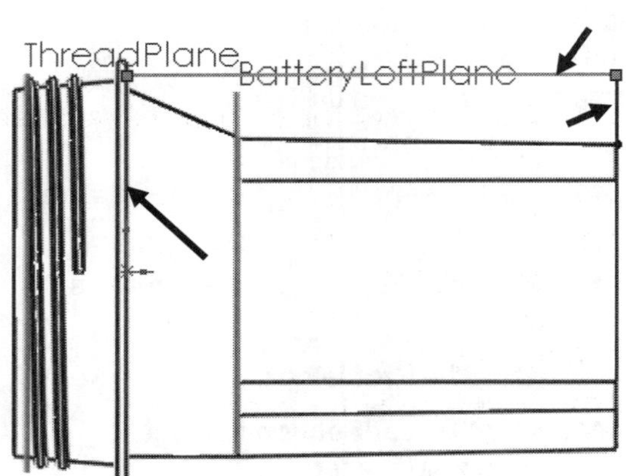

Insert a 2D Fillet.

457) Click **Sketch Fillet** Sketch Fillet.

458) Click the **upper right corner** of the sketch lines.

459) Enter **.500**, [**12.7**] for Radius.

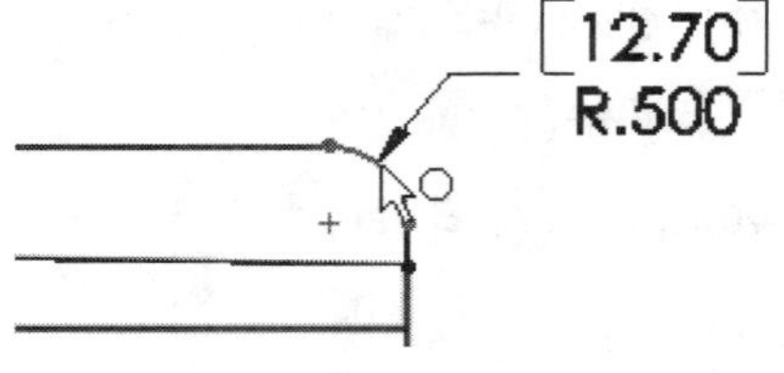

460) Click **OK** from the Sketch Fillet PropertyManager.

Add a Coincident Relation.

461) Click the **left end point** of the horizontal line.

462) Hold the **Ctrl** key down.

463) Click the **right vertical edge** of the Boss Stop.

464) Release the **Ctrl** key.

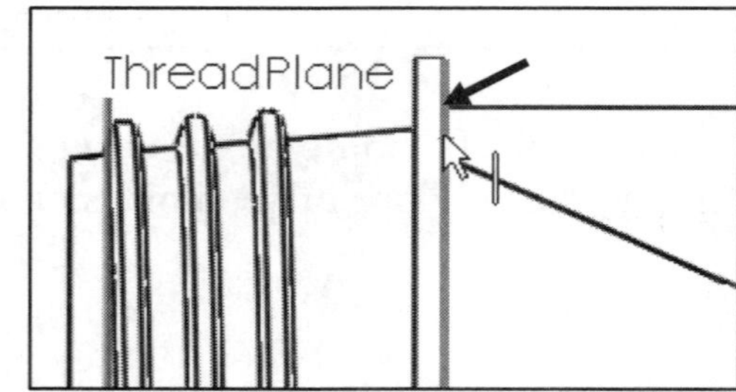

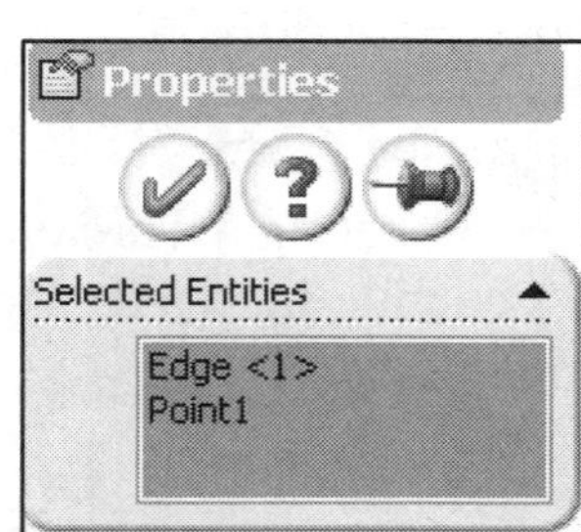

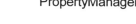

465) Click **Coincident** from the Add Relations box.

466) Click **OK** from the Properties PropertyManager.

Add an Intersection Relation

467) Click the **bottom end point** of the vertical line. Hold the **Ctrl** key down.

468) Click the **right vertical edge** of the Housing.

469) Click the **horizontal edge** of the Housing.

470) Release the **Ctrl** key.

471) Click **Intersection** from the Add Relations box.

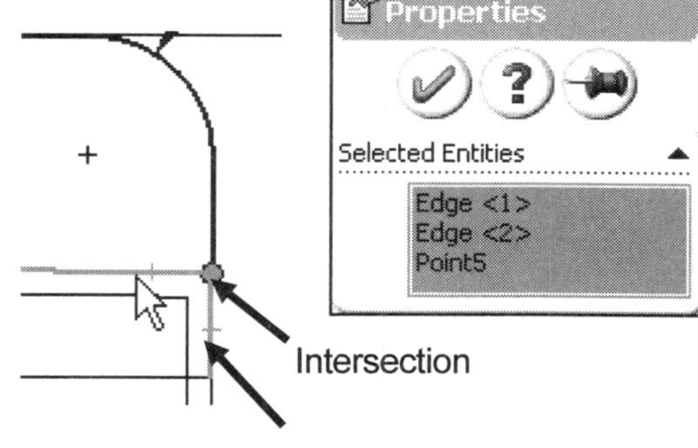

472) Click **OK** from the Properties PropertyManager.

Add a dimension.

473) Click **Smart Dimension** .

474) Click the **Origin**.

475) Click the **horizontal line**.

476) Click a **position** to the right.

477) Enter **2.500**, **[63.5]**.

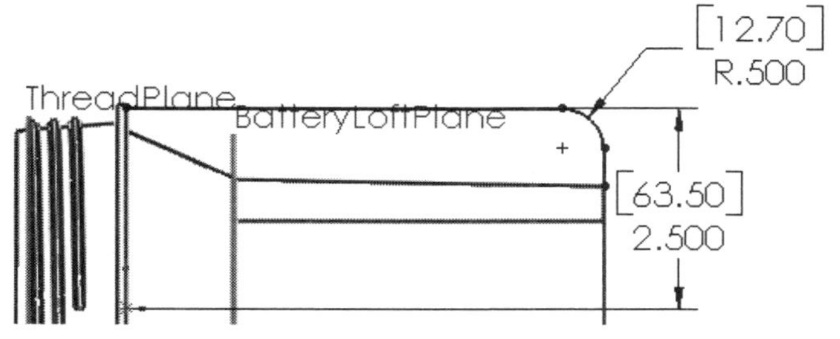

Close the Sketch.

478) Click **Exit Sketch** .

479) Rename **Sketch8** to **HandlePath**.

480) Click **Save**.

Create the Sweep Profile.

481) Click **Back view**.

482) Select the **back circular face** of the Boss-Stop feature.

483) Click **Sketch**.

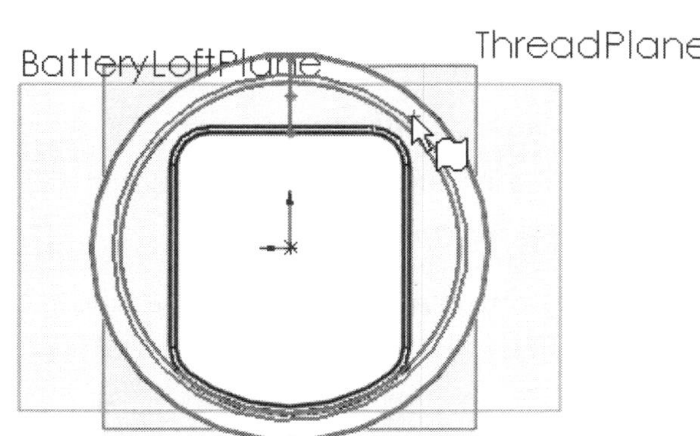

484) Click **Centerline** Centerl... .

485) Sketch a **vertical centerline** collinear with the Right Plane, coincident to the Origin.

486) Sketch a **horizontal centerline**. The left end point of the centerline is coincident with the vertical centerline on the Boss-Stop feature. Do not select existing feature geometry.

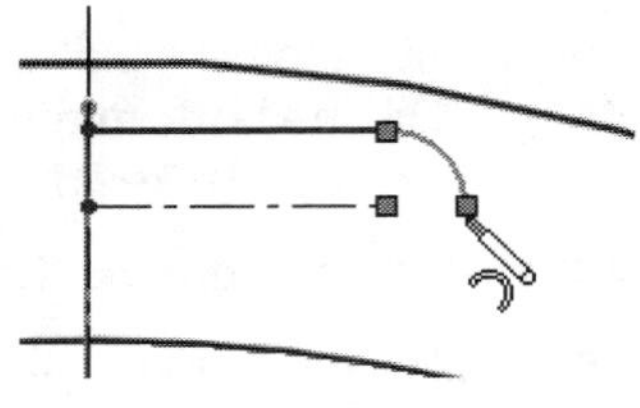

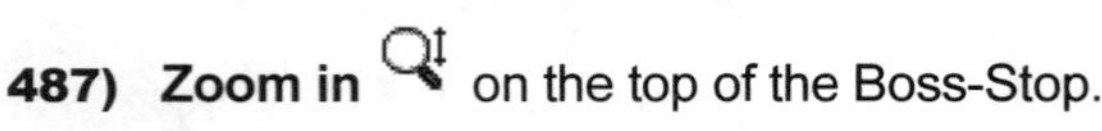

487) **Zoom in** on the top of the Boss-Stop.

488) Click **Line** Line .

489) Sketch a **line** above the horizontal centerline.

490) Click **Tangent Arc** Tangent Arc .

491) Sketch a **90º arc**.

492) Click **Tangent Arc** Tangent Arc to exit.

Add an Equal relation.

493) Click the **horizontal centerline**.

494) Hold the **Ctrl** key down.

495) Click the **horizontal line**.

496) Release the **Ctrl** key.

497) Click **Equal** = from the Add Relations box.

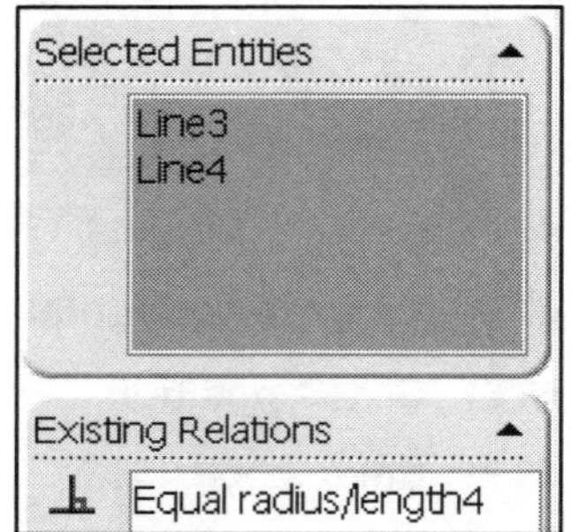

498) Click **OK** from the Properties PropertyManager.

Add a Horizontal Relation.

499) Click the **right endpoint** of the tangent arc.

500) Hold the **Ctrl** key down.

501) Click the **arc center point**.

502) Click the left **end point** of the centerline.

503) Release the **Ctrl** key.

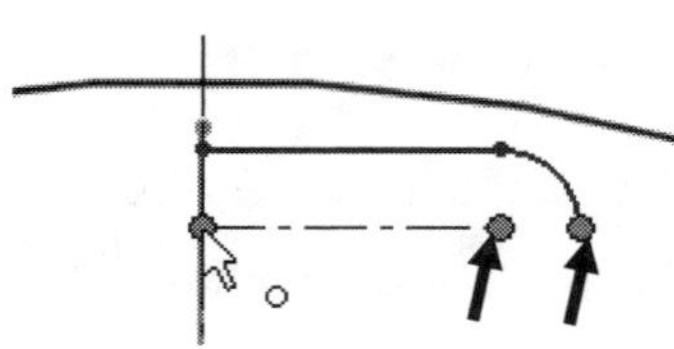

504) Click **Horizontal** — from the Add Relations box.

505) Click **OK** from the Properties PropertyManager.

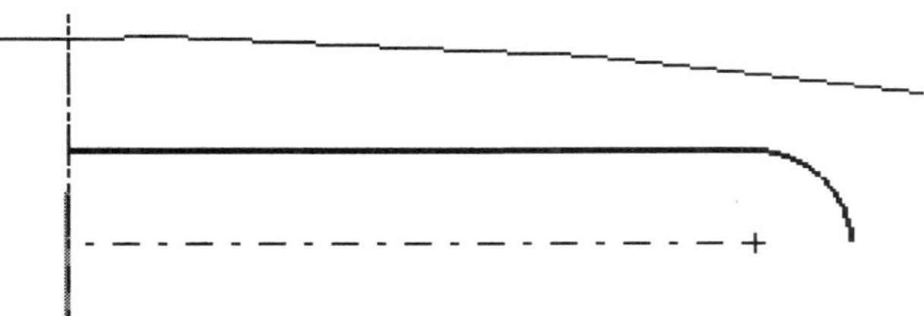

Mirror about the horizontal centerline.

506) Click **Mirror Entities** Mirror from the Sketch toolbar.

507) Click the **horizontal** line. Click the **90º arc**.

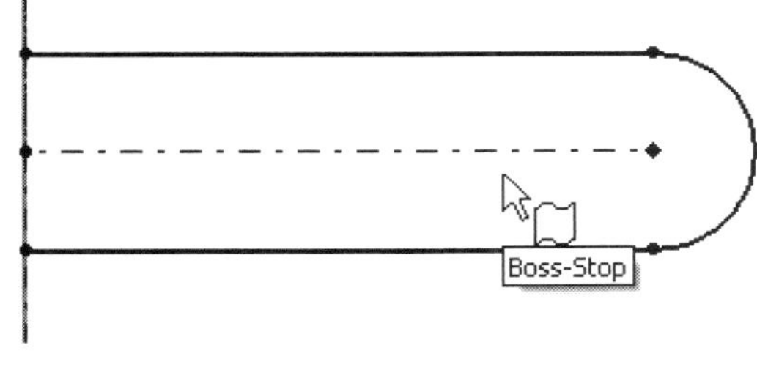

508) Click the **Mirror about** text box.

509) Click the **horizontal Centerline.**

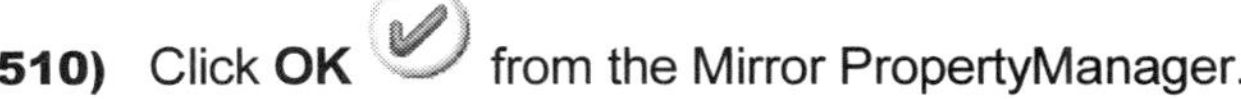

510) Click **OK** from the Mirror PropertyManager.

Mirror about the vertical centerline.

511) Click **Mirror Entities** Mirror from the Sketch toolbar.

512) Window Select the **two horizontal lines**, the **horizontal centerline** and the **90º arc** for Entities to mirror.

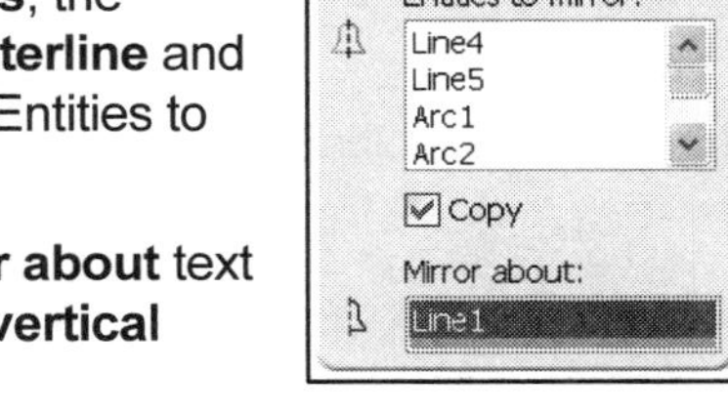

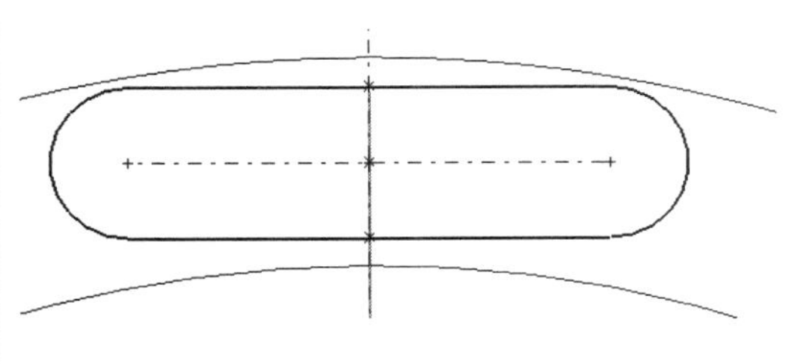

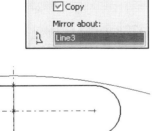

513) Click the **Mirror about** text box. Click the **vertical Centerline**.

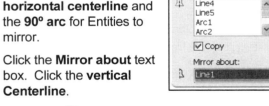

514) Click **OK** from the Mirror PropertyManager.

Add dimensions.

515) Click **Smart Dimension** Dimens....

516) Enter **1.000**, [**25.4**] between the arc center points.

517) Enter **.100**, [**2.54**] for Radius.

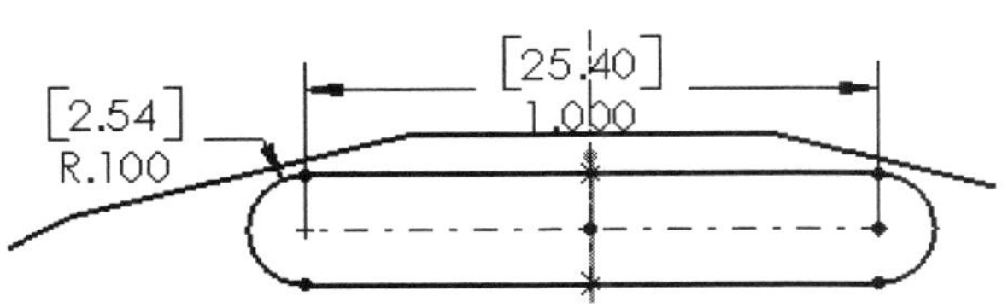

Add a Pierce Relation.

518) Right-click **Select**.

519) Click the **top midpoint** of the Sketch profile.

520) Click **Isometric view**.

521) Hold the **Ctrl** key down.

522) Click the **line** from the Handle Path.

523) Release the **Ctrl** key.

524) Click **Pierce** from the Add Relations box.

525) Click **OK** from the Properties PropertyManager.

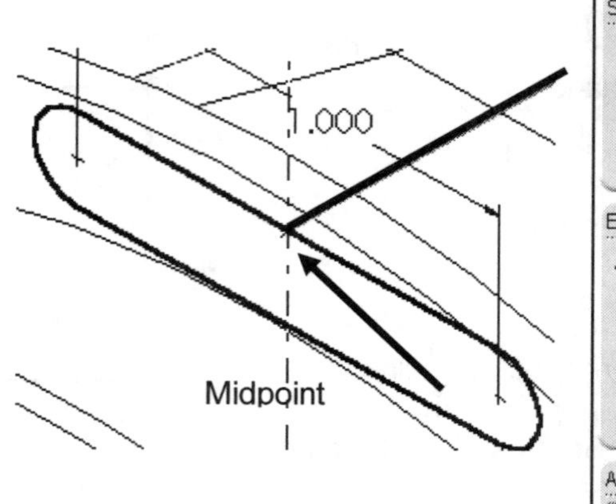

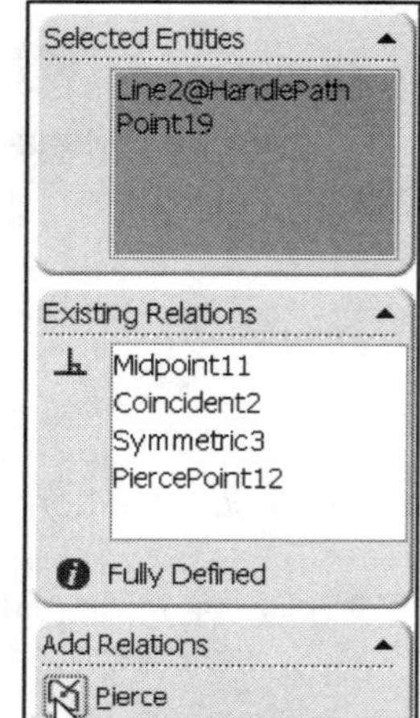

Close the Sketch.

526) Click **Exit Sketch** Exit Sketch.

527) Rename **Sketch9** to **HandleProfile**.

528) Click **Rebuild** from the Main menu.

529) **Hide** ThreadPlane.

530) **Hide** BatterlyLoftPlane.

Insert the Sweep feature.

531) Click **Sweep Boss/Base** Swept Boss/B... from the Features toolbar. HandleProfile is the Sweep profile.

532) Click the **Profile** text box.

533) Click **HandleProfile** from the FeatureManager.

534) Click the **Path** text box.

535) Click the **HandlePath** from the FeatureManager.

536) Click **OK** from the Sweep PropertyManager.

Profile and Path
HandleProfile
HandlePath

Fit the profile to the Graphics window.

537) Press the **f** key.

538) Click **Shaded With Edges**.

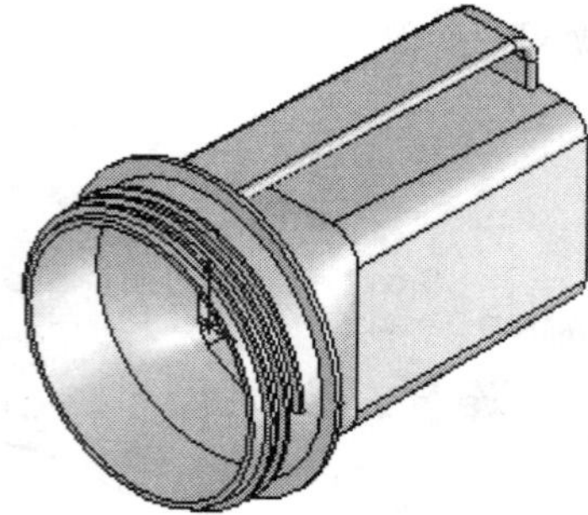

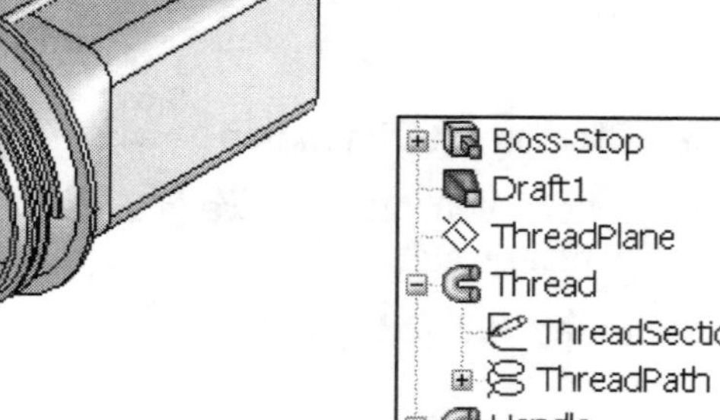

539) Rename **Sweep2** to **Handle**.

540) Click **Save** .

How does the Handle Sweep feature interact with other parts in the FLASHLIGHT assembly? Answer: The Handle requires an Extruded Cut to insert the SWITCH.

HOUSING Part-Extruded Cut Feature with UpToSurface

Create an Extruded Cut in the Handle for the SWITCH. Utilize the top face of the Handle for the sketch plane. Create a circular sketch centered on the Handle.

Utilize the UpToSurface option for End Condition. Select the inside surface of the HOUSING for the reference surface.

Activity: HOUSING Part-Extruded Cut Feature with UpToSurface

Select the Sketch Plane.

541) Click the **top face** of the Handle.

Insert the Sketch.

542) Click **Sketch** Sketch.

543) Click **Top view**.

544) Click **Circle** Circle.

545) Sketch a **circle** on the Handle near the front.

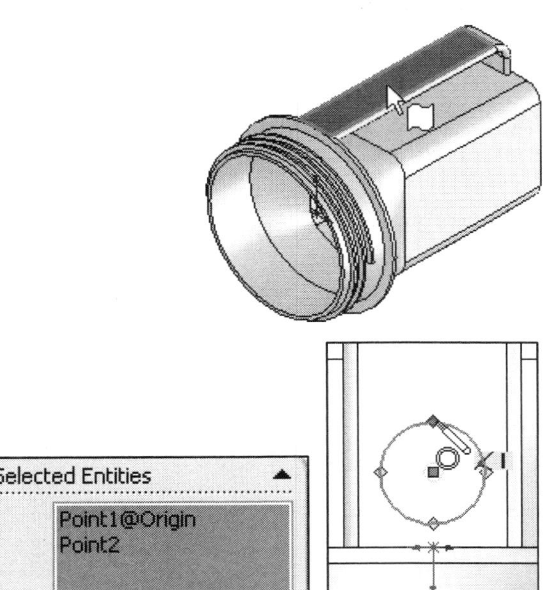

Add a Vertical Relation.

546) Right-click **Select**.

547) Click the **Origin**.

548) Hold the **Ctrl** key down.

549) Click the **center point** of the circle.

550) Release the **Ctrl** key.

551) Click **Vertical** | from the Add Relations box.

552) Click **OK** from the PropertyManager.

Add dimensions.

553) Click **Smart Dimension** Smart Dimens... .

554) Enter **.510**, [**12.95**] for diameter.

555) Enter **.450**, [**11.43**] for the distance from the Origin.

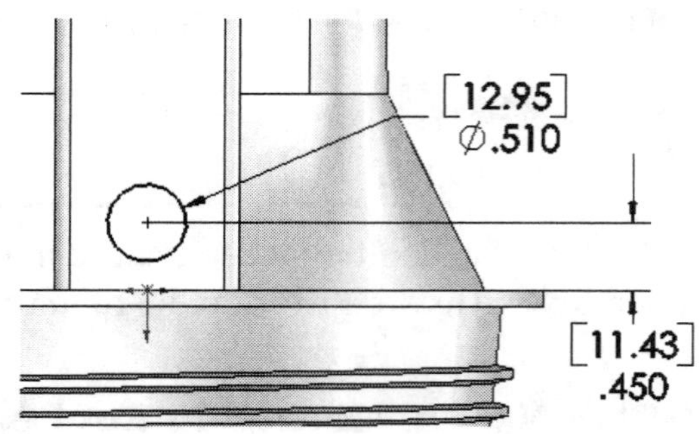

Insert an Extruded Cut feature.

556) **Rotate** the model to view the inside Shell1.

557) Click **Extruded Cut** Extruded Cut .

558) Click the **Up To Surface** option from the Type list box.

559) Click the **top inside face** of the Shell1.

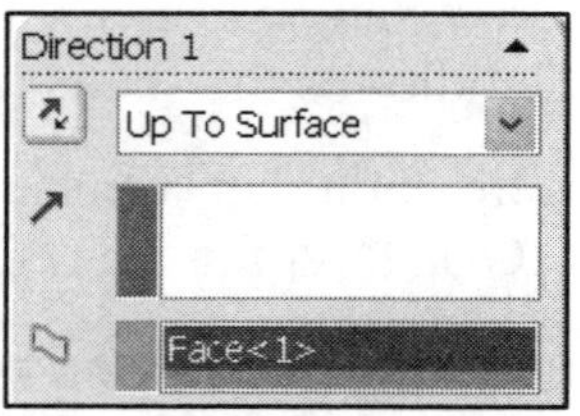

560) Click **OK** from the PropertyManager.

561) Rename **Cut-Extrude1** to **SwitchHole**.

562) Click **Isometric view** .

563) Click **Save** .

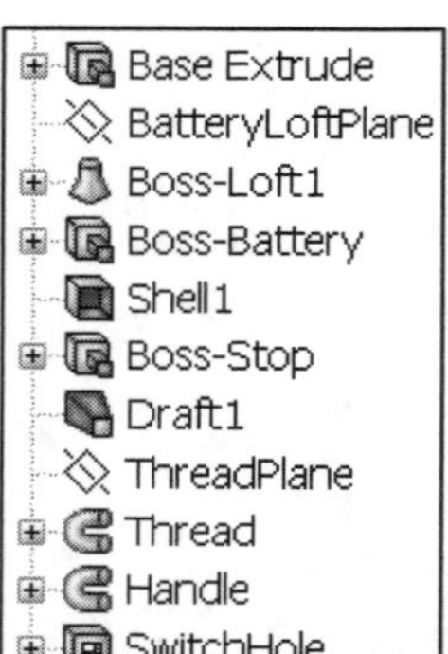

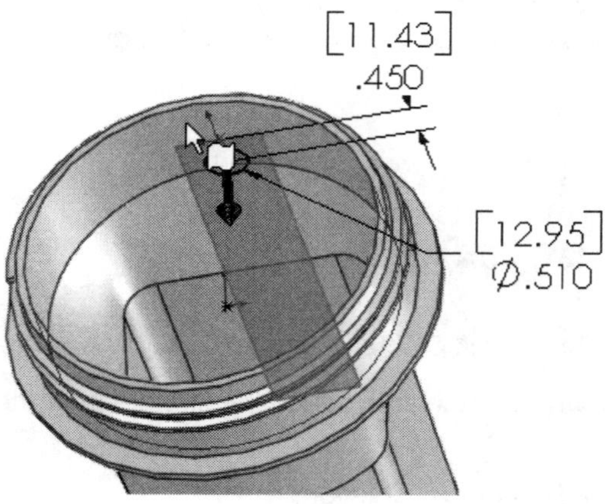

HOUSING Part-First Rib and Linear Pattern Feature

The Rib feature adds material between contours of existing geometry. Use Ribs to add structural integrity to a part.

A Rib requires:

- A Sketch.
- Thickness.
- Extrusion direction.

The first Rib profile is sketched on the Top plane. A 1° Draft Angle is required for manufacturing. Determine the Rib thickness by the manufacturing process and the material.

Note: Rule of thumb states that the Rib thickness is ½ the part wall thickness. The Rib thickness dimension is .100 inches [2.54mm] for illustration purposes.

The HOUSING requires multiple Ribs to support the BATTERY. A Linear Pattern creates multiple instances of a feature along a straight line. Create the Linear Pattern in two directions along the same vertical edge of the HOUSING.

Activity: HOUSING Part-First Rib and Linear Pattern Feature

Display all hidden lines.

564) Click **Hidden Lines Visible**.

Select the Sketch.

565) Click the **Top Plane** from the FeatureManager.

566) Click **Sketch** .

567) Click **Top view**.

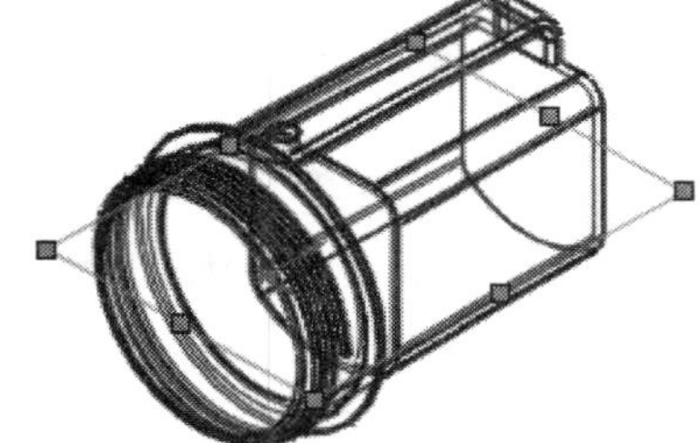

568) Click **Line** Line from the Sketch toolbar.

569) Sketch a **horizontal line**. The endpoints are located on either side of the Handle.

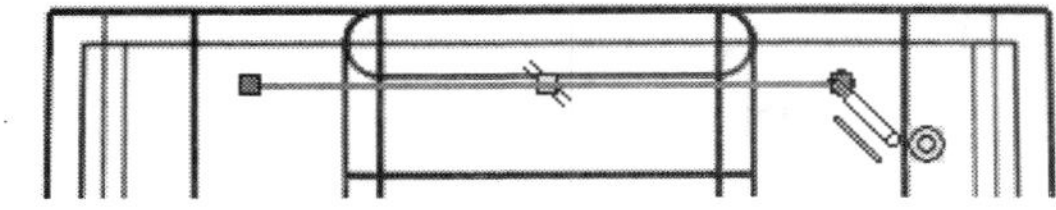

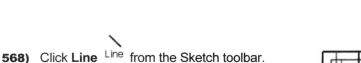

Add a dimension.

570) Click **Smart Dimension** .

571) Click the **inner back edge**.

572) Click the **horizontal line**.

573) Click a **position** to the right of the profile.

574) Enter **.175**, [**4.45**].

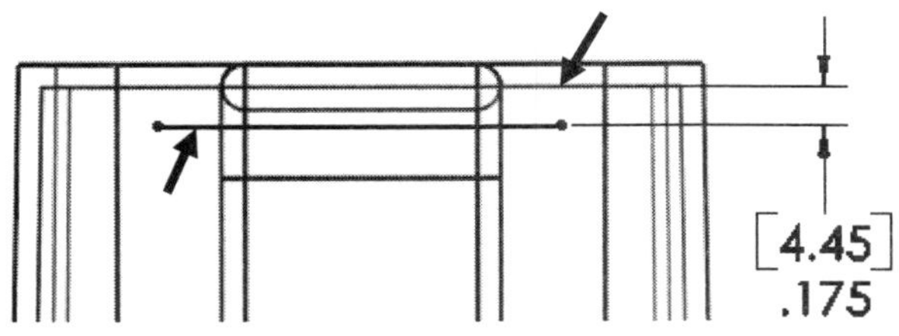

Insert a Rib feature.

575) Click **Rib** from the Features toolbar.

576) Click the **Both Sides** button.

577) Enter **.100**, [**2.54**] for Rib Thickness.

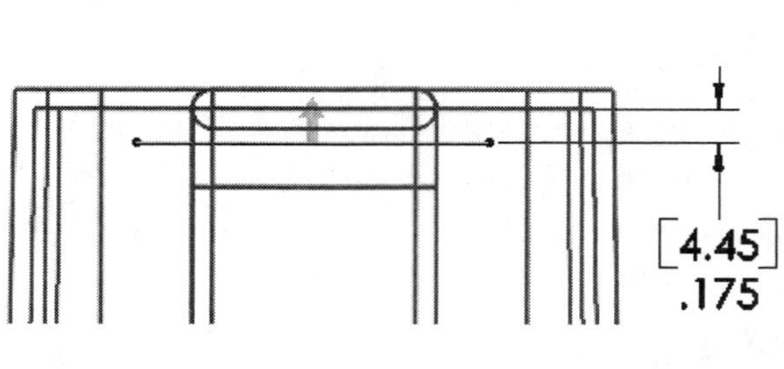

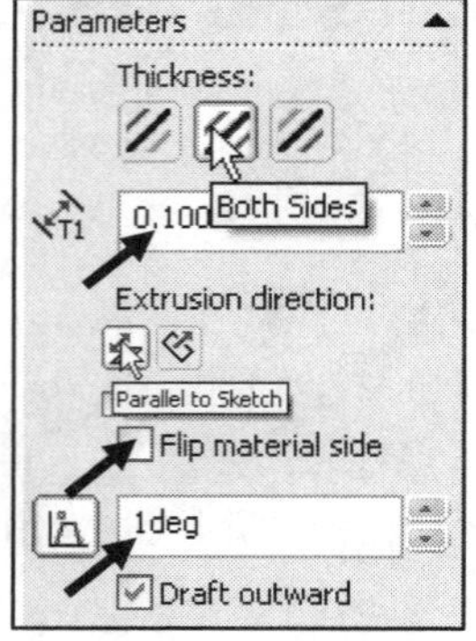

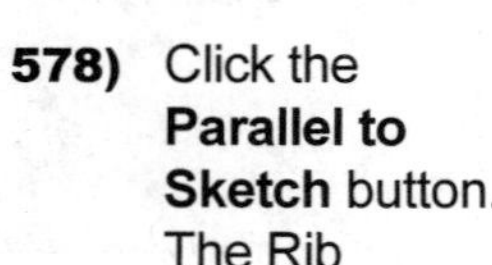

578) Click the **Parallel to Sketch** button. The Rib direction arrow points to the back. Flip the material side if required. Select the Flip material side check box if the direction arrow does not point towards the back.

579) Click the **Draft On/Off** button.

580) Enter **1** for Draft Angle.

581) Click **Front view**.

582) Click the **back inside face** of the HOUSING for the Body.

Rib pointing inwards

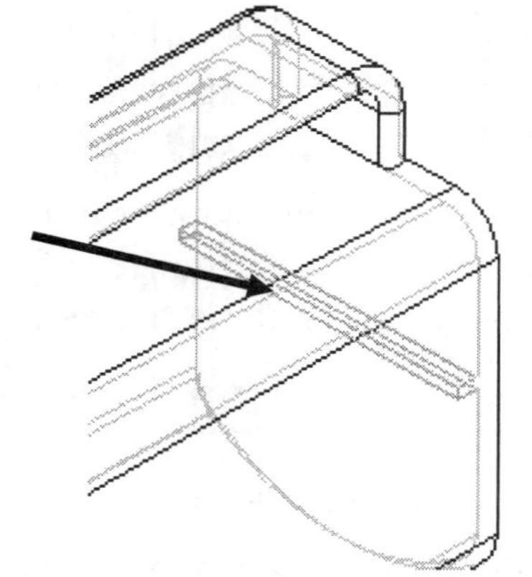

583) Click **OK** from the Rib PropertyManager.

584) Click **Isometric view**.

585) Click **Save**.

Existing geometry defines the Rib boundaries. The Rib does not penetrate through the wall.

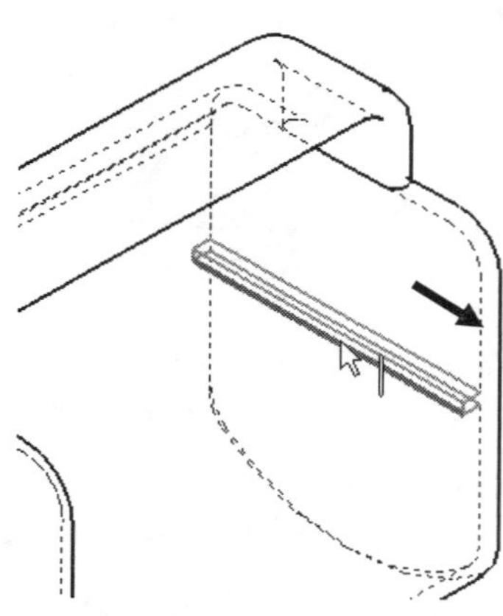

Insert the Linear Pattern feature.

586) **Zoom to Area** on Rib1.

587) Click **Rib1** from the FeatureManager.

588) Click **Linear Pattern** Linear Pattern. Rib1 is displayed in the Features to Pattern box.

589) Click the **Direction 1 Pattern Direction** text box.

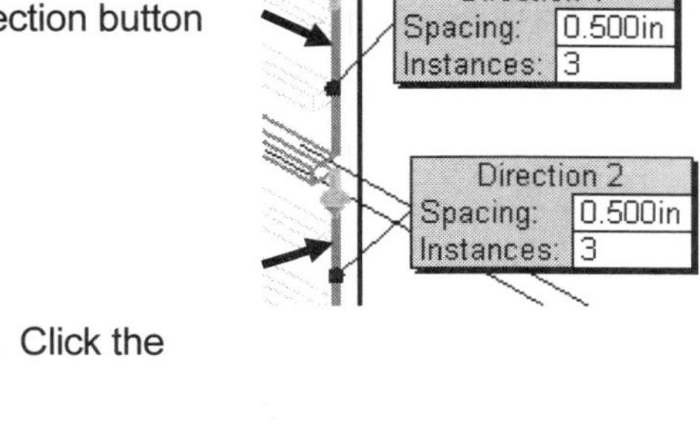

590) Click the **hidden upper back vertical edge** of Shell1. The direction arrow points upward. Click the Reverse direction button if required.

591) Enter **.500**, [**12.7**] for Spacing.

592) Enter **3** for Number of Instances.

593) Click the **Direction 2 Pattern Direction** text box.

594) Click the hidden **lower back vertical edge** of Shell1. Click the Reverse direction button if required.

595) Enter **.500**, [**12.7**] for Spacing.

596) Enter **3** for Number of Instances.

597) Select the **Pattern seed only** check box.

598) Drag the Linear Pattern **Scroll bar** downward to display the Options box.

599) Check **Geometry Pattern**.

600) Click **OK** from the Linear Pattern PropertyManager.

601) Click **Isometric view**.

602) Click **Save**.

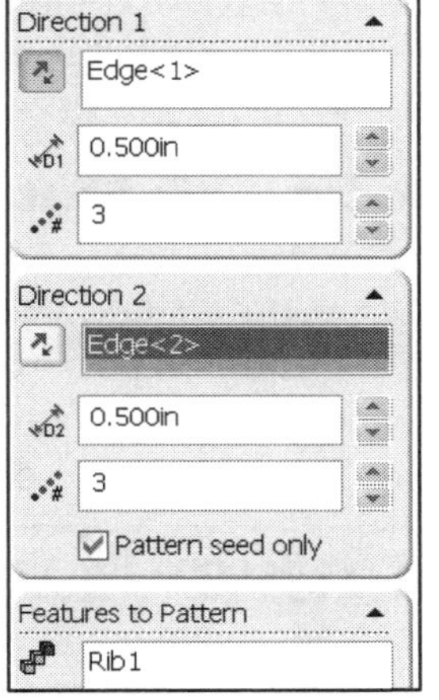

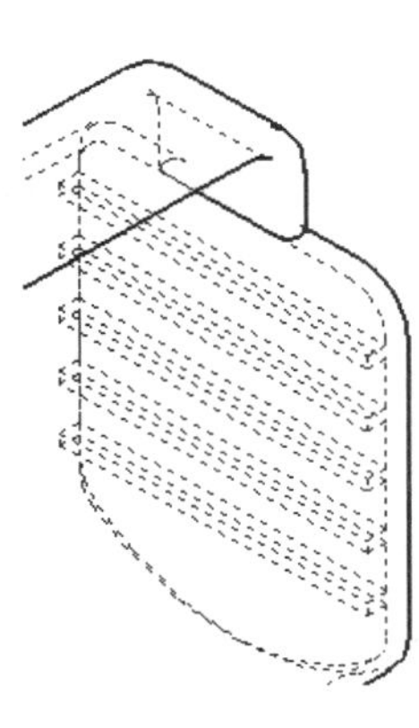

Utilize the Geometry Pattern option to efficiently create and rebuild patterns. Know when to check the Geometry pattern.

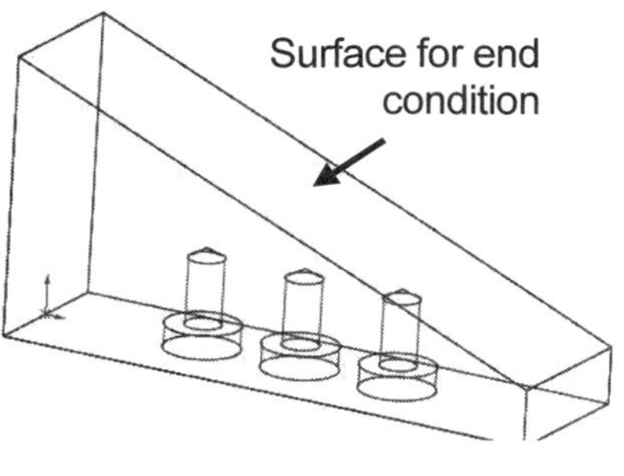

Check Geometry Pattern. You require an exact copy of the seed feature. Each instance is an exact copy of the faces and edges of the original feature. End conditions are not calculated. This option saves rebuild time.

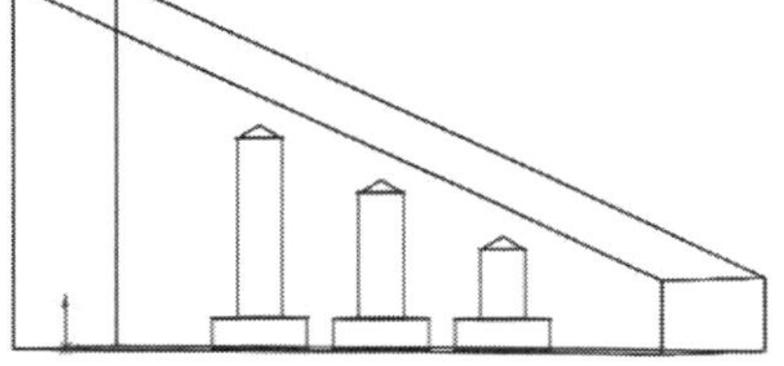

Uncheck Geometry Pattern. You require the end condition to vary. Each instance will have a different end condition. Each instance is offset from the selected surface by the same amount.

Suppress Patterns when not required. Patterns contain repetitive geometry that takes time to rebuild. Pattern features also clutter the part during the model creation process. Suppress patterns as you continue to create more complex features in the part. Unsuppress a feature to restore the display and load into memory for future calculations. Hide features to improve clarity. Show feature to display hidden features.

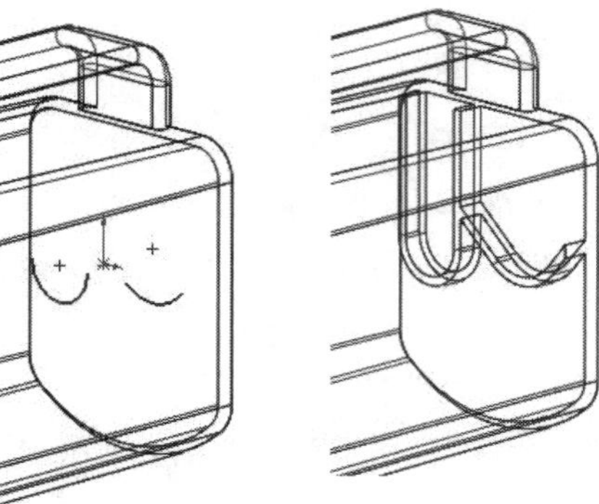

Rib sketches are not required to be fully defined. The Linear Rib option blends sketched geometry into existing contours of the model.

Example: Create an offset reference plane from the inside back face of the HOUSING.

Sketch two under defined arcs. Insert a Rib feature with the Linear option. The Rib extends to the Shell walls.

HOUSING Part-Second Rib Feature

The Second Rib feature supports and centers the BATTERY. The Rib is sketched on a reference plane created through a point on the Handle and parallel with the Right Plane. The Rib sketch references the Origin and existing geometry in the HOUSING. Utilize an Intersection and Coincident relation to define the sketch.

Activity: HOUSING Part-Second Rib Feature

Insert the plane.

603) Click **Wireframe**.

604) **Zoom to Area** on the back right side of the Handle.

605) Click **Insert**, **Reference Geometry**, **Plane** from the Main menu.

606) Click **Parallel Plane at Point**. The Point-Plane option requires a point and a Plane.

607) Click the **Right Plane** from the FeatureManager.

608) Click the **vertex** (point) at the back right of the handle.

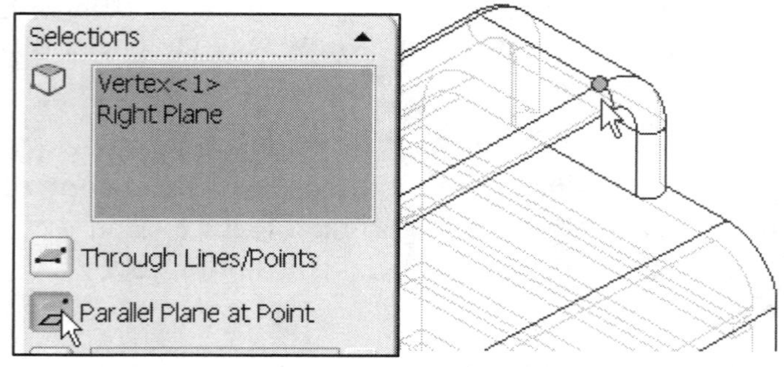

609) Click **OK** from the Plane PropertyManager.

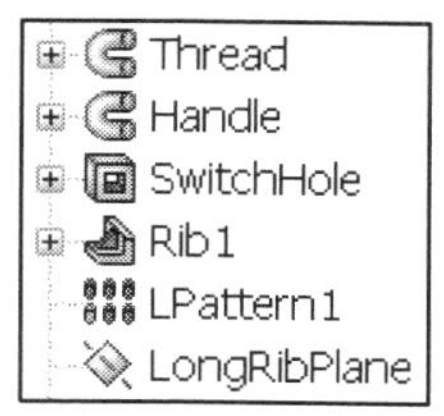

610) Rename **Plane1** to **LongRibPlane**.

Fit to the Graphics window.
611) Press the **f** key.

612) Click **Save** .

Create the second Rib.
613) **Show** the BatteryLoftPlane.

614) Click **LongRibPlane** for Sketch Plane.

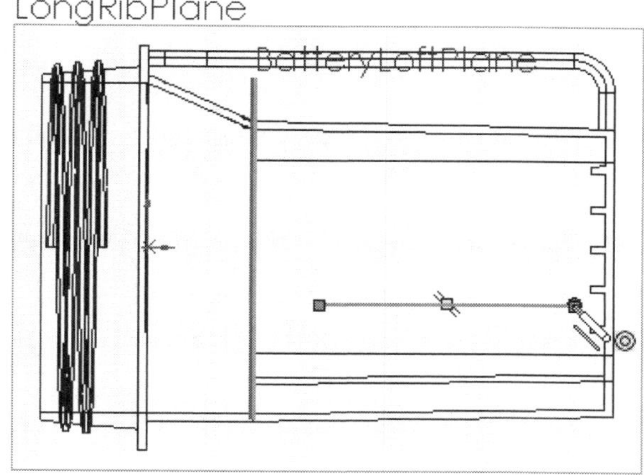

Insert the Sketch.

615) Click **Sketch** Sketch.

616) Click **Right view**.

617) Click **Line** Line. Sketch a **horizontal line**. Do not select the edges of the Shell1 feature.

Add a Coincident Relation.
618) Right-click **Select**.

619) Click the **left end point** of the horizontal sketch line.

620) Hold the **Ctrl** key down.

621) Click the **BatteryLoftPlane** from the FeatureManager.

622) Release the **Ctrl** key.

623) Click **Coincident**.

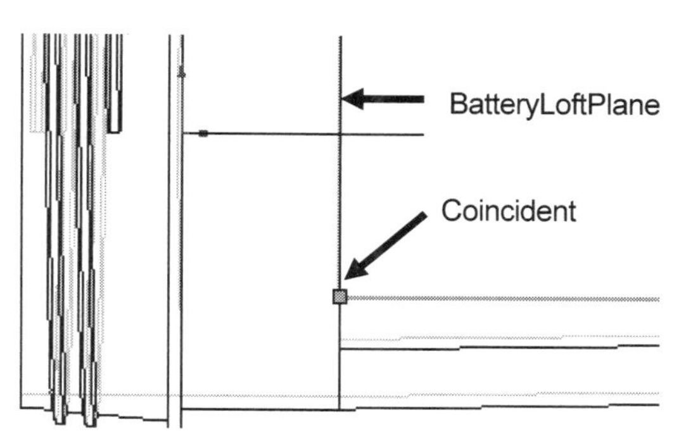

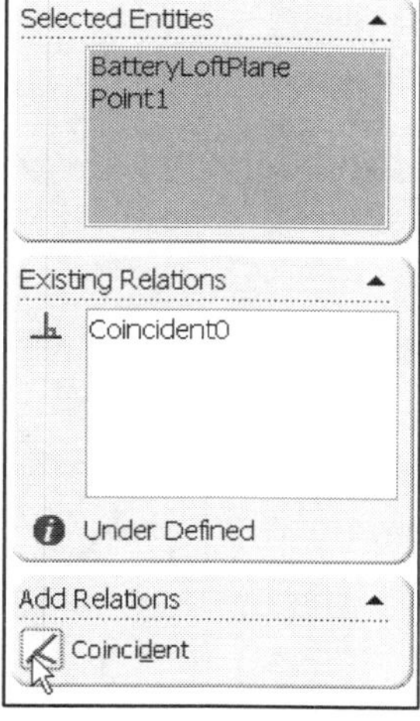

624) Click **OK** from the Properties PropertyManager.

Add a dimension.
625) Click **Smart Dimension** Smart Dimens... .

626) Click the **horizontal line**. Click **Origin**. Click a **position** for the vertical linear dimension text.

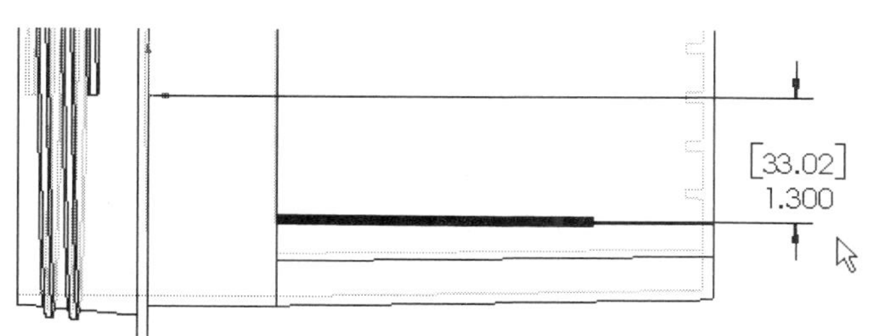

627) Enter **1.300**, [**33.02**].

When the sketch and reference geometry become complex, create dimensions by selecting reference Planes and the Origin in the FeatureManager.

Dimension the Rib from the Origin, not from an edge or surface for design flexibility. The Origin remains constant. Modify edges and surfaces with the Fillet feature.

Sketch an arc.

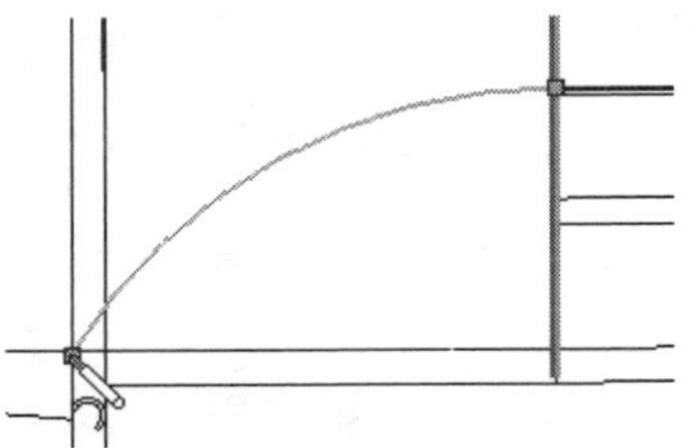

628) **Zoom to Area** on the horizontal Sketch line.

629) Click **Tangent Arc** Tangent Arc from the Sketch toolbar.

630) Click the **left end** of the horizontal line.

631) Click the **intersection** of the Shell1 and Boss Stop features.

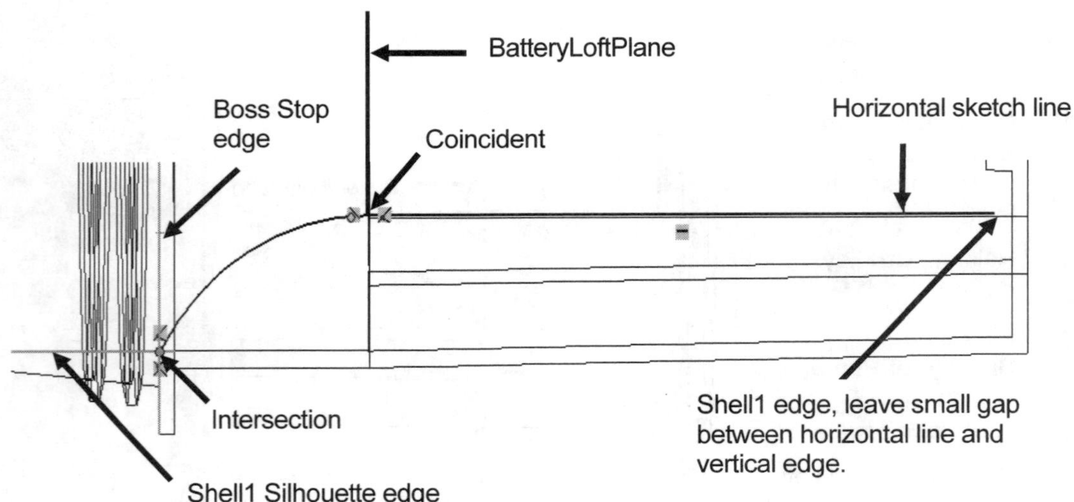

Add an Intersection Relation.

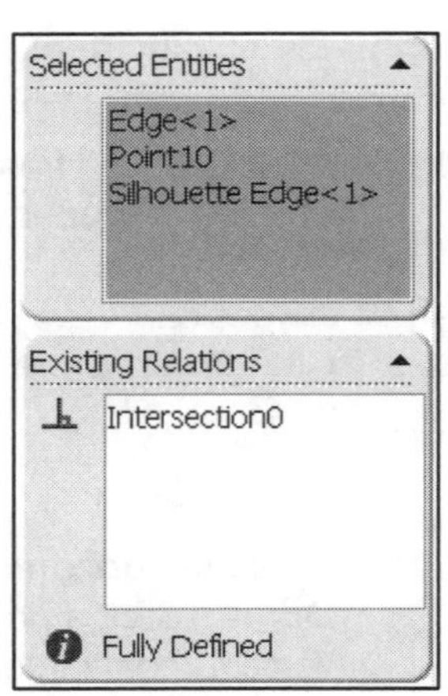

632) Right-click **Select**.

633) Click the **end point** of the arc.

634) Hold the **Ctrl** key down.

635) Click the **Shell1 Silhouette Edge** of the lower horizontal inside wall.

636) Click the left **vertical Boss-Stop edge**. Release the **Ctrl** key.

637) Click **Intersection**.

638) Click **OK** from the Properties PropertyManager.

Insert the Rib feature.

639) Click **Rib** from the Features toolbar.

640) Click the **Both Sides** button.

641) Enter **.075**, [**1.91**] for Rib Thickness.

642) Click the **Draft On/Off** button.

643) Enter **1** for Angle.

644) Click the **Draft outward** check box.

645) Click the **Flip material side** check box if required. The direction arrow points towards the bottom.

646) Click **OK** from the Rib PropertyManager.

647) Click **Isometric view**.

648) Click **Shaded With Edges**.

649) **Hide** LongRibPLane.

650) **Hide** BatteryLoftPlane.

651) Click **Save**.

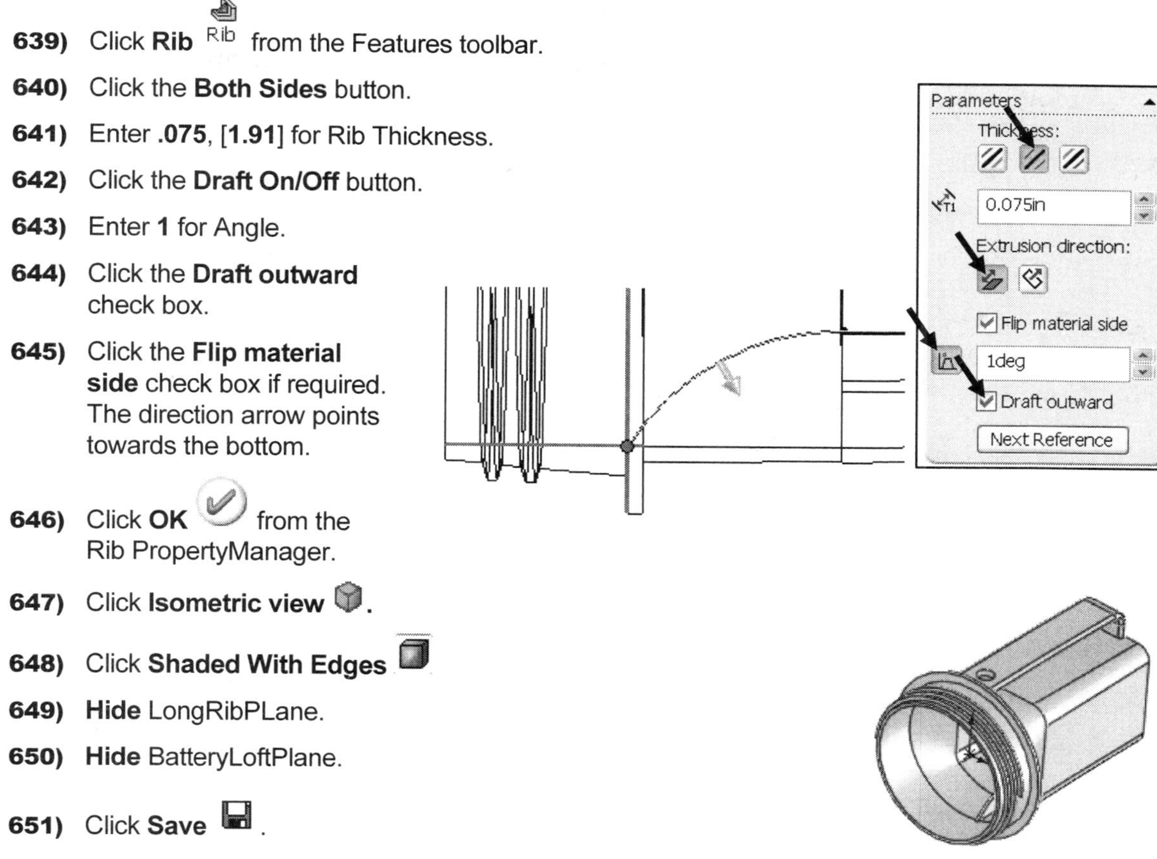

HOUSING Part-Mirror Feature

An additional Rib is required to support the BATTERY. Reuse features with the Mirror feature to create a Rib symmetric about the Right Plane.

The Mirror feature requires:

- Mirror Face or Plane reference.
- Features or Faces to Mirror.

Utilize the Mirror feature. Select the Right Plane for the Mirror Plane. Select the second Rib for the Features to Mirror.

Activity: HOUSING Part-Mirror Feature

Insert the Mirror feature.

652) Click **Mirror**  Mirror from the Features toolbar.

653) Click the **Mirror Face/Plane** text box.

654) Click **Right Plane** from the FeatureManager.

655) Click **Rib2** for Features to Mirror from the FeatureManager.

656) Click **OK** from the Mirror PropertyManager.

657) Click **Trimetric view**.

658) Click **Save**.

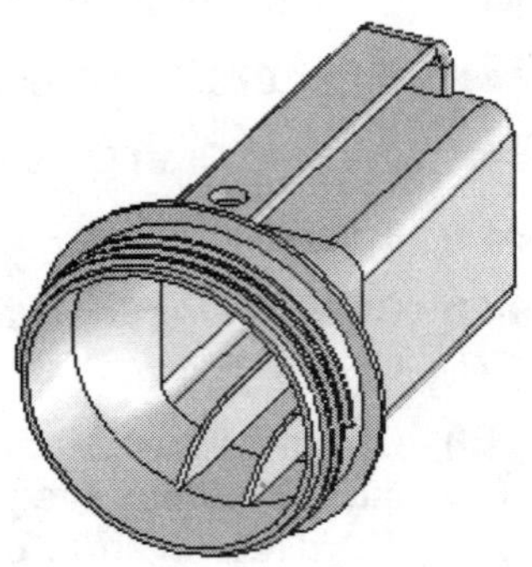

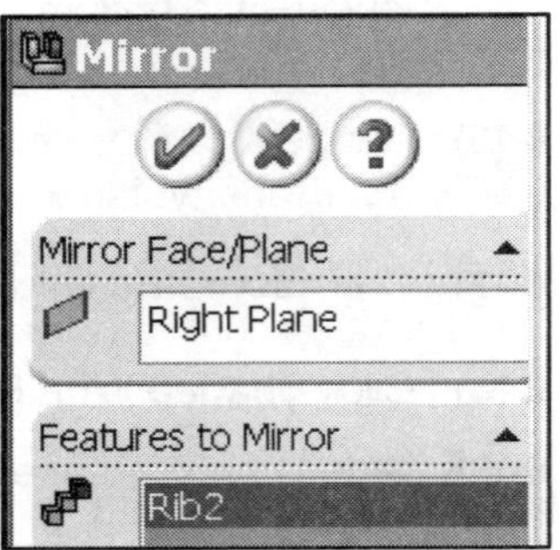

Close all parts.

659) Click **Window**, **Close All** from the Main menu.

The parts for the FLASHLIGHT are complete! Review the HOUSING before moving on to the FLASHLIGHT assembly.

Additional information on Extrude Base/Boss, Extrude Cut, Sweep, Loft, Helix/Spiral, Rib, Mirror and Reference Planes are found in SolidWorks Help Topics.

Review of the HOUSING Part.

The HOUSING utilized the Extruded Base feature with the Draft Angle option. The Loft feature was created to blend the circular face of the LENS with the rectangular face of the BATTERY. The Shell feature removed material with a constant wall thickness. The Draft feature utilized the front face as the Neutral plane.

You created a Thread similar to the LENSCAP Thread. The Thread profile was copied from the LENSCAP and inserted into the Top Plane of the HOUSING. The Extruded Cut feature was utilized to create a hole for the Switch. The Rib features were utilized in a Linear Pattern and Mirror feature.

Each feature has additional options that are applied to create different geometry. The Offset From Surface option creates an Extruded Cut on the curved surface of the HOUSING and LENSCAP. The Reverse offset and Translate surface options produce a cut depth constant throughout the curved surface.

Utilize Tools, Sketch Entities, Text to create the text profile on an Offset Plane.

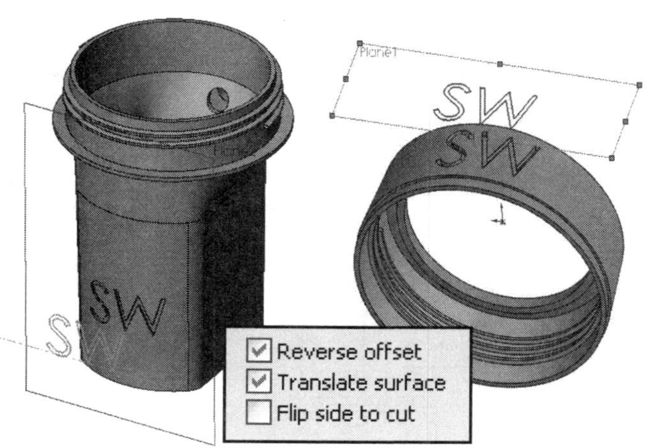

Example: Offset From Surface

Computer Aided Manufacturing Software such as CAM\Works contains machine-ready text fonts. Utilize the text fonts supported by your machine shop to save time.

FLASHLIGHT Assembly

Plan the Sub-assembly component layout diagram.

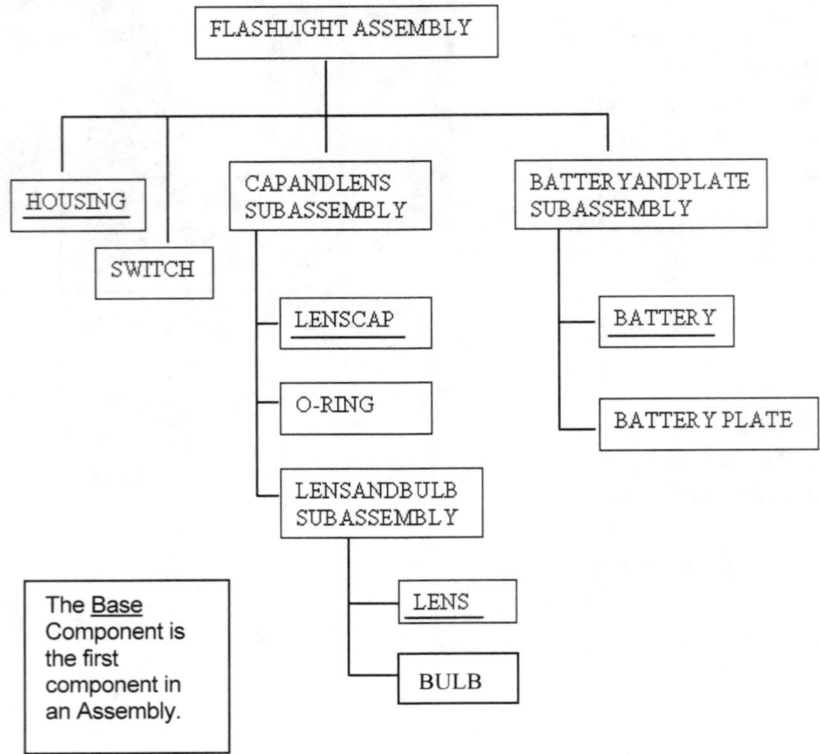

Assembly Layout Structure

The FLASHLIGHT assembly steps are as follows:

- Create the LENSANDBULB sub-assembly from the LENS and BULB components. The

  LENS is the Base component.

- Create the BATTERYANDPLATE sub-assembly from the BATTERY and BATTERYPLATE.

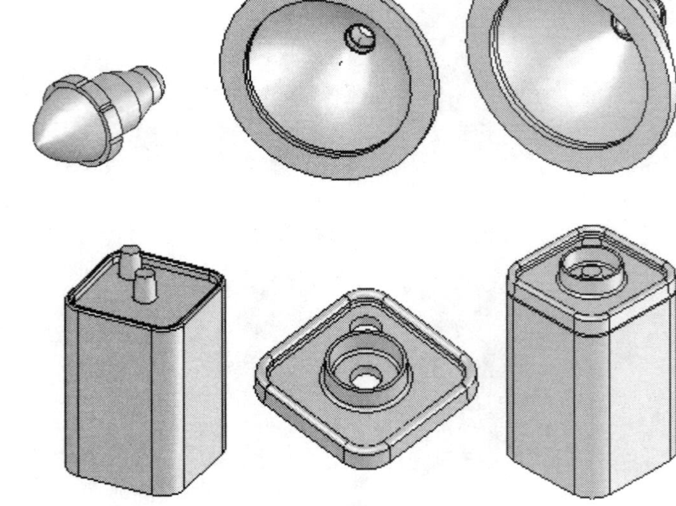

- Create the CAPANDLENS sub-assembly from the LENSCAP, O-RING and LENSANDBULB sub-assembly. The LENSCAP is the Base component.

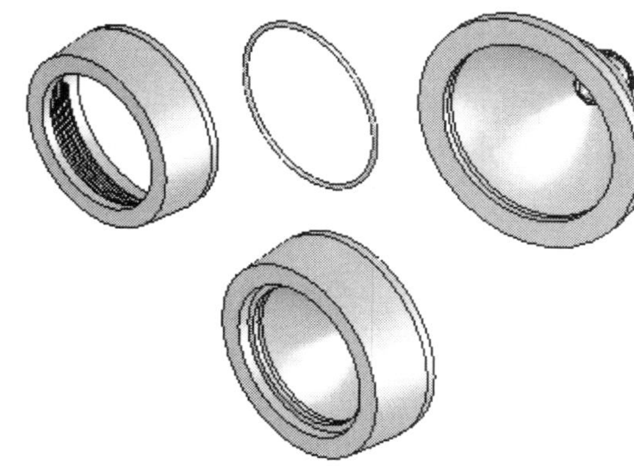

- Create the FLASHLIGHT assembly. The HOUSING is the Base component. Insert the SWITCH, CAPANDLENS and BATTERYANDPLATE.

- Modify the dimensions to complete the FLASHLIGHT assembly.

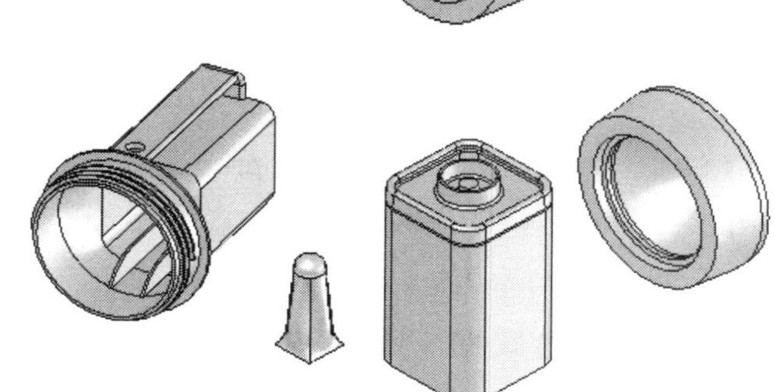

Assembly Template

An Assembly Document Template is the foundation of the assembly. The FLASHLIGHT assembly and its sub-assemblies require the Assembly Document Template. In Project 2, you created the ASM-MM-ANSI Template for the GUIDE-ROD. Create the ASM-IN-ANSI and ASM-MM-ISO Templates.

Save the "Click OK" step. Double-click on the Template icon to open the Template in one step instead of two. Double-click on a part or assembly name in the Open Dialog box to open the document.

LENSANDBULB Sub-assembly

Create the LENSANDBULB sub-assembly. Utilize three Coincident Mates to assemble the BULB component to the LENS component. When geometry is complex, select the Planes in the Mate Selection box.

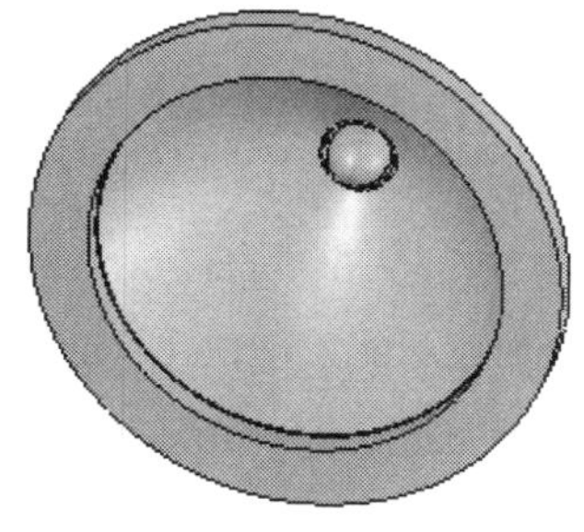

Suppress the Lens Shield feature to view all inside surfaces during the mate process.

Activity: Assembly Templates

Create an Assembly Template.

660) Click **File**, **New** from the Main menu. Double-click **Assembly** from the default Templates tab.

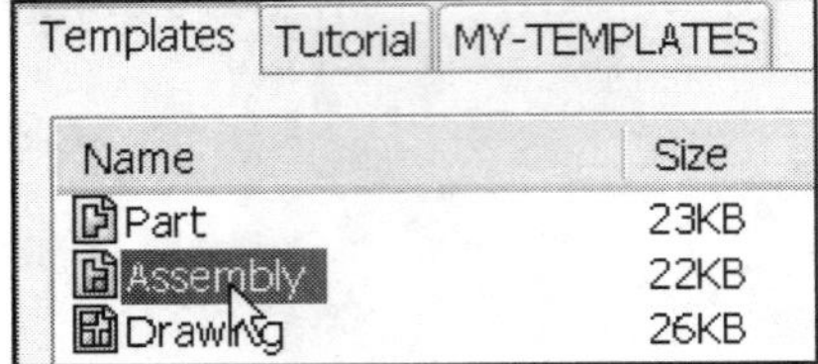

661) Click **Cancel** from the Insert Component PropertyManager.

Set the Assembly Document Template options.

662) Click **Tools**, **Options**, **Document Properties** tab from the Main menu.

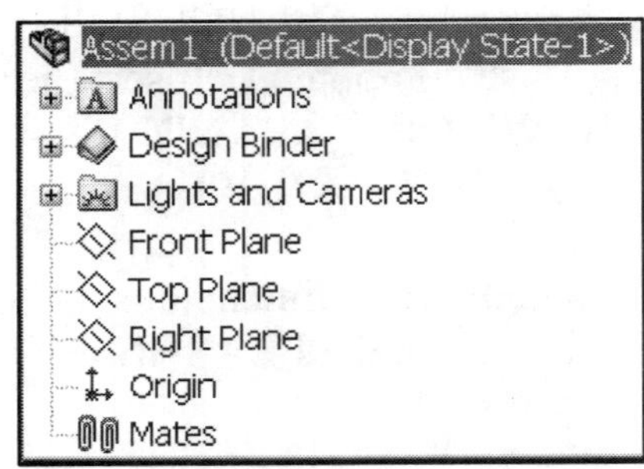

Create an English assembly template.

663) Select **ANSI** from the Detailing option.

664) Click **Units**. Click **IPS**.

665) Enter **3** in the Lengths units Decimal spin box.

666) Enter **0** for Angular units Decimal spin box.

667) Click **OK**.

Save the assembly template.

668) Click **File**, **Save As** from the Main menu. Click the **Assembly Template (*asmdot)** from the Save As type list box. Select **ENGDESIGN-W-SOLIDWORKS\MY-TEMPLATES** for Save in file folder.

669) Enter **ASM-IN-ANSI** in the file name text box.

670) Click **Save**.

Create a Metric assembly template.

671) Click **File**, **New** from the Main menu.

672) Double-click **Assembly** from the default Templates tab.

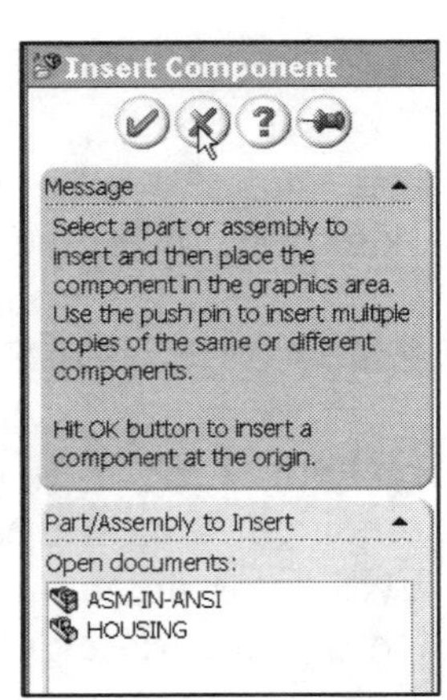

673) Click **Cancel** from the Insert Component PropertyManager.

Set the Assembly Document Template options.

674) Click **Tools**, **Options**, **Document Properties** tab from the Main menu.

675) Select **ISO** from the Detailing option.

676) Click **Units**.

677) Click **MMGS** from the Linear units list box.

678) Enter **2** in the Lengths units Decimal spin box.

679) Enter **0** for Angular units Decimal spin box.

680) Click **OK**.

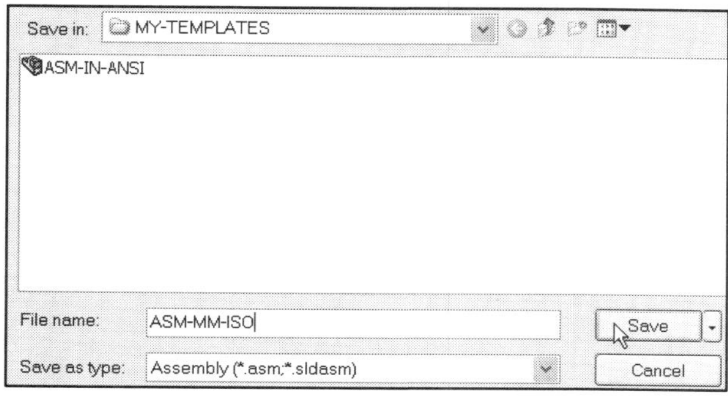

Save the assembly template.

681) Click **File**, **Save As** from the Main menu.

682) Click the **Assembly Template (*asmdot)** from the Save As type list box. Select **ENGDESIGN-W-SOLIDWORKS\MY-TEMPLATES** for Save in file folder.

683) Enter **ASM-MM-ISO** in the File name text box. Click **Save**.

Activity: LENSANDBULB Sub-assembly

Close all documents.

684) Click **Windows**, **Close All** from the Main menu.

Create the LENSANDBULB sub-assembly.

685) Click **File**, **New** from the Main menu. Click the **MY-TEMPLATES** tab. Double-click the **ASM-IN-ANSI [ASM-MM-ISO]**.

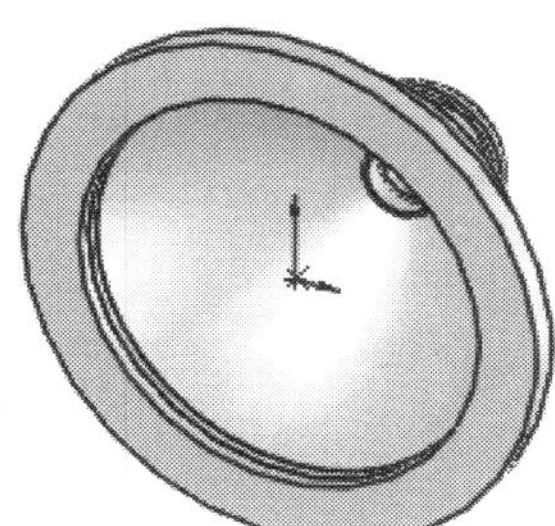

Insert the LENS.

686) Click **View**, check **Origin** from the Main menu,

687) Click **Browse**. Select **Part** for Files of type. Double-click **LENS** from the Open dialog box. Click the **Origin** of the Assembly. The mouse pointer displays the Insert Component fixed at the Origin icon. Click **Save**.

688) Select the **PROJECTS** folder.

689) Enter **LENSANDBULB** for File name.

690) Enter **LENS AND BULB ASSEMBLY** for Description. Click **Save**.

Insert the BULB.

691) Click **Insert Component** from the Assemblies toolbar. Click **Browse**.

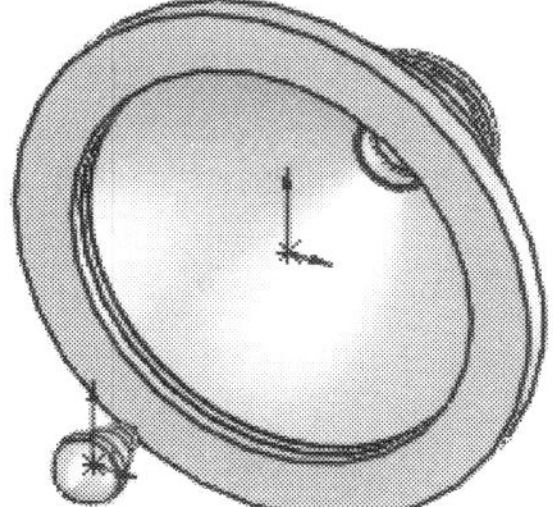

692) Double-click **BULB** from the Open dialog box. Click a **position** in front of the LENS. Click **Shaded With Edges**.

Fit to the Graphics window.

693) Press the **f** key.

Move the BULB.

694) Click and drag the **BULB** in the Graphics window.

695) Click a **position** in front of the LENS.

Save the LENSANDBULB.

696) Click **Save** .

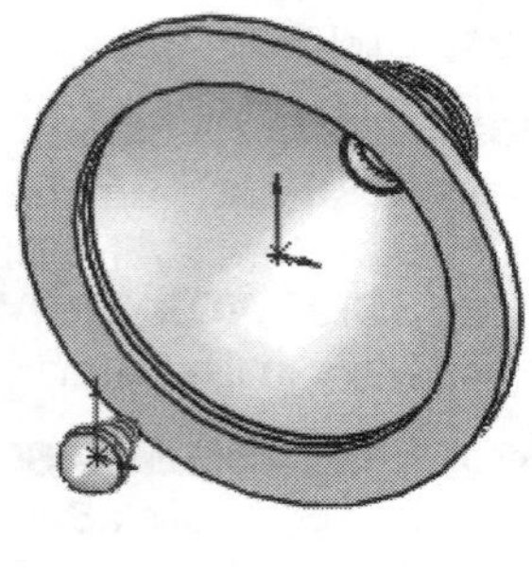

Suppress the LensShield feature.

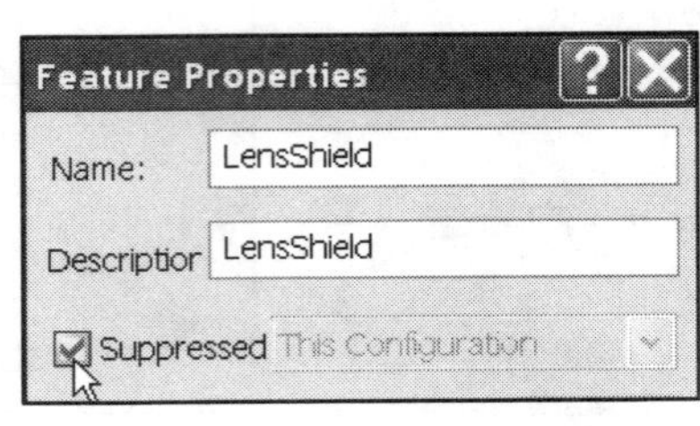

697) Expand **LENS** in the FeatureManager.

698) Right-click **LensShield** in the FeatureManager.

699) Click Feature Properties.

700) Check the **Suppressed** box.

701) Click **OK** from the Feature Properties box.

Insert a Coincident Mate.

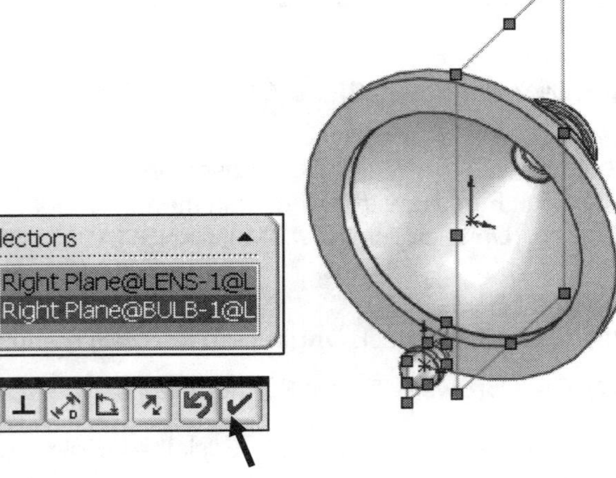

702) Click **Mate** from the Assemblies toolbar.

703) **Expand** the FeatureManager.

704) Click the **Right Plane** of the LENS from the FeatureManager.

705) Expand the **BULB** in the FeatureManager.

706) Click **Right Plane** of the BULB.

707) Click **Coincident** from the Pop-up menu.

708) Click **OK** .

Insert the second Coincident Mate.

709) Click the **Top Plane** of the LENS from the FeatureManager.

710) Click the **Top Plane** of the BULB from the FeatureManager.

711) Click **Coincident** .

712) Click **OK** .

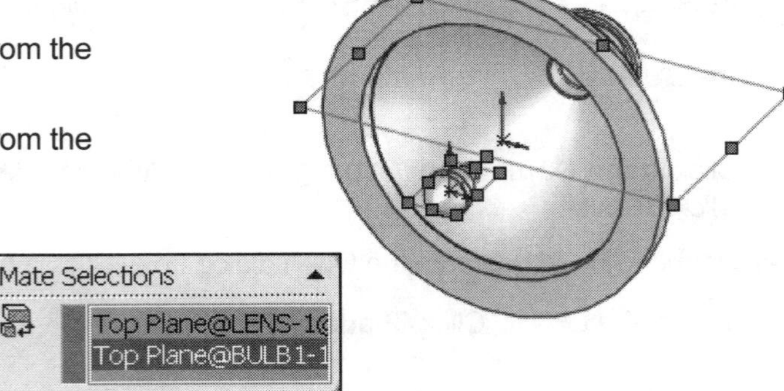

Select face geometry efficiently. Position the mouse pointer in the middle of the face. Do not position the mouse pointer near the edge of the face. Zoom in on geometry. Utilize the Face Selection Filter for narrow faces.

Activate the Face Selection Filter.

713) Press the **X** Shortcut key. The Filter icon is displayed.

Only faces are selected until the Face Selection Filter is deactivated. Select Clear All Filters from the Selection Filter Toolbar to deactivate all filters.

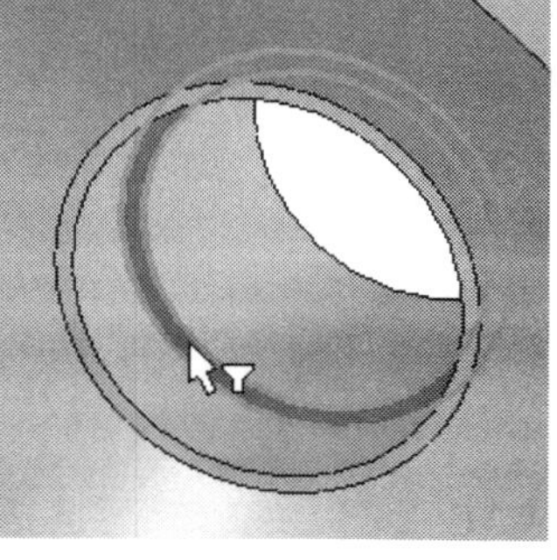

Insert a Coincident Mate.

714) **Zoom in** and **Rotate** on the Counterbore.

715) Select the **Counterbore face** of the LENS.

716) Click the **bottom flat face** of the BULB. Coincident is selected by default.

717) Click **OK**.

Mate Selections
Face<1>@LENS-1
Face<2>@BULB1-1

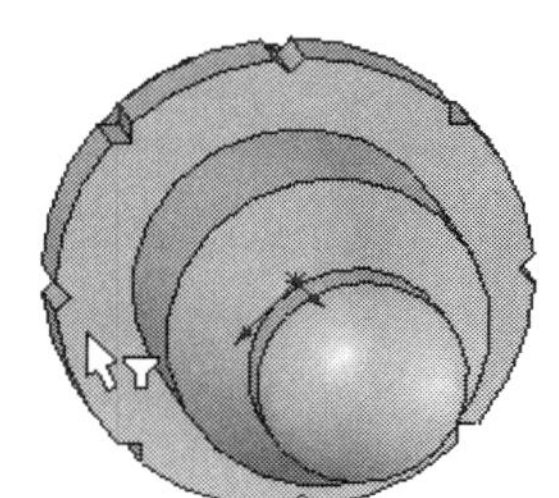

Close the Mate PropertyManager.

718) Click **OK** from the Mate PropertyManager. The LENSANDBULB is fully defined.

Clear the Face filter.

719) Press the **X** key.

Display the Mate types.

720) Expand **Mates** in the FeatureManager.

721) Click Right view.

Save the LENSANDBULB.

722) Click Isometric view.

723) Click **Save**.

724)

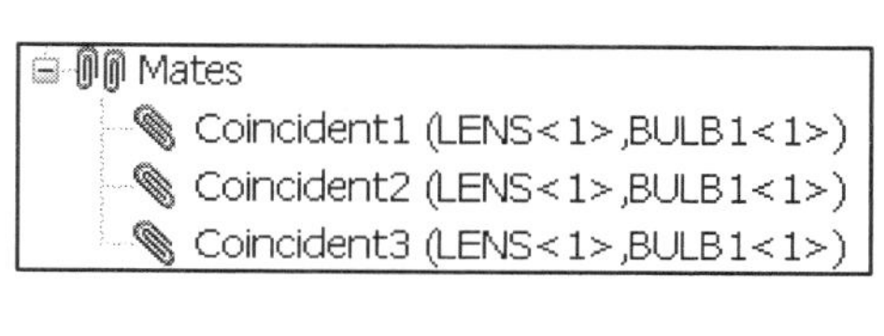

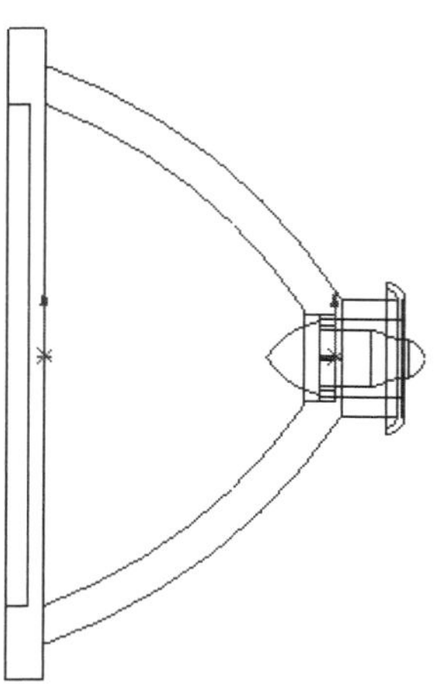

If the wrong face or edge is selected, click the face or edge again to remove it from the Mate Selections text box. Right-click Clear Selections to remove all geometry from the Mate Selections text box. To delete a Mate from the FeatureManager, right-click on the Mate, click Delete.

BATTERYANDPLATE Sub-assembly

Create the BATTERYANDPLATE sub-assembly. Utilize two Coincident Mates and one Concentric Mate to assemble the BATTERYPLATE component to the BATTERY component.

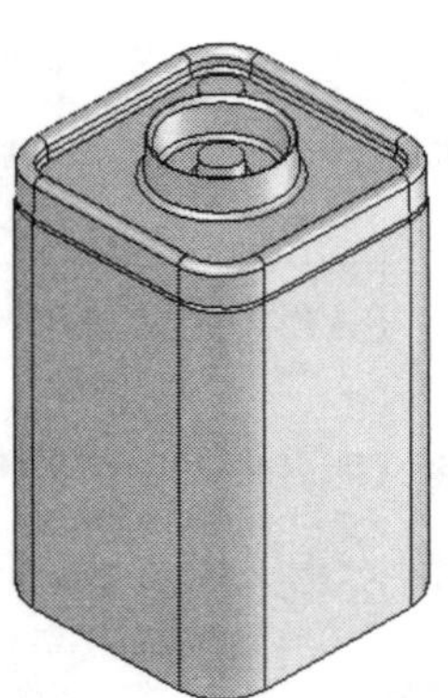

Note: Utilize the Selection Filter required. Select Planes from the FeatureManager when Selection Filters are activated.

Activity: BATTERYANDPLATE Sub-assembly

Create the BATTERYANDPLATE sub-assembly.

725) Click **File**, **New** from the Main menu.

726) Click the **MY-TEMPLATES** tab.

727) Double-click **ASM-IN-ANSI**.

Insert the BATTERY part.

728) Click **View**, check **Origin** from the Main menu.

729) Click **Browse** from the Insert Component PropertyManager.

730) Double-click **BATTERY** from the Open dialog box.

Place the BATTERY.

731) Click the **Origin** of the Assembly.

Save the BATTERYANDPLATE sub-assembly.

732) Click **Save**.

733) Select the **PROJECTS** file folder.

734) Enter **BATTERYANDPLATE** for File name.

735) Enter BATTERY AND PLATE FOR 6-VOLT FLASHLIGHT for Description.

736) Click **Save**.

Insert the BATTERYPLATE part.

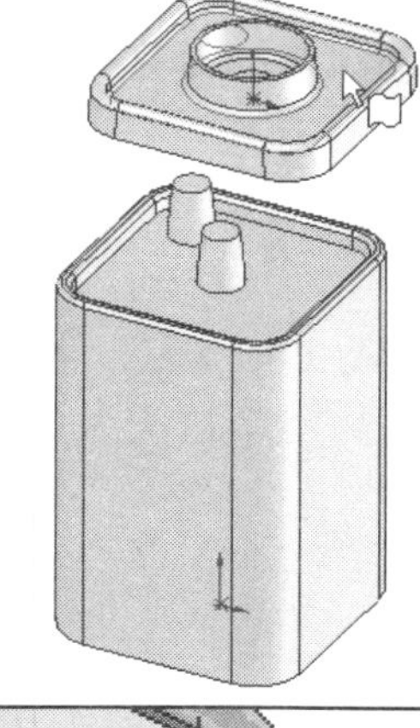

737) Click **Insert Component**  from the Assemblies toolbar.

738) Click **Browse**.

739) Double-click **BATTERYPLATE** from the Open dialog box.

740) Click a **position** above the BATTERY.

Insert a Coincident Mate.

741) Press the **Up Arrow** key, approximately 6 times to display the narrow outside bottom face of the BATTERYPLATE.

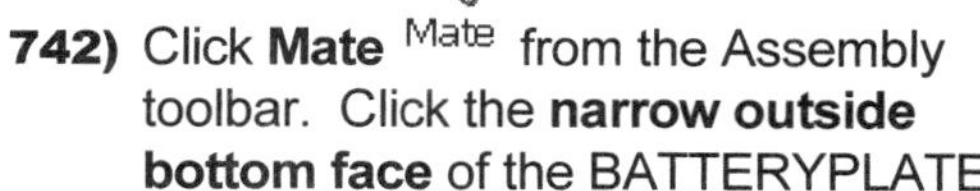

742) Click **Mate** from the Assembly toolbar. Click the **narrow outside bottom face** of the BATTERYPLATE.

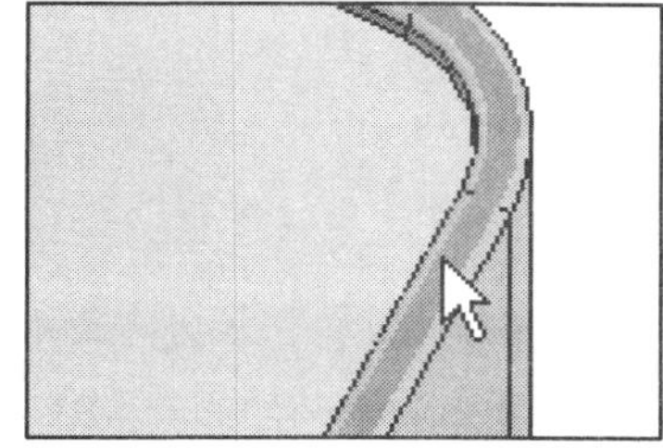

743) Press the **Down Arrow** key, approximately 8 times to display the top face of the BATTERY.

744) **Zoom In** on the top face.

745) Click the **top narrow flat face** of the BATTERY Base Extrude feature. Coincident is selected by default.

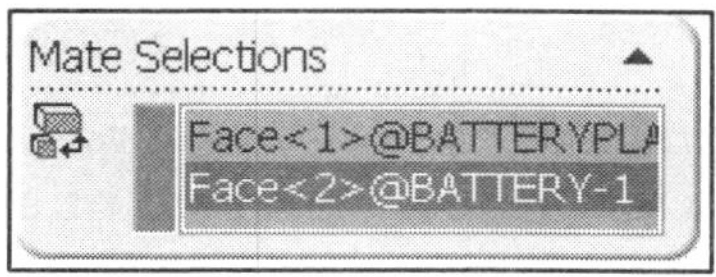

746) Click **OK**.

Insert a Coincident Mate.

747) Click the **Right Plane** of the BATTERY.

748) Click the **Right Plane** of the BATTERYPLATE. Coincident is selected by default.

749) Click **OK**.

Insert a Concentric Mate.

750) Click the **cylindrical face** Terminal feature of the BATTERY. Click the **cylindrical face** Holder feature of the BATTERYPLATE. Concentric is selected by default.

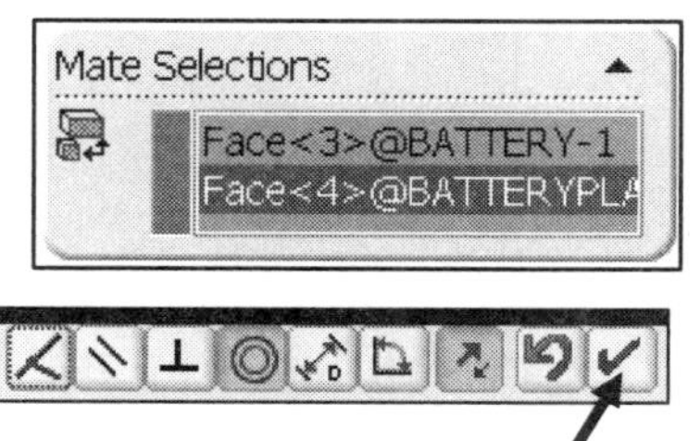

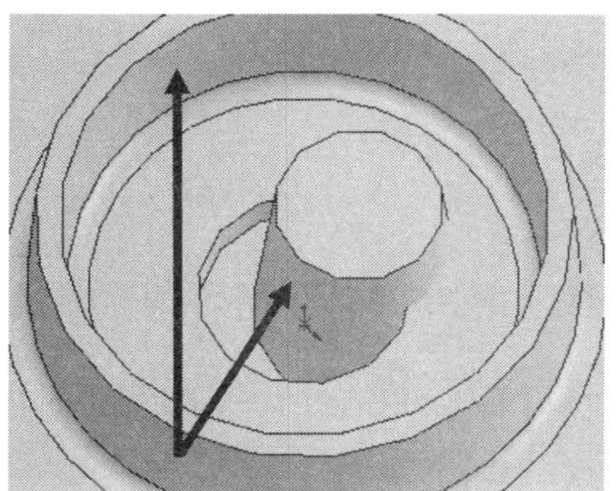

751) Click **OK**.

752) Click **OK** from the Mate PropertyManager.

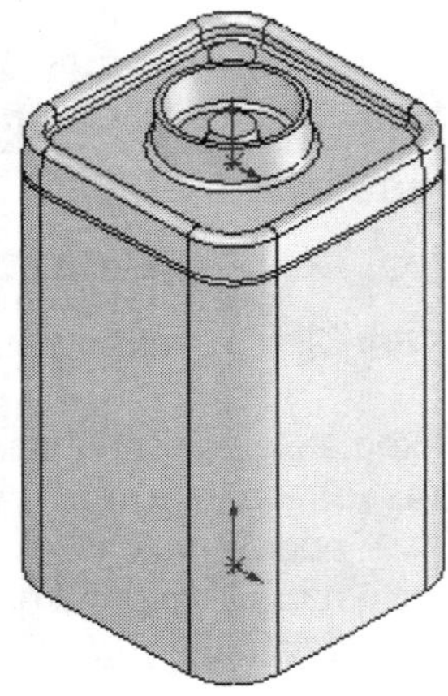

Save the BATTERYANDPLATE.

753) Click Isometric view .

754) Click **Save** .

CAPANDLENS Sub-assembly

Create the CAPANDLENS sub-assembly. Utilize two Coincident Mates and one Distance Mate to assemble the O-RING to the LENSCAP. Utilize three Coincident Mates to assemble the LENSANDBULB sub-assembly to the LENSCAP component.

Caution: Select the correct reference. Expand the LENSCAP and O-RING. Click the Right Plane within the LENSCAP. Click the Right Plane within the O-RING.

Activity: CAPANDLENS Sub-assembly

Create the CAPANDLENS sub-assembly.

755) Click **File**, **New** from the Main menu.

756) Click the **MY-TEMPLATES** tab.

757) Double-click **ASM-IN-ANSI**.

Insert the LENSCAP sub-assembly.

758) Click **View**, check **Origin** from the Main menu.

759) Click **Browse** from the Insert Component PropertyManager.

760) Double-click **LENSCAP** from the Open dialog box.

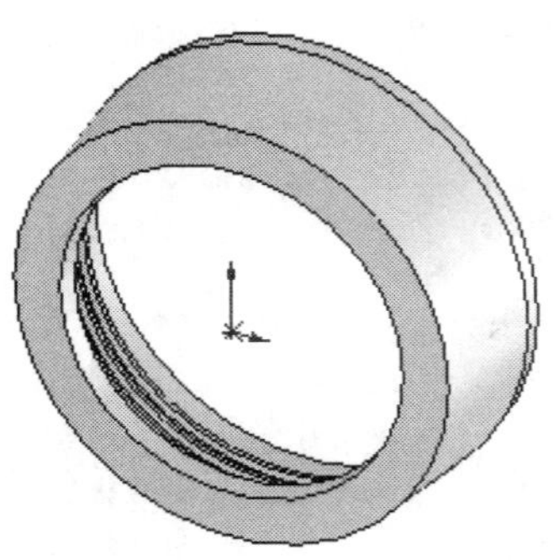

761) Click the **Origin** of the Assembly.

Save the CAPANDLENS assembly.

762) Click **Save** .

763) Select the **PROJECTS** file folder. Enter **CAPANDLENS** for File name.

764) Enter **LENSCAP AND LENS** for Description.

765) Click **Save**.

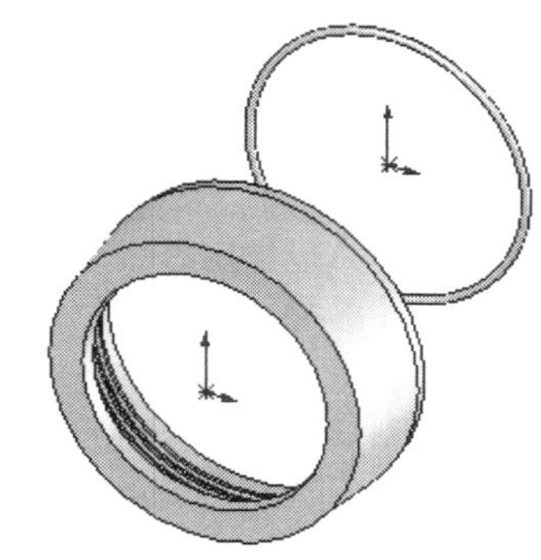

Insert the O-RING part.

766) Click **Insert Component** Insert Compo... from the Assembly toolbar.

767) Click **Browse**.

768) Double-click **O-RING** from the Open dialog box.

769) Click a **position** behind the LENSCAP.

Insert the LENSANDBULB assembly.

770) Click **Insert Component** Insert Compo... from the Assembly toolbar.

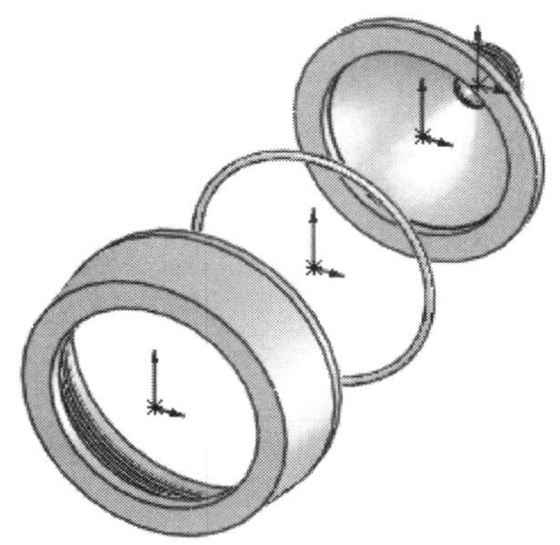

771) Click **Browse**. Select **Assembly** for Files of Type in the Open dialog box.

772) Double-click **LENSANDBULB**.

773) Click a **position** behind the O-RING.

774) Click Isometric view.

Move and Hide Components.

775) Click and drag the **O-RING** and **LENSANDBULB** to position equally spaced in the Graphics window.

776) Right-click **LENSANDBULB** in the FeatureManager.

777) Click **Hide** Hide.

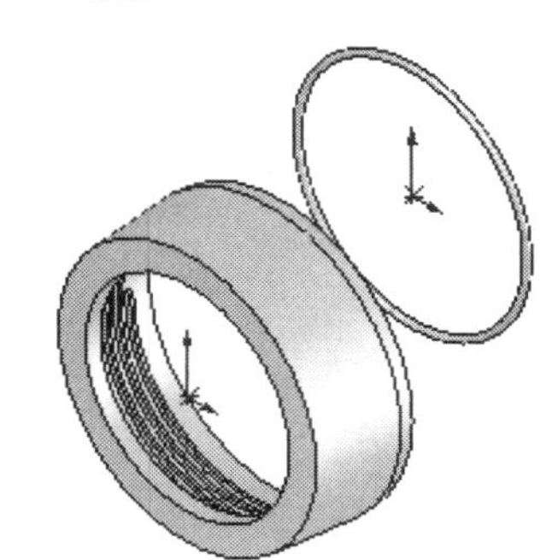

Insert three Mates between the LENSCAP and O-RING.

778) Click **Mate** Mate from the Assembly toolbar.

Insert a Coincident Mate.

779) Click the **Right Plane** of the LENSCAP in the FeatureManager.

780) Click the **Right Plane** of the O-RING in the FeatureManager.

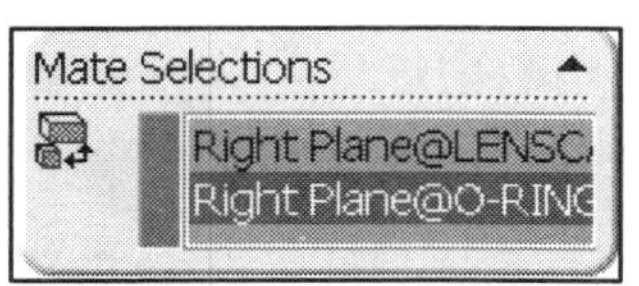

781) Click **Coincident**.

782) Click **OK**.

Insert a second Coincident Mate.

783) Click the **Top Plane** of the LENSCAP in the FeatureManager.

784) Click the **Top Plane** of the O-RING in the FeatureManager.

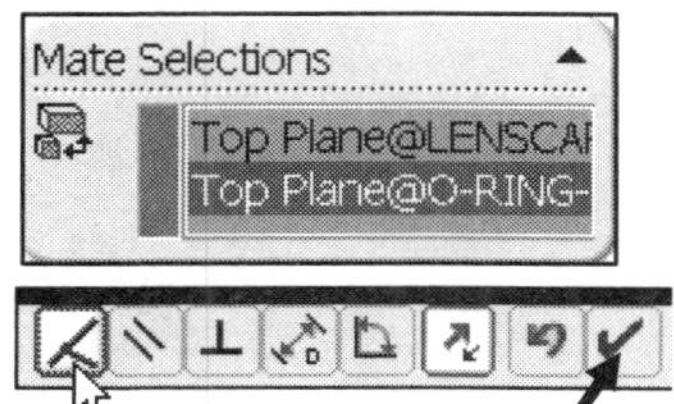

785) Click **Coincident**.

786) Click **OK**.

787)

Insert a Distance Mate.

788) Click the Shell1 **back inside face** of the LENSCAP.

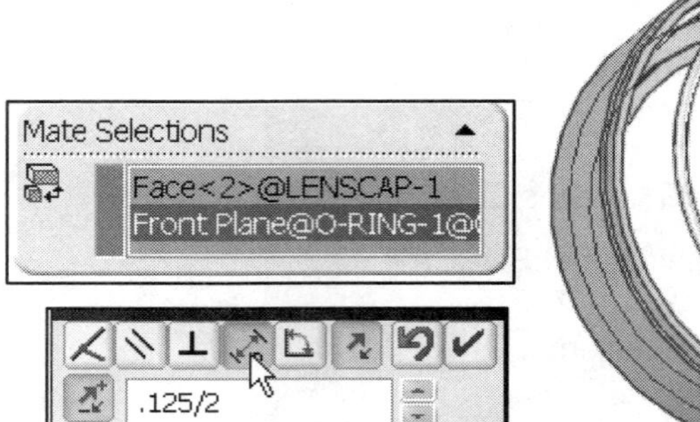

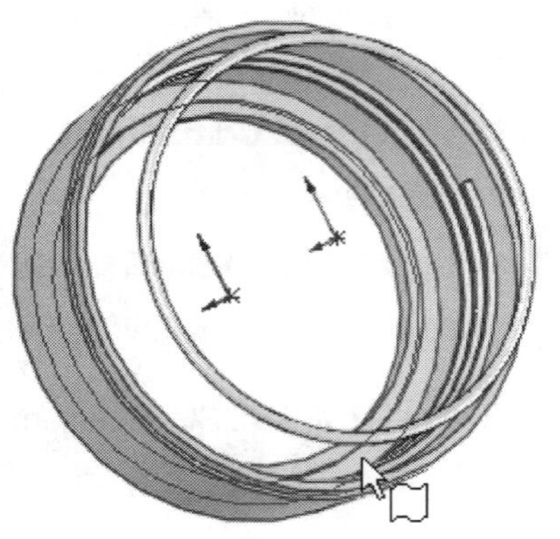

789) Click the **Front Plane** of the O-RING in the FeatureManager.

790) C lick **Distance**.

791) Enter .125/2in, [3.175/2mm].

792) Click **OK**.

793) Click **OK** from the Mate PropertyManager.

794) Click Isometric view .

795) Click **Save**.

How is the Distance Mate, .0625, [1.588] calculated? Answer:

O-RING Radius (.1250in/2) = .0625in.

O-RING Radius [3.175mm/2] = [1.5875].

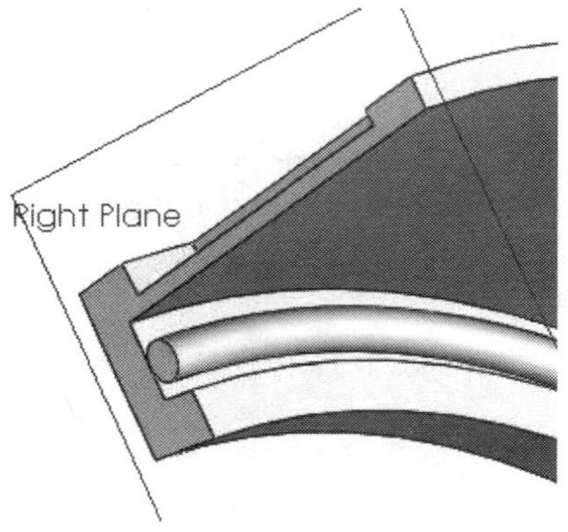

Utilize a Section View to locate internal geometry for mating and verify position of components.

Build flexibility into the Mate. The Distance Mate option offers additional flexibility over the Coincident Mate option. The Distance Mate value can be modified.

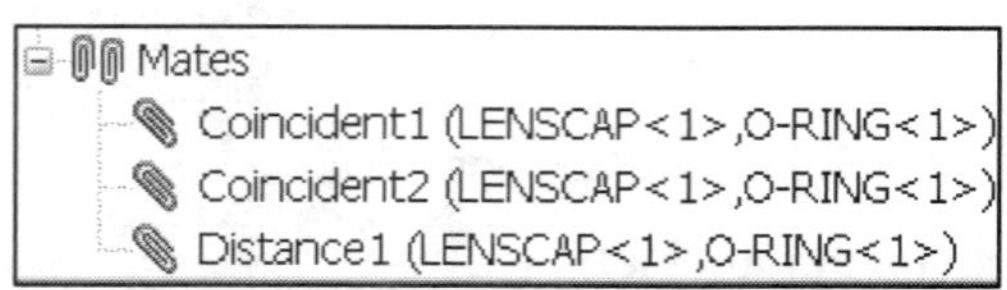

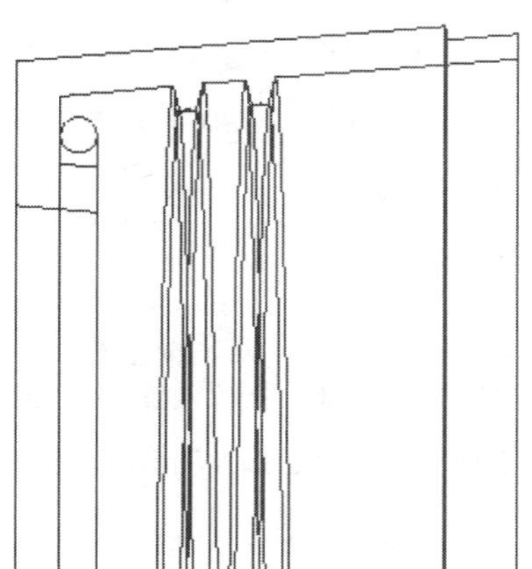

Show the LENSANDBULB.

796) Right-click **LENSANDBULB** in the FeatureManager.

797) Click **Show** Show

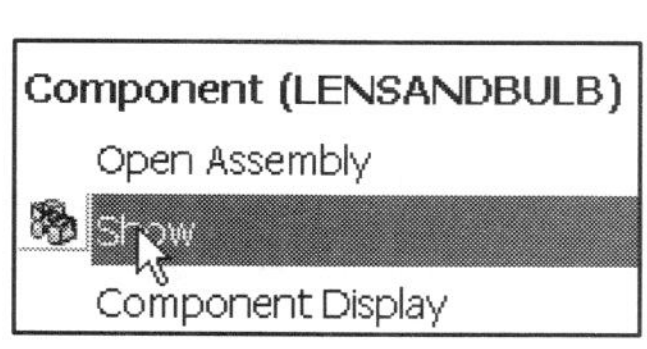

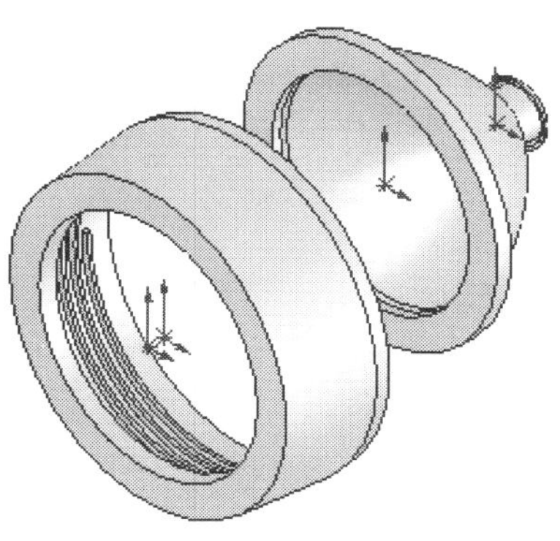

Fit the Model to the Graphics window.

798) Press the **f** key.

799) Click **Mate** .

Insert a Coincident Mate.

800) Click the **Right Plane** of the LENSCAP.

801) Click the **Right Plane** of the LENSANDBULB.

802) Click **Coincident**.

803) Click **OK**.

Insert a Coincident Mate.

804) Click the **Top Plane** of the LENSCAP.

805) Click the **Top Plane** of the LENSANDBULB.

806) Click **Coincident**.

807) Click **OK**.

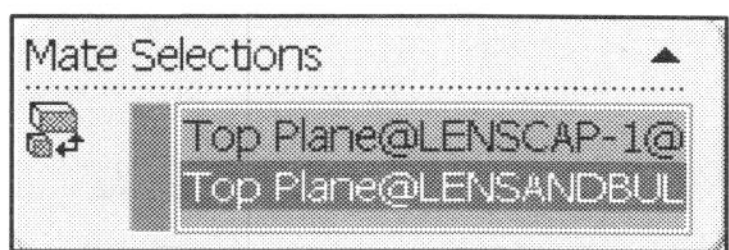

Insert a Coincident Mate.

808) Click the flat inside **narrow back face** of the LENSCAP.

809) Click the **front flat face** of the LENSANDBULB. Coincident is selected by default.

810) Click **OK**.

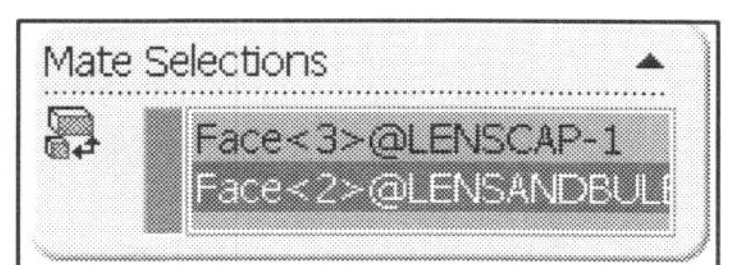

811) Click **OK** from the Mate PropertyManager.

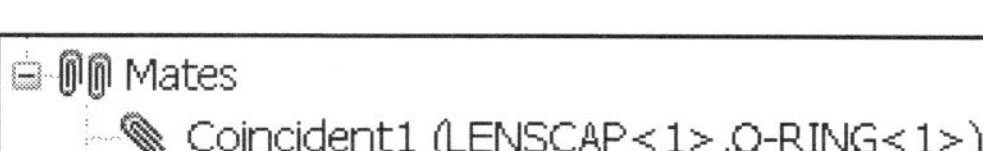

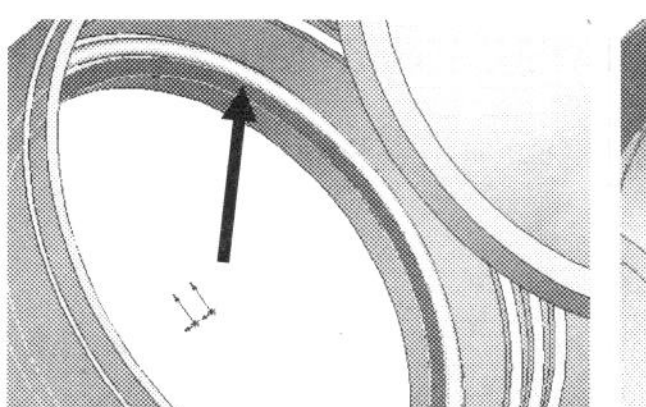

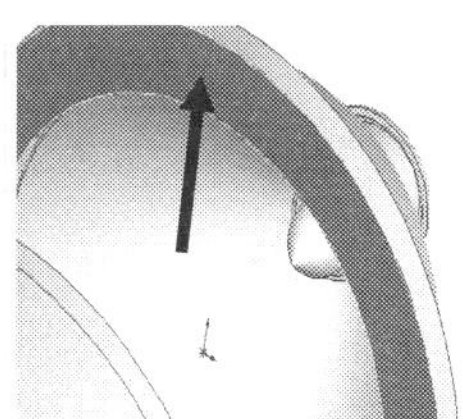

Confirm the location of the O-RING.

812) Click the **Right Plane** of the CAPANDLENS.

813) Click Section view.

814) Click Isometric view.

815) Check **Section 2**. Click the **Top Plane**.

816) Click **OK** from the Section View PropertyManager.

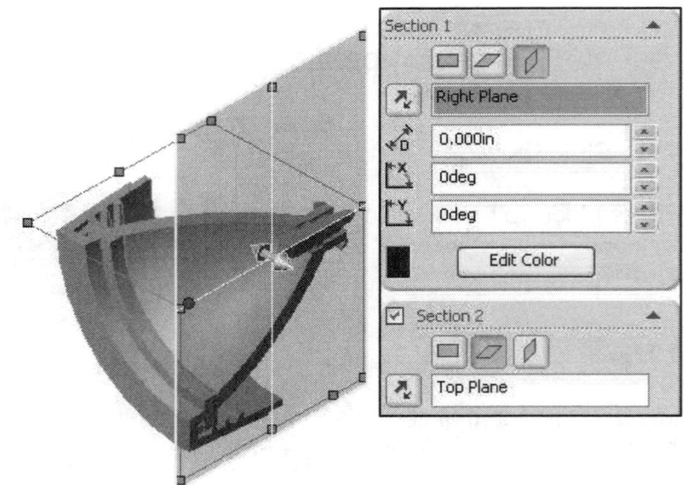

Save the CAPANDLENS sub-assembly.

817) Click Section view.

818) Click **Save**.

The LENSANDBULB, BATTERYANDPLATE, and CAPANDLENS sub-assemblies are complete. The components in each assembly are fully defined. No minus (-) sign or red error flags exist in the FeatureManager. Insert the sub-assemblies into the final FLASHLIGHT assembly.

FLASHLIGHT assembly

Create the FLASHLIGHT assembly. The HOUSING is the Base component. The FLASHLIGHT assembly mates the HOUSING to the SWITCH component. The FLASHLIGHT assembly mates the CAPANDLENS and BATTERYANDPLATE.

Activity: FLASHLIGHT Assembly

Create the FLASHLIGHT assembly.

819) Click **File**, **New** from the Main menu.

820) Click the **MY-TEMPLATES** tab.

821) Double-click the **ASM-IN-ANSI**.

Insert the HOUSING and SWITCH.

822) Click **View**, check **Origin** from the Main menu.

823) Click **Browse** from the Insert Component PropertyManager.

824) Select **Parts** for Files of Type.

825) Double-click **HOUSING** from the Open dialog box.

826) Click the **Origin** of the Assembly.

827) Click Insert Component Insert Compo... .

828) Click **Browse**.

829) Double-click **SWITCH** from the Open dialog box.

830) Click a **position** in front of the HOUSING.

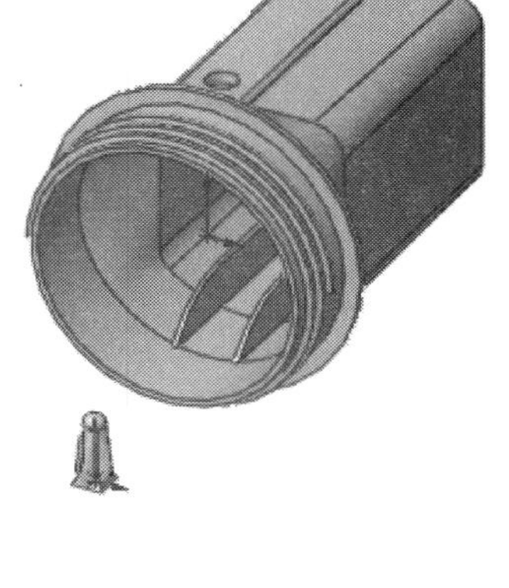

Save the FLASHLIGHT assembly.

831) Click **Save** .

832) Select the **PROJECTS** folder.

833) Enter **FLASHLIGHT** for File name.

834) Enter **FLASHLIGHT ASSEMBLY** for Description.

835) Click **Save**.

Insert a Coincident Mate.

836) Click **Mate** Mate .

837) Click the **Right Plane** of the HOUSING.

838) Click the **Right Plane** of the SWITCH.

839) Click **Coincident** .

840) Click **OK** .

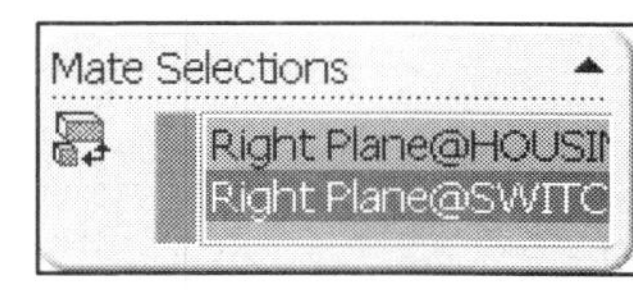

Insert a Coincident Mate.

841) Click **View**, check **Temporary** axis from the main menu.

842) Click the **Temporary axis** inside the Switch Hole of the HOUSING.

843) Click the **Front Plane** of the SWITCH.

844) Click **Coincident** .

845) Click **OK** .

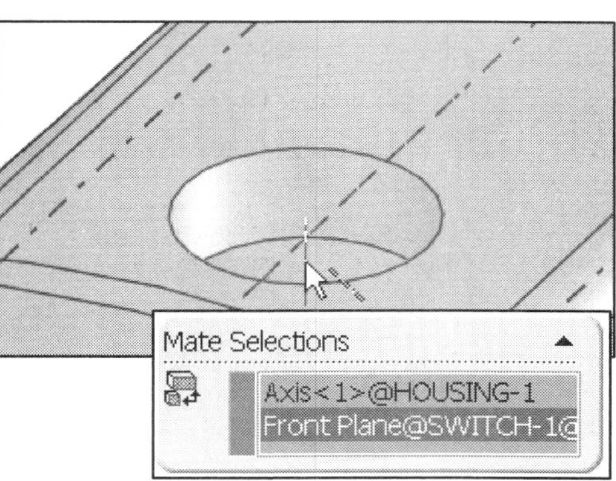

Insert a Distance Mate.

846) Click the **top face** of the Handle.

847) Click the **Vertex** on the Loft top face of the SWITCH.

848) Click **Distance** .

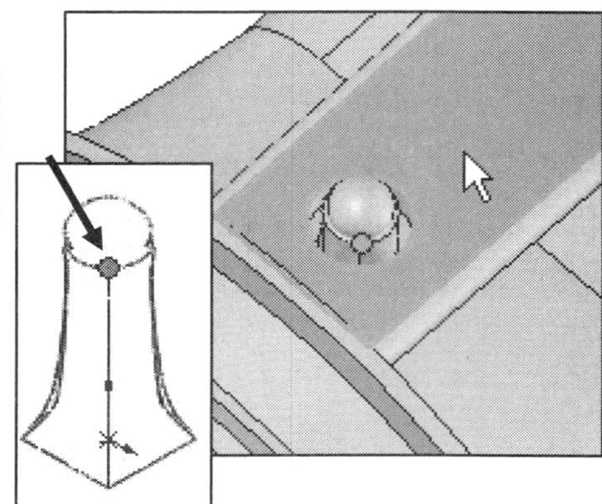

849) Enter **.100in**, [**2.54**]. Check Flip Direction if required. The inch value is converted to millimeters.

850) Click **OK** ✔.

851) Click **OK**  from the Mate PropertyManager.

Insert the CAPANDLENS assembly.

852) Click **View**, uncheck **Temporary Axis** from the Main menu.

853) Click Insert Component Insert Compo....

854) Click **Browse**.

855) Select **Assembly** for Files of Type.

856) Double-click **CAPANDLENS** from the Open dialog box.

Place the Assembly.

857) Click a **position** in front of the HOUSING.

858) Click **View**, uncheck **Origins** from the Main menu.

Insert Mates between the HOUSING component and the CAPANDLENS sub-assembly.

859) Click **Mate** Mate from the Assembly toolbar.

Insert a Coincident Mate.

860) Click the **Right Plane** of the HOUSING.

861) Click the **Right Plane** of the CAPANDLENS.

862) Click **Coincident**.

863) Click **OK** ✔.

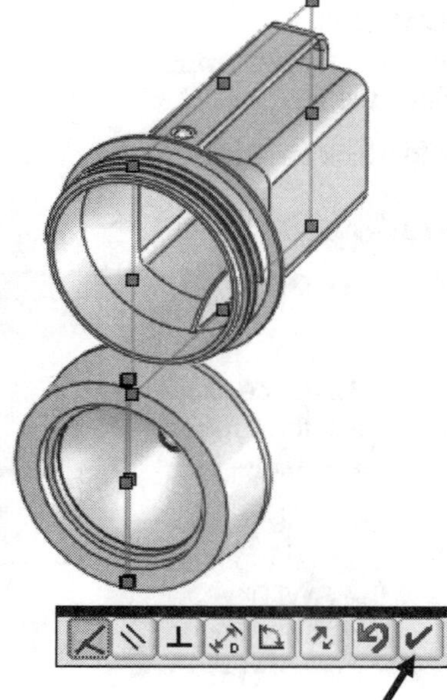

Insert a Coincident Mate.

864) Click the **Top Plane** of the HOUSING.

865) Click the **Top Plane** of the CAPANDLENS.

866) Click **Coincident**.

867) Click **OK**.

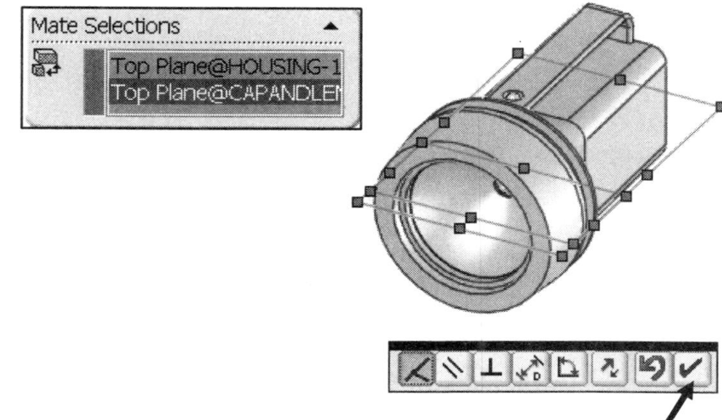

Insert a Coincident Mate.

868) Click the **front face of the Boss-Stop** on the HOUSING.

Rotate the view.

869) Press the **Left Arrow Key** to view the back face.

870) Click the **back face** of the CAPANDLENS.

871) Click Coincident.

872) Click **OK**.

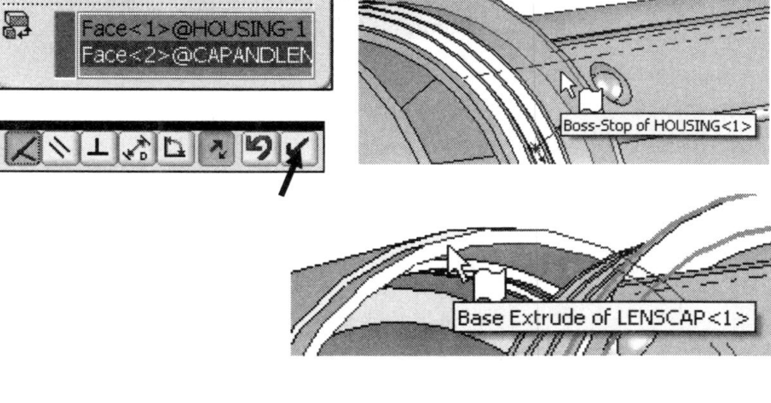

873) Click **OK** from the Mate PropertyManager.

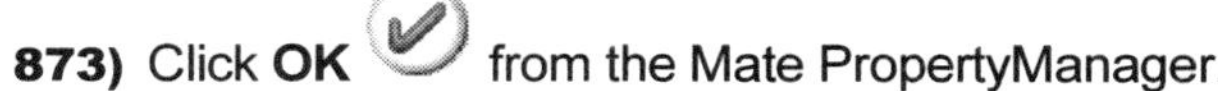

Save the FLASHLIGHT assembly.

874) Click Isometric view.

875) Click **Save**.

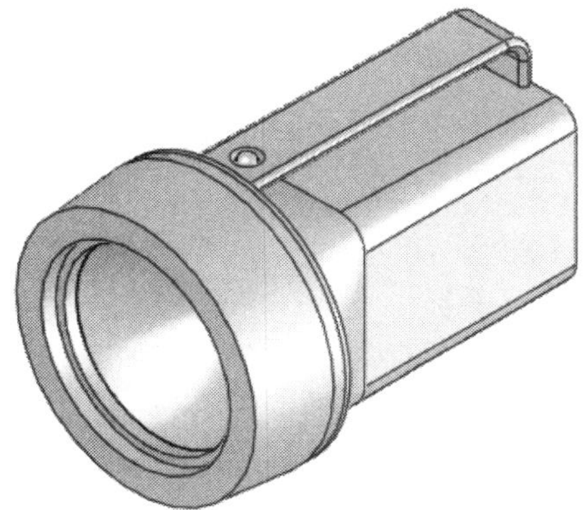

Insert the BATTERYANDPLATE sub-assembly.

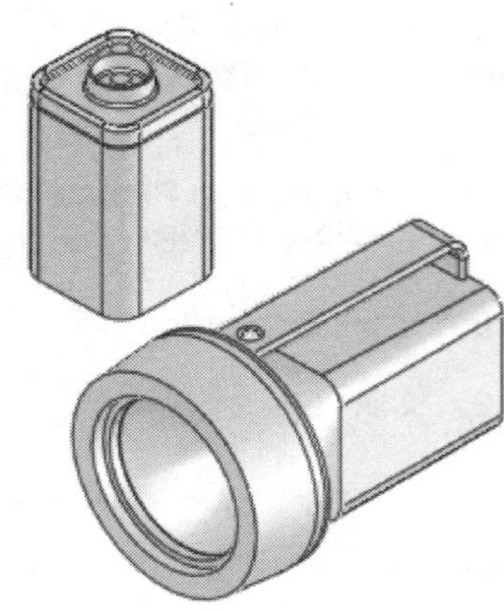

876) Click Insert Component  Insert Compo... .

877) Click **Browse**.

878) Select **Assembly** for Files of type.

879) Double-click **BATTERYANDPLATE** from the Open dialog box.

880) Click a **position** to the left of the HOUSING.

Rotate the part.

881) Click **BATTERYANDPLATE** in the FeatureManager.

882) Click **Rotate Component**  Rotate Compo... from the Assembly toolbar.

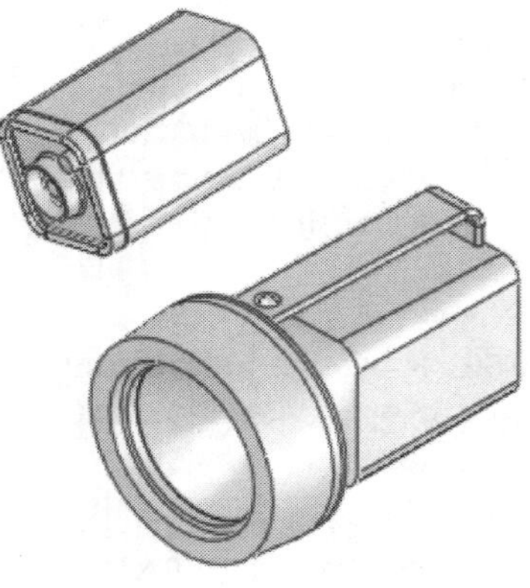

883) Rotate the **BATTERYANDPLATE** until it is approximately parallel with the HOUSING.

884) Click **OK** from the Rotate Component PropertyManager.

Insert a Coincident Mate.

885) Click **Mate** Mate .

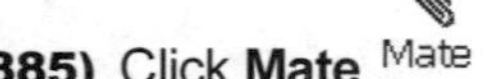

886) Click the **Right Plane** of the HOUSING.

887) Click the **Front Plane** of the BATTERYANDPLATE.

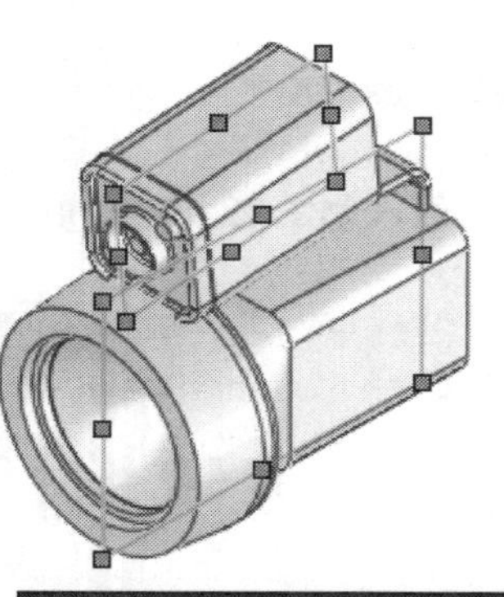

888) Click **Coincident**.

889) Click OK.

890) Move the **BATTERYANDYPLATE** in front of the HOUSING.

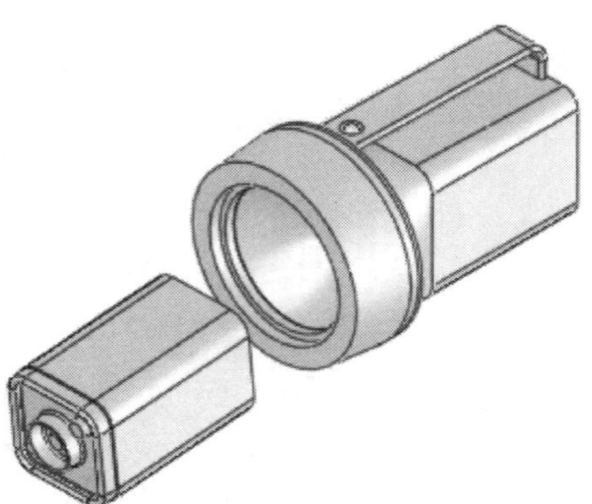

Insert a Coincident Mate.

891) Click the **Top Plane** of the HOUSING.

892) Click the **Right Plane** of the BATTERYANDPLATE.

893) Click **Coincident**.

894) Click **OK**.

895) Click **OK** from the Mate PropertyManager.

896) Display the Section view.

897) Click the **Right Plane** in the FLASHLIGHT Assembly FeatureManager.

898) Click Section view.

899) Click **OK** from the Section View PropertyManager.

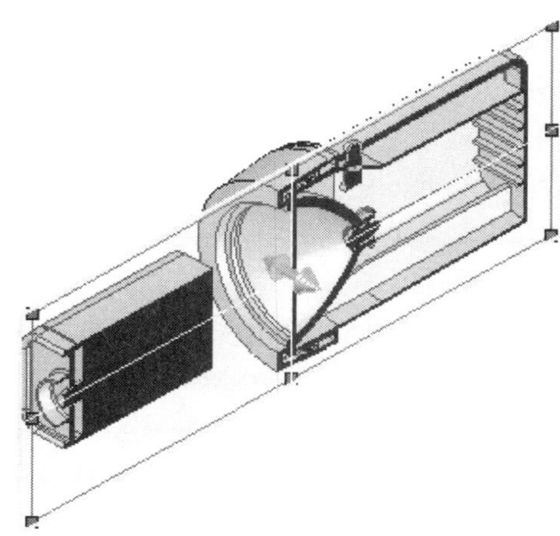

Move the BATTERYANDPLATE in front of the HOUSING.

900) Click and drag the **BATTERYANDPLATE** in front of the HOUSING.

Insert a Coincident Mate.

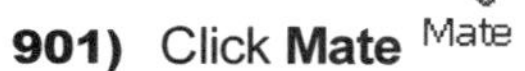

901) Click **Mate**.

902) Click the **back center Rib1 face** of the HOUSING.

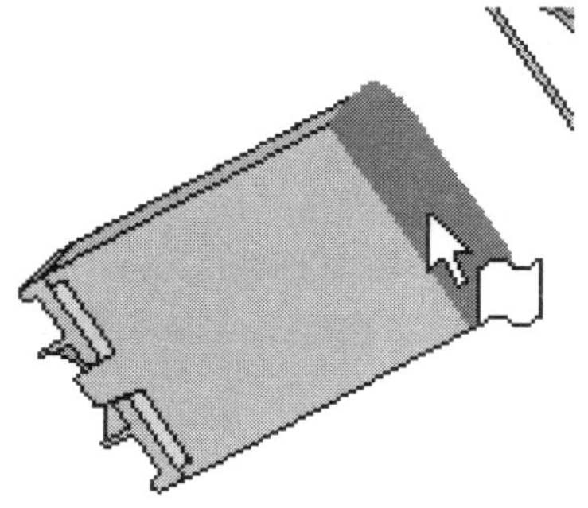

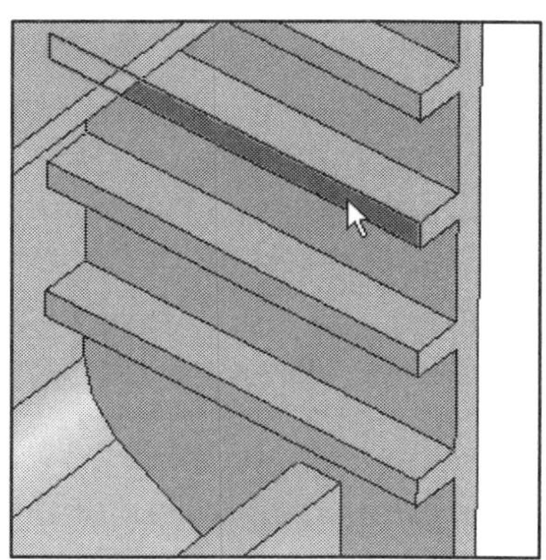

903) Click the **bottom face** of the BATTERYANDPLATE.

904) Click **Coincident**.

905) Click **OK**.

906) Click Isometric view.

907) Click **OK** from the Mate PropertyManager.

Display the Full view.

908) Click Section view .

Save the FLASHLIGHT.

909) Click **Save** .

910) Click **Yes** to update all components.

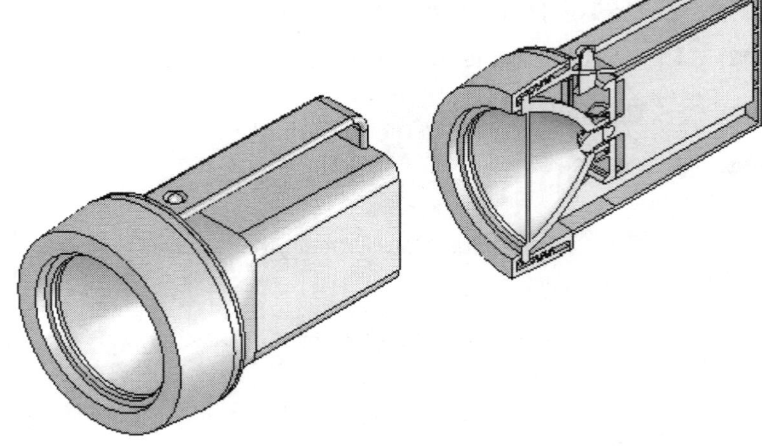

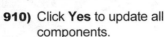

Additional information on Assembly, Move Component, Rotate Component, and Mates is available in SolidWorks Help Topics.

Refer to Help, Online Tutorial Assembly Mates exercise and Design Tables exercise for additional information.

Review of the FLASHLIGHT Assembly.

The FLASHLIGHT assembly consisted of the CAPANDLENS sub-assembly, BATTERYANDPLATE sub-assembly, HOUSING part and SWITCH part. The CAPANDLENS sub-assembly contained the BULBANDLENS sub-assembly, the O-RING and the LENSCAP part.

Through the Assembly Layout illustration you simplified the number of components into a series of smaller assemblies. You also enhanced your modeling techniques and skills.

You still have a few more areas to address. One of the biggest design issues in assembly modeling is interference. Let's investigate the FLASHLIGHT assembly.

Addressing Interference Issues

There is an interference issue between the FLASHLIGHT components. Address the design issue. Adjust Rib2 on the HOUSING. Test with the Interference Check command. The FLASHLIGHT assembly is illustrated in inches.

Activity: Addressing Interference Issues

Check for interference.

911) Click **Interference Detection** from the Assembly toolbar. Delete **FLASHLIGHT.SLDASM** from the Selected components box.

912) Click **BATTERYANDPLATE** from the FeatureManager.

913) Click **HOUSING** from the FeatureManager.

914) Click the **Calculate** button. The interference is displayed in red in the Graphics window. Click each **Interference** in the Results box to view the interference in red with Rib2 of the HOUSING.

915) Click **OK** from the Interference Detection PropertyManager.

Modify the Rib2 dimension.

916) Expand the **HOUSING** in the FeatureManager.

917) Double-click on the **Rib2** feature.

918) Click Hidden Lines Removed.

919) Double click **1.300**, [**33.02**].

920) Enter **1.350in**, [**34.29**].

921) Click Rebuild.

922) Click **OK**.

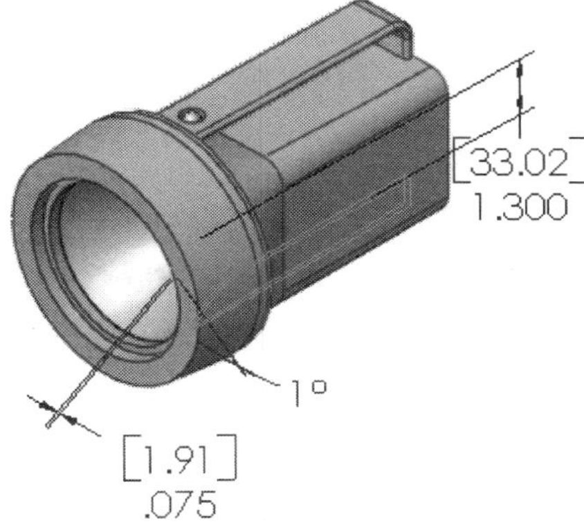

Recheck for Interference.

923) Click **Interference Detection** from the Assembly toolbar. The Interference dialog box is displayed.

924) Delete **FLASHLIGHT.SLDASM** from the Selected components box.

925) Click **BATTERYANDPLATE** from the FeatureManager.

926) Click **HOUSING** from the FeatureManager.

927) Click the **Calculate** button. No Interference is displayed in the Results box. The FLASHLIGHT design is complete.

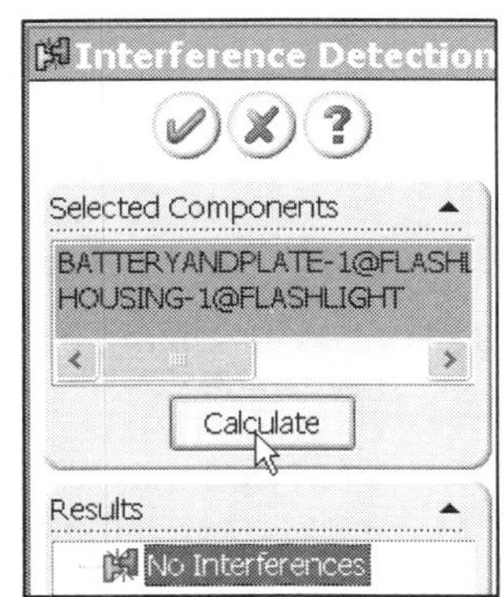

928) Click **OK** from the Interference Detection PropertyManager.

Save the FLASHLIGHT.

929) Click **Save** .

930) Click **YES** to the question, "Rebuild the assembly and update the components".

Export Files and eDrawings

You receive a call from the sales department. They inform you that the customer increased the initial order by 200,000 units. However, the customer requires a prototype to verify the design in six days. What do you do? Answer: Contact a Rapid Prototype supplier. You export three SolidWorks files:

- HOUSING.
- LENSCAP.
- BATTERYPLATE.

Use the Stereo Lithography (STL) format. Email the three files to a Rapid Prototype supplier. Example: Paperless Parts Inc. (www.paperlessparts.com). A Stereolithography (SLA) supplier provides physical models from 3D drawings. 2D drawings are not required. Export the HOUSING. SolidWorks eDrawings provides a facility for you to animate, view and create compressed documents to send to colleagues, customers and vendors. Publish an eDrawing of the FLASHLIGHT assembly.

Activity: Export Files and eDrawings

Open and Export the HOUSING.

931) Right-click on the **HOUSING** in the FLASHLIGHT Graphics window.

932) Click **Open Part**.

933) Click **File**, **Save As**. A warning message states that, "HOUSING.SLDPRT is being referenced by other open documents. Click **OK**.

934) Select **STL Files (*.stl)** from the Save as type drop down list. The Save dialog box displays new options.

935) Drag the **dialog box** to the left to view the Graphics window.

936) Click **Options** Options... in the lower right corner of the Save dialog box.

937) Check **Binary** from the Output as format box.

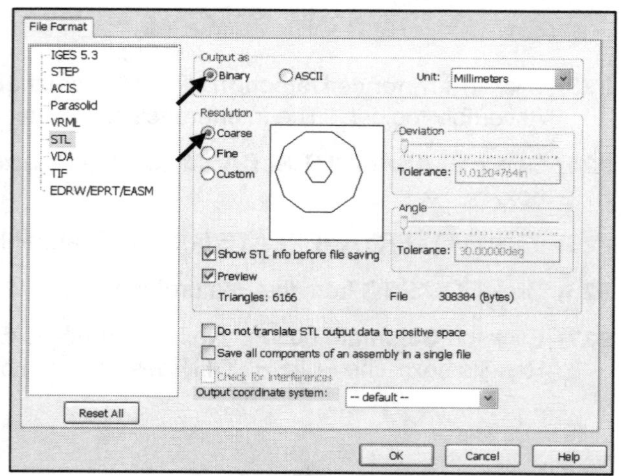

938) Click **Course** for Resolution.

Display the STL triangular faceted model.
939) Click **Preview**.

940) Drag the **dialog box** to the left to view the Graphics window.

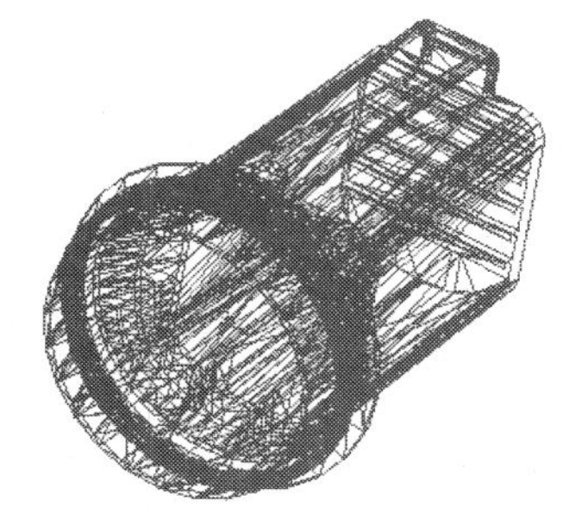

Create the binary STL file.
941) Click **OK** from the STL dialog box.

942) Click **Save** from the Save dialog box. A status report is provided.

943) Click **Yes**.

Publish an eDrawing and email the document to a colleague.

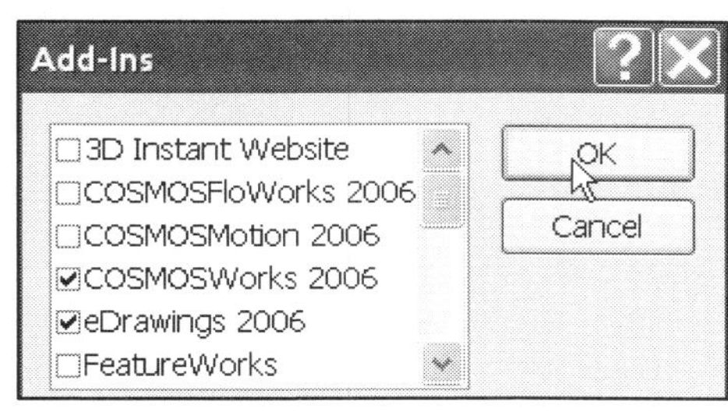

Create the eDrawing and animation.
944) Click **Tools**, **Add-ins**, **eDrawings 2006** from the Main menu.

945) Click **OK** from the Add-Ins box.

946)

947) Note: The eDrawings toolbar contains two icons.

View the eDrawing animation.

948) Click **eDrawing**  .

949) Click **Play** Play .

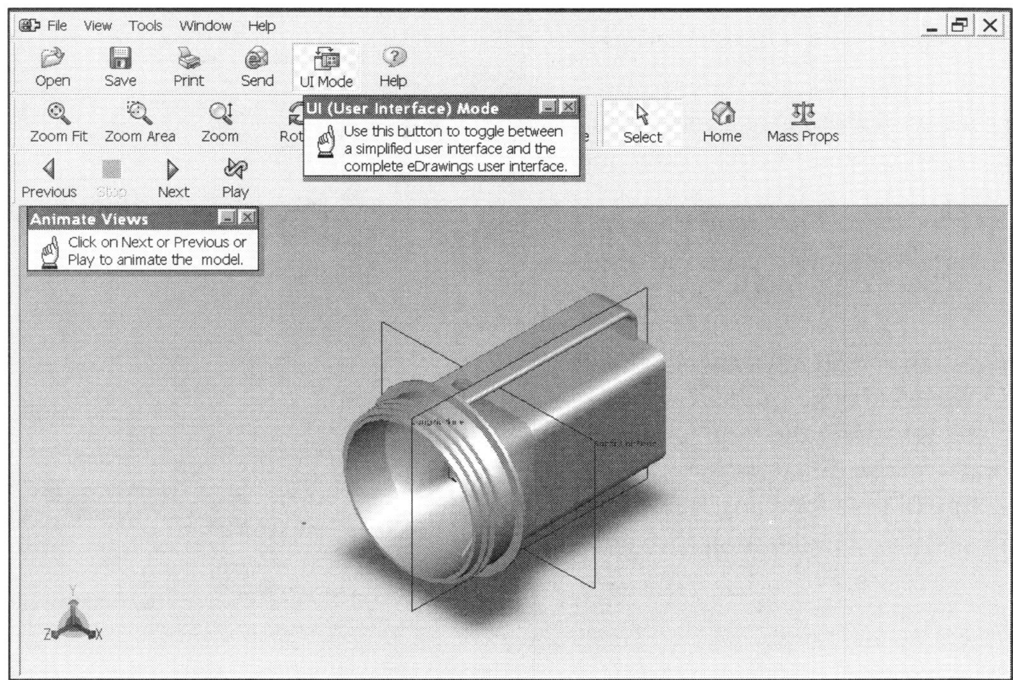

Stop the animation.

950) Click **Stop**  Stop.

Save the eDrawing.

951) Click **Save** Save from the eDrawing Main menu.

952) Select the **PROJECTS** folder.

953) Enter **FLASHLIGHT** for File name.

954) Click **Save**.

955) Click **Close** from the eDrawing screen.

It is time to go home. The telephone rings. The customer is ready to place the order. Tomorrow you will receive the purchase order.

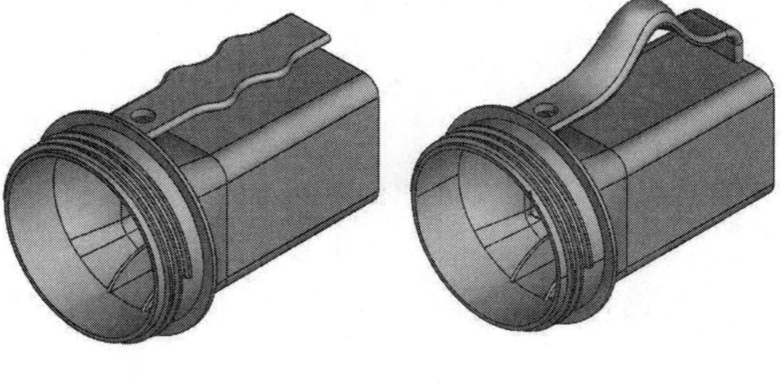

Guide Curves Deform

The customer also discusses a new purchase order that requires a major design change to the handle. You work with your industrial designer and discuss the two options. The first option utilizes Guide Curves on a Sweep feature.

The second option utilizes the Deform feature. These features are explored in a discussion on the multimedia CD contained in the text.

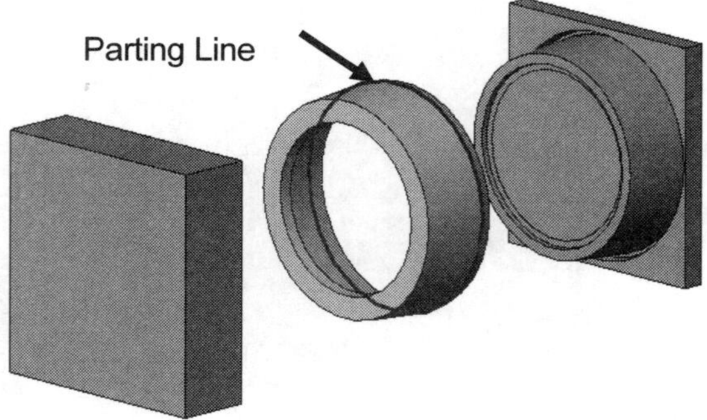

You contact your mold maker and send an eDrawing of the LENSCAP.

The mold maker recommends placing the parting line at the edge of the Revolved Cut surface and reversing the Draft Angle direction. The mold maker also recommends a snap fit versus a thread to reduce cost. The Core-Cavity mold tooling is explored in the project exercises.

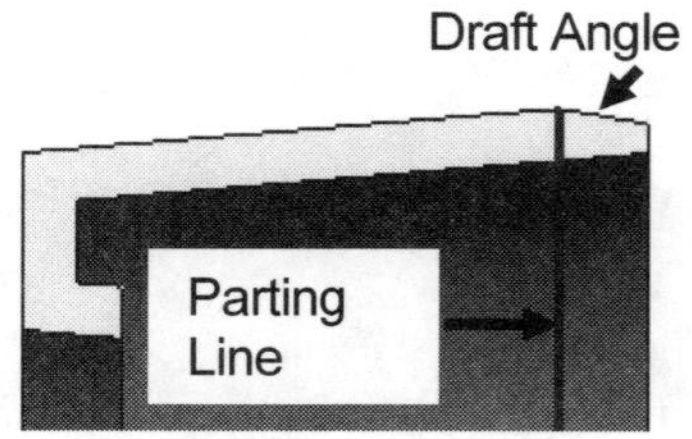

Additional information on Interference Detection, eDrawings, STL files (stereolithography), Guide Curves, Deform and Mold Tools are available in SolidWorks Help Topics.

Project Summary

The FLASHLIGHT assembly contains over 100 features, reference planes, sketches and components. You organized the features in each part. You developed an assembly layout structure to organize your components.

The O-RING utilized a Sweep Base feature. The SWITCH utilized a Loft Base feature. The simple Sweep feature requires two sketches: a path and a profile. A complex Sweep requires multiple sketches and Guide Curves. The Loft feature requires two or more sketches created on different planes.

The LENSCAP and HOUSING utilized a variety of features. You applied design intent to reuse geometry through Geometric Relationships, symmetry and patterns.

The assembly required an Assembly Template. You utilized the ASM-IN-ANSI Template to create the LENSANDBULB, CAPANDLENS, BATTERYANDPLATE and FLASHLIGHT assemblies.

You created an STL file of the Housing and an eDrawing of the FLASHLIGHT assembly to communicate with your vendor, mold maker and customer. Review the project exercises before moving on to Project 6.

Project Terminology

Assembly Component Layout Diagram: A diagram used to plan the top-level assembly organization. Organize parts into smaller subassemblies. Create a flow chart or manual sketch to classify components.

Component: A part or assembly inserted into a new assembly.

Draft: A feature used to add a specified draft angle to a face. You utilized a Draft feature with the Neutral Plane option.

eDrawings: A compressed document used to animate and view SolidWorks documents.

Extruded Thin Cut: A feature used to remove material by extruding an open profile.

Helix/Spiral Curve: A Helix is a curve with pitch. The Helix is created about an axis. You utilized a Helix Curve to create a thread for the LENSCAP.

Interference Detection: The amount of interference between components in an assembly is calculated with Tools, Interference Detection.

Loft: A feature used to blend two or more profiles on separate Planes. A Loft Boss adds material. A Loft Cut removes material. The HOUSING part utilized a Loft Boss feature to transition a circular profile of the LENSCAP to a square profile of the BATTERY.

Mates: A Mate is a geometric relationship between components in an assembly that constrain rotational and translational motion.

Mirror: The feature used to create a symmetric feature about a Mirror Plane. The Mirror feature created a second Rib, symmetric about the Right Plane.

Pattern: A Pattern creates one or more instances of a feature or group of features. A Circular Pattern creates instances of a seed feature about an axis of revolution. A Linear Pattern creates instances of a seed feature in a rectangular array, along one or two edges. The Linear Pattern was utilized to create multiple instances of the HOUSING Rib1 feature.

Plastic injection manufacturing: Review the fundamental design rules behind the plastic injection manufacturing process:

- Maintain a constant wall thickness. Inconsistent wall thickness creates stress. Utilize the Shell feature to create constant wall thickness.
- Create a radius on all corners. No sharp edges. Sharp edges create vacuum issues when removing the mold. Utilize the Fillet feature to remove sharp edges.
- Allow a minimum draft angle of 1 degree. Draft sides and internal ribs. Draft angles assist in removing the part from the mold. Utilize the Draft feature or Rib Draft angle option.

Revolved Cut Thin: A feature used to remove material by rotating a sketched open profile around a centerline.

Rib: A feature used to add material between contours of existing geometry. Use Ribs to add structural integrity to a part.

Shape: A feature used to deform a surface created by expanding, constraining, and tightening a selected surface. A deformed surface is flexible, much like a membrane.

Suppressed: A feature or component not loaded into memory. A feature is suppressed or unsuppressed. A component is suppressed or resolved. Suppress features and components to improve model rebuild time.

Stereo Lithography (STL) format: STL format is the type of file format requested by Rapid Prototype manufacturers.

Sweep: A Sweep Boss/Base feature adds material. A Sweep Cut removes material. A Sweep requires a profile sketch and a path sketch. A Sweep feature moves a profile along a path. The Sweep Boss tool is located on the Features toolbar. The Sweep Cut tool is located in the Insert menu.

Questions

1. Identify the function of the following features:
    - Sweep.
    - Revolved Cut Thin.
    - Loft.
    - Rib.
    - Draft.
    - Linear Pattern.
2. Describe a Suppressed feature. Why would you suppress a feature?
3. The Rib features require a Sketch, thickness and a ___________ direction.
4. What is a Pierce Relation?
5. Describe how to create a thread using the Sweep feature. Provide an example.
6. Explain how to create a Linear Pattern. Provide an example.
7. Identify two advantages of utilizing Convert Entities in a sketch to obtain the profile.
8. How is symmetry built into a: 1) Sketch , 2) Feature? Provide a few examples.
9. Define a Guide Curve. Identify the features that utilize Guide Curves.
10. Identify the differences between a Draft feature and the Draft Angle option in the Extruded Boss/Base feature.
11. Describe the differences between a Circular Pattern and a Linear Pattern.
12. Identify the advantages of the Convert Entities tool.
13. True or False. A Loft feature can only be inserted as the first feature in a part. Explain your answer.
14. A Sweep feature adds and removes material. Identify the location on the Main Pull down menu that contains the Sweep Cut feature. Hint: SolidWorks Help Topics.
15. Describe the difference between the Distance Mate option and the Coincident Mate option. Provide an example.

16. Review the Features toolbar. Identify the name of each feature.

A B C D E F G H I J K L M N O

A	B	C	D	E
F	G	H	I	J
K	L	M	N	O

Exercises

Exercise 5.1: QUATTRO-SEAL-O-RING Part.

Create the QUATTRO-SEAL-O-RING part as one Sweep feature.

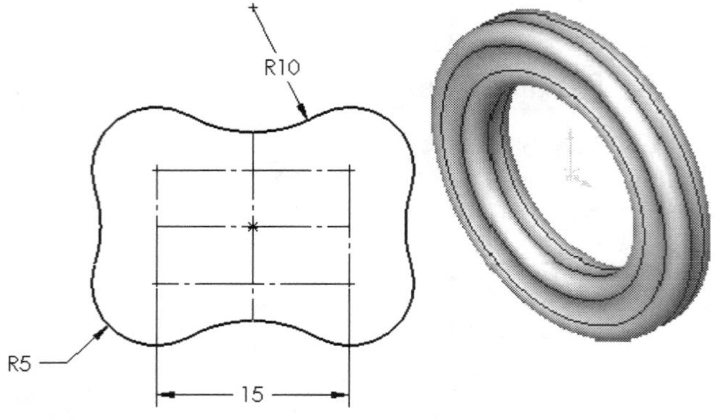

- Create a 100mm diameter Circle on the Front Plane for the path, Sketch1.
- Create the symmetric cross section on the Top Plane for the profile, Sketch2.

Exercise 5.2a: HOOK Part.

Create the HOOK part. The HOOK is created with a Sweep feature.

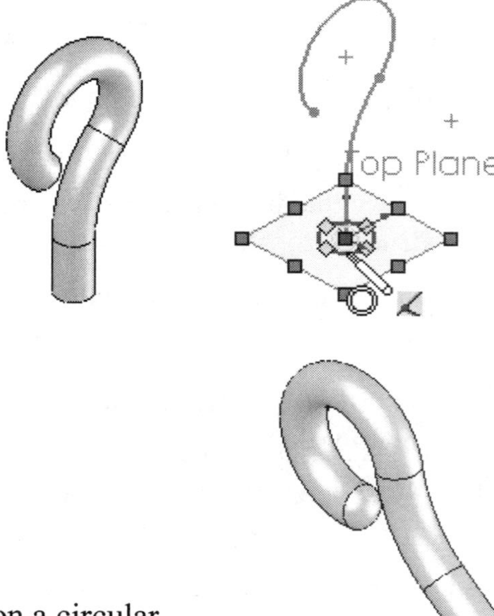

A Sweep feature adds material by moving a profile along a path. A simple Sweep feature requires two sketches. The first sketch is called the path. The second sketch is called the profile. The profile and path are sketched on perpendicular planes.

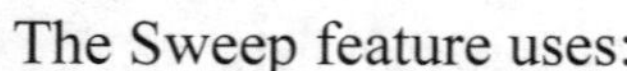

The Sweep feature uses:

- A path sketched on the Right Plane.
- A profile sketched on the Top Plane.

Utilize a Dome feature to create a spherical feature on a circular face. A Sweep Cut feature removes material.

Utilize a Sweep Cut feature to create the Thread for the HOOK part.

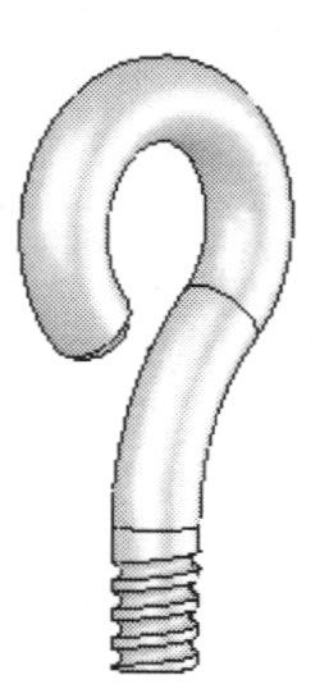

- Create the Sweep Path.
- Create the Sweep Profile.

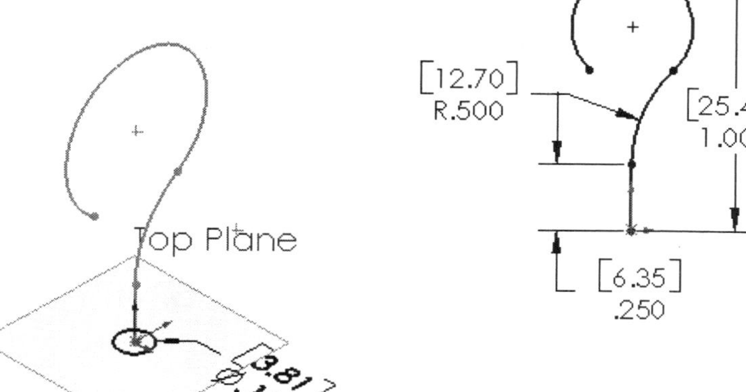

- Insert a Sweep feature.
- Use the Dome feature, .050 [1.27].

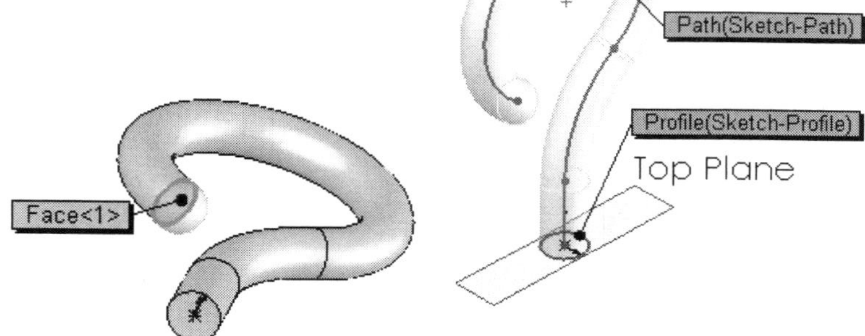

- Create the Threads. Sketch a circle ∅.020[.51mm] on the Right Plane for the Thread profile.
- Use Helix Curve feature for the path. Pitch 0.050 in, Revolution 4.0, Starting Angle 0.0 deg. Chamfer the bottom face.
- Create the Thread Profile.

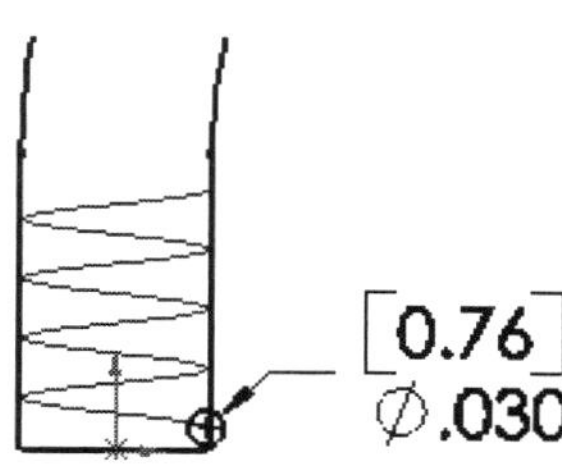

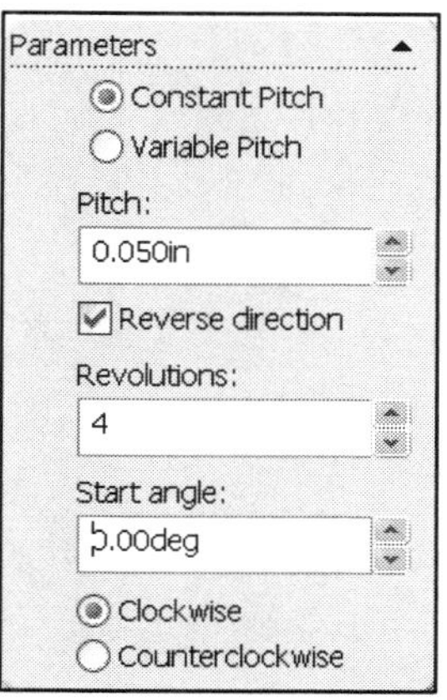

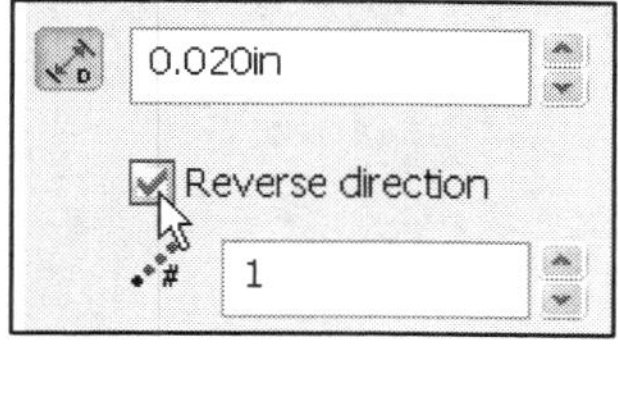

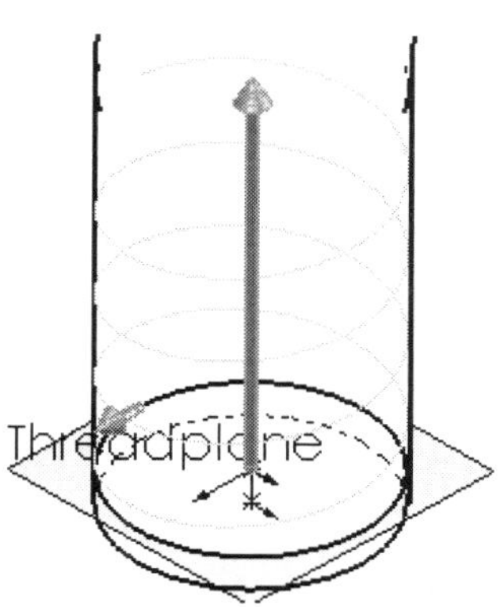

- Insert The Sweep Cut featue.

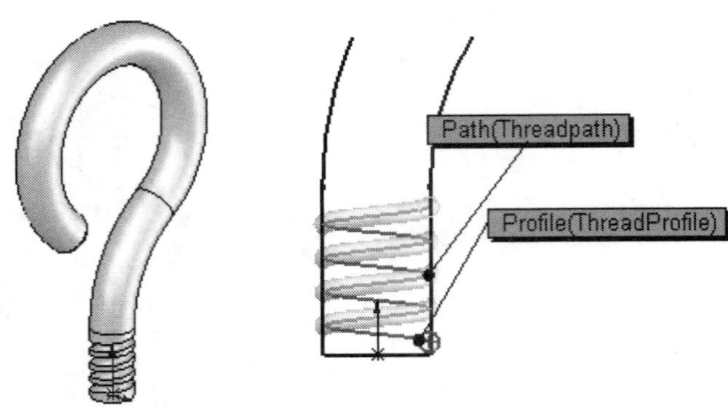

Exercise 5.2b: WEIGHT Part.

Create the WEIGHT part. Utilize the Loft Base Feature.

- The Top Plane and Plane 1 are 0.5 [12.7mm] apart.
- Sketch a rectangle 1.000 [25.40mm] x .750 [19.05] on the Top Plane.
- Sketch a square .500 [12.70mm]on Plane 1.
- Add a centered ∅.150 [3.81mm] Thru Hole.

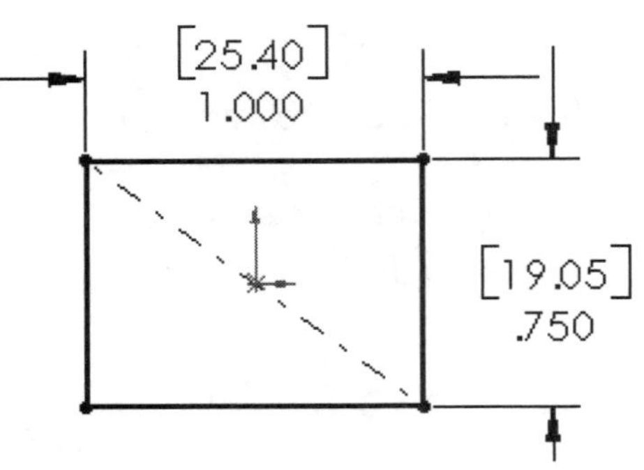

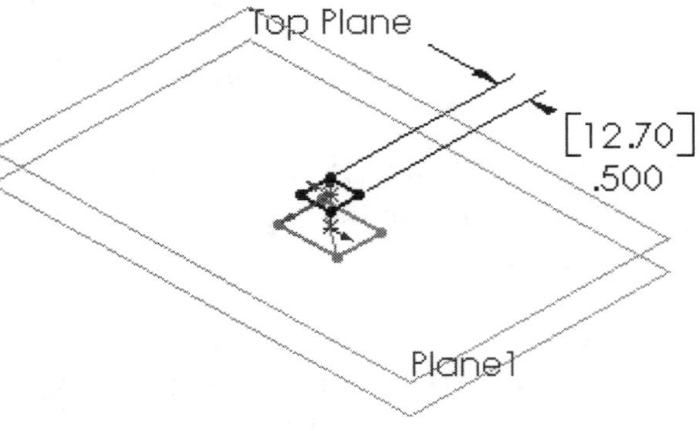

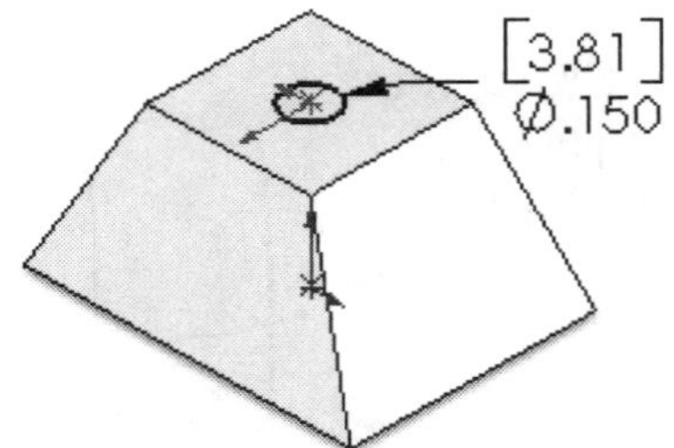

Exercise 5.2c: HOOK-WEIGHT Assembly.

Create the HOOK-WEIGHTassembly.

- Insert the HOOK part. Insert the WEIGHT part.

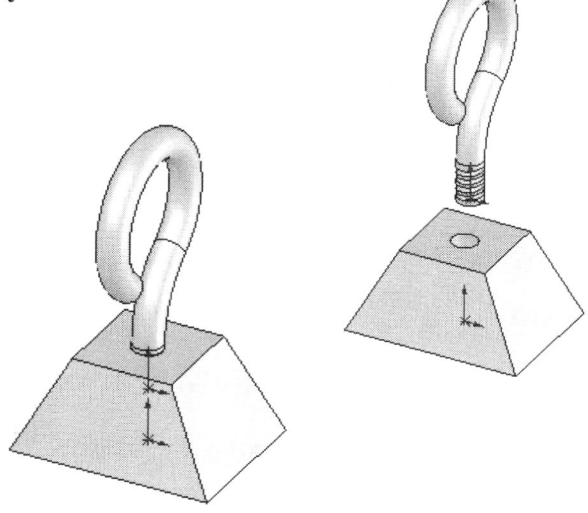

Exercise 5.3: SWEEP-CUT CASE

Create the CASE part.

- Utilize a Sweep Cut to remove material from the CASE. The profile for the Sweep Cut is a semi-circle.

- Dimensions are not provided. Design your case to hold pencils.

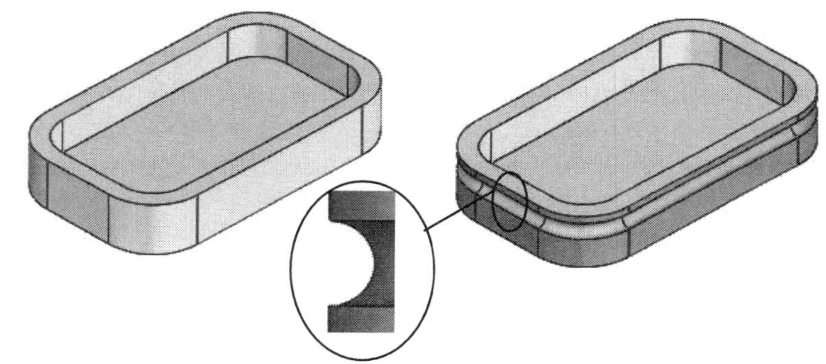

Exercise 5.4a: FLASHLIGHT DESIGN CHANGES.

Review the HOUSING. The HOUSING LongRibs are too thick. The current Ribs cause problems in the mold.

- Utilize ½ the Shell Thickness for the Ribs.

The HOUSING Handle is too short. A large human hand cannot comfortably hold the Handle.

- Redesign the Sweep path of the Handle.

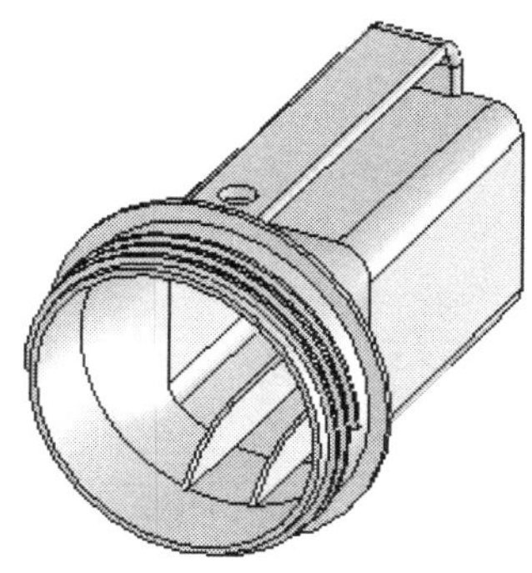

Exercise 5.4b: Exploded View Drawing.

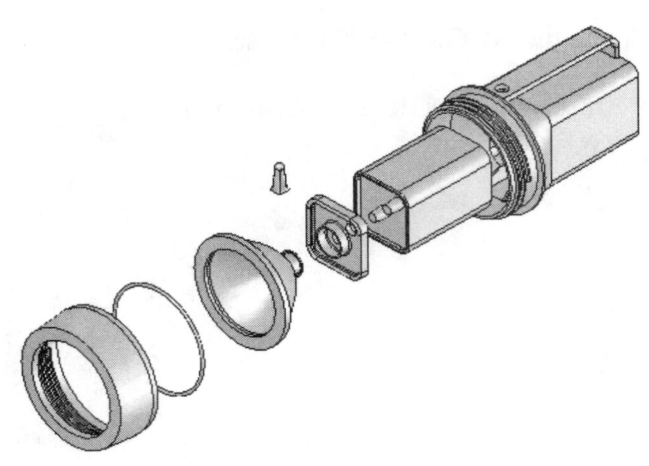

Create an Exploded View of the FLASHLIGHT assembly. Create a FLASHLIGHT assembly drawing.

- Utilize Custom Properties to add Part No. and Description for each FLASHLIGHT component.
- Insert a Bill of Materials into the drawing.

Exercise 5.4c: Core-Cavity Mold Tools.

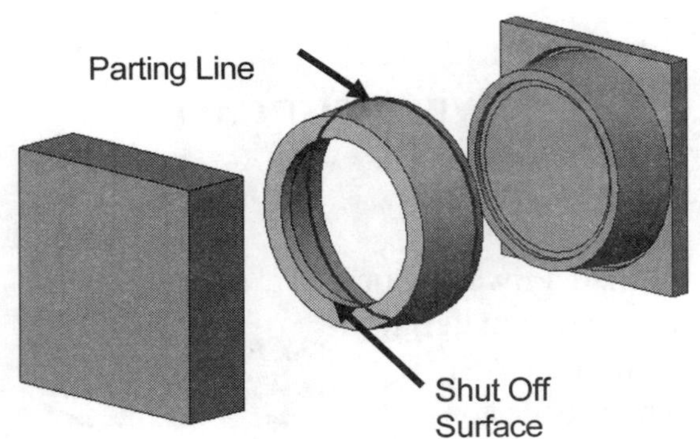

Redesign the LENSCAP to accommodate a more cost effective snap fit versus a Thread.

- Suppress the Thread feature.
- Modify the Revolved Thin Cut to create 3° Draft Angle away from the Parting Line.
- Create the Core and Cavity Mold Tools for the LENSCAP.
- Utilize the Front Cut for the Shut Off Surface.

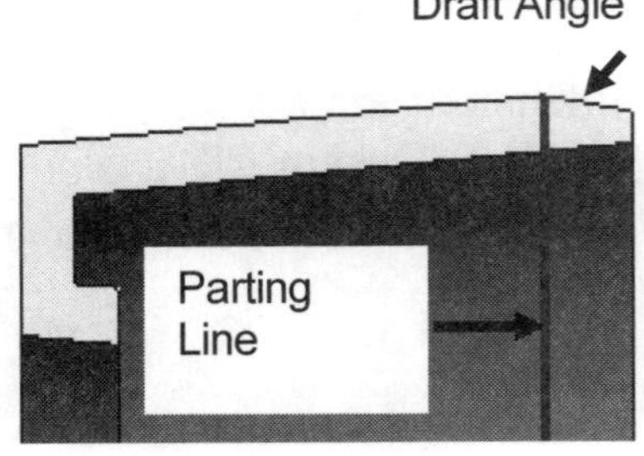

Exercise 5.5: Triangular Shaped Bottle.

A plastic BOTTLE is created from a variety of SolidWorks features.

- Create the shoulder of the BOTTLE with the Loft Base feature. Dimensions are not provided.

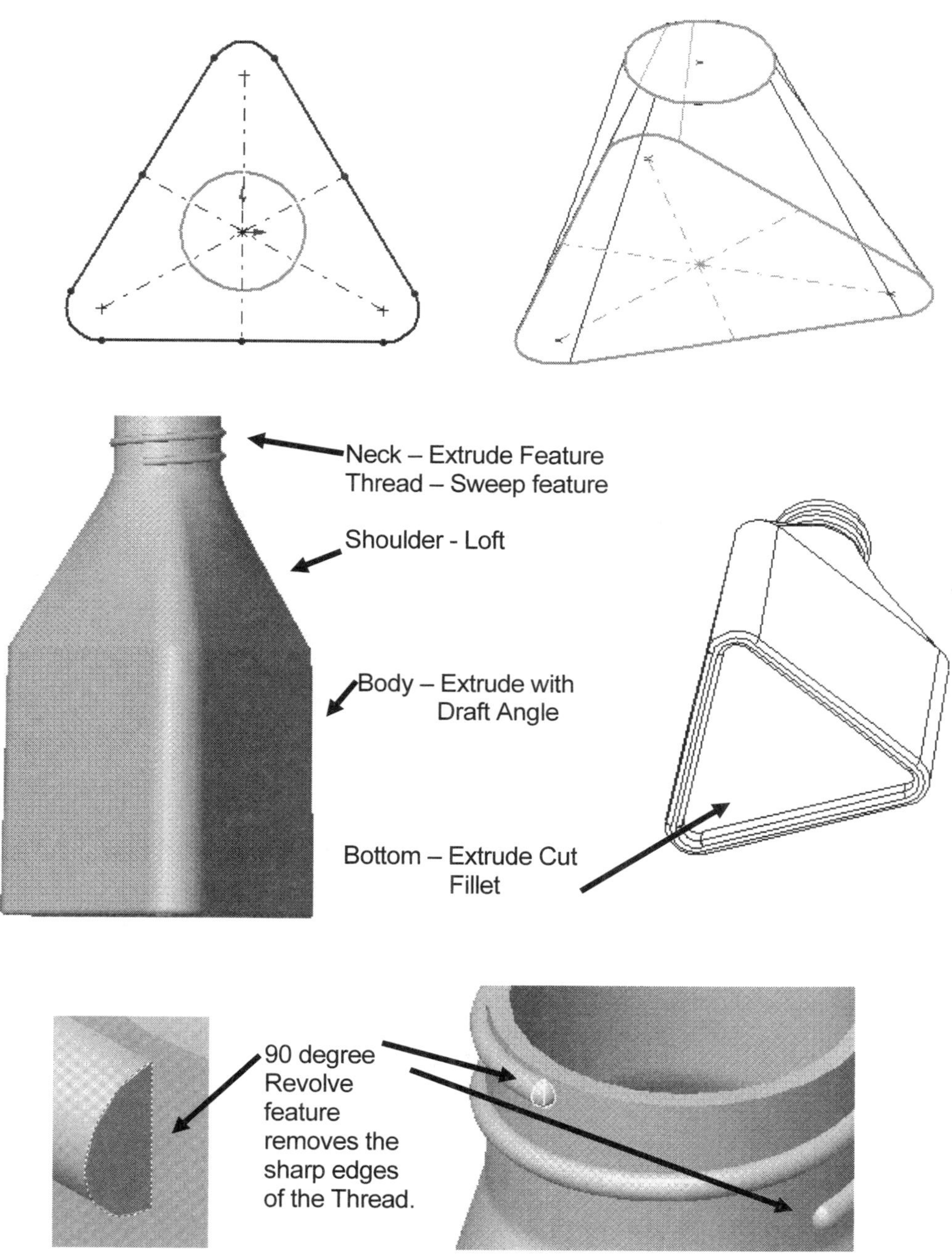

Exercise 5.6: WHEEL-AND-AXLE Assembly.

The WHEEL-AND-AXLE assembly is utilized to transform linear motion from the Pneumatic Linkage assembly (Exercise 2) into rotational motion of the WHEEL. The counter-clock wise rotational motion of the WHEEL is utilized to lift the applied WEIGHT.

The WHEEL-AND-AXLE assembly consists of the eleven unique parts:

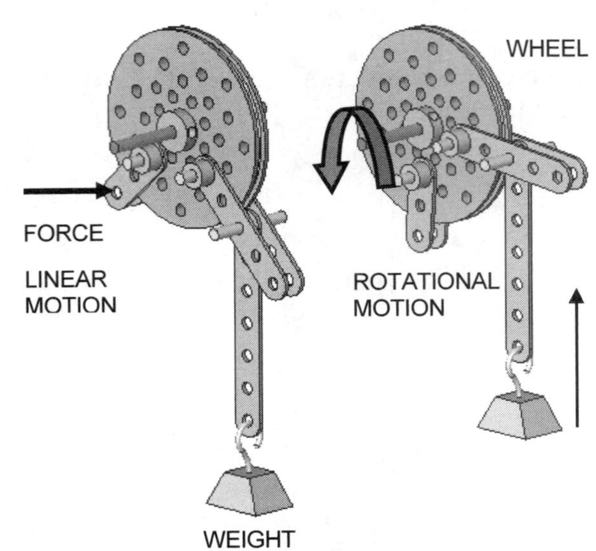

WHEEL-AND-AXLE Assembly
Courtesy of GEARS EDUCATIONAL SYSTEMS

The WEIGHT (Exercise 5.3b) and HOOK (Exercise 5.2) are components in the LINK-AND-HOOK subassembly. The other parts dimensions are provided. Read the entire exercise before you begin.

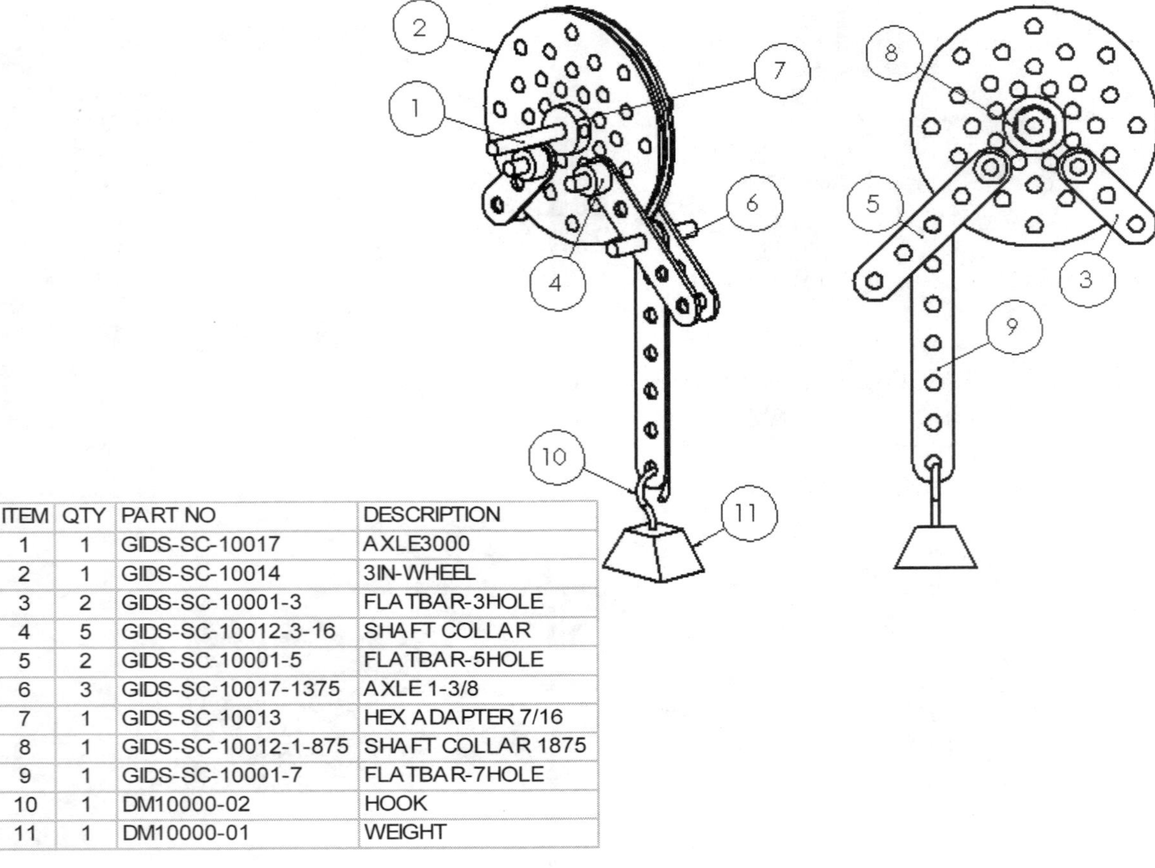

ITEM	QTY	PART NO	DESCRIPTION
1	1	GIDS-SC-10017	AXLE3000
2	1	GIDS-SC-10014	3IN-WHEEL
3	2	GIDS-SC-10001-3	FLATBAR-3HOLE
4	5	GIDS-SC-10012-3-16	SHAFT COLLAR
5	2	GIDS-SC-10001-5	FLATBAR-5HOLE
6	3	GIDS-SC-10017-1375	AXLE 1-3/8
7	1	GIDS-SC-10013	HEX ADAPTER 7/16
8	1	GIDS-SC-10012-1-875	SHAFT COLLAR 1875
9	1	GIDS-SC-10001-7	FLATBAR-7HOLE
10	1	DM10000-02	HOOK
11	1	DM10000-01	WEIGHT

Exercise 5.6a: AXLE Part.

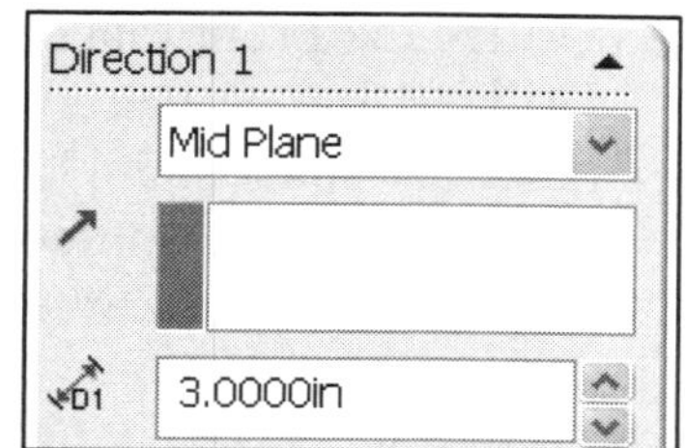

Two AXLEs parts are required for the WHEEL-AND-AXLE assembly:

1) AXLE3000 Part.

2) AXLE1375 Part.

- Create the AXLE3000. The AXLE3000 is a 3in [76.20mm] steel rod extruded with the MidPlane.

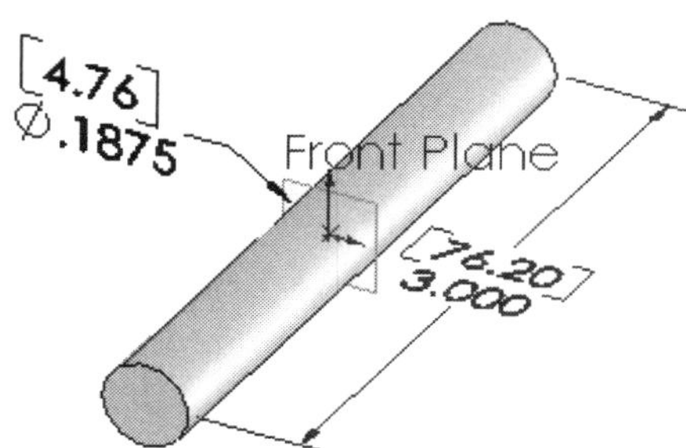

- The AXLE utilizes a ∅.1875 [4.76mm] circular sketch on the Front Plane. The Front Plane is utilized between the AXLE3000 and other mating components in the WHEEL-AND-AXLE assembly.

- Create the AXLE1375.

- Utilize the AXLE3000 and the File, Save As Option.

- Enter 1.375[34.93mm] for extruded depth.

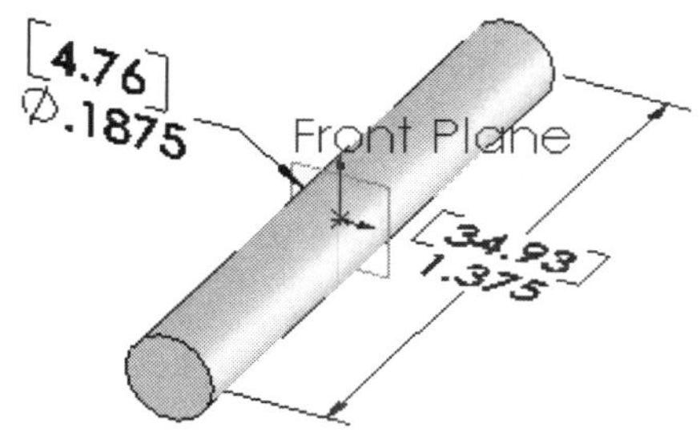

Exercise 5.6b: FLATBAR Part and Design Table.

Three FLATBAR parts are required for the WHEEL-AND-AXLE assembly:

1) FLATBAR–3HOLE Part.

2) FLATBAR–5HOLE Part.

3) FLATBAR–7HOLE Part.

The FLATBAR–3HOLE Part was created in Exercise 1.5c.

- Utilize the FLATBAR-3HOLE Part with a Design Table to create the FLATBAR-5HOLE and FLATBAR-7HOLE.

- Utilize the Front Plane for the Sketch Plane. Utilize a Linear Pattern for the holes. The holes are space .500[12.70mm] apart. The three parts are manufactured from 0.060in [1.5mm] Stainless Steel.

Exercise 5.6c: SHAFT COLLAR Part.

Create two SHAFT-COLLAR parts. Note A general SHAFT-COLLAR Part was created in Exercise 1.5b.

- Create the SHAFT-COLLAR-1875 part. Use the general SHAFT-COLLAR part with the File, Save As command. Enter SHAFT-COLLAR 1875 for file name.

- Create the SHAFT-COLLAR-5000 part. Use the general SHAFT-COLLAR part with the File, Save As command. Enter SHAFT-COLLAR-5000 for file name.

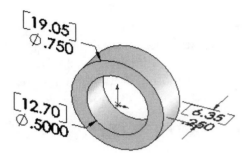

- Modify the feature dimensions for the SHAFT-COLLAR-5000 part. Utilize the Front Plane for the Sketch Plane.

    - The ID is .5000[12.70mm].

    - The OD is .750[19.05mm].

Exercise 5.6d: HEX ADAPTER Part.

Create a HEX ADAPTER part. The body of the HEX ADAPTER is a hexagonal shaped part.

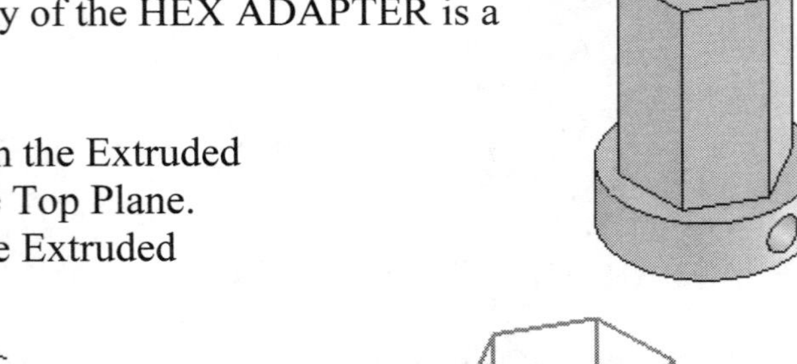

- Create the HEX-ADAPTER part with the Extruded Base feature. The sketch plane is the Top Plane. The Front and Right Plane creates the Extruded Base features.

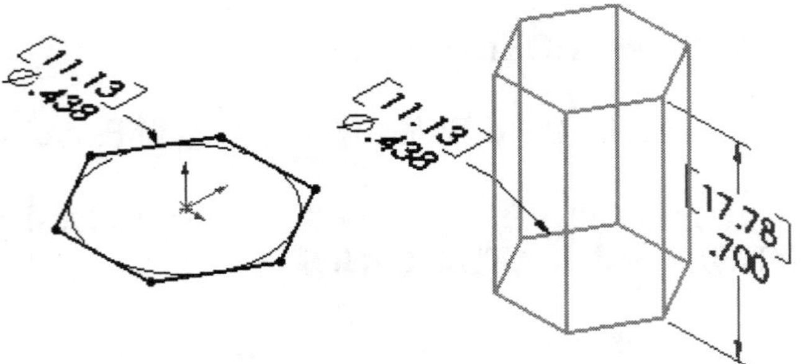

- Utilize the Hole Wizard to create an 8-32 UNC Tapped Hole on the Right Plane with the Through All option.

Create the base for the HEX-ADAPTER.

Use the Extrude Base feature.

- Create the set screw hole. Use the Extruded Cut feature.

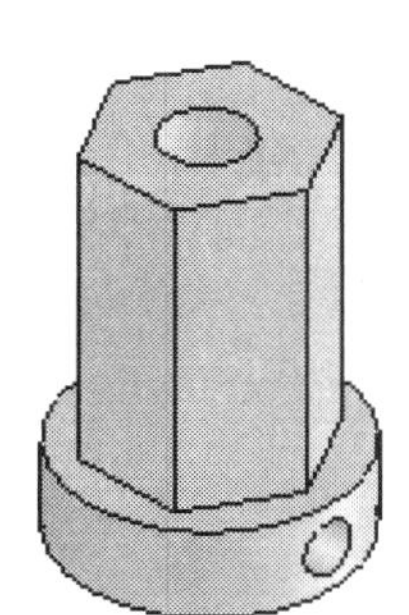

Exercise 5.6e: WHEEL Part.

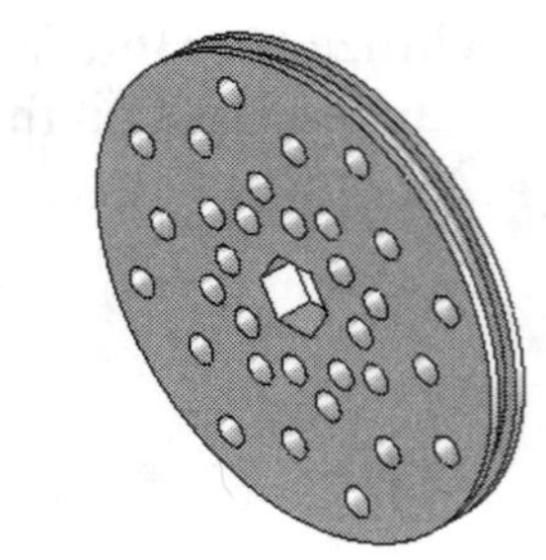

Create the WHEEL Part.

- Utilize a Extruded Base feature with the Depth of 0.25 [6.35mm] with the MidPlane option on the Front Plane. The Origin is located at the center of the WHEEL.

- Utilize a Revolved Cut feature to remove material from the WHEEL and create a groove.

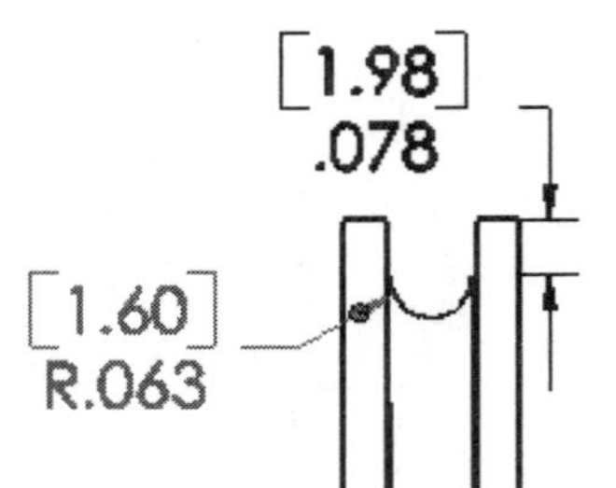

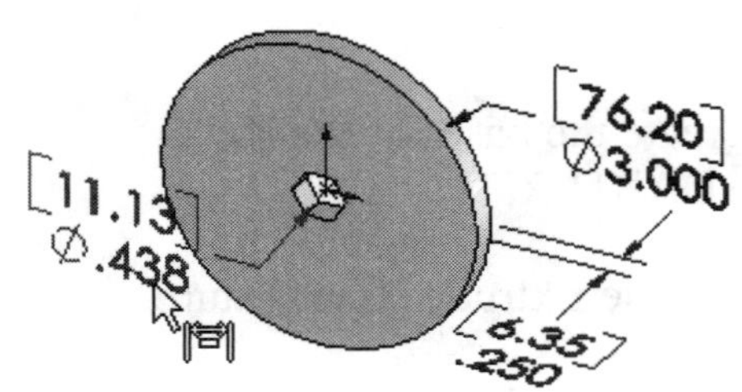

- The WHEEL contains a complex pattern of holes. Simplify the geometry by dividing the four holes into two Extruded Cut features. The first Extruded Cut feature contains two small circles sketched on two bolt circles. The bolt circles utilize construction geometry. Sketch two construction line bolt circles, 1.000[25.4mm] and 2.000[50.80mm].

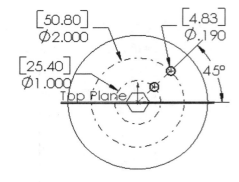

- Sketch a 45° centerline from the Origin to the second circle.

- The second Extruded Cut feature utilizes two small circles sketched on two bolt circles. The bolt circles utilize construction geometry.

- Utilize a Circular Pattern. The two Extruded Cut features are contained in one Circular Pattern. Revolve the Extruded Cut features about a Temporary Axis located at the center of the Hexagon.

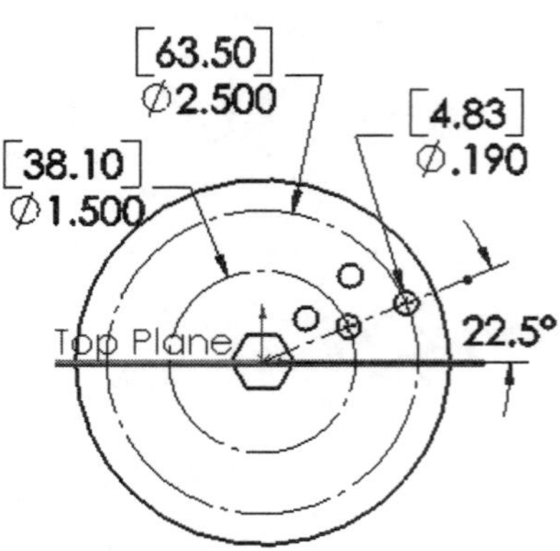

- Four bolt circles spaced 0.5[12.7mm] apart locate 8 - ∅.190[4.83mm] holes. Locate the first Extrude Cut seed hole on the first bolt circle and third bolt circle.

- Click the Top Plane and the Right Plane. Axis1 is positioned through the Hex Cut centered at the Origin.

- Drag the Axis1 handles outward to extend the length. Utilize the Reference Axis1 during the assembly mate process.

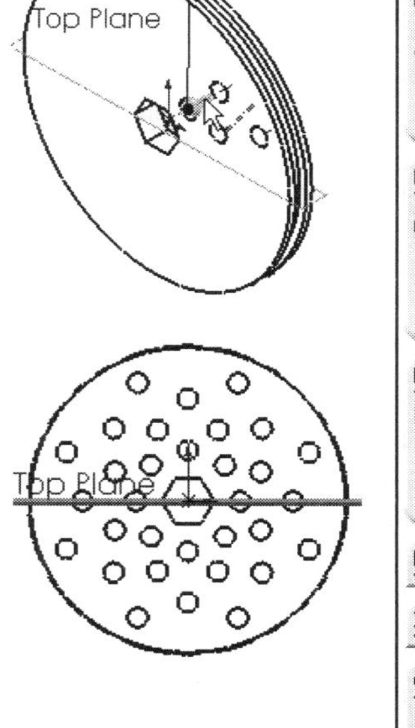

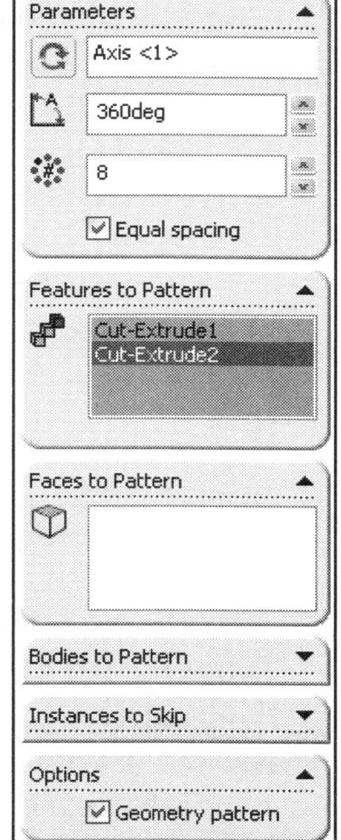

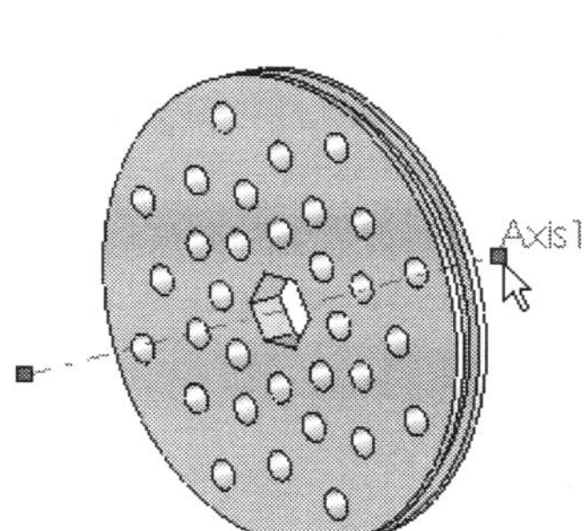

Exercise 5.6f: FLATBAR-SHAFT COLLAR assemblies.

Create two FLATBAR-SHAFT COLLAR assemblies:

1. FLATBAR-3HOLE-SHAFT COLLAR assembly. Use the SHAFT-COLLAR-1875 part with the FLATBAR-3HOLE part

2. FLATBAR-5HOLE-SHAFT COLLAR assembly. Use the SHAFT-COLLAR-1875 part with the FLATBAR-5HOLE part.

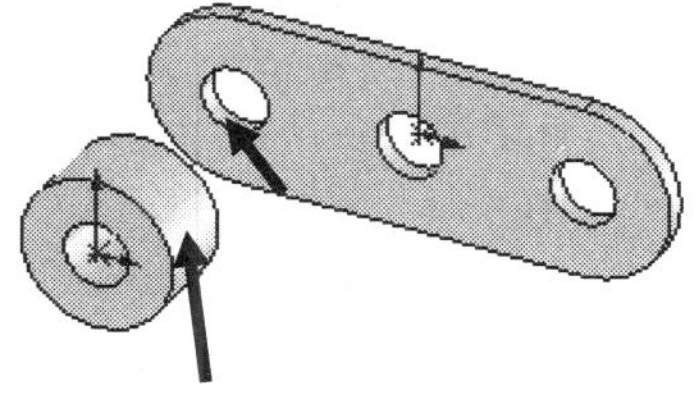

- Insert the FLATBAR-3HOLE part. The FLATBAR-3HOLE part is fixed to the Origin.

- Insert the SHAFT-COLLAR-1875. Create a Concentric Mate between the inside hole of the SHAFT-COLLAR-1875 with the first hole of the FLATBAR-3HOLE.

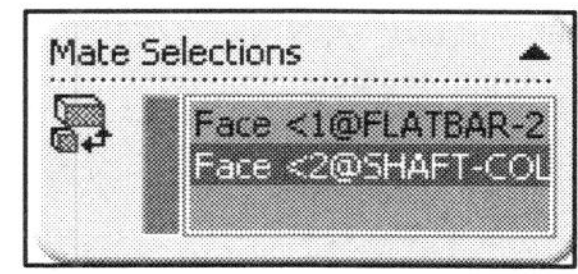

- Insert a Coincident Mate between the back face of the SHAFT-COLLAR-1875 and the front face of the FLATBAR-3HOLE.

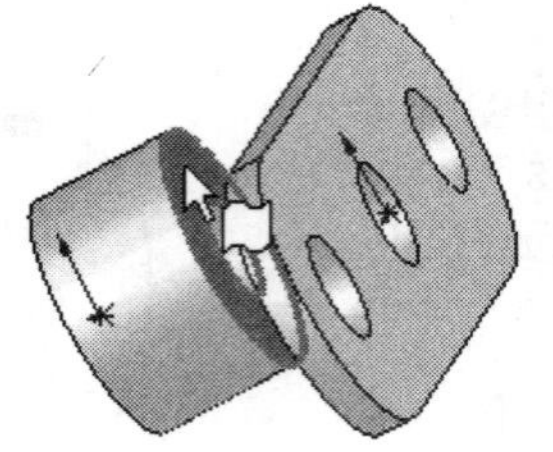

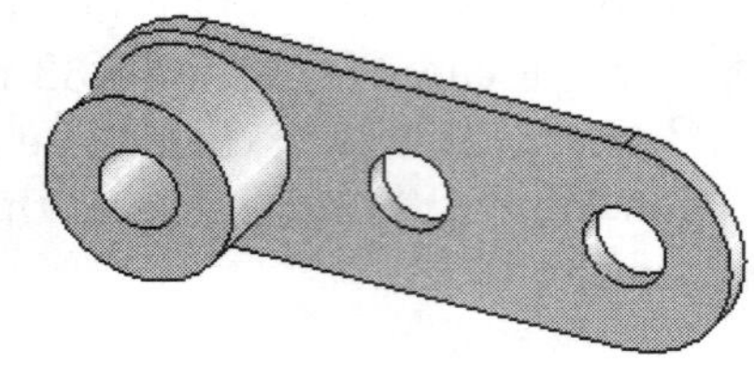

- Create the FLATBAR-5HOLE-SHAFT-COLLAR. Insert the FLATBAR-5HOLE-SHAFT-COLLAR assembly. Insert the FLATBAR-5HOLE. The FLATBAR-5HOLE part is fixed to the Origin.

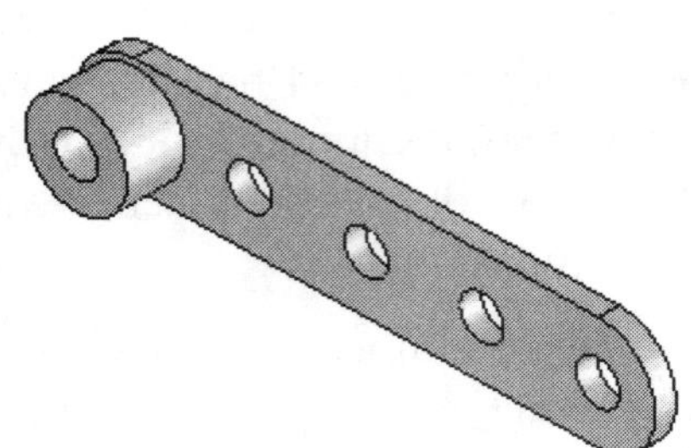

- Insert the SHAFT-COLLAR-1875. Create a Concentric Mate between the inside hole of the SHAFT-COLLAR-1875 with the first hole of the FLATBAR-5HOLE. Insert a Coincident Mate between the back face of the SHAFT-COLLAR-1875 and the front face of the FLATBAR-5HOLE.

Exercise 5.6g: LINK-AND-HOOK Assembly.

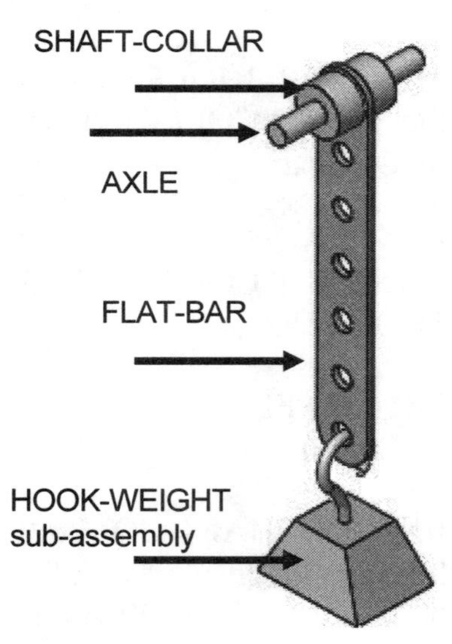

The LINK-AND-HOOK assembly combines the HOOK-WEIGHT sub-assembly and the SHAFT-COLLAR, AXLE and FLAT-BAR parts.

- Create a HOOK-WEIGHT sub-assembly. The HOOK and WEIGHT parts were developed in Project 3 Exercises.

- Create the FLAT-BAR part with a 7-Hole Linear Pattern. Insert the part.

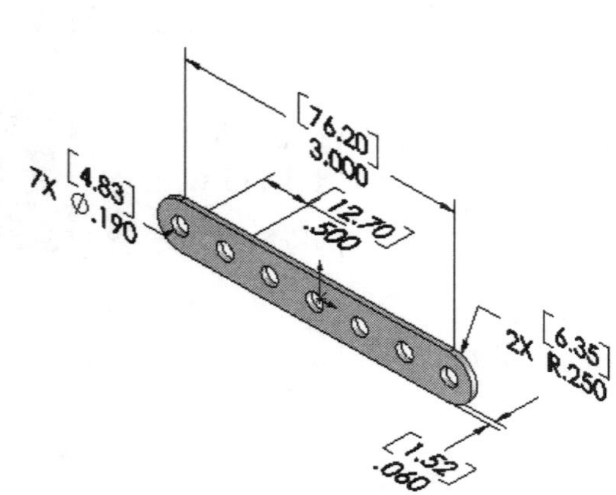

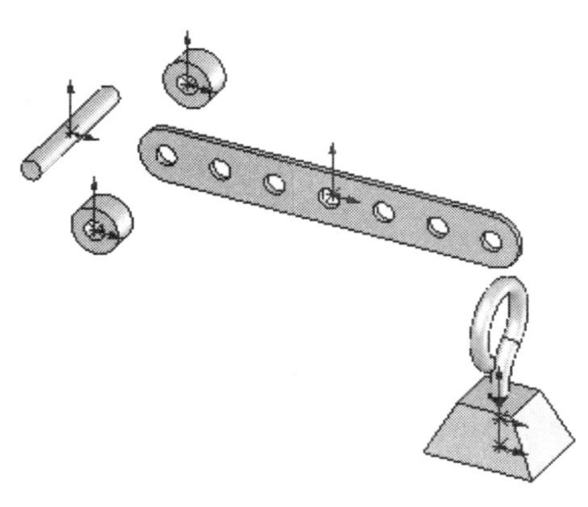

- Insert the HOOK-WEIGHT sub-assembly into the LINK-AND-HOOK assembly.
- Insert two SHAFT-COLLAR parts (Exercise 1.5b) and the AXLE part (Exercise 1.5a) into the assembly.

Note: There is more than one mating technique for this exercise. Incorporate symmetry into the assembly. Minimize components in the assembly FeatureManager; divide a large assembly into smaller sub-assemblies.

- Utilize the Design Library, Add File Location option. Browse and select the Project Folder that contains all your parts.
- Drag the parts from the Design Library into the assemblies.

Exercise 5.6h WHEEL-AND-AXLE Assembly.

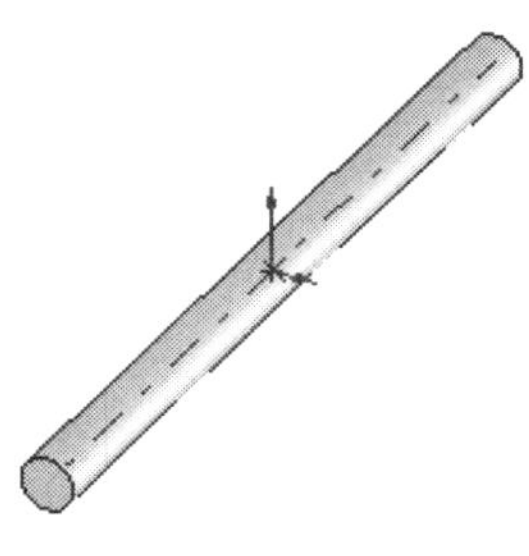

Create the WHEEL-AND-AXLE assembly. Insert the first component, the AXLE3000 part. The AXLE3000 is fixed to the Origin. Display the Temporary Axis.

- Insert the second component, the WHEEL part. Insert a Coincident Mate between the WHEEL Front Plane and the AXLE Front Plane. Insert a Coincident Mate between the WHEEL AXIS1 and the AXLE3000 Temporary Axis.
- The WHEEL is free to rotate about the AXLE3000. Utilize Rotate Component to rotate the WHEEL about AXIS1.

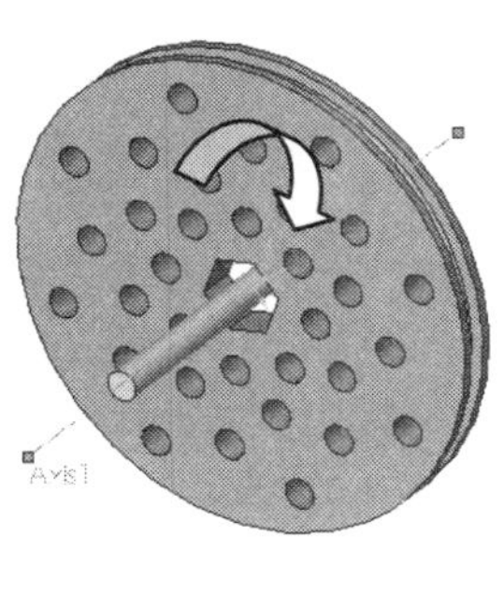

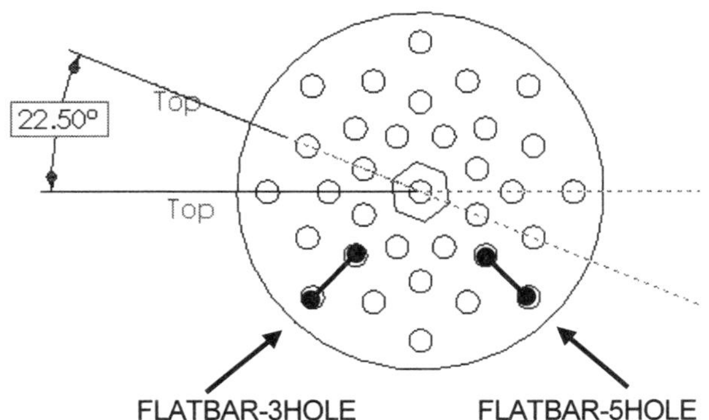

- Insert a 22.5° Angle Mate between the Top Plane of the WHEEL and the Top Plane of the WHEEL-AND-AXLE assembly.

The WHEEL is static and does not rotate. Rename Angle Mate to Wheel-Static. The Mate process is easier when parts do not rotate.

- Add parts with the Wheel-Static Angle Mate in the Resolved state. Suppress the Wheel-Static Angle Mate to simulate dynamic motion in the final step.

- Locate the mating holes on the WHEEL for the FLATBAR-3HOLE-SHAFT-COLLAR assembly and the FLATBAR-5HOLE-SHAFT-COLLAR assembly. Insert the FLATBAR-3HOLE-SHAFT-COLLAR assembly.

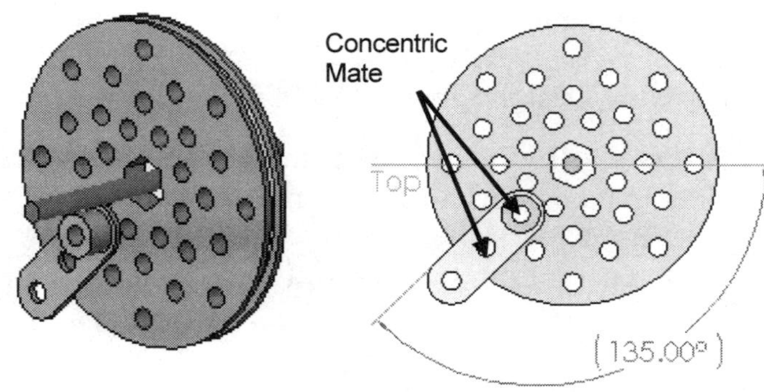

- Create a Concentric Mates with the first hole of the FLATBAR-3HOLE and the WHEEL hole located at 135° from the X-axis.

- Insert a Concentric Mate with the second hole of the FLATBAR-3HOLE and the WHEEL hole located at 135° from the X-axis.

- Insert a Coincident Mate between the back face of the FLAT-BAR-3HOLE-SHAFT-COLLAR and the front face of the WHEEL.

- Insert the FLATBAR-5HOLE-SHAFT-COLLAR assembly. Create two Concentric Mates and one Coincident Mate. The two FLATBARs are 90° apart.

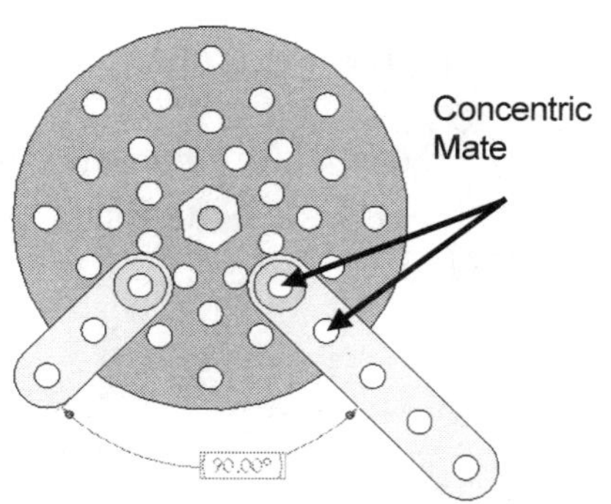

- Insert the second FLATBAR-3HOLE-SHAFT-COLLAR assembly coincident with the back face of the WHEEL. Add two Concentric Mates and one Coincident Mate.

- Insert the second FLATBAR-5OLE-SHAFT-COLLAR assembly coincident with the back face of the WHEEL. Add two Concentric Mates and one Coincident Mate.

- Insert the AXLE-1375 part. Create a Concentric Mate between the AXLE-1375 conical face and the left SHAFT-COLLAR hole. Create a Coincident Mate between the AXLE-1375 Front Plane and the WHEEL Front Plane. The AXLE-1375 is symmetric about the WHEEL Front Plane.

- Insert the AXLE-1375 part. Create a Concentric Mate between the AXLE-1375 conical face and the right SHAFT-COLLAR hole. Create a Coincident Mate between the AXLE-1375 Front Plane and the WHEEL Front Plane.

- Insert the HEX ADAPTER part. Insert a Concentric Mate between the Thru Hole and the AXLE-3000 shaft. Insert Parallel Mate between the edge of the HEX ADAPTER and the edge of the WHEEL hex cut.

- Insert a Coincident Mate between the bottom face of the HEX ADAPTER Base Extrude and the front face of the WHEEL

- Insert the SHAFT-COLLAR-5000 part. Create a Concentric Mate between the SHAFT-COLLAR-5000 and the AXLE3000.

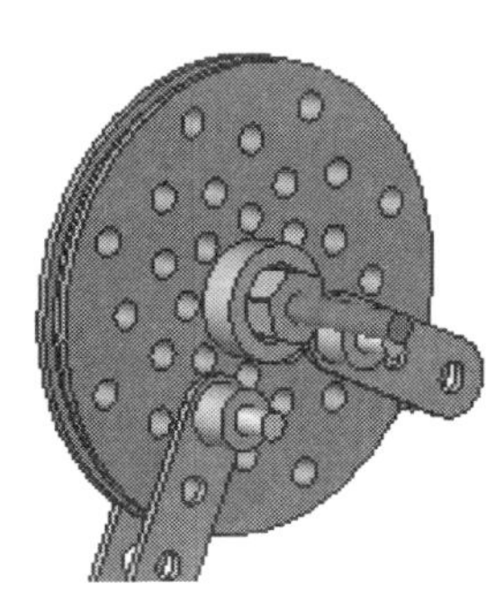

- Insert a Coincident Mate between the SHAFT-COLLAR-5000 back face and the WHEEL back face.
- Insert the LINK-AND-WEIGHT assembly. Insert a Concentric Mate between the AXLE-1375 and the 3rd hole of the FLATBAR-5HOLE.
- Insert a Coincident Mate between the LINK-AND-WEIGHT Front Plane and the WHEEL Front Plane.
- Insert a Parallel Mate between the LINK-AND-WEIGHT Top Plane and the WHEEL-AND-AXLE Top Plane. The WEIGHT will remain vertical during WHEEL rotate.
- Resolve the Wheel-Static Angle Mate. Apply a counter-clockwise Rotary Motor Simulation to the front face of the WHEEL. Play the simulation. The WHEEL rotates counter-clockwise and the WEIGHT translates in an upward vertical direction. Suppress the Rotary Motor.

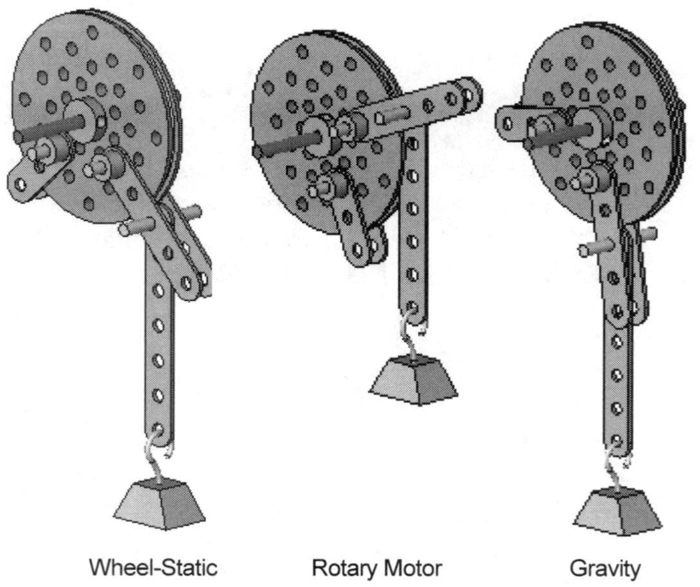

- Apply Gravity Simulation to the FLAT-BAR-7HOLE front face. Play the simulation. The WEIGHT translates in a downward vertical direction and the WHEEL rotates clockwise.
- Suppress the Wheel-Static Angle Mate. The WHEEL returns to the default rest position. The WHEEL-AND-AXLE assembly is complete.

Exercise 5.6i WHEEL-AND-AXLE Drawing.

Create the WHEEL-AND-AXLE drawing.

- Add PART NO. and DESCRIPTION Property Values to all parts. Insert a Bill of Materials.

Exercise 5.7: Industry Collaborative Exercise.

You now work with a team of engineers on a new industrial application. The senior engineer specifies a ½HP AC Motor. The Parts Department stocks the motor. Create the SPEED REDUCER Assembly. Safely reduce the input speed of the motor at a ratio of 30:1. An enclosed gear drive, called a Speed Reducer, safely reduces the speed of the motor. The enclosed gear drive is a purchased part. The Motor is fastened to the Speed Reducer.

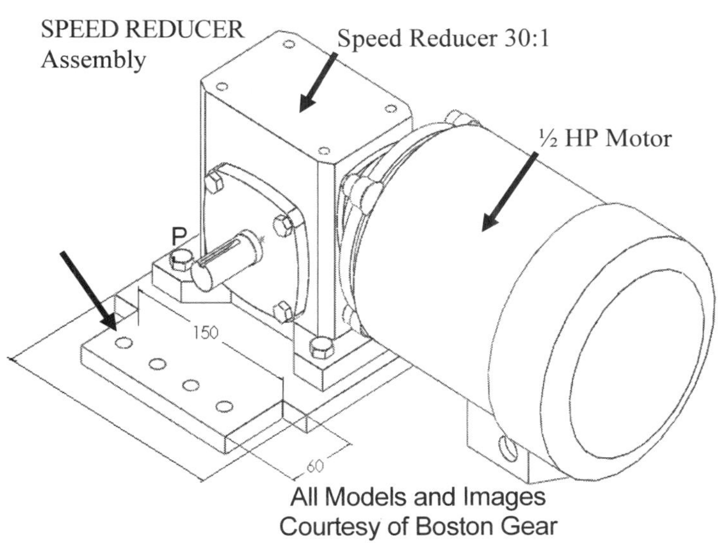

All Models and Images Courtesy of Boston Gear

Determine the parts to design. PLATE-SR contains a 150mm x 60mm notched section with 4 equally spaced holes. The Speed Reducer is mounted to the PLATE-SR with 4 fasteners. All holes on PLATE-SR use the same fastener.

You receive vendor information from the Purchasing Department. The ½ HP Motor is manufactured by Boston Gear, Quincy, MA. The Motor part number is FUTF. No drawings of the Motor exist in the Engineering Department.

- Invoke a web browser. Enter the URL: www.3DContentCentral.com.
- Enter your email address and password. If you are a new user to the web site, click the Register button and enter the requested information. You will be emailed with the required information.

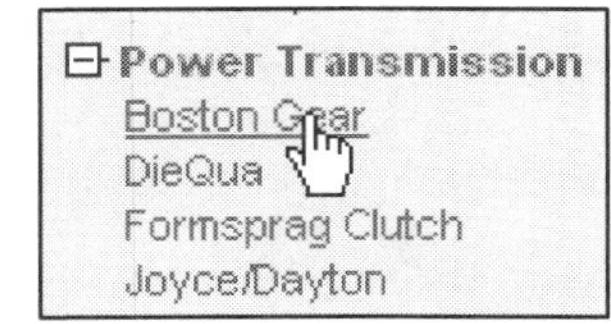

- Select Boston Gear from the Vendor list. Click Product Search.

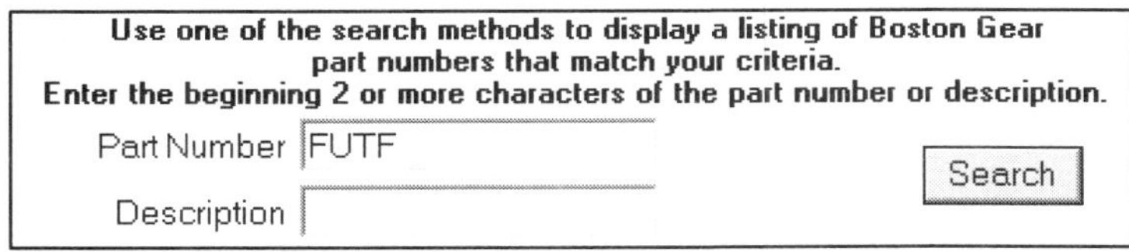

- Enter FUTF for Part Number.
- Click View Spec Sheet

View Product Table	Add to RFQ Cart	View Spec Sheet	Part Number	Product Family	Description
Table	Add	Spec	FUTF	AC MOTORS	AC MOTOR, TEFC, C-FACE

  to display the motor specification. Click the 3D CAD button to view and download the part.

- Click the 3D Formats button.
- Select the SolidWorks Assembly to download.
- Locate the Enclosed Speed Reducer. Click the Product Tree button.
- Click the Worm Gear Speed Reducers, Single Reduction Projecting O/P option.

Select Download Format

2D Formats:

Version: N/A Start Download

3D Formats: SolidWorks Part/Assembly (.sldprt)

Version: 2005 Start Download

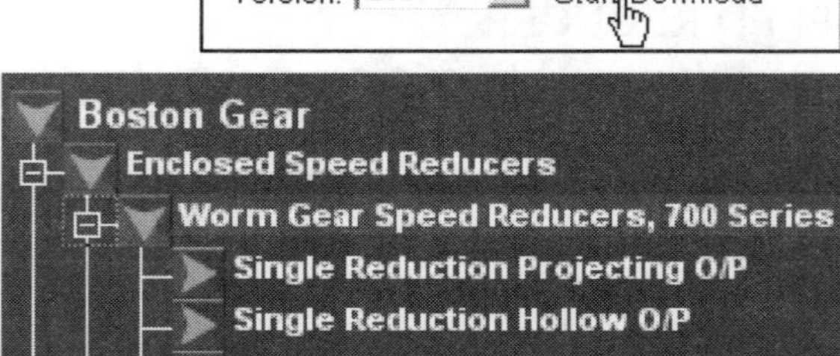

- Click the Type B – G icon in the second row.

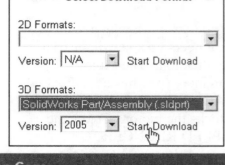

- Select ½ in the Motor HP (Class I) list box. Select 30 in the Ratio list box. Click Spec and the 3D CAD button to view the Speed Reducer specification and download the SolidWorks Assembly.

Add to RFQ Cart	View Spec Sheet	Part Number	Ratio	Torque Cap (LB-IN)	Bore Code	Motor HP (Class I)	Fan Cooled Rating?
Add	Spec	F718B-30-B5-G	30	440	B5 - 56C	1/2	NO

The Speed Reducer ships with HHCS (4) 3/8-16 x 1 inch, (Heavy Hex Cap Screw 3/8 inch diameter, 16 threads per inch, 1 inch length).

- Create a sub assembly between the Motor and Speed Reducer. Mate the 4 HHCS between the Motor and the Speed Reducer.
- Measure the size and location of the Speed Reducer mounting holes. Create the part, PLATE-SR. Create the SPEED REDUCER assembly. Mate the sub assembly to the PLATE-SR. Utilize fasteners from the SolidWorks/Toolbox or use the Flange Bolt from the Feature Palette. Create an assembly drawing and Bill of Materials.

Project 6

Top Down Assembly Modeling and Sheet Metal Parts

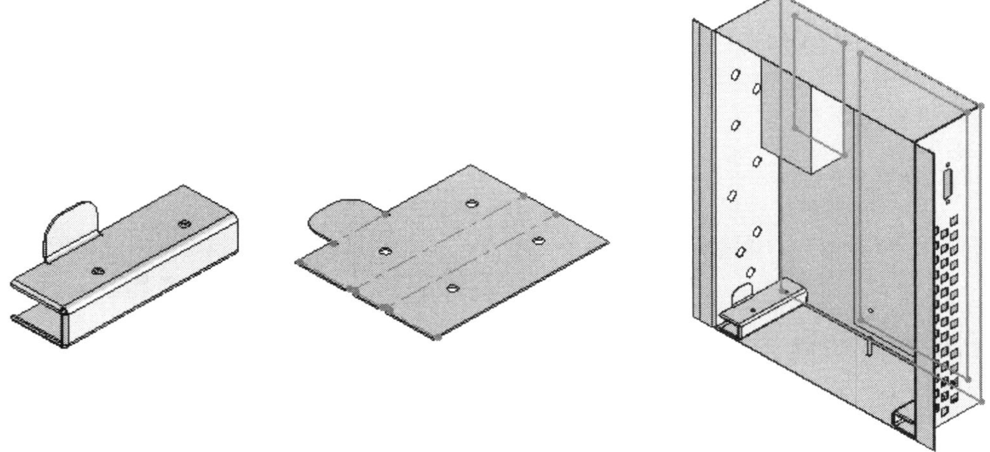

Below are the desired outcomes and usage competencies based on the completion of Project 6.

Project Desired Outcomes:	Usage Competencies:
• Three different BOX configurations: ○ Small. ○ Medium. ○ Large.	• Understanding of the Top Down assembly method and to develop components in-context. • Ability to import parts into an assembly. • Knowledge to develop a Design Table.
• CABINET drawing with two configurations: ○ Default – 3D formed state. ○ Flat – 2D flatten state.	• Ability to convert a solid part into a sheet metal part and insert sheet metal features. • Knowledge of sheet metal configurations in the drawing: 3D Formed and 2D Flat Pattern states.
• BRACKET part.	• Understanding of inserting sheet metal features: Base, Edge and Miter Flange, Hem, Flat Pattern.

Notes:

Project 6-Top Down Assembly Modeling and Sheet Metal Parts

Project Objective

Create three different BOX sizes utilizing the Top Down assembly modeling approach. The Top Down approach is a conceptual approach used to develop products from within the assembly. Major design requirements are translated into sub-assemblies or individual components and key relationships.

Model sheet metal components in their 3D formed state. Manufacture the sheet metal components in a flatten state. Control the formed state and flatten state through configurations.

Create the parameters and equations utilized to control the configurations in a Design Table.

On the completion of this project, you will be able to:

- Create a new Top Down assembly and Layout Sketch.
- Choose the best profile for the Layout Sketch.
- Choose the proper Sketch plane.
- Insert sheet metal bends to transform a solid part into a sheet metal part.
- Create a Linear Pattern of Holes.
- Insert IGES format PEM® self-clinching fasteners obtained from the Internet.
- Use a Component Pattern to maintain a relationship between the Holes and the fasteners.
- Set Document Properties and System Options.
- Create Link Values.
- Use and produce Equations.
- Insert a Sheetmetal Library feature and Forming Tool feature.
- Address manufacturing considerations.
- Create Relationships.
- Select the correct PEM® Fastener for the assembly.

- Open IGES models and save them as SolidWorks part files.
- Insert Assembly features.
- Replace Components in an assembly.
- Insert a Design Table.
- Create a sheet metal part by starting with a solid part and inserting a Shell feature, Rip feature and Insert Sheet Metal Bends feature.
- Create a sheet metal part by starting with a Base Flange feature.
- Use the following SolidWorks features:
  - Extruded Boss/Base.
  - Shell.
  - Hole Wizard.
  - Linear Pattern.
  - Component Pattern.
  - Rip.
  - Insert Sheet Metal Bends.
  - Base Flange.
  - Edge Flange.
  - Miter Flange.
  - Hem.
  - Jog.
  - Flat Pattern.
  - Mirror Components.
  - Assembly Feature, Hole.
  - Replace Component.

Project Situation

You now work for a different company. Life is filled with opportunities. You are part of a global project design team that is required to create a family of electrical boxes for general industrial use. You are the project manager.

You receive a customer request from the Sales department for three different size electrical boxes.

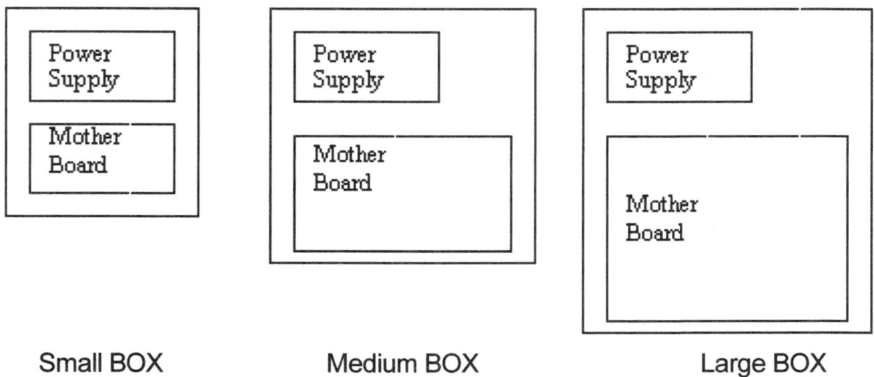

Delivery time to the customer is a concern. You work in a concurrent engineering environment.

Your company is expecting a sales order for 5,000 units in each requested BOX configuration.

The BOX contains the following key components:

- Power supply
- Motherboard

The size of the power supply is the same for all three boxes.

The size of the power supply is the constant.

The size of the BOX is a variable.

The available space for the motherboard is dependent on the size of the BOX.

The depth of the three boxes is 100mm.

You contact the customer to discuss and obtain design options and product specifications. Key customer requirements:

Three different BOX sizes:

- 300mm x 400mm x 100mm Small.
- 400mm x 500mm x 100mm Medium.
- 550mm x 600mm x100mm Large.
- Adequate spacing between the power supply, motherboard and internal walls.
- Field serviceable.

You are responsible to produce a sketched layout from the provided critical dimensions. You are also required to design the three boxes. The BOX is used in an outside environment.

Top Down Design Approach

Top down design approach is a conceptual approach used to develop products from within the assembly.

Major design requirements are translated into sub-assemblies or individual components and key relationships.

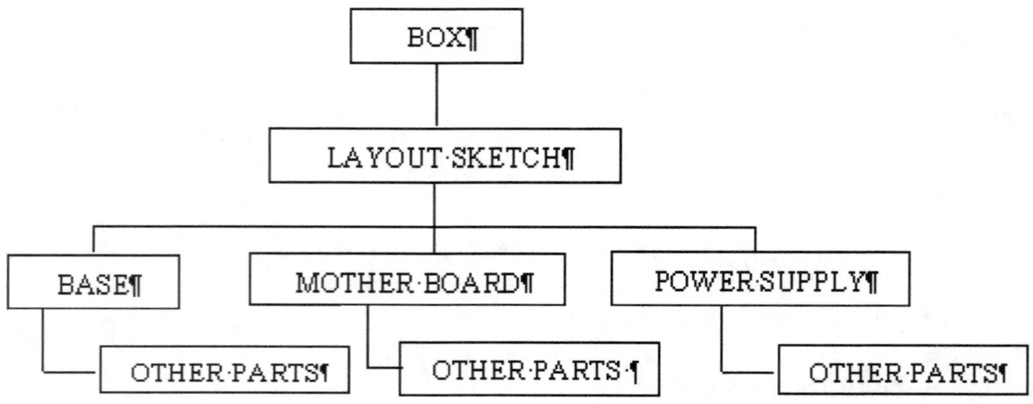

Conceptual Top down design approach

There are two Top Down design methods:

Method 1: Start with a Layout Sketch. Insert new components.

- The Layout Sketch specifies the location of the key components.
- Create or add additional components to complete the assembly.

Method 2: Start with a component. Insert new components.

- Additional components reference existing components in the assembly.

You will use a combination of the Top Down Method 1, Top Down Method 2 and Bottom Up approaches in the BOX assembly.

Consider the following in a preliminary design product specification:

- What are the major design components?
- The motherboard and power supply are the major design components.
- What are the key design constraints?

The customer specified three different BOX sizes. How does each part relate to the other? From experience and discussions with the electrical engineering department, a 25mm physical gap is required between the power supply and the motherboard. A 20mm physical gap is required between the internal components and the side of the BOX.

How will the customer use the product? The customer does not disclose the specific usage of the BOX. The customer is in a very competitive market.

What is the most cost-effective material for the product? Aluminum is cost-effective, strong, relatively easy to fabricate, corrosion resistant and non-magnetic.

Incorporate the design specifications into the BOX assembly. Use a Layout Sketch, solid parts and sheet metal parts. Obtain additional parts from your vendors.

BOX Assembly Overview

Create the Layout Sketch in the BOX assembly. Insert a new part, MOTHERBOARD. Convert edges from the Layout Sketch to develop the outline of the MOTHERBOARD. Use the outline sketch as the Extruded Base feature for the MOTHERBOARD component. An Extruded Boss locates a key electrical connector for a wire harness. Design the location of major electrical connections early in the assembly process.

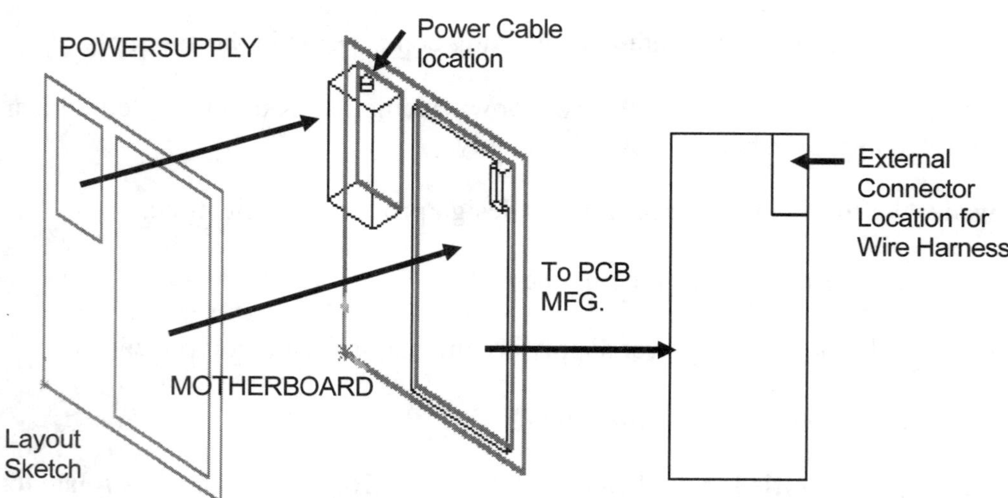

Export the MOTHERBOARD outline to CircuitWorks, a SolidWorks Gold Partner software application. Inform the Printed Circuit Board manufacturer the maximum size of the MOTHERBOARD and the location of the key electrical components.

Insert a new part, POWERSUPPLY. Convert edges from the Layout Sketch to develop the outline of the POWERSUPPLY.

Use the outline as the Extruded Base feature for the POWERSUPPLY component.

An Extruded Boss feature represents the location of the power cable.

Add additional features to complete the POWERSUPPLY.

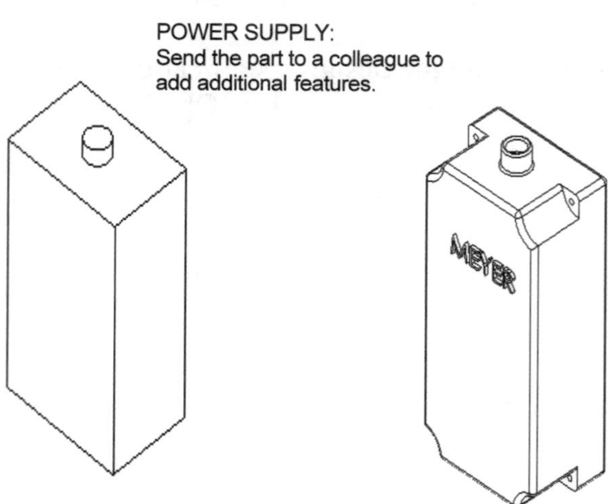

POWER SUPPLY:
Send the part to a colleague to add additional features.
MEYER

Insert a new part, CABINET. Convert edges from the Layout.

Use the outline sketch as the Extruded Base feature for the CABINET component.

Shell the Extruded feature. Add Rip features to the 4 CABINET corners.

Insert Sheet Metal Bends to transform a solid part into a sheet metal part.

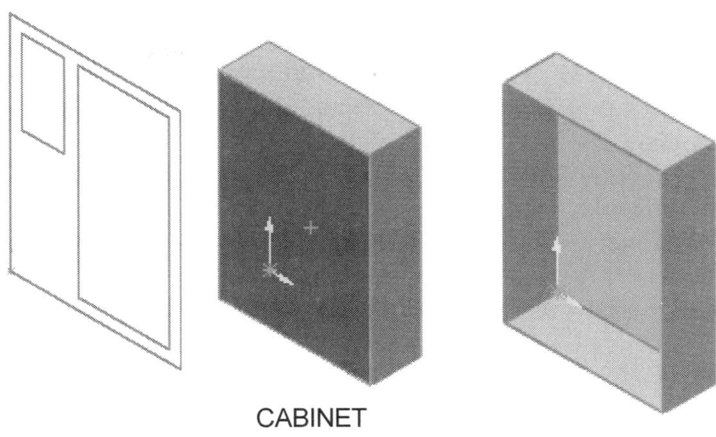

Sheet metal components utilize features to create flanges, cuts and forms.

Model sheet metal components in their 3D formed state.

Manufacture sheet metal components in their 2D flatten state.

Work with your sheet metal manufacturer. Discuss cost effective options.

Create a sketched pattern to add square cuts instead of formed louvers.

Create a Linear Pattern of Holes for the CABINET.

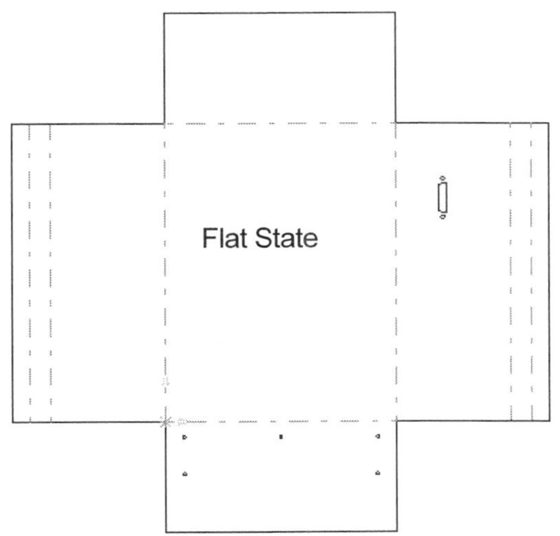

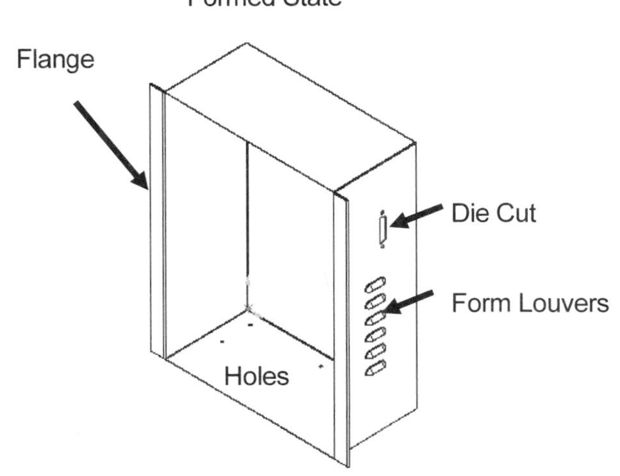

Insert IGES format PEM® self-clinching fasteners obtained from the Internet.

Use a Component Pattern to maintain a relationship between the Holes and the fasteners.

Utilize Replace Component to modify the M5 fastener to an M4 fastener.

Create Equations to control the Layout Sketch and Linear Pattern variables in the BOX assembly.

Insert a Design Table to create BOX assembly Configurations.

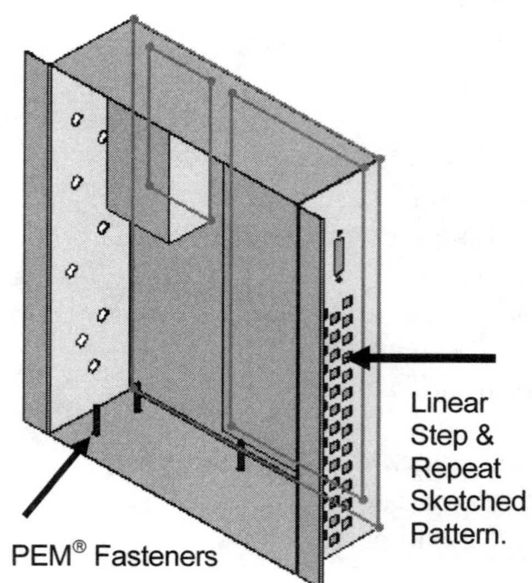

Insert a Sheet metal BRACKET In-context of the BOX assembly.

Utilize Mirror Components to create a right and left hand version of the BRACKET.

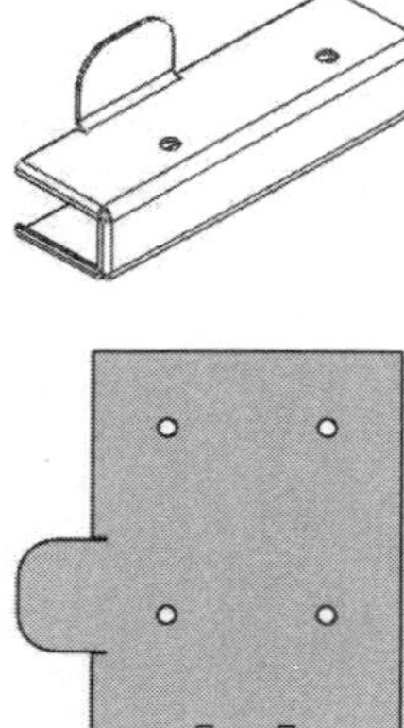

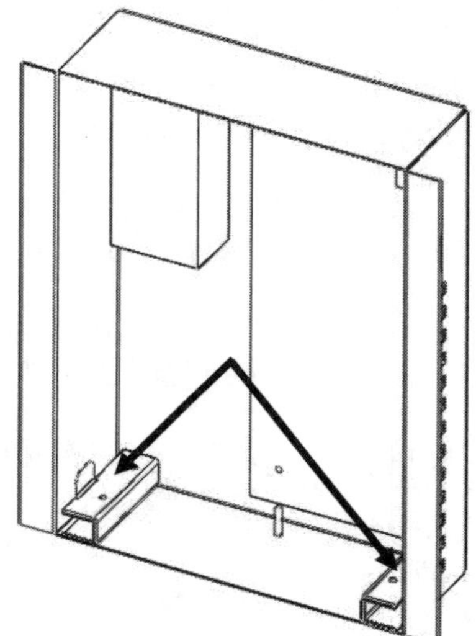

InPlace Mates and In-context Features

Top Down Assembly modeling techniques develop InPlace Mates. An InPlace Mate is a Coincident Mate between the Front Plane of the new component and the selected plane or selected face of the assembly.

The new component is fully positioned in an InPlace Mate. No additional mates are required. The component is now dependent on the assembly. The InPlace Mate creates an external reference. The component references geometry in the assembly.

If the referenced document changes, the dependent document changes. The InPlace Mates are listed under the Mates group in the FeatureManager

Mates
InPlace1 (Part1<1>,Front Plane)

In a Top Down assembly, you create In-context features. An In-context feature is a feature that references geometry from another component. The In-context feature has an external reference to that component. If you change geometry on the referenced component, the associated In-context feature also changes.

An In-context feature is indicated in the FeatureManager with the “>” symbol. The external references exist with the feature, sketch plane or sketch geometry. The update path to the referenced component is contained in the assembly. When the update path is not valid or the referenced component is not found the “?” symbol is displayed in the FeatureManager.

In the BOX assembly, develop InPlace Mates for the MOTHERBOARD, POWERSUPPLY and CABINET components.

Create external references with the Convert Entities Sketch tool and extracting geometry from the Layout Sketch of the BOX assembly.

Working with In-context features requires practice and time. Planning and selecting the correct reference and understanding how to incorporate changes are important. Explore various techniques using InPlace Mates and external references developed In-context of another component.

Assembly Modeling Techniques with InPlace Mates:
Plan the Top Down Design method. Start from a Layout Sketch or with a component in the assembly.
Prepare the references. Utilize descriptive feature names for referenced features and sketches.
Utilize InPlace Mates sparingly. Load all related components into memory to propagate changes. Do not use InPlace Mates for purchased parts or hardware.
Group references. Select references from one component at a time.
Ask questions! Will the part be used again in a different assembly? If the answer is yes, do not use InPlace Mates. If the answer is no, use InPlace Mates.
Will the part be used in physical dynamics or multiple configurations? If the answer is yes, do not use InPlace Mates.
Work in the Edit Component mode to obtain the required external references in the assembly. Create all non-referenced features in the part, not in the assembly.
Obtain knowledge of your company’s policy on InPlace Mates or develop one as part of an engineering standard.

Part Template and Assembly Template

The parts and assemblies in this project require Templates created in Project 1 and Project 2. The MY-TEMPLATES tab is located in the New dialog box. If your MY-TEMPLATES folder contains the ASM-MM-ANSI and PART-MM-ANSI Templates, skip the next few steps.

Activity: Part Template and Assembly Template

Create the Assembly Template for the BOX.

1) Click **File**, **New** from the Main menu.

2) Double-click **Templates**, **Assembly** Assembly. Click **Cancel** from the Insert Component PropertyManager.

Set the Assembly Document Template options.

3) Click **Tools**, **Options**, **Document Properties** from the Main menu.

4) Select **ANSI** [**ISO**] from the Dimensioning Standard option.

5) Click **Units**. Click **MMGS** from the Linear units list box.

6) Enter **2** in the Decimal places spin box.

7) Enter **0** in the Angular units Decimal places spin box. Click **OK**.

Save the assembly template.

8) Click **File**, **Save As**. Click the **Assembly Template (*.asmdot)** from the Save As type list box.

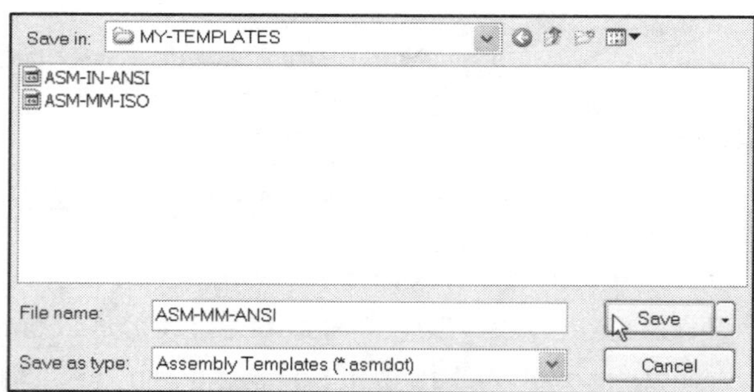

9) Select **ENGDESIGN-W-SOLIDWORKS\ MY-TEMPLATES** for the Save in file folder.

10) Enter **ASM-MM-ANSI, [ASM-MM-ISO]** in the File name text box.

11) Click **Save**.

Create the Part Template for the BOX.

12) Click **File**, **New** from the Main menu.

Double-click **Part** Part from the Templates tab.

13) Click **Tools**, **Options, Document Properties** tab from the Main menu.

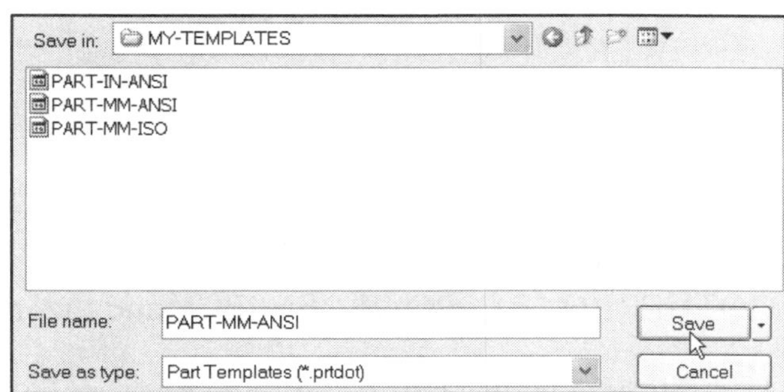

14) Select **ANSI** [**ISO**] from the Dimensioning standard drop down list.

Set the Units.

15) Click **Units**. Click **MMGS** from the Linear units list box. Enter **2** in the Decimal places spin box. Enter **0** for Angular units Decimal display. Click **OK**.

Save the Part Template.

16) Click **File**, **Save As** from the Main menu. Click **Part Templates (*.prtdot)** from the Save As type list box.

17) Select **ENGDESIGN-W-SOLIDWORKS\MY-TEMPLATES** for Save in file folder.

18) Enter **PART-MM-ANSI,[PART-MM-ISO]** in the File name text box. Click **Save**.

Display the MY-TEMPLATES tab.

19) Click **Tools**, **Options**, **File Locations** from the Main menu. Click **Add**.

20) Select **ENGDESIGN-W-SOLIDWORKS\MY-TEMPLATES** folder. Click **OK**.

Close All documents.

21) Click **Windows**, **Close All** from the Main menu.

BOX Assembly and Layout Sketch

The BOX assembly utilizes both the Top Down design approach and the Bottom up design approach. Begin the BOX assembly with a Layout Sketch.

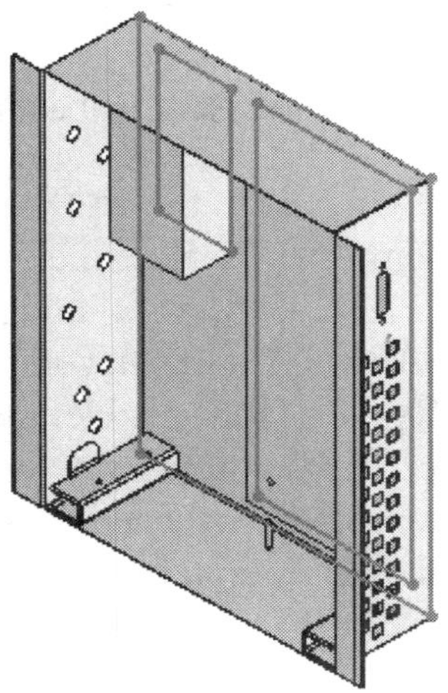

Create a New assembly named BOX. Insert a Layout Sketch to develop component space allocations and relations in the BOX assembly.

Add dimensions and relations to the Layout Sketch. Components and assemblies reference the Layout Sketch.

The BOX assembly contains the following key components:

- POWERSUPPLY
- MOTHERBOARD

The minimum physical spatial gap between the MOTHERBOARD and the POWERSUPPLY is 25mm. The minimum physical spatial gap between the MOTHERBOARD, POWERSUPPLY and the internal sheet metal BOX wall is 20mm.

After numerous discussions with the electrical engineer, you standardize on a POWERSUPPLY size: 150mm x 75mm x 50mm. You know the overall dimensions for the BOX, POWERSUPPLY and MOTHERBOARD. You also know the dimensional relationship between these components.

Now you must build these parameters into the design intent of the Layout Sketch. There is no symmetry between the major components. Locate the Layout Sketch with respect to the BOX assembly Origin.

Activity: Box Assembly and Layout Sketch

Create the BOX assembly.

22) Click **File**, **New** from the Main menu.

23) Click the **MY-TEMPLATES** tab.

24) Double-click the **ASM-MM-ANSI**. Assembly template.

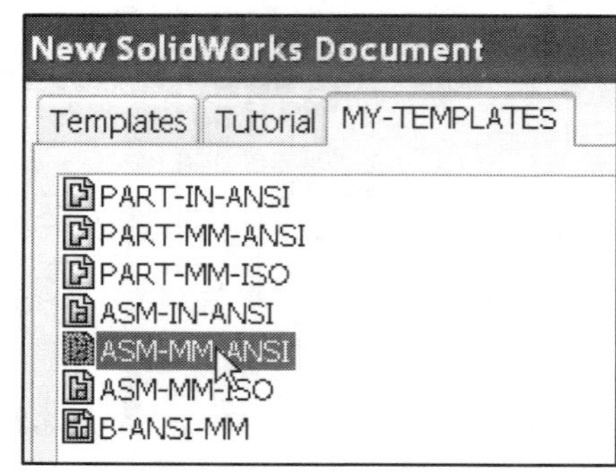

25) Click **Cancel** from the Insert Component PropertyManager.

Save the BOX assembly.

26) Click **Save**. Select **ENGDESIGN-W-SOLIDWORKS\PROJECTS** for the file folder.

27) Enter **BOX** in the file name box. Click **Save**.

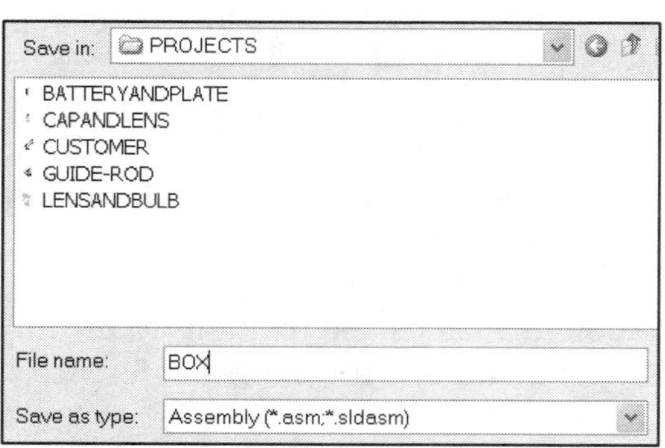

Each part in the BOX assembly requires a template. Utilize the PART-MM-ANSI [PART-MM-ISO] and ASM-MM-ANSI [ASM-MM-ISO] Templates. The Tools, System Options, Default Templates option prompts you to select a different document template. Otherwise, SolidWorks utilizes the default templates located in the \SolidWorks\data\templates folder.

Set the System Options.

28) Click **Tools**, **Options**, **Default Templates** from the Main menu.

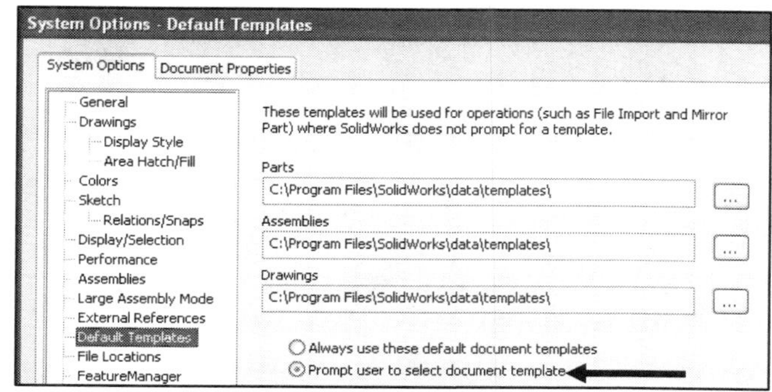

29) Click the **Prompt user** to select document template button.

30) Click **OK**.

The Layout Sketch is a sketch developed in the BOX assembly. The Layout Sketch contains the 2D relationships between all major components in the BOX assembly.

Select the Sketch Plane for the Layout Sketch.

31) Click **Front Plane** from the FeatureManager.

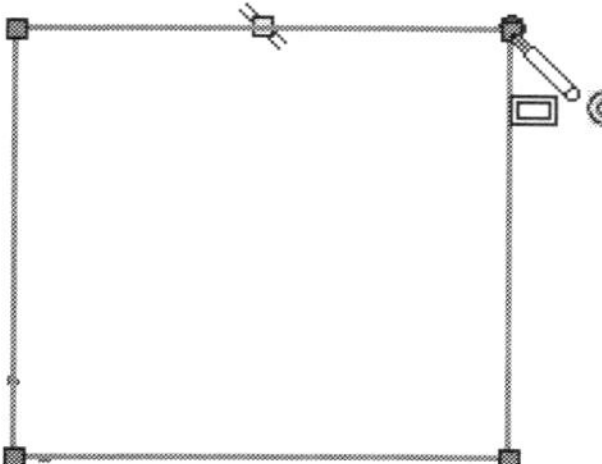

Sketch the profile of the BOX.

32) Click **Sketch** Sketch. Click **Rectangle** Rectan... from the Sketch toolbar. Sketch a **rectangle**. The first point is coincident with the Origin.

Add dimensions.

33) Click **Smart Dimension**  Smart Dimens... .

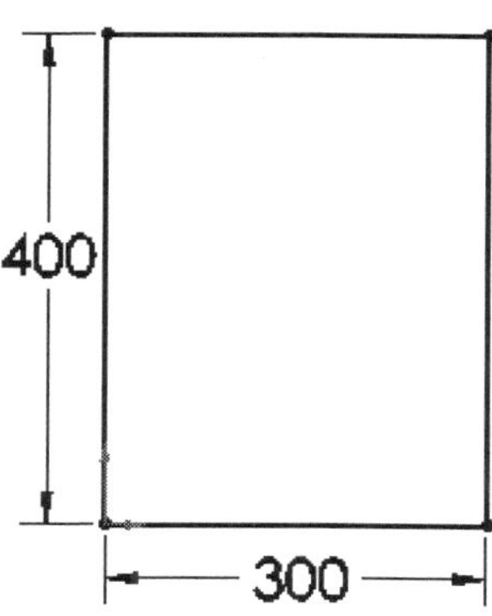

34) Click the **left vertical line**. Click a **position** to the left of the profile. Enter **400**. Click the **bottom horizontal line**. Click a **position** below the profile. Enter **300**.

Fit the model to the Graphics window.

35) Press the **f** key.

Sketch the profile for the POWER SUPPLY.

36) Click **Rectangle** Rectan... from the Sketch toolbar. Sketch a small **rectangle** inside the BOX.

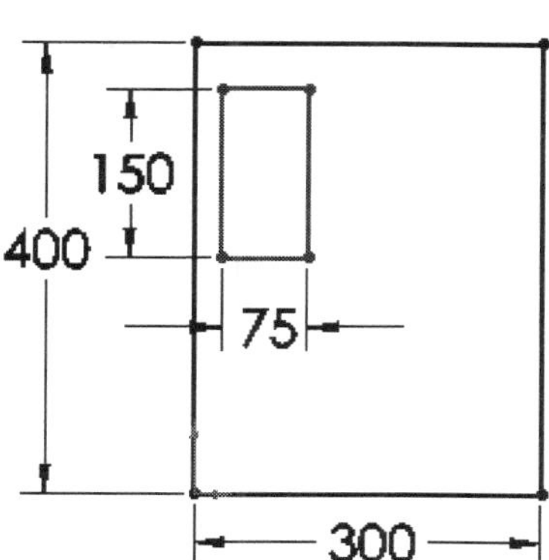

Add dimensions.

37) Click **Smart Dimension**  Smart Dimens... . Create a vertical dimension. Enter **150**. Create a horizontal dimension. Enter **75**.

Dimension the POWERSUPPLY 20mm from the left and top edges of the BOX.

38) Create a horizontal dimension. Click the BOX left **vertical edge**.

39) Click the POWERSUPPLY left **vertical edge**.

40) Click a **position** above the BOX. Enter **20**.

41) Create a vertical dimension. Click the BOX **top horizontal edge**.

42) Click the POWERSUPPLY **top horizontal edge**.

43) Click a **position** above and to the right of the BOX. Enter **20**.

Sketch the profile for the MOTHERBOARD.

44) Click **Rectangle** Rectan... from the Sketch toolbar.

45) Sketch a **rectangle** to the right of the POWERSUPPLY.

Add dimensions.

46) Click **Smart Dimension**  Smart Dimens... . Click the **left vertical edge** of the MOTHERBOARD. Click the **right vertical edge** of the POWERSUPPLY. Click a **position** above the BOX. Enter **25**.

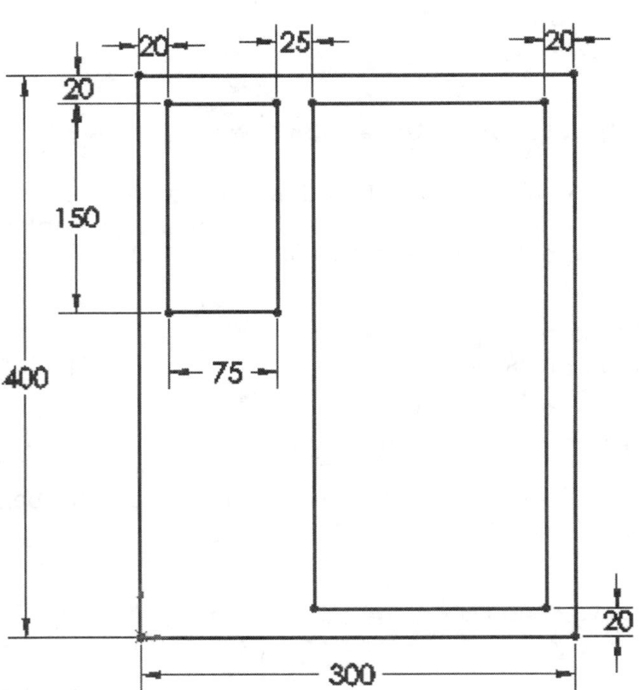

47) Click the horizontal **top edge** of the MOTHERBOARD. Click the horizontal **top edge** of the BOX. Click a position off the profile. Enter **20**.

48) Click the vertical **right edge** of the MOTHERBOARD. Click the vertical **right edge** of the BOX. Click a **position** above the Box. Enter **20**.

49) Click the horizontal **bottom edge** of the MOTHERBOARD. Click the horizontal **bottom edge** of the BOX.

50) Click a **position** to the right of the BOX. Enter **20**.

Note: Sketch1 is fully defined and is displayed in black. Insert a Collinear relation between the top lines of the two inside rectangles if required.

Close the Sketch.

51) Click **Exit Sketch**  .

52) Rename **Sketch1** to **Layout**.

Save the BOX assembly.

53) Click **Save** .

What happens when the size of the MOTHERBOARD changes? How do you insure that the BOX maintains the required 20mm spatial gap between the internal components and the BOX boundary? How do you design for future revisions? Answer: Through Link Values.

Link Values and Equations

Link Values are used to define equal relations. Create an equal relation between two or more sketched dimensions and or features with a Link Value. Link Values require a shared name. Mathematical expressions that define relationships between parameters and or dimensions are called Equations. Equations use shared names to control dimensions. Use Equations to connect values from sketches, features, patterns and various parts in an assembly.

Use Link Values within the same part. Use Equations in parts and assemblies, later in this project. The project goal is to create three boxes of different sizes. Insure that the models remain valid when dimensions change for various internal components. This is key! Link values and equations require feature dimensions. Utilize the Show Feature Dimensions option in the Annotations folder. The Annotations folder is the first entry in the FeatureManager. The variable Gap is the Link Value name common to all Layout Sketch dimensions with the value of 20.

Activity: Link Values and Equations

Display the dimensions.

54) Right-click the **Annotations** folder in the FeatureManager.

55) Click **Show Feature Dimensions**.

Insert a Link Value.

56) Right click on the lower right vertical dimension **20**.

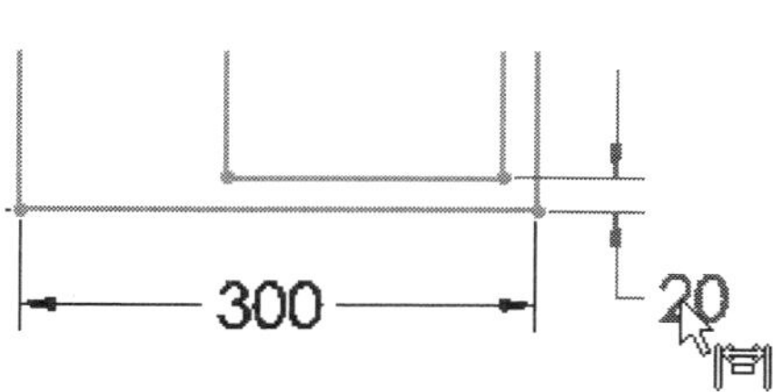

57) Click **Link Values**.

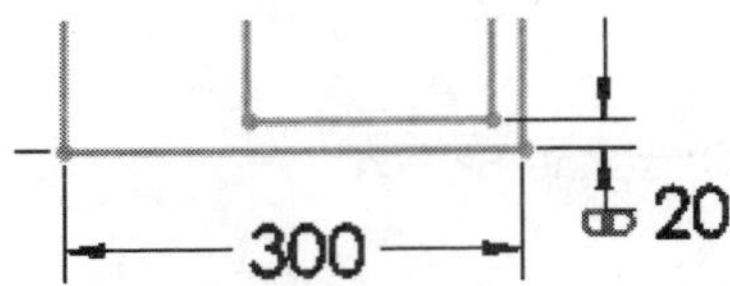

58) Enter **gap** in the Name text box in the Shared Values dialog box.

59) Click **OK**.

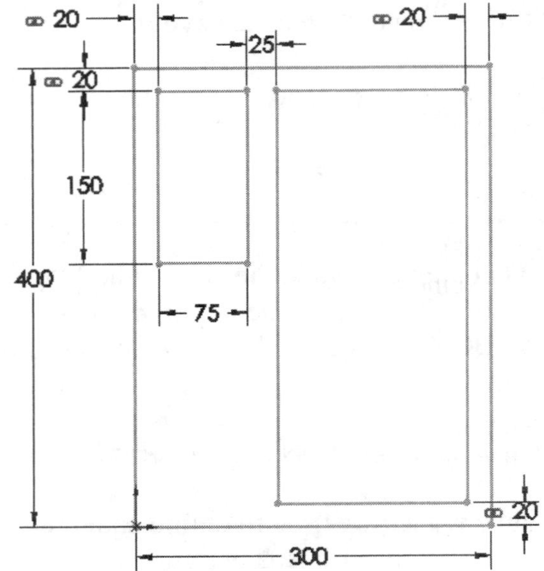

Link the remaining 20mm dimensions.

60) Right click on the upper vertical dimension **20**.

61) Hold the **Ctrl** key down.

62) Click the other **20** dimensions.

63) Click **Link Values**. The Shared Values dialog box is displayed.

64) Release the **Ctrl** key.

65) Click the **drop down arrow** from the Name text box.

66) Select **gap**.

67) Click **OK**.

Test the Link Values.

68) Double-click the lower right **20** dimension.

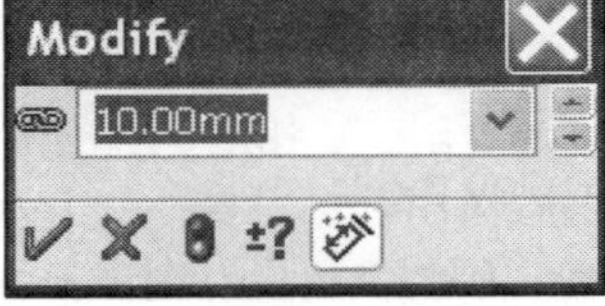

69) Enter **10**. Click **Rebuild**. The five Link Values change and display the Link symbol.

Return to the original value.

70) Double-click the lower right **10** dimension. Enter **20**.

71) Click **Rebuild**. Click the **Green Check mark** from the Mate Pop-up toolbar.

72) Click **OK** from the PropertyManager.

Note: All Link Values are equal to 20.

Save time when linking multiple dimensions. Hold the Ctrl key down. Select all dimensions to be linked. Right-click Link Value. Enter the variable Name. Release the Ctrl key.

Additional dimensions are required for Equations. Each dimension has a unique variable name. The names are used as Equation variables. The default names are based on the Sketch, Feature or Part. Feature names do not have to be changed. Rename variables for clarity when creating numerous Equations.

Rename the BOX assembly width and height. The full variable name is: "box-width@Layout". The system automatically appends Layout. If features are created or deleted in a different order, your variable names will be different.

Rename for overall box width.

73) Right-click the horizontal dimension, **300**.

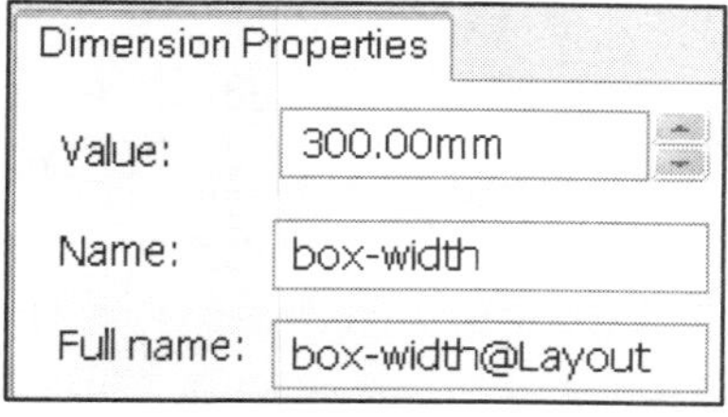

74) Click **Properties** Properties... .

75) Delete **D2** in the Name text box. Enter **box_width** in the Name text box.

76) Click **OK**.

Rename the overall box height.

77) Right-click the vertical dimension, **400**.

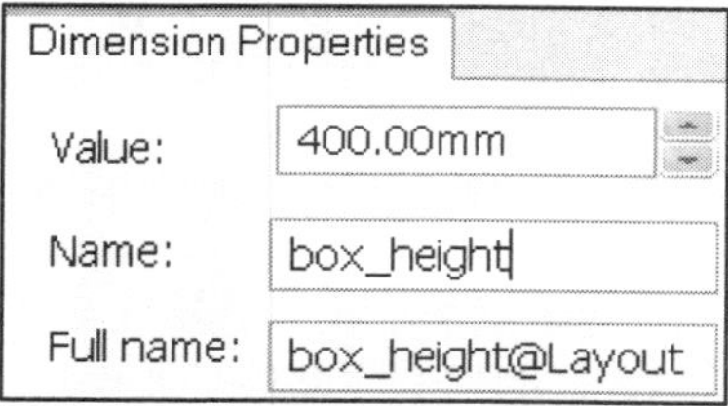

78) Click **Properties** Properties... .

79) Delete **D1** in the Name text box. Enter **box_height** in the Name text box. Click **OK**.

80) Click **OK** from the Dimension PropertyManager.

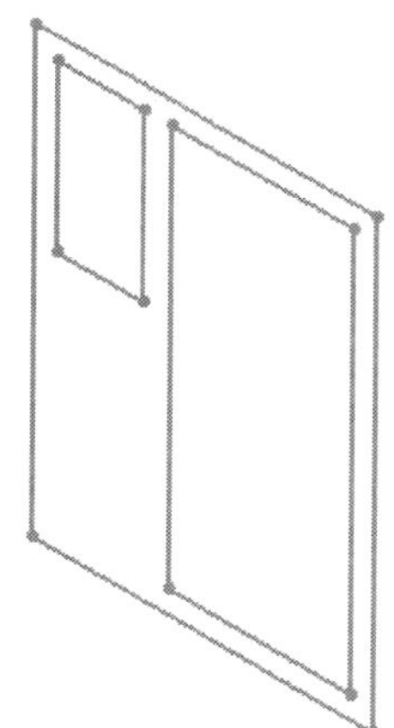

Display the Isometric view.

81) Click **Isometric view**.

Hide all dimensions.

82) Right-click the **Annotations** folder.

83) Uncheck **Show Feature Dimensions**.

Save the BOX assembly.

84) Click **Save**.

The Layout Sketch is complete. Develop the MOTHERBOARD part and the POWERSUPPLY part In-context of the BOX assembly Layout Sketch.

Select the BOX assembly Front Plane to create InPlace Mates. An InPlace Mate is a Coincident Mate developed between the Front Plane of the component and the selected plane in the assembly. Utilize Convert Entities and extract geometry from the Layout Sketch to create external references for both the MOTHERBOARD part and POWERSUPPLY part. Utilize Ctrl-Tab to switch between part and assembly windows.

MOTHERBOARD-Insert Component

The MOTHERBOARD requires the greatest amount of lead-time to design and manufacture. The outline of the MOTHERBOARD is created. Create the MOTHERBOARD component from the Layout Sketch.

An electrical engineer develops the Logic Diagram and Schematic required for the Printed Circuit Board (PCB). The MOTHERBOARD rectangular sketch represents the special constraints of a blank Printed Circuit Board (PCB).

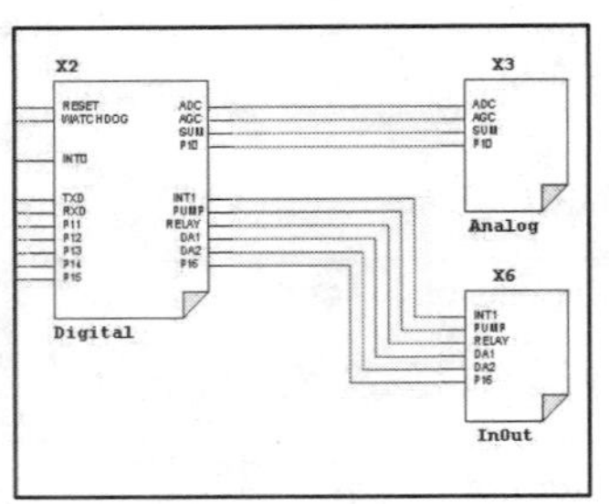

Logic Diagram (partial)

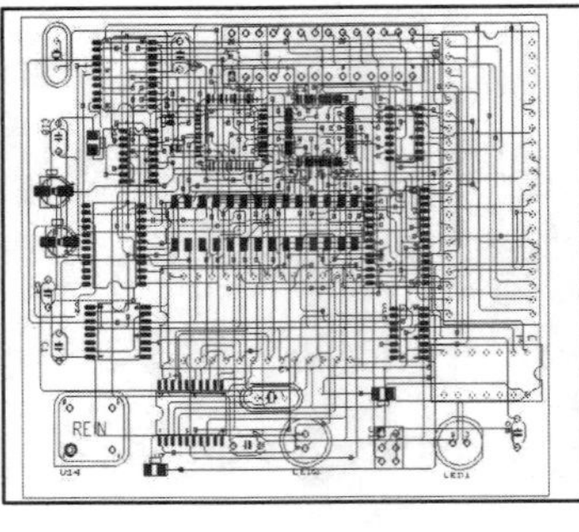

Schematic

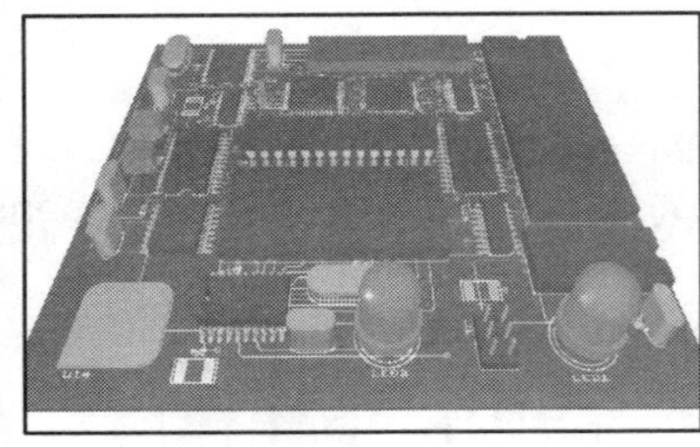

PCB

Courtesy of Electronic Workbench (www.electronicworkbench.com)

A rough design of a critical connector is located on the MOTHERBOARD in the upper right corner.

CircuitWorks software application from Zeal Solutions (www.circuitworks.co.uk) is a fully integrated data interface between SolidWorks and PCB Design systems.

As the project manager, your job is to create the board outline with the corresponding dimensions from the Layout Sketch. Export the MOTHERBOARD data in an industry-standard Intermediate Data Format (IDF) from SolidWorks.

The IDF file is sent to the PCB designer to populate the board with the correct 2D electronic components.

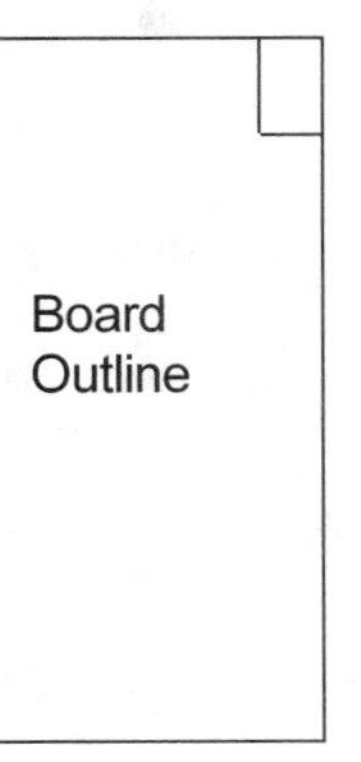

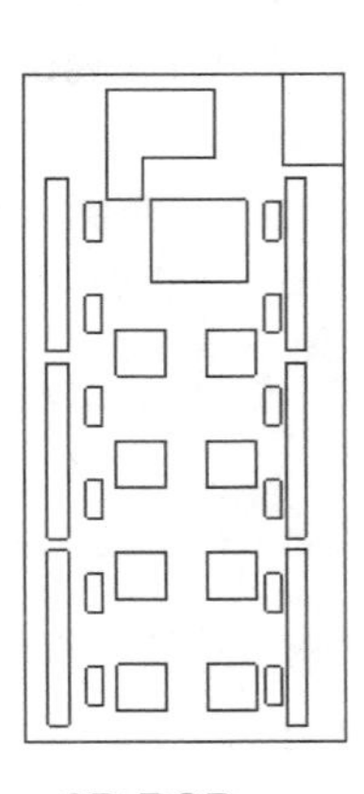

2D PCB

CircuitWorks utilizes industry-standard IDF files or PADS files, and produces the 3D SolidWorks assembly of the MOTHERBOARD. IDF and PADS are common file formats utilized in the PCB industry.

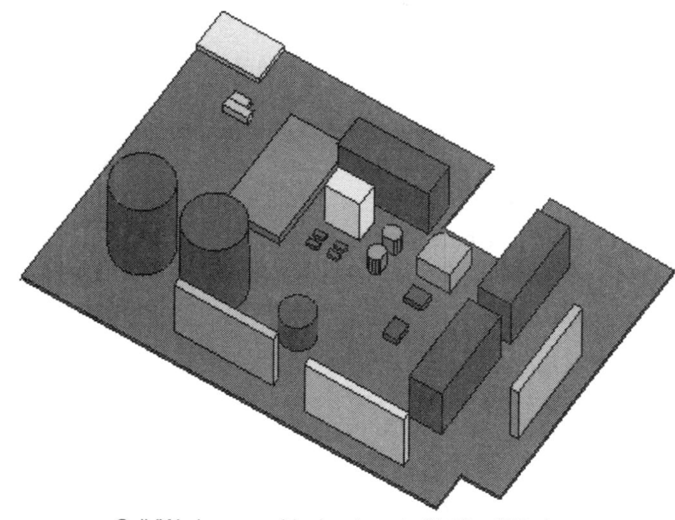

SolidWorks assembly developed with CircuitWorks
Courtesy of Computer Aided Products, Inc.

The MOTHERBOARD is fully populated with the components at the correct height. Your colleagues use the MOTHERBOARD assembly to develop other areas of the BOX assembly. An engineer develops the wire harness from the MOTHERBOARD to electrical components in the BOX.

A second engineer uses the 3D geometry from each electrical component on the MOTHERBOARD to create a heat sink.

As the project manager, you move components that interfere with other mechanical parts, cables and or wire harness. You distribute the updated information to your colleagues and manufacturing partners.

A new IDF file containing the component positions is provided to the PCB manufacturer for fabrication.

With SolidWorks Routing software application, you create a special type of sub-assembly that builds a path for electrical cables, pipes and tubes between components. SolidWorks Routing includes harness flattening and detailing capabilities to develop 2D harness manufacturing drawings from 3D electrical route assemblies. SolidWorks Routing contains a Cable/Wire Library and a Component Library. Additional information is available at www.solidworks.com.

Library Component from SolidWorks Routing

Continue with the BOX assembly design as the MOTHERBOARD is manufactured. Create a simplified MOTHERBOARD part In-context of the BOX assembly. Utilize the Layout Sketch in the BOX assembly.

Activity: MOTHERBOARD-Insert Component

Create the MOTHERBOARD component.

85) The BOX assembly is the open document. Click **Insert**, **Component**, **New Part** from the Main menu.

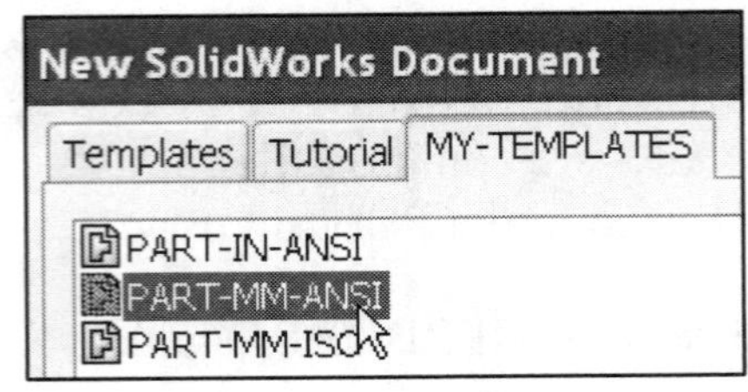

Select the Part Template.

86) Double-click **PART-MM-ANSI**.

Save the Part.

87) Enter **MOTHERBOARD** in the Filename text box. Note: Save in the **VENDOR-COMPONENTS** folder.

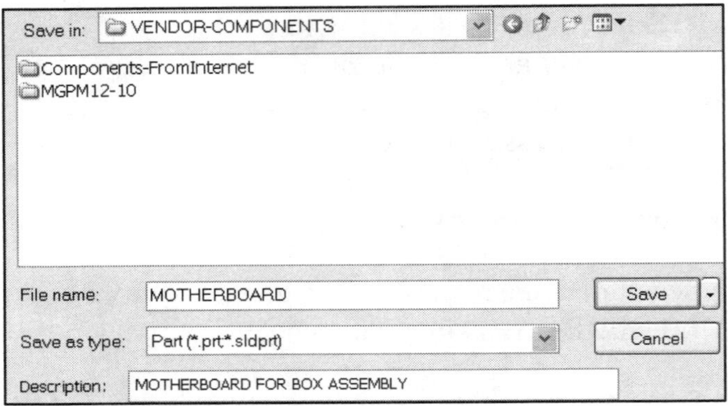

88) Enter **MOTHERBOARD FOR BOX ASSEMBLY** for Description. Click **Save**.

The Component Pointer is displayed on the mouse pointer. The MOTHERBOARD component is empty and requires a sketch plane. The Front Plane of the MOTHERBOARD component is mated with the Front plane of the BOX.

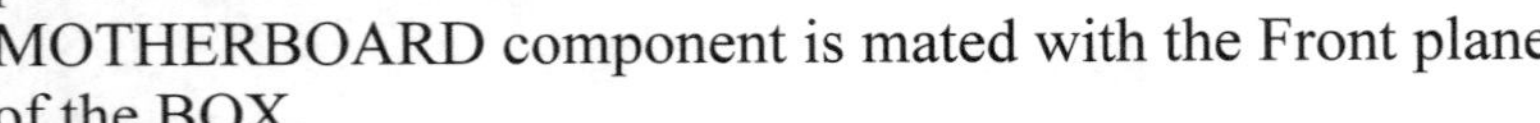

Select the Sketch Plane for the MOTHERBOARD.

89) Click the **Front Plane** of the BOX assembly FeatureManager.

90) Expand **MOTHERBOARD** in the FeatureManager. The MOTHERBOARD FeatureManager is displayed in light blue.

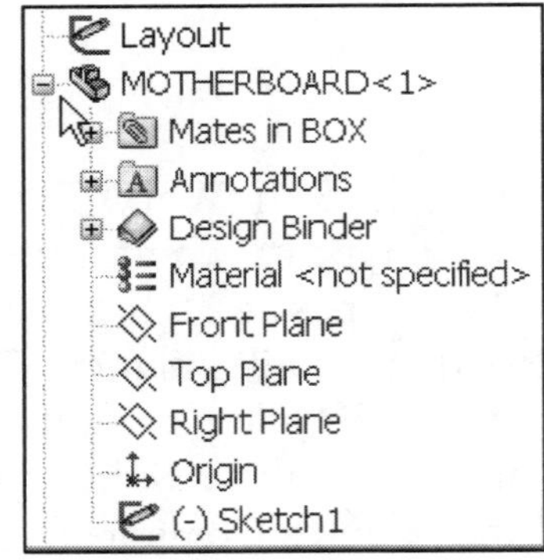

Components added In-context of the assembly automatically received an InPlace Mate within the Mates entry in the FeatureManager. An InPlace Mate is a Coincident Mate between the Front Plane of the MOTHERBOARD and the Front Plane of the BOX. The MOTHERBOARD entry is added to the FeatureManager. The system automatically selects Edit Component (Edit Compo...). The MOTHERBOARD text is displayed in blue to indicate that the component is actively being edited. The current Sketch plane is the Front Plane.

The system automatically selects the Sketch (Sketch) icon.

The current sketch name is (-) Sketch1. The document name displays:

SolidWorks 2006 - [Sketch1 of MOTHERBOARD -in- BOX *].

Create the Sketch.

91) Click the **right vertical edge** of the right inside rectangle.

92) Click **Convert Entities** Convert from the Sketch toolbar.

93) Click **closed contour** from the Resolve Ambiguity box.

94) Click **OK**. The outside perimeter of the Layout Sketch is the current Sketch.

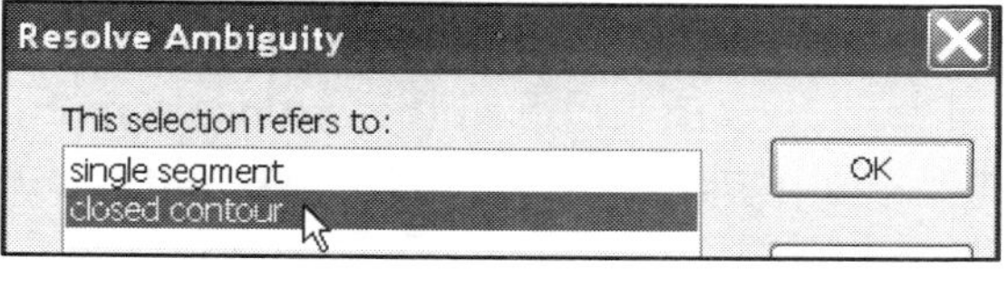

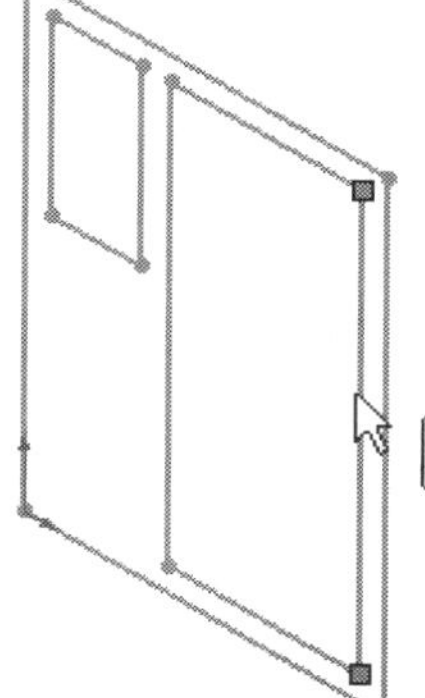

Display the Features Toolbar.

95) Click **Features** Features from the Control Area.

Insert the Extruded Base for the MOTHERBOARD.

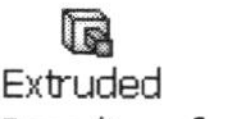

96) Click **Extruded Boss/Base** Extruded Boss/B.... from the Features toolbar.

97) Enter **10** for Depth.

98) Click **OK** from the Extrude PropertyManager.

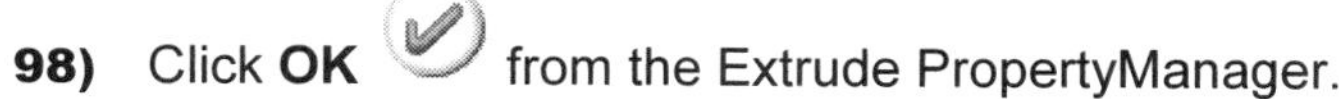

99) Rename **Extrude1** to **Base Extrude**.

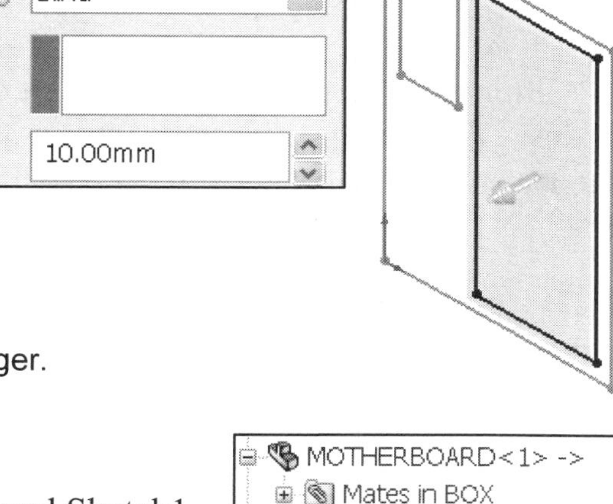

The MOTHERBOARD<1> ->, Base Extrude -> and Sketch1 -> contain the ">" symbol indicating external references to the BOX assembly. The Edit Component option acts as a switch between the assembly and the component edited in-context.

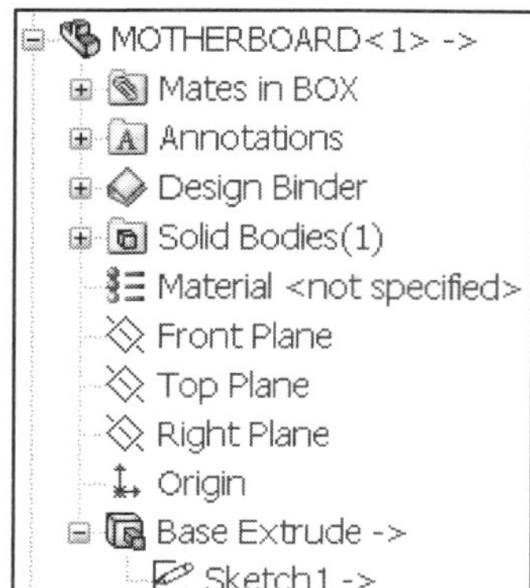

Return to the BOX assembly.

Return to the BOX assembly.

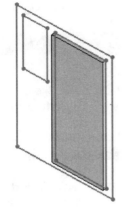

100) Click **Edit Component**  from the Assembly toolbar. The FeatureManager is displayed in black.

Fit the BOX to the Graphics window.
101) Press the **f** key.

Save the BOX assembly.
102) Click **Save**.

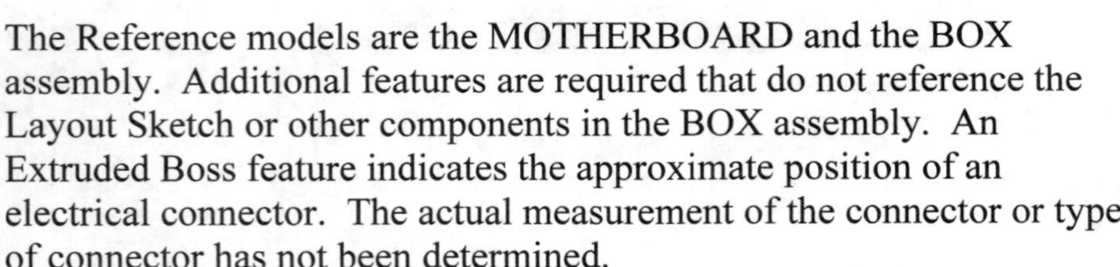

The Reference models are the MOTHERBOARD and the BOX assembly. Additional features are required that do not reference the Layout Sketch or other components in the BOX assembly. An Extruded Boss feature indicates the approximate position of an electrical connector. The actual measurement of the connector or type of connector has not been determined.

Perform the following steps to avoid unwanted assembly references:

1. Open the part from the assembly. 2. Add features. 3. Save the part.

4. Return to the assembly. 5. Save the assembly.

Utilize the f key to fit an In-context component to the Graphics window. An In-context component is not located at the part Origin. The In-context component is located at the Origin of the original assembly.

Insert the Extruded Boss for the MOTHERBOARD.
103) Right-click **MOTHERBOARD** in the FeatureManager.

104) Click **Open Part**.

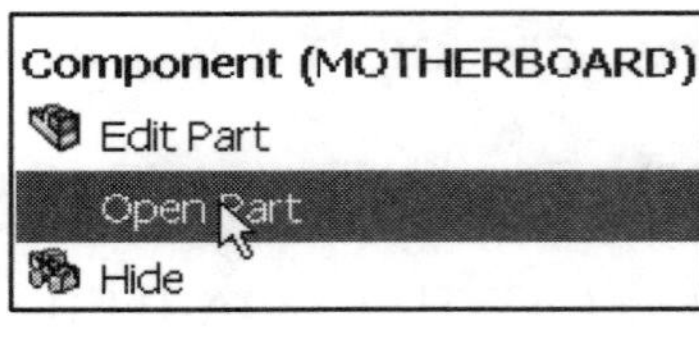

Fit the model to the Graphics window.
105) Press the **f** key.

Insert the Sketch.
106) Click the **front face** of Base Extrude. Click **Sketch**.

107) Click the outside **right vertical edge**. Hold the **Ctrl key** down. Click the **top horizontal edge**. Release the **Ctrl key**.

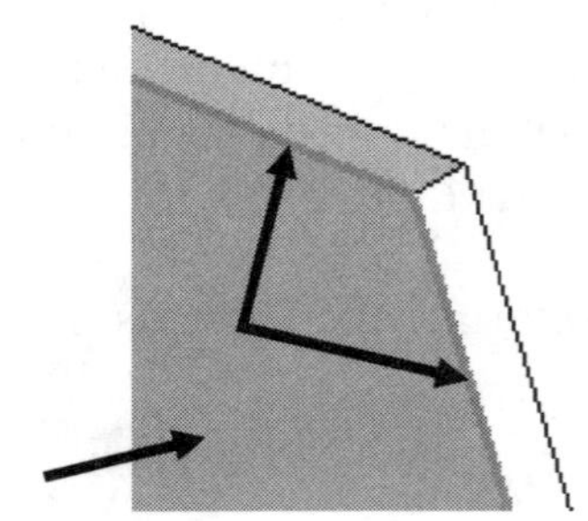

Front face

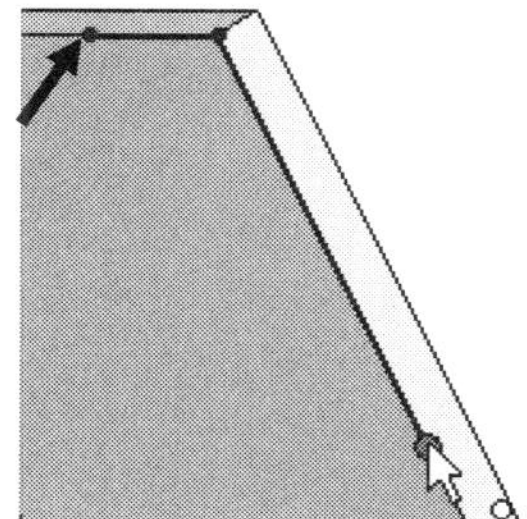

108) Click **Convert Entities** Convert from the Sketch toolbar. Drag the **bottom endpoint** of the convert line three quarters upward.

109) Drag the **left endpoint** of the converted line three quarters of the way to the right. Click **Front view** .

110) Click **Line** Line .

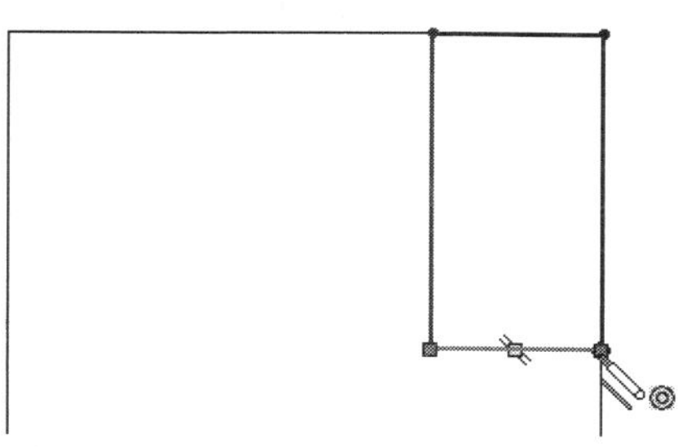

111) Sketch a **vertical line**.

112) Sketch a **horizontal line** to complete the rectangle.

Add dimensions.

113) Click **Smart Dimension** Smart Dimens... .

114) Enter **30** for the horizontal dimension.

115) Enter **50** for the vertical dimension.

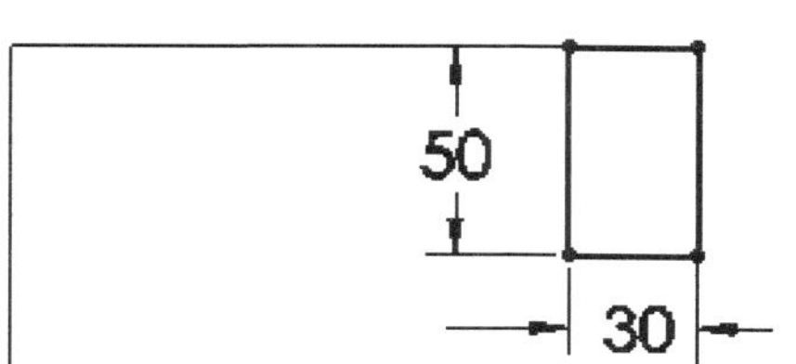

Extrude the Sketch.

116) Click **Features** Features , **Extruded Boss/Base** Extruded Boss/B... .

117) Enter **10** for Depth. Click **OK** from the Extrude PropertyManager.

118) Rename **Extrude2** to **Connector1**.

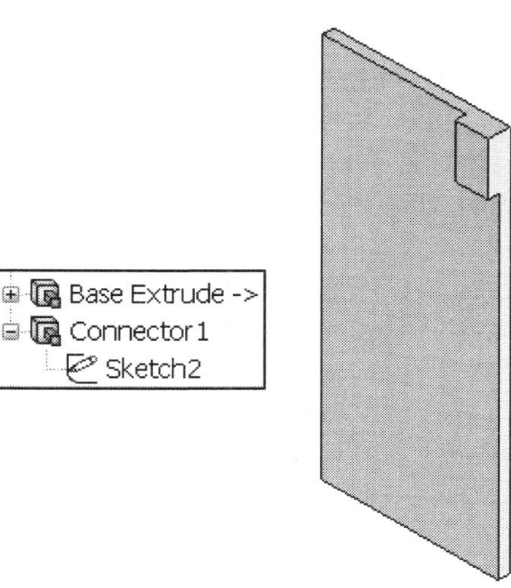

Display an Isometric view.

119) Click **Isometric view** .

120) Click **Save** .

Use color to indicate electrical connectors. Color the face of the Extruded Boss feature.

Color the Front face of Connector1.

121) Click the **Front face**. Click **Color** .

122) Select **yellow**. Click **OK** from the PropertyManager.

Save the MOTHERBOARD.

123) Click **Save**.

Return to the BOX assembly.

124) Press **Ctrl Tab**. Click **Yes** to rebuild the assembly.

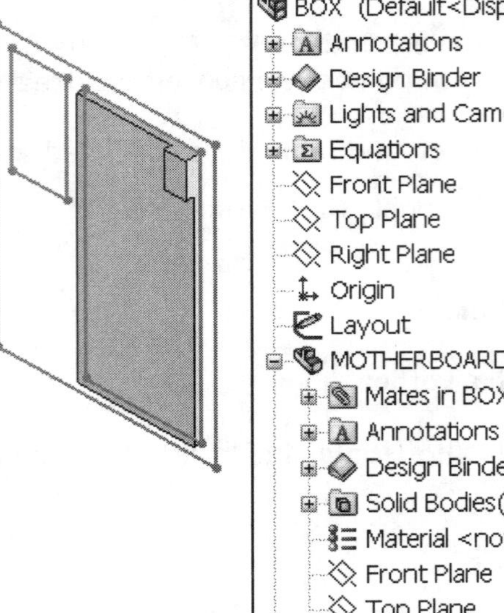

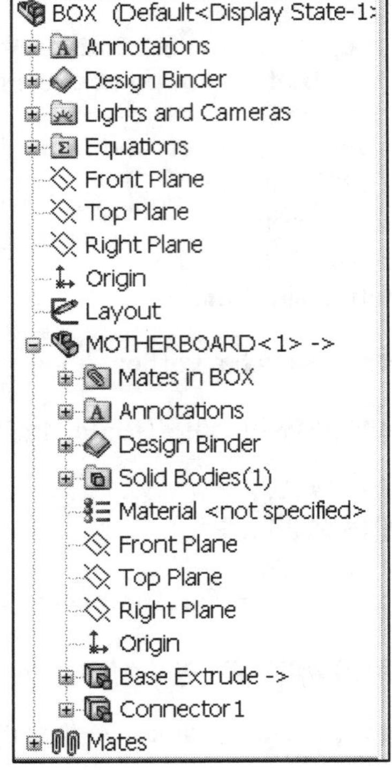

The MOTHERBOARD contains the new Connector1 Extruded Boss feature with the yellow Color Property. For now the MOTHERBOARD is complete. The POWERSUPPLY is the second key component to be defined In-context of the BOX assembly.

Locate external references. Open the BOX assembly before opening individual components referenced by the assembly when you start a new session of SolidWorks. The components load and locate their external references to the original assembly.

POWERSUPPLY-Insert Component

Create a simplified POWERSUPPLY part In-context of the BOX assembly. Utilize the Layout Sketch in the BOX assembly. Open the POWERSUPPLY part and insert an Extruded Boss to represent the connection to a cable.

Activity: POWERSUPPLY-Insert Component

Insert the POWERSUPPLY Component.

125) Click **Insert**, **Component**, **New Part** from the Main menu in the BOX assembly.

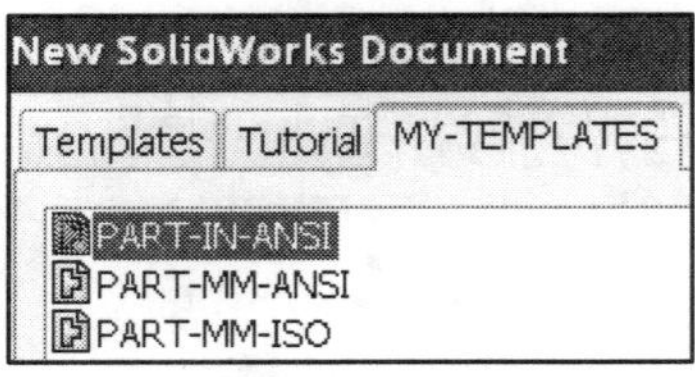

Select the Part Template.

126) Double-click the **PART-MM-ANSI** template icon.

Save the Part.

127) Select **ENGDESIGN-W-SOLIDWORKS\PROJECTS** for the file folder. Enter **POWERSUPPLY** in the Filename text box. Enter **POWERSUPPLY FOR BOX** for Description. Click **Save**.

The Component Pointer is displayed. The POWERSUPPLY component is empty and requires a sketch plane.

Select the Sketch Plane.

128) Click the **Front Plane** of the BOX in the FeatureManager. InPlace2 Mate is added to the BOX FeatureManager.

POWERSUPPLY<1>
Mates
InPlace1 (MOTHERBOARD<1>,Front Plane)
InPlace2 (POWERSUPPLY<1>,Front Plane)

The Front Plane of the POWERSUPPLY component is mated to the Front Plane of the BOX. Sketch1 of the POWERSUPPLY is the active sketch.

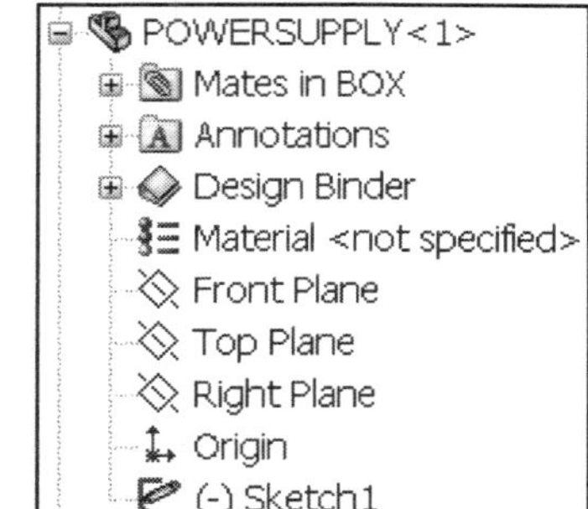

The system automatically selects Edit Component Edit Compo... .

The POWERSUPPLY entry in the FeatureManager is displayed in blue. The current Sketch plane is the Front Plane. The current sketch name is Sketch1. The name is indicated on the current document window title,

"Sketch1 of POWERSUPPLY - in- BOX."

POWERSUPPLY is the name of the component created In-context of the BOX assembly. Create the first Extruded Base feature In-context of the Layout Sketch.

Create the Sketch.

129) Click the **right vertical edge** of the POWERSUPPLY sketch.

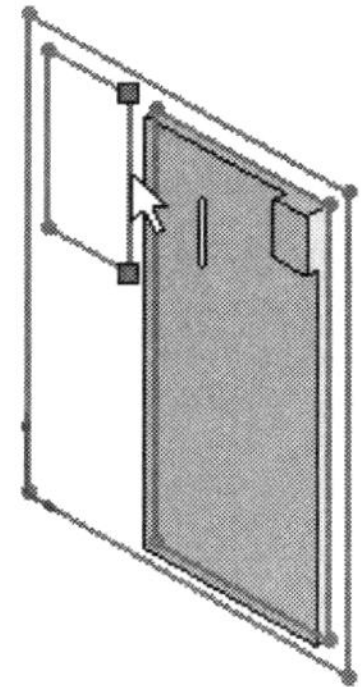

130) Click **Convert Entities** Convert from the Sketch toolbar. The Resolve Ambiguity dialog box is displayed.

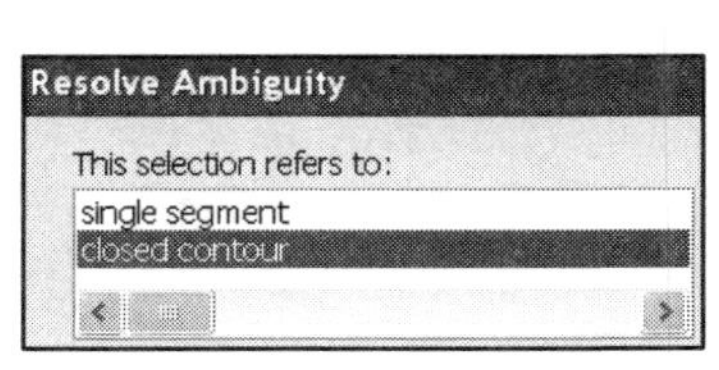

131) Click **closed contour**. Click **OK**.

Extrude the Sketch.

132) Click **Extruded Boss/Base** Extruded Boss/B... from the Features toolbar.

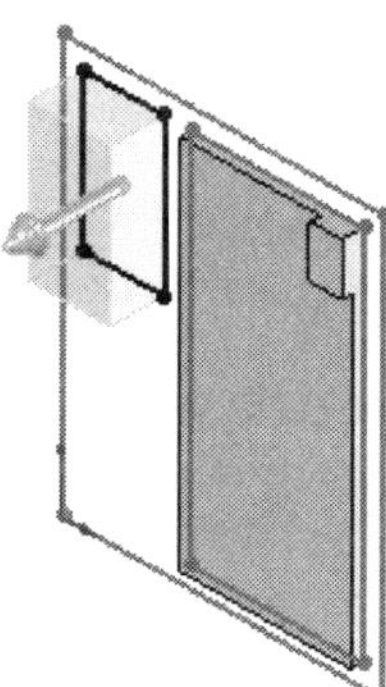

133) Enter **50** for Depth.

134) Click **OK** from the Extrude PropertyManager.

The POWERSUPPLY entry is displayed in blue. The part is being edited In-context of the BOX assembly.

Return to the BOX assembly.

135) Click **Edit Component** from the Assembly toolbar. The POWERSUPPLY is displayed in black.

Save the BOX assembly.

136) Click **Save**. Click **Yes** to save the referenced models.

The Extruded Boss feature represents the location of the cable that connects to the POWERSUPPLY. Think about where the cables and wire harness connects to key components. You do not have all of the required details for the cables.

In a concurrent engineering environment, create a simplified version early in the design process. No other information is required from the BOX assembly to create additional features for the POWERSUPPLY.

The design intent for the POWERSUPPLY is for the cable connection to be centered on the top face of the POWERSUPPLY. Utilize a centerline and Midpoint relation to construct the Extruded Boss feature centered on the top face. Open the POWERSUPPLY from the BOX assembly.

Open the POWERSUPPLY.

137) Right-click **POWERSUPPLY** in the Graphics window.

138) Click **Open Part**. Click **Top view**.

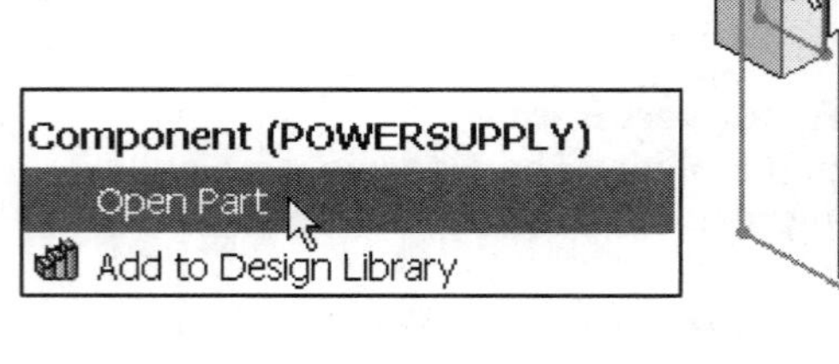

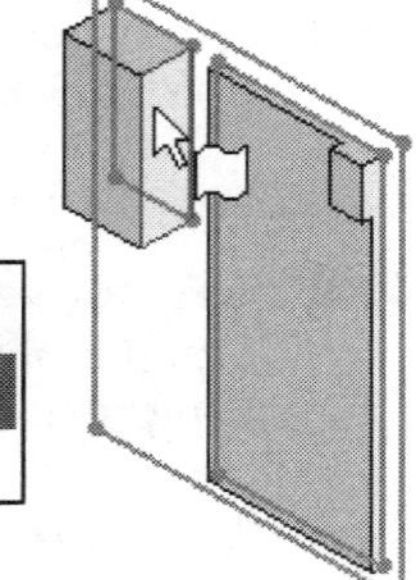

Create the Sketch.

139) Click the **top face** of Extrude1.

140) Click **Sketch**.

141) Click **Centerline**.

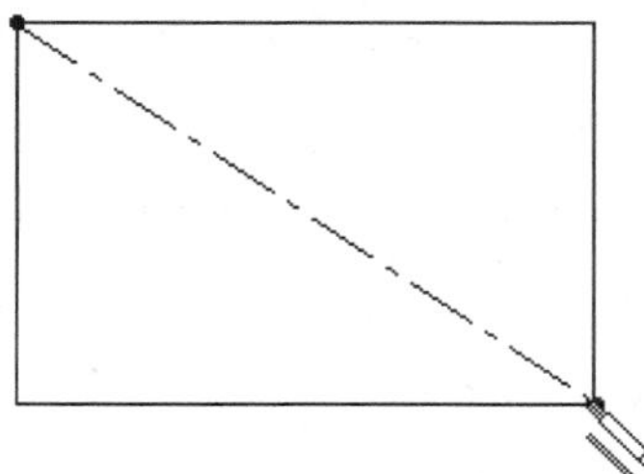

142) Sketch a diagonal **centerline**. Note: Align the endpoints with the corners of the POWERSUPPLY. The centerline is displayed in black.

Sketch a Circle.

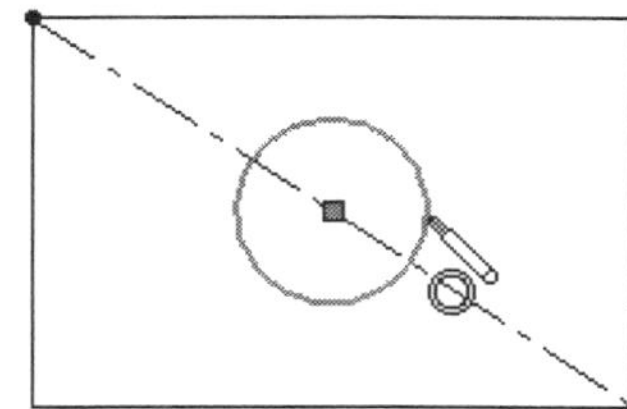

143) Click **Circle** Circle from the Sketch toolbar. Sketch a **circle**. Click the **Midpoint** of the Centerline for the center point of the circle.

Add a dimension.

144) Click **Smart Dimension**  Smart Dimens... . Click the **circumference** of the circle.

145) Click a **position** off the profile. Enter **15** for diameter. The circle is displayed in black.

Extrude the Sketch.

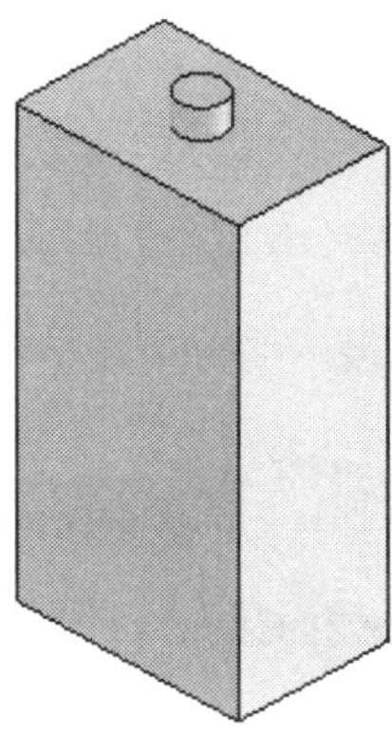

146) Click **Extruded Boss/Base**  Extruded Boss/B... from the Features toolbar.

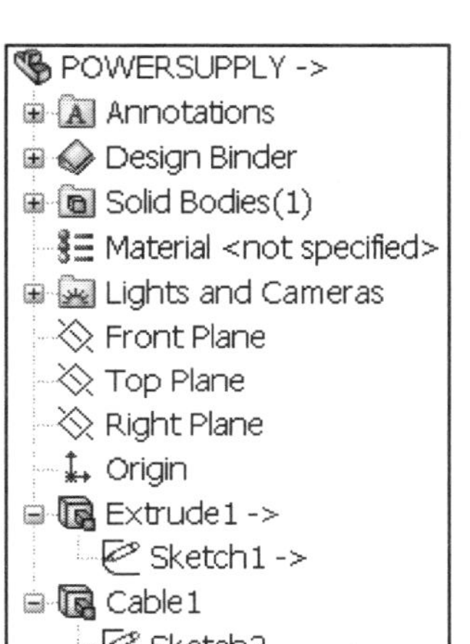

147) Enter **10** for Depth.

148) Click **OK** from the Extrude PropertyManager.

149) Rename **Extrude2** to **Cable1**.

150) Click **Isometric view** .

Save the POWERSUPPLY.

151) Click **Save**.

Return to the BOX assembly.

152) Press **Ctrl Tab**. Click **Yes** to update the assembly.

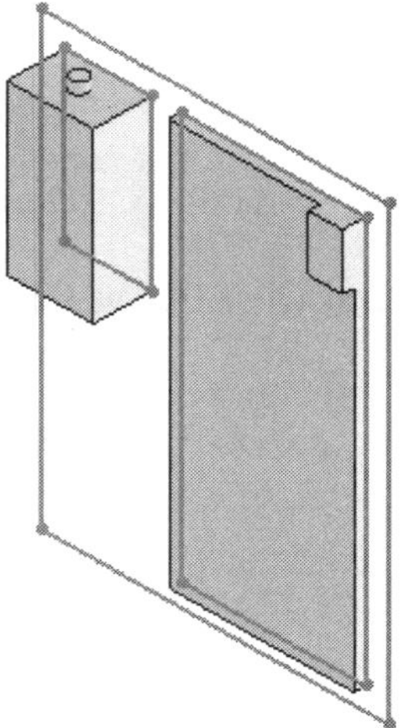

The POWERSUPPLY contains the new Extruded Boss feature, Cable1. Recall the initial design parameters. The requirement calls for three different size boxes. Test the Layout Sketch dimensions for the three configurations: Small, Medium and Large.

Does the Layout Sketch, MOTHERBOARD and POWERSUPPLY reflect the design intent of the BOX assembly? Review the next steps to confirm the original design intent.

Display all dimensions.

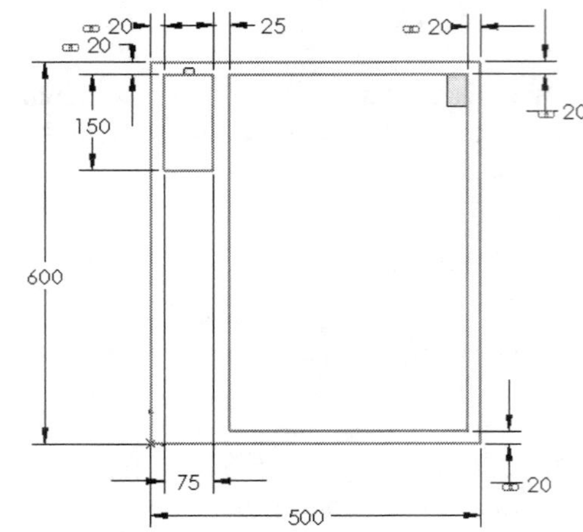

153) Click **Front view**.

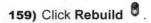

154) Right-click the **Annotations folder**.

155) Click **Show Feature Dimensions**.

156) Double-click **300**.

157) Enter **550** for the horizontal dimension. Double-click **400**.

158) Enter **600** for the vertical dimension.

159) Click **Rebuild**.

Return to the original dimensions.

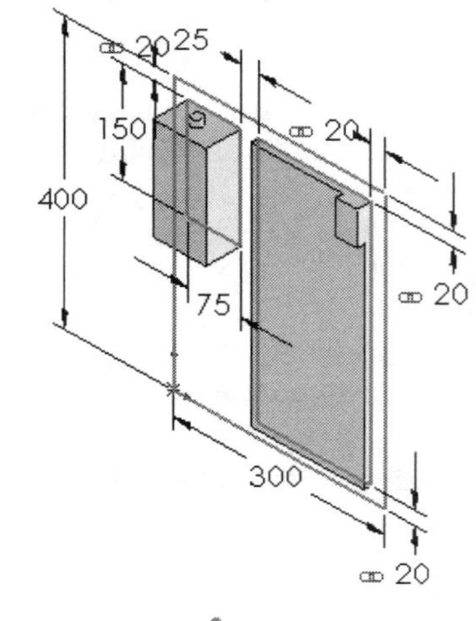

160) Double-click **550**. Enter **300** for width dimension.

161) Double-click **600**. Enter **400** for height dimension.

162) Click **Rebuild**. Click **Isometric view**.

163) Click **Save**.

Hide all dimensions.

164) Right-click the **Annotations folder**.

165) Uncheck **Show Feature Dimensions**.

Suppress the MOTHERBOARD and POWERSUPPLY.

166) Click **MOTHERBOARD** from the FeatureManager.

167) Hold the **Ctrl** key down.

168) Click **POWERSUPPLY**.

169) Right-click **Suppress**. Both components and their Mates are Suppressed.

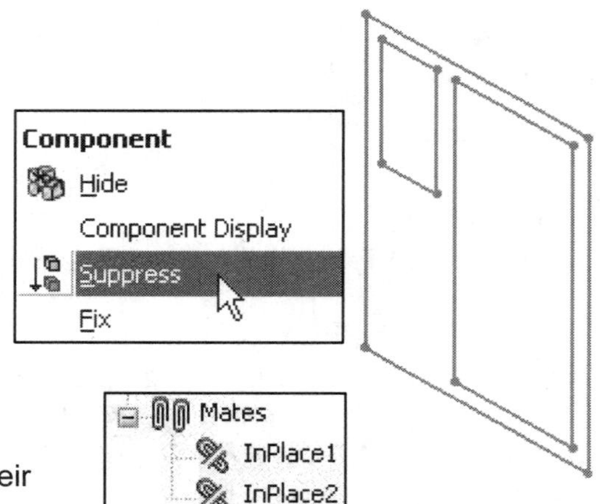

Electro-mechanical assemblies contain hundreds of parts. Suppress components saves rebuild time and simplifies the model. Only display the components and geometry required to create a new part or to mate a component.

Improve rebuild time and display performance for large assemblies. Review the System Options listed in Large Assembly Mode. Adjust the large assembly threshold to match your computer performance.

Check Remove detail during zoom/pan/rotate. Check Hide all planes, axes and sketches.

Review the System Option, Image Quality. Drag the resolution slider towards Low to improve computer performance.

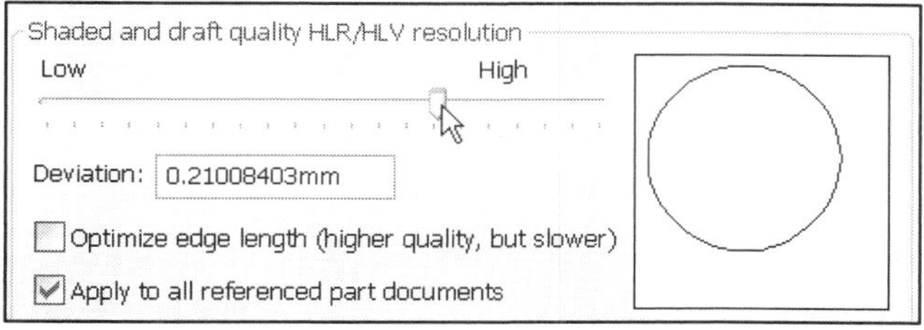

Additional details on Top Down Design, Layout Sketch, Link Value, In-context, External References, InPlace Mate, Edit Component and Large Assembly Mode are available in On-line help.

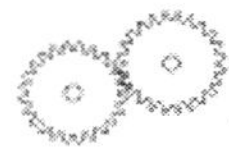

Review the BOX Assembly.

The BOX assembly utilized a Top Down design modeling approach by incorporating a Layout Sketch. The Layout Sketch consisted of 2D profiles and dimensions of the BOX, MOTHERBOARD and POWERSUPPLY.

The MOTHERBOARD was developed as a new part In-context of the BOX assembly. An InPlace Mate was created between the MOTHERBOARD Front Plane and the BOX assembly Front Plane. In the Edit Component mode, you extracted Layout Sketch geometry to create the first feature of the MOTHERBOARD part. The first feature, sketch and sketch plane contained external references to the BOX assembly.

The MOTHERBOARD was opened from the BOX assembly. Additional features were added to the MOTHERBOARD part. The POWERSUPPLY was developed as a new part In-context of the BOX assembly. The BOX assembly design intent and requirements were verified by modifying the dimensions to the different sizes of the BOX configurations.

The MOTHERBOARD and POWERSUPPLY are only two of numerous components in the BOX assembly. They are partially complete but represent the overall dimensions of the final component. Electro-Mechanical assemblies contain parts fabricated from sheet metal. Fabricate the CABINET and BRACKET for the BOX assembly from sheet metal.

Sheet Metal Overview

Sheet metal manufactures create sheet metal parts from a flat piece of raw material. To produce the final part, the material is cut, formed, and folded. In SolidWorks, the material thickness does not change.

Talk to colleagues. Talk to sheet metal manufacturers. Review other sheet metal parts previously designed by your company. You need to understand a few basic sheet metal definitions before starting the next parts, CABINET and BRACKET.

The CABINET begins as a solid part. The Shell feature determines the material thickness. The Rip feature removes material at the edges to prepare for sheet metal bends. The Insert Sheet Metal Bends feature transforms the solid part into a sheet metal part.

The BRACKET begins as a sheet metal part. The Base Flange feature is the first feature in a sheet metal part. Create the Base Flange from a sketch. The material thickness and bend radius of the Base Flange are applied to all other sheet metal features in the part.

There are two design states for sheet metal parts:

- Formed.
- Flat.

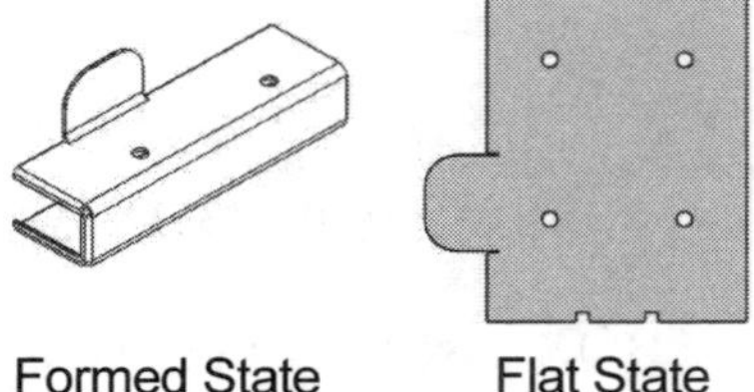

Formed State Flat State
BRACKET

Design the CABINET and BRACKET in the formed state. The Flatten feature creates the Flat Pattern for the manufactured flat state.

Sheet metal parts can be created from the flat state. Sketch a line on a face to indicate bend location. Insert the Sketched Bend feature to create the formed state.

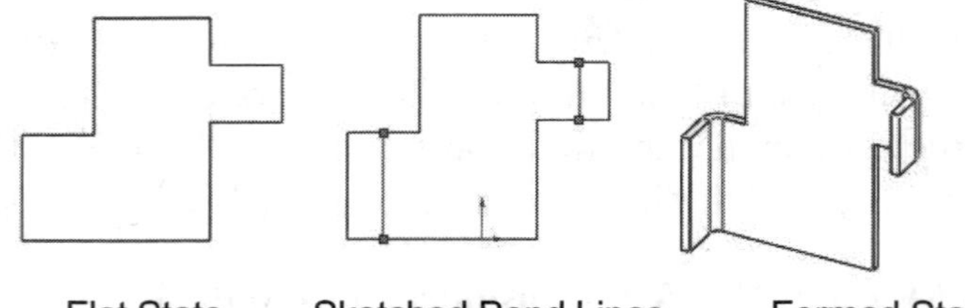

Flat State Sketched Bend Lines Formed State

Bends

Example: Use a flexible eraser, 50mm or longer. Bend the eraser in a U shape. The eraser displays tension and compression forces.

The area where there is no compression or tension is called the neutral axis or neutral bend line.

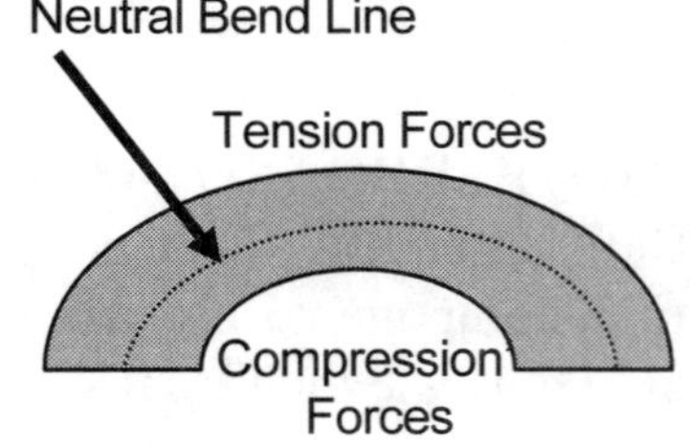

Eraser Example

Assume the material has no thickness. The length of the material formed into a 360° circle is the same as its circumference.

The length of a 90° bend would be ¼ of the circumference of a circle.

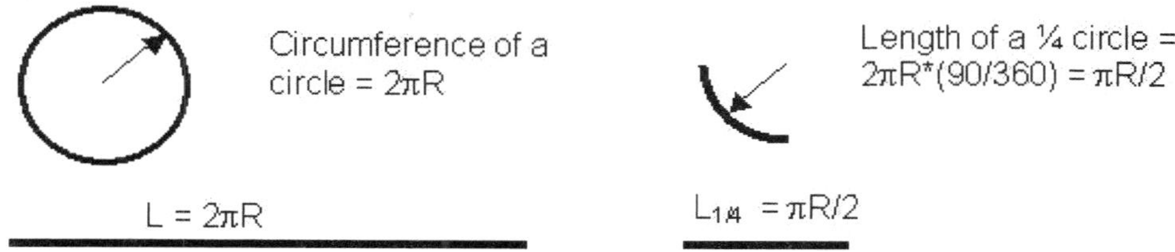

Length of 90° bend

In the real world, materials have thickness. Materials develop different lengths when formed in a bend depending on their thickness.

There are three major properties which determines the length of a bend:

- Bend radius.
- Material thickness.
- Bend angle.

The distance from the inside radius of the bend to the neutral bend line is labeled δ.

The symbol 'δ' is the Greek letter delta. The amount of flat material required to create a bend is greater than the inside radius and depends on the neutral bend line.

The true developed flat length L, is measured from the endpoints of the neutral bend line.

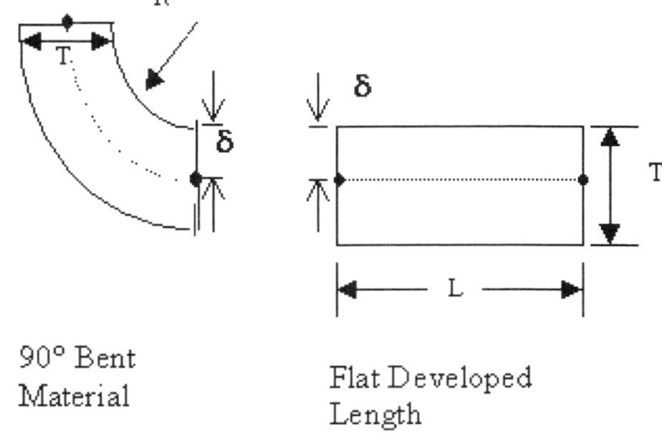

True developed flat length

Example:

T is the Material thickness.

Create a 90° bend with an inside radius of R:

$L = \frac{1}{2} \pi R + \delta T$

The ratio between δ and T is called the K-factor. Let K = 0.41 for Aluminum:

$K = \delta / T$

$\delta = KT = 0.41T$

$L = \frac{1}{2} \pi R + 0.41T$

U.S. Sheet metal shops use their own numbers.

Example:

One shop may use K = 0.41 for Aluminum, versus another shop uses K = 0.45.

Use tables, manufactures specifications or experience.

Save design time and manufacturing time. Work with your Sheet metal shop to know their K-factor. Material and their equipment produce different values. Build these values into the initial design.

Where do you obtain the material required for the Bend? The answer comes from the Sheet metal Flange position option. The four options are: Material Inside, Material Outside, Bend Outside and Bend from Virtual Sharp.

Material Inside: The outside edge of the Flange coincides with the fixed edge of the sheet metal feature.

Material Outside: The inside edge of the Flange coincides with the fixed edge of the sheet metal feature.

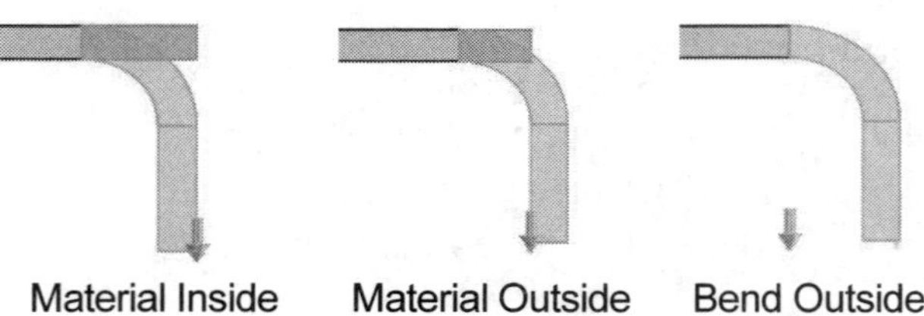

Bend Outside: The Flange is offset by the bend radius.

Bend from Virtual Sharp: The Flange maintains the dimension to the original edge and varies the bend material condition to automatically match with the flange's end condition.

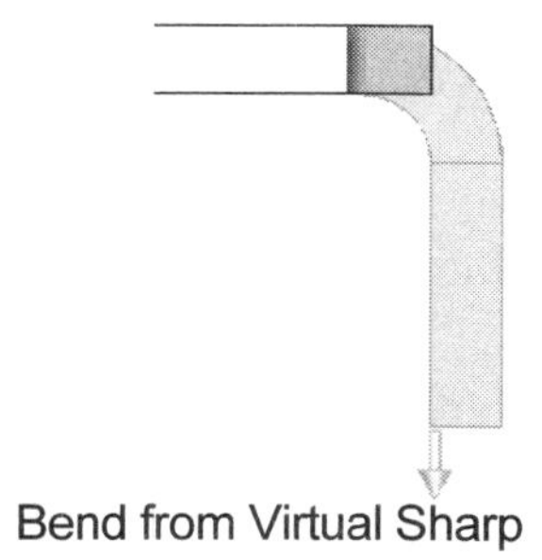

Relief

Sheet metal corners are subject to stress. Excess stress will tear material. Remove material to relieve stress with Auto Relief. The three options are: Rectangular, Tear and Obround.

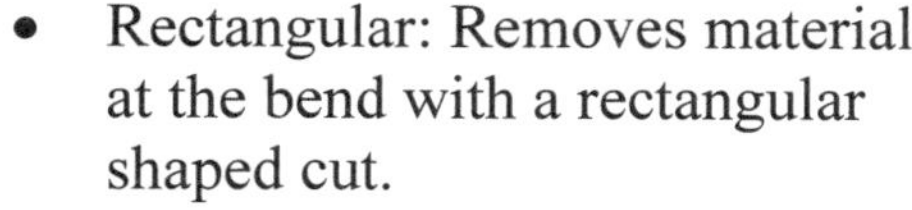

- Rectangular: Removes material at the bend with a rectangular shaped cut.

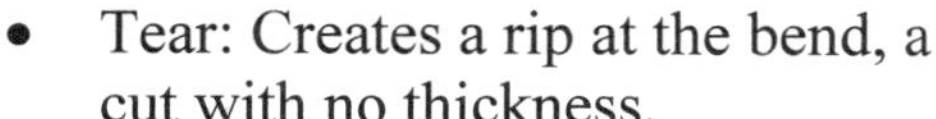

- Tear: Creates a rip at the bend, a cut with no thickness.

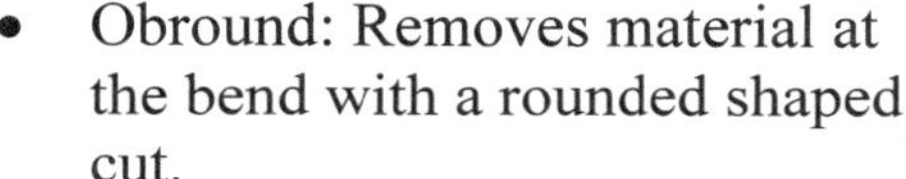

- Obround: Removes material at the bend with a rounded shaped cut.

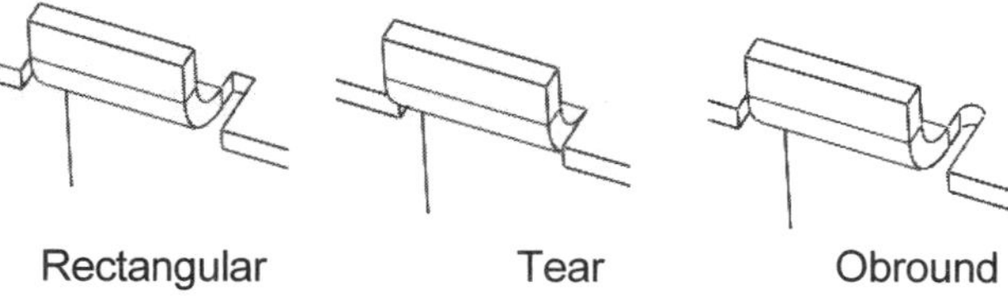

CABINET-Insert Component

Create the CABINET component inside the assembly and attach it to the Front Plane. The CABINET component references the Layout Sketch.

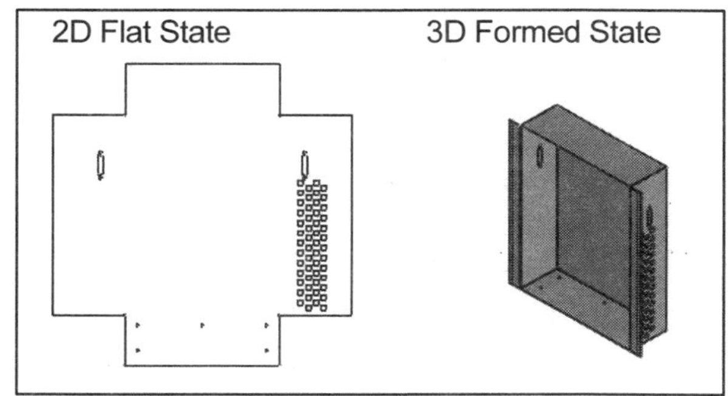

Create the CABINET component as a solid box. Shell the box to create the constant sheet metal thickness. Utilize the Rip feature to cut the solid edges. Utilize the Insert Bends feature to create a sheet metal part from a solid part.

Add additional sheet metal Edge Flange and Hem features. Add dies, louvers and cuts to complete the CABINET.

Utilize configurations to create the 3D formed state for the BOX assembly and the 2D flat state for the CABINET drawing.

Activity: CABINET-Insert Component

Insert the CABINET Component.

170) **Open** the BOX assembly.

171) Click **Insert**, **Component**, **New Part** from the Main menu.

Select the Part Template.

172) Double-click **PART-MM-ANSI** template.

Save the Part.

173) The Save As dialog box is displayed. Select **ENGDESIGN-W-SOLIDWORKS\PROJECTS** for the file folder. Enter **CABINET** in the Filename text box. Enter **CABINET FOR BOX** for Description.

174) Click **Save**.

The Component Pointer is displayed. The CABINET component is empty and requires a sketch plane. The Front Plane of the CABINET component is mated with the Front Plane of the BOX. CABINET is the name of the component created In-context of the BOX assembly.

Select the Sketch Plane.

175) Click the **Front Plane** of the BOX in the FeatureManager. The system automatically selects Sketch Sketch .

Create the Sketch.

176) Click the **right vertical edge** of the BOX.

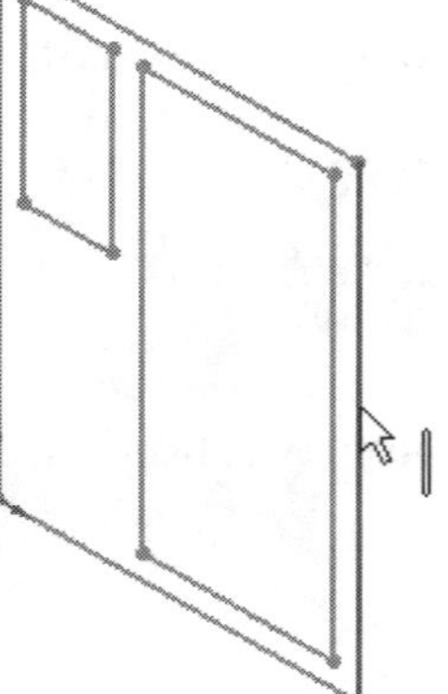

177) Click **Convert Entities** Convert . The Resolve Ambiguity dialog box is displayed.

178) Click **closed contour**.

179) Click **OK**. The outside perimeter is the current Sketch.

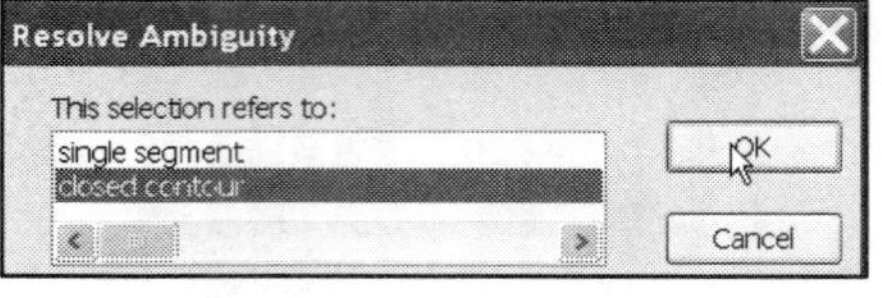

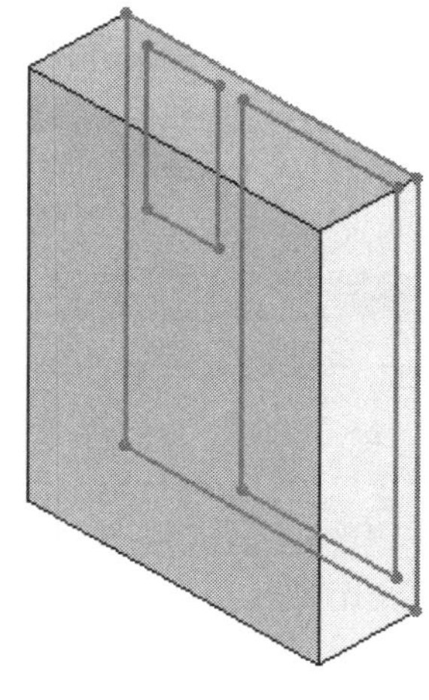

Extrude the Sketch.

180) Click **Extruded Boss/Base** .

181) Enter **100 Depth**.

182) Click **OK** from the Extrude PropertyManager.

Return to the BOX assembly.

183) Click **Edit Component**  from the Assembly toolbar.

Caution: Do not create unwanted geometry references. Open the part when creating features that require no references from the assembly. The features of the CABINET require no additional references from the BOX assembly, MOTHERBOARD or POWERSUPPLY.

Open the CABINET part.
184) Right-click **CABINET** from the FeatureManager.

185) Click **Open Part**.

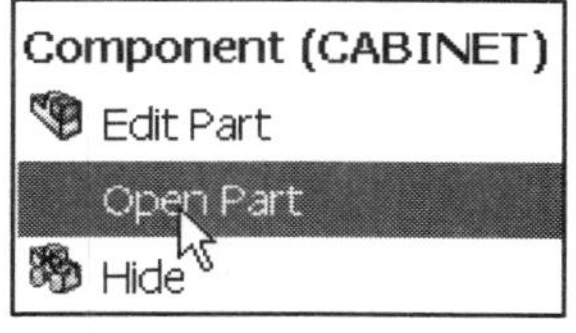

Fit the model to the Graphics window.
186) Press the **f** key.

187) Click the **Isometric view** .

Create the Shell.
188) Click the **front face** of the Extrude1 feature.

189) Click **Shell**  from the Features toolbar.

190) Check the **Shell outward** box.

191) Enter **1** mm for Thickness.

192) Click **OK** from the Shell PropertyManager.

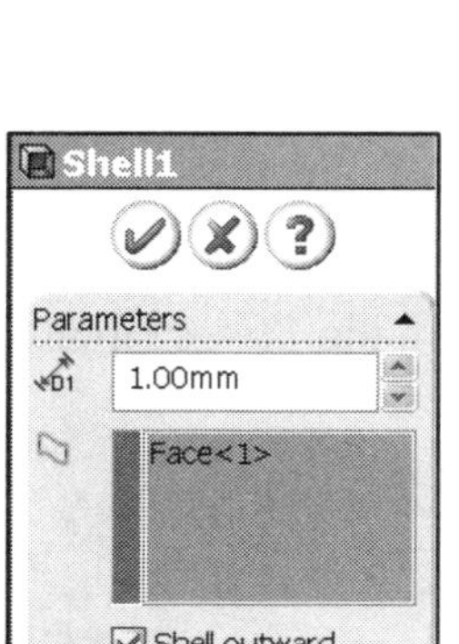

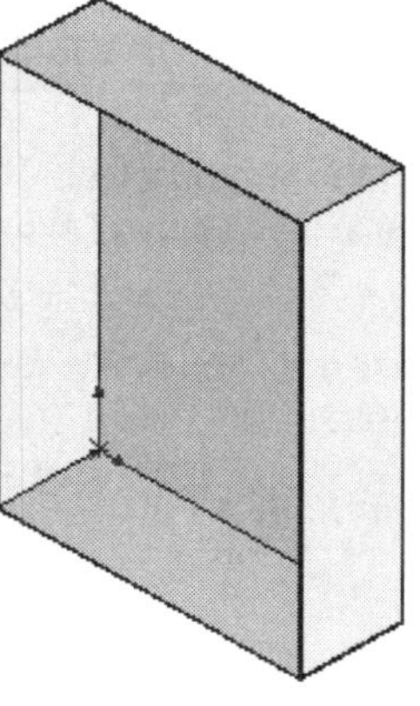

Display the Sheet metal toolbar in the Control Area.

193) Right-click in the **Control Area**. Click **Customize Menu**. Check **Sheet Metal**.

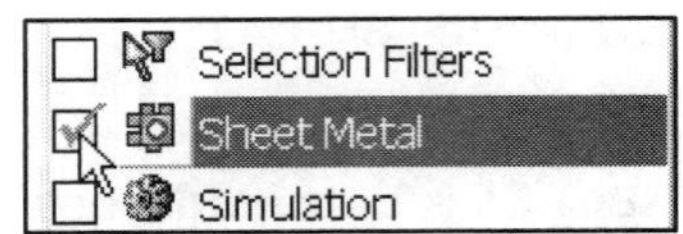

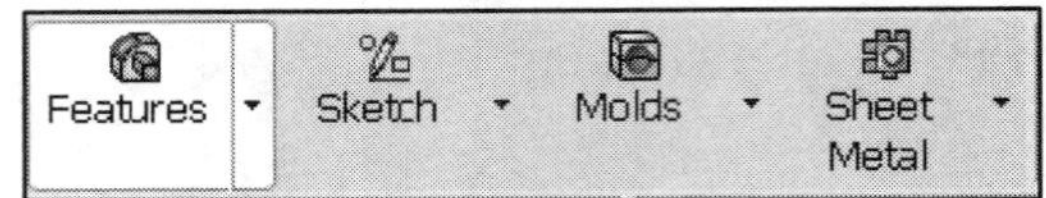

Maintain constant thickness. Sheet metal features only work with constant wall thickness. The Shell feature maintains constant wall thickness. The solid Extruded Base feature represents the overall size of the sheet metal CABINET. The CABINET part is solid. The Rip feature and Insert Sheet Metal Bends feature convert a shelled solid part into a sheet metal part.

CABINET-Rip Feature and Sheet Metal Bends

The Rip feature creates a cut of no thickness along the edges of the Extruded Base feature. Rip the Extruded Base feature along the four edges. The Bend feature creates sheet metal bends.

Specify bend parameters: bend radius, bend allowance and relief. Select the bottom face to remain fixed during bending and unbending. In the next example, you will create the Rip and the Insert Bend features in two steps. The Bends PropertyManager contains the Rip parameter. Utilize the Rip parameter to create a simple Rip and Bend in one step.

Activity: CABINET-Rip Feature and Sheet Metal Bends

Fit the model to the Graphics window.

194) Press the **f** key.

Insert a Rip. A Rip creates a gap between two edges in a sheet metal part.

195) Click **Rip** Rip from the Sheet Metal toolbar.

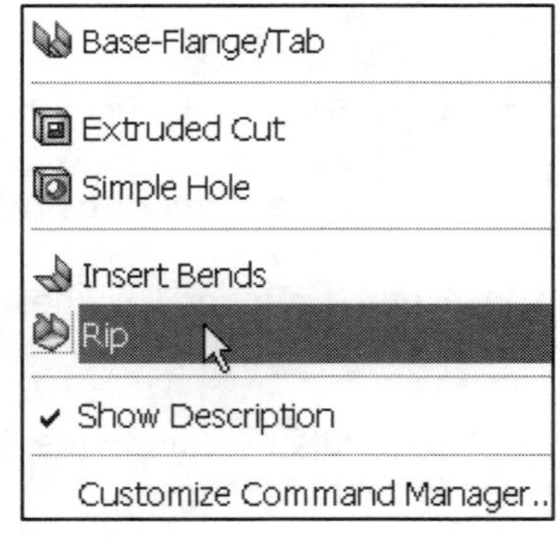

196) **Rotate** the part to view the inside edges.

197) Click **the inside lower left edge.**

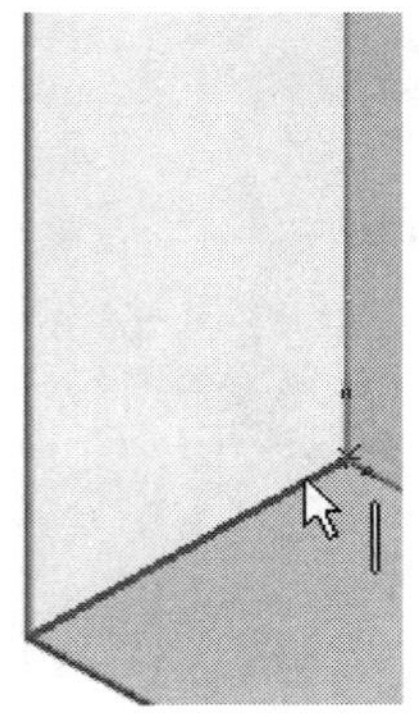

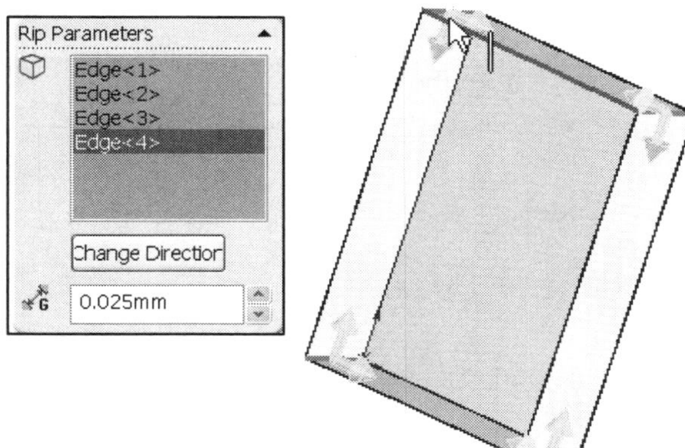

198) Click the **inside upper left edge**.

199) Click the **inside upper right edge**.

200) Click the **inside lower right edge**.

201) Click **OK** from the Rip PropertyManager.

202) Click **Isometric view**.

Insert the Sheet Metal Bends.

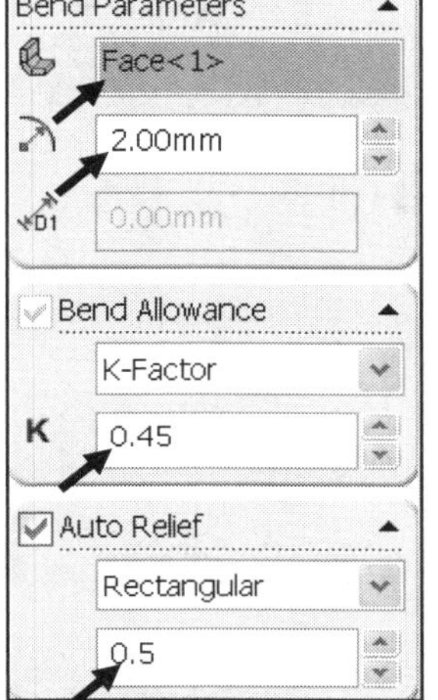

203) Click the inside **bottom face** to remain fixed.

204) Click **Insert Bends** Insert Bends from the Sheet metal toolbar.

205) Enter **2.00mm** for bend radius.

206) Enter **.45** for K-Factor. Enter **.5** for Rectangular Relief.

207) Click **OK** from the Bends PropertyManager.

208) Click **OK** to the message, "Auto relief cuts were made for one or more bends".

209) Zoom in on the Rectangular relief in the upper back corner.

Display the full view.

210) Click **Isometric** view. Click **Save**.

You just created your first sheet metal part. The .45 K-Factor is based on your machine shops parameters for Aluminum.

Save manufacturing cost and reduce setup time. A sheet metal manufacturer maintains a turret of standard relief tools for Rectangular and Obround relief. Obtain the dimensions of these tools to utilize in your design.

The CABINET part is in its 3D formed state. Display its 2D flat manufactured state. Test every feature to determine if the part can be manufactured as a sheet metal part. Alternate between 3D formed and 2D flat for every additional sheet metal feature you create. The Flatten feature alternates a sheet metal part between the flat state and formed state.

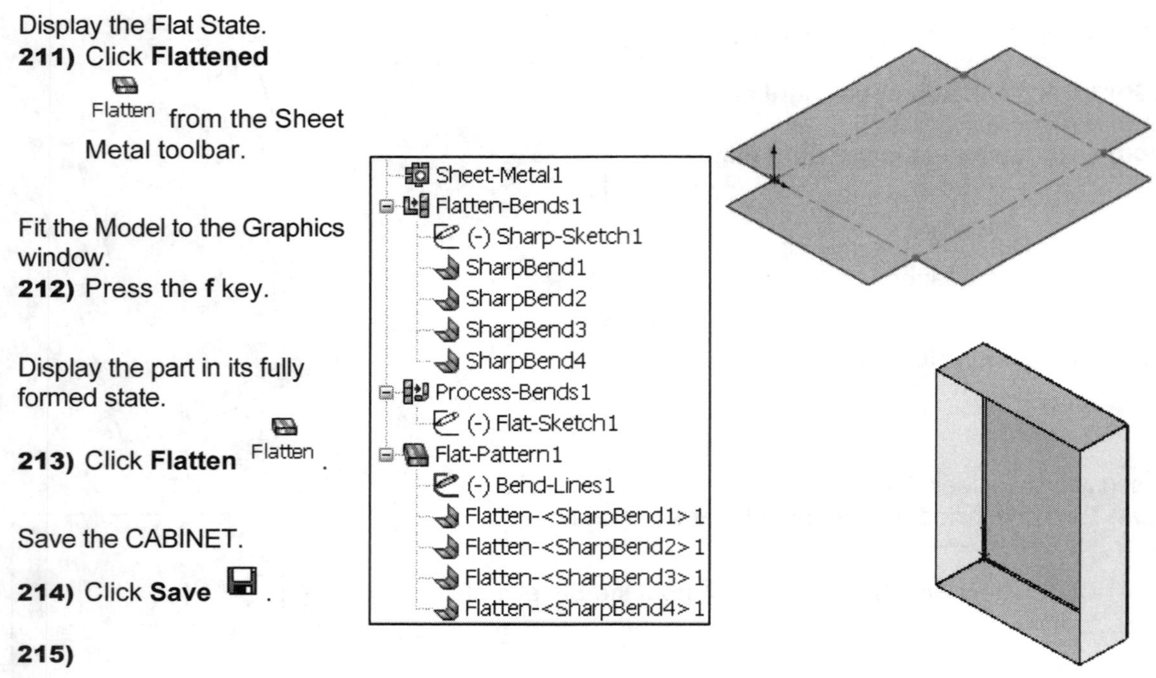

Display the Flat State.

211) Click **Flattened** Flatten from the Sheet Metal toolbar.

Fit the Model to the Graphics window.

212) Press the **f** key.

Display the part in its fully formed state.

213) Click **Flatten** Flatten.

Save the CABINET.

214) Click **Save**.

215)

Note: To return to the solid part, utilize the No Bends No Bends feature to roll back the model before the first sheet metal bend.

CABINET-Edge Flange

Create the right flange wall and left flange wall with the Edge Flange feature. The Edge Flange feature adds a wall to a selected edge of a sheet metal part.

Select the inside edges when creating bends.

Create the right hem and left hem with the Hem feature. The Hem feature folds back at an edge of a sheet metal part. A Hem can be open, closed, double or tear-drop.

Closed Open Tear Drop
Hem options

In the preliminary design stage, review Hem options with your sheet metal manufacturer.

Activity: CABINET-Edge Flange

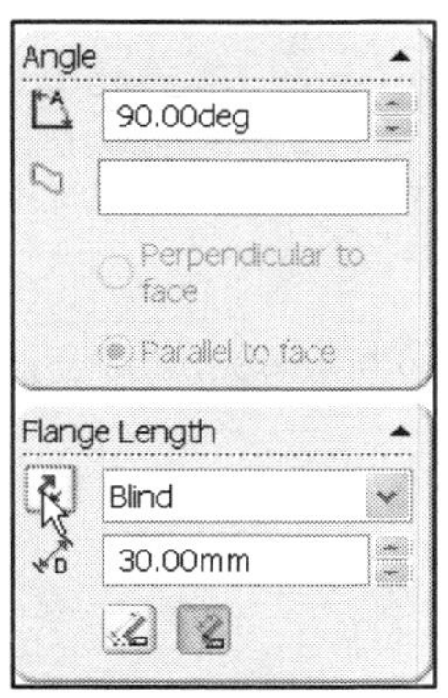

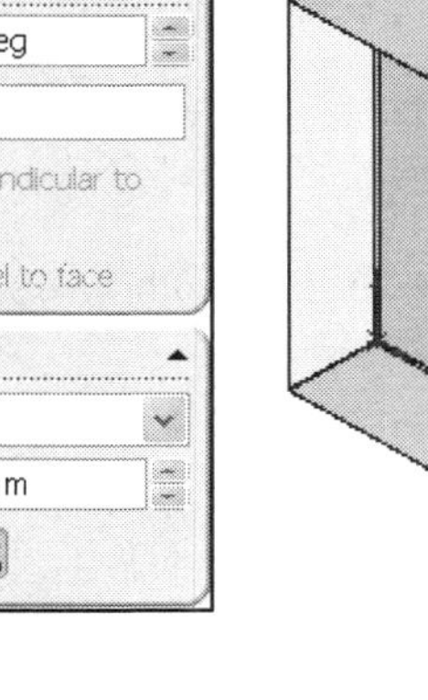

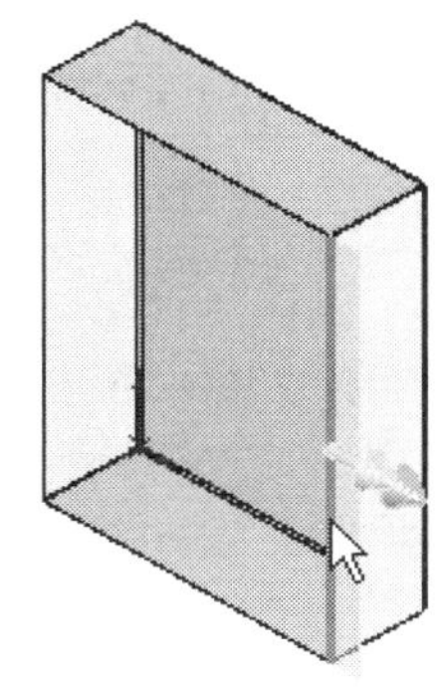

Insert the front right Flange.

216) Select the **front vertical right edge**.

217) Click **Edge Flange**  from the Sheet Metal toolbar.

218) Select **Blind** for Type. The feature direction arrow points towards the right.

219) Enter **30** for Length. Click the **Reverse Direction** button. The Direction arrow points towards the right. Accept all other defaults.

220) Click **OK** from the Edge-Flange PropertyManager.

Insert the right Hem.

221) Click **Front view**.

222) Select the **right edge** of the right flange.

223) Click **Hem** from the Sheet metal toolbar.

224) Click **Isometric view**.

225) Click the **Reverse Direction** button.

226) Enter **10** for Hem Length.

227) Enter **.10** for Gap Distance.

228) Click **OK** from the Hem PropertyManager.

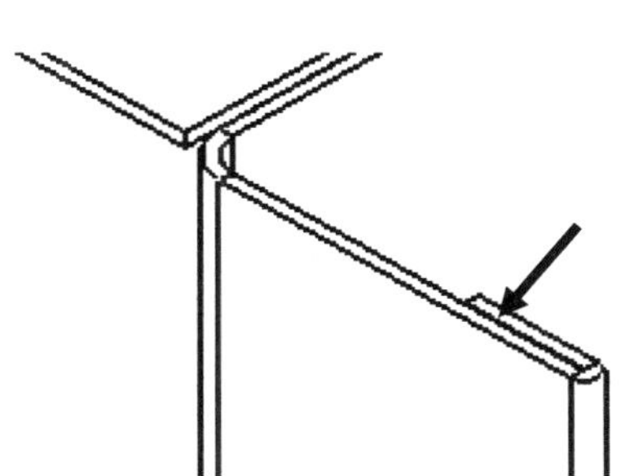

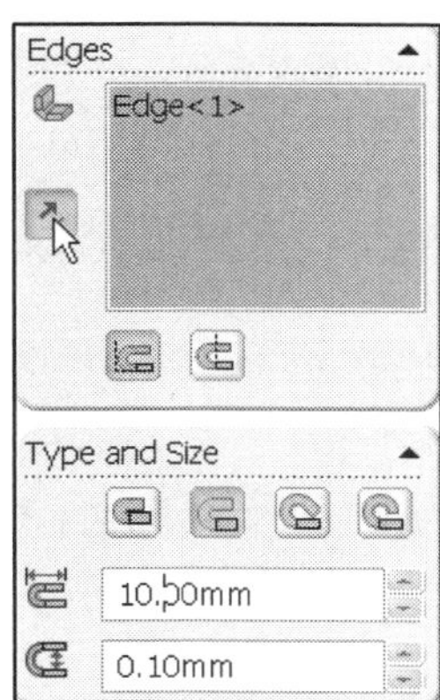

Insert the left Edge Flange wall.

229) Click **Front view**.

230) Select the **front vertical left edge**.

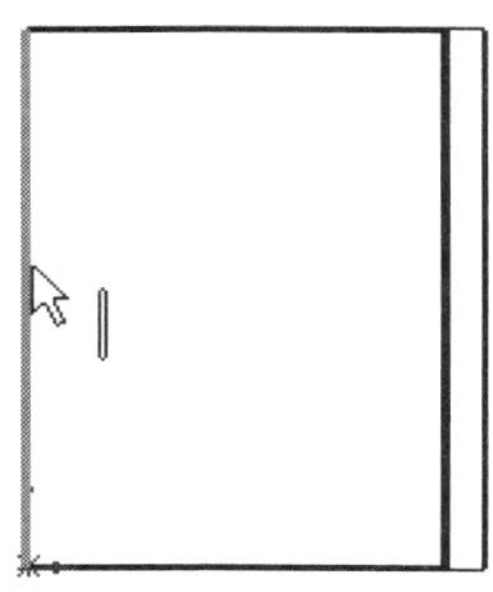

231) Click **Edge Flange** .

232) Select **Blind** for Type. The feature direction arrow points towards the left. Reverse the arrow direction if required.

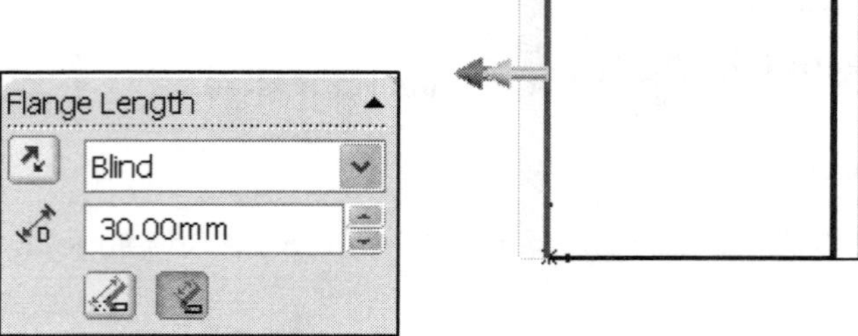

233) Enter **30** for Depth. Accept all other defaults.

234) Click **OK** from the Edge-Flange PropertyManager.

Insert the left edge Hem.

235) Select the **left edge** of the left flange.

236) Click **Isometric view**.

237) Click **Hem** from the Sheet metal toolbar.

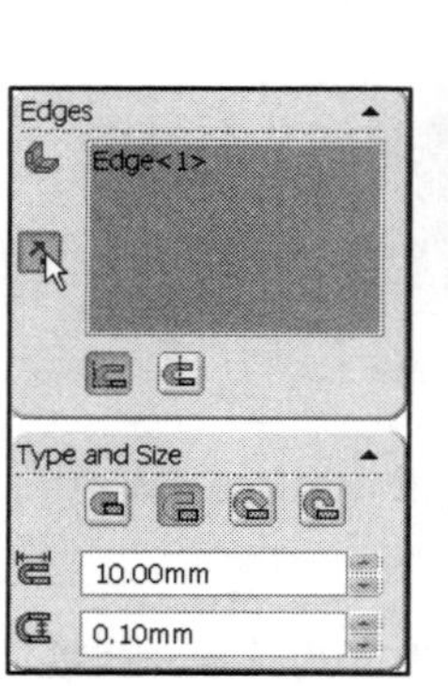

238) Click the **Reverse Direction** button.

239) Enter **.10** for Gap Distance.

240) Click **OK** from the Hem PropertyManager.

Display the part in its flat manufactured state and formed state.

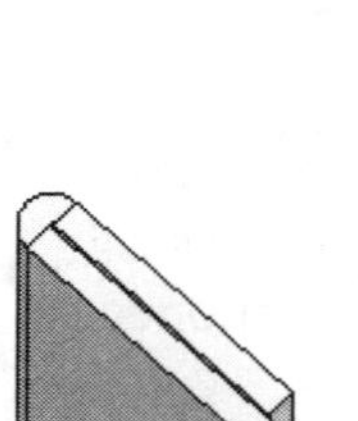

241) Click **Flatten** from the Sheet Metal toolbar.

242) Click **Top view**.

243) Click **Flatten** to display the part in its fully formed state.

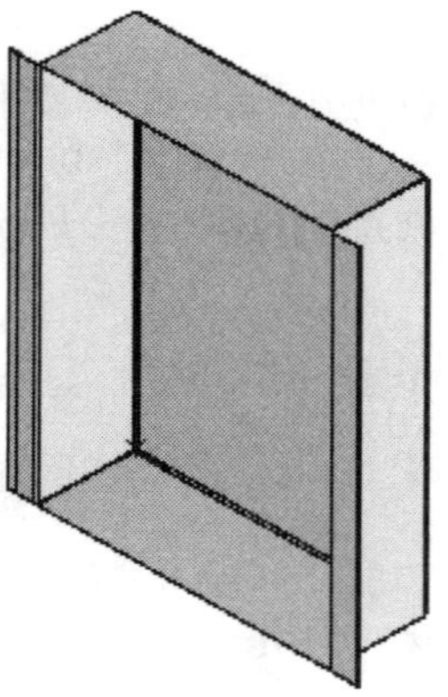

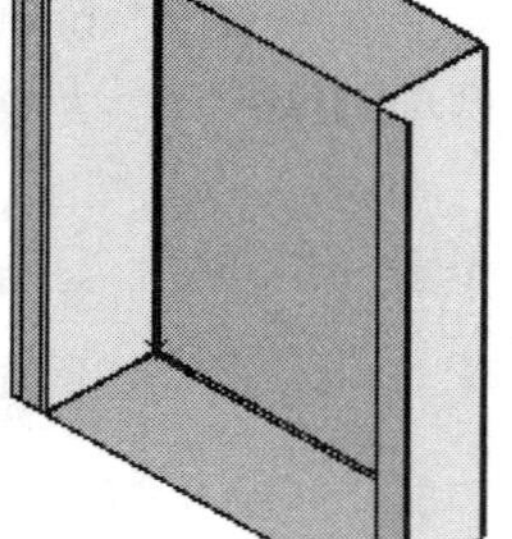

244) Click **Isometric view**.

245) Rename **Edge-Flange1** to **Edge-Flange1-Right**.

246) Rename **Edge-Flange2** to **Edge-Flange2-Left**.

247) Rename **Hem1** to **Hem1-Right**.

248) Rename **Hem2** to **Hem2-Left**.

Save the CABINET.

249) Click **Save**.

Simplify the FeatureManager. Sheet metal parts contain numerous flanges and hems. Rename features with descriptive names.

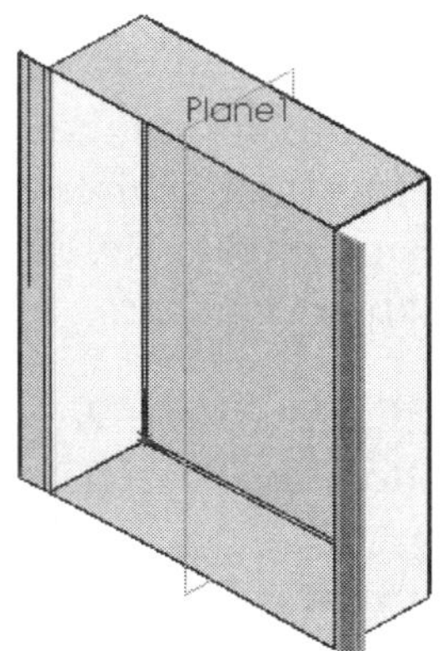

Save design time. Utilize Mirror Feature to mirror sheet metal features about a plane. Example: In a second design iteration, the Edge Flange1-Right and Hem1-Right are mirrored about Plane1.

The Mirror feature was not utilized in the CABINET. A Mirror Plane and Equations are required to determine the flange and hem locations.

Maintain the design intent. In the Top Down design process return to the Layout Sketch after inserting a new component to verify the assembly design intent.

Increase and decrease dimension values in the Layout Sketch. To avoid problems in a top level assembly, select the same face to remain fixed for the Flat Pattern and Bend/Unbend features. Save sheet metal parts in their 3D formed state.

The CABINET requires additional solid and sheet metal features. These features require no references in the BOX assembly. Work in the CABINET part.

CABINET-Hole Wizard and Linear Pattern

Sheet metal holes are created through a punch or drill process. Each process has advantages and disadvantages:

- Cost.
- Time.
- Accuracy.

Investigate a Linear Pattern of holes. Select a self-clinching threaded fastener that is inserted into the sheet metal during the manufacturing process. The fastener requires a thru hole in the sheet metal.

Holes should be of equal size and utilize common fasteners. Why? You need to insure a cost effect design that is price competitive. Your company must be profitable with their designs to insure financial stability and future growth.

Another important reason for fastener commonality and simplicity is the customer. The customer or service engineer does not want to supply a variety of tools for different fasteners.

A designer needs to be prepared for changes. You proposed two fasteners. Ask Purchasing to verify availability of each fastener. Select a M5 hole and wait for a return phone call from the Purchasing department to confirm. Design flexibility is key!

Dimension the hole position. Do not dimension to sheet metal bends. If the sheet metal manufacturer modifies the bend radius, the hole position does not maintain the design intent. Reference Hole1 dimensions by selecting the Origin in the FeatureManager.

Utilize the Hole Wizard feature to create a Thru Hole. Hole1 is positioned on the inside bottom face based on the selection point.

Activity: CABINET-Hole Wizard and Linear Pattern

Insert the first Hole.

250) **Open** the CABINET part.

Insert the Hole with the Hole Wizard.

251) Click the **inside bottom face**.

252) Click **Hole Wizard**  from the Features toolbar.

253) Click the **Hole** tab.

254) Select **ANSI Metric** for the Standard Property.

255) Select **M5.0** from the Size text box.

256) Select **Through All** for End Condition.

257) Click the **Positions** tab.

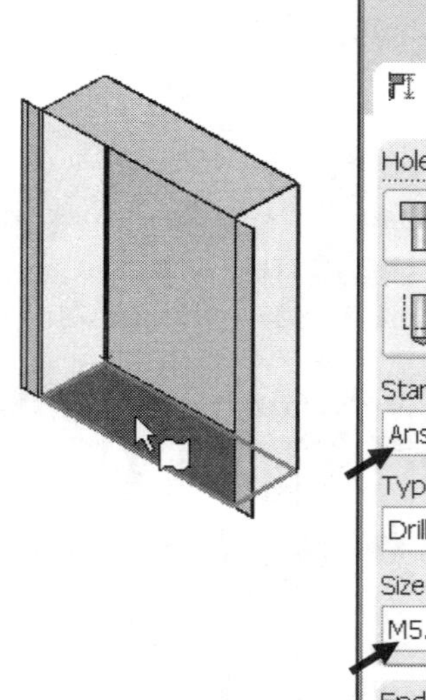

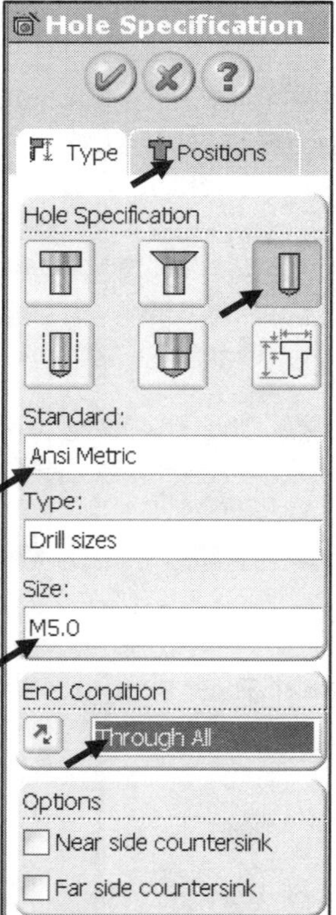

Dimension Hole1.

258) Click **Smart Dimension** Smart Dimens... .

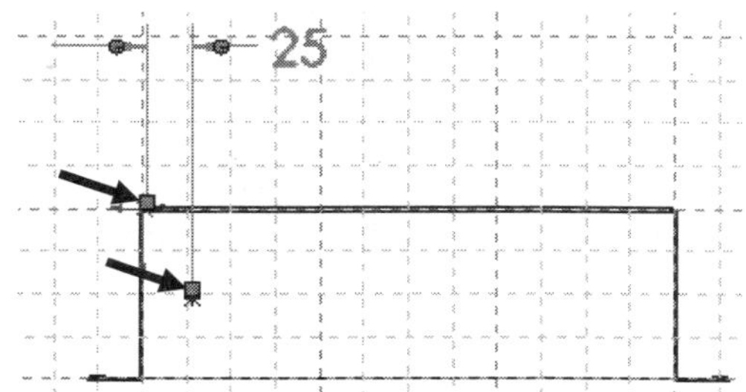

259) Click **Top view**. Click the **Origin** of the Extruded Base feature.

260) Click the Hole **center point**. Enter **25** for the horizontal dimension.

261) Expand the **CABINET** CABINET -> icon. Click the **Origin** from the FeatureManager.

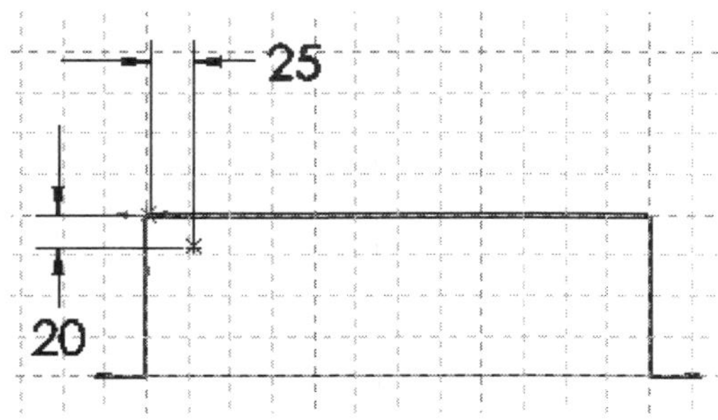

262) Click the Hole **center point**. Enter **20** for the vertical dimension.

263) Click **OK** from the Dimension PropertyManager. Click **OK** from the Hole-Position PropertyManager.

264) Click **Isometric view**.

265) Click **Save**.

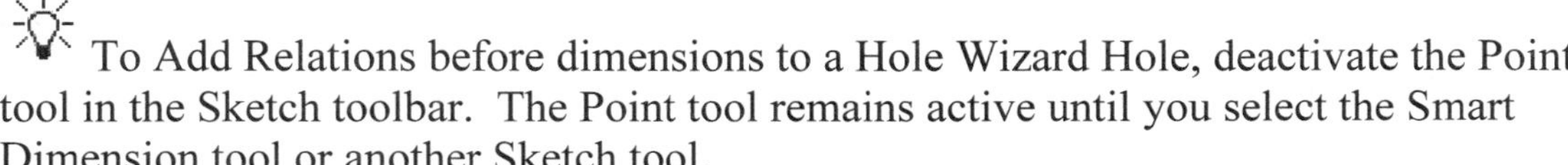

To Add Relations before dimensions to a Hole Wizard Hole, deactivate the Point tool in the Sketch toolbar. The Point tool remains active until you select the Smart Dimension tool or another Sketch tool.

Insert a Linear Pattern of Holes.

266) Click **Linear Pattern** Linear from the Features toolbar.

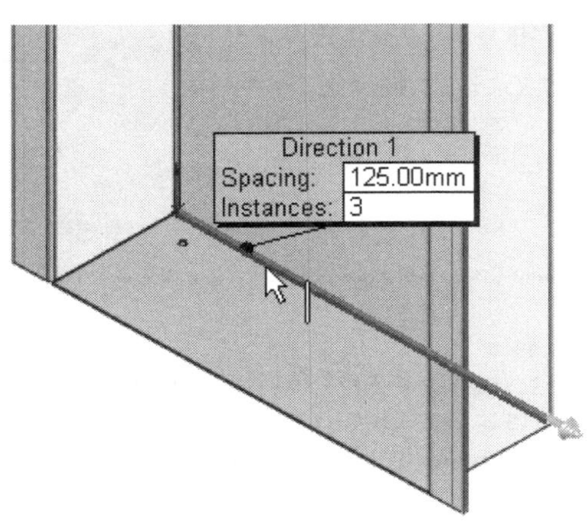

267) Click the **back inside edge** for the Direction 1 selected text box. The first direction arrow points to the right. Click the Reverse Direction button if required.

268) Enter **125** for Spacing.

269) Enter **3** for Number of Instances.

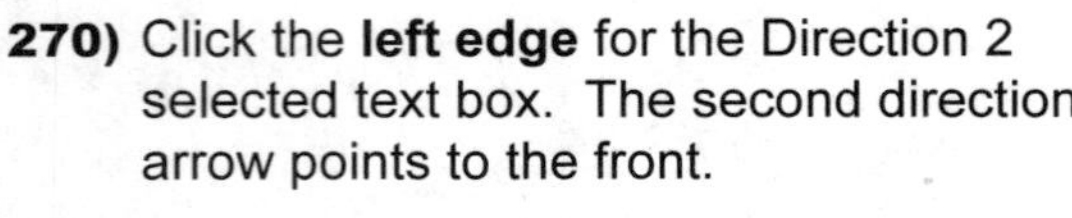

270) Click the **left edge** for the Direction 2 selected text box. The second direction arrow points to the front.

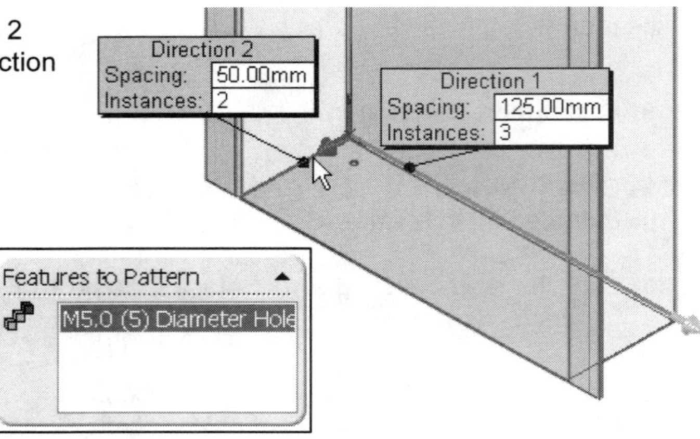

271) Enter **50** for Spacing.

272) Enter **2** for Number of Instances.

273) Click the **M5.0** from the FeatureManager.

Remove an Instance.

274) Click inside the **Instances to Skip** text box from the LPattern1 PropertyManager.

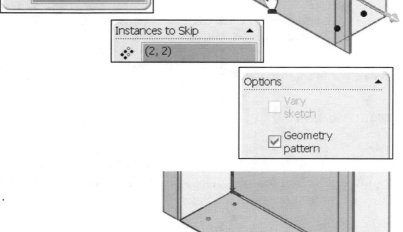

275) Click the **front middle hole** in the Graphics window.

276) Check the **Geometry pattern** check box.

277) Click **OK** from the Linear Pattern PropertyManager.

278) Click **Isometric view**.

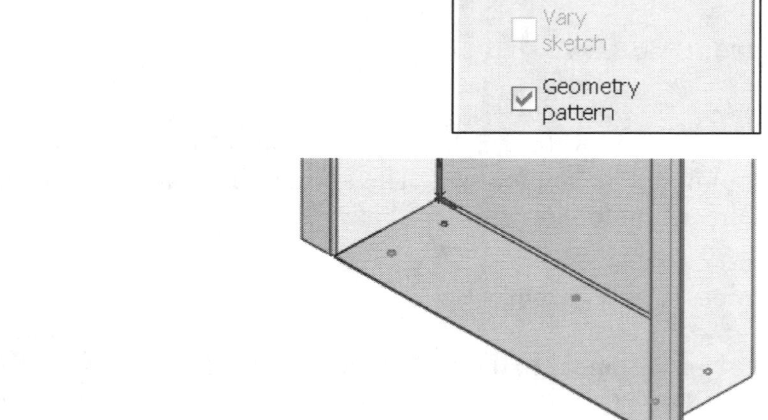

Save the CABINET.

279) Click **Save**.

Use the Geometry pattern option to improve system performance for sheet metal parts. The Geometry pattern option copies faces and edges of the seed feature. Type options such as Up to Surface are not copied.

The Instances to Skip option removes a selected instance from the pattern. The value (2, 2) represents the instance position in the first direction - second instance, second direction - second instance.

CABINET-Sheetmetal Library Feature

Sheet metal manufacturers utilize dies and forms to create specialty cuts and shapes. The Design Library contains information on dies and forms. The Design Library, features folder contains examples of predefined sheet metal shapes. Insert a die cut on the right wall of the CABINET. The die cut is for a data cable. The team will discuss sealing issues at a later date.

Activity: CABINET-Sheetmetal Library Feature

Insert a Sheetmetal Library Feature.

280) Check **View**, **Task Pane** from the Main menu.

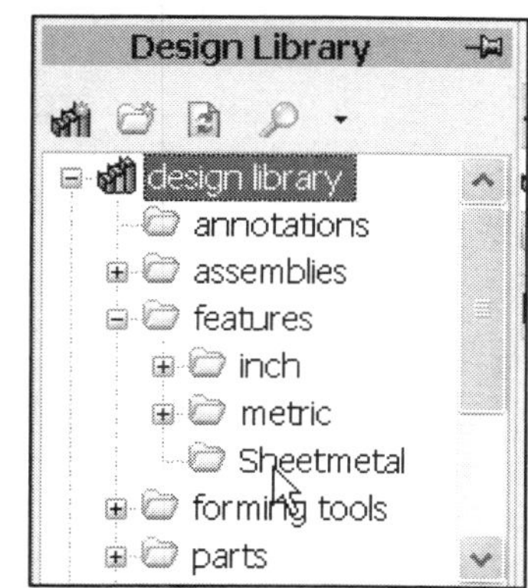

281) Click **design library**.

282) **Expand** Design Library.

283) **Expand** features.

284) Click the **Sheetmetal** folder.

285) Click and drag the **d-cutout** to the Graphics window.

286) Release the mouse button on the **right flange outside face** of the CABINET.

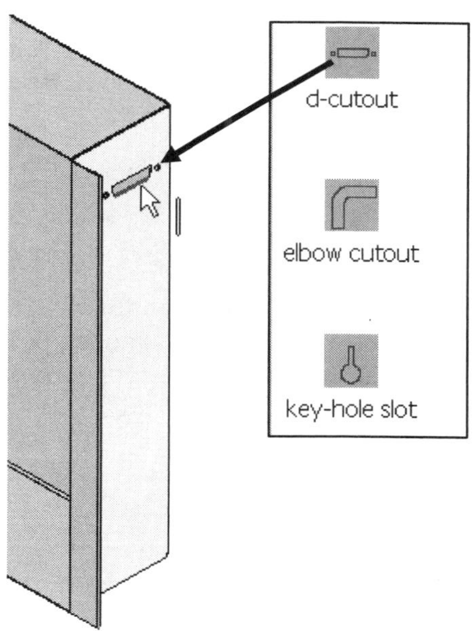

Edit the Sketch.

287) Click the **Edit Sketch** Edit Sketch button from the d-cutout PropertyManager. The Library Feature Profile dialog box is displayed. DO NOT SELECT THE FINISH BUTTON.

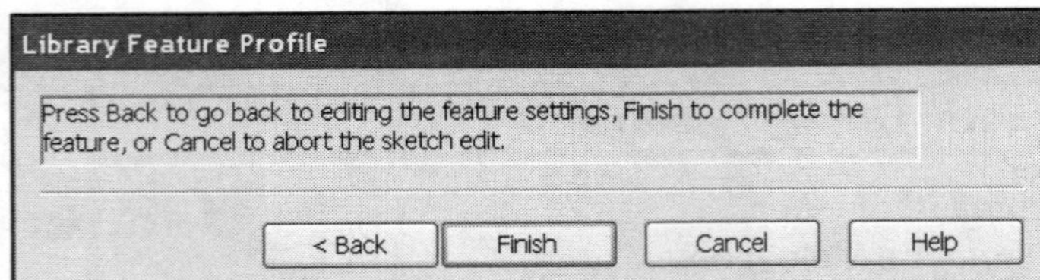

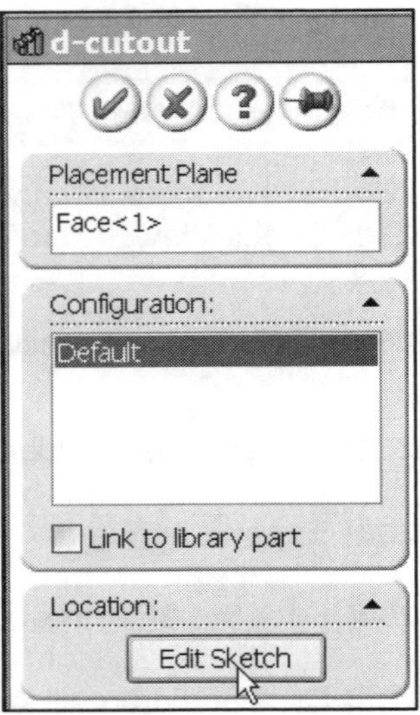

Rotate the d-cutout.

288) **Expand** CABINET in the Graphics Window.

289) Click **Tools**, **Sketch Tools**, **Modify** Modify... from the Main menu. The mouse pointer displays the modify move/rotate icon.

290) Right-click a **position** to the right of the sketch. Drag the mouse pointer counter clockwise to rotate the sketch 90°.

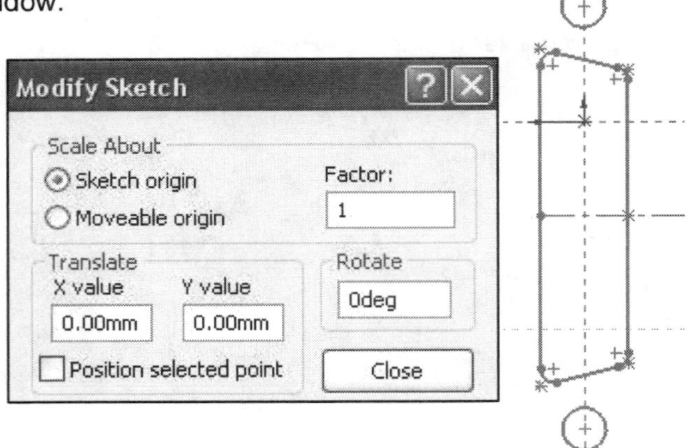

291) Click **Close**.

Display the Right view.

292) Click **Right view** .

293) Zoom to Area on the d-cutout.

Dimension the d-cutout.

294) Click **Smart Dimension** Smart Dimens....

Create a vertical dimension.

295) Click the **mid point** of the d-cutout.

296) Expand the **CABINET** CABINET -> FeatureManager.

297) Click the **Origin** of the CABINET from the FeatureManager.

298) Enter **320**.

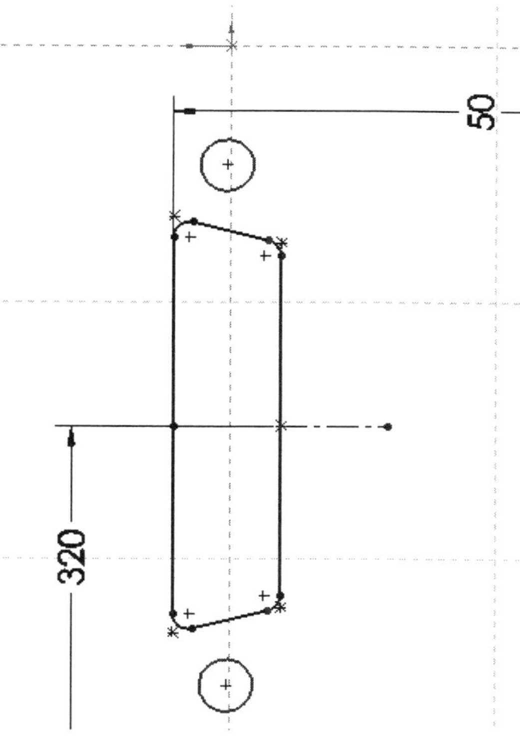

Create a horizontal dimension.

299) Click the **left vertical line** of the d-cutout.

300) Expand the **CABINET** CABINET -> FeatureManager.

301) Click the **Origin** of the CABINET from the FeatureManager.

302) Enter **50**.

303) Click **Finish**. The d-cutout entry is displayed in the FeatureManager.

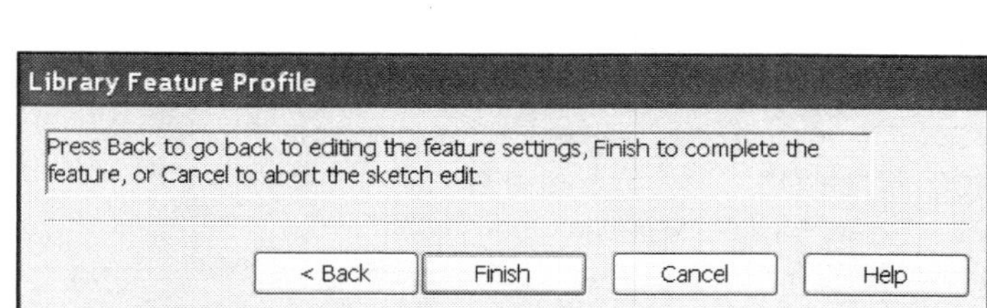

304) Click **Isometric view** .

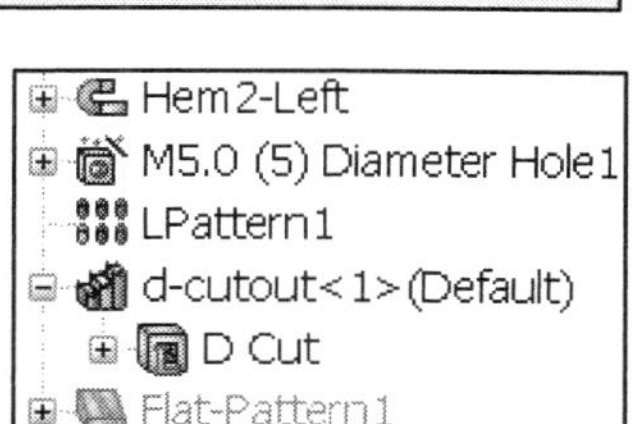

305) Click **Save** .

With thin sheet metal parts, select the dimension references with care. Use the Zoom and Rotate commands to view the correct edge. Use reference planes or the Origin to create dimensions. The Origin and planes do not change during the flat and formed states.

Save time with the Modify Sketch tool. Utilize the left and right mouse point positioned on the large black dots. The left button Pans and the right button Rotates. The center dot reorients the Origin of the sketch and Mirrors the sketch about y, x or both.

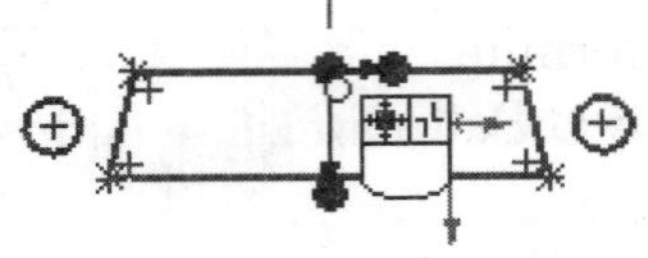

The d-cutout goes through the right and left side. Through All is the current Type option. This is not the design intent. Redefine the end condition through the right flange.

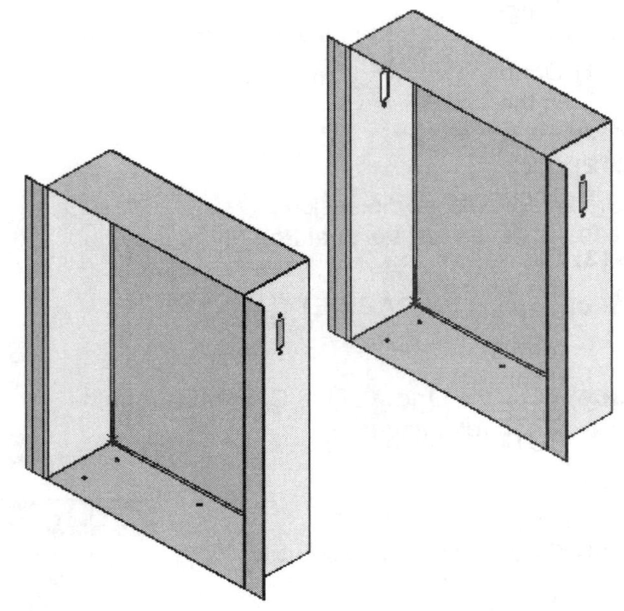

Modify the D-Cut End Condition.

306) Right-click **D Cut** D Cut in the FeatureManager.

307) Click **Edit Feature**. Click **Up To Next** from the End Condition drop down list.

308) Click **Isometric view**.

309) Click **OK** from the D Cut PropertyManager.

The D-Cut feature is positioned before the Flat Pattern1 icon in the FeatureManager. The D-Cut is incorporated into the Flat Pattern. The sheet metal manufacturing process is cost effective to perform cuts and holes in the flat state.

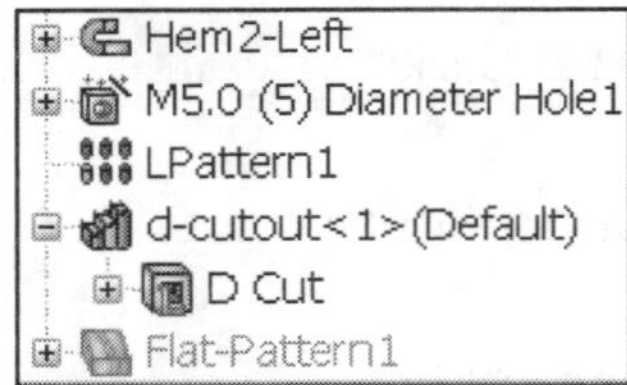

CABINET-Louver Forming Tool

Form features, such as louvers are added in the formed state. Formed features are normally more expensive than cut features. Louvers are utilized to direct air flow. The louvers are used to dissipate the heat created by the internal electronic components.

The forming tools folder contains numerous sheet metal forming shapes. In SolidWorks, the forming tools are inserted after the Bends are processed. Suppress forming tools in the Flat Pattern.

Activity: CABINET-Louver Forming Tool

Insert a Louver Forming Tool.

310) Press the right **Arrow key** approximately 5 times to display the inside right flange.

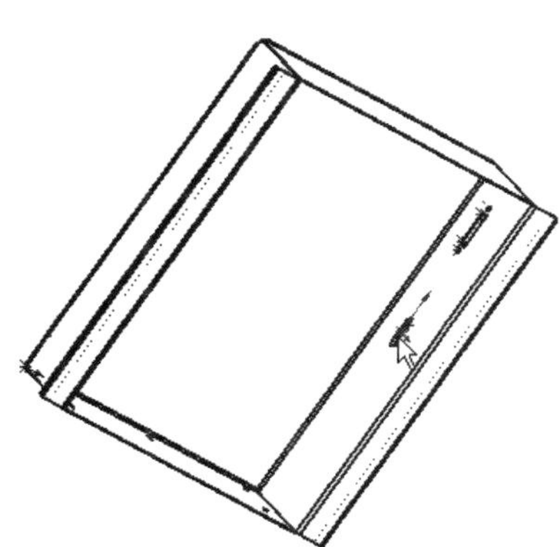

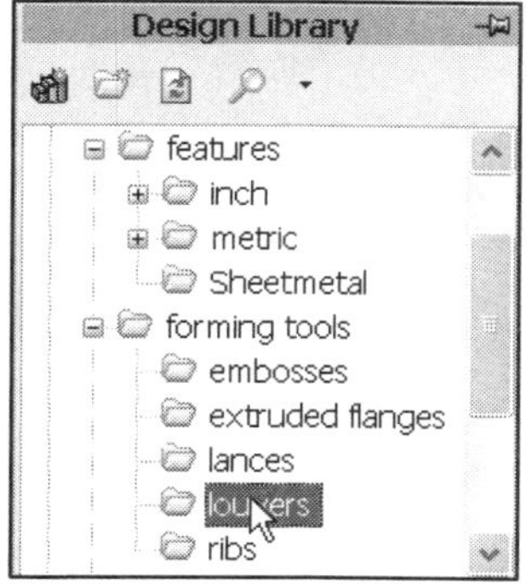

311) Double-click **forming tools** in the Design Library menu.

312) Click the **louvers** folder. The louver is displayed.

313) Click and drag the **louver** to the inside right flange of the CABINET. The Position form feature dialog box is displayed. Note: DO NOT SELECT THE FINISH BUTTON AT THIS TIME.

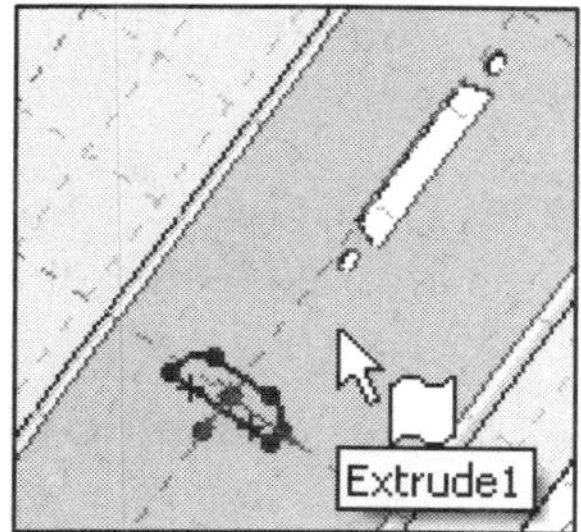

Rotate the Louver.

314) Click **Tools**, **Sketch Tools**, **Modify** Modify... from the Main menu. Right-click a **position** to the right of the sketch. Drag the mouse pointer clockwise to rotate the sketch 90°.

315) Click **Close**. Click **Right view**.

Dimension the Louver.

316) Click **Smart Dimension** .

317) Click the **Origin** of the CABINET in the FeatureManager.

318) Click the **horizontal centerline** of the Louver.

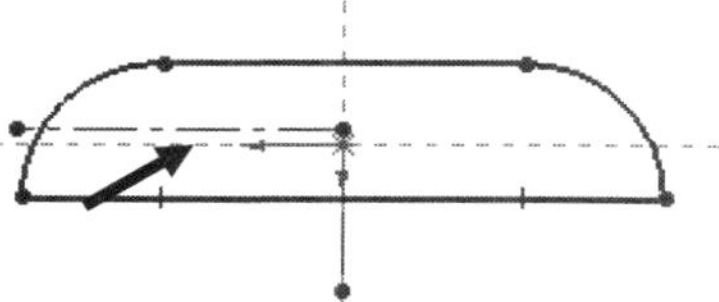

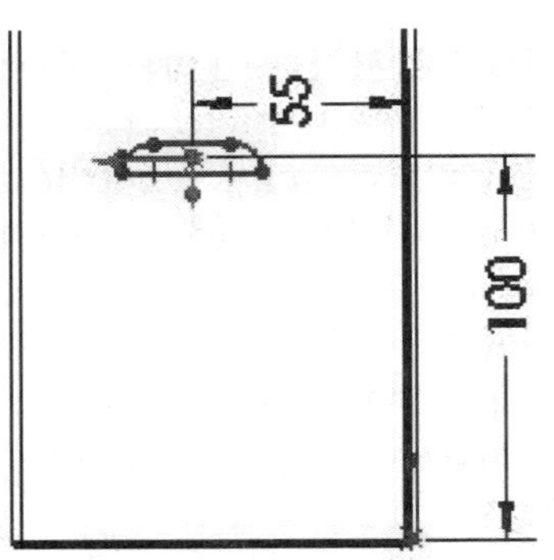

319) Enter **100** for the vertical dimension.

320) Click the **Origin** of the CABINET in the FeatureManager. Click the **vertical centerline** of the Louver.

321) Enter **55** for the horizontal dimension.

Display the Louver.

322) Click **Finish** Position Form Feature dialog box.

323) Press the **f** key.

Add a Linear Pattern of Louvers.

324) Click **Features** Features, **Linear Pattern** Linear. Click the **back vertical edge CABINET** for Direction 1.

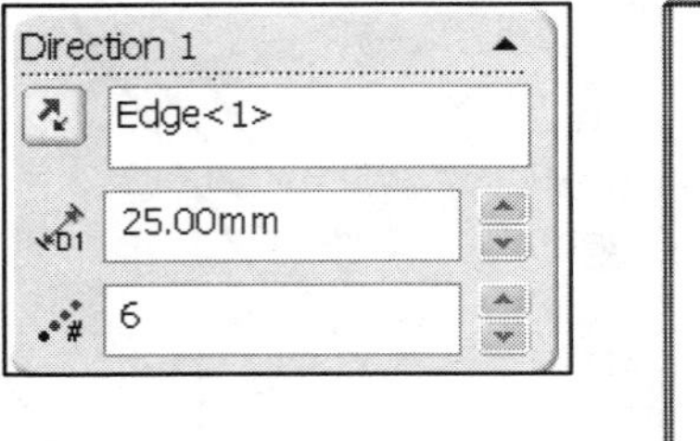

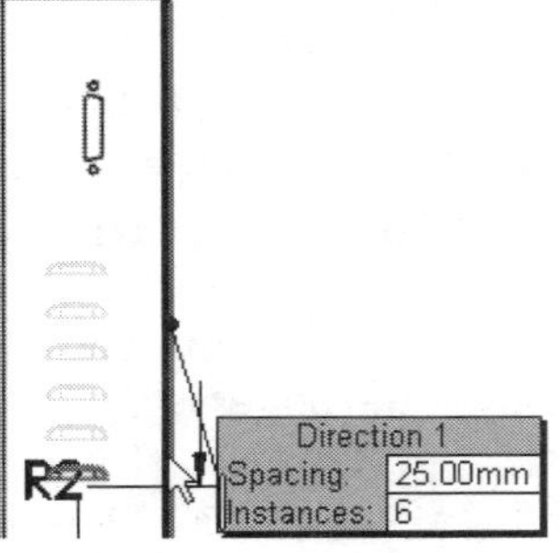

325) Enter **25** for Spacing. Enter **6** for Number of Instances. Flip the Direction arrow upward if required.

326) Click **OK** from the LPattern2 PropertyManager.

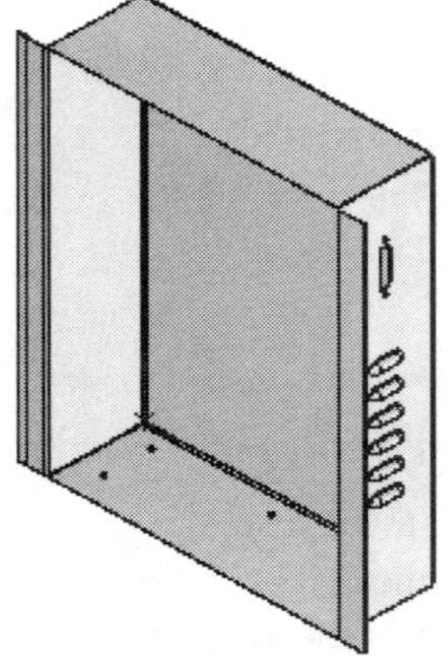

327) Click **Isometric view** .

Save the CABINET.

328) Click **Save** .

Manufacturing Considerations

How do you determine the size and shape of the louver form? Are additional die cuts or forms required in the project? Work with a sheet metal manufacturer. Ask questions. What are the standards? Identify the type of tooling in stock? Inquire on form advantages and disadvantages.

One company that has taken design and form information to the Internet is Lehi Sheetmetal, Westboro, MA. (www.lehisheetmetal.com).

Standard dies, punches and manufacturing equipment such as brakes and turrets are listed in the Engineering helpers section.

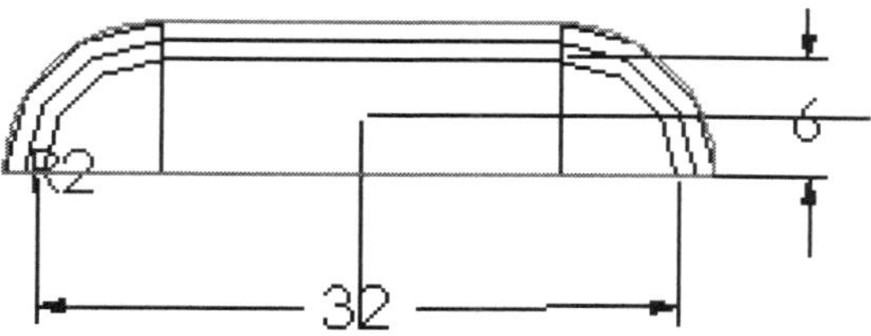

Dimensions are provided for their standard forms. The form tool you used for this project creates a 32mm x 6mm louver. The tool is commercially available.

Your manufacturer only stocks 3in., (75mm) and 4in., (100mm) louvers. Work with the sheet metal manufacturer to obtain a cost effective alternative. Create a pattern of standard square cuts to dissipate the heat.

If a custom form is required, most custom sheet metal manufacturers can accommodate your requirement. Example: Wilson Tool, Great Bear Lake, MN (www.wilsontool.com).

However, you will be charged for the tool. How do you select material? Consider the following:

- Strength
- Fit
- Bend Characteristics
- Weight
- Cost

All of these factors influence material selection. Raw aluminum is a commodity. Large manufacturers such as Alcoa and Reynolds sell to a material supplier, such as *Pierce Aluminum.

ALUMINUM SHEET
NON HEAT TREATABLE, 1100-0
QQ-A-250/1 ASTM B 209

All thickness and widths available from coil for custom blanks

SIZE IN INCHES	WGT/SHEET
.032 x 36 x 96	11.05
.040 x 36 x 96	13.82
.040 x 48 x 144	27.65
.050 x 36 x 96	17.28
.050 x 48 x 144	34.56
.063 x 36 x 96	21.77
.063 x 48 x 144	43.55
.080 x 36 x 96	27.65
.080 x 48 x 144	55.30
.090 x 36 x 144	46.66
.090 x 48 x 144	62.26
.100 x 36 x 96	34.56
.125 x 48 x 144	86.40
.125 x 60 x 144	108.00
.190 x 36 x 144	131.33

*Courtesy of Piece Aluminum Co, Inc.
Canton, MA

Pierce Aluminum in turn, sells material of different sizes and shapes to distributors and other manufacturers. Material is sold in sheets or cut to size in rolls. U.S. Sheet metal manufacturers work with standard 8ft – 12ft stock sheets. For larger quantities, the material is usually supplied in rolls. For a few cents more per pound, sheet metal manufacturers request the supplier to shear the material to a custom size.

Check Dual Dimensioning from Tools, Options Document Properties to display both Metric and English units. Do not waste raw material. Optimize flat pattern layout by knowing your sheet metal manufacturers equipment.

Discuss options for large cabinets that require multiple panels and welds. In Project 1, you were required to be cognizant of the manufacturing process for machined parts.

In Project 4 and 5 you created and purchased parts and recognized the Draft feature required to manufacture plastic parts.

Whether a sheet metal part is produced in or out of house, knowledge of the materials, forms and layout provides the best cost effective design to the customer.

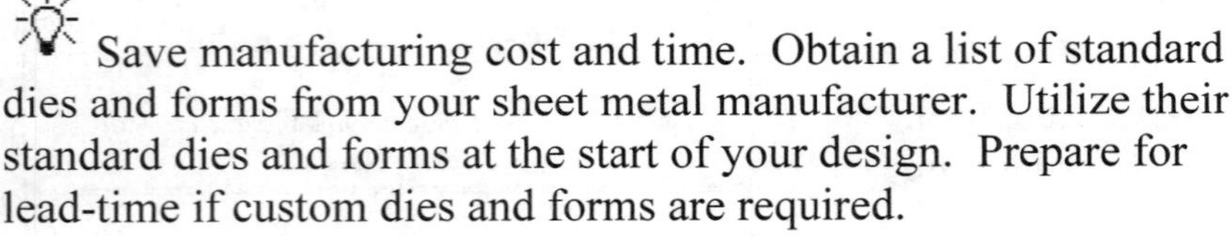

Save manufacturing cost and time. Obtain a list of standard dies and forms from your sheet metal manufacturer. Utilize their standard dies and forms at the start of your design. Prepare for lead-time if custom dies and forms are required.

You require both a protective and cosmetic finish for the Aluminum BOX. Review options with the sheet metal vendor. Parts are anodized. Black and clear anodized finishes are the most common. In harsh environments, parts are covered with a protective coating such as Teflon® or Halon®.

The finish adds thickness to the material. A few thousandths could cause problems in the assembly. Think about the finish before the design begins.

Your sheet metal manufacturer suggests a pattern of square cuts replace the Louvers for substantial cost savings.

Suppress the Louver. The Linear Pattern is a child of the Louver. The Linear Pattern is suppressed. Utilize the Sketch Linear Step and Repeat option.

Activity: Manufacturing Considerations-Sketch Linear Pattern

Suppress the Louver.

329) Right-click **louver1** from the FeatureManager.

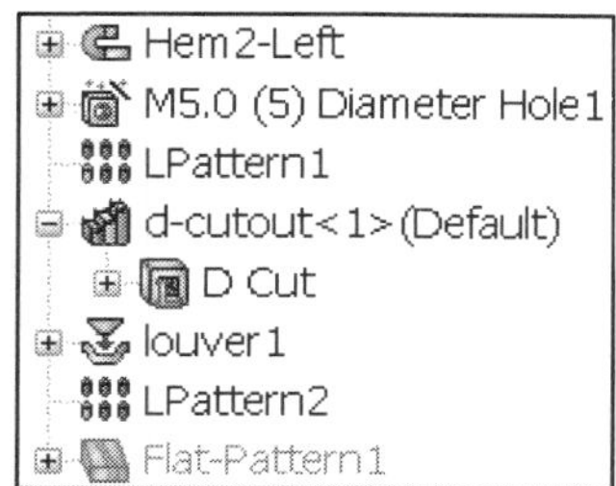

330) Click **Suppress** Suppress.

Sketch the profile of squares.

331) Click **Right view**.

332) Click the **CABINET right face** in the Graphics window.

333) Click **Sketch** Sketch.

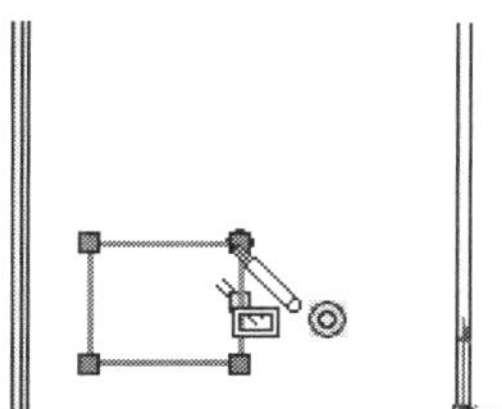

Create the first square.

334) Click **Rectangle** Rectan... . Sketch a **square** in the lower left corner.

Add dimensions.

335) Click **Smart Dimension** Smart Dimens... . Create a vertical and horizontal **10**mm dimension.

336) Click the **Origin**. Click the **bottom horizontal line** the square. Click a **position** to the left of the profile. Enter **10**.

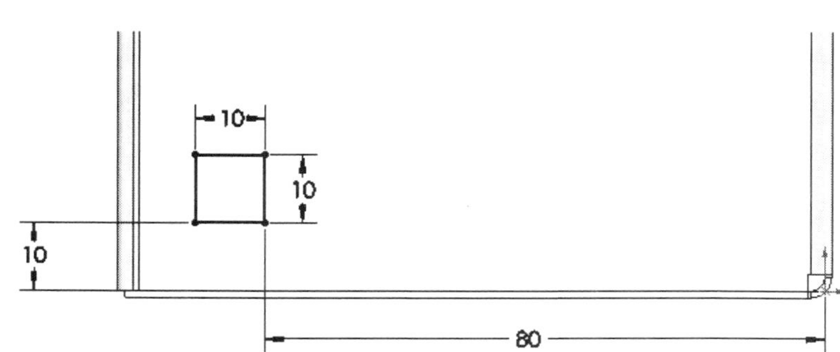

Create a horizontal dimension.

337) Click the **Origin** for the dimension reference.

338) Click the **right vertical line** of the square.

339) Click a position **below** the profile. Enter **80**.

Create a second square.

340) Click **Rectangle** Rectan... . Sketch a **square diagonal** to the right of the first square.

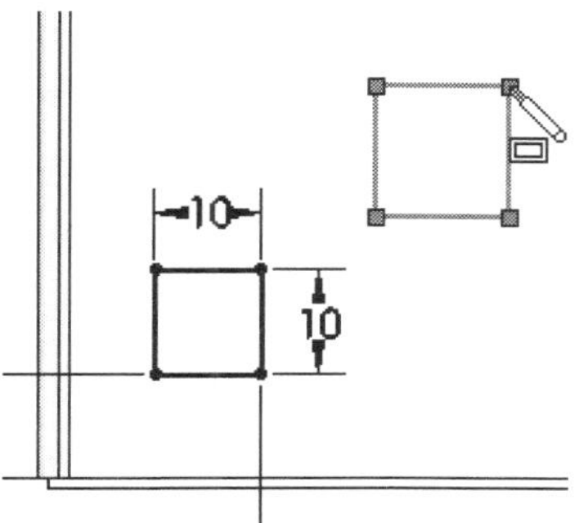

Create a horizontal dimension.

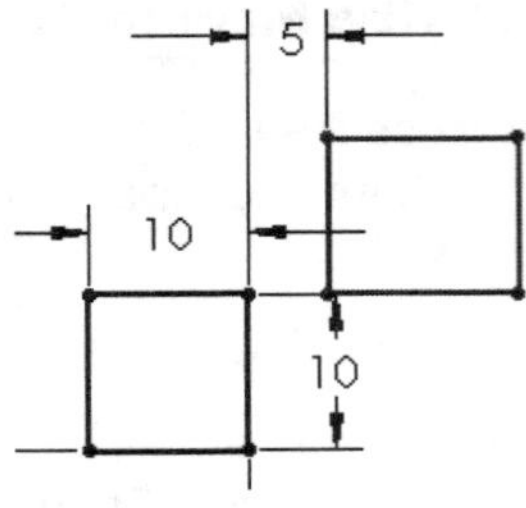

341) Click **Smart Dimension** Smart Dimens.... Click the **right vertical** line of the first box.

342) Click the **left vertical** line of the second box. Enter **5**.

Add an Equal Relation.

343) Right-click **Select**. Click the **top line** of the second square. Hold the **Ctrl key** down. Click the **left line** of the second square.

Release the **Ctrl** key. Click **Equal** =. Click **OK** from the PropertyManager.

Add an Equal Relation.

344) Click the **top horizontal line** of the first square. Hold the **Ctrl key** down. Click the **top horizontal line** of the second square. Release the **Ctrl** key.

345) Click **Equal**. Click **OK** from the PropertyManager.

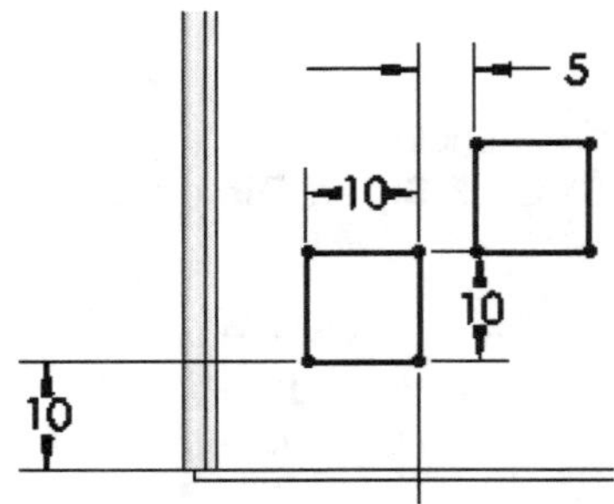

Add a Collinear Relation.

346) Click the **top horizontal line** of the first square. Hold the **Ctrl key** down. Click the **bottom horizontal line** of the second square.

347) Release the **Ctrl** key. Click **Collinear**. Click **OK** from the PropertyManager.

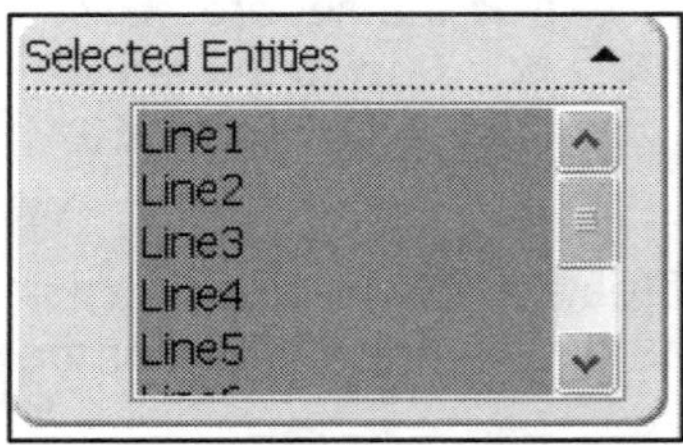

Repeat the Sketch.

348) Window-Select all **eight lines** of the two squares.

349) Click **Tools**, **Sketch Tools**, Linear Pattern... from the Main menu.

350) Enter **2** for Number for Direction1.

351) Enter **30** for Spacing for Direction1.

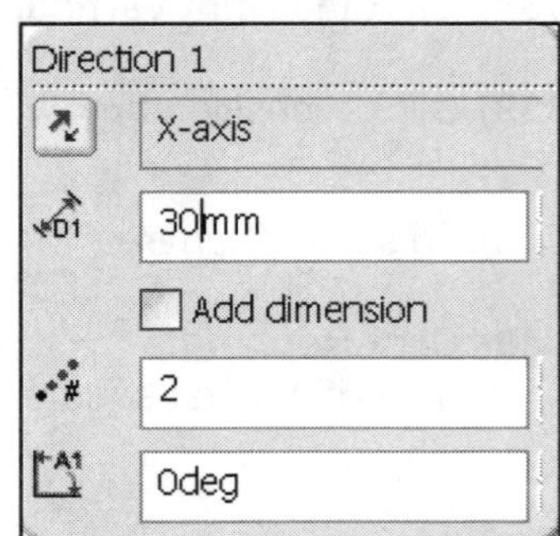

352) Enter **13** for Number for Direction2.

353) Press the **TAB** key.

354) Enter **20** for Spacing for Direction2.

355) Click **OK** from the Linear Pattern PropertyManager.

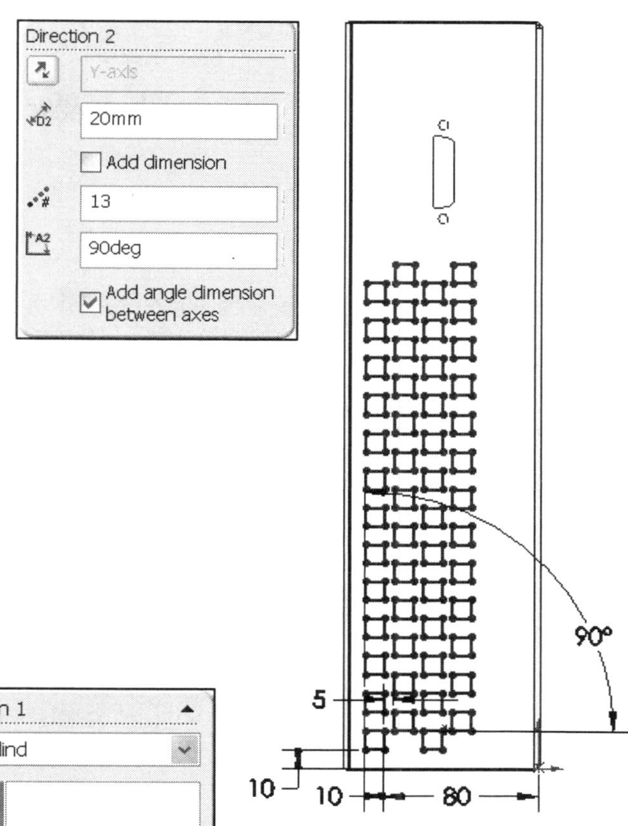

Extrude the sketch.

356) Click **Extruded Cut** from the Features toolbar.

357) Check **Link to thickness**.

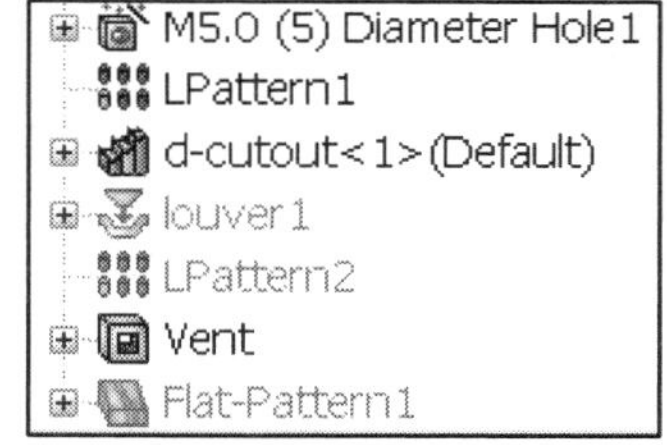

358) Click **OK** from the Cut-Extrude PropertyManager.

M5.0 (5) Diameter Hole1
LPattern1
d-cutout<1>(Default)
louver1
LPattern2
Vent
Flat-Pattern1

359) Click **Isometric view**.

360) Rename **Cut-Extrude2** to **Vent**.

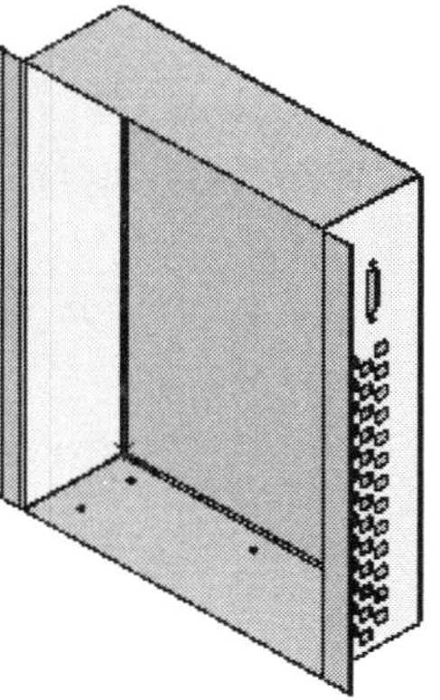

Save the CABINET in its formed state.

361) Click **Save**.

Before you utilize the Sketch Linear Pattern, determine the design intent of the pattern in the part and in a future assembly. If there are mating components, use Pattern features. Pattern features provide additional options compared to a simple sketch tool.

Additional Pattern Options

There are three additional feature Pattern options: Curve Driven Pattern, Sketch Driven Pattern and Table Driven Pattern.

- Curve Driven Pattern creates instances of the seed feature through a sketched curve or edge of a sketch.
- Sketch Driven Pattern creates instances of the seed feature though sketched points.
- Table Driven Pattern creates instances of the seed feature through X-Y coordinates in an existing table file or text file.

Utilize a Sketch Pattern for a random pattern. A Sketch Pattern requires a sketch and a feature. The Library Feature Sheetmetal folder contained the d-cutout and other common profiles utilized in sheet metal parts. Create a sketch with random Points on the CABINET left face. Insert sw-b212 and create a Sketch Pattern.

Activity: Additional Pattern Options-Sketch Driven Pattern

Create the sketch.

362) Click **Left view**. Click the **CABINET left face** for the sketch plane.

363) Click **Sketch** Sketch. Click **Point** Point from the Sketch toolbar.

364) Sketch a random series of **points** on the left face. Make a mental note of the first Point you select, the Point is required to constrain the sw-b212 sheet metal feature.

Close the Sketch.

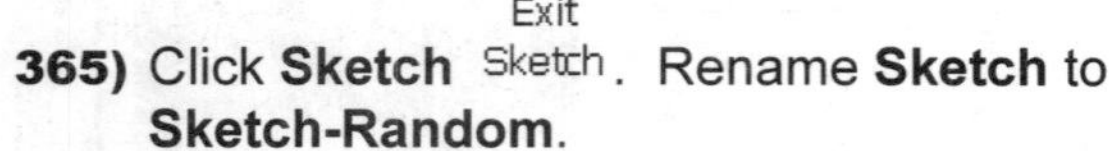

365) Click **Sketch** Exit Sketch. Rename **Sketch** to **Sketch-Random**.

366) **Rotate** the CABINET to view the inside left face. Click **Save**.

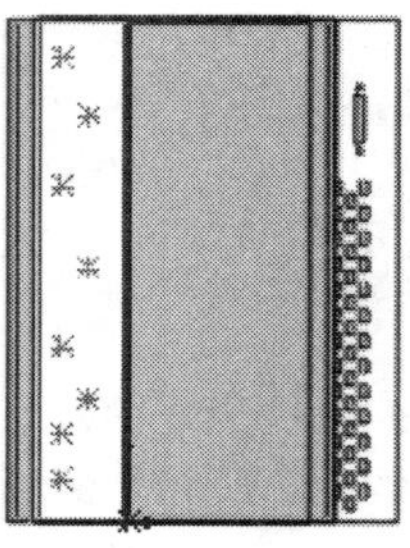

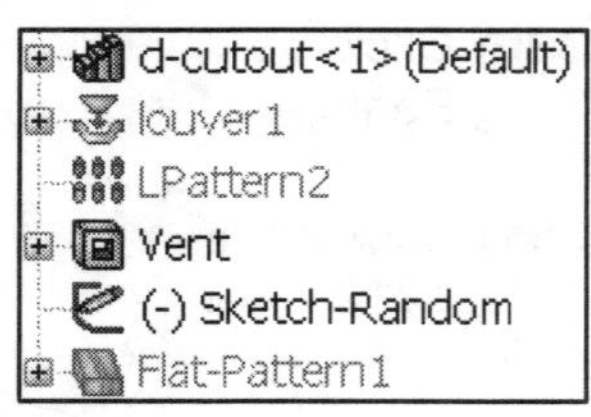

Insert the sw-b212 sheet metal tool.

367) **Expand** in the Design Library.

368) **Expand** features. Click the **Sheetmetal** folder.

369) Drag **sw-b212** sw-b212 to the inside left face of the CABINET.

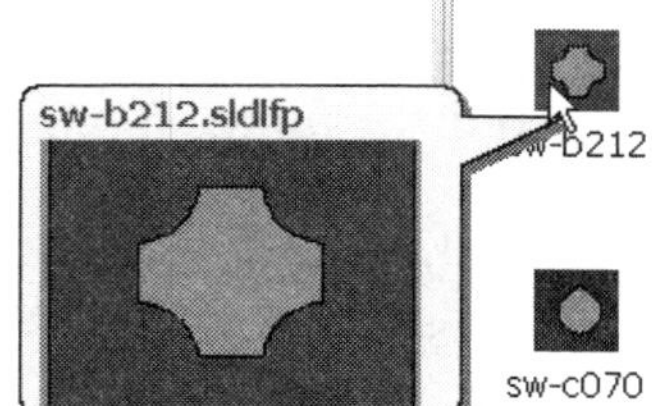

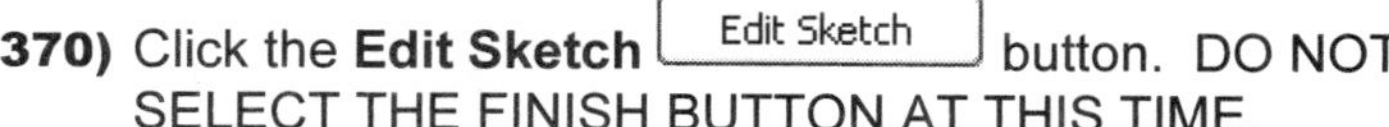

370) Click the **Edit Sketch** Edit Sketch button. DO NOT SELECT THE FINISH BUTTON AT THIS TIME.

Add a Midpoint Relation between the center point of the sw-b212 tool and the first random sketch point.

371) Click the **vertical centerline** of sw-b212.

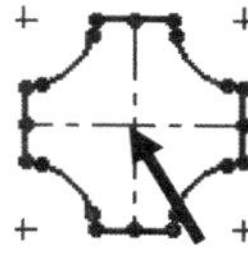

372) Hold the **Ctrl** key down. Click the **Point** of the first random sketch point. Release the **Ctrl** key.

373) Click **Midpoint** .

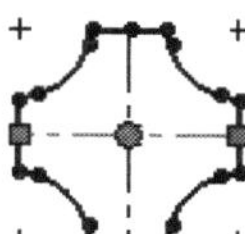

374) Click the **Finish** button.

Edit the End Condition.

375) Right-click **Cut-Extrude1** in the FeatureManager.

376) Click **Edit Feature**. Select **Blind** for End Condition.

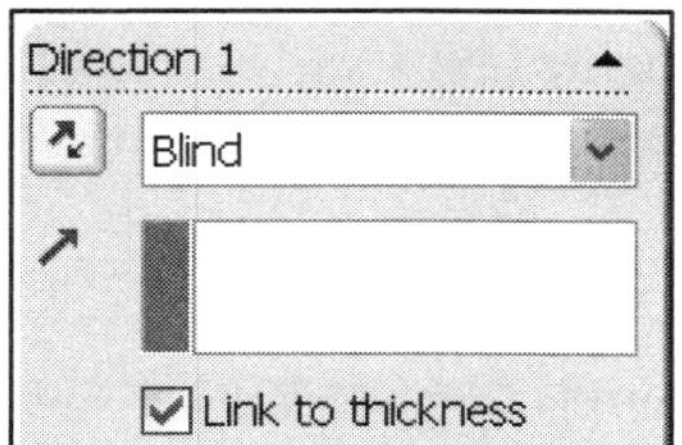

377) Check **Link to thickness**.

378) Click **OK** from the Cut-Extrude1 PropertyManager.

Insert the Sketch Pattern.

379) Click **Insert**, **Pattern/Mirror**, **Sketch Driven Pattern** Sketch Driven Pattern... from the Main menu.

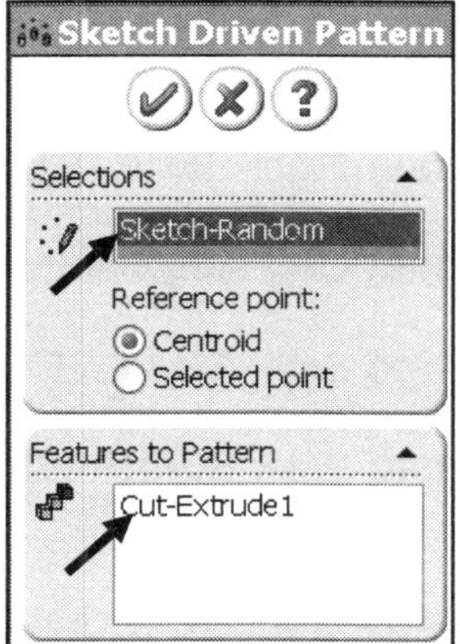

380) Click the **Reference Sketch** box. **Expand** the CABINET FeatureManager. Click **Sketch-Random** for Sketch.

381) Click the **Features to Pattern** box. Click **Cut-Extrude1** from sw-b212 in the FeatureManager

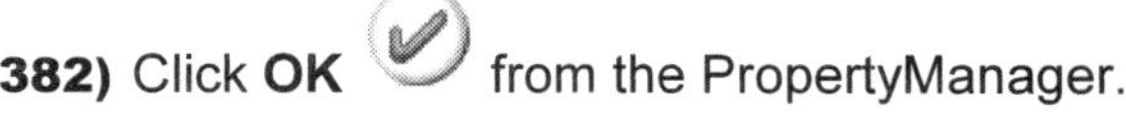

382) Click **OK** from the PropertyManager.

383) Click **Isometric view** . Click **Save** .

The Sketch Pattern is complete. Suppress the patterns when not required for future model development.

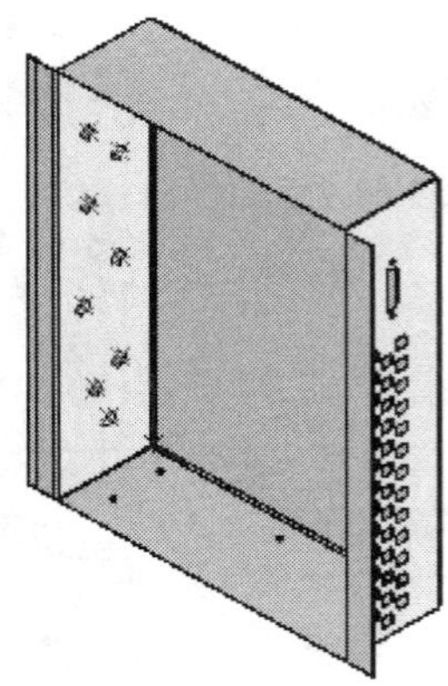

Utilize the Suppress option with configurations to save the formed and flat state of the CABINET.

CABINET-Formed and Flat States

How do you control the 3D formed state in the assembly and the 2D flat state in the drawing? Answer: Utilize configurations. A configuration is a variation of a part or assembly within a single document. Variations include different dimensions, features, and properties.

The BOX assembly requires the CABINET in the 3D formed state. Utilize the Default Configuration in the assembly.

The CABINET drawing requires the 2D flat state. The drawing requires a view with the Linear Pattern of square cuts and the random sketch pattern suppressed. Create a new configuration named NO-VENT. Suppress the patterns. Create a Derived configuration named NO-VENT-FLAT. Unsuppress the Flat Pattern feature to maintain the CABINET in its flat state. Create two configurations in the 3D formed and 2D flat state.

Activity: CABINET-Formed and Flat States

Display the ConfigurationManager.

384) Drag the **Split bar** down to divide the FeatureManager in half. Click the **ConfigurationManager** icon in the top half. The ConfigurationManager is displayed above the FeatureManager.

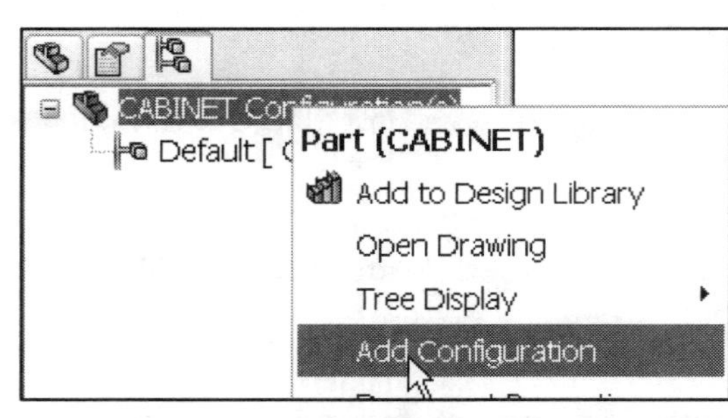

Add a Configuration.

385) Right-click **CABINET Configuration(s)**.

386) Click **Add Configuration**.

387) Enter **NO-VENT** for Configuration name.

388) Enter **SUPPRESS VENT CUTS** Description.

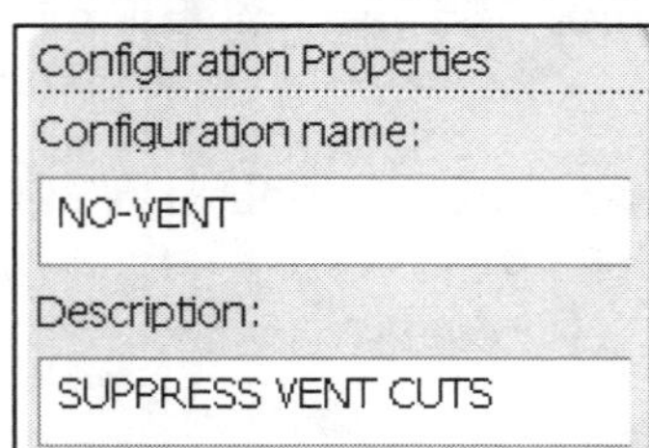

389) Click **OK** from the Add Configuration PropertyManager.

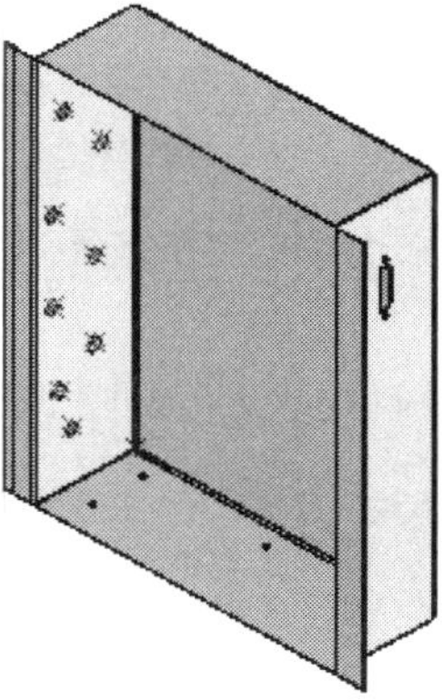

Suppress the Vent Extruded Cut feature.

390) Right-click **Vent** Vent from the FeatureManager.

391) Click **Suppress** Suppress.

The NO-VENT Configuration contains the suppressed Vent Extruded Cut feature. A Flat Pattern exists for the Default Configuration. The Flat Pattern Configuration is called a Derived Configuration.

Create a Flat Pattern Derived Configuration for the NO-VENT configuration. Unsuppress the Flat Pattern feature.

Create a Derived Configuration.

392) Right-click **NO-VENT[CABINET]** from the ConfigurationManager.

393) Click **Add Derived Configuration**.

394) Enter **NO-VENT-FLAT-PATTERN** for Configuration name.

CABINET Configuration(s) (NO-VENT-FLAT-P.
Default [CABINET]
NO-VENT [CABINET]
NO-VENT-FLAT-PATTERN [CABINET]

395) Click **OK** from the Add Configuration PropertyManager.

Unsuppress the Flat-Pattern1.

396) Right-click **Flat-Pattern1** Flat-Pattern1 from the CABINET FeatureManager.

397) Click **Unsuppress** Unsuppress to display the Flat State.

Hide the Random Sketch Points.

398) Right-click **Sketch Random** (-) Sketch Random in the FeatureManager. Click **Hide**.

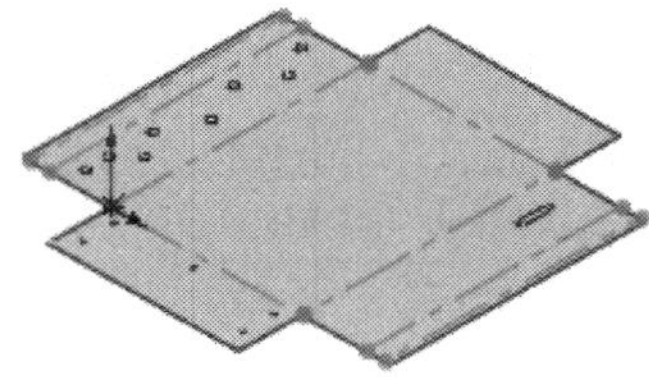

Display the four Configurations.

399) Double-click **Default [CABINET]** from the ConfigurationManager.

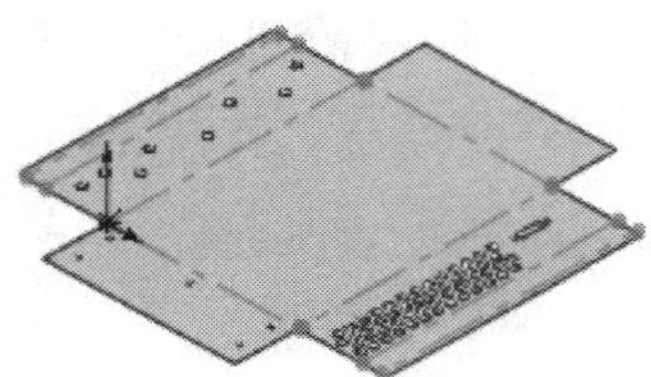

400) UnSuppress Flat-Pattern1 from the FeatureManager.

401) Double-click **NO-VENT [CABINET]**.

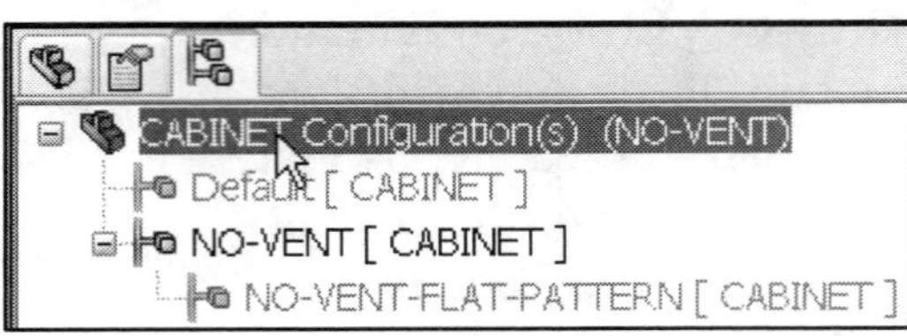

402) Double-click **NO-VENT-FLAT-PATTERN [CABINET]**.

403) Double-click **Default [CABINET]** to return to the Default Configuration.

404) Suppress Flat-Pattern1 from the FeatureManager.

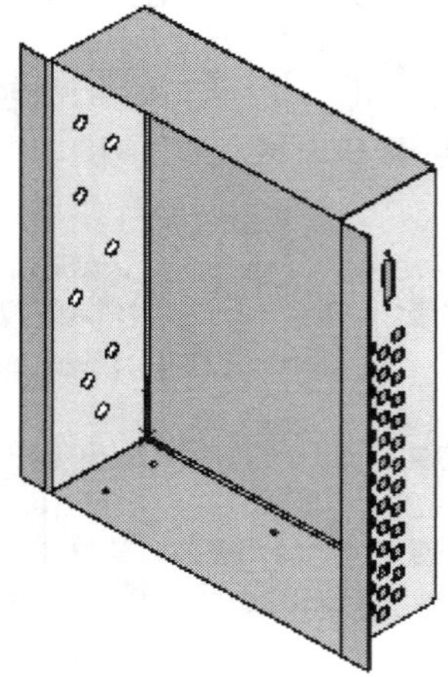

Save the CABINET.

405) Click **Save**.

CABINET-Sheet Metal Drawing with Configurations

Sheet metal drawings are produced in the flat state. Create a new C-size [A2] drawing size for the CABINET. Utilize the default SolidWorks Drawing Template. Insert the Top view into the drawing. Modify the Drawing View Properties from the Default configuration to the Flat configuration.

To create a multi configuration drawing, insert the Default configuration for Model View. Modify the View Properties in the drawing to change the configuration.

Activity: CABINET-Sheet Metal Drawing with Configurations

Open the CABINET.

406) Open the CABINET. The FeatureManager CABINET (Default)-> icon displays the Default configuration.

Create a new drawing.

407) Click **Make Drawing from Part/Assembly** from the Standard toolbar. Double-click **Drawing** from the Templates folder.

408) Select **C-Landscape** [**A2-Landscape**] for Sheet Format/Size.

409) Click **OK**. Model View is selected by default. The Front View outline of the CABINET is located on the cursor.

Insert the Isometric view.

410) Click **Single View**. Click **View orientation**.

411) Click ***Isometric** from the Orientation box.

412) Click a **position** on the right side of the drawing.

413) Click **OK** from the Drawing View1 PropertyManager.

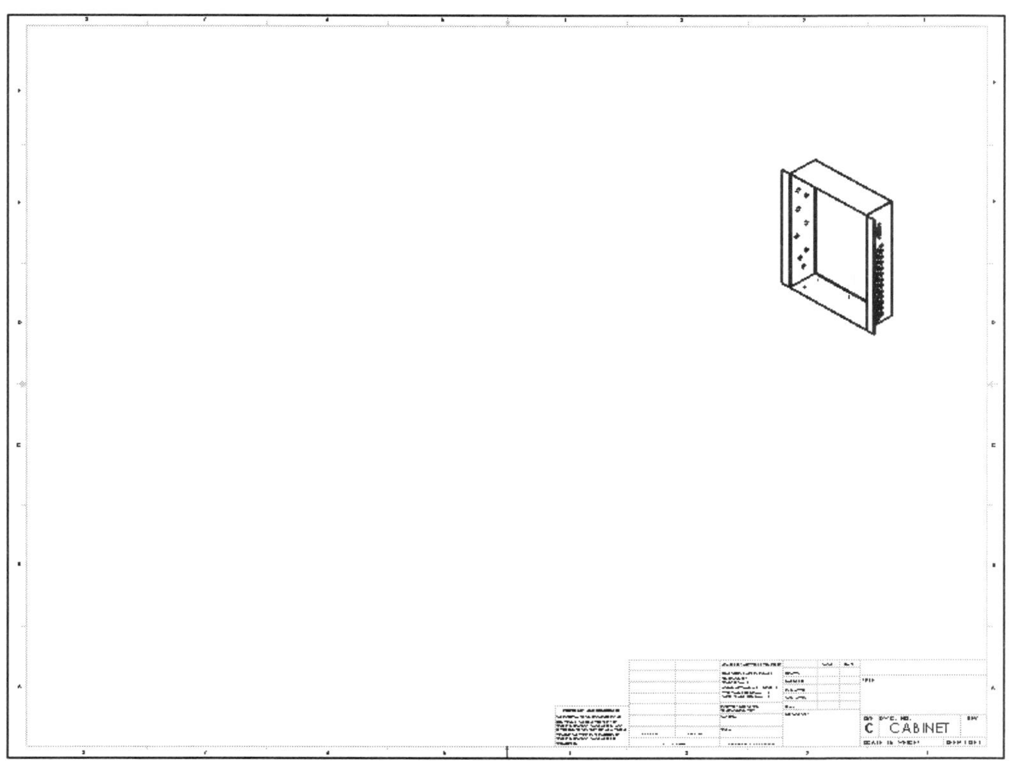

Insert the Default Flat pattern view.

414) Click **Model View**  from the Drawings toolbar.

415) Click **CABINET** from the Open documents box.

416) Click **Next**.

417) Click **View orientation**.

418) Click **Flat pattern** from the Orientation list.

419) Click a **position** on the left side of the drawing.

420) Click **OK**.

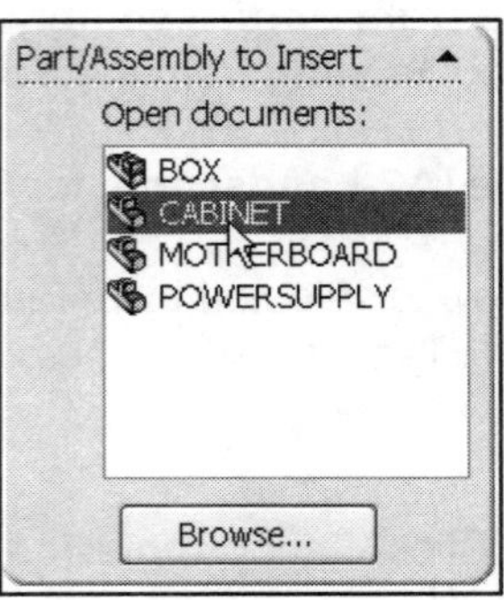

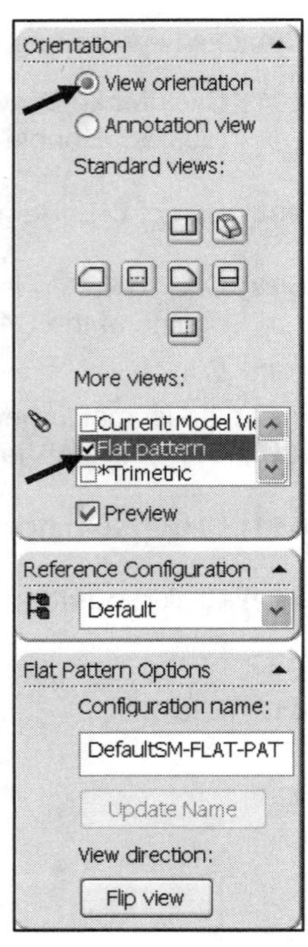

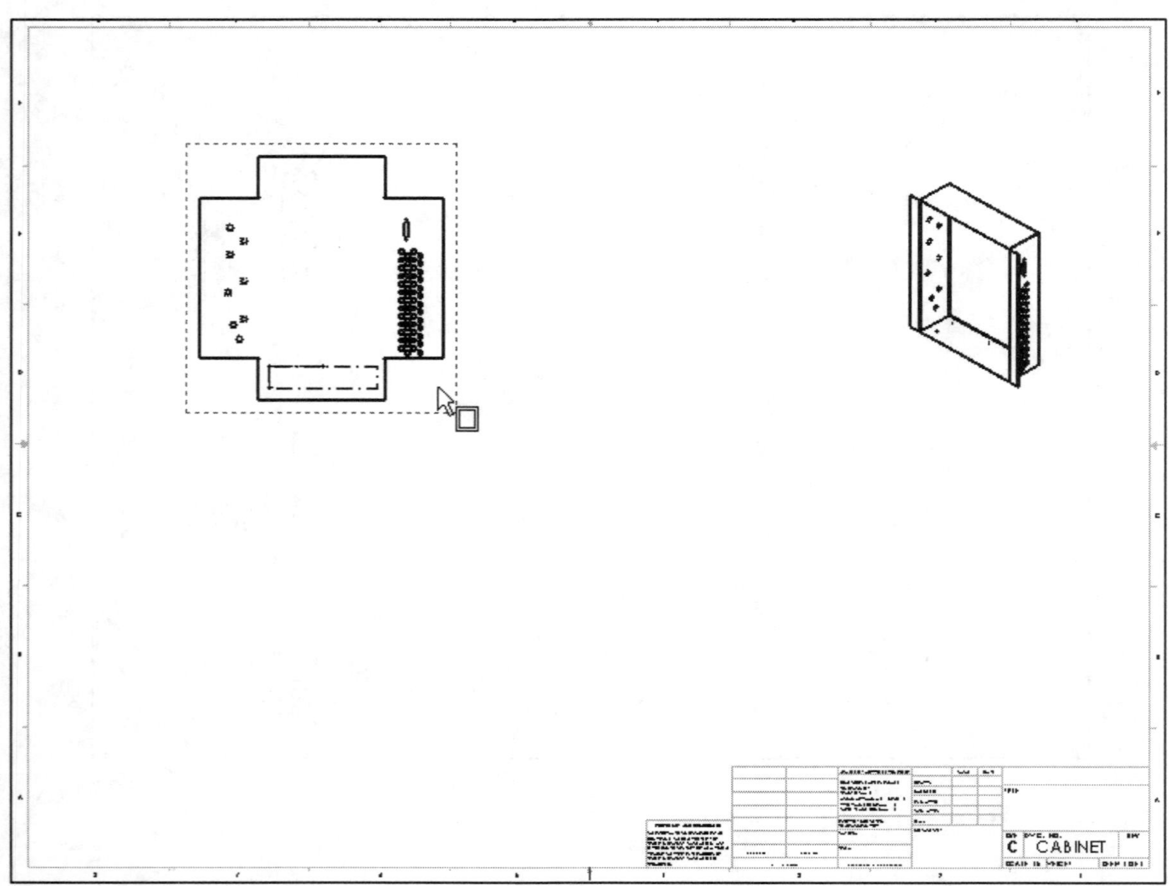

Copy and Paste the two views.

421) Click the **Isometric view boundary**.

422) Hold the **Ctrl** key down.

423) Click the **Flat pattern view boundary**.

424) Press **Ctrl C** to copy.

425) Click a **position** below the views.

426) Release the **Ctrl** key.

427) Click **Ctrl V** to paste.

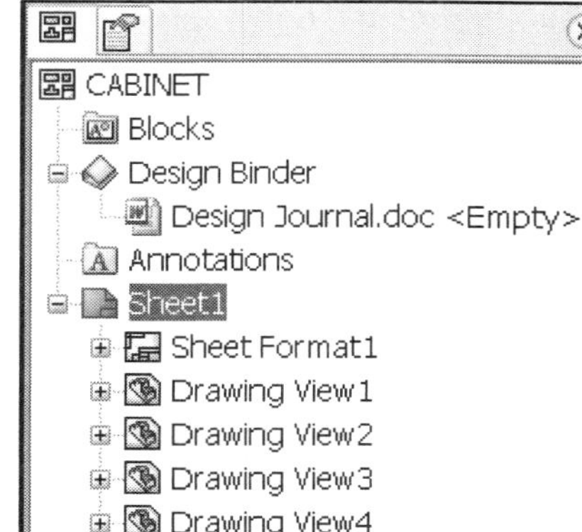

Hide Sketches, Points and Origins.

428) Click **View**, uncheck **Sketches** from the Main menu.

429) Click **View**, uncheck **Points** from the Main menu.

430) Click **View**, uncheck **Origins** from the Main menu.

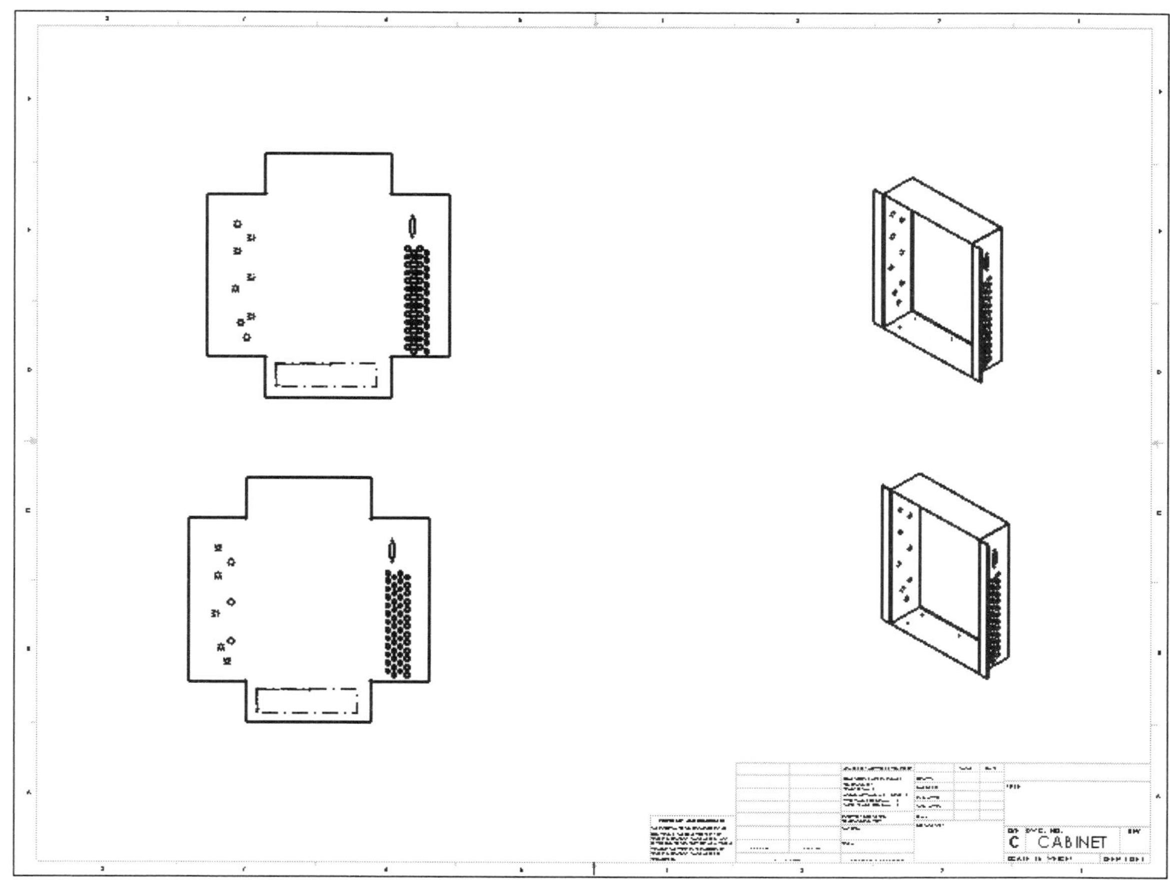

Modify the configurations.

431) Select the **lower left Flat pattern view in Sheet1**.

432) Right-click **Properties**.

433) Select **NO-VENT-FLAT-PATTERN** from the Configuration information drop down list.

434) Click **OK**.

435) Select the **lower right Isometric view**.

436) Right-click **Properties**.

437) Select **NO-VENT "SUPPRESS VENT CUTS"** from the Configuration information drop down list.

438) Click **OK**.

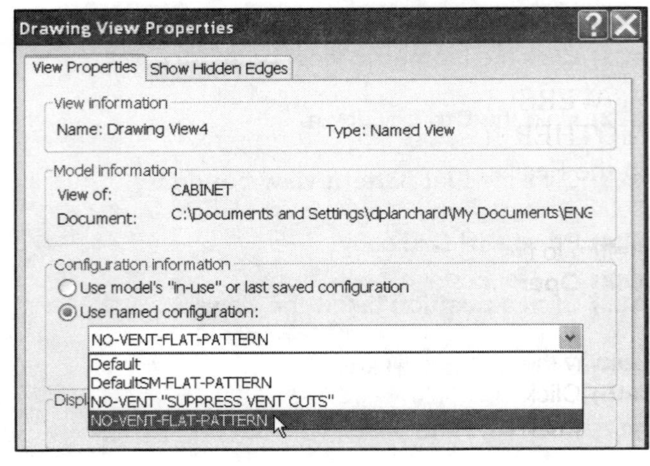

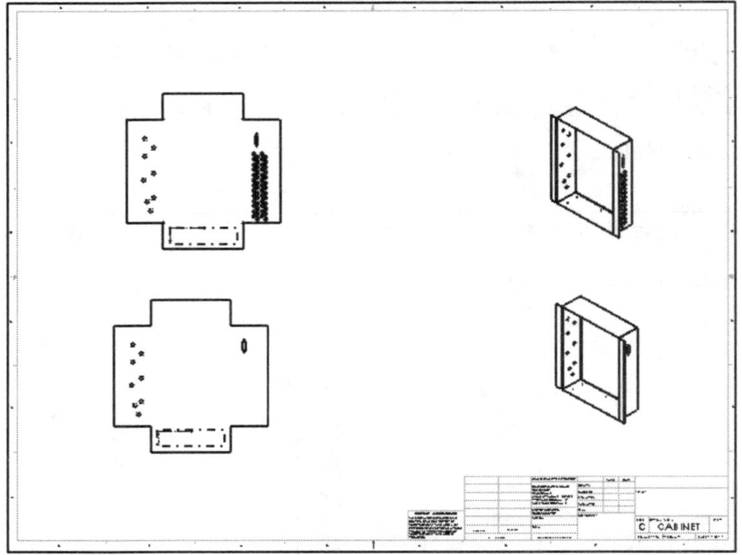

Note: Hide Origins, Planes and Sketches in drawing views. Insert centerlines to represent sheet metal bend lines. These activities are left as an exercise in the end of this project.

Save and Close the CABINET drawing.

439) Click **Save**.

440) Enter **CABINET** For File name.

441) Click **Save**.

442) Click **Yes**.

443) Click **File**, **Close** from the Main menu.

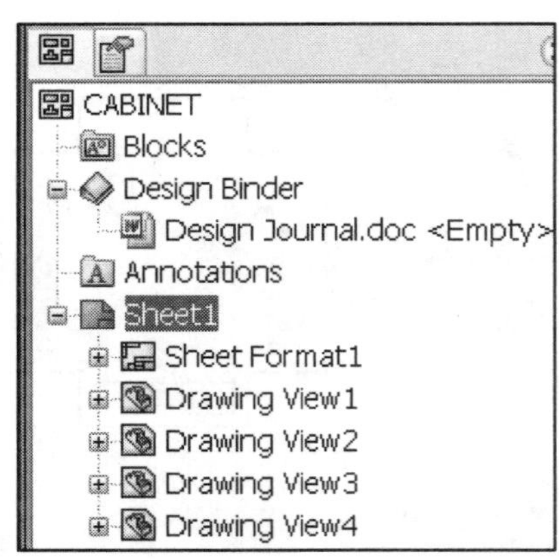

The CABINET is in the Default configuration.

Return to the BOX assembly. Review the BOX FeatureManager. The MOTHERBOARD and POWERSUPPLY are suppressed. Restore the MOTHERBOARD and POWERSUPPLY. Collapse entries in the FeatureManager.

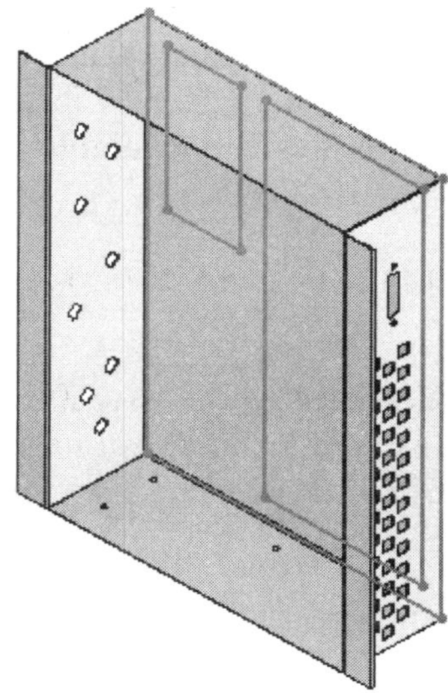

Return to the BOX assembly.

444) Open the BOX assembly.

Display the components.

445) Click the **MOTHERBOARD** in the BOX FeatureManager.

446) Hold the **Ctrl** key down.

447) Click on the **POWERSUPPLY** in the FeatureManager.

448) Right-click **Set to Resolved**.

449) Release the **Ctrl** key.

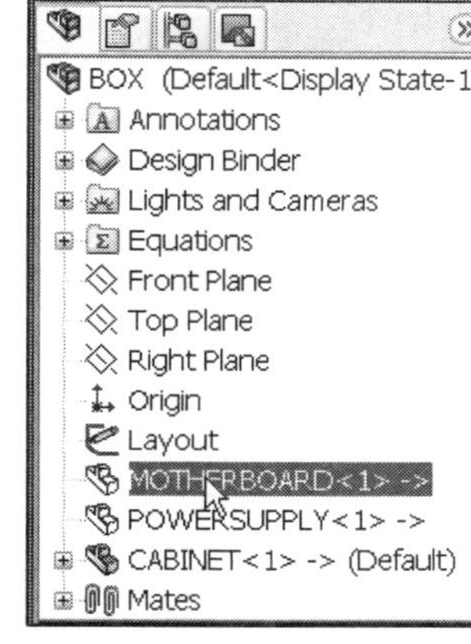

Save the BOX assembly.

450) Click **Save** .

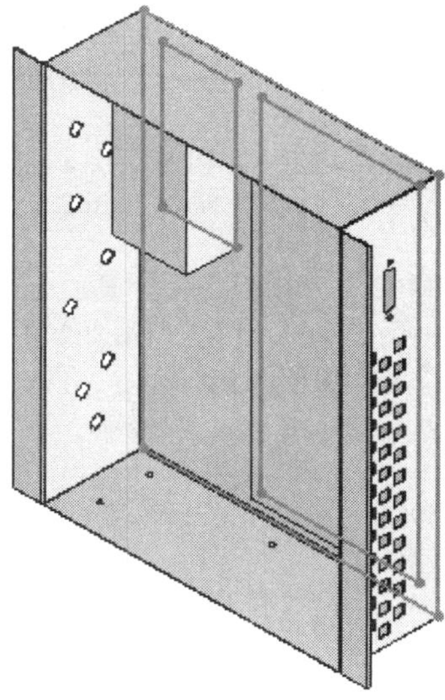

Work in SolidWorks from the design through the manufacturing process to avoid data conversion issues and decreased shop time. The SolidWorks Manufacturing Partner Network (www.solidworks.com) lists Sheet Metal manufacturers that utilize SolidWorks.

Additional details on Sheet Metal, Rip, Insert Bends, Flat Pattern, Forming Tools, Edge Flange, Hem, Library Feature, Linear Step and Repeat and Configuration Properties, are available in on-line Help.

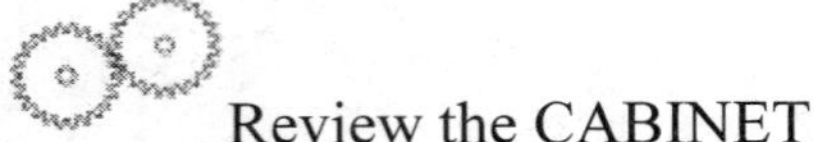

Review the CABINET.

You created the CABINET component inside the BOX assembly. The InPlace Mate inserted a coincident mate between the Front Plane of the CABINET and the Front Plane of the BOX. The CABINET component referenced the outside profile of the Layout Sketch.

The first feature of the CABINET was the Extruded Base feature that created a solid box. You utilized the Shell feature to create the constant wall thickness.

The Rip feature cut removed the solid edges. The Insert Bends feature created a sheet metal part from a solid part. The Flat Pattern feature displayed the sheet metal part in the manufactured 2D flat state.

The Edge Flange and Hem features were added to the right and left side of the CABINET. Sheet metal dies and form louvers were inserted from the Library Features.

The Sketch Linear Pattern was utilized to replace the form louvers with more cost effective cuts. You created a configuration to represent the 2D flat state for the CABINET drawing. The 3D formed state was utilized in the BOX assembly.

PEM® Fasteners and IGES components

The BOX assembly contains an additional support BRACKET that is fastened to the CABINET. To accommodate the new BRACKET, the Linear Pattern of 5 holes is added to the CABINET.

How do you fasten the BRACKET to the CABINET?

Answer: Utilize efficient and cost effective self-clinching fasteners. Example: PEM® Fasteners.

PEM® Fasteners, Examples

PEM® Fastening Systems, Danboro, PA USA manufactures self-clinching fasteners, called PEM® Fasteners.

PEM® Fasteners are used in numerous applications and are provided in a variety of shapes and sizes. IGES standard PEM® models are available at (www.pennfast.com) and are used in the following example.

Answer the following questions in order to select the correct PEM® Fastener for the assembly:

QUESTION:	ANSWER:
What is the material type?	Aluminum
What is the material thickness of the CABINET?	1mm
What is the material thickness of the BRACKET?	19mm
What standard size PEM® Fastener is available?	FHA-M5-30ZI
What is the hole diameter required for the CABINET?	5mm ± 0.08
What is the hole diameter required for the BRACKET?	5.6mm maximum
Total Thickness = CABINET Thickness + BRACKET Thickness + NUT Thickness Total Thickness = 1mm + 19mm + 5mm = 25mm (minimum)	25mm (minimum)

The selected PEM® Fastener for the project is the FHA-M5-30ZI.

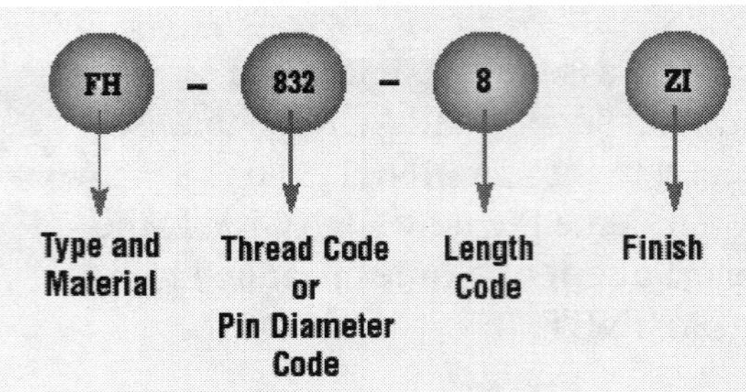

Part Number General Designation for PEM®

- **FHA** designates the stud type and material. Flush-head Aluminum
- **M5** designates the thread size.
- **30** designates length code: 30mm.
- **ZI** designates finish.

The overall dimensions of the FH PEM® Fasteners series are the same for various materials. Do not utilize PEM® Fasteners as a feature in the Flat State of a component. In the sheet metal manufacturing process, PEM® Fasteners are added after the material pattern has been fabricated.

Proper PEM® Fasteners material selection is critical. There are numerous grades of aluminum and stainless steel. Test the installation of the material fastener before final specification.

Note: When the fastener is pressed into ductile host metal, it displaces the host material around the mounting hole, causing metal to cold flow into a designed annular recess in the shank.

Ribs prevent the fastener from rotating in the host material once it has been properly inserted. The fasteners become a permanent part of the panel in which they are installed.

During the manufacturing process, a stud is installed by placing the fastener in a punched or drilled hole and squeezing the stud into place with a press. The squeezing action embeds the head of the stud flush into the sheet metal.

Obtain additional manufacturing information that directly affects the design.

Manufacturing Information:	**FH-M4ZI:**	**FH-M5ZI:**
Hole Size in sheet metal (CABINET).	4.0mm ± 0.8	5.0mm ± 0.8
Maximum Hole in attached parts (BRACKET).	4.6mm	5.6mm
Centerline to edge minimum distance. (from center point of hole to edge of CABINET)	7.2mm	7.2mm

Note: The following steps require access to the Internet with the ability to download files. The FH-M5-30ZI.zip and FH-M4-20ZI.zip parts are available on the Multimedia CD contained in the book. Part geometry for Aluminum and Stainless Steel fasteners is the same.

Activity: PEM® Fasteners and IGES Components

Obtain the PEM® fastener.

451) Enter the URL: http://www.pennfast.com.

452) Click **Fastening Products**.

453) Click **PEM Self-Clinching and Weld Fasteners for Sheet Metal**.

454) Enter **FH-M5-30ZI** in the Quick Search box.

Information Request
Fastening Products
Press & Installation Equipment
Technical Help & Learning Center
CAD File Library
Representatives & Distributors
Tradeshow Calendar
Complete (PDF) Literature Files

• AutoSpec® Solutio
New Products
Atlas™ Fasteners for One-Side Access Only Installation
AutoSpec® Solutions for the Automotive Industry
Custom Hardware Options
PEM® Cable/Wire Mounting Hardware
PEM® Connector Mounting Hardware
PEM® Panel Access Hardware
PEM® PC Board Broaching Fasteners
PEM® PC Board Surface Mount Fasteners
PEM® Self-Clinching and Weld Fasteners for Sheet Metal

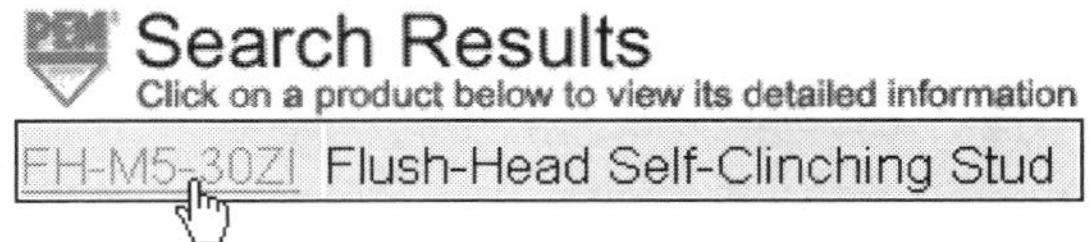

Search Results
Click on a product below to view its detailed information
FH-M5-30ZI Flush-Head Self-Clinching Stud

455) Click the **CAD** icon. Note: Login in. Enter **user name** and **password**. Register for a **user name** and **password** if you do not have one. They will be emailed to you.

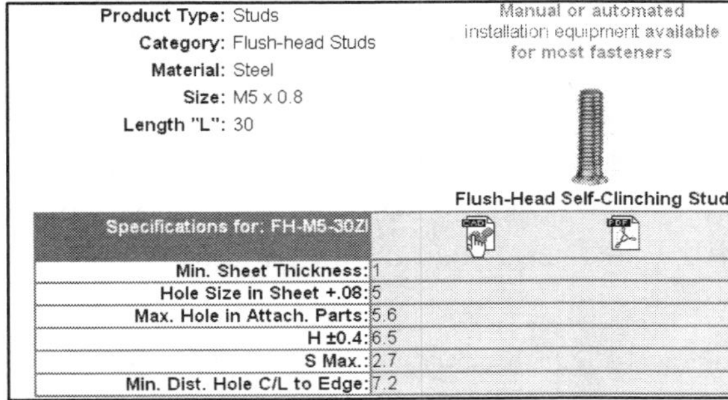

Product Type: Studs
Category: Flush-head Studs
Material: Steel
Size: M5 x 0.8
Length "L": 30
Manual or automated installation equipment available for most fasteners
Flush-Head Self-Clinching Stud
Specifications for: FH-M5-30ZI
Min. Sheet Thickness: 1
Hole Size in Sheet +.08: 5
Max. Hole in Attach. Parts: 5.6
H ±0.4: 6.5
S Max.: 2.7
Min. Dist. Hole C/L to Edge: 7.2

Download two different metric studs.

456) Click **FH-M5-30ZI**.

457) Click **Format/Options**.

458) Set Format: **IGES**. Set insert directly into: **SolidWorks 2005**. Note: At the time of this book, this was the highest version available from the website. Click **OK**.

459) Click **Download**. Save to the **COMPONENTS** folder.

460) Enter **FH-M4-25ZI** in the Search box.

461) Click **FH-M4-25ZI**. Click **Download**. Save to the **COMPONENTS** file folder.

462) Unzip the two files, **cr1527** and **cr1551**. Note: Unzip file names will be different each time you access this website.

463) Select the **ENGDESIGN-W-SOLIDWORKS\COMPONENTS** file folder to save the IGES files.

The IGES files, cr1527 and cr1551 are created and stored in the VENDOR-COMPONENT folder.

You will use the cr1551 file again. Note: You cannot insert an IGES component directly into the BOX assembly. Open the IGES model in SolidWorks. Save the model as a SolidWorks part file.

Open the IGES model.

464) Click **File**, **Open** from the Main menu.

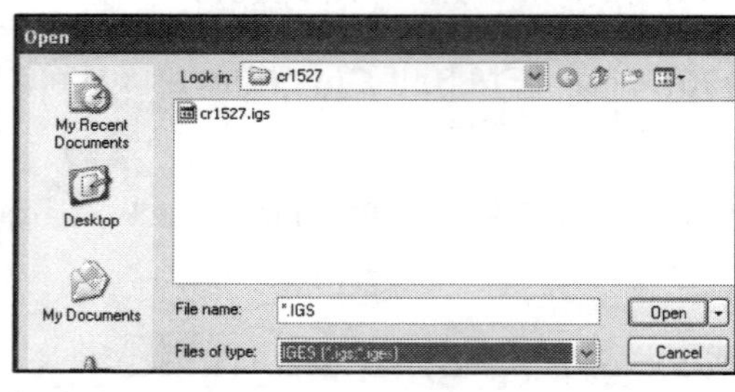

465) Select the **IGS** format from the drop down list. Select the **cr1527** folder.

466) Double-click **cr1527.igs** file. The system displays the Part Templates in the New dialog box.

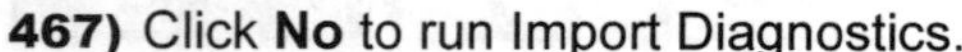

467) Click **No** to run Import Diagnostics.

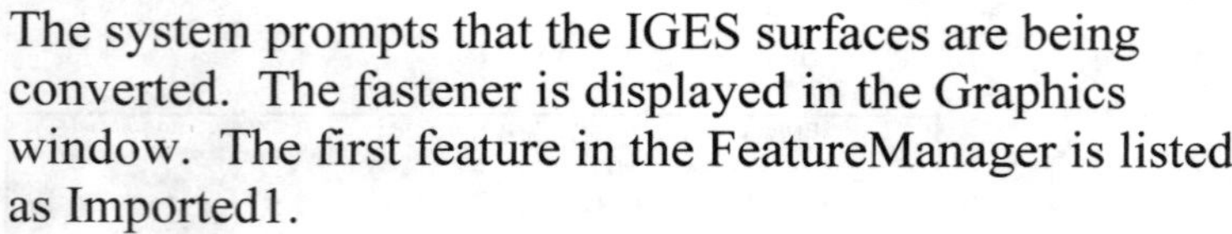

The system prompts that the IGES surfaces are being converted. The fastener is displayed in the Graphics window. The first feature in the FeatureManager is listed as Imported1.

Reference Imported1 geometry with dimensions. Convert faces and edges in the sketch when required. The FH-M5-30ZI part requires no modification.

Save cr1527 in a SolidWorks part file format.

468) Click **Save** .

469) Enter **FH-M5-30ZI** for File name.

470) Click **Save**.

Repeat the above procedure for cr1551 IGES model.

471) Open cr1151.IGS.

472) Click **Save**.

473) Enter **FH-M4-25ZI** in SolidWorks part file format.

474) Click **File**, **Close** from the Main menu. The FH-M5-25ZI remains open.

Insert the FH-M5-30ZI fastener into the BOX assembly.

475) Open the **Box** assembly.

476) Click **Insert**, **Component**, Existing Part/Assembly... from the Main menu.

477) Double-click **FH-M5-30ZI** in the Open documents box. Note: If FH-M5-30ZI is not open, click Browse to select FH-M5-30ZI.

478) Click inside the **Graphics window** in the inside bottom left corner near the seed feature of the Linear Pattern of Holes.

479) **Zoom to Area** on the Hole and fastener.

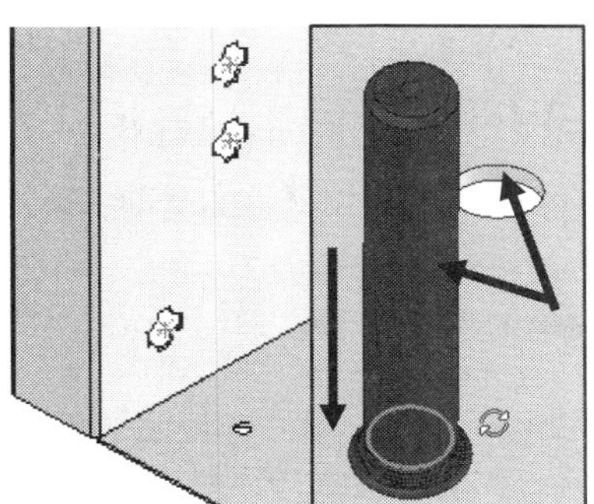

Rotate the FH-M5-30ZI component.

480) Click **Rotate Component** Rotate Compo... from the Assembly toolbar. Rotate the **FH-M5-30ZI** component until the head faces downward. Click **OK**.

Insert a Concentric Mate.

481) Click **Mate** Mate. Click the cylindrical **shaft** of the FH-M5-30ZI fastener. Click the cylindrical **face** of the back left **Hole**.

482) Click **Concentric** from the Pop-up menu.

483) Click **OK**.

Note: If required, click the Align/Anti Align button to flip the fastener.

Insert a Coincident Mate.

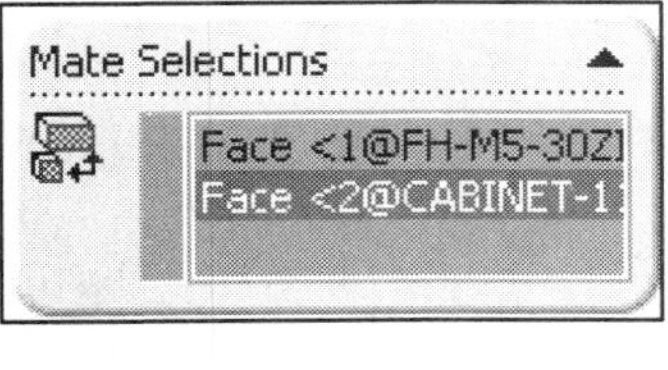

484) Press the **Up Arrow** key to rotate the model to display the head of the FH-M5-30ZI fastener. Click the **head face** of the FH-M5-30ZI fastener.

485) Click the **outside bottom face** of the CABINET. Click **Coincident** from the Pop-up menu.

486) Click **OK**.

Insert a Parallel Mate.

487) Expand the **BOX FeatureManager** icon.

488) Click the **Front plane** of the FH-M5-30ZI fastener. Click the **Right plane** of the CABINET. Click **Parallel** from the Pop-up menu.

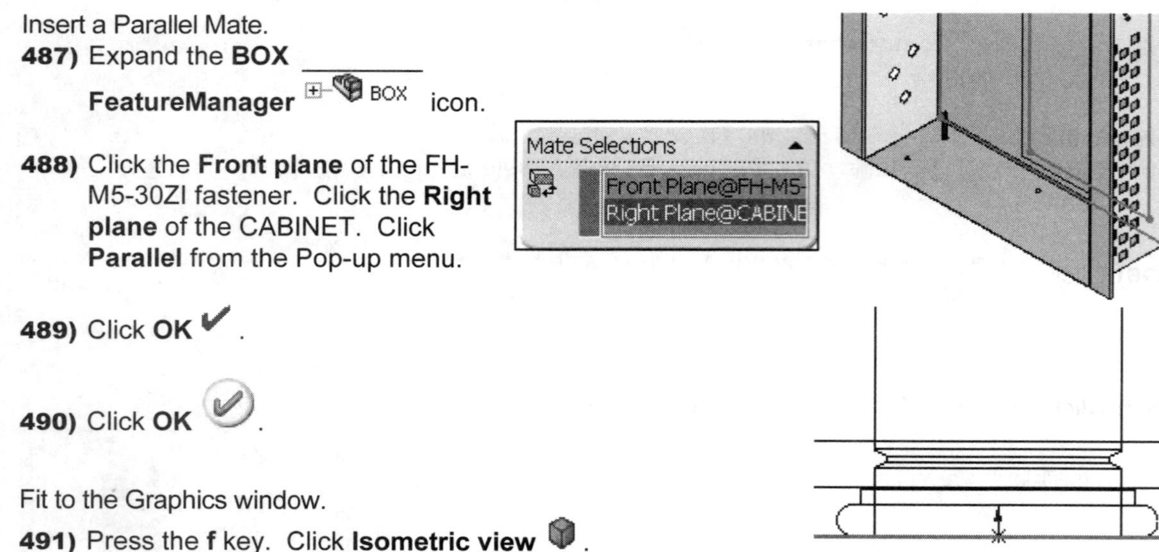

489) Click **OK**.

490) Click **OK**.

Fit to the Graphics window.

491) Press the **f** key. Click **Isometric view**.

492) Click **Save**.

Three Mates fully define the FH-M5-30ZI fastener. The PEM® fastener creates an interference fit with Hole1.

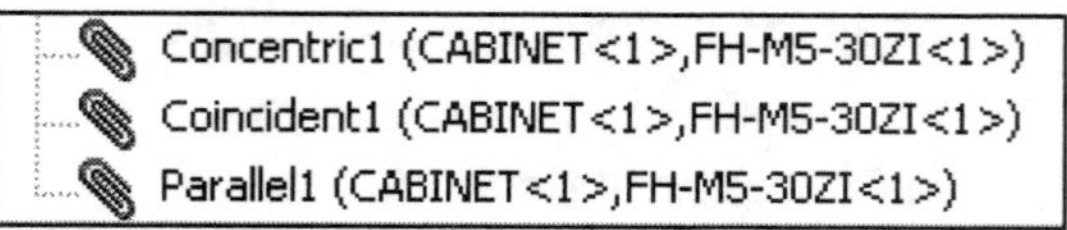

Derived Component Pattern

A Derived Component Pattern is a pattern that utilizes an existing component in an assembly and a driving feature from another component in the same assembly. Utilize a Component Pattern, Feature Driven option to create multiple copies of a component in an assembly. The FH-M5-30ZI references the Hole1 seed feature. The Component Pattern displays the five FH-M5-30ZI fasteners based on the CABINET LPattern1 feature.

Activity: Derived Component Pattern

Insert a Feature Driven Component Pattern.

493) Click **Insert**, **Component Pattern**, **Feature Driven** from the Main menu.

494) Click **FH-M5-30ZI** from the BOX FeatureManager for Components to Pattern. Click **inside** the Driving Feature box.

495) Click **CABINET\LPattern1** in the BOX FeatureManager.

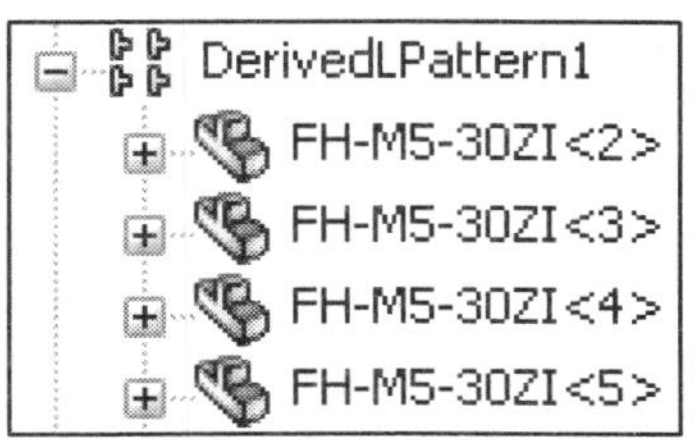

496) Click **OK**.

Expand the Derived LPattern1.

497) Click the **Plus** icon to the left of Derived LPattern1 in the FeatureManager.

498) Click **Isometric view**.

Save the BOX.

499) Click **Save**.

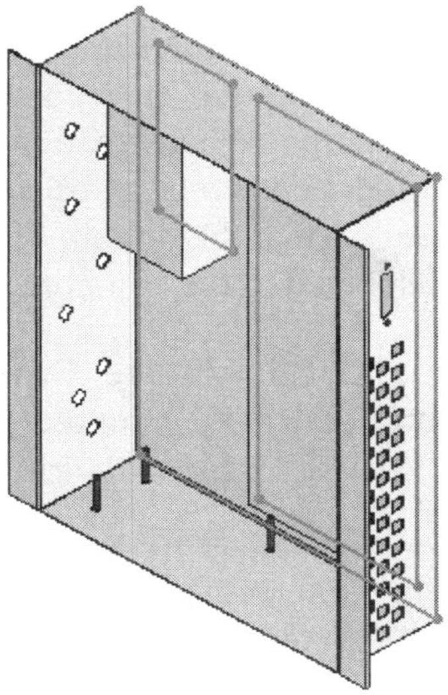

The additional FH-M5-30ZI instances are located under the Derived LPattern1 in the FeatureManager. The purchasing manager for your company determines that the FH-M5-30ZI fastener has a longer lead-time than the FH-M4-25ZI fastener.

The FH-M4-25 fastener is in stock. Time is critical. You ask the engineer creating the corresponding BRACKET if the FH-M4-25ZI fastener is a reliable substitute.

You place a phone call. You get voice mail. You send email. You wait for the engineer's response and create the next assembly feature.

The common PEM® fastener library is available in SolidWorks Toolbox.

How do you locate a hole for a fastener that has to go through multiple components in an assembly? Answer: Utilize an Assembly Hole feature.

MOTHERBOARD-Assembly Hole Feature

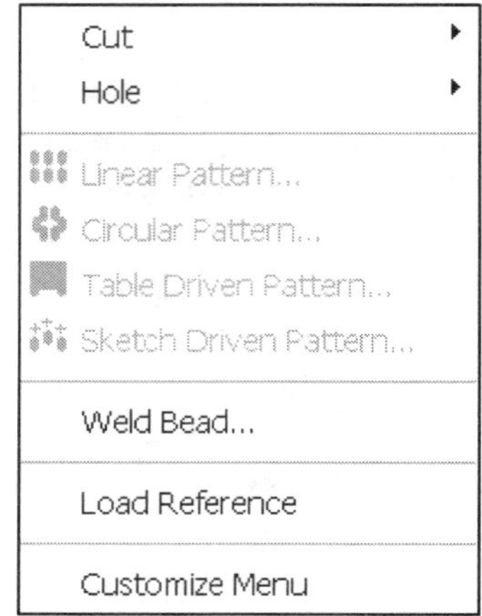

Assembly features are holes and cuts created in the assembly. Utilize Assembly features after components have been assembled. Assembly features include Cut, Hole, Linear Pattern, Circular Pattern Table Driven Pattern, Sketch Driven Pattern and Weld Bead. Create a Cut or Hole Assembly feature to activate the Assembly Feature Pattern options.

Assembly features are accessed through the Insert, Assembly Feature option. Insert an Assembly feature into the BOX assembly. When creating an Assembly feature, determine the components to be affected by the feature. Assembly features are listed at the bottom of the FeatureManager. They are not displayed in the components affected by the feature.

Additional holes are created through multiple components in the BOX assembly. A through Hole is required from the front of the MOTHERBOARD to the back of the CABINET. Since the Hole is an assembly feature, it is not displayed in the CABINET part.

Avoid Mate Errors. Utilize Mates to fully define components that are referenced by Assembly features. Use the Hole Wizard as an Assembly feature.

Activity: MOTHERBOARD-Assembly Hole Feature

Insert an Assembly feature with the Hole Wizard.

500) Click the **front face** of the MOTHERBOARD.

501) Click **Insert**, **Assembly Feature**, **Hole**, **Wizard** Wizard... from the Main menu.

502) Click the **Hole** icon.

503) Select **Ansi Metric**.

504) Select **M5.0** for size.

505) Click **Through All** for Hole Type Depth.

506) Click the **Positions** Tab.

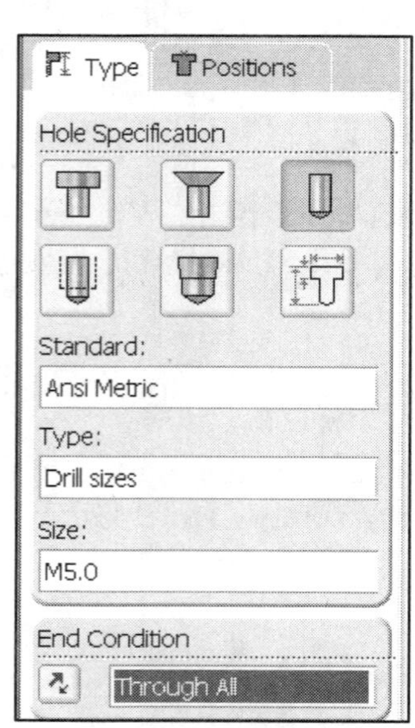

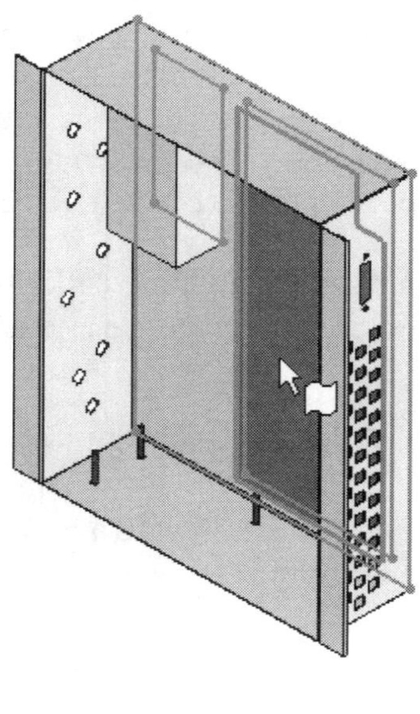

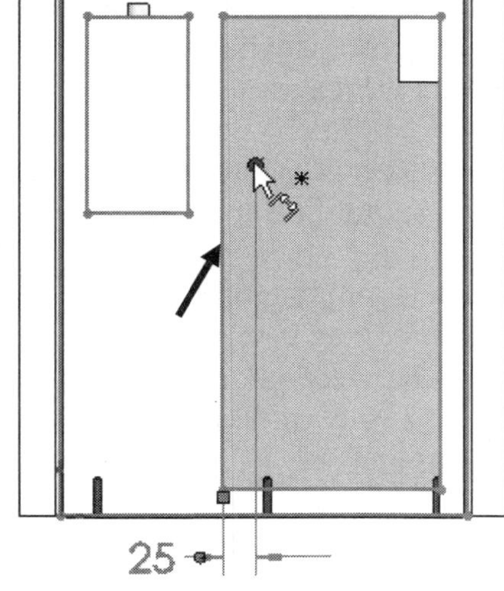

507) Click **Front view** .

Dimension the hole on the MOTHERBOARD.

508) Click **Smart Dimension** Dimens... .

Add a horizontal dimension.

509) Click the **left edge** of the MOTHERBOARD. Click the **center point** of the hole. Click a **position** below the profile.

510) Enter **25**.

Add a vertical dimension.

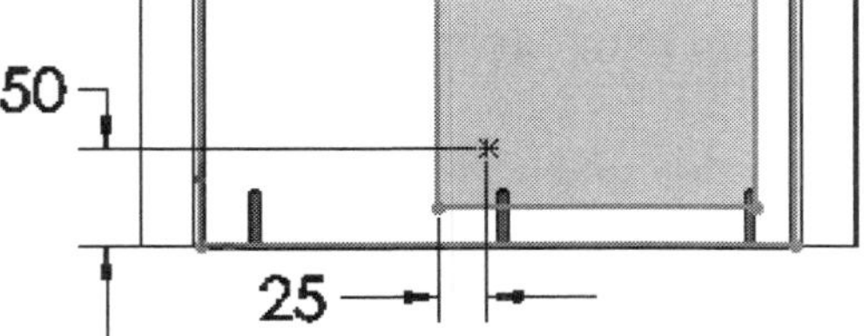

511) Click the **Origin** of the CABINET from the FeatureManager.

512) Click the **center point** of the hole.

513) Click a **position** to the left of the profile.

Enter **50**. Click **OK** from the Hole Position PropertyManager. The M5 hole is added to the FeatureManager.

Save the BOX.

514) Click **Isometric view** .

515) Click **Save** .

Close all parts and assemblies.

516) Click **Window**, **Close All** from the Main menu.

Assembly FeatureManager and External References

The FeatureManager contains numerous entries in an assembly. Understanding the organization of the components and their Mates is critical in creating an assembly without errors. Errors occur within features such as a radius that is too large to create a Fillet feature. When an error occurs in the assembly, the feature or component is labeled in red.

Mate errors occur when you select conflicting geometry such as a Coincident Mate and a Distance Mate with the same faces.

In the initial mating, undo a mate that causes an error. Mate errors occur later on in the design process when you suppress required components and features. Plan ahead to avoid problems.

Use reference planes for Mates that will not be suppressed.

When a component displays a '->' symbol, an external reference exists between geometry from the assembly or from another component.

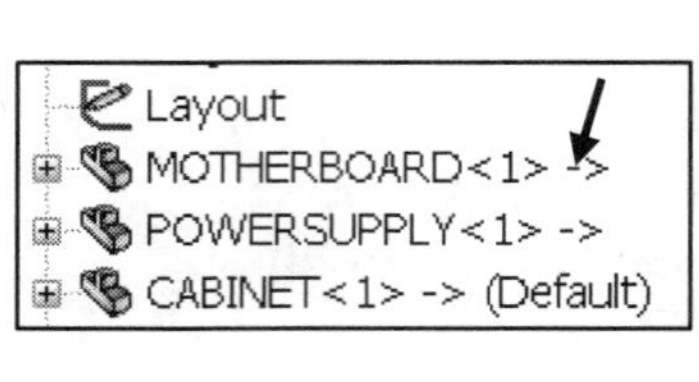

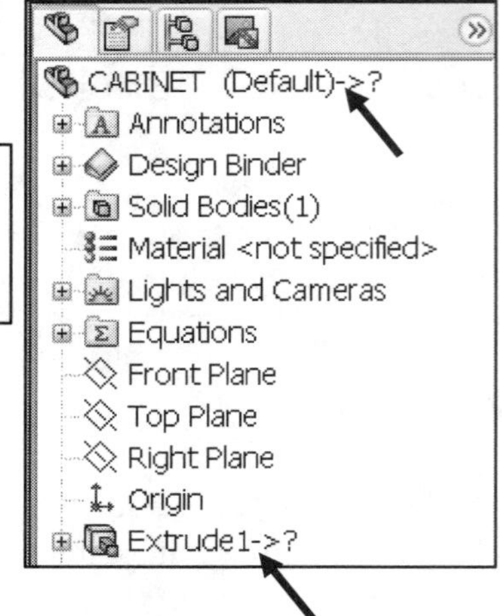

When the system does not locate referenced geometry, the part name displays a '->?' symbol to the right of the component name in the FeatureManager.

Explore external references in the next activity. Open the CABINET without opening the BOX assembly. The '->?' symbol is displayed after the part name.

Activity: Assembly FeatureManager and External References

Open the CABINET part.

517) Click **File**, **Open** from the Main menu.

518) Browse to **ENGDESIGN-W-SOLIDWORKS\PROJECTS**.

519) Click **Part** for Files of Type.

520) Double-click **CABINET**.

The CABINET cannot locate the referenced geometry BOX. The "->?" is displayed to the right of the CABINET name and Extrude1 in the FeatureManager.

Open the BOX assembly.

521) Click **File**, **Open**. Click **Assembly** for Files of Type.

522) Double-click **BOX**.

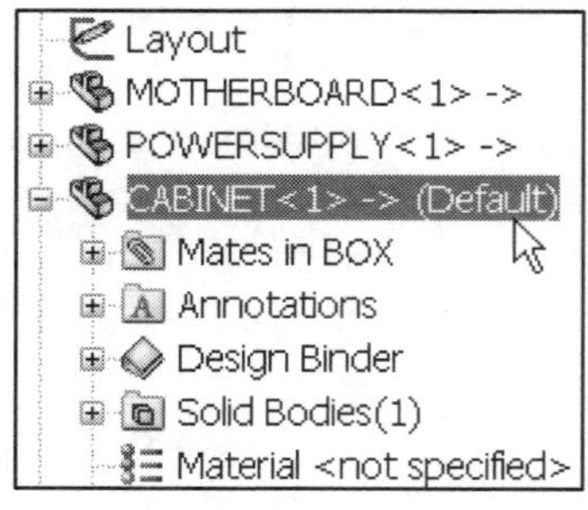

Reload the CABINET

523) Right-click **CABINET** in the FeatureManager. Click the **More arrow** at the bottom of the Pop-up menu.

524) Click **Reload** Reload. Click **OK** from the Reload dialog box.

525) Return to the CABINET assembly.

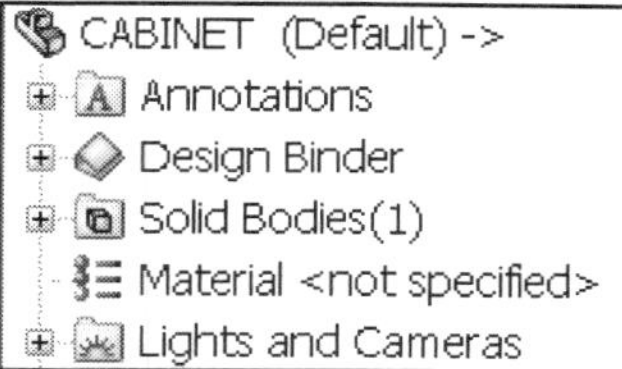

Save the CABINET.

526) Click **Save** .

The CABINET references the BOX assembly. The external references are resolved and the question marks are removed.

Replace Components

The Replace Components option replaces a component in the current assembly with another component. Replace a part with a new part or assembly or an assembly with a part. If multiple instances of a component exist, select the instances to replace.

The BRACKET engineer contacts you. You proceed to replace the FH-M5-30ZI fastener with the FH-M4-25ZI fastener. Use the Replace Components option to exchange the FH-M5-30ZI fastener with FH-M4-25ZI fastener in the BOX assembly.

Edit the Mates and select new Mate references. The Derived Component Pattern updates with the new fastener. Edit the CABINET and change the Hole size of the seed feature from M5 to M4. The CABINET Linear Pattern updates with the new Hole.

Before you replace Component-A in and assembly with Component-B, close Component-B. The Replace Component option produces an error message with open components. Example; Close the FH-M4-25ZI part before replacing the FH-M5-30ZI part in the current assembly.

Activity: Replace Components

Replace the FH-M5-30ZI component with the FH-M4-25ZI component.

527) Open the **BOX** assembly.

528) Right-click **FH-M5-30ZI** FH-M5-30ZI<1> from the FeatureManager.

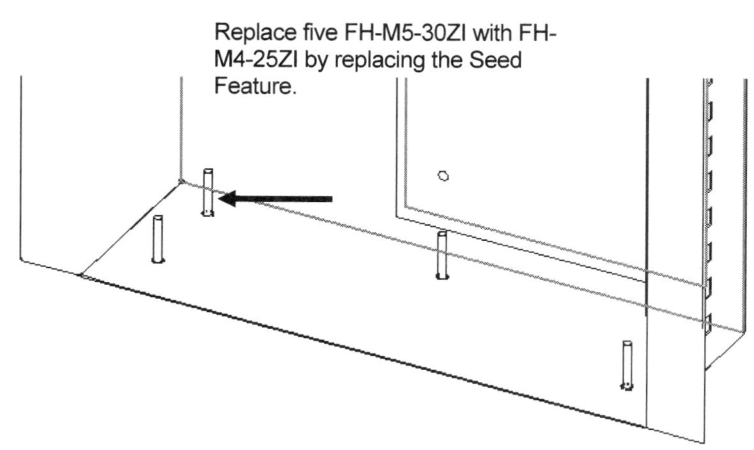

Replace five FH-M5-30ZI with FH-M4-25ZI by replacing the Seed Feature.

529) Click the **More arrow** at the bottom of the Pop-up menu.

530) Click **Replace Components** Replace Components.

531) Click **Browse**.

532) Double-click **FH-M4-25ZI**.

533) Click **OK**. Note: If the What's Wrong box is displayed. Click **Close** from the What's Wrong dialog box.

The five FH-M5-30ZI fasteners are replaced with the five FH-M4-25ZI fasteners. Two Mate Entity warning errors occur.

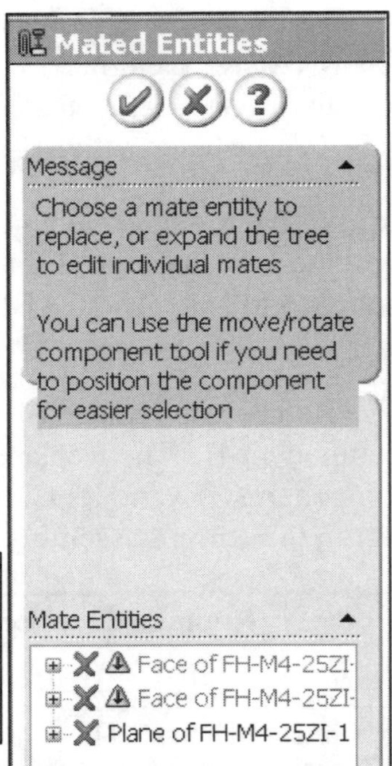

A red X is displayed on the Mated Entities PropertyManager. Redefine the Concentric Mate and Coincident Mate.

Select faces from the FH-M4-25ZI component.

Edit the Concentric Mate.

534) Expand the first **Mate Entry** Face of FH-M4-25ZI-1.

535) Double-click **Concentric1**.

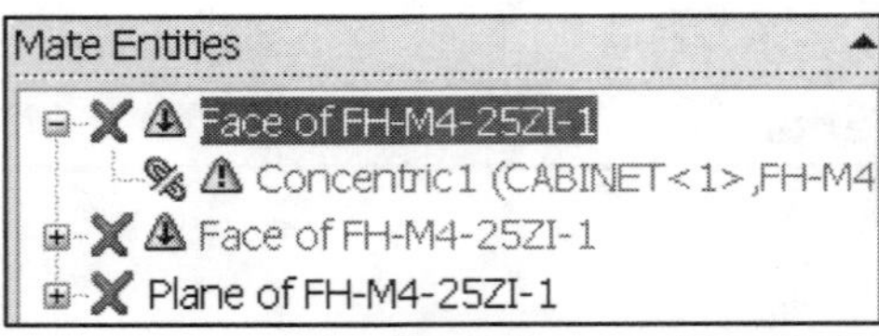

536) Click the **FH-M4-25ZI cylindrical face**. The Face is displayed in the Replacement Mate Entity box.

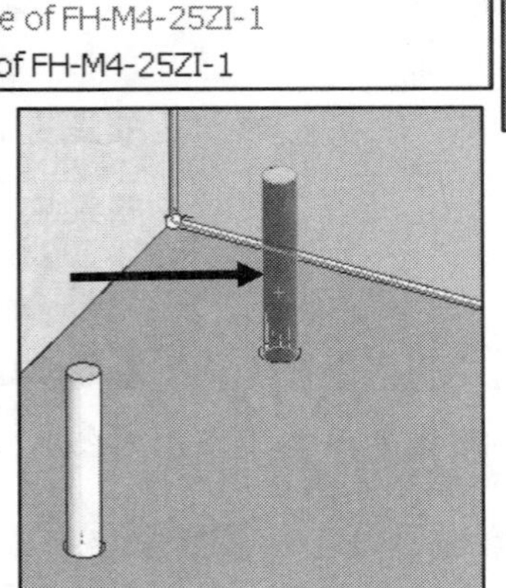

Edit the Coincident Mate.

537) Expand the second **Mate Entry**.

538) Click **Bottom view**.

539) Double-click **Coincident**.

540) Click the **FH-M4-25 bottom face**.

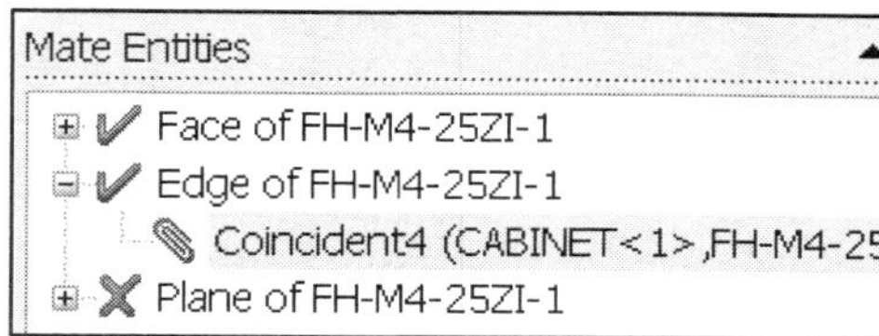

541) Click **OK** from the Mate Entities PropertyManager.

Edit the M5 Hole to an M4 Hole.

542) Click **CABINET** from the FeatureManager.

543) Click **Edit Component** Edit Compo... from the Assembly Toolbar. The CABINET entries are displayed in blue.

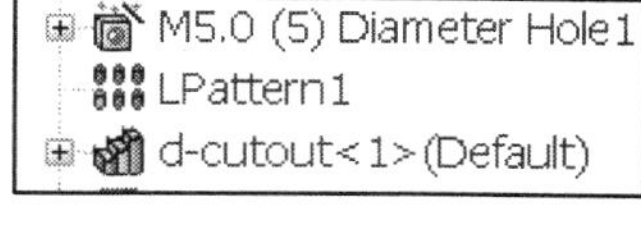

544) Expand CABINET in the FeatureManager. Right-click the **M5 Hole**. Click **Edit Feature**. The Hole Definition dialog box is displayed. Select **M4** for Size from the Hole dialog box.

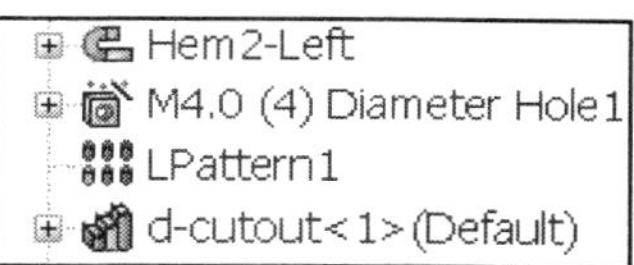

545) Click **OK** . The M4 Hole is displayed in the FeatureManager. Click **Edit Component** Edit Compo... from the Assembly Toolbar to return to the BOX assembly. The CABINET entries are displayed in black.

Save the BOX.

546) Click **Save**.

Note: The Hole of the CABINET requires a M4 hole 4mm ± 0.8. Add a limit dimension in the drawing and a revision note to document the change from an M5 to an M4. These actions are left as an exercise.

IGES imported geometry requires you to select new mate references during Replace Components. Utilize reference planes for Mate entities to save time. The Replace Components option attempts to replace all Mate entities. Reference planes provide the best security in replacing the appropriate Mate entity during the Replace Components option.

Equations

How do you insure that the fasteners remain symmetrical with the bottom of the BOX when the box-width dimension varies?

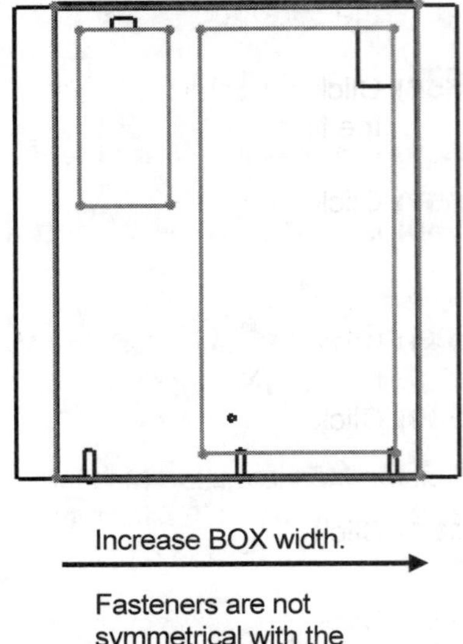

Increase BOX width.

Fasteners are not symmetrical with the bottom of the BOX.

Answer: With an Equation.

Equations use shared names to control dimensions.

Use Equations to connect values from sketches, features, patterns and various parts in an assembly.

Create an Equation. Each dimension has a unique variable name. The names are used as Equation variables. The default names are based on the Sketch, Feature or Part. Rename default names for clarity.

Resolve all Mate Errors before creating Equations. Mate Errors produce unpredictable results with parameters driven by Equations.

Activity: Equations

Display feature dimensions.

547) Drag the **Splitbar** downward to display the BOX FeatureManager.

548) Drag the **lower slide bar** downward to display the CABINET features.

549) Right-click the CABINET **Annotations folder**.

550) Check **Show Feature Dimensions**.

551) Display the **Front view**.

Edit the LPattern1 dimension Name.

552) Click the **125** dimension. Click **More Properties.**

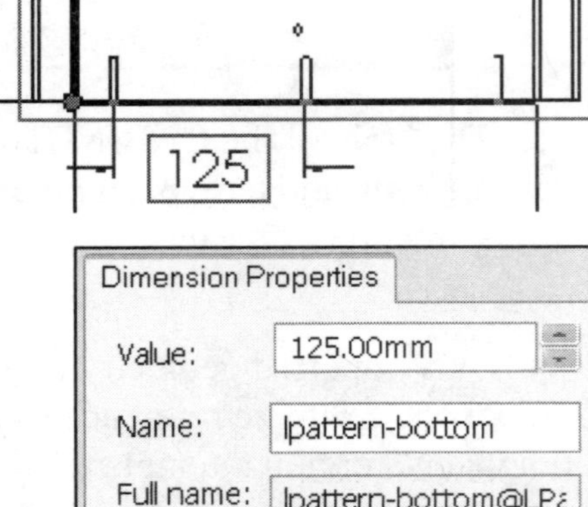

Rename the D3 dimension.

553) Enter **lpattern-bottom** for Name.

554) Click **OK**.

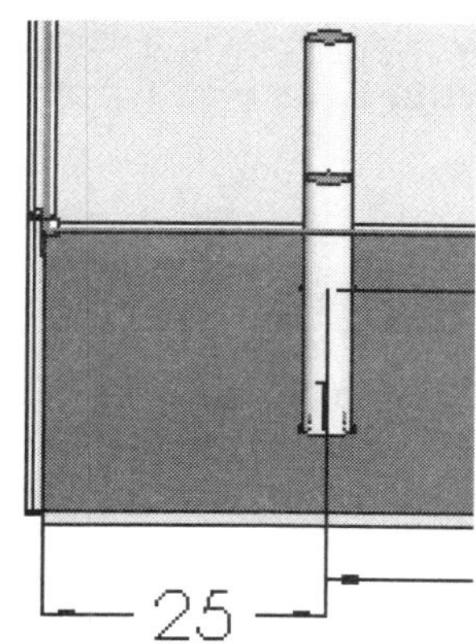

Edit the M4 Hole dimension Name.

555) Press the **Down Arrow key** approximately two times to display the back hole.

556) Click dimension **25**. 25 is the M4.0 Hole horizontal dimension in the lower left corner.

557) Click **More Properties**.

Rename the D1 dimension.

558) Enter **hole-bottom** for Name.

559) Click **OK**.

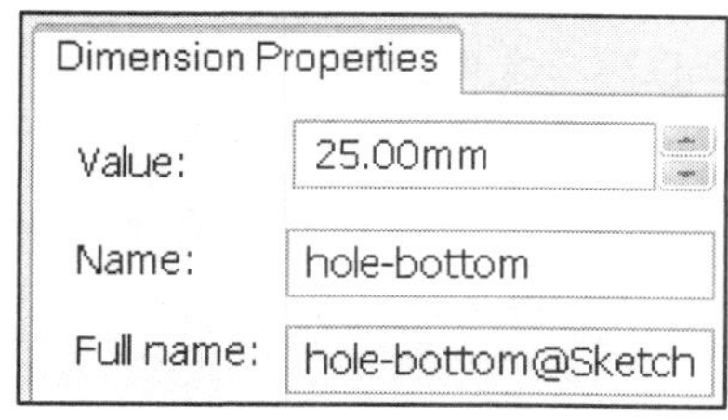

560) Click **OK** .

561) Click **Isometric view** .

Display the BOX feature dimensions.

562) Right-click the BOX **Annotations folder** in the BOX FeatureManager.

563) Check **Show Feature Dimensions**.

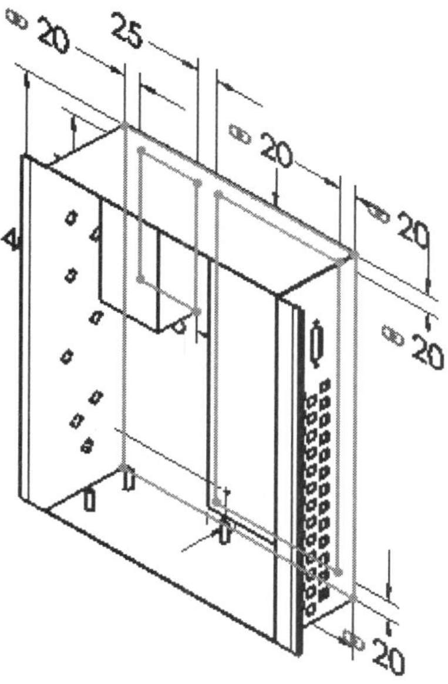

Create the first Equation.

564) Click **Front view** .

565) Click **Tools**, **Equations** Equations... from the Main menu. Line 1 displays the linked value, gap, the link icon and the value 20.

566) Click **Add** from the Equations dialog box.

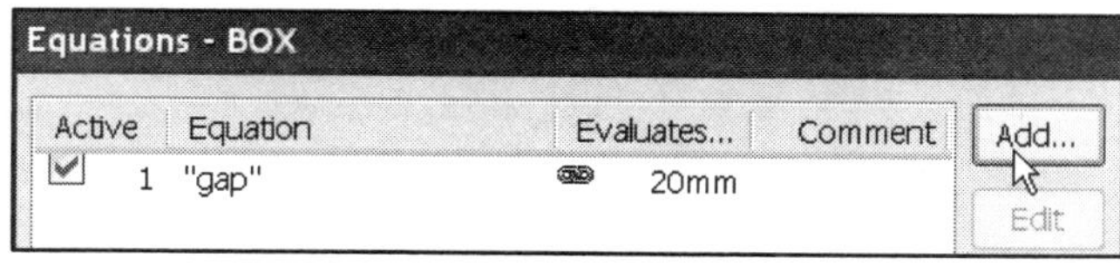

Create the first half of equation1.

567) Click the lpattern-bottom horizontal dimension, **125**. The variable "lpattern-bottom@Lpattern1@CABINET.Part" is added to the New Equation text box. Click **=** from the keypad.

Create the second half of equation1.

568) Enter **0.5* (** from the keypad.

"lpattern-bottom@LPattern1@CABINET.Part" = 0.5 * (

569) Click the box_width horizontal dimension, **300** from the Graphics window. The variable "box_width@layout" is added to the equation text box.

= 0.5 * ("box_widrh@Layout"

570) Enter **–2*** from the keypad.

= 0.5 * ("box_widrh@Layout" - 2 *

571) Click **Bottom view** .

box_widrh@Layout" - 2 * "hole-bottom@Sketch12@CABINET.Part"

572) Click the M4 hole-bottom dimension, **25**. The variable "hole-bottom@Sketch12@CABINET.Part" is add to the equation text box.

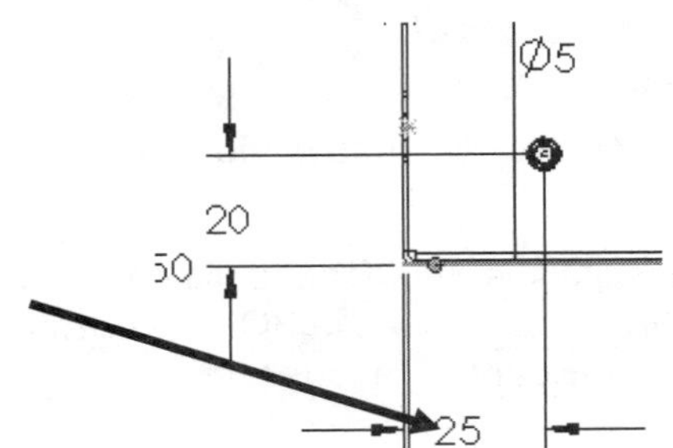

573) Enter **)** from the keypad.

Display the first equation.

574) Click **OK** from the Add Equation dialog box.

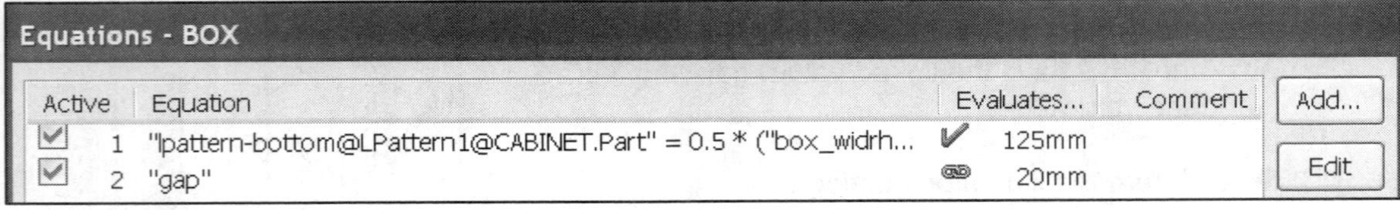

575) Click **OK** from the Equations box.

The Equation dialog box contains the complete equation. A green check mark placed in the first column indicates that the Equation is solved. The Equation evaluates to 125mm.

The Equation Σ icon, placed in front of the 125 dimension, indicates that an equation drives the value.

Remember the initial design parameters. There are three different size boxes. Remember the design intent. You build a Layout Sketch to control the different sizes.

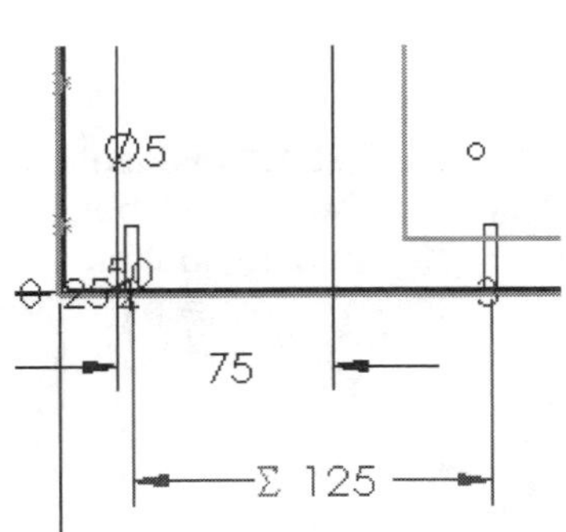

Test the equation by modify the Layout Sketch dimensions.

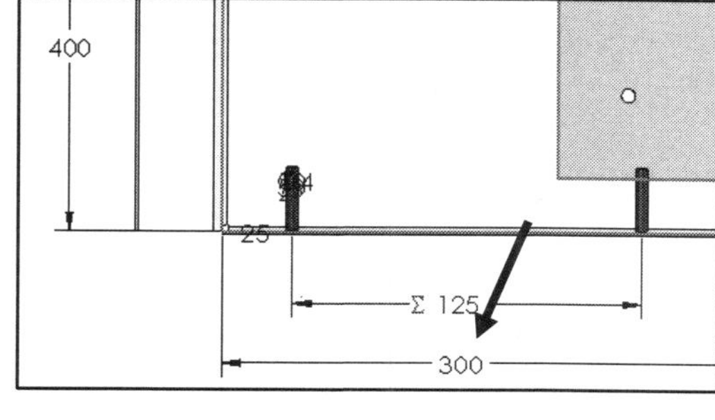

Verify the Equation. Modify the dimensions.

576) Click **Front view**.

577) Double-click the horizontal dimension box-width, **300**.

578) Enter **400**. Click **Rebuild**. The Equation dimension displays 175.

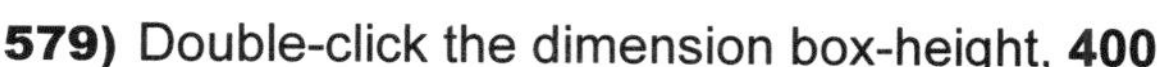

579) Double-click the dimension box-height, **400**.

580) Enter **500**. Click **Rebuild**.

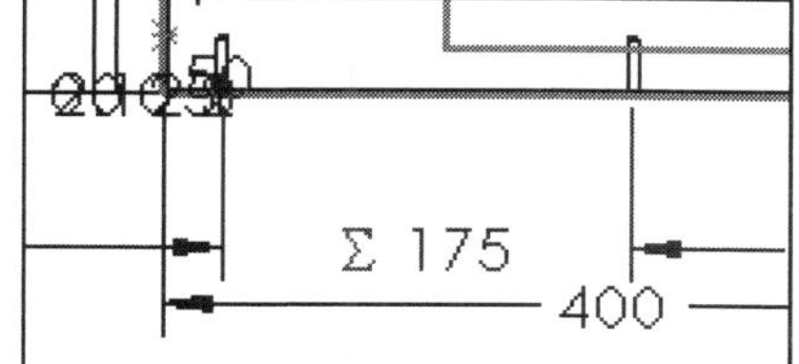

Return to the original dimensions.

581) Double-click on the horizontal dimension, **400**. Enter **300**.

582) Double-click the vertical dimension, **500**. Enter **400**.

583) Click **Rebuild**.

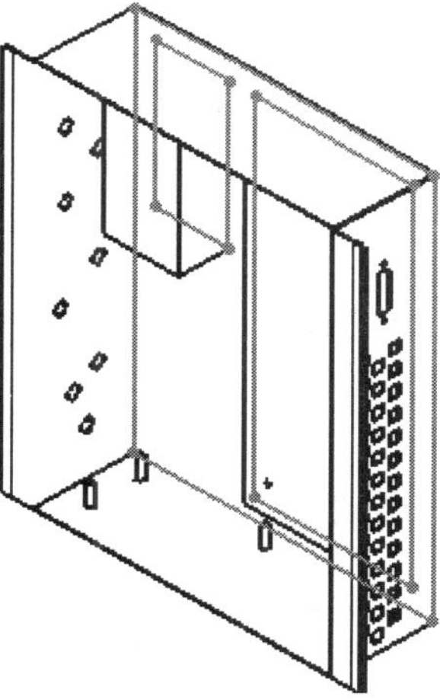

Hide the dimensions.

584) Right-click the **CABINET Annotations folder**, uncheck **Show Feature Dimension.**

585) Right-click the **BOX Annotations folder**, uncheck **Show Feature Dimension**.

Save the BOX.

586) Click **Isometric view**

587) Click **Save**.

The BOX assembly requires three configurations. Recall the CABINET drawing. You had two configurations that controlled the Flat Pattern feature state.

Now control dimensions, features and parts in an assembly. A Design Table is an efficient tool to control variations in assemblies and parts.

Design Tables

A Design Table is an Excel spreadsheet used to create multiple configurations in a part or assembly. Utilize the Design Table to create three configurations of the BOX assembly:

- Small
- Medium
- Large

Activity: Design Tables

Create the Design Table.

588) Click **Insert**, **Design Table** Design Table... from the Main menu. Accept the Auto-create default.

589) Click **OK** from the Design Table PropertyManager.

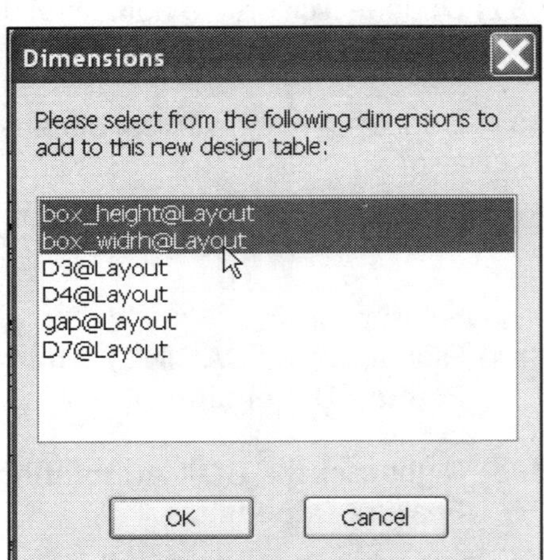

Select the input dimension.

590) Hold the **Ctrl** key down.

591) Click the **box_width@Layout** dimension.

592) Click the **box_height@Layout** dimension.

593) Release the **Ctrl** key.

594) Click **OK**.

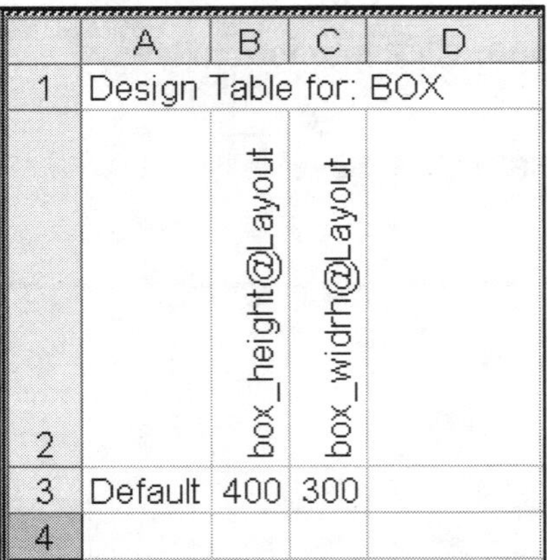

	A	B	C	D
1	Design Table for: BOX			
2		box_height@Layout	box_widrh@Layout	
3	Default	400	300	
4				

The input dimension names and default values are automatically entered into the Design Table.

The value Default is entered in Cell A3.

The value 400 is entered in Cell B3 for box_height and the value 300 is entered in Cell C3 for box_width.

Enter the three configuration names.

595) Click Cell **A4**. Enter **Small**.

596) Click Cell **A5**. Enter **Medium**.

597) Click Cell **A6**. Enter **Large**.

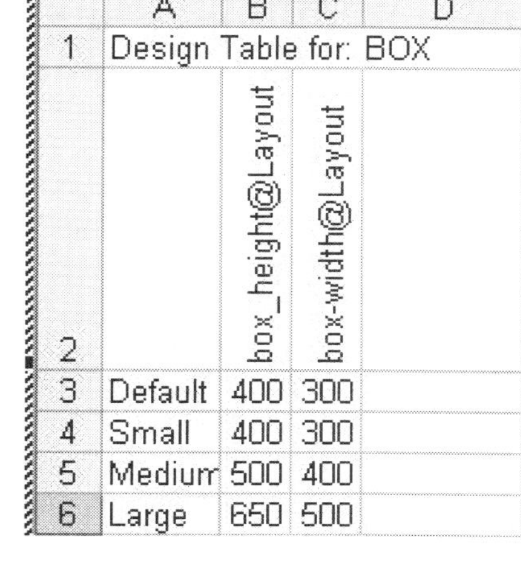

	A	B	C	D
1	Design Table for: BOX			
2		box_height@Layout	box-width@Layout	
3	Default	400	300	
4	Small	400	300	
5	Medium	500	400	
6	Large	650	500	

Enter the dimension values for the Small configuration.

598) Click Cell **B4**. Enter **400** for box_height. Click Cell **C4**. Enter **300** for box_width.

Enter the dimension values for the Medium configuration.

599) Click Cell **B5**. Enter **600**. Click Cell **C5**. Enter **400**.

Enter the dimension values for the Large configuration.

600) Click Cell **B6**. Enter **650**. Click Cell **C6**. Enter **500**.

Build the three configurations.

601) Click a **position** outside the EXCEL Design Table in the Graphics window.

602) Click **OK** to generate the configurations. The Design Table icon is displayed in the BOX FeatureManager.

Display the configurations.

603) Click the **Configuration Manager** icon.

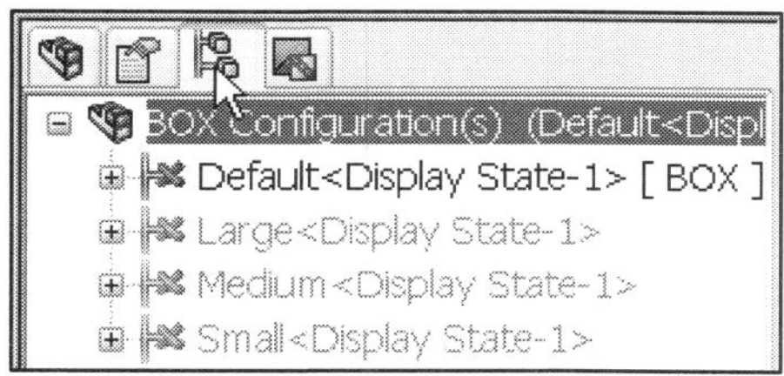

604) Double-click **Small**. Double-click **Medium**.

605) Double-click **Large**.

Return to the Default configuration.

606) Double-click **Default.**

Fit the model to the Graphics window.

607) Press the **f** key.

608) Click **Save** . Click **Yes**.

Expand the FeatureManager.

609) Click the **FeatureManager** icon.

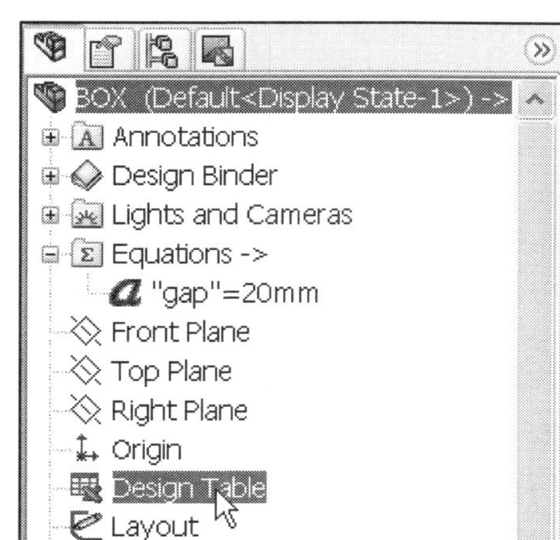

Edit to the Design Table.

610) Right-click **Design Table** from the BOX FeatureManager. Click **Edit Table**.

	A	B	C	D
1	Design Table for: BOX			
2		box_height@Layout	box-width@Layout	$State@POWERSUPPLY<1>
3	Default	400	300	R
4	Small	400	300	R
5	Medium	500	400	R
6	Large	650	500	S

611) Click **OK** from the Add Rows and Columns dialog box.

612) Click Cell **D2**. Enter **$State@POWERSUPPLY<1>**.

613) Click Cell **D3**. Enter **R** for Resolved.

614) Copy Cell **D3**. Select Cell **D4** and Cell **D5**. Click **Paste**. Click Cell **D6**. Enter **S** for Suppressed.

615) Update the configurations. Click a **position** outside the EXCEL Design Table. Click **OK**.

The Design Table component variables must match the FeatureManager names in order to create configurations. The Design Table variable $State@POWERSUPPLY<1> is exactly as displayed in the BOX FeatureManager. If the name in the BOX FeatureManager was P-SUPPLY<2> then the Design Table variable is $State@ P-SUPPLY<2>.

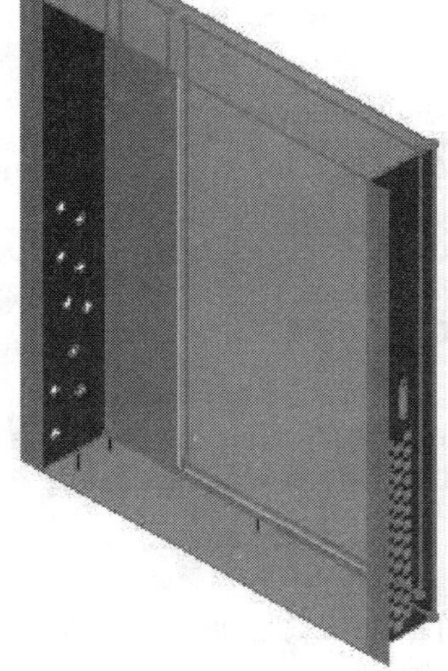

Display the Large Configuration.

616) Click the **Configuration Manager**. Double-click **Large** from the Configuration Manager. The POWERSUPPLY is suppressed in the Large configuration.

Return to the Default configuration.

617) Double-click **Default**.

Fit the model to the Graphics window.

618) Press the **f** key.

Save the BOX assembly.

619) Click **Save**. Click **Yes** to save the referenced documents.

Dimensions, Color, Configurations, Custom Properties and other variables are controlled through Design Tables. The engineer working on the sheet metal bracket had to visit another customer. As the project manager, it is up to you to get the job done. Create the sheet metal BRACKET in the next activity. The sheet metal BRACKET is created In-context to illustrate the Top Down Assembly Modeling process. Sheet metal parts are created in a Bottom Up approach and then inserted and mated in the assembly.

BRACKET Part-Sheet Metal Features

The CABINET was converted from a solid part to a sheet metal part by using Rip and Insert Bends. The sheet metal BRACKET part begins with the Base Flange. The Base Flange utilizes a U-shaped sketch profile. The material thickness and bend radius are set in the Base Flange.

Create the BRACKET In-context of the BOX assembly. The BRACKET references the inside bottom edge and left corner of the CABINET.

 Orient the Flat Pattern. The first sketched edge remains fixed with the Flatten tool.

Sketch the first line from left to right coincident with the inside bottom edge. The BRACKET is not symmetrical and requires a right hand and left hand version. Utilize Mirror Component to create a right-hand copy of the BRACKET.

Activity: BRACKET Part-Sheet Metal Features

Insert the BRACKET component.

620) Open the **BOX** assembly.

621) Click **Insert**, **Component**, **New Part** New Part... from the Main menu.

622) Click **OK**. Enter **BRACKET** for part name. Click **Save**.

623) Click the **Front Plane** from the BOX FeatureManager.

Sketch the profile for the Base Flange.

624) Click **Front view**.

625) Check **View**, **Temporary Axis** from the Main menu.

626) **Zoom to Area** on the front lower inside edge of the BOX.

627) Click **Line** Line.

628) Sketch a **horizontal line** collinear with the inside edge of the CABINET. Note: Sketch the horizontal line from left to right.

629) Sketch a **vertical line** and a **horizontal line** to complete the U-shaped profile.

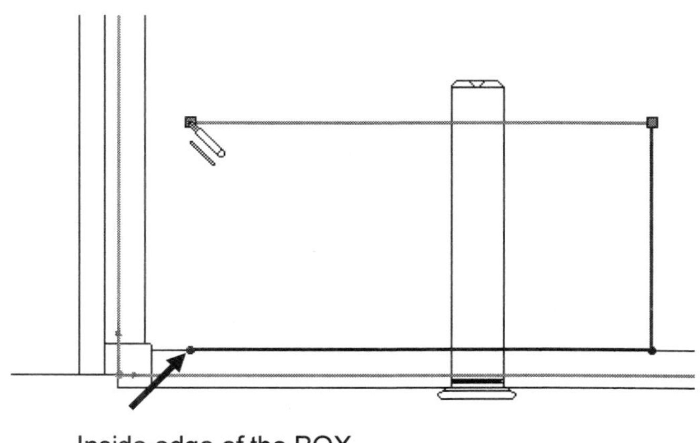

Inside edge of the BOX

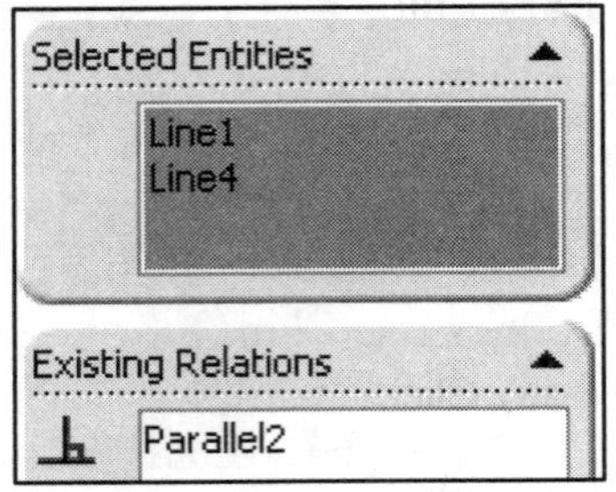

Add an Equal Relation.

630) Right-click **Select**. Click the **top horizontal** line. Hold the **Ctrl** key down. Click the **Bottom horizontal** line. Release the **Ctrl** key. Click **Equal** = . Click **OK** .

Note: The bottom horizontal line is displayed in black. The bottom line is Collinear with the inside bottom edge. Add a Collinear relation between the bottom line and the inside bottom edge if required.

Add dimensions.

631) Click **Smart Dimension** Smart Dimens... .

632) Click the **top horizontal line**. Click the **Top** of the fastener. Click a **position** to the right of the fastener.

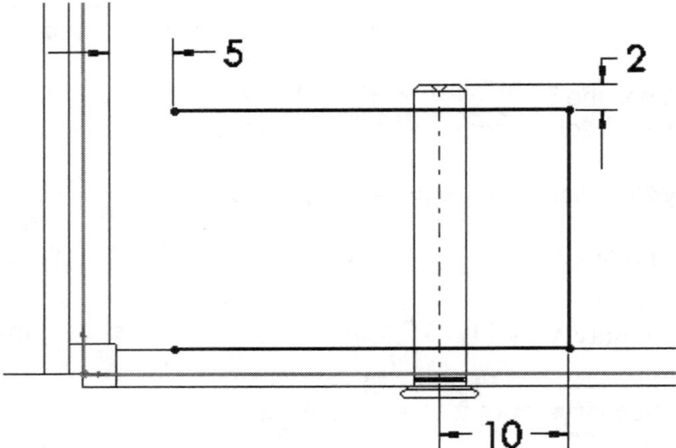

633) Enter **2**.

634) Click the **centerline** of the fastener. Click the **vertical line**. Click a **position** below the fastener.

635) Enter **10**.

636) Click the **left edge** of the CABINET. Click the **left end point** of the top horizontal line. Click a **position** above the profile.

637) Enter **5.**

Insert the Base Flange.

638) Click **Isometric view** .

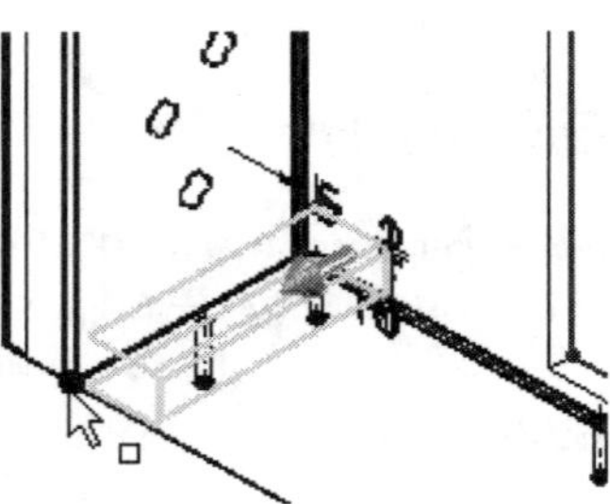

639) Click **Base Flange** Base-Fl... from the Sheet Metal toolbar.

640) Select **Up to Vertex** for Direction 1.

641) Click the CABINET **Extruded-Base front left vertex**.

642) Enter **1** for Thickness.

643) Enter **2** for Bend Radius.

644) Enter **.45** for K factor.

645) Click **OK**.

646) Click the **Front view**.

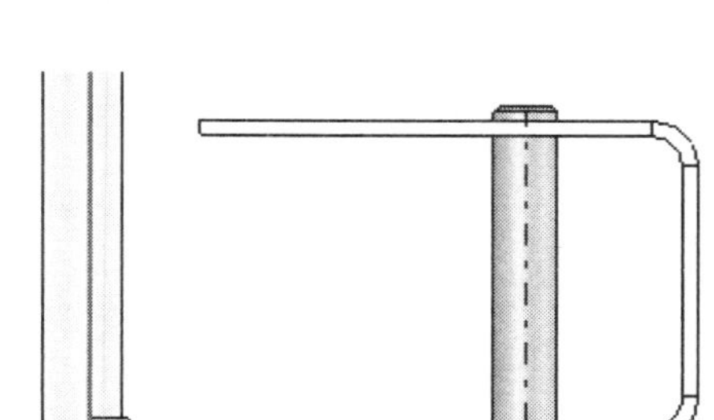

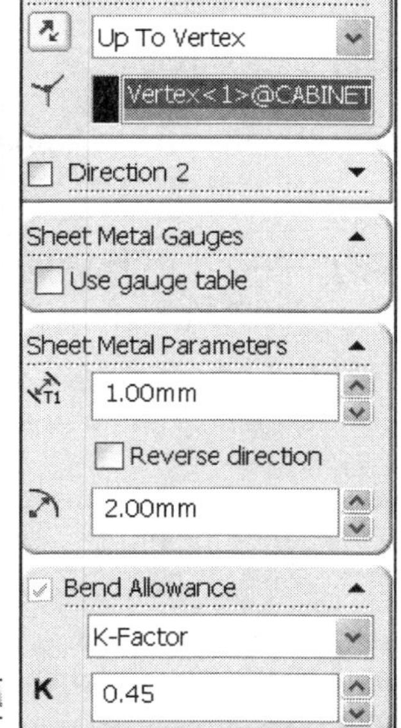

The PEM® fasteners protrude through the BRACKET in the BOX assembly.

Save the BOX assembly.

647) Click **Save**.

Open the BRACKET part from the BOX assembly.

648) Right-click the **BRACKET** in the Graphics window.

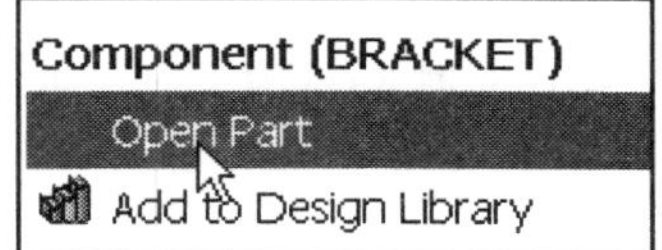

649) Click **Open Part**.

The BRACKET part contains no holes. The BRACKET requires two holes that reference the location of the fasteners. Utilize In-context Extruded Cut feature to locate the holes. Display Wireframe mode to view the fastener position. Allow for a 0.8mm clearance.

Activity: BRACKET Part-In-context Features

Insert the Extruded Cut feature in-context of the BOX assembly.

650) Open the **BOX** assembly. The Edit Component Edit Compo... icon is activated and the BRACKET entry in the FeatureManager is displayed in blue.

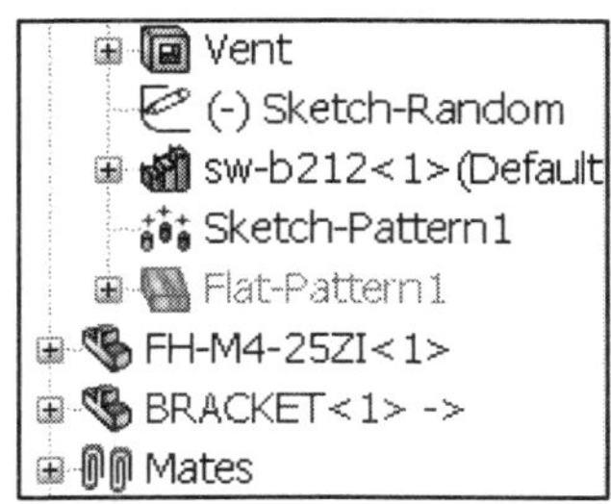

651) Press the **f** key.

652) **Rotate** to view the top face of the BRACKET.

653) Click the **BRACKET top face**.

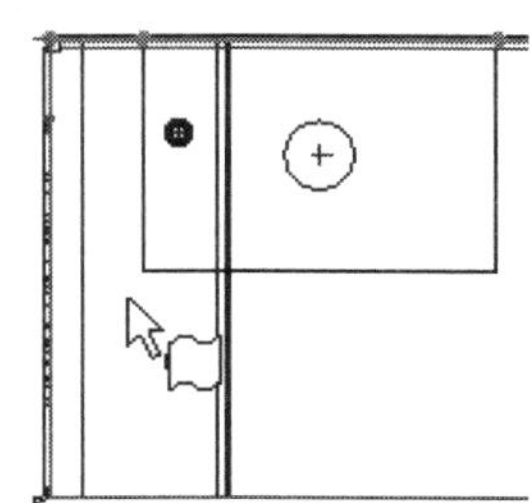

654) Click **Sketch** Sketch. Click **Top view**.

655) Click **Wireframe**.

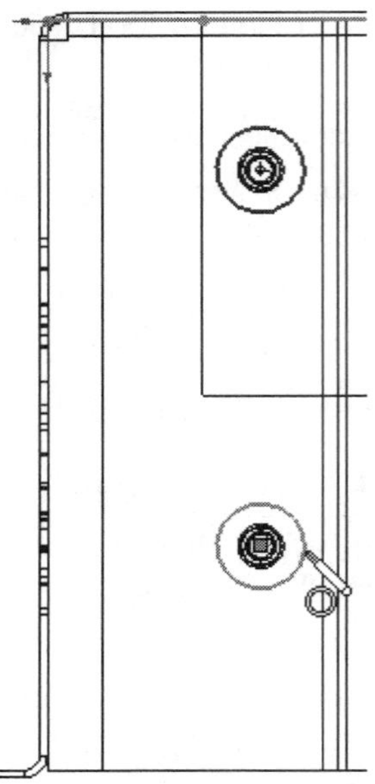

Sketch two circular profiles referencing the PEM center points.

656) Click **Circle** Circle.

657) Drag the **mouse pointer** over the center point of the top PEM circular edge to "wake up" the PEM center point.

658) Click the **PEM centerpoint**. Click a **position** to the right of the center point.

659) Drag the **mouse pointer** over the center point of the bottom PEM circular edge to "wake up" the PEM center point.

660) Click the **PEM center point**. Click a **position** to the right of the center point.

Add an Equal Relation.

661) Right-click **Select**.

662) Click the **circumference** of the top circle.

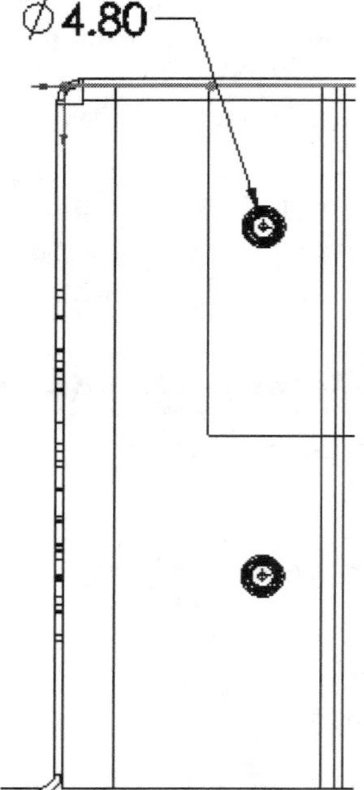

663) Hold the **Ctrl** key down.

664) Click the **circumference** of the bottom circle. Release the **Ctrl** key. Click **Equal**.

665) Click **OK**.

Add dimensions.

666) Click **Smart Dimension**  Smart Dimens.... Click the **circumference** of the top circle.

667) Click a **position** off the profile.

668) Enter **4.80**.

669) Click **Extruded Cut**  Extruded Cut from the Features toolbar.

670) Select **Through All** for Direction1.

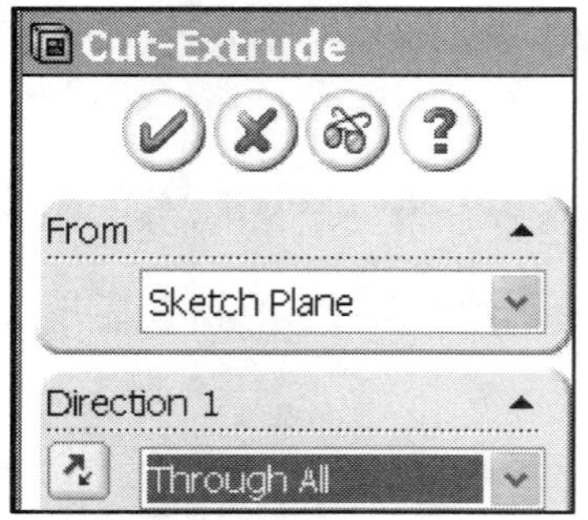

671) Click **OK** from the Cut-Extrude PropertyManager.

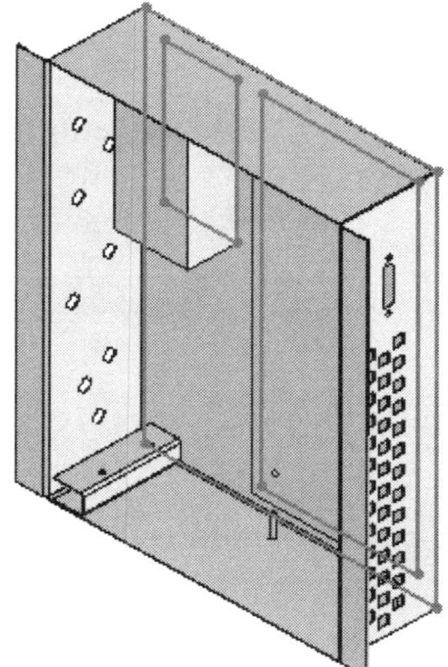

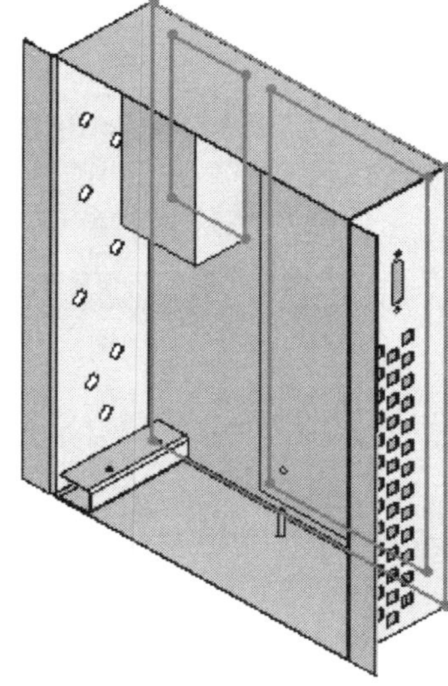

Return to the BOX assembly.

672) Click **Edit Component** Edit Compo... from the Assembly toolbar.

673) Click **Isometric view**. Click **Shaded With Edges**.

Save the Box assembly and its referenced components.

674) Click **Save**. Click **Yes**.

No additional references from the BOX components are required. The Edge Flange Tab, Break Corner and Miter Flange sheet metal features are developed in the BRACKET part.

The Edge Flange feature adds a flange on the selected edge. Edit the Flange Profile to create a 30 mm tab, 20 mm from the front face. The Tab requires fillet corners. The Break Corner feature adds fillets or chamfers to sheet metal edges.

Activity: BRACKET Part-Edge Flange Tab, Break Corner and Miter Flange Features

Open the BRACKET.

675) Right-click **BRACKET** in the Graphics window.

676) Click **Open Part**.

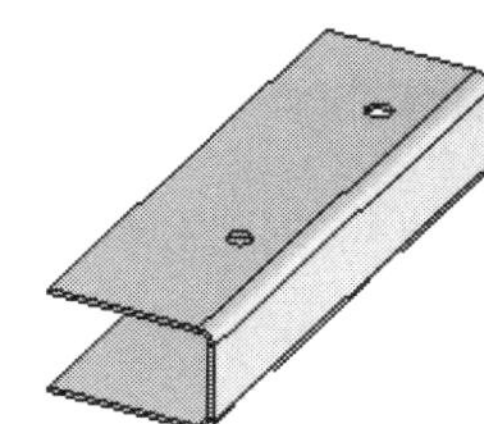

Display the 2D flat state.

677) Right-click **Flat-Pattern1** from the FeatureManager. Click **Unsuppress**.

Display the 3D formed state.

678) Right-click **Flat-Pattern1**. Click **Suppress**.

Insert a Tab using the Edge Flange features.

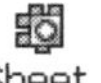

679) Click **Sheet Metal** Sheet Metal from the Control Area.

680) Click the **top left edge** of the BRACKET.

681) Click **Edge Flange** Edge Flange. Click a **position** above the BRACKET for direction.

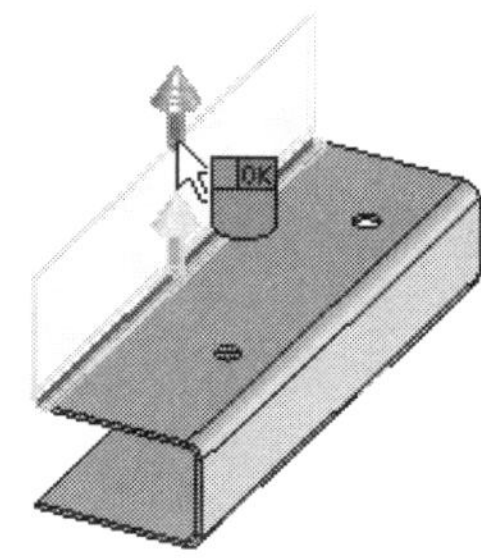

682) Enter **20** for Flange Length in the spin box.

683) Click **Edit Flange Profile** [Edit Flange Profile]. Do not click the Finish button at this time. Move the Profile Sketch dialog box off to the side of the Graphics window.

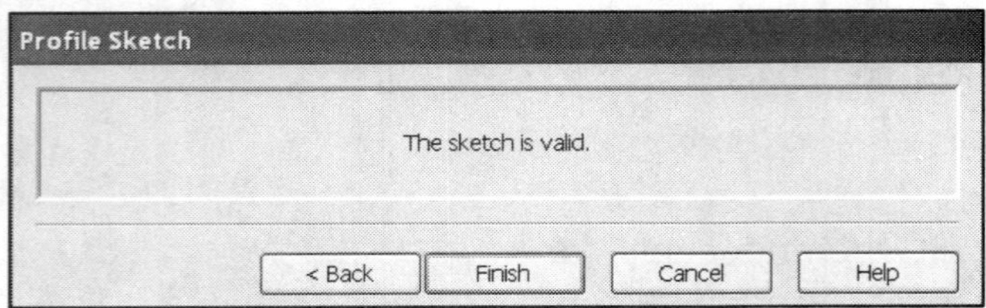

684) Drag the **left edge** towards the front Hole.

685) Drag the **right edge** towards the front Hole.

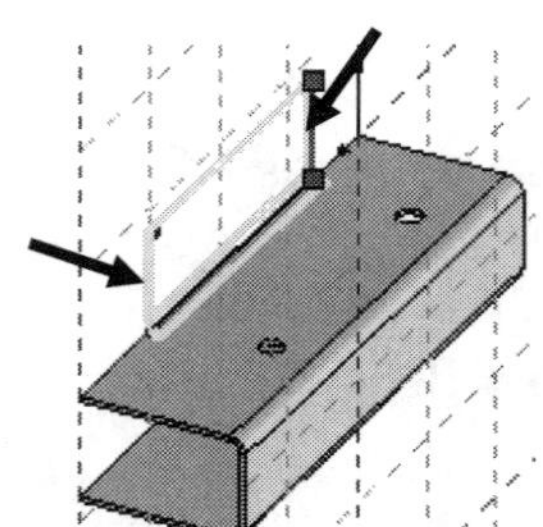

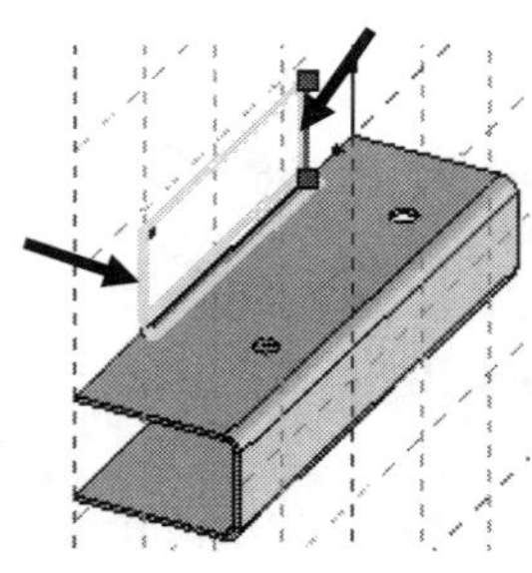

Add dimensions.

686) Click **Smart Dimension** Smart Dimens....

687) Click the **front left vertex** of Base-Flange1.

688) Click the **left vertical** line.

689) Click a **position** above the profile.

690) Enter **20**.

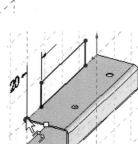

691) Click the **top horizontal** line.

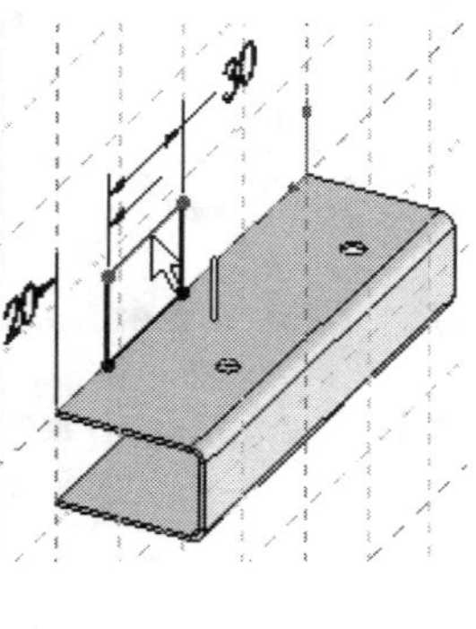

692) Click a **position** above the profile.

693) Enter **30**.

694) Click **Finish** from the Profile Sketch box.

695) Click **OK**.

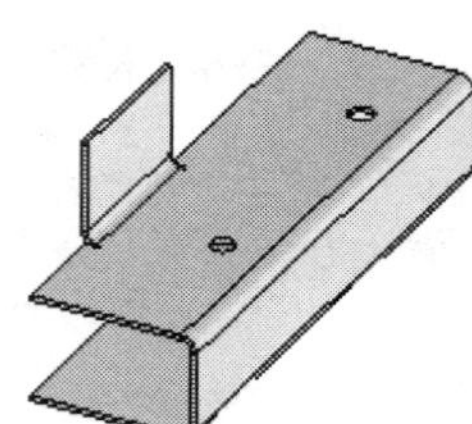

Insert the Break Corner.

696) Zoom in on the Tab.

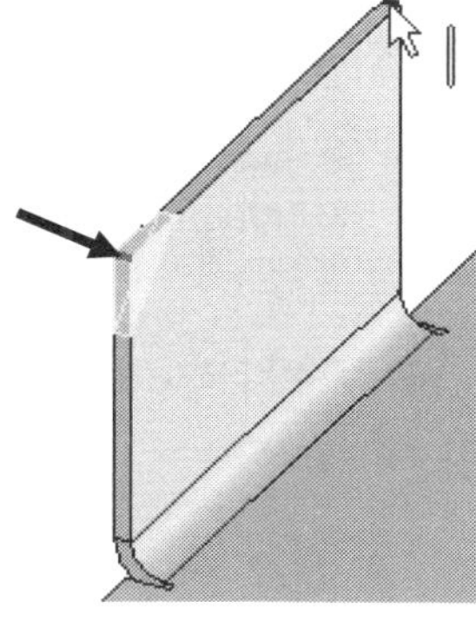

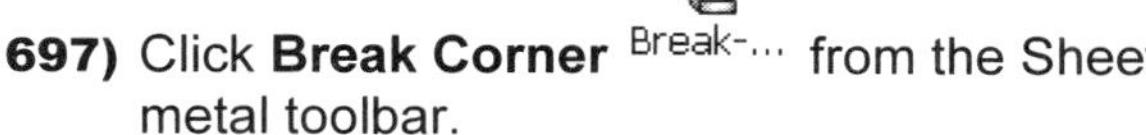

697) Click **Break Corner** Break-... from the Sheet metal toolbar.

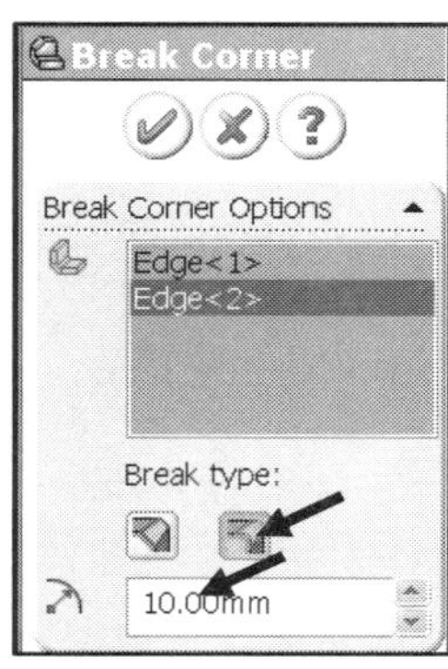

698) Click the small **front edge** of the flange

699) Click the small **back edge** of the flange.

700) Click **Fillet** for Break type.

701) Enter **10** for Radius.

702) Click **OK**.

703) Click **Save**.

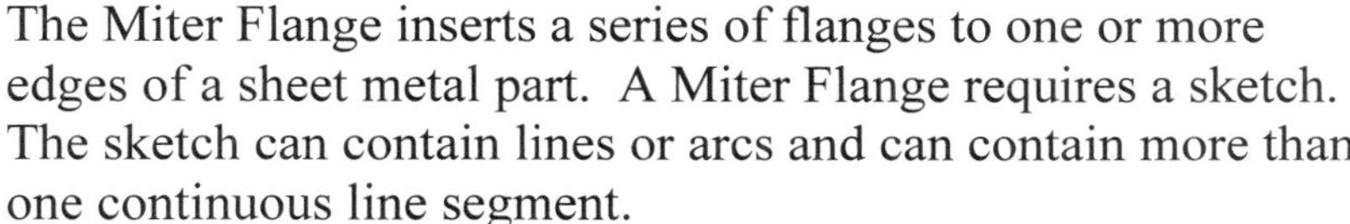

The Miter Flange inserts a series of flanges to one or more edges of a sheet metal part. A Miter Flange requires a sketch. The sketch can contain lines or arcs and can contain more than one continuous line segment.

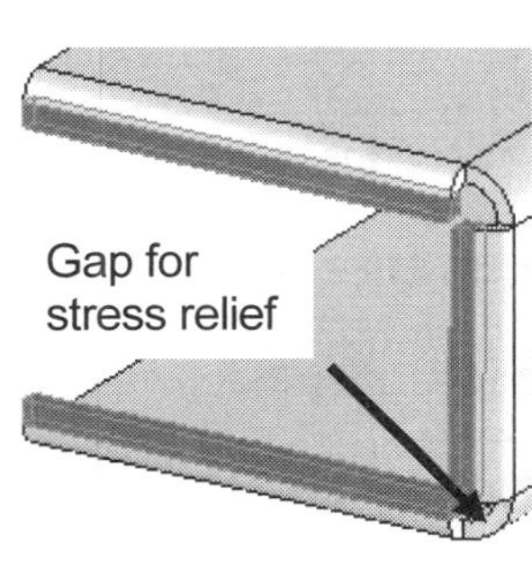

The sketch plane is normal (perpendicular) to the first edge, closest to the selection point. The geometry you create must be physically possible. New flanges cannot cross or deform. The current 2mm bend radius of the BRACKET is too small to insert a Miter Flange. Leave the area open for stress relief and utilize a Gap distance of 0.5 mm.

Insert the Miter Flange.

704) Click **Miter Flange** Miter Flange. from the Sheet metal toolbar.

705) Click the BRACKET **front inside edge**. Note: Click the edge close to the left side. The new sketch Origin is displayed in the left corner.

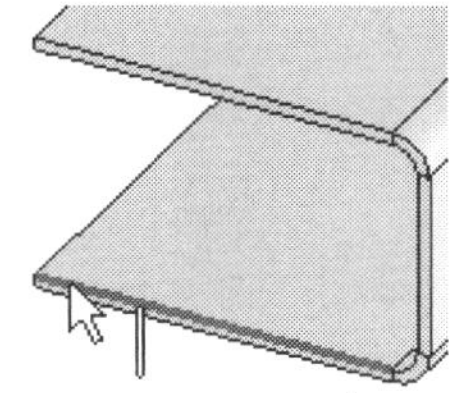

706) Zoom to Area on the left corner.

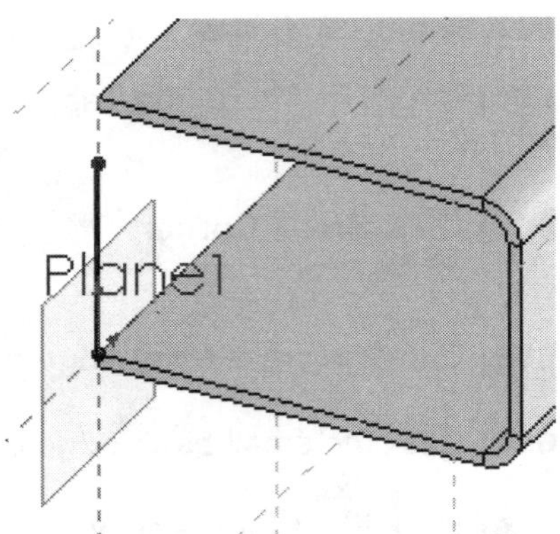

707) Click **Line** Line .

708) Sketch a **small vertical line** at the front inside left corner. The first point is coincident with the new sketch Origin.

Add dimensions.

709) Click **Smart Dimension**  Smart Dimens... .

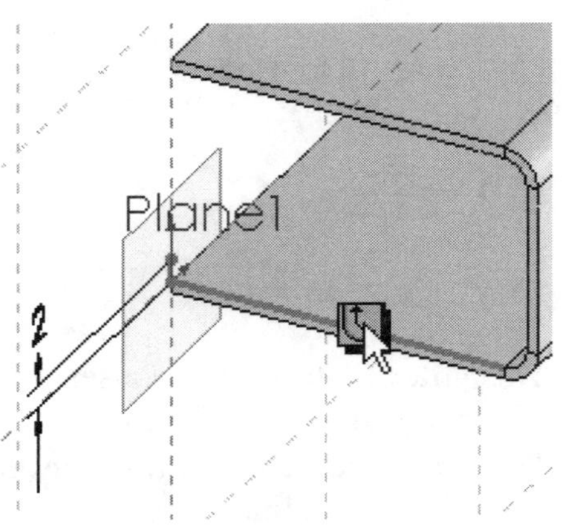

710) Click the **vertical line**.

711) Click a **position** to the left of the BRACKET.

712) Enter **2**.

713) Click **Exit Sketch**  Exit Sketch .

714) Click the **Propagate** icon to select inside tangent edges.

715) Uncheck **Use Default Radius**.

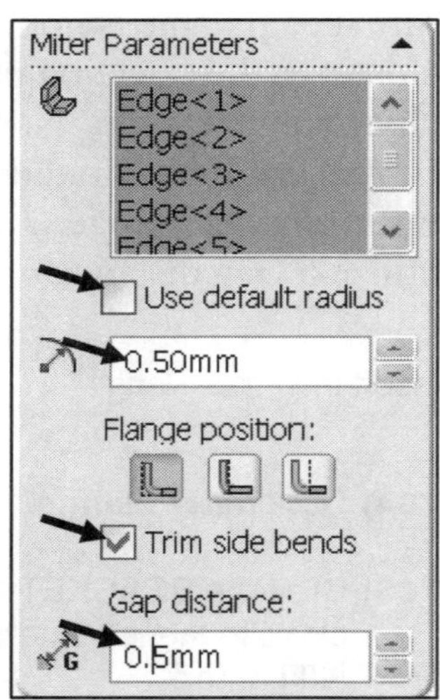

716) Enter **.5** for Bend Radius.

717) Check **Trim side bends**.

718) Enter **.5** for Rip Gap distance.

719) Click **OK** .

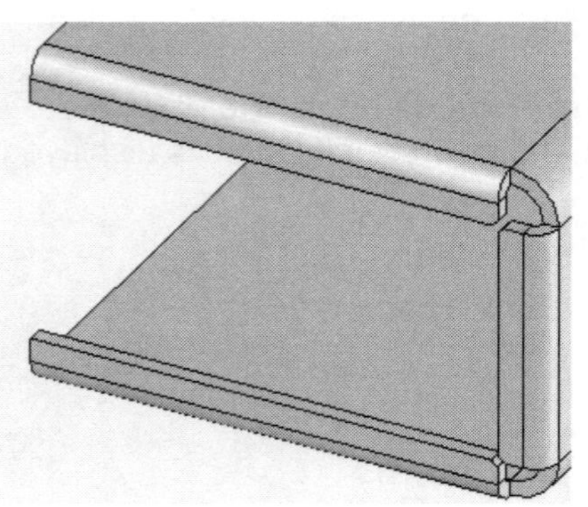

Display the flat and formed states.

720) Click **Isometric view** .

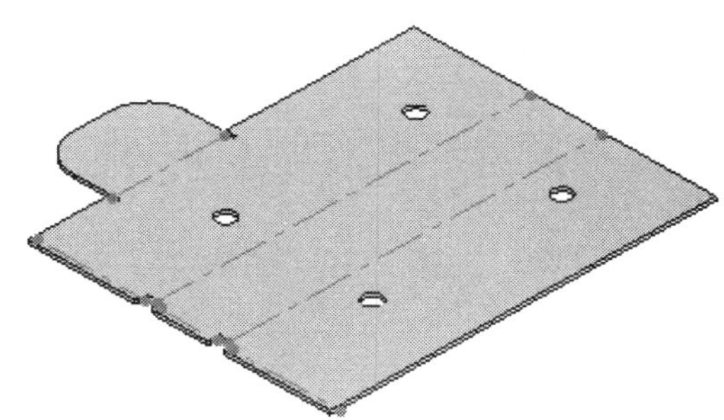

721) Click **Flatten** Flatten to display the 2D flat state.

722) Click **Flatten** Flatten to display the 3D formed state.

Save the BRACKET.

723) Click **Save** .

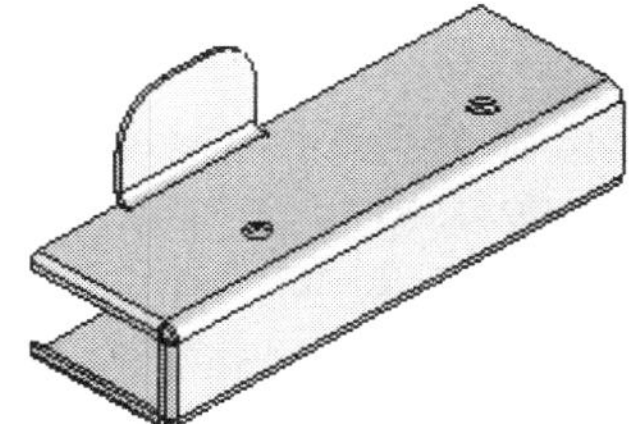

The Trim side bends option creates a Chamfer at the inside corners of the Miter Flange. Miter profiles produce various results. Combine lines and arcs for more complex miters.

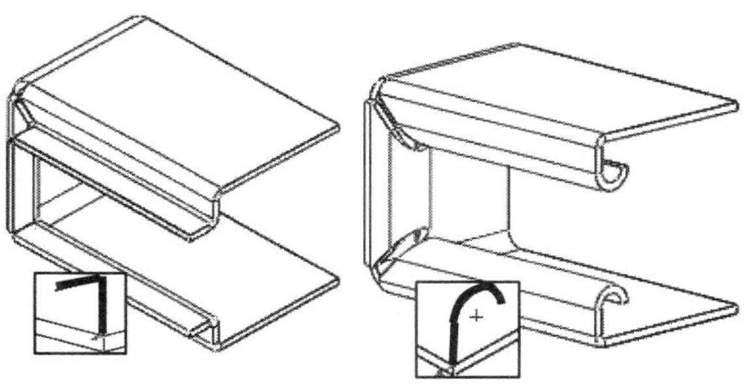

Covers are very common sheet metal parts. Covers protect equipment and operators from harm.

Utilize the Base Flange, Miter Flange, Close Corner and Edge Flange to create simple covers. Add Holes for fasteners. The Base Flange is a single sketched line that represents the area to be covered. Insert the Miter Flange and select the 4 edges on the top face. Utilize the Material Outside option for Flange position to add the walls to the outside of the Base Flange.

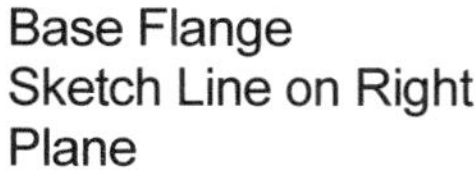

Base Flange
Sketch Line on Right Plane

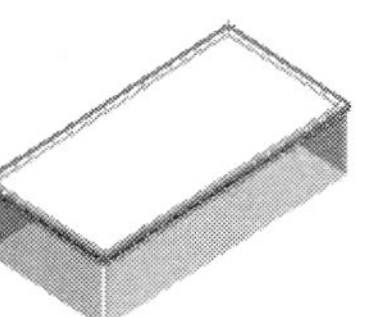

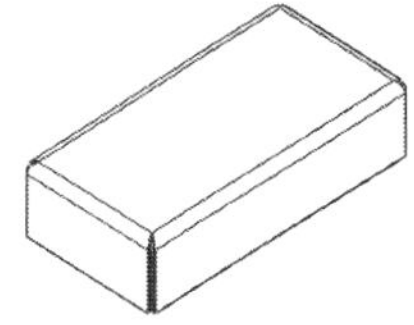

Miter Flange
Select 4 edges around the top face.

The Miter Flange creates a gap between the perpendicular walls. The Closed Corner extends the faces to eliminate the gap.

Create the Edge Flanges after the corners are closed.

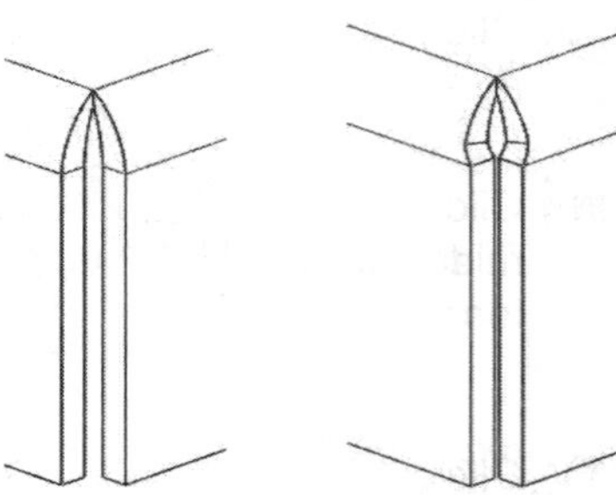

A Sketched Bend inserts a bend on a flat face or plane. The Sketch Bend requires a profile.

Holes and cuts are added to the cover. A hole or cut can cross a bend line.

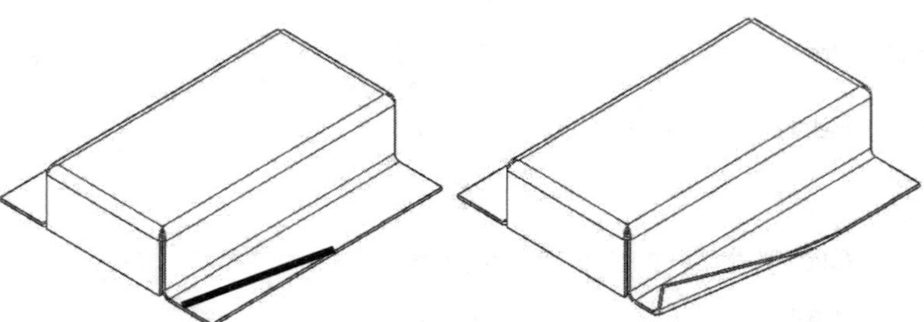

The Base Flange utilized the MidPlane option. Utilize the same plane to mirror the sets of holes.

There is plenty of time to develop additional sheet metal parts in the provided exercises at the end of the chapter.

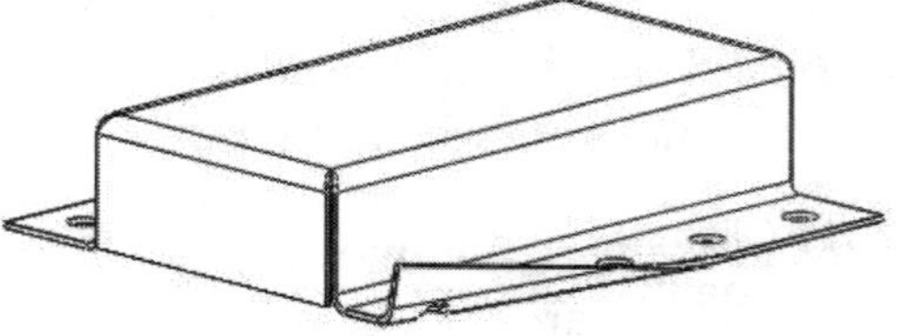

Return to the BOX assembly.

A second BRACKET is required for the right side of the CABINET. Design for the three configurations and reuse geometry.

BRACKET-Mirror Component

Insert a reference plane through the center PEM® fastener. The right side BRACKET requires a right hand version of the left side BRACKET. Utilize the Mirror Component option to create the mirrored right side BRACKET. Mate and modify the mirrored right side BRACKET.

Activity: BRACKET-Mirror Component

724) Open the **BOX** assembly.

Display Sketches, Planes and Temporary Axes.

725) Click **View**, check **Sketches** from the Main menu.

726) Click **View**, check **Planes** from the Main menu.

727) Click **View**, check **Temporary Axes** from the Main menu.

728) Zoom to Area on the top circular face of the middle PEM® fastener.

Insert a Reference Point.

729) Click **Insert**, **Reference Geometry**, **Point** Point... .

730) Click the **top circular edge** of the back middle fastener. The Reference Point is located at the center point of the top circle.

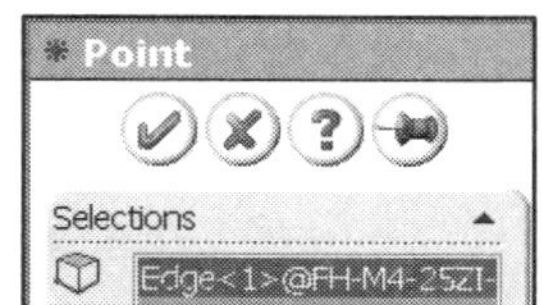

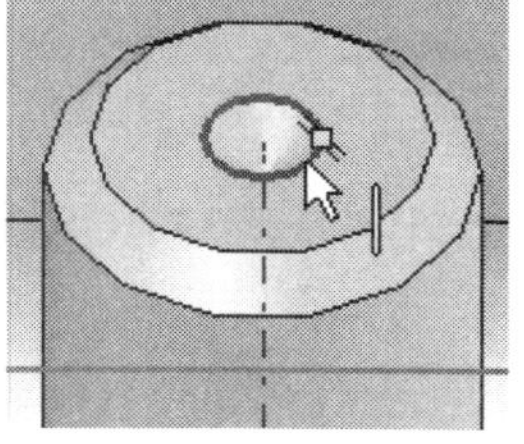

731) Click **OK** from the Point PropertyManager.

732) Press the **f** key.

733) Rename **Point1** to **Mirror Point**.

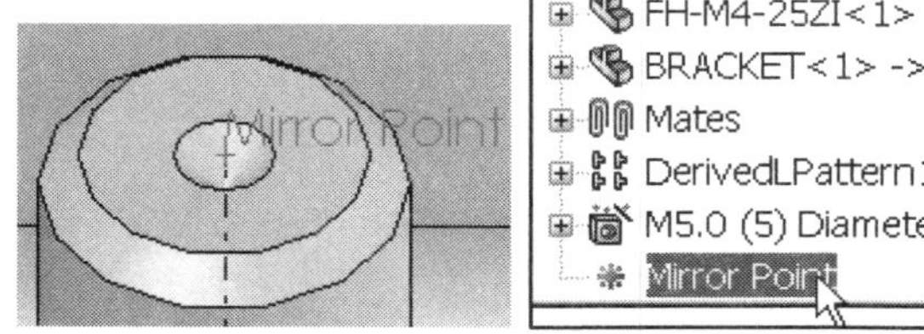

Insert a Reference Plane.

734) Click **Insert**, **Reference Geometry, Plane** Plane... from the Main menu.

735) Click **Parallel Plane at Point** Parallel Plane at Point.

736) Click the **Mirror Point** of the middle fastener from the FeatureManager.

737) Click the **Right Plane** in the BOX assembly from the FeatureManager.

738) Click **OK** from the Plane PropertyManager.

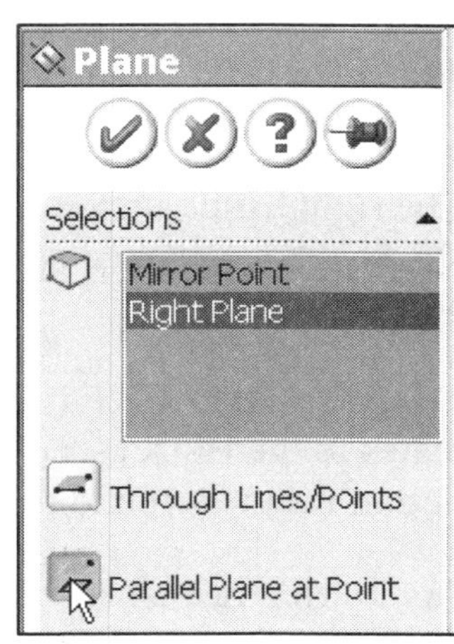

Fit the model to the Graphics window.

739) Press the **f** key.

740) Rename **PlANE1** to **Mirror PLANE**.

741) Click **Save** .

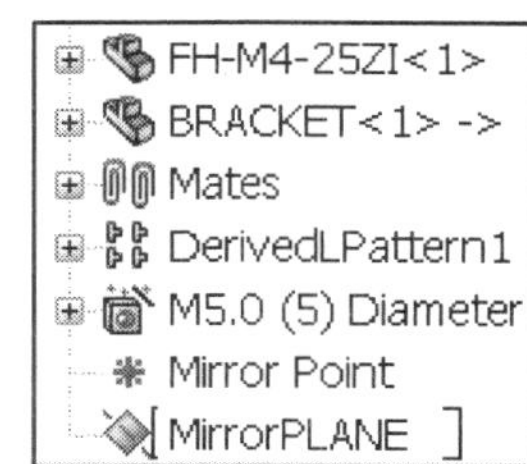

Display reference geometry in the Assembly. Utilize Short Cut keys to view sketches, planes and axis in the assembly. Reference geometry is not displayed by default.

Mirror the Component.

742) Click **Mirror Plane** from the FeatureManager.

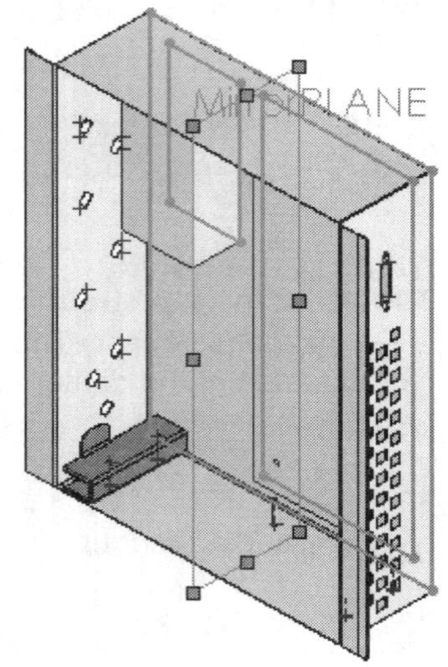

743) Click **Insert**, **Mirror Components** from the Main menu. The Mirror Plane is selected.

744) Click **BRACKET** from the BOX FeatureManager.

745) Check the **BRACKET-1** entry in the Component to Mirror box for left/right versions. The Recreate mates to new components box remains unchecked.

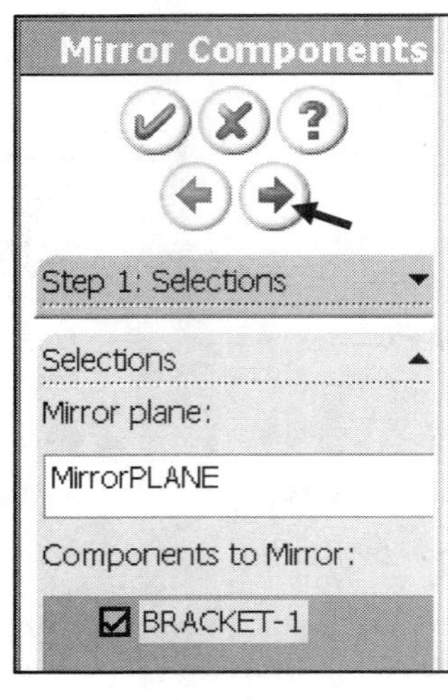

746) Click **Next**. Accept the default name for the new part, MirrorBRACKET.

747) Click **OK** from the Mirror Components PropertyManager.

The right hand version of the BRACKET is named MirrorBRACKET.

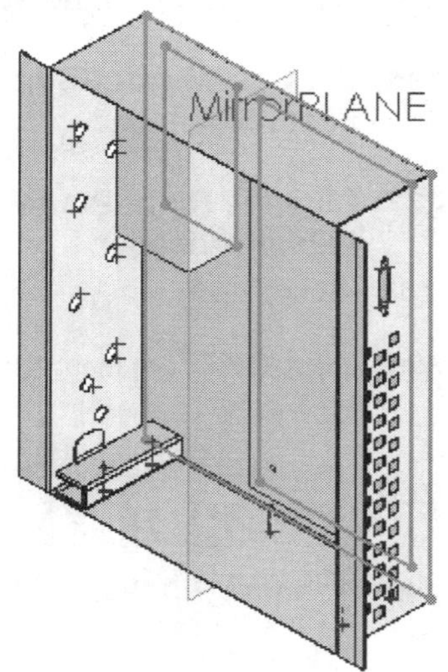

The MirrorBRACKET requires mates to the BOX assembly. Utilize the Mirror Component option for the left and right hand version.

An interference exists between the MOTHERBOARD and the MirrorBRACKET.

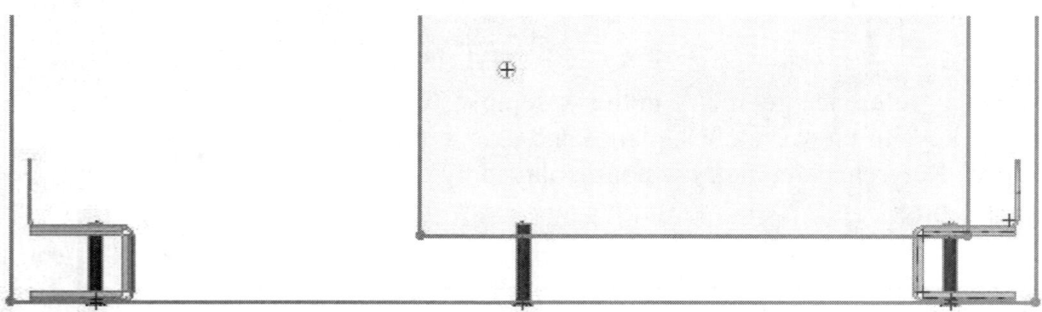

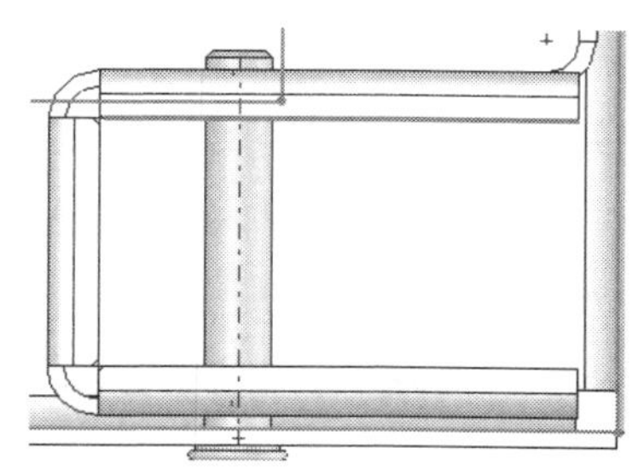

Move the MirrorBRACKET.

748) Click and drag the **MirrorBRACKET** downward to display the top cylindrical face of the PEM fasteners.

Mate the MirrorBRACKET.

749) Click **Mate** from the Assembly toolbar.

750) Click the **cylindrical face** of the front right fastener.

751) Click the **front hole** of the MirrorBRACKET.

752) Click **Concentric**.

753) Click **OK**.

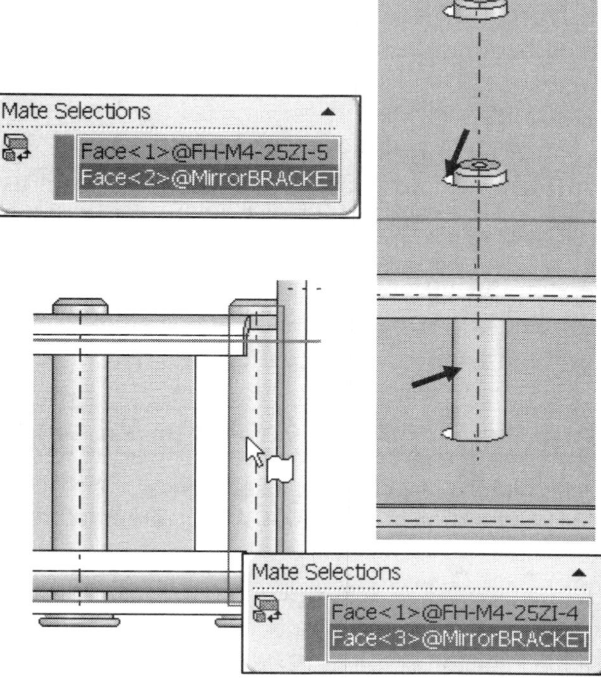

Insert a Concentric Mate.

754) Click the **cylindrical face** of the back right fastener.

755) Click the **back hole** of the MirrorBRACKET.

756) Click **Concentric**.

757) Click **OK**.

Insert a Coincident Mate.

758) Click **Front view**.

759) Drag the **MirrorBRACKET** upward.

760) **Rotate** the model to view the bottom face of the MirrorBRACKET. Click the **bottom face** of the MirrorBRACKET. Click **Isometric view**.

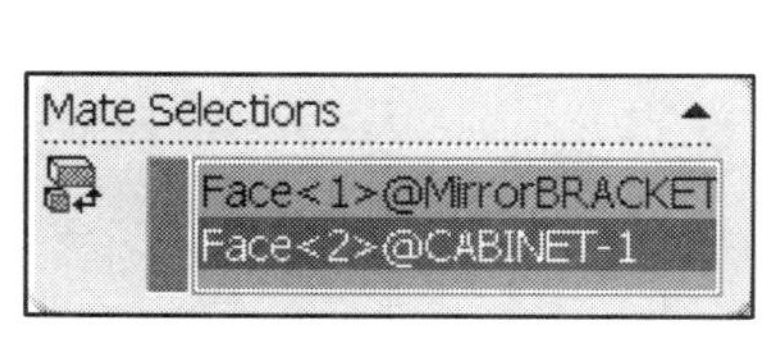

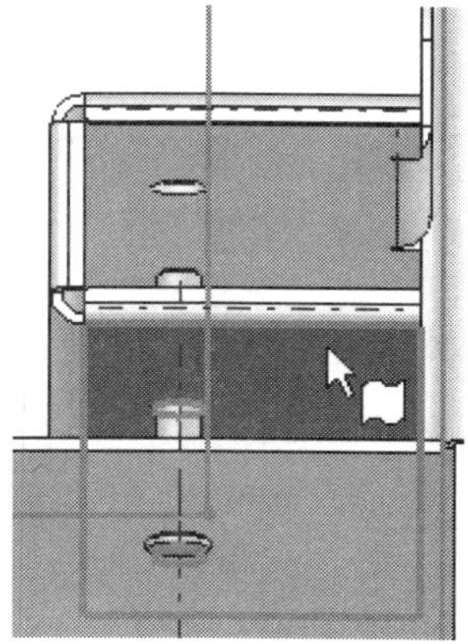

761) Click the **inside bottom face** of the CABINET. Click **Coincident**.

762) Click **OK**. Click **OK**.

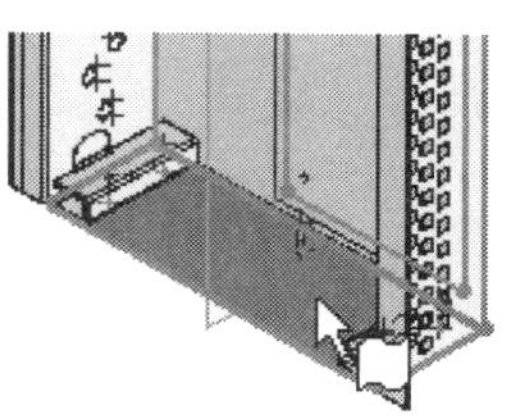

Save the BOX assembly.

763) Click **Save** . Click **Yes**.

MirrorBRACKET Part-Bends, Unfold and Fold and Jog Features

Open the MirrorBRACKET part. The MirrorBRACKET is not a sheet metal part. The MirrorBRACKET references only the BRACKET's geometry. The MirrorBRACKET must be manufactured in a 2D Flat State. Insert Sheet Metal Bends to create the Flat State.

Control the unfold/fold process. Insert an Extruded Cut across a bend radius. Utilize the Unfold and Fold features to flatten and form two bends. Perform cuts across bends after the Unfold. Utilize unfold/fold steps for additional complex sheet metal components.

Sketch the cut profile across the Bend Radius. The Extruded Cut is linked to the Thickness. A Jog feature creates a small, short bend. Insert a Jog feature to offset the right tab and to complete the MirrorBRACKET.

Activity: MirrorBRACKET Part-Bends, Unfold and Fold and Jog Features

Open MirrorBRACKET and Insert Bends.

764) Right-click **MirrorBRACKET** in the FeatureManager.

765) Click **Open Part**.

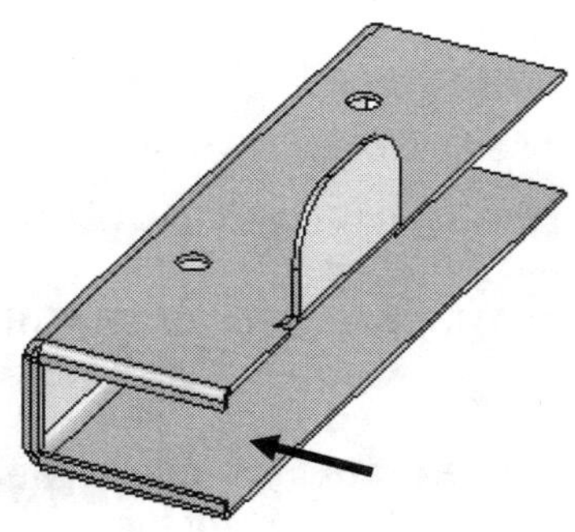

Fit the Model to the Graphics window.

766) Press the **f** key.

767) Click the **inside bottom face** for Fixed Face.

768) Click **Insert Bends** Insert Bends from the Sheet Metal toolbar.

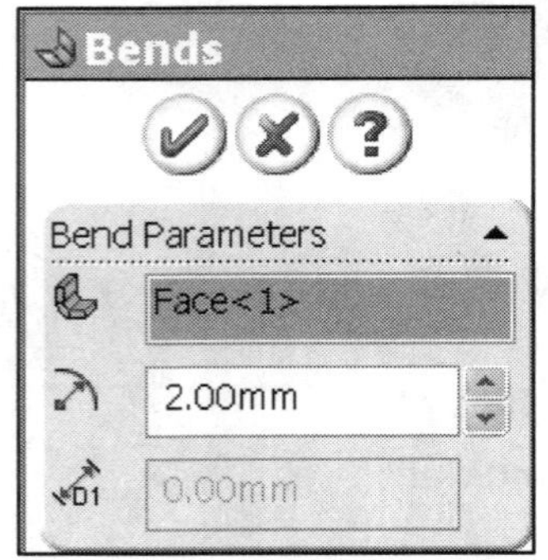

769) Click **OK** from the Bends PropertyManager.

Unfold two Bends.

770) Click **Unfold** Unfold .

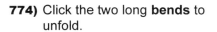

771) Zoom to Area on the right inside bottom face.

772) Click the right **inside bottom face** to remain fixed.

773) Rotate the **model** to view the two long bends.

774) Click the two long **bends** to unfold.

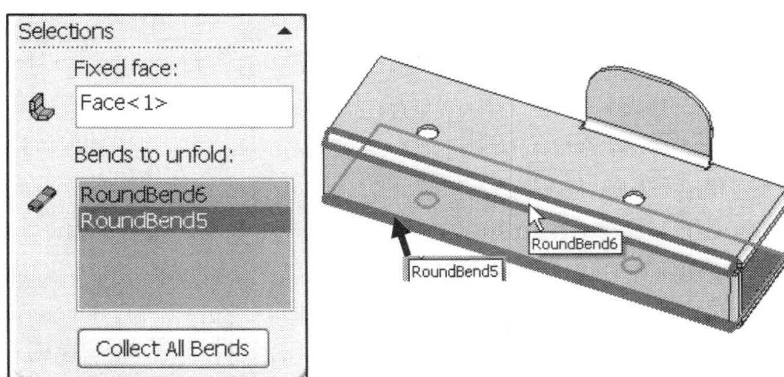

775) Click **OK** .

776) Click **Top view** .

Note: Only the selected two bends unfold. The Tab remains folded.

Create the Sketch for an Extruded Cut.

777) Click the **left top face**.

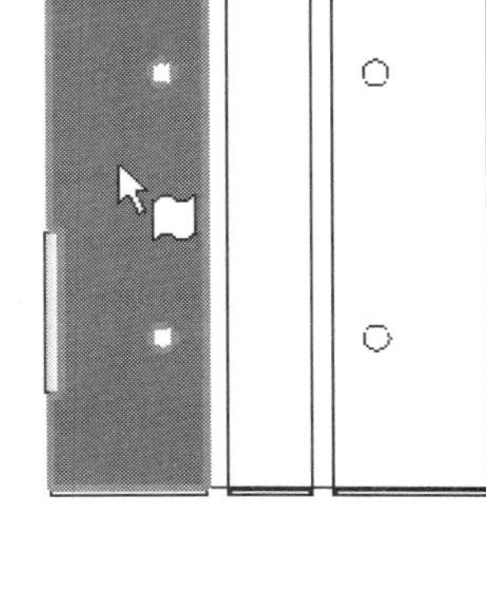

778) Click **Sketch** Sketch .

779) Click **Rectangle** Rectan... from the Sketch toolbar.

780) Click the **upper left corner** of the Mirror BRACKET.

781) Click a **position** coincident with the right bend line.

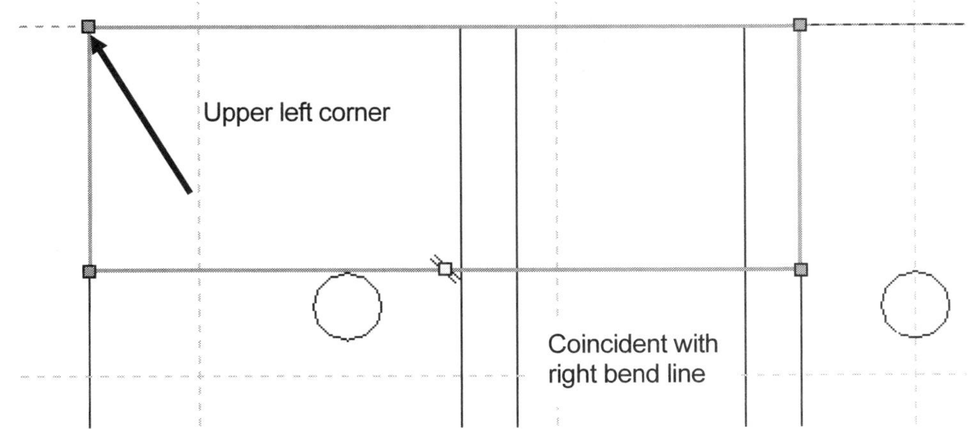

Add a dimension.

782) Click **Smart Dimension** Smart Dimens... .

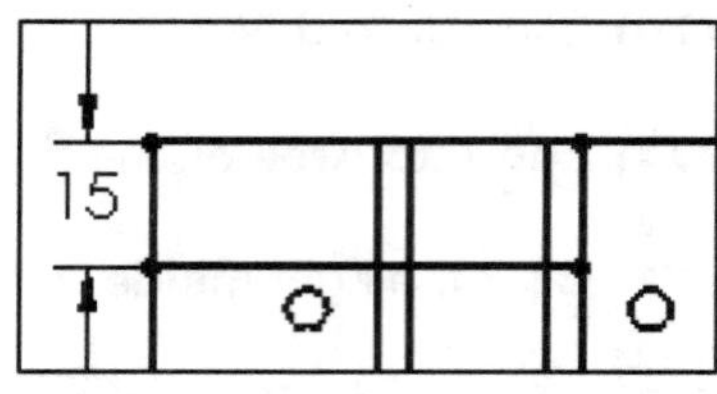

783) Click the **top horizontal edge** of the MirrorBRACKET.

784) Click the **bottom horizontal line** of the rectangle.

785) Enter **15**.

786) Click **OK** .

Extrude the Sketch

787) Click **Extruded Cut**  from the Sheet Metal toolbar.

788) Check **Link to Thickness**.

789) Click **OK** from the Cut-Extrude PropertyManager.

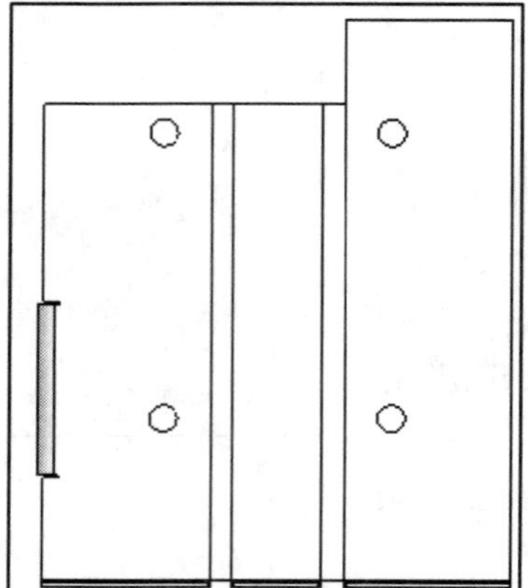

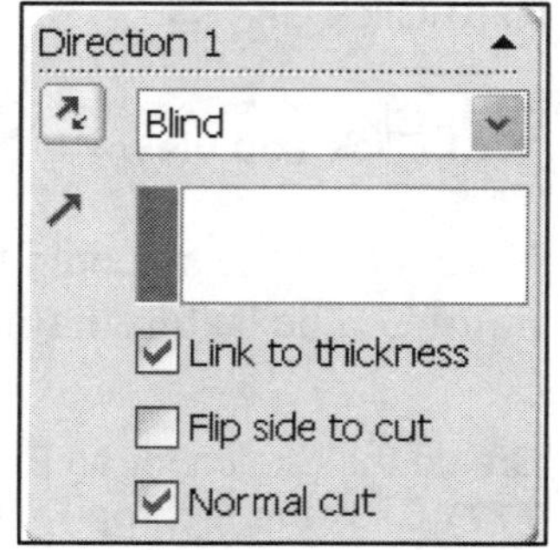

Fold the Bends.

790) Click **Fold** Fold from the Sheet Metal toolbar.

791) Click **Collect All Bends** in the Fold PropertyManager. All Unfolded bends are displayed in the Bends to fold box.

792) Click **OK** from the Fold PropertyManager.

793) Click **Isometric view** .

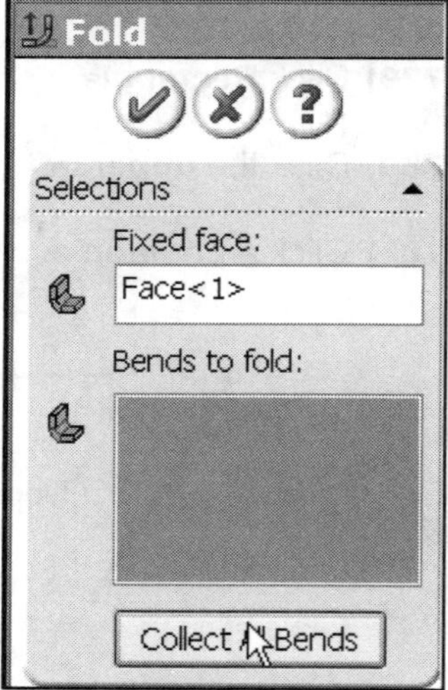

Insert a Jog.

794) Click the **front face** of the Tab.

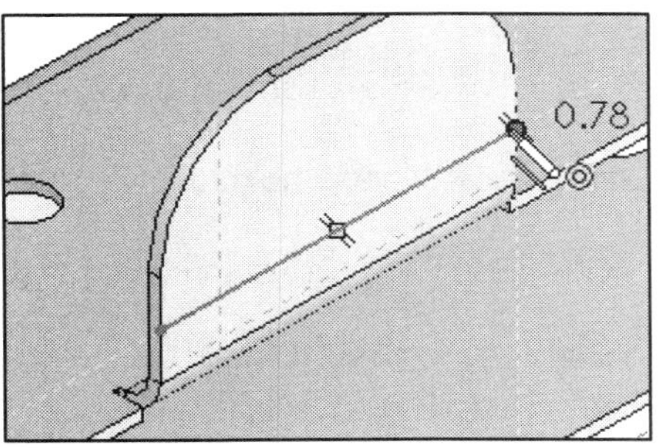

795) Click **Jog** .

796) Click **line** .

797) Sketch a **horizontal line** across the midpoints of the Tab.

798) Click **Exit Sketch** . Click the **Fixed Face** box.

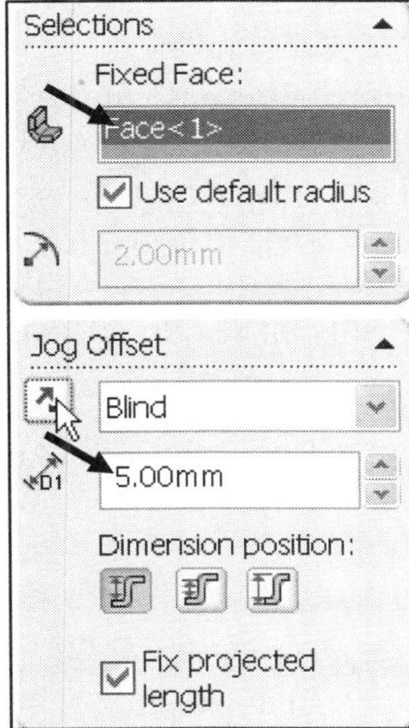

799) Click the **front face** of the tap below the horizontal line.

800) Enter **5** for Jog Offset Distance.

801) Click **Reverse Direction** . The Jog points to the left.

802) Click **OK** .

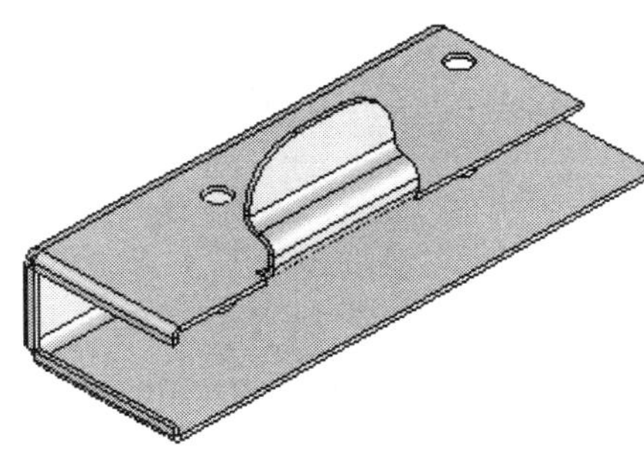

Display the Jog.

803) Use the **arrow keys** to rotate and view the Jog.

Display the flat/formed state.

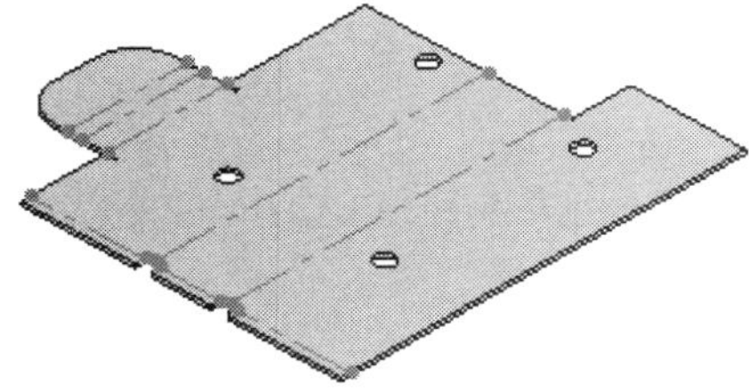

804) Click **Flatten** to display the flat state.

805) Click **Flatten** to display the formed state.

806) Click **Isometric view** .

807) Click **Save** .

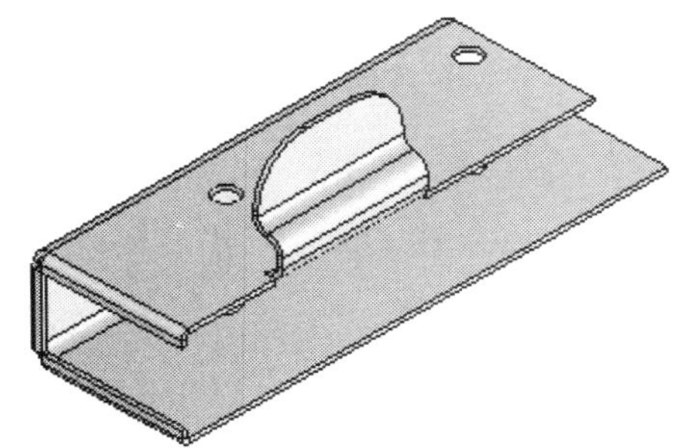

Return to the BOX assembly.

808) Press **Ctrl Tab**.

Save the BOX assembly.

809) Click **Save**.

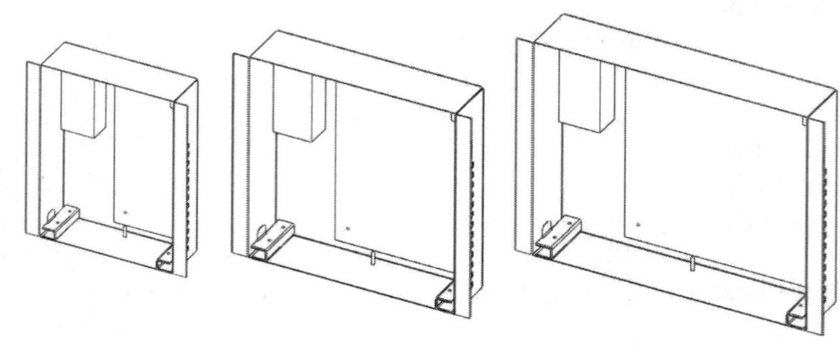

Note: The BRACKET and MirrorBRACKET remain centered around the Mirror Plane for the BOX assembly configurations. If the MirrorBRACKET is not centered for the Small, Medium and Large Configurations, Unsuppress the Mirror Point and Mirror Plane in the BOX FeatureManager. Unsuppress the Mates created for the MirrorBRACKET part.

The ConfigurationManager, Add Configuration, Advanced, Suppress new features and mates option controls the state of new features and mates in multiple configuration assemblies.

The BOX configurations are complete.

Fully define all sketches. Rebuild errors occur in a Top Down design approach if the sketches are not fully defined.

Additional details on IGES, Replace Component, Equations, Design Table and Configurations, Mirror Component and Sheet metal (Base Flange, Edge Flange, Miter Flange, Extruded Cut, Sketch Bend, Break Corner, Closed Corner, Hem, Fold, Unfold, Jog) are available in On-line Help. Index all Sheet metal features under the keyword, sheet metal.

Refer to the Help, Online Tutorial Sheet Metal exercise and Advanced Design Techniques for additional information.

Review the PEM® fasteners, Configurations and Sheet Metal features.

You obtained IGES format PEM® self-clinching fasteners from the Internet. IGES files are opened in SolidWorks and saved as part files. The PEM® fasteners were inserted into the BOX assembly seed Hole. You developed a Component Pattern for the fasteners that referenced the CABINET Linear Pattern of Holes.

You added an Assembly Cut feature to the BOX assembly. The Cut feature created a hole through the MOTHERBOARD and CABINET components.

Due to part availability, you utilized the Replace Components option to exchange the M5 fastener with the M4 fastener. The new mates were redefined to update the M4 fastener. The M4 fastener required the CABINET Holes to be modified from M5 to M4.

Equations controlled the location of the CABINET Holes based on the Layout Sketch dimensions. Variables in the Layout Sketch were inserted into a Design Table to create the BOX assembly Configurations: Small, Medium and Large.

The sheet metal BRACKET was created in-context of the BOX assembly and referenced the location of the PEM® fasteners. You inserted the Base Flange, Edge Flange and Miter Flange features.

The Mirror Components option was utilized to create a right hand version of the BRACKET. The MirrorBRACKET required Insert Bends, Fold/Unfold and an Extruded Cut across the Bends for manufacturing. The Jog feature provided an offset for the Tab by inserting two additional bends from one sketched line.

Project Summary

You created three different BOX sizes utilizing the Top down assembly modeling approach. The Top down design approach is a conceptual approach used to develop products from within the assembly.

The BOX assembly began with a Layout Sketch. The Layout Sketch built in relationships between 2D geometry that represented the MOTHERBOARD, POWERSUPPLY and CABINET components. These three components were developed In-context of the Layout Sketch. The components contain InPlace Mates and external references to the BOX assembly.

Additional Extruded features were inserted in the MOTHERBOARD and POWERSUPPLY parts.

The CABINET part developed an Extruded Base feature In-context of the BOX assembly. The Shell feature created a constant wall thickness for the solid part.

The Rip feature and Insert Bends feature were added to convert the solid part into a sheet metal part.

Sheet metal components utilized the Edge, Hem, Extruded Cut, Die Cuts, Forms and Flat Pattern features. Model sheet metal components in their 3D formed state. Manufacture sheet metal components in their 2D flatten state.

The Component Pattern maintained the relationship between the Cabinet Holes and the PEM® self-clinching fasteners. You utilized Replace Components to modify the M5 fastener to an M4 fastener. The new mates were redefined to update the M4 fastener.

Equations controlled the location of the Cabinet Holes. Variables in the Layout Sketch were inserted into a Design Table to create the BOX assembly Configurations: Small, Medium and Large.

The BRACKET was created utilizing sheet metal features: Base Flange, Edge Flange and Miter Flange. You utilized Mirror Components to create a right hand version, MirrorBRACKET. The MirrorBRACKET required Insert Bends and an Extruded Cut feature through the sheet metal bends.

The Mirror Plane built in the design intent for the BRACKET and MirrorBRACKET to remain centered for each BOX assembly configuration.

Sheet metal parts are created individually or In-context of an assembly.

Project Terminology

Assembly Feature: Features created in the assembly such as a hole or extrude. The Hole assembly feature was utilized to create a hole through 2 different components in the BOX assembly.

Bend Allowance (Radius): The arc length of the bend as measured along the neutral axis of the material.

CircuitWorks: CircuitWorks from Zeal Solutions (www.circuitworks.co.uk) is a fully integrated data interface between SolidWorks and PCB Design systems.

Derived Component Pattern: A pattern created inside the assembly. A Derived Pattern utilizes a component from the assembly. There are two methods to reference a Derived Pattern. Method 1 - Derived Pattern references a Linear or Circular feature pattern. Method 2 – Derived Pattern references a local pattern created in the assembly.

Design Table: A Design Table is an Excel spreadsheet used to create multiple configurations in a part or assembly. Utilize a Design Table to create the small, medium and large BOX configurations.

Equations: Mathematical expressions that define relationships between parameters and or dimensions are called Equations. Equations use shared names to control dimensions. Use Equations to connect values from sketches, features, patterns and various parts in an assembly. Use Equations in different parts and assemblies.

Extruded Boss/Base: Add material to the part. Utilize to create the CABINET as a solid part.

Flange: Adds a flange (wall) to a selected edge of a sheet metal part.

Flat Pattern: The flat manufactured state of a sheet metal part. It contains no bends.

Flattened: Creates the flat pattern for a sheet metal part. The Flattened feature toggles between the flat and formed state. A Flat configuration is created. Utilize the Flat configuration in the drawing to dimension the flat pattern.

Fold/Unfold: Flatten one or more bends to create an extruded cut across a bend.

Hem: Adds a hem to a selected edge of a sheet metal part.

Insert Sheet Metal Bends: Converts a solid part into a sheet metal part. Requires a fixed face or edge and a bend radius.

Jog: Adds an offset to a flange by creating 2 bends from one sketch line.

Layout Sketch: Specifies the location of the key components. Components and assemblies reference the Layout Sketch.

Link Values: Are used to define equal relations. Create an equal relation between two or more sketched dimensions and or features with a Link Value. Link Values require a shared name. Use Link Values within the same part.

Mirror Components: Creates a right/left hand version of component about a plane in an assembly.

Reload: Refreshes shared documents.

Replace: Substitutes one or more instances of a component with a closed different component in an assembly.

Rip: A Rip feature is a cut of 0 thickness. Utilize a Rip feature on the edges of a shelled box before inserting sheet metal bends

Shell: Creates a constant wall thickness for the CABINET Extruded Base. The Shell feature represents the thickness of the sheet metal utilized for the cabinet.

Suppressed: A feature that is not displayed. Hide features to improve clarity. Suppressed features to improve model Rebuild time.

Top Down design approach: A conceptual approach used to develop products from within the assembly. Major design requirements are translated into sub-assemblies or individual components and key relationships

Questions

1. What is a Top Down approach? When do you create a Layout Sketch?
2. How do you create a new component in-context of the assembly?
3. What is the difference between a Link Value and an Equation?
4. Name three characteristics unique to sheet metal parts.
5. Identify the indicator for a part in an Edit Component state.
6. Where should you position the Layout Sketch?
7. For a solid extruded block, what features do you add to create a sheet metal part?
8. Name the two primary states of a sheet metal part.
9. How do you insert a formed sheet metal feature such as a dimple or louver?
10. Identify the type of information that a sheet metal manufacturer provides.
11. What is an Assembly Feature?
12. What features are required before you create the Component Pattern in the assembly?
13. True or False. If you utilize Replace Component, you have to modify all the mate references.
14. Define a Design Table.
15. Identify the following Sheet Metal features.

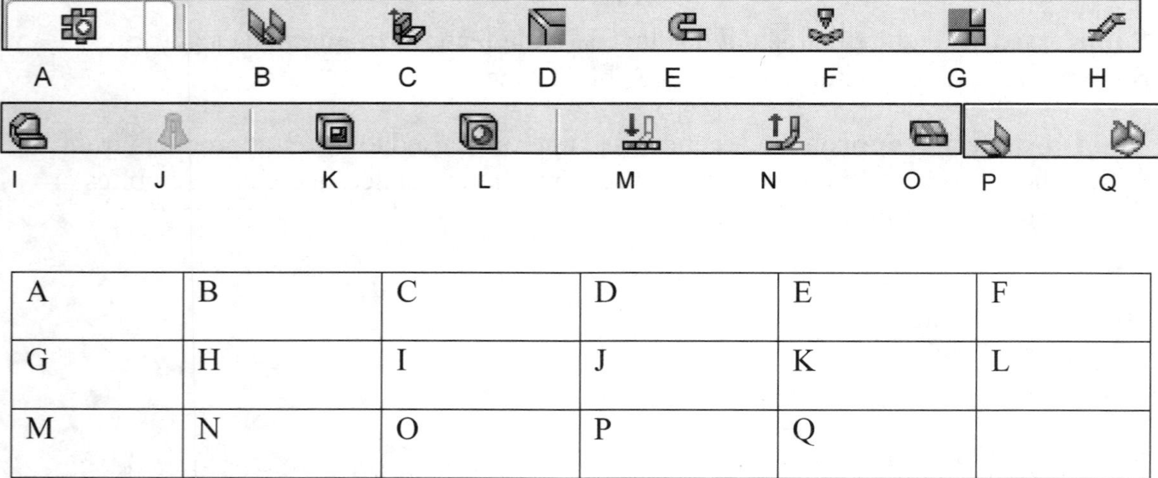

A	B	C	D	E	F
G	H	I	J	K	L
M	N	O	P	Q	

Exercises

Exercise 6.1: L-BRACKET Part.

Create the L-BRACKET Sheet metal parts.

- Create a family of sheet metal L-BRACKETS. L-BRACKETS are used in the construction industry.
- Create an eight hole L-BRACKET.
- Use Equations to control the hole spacing.

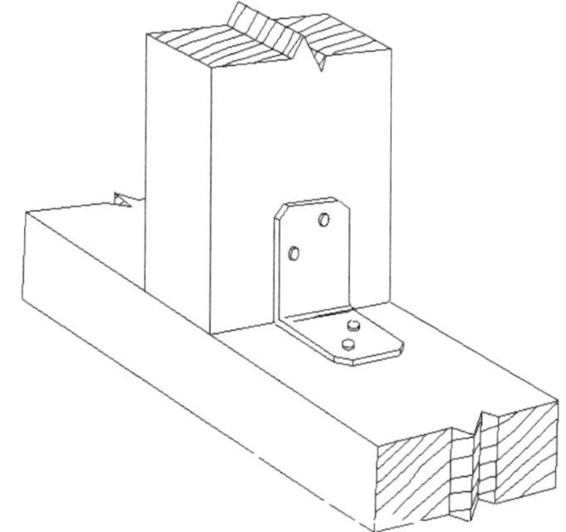

Stong-Tie Reinforcing Brackets
Courtesy of Simpson Strong Tie
Corporation of California

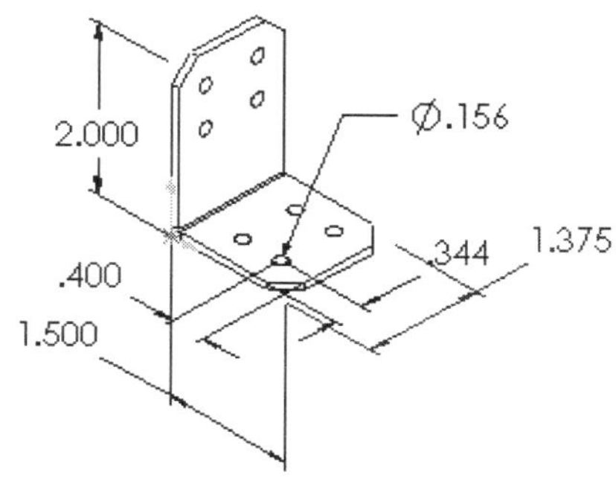

Review Design Tables in On-line Help and On-line Tutorial.

	A	B	C	D	E
1	Design Table for: lbracket				
2		height@Sketch1	width@Sketch1	depth@Base-Extrude-Thin	hole1dia@Sketch2
3	First Instance	2	1.5	1.375	0.156
4	Small2x1.5x1	2	1.5	1	0.156
5	Medium3x2x2	3	2	2	0.156
6	Large4x3x4	4	3	4	0.25

L-BRACKET DESIGN TABLE

- Create a Design Table for the L-Bracket.
- Rename the dimensions of the L-Bracket.
- Create a drawing that contains the flat state and formed state of the L-BRACKET.

Exercise 6.2: SHEET METAL SUPPORTS

Create the SHEET METAL SUPPORT parts. The following examples are courtesy of Strong Arm Corporation.

- Obtain additional engineering information regarding dimensions and bearing loads. Visit www.strongtie.com.

Similar parts can be located in local hardware and lumber stores. An actual physical model provides a great advantage in learning SolidWorks Sheet metal functionality.

- Estimate the length, width and depth dimensions. Beams are 2" x 4"(50mmx100mm), posts are 4" x 4"(100mmx100mm).

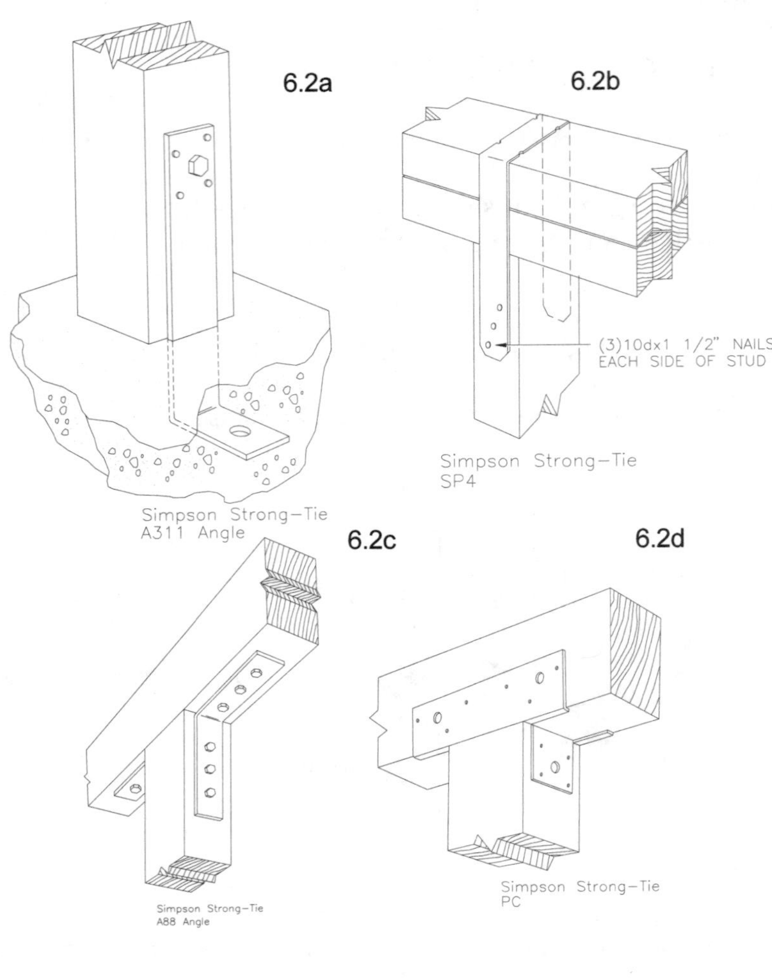

Exercise 6.3: SHEET METAL COVER.

Design a sheet metal COVER. Note: Dimensions are not provide for this exercise.

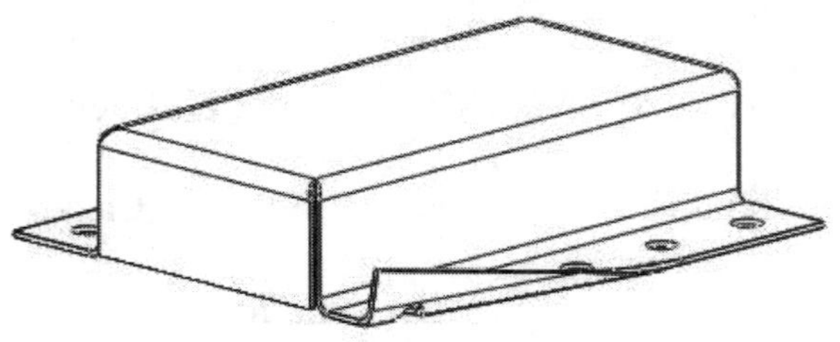

Exercise 6.4: LAYOUT SKETCH.

Create a Layout Sketch in the Assembly.

- Create a Layout Sketch for a Top down design in a new appliance or consumer electronics (refrigerator, stereo CD player).
- Identify the major components that define the assembly.
- Define important relationships with Equations and Link Values.

Exercise 6.5: TRIANGULAR SUPPORT Assembly.

Create the TRIANGULAR SUPPORT ASSEMBLY. The TRIANGULAR SUPPORT Assembly consists of the following parts:

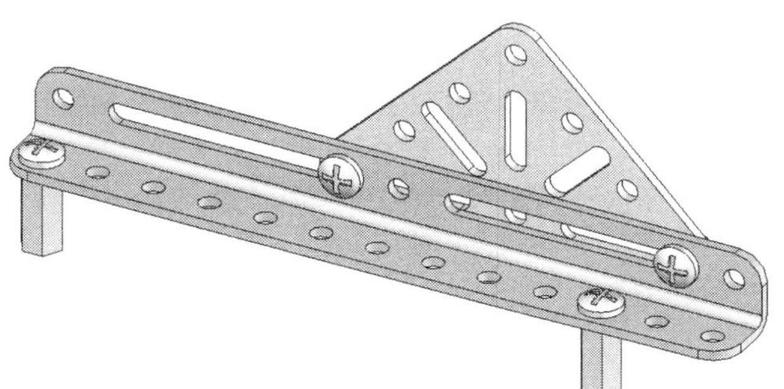

1. ANGLE-BRACKET-13HOLE
2. TRIANGLE
3. STANDOFF
4. MACHINE SCREW

Review all parts of this exercise.

Exercise 6.5a: ANGLE-BRACKET-13HOLE.

- Create the ANGLE-BRACKET-13HOLE. Note the ANGLE-BRACKET with 7 holes was created in the Chapter 4 exercises. The ANGLE-BRACKET-13HOLE is manufactured from .060 [1.5mm] Stainless Steel.
- Insert Sheet Metal Bends to flatten the part.

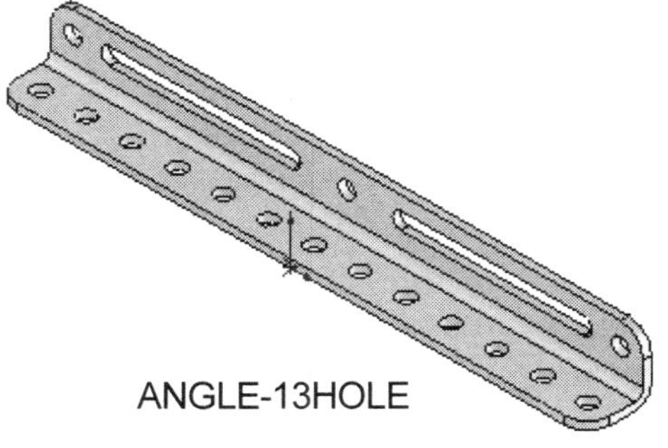

- Save the ANGLE-BRACKET-13HOLE in the 3D formed state.

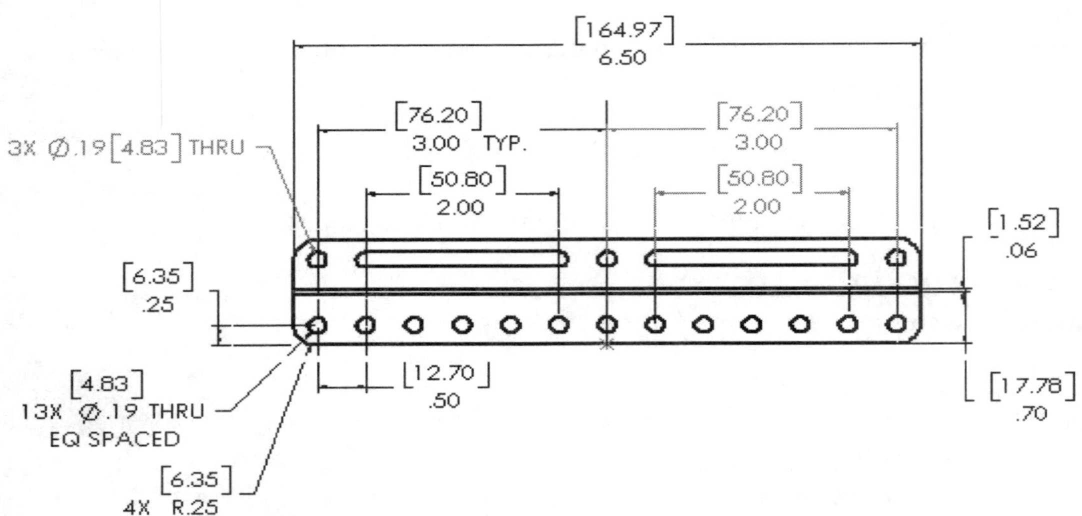

Exercise 6.5b: TRIANGLE.

The center points of the slots and holes locate key geometry for the TRIANGLE. Utilize sketched construction geometry to locate the center points. Construction geometry is not calculated in the extruded profile.

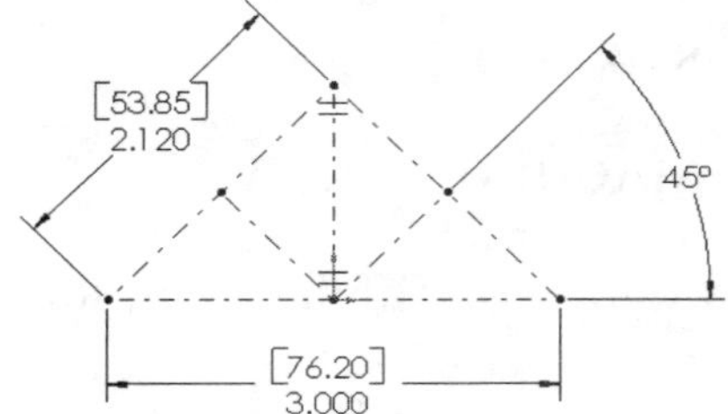

- Create the TRIANGLE on the Front Plane. The TRIANGLE is manufactured from .060 [1.5mm] Stainless Steel.
- Utilize the Sketch Offset tool and Sketch Fillet to create the sketch profile for the Extruded Base feature.
- Utilize Sketch Mirror and the Circle Sketch tools to create the Extruded Cut features.
- Utilize the Rectangle, Sketch Trim and Tangent Arc tools to create the Extruded Cut left bottom slot.
- Utilize the Mirror feature to create the right bottom slot.

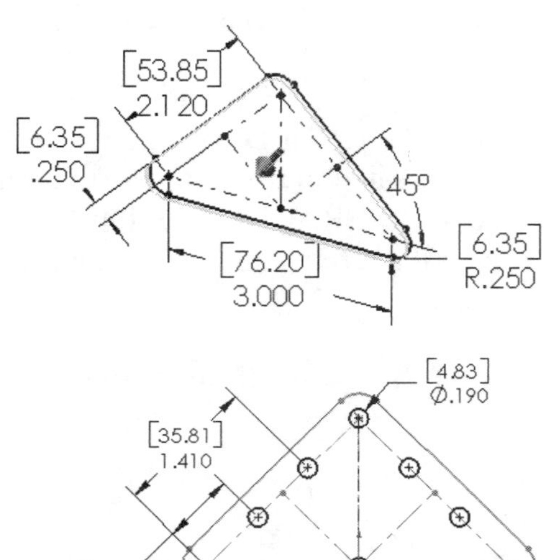

- Utilize the Parallelogram and Tangent Arc Sketch tools to create the Extruded Cut.
- Utilize the Circular Pattern to create the three radial slot cuts.

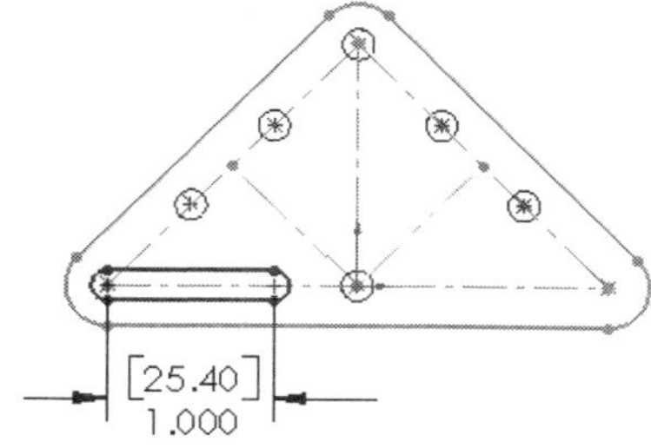

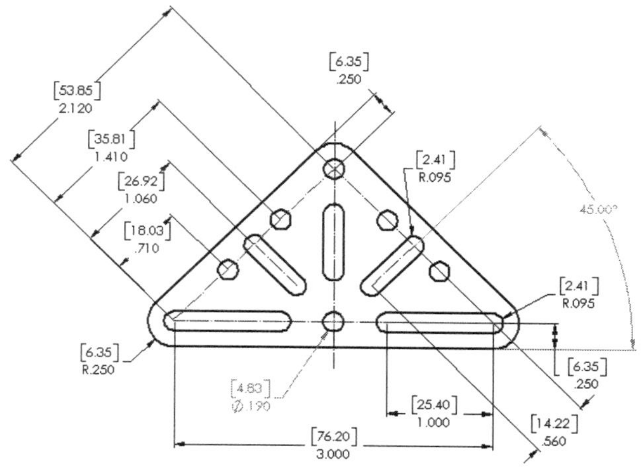

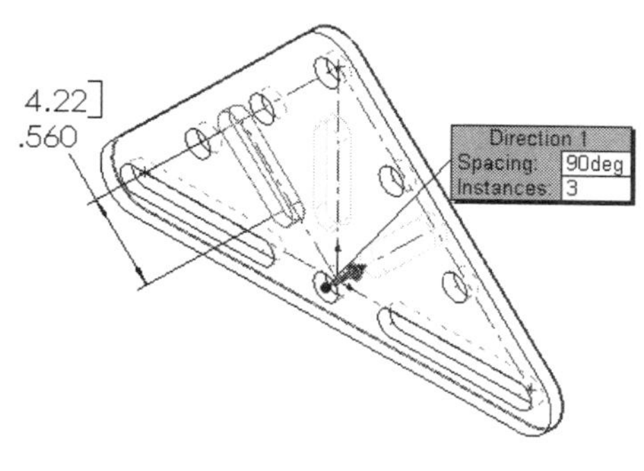

Exercise 6.5c: HEX-STANDOFF and machine SCREW.

Create the HEX-STANDOFF and SCREW parts.

- Utilize a 10-24 Tapped Hole.
- Utilize a 10-24 SCREW. Note the SCREW was created in Exercise 4.1e.
- For Metric sizes utilize an M5 Tapped Hole and an M5 Machine Screw.

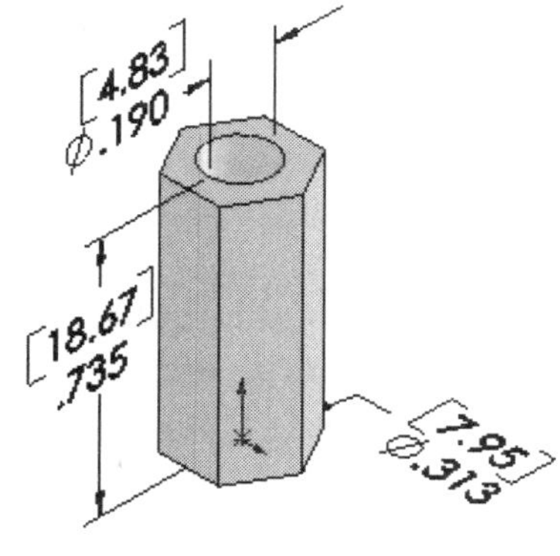

Exercise 6.5d: FRONT-SUPPORT ASSEMBLY.

The FRONT-SUPPORT assembly consists of the following parts:

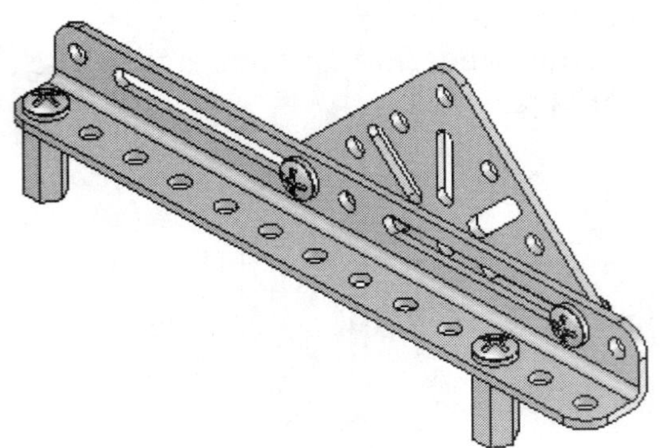

- ANGLE-BEACKET-13HOLE part.
- TRIANGLE part.
- HEX-STANDOFF part.
- SCREW part.

Insert the ANGLE-BEACKET-13HOLE part. The ANGLE-BEACKET-13HOLE part is fixed to the FRONT-SUPPORT Origin.

Insert the first HEX-STANDOFF part. Utilize Concentric and Coincident Mates to assemble the HEX-STANDOFF to the left hole of the ANGLE-13HOLE part.
Utilize a Parallel Mate.

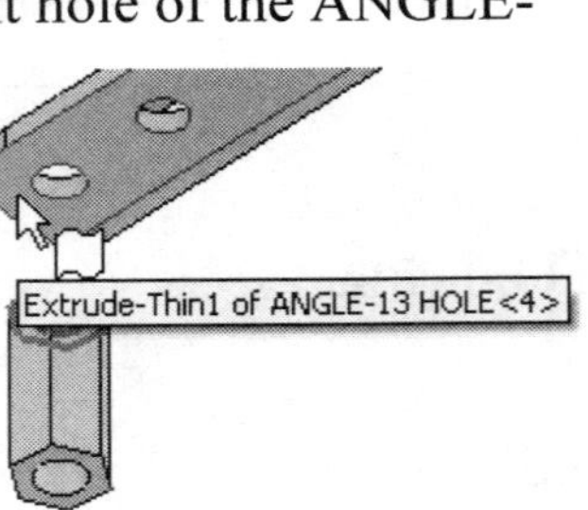

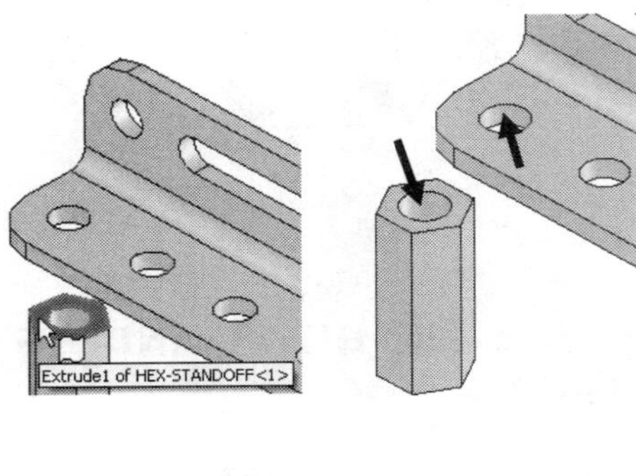

Insert the second HEX-STANDOFF part. Utilize Concentric and Coincident Mates to assemble the HEX-STANDOFF to the third hole from the right side.

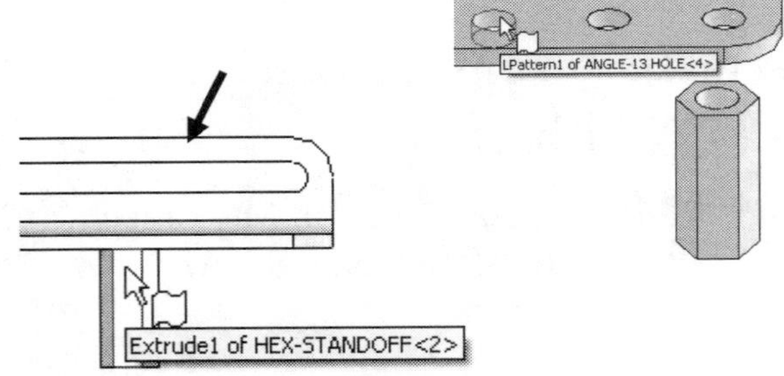

Insert the TRIANGLE part. Utilize Concentric, Distance and Parallel Mates to assemble the TRIANGLE.

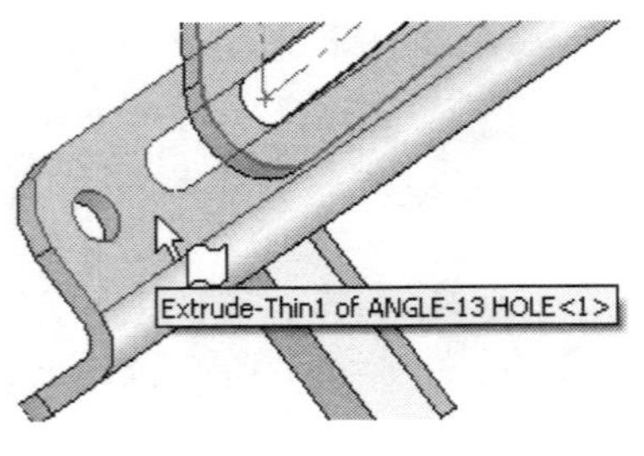

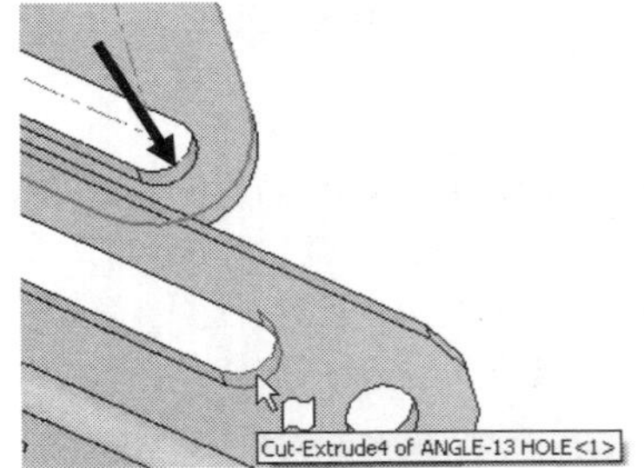

Insert the SCREW part. Utilize Concentric and Coincident Smart Mates to assemble the four SCREWS.

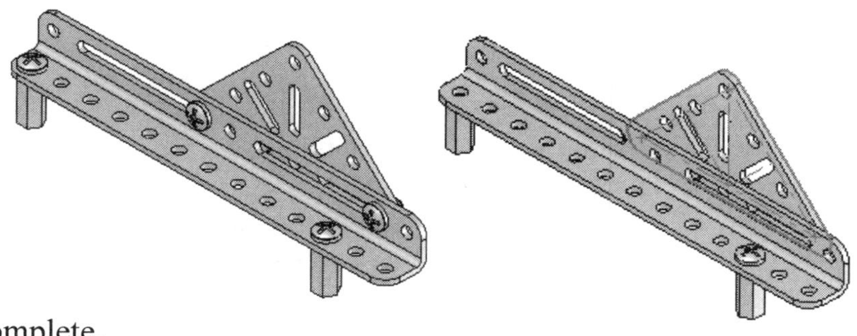

The TRIANGLE-SUPPORT Assembly is complete.

Exercise 6.5E: MIRROR-FRONT-SUPPORT ASSEMBLY.

Utilize Mirror Component to create a mirror of the FRONT-SUPPORT assembly.

- Create a Create a new plane, Plane1. Plane1 is offset 1.75[44.45mm] from the front face of the ANGLE-BRACKET-13HOLE.

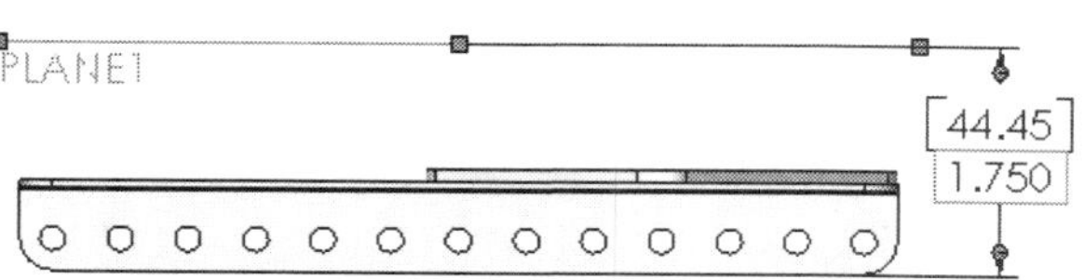

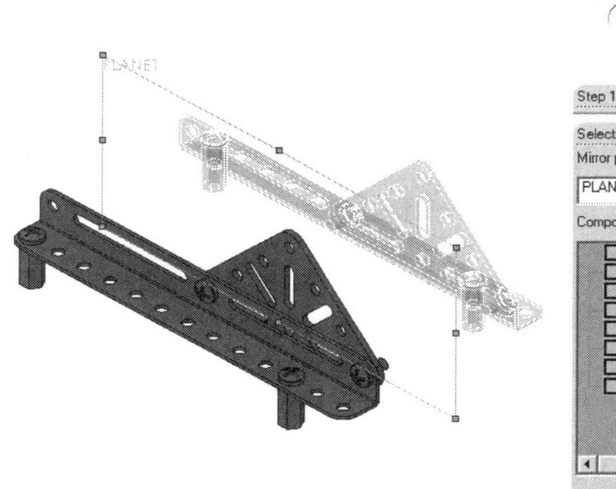

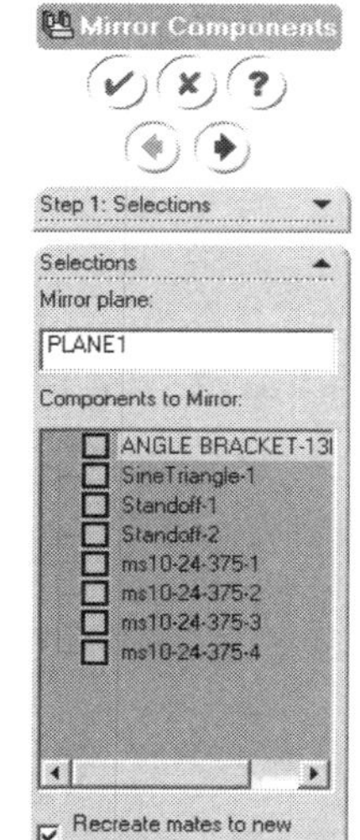

- Create a Concentric Mate and Coincident Mate for each MACHINE SCREW.
- Mirror all components about Plane1.
- Select Insert, Mirror Components. PLANE1 is the Mirror Plane.
- Select the ANGLE-BRACKET-13HOLE, TRIANGLE, STANDOFF<1>, STANDOFF<2>, and 4-MACHINE SCREWS from the FeatureManager.

- Check the Recreate mates to new components. If the mirror components are upside down, click the blue arrow.

- Select the Reorient Components button.

- Organize components in the FeatureManager. Group the MACHINE SCREWS. Drag each MACHINE SCREW to the bottom of FeatureManager. The 8-MACHINE SCREWs are listed sequentially. Select the eight MACHINE SCREWS. Right-click Add to New Folder. Enter hardware for folder name. All the MACHINE SCREWS are listed below the hardware folder.

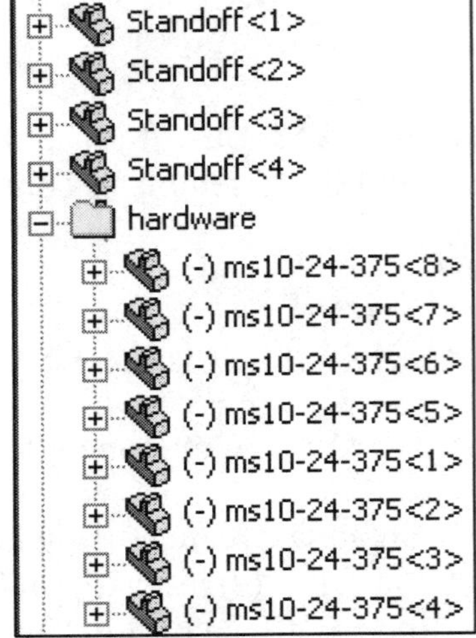

- Group the STANDOFFs. Drag STANDOFF<1> above STANDOFF<3>. Drag STANDOFF<2> below STANDOFF<1>. The four STANDOFFs are grouped together.

- Select the four STANDOFFs. Right-click Add to New Folder. Enter standoffs for folder name.

- All the STANDOFFs are listed below the standoffs folder.

- Suppress the hardware folder from the FeatureManager.

- The MIRROR-FRONT-TRIANGLE-SUPPORT Assembly is complete.

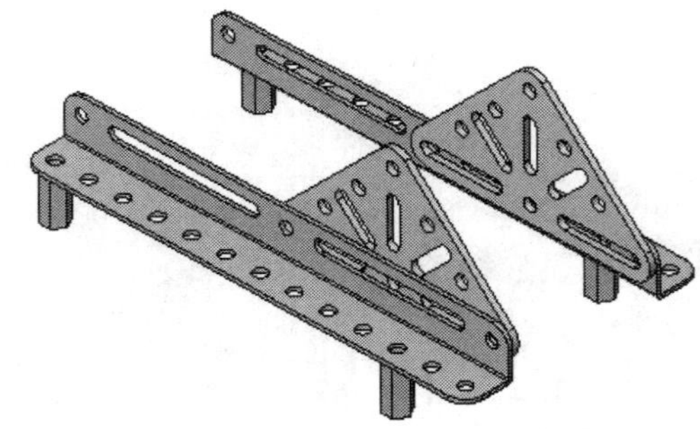

Exercise 6.6: PNEUMATIC TEST MODULE Assembly.

Create the PNEUMATIC TEST MODULE Assembly. The PNEUMATIC TEST MODULE Assembly utilizes 4 subassemblies created in previous exercises.

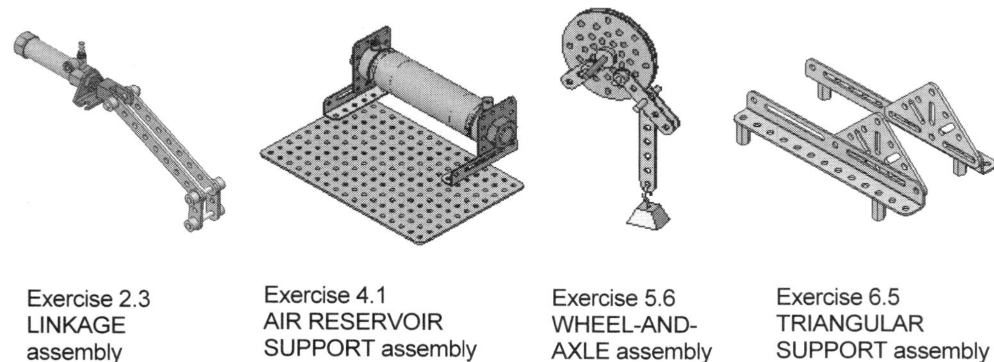

Exercise 2.3 LINKAGE assembly

Exercise 4.1 AIR RESERVOIR SUPPORT assembly

Exercise 5.6 WHEEL-AND-AXLE assembly

Exercise 6.5 TRIANGULAR SUPPORT assembly

Courtesy of SMC Corporation of America & Gears Educational Systems

Exercise 6.6a: Modify the LINKAGE Assembly.

- Modify the LINKAGE assembly. Delete components no longer required. Insert new components.
- Open the LINKAGE assembly.
- Delete the FLAT-BAR-3HOLE<1> and FLAT-BAR-3HOLE<2>.
- Delete AXLE<3>. Delete the SHAFT-COLLAR<5> and SHAFT-COLLAR<6>.

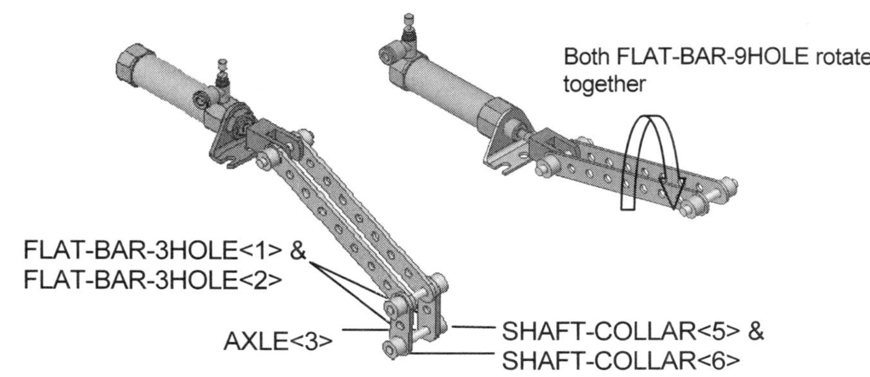

Insert the first STANDOFF part.

- Create a Concentric Mate between the Temporary Axis of the STANDOFF Tapped Hole and the Axis of the half Slot Cut.

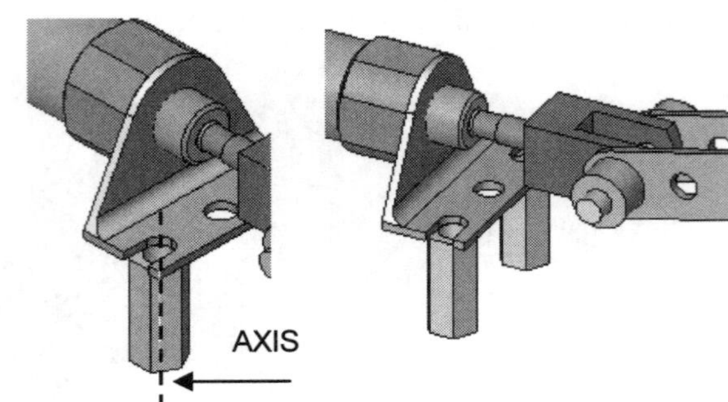

- Create a Coincident Mate between the STANDOFF top face and the BRACKET bottom face.
- Create a Parallel Mate between the STANDOFF front face and the BRACKET front face.
- Insert the second STANDOFF part. Create a Concentric, Coincident and Parallel Mate.
- Save the LINKAGE assembly.

Exercise 6.6b: Modify the WHEEL-AND-AXLE assembly.

- Open the WHEEL-AND-AXLE assembly. The WHEEL-AND-AXLE rotates in the PNEUMATIC TEST MODULE assembly.

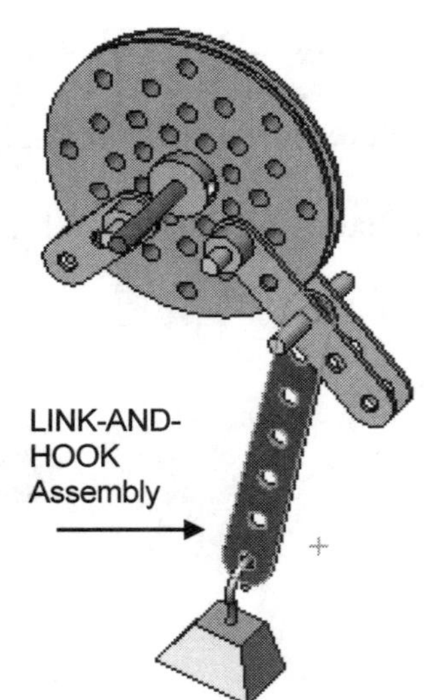

- Expand the Mates. Suppress the Parallel Mate for the LINK-AND-HOOK and WHEEL-AND-AXLE Top Plane. The LINK-AND-HOOK is free to rotate.
- Suppress the WHEEL-STATIC Angle Mate between the WHEEL Top Plane and the WHEEL-AND-AXLE Top Plane. The WHEEL is free to rotate.
- Save the WHEEL-AND-AXLE assembly.

Exercise 6.6c: PNEUMATIC TEST MODULE Assembly.

Create the PNEUMATIC TEST MODULE assembly.

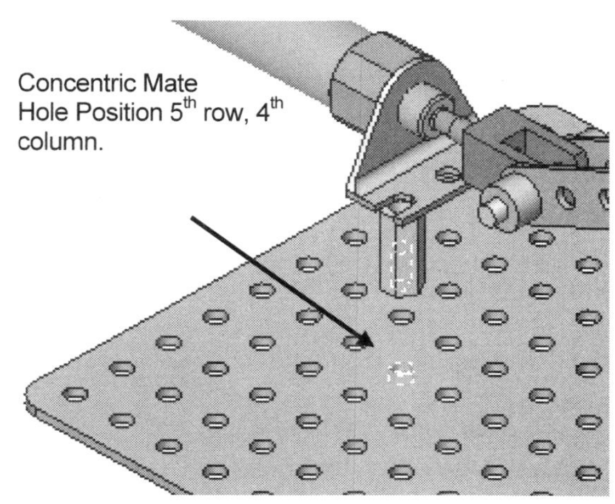

- Insert the AIR RESERVOIR SUPPORT assembly. The AIR RESERVOIR SUPPORT assembly is fixed to the Origin.
- Insert the LINKAGE assembly.
- Create a Coincident Mate between the front STANDOFF Tapped Hole and the 5th row, 4th column in the FLAT PLATE part.
- Create a Coincident Mate between the STANDOFF bottom face and the FLAT PLATE top face.
- Create a Parallel Mate between the LINKAGE Front plane and the PNEUMATIC TEST MODULE Front plane.

The LINKAGE assembly is fully defined and centered on the FLAT PLATE.

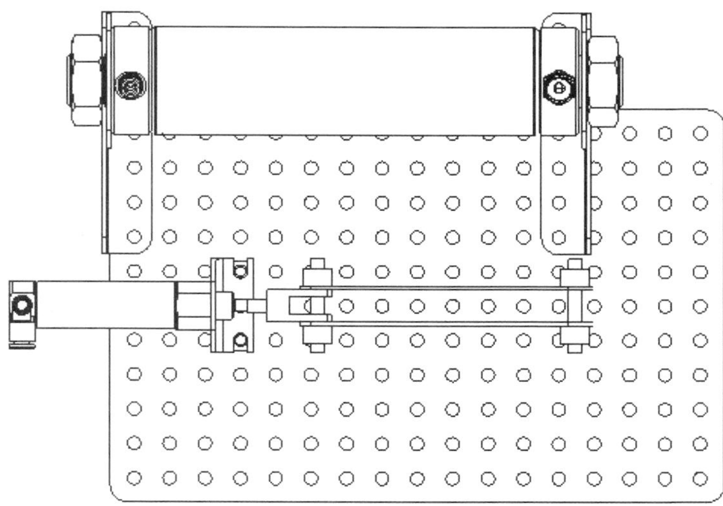

Components do not translate or rotate after insertion into the assembly. The LINKAGE assembly FLAT BARs do not rotate after insertion into the PNEUMATIC TEST MODULE assembly. The LINKAGE assembly is in the Rigid state.

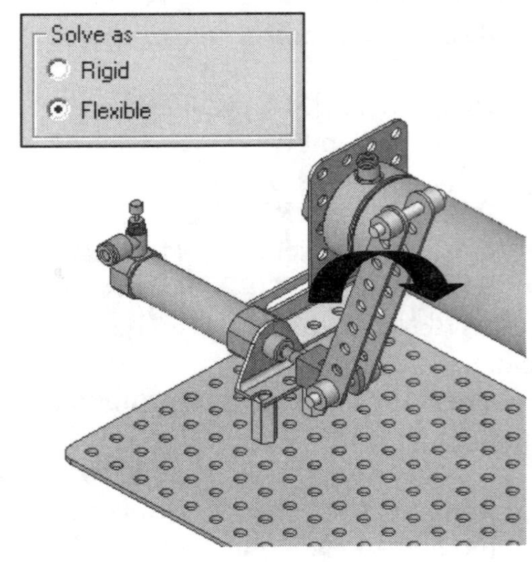

Remove the Rigid state.

- Select LINKAGE from the FeatureManager. Right-click Component Properties.
- Select Flexible for state in the Solve as box. The two FLATBAR-9HOLE in the LINKAGE assembly are free to rotate in the PNEUMATIC TEST MODULE assembly.
- Insert the WHEEL-AND-AXLE assembly.
- Create a Coincident Mate between the WHEEL-AND-AXLE Front plane and the LINKAGE assembly Front plane.
- Create as Concentric Mate between the WHEEL AXLE-3000 and the SINE-TRIANGLE top hole.
- Move the two FLAT-BAR-7HOLE downward.

Create a Concentric Mate between the LINKAGE right AXLE-1375 and the FLAT-BAR-3HOLE bottom left hole.

- Remove the Rigid state.
- Select WHEEL-AND-AXLE from the FeatureManager.
- Right-click Component Properties.

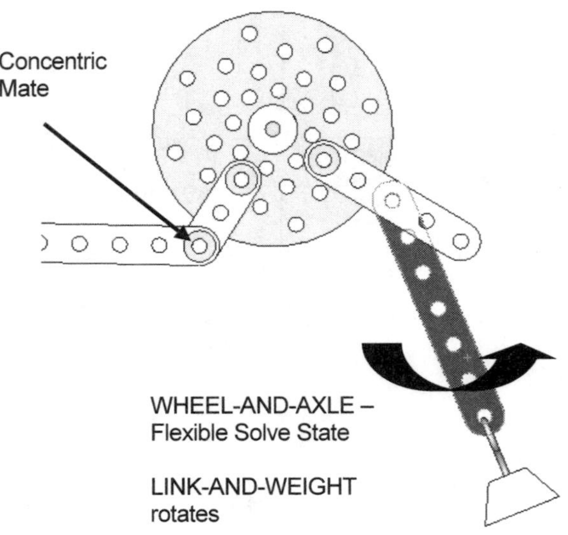

- Select Flexible for state in the Solve as box. The LINK-AND-WEIGHT assembly is free to rotate in the PNEUMATIC TEST MODULE assembly.
- Create a Parallel Mate.
- Select the WEIGHT top face.
- Select the PNEUMATIC TEST MODULE Top plane.

The WHEEL does not translate or rotate. The linear motion of the Air Cylinder determines the rotational motion of the WHEEL.

- Remove the Rigid state. Expand LINKAGE in the FeatureManager.
- Select AirCylinder from the FeatureManager.
- Right-click Component Properties.
- Select Flexible for state in the Solve as box.
- Expand NCJ22005Z-MP assembly. Expand the MateGroup1 folder.
- Click Stroke-Distance Mate.
- Right-click Suppress.
- Move the LINKAGE assembly. Right-click the ROD CLEVIS in the Graphics window.
- Click Move Component.
- Select By Delta XYZ. Enter 1.000 [25.4mm] for ΔX.

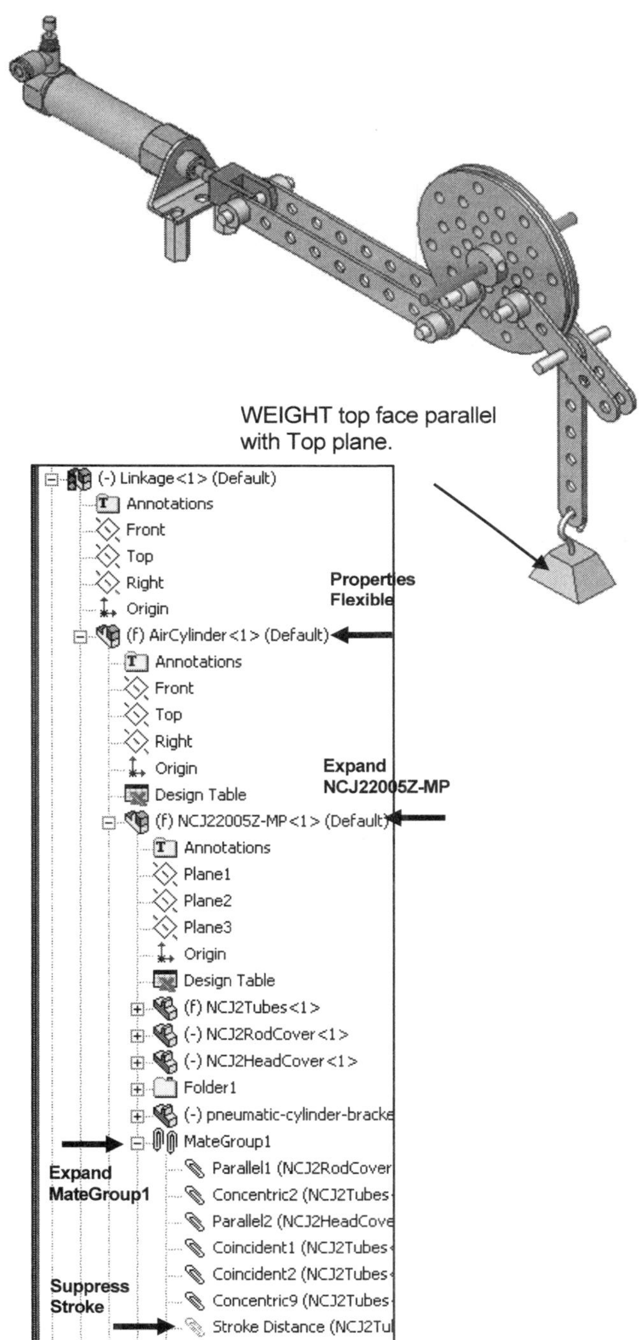

The AirCylinder Rod extends to the right. The WHEEL rotates and lifts the WEIGHT in a vertical direction.

- Save the PNEUMATIC TEST MODULE assembly.

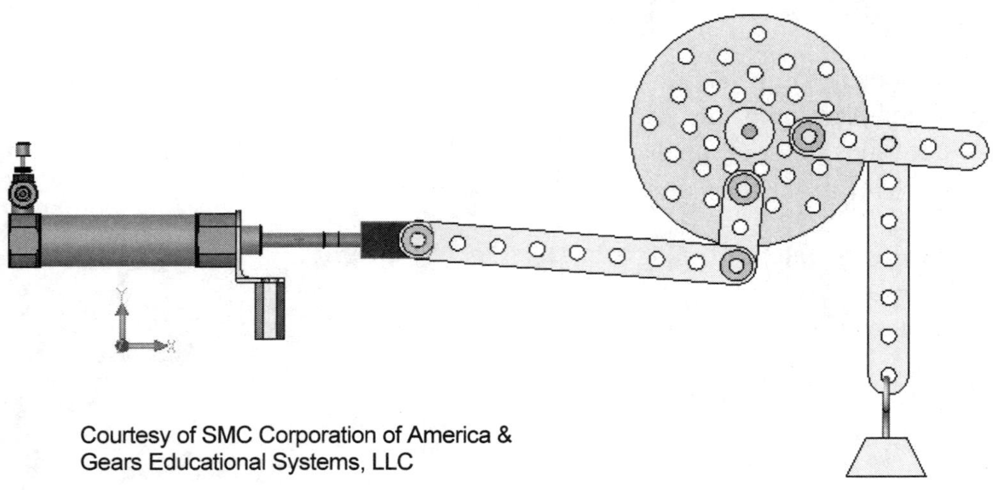

Courtesy of SMC Corporation of America &
Gears Educational Systems, LLC

Exercise 6.6d: SCHEMATIC DIAGRAM

Create the new drawing, SCHEMATIC DIAGRAM for the pneumatic components.

The pneumatic components utilized in the PNEUMATIC TEST MODULE Assembly are:

1. Air Reservoir
2. Regulator
3. ON/OFF/PURGE Valve – Mechanical 2/2
4. 3Way Solenoid Valve
5. Air Cylinder – Linear Actuator

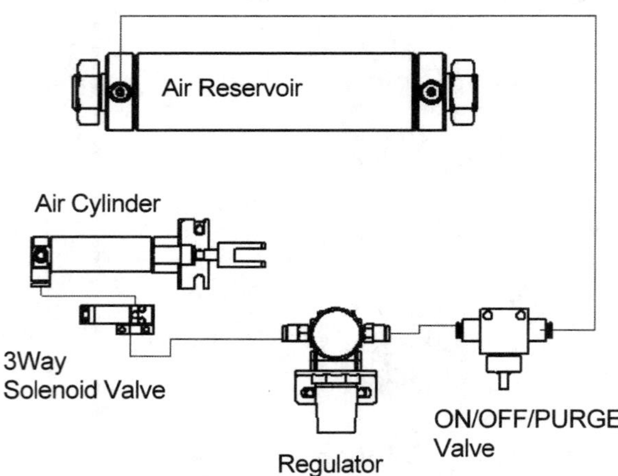

Pneumatic Components Diagram
Courtesy of SMC Corporation of America and
Gears Educational Systems.

ISO-1219 Pneumatic Symbols are created as SolidWorks Blocks. The Blocks are stored in the Exercise Pneumatic ISO Symbols folder in the files downloaded from the publisher's website.

- Utilize Insert, Block.
- Insert the Blocks into a B-size drawing.
- Enter 0.1 for Scale.
- Label each symbol.
- Utilize the Line tool to connect the pneumatic symbols.

Exercise 6-6e: PNEUMATIC TEST MODULE Assembly.

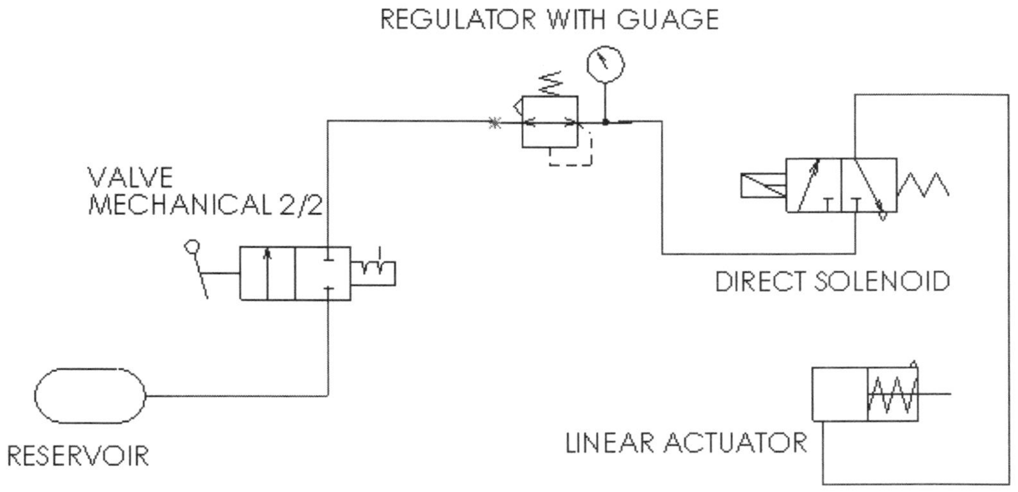

ISO-1219 Symbols
Courtesy of SMC Corporation of America

The PNEUMATIC TEST MODULE Assembly was partially completed in Exercise 6.5 and Exercise 6.6. Additional pneumatic components are required.

The Regulator utilizes a plastic knob to control the pressure from the Air Reservoir.

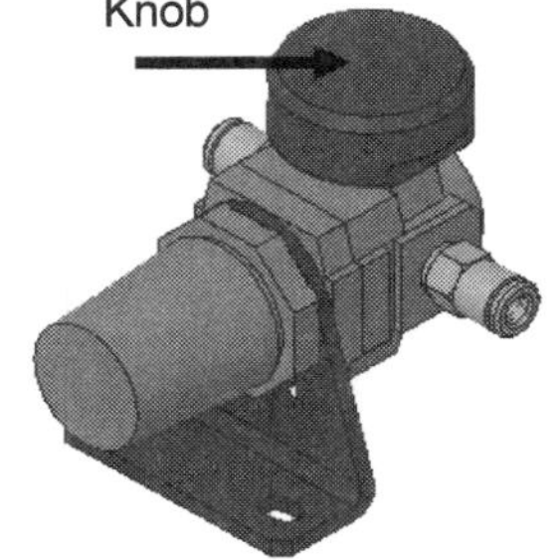

Regulator Assembly
Courtesy of SMC
Corporation of America

The Knob controls the Pressure at P2 by adjusting the screw loading on the setting Spring. The Main valve is held open, allowing flow from the inlet, P1 to the outlet, P2. When the air consumption rate drops, the force at P2 increases. This increase in force causes the Diaphragm to drop maintaining the constant pressure through the valve.

ON/OFF/PURGE Valve
Courtesy of SMC Corporation of America

Plastic components are utilized in a variety of applications. The ON/OFF/PURGE value utilizes plastic components for the Knob and Inlet and Outlet ports.

The ON/OFF/PURGE valve controls the airflow from the Regulator.

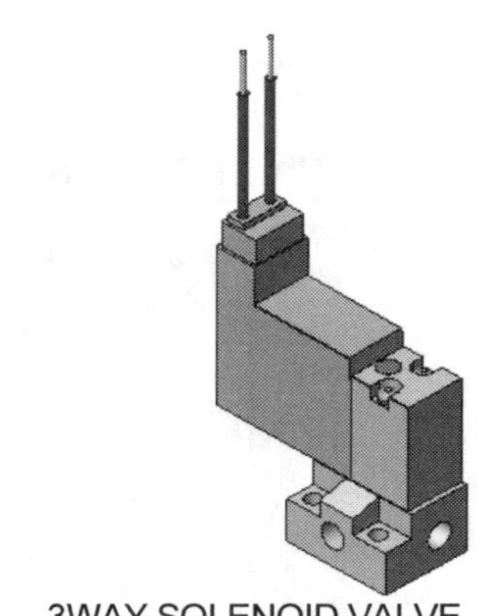

3WAY SOLENOID VALVE
Courtesy of SMC Corporation of America

The 3Way Solenoid value utilizes a plastic housing to protect the internal electronic components. The 3Way Solenoid value controls the electrical operation of to the Air Cylinder. The Solenoid acts like a switch.

Insert the following components into PNEUMATIC TEST MODULE Assembly:

1. ON/OFF/PURGE VALVE (Exercise 2.4).
2. REGULATOR.
3. SOLENOID.

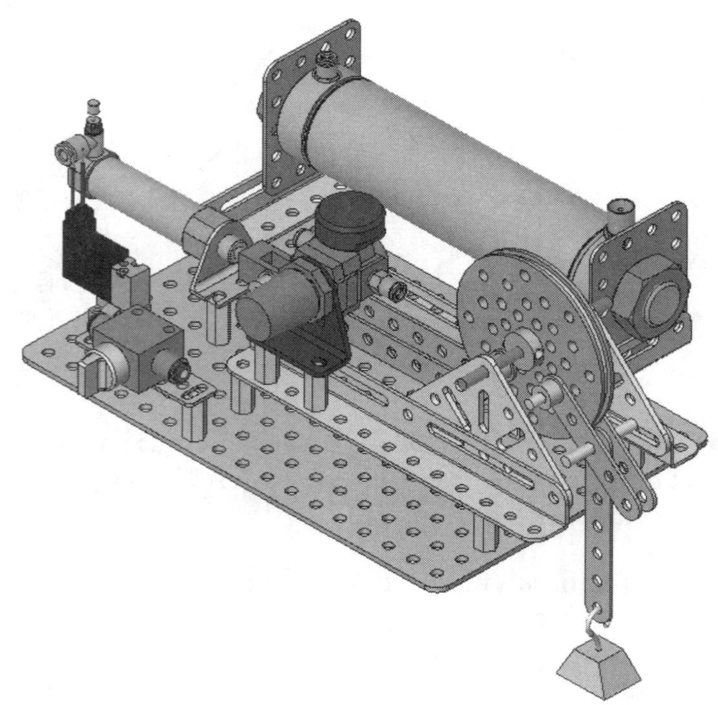

Exercise 6.6f: TUBING Part.

- Insert a new part, TUBING in-context of the PNEUMATIC TEST MODULE assembly. Utilize Insert, Component, New Part.
- Utilize the Sweep feature. There are four different paths between the air fittings. The start point and end point of each path references the air fittings between pneumatic components. The profile cross section is a 5/32[M5] circle.

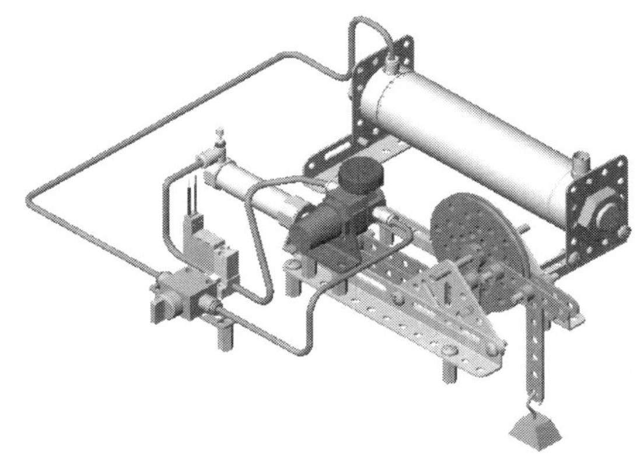

- Utilize reference planes to create sketched paths.
- Utilize on line help for information to create 3D sketches.

Note: Engineers utilize the SolidWorks Piping Add-In software application to efficiently create tubing, wiring and piping in assemblies.

Exercise 6.7: Industry Collaborative Exercise.

Create a new SolidWorks part from imported 2D geometry.

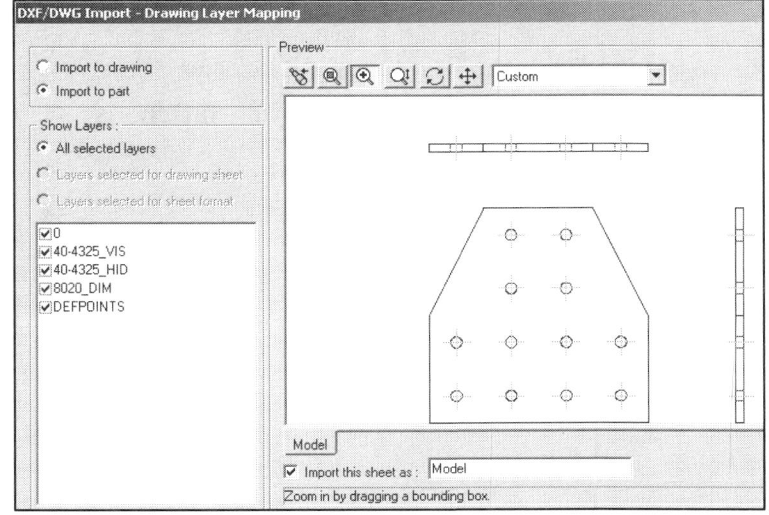

In Exercise 1.2 you created profiles from the company 80/20, Inc. (www.8020.net). Hundreds of .dwg (AutoCAD Drawing) and .dxf files (Drawing Exchange Format) exist on their web site. Many companies support .dwg or .dxf file format.

- Download the 2D .dwg library from www.8020.net (8Mb) or open the 40-4325 drawing from the files downloaded from the publisher's website.
- Open the part, 40-4325.dwg.
- Click Open.
- Select .dwg for File type.
- Click Import to Part.
- Click Next.
- Click Millimeters for Units.
- Click Finish.

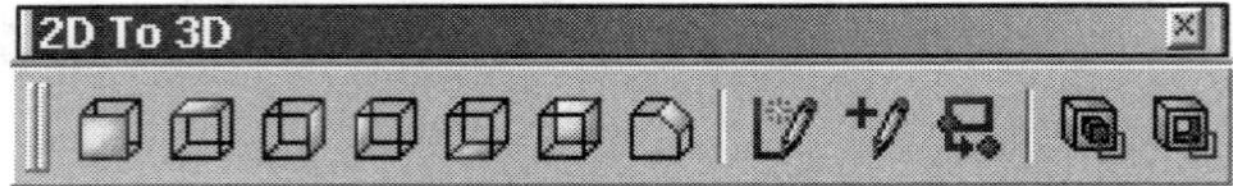

- Select a Part metric template from the New dialog box.

A New part is opened and the 2D Autocad geometry is inserted into Sketch1. The 2D to 3D Toolbar is displayed.

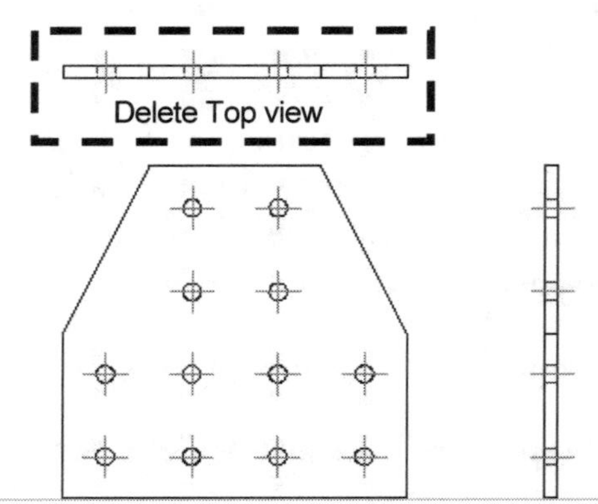

Model Courtesy of 80/20, Inc., Columbia City, IN USA.

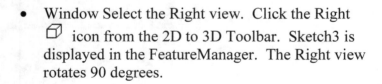

- Window Select the Top view. Delete the geometry.
- Define the views in Sketch1.
- Window Select the Front view.
- Click the Front icon from the 2D to 3D Toolbar. Sketch2 is displayed in the FeatureManager. Do not exit Sketch1.
- Window Select the Right view. Click the Right icon from the 2D to 3D Toolbar. Sketch3 is displayed in the FeatureManager. The Right view rotates 90 degrees.
- Align the Right view.
- Display the Isometric view. Click the lower left corner of the right view sketch.

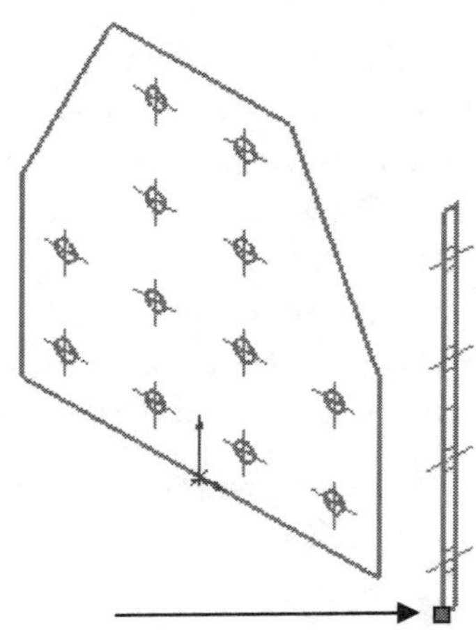

- Click Align Sketch icon from the 2D to 3D toolbar. The right view is aligned to the Front plane.

- Exit Sketch 1.

- Edit Sketch2.

- Right-click Edit Sketch.

- Click Extrude from the 2D to 3D toolbar. Click the right back vertex of the right view.

- Click OK to complete the Extruded-Base-Feature.

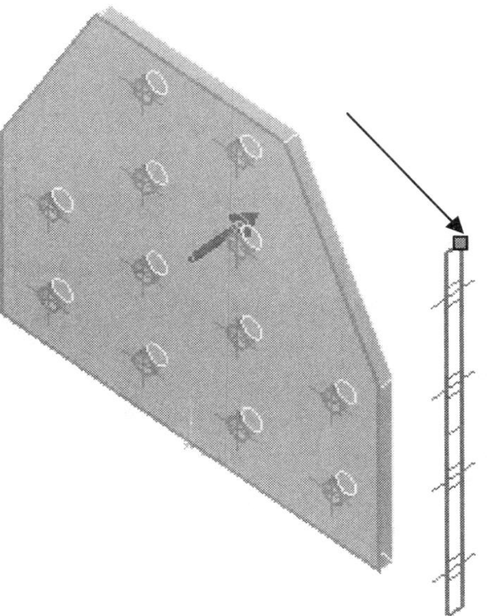

Sketch2 contains no dimensions and is under defined. The part geometry was generated from the .dwg file.

- Right-click Extrude1 in the FeatureManager.

- Click Edit Sketch.

- Utilize a Fix relation to fully define the Extruded Base sketch.

Exercise 6.8: Product Data Management (PDM).

Three months have passed. The BOX now contains hundreds of components. Many engineers and designers work to complete the project on time. How do you manage the parts, drawings and assemblies? PDM/Works is a project data management software application that runs inside SolidWorks.

The application is comprised of four major components:

Automated Revision Control.

Check In/Check Out of Vaulted Area for Security.

Support of Concurrent Engineering Activities.

Maintaining a History of Design Activities.

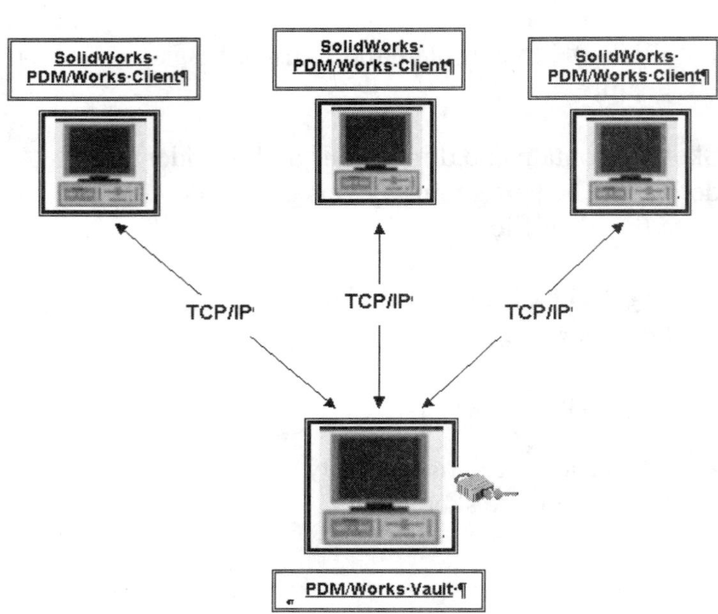

- Use the World Wide Web to research PDM four major components. How would PDM be used in the concurrent engineering application with the BOX assembly?
- Identify other departments in your company that would utilize a PDM system.

Exercise 6.9: **Industry Collaborative Exercise**.
MicroGroup®, Inc, Medway, MA (www.microgroup.com) is a tubing supplier and fabricator. MicroGroup® is a member of the SolidWorks Manufacturing Network.

- Invoke the SolidWorks web page (www.solidworks.com).
- Locate the Partners Manufacturing Network page.
- Search for tubing products to find the supplier, MicroGroup.

Tubing is measured by Outside Diameter OD and Inside Diameter ID.

- Develop a Design Table to represent the OD and ID of 3 different sizes.

Sizes			
MM	**Length**	**OD-Max**	**ID-Nominal**
M1	10	1	0.6
M4	15	4	3
M8	20	8	6

- Develop a TUBING drawing to contain three TUBING configurations.

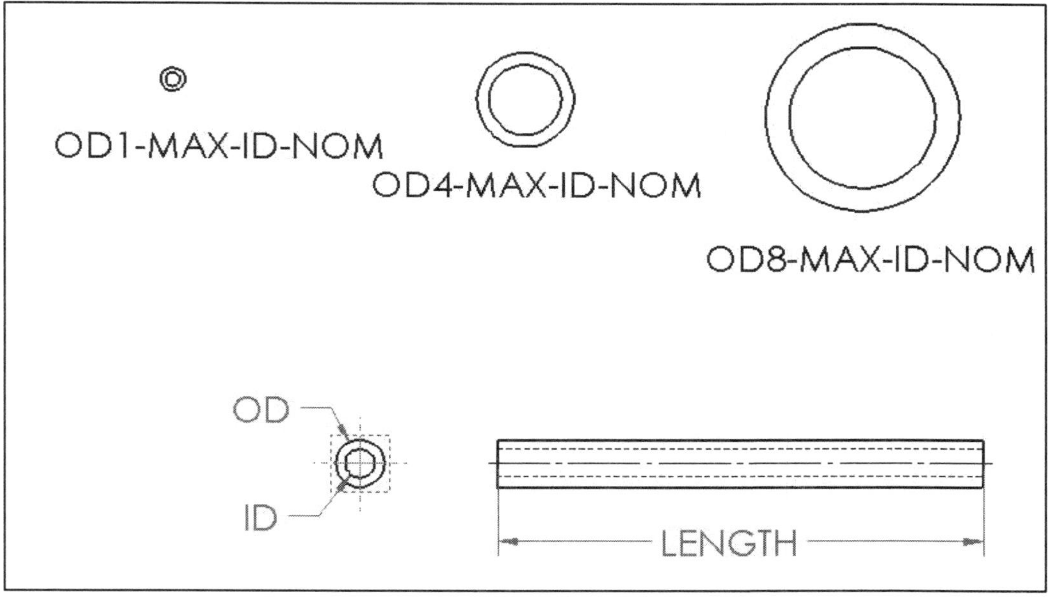

Exercise 6.10: **Industry Collaborative Exercise**.

Create a quality inspection CHECKING STATION assembly. Work with the team of manufacturing engineers. The quality inspection CHECKING STATION is comprised of four aluminum COREPLATEs.

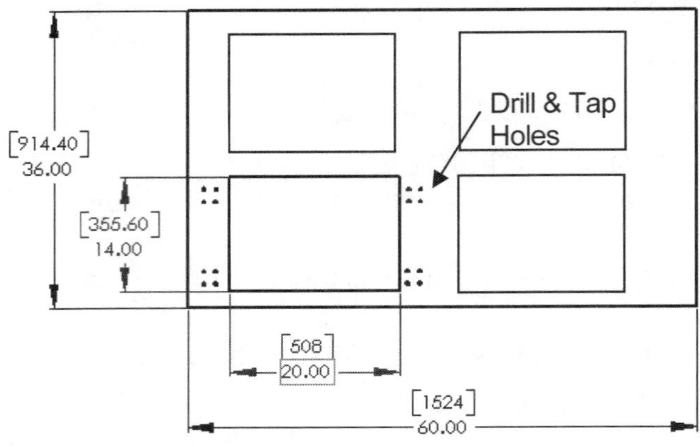

Each COREPLATE measures 20in. x 14in., (508mm x 355.6mm).

The COREPLATEs are clamped to a large steel TABLETOP 60in. x 36in., (1524mm x 914.4mm). The aluminum COREPLATEs are clamped to the TABLETOP during the checking process.

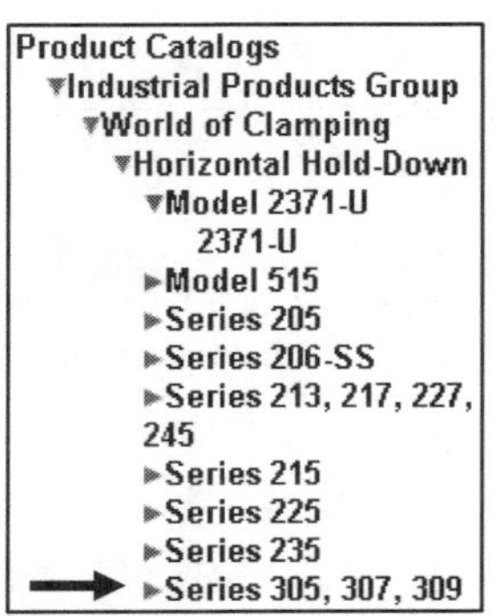

You require four holding CLAMPs mounted at the corners of the COREPLATE. Each compact CLAMP allows the quality inspector to operate in a tight area. Holes for the CLAMPs are drilled and tapped on the TABLETOP. The CLAMPs are fastened to the TABLETOP.

The senior manufacturing engineering on your team presents you with some initial calculations. The CLAMP requires a minimum holding capacity of 500 lb (340 daN).

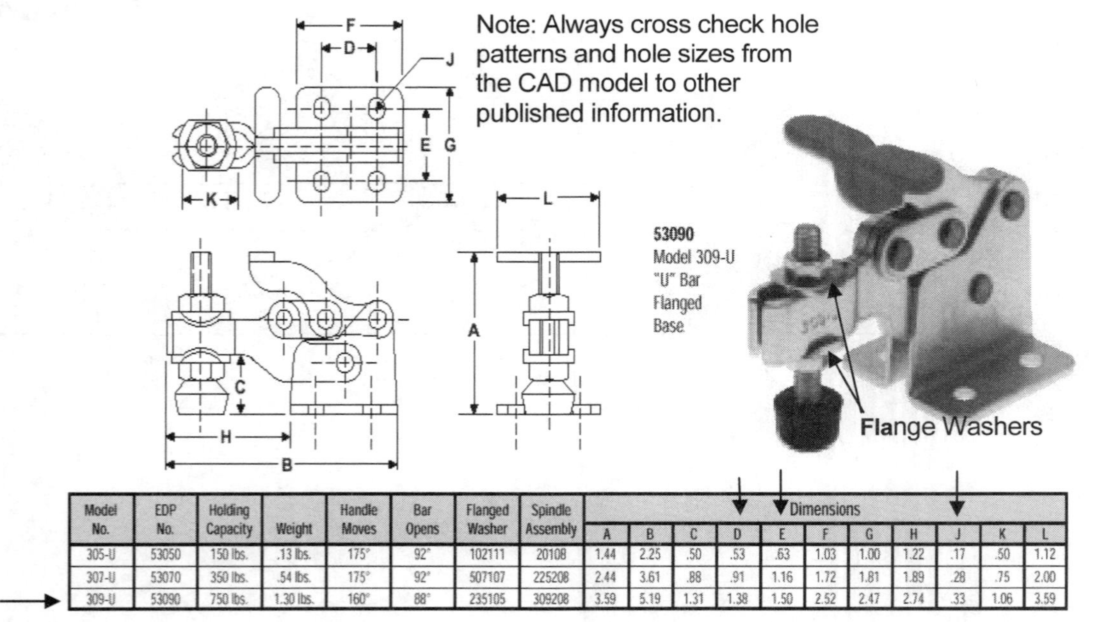

Model No.	EDP No.	Holding Capacity	Weight	Handle Moves	Bar Opens	Flanged Washer	Spindle Assembly	Dimensions A	B	C	D	E	F	G	H	J	K	L
305-U	53050	150 lbs.	.13 lbs.	175°	92°	102111	20108	1.44	2.25	.50	.53	.63	1.03	1.00	1.22	.17	.50	1.12
307-U	53070	350 lbs.	.54 lbs.	175°	92°	507107	225208	2.44	3.61	.88	.91	1.16	1.72	1.81	1.89	.28	.75	2.00
309-U	53090	750 lbs.	1.30 lbs.	160°	88°	235105	309208	3.59	5.19	1.31	1.38	1.50	2.52	2.47	2.74	.33	1.06	3.59

- Invoke a web browser. Enter the URL: www.destaco.com.

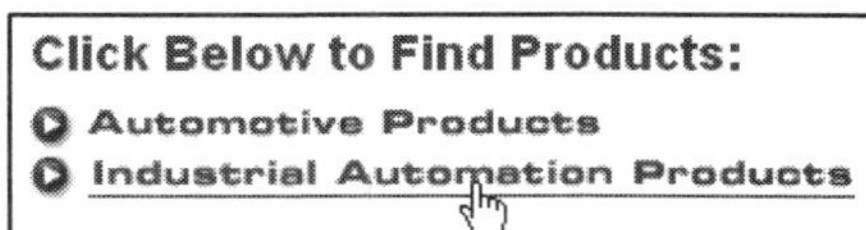

- Click Industrial Automation Products.
- Click DE-STA-CO Industrial Clamping Products.

DE-STA-CO Industrial Clamping Products
Vertical Handle Hold-down Action Clamps
Horizontal Handle Hold-down Action Clamps

Industrial Products

Heavy Duty Hold-down Action
Horizontal Hold-down

- Click Horizontal Hold-Down.
- Click Series 305, 307, 309 to view product information.

Series 235
Series 305, 307, 309
NEW Toggle Clamps

- Record the part numbers and hole dimensions. Download the components required to create the CLAMP-WASHER-SPINDLE sub assembly. Click 3D CAD Library . Download 305-U Clamp.
- Use the On-line Help to review the commands: Linear Pattern, Mirror, Mirror All, Component Pattern, Mirror Component.
- Manually sketch a plan of your assembly.
- Develop the Layout Sketch in the CHECKING STATION assembly.
- Create the components TABLETOP and COREPLATE from the Layout Sketch.
- Add the CLAMP-WASHER-SPINDLE sub assembly.

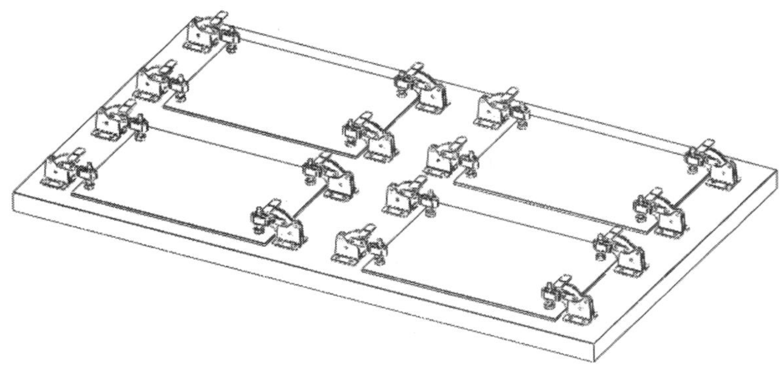

- Insert 4 SCREWs for each CLAMP.
- Create an assembly Drawing and a Bill of Materials for the CHECKING STATION.

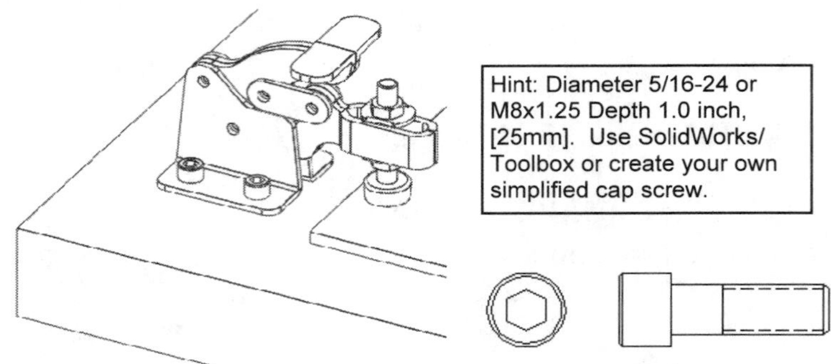

Hint: Diameter 5/16-24 or M8x1.25 Depth 1.0 inch, [25mm]. Use SolidWorks/ Toolbox or create your own simplified cap screw.

Exercise 6.11: Industry Collaborative Exercise.

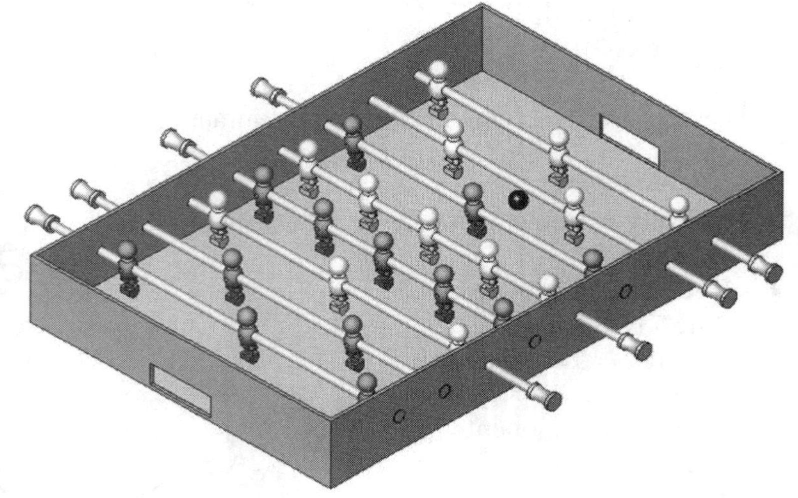

You are part of a team to develop a SOCCER PLAY TABLE Assembly. Partial dimensions have been provided.

Develop the assembly based on these design constraints.

- Research the World Wide Web.
- Utilize Tools, 3D Content Central and www.globalspec.com to find components such as handles, rods, caps and bushings. Answers will vary. Read all requirements first.

The SOCCERPLAYER is one part. The maximum dimensions are 50mm x 50mm x 165 mm.

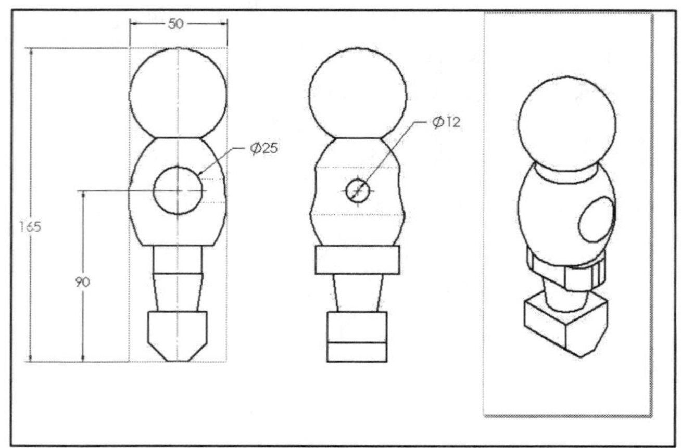

The BASE ROD Thru Hole is 25mm. The Screw Blind Hole is 12mm.

The 25mm BASE ROD part has a minimum length of 1200mm.

There are three different BASE RODs: 5HOLE, 3HOLE and 2HOLE. The BASE ROD is a component of the ROD-PLAYER subassemblies that contains a GRIPPER and an END CAP.

5 HOLE
3 HOLE
2 HOLE

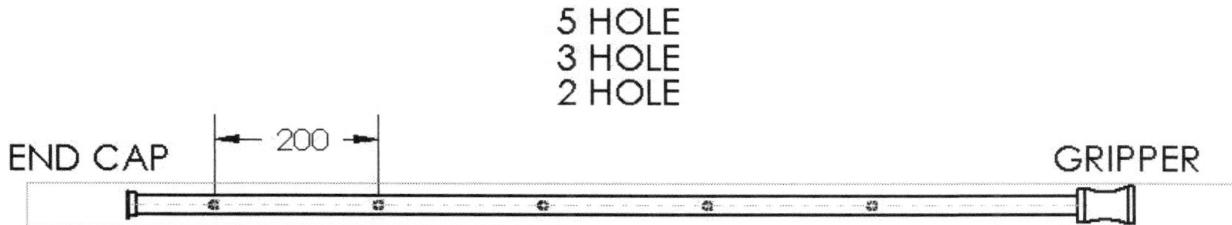

BASE ROD ∅ 25 MM x 1200MM (Minimum)

There are six subassemblies.

5PLAYER-HOME	5PLAYER-AWAY
3PLAYER-HOME	3PLAYER-AWAY
2PLAYER-HOME	2PLAYER-AWAY

The TABLE size is 1000mmx1500mmx200mm. The Thickness of the TABLE is 10mm. The spacing between the six subassemblies is 150mm. The Thru Holes in the TABLE contain a Bushing. The Thru Hole height is based upon the PLAYER size.

Plan the parts and assemblies before starting this project. Utilize individual parts and assemblies or create configurations with Design Tables.

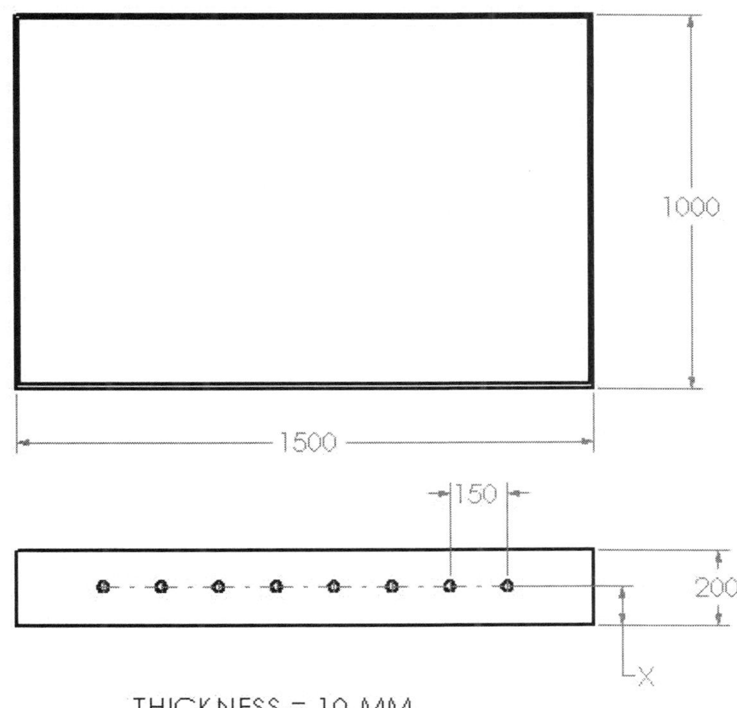

Notes:

Appendix

Engineering Changer Order (ECO)

D&M

Engineering Change Order

ECO # ______________
Page 1 of __

	☐	Hardware	Author
	☐	Software	Date
Product Line	☐	Quality	Authorized Mgr.
	☐	Tech Pubs	Date

Change Tested By

Reason for ECO(Describe the existing problem, symptom and impact on field)

D&M Part No.	Rev From/To	Part Description	Description	Owner

ECO Implementation/Class			Departments	Approvals	Date
All in Field	☐		Engineering		
All in Test	☐		Manufacturing		
All in Assembly	☐		Technical Support		
All in Stock	☐		Marketing		
All on Order	☐		DOC Control		
All Future	☐				
Material Disposition			ECO Cost		
Rework	☐		DO NOT WRITE BELOW THIS LINE(ECO BOARD ONLY)		
Scrap	☐		Effective Date		
Use as is	☐		Incorporated Date		
None	☐		Board Approval		
See Attached	☐		Board Date		

Feature Toolbar and Insert Menu

The Default Features Toolbar contains the features utilized in Project 1, Project 4 and Project 5 to create parts. Additional features and tools are available from the Insert menu. Project 4 utilized the Mold tools. Project 6 utilized the Sheet Metal.

A complete list of tools is available in Help, SolidWorks Help Topics, Toolbar. Review the Multimedia CD for additional examples from the default Features toolbar.

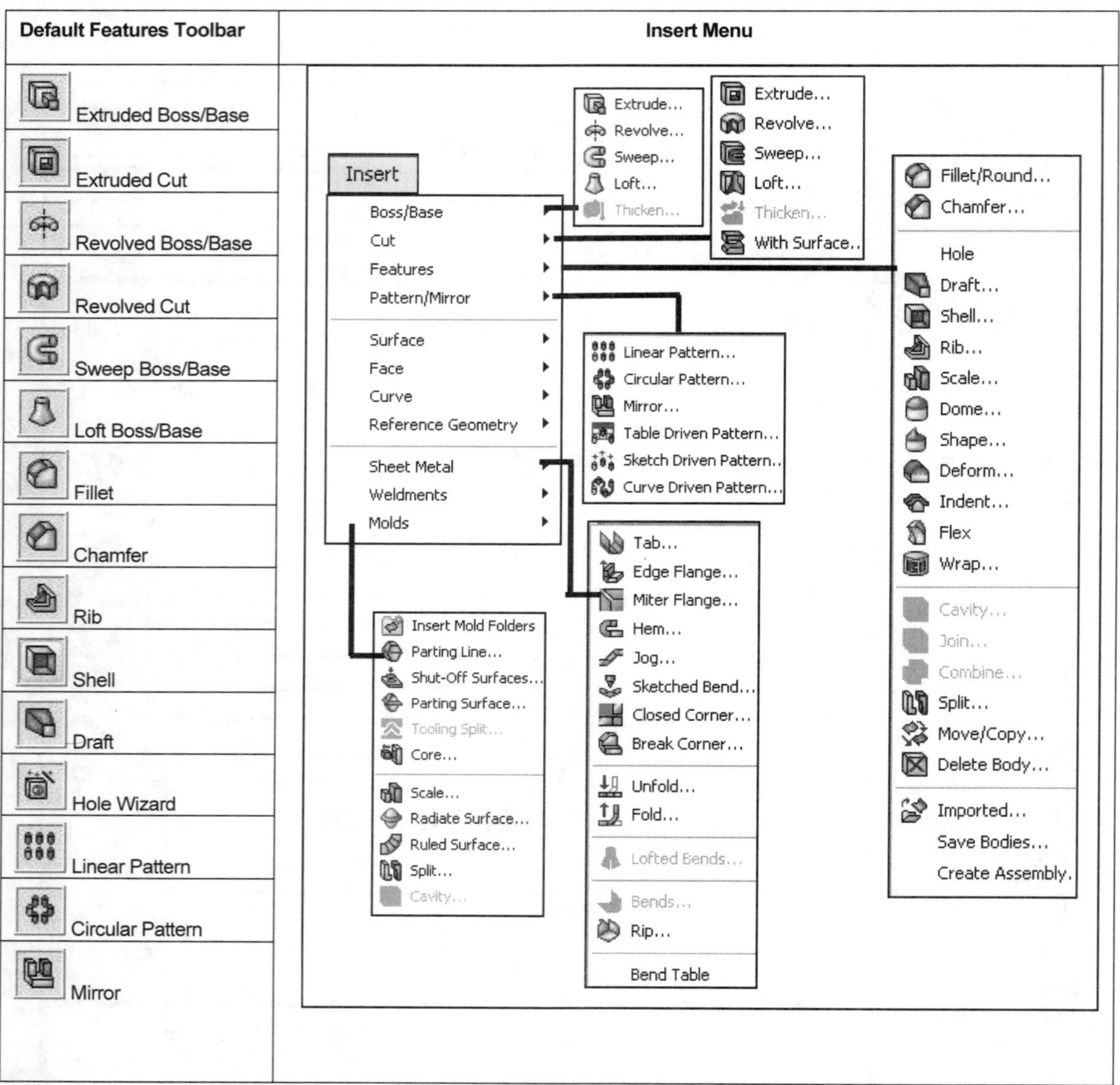

SolidWorks Keyboard Shortcuts

Listed below are the pre-defined keyboard shortcuts in SolidWorks:

Action:	**Key Combination:**
Model Views	
Rotate the model horizontally or vertically:	**Arrow** keys
Rotate the model horizontally or vertically 90 degrees.	**Shift** + **Arrow** keys
Rotate the model clockwise or counterclockwise	**Alt** + left of right **Arrow** keys
Pan the model	**Ctrl** + **Arrow** keys
Zoom in	**Shift + z**
Zoom out	**z**
Zoom to fit	**f**
Previous view	**Ctrl + Shift + z**
View Orientation	
View Orientation menu	**Spacebar**
Front view	**Ctrl + 1**
Back view	**Ctrl + 2**
Left view	**Ctrl + 3**
Right view	**Ctrl + 4**
Top view	**Ctrl + 5**
Bottom view	**Ctrl + 6**
Isometric view	**Ctrl + 7**
NormalTo view	**Ctrl + 8**
Selection Filters	
Filter edges	**e**
Filter vertices	**v**
Filter faces	**x**
Toggle Selection Filter toolbar	**F5**
Toggle selection filters on/off	**F6**
File menu items	
New SolidWorks document	**Ctrl + n**
Open document	**Ctrl + o**
Open From Web Folder	**Ctrl + w**
Make Drawing from Part	**Ctrl + d**
Make Assembly from Part	**Ctrl + a**
Save	**Ctrl +s**
Print	**Ctrl + p**
Additional shortcuts	
Access online help inside of PropertyManager or dialog box	**F1**
Rename an item in the FeatureManager design tree	**F2**
Rebuild the model	**Ctrl + b**
Force rebuild – Rebuild the model and all its features	**Ctrl + q**
Redraw the screen	**Ctrl + r**
Cycle between open SolidWorks document	**Ctrl + Tab**

Line to arc/arc to line in the Sketch	a
Undo	**Ctrl + z**
Redo	**Ctrl + y**
Cut	**Ctrl + x**
Copy	**Ctrl + c**
Additional shortcuts	
Paste	**Ctrl + v**
Delete	**Delete**
Next window	**Ctrl + F6**
Close window	**Ctrl + F4**
Selects all text inside an Annotations text box	**Ctrl + a**

In the Sketch, the Esc key unselects geometry items currently selected in the Properties box and Add Relations box. In the model, the Esc key closes the PropertyManager and cancels the selections.

Windows Shortcuts

Listed below are the pre-defined keyboard shortcuts in Microsoft Windows:

Action:	**Keyboard Combination:**
Open the Start menu	Windows Logo key
Open Windows Explorer	Windows Logo key + E
Minimize all open windows	Windows Logo key + M
Open a Search window	Windows Logo key + F
Open Windows Help	Windows Logo key + F1
Select multiple geometry items in a SolidWorks document	Ctrl key (Hold the Ctrl key down. Select items.) Release the Ctrl key.

Types of Decimal Dimensions ASME Y14.5M

This text follows the ASME Y14 Engineering Drawing and Related Documentation Practices for drawings. Display of dimensions and tolerances are as follows:

TYPES of DECIMAL DIMENSIONS (ASME Y14.5M)			
Description:	**Example: MM**	**Description:**	**Example: INCH**
Dimension is less than 1mm. Zero precedes the decimal point.	0.9 0.95	Dimension is less than 1 inch. Zero is not used before the decimal point.	.5 .56
Dimension is a whole number. Display no decimal point. Display no zero after decimal point.	19	Express dimension to the same number of decimal places as its tolerance.	1.750
Dimension exceeds a whole number by a decimal fraction of a millimeter. Display no zero to the right of the decimal.	11.5 11.51	Add zeros to the right of the decimal point. If the tolerance is expressed to 3 places, then the dimension contains 3 places to the right of the decimal point.	

Tolerance Display for INCH and METRIC DIMENSIONS (ASME Y14.5M)		
Display:	Inch:	Metric:
Dimensions less than 1	.5	0.5
Unilateral Tolerance	$1.417^{+.005}_{-.000}$	$36^{0}_{-0.5}$
Bilateral Tolerance	$1.417^{+.010}_{-.020}$	$36^{+0.25}_{-0.50}$
Limit Tolerance	.571 .463	14.50 11.50

Helpful On-Line Information

The SolidWorks URL: http://**www.solidworks.com** contains information on local resellers, Gold Partners, Solutions Partners, Manufacturing Partners and SolidWorks users groups.

The SolidWorks URL: http://www.3DContentCentral.com contains additional engineering electronic catalog information.

The SolidWorks web site provides links to sample designs, frequently asked questions and the independent News Group (comp.cad.solidworks).

Helpful on-line SolidWorks information is available from the following URLs:

http://www.mechengineer.com/snug/

Configuration information and other tips and tricks.

http://www.solidworktips.com

Helpful tips, tricks on SolidWorks and API.

Certified SolidWorks Professionals (CSWP) URLs provide additional helpful on-line information:

http://www.scottjbaugh.com	Scott J. Baugh
http://www.3-ddesignsolutions.com	Devon Sowell
http://www.zxys.com	Paul Salvador
http://www.mikejwilson.com	Mike J. Wilson
http://www.frontiernet.net/~mlombard	Matt Lombard
http://www.dimontegroup.com	Gene Dimonte & Ed Eaton

On-line tutorials are for educational purposes only. Tutorials are copyrighted by their respective owners.

INDEX

3DContentCentral 2-69
3MMCAPSCREW 2-60
3Point Arc 4-44
4MMCAPSCREW 2-39
80/20 Inc. 1-108

A

Add Derived Configuration 6-61
Advanced Mates 2-16
Advanced Mode 1-11
Animate Explode 2-54
Animation 2-56
Annotations Toolbar 3-8
ANSI 1-19, 1-43
Arrow Dimensions 3-9, 3-10
Arrows 1-49
ASME Y14.3M 1-28
Assembly Hole Feature 6-76
Assembly Modeling Approach 2-5
Assembly Template 5-63, 6-12
Auto Balloon 3-71
Auto Relief 6-35
Auxiliary View 3-30

B

Balloon Text 3-72
Balloons 3-71
B-ANSI-MM Drawing Template 3-21, 3-34
Base Feature 1-31
Base Flange 6-89, 6-90
BATTERY Part Extruded Base Feature 4-17
BATTERY Part Extruded Boss Feature 4-26
BATTERY Part Extruded Cut Feature 4-23
BATTERY Part Fillet Feature 4-22, 4-25
BATTERYANDPLATE Sub-assembly 5-68
BATTERYPLATE Part 4-33
BATTERYPLATE Part Extruded Boss Feature 4-36
BATTERYPLATE Part Fillet Feature 4-37
Bend angle 6-33
Bend from Virtual Sharp 6-34
Bend Outside 6-34
Bend radius 6-32
Bends 6-32
Bill of Materials 3-72
Bottom Up Design Approach 2-5
BOX Assembly 6-8
BOX Assembly Layout Sketch 6-13
BOX Assembly Link Values and Equations 6-17
BRACKET Part 6-89
BRACKET Part Base Flange 6-89
BRACKET Part Break Corner 6-93
BRACKET Part Edge Flange 6-93
BRACKET Part In-content Feature 6-91
BRACKET Part Mirror Component Feature 6-98
BRACKET Part Miter Flange 6-93
Break Corner 6-93
BULB Part 4-57
BULB Part Circular Pattern Feature 4-65
BULB Part Dome Feature 4-64
BULB Part Revolved Base Feature 4-58
BULB Part Revolved Boss Feature 4-60
BULB Part Revolved Cut Thin Feature 4-62
BULB Part Spline Sketch Tool Feature 4-60

C

CABINET Convert Entities Feature 6-35
CABINET Edge Flange 6-40
CABINET Extruded Base Feature 6-37
CABINET Formed and Flat States 6-60
CABINET HEM Feature 6-40
CABINET Hole Wizard Feature 6-43
CABINET Insert Component 6-35
CABINET Insert Sheet Metal Bends 6-38
CABINET Louver Forming Tool 6-51
CABINET Rip Feature 6-36
CABINET Sheetmetal Library Feature 6-47
CABINET Shell Feature 6-32
CAPANDLENS Sub-assembly 5-70
Center Marks 3-49
Centerlines 1-81, 1-84, 3-49
Centerpoint Arc 4-52
Chamfer Feature 1-62
Circle 1-47
Circle Feedback Symbol 1-47
Circle Split Line 3-71

CircuitWorks 6-20
Circular Pattern Feature 4-65
Clearance Fit 2-47
Close 1-15
Coincident Mate 2-16, 2-24, 2-44
Coincident Mate 5-66
Coincident Relation 1-61, 1-70
Collapse 2-14, 2-55
Collinear Relation 3-43
Collision Detection 2-30
Color and Optics 1-78
CommandManager 1-12, 1-13, 1-14
Company Logo 3-17
Company Name Property 3-6, 3-14
Component Pattern 2-62
Component Properties 3-28
Component States 2-15
Concentric Mate 5-69
Concentric SmartMate 2-44
ConfigurationManager 5-11
Control Area 1-13, 1-32
Convert Entities 1-63. 1-64
Convert Entities Sketch Tool 4-47
Copy the Assembly 2-80
Copy/Paste Function 1-70
Coradial 1-76
COSMOSXpress 2-84
Crop View 3-41
Curve Driven Pattern 6-58
CUSTOMER Assembly 2-74
Customizing Toolbars 4-68

D

Dangle 1-73, 1-75
Datum Planes 1-27
Delete 4-34
Derived Component Pattern 6-74
Design Changes 1-72
Design Checklist 4-70
Design Intent 4-6
Design Library 1-10, 2-32
Design Table 5-10
Detail Drawing 3-36
Detail View 3-33
Diameter dimension 1-45
Dimension Holes 3-46
Dimension Property box_height 6-19
Dimensioning Standards 1-19
Dimension Property box_width 6-19
Display Modes 1-41
Display with Parenthesis 3-45, 3-54
Distance Mate 5-72
Document Properties 1-19, 3-62
Dome Feature 4-64
Draft Analysis 4-73
Draft Angle 4-27
Draft Feature 5-41
Drawing Document Properties 3-62
Drawing Layers 3-11
Drawing Part Number 3-62
Drawing Template 3-5, 3-7
Drawing toolbar 3-24
Drawing View Properties 3-70
DWG. NO. Box 3-26
Dynamic Mirror Feature 1-83

E

Edge Flange 6-40
Edge Properties 3-28
Edit Feature 4-34
Edit Part 1-71
Edit Component 6-22
Edit Part Color 1-78
Edit Sheet Format 3-5
eDrawings 5-82
Elastic Modulus 2-85
Electronic Workbench 6-20
Endpoint 1-83
Engineering Change Order 3-60
Equal Relation 1-45, 1-47
Equal Relation 5-8
Equations 6-17, 6-82
Expand 2-14, 2-21
Exploded View 2-51, 2-53, 3-68
Export Files 5-82
Extrude the Sketch 6-25
Extruded Base 1-31, 1-59
Extruded Boss/Base 1-24
Extruded Cut 1-24, 1-64

F

Fasteners 1-43
Feedback Symbols 1-32, 1-46
Features 1-24, 1-34
FeatureManager 1-12, 2-14

Features Toolbar 1-13, 1-14
Feature Statistics 5-19
FHA-M5-30ZI Fastener 6-69
File Explorer 1-10
File Folder 1-7
File Locations 1-17
File Extension 1-22
File Management 1-7
Fillet Feature 1-24, 1-52
Filter Faces 2-23
First Angle Projection 1-30
Fit 2-47
FLASHLIGHT Assembly 5-62, 5-74
FLASHLIGHT Assembly Document Template 5-63
Flat State: 2D 6-32, 6-36
Flattened 6-40
Fold 6-102
Folders, FeatureManager 2-68
Format Layer 3-52
Forming Tool 6-51
Front Plane 1-27, 1-32
Font size 3-15
Formed State, 3D 6-32, 6-51
Front View 1-14
Full Round Fillet 4-37, 4-38

G

Gains Pressure slider 5-18
Gap in extension line 3-39
Gap Link Valve 6-18
Gears Educational Systems 1-109
General Notes 3-57
Graphics window 1-9
Gray area 1-13, 1-14
GUIDE Drawing 3-24
GUIDE Drawing Company Logo 3-17
GUIDE Drawing Document Properties 3-62
GUIDE Drawing General Notes 3-57
GUIDE Drawing Hole Callout 3-46
GUIDE Drawing Insert Model Items 3-38
GUIDE Drawing Move Dimensions 3-39
GUIDE Drawing Moving Views 3-27
GUIDE Drawing Parametric Notes 3-57
GUIDE Drawing Revision Table 3-60
GUIDE Drawing Save Sheet Format 3-20
GUIDE Drawing Sheet Format 3-13
GUIDE Drawing Sheet Properties 3-6, 3-9
GUIDE Drawing Template 3-20
GUIDE Drawing Title Block 3-12
GUIDE Part Dynamic Mirror Feature 1-83
GUIDE Part Extruded-Base Feature 1-83
GUIDE Part Insert an Additional Feature 3-55
GUIDE Part Linear Pattern Feature 1-94
GUIDE Part Materials Editor 1-96
GUIDE Part Mirror Feature 1-90
GUIDE Part Overview 1-81
GUIDE ROD Assembly 2-7
GUIDE-Part Mass Properties 1-96
GUIDE-ROD Assembly Collision Detection 2-30
GUIDE-ROD Assembly Component Mate 2-18
GUIDE-ROD Assembly Component Pattern 2-62
GUIDE-ROD Assembly Exploded View 3-68
GUIDE-ROD Assembly Redefining Mates 2-64
GUIDE-ROD Drawing Associative Part, Assembly and Drawing 3-77
GUIDE-ROD Drawing Bill of Materials 3-72

H

Handle 1-38
Helix/Spiral Feature 5-42
Help 1-15
Hem 6-40, 6-42
Hidden Dims 3-11
Hidden Lines Removed 1-41
Hidden Lines Visible 1-41
Hide 2-21, 2-66
Hole Callout 3-48
Hole Wizard Counterbore Feature 4-48
Hole Wizard Countersink Feature 1-24, 1-54,1-93
Horizontal Relation 1-34, 1-48
HOUSING Part 5-31
HOUSING Part Draft Feature 5-41
HOUSING Part Extruded Base Feature 5-33
HOUSING Part Extruded Boss Feature 5-38
HOUSING Part Extruded Cut Feature 5-51
HOUSING Part Helix/Spiral Curve 5-42
HOUSING Part Linear Pattern Feature 5-52
HOUSING Part Loft Boss Feature 5-34
HOUSING Part Mirror Feature 5-59
HOUSING Part Rib Feature 5-52
HOUSING Part Shell Feature 5-39
HOUSING Part Sweep Feature 5-42, 5-56

I

IGES Components 6-69
In-Context Features 6-10
Injection Molded Process, 4-32
InPlace Mates 6-11
Insert Bends Feature 6-89, 6-102
Insert Component 2-11, 2-12
Insert Model Items 3-38
Insert Sheet Metal Bends 6-38
Interference 2-58
Interference Fit 2-47
Intersection Relation 5-47
ISO 1-19
Isometric View 1-28, 1-43

J & K

Jog Feature 6-102
K-factor 6-39

L

Landscape 3-7
Layer Properties 3-11
Layer Toolbar 3-11
Lee Plastics, Inc. 4-32
LENS Part 4-42
LENS Part Revolved Boss Thin Feature 4-51
LENS Part Convert Entities Sketch Tool 4-47
LENS Part Extruded Boss Feature 4-47
LENS Part Extruded Boss Feature 4-54
LENS Part HoleWizard 4-48
LENS Part Offset Entities 4-54
LENS Part Revolved Base Feature 4-43
LENS Part Shell Feature 4-46
LENSANDBULB Sub-assembly 5-63
LENSCAP Part Extruded Base Feature 5-21
LENSCAP Part Extruded Cut Feature 5-21
LENSCAP Part Helix/Spiral Curve 5-25
LENSCAP Part Revolved Cut Thin Feature 5-24
LENSCAP Part Shell Feature 5-21
LENSCAP Part Sweep Feature 5-25
LENSCAP Part Thread Feature 5-25
Line 1-65, 1-83
Line Properties 1-34
Linear Component Pattern 2-64
Linear Dimension Symbol 1-39
Linear Motion 2-6
Linear Pattern Feature 1-94, 5-53
Link to Property 3-65
Link Values 6-17
Loft Base Feature 5-13
Louver 6-51

M

Machined Parts 1-26
Main Menu 1-12
Make Buy Decision 2-71
Manipulator Handle 2-51
Manufacturing Considerations 1-98
Manufacturing Design Issues 4-82
Mark for Drawing 1-37
Mass Density 1-96
Mass Properties 1-96
Mate Diagnostics 2-29
Mate Errors 2-26
Mate Flags 2-29
Mate Pop-up toolbar 2-19
Mate Types 2-16
Material Inside 6-34
Material Outside 6-34
Material Property 3-68
Material Thickness 6-32
Materials Editor 1-96
Materials Library 1-97
Mates 2-16
Mates: Redefining 2-64
Maximize Button 1-14
Measure 4-30
Midpoint Relation 5-15
Mirror Components 6-107
Mirror Entities 5-34
Mirror Feature 1-90
Mirror Point 6-99, 6106
MirrorBRACKET Part 6-98
MirrorBRACKET Part Fold Feature 6-102
MirrorBRACKET Part Insert Bends 6-102
MirrorBRACKET Part Jog Feature 6-102
MirrorBRACKET Part Unfold Feature 6-102
Miter Flange 6-93
MMGS 1-20
Model View 6-62
Modify Component Dimensions 2-31
Modify Dimension 1-39

Modify Sketch tool 6-50
Modify Text Box 1-35, 1-37
Mold Analysis 4-83
Mold Base 4-72
Mold Tooling 4-11, 4-72
MoldFlowXpress 4-83
Molds CommandManager 4-74
MOTHERBOARD Assembly Hole Feature 6-76
MOTHERBOARD Edit Component 6-22
MOTHERBOARD Extruded Boss 6-23
MOTHERBOARD Extruded-Base 6-22
MOTHERBOARD Insert Component 6-20
Move Dimensions 3-39
Move Dimensions to a different view 3-45
Move Views 3-27
Multi-body Parts 4-40
Multiple Radius Options 4-37

N

Named Views 1-68
New Assembly 2-8
New Drawing 3-7
New Part 1-11
New View 1-69
No Bends 6-40
NormalTo 1-61
Notes 3-57
Notes Layer 3-11
Novice Mode 1-11

O

Obround Relief 6-35
Offset Entities 4-23, 4-31
Online Tutorial 1-16
Orientation Menu 1-69
Origin 1-12
O-RING Part Design Table 5-9
O-RING Part Swept Boss/Base Feature 5-7
Orthographic Projection 1-26

P

Pan 1-43
Parallel Mate 2-21
Parallel Plane at Point 6-99
Parametric Notes 3-57
Part Color 1-78
Part Template 1-19, 1-20, 4-11, 6-12
Partial Auxiliary View 3-42
PART-IN-ANSI Template 4-14
Parting Lines 4-76
Parting Surfaces 4-77
PART-MM-ANSI Template 1-21
PART-MM-ISO 4-13
Paste 1-70
Pattern Options 6-58
PEM Fasteners 6-91
Perpendicular Relation 4-66
PhotoWorks 1-97, 1-112
Pierce Relation 5-49
Plane Offset 5-27
PLATE Part 1-23
PLATE Part Extruded-Base Feature 1-31
PLATE Part Extruded-Cut Feature 1-45
PLATE Part Fillet Feature 1-52
PLATE Part Hole Wizard 1-54
PLATE Part Modify Dimensions 1-40
PLATE Part Rename 1-39
Point 6-55
Poisson's ratio 2-89
Polygon 2-39
POWERSUPPLY Insert Component 6-26
Press Fit 2-47
Previous View 1-42
Primary datum plane 1-27
Principle Views 1-27
Product Data Management (PDM) 6-130
Propagate icon 6-96
Properties of the Sheet 3-27
Push Pin 1-69

Q & R

Rebuild 1-37
Rebuild Errors 1-73
Rectangle 1-32
Redefining Mates 2-64
Reference Planes 1-27
Reid Tool Supply Co 1-107
Relations 1-37, 1-45
Relief 6-35
Rename 1-39
Replace Component 6-79

Reset 1-37
Restore 1-37
Revision Table 3-60
Revolved Boss/Base Feature 4-51
Revolved Cut Feature 4-62
Revolved Cut Thin Feature 5-24
Rib Feature 5-53, 5-54,
Right-click Select 1-33
Rip Feature 6-37
ROD Part Chamfer Feature 1-62
ROD Part Convert Entities Sketch Tool 1-63
ROD Part Copy/Paste Function 1-69
ROD Part Design Changes 1-71
ROD Part Edit Color 1-78
ROD Part Extruded-Base Feature 1-59
ROD Part Extruded-Cut Feature 1-61
ROD Part Overview 1-57
ROD Part Rebuild Errors 1-73
ROD Part Rollback 1-71
Rollback Bar 1-72
Rotate 1-42
Rotate Component 2-22, 2-23
Rotational Motion 2-6

S

Save 1-21
Save As 4-34
Save As Copy 2-59
Save As Drawing Template 3-20
Save Sheet Format 3-20
Scale Feature for molded parts 4-77
Secondary datum plane 1-27
Section View 2-50
Select 1-33
Select Faces 1-78
Selected Entities 1-47
Selection Filters 2-23, 2-26
Set to Resolved 6-67
Shaded 1-42
Shaded with Edges 1-42
Shadows in Shaded Mode 1-42
Shape Feature 5-14, 5-18
Sheet Format 3-5, 3-13
Sheet Format dialog box 3-7
Sheet Landscape 3-7
Sheet Metal Bends 6-32
Sheet Metal Overview 6-32
Sheet Metal Toolbar 6-38
Sheet Properties 3-9
Shell Feature 5-21
Short Cut Keys 4-68
Show 2-26, 2-30
Show Component 5-73
Shut-off Surfaces 4-73, 4-77
Silhouette Edge 4-52
Sketch 1-24
Sketch Driven Pattern 6-58
Sketch Entities 1-75, 1-101
Sketch Relations 1-33
Sketch Toolbar 1-13, 1-33
Sketch Tools 1-33, 1-1-01
Smart Dimension 1-35
SmartMates 2-44
SMC Corporation of America 1-23, 1-113
Socket Head Cap Screw 2-39
SolidWorks Help 1-13
Spin Box Increments 1-36
Spline 4-61
Split Bar 2-54
Standard Mates 2-16
Standard Toolbar 1-12
Standard Views 1-14
Start SolidWorks 1-9
Suppress 6-29, 2-68
sw-b212 6-58
Sweep Boss/Base Feature 5-13, 5-34
Sweep Profile 5-46
SWITCH Part Loft Base Feature 5-13
SWITCH Part Loft Planes 5-14
SWITCH Part Shape Feature 5-18
System Options 1-17

T

Tips of the Day 1-9
Table Driven Pattern 6-58
Tangent Arc 1-90
Tangent Edge Visible 3-36
Tangent Relation 1-90, 5-16
Task Pane 1-9
Tear Relief 6-35
Templates 1-19
Temporary Axis 2-58, 2-64
Tertiary datum plane 1-27
Third Angle Projection 1-29

Thread Feature 5-42
Thumbnails 2-8
Title Block 3-13, 3-14, 3-62
Tolerance 2-47
Tolerance Block 3-15
Toolbox Library 2-70
Tooling Split 4-78
Top Down Model Approach 2-5, 6-6
Transition Fit 2-47, 2-51
Transparent Optical Property 4-56
Trim Entities 1-65, 4-66

U & V

Undo 1-33
Unfold 6-102
Units 1-6, 1-20
Unsuppress 6-58
Up to Vertex 6-90
UpToSurface Option 5-48
User Interface 1-12
Vertical Relation 4-52
View Modes 1-41
View Orientation 1-44, 1-68
View Port 1-41

W, X, Y, Z

Wireframe 1-41
Yield Strength 2-89
Zoom In/Out 1-42
Zoom to Area 1-42
Zoom to Fit 1-42
Zoom to Selection 1-42

Notes: